W9-AGN-689

HANDBOOK OF
THE NATIONS

ISSN 0194-3790

HANDBOOK OF THE NATIONS
Tenth Edition

A Brief Guide to the Economy,
Government, Land, Demographics,
Communications, and National Defense
Establishment of Each of 249 Nations
and Other Political Entities

Compiled and Published by
U.S. Central Intelligence Agency

Reissued by

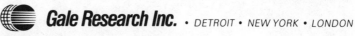 **Gale Research Inc.** · DETROIT · NEW YORK · LONDON

Bibliographic Note

Handbook of the Nations, Tenth Edition, is a reprint of *The World Factbook/1990*. *The World Factbook* (formerly called *National Basic Intelligence Factbook*) is produced annually (its predecessor was issued semiannually) by the Central Intelligence Agency, using data provided by various components of the Central Intelligence Agency, the Defense Intelligence Agency, the U.S. Bureau of Census, the Defense Nuclear Agency, the U.S. Coast Guard, the U.S. Department of State, and other government agencies. Information available to the compiling agency as of January 1, 1990, was used in preparing the base data for this issue; however, important political information was updated to March 30, 1990, and population estimates were made as of July 1, 1990.

The paper used in this publication meets the minimum requirements of American National Standard for Information Sciences—Permanence Paper for Printed Library Materials, ANSI Z39.48-1984. ∞™

ISSN 0194-3790
ISBN 0-8103-6923-0

Printed in the United States of America

Published simultaneously in the United Kingdom
by Gale Research International Limited
(An affiliated company of Gale Research Inc.)

Contents

FOREWORD

Handbook of the Nations, Tenth Edition, (originally titled *The World Factbook/1990*) was produced by the Central Intelligence Agency, an agency of the United States Government. It provides up-to-date listings on the land, people, government, economy, communications, and transportation systems and the armed forces of 249 countries and political entities of the world. It places these entries in context by adding a synoptic entry on the world as a whole.

Most of the information was revised as of January 1, 1990; however, major political developments were recorded up through March 30, 1990, and population estimates were projected to July 1, 1990. Population growth rates were estimated for mid-1990 through mid-1991. Military age figures, by country, were estimated for the period 1990-94.

Data sources

The Central Intelligence Agency compiles these data for publication, annually, by consulting its own perpetually-updated files, as well as those of the Defense Intelligence Agency, the Bureau of the Census, the Defense Nuclear Agency, the United States Coast Guard and the Foreign Broadcast Information Service. Sources also include the Navy Operational Intelligence Center and Maritime Administration (merchant marine data), Office of Territorial and International Affairs (Department of Interior), U.S. Board on Geographic Names, and the U.S. Department of State.

The entries

Entries are typically one to two pages in length, and in addition to key data, which is heavily statistical in nature, entries provide a small map to aid in recognition of the country and the general placement of its important cities. The small maps are referenced to a series of regional maps of the world, located at the back of the book.

Expansion

This tenth edition maintains and expands somewhat on the format changes which were initiated in the ninth edition. As with the ninth edition, it provides additional data under the *Economy* rubric, and supplies more data in the exports entries than before. *Birth* and *death* rates as well as the overall *fertility* and *infant mortality* rates can now be found under the *People* heading. The *Handbook* goes beyond its predecessors in expanding the leadership entry. This means that changes and additions, which boosted the ninth edition's size about one-third over previous editions, have all been retained while yet another twenty pages have been added. Instead of 366 pages, plus maps, edition number ten has 382 pages, plus maps. (Particulars of the tenth edition improvements are detailed under the *Notes* beginning on page xi.)

The material in this *Handbook*, not classified, but *not* provided directly to the public by the CIA, is made available in this publicly circulated edition so that students and private researchers may access it without undue difficulty.

Notes, Definitions, and Abbreviations

There have been some significant changes in this edition. In the Goverment section the former Branches entry has been replaced by three entries—Executive branch, Legislative branch, and Judicial branch. The Leaders entry now has subentries for Chief of State, Head of Government, and their deputies. The Elections entry has been completely redone with information for each branch of the national government, including the date for the last election, the date for the next election, results (percent of vote by candidate or party), and current distribution of seats by party. In the Economy section there is a new entry on Illicit drugs.

Abbreviations: (see Appendix B for international organizations)

avdp.	avoirdupois
c.i.f.	cost, insurance, and freight
CY	calendar year
DWT	deadweight ton
est.	estimate
Ex-Im	Export-Import Bank of the United States
f.o.b.	free on board
FRG	Federal Republic of Germany (West Germany)
FY	fiscal year
GDP	gross domestic product
GDR	German Democratic Republic (East Germany)
GNP	gross national product
GRT	gross register ton
km	kilometer
km²	square kilometer
kW	kilowatt
kWh	kilowatt-hour
m	meter
NA	not available
NEGL	negligible
nm	nautical mile
NZ	New Zealand
ODA	official development assistance
OOF	other official flows
PDRY	People's Democratic Republic of Yemen [Yemen (Aden) or South Yemen]
UAE	United Arab Emirates
UK	United Kingdom
US	United States
USSR	Union of Soviet Socialist Republics (Soviet Union)
YAR	Yemen Arab Republic [Yemen (Sanaa) or North Yemen]

Administrative divisions: The numbers, designatory terms, and first-order administrative divisions are generally those approved by the United States Board on Geographic Names (BGN) as of 5 April 1990. Changes that have been reported but not yet acted upon by BGN are noted.

Area: Total area is the sum of all land and water areas delimited by international boundaries and/or coastlines. Land area is the aggregate of all surfaces delimited by international boundaries and/or coastlines, excluding inland water bodies (lakes, reservoirs, rivers). Comparative areas are based on total area equivalents. Most entities are compared with the entire US or one of the 50 states. The smaller entities are compared with Washington, DC (178 km², 69 miles²) or The Mall in Washington, DC (0.59 km², 0.23 miles², 146 acres).

Birth rate: The average annual number of births during a year per 1,000 population at midyear. Also known as crude birth rate.

Contributors: Information was provided by the Bureau of the Census (Department of Commerce), Central Intelligence Agency, Defense Intelligence Agency, Defense Nuclear Agency, Department of State, Foreign Broadcast Information Service, Navy Operational Intelligence Center and Maritime Administration (merchant marine data), Office of Territorial and International Affairs (Department of the Interior), United States Board on Geographic Names, United States Coast Guard, and others.

Dates of information: In general, information available as of 1 January 1990 was used in the preparation of this edition. Population figures are estimates for 1 July 1990, with population growth rates estimated for mid-1990 through mid-1991. Major political events have been updated through 30 March 1990. Military age figures are average annual estimates for 1990-94.

Death rate: The average annual number of deaths during a year per 1,000 population at midyear. Also known as crude death rate.

Diplomatic representation: The US Government has diplomatic relations with 162 nations. There are only 144 US embassies, since some nations have US ambassadors accredited to them, but no physical US mission exists. The US has diplomatic relations with 149 of the 159 UN members—the exceptions are Albania, Angola, Byelorussia (constituent republic of the Soviet Union), Cambodia, Cuba, Iran, Vietnam, People's Democratic Republic of Yemen [Yemen (Aden) or South Yemen], Ukraine (constituent republic of the Soviet Union), and, obviously, the US itself. In addition, the US has diplomatic relations with 13 nations that are not in the UN—Andorra, Federated States of Micronesia, Kiribati, Liechtenstein, Marshall Islands, Monaco, Nauru, San Marino, South Korea, Switzerland, Tonga, Tuvalu, and the Vatican City. North Korea is not in the UN and the US does not have diplomatic relations with that nation. The US has not recognized the incorporation of Estonia, Latvia, and Lithuania into the Soviet Union and continues to accredit the diplomatic representatives of their last free governments.

Disputes: This category includes a wide variety of situations that range from traditional bilateral boundary disputes to unilateral claims of one sort or another. Every international land boundary dispute in the "Guide to International Boundaries," a map published by the Department of State, is included. References to other situations may also be included that are border- or frontier-relevant, such as maritime disputes, geopolitical questions, or irredentist issues. However, inclusion does not necessarily constitute official acceptance or recognition by the US Government.

Entities: Some of the nations, dependent areas, areas of special sovereignty, and governments included in this publication are not independent, and others are not officially recognized by the US Government. Nation refers to a people politically organized into a sovereign state with a definite territory. Dependent area refers to a broad category of political entities that are associated in some way with a nation. Names used for page headings are usually the short-form names as approved by the US Board on Geographic Names. The long-form name is included in the Government section and an entry of "none" indicates a long-form name does not exist. In some instances, no short-form name exists—then the long-form name must serve for all usages.
There are 249 entities in the *Handbook* that may be categorized as follows:

NATIONS

157 UN members (There are 159 members in the UN, but only 157 are included in *Handbook of the Nations* because Byelorussia and Ukraine are constituent republics of the Soviet Union.)

15 nations that are not members of the UN—Andorra, Federated States of Micronesia, Kiribati, Liechtenstein, Marshall Islands, Monaco, Namibia, Nauru, North Korea, San Marino, South Korea, Switzerland, Tonga, Tuvalu, Vatican City

OTHER

1 Taiwan

DEPENDENT AREAS

6 Australia—Ashmore and Cartier Islands, Christmas Island, Cocos (Keeling) Islands, Coral Sea Islands, Heard Island and McDonald Islands, Norfolk Island

2 Denmark—Faroe Islands, Greenland

16 France—Bassas da India, Clipperton Island, Europa Island, French Guiana, French Polynesia, French Southern and Antarctic Lands, Glorioso Islands, Guadeloupe, Juan de Nova Island, Martinique, Mayotte, New Caledonia, Reunion, St. Pierre and Miquelon, Tromelin Island, Wallis and Futuna

2 Netherlands—Aruba, Netherlands Antilles

3 New Zealand—Cook Islands, Niue, Tokelau

3 Norway—Bouvet Island, Jan Mayen, Svalbard

1 Portugal—Macau

16 United Kingdom—Anguilla, Bermuda, British Indian Ocean Territory, British Virgin Islands, Cayman Islands, Falkland Islands, Gibraltar, Guernsey, Hong Kong, Isle of Man, Jersey, Montserrat, Pitcairn Islands, St. Helena, South Georgia and the South Sandwich Islands, Turks and Caicos Islands

15 United States—American Samoa, Baker Island, Guam, Howland Island, Jarvis Island, Johnston Atoll, Kingman Reef, Midway Islands, Navassa Island, Northern Mariana Islands, Palmyra Atoll, Puerto Rico, Trust Territory of the Pacific Islands (Palau), Virgin Islands, Wake Island

MISCELLANEOUS

7 Antarctica, Gaza Strip, Iraq-Saudi Arabia Neutral Zone, Paracel Islands, Spratly Islands, West Bank, Western Sahara

OTHER ENTITIES

4 oceans—Arctic Ocean, Atlantic Ocean, Indian Ocean, Pacific Ocean

1 World
—
249 total

Notes: The US Government has not recognized the incorporation of Estonia, Latvia, and Lithuania into the Soviet Union as constituent republics during World War II. Those Baltic states are not members of the UN and are not included in the list of nations. The US Government does not recognize the four so-called "independent" homelands of Bophuthatswana, Ciskei, Transkei, and Venda in South Africa.

Gross domestic product (GDP): The value of all goods and services produced domestically.

Gross national product (GNP): The value of all goods and services produced domestically, plus income earned abroad, minus income earned by foreigners from domestic production.

GNP/GDP methodology: GNP/GDP dollar estimates for the OECD countries, the USSR, Eastern Europe, and a portion of the developing countries, are derived from *purchasing power parity (PPP)* calculations rather than from conversions at official currency exchange rates. The PPP methods involve the use of average price weights, which lie between the weights of the domestic and foreign price systems; using these weights US $100 converted into German marks by a PPP method will buy an equal amount of goods and services in both the US and Germany. One caution: the proportion of, say, military expenditures as a percent of GNP/GDP in local currency accounts may differ substantially from the proportion when GNP/GDP is expressed in PPP dollar terms, as, for example, when an observer estimates the dollar level of Soviet or Japanese military expenditures. Similarly, dollar figures for exports and imports reflect the price patterns of international markets rather than PPP price patterns.

Growth rate (population): The annual percent change in the population, resulting from a surplus (or deficit) of births over deaths and the balance of migrants entering and leaving a country. The rate may be positive or negative.

Illicit drugs: There are five categories of illicit drugs—narcotics, stimulants, depressants (sedatives), hallucinogens, and cannabis. These categories include many drugs legally produced and prescribed by doctors as well as those illegally produced and sold outside medical channels.

Cannabis (Cannabis sativa) is the common hemp plant, provides hallucinogens with some sedative properties, and includes marijuana (pot, Acapulco gold, grass, reefer), tetrahydrocannabinol (THC, Marinol), hashish (hash), and hashish oil (hash oil).

Coca (Erythroxylon coca) is a bush and the leaves contain the stimulant cocaine. Coca is not to be confused with cocoa which comes from cacao seeds and is used in making chocolate, cocoa, and cocoa butter.

Cocaine is a stimulant derived from the leaves of the coca bush.

Depressants (sedatives) are drugs that reduce tension and anxiety and include chloral hydrate, barbiturates (Amytal, Nembutal, Seconal, phenobarbital), benzodiazepines (Librium, Valium), methaqualone (Quaalude), glutethimide (Doriden), and others (Equanil, Placidyl, Valmid).

Drugs are any chemical substances that effect a physical, mental, emotional, or behavioral change in an individual.

Drug abuse is the use of any licit or illicit chemical substance that results in physical, mental, emotional, or behavioral impairment in an individual.

Hallucinogens are drugs that affect sensation, thinking, self-awareness, and emotion. Hallucinogens include LSD (acid, microdot), mescaline and peyote (mexc, buttons, cactus), amphetamine variants (PMA, STP, DOB), phencyclidine (PCP, angel dust, hog), phencyclidine analogues (PCE, PCPy, TCP), and others (psilocybin, psilocyn).

Hashish is the resinous exudate of the cannabis or hemp plant (Cannabis sativa).

Heroin is a semisynthetic derivative of morphine.

Marijuana is the dried leaves of the cannabis or hemp plant (Cannabis sativa).

Narcotics are drugs that relieve pain, often induce sleep, and refer to opium, opium derivatives, and synthetic substitutes. Natural narcotics include opium (paregoric, parepectolin), morphine (MS-Contin, Roxanol), codeine (Tylenol w/codeine, Empirin w/codeine, Robitussan A-C), and thebaine. Semisynthetic narcotics include heroin (horse, smack) and hydromorphone (Dilaudid). Synthetic narcotics include meperidine or Pethidine (Demerol, Mepergan), methadone (Dolophine, Methadose), and others (Darvon, Lomotil).

Opium is the milky exudate of the incised, unripe seedpod of the opium poppy.

Opium poppy (Papaver somniferum) is the source for many natural and semisynthetic narcotics.

Poppy straw concentrate is the alkaloid derived from the mature dried opium poppy.

Qat (kat, khat) is a stimulant from the buds or leaves of Catha edulis and is chewed or drunk as tea.

Stimulants are drugs that relieve mild depression, increase energy and activity, and include cocaine (coke, snow, crack), amphetamines (Desoxyn, Dexedrine), phenmetrazine (Preludin), methylphenidate (Ritalin), and others (Cylert, Sanorex, Tenuate).

Infant mortality rate: The number of deaths to infants under one year of age in a given year per 1,000 live births occurring in the same year.

Land use: Human use of the land surface is categorized as *arable land*—land cultivated for crops that are replanted after each harvest (wheat, maize, rice); *permanent crops*—land cultivated for crops that are not replanted after each harvest (citrus, coffee, rubber); *meadows and pastures*—land permanently used for herbaceous forage crops; *forest and woodland*—land under dense or open stands of trees; and *other*—any land type not specifically mentioned above (urban areas, roads, desert). The percentage figure for irrigated refers to the portion of the entire amount of land area that is artificially supplied with water.

Leaders: The chief of state is the titular leader of the country who represents the state at official and ceremonial functions but is not involved with the day-to-day activities of the government. The head of government is the administrative leader who manages the day-to-day activities of the government. In the UK, the monarch is the chief of state and the prime minister is the head of government. In the US, the President is both the chief of state and the head of government.

Life expectancy at birth: The average number of years to be lived by a group of people all born in the same year, if mortality at each age remains constant in the future.

Maritime claims: The proximity of neighboring states may prevent some national claims from being fully extended.

Merchant marine: All ships engaged in the carriage of goods. All commercial vessels (as opposed to all nonmilitary ships), which excludes tugs, fishing vessels, offshore oil rigs, etc. Also, a grouping of merchant ships by nationality or register.

Captive register—A register of ships maintained by a territory, possession, or colony primarily or exclusively for the use of ships owned in the parent country. Also referred to as an offshore register, the offshore equivalent of an internal register. Ships on a captive register will fly the same flag as the parent country, or a local variant of it, but will be subject to the maritime laws and taxation rules of the offshore territory. Although the nature of a captive register makes it especially desirable for ships owned in the parent country, just as in the internal register, the ships may also be owned abroad. The captive register then acts as a flag of convenience register, except that it is not the register of an independent state.

Flag of convenience register—A national register offering registration to a merchant ship not owned in the flag state. The major flags of convenience (FOC) attract ships to their register by virtue of low fees, low or nonexistent taxation of profits, and liberal manning requirements. True FOC registers are characterized by having relatively few of the ships registered actually owned in the flag state. Thus, while virtually any flag can be used for ships under a given set of circumstances, an FOC register is one where the majority of the merchant fleet is owned abroad. It is also referred to as an open register.

Flag state—The nation in which a ship is registered and which holds legal jurisdiction over operation of the ship, whether at home or abroad. Differences in flag state maritime legislation determine how a ship is manned and taxed and whether a foreign-owned ship may be placed on the register.

Internal register—A register of ships maintained as a subset of a national register. Ships on the internal register fly the national flag and have that nationality but are subject to a separate set of maritime rules from those on the main national register. These differences usually include lower taxation of profits, manning by foreign nationals, and, usually, ownership outside the flag state (when it functions as an FOC register). The Norwegian International Ship Register and Danish International Ship Register are the most notable examples of an internal register. Both have been instrumental in stemming flight from the national flag to flags of convenience and in attracting foreign-owned ships to the Norwegian and Danish flags.

Merchant ship—A vessel that carries goods against payment of freight. Commonly used to denote any nonmilitary ship but accurately restricted to commercial vessels only.

Register—The record of a ship's ownership and nationality as listed with the maritime authorities of a country. Also, the compendium of such individual ships' registrations. Registration of a ship provides it with a nationality and makes it subject to the laws of the country in which registered (the flag state) regardless of the nationality of the ship's ultimate owner.

Money figures: All are expressed in contemporaneous US dollars unless otherwise indicated.

Net migration rate: The balance between the number of persons entering and leaving a country during the year per 1,000 persons (based on midyear population). An excess of persons entering the country is referred to as net immigration (3.56 migrants/1,000 population); an excess of persons leaving the country as net emigration (−9.26 migrants/1,000 population).

Population: Figures are estimates from the Bureau of the Census based on statistics from population censuses, vital registration systems, or sample surveys pertaining to the recent past, and on assumptions about future trends.

Total fertility rate: The average number of children that would be born per woman if all women lived to the end of their childbearing years and bore children according to a given fertility rate at each age.

Years: All year references are for the calendar year (CY) unless indicated as fiscal year (FY).

Afjghanistan

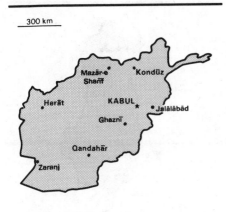

300 km

See regional map VIII

Geography

Total area: 647,500 km²; land area: 647,500 km²
Comparative area: slightly smaller than Texas
Land boundaries: 5,826 km total; China 76 km, Iran 936 km, Pakistan 2,430 km, USSR 2,384 km
Coastline: none—landlocked
Maritime claims: none—landlocked
Disputes: Pashtun question with Pakistan; Baloch question with Iran and Pakistan; periodic disputes with Iran over Helmand water rights; insurgency with Iranian and Pakistani involvement; traditional tribal rivalries
Climate: arid to semiarid; cold winters and hot summers
Terrain: mostly rugged mountains; plains in north and southwest
Natural resources: natural gas, crude oil, coal, copper, talc, barites, sulphur, lead, zinc, iron ore, salt, precious and semiprecious stones
Land use: 12% arable land; NEGL% permanent crops; 46% meadows and pastures; 3% forest and woodland; 39% other; includes NEGL% irrigated
Environment: damaging earthquakes occur in Hindu Kush mountains; soil degradation, desertification, overgrazing, deforestation, pollution
Note: landlocked

People

Population: 15,862,293 (July 1990), growth rate 7.7% (1990)
Birth rate: 44 births/1,000 population (1990)
Death rate: 18 deaths/1,000 population (1990)
Net migration rate: 51 migrants/1,000 population (1990); note—there are flows across the border in both directions, but data are fragmentary and unreliable

Infant mortality rate: 154 deaths/1,000 live births (1990)
Life expectancy at birth: 47 years male, 46 years female (1990)
Total fertility rate: 6.4 children born/woman (1990)
Nationality: noun—Afghan(s); adjective—Afghan
Ethnic divisions: 50% Pashtun, 25% Tajik, 9% Uzbek, 12-15% Hazara; minor ethnic groups include Chahar Aimaks, Turkmen, Baloch, and others
Religion: 74% Sunni Muslim, 15% Shi'a Muslim, 11% other
Language: 50% Pashtu, 35% Afghan Persian (Dari), 11% Turkic languages (primarily Uzbek and Turkmen), 4% thirty minor languages (primarily Balochi and Pashai); much bilingualism
Literacy: 12%
Labor force: 4,980,000; 67.8% agriculture and animal husbandry, 10.2% industry, 6.3% construction, 5.0% commerce, 10.7% services and other (1980 est.)
Organized labor: some small government-controlled unions

Government

Long-form name: Republic of Afghanistan
Type: authoritarian
Capital: Kabul
Administrative divisions: 30 provinces (velayat, singular—velāyat); Badakhshān, Bādghīs, Baghlān, Balkh, Bāmīān, Farāh, Fāryāb, Ghaznī, Ghowr, Helmand, Herāt, Jowzjān, Kābol, Kandahār, Kāpīsā, Konar, Kondoz, Laghmān, Lowgar, Nangarhār, Nīmrūz, Orūzgān, Paktīā, Paktīkā, Parvān, Samangān, Sar-e Pol, Takhār, Vardak, Zābol; note—there may be a new province of Nūrestān (Nuristan)
Independence: 19 August 1919 (from UK)
Constitution: adopted 30 November 1987
Legal system: has not accepted compulsory ICJ jurisdiction
National holiday: Anniversary of the Saur Revolution, 27 April (1978)
Executive branch: president, four vice presidents, prime minister, deputy prime minister, Council of Ministers (cabinet)
Legislative branch: bicameral National Assembly (Meli Shura) consists of an upper house or Senate (Sena) and a lower house or House of Representatives (Wolasi Jirgah)
Judicial branch: Supreme Court
Leaders: *Chief of State and Head of Government*—President (Mohammad) NAJIBULLAH (Ahmadzai) (since 30 November 1987); Chairman of the Council of Ministers Executive Committee Soltan Ali KESHTMAND (since 21 February 1989)
Political parties and leaders: only party—the People's Democratic Party of Afghanistan (PDPA) has two factions—the Par-

chami faction has been in power since December 1979 and members of the deposed Khalqi faction continue to hold some important posts mostly in the military and Ministry of Interior; nonparty figures hold some posts
Suffrage: universal, male ages 15-50
Elections: *Senate*—last held NA April 1988 (next to be held April 1991); results—PDPA is the only party; seats—(192 total, 115 elected) PDPA 115; *House of Representatives*—last held NA April 1988 (next to be held April 1993); results—PDPA is the only party; seats—(234 total) PDPA 184, 50 seats reserved for opposition
Communists: the PDPA claims 200,000 members (1988)
Other political or pressure groups: the military and other branches of internal security have been rebuilt by the USSR; insurgency continues throughout the country; widespread anti-Soviet and anti-regime sentiment and opposition on religious and political grounds
Member of: ADB, CCC, Colombo Plan, ESCAP, FAO, G-77, IAEA, IBRD, ICAO, IDA, IDB—Islamic Development Bank, IFAD, IFC, ILO, IMF, INTELSAT, ITU, NAM, UN, UNESCO, UPU, WFTU, WHO, WMO, WTO, WSG; suspended from OIC in January 1980
Diplomatic representation: Minister-Counselor, Chargé d'Affaires MIAGOL; Chancery at 2341 Wyoming Avenue NW, Washington DC 20008; telephone (202) 234-3770 or 3771; *US*—Chargé d'Affaires (vacant); Embassy at Ansari Wat, Wazir Akbar Khan Mina, Kabul; telephone 62230 through 62235 or 62436; note—US Embassy in Kabul was closed in January 1989
Flag: three equal horizontal bands of black (top), red, and green with the national coat of arms superimposed on the hoist side of the black and red bands; similar to the flag of Malawi which is shorter and bears a radiant, rising, red sun centered in the black band

Economy

Overview: Fundamentally, Afghanistan is an extremely poor, landlocked country, highly dependent on farming (wheat especially) and livestock raising (sheep and goats). Economic considerations, however, have played second fiddle to political and military upheavals, including the nine-year Soviet military occupation (ended 15 February 1989) and the continuing bloody civil war. Over the past decade, one-third of the population has fled the country, with Pakistan sheltering some 3 million refugees and Iran perhaps 2 million.

Afghanistan (continued)

Another 1 million have probably moved into and around urban areas within Afghanistan. Large numbers of bridges, buildings, and factories have been destroyed or damaged by military action or sabotage. Government claims to the contrary, gross domestic product almost certainly is lower than 10 years ago because of the loss of labor and capital and the disruption of trade and transport. Official claims indicate that agriculture grew by 0.7% and industry by 3.5% in 1988.

GDP: $3 billion, per capita $200; real growth rate 0% (1989 est.)

Inflation rate (consumer prices): over 50% (1989 est.)

Unemployment rate: NA%

Budget: revenues NA; expenditures $646.7 million, including capital expenditures of $370.2 million (FY87 est.)

Exports: $512 million (f.o.b., FY88); *commodities*—natural gas 55%, fruits and nuts 24%, handwoven carpets, wool, cotton, hides, and pelts; *partners*—mostly USSR and Eastern Europe

Imports: $996 million (c.i.f., FY88); *commodities*—food and petroleum products; *partners*—mostly USSR and Eastern Europe

External debt: $1.8 billion (December 1989 est.)

Industrial production: growth rate 6.2% (FY89 plan)

Electricity: 480,000 kW capacity; 1,470 million kWh produced, 100 kWh per capita (1989)

Industries: small-scale production of textiles, soap, furniture, shoes, fertilizer, and cement; handwoven carpets; natural gas, oil, coal, copper

Agriculture: largely subsistence farming and nomadic animal husbandry; cash products—wheat, fruits, nuts, karakul pelts, wool, mutton

Illicit drugs: an illicit producer of opium poppy and cannabis for the international drug trade; world's second largest opium producer (after Burma) and a major source of hashish

Aid: US commitments, including Ex-Im (FY70-88), $265 million; Western (non-US) countries, ODA and OOF bilateral commitments (1970-87), $419 million; OPEC bilateral aid (1979-89), $57 million; Communist countries (1970-88), $4.1 billion

Currency: afghani (plural—afghanis); 1 afghani (Af) = 100 puls

Exchange rates: afghanis (Af) per US$1—50.6 (fixed rate since 1982)

Fiscal year: 21 March-20 March

Communications

Railroads: 9.6 km (single track) 1.524-meter gauge from Kushka (USSR) to Towraghondī and 15.0 km from Termez (USSR) to Kheyrābād transshipment point on south bank of Amu Darya

Highways: 21,000 km total (1984); 2,800 km hard surface, 1,650 km bituminous-treated gravel and improved earth, 16,550 km unimproved earth and tracks

Inland waterways: total navigability 1,200 km; chiefly Amu Darya, which handles steamers up to about 500 metric tons

Pipelines: petroleum, oil, and lubricants pipelines—USSR to Bagrām and USSR to Shīndand; natural gas, 180 km

Ports: Shīr Khān and Kheyrābād (river ports)

Civil air: 2 TU-154, 2 Boeing 727, assorted smaller transports

Airports: 38 total, 34 usable; 9 with permanent-surface runways; none with runways over 3,659 m; 10 with runways 2,440-3,659 m; 15 with runways 1,220-2,439 m

Telecommunications: limited telephone, telegraph, and radiobroadcast services; television introduced in 1980; 31,200 telephones; stations—5 AM, no FM, 1 TV; 1 satellite earth station

Defense Forces

Branches: Armed Forces (Army; Air and Air Defense Forces); Border Guard Forces; National Police Force (Sarandoi); Ministry of State Security (WAD); Tribal Militia

Military manpower: males 15-49, 3,880,124; 2,080,725 fit for military service; 168,021 reach military age (22) annually

Defense expenditures: 9.1% of GDP (1984)

Albania

See regional map V

Geography

Total area: 28,750 km^2; land area: 27,400 km^2

Comparative area: slightly larger than Maryland

Land boundaries: 768 km total; Greece 282 km, Yugoslavia 486 km

Coastline: 362 km

Maritime claims:
Continental shelf: not specified
Territorial sea: 15 nm

Disputes: Kosovo question with Yugoslavia; Northern Epirus question with Greece

Climate: mild temperate; cool, cloudy, wet winters; hot, clear, dry summers; interior is cooler and wetter

Terrain: mostly mountains and hills; small plains along coast

Natural resources: crude oil, natural gas, coal, chromium, copper, timber, nickel

Land use: 21% arable land; 4% permanent crops; 15% meadows and pastures; 38% forest and woodland; 22% other; includes 1% irrigated

Environment: subject to destructive earthquakes; tsunami occur along southwestern coast; deforestation seems to be slowing

Note: strategic location along Strait of Otranto (links Adriatic Sea to Ionian Sea and Mediterranean Sea)

People

Population: 3,273,131 (July 1990), growth rate 1.9% (1990)

Birth rate: 25 births/1,000 population (1990)

Death rate: 5 deaths/1,000 population (1990)

Net migration rate: 0 migrants/1,000 population (1990)

Infant mortality rate: 52 deaths/1,000 live births (1990)

Life expectancy at birth: 72 years male, 78 years female (1990)

Total fertility rate: 3.0 children born/woman (1990)

Nationality: noun—Albanian(s); adjective—Albanian

Ethnic divisions: Albanian 90%, Greeks 8%, other 2% (Vlachs, Gypsies, Serbs, and Bulgarians) (1989 est.)

Religion: Albania claims to be the world's first atheist state; all churches and mosques were closed in 1967 and religious observances prohibited; pre-1967 estimates of religious affiliation—70% Muslim, 20% Albanian Orthodox, 10% Roman Catholic

Language: Albanian (Tosk is official dialect), Greek

Literacy: 75%

Labor force: 1,500,000 (1987); about 60% agriculture, 40% industry and commerce (1986)

Organized labor: Central Council of Albanian Trade Unions, 610,000 members

Government

Long-form name: People's Socialist Republic of Albania

Type: Communist state (Stalinist)

Capital: Tiranë

Administrative divisions: 26 districts (rrethe, singular—rreth); Berat, Dibrë, Durrës, Elbasan, Fier, Gjirokastër, Gramsh, Kolonjë, Korçë, Krujë, Kukës, Lezhë, Librazhd, Lushnjë, Mat, Mirditë, Përmet, Pogradec, Pukë, Sarandë, Shkodër, Skrapar, Tepelenë, Tiranë, Tropojë, Vlorë

Independence: 28 November 1912 (from Turkey); People's Socialist Republic of Albania declared 11 January 1946

Constitution: 27 December 1976

Legal system: judicial review of legislative acts only in the Presidium of the People's Assembly, which is not a true court; has not accepted compulsory ICJ jurisdiction

National holiday: Liberation Day, 29 November (1944)

Executive branch: president of the Presidium of the People's Assembly, three vice presidents, Presidium of the People's Assembly; chairman of the Council of Ministers, three deputy chairmen, Council of Ministers

Legislative branch: unicameral People's Assembly (Kuvëndi Popullor)

Judicial branch: Supreme Court

Leaders: *Chief of State*—President of the Presidium of the People's Assembly Ramiz ALIA (since 22 November 1982); *Head of Government*—Chairman of the Council of Ministers Adil ÇARÇANI (since 14 January 1982)

Political parties and leaders: only party—Albanian Workers Party, Ramiz Alia, first secretary

Suffrage: universal and compulsory at age 18

Elections: *President*—last held 19 February 1987 (next to be held February 1991); results—President Ramiz Alia was reelected without opposition; *People's Assembly*—last held 1 February 1987 (next to be held February 1991); results—Albanian Workers Party is the only party; seats—(250 total) Albanian Workers Party 250

Communists: 147,000 party members (November 1986)

Member of: CCC, CEMA (has not participated since rift with USSR in 1961), FAO, IAEA, IPU, ITU, UN, UNESCO, UNIDO, UPU, WFTU, WHO, WMO

Diplomatic representation: none—the US does not recognize the Albanian Government and has no diplomatic or consular relations with Albania; there is no third-power representation of Albanian interests in the US or of US interests in Albania

Flag: red with a black two-headed eagle in the center below a red five-pointed star outlined in yellow

Economy

Overview: As the poorest country in Europe, Albania's development lags behind even the least favored areas of the Yugoslav economy. The Stalinist-type economy operates on the principles of central planning and state ownership of the means of production. In recent years Albania has implemented limited economic reforms to stimulate its lagging economy, although they do not go nearly so far as current reforms in the USSR and Eastern Europe. Attempts at self-reliance and a policy of not borrowing from international lenders—sometimes overlooked in recent years—have greatly hindered the development of a broad economic infrastructure. Albania, however, possesses considerable mineral resources and is largely self-sufficient in food. Numerical estimates of Albanian economic activity are subject to an especially wide margin of error because the government is isolated and closemouthed.

GNP: $3.8 billion, per capita $1,200; real growth rate NA% (1989 est.)

Inflation rate (consumer prices): NA%

Unemployment rate: NA%

Budget: revenues $2.3 billion; expenditures $2.3 billion, including capital expenditures of NA (1989)

Exports: $378 million (f.o.b., 1987 est.); *commodities*—asphalt, bitumen, petroleum products, metals and metallic ores, electricity, oil, vegetables, fruits, tobacco; *partners*—Italy, Yugoslavia, FRG, Greece, Czechoslovakia, Poland, Romania, Bulgaria, Hungary

Imports: $255 million (f.o.b., 1987 est.); *commodities*—machinery, machine tools, iron and steel products, textiles, chemicals, pharmaceuticals; *partners*—Italy, Yugoslavia, FRG, Czechoslovakia, Romania, Poland, Hungary, Bulgaria, GDR

External debt: $NA

Industrial production: growth rate NA

Electricity: 1,630,000 kW capacity; 4,725 million kWh produced, 1,440 kWh per capita (1989)

Industries: food processing, textiles and clothing, lumber, oil, cement, chemicals, basic metals, hydropower

Agriculture: arable land per capita among lowest in Europe; one-half of work force engaged in farming; produces wide range of temperate-zone crops and livestock; claims self-sufficiency in grain output

Aid: none

Currency: lek (plural—lekë); 1 lek (L) = 100 qintars

Exchange rates: lekë (L) per US$1—8.00 (noncommercial fixed rate since 1986), 4.14 (commercial fixed rate since 1987)

Fiscal year: calendar year

Communications

Railroads: 543 km total; 509 1.435-meter standard gauge, single track and 34 km narrow gauge, single track (1988); line connecting Titograd (Yugoslavia) and Shkodër (Albania) completed August 1986

Highways: 16,700 km total; 6,700 km highway and roads, 10,000 km forest and agricultural

Inland waterways: 43 km plus Albanian sections of Lake Scutari, Lake Ohrid, and Lake Prespa

Pipelines: crude oil, 145 km; refined products, 55 km; natural gas, 64 km (1988)

Ports: Durrës, Sarandë, Vlorë

Merchant marine: 11 ships (1,000 GRT or over) totaling 52,886 GRT/75,993 DWT; includes 11 cargo

Airports: 12 total, 10 usable; more than 5 with permanent-surface runways; more than 5 with runways 2,440-3,659 m; 5 with runways 1,220-2,439 m

Telecommunications: stations—17 AM, 5 FM, 9 TV; 52,000 TV sets; 210,000 radios

Defense Forces

Branches: Albanian People's Army, Frontier Troops, Interior Troops, Albanian Coastal Defense Command, Air and Air Defense Force

Military manpower: males 15-49, 882,965; 729,635 fit for military service; 33,598 reach military age (19) annually

3

Albania (continued)

Defense expenditures: 1.1 billion leks, 11.3% of total budget (FY88); note—conversion of the military budget into US dollars using the official administratively set exchange rate would produce misleading results

Algeria

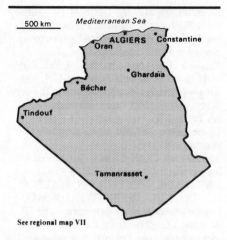

500 km | Mediterranean Sea

ALGIERS · Constantine
Oran

· Ghardaïa

· Béchar

· Tindouf

· Tamanrasset

See regional map VII

Geography

Total area: 2,381,740 km²; land area: 2,381,740 km²
Comparative area: slightly less than 3.5 times the size of Texas
Land boundaries: 6,343 km total; Libya 982 km, Mali 1,376 km, Mauritania 463 km, Morocco 1,559 km, Niger 956 km, Tunisia 965 km, Western Sahara 42 km
Coastline: 998 km
Maritime claims:
  Territorial sea: 12 nm
Disputes: Libya claims about 19,400 km² in southeastern Algeria
Climate: arid to semiarid; mild, wet winters with hot, dry summers along coast; drier with cold winters and hot summers on high plateau; sirocco is a hot, dust/sand-laden wind especially common in summer
Terrain: mostly high plateau and desert; some mountains; narrow, discontinuous coastal plain
Natural resources: crude oil, natural gas, iron ore, phosphates, uranium, lead, zinc
Land use: 3% arable land; NEGL% permanent crops; 13% meadows and pastures; 2% forest and woodland; 82% other; includes NEGL% irrigated
Environment: mountainous areas subject to severe earthquakes; desertification
Note: second largest country in Africa (after Sudan)

People

Population: 25,566,507 (July 1990), growth rate 2.8% (1990)
Birth rate: 37 births/1,000 population (1990)
Death rate: 9 deaths/1,000 population (1990)
Net migration rate: 0 migrants/1,000 population (1990)
Infant mortality rate: 87 deaths/1,000 live births (1990)

Life expectancy at birth: 61 years male, 64 years female (1990)
Total fertility rate: 5.4 children born/woman (1990)
Nationality: noun—Algerian(s); adjective—Algerian
Ethnic divisions: 99% Arab-Berber, less than 1% European
Religion: 99% Sunni Muslim (state religion); 1% Christian and Jewish
Language: Arabic (official), French, Berber dialects
Literacy: 52%
Labor force: 3,700,000; 40% industry and commerce, 24% agriculture, 17% government, 10% services (1984)
Organized labor: 16-19% of labor force claimed; General Union of Algerian Workers (UGTA) is the only labor organization and is subordinate to the National Liberation Front

Government

Long-form name: Democratic and Popular Republic of Algeria
Type: republic
Capital: Algiers
Administrative divisions: 31 provinces (wilayat, singular—wilaya); Adrar, Alger, Annaba, Batna, Béchar, Bejaïa, Biskra, Blida, Bouira, Constantine, Djelfa, El Asnam, Guelma, Jijel, Laghouat, Mascara, Médéa, Mostaganem, M'sila, Oran, Ouargla, Oum el Bouaghi, Saïda, Setif, Sidi Bel Abbès, Skikda, Tamanrasset, Tébessa, Tiaret, Tizi Ouzou, Tlemcen; note—there may now be 48 provinces with El Asnam abolished, and the addition of 18 new provinces named Ain Delfa, Ain Temouchent, Bordjbou, Boumerdes, Chlef, El Bayadh, El Oued, El Tarf, Illizi, Jijel, Khenchela, Mila, Naama, Relizane, Souk Ahras, Tindouf, Tipaza, Tissemsilt
Independence: 5 July 1962 (from France)
Constitution: 19 November 1976, effective 22 November 1976
Legal system: socialist, based on French and Islamic law; judicial review of legislative acts in ad hoc Constitutional Council composed of various public officials, including several Supreme Court justices; has not accepted compulsory ICJ jurisdiction
National holiday: Anniversary of the Revolution, 1 November (1954)
Executive branch: president, prime minister, Council of Ministers (cabinet)
Legislative branch: unicameral National People's Assembly (Assemblée Nationale Populaire)
Judicial branch: Supreme Court (Cour Suprême)
Leaders: *Chief of State*—President Chadli BENDJEDID (since 7 February 1979);

Head of Government—Prime Minister Mouloud HAMROUCHE (since 9 September 1989)

Political parties and leaders: National Liberation Front (FLN), Col. Chadli Bendjedid, chairman; Abdelhamid Mehri, secretary general; the government established a multiparty system in September 1989 and as of 1 February 1990 19 legal parties existed

Suffrage: universal at age 18

Elections: *President*—last held on 22 December 1988 (next to be held December 1993); results—President Bendjedid was reelected without opposition;
People's National Assembly—last held on 26 February 1987 (next to be held by February 1992); results—FLN was the only party; seats—(281 total) FLN 281; note—the government has promised to hold multiparty elections (municipal and wilaya) in June 1990, the first in Algerian history

Communists: 400 (est.); Communist party banned 1962

Member of: AfDB, AIOEC, Arab League, ASSIMER, CCC, FAO, G-77, GATT (de facto), IAEA, IBRD, ICAO, IDA, IDB—Islamic Development Bank, IFAD, ILO, IMF, IMO, INTELSAT, ILZSG, INTERPOL, IOOC, ITU, NAM, OAPEC, OAU, OIC, OPEC, UN, UNESCO, UPU, WHO, WIPO, WMO

Diplomatic representation: Ambassador Abderrahmane BENSID; Chancery at 2118 Kalorama Road NW, Washington DC 20008; telephone (202) 328-5300; *US*—Ambassador Christopher W. S. ROSS; Embassy at 4 Chemin Cheich Bachir Brahimi, Algiers (mailing address is B. P. Box 549, Alger-Gare, 16000 Algiers); telephone [213] (2) 601-425 or 255, 186; there is a US Consulate in Oran

Flag: two equal vertical bands of green (hoist side) and white with a red five-pointed star within a red crescent; the crescent, star, and color green are traditional symbols of Islam (the state religion)

Economy

Overview: The exploitation of oil and natural gas products forms the backbone of the economy. Algeria depends on hydrocarbons for nearly all of its export receipts, about 30% of government revenues, and nearly 25% of GDP. In 1973-74 the sharp increase in oil prices led to a booming economy that helped to finance an ambitious program of industrialization. Plunging oil and gas prices, combined with the mismanagement of Algeria's highly centralized economy, have brought the nation to its most serious social and economic crisis since independence. The government has promised far-reaching reforms, including giving public sector companies more autonomy, encouraging private-sector activity, boosting gas and nonhydrocarbon exports, and a major overhaul of the banking and financial systems. In 1988 the government started to implement a new economic policy to dismantle large state farms into privately operated units.

GDP: $54.1 billion, per capita $2,235; real growth rate −1.8% (1988)

Inflation rate (consumer prices): 5.9% (1988)

Unemployment rate: 19% (1988)

Budget: revenues $17.4 billion; expenditures $22.0 billion, including capital expenditures of $8.0 billion (1988)

Exports: $9.1 billion (f.o.b., 1989 est.); *commodities*—petroleum and natural gas 98%; *partners*—Netherlands, Czechoslovakia, Romania, Italy, France, US

Imports: $7.8 billion (f.o.b., 1989 est.); *commodities*—capital goods 35%, consumer goods 36%, food 20%; *partners*—France 25%, Italy 8%, FRG 8%, US 6-7%

External debt: $26.2 billion (December 1989)

Industrial production: growth rate 5.4% (1986)

Electricity: 4,333,000 kW capacity; 14,370 million kWh produced, 580 kWh per capita (1989)

Industries: petroleum, light industries, natural gas, mining, electrical, petrochemical, food processing

Agriculture: accounts for 8% of GDP and employs 24% of labor force; net importer of food—grain, vegetable oil, and sugar; farm production includes wheat, barley, oats, grapes, olives, citrus, fruits, sheep, and cattle

Aid: US commitments, including Ex-Im (FY70-85), $1.4 billion; Western (non-US) countries, ODA and OOF bilateral commitments (1970-87), $8.2 billion; OPEC bilateral aid (1979-89), $1.8 billion; Communist countries (1970-88), $2.7 billion

Currency: Algerian dinar (plural—dinars): 1 Algerian dinar (DA) = 100 centimes

Exchange rates: Algerian dinars (DA) per US$1—8.0086 (January 1990), 7.6086 (1989), 5.9148 (1988), 4.8497 (1987), 4.7023 (1986), 5.0278 (1985)

Fiscal year: calendar year

Communications

Railroads: 4,146 km total; 2,632 km standard gauge (1.435 m), 1,258 km 1.055-meter gauge, 256 km 1.000-meter gauge; 300 km electrified; 215 km double track

Highways: 80,000 km total; 60,000 km concrete or bituminous, 20,000 km gravel, crushed stone, unimproved earth

Pipelines: crude oil, 6,612 km; refined products, 298 km; natural gas, 2,948 km

Ports: Algiers, Annaba, Arzew, Bejaïa, Jijel, Mers el Kebir, Mostaganem, Oran, Skikda

Merchant marine: 75 ships (1,000 GRT or over) totaling 900,957 GRT/1,063,994 DWT; includes 5 passenger, 27 cargo, 2 vehicle carrier, 10 roll-on/roll-off cargo, 5 petroleum, oils, and lubricants (POL) tanker, 9 liquefied gas, 7 chemical tanker, 9 bulk, 1 specialized liquid cargo

Civil air: 42 major transport aircraft

Airports: 147 total, 136 usable; 53 with permanent-surface runways; 2 with runways over 3,660 m; 29 with runways 2,440-3,659 m; 68 with runways 1,220-2,439 m

Telecommunications: excellent domestic and international service in the north, sparse in the south; 693,000 telephones; stations—26 AM, no FM, 113 TV; 1,550,000 TV sets; 3,500,000 receiver sets; 6 submarine cables; coaxial cable or radio relay to Italy, France, Spain, Morocco, and Tunisia; satellite earth stations—1 Atlantic Ocean INTELSAT, 1 Indian Ocean INTELSAT, 1 Intersputnik, 1 ARABSAT, and 15 domestic

Defense Forces

Branches: Army, Navy, Air Force, National Gendarmerie

Military manpower: males 15-49, 5,886,334; 3,638,458 fit for military service; 293,476 reach military age (19) annually

Defense expenditures: 1.8% of GDP, or $974 million (1989 est.)

American Samoa
(territory of the US)

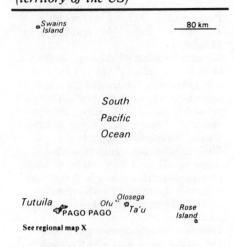

South
Pacific
Ocean

Tutuila   Ofu Olosega
         PAGO PAGO Ta'u   Rose
                               Island

See regional map X

Geography

Total area: 199 km²; land area: 199 km²
Comparative area: slightly larger than Washington, DC
Land boundaries: none
Coastline: 116 km
Maritime claims:
   Contiguous zone: 12 nm
   Continental shelf: 200 m
   Extended economic zone: 200 nm
   Territorial sea: 12 nm
Climate: tropical marine, moderated by southeast trade winds; annual rainfall averages 124 inches; rainy season from November to April, dry season from May to October; little seasonal temperature variation
Terrain: five volcanic islands with rugged peaks and limited coastal plains, two coral atolls
Natural resources: pumice and pumicite
Land use: 10% arable land; 5% permanent crops; 0% meadows and pastures; 75% forest and woodland; 10% other
Environment: typhoons common from December to March
Note: Pago Pago has one of the best natural deepwater harbors in the South Pacific Ocean, sheltered by shape from rough seas and protected by peripheral mountains from high winds; strategic location about 3,700 km south-southwest of Honolulu in the South Pacific Ocean about halfway between Hawaii and New Zealand

People

Population: 41,840 (July 1990), growth rate 2.9% (1990)
Birth rate: 41 births/1,000 population (1990)
Death rate: 4 deaths/1,000 population (1990)
Net migration rate: −8 immigrants/1,000 population (1990)

Infant mortality rate: 11 deaths/1,000 live births (1990)
Life expectancy at birth: 69 years male, 74 years female (1990)
Total fertility rate: 5.4 children born/woman (1990)
Nationality: noun—American Samoan(s); adjective—American Samoan
Ethnic divisions: 90% Samoan (Polynesian), 2% Caucasian, 2% Tongan, 6% other
Religion: about 50% Christian Congregationalist, 20% Roman Catholic, 30% mostly Protestant denominations and other
Language: Samoan (closely related to Hawaiian and other Polynesian languages) and English; most people are bilingual
Literacy: 99%
Labor force: 10,000; 48% government, 33% tuna canneries, 19% other (1986 est.)
Organized labor: NA
Note: about 65,000 American Samoans live in the States of California and Washington and 20,000 in Hawaii

Government

Long-form name: Territory of American Samoa
Type: unincorporated and unorganized territory of the US
Capital: Pago Pago
Administrative divisions: none (territory of the US)
Independence: none (territory of the US)
Constitution: ratified 1966, in effect 1967
National holiday: Flag Day, 17 April (1900)
Executive branch: US president, governor, lieutenant governor
Legislative branch: bicameral Legislature (Fono) consists of an upper house or Senate and a lower house or House of Representatives
Judicial branch: High Court
Leaders: *Chief of State*—President George BUSH (since 20 January 1989); Vice President Dan QUAYLE (since 20 January 1989);
Head of Government—Governor Peter Tali COLEMAN (since 20 January 1989); Lieutenant Governor Galea'i POUMELE (since NA 1989)
Suffrage: universal at age 18; indigenous inhabitants are US nationals, not US citizens
Elections: *Governor*—last held 7 November 1988 (next to be held November 1992); results—Peter T. Coleman was elected (percent of vote NA);
Senate—last held 7 November 1988 (next to be held November 1992); results—senators elected by county councils from 12 senate districts; seats—(18 total) number of seats by party NA;

House of Representatives—last held 7 November 1988 (next to be held November 1990); results—representatives popularly elected from 17 house districts; seats—(21 total, 20 elected and 1 nonvoting delegate from Swain's Island);
US House of Representatives—last held 19 November 1988 (next to be held November 1990); results—Eni R. F. H. Faleomavaega elected as a nonvoting delegate
Communists: none
Diplomatic representation: none (territory of the US)
Flag: blue with a white triangle edged in red that is based on the fly side and extends to the hoist side; a brown and white American bald eagle flying toward the hoist side is carrying two traditional Samoan symbols of authority, a staff and a war club
Note: administered by the US Department of Interior, Office of Territorial and International Affairs; indigenous inhabitants are US nationals, not citizens of the US

Economy

Overview: Economic development is strongly linked to the US, with which American Samoa does 90% of its foreign trade. Tuna fishing and tuna processing plants are the backbone of the private sector economy, with canned tuna the primary export. The tuna canneries are the second-largest employer, exceeded only by the government. Other economic activities include meat canning, handicrafts, dairy farming, and a slowly developing tourist industry. Tropical agricultural production provides little surplus for export.
GNP: $190 million, per capita $5,210; real growth rate NA% (1985)
Inflation rate (consumer prices): 4.3% (1989)
Unemployment rate: 13.4% (1986)
Budget: revenues $90.3 million; expenditures $93.15 million, including capital expenditures of $4.9 million (1988)
Exports: $288 million (f.o.b., 1987); *commodities*—canned tuna 93%; *partners*—US 99.6%
Imports: $346 million (c.i.f., 1987); *commodities*—building materials 18%, food 17%, petroleum products 14%; *partners*—US 72%, Japan 7%, NZ 7%, Australia 5%, other 9%
External debt: $NA
Industrial production: growth rate NA%
Electricity: 35,000 kW capacity; 70 million kWh produced, 1,720 kWh per capita (1989)
Industries: tuna canneries (largely dependent on foreign supplies of raw tuna)

6

Andorra

Agriculture: bananas, coconuts, vegetables, taro, breadfruit, yams, copra, pineapples, papayas
Aid: $20.1 million in operational funds and $5.8 million in construction funds for capital improvement projects from the US Department of Interior (1989)
Currency: US currency is used
Exchange rates: US currency is used
Fiscal year: 1 October-30 September

Communications

Railroads: small marine railroad in Pago Pago harbor
Highways: 350 km total; 150 km paved, 200 km unpaved
Ports: Pago Pago, Ta'u
Airports: 3 total, 3 usable; 1 with permanent-surface runways; none with runways over 3,659 m; 1 with runways 2,440 to 3,659 m (international airport at Tafuna, near Pago Pago); small airstrips on Ta'u and Ofu
Telecommunications: 6,500 telephones; stations—1 AM, no FM, 1 TV; good telex, telegraph, and facsimile services; 1 Pacific Ocean INTELSAT earth station

Defense Forces

Note: defense is the responsibility of the US

See regional map V

Geography

Total area: 450 km²; land area: 450 km²
Comparative area: slightly more than 2.5 times the size of Washington, DC
Land boundaries: 125 km total; France 60 km, Spain 65 km
Coastline: none—landlocked
Maritime claims: none—landlocked
Climate: temperate; snowy, cold winters and cool, dry summers
Terrain: rugged mountains dissected by narrow valleys
Natural resources: hydropower, mineral water, timber, iron ore, lead
Land use: 2% arable land; 0% permanent crops; 56% meadows and pastures; 22% forest and woodland; 20% other
Environment: deforestation, overgrazing
Note: landlocked

People

Population: 51,895 (July 1990), growth rate 2.6% (1990)
Birth rate: 12 births/1,000 population (1990)
Death rate: 4 deaths/1,000 population (1990)
Net migration rate: 18 migrants/1,000 population (1990)
Infant mortality rate: 7 deaths/1,000 live births (1990)
Life expectancy at birth: 74 years male, 81 years female (1990)
Total fertility rate: 1.3 children born/woman (1990)
Nationality: noun—Andorran(s); adjective—Andorran
Ethnic divisions: Catalan stock; 61% Spanish, 30% Andorran, 6% French, 3% other
Religion: virtually all Roman Catholic
Language: Catalan (official); many also speak some French and Castilian
Literacy: 100%
Labor force: NA
Organized labor: none

Government

Long-form name: Principality of Andorra
Type: unique coprincipality under formal sovereignty of president of France and Spanish bishop of Seo de Urgel, who are represented locally by officials called verguers
Capital: Andorra la Vella
Administrative divisions: 7 parishes (parròquies, singular—parròquia); Andorra, Canillo, Encamp, La Massana, Les Escaldes, Ordino, Sant Julià de Lòria
Independence: 1278
Constitution: none; some pareatges and decrees, mostly custom and usage
Legal system: based on French and Spanish civil codes; no judicial review of legislative acts; has not accepted compulsory ICJ jurisdiction
National holiday: Mare de Deu de Meritxell, 8 September
Executive branch: two co-princes (president of France, bishop of Seo de Urgel in Spain), two designated representatives (French veguer, Episcopal veguer), two permanent delegates (French prefect for the department of Pyrénées-Orientales, Spanish vicar general for the Seo de Urgel diocese), president of government, Executive Council
Legislative branch: unicameral General Council of the Valleys (Consell General de las Valls)
Judicial branch: civil cases—Supreme Court of Andorra at Perpignan (France) or the Ecclesiastical Court of the bishop of Seo de Urgel (Spain); criminal cases—Tribunal of the Courts (Tribunal des Cortes)
Leaders: *Chiefs of State*—French Co-Prince François MITTERRAND (since 21 May 1981), represented by Veguer de França Louis DEBLE; Spanish Episcopal Co-Prince Mgr. Joan MARTI y Alanís (since 31 January 1971), represented by Veguer Episcopal Francesc BADIA Batalla;
Head of Government—Josep PINTAT Solans (since NA 1984)
Political parties and leaders: political parties not yet legally recognized; traditionally no political parties but partisans for particular independent candidates for the General Council on the basis of competence, personality, and orientation toward Spain or France; various small pressure groups developed in 1972; first formal political party, Andorran Democratic Association, was formed in 1976 and reorganized in 1979 as Andorran Democratic Party
Suffrage: universal at age 18
Elections: *General Council of the Valleys*—last held 11 December 1989 (next to

7

Andorra *(continued)*

be held December 1993); results—percent of vote NA; seats—(28 total) number of seats by party NA
Communists: negligible
Member of: CCC, UNESCO
Diplomatic representation: Andorra has no mission in the US; *US*—includes Andorra within the Barcelona (Spain) Consular District and the US Consul General visits Andorra periodically; Consul General Ruth A. DAVIS; Consulate General at Via Layetana 33, Barcelona 3, Spain (mailing address APO NY 09286); telephone [34] (3) 319-9550
Flag: three equal vertical bands of blue (hoist side), yellow, and red with the national coat of arms centered in the yellow band; the coat of arms features a quartered shield; similar to the flag of Chad which does not have a national coat of arms in the center; also similar to the flag of Romania which has a national coat of arms featuring a mountain landscape below a red five-pointed star and the words *REPUBLICA SOCIALISTA ROMANIA* at the bottom

Economy

Overview: The mainstay of Andorra's economy is tourism. An estimated 12 million tourists visit annually, attracted by Andorra's duty-free status and by its summer and winter resorts. Agricultural production is limited by a scarcity of arable land, and most food has to be imported. The principal livestock activity is sheep raising. Manufacturing consists mainly of cigarettes, cigars, and furniture. The rapid pace of European economic integration is a potential threat to Andorra's advantages from its duty-free status.
GNP: $NA, per capita $NA; real growth rate NA%
Inflation rate (consumer prices): NA%
Unemployment rate: NA%
Budget: revenues $NA; expenditures $NA, including capital expenditures of $NA
Exports: $0.017 million (f.o.b., 1986); *commodities*—electricity; *partners*—France, Spain
Imports: $531 million (f.o.b., 1986); *commodities*—NA; *partners*—France, Spain
External debt: $NA
Industrial production: growth rate NA%
Electricity: 35,000 kW capacity; 140 million kWh produced, 2,800 kWh per capita (1989)
Industries: tourism (particularly skiing), sheep, timber, tobacco, smuggling, banking
Agriculture: sheep raising; small quantities of tobacco, rye, wheat, barley, oats, and some vegetables
Aid: none

Currency: French franc (plural—francs) and Spanish peseta (plural—pesetas); 1 French franc (F) = 100 centimes and 1 Spanish peseta (Pta) = 100 céntimos
Exchange rates: French francs (F) per US$1—5.7598 (January 1990), 6.3801 (1989), 5.9569 (1988), 6.0107 (1987), 6.9261 (1986), 8.9852 (1985); Spanish pesetas (Ptas) per US$1—109.69 (January 1990), 118.38 (1989), 116.49 (1988), 123.48 (1987), 140.05 (1986), 170.04 (1985)
Fiscal year: calendar year

Communications

Highways: 96 km
Telecommunications: international digital microwave network; international landline circuits to France and Spain; stations—1 AM, no FM, no TV; 17,700 telephones

Defense Forces

Note: defense is the responsibility of France and Spain

Angola

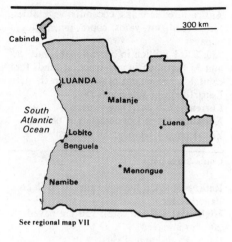

See regional map VII

Geography

Total area: 1,246,700 km²; land area: 1,246,700 km²
Comparative area: slightly less than twice the size of Texas
Land boundaries: 5,198 km total; Congo 201 km, Namibia 1,376 km, Zaire 2,511 km, Zambia 1,110 km
Coastline: 1,600 km
Maritime claims:
   Exclusive fishing zone: 200 nm
   Territorial sea: 20 nm
Disputes: civil war since independence on 11 November 1975
Climate: semiarid in south and along coast to Luanda; north has cool, dry season (May to October) and hot, rainy season (November to April)
Terrain: narrow coastal plain rises abruptly to vast interior plateau
Natural resources: petroleum, diamonds, iron ore, phosphates, copper, feldspar, gold, bauxite, uranium
Land use: 2% arable land; NEGL% permanent crops; 23% meadows and pastures; 43% forest and woodland; 32% other
Environment: locally heavy rainfall causes periodic flooding on plateau; desertification
Note: Cabinda is separated from rest of country by Zaire

People

Population: 8,534,483 (July 1990), growth rate 2.9% (1990)
Birth rate: 47 births/1,000 population (1990)
Death rate: 20 deaths/1,000 population (1990)
Net migration rate: 2 migrants/1,000 population (1990)
Infant mortality rate: 158 deaths/1,000 live births (1990)
Life expectancy at birth: 42 years male, 46 years female (1990)

Total fertility rate: 6.7 children born/
woman (1990)
Nationality: noun—Angolan(s);
adjective—Angolan
Ethnic divisions: 37% Ovimbundu, 25%
Kimbundu, 13% Bakongo, 2% Mestiço,
1% European
Religion: 47% indigenous beliefs, 38% Roman Catholic, 15% Protestant (est.)
Language: Portuguese (official); various
Bantu dialects
Literacy: 41%
Labor force: 2,783,000 economically active; 85% agriculture, 15% industry (1985
est.)
Organized labor: about 450,695 (1980)

Government

Long-form name: People's Republic of
Angola
Type: Marxist people's republic
Capital: Luanda
Administrative divisions: 18 provinces (províncias, singular—província); Bengo,
Benguela, Bié, Cabinda, Cuando
Cubango, Cuanza Norte, Cuanza Sul, Cunene, Huambo, Huíla, Luanda, Lunda
Norte, Lunda Sul, Malanje, Moxico, Namibe, Uíge, Zaire
Independence: 11 November 1975 (from
Portugal)
Constitution: 11 November 1975; revised
7 January 1978 and 11 August 1980
Legal system: based on Portuguese civil
law system and customary law, but being
modified along socialist lines
National holiday: Independence Day, 11
November (1975)
Executive branch: president, chairman of
the Council of Ministers, Council of Ministers (cabinet)
Legislative branch: unicameral National
People's Assembly
Judicial branch: Supreme Court (Tribunal
da Relacao)
Leaders: *Chief of State and Head of Government*—President José Eduardo dos
SANTOS (since 21 September 1979)
Political parties and leaders: only party—
Popular Movement for the Liberation of
Angola-Labor Party (MPLA-Labor
Party), José Eduardo dos Santos; National
Union for the Total Independence of
Angola (UNITA), lost to the MPLA with
Cuban military support in immediate
postindependence struggle, now carrying
out insurgency
Suffrage: universal adult at age NA
Elections: none held to date
Member of: ACP, AfDB, CCC, FAO, G-
77, GATT (de facto), ICAO, IFAD, ILO,
IMO, INTELSAT, ITU, NAM, OAU,
SADCC, UN, UNESCO, UNICEF,
UPU, WFTU, WHO, WMO

Diplomatic representation: none
Flag: two equal horizontal bands of red
(top) and black with a centered yellow emblem consisting of a five-pointed star
within half a cogwheel crossed by a machete (in the style of a hammer and sickle)

Economy

Overview: Subsistence agriculture provides
the main livelihood for 80-90% of the population, but accounts for only 10-20% of
GDP. Oil production is the most lucrative
sector of the economy, contributing about
50% to GDP. In recent years, however,
the impact of fighting an internal war has
severely affected the economy and food
has to be imported.
GDP: $5.0 billion, per capita $600; real
growth rate 9.2% (1988 est.)
Inflation rate (consumer prices): NA%
Unemployment rate: NA%
Budget: revenues NA; expenditures $2.7
billion, including capital expenditures of
NA (1986 est.)
Exports: $2.9 billion (f.o.b., 1989 est.);
commodities—oil, coffee, diamonds, sisal,
fish and fish products, timber, cotton;
partners—US, USSR, Cuba, Portugal,
Brazil
Imports: $2.5 billion (f.o.b., 1989 est.);
commodities—capital equipment
(machinery and electrical equipment),
food, vehicles and spare parts, textiles and
clothing, medicines; substantial military
deliveries; *partners*—US, USSR, Cuba,
Portugal, Brazil
External debt: $3.0 billion (1989)
Industrial production: growth rate NA%
Electricity: 506,000 kW capacity; 770 million kWh produced, 90 kWh per capita
(1989)
Industries: petroleum, mining (phosphate
rock, diamonds), fish processing, brewing,
tobacco, sugar, textiles, cement, food processing, building construction
Agriculture: cash crops—coffee, sisal,
corn, cotton, sugar, manioc, tobacco; food
crops—cassava, corn, vegetables, plantains, bananas, and other local foodstuffs;
disruptions caused by civil war and marketing deficiencies require food imports
Aid: US commitments, including Ex-Im
(FY70-88), $263 million; Western (non-
US) countries, ODA and OOF bilateral
commitments (1970-87), $903 million;
Communist countries (1970-88), $1.3 billion
Currency: kwanza (plural—kwanza); 1
kwanza (Kz) = 100 lwei
Exchange rates: kwanza (Kz) per US$1—
29.62 (fixed rate since 1976)
Fiscal year: calendar year

Communications

Railroads: 3,189 km total; 2,879 km
1.067-meter gauge, 310 km 0.600-meter
gauge; limited trackage in use because of
insurgent attacks; sections of the Benguela
Railroad closed because of insurgency
Highways: 73,828 km total; 8,577 km
bituminous-surface treatment, 29,350 km
crushed stone, gravel, or improved earth,
remainder unimproved earth
Inland waterways: 1,295 km navigable
Pipelines: crude oil, 179 km
Ports: Luanda, Lobito, Namibe, Cabinda
Merchant marine: 12 ships (1,000 GRT or
over) totaling 66,348 GRT/102,825 DWT;
includes 11 cargo, 1 petroleum, oils, and
lubricants (POL) tanker
Civil air: 27 major transport aircraft
Airports: 317 total, 184 usable; 28 with
permanent-surface runways; 1 with runways over 3,659 m; 12 with runways
2,440-3,659 m; 60 with runways 1,220-
2,439 m
Telecommunications: fair system of wire,
radio relay, and troposcatter routes; high
frequency used extensively for military/
Cuban links; 40,300 telephones; stations—
17 AM, 13 FM, 2 TV; 2 Atlantic Ocean
INTELSAT earth stations

Defense Forces

Branches: Army, Navy, Air Force/Air
Defense; paramilitary forces—People's
Defense Organization and Territorial
Troops, Frontier Guard, Popular Vigilance
Brigades
Military manpower: males 15-49,
2,049,295; 1,030,868 fit for military service; 90,877 reach military age (18) annually
Defense expenditures: NA

Anguilla
(dependent territory of the UK)

See regional map III

Geography

Total area: 91 km²; land area: 91 km²
Comparative area: about half the size of Washington, DC
Land boundaries: none
Coastline: 61 km
Maritime claims:
 Continental shelf: 200 meters or to depth of exploitation
 Exclusive fishing zone: 200 nm
 Territorial sea: 3 nm
Climate: tropical; moderated by northeast trade winds
Terrain: flat and low-lying island of coral and limestone
Natural resources: negligible; salt, fish, lobsters
Land use: NA% arable land; NA% permanent crops; NA% meadows and pastures; NA% forest and woodland; NA% other; mostly rock with sparse scrub oak, few trees, some commercial salt ponds
Environment: frequent hurricanes, other tropical storms (July to October)
Note: located 270 km east of Puerto Rico

People

Population: 6,883 (July 1990), growth rate 0.6% (1990)
Birth rate: 24 births/1,000 population (1990)
Death rate: 9 deaths/1,000 population (1990)
Net migration rate: −10 migrants/1,000 population (1990)
Infant mortality rate: 18 deaths/1,000 live births (1990)
Life expectancy at birth: 71 years male, 76 years female (1990)
Total fertility rate: 3.1 children born/woman (1990)
Nationality: noun—Anguillan(s); adjective—Anguillan
Ethnic divisions: mainly of black African descent

Religion: Anglican, Methodist, and Roman Catholic
Language: English (official)
Literacy: 80%
Labor force: 2,780 (1984)
Organized labor: NA

Government

Long-form name: none
Type: dependent territory of the UK
Capital: The Valley
Administrative divisions: none (dependent territory of the UK)
Independence: none (dependent territory of the UK)
Constitution: 1 April 1982
Legal system: based on English common law
National holiday: Anguilla Day, 30 May
Executive branch: British monarch, governor, chief minister, Executive Council (cabinet)
Legislative branch: unicameral House of Assembly
Judicial branch: High Court
Leaders: *Chief of State*—Queen ELIZABETH II (since 6 February 1952), represented by Governor Geoffrey O. WHITTAKER (since NA 1987);
Head of Government—Chief Minister Emile GUMBS (since NA March 1984, served previously from February 1977 to May 1980)
Political parties and leaders: Anguilla National Alliance (ANA), Emile Gumbs; Anguilla United Party (AUP), Ronald Webster; Anguilla Democratic Party (ADP), Victor Banks
Suffrage: universal at age 18
Elections: *House of Assembly*—last held 27 February 1989 (next to be held February 1994); results—percent of vote by party NA; seats—(11 total, 7 elected) ANA 3, AUP 2, ADP 1, independent 1
Communists: none
Member of: Commonwealth
Diplomatic representation: none (dependent territory of the UK)
Flag: two horizontal bands of white (top, almost triple width) and light blue with three orange dolphins in an interlocking circular design centered in the white band

Economy

Overview: Anguilla has few natural resources, and the economy depends heavily on lobster fishing, offshore banking, tourism, and remittances from emigrants. In recent years the economy has benefited from a boom in tourism. Development is planned to improve the infrastructure, particularly transport and tourist facilities, and also light industry. Improvement in

the economy has reduced unemployment from 40% in 1984 to about 5% in 1988.
GDP: $23 million, per capita $3,350 (1988 est.); real growth rate 8.2% (1988)
Inflation rate (consumer prices): 4.5% (1988 est.)
Unemployment rate: 5.0% (1988 est.)
Budget: revenues $9.0 million; expenditures $8.8 million, including capital expenditures of NA (1988 est.)
Exports: $NA; *commodities*—lobsters and salt; *partners*—NA
Imports: $NA; *commodities*—NA; *partners* —NA
External debt: $NA
Industrial production: growth rate NA%
Electricity: 3,000 kW capacity; 9 million kWh produced, 1,300 kWh per capita (1988)
Industries: tourism, boat building, salt, fishing (including lobster)
Agriculture: pigeon peas, corn, sweet potatoes, sheep, goats, pigs, cattle, poultry
Aid: Western (non-US) countries, ODA and OOF bilateral commitments (1970-87), $33 million
Currency: East Caribbean dollar (plural—dollars); 1 EC dollar (EC$) = 100 cents
Exchange rates: East Caribbean dollars (EC$) per US$1—2.70 (fixed rate since 1976)
Fiscal year: NA

Communications

Highways: 60 km surfaced
Ports: Road Bay, Blowing Point
Civil air: no major transport aircraft
Airports: 3 total, 3 usable; 1 with permanent-surface runways of 1,100 m (Wallblake Airport)
Telecommunications: modern internal telephone system; 890 telephones; stations—3 AM, 1 FM, no TV; radio relay link to island of St. Martin

Defense Forces

Note: defense is the responsibility of the UK

Antarctica

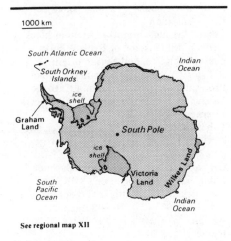

1000 km

South Atlantic Ocean
South Orkney Islands
Indian Ocean
ice shelf
Graham Land
South Pole
ice shelf
Victoria Land
Wilkes Land
South Pacific Ocean
Indian Ocean

See regional map XII

Geography

Total area: about 14,000,000 km^2; land area: about 14,000,000 km^2
Comparative area: slightly less than 1.5 times the size of the US; second-smallest continent (after Australia)
Land boundaries: see entry on **Disputes**
Coastline: 17,968 km
Maritime claims: see entry on **Disputes**
Disputes: Antarctic Treaty suspends all claims; sections (some overlapping) claimed by Argentina, Australia, Chile, France (Adélie Land), New Zealand (Ross Dependency), Norway (Queen Maud Land), and UK; Brazil claims a Zone of Interest; the US and USSR do not recognize the territorial claims of other nations and have made no claims themselves (but reserve the right to do so); no formal claims have been made in the sector between 90° west and 150° west
Climate: severe low temperatures vary with latitude, elevation, and distance from the ocean; East Antarctica colder than Antarctic Peninsula in the west; warmest temperatures occur in January along the coast and average slightly below freezing
Terrain: about 98% thick continental ice sheet, with average elevations between 2,000 and 4,000 meters; mountain ranges up to 5,000 meters high; ice-free coastal areas include parts of southern Victoria Land, Wilkes Land, and the scientific research areas of Graham Land and Ross Island on McMurdo Sound; glaciers form ice shelves along about half of coastline
Natural resources: coal and iron ore; chromium, copper, gold, nickel, platinum, and hydrocarbons have been found in small quantities along the coast; offshore deposits of oil and gas
Land use: 0% arable land; 0% permanent crops; 0% meadows and pastures; 0% forest and woodland; 100% other (98% ice, 2% barren rock)

Environment: mostly uninhabitable; katabatic (gravity) winds blow coastward from the high interior; frequent blizzards form near the foot of the plateau; cyclonic storms form over the ocean and move clockwise around the coast; during summer more solar radiation reaches the surface at the South Pole than is received at the Equator in an equivalent period; in October 1987 it was reported that the ozone shield, which protects the Earth's surface from harmful ultraviolet radiation, has dwindled to its lowest level ever over Antarctica; subject to active volcanism (Deception Island)
Note: the coldest continent

People

Population: no indigenous inhabitants; staffing of research stations varies seasonally
Summer (January) population—3,330; Argentina 179, Australia 216, Brazil 36, Chile 124, China 62, France 46, FRG 9, GDR 15, India 59, Italy 121, Japan 52, NZ 251, Poland 19, South Africa 102, South Korea 17, UK 72, Uruguay 47, US 1,250, USSR 653 (1986-87)
Winter (July) population—1,148 total; Argentina 149, Australia 82, Brazil 11, Chile 59, China 16, France 32, FRG 9, GDR 9, India 17, Japan 37, NZ 11, Poland 19, South Africa 15, UK 61, Uruguay 10, US 242, USSR 369 (1986-87)
Year-round stations—43 total; Argentina 7, Australia 3, Brazil 1, Chile 3, China 1, France 1, FRG 1, GDR 1, India 1, Japan 2, NZ 1, Poland 1, South Africa 1, South Korea 1, UK 6, Uruguay 1, US 3, USSR 8 (1986-87)
Summer only stations—26 total; Argentina 3, Australia 3, Chile 4, Italy 1, Japan 1, NZ 2, South Africa 2, US 4, USSR 6 (1986-87)

Government

Long-form name: none
Type: The Antarctic Treaty, signed on 1 December 1959 and entered into force on 23 June 1961, established, for at least 30 years, a legal framework for peaceful use, scientific research, and suspension of territorial claims. Administration is carried out through consultative member meetings—the 14th and last meeting was held in Rio de Janeiro (Brazil) in October 1987.
Consultative (voting) members include claimant nations (they claim portions of Antarctica as national territory and some claims overlap) and nonclaimant nations (they have made no claims to Antarctic territory, although the US and USSR have reserved the right to do so and do

not recognize the claims of others); the year in parentheses indicates when an acceding nation was voted to full consultative (voting) status, while no date indicates an original 1959 treaty signatory. Claimant nations are—Argentina, Australia, Chile, France, New Zealand, Norway, and the UK. Nonclaimant nations are—Belgium, Brazil (1983), China (1985), FRG (1981), GDR (1987), India (1983), Italy (1987), Japan, Poland (1977), South Africa, Uruguay (1985), US, and the USSR.
Acceding (nonvoting) members, with year of accession in parenthesis, are—Austria (1987), Bulgaria (1978), Cuba (1984), Czechoslovakia (1962), Denmark (1965), Finland (1984), Greece (1987), Hungary (1984), Netherlands (1987), North Korea (1987), Papua New Guinea (1981), Peru (1981), Romania (1971), South Korea (1986), Spain (1982), and Sweden (1984).
Antarctic Treaty Summary: Article 1—area to be used for peaceful purposes only and military activity, such as weapons testing, is prohibited, but military personnel and equipment may be used for scientific purposes; Article 2—freedom of scientific investigation and cooperation shall continue; Article 3—free exchange of information and personnel; Article 4—does not recognize, dispute, or establish territorial claims and no new claims shall be asserted while the treaty is in force; Article 5—prohibits nuclear explosions or disposal of radioactive wastes; Article 6—includes under the treaty all land and ice shelves south of 60° 00′ south, but that the water areas be covered by international law; Article 7—treaty-state observers have free access, including aerial observation, to any area and may inspect all stations, installations, and equipment; advance notice of all activities and the introduction of military personnel must be given; Article 8—allows for jurisdiction over observers and scientists by their own states; Article 9—frequent consultative meetings take place among member nations and acceding nations given consultative status; Article 10—treaty states will discourage activities by any country in Antarctica that are contrary to the treaty; Article 11—disputes to be settled peacefully by the parties concerned or, ultimately, by the ICJ; Articles 12, 13, 14—deal with upholding, interpreting, and amending the treaty among involved nations.
Other agreements: Convention on the Conservation of Antarctic Marine Living Resources; Convention for the Conservation of Antarctic Seals; a mineral resources agreement is currently undergoing ratification by the Antarctic Treaty consultative parties

11

Antarctica (continued)

Economy

Overview: No economic activity at present except for fishing off the coast and small-scale tourism, both based abroad. Exploitation of mineral resources will be held back by technical difficulties, high costs, and objections by environmentalists.

Communications

Airports: 39 total; 25 usable; none with permanent surface runways; 3 with runways over 3,659 m; 6 with runways 2,440-3,659 m; 4 with runways 1,220-2,439 m
Ports: none; offshore anchorage only

Defense Forces

Note: none; Article 7 of the Antarctic Treaty states that advance notice of all activities and the introduction of military personnel must be given

Antigua and Barbuda

20 km

Barbuda

Caribbean Sea

SAINT JOHN'S · *Antigua*

● *Redonda*

See regional map III

Geography

Total area: 440 km²; land area: 440 km²; includes Redonda
Comparative area: slightly less than 2.5 times the size of Washington, DC
Land boundaries: none
Coastline: 153 km
Maritime claims:
Contiguous zone: 24 nm
Extended economic zone: 200 nm
Territorial sea: 12 nm
Climate: tropical marine; little seasonal temperature variation
Terrain: mostly low-lying limestone and coral islands with some higher volcanic areas
Natural resources: negligible; pleasant climate fosters tourism
Land use: 18% arable land; 0% permanent crops; 7% meadows and pastures; 16% forest and woodland; 59% other
Environment: subject to hurricanes and tropical storms (July to October); insufficient freshwater resources; deeply indented coastline provides many natural harbors
Note: 420 km east-southeast of Puerto Rico

People

Population: 63,726 (July 1990), growth rate 0.3% (1990)
Birth rate: 18 births/1,000 population (1990)
Death rate: 6 deaths/1,000 population (1990)
Net migration rate: −10 migrants/1,000 population (1990)
Infant mortality rate: 23 deaths/1,000 live births (1990)
Life expectancy at birth: 70 years male, 74 years female (1990)
Total fertility rate: 1.7 children born/woman (1990)

Nationality: noun—Antiguan(s); adjective—Antiguan
Ethnic divisions: almost entirely of black African origin; some of British, Portuguese, Lebanese, and Syrian origin
Religion: Anglican (predominant), other Protestant sects, some Roman Catholic
Language: English (official), local dialects
Literacy: 90% (est.)
Labor force: 30,000; 82% commerce and services, 11% agriculture, 7% industry (1983)
Organized labor: Antigua and Barbuda Public Service Association (ABPSA), membership 500; Antigua Trades and Labor Union (ATLU), 10,000 members; Antigua Workers Union (AWU), 10,000 members (1986 est.)

Government

Long-form name: none
Type: parliamentary democracy
Capital: Saint John's
Administrative divisions: 6 parishes and 2 dependencies*; Barbuda*, Redonda*, Saint George, Saint John, Saint Mary, Saint Paul, Saint Peter, Saint Philip
Independence: 1 November 1981 (from UK)
Constitution: 1 November 1981
Legal system: based on English common law
National holiday: Independence Day, 1 November (1981)
Executive branch: British monarch, governor general, prime minister, deputy prime minister, Cabinet
Legislative branch: bicameral Parliament consists of an upper house or Senate and a lower house or House of Representatives
Judicial branch: Eastern Caribbean Supreme Court
Leaders: *Chief of State*—Queen ELIZABETH II (since 6 February 1952), represented by Governor General Sir Wilfred Ebenezer JACOBS (since 1 November 1981, previously Governor since 1976);
Head of Government—Prime Minister Vere Cornwall BIRD, Sr. (since NA 1976); Deputy Prime Minister Lester BIRD (since NA 1976)
Political parties and leaders: Antigua Labor Party (ALP), Vere C. Bird, Sr., Lester Bird; United National Democratic Party (UNDP), Dr. Ivor Heath
Suffrage: universal at age 18
Elections: *House of Representatives*—last held 9 March 1989 (next to be held 1994); results—percentage of vote by party NA; seats—(17 total) ALP 15, UNDP 1, independent 1
Communists: negligible
Other political or pressure groups: Antigua Caribbean Liberation Movement (ACLM), a small leftist nationalist group

led by Leonard (Tim) Hector; Antigua Trades and Labor Union (ATLU), headed by Noel Thomas
Member of: ACP, CARICOM, Commonwealth, FAO, G-77, IBRD, ICAO, ILO, IMF, ISO, OAS, UN, UNESCO, WHO, WMO
Diplomatic representation: Ambassador Edmund Hawkins LAKE; Chancery at Suite 2H, 3400 International Drive NW, Washington DC 20008; telephone (202) 362-5211 or 5166, 5122, 5225; there is an Antiguan Consulate in Miami; *US*—the US Ambassador to Barbados is accredited to Antigua and Barbuda, and in his absence, the Embassy is headed by Chargé d'Affaires Roger R. GAMBLE; Embassy at Queen Elizabeth Highway, Saint John's (mailing address is FPO Miami 34054); telephone (809) 462-3505 or 3506
Flag: red with an inverted isosceles triangle based on the top edge of the flag; the triangle contains three horizontal bands of black (top), light blue, and white with a yellow rising sun in the black band

Economy

Overview: The economy is primarily service oriented, with tourism the most important determinant of economic performance. During the period 1983-87, real GDP expanded at an annual average rate of 8%. Tourism's contribution to GDP, as measured by value added in hotels and restaurants, rose from about 14% in 1983 to 17% in 1987, and stimulated growth in other sectors—particularly in construction, communications, and public utilities. During the same period the combined share of agriculture and manufacturing declined from 12% to less than 10%. Antigua and Barbuda is one of the few areas in the Caribbean experiencing a labor shortage in some sectors of the economy.
GDP: $353.5 million, per capita $5,550; real growth rate 6.2% (1989 est.)
Inflation rate (consumer prices): 7.1% (1988 est.)
Unemployment rate: 5.0% (1988 est.)
Budget: revenues $77 million; expenditures $81 million, including capital expenditures of $13 million (1988 est.)
Exports: $30.4 million (f.o.b., 1988 est.); *commodities*—petroleum products 46%, manufactures 29%, food and live animals 14%, machinery and transport equipment 11%; *partners*—Trinidad and Tobago 40%, Barbados 8%, US 0.3%
Imports: $302.1 million (c.i.f., 1988 est.); *commodities*—food and live animals, machinery and transport equipment, manufactures, chemicals, oil; *partners*—US 27%, UK 14%, CARICOM 7%, Canada 4%, other 48%
External debt: $245.4 million (1987)

Industrial production: growth rate 10% (1987)
Electricity: 49,000 kW capacity; 90 million kWh produced, 1,410 kWh per capita (1989)
Industries: tourism, construction, light manufacturing (clothing, alcohol, household appliances)
Agriculture: accounts for 4% of GDP; expanding output of cotton, fruits, vegetables, and livestock sector; other crops—bananas, coconuts, cucumbers, mangoes; not self-sufficient in food
Aid: Western (non-US) countries, ODA and OOF bilateral commitments (1970-87), $40 million
Currency: East Caribbean dollar (plural—dollars); 1 EC dollar (EC$) = 100 cents
Exchange rates: East Caribbean dollars (EC$) per US$1—2.70 (fixed rate since 1976)
Fiscal year: 1 April-31 March

Communications

Railroads: 64 km 0.760-meter narrow gauge and 13 km 0.610-meter gauge used almost exclusively for handling sugarcane
Highways: 240 km
Ports: St. John's
Merchant marine: 80 ships (1,000 GRT or over) totaling 307,315 GRT/501,552 DWT; includes 50 cargo, 4 refrigerated cargo, 8 container, 8 roll-on/roll-off cargo, 2 petroleum, oils, and lubricants (POL) tanker, 5 chemical tanker, 2 liquefied gas, 1 short-sea passenger; note—a flag of convenience registry
Civil air: 10 major transport aircraft
Airports: 3 total, 3 usable; 2 with permanent-surface runways; 1 with runways 2,440-3,659 m; 2 with runways less than 2,440 m
Telecommunications: good automatic telephone system; 6,700 telephones; tropospheric scatter links with Saba and Guadeloupe; stations—4 AM, 2 FM, 2 TV, 2 shortwave; 1 coaxial submarine cable; 1 Atlantic Ocean INTELSAT earth station

Defense Forces

Branches: Antigua and Barbuda Defense Force, Royal Antigua and Barbuda Police Force (includes the Coast Guard)
Military manpower: NA
Defense expenditures: NA

Arctic Ocean

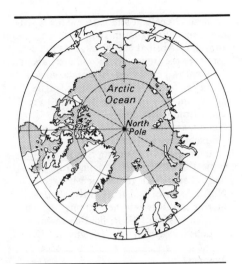

Geography

Total area: 14,056,000 km²; includes Baffin Bay, Barents Sea, Beaufort Sea, Chukchi Sea, East Siberian Sea, Greenland Sea, Hudson Bay, Hudson Strait, Kara Sea, Laptev Sea, and other tributary water bodies
Comparative area: slightly more than 1.5 times the size of the US; smallest of the world's four oceans (after Pacific Ocean, Atlantic Ocean, and Indian Ocean)
Coastline: 45,389 km
Climate: persistent cold and relatively narrow annual temperature ranges; winters characterized by continuous darkness, cold and stable weather conditions, and clear skies; summers characterized by continuous daylight, damp and foggy weather, and weak cyclones with rain or snow
Terrain: central surface covered by a perennial drifting polar icepack which averages about 3 meters in thickness, although pressure ridges may be three times that size; clockwise drift pattern in the Beaufort Gyral Stream, but nearly straight line movement from the New Siberian Islands (USSR) to Denmark Strait (between Greenland and Iceland); the ice pack is surrounded by open seas during the summer, but more than doubles in size during the winter and extends to the encircling land masses; the ocean floor is about 50% continental shelf (highest percentage of any ocean) with the remainder a central basin interrupted by three submarine ridges (Alpha Cordillera, Nansen Cordillera, and Lomonsov Ridge); maximum depth is 4,665 meters in the Fram Basin
Natural resources: sand and gravel aggregates, placer deposits, polymetallic nodules, oil and gas fields, fish, marine mammals (seals, whales)
Environment: endangered marine species include walruses and whales; ice islands occasionally break away from northern Ellesmere Island; icebergs calved from

western Greenland and extreme northeastern Canada; maximum snow cover in March or April about 20 to 50 centimeters over the frozen ocean and lasts about 10 months; permafrost in islands; virtually icelocked from October to June; fragile ecosystem slow to change and slow to recover from disruptions or damage
Note: major chokepoint is the southern Chukchi Sea (northern access to the Pacific Ocean via the Bering Strait); ships subject to superstructure icing from October to May; strategic location between North America and the USSR; shortest marine link between the extremes of eastern and western USSR; floating research stations operated by the US and USSR

Economy

Overview: Economic activity is limited to the exploitation of natural resources, including crude oil, natural gas, fishing, and sealing.

Communications

Ports: Churchill (Canada), Murmansk (USSR), Prudhoe Bay (US)
Telecommunications: no submarine cables
Note: sparse network of air, ocean, river, and land routes; the Northwest Passage (North America) and Northern Sea Route (Asia) are important waterways

Argentina

See regional map IV

Geography

Total area: 2,766,890 km²; land area: 2,736,690 km²
Comparative area: slightly more than four times the size of Texas
Land boundaries: 9,665 km total; Bolivia 832 km, Brazil 1,224 km, Chile 5,150 km, Paraguay 1,880 km, Uruguay 579 km
Coastline: 4,989 km
Maritime claims:
  Continental shelf: 200 meters or to depth of exploitation
  Territorial sea: 200 nm (overflight and navigation permitted beyond 12 nm)
Disputes: short section of the boundary with Uruguay is in dispute; short section of the boundary with Chile is indefinite; claims British-administered Falkland Islands (Islas Malvinas); claims British-administered South Georgia and the South Sandwich Islands; territorial claim in Antarctica
Climate: mostly temperate; arid in southeast; subantarctic in southwest
Terrain: rich plains of the Pampas in northern half, flat to rolling plateau of Patagonia in south, rugged Andes along western border
Natural resources: fertile plains of the pampas, lead, zinc, tin, copper, iron ore, manganese, crude oil, uranium
Land use: 9% arable land; 4% permanent crops; 52% meadows and pastures; 22% forest and woodland; 13% other; includes 1% irrigated
Environment: Tucumán and Mendoza areas in Andes subject to earthquakes; pamperos are violent windstorms that can strike Pampas and northeast; irrigated soil degradation; desertification; air and water pollution in Buenos Aires
Note: second-largest country in South America (after Brazil); strategic location relative to sea lanes between South Atlantic and South Pacific Oceans (Strait of Magellan, Beagle Channel, Drake Passage)

People

Population: 32,290,966 (July 1990), growth rate 1.2% (1990)
Birth rate: 20 births/1,000 population (1990)
Death rate: 9 deaths/1,000 population (1990)
Net migration rate: NEGL migrants/1,000 population (1990)
Infant mortality rate: 32 deaths/1,000 live births (1990)
Life expectancy at birth: 67 years male, 74 years female (1990)
Total fertility rate: 2.8 children born/woman (1990)
Nationality: noun—Argentine(s); adjective—Argentine
Ethnic divisions: 85% white, 15% mestizo, Indian, or other nonwhite groups
Religion: 90% nominally Roman Catholic (less than 20% practicing), 2% Protestant, 2% Jewish, 6% other
Language: Spanish (official), English, Italian, German, French
Literacy: 94%
Labor force: 10,900,000; 12% agriculture, 31% industry, 57% services (1985 est.)
Organized labor: 3,000,000; 28% of labor force

Government

Long-form name: Argentine Republic
Type: republic
Capital: Buenos Aires (tentative plans to move to Viedma by 1990 indefinitely postponed)
Administrative divisions: 22 provinces (provincias, singular—provincia), 1 national territory* (territorio nacional), and 1 district** (distrito); Buenos Aires, Catamarca, Chaco, Chubut, Córdoba, Corrientes, Distrito Federal**, Entre Ríos, Formosa, Jujuy, La Pampa, La Rioja, Mendoza, Misiones, Neuquén, Río Negro, Salta, San Juan, San Luis, Santa Cruz, Santa Fe, Santiago del Estero, Tierra del Fuego and Antártida e Islas del Atlántico Sur*, Tucumán
Independence: 9 July 1816 (from Spain)
Constitution: 1 May 1853
Legal system: mixture of US and West European legal systems; has not accepted compulsory ICJ jurisdiction
National holiday: National Day, 25 May (1810)
Executive branch: president, vice president, Cabinet
Legislative branch: bicameral National Congress (Congreso Nacional) consists of an upper chamber or Senate (Senado) and

a lower chamber or Chamber of Deputies (Camera de Diputados)

Judicial branch: Supreme Court (Corte Suprema)

Leaders: *Chief of State and Head of Government*—President Carlos Saúl MENEM (since 8 July 1989); Vice President Eduardo DUHALDE (since 8 July 1989)

Political parties and leaders: Justicialist Party (JP), Antonio Cafiero, Peronist umbrella political organization; Radical Civic Union (UCR), Raúl Alfonsín, moderately left of center; Union of the Democratic Center (UCEDE), Alvaro Alsogaray, conservative party; Intransigent Party (PI), Dr. Oscar Alende, leftist party; several provincial parties

Suffrage: universal at age 18

Elections: *President*—last held 14 May 1989 (next to be held May 1995); results—Carlos Saúl Menem was elected; *Chamber of Deputies*—last held 14 May 1989 (next to be held May 1991); results—JP 47%, UCR 30%, UDC 7%, other 16%; seats—(254 total); JP 122, UCR 93, UDC 11, other 28

Communists: some 70,000 members in various party organizations, including a small nucleus of activists

Other political or pressure groups: Peronist-dominated labor movement, General Confederation of Labor (Peronist-leaning umbrella labor organization), Argentine Industrial Union (manufacturers' association), Argentine Rural Society (large landowners' association), business organizations, students, the Roman Catholic Church, the Armed Forces

Member of: CCC, FAO, G-77, GATT, Group of Eight, IADB, IAEA, IBRD, ICAC, ICAO, IDA, IDB—Inter-American Development Bank, IFAD, IFC, IHO, ILO, IMF, IMO, INTELSAT, INTERPOL, IOOC, ISO, ITU, IWC—International Whaling Commission, IWC—International Wheat Council, LAIA, NAM, OAS, PAHO, SELA, UN, UNESCO, UPU, WFTU, WHO, WMO, WTO, WSG

Diplomatic representation: Ambassador Guido Jose Maria DI TELLA; Chancery at 1600 New Hampshire Avenue NW, Washington DC 20009; telephone 202) 939-6400 through 6403; there are Argentine Consulates General in Houston, Miami, New Orleans, New York, San Francisco, and San Juan (Puerto Rico), and Consulates in Baltimore, Chicago, and Los Angeles; *US*—Ambassador Terence A. TODMAN; Embassy at 4300 Colombia, 1425 Buenos Aires (mailing address is APO Miami 34034); telephone [54] (1) 774-7611 or 8811, 9911

Flag: three equal horizontal bands of light blue (top), white, and light blue; centered in the white band is a radiant yellow sun with a human face known as the Sun of May

Economy

Overview: Argentina is rich in natural resources, and has a highly literate population, an export-oriented agricultural sector, and a diversified industrial base. Nevertheless, the economy has encountered major problems in recent years, leading to a recession in 1988-89. Economic growth slowed to 2.0% in 1987 and to −1.8% in 1988; a sharp decline of −5.5% has been estimated for 1989. A widening public-sector deficit and a multidigit inflation rate has dominated the economy over the past three years, reaching about 5,000% in 1989. Since 1978, Argentina's external debt has nearly doubled to $60 billion, creating severe debt-servicing difficulties and hurting the country's creditworthiness with international lenders.

GNP: $72.0 billion, per capita $2,217; real growth rate −5.5% (1989 est.)

Inflation rate (consumer prices): 4,925% (1989)

Unemployment rate: 8.5% (1989 est.)

Budget: revenues $11.5 billion; expenditures $13.0 billion, including capital expenditures of $0.93 billion (1988)

Exports: $9.6 billion (f.o.b., 1989); *commodities*—meat, wheat, corn, oilseed, hides, wool; *partners*—US 14%, USSR, Italy, Brazil, Japan, Netherlands

Imports: $4.3 billion (c.i.f., 1989); *commodities*—machinery and equipment, chemicals, metals, fuels and lubricants, agricultural products; *partners*—US 25%, Brazil, FRG, Bolivia, Japan, Italy, Netherlands

External debt: $60 billion (December 1989)

Industrial production: growth rate −8% (1989)

Electricity: 16,449,000 kW capacity; 46,590 million kWh produced, 1,460 kWh per capita (1989)

Industries: food processing (especially meat packing), motor vehicles, consumer durables, textiles, chemicals and petrochemicals, printing, metallurgy, steel

Agriculture: accounts for 15% of GNP (including fishing); produces abundant food for both domestic consumption and exports; among world's top five exporters of grain and beef; principal crops—wheat, corn, sorghum, soybeans, sugar beets; 1987 fish catch estimated at 500,000 tons

Aid: US commitments, including Ex-Im (FY70-88), $1.0 billion; Western (non-US) countries, ODA and OOF bilateral commitments (1970-87), $3.6 billion; Communist countries (1970-88), $718 million

Currency: austral (plural—australes); 1 austral (₳) = 100 centavos

Exchange rates: australes (₳) per US$1—1,930 (December 1989), 8.7526 (1988), 2.1443 (1987), 0.9430 (1986), 0.6018 (1985)

Fiscal year: calendar year

Communications

Railroads: 34,172 km total (includes 169 km electrified); includes a mixture of 1.435-meter standard gauge, 1.676-meter broad gauge, 1.000-meter gauge, and 0.750-meter gauge

Highways: 208,350 km total; 47,550 km paved, 39,500 km gravel, 101,000 km improved earth, 20,300 km unimproved earth

Inland waterways: 11,000 km navigable

Pipelines: 4,090 km crude oil; 2,900 km refined products; 9,918 km natural gas

Ports: Bahia Blanca, Buenos Aires, Necochea, Rio Gallegos, Rosario, Santa Fe

Merchant marine: 131 ships (1,000 GRT or over) totaling 1,693,540 GRT/2,707,079 DWT; includes 45 cargo, 6 refrigerated cargo, 6 container, 1 roll-on/roll-off cargo, 1 railcar carrier, 48 petroleum, oils, and lubricants (POL) tanker, 2 chemical tanker, 4 liquefied gas, 18 bulk

Civil air: 54 major transport aircraft

Airports: 1,799 total, 1,617 usable; 132 with permanent-surface runways; 1 with runways over 3,659 m; 30 with runways 2,440-3,659 m; 335 with runways 1,220-2,439 m

Telecommunications: extensive modern system; 2,650,000 telephones (12,000 public telephones); radio relay widely used; stations—171 AM, no FM, 231 TV, 13 shortwave; 2 Atlantic Ocean INTELSAT earth stations; domestic satellite network has 40 stations

Defense Forces

Branches: Argentine Army, Navy of the Argentine Republic, Argentine Air Force, National Gendarmerie, Argentine Naval Prefecture, National Aeronautical Police

Military manpower: males 15-49, 7,860,054; 6,372,189 fit for military service; 277,144 reach military age (20) annually

Defense expenditures: 1.4% of GNP (1987)

Aruba
(part of the Dutch realm)

Caribbean Sea

Druif

ORANJESTAD

Santa Cruz

Sint Nicolaas

10 km

See regional map III

Geography

Total area: 193 km²; land area: 193 km²
Comparative area: slightly larger than Washington, DC
Land boundaries: none
Coastline: 68.5 km
Maritime claims:
Exclusive fishing zone: 12 nm
Territorial sea: 12 nm
Climate: tropical marine; little seasonal temperature variation
Terrain: flat with a few hills; scant vegetation
Natural resources: negligible; white sandy beaches
Land use: 0% arable land; 0% permanent crops; 0% meadows and pastures; 0% forest and woodland; 100% other
Environment: lies outside the Caribbean hurricane belt
Note: 28 km north of Venezuela

People

Population: 62,656 (July 1990), growth rate 0.2% (1990)
Birth rate: 16 births/1,000 population (1990)
Death rate: 6 deaths/1,000 population (1990)
Net migration rate: −8 migrants/1,000 population (1990)
Infant mortality rate: 8 deaths/1,000 live births (1990)
Life expectancy at birth: 72 years male, 80 years female (1990)
Total fertility rate: 1.8 children born/ woman (1990)
Nationality: noun—Aruban(s); adjective— Aruban
Ethnic divisions: 80% mixed European/ Caribbean Indian
Religion: 82% Roman Catholic, 8% Protestant; also small Hindu, Muslim, Confucian, and Jewish minority

Language: Dutch (official), Papiamento (a Spanish, Portuguese, Dutch, English dialect), English (widely spoken), Spanish
Literacy: 95%
Labor force: NA, but most employment is in the tourist industry (1986)
Organized labor: Aruban Workers' Federation (FTA)

Government

Long-form name: none
Type: part of the Dutch realm—full autonomy in internal affairs obtained in 1986 upon separation from the Netherlands Antilles
Capital: Oranjestad
Administrative divisions: none (self-governing part of the Netherlands)
Independence: planned for 1996
Constitution: 1 January 1986
Legal system: based on Dutch civil law system, with some English common law influence
National holiday: Flag Day, 18 March
Executive branch: Dutch monarch, governor, prime minister, Council of Ministers (cabinet)
Legislative branch: unicameral Parliament (Staten)
Judicial branch: Joint High Court of Justice
Leaders: *Chief of State*—Queen BEATRIX Wilhelmina Armgard (since 30 April 1980), represented by Governor General Felipe B. TROMP (since 1 January 1986);
Head of Government—Prime Minister Nelson ODUBER (since NA February 1989)
Political parties and leaders: Electoral Movement Party (MEP), Nelson Oduber; Aruban People's Party (AVP), Henny Eman; National Democratic Action (ADN), Pedro Charro Kelly; New Patriotic Party (PPN), Eddy Werlemen; Aruban Patriotic Party (PPA), Benny Nisbet; Aruban Democratic Party (PDA), Leo Berlinski; Democratic Action 86 (AD'86), Arturo Oduber; governing coalition includes the MEP, PPA, and ADN
Suffrage: universal at age 18
Elections: *Parliament*—last held 6 January 1989 (next to be held by January 1993); results—percent of vote by party NA; seats—(21 total) MEP 10, AVP 8, ADN 1, PPN 1, PPA 1
Diplomatic representation: none (self-governing part of the Netherlands)
Flag: blue with two narrow horizontal yellow stripes across the lower portion and a red, four-pointed star outlined in white in the upper hoist-side corner

Economy

Overview: Tourism is the mainstay of the economy. In 1985 the economy suffered a severe blow when Exxon closed its refinery, a major source of employment and foreign exchange earnings. Economic collapse was prevented by soft loans from the Dutch Government and by a booming tourist industry. Hotel capacity expanded by 20% between 1985 and 1987 and is projected to more than double by 1990. Unemployment has steadily declined from about 20% in 1986 to about 3% in 1988.
GDP: $620 million, per capita $10,000; real growth rate 16.7% (1988 est.)
Inflation rate (consumer prices): 4% (1988 est.)
Unemployment rate: 3% (1988 est.)
Budget: revenues $145 million; expenditures $185 million, including capital expenditures of $42 million (1988)
Exports: $47.5 million (f.o.b., 1988 est.); *commodities*—mostly petroleum products; *partners*—US 64%, EC
Imports: $296.0 million (c.i.f., 1988 est.); *commodities*—food, consumer goods, manufactures; *partners*—US 8%, EC
External debt: $81 million (1987)
Industrial production: growth rate −20% (1984)
Electricity: 310,000 kW capacity; 945 million kWh produced, 15,120 kWh per capita (1989)
Industries: tourism, transshipment facilities
Agriculture: poor quality soils and low rainfall limit agricultural activity to the cultivation of aloes
Aid: none
Currency: Aruban florin (plural—florins); 1 Aruban florin (Af.) = 100 cents
Exchange rates: Aruban florins (Af.) per US$1—1.7900 (fixed rate since 1986)
Fiscal year: calendar year

Communications

Ports: Oranjestad, Sint Nicolaas
Airfield: government-owned airport east of Oranjestad
Telecommunications: generally adequate; extensive interisland radio relay links; 72,168 telephones; stations—4 AM, 4 FM, 1 TV; 1 sea cable to St. Maarten

Defense Forces

Note: defense is the responsibility of the Netherlands until 1996

Ashmore and Cartier Islands

(territory of Australia)

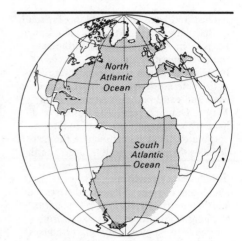

See regional map X

Geography

Total area: 5 km²; land area: 5 km²; includes Ashmore Reef (West, Middle, and East Islets) and Cartier Island
Comparative area: about 8.5 times the size of The Mall in Washington, DC
Land boundaries: none
Coastline: 74.1 km
Maritime claims:
Contiguous zone: 12 nm
Continental shelf: 200 meters or to depth of exploration
Exclusive fishing zone: 200 nm
Territorial sea: 3 nm
Climate: tropical
Terrain: low with sand and coral
Natural resources: fish
Land use: 0% arable land; 0% permanent crops; 0% meadows and pastures; 0% forest and woodland; 100% other—grass and sand
Environment: surrounded by shoals and reefs; Ashmore Reef National Nature Reserve established in August 1983
Note: located in extreme eastern Indian Ocean between Australia and Indonesia 320 km off the northwest coast of Australia

People

Population: no permanent inhabitants; seasonal caretakers

Government

Long-form name: Territory of Ashmore and Cartier Islands
Type: territory of Australia administered by the Australian Ministry for Territories and Local Government
Administrative divisions: none (territory of Australia)
Legal system: relevant laws of the Northern Territory of Australia

Note: administered by the Australian Minister for Arts, Sports, the Environment, Tourism, and Territories Graham Richardson
Diplomatic representation: none (territory of Australia)

Economy

Overview: no economic activity

Communications

Ports: none; offshore anchorage only

Defense Forces

Note: defense is the responsibility of Australia; periodic visits by the Royal Australian Navy and Royal Australian Air Force

Atlantic Ocean

Geography

Total area: 82,217,000 km²; includes Baltic Sea, Black Sea, Caribbean Sea, Davis Strait, Denmark Strait, Drake Passage, Gulf of Mexico, Mediterranean Sea, North Sea, Norwegian Sea, Weddell Sea, and other tributary water bodies
Comparative area: slightly less than nine times the size of the US; second-largest of the world's four oceans (after the Pacific Ocean, but larger than Indian Ocean or Arctic Ocean)
Coastline: 111,866 km
Climate: tropical cyclones (hurricanes) develop off the coast of Africa near Cape Verde and move westward into the Caribbean Sea; hurricanes can occur from May to December, but are most frequent from August to November
Terrain: surface usually covered with sea ice in Labrador Sea, Denmark Strait, and Baltic Sea from October to June; clockwise warm water gyre (broad, circular system of currents) in the north Atlantic, counterclockwise warm water gyre in the south Atlantic; the ocean floor is dominated by the Mid-Atlantic Ridge, a rugged north-south centerline for the entire Atlantic basin; maximum depth is 8,605 meters in the Puerto Rico Trench
Natural resources: oil and gas fields, fish, marine mammals (seals and whales), sand and gravel aggregates, placer deposits, polymetallic nodules, precious stones
Environment: endangered marine species include the manatee, seals, sea lions, turtles, and whales; municipal sludge pollution off eastern US, southern Brazil, and eastern Argentina; oil pollution in Caribbean Sea, Gulf of Mexico, Lake Maracaibo, Mediterranean Sea, and North Sea; industrial waste and municipal sewage pollution in Baltic Sea, North Sea, and Mediterranean Sea; icebergs common in Davis Strait, Denmark Strait, and the northwestern Atlantic from February to

Atlantic Ocean *(continued)*

August and have been spotted as far south as Bermuda and the Madeira Islands; icebergs from Antarctica occur in the extreme southern Atlantic
Note: ships subject to superstructure icing in extreme north Atlantic from October to May and extreme south Atlantic from May to October; persistent fog can be a hazard to shipping from May to September; major choke points include the Dardanelles, Strait of Gibraltar, access to the Panama and Suez Canals; strategic straits include the Dover Strait, Straits of Florida, Mona Passage, The Sound (Øresund), and Windward Passage; north Atlantic shipping lanes subject to icebergs from February to August; the Equator divides the Atlantic Ocean into the North Atlantic Ocean and South Atlantic Ocean

Economy

Overview: Economic activity is limited to exploitation of natural resources, especially fish, dredging aragonite sands (The Bahamas), and crude oil and natural gas production (Caribbean Sea and North Sea).

Communications

Ports: Alexandria (Egypt), Algiers (Algeria), Antwerp (Belgium), Barcelona (Spain), Buenos Aires (Argentina), Casablanca (Morocco), Colon (Panama), Copenhagen (Denmark), Dakar (Senegal), Gdansk (Poland), Hamburg (FRG), Helsinki (Finland), Las Palmas (Canary Islands, Spain), Le Havre (France), Leningrad (USSR), Lisbon (Portugal), London (UK), Marseille (France), Montevideo (Uruguay), Montreal (Canada), Naples (Italy), New Orleans (US), New York (US), Oran (Algeria), Oslo (Norway), Piraeus (Greece), Rio de Janeiro (Brazil), Rotterdam (Netherlands), Stockholm (Sweden)
Telecommunications: numerous submarine cables with most between continental Europe and the UK, North America and the UK, and in the Mediterranean; numerous direct links across Atlantic via INTELSAT satellite network
Note: Kiel Canal and St. Lawrence Seaway are two important waterways

Australia

Timor Sea
Indian Ocean
Darwin
Coral Sea
Alice Springs
Brisbane
Perth
Great Australian Bight
Adelaide
Sydney
CANBERRA
Melbourne
Tasman Sea
Indian Ocean
Tasmania
1000 km

See regional map X

Geography

Total area: 7,686,850 km^2; land area: 7,617,930 km^2; includes Macquarie Island
Comparative area: slightly smaller than the US
Land boundaries: none
Coastline: 25,760 km
Maritime claims:
  Contiguous zone: 12 nm
  Continental shelf: 200 meters or to depth of exploitation
  Exclusive fishing zone: 200 nm
  Territorial sea: 3 nm
Disputes: territorial claim in Antarctica (Australian Antarctic Territory)
Climate: generally arid to semiarid; temperate in south and east; tropical in north
Terrain: mostly low plateau with deserts; fertile plain in southeast
Natural resources: bauxite, coal, iron ore, copper, tin, silver, uranium, nickel, tungsten, mineral sands, lead, zinc, diamonds, natural gas, crude oil
Land use: 6% arable land; NEGL% permanent crops; 58% meadows and pastures; 14% forest and woodland; 22% other; includes NEGL% irrigated
Environment: subject to severe droughts and floods; cyclones along coast; limited freshwater availability; irrigated soil degradation; regular, tropical, invigorating, sea breeze known as the doctor occurs along west coast in summer; desertification
Note: world's smallest continent but sixth-largest country

People

Population: 16,923,478 (July 1990), growth rate 1.3% (1990)
Birth rate: 15 births/1,000 population (1990)
Death rate: 8 deaths/1,000 population (1990)

Net migration rate: 6 migrants/1,000 population (1990)
Infant mortality rate: 8 deaths/1,000 live births (1990)
Life expectancy at birth: 73 years male, 80 years female (1990)
Total fertility rate: 1.8 children born/woman (1990)
Nationality: noun—Australian(s); adjective—Australian
Ethnic divisions: 95% Caucasian, 4% Asian, 1% Aboriginal and other
Religion: 26.1% Anglican, 26.0% Roman Catholic, 24.3% other Christian
Language: English, native languages
Literacy: 98.5%
Labor force: 7,700,000; 33.8% finance and services, 22.3% public and community services, 20.1% wholesale and retail trade, 16.2% manufacturing and industry, 6.1% agriculture (1987)
Organized labor: 62% of labor force (1986)

Government

Long-form name: Commonwealth of Australia
Type: federal parliamentary state
Capital: Canberra
Administrative divisions: 6 states and 2 territories*; Australian Capital Territory*, New South Wales, Northern Territory*, Queensland, South Australia, Tasmania, Victoria, Western Australia
Dependent areas: Ashmore and Cartier Islands, Christmas Island, Cocos (Keeling) Islands, Coral Sea Islands, Heard Island and McDonald Islands, Norfolk Island
Independence: 1 January 1901 (federation of UK colonies)
Constitution: 9 July 1900, effective 1 January 1901
Legal system: based on English common law; accepts compulsory ICJ jurisdiction, with reservations
National holiday: Australia Day (last Monday in January), 29 January 1990
Executive branch: British monarch, governor general, prime minister, deputy prime minister, Cabinet
Legislative branch: bicameral Federal Parliament consists of an upper house or Senate and a lower house or House of Representatives
Judicial branch: High Court
Leaders: *Chief of State*—Queen ELIZABETH II (since February 1952), represented by Governor General William George HAYDEN (since NA February 1989);
Head of Government—Prime Minister Robert James Lee HAWKE (since 11 March 1983); Deputy Prime Minister Paul KEATING (since 3 April 1990)

Political parties and leaders:
government—Australian Labor Party, Robert Hawke; *opposition*—Liberal Party, Andrew Peacock; National Party, Charles Blunt; Australian Democratic Party, Janine Haines

Suffrage: universal and compulsory at age 18

Elections: *Senate*—last held 11 July 1987 (next to be held by 12 May 1990); results—Labor 43%, Liberal-National 42%, Australian Democrats 8%, independents 2%; seats—(76 total) Labor 32, Liberal-National 34, Australian Democrats 7, independents 3;
House of Representatives—last held 24 March 1990 (next to be held by November 1993); results—Labor 39.7%, Liberal-National 43%, Australian Democrats and independents 11.1%; seats—(148 total) Labor 78, Liberal-National 69, independent 1

Communists: 4,000 members (est.)

Other political or pressure groups: Australian Democratic Labor Party (anti-Communist Labor Party splinter group); Peace and Nuclear Disarmament Action (Nuclear Disarmament Party splinter group)

Member of: ADB, AIOEC, ANZUS, CCC, CIPEC (associate), Colombo Plan, Commonwealth, DAC, ESA, ESCAP, FAO, GATT, IAEA, IATP, IBA, IBRD, ICAC, ICAO, ICO, IDA, IEA, IFAD, IFC, IHO, ILO, ILZSG, IMF, IMO, INTELSAT, INTERPOL, IOOC, IPU, IRC, ISO, ITC, ITU, IWC—International Whaling Commission, IWC—International Wheat Council, OECD, SPF, UN, UNESCO, UPU, WHO, WIPO, WMO, WSG

Diplomatic representation: Ambassador Michael J. COOK; Chancery at 1601 Massachusetts Avenue NW, Washington DC 20036; telephone (202) 797-3000; there are Australian Consulates General in Chicago, Honolulu, Houston, Los Angeles, New York, Pago Pago (American Samoa), and San Francisco; *US*—Ambassador Melvin F. SEMBLER; Moonah Place, Yarralumla, Canberra, Australian Capital Territory 2600 (mailing address is APO San Francisco 6404); telephone [61] (62) 705000; there are US Consulates General in Melbourne, Perth, and Sydney, and a Consulate in Brisbane

Flag: blue with the flag of the UK in the upper hoist-side quadrant and a large seven-pointed star in the lower hoist-side quadrant; the remaining half is a representation of the Southern Cross constellation in white with one small five-pointed star and four, larger, seven-pointed stars

Economy

Overview: Australia has a prosperous Western-style capitalist economy, with a per capita GNP comparable to levels in industrialized West European countries. Rich in natural resources, Australia is a major exporter of agricultural products, minerals, metals, and fossil fuels. Of the top 25 exports, 21 are primary products, so that, as happened during 1983-84, a downturn in world commodity prices can have a big impact on the economy. The government is pushing for increased exports of manufactured goods but competition in international markets will be severe.

GNP: $240.8 billion, per capita $14,300; real growth rate 4.1% (1989 est.)

Inflation rate (consumer prices): 8.0% (1989)

Unemployment rate: 6.0% (December 1989)

Budget: revenues $76.3 billion; expenditures $69.1 billion, including capital expenditures of NA (FY90 est.)

Exports: $43.2 billion (f.o.b., FY89); *commodities*—wheat, barley, beef, lamb, dairy products, wool, coal, iron ore; *partners*—Japan 26%, US 11%, NZ 6%, South Korea 4%, Singapore 4%, USSR 3%

Imports: $48.6 billion (c.i.f., FY89); *commodities*—manufactured raw materials, capital equipment, consumer goods; *partners*—US 22%, Japan 22%, UK 7%, FRG 6%, NZ 4% (1984)

External debt: $111.6 billion (September 1989)

Industrial production: growth rate 5.6% (FY88)

Electricity: 38,000,000 kW capacity; 139,000 million kWh produced, 8,450 kWh per capita (1989)

Industries: mining, industrial and transportation equipment, food processing, chemicals, steel, motor vehicles

Agriculture: accounts for 5% of GNP and 37% of export revenues; world's largest exporter of beef and wool, second-largest for mutton, and among top wheat exporters; major crops—wheat, barley, sugarcane, fruit; livestock—cattle, sheep, poultry

Aid: donor—ODA and OOF commitments (1970-87), $8.8 billion

Currency: Australian dollar (plural—dollars); 1 Australian dollar ($A) = 100 cents

Exchange rates: Australian dollars ($A) per US$1—1.2784 (January 1990), 1.2618 (1989), 1.2752 (1988), 1.4267 (1987), 1.4905 (1986), 1.4269 (1985)

Fiscal year: 1 July-30 June

Communications

Railroads: 40,478 km total; 7,970 km 1.600-meter gauge, 16,201 km 1.435-meter standard gauge, 16,307 km 1.067-meter gauge; 183 km dual gauge; 1,130 km electrified; government owned (except for a few hundred kilometers of privately owned track) (1985)

Highways: 837,872 km total; 243,750 km paved, 228,396 km gravel, crushed stone, or stabilized soil surface, 365,726 km unimproved earth

Inland waterways: 8,368 km; mainly by small, shallow-draft craft

Pipelines: crude oil, 2,500 km; refined products, 500 km; natural gas, 5,600 km

Ports: Adelaide, Brisbane, Cairns, Darwin, Devonport, Fremantle, Geelong, Hobart, Launceston, Mackay, Melbourne, Sydney, Townsville

Merchant marine: 77 ships (1,000 GRT or over) totaling 2,300,049 GRT/3,493,802 DWT; includes 2 short-sea passenger, 7 cargo, 5 container, 10 roll-on/roll-off cargo, 17 petroleum, oils, and lubricants (POL) tanker, 2 chemical tanker, 3 liquefied gas, 1 combination ore/oil, 1 livestock carrier, 29 bulk

Civil air: around 150 major transport aircraft

Airports: 564 total, 524 usable; 235 with permanent-surface runways, 2 with runways over 3,659 m; 20 with runways 2,440-3,659 m; 311 with runways 1,220-2,439 m

Telecommunications: good international and domestic service; 8.7 million telephones; stations—258 AM, 67 FM, 134 TV; submarine cables to New Zealand, Papua New Guinea, and Indonesia; domestic satellite service; satellite stations—4 Indian Ocean INTELSAT, 6 Pacific Ocean INTELSAT earth stations

Defense Forces

Branches: Royal Australian Navy, Australian Army, Royal Australian Air Force

Military manpower: males 15-49, 4,588,750; 4,009,127 fit for military service; 136,042 reach military age (17) annually

Defense expenditures: NA

Austria

150 km

See regional map V

Geography

Total area: 83,850 km²; land area: 82,730 km²

Comparative area: slightly smaller than Maine

Land boundaries: 2,640 km total; Czechoslovakia 548 km, Hungary 366 km, Italy 430 km, Liechtenstein 37 km, Switzerland 164 km, FRG 784 km, Yugoslavia 311 km

Coastline: none—landlocked

Maritime claims: none—landlocked

Disputes: South Tyrol question with Italy

Climate: temperate; continental, cloudy; cold winters with frequent rain in lowlands and snow in mountains; cool summers with occasional showers

Terrain: mostly mountains with Alps in west and south; mostly flat, with gentle slopes along eastern and northern margins

Natural resources: iron ore, crude oil, timber, magnesite, aluminum, lead, coal, lignite, copper, hydropower

Land use: 17% arable land; 1% permanent crops; 24% meadows and pastures; 39% forest and woodland; 19% other; includes NEGL% irrigated

Environment: because of steep slopes, poor soils, and cold temperatures, population is concentrated on eastern lowlands

Note: landlocked; strategic location at the crossroads of central Europe with many easily traversable Alpine passes and valleys; major river is the Danube

People

Population: 7,644,275 (July 1990), growth rate 0.3% (1990)

Birth rate: 12 births/1,000 population (1990)

Death rate: 11 deaths/1,000 population (1990)

Net migration rate: 2 migrants/1,000 population (1990)

Infant mortality rate: 6 deaths/1,000 live births (1990)

Life expectancy at birth: 73 years male, 80 years female (1990)

Total fertility rate: 1.5 children born/woman (1990)

Nationality: noun—Austrian(s); adjective—Austrian

Ethnic divisions: 99.4% German, 0.3% Croatian, 0.2% Slovene, 0.1% other

Religion: 85% Roman Catholic, 6% Protestant, 9% other

Language: German

Literacy: 98%

Labor force: 3,037,000; 56.4% services, 35.4% industry and crafts, 8.1% agriculture and forestry; an estimated 200,000 Austrians are employed in other European countries; foreign laborers in Austria number 177,840, about 6% of labor force (1988)

Organized labor: 1,672,820 members of Austrian Trade Union Federation (1984)

Government

Long-form name: Republic of Austria

Type: federal republic

Capital: Vienna

Administrative divisions: 9 states (bundesländer, singular—bundesland); Burgenland, Kärnten, Niederösterreich, Oberösterreich, Salzburg, Steiermark, Tirol, Vorarlberg, Wien

Independence: 12 November 1918 (from Austro-Hungarian Empire)

Constitution: 1920, revised 1929 (reinstated 1945)

Legal system: civil law system with Roman law origin; judicial review of legislative acts by a Constitutional Court; separate administrative and civil/penal supreme courts; has not accepted compulsory ICJ jurisdiction

National holiday: National Day, 26 October (1955)

Executive branch: president, chancellor, vice chancellor, Council of Ministers (cabinet)

Legislative branch: bicameral Federal Assembly (Bundesversammlung) consists of an upper council or Federal Council (Bundesrat) and a lower council or National Council (Nationalrat)

Judicial branch: Supreme Judicial Court (Oberster Gerichtshof) for civil and criminal cases, Administrative Court (Verwaltungsgerichtshof) for bureaucratic cases, Constitutional Court (Verfassungsgerichtshof) for constitutional cases

Leaders: *Chief of State*—President Kurt WALDHEIM (since 8 July 1986); *Head of Government*—Chancellor Franz VRANITZKY (since 16 June 1986); Vice Chancellor Josef RIEGLER (since 19 May 1989)

Political parties and leaders: Socialist Party of Austria (SPÖ), Franz Vranitzky, chairman; Austrian People's Party (ÖVP), Josef Riegler, chairman; Freedom Party of Austria (FPÖ), Jörg Haider, chairman; Communist Party (KPÖ), Franz Muhri, chairman; Green Alternative List (GAL), Andreas Wabl, chairman

Suffrage: universal at age 19; compulsory for presidential elections

Elections: *President*—last held 8 June 1986 (next to be held May 1992); results of Second Ballot—Dr. Kurt Waldheim 53.89%, Dr. Kurt Steyrer 46.11%; *Federal Council*—last held 23 November 1986 (next to be held November 1990); results—percent of vote by party NA; seats—(63 total) ÖVP 32, SPÖ 30, FPÖ 1; *National Council*—last held 23 November 1986 (next to be held November 1990); results—SPO 43.1%, ÖVP 41.3%, FPÖ 9.7%, GAL 4.8%, KPÖ 0.7%, other 0.32%; seats—(183 total) SPO 80, ÖVP 77, FPO 18, GAL 8

Communists: membership 15,000 est.; activists 7,000-8,000

Other political or pressure groups: Federal Chamber of Commerce and Industry; Austrian Trade Union Federation (primarily Socialist); three composite leagues of the Austrian People's Party (ÖVP) representing business, labor, and farmers; ÖVP-oriented League of Austrian Industrialists; Roman Catholic Church, including its chief lay organization, Catholic Action

Member of: ADB, Council of Europe, CCC, DAC, ECE, EFTA, EMA, ESA, FAO, GATT, IAEA, IDB—Inter-American Development Bank, IBRD, ICAC, ICAO, IDA, IEA, IFAD, IFC, ILO, ILZSG, IMF, IMO, INTELSAT, INTERPOL, ITU, IWC—International Wheat Council, OECD, UN, UNESCO, UPU, WFTU, WHO, WIPO, WMO, WTO, WSG; Austria is neutral and is not a member of NATO or the EC

Diplomatic representation: Ambassador Friedrich HOESS; Embassy at 2343 Massachusetts Avenue NW, Washington DC 20008; telephone (202) 483-4474; there are Austrian Consulates General in Chicago, Los Angeles, and New York; *US*—Ambassador Henry A. GRUNWALD; Embassy at Boltzmanngasse 16, A-1091, Vienna (mailing address is APO New York 09108); telephone [43] (222) 31-55-11; there is a US Consulate General in Salzburg

Flag: three equal horizontal bands of red (top), white, and red

20

Economy

Overview: Austria boasts a prosperous and stable capitalist economy with a sizable proportion of nationalized industry and extensive welfare benefits. Thanks to an excellent raw material endowment, a technically skilled labor force, and strong links with West German industrial firms, Austria has successfully occupied specialized niches in European industry and services (tourism, banking) and produces almost enough food to feed itself with only 8% of the labor force in agriculture. Living standards are roughly comparable with the large industrial countries of Western Europe. Problems for the 1990s include an aging population and the struggle to keep welfare benefits within budget capabilities.
GDP: $103.2 billion, per capita $13,600; real growth rate 4.2% (1989 est.)
Inflation rate (consumer prices): 2.7% (1989)
Unemployment: 4.8% (1989)
Budget: revenues $34.2 billion; expenditures $39.5 billion, including capital expenditures of NA (1988)
Exports: $31.2 billion (f.o.b., 1989); *commodities*—machinery and equipment, iron and steel, lumber, textiles, paper products, chemicals; *partners*—FRG 35%, Italy 10%, Eastern Europe 9%, Switzerland 7%, US 4%, OPEC 3%
Imports: $37.9 billion (c.i.f., 1989); *commodities*—petroleum, foodstuffs, machinery and equipment, vehicles, chemicals, textiles and clothing, pharmaceuticals; *partners*—FRG 44%, Italy 9%, Eastern Europe 6%, Switzerland 5%, US 4%, USSR 2%
External debt: $12.4 billion (December 1987)
Industrial production: growth rate 5.8% (1989 est.)
Electricity: 17,562,000 kW capacity; 49,290 million kWh produced, 6,500 kWh per capita (1989)
Industries: foods, iron and steel, machines, textiles, chemicals, electrical, paper and pulp, tourism, mining
Agriculture: accounts for 4% of GDP (including forestry); principal crops and animals—grains, fruit, potatoes, sugar beets, sawn wood, cattle, pigs poultry; 80-90% self-sufficient in food
Aid: donor—ODA and OOF commitments (1970-87), $1.7 billion
Currency: Austrian schilling (plural—schillings); 1 Austrian schilling (S) = 100 groschen
Exchange rates: Austrian schillings (S) per US$1—11.907 (January 1990), 13.231 (1989), 12.348 (1988), 12.643 (1987), 15.267 (1986), 20.690 (1985)
Fiscal year: calendar year

Communications

Railroads: 6,028 km total; 5,388 km government owned and 640 km privately owned (1.435- and 1.000-meter gauge); 5,403 km 1.435-meter standard gauge of which 3,051 km is electrified and 1,520 km is double tracked; 363 km 0.760-meter narrow gauge of which 91 km is electrified
Highways: 95,412 km total; 34,612 are the primary network (including 1,012 km of autobahn, 10,400 km of federal, and 23,200 km of provincial roads); of this number, 21,812 km are paved and 12,800 km are unpaved; in addition, there are 60,800 km of communal roads (mostly gravel, crushed stone, earth)
Inland waterways: 446 km
Ports: Vienna, Linz (river ports)
Merchant marine: 29 ships (1,000 GRT or over) totaling 209,311 GRT/366,401 DWT; includes 23 cargo, 1 container, 5 bulk
Pipelines: 554 km crude oil; 2,611 km natural gas; 171 km refined products
Civil air: 25 major transport aircraft
Airports: 55 total, 54 usable; 19 with permanent-surface runways; none with runways over 3,659 m; 5 with runways 2,440-3,659 m; 4 with runways 1,220-2,439 m
Telecommunications: highly developed and efficient; 4,014,000 telephones; extensive TV and radiobroadcast systems; stations—6 AM, 21 (544 repeaters) FM, 47 (867 repeaters) TV; satellite stations operating in INTELSAT 1 Atlantic Ocean earth station and 1 Indian Ocean earth station and EUTELSAT systems

Defense Forces

Branches: Army, Flying Division
Military manpower: males 15-49, 1,970,189; 1,656,228 fit for military service; 50,090 reach military age (19) annually
Defense expenditures: 1.1% of GDP, or $1.1 billion (1989 est.)

The Bahamas

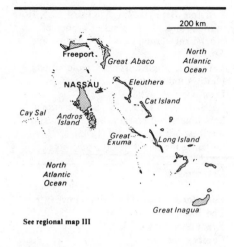

200 km

See regional map III

Geography

Total area: 13,940 km²; land area: 10,070 km²
Comparative area: slightly larger than Connecticut
Land boundaries: none
Coastline: 3,542 km
Maritime claims:
Continental shelf: 200 meters or to depth of exploitation
Exclusive fishing zone: 200 nm
Territorial sea: 3 nm
Climate: tropical marine; moderated by warm waters of Gulf Stream
Terrain: long, flat coral formations with some low rounded hills
Natural resources: salt, aragonite, timber
Land use: 1% arable land; NEGL% permanent crops; NEGL% meadows and pastures; 32% forest and woodland; 67% other
Environment: subject to hurricanes and other tropical storms that cause extensive flood damage
Note: strategic location adjacent to US and Cuba; extensive island chain

People

Population: 246,491 (July 1990), growth rate 1.2% (1990)
Birth rate: 17 births/1,000 population (1990)
Death rate: 6 deaths/1,000 population (1990)
Net migration rate: 0 migrants/1,000 population (1990)
Infant mortality rate: 21 deaths/1,000 live births (1990)
Life expectancy at birth: 68 years male, 75 years female (1990)
Total fertility rate: 1.9 children born/woman (1990)
Nationality: noun—Bahamian(s); adjective—Bahamian
Ethnic divisions: 85% black, 15% white

The Bahamas (continued)

Religion: Baptist 29%, Anglican 23%, Roman Catholic 22%, smaller groups of other Protestants, Greek Orthodox, and Jews

Language: English; some Creole among Haitian immigrants

Literacy: 95% (1986)

Labor force: 132,600; 30% government, 25% hotels and restaurants, 10% business services, 5% agriculture (1986)

Organized labor: 25% of labor force

Government

Long-form name: The Commonwealth of The Bahamas

Type: commonwealth

Capital: Nassau

Administrative divisions: 21 districts; Abaco, Acklins Island, Andros Island, Berry Islands, Biminis, Cat Island, Cay Lobos, Crooked Island, Eleuthera, Exuma, Grand Bahama, Harbour Island, Inagua, Long Cay, Long Island, Mayaguana, New Providence, Ragged Island, Rum Cay, San Salvador, Spanish Wells

Independence: 10 July 1973 (from UK)

Constitution: 10 July 1973

Legal system: based on English common law

National holiday: Independence Day, 10 July (1973)

Executive branch: British monarch, governor general, prime minister, deputy prime minister, Cabinet

Legislative branch: bicameral Parliament consists of an upper house or Senate and a lower house or House of Assembly

Judicial branch: Supreme Court

Leaders: *Chief of State*—Queen ELIZABETH II (since 6 February 1952), represented by Acting Governor General Sir Henry TAYLOR (since 26 June 1988); *Head of Government*—Prime Minister Sir Lynden Oscar PINDLING (since 16 January 1967)

Political parties and leaders: Progressive Liberal Party (PLP), Sir Lynden O. Pindling; Free National Movement (FNM), Cecil Wallace-Whitfield

Suffrage: universal at age 18

Elections: *House of Assembly*—last held 19 June 1987 (next to be held by June 1992); results—percent of vote by party NA; seats—(49 total) PLP 31, FNM 16, independents 2

Communists: none known

Other political or pressure groups: Vanguard Nationalist and Socialist Party (VNSP), a small leftist party headed by Lionel Carey; Trade Union Congress (TUC), headed by Arlington Miller

Member of: ACP, CARICOM, CCC, CDB, Commonwealth, FAO, G-77, GATT (de facto), IBRD, ICAO, IDB—Inter-American Development Bank, ILO, IMF, IMO, INTELSAT, INTERPOL, ITU, NAM, OAS, PAHO, UN, UNESCO, UPU, WHO, WIPO, WMO, WTO

Diplomatic representation: Ambassador Margaret E. MCDONALD; Chancery at Suite 865, 600 New Hampshire Avenue NW, Washington DC 20037; telephone (202) 944-3390; there are Bahamian Consulates General in Miami and New York; *US*—Ambassador Chic HECHT; Embassy at Mosmar Building, Queen Street, Nassau (mailing address is P. O. Box N-8197, Nassau); telephone (809) 322-1181 or 328-2206

Flag: three equal horizontal bands of aquamarine (top), gold, and aquamarine with a black equilateral triangle based on the hoist side

---

Economy

Overview: The Bahamas is a stable, middle-income developing nation whose economy is based primarily on tourism and offshore banking. Tourism alone provides about 50% of GDP and directly or indirectly employs about 50,000 people or 40% of the local work force. The economy has boomed in recent years, aided by a steady annual increase in the number of tourists. The per capita GDP of over $9,800 is one of the highest in the region.

GDP: $2.4 billion, per capita $9,875; real growth rate 2.0% (1988 est.)

Inflation rate (consumer prices): 4.1% (1988)

Unemployment: 12% (1986)

Budget: revenues $555 million; expenditures $702 million, including capital expenditures of $138 million (1989 est.)

Exports: $733 million (f.o.b., 1987); *commodities*—pharmaceuticals, cement, rum, crawfish; *partners*—US 90%, UK 10%

Imports: $1.7 billion (c.i.f., 1987); *commodities*—foodstuffs, manufactured goods, mineral fuels; *partners*—Iran 30%, Nigeria 20%, US 10%, EC 10%, Gabon 10%

External debt: $1.5 billion (September 1988)

Industrial production: growth rate NA%

Electricity: 368,000 kW capacity; 857 million kWh produced, 3,470 kWh per capita (1989)

Industries: banking, tourism, cement, oil refining and transshipment, salt production, rum, aragonite, pharmaceuticals, spiral weld, steel pipe

Agriculture: accounts for less than 5% of GDP; dominated by small-scale producers; principal products—citrus fruit, vegetables, poultry; large net importer of food

Aid: US commitments, including Ex-Im (FY70-80), $42 million; Western (non-US) countries, ODA and OOF bilateral commitments (1970-87), $344 million

Currency: Bahamian dollar (plural—dollars); 1 Bahamian dollar (B$) = 100 cents

Exchange rates: Bahamian dollar (B$) per US$1—1.00 (fixed rate)

Fiscal year: calendar year

Communications

Highways: 2,400 km total; 1,350 km paved, 1,050 km gravel

Ports: Freeport, Nassau

Merchant marine: 533 ships (1,000 GRT or over) totaling 11,684,123 GRT/ 19,574,532 DWT; includes 26 passenger, 15 short-sea passenger, 121 cargo, 40 roll-on/roll-off cargo, 42 refrigerated cargo, 16 container, 6 car carrier, 123 petroleum, oils, and lubricants (POL) tanker, 6 liquefied gas, 19 combination ore/oil, 29 chemical tanker, 1 specialized tanker, 86 bulk, 3 combination bulk; note—a flag of convenience registry

Civil air: 9 major transport aircraft

Airports: 59 total, 57 usable; 31 with permanent-surface runways; none with runways over 3,659 m; 3 with runways 2,440-3,659 m; 25 with runways 1,220-2,439 m

Telecommunications: highly developed; 99,000 telephones in totally automatic system; tropospheric scatter and submarine cable links to Florida; stations—3 AM, 2 FM, 1 TV; 3 coaxial submarine cables;1 Atlantic Ocean INTELSAT earth station

---

Defense Forces

Branches: Royal Bahamas Defense Force (a coast guard element only), Royal Bahamas Police Force

Military manpower: NA

Defense expenditures: NA

Bahrain

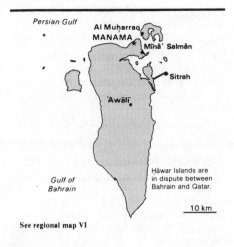

Persian Gulf

Al Muḥarraq
MANAMA
Mīnā' Salmān
Sitrah
'Awālī

Gulf of Bahrain

Ḥawar Islands are in dispute between Bahrain and Qatar.

10 km

See regional map VI

Geography

Total area: 620 km²; land area: 620 km²
Comparative area: slightly less than 3.5 times the size of Washington, DC
Land boundaries: none
Coastline: 161 km
Maritime claims:
Continental shelf: not specific
Territorial sea: 3 nm
Disputes: territorial dispute with Qatar over the Ḥawar Islands
Climate: arid; mild, pleasant winters; very hot, humid summers
Terrain: mostly low desert plain rising gently to low central escarpment
Natural resources: oil, associated and nonassociated natural gas, fish
Land use: 2% arable land; 2% permanent crops; 6% meadows and pastures; 0% forest and woodland; 90% other; includes NEGL% irrigated
Environment: subsurface water sources being rapidly depleted (requires development of desalination facilities); dust storms; desertification
Note: proximity to primary Middle Eastern crude oil sources and strategic location in Persian Gulf through which much of Western world's crude oil must transit to reach open ocean

People

Population: 520,186 (July 1990), growth rate 3.2% (1990)
Birth rate: 28 births/1,000 population (1990)
Death rate: 3 deaths/1,000 population (1990)
Net migration rate: 8 migrants/1,000 population (1990)
Infant mortality rate: 19 deaths/1,000 live births (1990)
Life expectancy at birth: 71 years male, 76 years female (1990)

Total fertility rate: 4.1 children born/woman (1990)
Nationality: noun—Bahraini(s); adjective—Bahraini
Ethnic divisions: 63% Bahraini, 13% Asian, 10% other Arab, 8% Iranian, 6% other
Religion: Muslim (70% Shi'a, 30% Sunni)
Language: Arabic (official); English also widely spoken; Farsi, Urdu
Literacy: 40%
Labor force: 140,000; 42% of labor force is Bahraini; 85% industry and commerce, 5% agriculture, 5% services, 3% government (1982)
Organized labor: General Committee for Bahrain Workers exists in only eight major designated companies

Government

Long-form name: State of Bahrain
Type: traditional monarchy
Capital: Manama
Administrative divisions: 11 municipalities (baladīyat, singular—baladīyah); Al Ḥadd, Al Manāmah, Al Minṭaqah al Gharbīyah, Al Minṭaqah al Wusṭā, Al Minṭaqah ash Shamālīyah, Al Muḥarraq, Ar Rifā' wa al Minṭaqah al Janūbīyah, Jidd Ḥafṣ, Madīnat 'Isá, Minṭaqat Juzur Ḥawār, Sitrah
Independence: 15 August 1971 (from UK)
Constitution: 26 May 1973, effective 6 December 1973
Legal system: based on Islamic law and English common law
National holiday: National Day, 16 December
Executive branch: amir, crown prince and heir apparent, prime minister, Cabinet
Legislative branch: unicameral National Assembly was dissolved 26 August 1975 and legislative powers were assumed by the Cabinet
Judicial branch: High Civil Appeals Court
Leaders: *Chief of State*—Amir 'Isa bin Salman Al KHALIFA (since 2 November 1961); Heir Apparent Hamad bin 'Isa Al KHALIFA (son of Amir; born 28 January 1950);
Head of Government—Prime Minister Khalifa bin Salman Al KHALIFA, (since 19 January 1970)
Political parties and pressure groups: political parties prohibited; several small, clandestine leftist and Shi'a fundamentalist groups are active
Suffrage: none
Elections: none
Communists: negligible
Member of: Arab League, FAO, G-77, GATT (de facto), GCC, IBRD, ICAO, IDB—Islamic Development Bank, ILO,

IMF, IMO, INTERPOL, ITU, NAM, OAPEC, OIC, UN, UNESCO, UPU, WHO
Diplomatic representation: Ambassador Ghazi Muhammad AL-QUSAYBI; Chancery at 3502 International Drive NW, Washington DC 20008; telephone (202) 342-0741 or 342-0742; there is a Bahraini Consulate General in New York; *US*—Ambassador Dr. Charles W. HOSTLER; Embassy at Shaikh Isa Road, Manama (mailing address is P. O. 26431, Manama, or FPO New York 09526); telephone [973] 714151 through 714153
Flag: red with a white serrated band (eight white points) on the hoist side

Economy

Overview: The oil price decline in recent years has had an adverse impact on the economy. Petroleum production and processing account for about 85% of export receipts, 60% of government revenues, and 20% of GDP. In 1986 soft oil-market conditions led to a 5% drop in GDP, in sharp contrast wit the 5% average annual growth rate during the early 1980s. The slowdown in economic activity, however, has helped to check the inflation of the 1970s. The government's past economic diversification efforts have moderated the severity of the downturn but failed to offset oil and gas revenue losses.
GDP: $3.5 billion, per capita $7,550 (1987); real growth rate 0% (1988)
Inflation rate (consumer prices): 0.3% (1988)
Unemployment: 8-10% (1989)
Budget: revenues $1,136 million; expenditures $1,210 million, including capital expenditures of $294 million (1987)
Exports: $2.4 billion (f.o.b., 1988 est.); *commodities*—petroleum 80%, aluminum 7%, other 13%; *partners*—US, UAE, Japan, Singapore, Saudi Arabia
Imports: $2.5 billion (f.o.b., 1988 est.); *commodities*—nonoil 59%, crude oil 41%; *partners*—UK, Saudi Arabia, US, Japan
External debt: $1.1 billion (December 1989 est.)
Industrial production: growth rate −3.1% (1987)
Electricity: 1,652,000 kW capacity; 6,000 million kWh produced, 12,800 kWh per capita (1989)
Industries: petroleum processing and refining, aluminum smelting, offshore banking, ship repairing
Agriculture: including fishing, accounts for less than 2% of GDP; not self-sufficient in food production; heavily subsidized sector produces fruit, vegetables, poultry, dairy products, shrimp, and fish; fish catch 9,000 metric tons in 1987

Bahrain (continued)

Aid: US commitments, including Ex-Im (FY70-79), $24 million; Western (non-US) countries, ODA and OOF bilateral Commitments (1970-87), $28 million; OPEC bilateral aid (1979-89), $9.8 billion
Currency: Bahraini dinar (plural—dinars); 1 Bahraini dinar (BD) = 1,000 fils
Exchange rates: Bahraini dinars (BD) per US$1—0.3760 (fixed rate)
Fiscal year: calendar year

Communications

Highways: 200 km bituminous surfaced, including 25 km bridge-causeway to Saudi Arabia opened in November 1986; NA km natural surface tracks
Ports: Mina Salman, Mina al Manamah, Sitrah
Merchant marine: 1 cargo and 1 bulk (1,000 GRT or over) totaling 28,621 GRT/ 44,137 DWT
Pipelines: crude oil, 56 km; refined products, 16 km; natural gas, 32 km
Civil air: 24 major transport aircraft
Airports: 3 total, 3 usable; 2 with permanent-surface runways; 2 with runways over 3,659 m; 1 with runways 1,220-2,439 m
Telecommunications: excellent international telecommunications; adequate domestic services; 98,000 telephones; stations—2 AM, 1 FM, 2 TV; satellite earth stations—1 Atlantic Ocean INTELSAT, 1 Indian Ocean INTELSAT, 1 ARABSAT; tropospheric scatter and microwave to Qatar, UAE, Saudi Arabia; submarine cable to Qatar and UAE

Defense Forces

Branches: Army (Defense Force), Navy, Air Force
Military manpower: males 15-49, 183,580; 102,334 fit for military service
Defense expenditures: 5% of GDP, or $194 million (1990 est.)

Baker Island
(territory of the US)

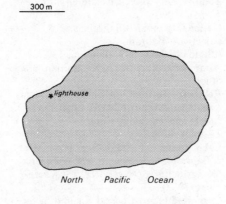

See regional map X

Geography

Total area: 1.4 km²; land area: 1.4 km²
Comparative area: about 2.3 times the size of The Mall in Washington, DC
Land boundaries: none
Coastline: 4.8 km
Maritime claims:
  Contiguous zone: 12 nm
  Continental shelf: 200 m
  Extended economic zone: 200 nm
  Territorial sea: 12 nm
Climate: equatorial; scant rainfall, constant wind, burning sun
Terrain: low, nearly level coral island surrounded by a narrow fringing reef
Natural resources: guano (deposits worked until 1891)
Land use: 0% arable land; 0% permanent crops; 0% meadows and pastures; 0% forest and woodland; 100% other
Environment: treeless, sparse and scattered vegetation consisting of grasses, prostrate vines, and low growing shrubs; lacks fresh water; primarily a nesting, roosting, and foraging habitat for seabirds, shorebirds, and marine wildlife
Note: remote location 2,575 km southwest of Honolulu in the North Pacific Ocean, just north of the Equator, about halfway between Hawaii and Australia

People

Population: uninhabited
Note: American civilians evacuated in 1942 after Japanese air and naval attacks during World War II; occupied by US military during World War II, but abandoned after the war; public entry is by special-use permit only and generally restricted to scientists and educators; a cemetery and cemetery ruins located near the middle of the west coast

Government

Long-form name: none
Type: unincorporated territory of the US administered by the Fish and Wildlife Service of the US Department of the Interior as part of the National Wildlife Refuge system

Economy

Overview: no economic activity

Communications

Ports: none; offshore anchorage only, one boat landing area along the the middle of the west coast
Airports: 1 abandoned World War II runway of 1,665 m
Note: there is a day beacon near the middle of the west coast

Defense Forces

Note: defense is the responsibility of the US; visited annually by the US Coast Guard

Bangladesh

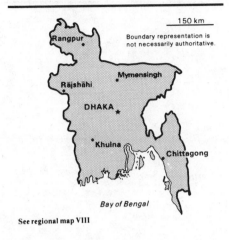

Boundary representation is not necessarily authoritative.

150 km

Bay of Bengal

See regional map VIII

Geography

Total area: 144,000 km²; land area: 133,910 km²

Comparative area: slightly smaller than Wisconsin

Land boundaries: 4,246 km total; Burma 193 km, India 4,053 km

Coastline: 580 km

Maritime claims:
Contiguous zone: 18 nm
Continental shelf: up to outer limits of continental margin
Extended economic zone: 200 nm
Territorial sea: 12 nm

Disputes: a portion of the boundary with India is in dispute; water sharing problems with upstream riparian India over the Ganges

Climate: tropical; cool, dry winter (October to March); hot, humid summer (March to June); cool, rainy monsoon (June to October)

Terrain: mostly flat alluvial plain; hilly in southeast

Natural resources: natural gas, uranium, arable land, timber

Land use: 67% arable land; 2% permanent crops; 4% meadows and pastures; 16% forest and woodland; 11% other; includes 14% irrigated

Environment: vulnerable to droughts; much of country routinely flooded during summer monsoon season; overpopulation; deforestation

Note: almost completely surrounded by India

People

Population: 118,433,062 (July 1990), growth rate 2.8% (1990)

Birth rate: 42 births/1,000 population (1990)

Death rate: 14 deaths/1,000 population (1990)

Net migration rate: 0 migrants/1,000 population (1990)

Infant mortality rate: 136 deaths/1,000 live births (1990)

Life expectancy at birth: 54 years male, 53 years female (1990)

Total fertility rate: 5.7 children born/ woman (1990)

Nationality: noun—Bangladeshi(s); adjective—Bangladesh

Ethnic divisions: 98% Bengali; 250,000 Biharis, and less than 1 million tribals

Religion: 83% Muslim, about 16% Hindu, less than 1% Buddhist, Christian, and other

Language: Bangla (official), English widely used

Literacy: 29% (39% men, 18% women)

Labor force: 35,100,000; 74% agriculture, 15% services, 11% industry and commerce; extensive export of labor to Saudi Arabia, UAE, Oman, and Kuwait (FY86)

Organized labor: 3% of labor force belongs to 2,614 registered unions (1986 est.)

Government

Long-form name: People's Republic of Bangladesh

Type: republic

Capital: Dhaka

Administrative divisions: 64 districts (zilla-gulo, singular—zilla); Bāgerhāt, Bāndarban, Barisāl, Bhola, Bogra, Borguna, Brāhmanbāria, Chāndpur, Chapai Nawābganj, Chattagram, Chuādānga, Comilla, Cox's Bāzār, Dhaka, Dinājpur, Farīdpur, Feni, Gaibandha, Gāzipur, Gopālganj, Habiganj, Jaipurhāt, Jamālpur, Jessore, Jhālakāti, Jhenaidah, Khagrāchari, Khulna, Kishorganj, Kurīgrām, Kushtia, Laksmipur, Lāl-monirhāt, Mādārīpur, Māgura, Mānikganj, Meherpur, Moulavibāzār, Munshiganj, Mymensingh, Naogaon, Narail, Nārāyanganj, Narsingdi, Nator, Netrakona, Nilphāmāri, Noākhāli, Pābna, Panchāgar, Parbattya Chattagram, Patuākhāli, Pirojpur, Rājbāri, Rājshāhi, Rangpur, Sātkhira, Shariyatpur, Sherpur, Sirājganj, Sunāmganj, Sylhet, Tangail, and Thākurgaon

Independence: 16 December 1971 (from Pakistan; formerly East Pakistan)

Constitution: 4 November 1972, effective 16 December 1972, suspended following coup of 24 March 1982, restored 10 November 1986

Legal system: based on English common law

National holiday: Independence Day, 26 March (1971)

Executive branch: president, vice president, prime minister, three deputy prime ministers, Council of Ministers (cabinet)

Legislative branch: unicameral Parliament (Jatiya Sangsad)

Judicial branch: Supreme Court

Leaders: *Chief of State*—President Hussain Mohammad ERSHAD (since 11 December 1983, elected 15 October 1986); Vice President Moudad AHMED (since 12 August 1989);

Head of Government—Prime Minister Qazi Zafar AHMED (since 12 August 1989)

Political parties and leaders: Jatiyo Party, Hussain Mohammad Ershad; Bangladesh Nationalist Party, Begum Ziaur Rahman; Awami League, Sheikh Hasina Wazed; United People's Party, Kazi Zafar Ahmed; Democratic League, Khondakar Mushtaque Ahmed; Muslim League, Khan A. Sabur; Jatiyo Samajtantrik Dal (National Socialist Party), M. A. Jalil; Bangladesh Communist Party (pro-Soviet), Saifuddin Ahmed Manik; Jamaat-E-Islami, Ali Khan

Suffrage: universal at age 18

Elections: *President*—last held 15 October 1986 (next to be held October 1991); results—President Hussain Mohammad Ershad received 83.5% of vote;

Parliament—last held 3 March 1988 (next to be held March 1993); results—percent of vote by party NA; seats—(330 total, 300 elected and 30 seats reserved for women) Jatiyo Party won 256 out of 300 seats

Communists: 5,000 members (1987 est.)

Member of: ADB, CCC, Colombo Plan, Commonwealth, ESCAP, FAO, G-77, GATT, IAEA, IBRD, ICAO, IDA, IDB—Islamic Development Bank, IFAD, IFC, ILO, IMF, IMO, INTELSAT, INTERPOL, IRC, ITU, NAM, OIC, SAARC, UN, UNCTAD, UNESCO, UPU, WHO, WFTU, WMO, WTO

Diplomatic representation: Ambassador A. H. S. Ataul KARIM; Chancery at 2201 Wisconsin Avenue NW, Washington DC 20007; telephone (202) 342-8372 through 8376; there is a Bangladesh Consulate General in New York; *US*—Ambassador Willard A. DE PREE; Embassy at Diplomatic Enclave, Madani Avenue, Baridhara Model Town, Dhaka (mailing address is G. P. O. Box 323, Ramna, Dhaka); telephone [88] (2) 608170

Flag: green with a large red disk slightly to the hoist side of center; green is the traditional color of Islam

Economy

Overview: The economy is based on the output of a narrow range of agricultural products, such as jute, which is the main cash crop and major source of export earnings. Bangladesh is hampered by a relative lack of natural resources, a rapid

Bangladesh (continued)

population growth of 2.8% a year and a limited infrastructure, and it is highly vulnerable to natural disasters. Despite these constraints, real GDP averaged about 3.8% annually during 1985-88. One of the poorest nations in the world, alleviation of poverty remains the cornerstone of the government's development strategy. The agricultural sector contributes over 50% to GDP and 75% to exports, and employs over 74% of the labor force. Industry accounts for about 10% of GDP.

GDP: $20.6 billion, per capita $180; real growth rate 2.1% (FY89 est.)

Inflation rate (consumer prices): 8-10% (FY89 est.)

Unemployment rate: 30% (FY88 est.)

Budget: revenues $1.8 billion; expenditures $3.3 billion, including capital expenditures of $1.7 billion (FY89)

Exports: $1.3 billion (f.o.b., FY89 est.); *commodities*—jute, tea, leather, shrimp, manufacturing; *partners*—US 25%, Western Europe 22%, Middle East 9%, Japan 8%, Eastern Europe 7%

Imports: $3.1 billion (c.i.f., FY89 est.); *commodities*—food, petroleum and other energy, nonfood consumer goods, semiprocessed goods, and capital equipment; *partners*—Western Europe 18%, Japan 14%, Middle East 9%, US 8%

External debt: $10.4 billion (December 1989)

Industrial production: growth rate 5.4% (FY89 est.)

Electricity: 1,700,000 kW capacity; 4,900 million kWh produced, 40 kWh per capita (1989)

Industries: jute manufacturing, food processing, cotton textiles, petroleum, urea fertilizer

Agriculture: accounts for about 50% of GDP and 74% of both employment and exports; imports 10% of food grain requirements; world's largest exporter of jute; commercial products—jute, rice, wheat, tea, sugarcane, potatoes, beef, milk, poultry; shortages include wheat, vegetable oils and cotton; fish catch 778,000 metric tons in 1986

Aid: US commitments, including Ex-Im (FY70-87), $3.2 billion; Western (non-US) countries, ODA and OOF bilateral commitments (1980-87), $9.5 billion; OPEC bilateral aid (1979-89), $652 million; Communist countries (1970-88), $1.5 billion

Currency: taka (plural—taka); 1 taka (Tk) = 100 paise

Exchange rates: taka (Tk) per US$1—32.270 (January 1990), 32.270 (1989), 31.733 (1988), 30.950 (1987), 30.407 (1986), 27.995 (1985)

Fiscal year: 1 July-30 June

Communications

Railroads: 2,892 km total (1986); 1,914 km 1.000 meter gauge, 978 km 1.676 meter broad gauge

Highways: 7,240 km total (1985); 3,840 km paved, 3,400 km unpaved

Inland waterways: 5,150-8,046 km navigable waterways (includes 2,575-3,058 km main cargo routes)

Ports: Chittagong, Chalna

Merchant marine: 47 ships (1,000 GRT or over) totaling 331,568 GRT/493,935 DWT; includes 38 cargo, 2 petroleum, oils, and lubricants (POL) tanker, 3 refrigerated cargo, 1 roll-on/roll-off, 3 bulk

Pipelines: 650 km natural gas

Civil air: 15 major transport aircraft

Airports: 16 total, 13 usable; 13 with permanent-surface runways; none with runways over 3,659 m; 4 with runways 2,440-3,659 m; 7 with runways 1,220-2,439 m

Telecommunications: adequate international radio communications and landline service; fair domestic wire and microwave service; fair broadcast service; 182,000 telephones; stations—9 AM, 6 FM, 11 TV; 2 Indian Ocean INTELSAT satellite earth stations

Defense Forces

Branches: Army, Navy, Air Force; paramilitary forces—Bangladesh Rifles, Bangladesh Ansars, Armed Police Reserve, Coastal Police

Military manpower: males 15-49, 28,110,802; 16,686,644 fit for military service

Defense expenditures: 1.5% of GDP, or $309 million (FY90 est.)

Barbados

See regional map III

Geography

Total area: 430 km²; land area: 430 km²

Comparative area: slightly less than 2.5 times the size of Washington, DC

Land boundaries: none

Coastline: 97 km

Maritime claims:
Extended economic zone: 200 nm
Territorial sea: 12 nm

Climate: tropical; rainy season (June to October)

Terrain: relatively flat; rises gently to central highland region

Natural resources: crude oil, fishing, natural gas

Land use: 77% arable land; 0% permanent crops; 9% meadows and pastures; 0% forest and woodland; 14% other

Environment: subject to hurricanes (especially June to October)

Note: easternmost Caribbean island

People

Population: 262,688 (July 1990), growth rate 0.6% (1990)

Birth rate: 18 births/1,000 population (1990)

Death rate: 8 deaths/1,000 population (1990)

Net migration rate: −5 migrants/1,000 population (1990)

Infant mortality rate: 16 deaths/1,000 live births (1990)

Life expectancy at birth: 73 years male, 77 years female (1990)

Total fertility rate: 2.1 children born/woman (1990)

Nationality: noun—Barbadian(s); adjective—Barbadian

Ethnic divisions: 80% African, 16% mixed, 4% European

Religion: 70% Anglican, 9% Methodist, 4% Roman Catholic, 17% other, including Moravian

Language: English

Literacy: 99%
Labor force: 112,300; 37% services and government; 22% commerce, 22% manufacturing and construction; 9% transportation, storage, communications, and financial institutions; 8% agriculture; 2% utilities (1985 est.)
Organized labor: 32% of labor force

Government

Long-form name: none
Type: parliamentary democracy
Capital: Bridgetown
Administrative divisions: 11 parishes; Christ Church, Saint Andrew, Saint George, Saint James, Saint John, Saint Joseph, Saint Lucy, Saint Michael, Saint Peter, Saint Philip, Saint Thomas; note—there may a new city of Bridgetown
Independence: 30 November 1966 (from UK)
Constitution: 30 November 1966
Legal system: English common law; no judicial review of legislative acts
National holiday: Independence Day, 30 November (1966)
Executive branch: British monarch, governor general, prime minister, deputy prime minister, Cabinet
Legislative branch: bicameral Parliament consists of an upper house or Senate and a lower house or House of Assembly
Judicial branch: Supreme Court of Judicature
Leaders: *Chief of State*—Queen ELIZABETH II (since 6 February 1952), represented by Governor General Sir Hugh SPRINGER (since 24 February 1984); *Head of Government*—Prime Minister Lloyd Erskine SANDIFORD (since 2 June 1987)
Political parties and leaders: Democratic Labor Party (DLP), Erskine Sandiford; Barbados Labor Party (BLP), Henry Forde; National Democratic Party (NDP), Richie Haynes
Suffrage: universal at age 18
Elections: *House of Assembly*—last held 28 May 1986 (next to be held by May 1991); results—DLP 59.4%, BLP 40.6%; seats—(27 total) DLP 24, BLP 3; note—a split in the DLP in February 1989 resulted in the formation of the NDP, changing the status of seats to DLP 20, NDP 4, BLP 3
Communists: negligible
Other political or pressure groups: Industrial and General Workers Union, Bobby Clarke; People's Progressive Movement, Eric Sealy; Workers' Party of Barbados, Dr. George Belle
Member of: ACP, CARICOM, Commonwealth, FAO, G-77, GATT, IADB, IBRD, ICAO, IDB—Inter-American Development Bank, IFAD, IFC, ILO, IMF,

IMO, INTELSAT, INTERPOL, ISO, ITU, IWC—International Wheat Council, NAM, OAS, PAHO, SELA, UN, UNESCO, UPU, WHO, WMO
Diplomatic representation: Ambassador Sir William DOUGLAS; Chancery at 2144 Wyoming Avenue NW, Washington DC 20008; telephone (202) 939-9200 through 9202; there is a Barbadian Consulate General in New York and a Consulate in Los Angeles; *US*—Ambassador-nominee G. Philip HUGHES; Embassy at Canadian Imperial Bank of Commerce Building, Broad Street, Bridgetown (mailing address is P. O. Box 302, Bridgetown or FPO Miami 34054); telephone (809) 436-4950 through 4957
Flag: three equal vertical bands of blue (hoist side), yellow, and blue with the head of a black trident centered on the gold band; the trident head represents independence and a break with the past (the colonial coat of arms contained a complete trident)

Economy

Overview: A per capita income of $5,250 gives Barbados the highest standard of living of all the small island states of the eastern Caribbean. Historically, the economy was based on the cultivation of sugarcane and related activities. In recent years, however, the economy has diversified into manufacturing and tourism. The tourist industry is now a major employer of the labor force and a primary source of foreign exchange. A high unemployment rate of about 19% in 1988 remains one of the most serious economic problems facing the country.
GDP: $1.3 billion, per capita $5,250 (1988 est.); real growth rate 3.7% (1989 est.)
Inflation rate (consumer prices): 4.7% (1988)
Unemployment: 18.6% (1988)
Budget: revenues $476 million; expenditures $543 million, including capital expenditures of $94 million (FY86)
Exports: $173 million (f.o.b., 1988); *commodities*—sugar and molasses, electrical components, clothing, rum, machinery and transport equipment; *partners:* US 30%, CARICOM, UK, Puerto Rico, Canada
Imports: $582 million (c.i.f., 1988); *commodities*—foodstuffs, consumer durables, raw materials, crude oil; *partners*—US 34%, CARICOM, Japan, UK, Canada
External debt: $635 million (December 1989 est.)
Industrial production: growth rate −5.4% (1987 est.)
Electricity: 132,000 kW capacity; 460 million kWh produced, 1,780 kWh per capita (1989)

Industries: tourism, sugar, light manufacturing, component assembly for export
Agriculture: accounts for 10% of GDP; major cash crop is sugarcane; other crops—vegetables and cotton; not self-sufficient in food
Aid: US commitments, including Ex-Im (FY70-84), $14 million; Western (non-US) countries, ODA and OOF bilateral commitments (1970-87), $144 million
Currency: Barbadian dollars (plural—dollars); 1 Barbadian dollar (Bds$) = 100 cents
Exchange rates: Barbadian dollars (Bds$) per US$1—2.0113 (fixed rate)
Fiscal year: 1 April-31 March

Communications

Highways: 1,570 km total; 1,475 km paved, 95 km gravel and earth
Ports: Bridgetown
Merchant marine: 2 cargo ships (1,000 GRT or over) totaling 3,200 GRT/7,338 DWT
Civil air: 2 major transport aircraft
Airports: 1 with permanent-surface runways 2,440-3,659 m
Telecommunications: islandwide automatic telephone system with 89,000 telephones; tropospheric scatter link to Trinidad and St. Lucia; stations—3 AM, 2 FM, 2 (1 is pay) TV; 1 Atlantic Ocean INTELSAT earth station

Defense Forces

Branches: Barbados Defense Force, Royal Barbados Police Force
Military manpower: males 15-49, 67,677; 47,566 fit for military service, no conscription
Defense expenditures: 0.6% of GDP (1986)

27

Bassas da India
(French possession)

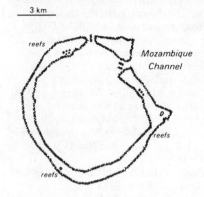

3 km

reefs

Mozambique Channel

reefs

reefs

See regional map VII

Geography

Total area: undetermined
Comparative area: undetermined
Land boundaries: none
Coastline: 35.2 km
Maritime claims:
Contiguous zone: 12 nm
Continental shelf: 200 meters or to depth of exploitation
Extended economic zone: 200 nm
Territorial sea: 12 nm
Disputes: claimed by Madagascar
Climate: tropical
Terrain: a volcanic rock 2.4 m high
Natural resources: none
Land use: 0% arable land; 0% permanent crops; 0% meadows and pastures; 0% forest and woodland; 100% other (rock)
Environment: surrounded by reefs; subject to periodic cyclones
Note: navigational hazard since it is usually under water during high tide; located in southern Mozambique Channel about halfway between Africa and Madagascar

People

Population: uninhabited

Government

Long-form name: none
Type: French possession administered by Commissioner of the Republic Daniel CONSTANTIN, resident in Reunion

Economy

Overview: no economic activity

Communications

Ports: none; offshore anchorage only

Defense Forces

Note: defense is the responsibility of France

Belgium

50 km

North Sea

Oostende   Antwerp
Kortrijk   BRUSSELS
Mons   Liège
Charleroi
Bastogne

See regional map V

Geography

Total area: 30,510 km^2; land area: 30,230 km^2
Comparative area: slightly larger than Maryland
Land boundaries: 1,385 km total; France 620 km, Luxembourg 148 km, Netherlands 450 km, FRG 167 km
Coastline: 64 km
Maritime claims:
Continental shelf: not specific
Exclusive fishing zone: equidistant line with neighbors (extends about 68 km from coast)
Territorial sea: 12 nm
Climate: temperate; mild winters, cool summers; rainy, humid, cloudy
Terrain: flat coastal plains in northwest, central rolling hills, rugged mountains of Ardennes Forest in southeast
Natural resources: coal, natural gas
Land use: 24% arable land; 1% permanent crops; 20% meadows and pastures; 21% forest and woodland; 34% other; includes NEGL% irrigated
Environment: air and water pollution
Note: majority of West European capitals within 1,000 km of Brussels; crossroads of Western Europe; Brussels is the seat of the EC

People

Population: 9,909,285 (July 1990), growth rate 0.1% (1990)
Birth rate: 12 births/1,000 population (1990)
Death rate: 11 deaths/1,000 population (1990)
Net migration rate: 0 migrants/1,000 population (1990)
Infant mortality rate: 6 deaths/1,000 live births (1990)
Life expectancy at birth: 73 years male, 80 years female (1990)

Total fertility rate: 1.6 children born/woman (1990)
Nationality: noun—Belgian(s); adjective—Belgian
Ethnic divisions: 55% Fleming, 33% Walloon, 12% mixed or other
Religion: 75% Roman Catholic; remainder Protestant or other
Language: 56% Flemish (Dutch), 32% French, 1% German; 11% legally bilingual; divided along ethnic lines
Literacy: 98%
Labor force: 4,000,000; 58% services, 37% industry, 5% agriculture (1987)
Organized labor: 70% of labor force

Government

Long-form name: Kingdom of Belgium
Type: constitutional monarchy
Capital: Brussels
Administrative divisions: 9 provinces (French—provinces, singular—province; Flemish—provinciën, singular—provincie); Antwerpen, Brabant, Hainaut, Liège, Limburg, Luxembourg, Namur, Oost-Vlaanderen, West-Vlaanderen
Independence: 4 October 1830 (from the Netherlands)
Constitution: 7 February 1831, last revised 8-9 August 1980; the government is in the process of revising the Constitution, with the aim of federalizing the Belgian state
Legal system: civil law system influenced by English constitutional theory; judicial review of legislative acts; accepts compulsory ICJ jurisdiction, with reservations
National holiday: National Day, 21 July (ascension of King Leopold to the throne in 1831)
Executive branch: monarch, prime minister, five deputy prime ministers, Cabinet
Legislative branch: bicameral Parliament consists of an upper chamber or Senate (Flemish—Senaat, French—Sénat) and a lower chamber or Chamber of Representatives (Flemish—Kamer van Volksvertegenwoordigers, French—Chambre des Représentants)
Judicial branch: Supreme Court of Justice (Flemish—Hof van Cassatie, French—Cour de Cassation)
Leaders: *Chief of State*—King BAUDOUIN I (since 17 July 1951); Heir Apparent Prince ALBERT of Liège (brother of the King; born 6 June 1934);
Head of Government—Prime Minister Wilfried MARTENS, (since April 1979, with a 10-month interruption in 1981)
Political parties and leaders: Flemish Social Christian (CVP), Herman van Rompuy, president; Walloon Social Christian (PSC), Gérard Deprez, president; Flemish Socialist (SP), Frank Vandenbroucke, president; Walloon Socialist (PS), Guy Spitaels, president; Flemish Liberal

(PVV), Guy Verhofstadt, president; Walloon Liberal (PRL), Antoine Duquesne, president; Francophone Democratic Front (FDF), Georges Clerfayt, president; Volksunie (VU), Jaak Gabriels, president; Communist Party (PCB), Louis van Geyt, president; Vlaams Blok (VB), Karel Dillen; other minor parties

Suffrage: universal and compulsory at age 18

Elections: *Senate*—last held 13 December 1987 (next to be held December 1991); results—CVP 19.2%, PS 15.7%, SP 14.7%, PVV 11.3%, PRL 9.3%, VU 8.1%, PSC 7.8%, ECOLO-AGALEV 7.7%, VB 2.0%, VDF 1.3%, other 1.96%; seats—(106 total) CVP 22, PS 20, SP 17, PRL 12, PVV 11, PSC 9, VU 8, ECOLO-AGALEV 5, VB 1, FDF 1; *Chamber of Representatives*—last held 13 December 1987 (next to be held December 1991); results—CVP 19.45%, PS 15.66%, SP 14.88%, PVV 11.55%, PRL 9.41%, PSC 8.01%, VU 8.05%, ECOLO-AGALEV 7.05%, VB 1.90%, FDF 1.16%, other 2.88%; seats—(212 total) CVP 43, PS 40, SP 32, PVV 25, PRL 23, PSC 19, VU 16, ECOLO-AGALEV 9, FDF 3, VB 2

Communists: under 5,000 members (December 1985 est.)

Other political or pressure groups: Christian and Socialist Trade Unions; Federation of Belgian Industries; numerous other associations representing bankers, manufacturers, middle-class artisans, and the legal and medical professions; various organizations represent the cultural interests of Flanders and Wallonia; various peace groups such as the Flemish Action Committee Against Nuclear Weapons and Pax Christi

Member of: ADB, Benelux, BLEU, CCC, Council of Europe, DAC, EC, ECE, ECOSOC, EIB, EMS, ESA, GATT, IAEA, IBRD, ICAC, ICAO, ICES, ICO, IDA, IDB—Inter-American Development Bank, IEA, IFAD, IFC, ILO, ILZSG, IMF, IMO, INTELSAT, INTERPOL, IOOC, IPU, ITC, ITU, NATO, OAS (observer), OECD, UN, UNESCO, UPU, WEU, WHO, WIPO, WMO, WSG

Diplomatic representation: Ambassador Herman DEHENNIN; Chancery at 3330 Garfield Street NW, Washington DC 20008; telephone (202) 333-6900; there are Belgian Consulates General in Atlanta, Chicago, Houston, Los Angeles, and New York; *US*—Ambassador Maynard W. GLITMAN; Embassy at 27 Boulevard du Regent, B-1000 Brussels (mailing address is APO New York 09667); telephone [32] (2) 513-3830; there is a US Consulate General in Antwerp

Flag: three equal vertical bands of black (hoist side), yellow, and red; the design was based on the flag of France

Economy

Overview: This small private-enterprise economy has capitalized on its central geographic location, highly developed transport network, and diversified industrial and commercial base. Industry is concentrated mainly in the populous Flemish area in the north, although the government is encouraging reinvestment in the southern region of Walloon. With few natural resources Belgium must import essential raw materials, making its economy closely dependent on the state of world markets. In 1988 over 70% of trade was with other EC countries. During the period 1986-88 the economy profited from falling oil prices and a lower dollar, which helped to improve the terms of trade. Real GDP grew by an average of 3.5% in 1986-89, up from 1.5% in 1985. However, a large budget deficit and 10% unemployment cast a shadow on the economy.

GDP: $136.0 billion, per capita $13,700; real growth rate 4.5% (1989 est.)

Inflation rate (consumer prices): 3.6% (1989 est.)

Unemployment rate: 9.7% est. (1989 est.)

Budget: revenues $45.0 billion; expenditures $55.3 billion, including capital expenditures of NA (1989)

Exports: $100.3 billion (f.o.b., 1989) Belgium-Luxembourg Economic Union; *commodities*—iron and steel, transportation equipment, tractors, diamonds, petroleum products; *partners*—EC 74%, US 5%, Communist countries 2% (1988)

Imports: $100.1 billion (c.i.f., 1989) Belgium-Luxembourg Economic Union; *commodities*—fuels, grains, chemicals, foodstuffs; *partners*—EC 72%, US 5%, oil-exporting less developed countries 4%, Communist countries 3% (1988)

External debt: $27.5 billion (1988)

Industrial production: growth rate 6.4% (1988)

Electricity: 17,325,000 kW capacity; 62,780 million kWh produced, 6,350 kWh per capita (1989)

Industries: engineering and metal products, processed food and beverages, chemicals, basic metals, textiles, glass, petroleum, coal

Agriculture: accounts for 2% of GDP; emphasis on livestock production—beef, veal, pork, milk; major crops are sugar beets, fresh vegetables, fruits, grain, and tobacco; net importer of farm products

Aid: donor—ODA and OOF commitments (1970-87), $4.3 billion

Currency: Belgian franc (plural—francs); 1 Belgian franc (BF) = 100 centimes

Exchange rates: Belgian francs (BF) per US$1—35.468 (January 1990), 39.404 (1989), 36.768 (1988), 37.334 (1987), 44.672 (1986), 59.378 (1985)

Fiscal year: calendar year

Communications

Railroads: Belgian National Railways (SNCB) operates 3,667 km 1.435-meter standard gauge, government owned; 2,563 km double track; 1,978 km electrified; 191 km 1.000-meter gauge, government owned and operated

Highways: 103,396 km total; 1,317 km limited access, divided autoroute; 11,717 km national highway; 1,362 km provincial road; about 38,000 km paved and 51,000 km unpaved rural roads

Inland waterways: 2,043 km (1,528 km in regular commercial use)

Ports: Antwerp, Brugge, Gent, Oostende, Zeebrugge, 1 secondary, and 1 minor maritime; 11 inland

Merchant marine: 67 ships (1,000 GRT or over) totaling 1,854,898 GRT/3,071,637 DWT; includes 1 short-sea passenger, 10 cargo, 6 roll-on/roll-off, 6 container, 7 petroleum, oils, and lubricants (POL) tanker, 6 liquefied gas, 3 combination ore/oil, 9 chemical tanker, 13 bulk, 6 combination bulk

Pipelines: refined products 1,167 km; crude 161 km; natural gas 3,300 km

Civil air: 47 major transport aircraft

Airports: 42 total, 42 usable; 24 with permanent-surface runways; none with runways over 3,659 m; 14 with runways 2,440-3,659 m; 3 with runways 1,220-2,439 m

Telecommunications: excellent domestic and international telephone and telegraph facilities; 4,560,000 telephones; stations—8 AM, 19 FM (41 relays), 25 TV (10 relays); 5 submarine cables; satellite earth stations operating in INTELSAT 3 Atlantic Ocean and EUTELSAT systems

Defense Forces

Branches: Army, Navy, Air Force

Military manpower: males 15-49, 2,512,681; 2,114,701 fit for military service; 66,758 reach military age (19) annually

Defense expenditures: 2.7% of GDP, or $3.7 billion (1989 est.)

Belize

75 km

See regional map III

Geography

Total area: 22,960 km²; land area: 22,800 km²
Comparative area: slightly larger than Massachusetts
Land boundaries: 516 km total; Guatemala 266 km, Mexico 250 km
Coastline: 386 km
Maritime claims:
Territorial sea: 3 nm
Disputes: claimed by Guatemala, but boundary negotiations are under way
Climate: tropical; very hot and humid; rainy season (May to February)
Terrain: flat, swampy coastal plain; low mountains in south
Natural resources: arable land potential, timber, fish
Land use: 2% arable land; NEGL% permanent crops; 2% meadows and pastures; 44% forest and woodland; 52% other; includes NEGL% irrigated
Environment: frequent devastating hurricanes (September to December) and coastal flooding (especially in south); deforestation
Note: national capital moved 80 km inland from Belize City to Belmopan because of hurricanes; only country in Central America without a coastline on the North Pacific Ocean

People

Population: 219,737 (July 1990), growth rate 3.7% (1990)
Birth rate: 38 births/1,000 population (1990)
Death rate: 6 deaths/1,000 population (1990)
Net migration rate: 4 migrants/1,000 population (1990)
Infant mortality rate: 35 deaths/1,000 live births (1990)
Life expectancy at birth: 67 years male, 72 years female (1990)

Total fertility rate: 4.8 children born/woman (1990)
Nationality: noun—Belizean(s); adjective—Belizean
Ethnic divisions: 39.7% Creole, 33.1% Mestizo, 9.5% Maya, 7.6% Garifuna, 2.1% East Indian, 8.0% other
Religion: 60% Roman Catholic; 40% Protestant (Anglican, Seventh-Day Adventist, Methodist, Baptist, Jehovah's Witnesses, Mennonite)
Language: English (official), Spanish, Maya, Garifuna (Carib)
Literacy: 93% (est.)
Labor force: 51,500; 30.0% agriculture, 16.0% services, 15.4% government, 11.2% commerce, 10.3% manufacturing; shortage of skilled labor and all types of technical personnel (1985)
Organized labor: 30% of labor force; 11 unions currently active

Government

Long-form name: none
Type: parliamentary
Capital: Belmopan
Administrative divisions: 6 districts; Belize, Cayo, Corozal, Orange Walk, Stann Creek, Toledo
Independence: 21 September 1981 (from UK; formerly British Honduras)
Constitution: 21 September 1981
Legal system: English law
National holiday: Independence Day, 21 September
Executive branch: British monarch, governor general, prime minister, deputy prime minister, Cabinet
Legislative branch: bicameral National Assembly consists of an upper house or Senate and a lower house or House of Representatives
Judicial branch: Supreme Court
Leaders: *Chief of State*—Queen ELIZABETH II (since 6 February 1952), represented by Governor General Dame Elmira Minita GORDON (since 21 September 1981);
Head of Government—Prime Minister George Cadle PRICE (since 4 September 1989)
Political parties and leaders: People's United Party (PUP), George Price, Florencio Marin, Said Musa; United Democratic Party (UDP), Manuel Esquivel, Curl Thompson, Dean Barrow; Belize Popular Party (BPP), Louis Sylvestre
Suffrage: universal at age 18
Elections: *National Assembly*—last held 4 September 1989 (next to be held September 1994); results—percent of vote by party NA; seats—(28 total) PUP 15 seats, UDP 13 seats; note—in January 1990 one member expelled from UDP joined PUP, making the seat count 16 PUP, UDP 12

Communists: negligible
Other political or pressure groups: Society for the Promotion of Education and Research (SPEAR) headed by former PUP minister; United Workers Front
Member of: ACP, CARICOM, CDB, Commonwealth, FAO, GATT, IBRD, IDA, IFAD, IFC, ILO, IMF, G-77, ISO, ITU, UN, UNESCO, UPU, WHO, WMO
Diplomatic representation: Ambassador Edward A. LAING; Chancery at Suite 2J, 3400 International Drive NW, Washington DC 20008; telephone (202) 363-4505; *US*—Ambassador Robert G. RICH, Jr.; Embassy at Gabourel Lane and Hutson Street, Belize City (mailing address is P. O. Box 286, Belize City); telephone [501] 77161 through 77163
Flag: blue with a narrow red stripe along the top and the bottom edges; centered is a large white disk bearing the coat of arms; the coat of arms features a shield flanked by two workers with a mahogany tree at the top and the related motto *SUB UMBRA FLOREO* (I Flourish in the Shade) on a scroll at the bottom, all encircled by a green garland

Economy

Overview: The economy is based primarily on agriculture and merchandising. Agriculture accounts for more than 30% of GDP and provides 75% of export earnings, while sugar, the chief crop, accounts for almost 40% of hard currency earnings. The US, Belize's main trading partner, is assisting in efforts to reduce dependency on sugar with an agricultural diversification program. In 1987 the drop in income from sugar sales to the US because of quota reductions was almost totally offset by higher world prices for sugar.
GDP: $225.6 million, per capita $1,285; real growth rate 6% (1989 est.)
Inflation rate (consumer prices): 1.5% (1988)
Unemployment rate: 14% (1988 est.)
Budget: revenues $94.6 million; expenditures $74.3 million, including capital expenditures of $33.9 million (1988 est.)
Exports: $120 million (f.o.b., 1988); *commodities*—sugar, clothing, seafood, molasses, citrus, wood and wood products; *partners*—US 47%, UK, Trinidad and Tobago, Canada (1987)
Imports: $176 million (c.i.f., 1988); *commodities*—machinery and transportation equipment, food, manufactured goods, fuels, chemicals, pharmaceuticals; *partners*—US 55%, UK, Netherlands Antilles, Mexico (1987)
External debt: $140 million (December 1988)

Industrial production: growth rate 6% (1988)
Electricity: 34,000 kW capacity; 88 million kWh produced, 500 kWh per capita (1989)
Industries: sugar refining, clothing, timber and forest products, furniture, rum, soap, beverages, cigarettes, tourism
Agriculture: accounts for 30% of GDP (including fish and forestry); commercial crops include sugarcane, bananas, coca, citrus fruits; expanding output of lumber and cultured shrimp; net importer of basic foods
Illicit drugs: an illicit producer of cannabis for the international drug trade; eradication program cut marijuana production from 200 metric tons in 1987 to 66 metric tons in 1989; transshipment point for cocaine
Aid: US commitments, including Ex-Im (FY70-88), $94 million; Western (non-US) countries, ODA and OOF bilateral commitments (1970-87), $194 million
Currency: Belizean dollar (plural—dollars); 1 Belizean dollar (Bz$) = 100 cents
Exchange rates: Belizean dollars (Bz$) per US$1—2.00 (fixed rate)
Fiscal year: 1 April-31 March

Communications

Highways: 2,575 km total; 340 km paved, 1,190 km gravel, 735 km improved earth, and 310 km unimproved earth
Inland waterways: 825 km river network used by shallow-draft craft; seasonally navigable
Ports: Belize City, Belize City Southwest
Civil air: no major transport aircraft
Airports: 38 total, 30 usable; 4 with permanent-surface runways; none with runways over 2,439 m; 2 with runways 1,220-2,439 m
Telecommunications: 8,650 telephones; above-average system based on radio relay; stations—6 AM, 5 FM, 1 TV, 1 shortwave; 1 Atlantic Ocean INTELSAT earth station

Defense Forces

Branches: British Forces Belize, Belize Defense Force, Police Department
Military manpower: males 15-49, 50,988; 30,502 fit for military service; 2,500 reach military age (18) annually
Defense expenditures: 2.0% of GDP, or $4.6 million (1989 est.)

Benin

150 km

Malanville

Natitingou

Parakou

Abomey

Cotonou PORTO-NOVO

Bight of Benin

See regional map VII

Geography

Total area: 112,620 km^2; land area: 110,620 km^2
Comparative area: slightly smaller than Pennsylvania
Land boundaries: 1,989 km total; Burkina 306 km, Niger 266 km, Nigeria 773 km, Togo 644 km
Coastline: 121 km
Maritime claims:
  Territorial sea: 200 nm
Climate: tropical; hot, humid in south; semiarid in north
Terrain: mostly flat to undulating plain; some hills and low mountains
Natural resources: small offshore oil deposits, limestone, marble, timber
Land use: 12% arable land; 4% permanent crops; 4% meadows and pastures; 35% forest and woodland; 45% other; includes NEGL% irrigated
Environment: hot, dry, dusty harmattan wind may affect north in winter; deforestation; desertification
Note: recent droughts have severely affected marginal agriculture in north; no natural harbors

People

Population: 4,673,964 (July 1990), growth rate 3.3% (1990)
Birth rate: 50 births/1,000 population (1990)
Death rate: 16 deaths/1,000 population (1990)
Net migration rate: NEGL migrants/1,000 population (1990)
Infant mortality rate: 121 deaths/1,000 live births (1990)
Life expectancy at birth: 48 years male, 52 years female (1990)
Total fertility rate: 7.1 children born/woman (1990)
Nationality: noun—Beninese (sing., pl.); adjective—Beninese

Ethnic divisions: 99% African (42 ethnic groups, most important being Fon, Adja, Yoruba, Bariba); 5,500 Europeans
Religion: 70% indigenous beliefs, 15% Muslim, 15% Christian
Language: French (official); Fon and Yoruba most common vernaculars in south; at least six major tribal languages in north
Literacy: 25.9%
Labor force: 1,900,000 (1987); 60% agriculture, 38% transport, commerce, and public services, less than 2% industry; 49% of population of working age (1985)
Organized labor: about 75% of wage earners

Government

Long-form name: Republic of Benin
Type: dropped Marxism-Leninism December 1989; democratic reforms adopted February 1990; transition to multiparty system by 1991 planned
Capital: Porto-Novo (official), Cotonou (de facto)
Administrative divisions: 6 provinces; Atakora, Atlantique, Borgou, Mono, Ouémé, Zou
Independence: 1 August 1960 (from France; formerly Dahomey)
Constitution: 23 May 1977 (nullified 1 March 1990); new constitution to be drafted by April 1990
Legal system: based on French civil law and customary law; has not accepted compulsory ICJ jurisdiction
National holiday: National Day, 30 November (1975)
Executive branch: president, prime minister, cabinet
Legislative branch: unicameral National Revolutionary Assembly (Assemblée Nationale Révolutionnaire) dissolved 1 March 1990 and replaced by a 24-member interim High Council of the Republic during the transition period
Judicial branch: Central People's Court (Cour Central Populaire)
Leaders: *Chief of State and Head of Government*—President Mathieu KEREKOU (since 27 October 1972)
Political parties and leaders: only party—People's Revolutionary Party of Benin (PRPB), President Mathieu Kérékou, chairman of the Central Committee
Suffrage: universal at age 18
Elections: *President*—last held July 1989 (next to be held July 1994); results—President Mathieu Kérékou was reelected by the National Revolutionary Assembly; *National Revolutionary Assembly*—dissolved 1 March 1990 and replaced by a 24-member interim High Council of the

Benin (continued)

Republic with legislative elections for new institutions planned for February 1991
Communists: dropped Marxism-Leninism December 1989
Member of: ACP, AfDB, CEAO, EAMA, ECA, ECOWAS, Entente, FAO, G-77, GATT, IBRD, ICAO, ICO, IDA, IFAD, ILO, IMF, IMO, INTELSAT, INTERPOL, ITU, NAM, Niger River Commission, OAU, OCAM, UN, UNESCO, UPU, WFTU, WHO, WIPO, WMO, WTO
Diplomatic representation: Ambassador Theophile NATA; Chancery at 2737 Cathedral Avenue NW, Washington DC 20008; telephone (202) 232-6656; *US*—Ambassador Harriet ISOM; Embassy at Rue Caporal Anani Bernard, Cotonou (mailing address is B. P. 2012, Cotonou); telephone [229] 30-06-50
Flag: green with a red five-pointed star in the upper hoist-side corner

Economy

Overview: Benin is one of the least developed countries in the world because of limited natural resources and a poorly developed infrastructure. Agriculture accounts for almost 45% of GDP, employs about 60% of the labor force, and generates a major share of foreign exchange earnings. The industrial sector contributes only about 15% to GDP and employs 2% of the work force. Persistently low prices in recent years have limited hard currency earnings from Benin's major exports of agricultural products and crude oil.
GDP: $1.7 billion, per capita $335; real growth rate 1.8% (1988)
Inflation rate (consumer prices): 4.3% (1988)
Unemployment: NA
Budget: revenues $168 million; expenditures $317 million, including capital expenditures of $97 million (1989)
Exports: $226 million (f.o.b., 1988); *commodities*—crude oil, cotton, palm products, cocoa; *partners*—FRG 36%, France 16%, Spain 14%, Italy 8%, UK 7%
Imports: $413 million (f.o.b., 1988); *commodities*—foodstuffs, beverages, tobacco, petroleum products, intermediate goods, capital goods, light consumer goods; *partners*—France 34%, Netherlands 10%, Japan 7%, Italy 6%, US 5%
External debt: $1.0 billion (December 1989 est.)
Industrial production: growth rate −0.7% (1988)
Electricity: 28,000 kW capacity; 24 million kWh produced, 5 kWh per capita (1989)
Industries: palm oil and palm kernel oil processing, textiles, beverages, petroleum

Agriculture: small farms produce 90% of agricultural output; production is dominated by food crops—corn, sorghum, cassava, beans, and rice; cash crops include cotton, palm oil, and peanuts; poultry and livestock output has not kept up with consumption
Aid: US commitments, including Ex-Im (FY70-88), $41 million; Western (non-US) countries, ODA and OOF bilateral commitments (1970-87), $1.0 billion; OPEC bilateral aid (1979-89), $19 million; Communist countries (1970-88), $101 million
Currency: Communauté Financière Africaine franc (plural—francs); 1 CFA franc (CFAF) = 100 centimes
Exchange rates: Communauté Financière Africaine francs (CFAF) per US$1—287.99 (January 1990), 319.01 (1989), 297.85 (1988), 300.54 (1987), 346.30 (1986), 449.26 (1985)
Fiscal year: calendar year

Communications

Railroads: 578 km, all 1.000-meter gauge, single track
Highways: 5,050 km total; 920 km paved, 2,600 laterite, 1,530 km improved earth
Inland waterways: navigable along small sections, important only locally
Ports: Cotonou
Merchant marine: 1 cargo ship (1,000 GRT or over) of 2,999 GRT/4,407 DWT
Civil air: 3 major transport aircraft
Airports: 6 total, 5 usable; 1 with permanent-surface runways; none with runways over 2,439 m; 4 with runways 1,220-2,439 m
Telecommunications: fair system of open wire, submarine cable, and radio relay; 16,200 telephones; stations—2 AM, 2 FM, 1 TV; 1 Atlantic Ocean INTELSAT satellite earth station

Defense Forces

Branches: Army, Navy, Air Force
Military manpower: eligible 15-49, 2,015,206; of the 950,921 males 15-49, 486,620 are fit for military service; of the 1,064,285 females 15-49, 537,049 are fit for military service; about 55,550 males and 53,663 females reach military age (18) annually; both sexes are liable for military service
Defense expenditures: 1.7% of GDP, or $28.9 million (1988 est.)

Bermuda
(dependent territory of the UK)

See regional map II

Geography

Total area: 50 km²; land area: 50 km²
Comparative area: about 0.3 times the size of Washington, DC
Land boundaries: none
Coastline: 103 km
Maritime claims:
  Continental shelf: 200 meters or to depth of exploitation
  Exclusive fishing zone: 200 nm
  Territorial sea: 12 nm
Climate: subtropical; mild, humid; gales, strong winds common in winter
Terrain: low hills separated by fertile depressions
Natural resources: limestone, pleasant climate fostering tourism
Land use: 0% arable land; 0% permanent crops; 0% meadows and pastures; 20% forest and woodland; 80% other
Environment: ample rainfall, but no rivers or freshwater lakes; consists of about 360 small coral islands
Note: 1,050 km east of North Carolina; some reclaimed land leased by US Government

People

Population: 58,337 (July 1990), growth rate 1.5% (1990)
Birth rate: 15 births/1,000 population (1990)
Death rate: 7 deaths/1,000 population (1990)
Net migration rate: −6 migrants/1,000 population (1990)
Infant mortality rate: 12 deaths/1,000 live births (1990)
Life expectancy at birth: 72 years male, 78 years female (1990)
Total fertility rate: 1.7 children born/woman (1990)
Nationality: noun—Bermudian(s); adjective—Bermudian

Ethnic divisions: 61% black, 39% white and other
Religion: 37% Anglican, 14% Roman Catholic, 10% African Methodist Episcopal (Zion), 6% Methodist, 5% Seventh-Day Adventist, 28% other
Language: English
Literacy: 98%
Labor force: 32,000; 25% clerical, 22% services, 21% laborers, 13% professional and technical, 10% administrative and managerial, 7% sales, 2% agriculture and fishing (1984)
Organized labor: 8,573 members (1985); largest union is Bermuda Industrial Union

Government

Long-form name: none
Type: dependent territory of the UK
Capital: Hamilton
Administrative divisions: 9 parishes and 2 municipalities*; Devonshire, Hamilton, Hamilton*, Paget, Pembroke, Saint George*, Saint George's, Sandys, Smiths, Southampton, Warwick
Independence: none (dependent territory of the UK)
Constitution: 8 June 1968
Legal system: English law
National holiday: Bermuda Day, 22 May
Executive branch: British monarch, governor, deputy governor, premier, deputy premier, Executive Council (cabinet)
Legislative branch: bicameral Parliament consists of an upper house or Senate and a lower house or House of Assembly
Judicial branch: Supreme Court
Leaders: *Chief of State*—Queen ELIZABETH II (since 6 February 1952), represented by Governor Sir Desmond LANGLEY (since NA October 1988);
Head of Government—Premier John William David SWAN (since NA January 1982)
Political parties and leaders: United Bermuda Party (UBP), John W. D. Swan; Progressive Labor Party (PLP), Frederick Wade; National Liberal Party (NLP), Gilbert Darrell
Suffrage: universal at age 21
Elections: *House of Assembly*—last held 9 February 1989 (next to be held by February 1994); results—percent of vote by party NA; seats—(40 total) UBP 23, PLP 15, NLP 1, other 1
Communists: negligible
Other political or pressure groups: Bermuda Industrial Union (BIU), headed by Ottiwell Simmons
Member of: INTERPOL, WHO
Diplomatic representation: as a dependent territory of the UK, Bermuda's interests in the US are represented by the UK; *US*—Consul General James M. MEDAS; Consulate General at Vallis Building, Par-

la-Ville Road (off Front Street West), Hamilton (mailing address is P. O. Box 325, Hamilton, or FPO New York 09560); telephone (809) 295-1342
Flag: red with the flag of the UK in the upper hoist-side quadrant and the Bermudian coat of arms (white and blue shield with a red lion holding a scrolled shield showing the sinking of the ship Sea Venture off Bermuda in 1609) centered on the outer half of the flag

Economy

Overview: Bermuda enjoys one of the highest per capita incomes in the world, having successfully exploited its location by providing luxury tourist facilities and financial services. The tourist industry attracts more than 90% of its business from North America. The industrial sector is small, and agriculture is severely limited by a lack of suitable land. About 80% of food needs are imported.
GDP: $1.3 billion, per capita $23,000; real growth rate 2.0% (1989 est.)
Inflation rate (consumer prices): 4.8% (1988)
Unemployment: 2.0% (1988)
Budget: revenues $280 million; expenditures $279 million, including capital expenditures of $34 million (FY89 est.)
Exports: $23 million (f.o.b.,1985); *commodities*—semitropical produce, light manufactures; *partners*—US 25%, Italy 25%, UK 14%, Canada 5%, other 31%
Imports: $402 million (c.i.f., 1985); *commodities*—fuel, foodstuffs, machinery; *partners*—US 58%, Netherlands Antilles 9%, UK 8%, Canada 6%, Japan 5%, other 14%
External debt: NA
Industrial production: growth rate NA%
Electricity: 134,000 kW capacity; 446 million kWh produced, 7,680 kWh per capita (1989)
Industries: tourism, finance, structural concrete products, paints, pharmaceuticals, ship repairing
Agriculture: accounts for less than 1% of GDP; most basic foods must be imported; produces bananas, vegetables, citrus fruits, flowers, dairy products
Aid: US commitments, including Ex-Im (FY70-81), $34 million; Western (non-US) countries, ODA and OOF bilateral commitments (1970-87), $267 million
Currency: Bermudian dollar (plural—dollars); 1 Bermudian dollar (Bd$) = 100 cents
Exchange rates: Bermudian dollar (Bd$) per US$1—1.0000 (fixed rate)
Fiscal year: 1 April-31 March

Communications

Highways: 210 km public roads, all paved (about 400 km of private roads)
Ports: Freeport, Hamilton, St. George
Merchant marine: 93 ships (1,000 GRT or over) totaling 4,163,947 GRT/7,744,319 DWT; includes 2 short-sea passenger, 10 cargo, 4 refrigerated cargo, 5 container, 10 roll-on/roll-off, 27 petroleum, oils, and lubricants (POL) tanker, 4 chemical tanker, 1 combination ore/oil, 10 liquefied gas, 20 bulk; note—a flag of convenience registry
Civil air: 16 major transport aircraft
Airports: 1 with permanent-surface runways 2,440-3,659 m
Telecommunications: modern with fully automatic telephone system; 46,290 telephones; stations—5 AM, 3 FM, 2 TV; 3 submarine cables; 2 Atlantic Ocean INTELSAT earth stations

Defense Forces

Note: defense is the responsibility of the UK

Bhutan

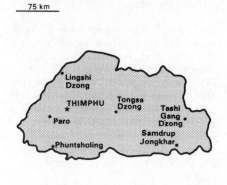

75 km

See regional map VIII

Geography

Total area: 47,000 km²; land area: 47,000 km²
Comparative area: slightly more than half the size of Indiana
Land boundaries: 1,075 km total; China 470 km, India 605 km
Coastline: none—landlocked
Maritime claims: none—landlocked
Climate: varies; tropical in southern plains; cool winters and hot summers in central valleys; severe winters and cool summers in Himalayas
Terrain: mostly mountainous with some fertile valleys and savanna
Natural resources: timber, hydropower, gypsum, calcium carbide
Land use: 2% arable land; NEGL% permanent crops; 5% meadows and pastures; 70% forest and woodland; 23% other
Environment: violent storms coming down from the Himalayas were the source of the country name which translates as Land of the Thunder Dragon
Note: landlocked; strategic location between China and India; controls several key Himalayan mountain passes

People

Population: 1,565,969 (July 1990), growth rate 2.0% (1990)
Birth rate: 37 births/1,000 population (1990)
Death rate: 17 deaths/1,000 population (1990)
Net migration rate: 0 migrants/1,000 population (1990)
Infant mortality rate: 137 deaths/1,000 live births (1990)
Life expectancy at birth: 50 years male, 48 years female (1990)
Total fertility rate: 5.0 children born/woman (1990)
Nationality: noun—Bhutanese (sing., pl.); adjective—Bhutanese

Ethnic divisions: 60% Bhote, 25% ethnic Nepalese, 15% indigenous or migrant tribes
Religion: 75% Lamaistic Buddhism, 25% Indian- and Nepalese-influenced Hinduism
Language: Bhotes speak various Tibetan dialects—most widely spoken dialect is Dzongkha (official); Nepalese speak various Nepalese dialects
Literacy: 5%
Labor force: NA; 95% agriculture, 1% industry and commerce; massive lack of skilled labor (1983)
Organized labor: not permitted

Government

Long-form name: Kingdom of Bhutan
Type: monarchy; special treaty relationship with India
Capital: Thimphu
Administrative divisions: 3 regions and 1 division*; Central Bhutan, Eastern Bhutan, Southern Bhutan*, Western Bhutan; note—there may now be 18 districts (dzong, singular and plural) named Bumthang, Chhukha, Chirang, Daga, Geylegphug, Ha, Lhuntshi, Mongar, Paro, Pemagatsel, Punakha, Samchi, Samdrup Jongkhar, Shemgang, Tashigang, Thimphu, Tongsa, Wangdiphodrang
Independence: 8 August 1949 (from India)
Constitution: no written constitution or bill of rights
Legal system: based on Indian law and English common law; has not accepted compulsory ICJ jurisdiction
National holiday: National Day (Ugyen Wangchuck became first hereditary king), 17 December (1907)
Executive branch: monarch, chairman of the Royal Advisory Council, Royal Advisory Council (Lodoi Tsokde), chairman of the Council of Ministers, Council of Ministers (Lhengye Shungtsog)
Legislative branch: unicameral National Assembly (Tshogdu)
Judicial branch: High Court
Leaders: *Chief of State and Head of Government*—King Jigme Singye WANGCHUCK (since 24 July 1972)
Political parties: no legal parties
Suffrage: each family has one vote in village-level elections
Elections: no national elections
Communists: no overt Communist presence
Other political or pressure groups: Buddhist clergy, Indian merchant community, ethnic Nepalese organizations
Member of: ADB, Colombo Plan, ESCAP, FAO, G-77, IBRD, IDA, IFAD, IMF, NAM, SAARC, UNESCO, UPU, UN, WHO

Diplomatic representation: no formal diplomatic relations, although informal contact is maintained between the Bhutanese and US Embassies in New Delhi (India); the Bhutanese mission to the UN in New York has consular jurisdiction in the US
Flag: divided diagonally from the lower hoist side corner; the upper triangle is orange and the lower triangle is red; centered along the dividing line is a large black and white dragon facing away from the hoist side

Economy

Overview: The economy is based on agriculture and forestry, which provide the main livelihood for 90% of the population and account for about 50% of GDP. One of the world's least developed countries, rugged mountains dominate and make the building of roads and other infrastructure difficult and expensive. Bhutan's hydropower potential and its attraction for tourists are its most important natural resources.
GDP: $273 million, per capita $199; real growth rate 6.3% (1988 est.)
Inflation rate (consumer prices): 10% (1989 est.)
Unemployment: NA
Budget: revenues $99 million; expenditures $128 million, including capital expenditures of $65 million (FY89 est.)
Exports: $70.9 million (f.o.b., FY89); *commodities*—cardamon, gypsum, timber, handicrafts, cement, fruit; *partners*—India 93%
Imports: $138.3 million (c.i.f., FY89 est.); *commodities*—fuel and lubricants, grain, machinery and parts, vehicles, fabrics; *partners*—India 67%
External debt: $70.1 million (FY89 est.)
Industrial production: growth rate −12.4% (1988 est.)
Electricity: 353,000 kW capacity; 2,000 million kWh produced, 1,300 kWh per capita (1989)
Industries: cement, chemical products, mining, distilling, food processing, handicrafts
Agriculture: accounts for 50% of GDP; based on subsistence farming and animal husbandry; self-sufficient in food except for foodgrains; other production—rice, corn, root crops, citrus fruit, dairy, and eggs
Aid: Western (non-US) countries, ODA and OOF bilateral commitments (1970-87), $85.8 million; OPEC bilateral aid (1979-89), $11 million
Currency: ngultrum (plural—ngultrum); 1 ngultrum (Nu) = 100 chetrum; note—Indian currency is also legal tender
Exchange rates: ngultrum (Nu) per US$1—16.965 (January 1990), 16.226

Bolivia

(1989), 13.917 (1988), 12.962 (1987),
12.611 (1986), 12.369 (1985); note—the
Bhutanese ngultrum is at par with the
Indian rupee
Fiscal year: 1 July-30 June

Communications

Highways: 1,304 km total; 418 km surfaced, 515 km improved, 371 km unimproved earth
Civil air: 1 jet, 2 prop
Airports: 2 total, 2 usable; 1 with
permanent-surface runways; none with
runways over 2,439 m; 2 with runways
1,220-2,439 m
Telecommunications: inadequate; 1,890
telephones (1985); 15,000 radio receivers
(1987 est.); 85 TV sets (1985); stations—
20 AM, no FM, no TV

Defense Forces

Branches: Royal Bhutan Army
Military manpower: males 15-49, 389,142;
208,231 fit for military service; 17,203
reach military age (18) annually
Defense expenditures: NA

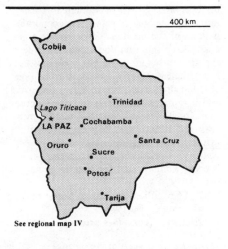

See regional map IV

Geography

Total area: 1,098,580 km^2; land area:
1,084,390 km^2
Comparative area: slightly less than three
times the size of Montana
Land boundaries: 6,743 km total; Argentina 832 km, Brazil 3,400 km, Chile 861
km, Paraguay 750 km, Peru 900 km
Coastline: none—landlocked
Maritime claims: none—landlocked
Disputes: has wanted a sovereign corridor
to the South Pacific Ocean since the Atacama area was lost to Chile in 1884; dispute with Chile over Río Lauca water
rights
Climate: varies with altitude; humid and
tropical to cold and semiarid
Terrain: high plateau, hills, lowland plains
Natural resources: tin, natural gas, crude
oil, zinc, tungsten, antimony, silver, iron
ore, lead, gold, timber
Land use: 3% arable land; NEGL% permanent crops; 25% meadows and pastures;
52% forest and woodland; 20% other; includes NEGL% irrigated
Environment: cold, thin air of high plateau
is obstacle to efficient fuel combustion;
overgrazing; soil erosion; desertification
Note: landlocked; shares control of Lago
Titicaca, world's highest navigable lake,
with Peru

People

Population: 6,706,854 (July 1990), growth
rate 2.1% (1990)
Birth rate: 35 births/1,000 population
(1990)
Death rate: 13 deaths/1,000 population
(1990)
Net migration rate: −1 migrant/1,000
population (1990)
Infant mortality rate: 125 deaths/1,000
live births (1990)
Life expectancy at birth: 52 years male,
56 years female (1990)

Total fertility rate: 4.7 children born/
woman (1990)
Nationality: noun—Bolivian(s); adjective
Bolivian
Ethnic divisions: 30% Quechua, 25% Aymara, 25-30% mixed, 5-15% European
Religion: 95% Roman Catholic; active
Protestant minority, especially Evangelical
Methodist
Language: Spanish, Quechua, and Aymara (all official)
Literacy: 63%
Labor force: 1,700,000; 50% agriculture,
26% services and utilities, 10% manufacturing, 4% mining, 10% other (1983)
Organized labor: 150,000-200,000, concentrated in mining, industry, construction,
and transportation; mostly organized under Bolivian Workers' Central (COB) labor federation

Government

Long-form name: Republic of Bolivia
Type: republic
Capital: La Paz (seat of government); Sucre (legal capital and seat of judiciary)
Administrative divisions: 9 departments
(departamentos, singular—departamento);
Chuquisaca, Cochabamba, El Beni, La
Paz, Oruro, Pando, Potosí, Santa Cruz,
Tarija
Independence: 6 August 1825 (from Spain)
Constitution: 2 February 1967
Legal system: based on Spanish law and
Code Napoleon; has not accepted compulsory ICJ jurisdiction
National holiday: Independence Day, 6
August (1825)
Executive branch: president, vice president, Cabinet
Legislative branch: bicameral National
Congress (Congreso Nacional) consists of
an upper chamber or Senate (Senado) and
a lower chamber or Chamber of Deputies
(Cámara de Diputados)
Judicial branch: Supreme Court (Corte
Suprema)
Leaders: *Chief of State and Head of Government*—President Jaime PAZ Zamora
(since 6 August 1989); Vice President Luis
OSSIO Sanjines (since 6 August 1989)
Political parties and leaders: Movement of
the Revolutionary Left (MIR), Jaime Paz
Zamora; Nationalist Democratic Action
(ADN), Hugo Banzer Suárez; Nationalist
Revolutionary Movement (MNR), Gonzalo Sánchez de Lozada; United Left (IU),
coalition of leftist parties which includes
Free Bolivia Movement (MBL), led by
Antonio Aranibar, Patriotic National
Convergency Axis (EJE-P) led by Walter
Delgadillo, and Bolivian Communist Party
(PCB) led by Humberto Ramirez; Conscience of the Fatherland (CONDEPA),

Bolivia *(continued)*

Carlos Palenque Avilés; Revolutionary Vanguard-9th of April (VR-9), Carlos Serrate Reich
Suffrage: universal and compulsory at age 18 (married) or 21 (single)
Elections: *President*—last held 7 May 1989 (next to be held May 1993); results—Gonzalo Sánchez de Lozada (MNR) 23%, Hugo Banzer Suárez (ADN) 22%, Jaime Paz Zamora (MIR) 19%; no candidate received a majority of the popular vote; Jaime Paz Zamora (MIR) formed a coalition with Hugo Banzer (ADN); with ADN support Paz Zamora won the congressional runoff election on 4 August and was inaugurated on 6 August; *Senate*—last held 7 May 1989 (next to be held May 1993); results—percent of vote NA; seats (27 total) MNR 9, ADN 8, MIR 8, CONDEPA 2; *Chamber of Deputies*—last held 7 May 1989 (next to be held May 1993); results—percent of vote by party NA; seats (130 total) MNR 40, ADN 38, MIR 30, IU 10, CONDEPA 9, VR-9 3
Member of: FAO, G-77, IADB, IAEA, IATP, IBRD, ICAO, ICO, IDA, IDB—Inter-American Development Bank, IFAD, IFC, ILO, IMF, INTELSAT, INTERPOL, ISO, ITC, ITU, IWC—International Wheat Council, LAIA, NAM, OAS, PAHO, SELA, UN, UNESCO, UPU, WHO, WMO, WTO
Diplomatic representation: Ambassador Jorge CRESPO; Chancery at 3014 Massachusetts Avenue NW, Washington DC 20008; telephone (202) 483-4410 through 4412; there are Bolivian Consulates General in Houston, Los Angeles, Miami, New Orleans, New York, and San Francisco; *US*—Ambassador Robert GELBARD; Embassy at Banco Popular del Peru Building, corner of Calles Mercado y Colon, La Paz (mailing address is P. O. Box 425, La Paz, or APO Miami 34032); telephone [591] (2) 350251 or 350120
Flag: three equal horizontal bands of red (top), yellow, and green with the coat of arms centered on the yellow band; similar to the flag of Ghana, which has a large black five-pointed star centered in the yellow band

Economy

Overview: The Bolivian economy steadily deteriorated between 1980 and 1985 as La Paz financed growing budget deficits by expanding the money supply and inflation spiraled—peaking at 11,700%. An austere orthodox economic program adopted by newly elected President Paz Estenssoro in 1985, however, succeeded in reducing inflation to between 10% and 20% annually during 1987 and 1989, eventually restart-

ing economic growth. President Paz Zamora has pledged to retain the economic policies of the previous government in order to keep inflation down and continue the growth begun under his predecessor. Nevertheless, Bolivia continues to be one of the poorest countries in Latin America, and it remains vulnerable to price fluctuations for its limited exports—mainly minerals and natural gas. Moreover, for many farmers, who constitute half of the country's work force, the main cash crop is coca, which is sold for cocaine processing.
GNP: $4.6 billion, per capita $660; real growth rate 2.8% (1988)
Inflation rate (consumer prices): 15.5% (1989)
Unemployment rate: 20.7% (1988)
Budget: revenues $2,867 million; expenditures $2,867 million, including capital expenditures of $663 million (1987)
Exports: $634 million (f.o.b., 1989); *commodities*—metals 45%, natural gas 32%, coffee, soybeans, sugar, cotton, timber, and illicit drugs; *partners*—US 23%, Argentina
Imports: $786 million (c.i.f., 1989); *commodities*—food, petroleum, consumer goods, capital goods; *partners*—US 15%
External debt: $5.7 billion (December 1989)
Industrial production: growth rate 8.1% (1987)
Electricity: 817,000 kW capacity; 1,728 million kWh produced, 260 kWh per capita (1989)
Industries: mining, smelting, petroleum, food and beverage, tobacco, handicrafts, clothing; illicit drug industry reportedly produces the largest revenues
Agriculture: accounts for 20% of GDP (including forestry and fisheries); principal commodities—coffee, coca, cotton, corn, sugarcane, rice, potatoes, timber; self-sufficient in food
Illicit drugs: world's second-largest producer of coca (after Peru) with an estimated 54,000 hectares under cultivation; government considers all but 12,000 hectares illicit and subject to eradication; intermediate coca products and cocaine exported to or through Colombia and Brazil to the US and other international drug markets
Aid: US commitments, including Ex-Im (FY70-88), $909 million; Western (non-US) countries, ODA and OOF bilateral commitments (1970-87), $1.4 billion; Communist countries (1970-88), $340 million
Currency: boliviano (plural—bolivianos); 1 boliviano ($B) = 100 centavos

Exchange rates: bolivianos ($B) per US$1—2.6917 (1989), 2.3502 (1988), 2.0549 (1987), 1.9220 (1986), 0.4400 (1985)
Fiscal year: calendar year

Communications

Railroads: 3,675 km total; 3,643 km 1.000-meter gauge and 32 km 0.760-meter gauge, all government owned, single track
Highways: 38,836 km total; 1,300 km paved, 6,700 km gravel, 30,836 km improved and unimproved earth
Inland waterways: 10,000 km of commercially navigable waterways
Pipelines: crude oil 1,800 km; refined products 580 km; natural gas 1,495 km
Ports: none; maritime outlets are Arica and Antofagasta in Chile and Matarani in Peru
Merchant marine: 2 cargo ships (1,000 GRT or over) totaling 14,051 GRT/22,155 DWT; note—1 is owned by the Bolivian Navy
Civil air: 56 major transport aircraft
Airports: 636 total, 551 usable; 9 with permanent-surface runways; 1 with runways over 3,659 m; 8 with runways 2,440-3,659 m; 110 with runways 1,220-2,439 m
Telecommunications: radio relay system being expanded; improved international services; 144,300 telephones; stations—129 AM, no FM, 43 TV, 68 shortwave; 1 Atlantic Ocean INTELSAT earth station

Defense Forces

Branches: Bolivian Army, Bolivian Navy, Bolivian Air Force (literally, the Army of the Nation, the Navy of the Nation, the Air Force of the Nation)
Military manpower: males 15-49, 1,629,154; 1,060,187 fit for military service; 70,528 reach military age (19) annually
Defense expenditures: 3% of GNP (1987)

Botswana

See regional map VII

Geography

Total area: 600,370 km²; land area: 585,370 km²
Comparative area: slightly smaller than Texas
Land boundaries: 4,013 km total; Namibia 1,360 km, South Africa 1,840 km, Zimbabwe 813 km
Coastline: none—landlocked
Maritime claims: none—landlocked
Disputes: short section of the boundary with Namibia is indefinite; quadripoint with Namibia, Zambia, and Zimbabwe is in disagreement
Climate: semiarid; warm winters and hot summers
Terrain: predominately flat to gently rolling tableland; Kalahari Desert in southwest
Natural resources: diamonds, copper, nickel, salt, soda ash, potash, coal, iron ore, silver, natural gas
Land use: 2% arable land; 0% permanent crops; 75% meadows and pastures; 2% forest and woodland; 21% other; includes NEGL% irrigated
Environment: rains in early 1988 broke six years of drought that had severely affected the important cattle industry; overgrazing; desertification
Note: landlocked; very long boundary with South Africa

People

Population: 1,224,527 (July 1990), growth rate 2.8% (1990)
Birth rate: 37 births/1,000 population (1990)
Death rate: 9 deaths/1,000 population (1990)
Net migration rate: 0 migrants/1,000 population (1990)
Infant mortality rate: 43 deaths/1,000 live births (1990)

Life expectancy at birth: 58 years male, 64 years female (1990)
Total fertility rate: 4.8 children born/woman (1990)
Nationality: noun and adjective—Motswana (singular), Batswana (plural)
Ethnic divisions: 95% Batswana; about 4% Kalanga, Basarwa, and Kgalagadi; about 1% white
Religion: 50% indigenous beliefs, 50% Christian
Language: English (official), Setswana
Literacy: 60%
Labor force: 400,000; 163,000 formal sector employees, most others are engaged in cattle raising and subsistence agriculture (1988 est.); 19,000 are employed in various mines in South Africa (1988)
Organized labor: 19 trade unions

Government

Long-form name: Republic of Botswana
Type: parliamentary republic
Capital: Gaborone
Administrative divisions: 10 districts; Central, Chobe, Ghanzi, Kgalagadi, Kgatleng, Kweneng, Ngamiland, North-East, South-East, Southern; note—in addition, there may now be 4 town councils named Francistown, Gaborone, Lobaste, Selebi-Pikwe
Independence: 30 September 1966 (from UK; formerly Bechuanaland)
Constitution: March 1965, effective 30 September 1966
Legal system: based on Roman-Dutch law and local customary law; judicial review limited to matters of interpretation; has not accepted compulsory ICJ jurisdiction
National holiday: Botswana Day, 30 September (1966)
Executive branch: president, vice president, Cabinet
Legislative branch: bicameral Parliament consists of an upper house or House of Chiefs and a lower house or National Assembly
Judicial branch: High Court, Court of Appeal
Leaders: *Chief of State and Head of Government*—President Quett K. J. MASIRE (since 13 July 1980); Vice President Peter S. MMUSI (since 3 January 1983)
Political parties and leaders: Botswana Democratic Party (BDP), Quett Masire; Botswana National Front (BNF), Kenneth Koma; Botswana People's Party (BPP), Knight Maripe; Botswana Independence Party (BIP), Motsamai Mpho; Botswana Progressive Union (BPU), Daniel Kwele
Suffrage: universal at age 21
Elections: *President*—last held 7 October 1989 (next to be held October 1994); results—President Quett K. J. Masire was reelected by the National Assembly;

National Assembly—last held 7 October 1989 (next to be held October 1994); results—percent of vote by party NA; seats—(34 total, 30 elected) BDP 31, BNF 3
Communists: no known Communist organization; Koma of BNF has long history of Communist contacts
Member of: ACP, AfDB, CCC, Commonwealth, FAO, G-77, GATT (de facto), IBRD, ICAO, IDA, IFAD, IFC, ILO, IMF, INTERPOL, ITU, NAM, OAU, Southern African Customs Union, SADCC, UN, UNESCO, UPU, WHO, WMO
Diplomatic representation: Ambassador Botsweletse Kingsley SEBELE; Chancery at Suite 404, 4301 Connecticut Avenue NW, Washington DC 20008; telephone (202) 244-4990 or 4991; *US*—Ambassador (vacant); Deputy Chief of Mission Johnnie CARSON; Embassy at Botswana Road, Gaborone (mailing address is P. O. Box 90, Gaborone); telephone [267] 353982 through 353984
Flag: light blue with a horizontal white-edged black stripe in the center

Economy

Overview: The economy has historically been based on cattle raising and crops. Agriculture today provides a livelihood for over 80% of the population, but produces only about 50% of food needs and contributes a small 5% to GDP. The driving force behind the rapid economic growth of the 1970s and 1980s has been the mining industry. This sector, mostly on the strength of diamonds, has gone from generating 25% of GDP in 1980 to over 50% in 1988. No other sector has experienced such growth, especially not that of the agricultural sector, which is plagued by erratic rainfall and poor soils. The unemployment rate remains a problem at 25%. A scarce resource base limits diversification into labor-intensive industries.
GDP: $1.87 billion, per capita $1,600; real growth rate 8.4% (FY88)
Inflation rate (consumer prices): 11.45% (1989)
Unemployment rate: 25% (1987)
Budget: revenues $1,235 million; expenditures $1,080 million, including capital expenditures of NA (FY90 est.)
Exports: $1.3 billion (f.o.b., 1988); *commodities*—diamonds 88%, copper and nickel 5%, meat 4%, cattle, animal products; *partners*—Switzerland, US, UK, other EC-associated members of Southern African Customs Union
Imports: $1.1 billion (c.i.f., 1988); *commodities*—foodstuffs, vehicles, textiles, petroleum products;

37

Botswana (continued)

partners—Switzerland, US, UK, other EC-associated members of Southern African Customs Union
External debt: $700 million (December 1989 est.)
Industrial production: growth rate 16.8% (FY86)
Electricity: 217,000 kW capacity; 630 million kWh produced, 510 kWh per capita (1989)
Industries: livestock processing; mining of diamonds, copper, nickel, coal, salt, soda ash, potash; tourism
Agriculture: accounts for only 5% of GDP; subsistence farming predominates; cattle raising supports 50% of the population; must import large share of food needs
Aid: US commitments, including Ex-Im (FY70-88), $242 million; Western (non-US) countries, ODA and OOF bilateral commitments (1970-87), $1.6 billion; OPEC bilateral aid (1979-89), $43 million; Communist countries (1970-88), $24 million
Currency: pula (plural—pula); 1 pula (P) = 100 thebe
Exchange rates: pula (P) per US$1— 1.8734 (January 1990), 2.0125 (1989), 1.8159 (1988), 1.6779 (1987), 1.8678 (1986), 1.8882 (1985)
Fiscal year: 1 April-31 March

Communications

Railroads: 712 km 1.0 67-meter gauge
Highways: 11,514 km total; 1,600 km paved; 1,700 km crushed stone or gravel, 5,177 km improved earth, 3,037 km unimproved earth
Civil air: 6 major transport aircraft
Airports: 99 total, 87 usable; 8 with permanent-surface runways; none with runways over 3,659 m; 2 with runways 2,440-3,659 m; 23 with runways 1,220-2,439 m
Telecommunications: the small system is a combination of open-wire lines, radio relay links, and a few radiocommunication stations; 17,900 telephones; stations—2 AM, 3 FM, no TV; 1 Indian Ocean INTELSAT earth station

Defense Forces

Branches: Army, Air Wing, Botswana Police
Military manpower: males 15-49, 249,480; 131,304 fit for military service; 14,363 reach military age (18) annually
Defense expenditures: 2.2% of GNP (1987)

Bouvet Island
(territory of Norway)

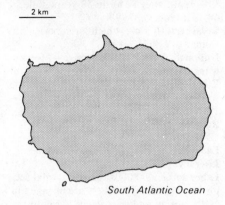

2 km

South Atlantic Ocean

See regional map XII

Geography

Total area: 58 km²; land area: 58 km²
Comparative area: about 0.3 times the size of Washington, DC
Land boundaries: none
Coastline: 29.6 km
Maritime claims:
Contiguous zone: 10 nm
Continental shelf: 200 meters or to depth of exploitation
Extended economic zone: 200 nm
Territorial sea: 4 nm
Climate: antarctic
Terrain: volcanic; maximum elevation about 800 meters; coast is mostly inaccessible
Natural resources: none
Land use: 0% arable land; 0% permanent crops; 0% meadows and pastures; 0% forest and woodland; 100% other
Environment: covered by glacial ice
Note: located in the South Atlantic Ocean 2,575 km south-southwest of the Cape of Good Hope, South Africa

People

Population: uninhabited

Government

Long-form name: none
Type: territory of Norway

Economy

Overview: no economic activity

Communications

Ports: none; offshore anchorage only
Telecommunications: automatic meteorological station

Defense Forces

Note: defense is the responsibility of Norway

Brazil

North Atlantic Ocean
Belém
Manaus
São Luís
Rio Branco
Recife
Cuiabá
Salvador
BRASÍLIA
Belo Horizonte
Corumbá
Rio de Janeiro
São Paulo
Boundary representation is not necessarily authoritative.
South Atlantic Ocean
Pôrto Alegre

1000 km

See regional map IV

Geography

Total area: 8,511,965 km²; land area: 8,456,510 km²; includes Arquipélago de Fernando de Noronha, Atol das Rocas, Ilha da Trindade, Ilhas Martin Vaz, and Penedos de São Pedro e São Paulo
Comparative area: slightly smaller than the US
Land boundaries: 14,691 km total; Argentina 1,224 km, Bolivia 3,400 km, Colombia 1,643 km, French Guiana 673 km, Guyana 1,119 km, Paraguay 1,290 km, Peru 1,560 km, Suriname 597 km, Uruguay 985 km, Venezuela 2,200 km
Coastline: 7,491 km
Maritime claims:
Continental shelf: 200 meters or to depth of exploitation
Exclusive fishing zone: 200 nm
Territorial sea: 200 nm
Disputes: short section of the boundary with Paraguay (just west of Guaíra Falls on the Rio Paraná) is in dispute; two short sections of boundary with Uruguay are in dispute (Arroyo de la Invernada area of the Rio Quaraí and the islands at the confluence of the Rio Quaraí and the Uruguay); claims a Zone of Interest in Antarctica
Climate: mostly tropical, but temperate in south
Terrain: mostly flat to rolling lowlands in north; some plains, hills, mountains, and narrow coastal belt
Natural resources: iron ore, manganese, bauxite, nickel, uranium, phosphates, tin, hydropower, gold, platinum, crude oil, timber
Land use: 7% arable land; 1% permanent crops; 19% meadows and pastures; 67% forest and woodland; 6% other; includes NEGL% irrigated
Environment: recurrent droughts in northeast; floods and frost in south; deforestation in Amazon basin; air and water pollution in Rio de Janeiro and São Paulo

Note: largest country in South America; shares common boundaries with every South American country except Chile and Ecuador

People

Population: 152,505,077 (July 1990), growth rate 1.9% (1990)
Birth rate: 26 births/1,000 population (1990)
Death rate: 7 deaths/1,000 population (1990)
Net migration rate: 0 migrants/1,000 population (1990)
Infant mortality rate: 69 deaths/1,000 live births (1990)
Life expectancy at birth: 62 years male, 68 years female (1990)
Total fertility rate: 3.1 children born/woman (1990)
Nationality: noun—Brazilian(s); adjective—Brazilian
Ethnic divisions: Portuguese, Italian, German, Japanese, black, Amerindian; 55% white, 38% mixed, 6% black, 1% other
Religion: 90% Roman Catholic (nominal)
Language: Portuguese (official), Spanish, English, French
Literacy: 76%
Labor force: 57,000,000 (1989 est.); 42% services, 31% agriculture, 27% industry
Organized labor: 13,000,000 dues paying members (1989 est.)

Government

Long-form name: Federative Republic of Brazil
Type: federal republic
Capital: Brasília
Administrative divisions: 24 states (estados, singular—estado), 2 territories* (territórios, singular—território), and 1 federal district** (distrito federal); Acre, Alagoas, Amapá*, Amazonas, Bahia, Ceará, Distrito Federal**, Espírito Santo, Goiás, Maranhão, Mato Grosso, Mato Grosso do Sul, Minas Gerais, Pará, Paraíba, Paraná, Pernambuco, Piauí, Rio de Janeiro, Rio Grande do Norte, Rio Grande do Sul, Rondônia, Roraima*, Santa Catarina, São Paulo, Sergipe, Tocantins; note—the territories of Amapá and Roraima will become states on 15 March 1991
Independence: 7 September 1822 (from Portugal)
Constitution: 5 October 1988
Legal system: based on Latin codes; has not accepted compulsory ICJ jurisdiction
National holiday: Independence Day, 7 September (1822)
Executive branch: president, vice president, Cabinet

Legislative branch: bicameral National Congress (Congresso Nacional) consists of an upper chamber or Senate (Senado) and a lower chamber or Chamber of Deputies (Cámara dos Deputados)
Judicial branch: Supreme Federal Tribunal
Leaders: *Chief of State and Head of Government*—President Fernando Affonso COLLOR de Mello (since 15 March 1990); Vice President Itamar FRANCO (since 15 March 1990)
Political parties and leaders: National Reconstruction Party (PRN), Daniel Tourinho, president; Brazilian Democratic Movement Party (PMDB), Ulysses Guimarães, president; Liberal Front Party (PFL), Hugo Napoleão, president; Workers' Party (PT), Luis Ignácio (Lula) da Silva, president; Brazilian Labor Party (PTB), Luiz Gonzaga de Paiva Muniz, president; Democratic Labor Party (PDT), Doutel de Andrade, president; Democratic Social Party (PDS), Jarbas Passarinho, president; Brazilian Social Democracy Party (PSDB), Mário Covas, president; Brazilian Communist Party (PCB), Salomão Malina, secretary general; Communist Party of Brazil (PCdoB), João Amazonas, president
Suffrage: voluntary at age 16; compulsory between ages 18 and 70; voluntary at age 70
Elections: *President*—last held 15 November 1989, with runoff on 17 December 1989 (next to be held November 1994); results—Fernando Collor de Mello 53%, Luis Inácio da Silva 47%; first free, direct presidential election since 1960; *Senate*—last held 15 November 1986 (next to be held 3 October 1990); results—PMDB 60%, PFL 21%, PDS 8%, PDT 3%, others 8%; seats—(66 total) PMDB 43, PFL 15, PDS 6, PDT 2, others 6; note—as of 1990 Senate has 75 seats; *Chamber of Deputies*—last held 15 November 1986 (next to be held 3 October 1990); results—PMDB 53%, PFL 23%, PDS 7%, PDT 5%, other 12%; seats—(495 total) PMDB 258, PFL 114, PDS 33, PDT 24, others 58; note—as of 1990 Chamber of Deputies has 570 seats
Communists: about 30,000
Other political or pressure groups: left wing of the Catholic Church and labor unions allied to leftist Worker's Party are critical of government's social and economic policies
Member of: CCC, FAO, G-77, GATT, Group of Eight, IADB, IAEA, IBRD, ICAC, ICAO, ICO, IDA, IDB—Inter-American Development Bank, IFAD, IFC, IHO, ILO, IMF, IMO, INTELSAT, IPU, IRC, ISO, ITU, IWC—International Wheat Council, OAS,

PAHO, SELA, UN, UNESCO, UPU, WHO, WIPO, WMO, WTO
Diplomatic representation: Ambassador Marcilio Marques MOREIRA; Chancery at 3006 Massachusetts Avenue NW, Washington DC 20008; telephone (202) 745-2700; there are Brazilian Consulates General in Atlanta, Chicago, Los Angeles, Miami, New Orleans, and New York, and Consulates in Dallas, Houston, and San Francisco; *US*—Ambassador Richard MELTON; Embassy at Avenida das Nocoes, Lote 3, Brasilia, Distrito Federal (mailing address is APO Miami 34030); telephone [55] (6) 321-7272; there are US Consulates General in Rio de Janeiro and São Paulo, and Consulates in Pôrto Alegre and Recife
Flag: green with a large yellow diamond in the center bearing a blue celestial globe with 23 white five-pointed stars (one for each state) arranged in the same pattern as the night sky over Brazil; the globe has a white equatorial band with the motto *ORDEM E PROGRESSO* (Order and Progress)

Economy

Overview: The economy, a mixture of private enterprises of all sizes and extensive government intervention, experienced enormous difficulties in the late 1980s, notably declining real growth, runaway inflation, foreign debt obligations of more than $100 billion, and uncertain economic policy. Government intervention includes trade and investment restrictions, wage/price controls, interest and exchange rate controls, and extensive tariff barriers. Ownership of major industrial facilities is divided among private interests, the government, and multinational companies. Ownership in agriculture likewise is varied, with the government intervening in the politically sensitive issues involving large landowners and the masses of poor peasants. In consultation with the IMF, the Brazilian Government has initiated several programs over the last few years to ameliorate the stagnation and foreign debt problems. None of these has given more than temporary relief. The strategy of the new Collor government is to increase the pace of privatization, encourage foreign trade and investment, and establish a more realistic exchange rate. One long-run strength is the existence of vast natural resources.
GDP: $377 billion, per capita $2,500; real growth rate 3% (1989 est.)
Inflation rate (consumer prices): 1,765% (1989)
Unemployment rate: 2.5% (December 1989)

Brazil (continued)

Budget: revenues $27.8 billion; expenditures $40.1 billion, including capital expenditures of $8.8 billion (1986)
Exports: $34.2 billion (1989 est.); *commodities*—coffee, metallurgical products, chemical products, foodstuffs, iron ore, automobiles and parts; *partners*—US 28%, EC 26%, Latin America 11%, Japan 6% (1987)
Imports: $18.0 billion (1989 est.); *commodities*—crude oil, capital goods, chemical products, foodstuffs, coal; *partners*—Middle East and Africa 24%, EC 22%, US 21%, Latin America 12%, Japan 6% (1987)
External debt: $109 billion (December 1989)
Industrial production: growth rate 3.2% (1989 est.)
Electricity: 52,865,000 kW capacity; 202,280 million kWh produced, 1,340 kWh per capita (1989)
Industries: textiles and other consumer goods, shoes, chemicals, cement, lumber, iron ore, steel, motor vehicles and auto parts, metalworking, capital goods, tin
Agriculture: accounts for 12% of GDP; world's largest producer and exporter of coffee and orange juice concentrate and second-largest exporter of soybeans; other products—rice, corn, sugarcane, cocoa, beef; self-sufficient in food, except for wheat
Illicit drugs: illicit producer of cannabis and coca, mostly for domestic consumption; government has an active eradication program to control cannabis and coca cultivation
Aid: US commitments, including Ex-Im (FY70-88), $2.5 billion; Western (non-US) countries, ODA and OOF bilateral commitments (1970-87), $9.5 billion; OPEC bilateral aid (1979-89), $284 million; Communist countries (1970-88), $1.3 billion
Currency: novo cruzado (plural—novos cruzados); 1 novo cruzado (NCr$) = 100 centavos
Exchange rates: novos cruzados (NCr$) per US$1—2.83392 (1989), 0.26238 (1988), 0.03923 (1987), 0.01366 (1986), 0.00620 (1985); note— 25 tourist/parallel rate (December 1989)
Fiscal year: calendar year

Communications

Railroads: 29,694 km total; 25,268 km 1.000-meter gauge, 4,339 km 1.600-meter gauge, 74 km mixed 1.600-1.000-meter gauge, 13 km 0.760-meter gauge; 2,308 km electrified
Highways: 1,448,000 km total; 48,000 km paved, 1,400,000 km gravel or earth
Inland waterways: 50,000 km navigable

Pipelines: crude oil, 2,000 km; refined products, 3,804 km; natural gas, 1,095 km
Ports: Belém, Fortaleza, Ilhéus, Manaus, Paranagua, Porto Alegre, Recife, Rio de Janeiro, Rio Grande, Salvador, Santos
Merchant marine: 271 ships (1,000 GRT or over) totaling 5,855,708 GRT/ 9,909,097 DWT; includes 2 passenger-cargo, 68 cargo, 1 refrigerated cargo, 12 container, 9 roll-on/roll-off, 56 petroleum, oils, and lubricants (POL) tanker, 15 chemical tanker, 10 liquefied gas, 14 combination ore/oil, 82 bulk, 2 combination bulk
Civil air: 176 major transport aircraft
Airports: 3,774 total, 3,106 usable; 386 with permanent-surface runways; 2 with runways over 3,659 m; 21 with runways 2,240-3,659 m; 503 with runways 1,220-2,439 m
Telecommunications: good system; extensive radio relay facilities; 9.86 million telephones; stations—1,223 AM, no FM, 112 TV, 151 shortwave; 3 coaxial submarine cables 3 Atlantic Ocean INTELSAT earth stations with total of 3 antennas; 64 domestic satellite stations

Defense Forces

Branches: Brazilian Army, Navy of Brazil, Brazilian Air Force
Military manpower: males 15-49, 39,620,936; 26,752,307 fit for military service; 1,617,378 reach military age (18) annually
Defense expenditures: 0.6% of GDP, or $2.3 billion (1989 est.)

British Indian Ocean Territory
(dependent territory of the UK)

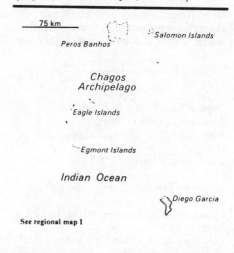

See regional map I

Geography

Total area: 60 km^2; land area: 60 km^2
Comparative area: about 0.3 times the size of Washington, DC
Land boundaries: none
Coastline: 698 km
Maritime claims:
  Territorial sea: 3 nm
Disputes: Diego Garcia is claimed by Mauritius
Climate: tropical marine; hot, humid, moderated by trade winds
Terrain: flat and low (up to 4 meters in elevation)
Natural resources: coconuts, fish
Land use: 0% arable land; 0% permanent crops; 0% meadows and pastures; 0% forest and woodland; 100% other
Environment: archipelago of 2,300 islands
Note: Diego Garcia, largest and southernmost island, occupies strategic location in central Indian Ocean

People

Population: no permanent civilian population; formerly about 3,000 islanders
Ethnic divisions: civilian inhabitants, known as the Ilois, evacuated to Mauritius before construction of UK and US defense facilities

Government

Long-form name: British Indian Ocean Territory (no short-form name); abbreviated BIOT
Type: dependent territory of the UK
Capital: none
Leaders: *Chief of State*—Queen ELIZABETH II (since 6 February 1952); *Head of Government*—Commissioner R. EDIS (since NA 1988), Administrator Robin CROMPTON (since NA 1988); note—both officials reside in the UK

Diplomatic representation: none (dependent territory of the UK)
Flag: the flag of the UK is used

Economy

Overview: All economic activity is concentrated on the largest island of Diego Garcia, where joint UK-US defense facilities are located. Construction projects and various services needed to support the military installations are done by military and contract employees from the UK and US. There are no industrial or agricultural activities on the islands.
Electricity: provided by the US military

Communications

Highways: short stretch of paved road between port and airfield on Diego Garcia
Ports: Diego Garcia
Airports: 1 with permanent-surface runways over 3,659 m on Diego Garcia
Telecommunications: minimal facilities; stations (operated by the US Navy)—1 AM, 1 FM, 1 TV; 1 Atlantic Ocean INTELSAT earth station

Defense Forces

Note: defense is the responsibility of the UK

British Virgin Islands
(dependent territory of the UK)

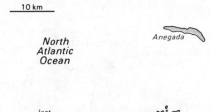

See regional map III

Geography

Total area: 150 km²; land area: 150 km²
Comparative area: about 0.8 times the size of Washington, DC
Coastline: 80 km
Maritime claims:
  Continental shelf: 200 meters or to depth of exploitation
  Exclusive fishing zone: 200 nm
  Territorial sea: 3 nm
Climate: subtropical; humid; temperatures moderated by trade winds
Terrain: coral islands relatively flat; volcanic islands steep, hilly
Natural resources: negligible
Land use: 20% arable land; 7% permanent crops; 33% meadows and pastures; 7% forest and woodland; 33% other
Environment: subject to hurricanes and tropical storms from July to October
Note: strong ties to nearby US Virgin Islands and Puerto Rico

People

Population: 12,258 (July 1990), growth rate 1.1% (1990)
Birth rate: 20 births/1,000 population (1990)
Death rate: 5 deaths/1,000 population (1990)
Net migration rate: −3 migrants/1,000 population (1990)
Infant mortality rate: 14 deaths/1,000 live births (1990)
Life expectancy at birth: 71 years male, 77 years female (1990)
Total fertility rate: 2.2 children born/woman (1990)
Nationality: noun—British Virgin Islander(s); adjective—British Virgin Islander
Ethnic divisions: over 90% black, remainder of white and Asian origin

Religion: majority Methodist; others include Anglican, Church of God, Seventh-Day Adventist, Baptist, and Roman Catholic
Language: English (official)
Literacy: 98%
Labor force: 4,911 (1980)
Organized labor: NA

Government

Long-form name: none
Type: dependent territory of the UK
Capital: Road Town
Administrative divisions: none (dependent territory of the UK)
Independence: none (dependent territory of the UK)
Constitution: 1 June 1977
Legal system: English law
National holiday: Territory Day, 1 July
Executive branch: British monarch, governor, chief minister, Executive Council (cabinet)
Legislative branch: unicameral Legislative Council
Judicial branch: Eastern Caribbean Supreme Court
Leaders: *Chief of State*—Queen ELIZABETH II (since 6 February 1952), represented by Governor John Mark Ambrose HERDMAN (since NA 1986);
Head of Government—Chief Minister H. Lavity STOUTT (since NA 1986)
Political parties and leaders: United Party (UP), Conrad Maduro; Virgin Islands Party (VIP), H. Lavity Stoutt; Independent People's Movement (IPM), Cyril B. Romney
Suffrage: universal at age 18
Elections: *Legislative Council*—last held 30 September 1986 (next to be held by September 1991); results—percent of vote by party NA; seats—(9 total) UP 2, VIP 5, IPM 2
Communists: probably none
Member of: Commonwealth
Diplomatic representation: none (dependent territory of the UK)
Flag: blue with the flag of the UK in the upper hoist-side quadrant and the Virgin Islander coat of arms centered in the outer half of the flag; the coat of arms depicts a woman flanked on either side by a vertical column of six oil lamps above a scroll bearing the Latin word *VIGILATE* (Be Watchful)

Economy

Overview: The economy is highly dependent on the tourist industry, which generates about 21% of the national income. In 1985 the government offered offshore registration to companies wishing to incorporate in the islands, and, in consequence,

41

British Virgin Islands (continued)

incorporation fees generated about $2 million in 1987. Livestock raising is the most significant agricultural activity. The islands' crops, limited by poor soils, are unable to meet food requirements.
GDP: $106.7 million, per capita $8,900; real growth rate 2.5% (1987)
Inflation rate (consumer prices): 1.7% (January 1987)
Unemployment rate: NA%
Budget: revenues $26.2 million; expenditures $25.4 million, including capital expenditures of $NA (1988 est.)
Exports: $2.3 million (f.o.b., 1985); *commodities*—rum, fresh fish, gravel, sand, fruits, animals; *partners*—Virgin Islands (US), Puerto Rico, US
Imports: $72.0 million (c.i.f., 1985); *commodities*—building materials, automobiles, foodstuffs, machinery; *partners*—Virgin Islands (US), Puerto Rico, US
External debt: $4.5 million (1985)
Industrial production: growth rate −4.0% (1985)
Electricity: 13,500 kW capacity; 59 million kWh produced, 4,870 kWh per capita (1989)
Industries: tourism, light industry, construction, rum, concrete block, offshore financial center
Agriculture: livestock (including poultry), fish, fruit, vegetables
Aid: NA
Currency: US currency is used
Exchange rates: US currency is used
Fiscal year: 1 April-31 March

Communications

Highways: 106 km motorable roads (1983)
Ports: Road Town
Airports: 3 total, 3 usable; 2 with permanent-surface runways less than 1,220 m
Telecommunications: 3,000 telephones; worldwide external telephone service; submarine cable communication links to Bermuda; stations—1 AM, no FM, 1 TV

Defense Forces

Note: defense is the responsibility of the UK

Brunei

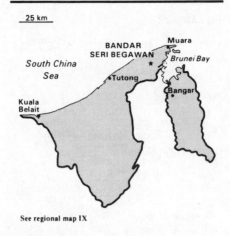

See regional map IX

Geography

Total area: 5,770 km^2; land area: 5,270 km^2
Comparative area: slightly larger than Delaware
Land boundary: 381 km with Malaysia
Coastline: 161 km
Maritime claims:
  Exclusive fishing zone: 200 nm
  Territorial sea: 12 nm
Disputes: may wish to purchase the Malaysian salient that divides the country
Climate: tropical; hot, humid, rainy
Terrain: flat coastal plain rises to mountains in east; hilly lowland in west
Natural resources: crude oil, natural gas, timber
Land use: 1% arable land; 1% permanent crops; 1% meadows and pastures; 79% forest and woodland; 18% other; includes NEGL% irrigated
Environment: typhoons, earthquakes, and severe flooding are rare
Note: close to vital sea lanes through South China Sea linking Indian and Pacific Oceans; two parts physically separated by Malaysia; almost an enclave of Malaysia

People

Population: 372,108 (July 1990), growth rate 7.1% (1990)
Birth rate: 23 births/1,000 population (1990)
Death rate: 4 deaths/1,000 population (1990)
Net migration rate: 52 migrants/1,000 population (1990)
Infant mortality rate: 10 deaths/1,000 live births (1990)
Life expectancy at birth: 74 years male, 77 years female (1990)
Total fertility rate: 2.9 children born/woman (1990)

Nationality: noun—Bruneian(s); adjective—Bruneian
Ethnic divisions: 64% Malay, 20% Chinese, 16% other
Religion: 60% Muslim (official); 8% Christian; 32% Buddhist and indigenous beliefs
Language: Malay (official), English, and Chinese
Literacy: 45%
Labor force: 89,000 (includes members of the Army); 33% of labor force is foreign (1988); 50.4% production of oil, natural gas, and construction; 47.6% trade, services, and other; 2.0% agriculture, forestry, and fishing (1984)
Organized labor: 2% of labor force

Government

Long-form name: Negara Brunei Darussalam
Type: constitutional sultanate
Capital: Bandar Seri Begawan
Administrative divisions: 4 districts (daerah-daerah, singular—daerah); Belait, Brunei and Muara, Temburong, Tutong
Independence: 1 January 1984 (from UK)
Constitution: 29 September 1959 (some provisions suspended under a State of Emergency since December 1962, others since independence on 1 January 1984)
Legal system: based on Islamic law
National holiday: National Day, 23 February (1984)
Executive branch: sultan, prime minister, Council of Cabinet Ministers
Legislative branch: unicameral Legislative Council (Majlis Masyuarat Megeri)
Judicial branch: Supreme Court
Leaders: *Chief of State and Head of Government*—Sultan and Prime Minister Sir Muda HASSANAL BOLKIAH Mu'izzaddin Waddaulah (since 5 October 1967)
Political parties and leaders: Brunei National United Party (inactive), Anak Hasanuddin, chairman; Brunei National Democratic Party (the first legal political party and now banned) Abdul Latif bin Abdul Hamid, chairman
Suffrage: none
Elections: *Legislative Council*—last held in March 1962; in 1970 the Council was changed to an appointive body by decree of the sultan and no elections are planned
Communists: probably none
Member of: ASEAN, ESCAP (associate member), IMO, INTERPOL, OIC, UN
Diplomatic representation: Ambassador Dato Paduka Haji MOHAMED SUNI bin Haji Idris; Chancery at 2600 Virginia Avenue NW, Washington DC 20037; telephone (202) 342-0159; *US*—Ambassador Christopher H. PHILLIPS; Embassy at Teck Guan Plaza (corner of Jalan McArthur), Bandar Seri Begawan (mailing ad-

dress is P. O. Box 2991, Bandar Seri Begawan); telephone [673] (2) 29670
Flag: yellow with two diagonal bands of white (top, almost double width) and black starting from the upper hoist side; the national emblem in red is superimposed at the center; the emblem includes a swallow-tailed flag on top of a winged column within an upturned crescent above a scroll and flanked by two upraised hands

Economy

Overview: The economy is a mixture of foreign and domestic entrepreneurship, government regulation and welfare measures, and village tradition. It is almost totally supported by exports of crude oil and natural gas, with revenues from the petroleum sector accounting for more than 70% of GDP. Per capita GDP of $9,600 is among the highest in the Third World, and substantial income from overseas investment supplements domestic production. The government provides for all medical services and subsidizes food and housing.
GDP: $3.3 billion, per capita $9,600; real growth rate 2.5% (1989 est.)
Inflation rate (consumer prices): 2.5% (1989 est.)
Unemployment: 2.5%, shortage of skilled labor (1989 est.)
Budget: revenues $1.2 billion (1987); expenditures $1.6 billion, including capital expenditures of NA (1989 est.)
Exports: $2.07 billion (f.o.b., 1987); *commodities*—crude oil, liquefied natural gas, petroleum products; *partners*—Japan 55% (1986)
Imports: $800 million (c.i.f., 1987); *commodities*—machinery and transport equipment, manufactured goods; food, beverages, tobacco; consumer goods; *partners*—Singapore 31%, US 20%, Japan 6% (1986)
External debt: none
Industrial production: growth rate NA%
Electricity: 310,000 kW capacity; 890 million kWh produced, 2,580 kWh per capita (1989)
Industries: petroleum, liquefied natural gas, construction
Agriculture: imports about 80% of its food needs; principal crops and livestock include rice, cassava, bananas, buffaloes, and pigs
Aid: US commitments, including Ex-Im (FY70-87), $20.6 million; Western (non-US) countries, ODA and OOF bilateral commitments (1970-87), $143.7 million
Currency: Bruneian dollar (plural—dollars); 1 Bruneian dollar (B$) = 100 cents
Exchange rates: Bruneian dollars (B$) per US$1—1.8895 (January 1990), 1.9503 (1989), 2.0124 (1988), 2.1060 (1987),

2.1774 (1986), 2.2002 (1985); note—the Bruneian dollar is at par with the Singapore dollar
Fiscal year: calendar year

Communications

Railroads: 13 km 0.610-meter narrow-gauge private line
Highways: 1,090 km total; 370 km paved (bituminous treated) and another 52 km under construction, 720 km gravel or unimproved
Inland waterways: 209 km; navigable by craft drawing less than 1.2 meters
Ports: Kuala Belait, Muara
Merchant marine: 7 liquefied gas carriers (1,000 GRT or over) totaling 348,476 GRT/340,635 DWT
Pipelines: crude oil, 135 km; refined products, 418 km; natural gas, 920 km
Civil air: 4 major transport aircraft (3 Boeing 757-200, 1 Boeing 737-200)
Airports: 2 total, 2 usable; 1 with permanent-surface runways; 1 with runway over 3,659 m; 1 with runway 1,406 m
Telecommunications: service throughout country is adequate for present needs; international service good to adjacent Malaysia; radiobroadcast coverage good; 33,000 telephones (1987); stations—4 AM/FM, 1 TV; 74,000 radio receivers (1987); satellite earth stations—1 Indian Ocean INTELSAT and 1 Pacific Ocean INTELSAT

Defense Forces

Branches: Royal Brunei Armed Forces, including air wing, navy, and ground forces; British Gurkha Battalion; Royal Brunei Police; Gurkha Reserve Unit
Military manpower: males 15-49, 104,398; 60,242 fit for military service; 3,106 reach military age (18) annually
Defense expenditures: $197.6 million, 17% of central government budget (FY86)

Bulgaria

See regional map V

Geography

Total area: 110,910 km^2; land area: 110,550 km^2
Comparative area: slightly larger than Tennessee
Land boundaries: 1,881 km total; Greece 494 km, Romania 608 km, Turkey 240 km, Yugoslavia 539 km
Coastline: 354 km
Maritime claims:
  Contiguous zone: 24 nm
  Extended economic zone: 200 nm
  Territorial sea: 12 nm
Disputes: Macedonia question with Greece and Yugoslavia
Climate: temperate; cold, damp winters; hot, dry summers
Terrain: mostly mountains with lowlands in north and south
Natural resources: bauxite, copper, lead, zinc, coal, timber, arable land
Land use: 34% arable land; 3% permanent crops; 18% meadows and pastures; 35% forest and woodland; 10% other; includes 11% irrigated
Environment: subject to earthquakes, landslides; deforestation; air pollution
Note: strategic location near Turkish Straits; controls key land routes from Europe to Middle East and Asia

People

Population: 8,933,544 (July 1990), growth rate −0.3% (1990)
Birth rate: 13 births/1,000 population (1990)
Death rate: 12 deaths/1,000 population (1990)
Net migration rate: −4 migrants/1,000 population (1990)
Infant mortality rate: 13 deaths/1,000 live births (1990)
Life expectancy at birth: 69 years male, 76 years female (1990)

43

Bulgaria (continued)

Total fertility rate: 1.9 children born/
woman (1990)
Nationality: noun—Bulgarian(s); adjec-
tive—Bulgarian
Ethnic divisions: 85.3% Bulgarian, 8.5%
Turk, 2.6% Gypsy, 2.5% Macedonian,
0.3% Armenian, 0.2% Russian, 0.6% other
Religion: religious background of popula-
tion is 85% Bulgarian Orthodox, 13%
Muslim, 0.8% Jewish, 0.7% Roman Cath-
olic, 0.5% Protestant, Gregorian-Arme-
nian, and other
Language: Bulgarian; secondary languages
closely correspond to ethnic breakdown
Literacy: 95% (est.)
Labor force: 4,300,000; 33% industry,
20% agriculture, 47% other (1987)
Organized labor: all workers are members
of the Central Council of Trade Unions
(CCTU); Pod Krepa (Support), an inde-
pendent trade union, legally registered in
January 1990

Government

Long-form name: People's Republic of
Bulgaria
Type: Communist state, but democratic
elections planned for 1990
Capital: Sofia
Administrative divisions: 8 provinces
(oblasti, singular—oblast) and 1 city*
(grad); Burgas, Grad Sofiya*, Khaskovo,
Lovech, Mikhaylovgrad, Plovdiv, Razgrad,
Sofiya, Varna
Independence: 22 September 1908 (from
Ottoman Empire)
Constitution: 16 May 1971, effective 18
May 1971
Legal system: based on civil law system,
with Soviet law influence; judicial review
of legislative acts in the State Council;
has accepted compulsory ICJ jurisdiction
National holiday: Anniversary of the So-
cialist Revolution in Bulgaria, 9 Septem-
ber (1944)
Executive branch: president, chairman of
the Council of Ministers, four deputy
chairmen of the Council of Ministers,
Council of Ministers
Legislative branch: unicameral National
Assembly (Narodno Sobranyie)
Judicial branch: Supreme Court
Leaders: *Chief of State*—President Petur
Toshev MLADENOV (chairman of the
State Council since 11 November 1989;
became president on 3 April 1990 when
the State Council was abolished);
Head of Government—Chairman of the
Council of Ministers Andrey LUKANOV
(since 3 February 1990); Deputy Chair-
man of the Council of Ministers Chudo-
mir Asenov ALEKSANDROV (since 8
February 1990); Deputy Chairman of the
Council of Ministers Belcho Antonov
BELCHEV (since 8 February 1990); Dep-

uty Chairman of the Council of Ministers
Konstantin Dimitrov KOSEV (since 8
February 1990); Deputy Chairman of the
Council of Ministers Nora Krachunova
ANANIEVA (since 8 February 1990)
Political parties and leaders: Bulgarian
Communist Party (BKP), Aleksandur Li-
lov, chairman; Bulgarian National Agrar-
ian Union (BZNS), Angel Angelov Dimi-
trov, secretary of Permanent Board;
Bulgarian Social Democratic Party, Petur
Dentlieu; Green Party; Christian Demo-
crats; Radical Democratic Party; others
forming
Suffrage: universal and compulsory at age
18
Elections: *Chairman of the State Council*—last held 17 June 1986 (next to be
held May 1990); results—Todor Zhivkov
reelected but was replaced by Petur
Toshev Mladenov on 11 November 1989;
National Assembly—last held 8 June
1986 (next to be held May 1990);
results—percent of vote by party NA;
seats—(400 total) BKP 276, BZNS 99,
others 25
Communists: 932,055 party members
(April 1986)
Other political or pressure groups: Union
of Democratic Forces (umbrella organization for opposition groups); Ecoglenost,
Podkrepa Independent Trade Union, Fa-
therland Front, Communist Youth Union,
Central Council of Trade Unions, Na-
tional Committee for Defense of Peace,
Union of Fighters Against Fascism and
Capitalism, Committee of Bulgarian
Women, All-National Committee for
Bulgarian-Soviet Friendship; Union of
Democratic Forces, a coalition of about a
dozen dissident groups; numerous regional
and national interest groups with various
agendas
Member of: CCC, CEMA, FAO, IAEA,
IBEC, ICAO, ILO, ILZSG, IMO, IPU,
ITC, ITU, IWC—International Wheat
Council, UN, UNESCO, UPU, Warsaw
Pact WFTU, WHO, WIPO, WMO,
WTO
Diplomatic representation: Ambassador
Velichko Filipov VELICHKOV; Chancery
at 1621 22nd Street NW, Washington DC
20008; telephone (202) 387-7969; *US*—
Ambassador Sol POLANSKY; Embassy
at 1 Alexander Stamboliski Boulevard,
Sofia (mailing address is APO New York
09213); telephone [359] (2) 88-48-01
through 05
Flag: three equal horizontal bands of
white (top), green, and red with the national emblem on the hoist side of the
white stripe; the emblem contains a rampant lion within a wreath of wheat ears
below a red five-pointed star and above a

ribbon bearing the dates 681 (first Bulgarian state established) and 1944 (liberation
from Nazi control)

Economy

Overview: Growth in the sluggish Bulgarian economy fell to the 2% annual level in
the 1980s, and by 1989 Sofia's foreign
debt had skyrocketed to $10 billion—giv
ing a debt service ratio of more than 40%
of hard currency earnings. The
post-Zhivkov regime faces major problems
of renovating an aging industrial plant,
keeping abreast of rapidly unfolding tech-
nological developments, investing in additional energy capacity (the portion of electric power from nuclear energy reached
37% in 1988), and motivating workers, in
part by giving them a share in the earnings of their enterprises. A major decree
of January 1989 summarized and
extended the government's economic restructuring efforts, which include a partial
decentralization of controls over production decisions and foreign trade. The new
regime promises more extensive reforms
and eventually a market economy. But the
ruling group cannot (so far) bring itself to
give up ultimate control over economic
affairs exercised through the vertical Party/
ministerial command structure. Reforms
have not led to improved economic performance, in particular the provision of more
and better consumer goods. A further
blow to the economy was the exodus of
310,000 ethnic Turks in mid-1989, which
caused temporary shortages of skilled labor in glassware, aluminum, and other
industrial plants and in tobacco fields.
GNP: $51.2 billion, per capita $5,710; real
growth rate –0.1% (1989 est.)
Inflation rate (consumer prices): 12%
(1989)
Unemployment rate: NA%
Budget: revenues $26 billion; expenditures
$28 billion, including capital expenditures
of $NA billion (1988)
Exports: $20.3 billion (f.o.b., 1988); *com-
modities*—machinery and equipment
60.5%; agricultural products 14.7%; manufactured consumer goods 10.6%; fuels,
minerals, raw materials, and metals 8.5%;
other 5.7%; *partners*—Socialist countries
82.5% (USSR 61%, GDR 5.5%, Czechoslovakia 4.9%); developed countries 6.8%
(FRG 1.2%, Greece 1.0%); less developed
countries 10.7% (Libya 3.5%, Iraq 2.9%)
Imports: $21.0 billion (f.o.b., 1988); *com-
modities*—fuels, minerals, and raw materials 45.2%; machinery and equipment
39.8%; manufactured consumer goods
4.6%; agricultural products 3.8%; other

6.6%; *partners*—Socialist countries 80.5% (USSR 57.5%, GDR 5.7%), developed countries 15.1% (FRG 4.8%, Austria 1.6%); less developed countries 4.4% (Libya 1.0%, Brazil 0.9%)
External debt: $10 billion (1989)
Industrial production: growth rate 0.9% (1988)
Electricity: 11,500,000 kW capacity; 45,000 million kWh produced, 5,000 kWh per capita (1989)
Industries: food processing, machine and metal building, electronics, chemicals
Agriculture: accounts for 15% of GNP; climate and soil conditions support livestock raising and the growing of various grain crops, oilseeds, vegetables, fruits and tobacco; more than one-third of the arable land devoted to grain; world's fourth-largest tobacco exporter; surplus food producer
Aid: donor—$1.6 billion in bilateral aid to non-Communist less developed countries (1956-88)
Currency: lev (plural—leva); 1 lev (Lv) = 100 stotinki
Exchange rates: leva (Lv) per US$1—0.84 (1989), 0.82 (1988), 0.90 (1987), 0.95 (1986), 1.03 (1985)
Fiscal year: calendar year

Communications

Railroads: 4,294 km total, all government owned (1986); 4,049 km 1.435-meter standard gauge, 245 km narrow gauge; 908 km double track; 2,342 km electrified
Highways: 37,397 km total; 33,352 km hard surface (including 228 km superhighways); 4,045 km earth roads (1986)
Inland waterways: 470 km (1986)
Pipelines: crude, 193 km; refined product, 418 km; natural gas, 1,400 km (1986)
Ports: Burgas, Varna, Varna West; river ports are Ruse, Vidin, and Lom on the Danube
Merchant marine: 108 ships (1,000 GRT and over) totaling 1,240,204 GRT/ 1,872,723 DWT; includes 2 short-sea passenger, 32 cargo, 2 container, 1 passenger-cargo training, 5 roll-on/roll-off, 16 petroleum, oils, and lubricants (POL) tanker, 2 railcar carriers, 48 bulk
Civil air: 65 major transport aircraft
Airports: 380 total, 380 usable; about 120 with permanent-surface runways; 20 with runways 2,440-3,659 m; 20 with runways 1,220-2,439 m
Telecommunications: stations—15 AM, 16 FM, 13 TV; 1 Soviet TV relay; 2,100,000 TV sets; 2,100,000 radio receivers; at least 1 satellite earth station

Defense Forces

Branches: Bulgarian People's Army, Frontier Troops, Air and Air Defense Forces, Bulgarian Navy
Military manpower: males 15-49, 2,177,404; 1,823,111 fit for military service; 66,744 reach military age (19) annually
Defense expenditures: 1.6051 billion leva (1989); note—conversion of the military budget into US dollars using the official administratively set exchange rate would produce misleading results

Burkina

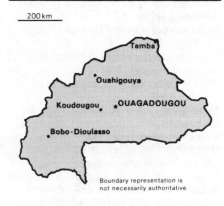

200 km

Boundary representation is not necessarily authoritative.

See regional map VII

Geography

Total area: 274,200 km^2; land area: 273,800 km^2
Comparative area: slightly larger than Colorado
Land boundaries: 3,192 km total; Benin 306 km, Ghana 548 km, Ivory Coast 584 km, Mali 1,000 km, Niger 628 km, Togo 126 km
Coastline: none—landlocked
Maritime claims: none—landlocked
Disputes: the disputed international boundary between Burkina and Mali was submitted to the International Court of Justice (ICJ) in October 1983 and the ICJ issued its final ruling in December 1986, which both sides agreed to accept; Burkina and Mali are proceeding with boundary demarcation, including the tripoint with Niger
Climate: tropical; warm, dry winters; hot, wet summers
Terrain: mostly flat to dissected, undulating plains; hills in west and southeast
Natural resources: manganese, limestone, marble; small deposits of gold, antimony, copper, nickel, bauxite, lead, phosphates, zinc, silver
Land use: 10% arable land; NEGL% permanent crops; 37% meadows and pastures; 26% forest and woodland; 27% other; includes NEGL% irrigated
Environment: recent droughts and desertification severely affecting marginal agricultural activities, population distribution, economy; overgrazing; deforestation
Note: landlocked

People

Population: 9,077,828 (July 1990), growth rate 3.1% (1990)
Birth rate: 50 births/1,000 population (1990)
Death rate: 17 deaths/1,000 population (1990)

Burkina (continued)

Net migration rate: −3 migrants/1,000 population (1990)
Infant mortality rate: 121 deaths/1,000 live births (1990)
Life expectancy at birth: 51 years male, 52 years female (1990)
Total fertility rate: 7.2 children born/woman (1990)
Nationality: noun—Burkinabe; adjective—Burkinabe
Ethnic divisions: more than 50 tribes; principal tribe is Mossi (about 2.5 million); other important groups are Gurunsi, Senufo, Lobi, Bobo, Mande, and Fulani
Religion: 65% indigenous beliefs, about 25% Muslim, 10% Christian (mainly Roman Catholic)
Language: French (official); tribal languages belong to Sudanic family, spoken by 90% of the population
Literacy: 13.2%
Labor force: 3,300,000 residents; 30,000 are wage earners; 82% agriculture, 13% industry, 5% commerce, services, and government; 20% of male labor force migrates annually to neighboring countries for seasonal employment (1984); 44% of population of working age (1985)
Organized labor: four principal trade union groups represent less than 1% of population

Government

Long-form name: Burkina Faso
Type: military; established by coup on 4 August 1983
Capital: Ouagadougou
Administrative divisions: 30 provinces; Bam, Bazéga, Bougouriba, Boulgou, Boulkiemdé, Ganzourgou, Gnagna, Gourma, Houet, Kadiogo, Kénédougou, Komoé, Kossi, Kouritenga, Mouhoun, Namentenga, Naouri, Oubritenga, Oudalan, Passore, Poni, Sanguié, Sanmatenga, Séno, Sissili, Soum, Sourou, Tapoa, Yatenga, Zoundwéogo
Independence: 5 August 1960 (from France; formerly Upper Volta)
Constitution: none; constitution of 27 November 1977 was abolished following coup of 25 November 1980
Legal system: based on French civil law system and customary law
National holiday: Anniversary of the Revolution, 4 August (1983)
Executive branch: chairman of the Popular Front, Council of Ministers
Legislative branch: unicameral National Assembly (Assemblée Nationale) was dissolved on 25 November 1980
Judicial branch: Appeals Court
Leaders: *Chief of State and Head of Government*—Chairman of the Popular Front Captain Blaise COMPAORE (since 15 October 1987)

Political parties and leaders: all political parties banned following November 1980 coup
Suffrage: none
Elections: the National Assembly was dissolved 25 November 1980 and no elections are scheduled
Communists: small Communist party front group; some sympathizers
Other political or pressure groups: committees for the defense of the revolution, watchdog/political action groups throughout the country in both organizations and communities
Member of: ACP, AfDB, CCC, CEAO, EAMA, ECA, EIB (associate), Entente, FAO, GATT, G-77, IBRD, ICAO, IDA, IDB—Islamic Development Bank, IFAD, IFC, ILO, IMF, INTELSAT, INTERPOL, IPU, IRC, ITU, NAM, Niger River Commission, OAU, OCAM, OIC, UN, UNESCO, UPU, WCL, WFTU, WHO, WIPO, WMO, WTO
Diplomatic representation: Ambassador Paul Désiré KABORE; Chancery at 2340 Massachusetts Avenue NW, Washington DC 20008; telephone (202) 332-5577 or 6895; *US*—Ambassador David H. SHINN; Embassy at Avenue Raoul Follerau, Ouagadougou (mailing address is B. P. 35, Ouagadougou); telephone [226] 30-67-23 through 25
Flag: two equal horizontal bands of red (top) and green with a yellow five-pointed star in the center; uses the popular pan-African colors of Ethiopia

Economy

Overview: One of the poorest countries in the world, Burkina has a high population density, few natural resources, and relatively infertile soil. Economic development is hindered by a poor communications network within a landlocked country. Agriculture provides about 40% of GDP and is entirely of a subsistence nature. Industry, dominated by unprofitable government-controlled corporations, accounted for 13% of GDP in 1985.
GDP: $1.43 billion, per capita $170; real growth rate 7.7% (1988)
Inflation rate (consumer prices): 4.3% (1988)
Unemployment rate: NA%
Budget: revenues $422 million; expenditures $516 million, including capital expenditures of $25 million (1987)
Exports: $249 million (f.o.b., 1988); *commodities*—oilseeds, cotton, live animals, gold; *partners*—EC 42% (France 30%, other 12%), Taiwan 17%, Ivory Coast 15% (1985)
Imports: $591 million (f.o.b., 1988); *commodities*—grain, dairy products, petro-

leum, machinery; *partners*—EC 37% (France 23%, other 14%), Africa 31%, US 15% (1985)
External debt: $969 million (December 1988)
Industrial production: growth rate 7.1% (1985)
Electricity: 121,000 kW capacity; 320 million kWh produced, 37 kWh per capita (1989)
Industries: agricultural processing plants; brewery, cement, and brick plants; a few other small consumer goods enterprises
Agriculture: cash crops—peanuts, shea nuts, sesame, cotton; food crops—sorghum, millet, corn, rice; livestock; not self-sufficient in food grains
Aid: US commitments, including Ex-Im (FY70-88), $271 million; Western (non-US) countries, ODA and OOF bilateral commitments (1970-87), $2.5 billion; Communist countries (1970-88), $94 million
Currency: Communauté Financière Africaine franc (plural—francs); 1 CFA franc (CFAF) = 100 centimes
Exchange rates: CFA francs (CFAF) per US$1—284.55 (January 1990), 319.01 (1989), 297.85 (1988), 300.54 (1987), 346.30 (1986), 449.26 (1985)
Fiscal year: calendar year

Communications

Railroads: 620 km total; 520 km Ouagadougou to Ivory Coast border and 100 km Ouagadougou to Kaya; all 1.00-meter gauge and single track
Highways: 16,500 km total; 1,300 km paved, 7,400 km improved, 7,800 km unimproved (1985)
Civil air: 2 major transport aircraft
Airports: 50 total, 43 usable; 2 with permanent-surface runways; none with runways over 3,659 m; 2 with runways 2,440-3,659 m; 7 with runways 1,220-2,439 m
Telecommunications: all services only fair; radio relay, wire, and radio communication stations in use; 13,900 telephones; stations—2 AM, 2 FM, 2 TV; 1 Atlantic Ocean INTELSAT earth station

Defense Forces

Branches: Army, Air Force
Military manpower: males 15-49, 1,775,143; 904,552 fit for military service; no conscription
Defense expenditures: 3.1% of GDP (1987)

Burma

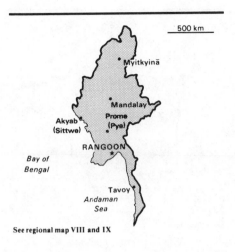

See regional map VIII and IX

Geography

Total area: 678,500 km²; land area: 657,740 km²
Comparative area: slightly smaller than Texas
Land boundaries: 5,876 km total; Bangladesh 193 km, China 2,185 km, India 1,463 km, Laos 235 km, Thailand 1,800 km
Coastline: 1,930 km
Maritime claims:
  Contiguous zone: 24 nm
  Continental shelf: edge of continental margin or 200 nm
  Extended economic zone: 200 nm
  Territorial sea: 12 nm
Climate: tropical monsoon; cloudy, rainy, hot, humid summers (southwest monsoon, June to September); less cloudy, scant rainfall, mild temperatures, lower humidity during winter (northeast monsoon, December to April)
Terrain: central lowlands ringed by steep, rugged highlands
Natural resources: crude oil, timber, tin, antimony, zinc, copper, tungsten, lead, coal, some marble, limestone, precious stones, natural gas
Land use: 15% arable land; 1% permanent crops; 1% meadows and pastures; 49% forest and woodland; 34% other; includes 2% irrigated
Environment: subject to destructive earthquakes and cyclones; flooding and landslides common during rainy season (June to September); deforestation
Note: strategic location near major Indian Ocean shipping lanes

People

Population: 41,277,389 (July 1990), growth rate 2.0% (1990)
Birth rate: 33 births/1,000 population (1990)

Death rate: 13 deaths/1,000 population (1990)
Net migration rate: 0 migrants/1,000 population (1990)
Infant mortality rate: 97 deaths/1,000 live births (1990)
Life expectancy at birth: 53 years male, 56 years female (1990)
Total fertility rate: 4.2 children born/woman (1990)
Nationality: noun—Burmese; adjective—Burmese
Ethnic divisions: 68% Burman, 9% Shan, 7% Karen, 4% Rakhine, 3% Chinese, 2% Mon, 2% Indian, 5% other
Religion: 85% Buddhist, 15% animist beliefs, Muslim, Christian, or other
Language: Burmese; minority ethnic groups have their own languages
Literacy: 78%
Labor force: 16,036,000; 65.2% agriculture, 14.3% industry, 10.1% trade, 6.3% government, 4.1% other (FY89 est.)
Organized labor: Workers' Asiayone (association), 1,800,000 members, and Peasants' Asiayone, 7,600,000 members

Government

Long-form name: Union of Burma; note—the local official name is Pyidaungzu Myanma Naingngandaw which has been translated as Union of Myanma or Union of Myanmar
Type: military government
Capital: Rangoon (sometimes translated as Yangon)
Administrative divisions: 7 divisions* (yin-mya, singular—yin) and 7 states (pyine-mya, singular—pyine); Chin State, Irrawaddy*, Kachin State, Karan State, Kayah State, Magwe*, Mandalay*, Mon State, Pegu*, Rakhine State, Rangoon*, Sagaing*, Shan State, Tenasserim*
Independence: 4 January 1948 (from UK)
Constitution: 3 January 1974 (suspended since 18 September 1988)
Legal system: martial law in effect throughout most of the country; has not accepted compulsory ICJ jurisdiction
National holiday: Independence Day, 4 January (1948)
Executive branch: chairman of the State Law and Order Restoration Council, State Law and Order Restoration Council
Legislative branch: unicameral People's Assembly (Pyithu Hluttaw) was dissolved after the coup of 18 September 1988
Judicial branch: Council of People's Justices was abolished after the coup of 18 September 1988
Leaders: *Chief of State and Head of Government*—Chairman of the State Law and Order Restoration Council and Prime Minister Gen. SAW MAUNG (since 18 September 1988)

Political parties and leaders: National League for Democracy, U Tin Oo and Aung San Suu Kyi; League for Democracy and Peace, U Nu; National Unity Party (promilitary); over 100 other parties
Suffrage: universal at age 18
Elections: *People's Assembly*—last held 6-20 October 1985, but dissolved after the coup of 18 September 1988; next scheduled 27 May 1990); results—percent of vote by party NA; seats—(NA total) number of seats by party NA
Communists: several hundred, est., primarily as an insurgent group on the northeast frontier
Other political or pressure groups: Kachin Independence Army; Karen National Union, several Shan factions (all insurgent groups); Burmese Communist Party (BCP)
Member of: ADB, Colombo Plan, ESCAP, FAO, G-77, GATT, IAEA, IBRD, ICAO, IDA, IFC, IHO, ILO, IMF, IMO, INTERPOL, IRC, ITU, UN, UNESCO, UPU, WHO, WMO
Diplomatic representation: Ambassador U MYO AUNG; Chancery at 2300 S Street NW, Washington DC 20008; telephone (202) 332-9044 through 9046; there is a Burmese Consulate General in New York; *US*—Ambassador Burton LEVIN; Embassy at 581 Merchant Street, Rangoon (mailing address is G. P. O. Box 521, Rangoon or Box B, APO San Francisco 96346); telephone 82055 or 82181
Flag: red with a blue rectangle in the upper hoist-side corner bearing, all in white, 14 five-pointed stars encircling a cogwheel containing a stalk of rice; the 14 stars represent the 14 administrative divisions

Economy

Overview: Burma is one of the poorest countries in Asia, with a per capita GDP of about $280. The government reports negligible growth for FY88. The nation has been unable to achieve any significant improvement in export earnings because of falling prices for many of its major commodity exports. For rice, traditionally the most important export, the drop in world prices has been accompanied by shrinking markets and a smaller volume of sales. In 1985 teak replaced rice as the largest export and continues to hold this position. The economy is heavily dependent on the agricultural sector, which generates about 40% of GDP and provides employment for more than 65% of the work force.
GDP: $11.0 billion, per capita $280; real growth rate 0.2% (FY88 est.)
Inflation rate (consumer prices): 22.6% (FY89 est.)
Unemployment rate: 10.4% in urban areas (FY87)

Burma (continued)

Budget: revenues $4.9 billion; expenditures $5.0 billion, including capital expenditures of $0.7 billion (FY89 est.)
Exports: $311 million (f.o.b., FY88 est.) *commodities*—teak, rice, oilseed, metals, rubber, gems; *partners*—Southeast Asia, India, China, EC, Africa
Imports: $536 million (c.i.f., FY88 est.) *commodities*—machinery, transport equipment, chemicals, food products; *partners*—Japan, EC, CEMA, China, Southeast Asia
External debt: $5.6 billion (December 1989 est.)
Industrial production: growth rate −1.5% (FY88)
Electricity: 950,000 kW capacity; 2,900 million kWh produced, 70 kWh per capita (1989)
Industries: agricultural processing; textiles and footwear; wood and wood products; petroleum refining; mining of copper, tin, tungsten, iron; construction materials; pharmaceuticals; fertilizer
Agriculture: accounts for about 40% of GDP (including fish and forestry); self-sufficient in food; principal crops—paddy rice, corn, oilseed, sugarcane, pulses; world's largest stand of hardwood trees; rice and teak account for 55% of export revenues; 1985 fish catch of 644 million metric tons
Illicit drugs: world's largest illicit producer of opium poppy and minor producer of cannabis for the international drug trade; opium production is on the increase as growers respond to the collapse of Rangoon's antinarcotic programs
Aid: US commitments, including Ex-Im (FY70-88), $158 million; Western (non-US) countries, ODA and OOF bilateral commitments (1970-87), $3.8 billion; Communist countries (1970-88), $424 million
Currency: kyat (plural—kyats); 1 kyat (K) = 100 pyas
Exchange rates: kyats (K) per US$1—6.5188 (January 1990), 6.7049 (1989), 6.3945 (1988), 6.6535 (1987), 7.3304 (1986), 8.4749 (1985)
Fiscal year: 1 April-31 March

Communications

Railroads: 3,991 km total, all government owned; 3,878 km 1.000-meter gauge, 113 km narrow-gauge industrial lines; 362 km double track
Highways: 27,000 km total; 3,200 km bituminous, 17,700 km improved earth or gravel, 6,100 km unimproved earth
Inland waterways: 12,800 km; 3,200 km navigable by large commercial vessels
Pipelines: crude, 1,343 km; natural gas, 330 km
Ports: Rangoon, Moulmein, Bassein

Merchant marine: 45 ships (1,000 GRT or over) totaling 595,814 GRT/955,924 DWT; includes 3 passenger-cargo, 15 cargo, 2 roll-on/roll-off, 1 vehicle carrier, 1 container, 2 petroleum, oils, and lubricants (POL) tanker, 5 chemical, 16 bulk
Civil air: 17 major transport aircraft (including 3 helicopters)
Airports: 88 total, 81 usable; 29 with permanent-surface runways; none with runways over 3,659 m; 3 with runways 2,440-3,659 m; 37 with runways 1,220-2,439 m
Telecommunications: meets minimum requirements for local and intercity service; international service is good; radiobroadcast coverage is limited to the most populous areas; 53,000 telephones (1986); stations—2 AM, 1 FM, 1 TV (1985); 1 Indian Ocean INTELSAT earth station

Defense Forces

Branches: Army, Navy, Air Force
Military manpower: eligible 15-49, 20,294,848; of the 10,135,886 males 15-49, 5,438,196 are fit for military service; of the 10,158,962 females 15-49, 5,437,518 are fit for military service; 434,200 males and 423,435 females reach military age (18) annually; both sexes are liable for military service
Defense expenditures: $315.0 million, 21.0% of central government budget (FY88)

Burundi

See regional map VII

Geography

Total area: 27,830 km²; land area: 25,650 km²
Comparative area: slightly larger than Maryland
Land boundaries: 974 km total; Rwanda 290 km, Tanzania 451 km, Zaire 233 km
Coastline: none—landlocked
Maritime claims: none—landlocked
Climate: temperate; warm; occasional frost in uplands
Terrain: mostly rolling to hilly highland; some plains
Natural resources: nickel, uranium, rare earth oxide, peat, cobalt, copper, platinum (not yet exploited), vanadium
Land use: 43% arable land; 8% permanent crops; 35% meadows and pastures; 2% forest and woodland; 12% other; includes NEGL% irrigated
Environment: soil exhaustion; soil erosion; deforestation
Note: landlocked; straddles crest of the Nile-Congo watershed

People

Population: 5,645,997 (July 1990), growth rate 3.2% (1990)
Birth rate: 47 births/1,000 population (1990)
Death rate: 15 deaths/1,000 population (1990)
Net migration rate: 0 migrants/1,000 population (1990)
Infant mortality rate: 111 deaths/1,000 live births (1990)
Life expectancy at birth: 50 years male, 54 years female (1990)
Total fertility rate: 7.0 children born/woman (1990)
Nationality: noun—Burundian(s); adjective—Burundi
Ethnic divisions: Africans—85% Hutu (Bantu), 14% Tutsi (Hamitic), 1% Twa (Pygmy); other Africans include about

70,000 refugees, mostly Rwandans and Zairians; non-Africans include about 3,000 Europeans and 2,000 South Asians
Religion: about 67% Christian (62% Roman Catholic, 5% Protestant), 32% indigenous beliefs, 1% Muslim
Language: Kirundi and French (official); Swahili (along Lake Tanganyika and in the Bujumbura area)
Literacy: 33.8%
Labor force: 1,900,000 (1983 est.); 93.0% agriculture, 4.0% government, 1.5% industry and commerce, 1.5% services; 52% of population of working age (1985)
Organized labor: sole group is the Union of Burundi Workers (UTB); by charter, membership is extended to all Burundi workers (informally); figures denoting active membership unobtainable

Government

Long-form name: Republic of Burundi
Type: republic
Capital: Bujumbura
Administrative divisions: 15 provinces; Bubanza, Bujumbura, Bururi, Cankuzo, Cibitoke, Gitega, Karuzi, Kayanza, Kirundo, Makamba, Muramvya, Muyinga, Ngozi, Rutana, Ruyigi
Independence: 1 July 1962 (from UN trusteeship under Belgian administration)
Constitution: 20 November 1981; suspended following the coup of 3 September 1987
Legal system: based on German and Belgian civil codes and customary law; has not accepted compulsory ICJ jurisdiction
National holiday: Independence Day, 1 July (1962)
Executive branch: president, Military Committee for National Salvation, prime minister, Council of Ministers
Legislative branch: unicameral National Assembly (Assemblée Nationale) was dissolved following the coup of 3 September 1987
Judicial branch: Supreme Court (Cour Supréme)
Leaders: *Chief of State*—President Pierre BUYOYA (since 9 September 1987); *Head of Government* Prime Minister Adrien SIBOMANA (since 26 October 1988)
Political parties and leaders: only party—National Party of Unity and Progress (UPRONA), a Tutsi-led party, Libere Bararunyeretse, coordinator of the National Permanent Secretariat
Suffrage: universal adult at age NA
Elections: *National Assembly*—dissolved after the coup of 3 September 1987; no elections are planned
Communists: no Communist party
Member of: ACP, AfDB, CCC, EAMA, ECA, FAO, G-77, GATT, IBRD, ICAO, ICO, IDA, IFAD, IFC, ILO, IMF, INTERPOL, ITU, NAM, OAU, UN, UNESCO, UPU, WHO, WIPO, WMO, WTO
Diplomatic representation: Ambassador Julien KAVAKURE; Chancery at Suite 212, 2233 Wisconsin Avenue NW, Washington DC 20007; telephone (202) 342-2574; *US*—Ambassador Cynthia Shepherd PERRY; Embassy at Avenue du Zaire, Bujumbura (mailing address is B. P. 1720, Bujumbura); telephone 234-54 through 56
Flag: divided by a white diagonal cross into red panels (top and bottom) and green panels (hoist side and outer side) with a white disk superimposed at the center bearing three red six-pointed stars outlined in green arranged in a triangular design (one star above, two stars below)

Economy

Overview: A landlocked, resource-poor country in an early stage of economic development, Burundi is predominately agricultural with only a few basic industries. Its economic health is dependent on the coffee crop, which accounts for an average 90% of foreign exchange earnings each year. The ability to pay for imports therefore continues to rest largely on the vagaries of the climate and the international coffee market.
GDP: $1.3 billion, per capita $255; real growth rate 2.8% (1988)
Inflation rate (consumer prices): 4.4% (1988 est.)
Unemployment rate: NA%
Budget: revenues $213 million; expenditures $292 million, including capital expenditures of $131 million (1988 est.)
Exports: $128 million (f.o.b., 1988); *commodities*—coffee 88%, tea, hides and skins; *partners*—EC 83%, US 5%, Asia 2%
Imports: $204 million (c.i.f., 1988); *commodities*—capital goods 31%, petroleum products 15%, foodstuffs, consumer goods; *partners*—EC 57%, Asia 23%, US 3%
External debt: $795 million (December 1989 est.)
Industrial production: real growth rate 5.1% (1986)
Electricity: 51,000 kW capacity; 105 million kWh produced, 19 kWh per capita (1989)
Industries: light consumer goods such as blankets, shoes, soap; assembly of imports; public works construction; food processing
Agriculture: accounts for 60% of GDP; 90% of population dependent on subsistence farming; marginally self-sufficient in food production; cash crops—coffee, cotton, tea; food crops—corn, sorghum, sweet potatoes, bananas, manioc; livestock—meat, milk, hides, and skins
Aid: US commitments, including Ex-Im (FY70-88), $68 million; Western (non-US) countries, ODA and OOF bilateral commitments (1970-87), $10 billion; OPEC bilateral aid (1979-89), $32 million; Communist countries (1970-88), $175 million
Currency: Burundi franc (plural—francs); 1 Burundi franc (FBu) = 100 centimes
Exchange rates: Burundi francs (FBu) per US$1—176.20 (January 1990), 158.67 (1989), 140.40 (1988), 123.56 (1987), 114.17 (1986), 120.69 (1985)
Fiscal year: calendar year

Communications

Highways: 5,900 km total; 400 km paved, 2,500 km gravel or laterite, 3,000 km improved or unimproved earth
Inland waterways: Lake Tanganyika
Ports: Bujumbura (lake port) connects to transportation systems of Tanzania and Zaire
Civil air: 1 major transport aircraft
Airports: 8 total, 7 usable; 1 with permanent-surface runways; none with runways over 3,659 m; 1 with runways 2,440-3,659 m; none with runways 1,220 to 2,439 m
Telecommunications: sparse system of wire, radiocommunications, and low-capacity radio relay links; 8,000 telephones; stations—2 AM, 2 FM, 1 TV; 1 Indian Ocean INTELSAT earth station

Defense Forces

Branches: Army (includes naval and air units); paramilitary Gendarmerie
Military manpower: males 15-49, 1,230,559; 642,927 fit for military service; 61,418 reach military age (16) annually
Defense expenditures: 3.1% of GDP (1987)

Cambodia

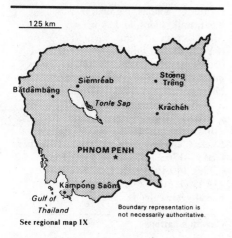

125 km

See regional map IX

Boundary representation is not necessarily authoritative.

Geography

Total area: 181,040 km²; land area: 176,520 km²
Comparative area: slightly smaller than Oklahoma
Land boundaries: 2,572 km total; Laos 541 km, Thailand 803 km, Vietnam 1,228 km
Coastline: 443 km
Maritime claims:
Contiguous zone: 24 nm
Continental shelf: 200 nm
Extended economic zone: 200 nm
Territorial sea: 12 nm
Disputes: offshore islands and three sections of the boundary with Vietnam are in dispute; maritime boundary with Vietnam not defined; occupied by Vietnam on 25 December 1978
Climate: tropical; rainy, monsoon season (May to October); dry season (December to March); little seasonal temperature variation
Terrain: mostly low, flat plains; mountains in southwest and north
Natural resources: timber, gemstones, some iron ore, manganese, phosphates, hydropower potential
Land use: 16% arable land; 1% permanent crops; 3% meadows and pastures; 76% forest and woodland; 4% other; includes 1% irrigated
Environment: a land of paddies and forests dominated by Mekong River and Tonle Sap
Note: buffer between Thailand and Vietnam

People

Population: 6,991,107 (July 1990), growth rate 2.2% (1990)
Birth rate: 39 births/1,000 population (1990)
Death rate: 16 deaths/1,000 population (1990)
Net migration rate: 0 migrants/1,000 population (1990)
Infant mortality rate: 128 deaths/1,000 live births (1990)
Life expectancy at birth: 47 years male, 50 years female (1990)
Total fertility rate: 4.5 children born/woman (1990)
Nationality: noun—Cambodian(s); adjective—Cambodian
Ethnic divisions: 90% Khmer (Cambodian), 5% Chinese, 5% other minorities
Religion: 95% Theravada Buddhism, 5% other
Language: Khmer (official), French
Literacy: 48%
Labor force: 2.5-3.0 million; 80% agriculture (1988 est.)
Organized labor: Kampuchea Federation of Trade Unions (FSC); under government control

Government

Long-form name: none
Type: disputed between the Coalition Government of Democratic Kampuchea (CGDK) led by Prince NORODOM SIHANOUK and the People's Republic of Kampuchea (PRK) led by HENG SAMRIN
Capital: Phnom Penh
Administrative divisions: 18 provinces (khêt, singular and plural) and 1 autonomous municipality* (rottatheanei, singular and plural); Bătdâmbâng, Kâmpóng Cham, Kâmpóng Chhnăng, Kâmpóng Spoe, Kâmpóng Thum, Kâmpôt, Kândal, Kaôh Kŏng, Krâchéh, Môndól Kiri, Phnum Pénh*, Poŭthĭsăt, Preăh Vihéar, Prey Vêng, Rôtânôkiri, Siĕmréab-Otdâr Méanchey, Stŏeng Trêng, Svay Riĕng, Takêv; note—there may be a new province of Banteay Méanchey and Siĕmréab-Otdâr Méanchey may have been divided into two provinces named Siĕmréab and Otdâr Méanchey
Independence: 9 November 1953 (from France)
Constitution: 27 June 1981
National holidays: CGDK—Independence Day, 17 April (1975); PRK—Liberation Day, 7 January (1979)
Executive branch: CGDK—president, prime minister; PRK—chairman of the Council of State, Council of State, chairman of the Council of Ministers, Council of Ministers
Legislative branch: CGDK—none; PRK—unicameral National Assembly
Judicial branch: CGDK—none; PRK—Supreme People's Court
Leaders: *Chief of State*—CGDK—President Prince NORODOM SIHANOUK (since NA July 1982); PRK—Chairman of the Council of State HENG SAMRIN (since 27 June 1981);
Head of Government—CGDK—Prime Minister SON SANN (since NA July 1982); PRK—Chairman of the Council of Ministers HUN SEN (since 14 January 1985)
Political parties and leaders: CGDK—three resistance groups including Democratic Kampuchea (DK, also known as the Khmer Rouge) under Khieu Samphan, Khmer People's National Liberation Front (KPNLF) under Son Sann, and National United Front for an Independent, Neutral, Peaceful, and Cooperative Cambodia (FUNCINPEC) under Prince Norodom Sihanouk; PRK—Kampuchean People's Revolutionary Party (KPRP) led by Heng Samrin
Suffrage: universal at age 18
Elections: CGDK—none; PRK—*National Assembly*—last held 1 May 1981; in February 1986 the Assembly voted to extend its term for five years (next to be held by March 1990); results—KPRP is the only party; seats—(123 total) KPRP 123
Member of: ADB, Colombo Plan, ESCAP, FAO, G-77, GATT (de facto), IAEA, IBRD, ICAO, IDA, ILO, IMF, IMO, INTERPOL, IRC, ITU, Mekong Committee (inactive), NAM, UN, UNESCO, UPU, WFTU, WHO, WMO, WTO for CGDK; none for PRK
Diplomatic representation: none
Flag: CGDK—red with the yellow silhouette of a stylized three-towered temple representing Angkor Wat in the center; Non-Communists—three horizontal bands of blue, red (double width), and blue with a white stylized temple representing Angkor Wat centered on the red band; PRK—red with the yellow silhouette of a stylized five-towered temple representing Angkor Wat in the center

Economy

Overview: Cambodia is a desperately poor country whose economic development has been stymied by deadly political infighting. The economy is based on agriculture and related industries. Over the past decade Cambodia has been slowly recovering from its near destruction by war and political upheaval. It still remains, however, one of the world's poorest countries, with an estimated per capita GDP of about $130. The food situation is precarious; during the 1980s famine has been averted only through international relief. In 1986 the production level of rice, the staple food crop, was able to meet only 80% of domestic needs. The biggest success of the nation's recovery program

has been in new rubber plantings and in fishing. Industry, other than rice processing, is almost nonexistent. Foreign trade is primarily with the USSR and Vietnam. Statistical data on the economy continues to be sparse and unreliable.
GDP: $890 million, per capita $130; real growth rate 0% (1989 est.)
Unemployment rate: NA%
Budget: revenues $NA; expenditures $NA, including capital expenditures of $NA
Inflation rate (consumer prices): NA%
Exports: $32 million (f.o.b., 1988); *commodities*—natural rubber, rice, pepper, wood; *partners*—Vietnam, USSR, Eastern Europe, Japan, India
Imports: $147 million (c.i.f., 1988); *commodities*—international food aid; fuels, consumer goods; *partners*—Vietnam, USSR, Eastern Europe, Japan, India
External debt: $600 million (1989)
Industrial production: growth rate NA%
Electricity: 126,000 kW capacity; 150 million kWh produced, 21 kWh per capita (1989)
Industries: rice milling, fishing, wood and wood products, rubber, cement, gem mining
Agriculture: mainly subsistence farming except for rubber plantations; main crops—rice, rubber, corn; food shortages—rice, meat, vegetables, dairy products, sugar, flour
Aid: US commitments, including Ex-Im (FY70-88), $719 million; Western (non-US) countries (1970-85), $270 million; Communist countries (1970-88), $950 million
Currency: riel (plural—riels); 1 riel (CR) = 100 sen
Exchange rates: riels (CR) per US$1—218 (November 1989) 100.00 (1987), 30.00 (1986), 7.00 (1985)
Fiscal year: calendar year

Communications

Railroads: 612 km 1.000-meter gauge, government owned
Highways: 13,351 km total; 2,622 km bituminous; 7,105 km crushed stone, gravel, or improved earth; 3,624 km unimproved earth; some roads in disrepair
Inland waterways: 3,700 km navigable all year to craft drawing 0.6 meters; 282 km navigable to craft drawing 1.8 meters
Ports: Kâmpóng Saôm, Phnom Penh
Airports: 22 total, 9 usable; 6 with permanent-surface runways; none with runways over 3,659 m; 2 with runways 2,440-3,659 m; 4 with runways 1,220-2,439 m
Telecommunications: service barely adequate for government requirements and virtually nonexistent for general public;

international service limited to Vietnam and other adjacent countries; stations—1 AM, no FM, 1 TV

Defense Forces

Branches: PRK—People's Republic of Kampuchea Armed Forces; Communist resistance forces—National Army of Democratic Kampuchea (Khmer Rouge); non-Communist resistance forces—Sihanoukist National Army (ANS) and Khmer People's National Liberation Front (KPNLF)
Military manpower: males 15-49, 1,857,129; 1,025,456 fit for military service; 61,649 reach military age (18) annually
Defense expenditures: NA

Cameroon

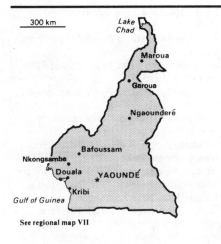

See regional map VII

Geography

Total area: 475,440 km^2; land area: 469,440 km^2
Comparative area: slightly larger than California
Land boundaries: 4,591 km total; Central African Republic 797 km, Chad 1,094 km, Congo 523 km, Equatorial Guinea 189 km, Gabon 298 km, Nigeria 1,690 km
Coastline: 402 km
Maritime claims:
  Continental shelf: not specific
  Territorial sea: 50 nm
Disputes: exact locations of the Chad-Niger-Nigeria and Cameroon-Chad-Nigeria tripoints in Lake Chad have not been determined, so the boundary has not been demarcated and border incidents have resulted; Nigerian proposals to re-open maritime boundary negotiations and redemarcate the entire land boundary have been rejected by Cameroon
Climate: varies with terrain from tropical along coast to semiarid and hot in north
Terrain: diverse with coastal plain in southwest, dissected plateau in center, mountains in west, plains in north
Natural resources: crude oil, bauxite, iron ore, timber, hydropower potential
Land use: 13% arable land; 2% permanent crops; 18% meadows and pastures; 54% forest and woodland; 13% other; includes NEGL% irrigated
Environment: recent volcanic activity with release of poisonous gases; deforestation; overgrazing; desertification
Note: sometimes referred to as the hinge of Africa

People

Population: 11,092,470 (July 1990), growth rate 2.7% (1990)
Birth rate: 42 births/1,000 population (1990)

Death rate: 15 deaths/1,000 population (1990)
Net migration rate: 0 migrants/1,000 population (1990)
Infant mortality rate: 120 deaths/1,000 live births (1990)
Life expectancy at birth: 49 years male, 53 years female (1990)
Total fertility rate: 5.7 children born/woman (1990)
Nationality: noun—Cameroonian(s); adjective—Cameroonian
Ethnic divisions: over 200 tribes of widely differing background; 31% Cameroon Highlanders, 19% Equatorial Bantu, 11% Kirdi, 10% Fulani, 8% Northwestern Bantu, 7% Eastern Nigritic, 13% other African, less than 1% non-African
Religion: 51% indigenous beliefs, 33% Christian, 16% Muslim
Language: English and French (official), 24 major African language groups
Literacy: 56.2%
Labor force: NA; 74.4% agriculture, 11.4% industry and transport, 14.2% other services (1983); 50% of population of working age (15-64 years) (1985)
Organized labor: under 45% of wage labor force

Government

Long-form name: Republic of Cameroon
Type: unitary republic; one-party presidential regime
Capital: Yaoundé
Administrative divisions: 10 provinces; Adamaoua, Centre, Est, Extrême-Nord, Littoral, Nord, Nord-Ouest, Ouest, Sud, Sud-Ouest
Independence: 1 January 1960 (from UN trusteeship under French administration; formerly French Cameroon)
Constitution: 20 May 1972
Legal system: based on French civil law system, with common law influence; has not accepted compulsory ICJ jurisdiction
National holiday: National Day, 20 May (1972)
Executive branch: president, Cabinet
Legislative branch: unicameral National Assembly (Assemblée Nationale)
Judicial branch: Supreme Court
Leaders: *Chief of State and Head of Government* President Paul BIYA (since 6 November 1982)
Political parties and leaders: only party—Cameroon People's Democratic Movement (RDPC), Paul Biya, president
Suffrage: universal at age 21
Elections: *President*—last held 24 April 1988 (next to be held April 1993); results—President Paul Biya reelected without opposition;
National Assembly—last held 24 April 1988 (next to be held April 1993);

results—RDPC is the only party; seats—(180 total) RDPC 180
Communists: no Communist party or significant number of sympathizers
Other political or pressure groups: Cameroon People's Union (UPC), remains an illegal group with its factional leaders in exile
Member of: ACP, AfDB, CCC, EAMA, ECA, EIB (associate), FAO, G-77, GATT, IAEA, IBRD, ICAC, ICAO, ICO, IDA, IDB—Islamic Development Bank, IFAD, IFC, ILO, IMF, IMO, INTELSAT, INTERPOL, IPU, ISO, ITU, Lake Chad Basin Commission, NAM, Niger River Commission, OAU, OIC, UDEAC, UN, UNESCO, UPU, WHO, WIPO, WMO, WTO
Diplomatic representation: Ambassador Paul PONDI; Chancery at 2349 Massachusetts Avenue NW, Washington DC 20008; telephone (202) 265-8790 through 8794; *US*—Ambassador Frances COOK; Embassy at Rue Nachtigal, Yaounde (mailing address is B. P. 817, Yaounde); telephone [237] 234014; there is a US Consulate General in Douala
Flag: three equal vertical bands of green (hoist side), red, and yellow with a yellow five-pointed star centered in the red band; uses the popular pan-African colors of Ethiopia

Economy

Overview: Over the past decade the economy has registered a remarkable performance because of the development of an offshore oil industry. Real GDP growth annually averaged 10% from 1978 to 1985. In 1986 Cameroon had one of the highest levels of income per capita in tropical Africa, with oil revenues picking up the slack as growth in other sectors softened. Because of the sharp drop in oil prices, however, the economy is now experiencing serious budgetary difficulties and balance-of-payments disequalibrium. Oil reserves currently being exploited will be depleted in the early 1990s, so ways must be found to boost agricultural and industrial exports in the medium term. The Sixth Cameroon Development Plan (1986-91) stresses balanced development and designates agriculture as the basis of the country's economic future.
GDP: $12.9 billion, per capita $955; real growth rate −8.6% (1988)
Inflation rate (consumer prices): 8.6% (FY88)
Unemployment rate: 7% (1985)
Budget: revenues $2.17 billion; expenditures $2.17 billion, including capital expenditures of $833 million (FY88)
Exports: $2.0 billion (f.o.b., 1988); *commodities*—petroleum products 56%,

coffee, cocoa, timber, manufactures; *partners*—EC (particularly the Netherlands) about 50%, US 3%
Imports: $2.3 billion (c.i.f., 1988); *commodities*—machines and electrical equipment, transport equipment, chemical products, consumer goods; *partners*—France 42%, Japan 7%, US 4%
External debt: $4.9 billion (December 1989 est.)
Industrial production: growth rate −6.4% (FY87)
Electricity: 752,000 kW capacity; 2,940 million kWh produced, 270 kWh per capita (1989)
Industries: crude oil products, small aluminum plant, food processing, light consumer goods industries, sawmills
Agriculture: the agriculture and forestry sectors provide employment for the majority of the population, contributing nearly 25% to GDP and providing a high degree of self-sufficiency in staple foods; commercial and food crops include coffee, cocoa, timber, cotton, rubber, bananas, oilseed, grains, livestock, root starches
Aid: US commitments, including Ex-Im (FY70-88), $400 million; Western (non-US) countries, ODA and OOF bilateral commitments (1970-87), $3.9 billion; OPEC bilateral aid (1979-89), $29 million; Communist countries (1970-88), $120 million
Currency: Communauté Financière Africaine franc (plural—francs); 1 CFA franc (CFAF) = 100 centimes
Exchange rates: Communauté Financière Africaine francs (CFAF) per US$1—287.99 (January 1990), 319.01 (1989), 297.85 (1988), 300.54 (1987), 346.30 (1986), 449.26 (1985)
Fiscal year: 1 July-30 June

Communications

Railroads: 1,003 km total; 858 km 1.000-meter gauge, 145 km 0.600-meter gauge
Highways: about 65,000 km total; includes 2,682 km bituminous, 30,000 km unimproved earth, 32,318 km gravel, earth, and improved earth
Inland waterways: 2,090 km; of decreasing importance
Ports: Douala
Merchant marine: 2 cargo ships (1,000 GRT or over) totaling 24,122 GRT/33,509 DWT
Civil air: 5 major transport aircraft
Airports: 61 total, 54 usable; 10 with permanent-surface runways; none with runways over 3,659 m; 5 with runways 2,440-3,659 m; 22 with runways 1,220-2,439 m
Telecommunications: good system of open wire, cable, troposcatter, and radio relay;

Canada

26,000 telephones; stations—10 AM, 1 FM, 1 TV; 2 Atlantic Ocean INTELSAT earth stations

Defense Forces

Branches: Army, Navy, Air Force; paramilitary Gendarmerie
Military manpower: males 15-49, 2,553,867; 1,286,831 fit for military service; 121,773 reach military age (18) annually
Defense expenditures: 1.7% of GDP, or $219 million (1990 est.)

See regional map II

Geography

Total area: 9,976,140 km²; land area: 9,220,970 km²
Comparative area: slightly larger than US
Land boundaries: 8,893 km with US (includes 2,477 km with Alaska)
Coastline: 243,791 km
Maritime claims:
  Continental shelf: 200 meters or to depth of exploitation
  Exclusive fishing zone: 200 nm
  Territorial sea: 12 nm
Disputes: maritime boundary disputes with France (St. Pierre and Miquelon) and US
Climate: varies from temperate in south to subarctic and arctic in north
Terrain: mostly plains with mountains in west and lowlands in southeast
Natural resources: nickel, zinc, copper, gold, lead, molybdenum, potash, silver, fish, timber, wildlife, coal, crude oil, natural gas
Land use: 5% arable land; NEGL% permanent crops; 3% meadows and pastures; 35% forest and woodland; 57% other; includes NEGL% irrigated
Environment: 80% of population concentrated within 160 km of US border; continuous permafrost in north a serious obstacle to development
Note: second-largest country in world (after USSR); strategic location between USSR and US via north polar route

People

Population: 26,538,229 (July 1990), growth rate 1.1% (1990)
Birth rate: 14 births/1,000 population (1990)
Death rate: 7 deaths/1,000 population (1990)
Net migration rate: 5 migrants/1,000 population (1990)

Infant mortality rate: 7 deaths/1,000 live births (1990)
Life expectancy at birth: 74 years male, 81 years female (1990)
Total fertility rate: 1.7 children born/woman (1990)
Nationality: noun—Canadian(s); adjective—Canadian
Ethnic divisions: 40% British Isles origin, 27% French origin, 20% other European, 1.5% indigenous Indian and Eskimo
Religion: 46% Roman Catholic, 16% United Church, 10% Anglican
Language: English and French (both official)
Literacy: 99%
Labor force: 13,380,000; services 75%, manufacturing 14%, agriculture 4%, construction 3%, other 4% (1988)
Organized labor: 30.6% of labor force; 39.6% of nonagricultural paid workers

Government

Long-form name: none
Type: confederation with parliamentary democracy
Capital: Ottawa
Administrative divisions: 10 provinces and 2 territories*; Alberta, British Columbia, Manitoba, New Brunswick, Newfoundland, Northwest Territories*, Nova Scotia, Ontario, Prince Edward Island, Quebec, Saskatchewan, Yukon Territory*
Independence: 1 July 1867 (from UK)
Constitution: amended British North America Act 1867 patriated to Canada 17 April 1982; charter of rights and unwritten customs
Legal system: based on English common law, except in Quebec, where civil law system based on French law prevails; accepts compulsory ICJ jurisdiction, with reservations
National holiday: Canada Day, 1 July (1867)
Executive branch: British monarch, governor general, prime minister, deputy prime minister, Cabinet
Legislative branch: bicameral Parliament consists of an upper house or Senate and a lower house or House of Commons
Judicial branch: Supreme Court
Leaders: *Chief of State*—Queen ELIZABETH II (since 6 February 1952), represented by Governor General Raymond John HNATSHYN (since 29 January 1990);
Head of Government—Prime Minister (Martin) Brian MULRONEY (since 4 September 1984); Deputy Prime Minister Donald Frank MAZANKOWSKI (since NA June 1986)

Political parties and leaders: Progressive Conservative, Brian Mulroney; Liberal, John Turner; New Democratic, Audrey McLaughlin
Suffrage: universal at age 18
Elections: *House of Commons*—last held 21 November 1988 (next to be held by November 1993); results—Progressive Conservative 43.0%, Liberal 32%, New Democratic Party 20%, other 5%; seats—(295 total) Progressive Conservative 170, Liberal 82, New Democratic Party 43
Communists: 3,000
Member of: ADB, CCC, Colombo Plan, Commonwealth, DAC, FAO, GATT, IAEA, IBRD, ICAO, ICES, ICO, IDA, IDB—Inter-American Development Bank, IEA, IFAD, IFC, IHO, ILO, ILZSG, IMF, IMO, INTELSAT, INTERPOL, IPU, ISO, ITC, ITU, IWC—International Whaling Commission, IWC—International Wheat Council, NATO, OAS, OECD, PAHO, UN, UNCTAD, UNESCO, UPU, WHO, WIPO, WMO, WSG
Diplomatic representation: Ambassador Derek BURNEY; Chancery at 1746 Massachusetts Avenue NW, Washington DC 20036; telephone (202) 785-1400; there are Canadian Consulates General in Atlanta, Boston, Buffalo, Chicago, Cleveland, Dallas, Detroit, Los Angeles, Minneapolis, New York, Philadelphia, San Francisco, and Seattle; *US*—Ambassador Edward N. NEY; Embassy at 100 Wellington Street, K1P 5T1, Ottawa (mailing address is P. O. Box 5000, Ogdensburg, NY 13669); telephone (613) 238-5335; there are US Consulates General in Calgary, Halifax, Montreal, Quebec, Toronto, and Vancouver
Flag: three vertical bands of red (hoist side), white (double width, square), and red with a red maple leaf centered in the white band

Economy

Overview: As an affluent, high-tech industrial society, Canada today closely resembles the US in per capita output, market-oriented economic system, and pattern of production. Since World War II the impressive growth of the manufacturing, mining, and service sectors has transformed the nation from a largely rural economy into one primarily industrial and urban. In the 1980s Canada registered one of the highest rates of growth among the OECD nations, averaging about 4%. With its great natural resources, skilled labor force, and modern capital plant, Canada has excellent economic prospects.
GDP: $513.6 billion, per capita $19,600; real growth rate 2.9% (1989 est.)

Inflation rate (consumer prices): 5.0% (1989)
Unemployment rate: 7.5% (1989)
Budget: revenues $79.2 billion; expenditures $102.0 billion, including capital expenditures of $1.8 billion (FY88 est.)
Exports: $127.2 billion (f.o.b., 1989); *commodities*—newsprint, wood pulp, timber, grain, crude petroleum, natural gas, ferrous and nonferrous ores, motor vehicles; *partners*—US, Japan, UK, FRG, other EC, USSR
Imports: $116.5 billion (c.i.f., 1989); *commodities*—processed foods, beverages, crude petroleum, chemicals, industrial machinery, motor vehicles, durable consumer goods, electronic computers; *partners*—US, Japan, UK, FRG, other EC, Taiwan, South Korea, Mexico
External debt: $247 billion (1987)
Industrial production: growth rate 2.3% (1989)
Electricity: 103,746,000 kW capacity; 472,580 million kWh produced, 17,960 kWh per capita (1989)
Industries: processed and unprocessed minerals, food products, wood and paper products, transportation equipment, chemicals, fish products, petroleum and natural gas
Agriculture: accounts for 3% of GDP; one of the world's major producers and exporters of grain (wheat and barley); key source of US agricultural imports; large forest resources cover 35% of total land area; commercial fisheries provide annual catch of 1.5 million metric tons, of which 75% is exported
Illicit drugs: illicit producer of cannabis for the domestic drug market
Aid: donor—ODA and OOF commitments (1970-87), $2.2 billion
Currency: Canadian dollar (plural—dollars); 1 Canadian dollar (Can$) = 100 cents
Exchange rates: Canadian dollars (Can$) per US$1—1.1714 (January 1990), 1.1840 (1989), 1.2307 (1988), 1.3260 (1987), 1.3895 (1986), 1.3655 (1985)
Fiscal year: 1 April-31 March

Communications

Railroads: 80,095 km total; 79,917 km 1.435-meter standard gauge (includes 129 km electrified); 178 km 0.915-meter narrow gauge (mostly unused); two major transcontinental freight railway systems—Canadian National (government owned) and Canadian Pacific Railway; passenger service—VIA (government operated)
Highways: 884,272 km total; 712,936 km surfaced (250,023 km paved), 171,336 km earth
Inland waterways: 3,000 km, including St. Lawrence Seaway

Pipelines: oil, 23,564 km total crude and refined; natural gas, 74,980 km
Ports: Halifax, Montreal, Quebec, Saint John (New Brunswick), St. John's (Newfoundland), Toronto, Vancouver
Merchant marine: 78 ships (1,000 GRT or over) totaling 555,749 GRT/774,914 DWT; includes 1 passenger, 5 short-sea passenger, 2 passenger-cargo, 12 cargo, 2 railcar carrier, 1 refrigerated cargo, 8 roll-on/roll-off, 1 container, 29 petroleum, oils, and lubricants (POL) tanker, 6 chemical tanker, 1 specialized tanker, 10 bulk; note—does not include ships used exclusively in the Great Lakes ships
Civil air: 636 major transport aircraft; Air Canada is the major carrier
Airports: 1,359 total, 1,117 usable; 442 with permanent-surface runways; 4 with runways over 3,659 m; 30 with runways 2,440-3,659 m; 322 with runways 1,220-2,439 m
Telecommunications: excellent service provided by modern media; 18.0 million telephones; stations—900 AM, 29 FM, 53 (1,400 repeaters) TV; 5 coaxial submarine cables; over 300 satellite earth stations operating in INTELSAT (including 4 Atlantic Ocean and 1 Pacific Ocean) and domestic systems

Defense Forces

Branches: Mobile Command, Maritime Command, Air Command, Communications Command, Canadian Forces Europe, Training Commands
Military manpower: males 15-49, 7,174,119; 6,251,492 fit for military service; 187,894 reach military age (17) annually
Defense expenditures: 2.0% of GDP, or $10 billion (1989 est.)

Cape Verde

Ilhas do Barlavento

Santo Antão • Mindelo • Santa Luzia • São Vicente • São Nicolau • Sal • Boa Vista

75 km

North Atlantic Ocean

Ilhas do Sotavento

Brava • Fogo • São Tiago • PRAIA • Maio

See regional map VII

Geography

Total area: 4,030 km²; land area: 4,030 km²
Comparative area: slightly larger than Rhode Island
Land boundaries: none
Coastline: 965 km
Maritime claims: (measured from claimed archipelagic baselines)
  Extended economic zone: 200 nm
  Territorial sea: 12 nm
Climate: temperate; warm, dry, summer precipitation very erratic
Terrain: steep, rugged, rocky, volcanic
Natural resources: salt, basalt rock, pozzolana, limestone, kaolin, fish
Land use: 9% arable land; NEGL% permanent crops; 6% meadows and pastures; NEGL% forest and woodland; 85% other; includes 1% irrigated
Environment: subject to prolonged droughts; harmattan wind can obscure visibility; volcanically and seismically active; deforestation; overgrazing
Note: strategic location 500 km from African coast near major north-south sea routes; important communications station; important sea and air refueling site

People

Population: 374,984 (July 1990), growth rate 3.0% (1990)
Birth rate: 49 births/1,000 population (1990)
Death rate: 11 deaths/1,000 population (1990)
Net migration rate: −8 migrants/1,000 population (1990)
Infant mortality rate: 65 deaths/1,000 live births (1990)
Life expectancy at birth: 59 years male, 63 years female (1990)
Total fertility rate: 6.7 children born/woman (1990)

Nationality: noun—Cape Verdean(s); adjective—Cape Verdean
Ethnic divisions: about 71% Creole (mulatto), 28% African, 1% European
Religion: Roman Catholicism fused with indigenous beliefs
Language: Portuguese and Crioulo, a blend of Portuguese and West African words
Literacy: 48% (1986)
Labor force: 102,000 (1985 est.); 57% agriculture (mostly subsistence), 29% services, 14% industry (1981); 51% of population of working age (1985)
Organized labor: Trade Unions of Cape Verde Unity Center (UNTC-CS) closely associated with ruling party

Government

Long-form name: Republic of Cape Verde
Type: republic
Capital: Praia
Administrative divisions: 12 districts (concelhos, singular—concelho); Boa Vista, Brava, Fogo, Maio, Paul, Praia, Ribeira Grande, Sal, Santa Catarina, São Nicolau, São Vicente, Tarrafal; there may be 2 new districts named Porto Novo and Santa Cruz
Independence: 5 July 1975 (from Portugal)
Constitution: 7 September 1980, amended 12 February 1981 and December 1988
National holiday: Independence Day, 5 July (1975)
Executive branch: president, prime minister, deputy minister, Council of Ministers (cabinet)
Legislative branch: unicameral National People's Assembly (Assembléia Nacional Popular)
Judicial branch: Supreme Tribunal of Justice (Supremo Tribunal de Justiạ)
Leaders: *Chief of State*—President Aristides María PEREIRA (since 5 July 1975);
Head of Government—Prime Minister Pedro Verona Rodrigues PIRES, (since 5 July 1975); Deputy Minister Aguinaldo Liboa RAMOS (since NA February 1990)
Political parties and leaders: only party—African Party for Independence of Cape Verde (PAICV), Aristides María Pereira, secretary general
Suffrage: universal at age 15
Elections: *President*—last held 13 January 1986 (next to be held January 1991); results—President Aristides María Pereira (PAICV) was reelected without opposition; *National People's Assembly*—last held 7 December 1985 (next to be held December 1990); results—PAICV is the only party; seats—(83 total) PAICV 83
Communists: a few Communists and some sympathizers

Member of: ACP, AfDB, ECA, ECOWAS, FAO, G-77, GATT (de facto), IBRD, ICAO, IDA, IFAD, IFC, ILO, IMF, IMO, IPU, ITU, NAM, OAU, UN, UNESCO, UPU, WHO, WMO
Diplomatic representation: Ambassador José Luis FERNANDES LOPES; Chancery at 3415 Massachusetts Avenue NW, Washington DC 20007; telephone (202) 965-6820; there is a Cape Verdean Consulate General in Boston; *US*—Ambassador Terry McNAMARA; Embassy at Rua Hojl Ya Yenna 81, Praia (mailing address is C. P. 201, Praia); telephone [238] 614-363 or 253
Flag: two equal horizontal bands of yellow (top) and green with a vertical red band on the hoist side; in the upper portion of the red band is a black five-pointed star framed by two corn stalks and a yellow clam shell; uses the popular pan-African colors of Ethiopia; similar to the flag of Guinea-Bissau which is longer and has an unadorned black star centered in the red band

Economy

Overview: Cape Verde's low per capita GDP reflects a poor natural resource base, a 17-year drought, and a high birth rate. The economy is service oriented, with commerce, transport, and public services accounting for 60% of GDP during the period 1984-86. Although nearly 70% of the population lives in rural areas, agriculture's share of GDP is only 16%; the fishing and manufacturing sectors are 4% each. About 90% of food must be imported. The fishing potential of the islands is not fully exploited (the fish catch—mostly lobster and tuna—came to only 10,000 tons in 1985). Cape Verde annually runs a high trade deficit, financed by remittances from emigrants, cash grants, food aid, and foreign loans.
GDP: $158 million, per capita $494; real growth rate 6.1% (1987)
Inflation rate (consumer prices): 3.8% (1987)
Unemployment rate: 25% (1988)
Budget: revenues $80 million; expenditures $87 million, including capital expenditures of $45 million (1988 est.)
Exports: $8.9 million (f.o.b., 1987); *commodities*—fish, bananas, salt; *partners*—Portugal, Angola, Algeria, Belgium/Luxembourg, Italy
Imports: $124 million (c.i.f., 1987); *commodities*—petroleum, foodstuffs, consumer goods, industrial products; *partners*—Portugal, Netherlands, Spain, France, US, FRG
External debt: $140 million (December 1988)

Cape Verde (continued)

Industrial production: growth rate 0% (1986 est.)
Electricity: 14,000 kW capacity; 18 million kWh produced, 50 kWh per capita (1989)
Industry: fish processing, salt mining, clothing factories, ship repair
Agriculture: accounts for 16% of GDP; largely subsistence farming; bananas are the only export crop; other crops—corn, beans, sweet potatoes, coffee; growth potential of agricultural sector limited by poor soils and limited rainfall; annual food imports required; fish catch provides for both domestic consumption and small exports
Aid: US commitments, including Ex-Im (FY75-88), $83 million; Western (non-US) countries, ODA and OOF bilateral commitments (1970-87), $540 million; OPEC bilateral aid (1979-89), $12 million; Communist countries (1970-88), $36 million
Currency: Cape Verdean escudo (plural—escudos); 1 Cape Verdean escudo (CVEsc) = 100 centavos
Exchange rates: Cape Verdean escudos (CVEsc) per US$1—72.31 (February 1990), 74.86 (December 1989), 72.01 (1988), 72.5 (1987), 76.56 (1986), 85.38 (1985)
Fiscal year: calendar year

Communications

Ports: Mindelo and Praia
Merchant marine: 5 cargo ships (1,000 GRT or over) totaling 9,308 GRT/16,172 DWT
Civil air: 2 major transport aircraft
Airports: 6 total, 6 usable; 4 with permanent-surface runways; none with runways over 3,659 m; 1 with runways 2,440-3,659 m; 4 with runways 1,220-2,439 m
Telecommunications: interisland radio relay system, high-frequency radio to mainland Portugal and Guinea-Bissau; 1,740 telephones; stations—5 AM, 1 FM, 1 TV; 2 coaxial submarine cables; 1 Atlantic Ocean INTELSAT earth station

Defense Forces

Branches: People's Revolutionary Armed Forces (FARP); Army, Navy, and Air Force are separate components of FARP
Military manpower: males 15-49, 68,776; 40,731 fit for military service
Defense expenditures: 11.8% of GDP (1981)

Cayman Islands
(dependent territory of the UK)

50 km

Caribbean Sea

Cayman Brac

Little Cayman

Grand Cayman
GEORGE TOWN

Caribbean Sea

See regional map III

Geography

Total area: 260 km²; land area: 260 km²
Comparative area: slightly less than 1.5 times the size of Washington, DC
Land boundaries: none
Coastline: 160 km
Maritime claims:
 Exclusive fishing zone: 200 nm
 Territorial sea: 3 nm
Climate: tropical marine; warm, rainy summers (May to October) and cool, relatively dry winters (November to April)
Terrain: low-lying limestone base surrounded by coral reefs
Natural resources: fish, climate and beaches that foster tourism
Land use: 0% arable land; 0% permanent crops; 8% meadows and pastures; 23% forest and woodland; 69% other
Environment: within the Caribbean hurricane belt
Note: important location between Cuba and Central America

People

Population: 26,356 (July 1990), growth rate 4.3% (1990)
Birth rate: 14 births/1,000 population (1990)
Death rate: 5 deaths/1,000 population (1990)
Net migration rate: 33 migrants/1,000 population (1990)
Infant mortality rate: 10 deaths/1,000 live births (1990)
Life expectancy at birth: 74 years male, 80 years female (1990)
Total fertility rate: 1.5 children born/woman (1990)
Nationality: noun—Caymanian(s); adjective—Caymanian
Ethnic divisions: 40% mixed, 20% white, 20% black, 20% expatriates of various ethnic groups

Religion: United Church (Presbyterian and Congregational), Anglican, Baptist, Roman Catholic, Church of God, other Protestant denominations
Language: English
Literacy: 98%
Labor force: 8,061; 18.7% service workers, 18.6% clerical, 12.5% construction, 6.7% finance and investment, 5.9% directors and business managers (1979)
Organized labor: Global Seaman's Union; Cayman All Trade Union

Government

Long-form name: none
Type: dependent territory of the UK
Capital: George Town
Administrative divisions: 12 districts; Bodden Town, Creek, East End, George Town, Jacksons, North Side, Prospect, South Town, Spot Bay, Stake Bay, West Bay, West End
Independence: none (dependent territory of the UK)
Legal system: British common law and local statutes
Constitution: 1959, revised 1972
National holiday: Constitution Day (first Monday in July), 3 July 1989
Executive branch: British monarch, governor, Executive Council (cabinet)
Legislative branch: unicameral Legislative Assembly
Judicial branch: Grand Court, Cayman Islands Court of Appeal
Leaders: *Chief of State*—Queen ELIZABETH II (since 6 February 1952), represented by Governor Alan James SCOTT (since NA 1987);
Head of Government—Governor and President of the Executive Council Alan James SCOTT (since NA 1987)
Political parties and leaders: no formal political parties
Suffrage: universal at age 18
Elections: *Legislative Assembly*—last held NA November 1988 (next to be held November 1992); results—percent of vote NA; seats—(15 total, 12 elected)
Communists: none
Member of: Commonwealth
Diplomatic representation: as a dependent territory of the UK, Caymanian interests in the US are represented by the UK; *US*—none
Flag: blue with the flag of the UK in the upper hoist-side quadrant and the Caymanian coat of arms on a white disk centered on the outer half of the flag; the coat of arms includes a pineapple and turtle above a shield with three stars (representing the three islands) and a scroll at the bottom bearing the motto *HE HATH FOUNDED IT UPON THE SEAS*

Economy

Overview: The economy depends heavily on tourism (70% of GDP and 75% of export earnings) and offshore financial services, with the tourist industry aimed at the luxury market and catering mainly to visitors from North America. About 90% of the islands' food and consumer goods needs must be imported. The Caymanians enjoy one of the highest standards of living in the region.

GDP: $238 million, per capita $10,000 (1989 est.); real growth rate 12% (1987 est.)

Inflation rate (consumer prices): 2.4% (1986)

Unemployment rate: NA%

Budget: revenues $46.2 million; expenditures $47.0 million, including capital expenditures of $9.1 million (1986)

Exports: $2.2 million (f.o.b., 1986 est.); *commodities*—turtle products, manufactured consumer goods; *partners*—mostly US

Imports: $134 million (c.i:f., 1986 est.); *commodities*—foodstuffs, manufactured goods; *partners*—US, Trinidad and Tobago, UK, Netherlands Antilles, Japan

External debt: $15 million (1986)

Industrial production: growth rate NA%

Electricity: 59,000 kW capacity; 213 million kWh produced, 8,960 kWh per capita (1989)

Industries: tourism, banking, insurance and finance, real estate and construction

Agriculture: minor production of vegetables, fruit, livestock; turtle farming

Aid: US commitments, including Ex-Im (FY70-87), $26.7 million; Western (non-US) countries, ODA and OOF bilateral commitments (1970-87), $32.2 million

Currency: Caymanian dollar (plural—dollars); 1 Caymanian dollar (CI$) = 100 cents

Exchange rates: Caymanian dollars (CI$) per US$1—0.835 (fixed rate)

Fiscal year: 1 April-31 March

Communications

Highways: 160 km of main roads

Ports: George Town, Cayman Brac

Merchant marine: 32 ships (1,000 GRT or over) totaling 355,055 GRT/576,622 DWT; includes 1 passenger-cargo, 8 cargo, 8 roll-on/roll-off cargo, 4 petroleum, oils, and lubricants (POL) tanker, 1 chemical tanker, 1 specialized tanker, 1 liquefied gas carrier, 8 bulk; note—a flag of convenience registry

Airports: 3 total; 3 usable; 2 with permanent-surface runways; none with runways over 2,439 m; 2 with runways 1,220-2,439 m

Telecommunications: 35,000 telephones; telephone system uses 1 submarine coaxial cable and 1 Atlantic Ocean INTELSAT earth station to link islands and access international services; stations—2 AM, 1 FM, no TV

Defense Forces

Note: defense is the responsibility of the UK

Central African Republic

See regional map VII

Geography

Total area: 622,980 km²; land area: 622,980 km²

Comparative area: slightly smaller than Texas

Land boundaries: 5,203 km total; Cameroon 797 km, Chad 1,197 km, Congo 467 km, Sudan 1,165 km, Zaire 1,577 km

Coastline: none—landlocked

Maritime claims: none—landlocked

Climate: tropical; hot, dry winters; mild to hot, wet summers

Terrain: vast, flat to rolling, monotonous plateau; scattered hills in northeast and southwest

Natural resources: diamonds, uranium, timber, gold, oil

Land use: 3% arable land; NEGL% permanent crops; 5% meadows and pastures; 64% forest and woodland; 28% other

Environment: hot, dry, dusty harmattan winds affect northern areas; poaching has diminished reputation as one of last great wildlife refuges; desertification

Note: landlocked; almost the precise center of Africa

People

Population: 2,877,365 (July 1990), growth rate 2.6% (1990)

Birth rate: 44 births/1,000 population (1990)

Death rate: 18 deaths/1,000 population (1990)

Net migration rate: 0 migrants/1,000 population (1990)

Infant mortality rate: 141 deaths/1,000 live births (1990)

Life expectancy at birth: 45 years male, 48 years female (1990)

Total fertility rate: 5.6 children born/woman (1990)

Nationality: noun—Central African(s); adjective—Central African

Central African Republic
(continued)

Ethnic divisions: about 80 ethnic groups, the majority of which have related ethnic and linguistic characteristics; 34% Baya, 27% Banda, 10% Sara, 21% Mandjia, 4% Mboum, 4% M'Baka; 6,500 Europeans, of whom 3,600 are French
Religion: 24% indigenous beliefs, 25% Protestant, 25% Roman Catholic, 15% Muslim, 11% other; animistic beliefs and practices strongly influence the Christian majority
Language: French (official); Sangho (lingua franca and national language); Arabic, Hunsa, Swahili
Literacy: 40.2%
Labor force: 775,413 (1986 est.); 85% agriculture, 9% commerce and services, 3% industry, 3% government; about 64,000 salaried workers; 55% of population of working age (1985)
Organized labor: 1% of labor force

Government

Long-form name: Central African Republic (no short-form name); abbreviated CAR
Type: republic, one-party presidential regime since 1986
Capital: Bangui
Administrative divisions: 14 prefectures (préfectures, singular—préfecture) and 2 economic prefectures* (préfectures économiques, singular—préfecture économique); Bamingui-Bangoran, Basse-Kotto, Gribingui*, Haute-Kotto, Haute-Sangha, Haut-Mbomou, Kémo-Gribingui, Lobaye, Mbomou, Nana-Mambéré, Ombella-Mpoko, Ouaka, Ouham, Ouham-Pendé, Sangha*, Vakaga; note—there may be a new autonomous commune of Bangui
Independence: 13 August 1960 (from France; formerly Central African Empire)
Constitution: 21 November 1986
Legal system: based on French law
National holiday: National Day (proclamation of the republic), 1 December (1958)
Executive branch: president, Council of Ministers (cabinet)
Legislative branch: bicameral Congress consists of an upper house or Economic and Regional Council (Conseil Economique et Régional) and a lower house or National Assembly (Assemblée Nationale)
Judicial branch: Supreme Court (Cour Suprême)
Leaders: *Chief of State and Head of Government*—President André-Dieudonné KOLINGBA (since 1 September 1981)

Political parties and leaders: only party—Centrafrican Democrtic Rally Party (RDC), André-Dieudonné Kolingba
Suffrage: universal at age 21
Elections: *President*—last held 21 November 1986 (next to be held November 1993); results—President Kolingba was reelected without opposition;
National Assembly—last held 31 July 1987 (next to be held July 1992); results—RDC is the only party; seats—(total) RDC 52
Communists: small number of Communist sympathizers
Member of: ACP, AfDB, CCC, Conference of East and Central African States, EAMA, ECA, FAO, G-77, GATT, IBRD, ICAO, ICO, IDA, IFAD, ILO, IMF, INTELSAT, INTERPOL, ITU, NAM, OAU, OCAM, UDEAC, UN, UNESCO, UPU, WHO, WIPO, WMO
Diplomatic representation: Ambassador Jean-Pierre SOHAHONG-KOMBET; Chancery at 1618 22nd Street NW, Washington DC 20008; telephone (202) 483-7800 or 7801; *US*—Ambassador Daniel H. SIMPSON; Embassy at Avenue du President David Dacko, Bangui (mailing address is B. P. 924, Bangui); telephone 61-02-00 or 61-25-78, 61-43-33
Flag: four equal horizontal bands of blue (top), white, green, and yellow with a vertical red band in center; there is a yellow five-pointed star on the hoist side of the blue band

Economy

Overview: The Central African Republic (CAR) is one of the poorest countries in Africa, with a per capita income of roughly $450 in 1988. Subsistence agriculture, including forestry, is the backbone of the economy, with over 70% of the population living in the countryside. In 1988 the agricultural sector generated about 40% of GDP, mining and manufacturing 14%, utilities and construction 4%, and services 41%. Agricultural products accounted for about 60% of export earnings and the diamond industry for 30%. Important constraints to economic development include the CAR's landlocked position, a poor transportation infrastructure, and a weak human resource base. Multilateral and bilateral development assistance plays a major role in providing capital for new investment.
GDP: $1.27 billion, per capita $453; real growth rate 2.0% (1988 est.)

Inflation rate (consumer prices): −4.2% (1988 est.)
Unemployment rate: 30% in Bangui (1988 est.)
Budget: revenues $132 million; current expenditures $305 million, including capital expenditures of $NA million (1989 est.)
Exports: $138 million (f.o.b., 1988 est.); *commodities*—diamonds, cotton, coffee, timber, tobacco; *partners*—France, Belgium, Italy, Japan, US
Imports: $285 million (c.i.f., 1988 est.); *commodities*—food, textiles, petroleum products, machinery, electrical equipment, motor vehicles, chemicals, pharmaceuticals, consumer goods, industrial products; *partners*—France, other EC, Japan, Algeria, Yugoslavia
External debt: $660 million (December 1989)
Industrial production: 1.9% (1987 est.)
Electricity: 35,000 kW capacity; 84 million kWh produced, 30 kWh per capita (1989)
Industries: sawmills, breweries, diamond mining, textiles, footwear, assembly of bicycles and motorcycles
Agriculture: accounts for 40% of GDP; self-sufficient in food production except for grain; commercial crops—cotton, coffee, tobacco, timber; food crops—manioc, yams, millet, corn, bananas
Aid: US commitments, including Ex-Im (FY70-88), $44 million; Western (non-US) countries, ODA and OOF bilateral commitments (1970-87), $1.3 billion; OPEC bilateral aid (1979-89), $6 million; Communist countries (1970-88), $38 million
Currency: Communauté Financière Africaine franc (plural—francs); 1 CFA franc (CFAF) = 100 centimes
Exchange rates: Communauté Financière Africaine francs (CFAF) per US$1— 287.99 (January 1990), 319.01 (1989), 297.85 (1988), 300.54 (1987), 346.30 (1986), 449.26 (1985)
Fiscal year: calendar year

Communications

Highways: 22,000 km total; 458 km bituminous, 10,542 km improved earth, 11,000 unimproved earth
Inland waterways: 800 km; traditional trade carried on by means of shallow-draft dugouts; Oubangui is the most important river
Civil air: 2 major transport aircraft
Airports: 66 total, 49 usable; 4 with permanent-surface runways; none with runways over 3,659 m; 2 with runways 2,440-3,659 m; 22 with runways 1,220-2,439 m

Chad

Telecommunications: fair system; network relies primarily on radio relay links, with low-capacity, low-powered radiocommunication also used; 6,000 telephones; stations—1 AM, 1 FM, 1 TV; 1 Atlantic Ocean INTELSAT earth station

Defense Forces

Branches: Army, Air Force
Military manpower: males 15-49, 642,207; 335,863 fit for military service
Defense expenditures: 1.8% of GDP, or $23 million (1989 est.)

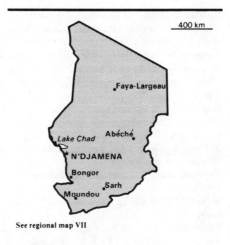

See regional map VII

Geography

Total area: 1,284,000 km²; land area: 1,259,200 km²
Comparative area: slightly more than three times the size of California
Land boundaries: 5,968 km total; Cameroon 1,094 km, Central African Republic 1,197 km, Libya 1,055 km, Niger 1,175 km, Nigeria 87 km, Sudan 1,360 km
Coastline: none—landlocked
Maritime claims: none—landlocked
Disputes: Libya claims and occupies a small portion of the Aozou Strip in far north; exact locations of the Chad-Niger-Nigeria and Cameroon-Chad-Nigeria tripoints in Lake Chad have not been determined—since the boundary has not been demarcated, border incidents have resulted
Climate: tropical in south, desert in north
Terrain: broad, arid plains in center, desert in north, mountains in northwest, lowlands in south
Natural resources: small quantities of crude oil (unexploited but exploration beginning), uranium, natron, kaolin, fish (Lake Chad)
Land use: 2% arable land; NEGL% permanent crops; 36% meadows and pastures; 11% forest and woodland; 51% other; includes NEGL% irrigated
Environment: hot, dry, dusty harmattan winds occur in north; drought and desertification adversely affecting south; subject to plagues of locusts
Note: landlocked; Lake Chad is the most significant water body in the Sahel

People

Population: 5,017,431 (July 1990), growth rate 2.1% (1990)
Birth rate: 42 births/1,000 population (1990)
Death rate: 22 deaths/1,000 population (1990)

Net migration rate: NEGL migrants/1,000 population (1990)
Infant mortality rate: 136 deaths/1,000 live births (1990)
Life expectancy at birth: 38 years male, 40 years female (1990)
Total fertility rate: 5.3 children born/woman (1990)
Nationality: noun—Chadian(s); adjective—Chadian
Ethnic divisions: some 200 distinct ethnic groups, most of whom are Muslims (Arabs, Toubou, Fulbe, Kotoko, Hausa, Kanembou, Baguirmi, Boulala, and Maba) in the north and center and non-Muslims (Sara, Ngambaye, Mbaye, Goulaye, Moudang, Moussei, Massa) in the south; some 150,000 nonindigenous, of whom 1,000 are French
Religion: 44% Muslim, 33% Christian, 23% indigenous beliefs, animism
Language: French and Arabic (official); Sara and Sango in south; more than 100 different languages and dialects are spoken
Literacy: 25.3%
Labor force: NA; 85% agriculture (engaged in unpaid subsistence farming, herding, and fishing)
Organized labor: about 20% of wage labor force

Government

Long-form name: Republic of Chad
Type: republic
Capital: N'Djamena
Administrative divisions: 14 prefectures (préfectures, singular—préfecture); Batha, Biltine, Borkou-Ennedi-Tibesti, Chari-Baguirmi, Guéra, Kanem, Lac, Logone Occidental, Logone Oriental, Mayo-Kébbi, Moyen-Chari, Ouaddaï, Salamat, Tandjilé
Independence: 11 August 1960 (from France)
Constitution: 22 December 1989
Legal system: based on French civil law system and Chadian customary law; has not accepted compulsory ICJ jurisdiction
National holiday: National Day (founding of the Third Republic), 7 June (1982)
Executive branch: president, Council of Ministers (cabinet)
Legislative branch: unicameral National Consultative Council (Conseil National Consultatif)
Judicial branch: Court of Appeal
Leaders: *Chief of State and Head of Government*—President Hissein HABRE (since 19 June 1982)
Political parties and leaders: National Union for Independence and Revolution (UNIR) established June 1984 with Habré as President; numerous dissident groups

Chad *(continued)*

(most significant opponents have returned to the government since mid-1986)

Suffrage: universal at age NA

Elections: *President*—last held 10 December 1989 (next to be held December 1996); results—President Habré was re-elected without opposition

Communists: no front organizations or underground party; probably a few Communists and some sympathizers

Other political or pressure groups: NA

Member of: ACP, AfDB, CEAO, Conference of East and Central African States, EAMA, ECA, EC (associate), FAO, G-77, GATT, IBRD, ICAC, ICAO, IDA, IDB—Islamic Development Bank, IFAD, ILO, IMF, INTELSAT, INTERPOL, ITU, Lake Chad Basin Commission, NAM, OAU, OCAM, OIC, UN, UNESCO, UPU, WHO, WIPO, WMO

Diplomatic representation: Ambassador Mahamat Ali ADOUM; Chancery at 2002 R Steet NW, Washington DC 20009; telephone (202) 462-4009; *US*—Ambassador (vacant); Chargé d'Affaires, Julius WALKER; Embassy at Avenue Felix Eboue, N'Djamena (mailing address is B. P. 413, N'Djamena); telephone [235] (51) 32-69 or 35-13, 28-62, 23-29, 32-29, 30-94, 28-47

Flag: three equal vertical bands of blue (hoist side), yellow, and red; similar to the flag of Andorra which has a national coat of arms featuring a quartered shield centered in the yellow band; also similar to the flag of Romania which has a national coat of arms featuring a mountain landscape centered in the yellow band; design was based on the flag of France

Economy

Overview: The climate, geographic location, and lack of infrastructure and natural resources potential make Chad one of the most underdeveloped countries in the world. Its economy is slowly recovering from the ravaging effects of prolonged civil war, conflict with Libya, drought, and food shortages. In 1986 real GDP returned to its 1977 level, with cotton, the major cash crop, accounting for 43% of exports. Over 80% of the work force is employed in subsistence farming and fishing. Industry is based almost entirely on the processing of agricultural products, including cotton, sugarcane, and cattle. Chad is still highly dependent on foreign aid, with its economy in trouble and many regions suffering from shortages.

GDP: $902 million, per capita $190; real growth rate 7.0% (1988)

Inflation rate (consumer prices): −3.0% (1987)

Unemployment rate: NA

Budget: revenues $61 million; expenditures $85 million, including capital expenditures of NA (1988 est.)

Exports: $432 million (f.o.b., 1988); *commodities*—cotton 43%, cattle 35%, textiles 5%, fish; *partners*—France, Nigeria, Cameroon

Imports: $214 million (c.i.f., 1988); *commodities*—machinery and transportation equipment 39%, industrial goods 20%, petroleum products 13%, foodstuffs 9%; *partners*—US, France

External debt: $360 million (December 1989)

Industrial production: growth rate −7.0% (1986)

Electricity: 38,000 kW capacity; 70 million kWh produced, 14 kWh per capita (1989)

Industries: cotton textile mills, slaughterhouses, brewery, natron (sodium carbonate)

Agriculture: accounts for 45% of GDP; largely subsistence farming; cotton most important cash crop; food crops include sorghum, millet, peanuts, rice, potatoes, manioc; livestock—cattle, sheep, goats, camels; self-sufficient in food in years of adequate rainfall

Aid: US commitments, including Ex-Im (FY70-88), $178 million; Western (non-US) countries, ODA and OOF bilateral commitments (1970-87), $1.2 billion; OPEC bilateral aid (1979-89), $28 million; Communist countries (1970-88), $71 million

Currency: Communauté Financière Africaine franc (plural—francs); 1 CFA franc (CFAF) = 100 centimes

Exchange rates: Communauté Financière Africaine francs (CFAF) per US$1—287.99 (January 1990), 319.01 (1989), 297.85 (1988), 300.54 (1987), 346.30 (1986), 449.26 (1985)

Fiscal year: calendar year

Communications

Highways: 31,322 km total; 32 km bituminous; 7,300 km gravel and laterite; remainder unimproved

Inland waterways: 2,000 km navigable

Civil air: 3 major transport aircraft

Airports: 71 total, 55 usable; 4 with permanent-surface runways; none with runways over 3,659 m; 3 with runways 2,440-3,659 m; 24 with runways 1,220-2,439 m

Telecommunications: fair system of radiocommunication stations for intercity links; 5,000 telephones; stations—3 AM, 1 FM, limited TV service; many facilities are inoperative; 1 Atlantic Ocean INTELSAT earth station

Defense Forces

Branches: Army, Air Force, paramilitary Gendarmerie, Presidential Guard

Military manpower: males 15-49, 1,163,312; 603,923 fit for military service; 50,255 reach military age (20) annually

Defense expenditures: 3.5% of GDP (1987)

Chile

South Pacific Ocean

Easter and Sala y Gomez islands are not shown.

Boundary representation is not necessarily authoritative.

See regional map IV

Geography

Total area: 756,950 km²; land area: 748,800 km²; includes Isla de Pascua (Easter Island) and Isla Sala y Gómez
Comparative area: slightly smaller than twice the size of Montana
Land boundaries: 6,171 km total; Argentina 5,150 km, Bolivia 861 km, Peru 160 km
Coastline: 6,435 km
Maritime claims:
  Contiguous zone: 24 nm
  Continental shelf: 200 nm
  Exclusive fishing zone: 200 nm
  Territorial sea: 12 nm
Disputes: short section of the southern boundary with Argentina is indefinite; Bolivia has wanted a sovereign corridor to the South Pacific Ocean since the Atacama area was lost to Chile in 1884; dispute with Bolivia over Río Lauca water rights; territorial claim in Antarctica (Chilean Antarctic Territory) partially overlaps Argentine claim
Climate: temperate; desert in north; cool and damp in south
Terrain: low coastal mountains; fertile central valley; rugged Andes in east
Natural resources: copper, timber, iron ore, nitrates, precious metals, molybdenum
Land use: 7% arable land; NEGL% permanent crops; 16% meadows and pastures; 21% forest and woodland; 56% other; includes 2% irrigated
Environment: subject to severe earthquakes, active volcanism, tsunami; Atacama Desert one of world's driest regions; desertification
Note: strategic location relative to sea lanes between Atlantic and Pacific Oceans (Strait of Magellan, Beagle Channel, Drake Passage)

People

Population: 13,082,842 (July 1990), growth rate 1.6% (1990)
Birth rate: 21 births/1,000 population (1990)
Death rate: 6 deaths/1,000 population (1990)
Net migration rate: 0 migrants/1,000 population (1990)
Infant mortality rate: 18 deaths/1,000 live births (1990)
Life expectancy at birth: 70 years male, 77 years female (1990)
Total fertility rate: 2.5 children born/woman (1990)
Nationality: noun—Chilean(s); adjective—Chilean
Ethnic divisions: 95% European and European-Indian, 3% Indian, 2% other
Religion: 89% Roman Catholic, 11% Protestant, and small Jewish population
Language: Spanish
Literacy: 94%
Labor force: 3,840,000; 38.6% services (including 12% government), 31.3% industry and commerce; 15.9% agriculture, forestry, and fishing; 8.7% mining; 4.4% construction (1985)
Organized labor: 10% of labor force (1989)

Government

Long-form name: Republic of Chile
Type: republic
Capital: Santiago
Administrative divisions: 13 regions (regiones, singular—región); Aisén del General Carlos Ibáñez del Campo, Antofagasta, Araucania, Atacama, Bíobío, Coquimbo, Libertador General Bernardo O'Higgins, Los Lagos, Magallanes y Antártica Chilena, Maule, Región Metropolitana, Tarapacá, Valparaiso
Independence: 18 September 1810 (from Spain)
Constitution: 11 September 1980, effective 11 March 1981; amended 30 July 1989
Legal system: based on Code of 1857 derived from Spanish law and subsequent codes influenced by French and Austrian law; judicial review of legislative acts in the Supreme Court; has not accepted compulsory ICJ jurisdiction
National holiday: Independence Day, 18 September (1810)
Executive branch: president, Cabinet
Legislative branch: bicameral National Congress (Congreso Nacional) consisting of an upper house or Senate and a lower house or Chamber of Deputies
Judicial branch: Supreme Court (Corte Suprema)
Leaders: *Chief of State and Head of Government*—President Patricio AYLWIN (since 11 March 1990)

Political parties and leaders: National Renovation (RN), Sergio Jarpa, president; Radical Party (PR), Enrique Silva Cimma; Social Democratic Party (PSD), Eugenio Velasco; Christian Democratic Party (PDC), Andrés Zaldivar; Party for Democracy, Ricardo Lagos; Socialist Party, Clodomiro Almeyda; other parties are Movement of United Popular Action (MAPU), Victor Barrueto; Christian Left (IC), Luis Maira; Communist Party of Chile (PCCh), Volodia Teitelboim; Movement of the Revolutionary Left (MIR) is splintered, no single leader; several leftist and far left parties formed a new coalition in November 1988 with Luis Maira as president; the 17-party Concertation of Parties for Democracy backed Patricio Aylwin's presidential candidacy in December 1989
Suffrage: universal and compulsory at age 18
Elections: *President*—last held 14 December 1989 (next to be held December 1993 or January 1994); results—Patricio Aylwin 55.2%, Hernan Büchi 29.4%, other 15.4%;
Senate—last held 14 December 1989 (next to be held December 1993 or January 1994); seats—(47 total, 38 elected) 17-party Concertation of Parties for Democracy 22;
Chamber of Deputies—last held 14 December 1989 (next to be held December 1993 or January 1994); seats—(120 total) Concertation of Parties for Democracy 69
Communists: 120,000 when PCCh was legal in 1973; 50,000 (est.) active militants
Other political or pressure groups: revitalized university student federations at all major universities dominated by opposition political groups; labor—United Labor Central (CUT) includes trade unionists from the country's five-largest labor confederations; Roman Catholic Church
Member of: CCC, CIPEC, ECOSOC, FAO, G-77, GATT, IADB, IAEA, IBRD, ICAO, IDA, IDB—Inter-American Development Bank, IFAD, IFC, IHO, ILO, IMF, IMO, INTELSAT, INTERPOL, IPU, ITU, LAIA, OAS, PAHO, SELA, UN, UNESCO, UPU, WHO, WIPO, WMO, WSG, WTO
Diplomatic representation: Ambassador Octavio ERRAZURIZ; Chancery at 1732 Massachusetts Avenue NW, Washington DC 20036; telephone (202) 785-1746; there are Chilean Consulates General in Chicago, Houston, Los Angeles, Miami, New York, and San Francisco; *US*—Ambassador Charles A. GILLESPIE, Jr.; Embassy at Codina Building, 1343 Agustinas, Santiago (mailing address is APO Miami 34033); telephone [56] (2) 710133 or 710190, 710326, 710375

Chile *(continued)*

Flag: two equal horizontal bands of white (top) and red; there is a blue square the same height as the white band at the hoist-side end of the white band; the square bears a white five-pointed star in the center; design was based on the US flag

Economy

Overview: In 1989 the economy grew at the rate of 9.9%, reflecting substantial growth in industry, agriculture, and construction. Copper accounts for nearly 50% of export revenues; Chile's economic wellbeing thus remains highly dependent on international copper prices. Unemployment and inflation rates have declined from their peaks in 1982 to 5.3% and 21.4%, respectively, in 1989. The major long-term economic problem is how to sustain growth in the face of political uncertainties.

GDP: $25.3 billion, per capita $1,970; real growth rate 9.9% (1989)

Inflation rate (consumer prices): 21.4% (1989)

Unemployment rate: 5.3% (1989)

Budget: revenues $4.9 billion; expenditures $5.1 billion, including capital expenditures of $0.6 billion (1986)

Exports: $7.0 billion (f.o.b., 1988); *commodities*—copper 48%, industrial products 33%, molybdenum, iron ore, wood pulp, fishmeal, fruits; *partners*—EC 34%, US 22%, Japan 10%, Brazil 7%

Imports: $4.7 billion (f.o.b., 1988); *commodities*—petroleum, wheat, capital goods, spare parts, raw materials; *partners*—EC 23%, US 20%, Japan 10%, Brazil 9%

External debt: $16.3 billion (December 1989)

Industrial production: growth rate 7.4% (1989)

Electricity: 4,044,000 kW capacity; 17,710 million kWh produced, 1,380 kWh per capita (1989)

Industries: copper, other minerals, foodstuffs, fish processing, iron and steel, wood and wood products

Agriculture: accounts for about 8% of GDP (including fishing and forestry); major exporter of fruit, fish, and timber products; major crops—wheat, corn, grapes, beans, sugar beets, potatoes, deciduous fruit; livestock products—beef, poultry, wool; self-sufficient in most foods; 1986 fish catch of 5.6 million metric tons net agricultural importer

Aid: US commitments, including Ex-Im (FY70-88), $521 million; Western (non-US) countries, ODA and OOF bilateral commitments (1970-87), $1.3 billion; Communist countries (1970-88), $386 million

Currency: Chilean peso (plural—pesos); 1 Chilean peso (Ch$) = 100 centavos

Exchange rates: Chilean pesos (Ch$) per US$1—296.68 (January 1990), 267.16 (1989), 245.05 (1988), 219.54 (1987), 193.02 (1986), 161.08 (1985)

Fiscal year: calendar year

Communications

Railroads: 8,613 km total; 4,257 km 1.676-meter gauge, 135 km 1.435-meter standard gauge, 4,221 km 1.000-meter gauge; electrification, 1,578 km 1.676-meter gauge, 76 km 1.000-meter gauge

Highways: 79,025 km total; 9,913 km paved, 33,140 km gravel, 35,972 km improved and unimproved earth (1984)

Inland waterways: 725 km

Pipelines: crude oil, 755 km; refined products, 785 km; natural gas, 320 km

Ports: Antofagasta, Iquique, Puerto Montt, Punta Arenas, Valparaiso, San Antonio, Talcahuano, Arica

Merchant marine: 35 ships (1,000 GRT or over) totaling 498,354 GRT/804,809 DWT; includes 13 cargo, 1 refrigerated cargo, 3 roll-on/roll-off cargo, 2 petroleum, oils, and lubricants (POL) tanker, 1 chemical tanker, 2 liquefied gas, 3 combination ore/oil, 10 bulk; note—in addition, 1 naval tanker and 1 military transport are sometimes used commercially

Civil air: 22 major transport aircraft

Airports: 392 total, 352 usable; 49 with permanent-surface runways; none with runways over 3,659 m; 11 with runways 2,440-3,659 m; 57 with runways 1,220-2,439 m

Telecommunications: modern telephone system based on extensive radio relay facilities; 768,000 telephones; stations—159 AM, no FM, 131 TV, 11 shortwave; satellite stations—2 Atlantic Ocean INTELSAT and 3 domestic

Defense Forces

Branches: Army of the Nation, National Navy, Air Force of the Nation, Carabineros of Chile

Military manpower: males 15-49, 3,491,854; 2,610,048 fit for military service; 118,569 reach military age (19) annually

Defense expenditures: 4.0% of GDP (1987)

China
(also see separate Taiwan entry)

1200 km

Boundary representation is not necessarily authoritative.

See regional map VIII

Geography

Total area: 9,596,960 km^2; land area: 9,326,410 km^2

Comparative area: slightly larger than the US

Land boundaries: 23,213.34 km total; Afghanistan 76 km, Bhutan 470 km, Burma 2,185 km, Hong Kong 30 km, India 3,380 km, North Korea 1,416 km, Laos 423 km, Macau 0.34 km, Mongolia 4,673 km, Nepal 1,236 km, Pakistan 523 km, USSR 7,520 km, Vietnam 1,281 km

Coastline: 14,500 km

Maritime claims:

Territorial sea: 12 nm

Disputes: boundary with India; bilateral negotiations are under way to resolve four disputed sections of the boundary with the USSR (Pamir, Argun, Amur, and Khabarovsk areas); a short section of the boundary with North Korea is indefinite; Hong Kong is scheduled to become a Special Administrative Region in 1997; Portuguese territory of Macau is scheduled to become a Special Administrative Region in 1999; sporadic border clashes with Vietnam; involved in a complex dispute over the Spratly Islands with Malaysia, Philippines, Taiwan, and Vietnam; maritime boundary dispute with Vietnam in the Gulf of Tonkin; Paracel Islands occupied by China, but claimed by Vietnam and Taiwan; claims Japanese-administered Senkaku-shotō (Senkaku Islands)

Climate: extremely diverse; tropical in south to subarctic in north

Terrain: mostly mountains, high plateaus, deserts in west; plains, deltas, and hills in east

Natural resources: coal, iron ore, crude oil, mercury, tin, tungsten, antimony, manganese, molybdenum, vanadium, magnetite, aluminum, lead, zinc, uranium, world's largest hydropower potential

Land use: 10% arable land; NEGL% permanent crops; 31% meadows and pastures; 14% forest and woodland; 45% other; includes 5% irrigated

Environment: frequent typhoons (about five times per year along southern and eastern coasts), damaging floods, tsunamis, earthquakes; deforestation; soil erosion; industrial pollution; water pollution; desertification

Note: world's third-largest country (after USSR and Canada)

People

Population: 1,118,162,727 (July 1990), growth rate 1.4% (1990)

Birth rate: 22 births/1,000 population (1990)

Death rate: 7 deaths/1,000 population (1990)

Net migration rate: 0 migrants/1,000 population (1990)

Infant mortality rate: 34 deaths/1,000 live births (1990)

Life expectancy at birth: 67 years male, 69 years female (1990)

Total fertility rate: 2.3 children born/woman (1990)

Nationality: noun—Chinese (sing., pl.); adjective—Chinese

Ethnic divisions: 93.3% Han Chinese; 6.7% Zhuang, Uygur, Hui, Yi, Tibetan, Miao, Manchu, Mongol, Buyi, Korean, and other nationalities

Religion: officially atheist, but traditionally pragmatic and eclectic; most important elements of religion are Confucianism, Taoism, and Buddhism; about 2-3% Muslim, 1% Christian

Language: Standard Chinese (Putonghua) or Mandarin (based on the Beijing dialect); also Yue (Cantonese), Wu (Shanghainese), Minbei (Fuzhou), Minnan (Hokkien-Taiwanese), Xiang, Gan, Hakka dialects, and minority languages (see ethnic divisions)

Literacy: over 75%

Labor force: 513,000,000; 61.1% agriculture and forestry, 25.2% industry and commerce, 4.6% construction and mining, 4.5% social services, 4.6% other (1986 est.)

Organized labor: All-China Federation of Trade Unions (ACFTU) follows the leadership of the Chinese Communist Party; membership over 80 million or about 65% of the urban work force (1985)

Government

Long-form name: People's Republic of China; abbreviated PRC

Type: Communist Party-led state

Capital: Beijing

Administrative divisions: 23 provinces (sheng, singular and plural), 5 autonomous regions* (zizhiqu, singular and plural), and 3 municipalities** (shi, singular and plural); Anhui, Beijing**, Fujian, Gansu, Guangdong, Guangxi*, Guizhou, Hainan, Hebei, Heilongjiang, Henan, Hubei, Hunan, Jiangsu, Jiangxi, Jilin, Liaoning, Nei Mongol*, Ningxia*, Qinghai, Shaanxi, Shandong, Shanghai**, Shanxi, Sichuan, Tianjin**, Xinjiang*, Xizang*, Yunnan, Zhejiang; note—China considers Taiwan its 23rd province

Independence: unification under the Qin (Ch'in) Dynasty 221 BC, Qing (Ch'ing or Manchu) Dynasty replaced by the Republic on 12 February 1912, People's Republic established 1 October 1949

Constitution: 4 December 1982

Legal system: a complex amalgam of custom and statute, largely criminal law; rudimentary civil code in effect since 1 January 1987; new legal codes in effect since 1 January 1980; continuing efforts are being made to improve civil, administrative, criminal, and commercial law

National holiday: National Day, 1 October (1949)

Executive branch: president, vice president, premier, three vice premiers, State Council, Central Military Commission (de facto)

Legislative branch: unicameral National People's Congress (Quanguo Renmin Daibiao Dahui)

Judicial branch: Supreme People's Court

Leaders: *Chief of State and Head of Government (de facto)*—DENG Xiaoping (since mid-1977);

Chief of State—President YANG Shangkun (since 8 April 1988); Vice President WANG Zhen (since 8 April 1988);

Head of Government—Premier LI Peng (Acting Premier since 24 November 1987, Premier since 9 April 1988); Vice Premier YAO Yilin (since 2 July 1979); Vice Premier TIAN Jiyun (since 20 June 1983); Vice Premier WU Xueqian (since 12 April 1988)

Political parties and leaders: only party—Chinese Communist Party (CCP), Jiang Zemin, general secretary of the Central Committee

Suffrage: universal at age 18

Elections: *President*—last held 8 April 1988 (next to be held March 1993); Yang Shangkun was elected by the Seventh National People's Congress;

National People's Congress—last held NA March 1988 (next to be held March 1993); results—CCP is the only party; seats—(2,970 total) CCP 2,970 (indirectly elected)

Communists: about 45,000,000 party members (1986)

Other political or pressure groups: such meaningful opposition as exists consists of loose coalitions, usually within the party and government organization, that vary by issue

Member of: ADB, CCC, ESCAP, FAO, IAEA, IBRD, ICAO, IDA, IFAD, IFC, IHO, ILO, IMF, IMO, INTELSAT, ITU, UN, UNESCO, UPU, WFTU, WHO, WIPO, WMO

Diplomatic representation: Ambassador ZHU Qizhen; Chancery at 2300 Connecticut Avenue NW, Washington DC 20008; telephone (202) 328-2500 through 2502; there are Chinese Consulates General in Chicago, Houston, New York, and San Francisco; *US*—Ambassador James R. LILLEY; Embassy at Xiu Shui Bei Jie 3, Beijing (mailing address is FPO San Francisco 96655); telephone [86] (1) 532-3831; there are US Consulates General in Chengdu, Guangzhou, Shanghai, and Shenyang

Flag: red with a large yellow five-pointed star and four smaller yellow five-pointed stars (arranged in a vertical arc toward the middle of the flag) in the upper hoist-side corner

Economy

Overview: Beginning in late 1978 the Chinese leadership has been trying to move the economy from the sluggish Soviet-style centrally planned economy to a more productive and flexible economy with market elements—but still within the framework of monolithic Communist control. To this end the authorities have switched to a system of household responsibility in agriculture in place of the old collectivization, increased the authority of local officials and plant managers in industry, permitted a wide variety of small-scale enterprise in services and light manufacturing, and opened the foreign economic sector to increased trade and joint ventures. The most gratifying result has been a strong spurt in production, particularly in agriculture in the early 1980s. Otherwise, the leadership has often experienced in its hybrid system the worst results of socialism (bureaucracy, lassitude, corruption) and of capitalism (windfall gains and stepped-up inflation). Beijing thus has periodically backtracked, retightening central controls at intervals and thereby undermining the credibility of the reform process. Open inflation and excess demand continue to plague the economy, and political repression, following the crackdown at Tiananmen in mid-1989, has curtailed tourism, foreign aid, and new investment by foreign firms. Popular resistance and changes in central policy have weakened China's population control program, which is essential to the nation's long-term economic viability.

China (continued)

GNP: $NA, per capita $NA; real growth rate 4% (1989 est.)
Inflation rate (consumer prices): 19.5% (1989)
Unemployment rate: 3.0% in urban areas (1989)
Budget: revenues $NA; expenditures $NA, including capital expenditures of $NA
Exports: $52.5 billion (f.o.b., 1989); *commodities*—manufactured goods, agricultural products, oilseeds, grain (rice and corn), oil, minerals; *partners*—Hong Kong, US, Japan, USSR, Singapore, FRG (1989)
Imports: $59.1 billion (c.i.f., 1989); *commodities*—grain (mostly wheat), chemical fertilizer, steel, industrial raw materials, machinery, equipment; *partners*—Hong Kong, Japan, US, FRG, USSR (1989)
External debt: $51 billion (1989 est.)
Industrial production: growth rate 8.0% (1989)
Electricity: 110,000,000 kW capacity; 560,000 million kWh produced, 500 kWh per capita (1989)
Industries: iron, steel, coal, machine building, armaments, textiles, petroleum
Agriculture: accounts for 26% of GNP; among the world's largest producers of rice, potatoes, sorghum, peanuts, tea, millet, barley, and pork; commercial crops include cotton, other fibers, and oilseeds; produces variety of livestock products; basically self-sufficient in food; fish catch of 8 million metric tons in 1986
Aid: US commitments, including Ex-Im (FY70-87), $220.7 million; Western (non-US) countries, ODA and OOF bilateral commitments (1970-87), $11.1 billion
Currency: yuan (plural—yuan); 1 yuan (¥) = 10 jiao
Exchange rates: yuan (¥) per US$1— 4.7221 (January 1990), 3.7651 (1989), 3.7221 (1988), 3.7221 (1987), 3.4528 (1986), 2.9367 (1985)
Fiscal year: calendar year

Communications

Railroads: total about 54,000 km common carrier lines; 53,400 km 1.435-meter standard gauge; 600 km 1.000-meter gauge; all single track except 11,200 km double track on standard-gauge lines; 6,500 km electrified; 10,000 km industrial lines (gauges range from 0.762 to 1.067 meters)
Highways: about 980,000 km all types roads; 162,000 km paved roads, 617,200 km gravel/improved earth roads, 200,800 km unimproved natural earth roads and tracks
Inland waterways: 138,600 km; about 109,800 km navigable
Pipelines: crude, 6,500 km; refined products, 1,100 km; natural gas, 6,200 km

Ports: Dalian, Guangzhou, Huangpu, Qingdao, Qinhuangdao, Shanghai, Xingang, Zhanjiang, Ningbo
Merchant marine: 1,373 ships (1,000 GRT or over) totaling 13,303,685 GRT/ 20,092,833 DWT; includes 25 passenger, 41 short-sea passenger, 17 passenger-cargo, 7 cargo/training, 766 cargo, 10 refrigerated cargo, 65 container, 17 roll-on/roll-off cargo, 3 multifunction barge carriers, 173 petroleum, oils, and lubricants (POL) tanker, 9 chemical tanker, 237 bulk, 2 vehicle carrier, 1 liquefied gas; note—China beneficially owns an additional 175 ships (1,000 GRT or over) totaling approximately 5,380,415 DWT that operate under the registry of Panama, UK, Hong Kong, Liberia, and Malta
Airports: 330 total, 330 usable; 260 with permanent-surface runways; fewer than 10 with runways over 3,500 m; 90 with runways 2,440-3,659 m; 200 with runways 1,220-2,439 m
Telecommunications: domestic and international services are increasingly available for private use; unevenly distributed internal system serves principal cities, industrial centers, and most townships; 11,000,000 telephones (December 1989); stations—274 AM, unknown FM, 202 (2,050 relays) TV; more than 215 million radio receivers; 75 million TVs; satellite earth stations—4 Pacific Ocean INTELSAT, 1 Indian Ocean INTELSAT, and 55 domestic

Defense Forces

Branches: Chinese People's Liberation Army (CPLA), CPLA Navy (including Marines), CPLA Air Force
Military manpower: males 15-49, 330,353,665; 184,515,412 fit for military service; 11,594,366 reach military age (18) annually
Defense expenditures: $5.28 billion (1988)

Christmas Island
(territory of Australia)

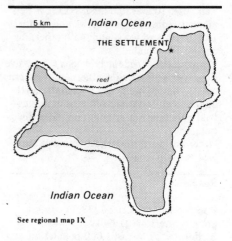

See regional map IX

Geography

Total area: 135 km²; land area: 135 km²
Comparative area: about 0.8 times the size of Washington, DC
Land boundaries: none
Coastline: 138.9 km
Maritime claims:
  Contiguous zone: 12 nm
  Continental shelf: 200 meters or to depth of exploitation
  Exclusive fishing zone: 200 nm
  Territorial sea: 3 nm
Climate: tropical; heat and humidity moderated by trade winds
Terrain: steep cliffs along coast rise abruptly to central plateau
Natural resources: phosphate
Land use: 0% arable land; 0% permanent crops; 0% meadows and pastures; 0% forest and woodland; 100% other
Environment: almost completely surrounded by a reef
Note: located along major sea lanes of Indian Ocean

People

Population: 2,278 (July 1990), growth rate 0.0% (1990)
Birth rate: NA births/1,000 population (1990)
Death rate: NA deaths/1,000 population (1990)
Net migration rate: NA migrants/1,000 population (1990)
Infant mortality rate: NA deaths/1,000 live births (1990)
Life expectancy at birth: NA years male, NA years female (1990)
Total fertility rate: NA children born/ woman (1990)
Nationality: noun—Christmas Islander(s), adjective—Christmas Island
Ethnic divisions: 61% Chinese, 25% Malay, 11% European, 3% other; no indigenous population

Religion: NA
Language: English
Literacy: NA%
Labor force: NA; all workers are employees of the Phosphate Mining Company of Christmas Island, Ltd.
Organized labor: NA

Government

Long-form name: Territory of Christmas Island
Type: territory of Australia
Capital: The Settlement
Administrative divisions: none (territory of Australia)
Independence: none (territory of Australia)
Constitution: Christmas Island Act of 1958
Legal system: under the authority of the governor general of Australia
National holiday: NA
Executive branch: British monarch, governor general of Australia, administrator, Advisory Council (cabinet)
Legislative branch: none
Judicial branch: none
Leaders: *Chief of State*—Queen ELIZABETH II (since 6 February 1952); *Head of Government*—Administrator A. D. TAYLOR (since NA)
Communists: none
Diplomatic representation: none (territory of Australia)
Flag: the flag of Australia is used

Economy

Overview: Phosphate mining is the only significant economic activity, but in November 1987 the Australian Government announced that the mine would be closed because of labor unrest. Plans are under way to build a casino and hotel to develop tourism.
GDP: $NA, per capita $NA; real growth rate NA%
Inflation rate (consumer prices): NA%
Unemployment rate: 0%
Budget: revenues $NA; expenditures $NA, including capital expenditures of $NA
Exports: $NA; *commodities*—phosphate; *partners*—Australia, NZ
Imports: $NA; *commodities*—NA; *partners*—NA
External debt: $NA
Industrial production: growth rate NA%
Electricity: 11,000 kW capacity; 38 million kWh produced, 16,680 kWh per capita (1989)
Industries: phosphate extraction (near depletion)
Agriculture: NA
Aid: none
Currency: Australian dollar (plural—dollars); 1 Australian dollar ($A) = 100 cents

Exchange rates: Australian dollars ($A) per US$1—1.2784 (January 1990), 1.2618 (1989), 1.2752 (1988), 1.4267 (1987), 1.4905 (1986), 1.4269 (1985)
Fiscal year: 1 July-30 June

Communications

Ports: Flying Fish Cove
Airports: 1 usable with permanent-surface runway 1,220-2,439 m
Telecommunications: 4,000 radios (1982)

Defense Forces

Note: defense is the responsibility of Australia

Clipperton Island
(French possession)

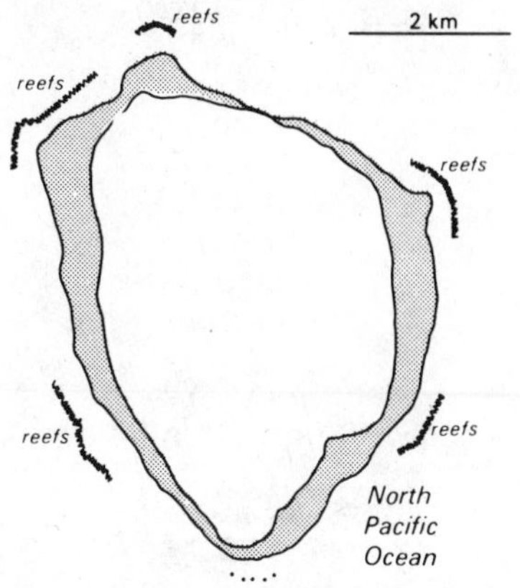

See regional map I

Geography

Total area: undetermined
Comparative area: undetermined
Land boundaries: none
Coastline: 11.1 km
Maritime claims:
  Contiguous zone: 12 nm
  Continental shelf: 200 meters or to depth of exploitation
  Extended economic zone: 200 nm
  Territorial sea: 12 nm
Climate: tropical
Terrain: coral atoll
Natural resources: none
Land use: 0% arable land; 0% permanent crops; 0% meadows and pastures; 0% forest and woodland; 100% other (coral)
Environment: reef about 8 km in circumference
Note: located 1,120 km southwest of Mexico in the North Pacific Ocean

People

Population: uninhabited

Government

Long-form name: none
Type: French possession administered by High Commissioner of the Republic Jean MONTPEZAT, resident in French Polynesia

Economy

Overview: no economic activity

Communications

Ports: none; offshore anchorage only

Defense Forces

Note: defense is the responsibility of France

65

Cocos (Keeling) Islands

(territory of Australia)

10 km

North Keeling Island

Indian Ocean

Horsburgh Island

reefs

Direction Island

reefs

Home Island

South Keeling Islands

West Island

reefs

South Island

See regional map IX

Geography

Total area: 14 km²; land area: 14 km²; main islands are West Island and Home Island

Comparative area: about 24 times the size of The Mall in Washington, DC

Land boundaries: none

Coastline: 42.6 km

Maritime claims:

Contiguous zone: 12 nm

Continental shelf: 200 meters or to depth of exploitation

Exclusive fishing zone: 200 nm

Territorial sea: 3 nm

Climate: pleasant, modified by the southeast trade winds for about nine months of the year; moderate rainfall

Terrain: flat, low-lying coral atolls

Natural resources: fish

Land use: 0% arable land; 0% permanent crops; 0% meadows and pastures; 0% forest and woodland; 100% other

Environment: two coral atolls thickly covered with coconut palms and other vegetation

Note: located 1,070 km southwest of Sumatra (Indonesia) in the Indian Ocean about halfway between Australia and Sri Lanka

People

Population: 670 (July 1990), growth rate 2.1% (1990)

Birth rate: NA births/1,000 population (1990)

Death rate: NA deaths/1,000 population (1990)

Net migration rate: NA migrants/1,000 population (1990)

Infant mortality rate: NA deaths/1,000 live births (1990)

Life expectancy at birth: NA years male, NA years female (1990)

Total fertility rate: NA children born/woman (1990)

Nationality: noun—Cocos Islander(s); adjective—Cocos Islander(s)

Ethnic divisions: mostly Europeans on West Island and Cocos Malays on Home Island

Religion: NA

Language: English

Literacy: NA%

Labor force: NA

Organized labor: none

Government

Long-form name: Territory of Cocos (Keeling) Islands

Type: territory of Australia

Capital: West Island

Administrative divisions: none (territory of Australia)

Independence: none (territory of Australia)

Constitution: Cocos (Keeling) Islands Act of 1955

Legal system: based upon the laws of Australia and local laws

National holiday: NA

Executive branch: British monarch, governor general of Australia, administrator, chairman of the Islands Council

Legislative branch: unicameral Islands Council

Judicial branch: Supreme Court

Leaders: *Chief of State*—Queen ELIZABETH II (since 6 February 1952);

Head of Government—Administrator D. LAWRIE (since NA 1989); Chairman of the Islands Council Parson Bin YAPAT (since NA)

Suffrage: NA

Elections: NA

Diplomatic representation: none (territory of Australia)

Flag: the flag of Australia is used

Economy

Overview: Grown throughout the islands, coconuts are the sole cash crop. Copra and fresh coconuts are the major export earners. Small local gardens and fishing contribute to the food supply, but additional food and most other necessities must be imported from Australia.

GNP: $NA, per capita $NA; real growth rate NA%

Inflation rate (consumer prices): NA%

Unemployment: NA

Budget: revenues $NA; expenditures $NA, including capital expenditures of $NA

Exports: $NA; *commodities*—copra; *partners*—Australia

Imports: $NA; *commodities*—foodstuffs; *partners*—Australia

External debt: $NA

Industrial production: growth rate NA%

Electricity: NA kW capacity; NA million kWh produced, NA kWh per capita

Industries: copra products

Agriculture: gardens provide vegetables, bananas, pawpaws, coconuts

Aid: none

Currency: Australian dollar (plural—dollars); 1 Australian dollar ($A) = 100 cents

Exchange rates: Australian dollars ($A) per US$1—1.2784 (January 1990), 1.2618 (1989), 1.2752 (1988), 1.4267 (1987), 1.4905 (1986), 1.4269 (1985)

Fiscal year: 1 July-30 June

Communications

Ports: none; lagoon anchorage only

Airports: 1 airfield with permanent-surface runway, 2,440-3,659 m; airport on West Island is a link in service between Australia and South Africa

Telecommunications: 250 radios (1985); linked by telephone, telex, and facsimile communications via satellite with Australia; stations—1 AM, no FM, no TV

Defense Forces

Note: defense is the responsibility of Australia

Colombia

Caribbean Sea
Barranquilla
Cartagena
Cúcuta
Medellín
Puerto Carreño
BOGOTÁ
North Pacific Ocean
Buenaventura
Cali
Pasto
Mitú
Leticia

400 km

Providencia, Malpelo, and San Andrés islands are not shown.
See regional map III and IV

Geography

Total area: 1,138,910 km²; land area: 1,038,700 km²; includes Isla de Malpelo, Roncador Cay, Serrana Bank, and Serranilla Bank
Comparative area: slightly less than three times the size of Montana
Land boundaries: 7,408 km total; Brazil 1,643 km, Ecuador 590 km, Panama 225 km, Peru 2,900, Venezuela 2,050 km
Coastline: 3,208 km total (1,448 km North Pacific Ocean; 1,760 Caribbean Sea)
Maritime claims:
Continental shelf: not specified
Extended economic zone: 200 nm
Territorial sea: 12 nm
Disputes: maritime boundary dispute with Venezuela in the Gulf of Venezuela; territorial dispute with Nicaragua over Archipelago de San Andres y Providencia and Quita Sueno Bank
Climate: tropical along coast and eastern plains; cooler in highlands
Terrain: mixture of flat coastal lowlands, plains in east, central highlands, some high mountains
Natural resources: crude oil, natural gas, coal, iron ore, nickel, gold, copper, emeralds
Land use: 4% arable land; 2% permanent crops; 29% meadows and pastures; 49% forest and woodland; 16% other; includes NEGL% irrigated
Environment: highlands subject to volcanic eruptions; deforestation; soil damage from overuse of pesticides; periodic droughts
Note: only South American country with coastlines on both North Pacific Ocean and Caribbean Sea

People

Population: 33,076,188 (July 1990), growth rate 2.1% (1990)
Birth rate: 27 births/1,000 population (1990)

Death rate: 5 deaths/1,000 population (1990)
Net migration rate: NEGL migrants/1,000 population (1990)
Infant mortality rate: 38 deaths/1,000 live births (1990)
Life expectancy at birth: 68 years male, 73 years female (1990)
Total fertility rate: 2.9 children born/woman (1990)
Nationality: noun—Colombian(s); adjective—Colombian
Ethnic divisions: 58% mestizo, 20% white, 14% mulatto, 4% black, 3% mixed black-Indian, 1% Indian
Religion: 95% Roman Catholic
Language: Spanish
Literacy: 88% (1987 est.), Indians about 40%
Labor force: 11,000,000 (1986); 53% services, 26% agriculture, 21% industry (1981)
Organized labor: 1,400,000 members (1987), about 12% of labor force; the Communist-backed Unitary Workers Central or CUT is the largest labor organization, with about 725,000 members (including all affiliate unions)

Government

Long-form name: Republic of Colombia
Type: republic; executive branch dominates government structure
Capital: Bogotá
Administrative divisions: 23 departments (départamentos, singular—départamento), 5 commissariats* (comisarías, singular—comisaría), and 4 intendancies** (intendencias, singular—intendencia); Amazonas*, Antioquia, Arauca**, Atlántico, Bolívar, Boyacá, Caldas, Caquetá, Casanare**, Cauca, Cesar, Chocó, Córdoba, Cundinamarca, Guainía*, Guaviare*, Huila, La Guajira, Magdalena, Meta, Nariño, Norte de Santander, Putumayo**, Quindío, Risaralda, San Andrés y Providencia**, Santander, Sucre, Tolima, Valle del Cauca, Vaupés*, Vichada*; note—there may be a new special district (distrito especial) named Bogotá
Independence: 20 July 1810 (from Spain)
Constitution: 4 August 1886, with amendments codified in 1946 and 1968
Legal system: based on Spanish law; judicial review of legislative acts in the Supreme Court; accepts compulsory ICJ jurisdiction, with reservations
National holiday: Independence Day, 20 July (1810)
Executive branch: president, presidential designate, cabinet
Legislative branch: bicameral Congress (Congreso) consists of an upper chamber

or Senate (Senado) and a lower chamber or Chamber of Representatives (Cámara de Representants)
Judicial branch: Supreme Court of Justice (Corte Suprema de Justica)
Leaders: *Chief of State and Head of Government*—President Virgilio BARCO Vargas (since 7 August 1986; term ends August 1990); Presidential Designate Víctor MOSQUERA Chaux (since 13 October 1986)
Political parties and leaders: Liberal Party—Virgilio Barco Vargas, Alfonso Lopez Michelson, Julio Cesar Turbay; Cesar Gaviria is the Liberal Party presidential candidate; Conservative Party—Misael Pastrana Borrero, Alvaro Gómez Hurtado; Rodrigo Lloredo, Conservative Party presidential candidate; Patriotic Union (UP), is a legal political party formed by Revolutionary Armed Forces of Colombia (FARC) and Colombian Communist Party (PCC), Bernardo Jaramillo Ossa is the UP presidential candidate
Suffrage: universal at age 18
Elections: *President*—last held 25 May 1986 (next to be held 27 May 1990); results—Virgilio Barco Vargas 59%, Alvaro Gomez Hurtado 36%, Jaime Pardo Leal 4% (assassinated in October 1987), others 1%;
Senate—last held 11 March 1990 (next to be held March 1994); results—percent of vote by party NA; seats—(114 total) Liberal 68, Conservative 45, UP 1;
House of Representatives last held 11 March 1990 (next to be held March 1994); results—percent of vote by party NA; seats—(199 total) Liberal 107, Conservative 82, UP 10
Communists: 18,000 members (est.), including Communist Party Youth Organization (JUCO)
Other political or pressure groups: Colombian Communist Party (PCC), Gilberto Vieira White; Communist Party/Marxist-Leninist (PCC/ML), Chinese-line Communist Party; Revolutionary Armed Forces of Colombia (FARC); National Liberation Army (ELN); People's Liberation Army (EPL); 19th of April Movement (M-19)
Member of: FAO, G-77, GATT, Group of Eight, IADB, IAEA, IBRD, ICAC, ICAO, ICO, IDA, IDB—Inter-American Development Bank, IFAD, IFC, IHO, ILO, IMF, IMO, INTELSAT, INTERPOL, IRC, ISO, ITU, LAIA, NAM, OAS, PAHO, SELA, UN, UNESCO, UPEB, UPU, WFTU, WHO, WIPO, WMO, WSG, WTO
Diplomatic representation: Ambassador Victor MOSQUERA; Chancery at 2118 Leroy Place NW, Washington DC 20008; telephone (202) 387-8338; there are

Colombia (continued)

Colombian Consulates General in Chicago, Houston, Miami, New Orleans, New York, San Francisco, and San Juan (Puerto Rico), and Consulates in Atlanta, Boston, Detroit, Ft. Lauderdale, Los Angeles, San Diego, and Tampa; US— Ambassador Thomas E. McNAMARA; Embassy at Calle 38, No.8-61, Bogotá (mailing address is APO Miami 34038); telephone [57] (1) 285-1300 or 1688; there is a US Consulate in Barranquilla
Flag: three horizontal bands of yellow (top, double-width), blue, and red; similar to the flag of Ecuador which is longer and bears the Ecuadorian coat of arms superimposed in the center

Economy

Overview: Economic activity has slowed gradually since 1986, but growth rates remain high by Latin American standards. Conservative economic policies have encouraged investment and kept inflation and unemployment under 30% and 10%, respectively. The rapid development of oil, coal, and other nontraditional industries over the past four years has helped to offset the decline in coffee prices—Colombia's major export. The collapse of the International Coffee Agreement in the summer of 1989, a troublesome rural insurgency, and drug-related violence dampen prospects for future growth.
GDP: $35.4 billion, per capita $1,110; real growth rate 3.7% (1988)
Inflation rate (consumer prices): 27% (1989 est.)
Unemployment rate: 9.0% (1989 est.)
Budget: revenues $4.39 billion; current expenditures $3.93 billion, capital expenditures $1.03 billion (1989 est.)
Exports: $5.76 billion (f.o.b., 1989 est.); *commodities*—coffee 30%, petroleum 24%, coal, bananas, fresh cut flowers; *partners*—US 36%, EC 21%, Japan 5%, Netherlands 4%, Sweden 3%
Imports: $5.02 billion (c.i.f., 1989 est.); *commodities*—industrial equipment, transportation equipment, foodstuffs, chemicals, paper products; *partners*—US 34%, EC 16%, Brazil 4%, Venezuela 3%, Japan 3%
External debt: $17.5 billion (1989)
Industrial production: growth rate 2.0% (1989 est.)
Electricity: 9,250,000 kW capacity; 35,364 million kWh produced, 1,110 kWh per capita (1989)
Industries: textiles, food processing, oil, clothing and footwear, beverages, chemicals, metal products, cement; mining— gold, coal, emeralds, iron, nickel, silver, salt

Agriculture: accounts for 22% of GDP; crops make up two-thirds and livestock one-third of agricultural output; climate and soils permit a wide variety of crops, such as coffee, rice, tobacco, corn, sugarcane, cocoa beans, oilseeds, vegetables; forest products and shrimp farming are becoming more important
Illicit drugs: major illicit producer of cannabis and coca for the international drug trade; key supplier of marijuana and cocaine to the US and other international drug markets; drug production and trafficking accounts for an estimated 4% of GDP and 28% of foreign exchange earnings
Aid: US commitments, including Ex-Im (FY70-88), $1.6 billion; Western (non-US) countries, ODA and OOF bilateral commitments (1970-87), $2.9 billion; Communist countries (1970-88), $399 million
Currency: Colombian peso (plural—pesos); 1 Colombian peso (Col$) = 100 centavos
Exchange rates: Colombian pesos (Col$) per US$1—439.68 (January 1990), 382.57 (1989), 299.17 (1988), 242.61 (1987), 194.26 (1986), 142.31 (1985)
Fiscal year: calendar year

Communications

Railroads: 3,563 km, all 0.914-meter gauge, single track
Highways: 75,450 km total; 9,350 km paved, 66,100 km earth and gravel surfaces
Inland waterways: 14,300 km, navigable by river boats
Pipelines: crude oil, 3,585 km; refined products, 1,350 km; natural gas, 830 km; natural gas liquids, 125 km
Ports: Barranquilla, Buenaventura, Cartagena, Covenas, San Andres, Santa Marta, Tumaco
Merchant marine: 34 ships (1,000 GRT or over) totaling 334,854 GRT/487,438 DWT; includes 23 cargo, 1 chemical tanker, 1 petroleum, oils, and lubricants (POL) tanker, 9 bulk
Civil air: 106 major transport aircraft
Airports: 673 total, 622 usable; 66 with permanent-surface runways; 1 with runways over 3,659 m; 10 with runways 2,440-3,659 m; 124 with runways 1,220-2,439 m
Telecommunications: nationwide radio relay system; 1,890,000 telephones; stations—413 AM, no FM, 33 TV, 28 shortwave 2 Atlantic Ocean INTELSAT earth stations with 2 antennas and 11 domestic satellite stations

Defense Forces

Branches: armed forces include Police (Policia Nacional) and military—Army (Ejercito Nacional), Air Force (Fuerza Aerea de Colombia), Navy (Armada Nacional)
Military manpower: males 15-49, 8,768,072; 5,953,729 fit for military service; 354,742 reach military age (18) annually
Defense expenditures: 1.9% of GDP, or $700 million (1990 est.)

Comoros

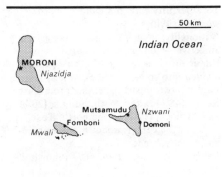

50 km

Indian Ocean

MORONI ★
Njazidja

Mutsamudu *Nzwani*
Fomboni ● *Domoni*
Mwali ●

Mozambique Channel

See regional map VII

Geography

Total area: 2,170 km²; land area: 2,170 km²
Comparative area: slightly more than 12 times the size of Washington, DC
Land boundaries: none
Coastline: 340 km
Maritime claims:
 Extended economic zone: 200 nm
 Territorial sea: 12 nm
Disputes: claims French-administered Mayotte
Climate: tropical marine; rainy season (November to May)
Terrain: volcanic islands, interiors vary from steep mountains to low hills
Natural resources: negligible
Land use: 35% arable land; 8% permanent crops; 7% meadows and pastures; 16% forest and woodland; 34% other
Environment: soil degradation and erosion; deforestation; cyclones possible during rainy season
Note: important location at northern end of Mozambique Channel

People

Population: 460,188 (July 1990), growth rate 3.5% (1990)
Birth rate: 48 births/1,000 population (1990)
Death rate: 12 deaths/1,000 population (1990)
Net migration rate: 0 migrants/1,000 population (1990)
Infant mortality rate: 89 deaths/1,000 live births (1990)
Life expectancy at birth: 54 years male, 58 years female (1990)
Total fertility rate: 7.0 children born/woman (1990)
Nationality: noun—Comoran(s); adjective—Comoran
Ethnic divisions: Antalote, Cafre, Makoa, Oimatsaha, Sakalava

Religion: 86% Sunni Muslim, 14% Roman Catholic
Language: Shaafi Islam (a Swahili dialect), Malagasy, French
Literacy: 15%
Labor force: 140,000 (1982); 80% agriculture, 3% government; 51% of population of working age (1985)
Organized labor: NA

Government

Long-form name: Federal Islamic Republic of the Comoros
Type: independent republic
Capital: Moroni
Administrative divisions: 3 islands; Anjouan, Grande Comore, Moheli; note—there may also be 4 municipalities named Domoni, Fomboni, Moroni, and Mutsamudu
Independence: 6 July 1975 (from France)
Constitution: 1 October 1978, amended October 1982 and January 1985
Legal system: French and Muslim law in a new consolidated code
National holiday: Independence Day, 6 July (1975)
Executive branch: president, Council of Ministers (cabinet)
Legislative branch: unicameral Federal Assembly (Assemblée Fédérale)
Judicial branch: Supreme Court (Cour Suprême)
Leaders: *Chief of State and Head of Government*—President Said Mohamed DJOHAR (since 11 March 1990)
Political parties: Comoran Union for Progress (Udzima), Said Mohamed Djohar, president; National Union for Democracy (UNDC), Mohamed Taki
Suffrage: universal at age 18
Elections: *President*—last held 11 March 1990 (next to be held March 1996); results—Said Mohamed Djohar (Udzima) 55%; Mohamed Taki Abdulkarim (UNDC) 45%;
Federal Assembly—last held 22 March 1987 (next to be held March 1992); results—percent of vote by party NA; seats—(42 total) Udzima 42
Member of: ACP, AfDB, FAO, G-77, IBRD, IDA, IDB—Islamic Development Bank, IFAD, ILO, IMF, ITU, NAM, OAU, OIC, UN, UNESCO, UPU, WHO, WMO
Diplomatic representation: Ambassador Amini Ali MOUMIN; Chancery (temporary) at the Comoran Permanent Mission to the UN, 336 East 45th Street, 2nd Floor, New York, NY 10017; telephone (212) 972-8010; *US*—Ambassador Howard K. WALKER, resides in Antananarivo (Madagascar); Embassy at address NA, Moroni (mailing address B. P. 1318, Moroni); telephone 73-12-03

Flag: green with a white crescent placed diagonally (closed side of the crescent points to the upper hoist-side corner of the flag); there are four white five-pointed stars placed in a line between the points of the crescent; the crescent, stars, and color green are traditional symbols of Islam; the four stars represent the four main islands of the archipelago—Mwali, Njazidja, Nzwani, and Mayotte (which is a territorial collectivity of France, but claimed by the Comoros)

Economy

Overview: One of the world's poorest countries, Comoros is made up of several islands that have poor transportation links, a young and rapidly increasing population, and few natural resources. The low educational level of the labor force contributes to a low level of economic activity, high unemployment, and a heavy dependence on foreign technical assistance. Agriculture, including fishing and forestry, is the leading sector of the economy. It contributes about 40% to GDP, employs 80% of the labor force, and provides most of the exports. The country is not self-sufficient in food production, and rice, the main staple, accounts for 90% of imports. During the period 1982-86 the industrial sector grew at an annual average rate of 5.3%, but its contribution to GDP was less than 4% in 1986. Despite major investment in the tourist industry, which accounts for about 25% of GDP, growth has stagnated since 1983.
GDP: $207 million, per capita $475; real growth rate 0.1% (1988 est.)
Inflation rate (consumer prices): 8.3% (1986)
Unemployment rate: over 16% (1988 est.)
Budget: revenues $75.2 million; expenditures $77.9 million, including capital expenditures of $4.8 million (1988 est.)
Exports: $12 million (f.o.b., 1987); *commodities*—vanilla, cloves, perfume oil, copra; *partners*—US 53%, France 41%, Africa 4%, FRG 2%
Imports: $52 million (c.i.f., 1987); *commodities*—rice and other foodstuffs, cement, petroleum products, consumer goods; *partners*—Europe 62% (France 22%, other 40%), Africa 5%, Pakistan, China
External debt: $238 million (December 1988)
Industrial production: growth rate 3.4% (1988 est.)
Electricity: 16,000 kW capacity; 24 million kWh produced, 55 kWh per capita (1989)
Industries: perfume distillation
Agriculture: accounts for 40% of GDP; most of population works in subsistence

Comoros (continued)

agriculture and fishing; plantations produce cash crops for export—vanilla, cloves, perfume essences, and copra; principal food crops—coconuts, bananas, cassava; world's leading producer of essence of ylang-ylang (for perfumes) and second-largest producer of vanilla; large net food importer

Aid: US commitments, including Ex-Im (FY80-88), $9 million; Western (non-US) countries, ODA and OOF bilateral commitments (1970-87), $371 million; OPEC bilateral aid (1979-89), $22 million; Communist countries (1970-88), $18 million

Currency: Comoran franc (plural—francs); 1 Comoran franc (CF) = 100 centimes

Exchange rates: Comoran francs (CF) per US$1—287.99 (January 1990), 319.01 (1989), 297.85 (1988), 300.54 (1987), 346.30 (1986), 449.26 (1985); note—linked to the French franc at 50 to 1 French franc

Fiscal year: calendar year

Communications

Highways: 750 km total; about 210 km bituminous, remainder crushed stone or gravel

Ports: Mutsamudu, Moroni

Civil air: 4 major transport aircraft

Airports: 4 total, 4 usable; 4 with permanent-surface runways; none with runways over 3,659 m; 1 with runways 2,440-3,659 m; 3 with runways 1,220-2,439 m

Telecommunications: sparse system of radio relay and high-frequency radio communication stations for interisland and external communications to Madagascar and Reunion; over 1,800 telephones; stations—2 AM, 1 FM, 1 TV

Defense Forces

Branches: Army, Presidential Guard, Gendarmerie

Military manpower: males 15-49, 97,504; 58,274 fit for military service

Defense expenditures: 3% of GDP (1981)

Congo

_200 km_

Ouesso

Owando

Djambala

Loubomo · BRAZZAVILLE

Kayes
Pointe-
Noire

Gulf of Guinea

See regional map VII

Geography

Total area: 342,000 km^2; land area: 341,500 km^2

Comparative area: slightly smaller than Montana

Land boundaries: 5,504 km total; Angola 201 km, Cameroon 523 km, Central African Republic 467 km, Gabon 1,903 km, Zaire 2,410 km

Coastline: 169 km

Maritime claims:

Territorial sea: 200 nm

Disputes: long section with Zaire along the Congo River is indefinite (no division of the river or its islands has been made)

Climate: tropical; rainy season (March to June); dry season (June to October); constantly high temperatures and humidity; particularly enervating climate astride the Equator

Terrain: coastal plain, southern basin, central plateau, northern basin

Natural resources: petroleum, timber, potash, lead, zinc, uranium, copper, phosphates, natural gas

Land use: 2% arable land; NEGL% permanent crops; 29% meadows and pastures; 62% forest and woodland; 7% other

Environment: deforestation; about 70% of the population lives in Brazzaville, Pointe Noire, or along the railroad between them

People

Population: 2,242,274 (July 1990), growth rate 3.0% (1990)

Birth rate: 43 births/1,000 population (1990)

Death rate: 14 deaths/1,000 population (1990)

Net migration rate: 0 migrants/1,000 population (1990)

Infant mortality rate: 110 deaths/1,000 live births (1990)

Life expectancy at birth: 52 years male, 55 years female (1990)

Total fertility rate: 5.8 children born/woman (1990)

Nationality: noun—Congolese (sing., pl.); adjective—Congolese or Congo

Ethnic divisions: about 15 ethnic groups divided into some 75 tribes, almost all Bantu; most important ethnic groups are Kongo (48%) in the south, Sangha (20%) and M'Bochi (12%) in the north, Teke (17%) in the center; about 8,500 Europeans, mostly French

Religion: 50% Christian, 48% animist, 2% Muslim

Language: French (official); many African languages with Lingala and Kikongo most widely used

Literacy: 62.9%

Labor force: 79,100 wage earners; 75% agriculture, 25% commerce, industry, and government; 51% of population of working age; 40% of population economically active (1985)

Organized labor: 20% of labor force (1979 est.)

Government

Long-form name: People's Republic of the Congo

Type: people's republic

Capital: Brazzaville

Administrative divisions: 9 regions (régions, singular—région); Bouenza, Cuvette, Kouilou, Lékoumou, Likouala, Niari, Plateaux, Pool, Sangha; note—there may be a new capital district of Brazzaville

Independence: 15 August 1960 (from France; formerly Congo/Brazzaville)

Constitution: 8 July 1979

Legal system: based on French civil law system and customary law

National holiday: National Day, 15 August (1960)

Executive branch: president, prime minister, Council of Ministers (cabinet)

Legislative branch: unicameral People's National Assembly (Assemblée Nationale Populaire)

Judicial branch: Supreme Court (Cour Suprême)

Leaders: _Chief of State and Head of Government_—President Denis SASSOU-NGUESSO (since 8 February 1979); Prime Minister Alphonse POATY-SOUCHLATY (since 6 August 1989)

Political parties and leaders: only party—Congolese Labor Party (PCT), President Denis Sassou-Nguesso, leader

Suffrage: universal at age 18

Elections: _President_—last held 26-31 July 1989 (next to be held July 1993); results—President Sassou-Nguesso unanimously reelected leader of the PCT by the Party Congress, which automatically makes him president;

People's National Assembly—last held 24 September 1989 (next to be held 1993); results—PCT is the only party; seats—(153 total) single list of candidates nominated by the PCT
Communists: unknown number of Communists and sympathizers
Other political or pressure groups: Union of Congolese Socialist Youth (UJSC), Congolese Trade Union Congress (CSC), Revolutionary Union of Congolese Women (URFC), General Union of Congolese Pupils and Students (UGEEC)
Member of: ACP, AfDB, CCC, Conference of East and Central African States, EAMA, ECA, EIB (associate), FAO, G-77, GATT, IBRD, ICAO, ICO, IDA, IFAD, IFC, ILO, IMF, IMO, INTELSAT, INTERPOL, ITU, NAM, OAU, UDEAC, UEAC, UN, UNESCO, UPU, WFTU, WHO, WIPO, WMO
Diplomatic representation: Ambassador Benjamin BOUNKOULOU; Chancery at 4891 Colorado Avenue NW, Washington DC 20011; telephone (202) 726-5500; *US*—Ambassador Leonard G. SHURTLEFF; Embassy at Avenue Amilcar Cabral, Brazzaville (mailing address is B. P. 1015, Brazzaville, or Box C, APO New York 09662-0006); telephone 83-20-70 or 83-26-24
Flag: red with the national emblem in the upper hoist-side corner; the emblem includes a yellow five-pointed star above a crossed hoe and hammer (like the hammer and sickle design) in yellow, flanked by two curved green palm branches; uses the popular pan-African colors of Ethiopia

Economy

Overview: Oil has supplanted forestry as the mainstay of the economy, providing about two-thirds of government revenues and exports. In the early 1980s rapidly rising oil revenues enabled Congo to finance large-scale development projects with growth averaging 5% annually, one of the highest rates in Africa. The world decline in oil prices, however, has forced the government to launch an austerity program to cope with declining receipts and mounting foreign debts.
GDP: $2.2 billion, per capita $1,000; real growth rate −3% (1988 est.)
Inflation rate (consumer prices): 1.5% (1988)
Unemployment rate: NA%
Budget: revenues $382 million; expenditures $575 million, including capital expenditures of $118 million (1988)
Exports: $912 million (f.o.b., 1987); *commodities*—crude petroleum 72%, lumber, plywood, coffee, cocoa, sugar, diamonds; *partners*—US, France, other EC

Imports: $494.4 million (c.i.f., 1987); *commodities*—foodstuffs, consumer goods, intermediate manufactures, capital equipment; *partners*—France, Italy, other EC, US, FRG, Spain, Japan, Brazil
External debt: $4.5 billion (December 1988)
Industrial production: growth rate −5.9% (1987)
Electricity: 133,000 kW capacity; 300 million kWh produced, 130 kWh per capita (1989)
Industries: crude oil, cement, sawmills, brewery, sugar mill, palm oil, soap, cigarettes
Agriculture: accounts for 11% of GDP (including fishing and forestry); cassava accounts for 90% of food output; other crops—rice, corn, peanuts, vegetables; cash crops include coffee and cocoa; forest products important export earner; imports over 90% of food needs
Aid: US commitments, including Ex-Im (FY70-88), $56 million; Western (non-US) countries, ODA and OOF bilateral commitments (1970-87), $2.1 billion; OPEC bilateral aid (1979-89), $15 million; Communist countries (1970-88), $338 million
Currency: Communauté Financière Africaine franc (plural—francs); 1 CFA franc (CFAF) = 100 centimes
Exchange rates: Communauté Financière Africaine francs (CFAF) per US$1—287.99 (January 1990), 319.01 (1989), 297.85 (1988), 300.54 (1987), 346.30 (1986), 449.26 (1985)
Fiscal year: calendar year

Communications

Railroads: 797 km, 1.067-meter gauge, single track (includes 285 km that are privately owned)
Highways: 12,000 km total; 560 km bituminous surface treated; 850 km gravel, laterite; 5,350 km improved earth; 5,240 km unimproved roads
Inland waterways: the Congo and Ubangi (Oubangui) Rivers provide 1,120 km of commercially navigable water transport; the rest are used for local traffic only
Pipelines: crude oil 25 km
Ports: Pointe-Noire (ocean port), Brazzaville (river port)
Civil air: 4 major transport aircraft
Airports: 51 total, 46 usable; 5 with permanent-surface runways; none with runways over 3,659 m; 1 with runways 2,440-3,659 m; 17 with runways 1,220-2,439 m

Telecommunications: services adequate for government use; primary network is composed of radio relay routes and coaxial cables; key centers are Brazzaville, Pointe-Noire, and Loubomo; 18,100 telephones; stations—3 AM, 1 FM, 4 TV; 1 Atlantic Ocean satellite station

Defense Forces

Branches: Army, Navy, Air Force, paramilitary National People's Militia
Military manpower: males 15-49, 492,419; 250,478 fit for military service; 23,622 reach military age (20) annually
Defense expenditures: 4.6% of GDP (1987)

Cook Islands
(free association with New Zealand)

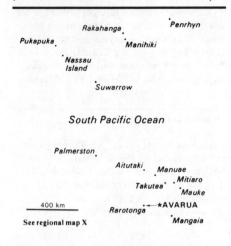

Rakahanga · Penrhyn
Pukapuka · Manihiki
Nassau Island ·
Suwarrow ·

South Pacific Ocean

Palmerston ·
Aitutaki · Manuae
Takutea · Mitiaro
· Mauke
400 km
Rarotonga → ★AVARUA
See regional map X · Mangaia

Geography

Total area: 240 km²; land area: 240 km²
Comparative area: slightly less than 1.5 times the size of Washington, DC
Land boundaries: none
Coastline: 120 km
Maritime claims:
Continental shelf: 200 meters or edge of continental margin
Extended economic zone: 200 nm
Territorial sea: 12 nm
Climate: tropical; moderated by trade winds
Terrain: low coral atolls in north; volcanic, hilly islands in south
Natural resources: negligible
Land use: 4% arable land; 22% permanent crops; 0% meadows and pastures; 0% forest and woodland; 74% other
Environment: subject to typhoons from November to March
Note: located 4,500 km south of Hawaii in the South Pacific Ocean

People

Population: 18,187 (July 1990), growth rate 0.5% (1990)
Birth rate: 22 births/1,000 population (1990)
Death rate: 7 deaths/1,000 population (1990)
Net migration rate: −10 migrants/1,000 population (1990)
Infant mortality rate: 24 deaths/1,000 live births (1990)
Life expectancy at birth: 66 years male, 72 years female (1990)
Total fertility rate: 3.5 children born/woman (1990)
Nationality: noun—Cook Islander(s); adjective—Cook Islander
Ethnic divisions: 81.3% Polynesian (full blood), 7.7% Polynesian and European, 7.7% Polynesian and other, 2.4% European, 0.9% other

Religion: Christian, majority of populace members of Cook Islands Christian Church
Language: English
Literacy: NA%
Labor force: 5,810; agriculture 29%, government 27%, services 25%, industry 15%, and other 4% (1981)
Organized labor: NA

Government

Long-form name: none
Type: self-governing in free association with New Zealand; Cook Islands fully responsible for internal affairs; New Zealand retains responsibility for external affairs, in consultation with the Cook Islands
Capital: Avarua
Administrative divisions: none
Independence: became self-governing in free association with New Zealand on 4 August 1965 and has the right at any time to move to full independence by unilateral action
Constitution: 4 August 1965
National holiday: NA
Executive branch: British monarch, representative of the UK, representative of New Zealand, prime minister, deputy prime minister, Cabinet
Legislative branch: unicameral Parliament; note—the unicameral House of Arikis (chiefs) advises on traditional matters, but has no legislative powers
Judicial branch: High Court
Leaders: *Chief of State*—Queen ELIZABETH II (since 6 February 1952); Representative of the UK Sir Tangaroa TANGAROA (since NA); Representative of New Zealand Adrian SINCOCK (since NA);
Head of Government—Prime Minister Geoffrey HENRY (since NA February 1989); Deputy Prime Minister Inatio AKARURU (since NA)
Political parties and leaders: Cook Islands Party, Geoffrey Henry; Democratic Tumu Party, Vincent Ingram; Democratic Party, Dr. Vincent Pupuke Robati; Cook Islands Labor Party, Rena Jonassen; Cook Islands People's Party, Sadaraka Sadaraka
Suffrage: universal adult at age NA
Elections: *Parliament*—last held 19 January 1989 (next to be held by January 1994); results—percent of vote by party NA; seats—(24 total) Cook Islands Party 12, Democratic Tumu Party 2, opposition coalition (including Democratic Party) 9, independent 1
Member of: ADB, ESCAP (associate member), IDA, IFC, IMF, SPF
Diplomatic representation: none (self-governing in free association with New Zealand)

Flag: blue with the flag of the UK in the upper hoist-side quadrant and a large circle of 15 white five-pointed stars (one for every island) centered in the outer half of the flag

Economy

Overview: Agriculture provides the economic base. The major export earners are fruit, copra, and clothing. Manufacturing activities are limited to a fruit-processing plant and several clothing factories. Economic development is hindered by the isolation of the islands from foreign markets and a lack of natural resources and good transportation links. A large trade deficit is annually made up for by remittances from emigrants and from foreign aid. Current economic development plans call for exploiting the tourism potential and expanding the fishing industry.
GDP: $40.0 million, per capita $2,200 (1988 est.); real growth rate 5.3% (1986-88 est.)
Inflation rate (consumer prices): 8.0% (1988)
Unemployment rate: NA%
Budget: revenues $33.8 million; expenditures $34.4 million, including capital expenditures of $NA (1990 est.)
Exports: $4.0 million (f.o.b., 1988); *commodities*—copra, fresh and canned fruit, clothing; *partners*—NZ 80%, Japan
Imports: $38.7 million (c.i.f., 1988); *commodities*—foodstuffs, textiles, fuels, timber; *partners*—NZ 49%, Japan, Australia, US
External debt: $NA
Industrial production: growth rate NA%
Electricity: 4,800 kW capacity; 15 million kWh produced, 830 kWh per capita (1989)
Industries: fruit processing, tourism
Agriculture: export crops—copra, citrus fruits, pineapples, tomatoes, bananas; subsistence crops—yams, taro
Aid: Western (non-US) countries, ODA and OOF bilateral commitments (1970-89), $128 million
Currency: New Zealand dollar (plural—dollars); 1 New Zealand dollar (NZ$) = 100 cents
Exchange rates: New Zealand dollars (NZ$) per US$1—1.6581 (January 1990), 1.6708 (1989), 1.5244 (1988), 1.6886 (1987), 1.9088 (1986), 2.0064 (1985)
Fiscal year: 1 April-31 March

Communications

Highways: 187 km total (1980); 35 km paved, 35 km gravel, 84 km improved earth, 33 km unimproved earth
Ports: Avatiu
Civil air: no major transport aircraft

Airports: 7 total, 5 usable; 1 with permanent-surface runways; none with runways over 2,439 m; 3 with runways 1,220-2,439 m
Telecommunications: stations—2 AM, no FM, no TV; 10,000 radio receivers; 2,052 telephones; 1 Pacific Ocean INTELSAT earth station

Defense Forces

Note: defense is the responsibility of New Zealand

Coral Sea Islands
(territory of Australia)

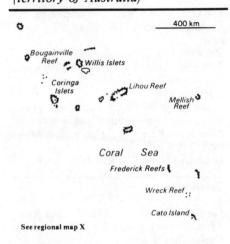

See regional map X

Geography

Total area: undetermined; includes numerous small islands and reefs scattered over a sea area of about 1 million km², with Willis Islets the most important
Comparative area: undetermined
Land boundaries: none
Coastline: 3,095 km
Maritime claims:
  Contiguous zone: 12 nm
  Continental shelf: 200 meters or to depth of exploitation
  Exclusive fishing zone: 200 nm
  Territorial sea: 3 nm
Climate: tropical
Terrain: sand and coral reefs and islands (or cays)
Natural resources: negligible
Land use: 0% arable land; 0% permanent crops; 0% meadows and pastures; 0% forest and woodland; 100% other, mostly grass or scrub cover; Lihou Reef Reserve and Coringa-Herald Reserve were declared National Nature Reserves on 3 August 1982
Environment: subject to occasional tropical cyclones; no permanent fresh water; important nesting area for birds and turtles
Note: the islands are located just off the northeast coast of Australia in the Coral Sea

People

Population: 3 meteorologists

Government

Long-form name: Coral Sea Islands Territory
Type: territory of Australia administered by the Minister for Arts, Sport, the Environment, Tourism, and Territories Graham Richardson
Flag: the flag of Australia is used

Economy

Overview: no economic activity

Communications

Ports: none; offshore anchorages only

Defense Forces

Note: defense is the responsibility of Australia; visited regularly by the Royal Australian Navy; Australia has control over the activities of visitors

Costa Rica

100 km

Cabo Gracias
a Dios

Liberia

Caribbean
Sea

Nicoya

Puntarenas

Puerto
Limón

SAN JOSÉ

San Isidro

North Pacific Ocean

Golfito

Isla del Coco
is not shown.

See regional map III

Geography

Total area: 51,100 km²; land area: 50,660 km²; includes Isla del Coco
Comparative area: slightly smaller than West Virginia
Land boundaries: 639 km total; Nicaragua 309 km, Panama 330 km
Coastline: 1,290 km
Maritime claims:
Continental shelf: 200 nm
Extended economic zone: 200 nm
Territorial sea: 12 nm
Climate: tropical; dry season (December to April); rainy season (May to November)
Terrain: coastal plains separated by rugged mountains
Natural resources: hydropower potential
Land use: 6% arable land; 7% permanent crops; 45% meadows and pastures; 34% forest and woodland; 8% other; includes 1% irrigated
Environment: subject to occasional earthquakes, hurricanes along Atlantic coast; frequent flooding of lowlands at onset of rainy season; active volcanoes; deforestation; soil erosion

People

Population: 3,032,795 (July 1990), growth rate 2.6% (1990)
Birth rate: 28 births/1,000 population (1990)
Death rate: 4 deaths/1,000 population (1990)
Net migration rate: 2 migrants/1,000 population (1990)
Infant mortality rate: 16 deaths/1,000 live births (1990)
Life expectancy at birth: 74 years male, 79 years female (1990)
Total fertility rate: 3.3 children born/woman (1990)
Nationality: noun—Costa Rican(s); adjective—Costa Rican

Ethnic divisions: 96% white (including mestizo), 2% black, 1% Indian, 1% Chinese
Religion: 95% Roman Catholic
Language: Spanish (official), English spoken around Puerto Limón
Literacy: 93%
Labor force: 868,300; industry and commerce 35.1%, government and services 33%, agriculture 27%, other 4.9% (1985 est.)
Organized labor: 15.1% of labor force

Government

Long-form name: Republic of Costa Rica
Type: democratic republic
Capital: San José
Administrative divisions: 7 provinces (provincias, singular—provincia); Alajuela, Cartago, Guanacaste, Heredia, Limón, Puntarenas, San José
Independence: 15 September 1821 (from Spain)
Constitution: 9 November 1949
Legal system: based on Spanish civil law system; judicial review of legislative acts in the Supreme Court; has not accepted compulsory ICJ jurisdiction
National holiday: Independence Day, 15 September (1821)
Executive branch: president, two vice presidents, Cabinet
Legislative branch: unicameral Legislative Assembly (Asamblea Legislativa)
Judicial branch: Supreme Court (Corte Suprema)
Leaders: *Chief of State and Head of Government*—President Rafael Angel CALDERON Fournier (since 8 May 1990); First Vice President German SERRANO Pinto (since 8 May 1990); Second Vice President Arnoldo LOPEZ Echandi (since 8 May 1990)
Political parties and leaders: National Liberation Party (PLN), Carlos Manuel Castillo; Social Christian Unity Party (PUSC), Rafael Angel Calderón Fournier; Marxist Popular Vanguard Party (PVP), Humberto Vargas Carbonell; New Republic Movement (MNR), Sergio Erick Ardón; Progressive Party (PP), Javier Solis; People's Party of Costa Rica (PPC), Lenin Chacon Vargas; Radical Democratic Party (PRD), Juan José Echeverría Brealey
Suffrage: universal and compulsory at age 18
Elections: *President*—last held 4 February 1990 (next to be held February 1994); results—Rafael Calderón Fournier 51%, Carlos Manuel Castillo 47%;
Legislative Assembly—last held 4 February 1990 (next to be held February 1994); results—percent of vote by party NA;

seats—(57 total) PUSC 29, PLN 25, PVP/PPC 1, regional parties 2
Communists: 7,500 members and sympathizers
Other political or pressure groups: Costa Rican Confederation of Democratic Workers (CCTD; Liberation Party affiliate), Confederated Union of Workers (CUT; Communist Party affiliate), Authentic Confederation of Democratic Workers (CATD; Communist Party affiliate), Chamber of Coffee Growers, National Association for Economic Development (ANFE), Free Costa Rica Movement (MCRL; rightwing militants), National Association of Educators (ANDE)
Member of: CACM, FAO, G-77, IADB, IAEA, IBRD, ICAO, ICO, IDA, IDB—Inter-American Development Bank, IFAD, IFC, ILO, IMF, IMO, INTELSAT, INTERPOL, IPU, ITU, IWC—International Wheat Council, OAS, ODECA, PAHO, SELA, UN, UNESCO, UPEB, UPU, WHO, WMO, WTO
Diplomatic representation: Ambassador Danilo JIMENEZ; Chancery at Suite 211, 1825 Connecticut Avenue NW, Washington DC 20009; telephone (202) 234-2945 through 2947; there are Costa Rican Consulates General at Albuquerque, Boston, Houston, Los Angeles, Miami, New Orleans, New York, San Antonio, San Diego, San Francisco, San Juan (Puerto Rico), and Tampa, and Consulates in Austin, Buffalo, Honolulu, and Raleigh; *US*—Ambassador (vacant); Embassy at Pavas Road, San Jose (mailing address is APO Miami 34020); telephone [506] 33-11-55
Flag: five horizontal bands of blue (top), white, red (double width), white, and blue with the coat of arms in a white disk on the hoist side of the red band

Economy

Overview: In 1988 the economy grew at a 3.8% rate, a drop from the 5.1% of the previous year. Gains in agricultural production (on the strength of good coffee and banana crops) and in construction, were partially offset by declines in the rates of growth for the industry and commerce sectors. In 1988 consumer prices rose by nearly 21% followed by a 10% rise in 1989. Unemployment is officially reported at about 6%, but much underemployment remains. External debt, on a per capita basis, is among the world's highest.
GDP: $4.7 billion, per capita $1,630; real growth rate 3.8% (1988)
Inflation rate (consumer prices): 10% (1989)
Unemployment rate: 5.5% (March 1989)

Budget: revenues $719 million; expenditures $808 million, including capital expenditures of $103 million (1988)
Exports: $1.3 billion (f.o.b., 1988); *commodities*—coffee, bananas, textiles, sugar; *partners*—US 75%, FRG, Guatemala, Netherlands, UK, Japan
Imports: $1.4 billion (c.i.f., 1988); *commodities*—petroleum, machinery, consumer durables, chemicals, fertilizer, foodstuffs; *partners*—US 35%, Japan, Guatemala, FRG
External debt: $4.5 billion (1989)
Industrial production: growth rate 2.1% (1988)
Electricity: 909,000 kW capacity; 2,928 million kWh produced, 990 kWh per capita (1989)
Industries: food processing, textiles and clothing, construction materials, fertilizer
Agriculture: accounts for 20-25% of GDP and 70% of exports; cash commodities—coffee, beef, bananas, sugar; other food crops include corn, rice, beans, potatotes; normally self-sufficient in food except for grain; depletion of forest resources resulting in lower timber output
Illicit drugs: illicit production of cannabis on small scattered plots; transshipment country for cocaine from South America
Aid: US commitments, including Ex-Im (FY70-88), $1.3 billion; Western (non-US) countries, ODA and OOF bilateral commitments (1970-87), $706 million; Communist countries (1971-88), $27 million
Currency: Costa Rican colón (plural—colones); 1 Costa Rican colón (C) = 100 céntimos
Exchange rates: Costa Rican colones (C) per US$1—84.689 (January 1990), 81.504 (1989), 75.805 (1988), 62.776 (1987), 55.986 (1986), 50.453 (1985)
Fiscal year: calendar year

Communications

Railroads: 950 km total, all 1.067-meter gauge; 260 km electrified
Highways: 15,400 km total; 7,030 km paved, 7,010 km gravel, 1,360 km unimproved earth
Inland waterways: about 730 km, seasonally navigable
Pipelines: refined products, 176 km
Ports: Puerto Limon, Caldera, Golfito, Moin, Puntarenas
Merchant marine: 2 cargo ships (1,000 GRT or over) totaling 4,279 GRT/6,602 DWT
Civil air: 9 major transport aircraft
Airports: 193 total, 177 usable; 25 with permanent-surface runways; none with runways over 3,659 m; 1 with runways 2,440-3,659 m; 11 with runways 1,220-2,439 m

Telecommunications: very good domestic telephone service; 292,000 telephones; connection into Central American Microwave System; stations—71 AM, no FM, 18 TV, 13 shortwave; 1 Atlantic Ocean INTELSAT earth station

---

Defense Forces

Branches: Civil Guard, Rural Assistance Guard; note—Constitution prohibits armed forces
Military manpower: males 15-49, 785,429; 530,986 fit for military service; 31,899 reach military age (18) annually
Defense expenditures: 0.6% of GDP (1987)

Cuba

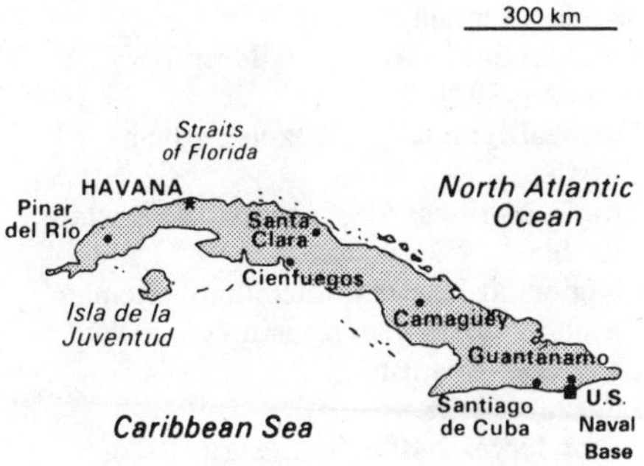

300 km

See regional map III

Geography

Total area: 110,860 km²; land area: 110,860 km²
Comparative area: slightly smaller than Pennsylvania
Land boundary: 29.1 km with US Naval Base at Guantánamo; note—Guantánamo is leased and as such remains part of Cuba
Coastline: 3,735 km
Maritime claims:
  Extended economic zone: 200 nm
  Territorial sea: 12 nm
Disputes: US Naval Base at Guantánamo is leased to US and only mutual agreement or US abandonment of the area can terminate the lease
Climate: tropical; moderated by trade winds; dry season (November to April); rainy season (May to October)
Terrain: mostly flat to rolling plains with rugged hills and mountains in the southeast
Natural resources: cobalt, nickel, iron ore, copper, manganese, salt, timber, silica
Land use: 23% arable land; 6% permanent crops; 23% meadows and pastures; 17% forest and woodland; 31% other; includes 10% irrigated
Environment: averages one hurricane every other year
Note: largest country in Caribbean; 145 km south of Florida

People

Population: 10,620,099 (July 1990), growth rate 1.1% (1990)
Birth rate: 18 births/1,000 population (1990)
Death rate: 7 deaths/1,000 population (1990)
Net migration rate: −1 migrant/1,000 population (1990)
Infant mortality rate: 12 deaths/1,000 live births (1990)

Life expectancy at birth: 73 years male, 78 years female (1990)
Total fertility rate: 1.9 children born/woman (1990)
Nationality: noun—Cuban(s); adjective—Cuban
Ethnic divisions: 51% mulatto, 37% white, 11% black, 1% Chinese
Religion: at least 85% nominally Roman Catholic before Castro assumed power
Language: Spanish
Literacy: 98.5%
Labor force: 3,400,000 in state sector; 30% services and government, 22% industry, 20% agriculture, 11% commerce, 10% construction, 7% transportation and communications (1988); economically active population 4,500,000 (1987)
Organized labor: Workers Central Union of Cuba (CTC), only labor federation approved by government; 2,910,000 members; the CTC is an umbrella organization composed of 17 member unions

Government

Long-form name: Republic of Cuba
Type: Communist state
Capital: Havana
Administrative divisions: 14 provinces (provincias, singular—provincia) and 1 special municipality* (municipio especial); Camagüey, Ciego de Avila, Cienfuegos, Ciudad de La Habana, Granma, Guantánamo, Holguín, Isla de la Juventud*, La Habana, Las Tunas, Matanzas, Pinar del Río, Sancti Spíritus, Santiago de Cuba, Villa Clara
Independence: 20 May 1902 (from Spain 10 December 1898; administered by the US from 1898 to 1902)
Constitution: 24 February 1976
Legal system: based on Spanish and American law, with large elements of Communist legal theory; does not accept compulsory ICJ jurisdiction
National holiday: Revolution Day, 1 January (1959)
Executive branch: president of the Council of State, first vice president of the Council of State, Council of State, president of the Council of Ministers, first vice president of the Council of Ministers, Council of Ministers
Legislative branch: unicameral National Assembly of the People's Power (Asamblea Nacional del Poder Popular)
Judicial branch: People's Supreme Court
Leaders: *Chief of State and Head of Government*—President of the Council of State and President of the Council of Ministers Fidel CASTRO Ruz (became Prime Minister in January 1959 and President since 2 December 1976); First Vice President of the Council of State and

First Vice President of the Council of Ministers Gen. Raúl CASTRO Ruz (since 2 December 1976)
Political parties and leaders: only party—Cuban Communist Party (PCC), Fidel Castro Ruz, first secretary
Suffrage: universal at age 16
Elections: *National Assembly of the People's Power*—last held NA December 1986 (next to be held December 1991); results—PCC is the only party; seats—(510 total) PCC 510 (indirectly elected)
Communists: about 600,000 full and candidate members
Member of: CEMA, ECLA, FAO, G-77, GATT, IADB (nonparticipant), IAEA, IBEC, ICAO, IFAD, ICO, IHO, ILO, IMO, IRC, ISO, ITU, IWC—International Wheat Council, NAM, OAS (nonparticipant), PAHO, SELA, UN, UNESCO, UNIDO, UPU, WFTU, WHO, WIPO, WMO, WSG, WTO
Diplomatic representation: none; protecting power in the US is Czechoslovakia—Cuban Interests Section; Counselor José Antonio Arbesu FRAGA; 2630 and 2639 16th Street NW, Washington DC 20009; telephone (202) 797-8518 or 8519, 8520, 8609, 8610; *US*—protecting power in Cuba is Switzerland—US Interests Section; Principal Officer John J. TAYLOR; Calzada entre L y M, Vedado Seccion, Havana; telephone 320551 or 320543
Flag: five equal horizontal bands of blue (top and bottom) alternating with white; a red equilateral triangle based on the hoist side bears a white five-pointed star in the center

Economy

Overview: The Soviet-style economy, centrally planned and largely state owned, is highly dependent on the agricultural sector and foreign trade. Sugar provides about 75% of export revenues and is mostly exported to the USSR and other CEMA countries. The economy has stagnated since 1985 under a program that has deemphasized material incentives in the workplace, abolished farmers' informal produce markets, and raised prices of government-supplied goods and services. Castro has complained that the ongoing CEMA reform process has interfered with the regular flow of goods to Cuba. Recently the government has been trying to increase trade with Latin America and China. Cuba has had difficulty servicing its foreign debt since 1982. The government currently is encouraging foreign investment in tourist facilities. Other investment priorities include sugar, basic foods, and nickel. The annual $4 billion Soviet subsidy, a main prop to Cuba's threadbare

economy, may be cut in view of the USSR's mounting economic problems.
GNP: $20.9 billion, per capita $2,000; real growth rate −1% (1989 est.)
Inflation rate (consumer prices): NA%
Unemployment: 6% overall, 10% for women (1989)
Budget: revenues $11.7 billion; expenditures $13.5 billion, including capital expenditures of $NA (1989 est.)
Exports: $5.5 billion (f.o.b., 1988); *commodities*—sugar, nickel, shellfish, citrus, tobacco, coffee; *partners*—USSR 67%, GDR 6%, China 4% (1988)
Imports: $7.6 billion (c.i.f., 1988); *commodities*—capital goods, industrial raw materials, food, petroleum; *partners*—USSR 71%, other Communist countries 15% (1988)
External debt: $6.8 billion (convertible currency, July 1989)
Industrial production: 3% (1988)
Electricity: 3,991,000 kW capacity; 14,972 million kWh produced, 1,425 kWh per capita (1989)
Industries: sugar milling, petroleum refining, food and tobacco processing, textiles, chemicals, paper and wood products, metals (particularly nickel), cement, fertilizers, consumer goods, agricultural machinery
Agriculture: accounts for 11% of GNP (including fishing and forestry); key commercial crops—sugarcane, tobacco, and citrus fruits; other products—coffee, rice, potatoes, meat, beans; world's largest sugar exporter; not self-sufficient in food
Aid: Western (non-US) countries, ODA and OOF bilateral commitments (1970-87), $657.5 million; Communist countries (1970-88), $13.5 billion
Currency: Cuban peso (plural—pesos); 1 Cuban peso (Cu$) = 100 centavos
Exchange rates: Cuban pesos (Cu$) per US$1—1.0000 (linked to the US dollar)
Fiscal year: calendar year

Communications

Railroads: 14,925 km total; Cuban National Railways operates 5,295 km of 1.435-meter gauge track; 199 km electrified; 9,630 km of sugar plantation lines of 0.914-1.435-meter gauge
Highways: about 21,000 km total; 9,000 km paved, 12,000 km gravel and earth surfaced
Inland waterways: 240 km
Ports: Cienfuegos, Havana, Mariel, Matanzas, Santiago de Cuba; 7 secondary, 35 minor
Merchant marine: 91 ships (1,000 GRT or over) totaling 701,418 GRT/1,014,014 DWT; includes 62 cargo, 7 refrigerated cargo, 3 cargo/training, 10 petroleum, oils, and lubricants (POL) tanker, 1 chem-

ical tanker, 2 liquefied gas, 6 bulk; note—Cuba beneficially owns an additional 34 ships (1,000 GRT and over) totaling 475,864 DWT under the registry of Panama, Cyprus, and Malta
Civil air: 59 major transport aircraft
Airports: 197 total, 168 usable; 72 with permanent-surface runways; 2 with runways over 3,659 m; 14 with runways 2,440-3,659 m; 17 with runways 1,220-2,439 m
Telecommunications: stations—150 AM, 5 FM, 58 TV; 1,530,000 TV sets; 2,140,000 radio receivers; 1 Atlantic Ocean INTELSAT earth station

Defense Forces

Branches: Revolutionary Armed Forces (Ground Forces, Revolutionary Navy, Air and Air Defense Force), Ministry of Interior Special Troops, Border Guard Troops, Territorial Militia Troops, Youth Labor Army
Military manpower: eligible 15-49, 6,027,131; of the 3,024,385 males 15-49, 1,897,175 are fit for military service; of the 3,002,746 females 15-49, 1,879,471 are fit for military service; 96,319 males and 92,765 females reach military age (17) annually
Defense expenditures: about 6% of GNP, or $1.2- $1.4 billion (1989 est.)

Cyprus

Mediterranean Sea

See regional map VI

Geography

Total area: 9,250 km²; land area: 9,240 km²
Comparative area: about 0.7 times the size of Connecticut
Land boundaries: none
Coastline: 648 km
Maritime claims:
Continental shelf: 200 meters or to depth of exploitation
Territorial sea: 12 nm
Disputes: 1974 hostilities divided the island into two de facto autonomous areas—a Greek area controlled by the Cypriot Government (60% of the island's land area) and a Turkish-Cypriot area (35% of the island) that are separated by a narrow UN buffer zone; in addition, there are two UK sovereign base areas (about 5% of the island's land area)
Climate: temperate, Mediterranean with hot, dry summers and cool, wet winters
Terrain: central plain with mountains to north and south
Natural resources: copper, pyrites, asbestos, gypsum, timber, salt, marble, clay earth pigment
Land use: 40% arable land; 7% permanent crops; 10% meadows and pastures; 18% forest and woodland; 25% other; includes 10% irrigated (most irrigated lands are in the Turkish-Cypriot area of the island)
Environment: moderate earthquake activity; water resource problems (no natural reservoir catchments, seasonal disparity in rainfall, and most potable resources concentrated in the Turkish-Cypriot area)

People

Population: 707,776 (July 1990), growth rate 1.0% (1990)
Birth rate: 19 births/1,000 population (1990)
Death rate: 8 deaths/1,000 population (1990)

Net migration rate: 0 migrants/1,000 population (1990)
Infant mortality rate: 10 deaths/1,000 live births (1990)
Life expectancy at birth: 73 years male, 78 years female (1990)
Total fertility rate: 2.4 children born/woman (1990)
Nationality: noun—Cypriot(s); adjective—Cypriot
Ethnic divisions: 78% Greek; 18% Turkish; 4% other
Religion: 78% Greek Orthodox; 18% Muslim; 4% Maronite, Armenian, Apostolic, and other
Language: Greek, Turkish, English
Literacy: 99% (est.)
Labor force: Greek area—251,406; 42% services, 33% industry, 22% agriculture; Turkish area—NA (1986)
Organized labor: 156,000 (1985 est.)

Government

Long-form name: Republic of Cyprus
Type: republic; a disaggregation of the two ethnic communities inhabiting the island began after the outbreak of communal strife in 1963; this separation was further solidified following the Turkish invasion of the island in July 1974, which gave the Turkish Cypriots de facto control in the north; Greek Cypriots control the only internationally recognized government; on 15 November 1983 Turkish Cypriot President Rauf Denktash declared independence and the formation of a Turkish Republic of Northern Cyprus, which has been recognized only by Turkey; both sides publicly call for the resolution of intercommunal differences and creation of a new federal system of government
Capital: Nicosia
Administrative divisions: 6 districts; Famagusta, Kyrenia, Larnaca, Limassol, Nicosia, Paphos
Independence: 16 August 1960 (from UK)
Constitution: 16 August 1960; negotiations to create the basis for a new or revised constitution to govern the island and to better relations between Greek and Turkish Cypriots have been held intermittently; in 1975 Turkish Cypriots created their own Constitution and governing bodies within the Turkish Federated State of Cyprus, which was renamed the Turkish Republic of Northern Cyprus in 1983; a new Constitution for the Turkish area passed by referendum in May 1985
Legal system: based on common law, with civil law modifications
National holiday: Independence Day, 1 October
Executive branch: president, Council of Ministers (cabinet); note—there is a presi-

dent, prime minister, and Council of Ministers (cabinet) in the Turkish area

Legislative branch: unicameral House of Representatives (Vouli Antiprosópon); note—there is a unicameral Assembly of the Republic (Cumhuriyet Meclisi) in the Turkish area

Judicial branch: Supreme Court; note—there is also a Supreme Court in the Turkish area

Leaders: *Chief of State and Head of Government*—President George VASSILIOU (since February 1988); note—Rauf R. DENKTAŞ was proclaimed President of the Turkish area on 13 February 1975

Political parties and leaders: *Greek Cypriot*—Progressive Party of the Working People (AKEL; Communist Party), Dimitrios Christotias, Democratic Rally (DESY), Glafkos Clerides; Democratic Party (DEKO), Spyros Kyprianou; United Democratic Union of the Center (EDEK), Vassos Lyssarides;
Turkish area—National Unity Party (NUP), Dervis Eroglu; Communal Liberation Party (CLP), Ismail Bozkurt; Republican Turkish Party (RTP), Ozker Ozgur; New Birth Party (NBP), Aytac Besheshler; New Cyprus savey (NCP), Alpay Durduran

Suffrage: universal at age 18

Elections: *President*—last held 14 February and 21 February 1988 (next to be held February 1993); results—George Vassiliou 52%, Glafkos Clerides 48%;
House of Representatives—last held 8 December 1985 (next to be held December 1990); results—Democratic Rally 33.56%, Democratic Party 27.65%, AKEL 27.43%, EDEK 11.07%; seats—(56 total) Democratic Rally 19, Democratic Party 16, AKEL (Communist) 15, EDEK 6;
Turkish Area: President—last held 9 June 1985 (next to be held June 1990); results—Rauf Denktash 70%;
Turkish Area: Legislative Assembly—last held 23 June 1985 (next to be held June 1990); results—percent of vote by party NA; seats—(50 total) National Unity Party (conservative) 24, Republican Turkish Party (Communist) 12, Communal Liberation Party (center-right) 10, New Birth Party 4

Communists: about 12,000

Other political or pressure groups: United Democratic Youth Organization (EDON; Communist controlled); Union of Cyprus Farmers (EKA; Communist controlled); Cyprus Farmers Union (PEK; pro-West); Pan-Cyprian Labor Federation (PEO; Communist controlled); Confederation of Cypriot Workers (SEK; pro-West); Federation of Turkish Cypriot Labor Unions (Turk-Sen); Confederation of Revolutionary Labor Unions (Dev-Is)

Member of: CCC, Commonwealth, Council of Europe, FAO, G-77, GATT, IAEA, IBRD, ICAO, ICO, IDA, IFAD, IFC, ILO, IMF, IMO, INTELSAT, INTERPOL, ITU, NAM, UN, UNESCO, UPU, WFTU, WHO, WMO, WTO; Turkish Federated State of Cyprus—OIC (observer)

Diplomatic representation: Ambassador Michael E. SHERIFIS; Chancery at 2211 R Street NW, Washington DC 20008; telephone (202) 462-5772; there is a Cypriot Consulate General in New York; *US*—(vacant); Embassy at the corner of Therissos Street and Dositheos Street, Nicosia (mailing address is FPO New York 09530); telephone [357] (2) 465151

Flag: white with a copper-colored silhouette of the island (the name Cyprus is derived from the Greek word for copper) above two green crossed olive branches in the center of the flag; the branches symbolize the hope for peace and reconciliation between the Greek and Turkish communities

Economy

Overview: These data are for the area controlled by the Republic of Cyprus (information on the northern Turkish-Cypriot area is sparse). The economy is small, diversified, and prosperous. Industry contributes about 28% to GDP and employs 35% of the labor force, while the service sector contributes about 55% to GDP and employs 40% of the labor force. Rapid growth in exports of agricultural and manufactured products and in tourism have played important roles in the average 6% rise in GDP in recent years. While this growth put considerable pressure on prices and the balance of payments, the inflation rate has remained low and the balance-of-payments deficit manageable.

GDP: $4.2 billion, per capita $6,100; real growth rate 6.9% (1988 est.)

Inflation rate (consumer prices): 3.9% (1989 est.)

Unemployment rate: 2.8% (1988)

Budget: revenues $1.2 billion; expenditures $1.4 billion, including capital expenditures of $178 million (1989 est.)

Exports: $767 million (f.o.b., 1988); *commodities*—citrus, potatoes, grapes, wine, cement, clothing and shoes; *partners*—Middle East and North Africa 37%, UK 27%, other EC 11%, US 2%

Imports: $1.9 billion (c.i.f., 1988); *commodities*—consumer goods 23%, petroleum and lubricants 12%, food and feed grains, machinery; *partners*—EC 60%, Middle East and North Africa 7%, US 4%

External debt: $2.8 billion (1988)

Industrial production: growth rate 6.5% (1988)

Electricity: 620,000 kW capacity; 1,770 million kWh produced, 2,530 kWh per capita (1989)

Industries: mining (iron pyrites, gypsum, asbestos); manufactured products—beverages, footwear, clothing, and cement—are principally for local consumption

Agriculture: accounts for 8% of GDP and employs 22% of labor force; major crops—potatoes, vegetables, barley, grapes, olives, and citrus fruits; vegetables and fruit provide 25% of export revenues

Aid: US commitments, including Ex-Im (FY70-88), $272 million; Western (non-US) countries, ODA and OOF bilateral commitments (1970-87), $223 million; OPEC bilateral aid (1979-89), $62 million; Communist countries (1970-88), $24 million

Currency: Cypriot pound (plural—pounds) and in Turkish area, Turkish lira (plural—liras); 1 Cypriot pound (£C) = 100 cents and 1 Turkish lira (TL) = 100 kuruş

Exchange rates: Cypriot pounds (£C) per US$1—0.4854 (January 1990), 0.4933 (1989), 0.4663 (1988), 0.4807 (1987), 0.5167 (1986), 0.6095 (1985); in Turkish area, Turkish liras (TL) per US$1—2,314.7 (November 1989), 1,422.3 (1988), 857.2 (1987), 674.5 (1986), 522.0 (1985)

Fiscal year: calendar year

Communications

Highways: 10,780 km total; 5,170 km bituminous surface treated; 5,610 km gravel, crushed stone, and earth

Ports: Famagusta, Kyrenia, Larnaca, Limassol, Paphos

Merchant marine: 1,100 ships (1,000 GRT or over) totaling 18,093,340 GRT/ 32,148,550 DWT; includes 1 passenger, 12 short-sea passenger, 2 passenger-cargo, 434 cargo, 61 refrigerated cargo, 18 roll-on/roll-off cargo, 40 container, 94 petroleum, oils, and lubricants (POL) tanker, 1 specialized cargo, 3 liquefied gas, 13 chemical tanker, 29 combination ore/oil, 341 bulk, 3 vehicle carrier, 48 combination bulk carrier; note—a flag of convenience registry; Cuba owns at least 20 of these ships and Yugoslavia owns 1

Civil air: 8 major transport aircraft

Airports: 13 total, 13 usable; 10 with permanent-surface runways; none with runways over 3,659 m; 7 with runways 2,440-3,659 m; 2 with runways 1,220-2,439 m

Czechoslovakia

Telecommunications: excellent in the area controlled by the Cypriot Government (Greek area), moderately good in the Turkish-Cypriot administered area; 210,000 telephones; stations—13 AM, 7 (7 repeaters) FM, 2 (40 repeaters) TV; tropospheric scatter circuits to Greece and Turkey; 3 submarine coaxial cables; satellite earth stations—INTELSAT, 1 Atlantic Ocean and 1 Indian Ocean, and EUTELSAT systems

Defense Forces

Branches: Cyprus National Guard; Turkish area—Turkish Cypriot Security Force
Military manpower: males 15-49, 180,946; 125,044 fit for military service; 5,083 reach military age (18) annually
Defense expenditures: 2% of GDP, or $84 million (1990 est.)

See regional map V

Geography

Total area: 127,870 km²; land area: 125,460 km²
Comparative area: slightly larger than New York State
Land boundaries: 3,446 km total; Austria 548 km, GDR 459 km, Hungary 676 km, Poland 1,309 km, USSR 98 km, FRG 356 km
Coastline: none—landlocked
Maritime claims: none—landlocked
Disputes: Nagymaros Dam dispute with Hungary
Climate: temperate; cool summers; cold, cloudy, humid winters
Terrain: mixture of hills and mountains separated by plains and basins
Natural resources: coal, timber, lignite, uranium, magnesite, iron ore, copper, zinc
Land use: 40% arable land; 1% permanent crops; 13% meadows and pastures; 37% forest and woodland; 9% other; includes 1% irrigated
Environment: infrequent earthquakes; acid rain; water pollution; air pollution
Note: landlocked; strategically located astride some of oldest and most significant land routes in Europe; Moravian Gate is a traditional military corridor between the North European Plain and the Danube in central Europe

People

Population: 15,683,234 (July 1990), growth rate 0.3% (1990)
Birth rate: 14 births/1,000 population (1990)
Death rate: 11 deaths/1,000 population (1990)
Net migration rate: NEGL migrants/ 1,000 population (1990)
Infant mortality rate: 11 deaths/1,000 live births (1990)
Life expectancy at birth: 69 years male, 76 years female (1990)

Total fertility rate: 2.0 children born/ woman (1990)
Nationality: noun—Czechoslovak(s); adjective—Czechoslovak
Ethnic divisions: 64.3% Czech, 30.5% Slovak, 3.8% Hungarian, 0.4% German, 0.4% Polish, 0.3% Ukrainian, 0.1% Russian, 0.2% other (Jewish, Gypsy)
Religion: 50% Roman Catholic, 20% Protestant, 2% Orthodox, 28% other
Language: Czech and Slovak (official), Hungarian
Literacy: 99%
Labor force: 8,200,000 (1987); 36.9% industry, 12.3% agriculture, 50.8% construction, communications, and other (1982)
Organized labor: Revolutionary Trade Union Movement (ROH), formerly regime-controlled; other industry-specific strike committees; new independent trade unions forming

Government

Long-form name: Czechoslovak Socialist Republic; abbreviated CSSR; note—on 23 March 1990 the name was changed to Czechosovak Federative Republic; because of Slovak concerns about their status in the Federation, the Federal Assembly approved the name Czech and Slovak Federative Republic on 20 April 1990
Type: in transition from Communist state to republic
Capital: Prague
Administrative divisions: 2 socialist republics (socialistické republiky, singular—socialistická republika); Česká Socialistická Republika, Slovenská Socialistická Republika
Independence: 18 October 1918 (from Austro-Hungarian Empire)
Constitution: 11 July 1960; amended in 1968 and 1970; new constitution under review (1 January 1990)
Legal system: civil law system based on Austro-Hungarian codes, modified by Communist legal theory; no judicial review of legislative acts; has not accepted compulsory ICJ jurisdiction
National holiday: National Holiday of the Republic (Anniversary of the Liberation), 9 May (1945)
Executive branch: president, prime minister, Cabinet
Legislative branch: bicameral Federal Assembly (Federální Shromáždění) consists of an upper house or House of Nations (Sněmovna Národu) and a lower house or House of the People (Sněmovna Lidu)
Judicial branch: Supreme Court
Leaders: *Chief of State*—President Vaclav HAVEL (since 28 December 1989); *Head of Government*—Premier Marián CALFA (since 10 December 1989); First Deputy Premier Valtr KOMAREK (since

7 December 1989); Jan
CARNOGURSKY (since 7 December
1989)

Political parties and leaders: Civic Forum,
since December 1989 leading political
force, loose coalition of former opposition-
ists headed by President Vaclav Havel;
Communist Party of Czechoslovakia
(KSC), Ladislav Adamec, chairman (since
20 December 1989); KSC toppled from
power in November 1989 by massive anti-
regime demonstrations, minority role in
coalition government since 10 December
1989

Suffrage: universal at age 18

Elections: *President*—last held 22 May
1985 (next to be held 8 June 1990; will be
a free election); results—Gustáv Husak
was reelected without opposition;
Federal Assembly—last held 23 and 24
May 1986 (next to be held 8 June 1990;
will be a free election); results—KSC was
the only party; seats—(350 total) KSC
350

Communists: 1.71 million party members
(April 1988) and falling

Other political groups: Czechoslovak Socialist Party, Czechoslovak People's Party,
Slovak Freedom Party, Slovak Revival
Party, Christian Democratic Party; more
than 40 political groups are expected to
field candidates for the 8 June 1990 election

Member of: CCC, CEMA, FAO, GATT,
IAEA, IBEC, ICAO, ICO, ILO, ILZSG,
IMO, IPU, ISO, ITC, ITU, UN,
UNESCO, UPU, Warsaw Pact, WFTU,
WHO, WIPO, WMO, WSG, WTO

Diplomatic representation: Ambassador
Rita KLIMOVA; Chancery at 3900 Lin-
nean Avenue NW, Washington DC
20008; telephone (202) 363-6315 or 6316;
US—Ambassador Shirley Temple
BLACK; Embassy at Trziste 15-12548,
Prague (mailing address is APO New
York 09213); telephone [42] (2) 53 6641
through 6649

Flag: two equal horizontal bands of white
(top) and red with a blue isosceles triangle
based on the hoist side

Economy

Overview: Czechoslovakia is highly industrialized and has a well-educated and
skilled labor force. Its industry, transport,
energy sources, banking, and most other
means of production are state owned. The
country is deficient, however, in energy
and many raw materials. Moreover, its
aging capital plant lags well behind West
European standards. Industry contributes
over 50% to GNP and construction 10%.
About 95% of agricultural land is in col-
lectives or state farms. The centrally
planned economy has been tightly linked
in trade (80%) to the USSR and Eastern
Europe. Growth has been sluggish, averaging less than 2% in the period 1982-89.
GNP per capita ranks next to the GDR as
the highest in the Communist countries.
As in the rest of Eastern Europe, the
sweeping political changes of 1989 have
been disrupting normal channels of supply
and compounding the government's economic problems. Czechoslovakia is beginning the difficult transition from a command to a market economy.

GNP: $123.2 billion, per capita $7,878;
real growth rate 1.0% (1989 est.)

Inflation rate (consumer prices): 1.5%
(1989)

Unemployment rate: 0.9% (1987)

Budget: revenues $22.4 billion; expendi-
tures $21.9 billion, including capital ex-
penditures of $3.7 billion (1986 state bud-
get)

Exports: $24.5 billion (f.o.b., 1988); *com-
modities*—machinery and equipment
58.5%; industrial consumer goods 15.2%;
fuels, minerals, and metals 10.6%; agricultural and forestry products 6.1%, other
products 15.2%; *partners*—USSR, GDR,
Poland, Hungary, FRG, Yugoslavia, Austria, Bulgaria, Romania, US

Imports: $23.5 billion (f.o.b., 1988); *com-
modities*—machinery and equipment
41.6%; fuels, minerals, and metals 32.2%;
agricultural and forestry products 11.5%;
industrial consumer goods 6.7%; other
products 8.0%; *partners*—USSR, GDR,
Poland, Hungary, FRG, Yugoslavia, Austria, Bulgaria, Romania, US

External debt: $7.4 billion, hard currency
indebtedness (1989)

Industrial production: growth rate 2.1%
(1988)

Electricity: 22,955,000 kW capacity;
85,000 million kWh produced, 5,410 kWh
per capita (1989)

Industries: iron and steel, machinery and
equipment, cement, sheet glass, motor vehicles, armaments, chemicals, ceramics,
wood, paper products, footwear

Agriculture: accounts for 15% of GNP
(includes forestry); largely self-sufficient in
food production; diversified crop and livestock production, including grains, potatoes, sugar beets, hops, fruit, hogs, cattle,
and poultry; exporter of forest products

Aid: donor—$4.2 billion in bilateral aid to
non-Communist less developed countries
(1954-88)

Currency: koruna (plural—koruny); 1 koruna (Kč) = 100 haleřu

Exchange rates: koruny (Kčs) per US$1—
17.00 (March 1990), 10.00 (1989), 5.63
(1988), 5.43 (1987), 5.95 (1986), 6.79
(1985), 6.65 (1984)

Fiscal year: calendar year

Communications

Railroads: 13,116 km total; 12,868 km
1.435-meter standard gauge, 102 km
1.524-meter broad gauge, 146 km 0.750-
and 0.760-meter narrow gauge; 2,854 km
double track; 3,530 km electrified; government owned (1986)

Highways: 73,805 km total; including 489
km superhighway (1986)

Inland waterways: 475 km (1986); the Elbe
(Labe) is the principal river

Pipelines: crude oil, 1,448 km; refined
products, 1,500 km; natural gas, 8,000 km

Ports: maritime outlets are in Poland
(Gdynia, Gdansk, Szczecin), Yugoslavia
(Rijeka, Koper), FRG (Hamburg), GDR
(Rostock); principal river ports are Prague
on the Vltava, Děčín on the Elbe (Labe),
Komárno on the Danube, Bratislava on
the Danube

Merchant marine: 21 ships (1,000 GRT or
over) totaling 208,471 GRT/ 308,072
DWT; includes 15 cargo, 6 bulk

Civil air: 40 major transport aircraft

Airports: 158 total, 158 usable; 40 with
permanent-surface runways; 19 with runways 2,440-3,659 m; 37 with runways
1,220-2,439 m

Telecommunications: stations—58 AM, 16
FM, 45 TV; 14 Soviet TV relays;
4,360,000 TV sets; 4,208,538 radio receivers; at least 1 satellite earth station

Defense Forces

Branches: Czechoslovak People's Army,
Frontier Guard, Air and Air Defense
Forces

Military manpower: males 15-49,
4,019,311; 3,076,735 fit for military service; 137,733 reach military age (18) annually

Defense expenditures: 28.4 billion koruny,
7% of total budget (1989); note—conversion of the military budget into US dollars
using the official administratively set exchange rate would produce misleading
results

Denmark

Skagerrak

100 km

Faroe Islands and Greenland are separate entries.

Skagen

Ålborg

Kattegat

Århus

COPENHAGEN

Esbjerg

Sjælland

Fyn

Bornholm

Odense

Åbenrå

Møn

Baltic Sea

Lolland

Falster

See regional map V

Geography

Total area: 43,070 km²; land area: 42,370 km²; includes the island of Bornholm in the Baltic Sea and the rest of metropolitan Denmark, but excludes the Faroe Islands and Greenland
Comparative area: slightly more than twice the size of Massachusetts
Land boundaries: 68 km with FRG
Coastline: 3,379 km
Maritime claims:
Contiguous zone: 4 nm
Continental shelf: 200 meters or to depth of exploitation
Exclusive fishing zone: 200 nm
Territorial sea: 3 nm
Disputes: Rockall continental shelf dispute involving Iceland, Ireland, and the UK (Ireland and the UK have signed a boundary agreement in the Rockall area); Denmark has challenged Norway's maritime claims between Greenland and Jan Mayen
Climate: temperate; humid and overcast; mild, windy winters and cool summers
Terrain: low and flat to gently rolling plains
Natural resources: crude oil, natural gas, fish, salt, limestone
Land use: 61% arable land; NEGL% permanent crops; 6% meadows and pastures; 12% forest and woodland; 21% other; includes 9% irrigated
Environment: air and water pollution
Note: controls Danish Straits linking Baltic and North Seas

People

Population: 5,131,217 (July 1990), growth rate NEGL% (1990)
Birth rate: 12 births/1,000 population (1990)
Death rate: 11 deaths/1,000 population (1990)
Net migration rate: NEGL migrants/1,000 population (1990)

Infant mortality rate: 6 deaths/1,000 live births (1990)
Life expectancy at birth: 73 years male, 79 years female (1990)
Total fertility rate: 1.6 children born/woman (1990)
Nationality: noun—Dane(s); adjective—Danish
Ethnic divisions: Scandinavian, Eskimo, Faroese, German
Religion: 97% Evangelical Lutheran, 2% other Protestant and Roman Catholic, 1% other
Language: Danish, Faroese, Greenlandic (an Eskimo dialect); small German-speaking minority
Literacy: 99%
Labor force: 2,760,000; 51% services, 34% industry, 8% government, 7% agriculture, forestry, and fishing (1988)
Organized labor: 65% of labor force

Government

Long-form name: Kingdom of Denmark
Type: constitutional monarchy
Capital: Copenhagen
Administrative divisions: metropolitan Denmark—14 counties (amter, singular—amt) and 1 city* (stad); Århus, Bornholm, Frederiksborg, Fyn, København, Nordjylland, Ribe, Ringkøbing, Roskilde, Sønderjylland, Staden København*, Storstrøm, Vejle, Vestsjaelland, Viborg; note—see separate entries for the Faroe Islands and Greenland which are part of the Danish realm and self-governing administrative divisions
Independence: became a constitutional monarchy in 1849
Constitution: 5 June 1953
Legal system: civil law system; judicial review of legislative acts; accepts compulsory ICJ jurisdiction, with reservations
National holiday: Birthday of the Queen, 16 April (1940)
Executive branch: monarch, heir apparent, prime minister, Cabinet
Legislative branch: unicameral Parliament (Folketing)
Judicial branch: Supreme Court
Leaders: *Chief of State*—Queen MARGRETHE II (since January 1972); Heir Apparent Crown Prince FREDERIK, elder son of the Queen (born 26 May 1968); *Head of Government*—Prime Minister Poul SCHLÜTER (since 10 September 1982)
Political parties and leaders: Social Democratic, Svend Auken; Liberal, Uffe Ellemann-Jensen; Conservative, Poul Schlüter; Radical Liberal, Niels Helveg Petersen; Socialist People's, Gert Petersen; Communist, Ole Sohn; Left Socialist, Elizabeth Brun Olesen; Center Democratic, Mimi Stilling Jakobsen; Christian Peo-

ple's, Flemming Kofoed-Svendsen; Justice, Poul Gerhard Kristiansen; Progress Party, Aage Brusgaard; Socialist Workers Party, leader NA; Communist Workers' Party (KAP); Common Course, Preben Møller Hansen; Green Party, Inger Borlehmann
Suffrage: universal at age 21
Elections: *Parliament*—last held 10 May 1988 (next to be held by May 1992); results—Social Democratic 29.9%, Conservative 19.3%, Socialist People's 13.0%, Liberal 11.8%, Radical Liberal 9.0%, Center Democratic 5.6%, Christian People's 2.0%, Common Course 2.7%, other 6.7%; seats—(175 total; includes 2 from Greenland and 2 from the Faroe Islands) Social Democratic 55, Conservative 35, Socialist People's 24, Liberal 22, Progress 16, Radical Liberal 10, Center Democratic 9, Christian People's 4
Member of: ADB, CCC, Council of Europe, DAC, EC, EMS, ESA, FAO, GATT, IAEA, IBRD, ICAC, ICAO, ICES, ICO, IDA, IDB, Inter-American Development Bank, IEA, IFAD, IFC, IHO, ILO, ILZSG, IMF, IMO, INTELSAT, INTERPOL, IPU, ISO, ITC, ITU, IWC—International Wheat Council, NATO, Nordic Council, OECD, UN, UNESCO, UPU, WHO, WIPO, WMO, WSG
Diplomatic representation: Ambassador Peter Pedersen DYVIG; Chancery at 3200 Whitehaven Street NW, Washington DC 20008; telephone (202) 234-4300; there are Danish Consulates General at Chicago, Houston, Los Angeles, and New York; *US*—Ambassador Keith L. BROWN; Embassy at Dag Hammarskjolds Alle 24, 2100 Copenhagen O (mailing address is APO New York 09170); telephone [45] (31) 42 31 44
Flag: red with a white cross that extends to the edges of the flag; the vertical part of the cross is shifted to the hoist side and that design element of the *Dannebrog* (Danish flag) was subsequently adopted by the other Nordic countries of Finland, Iceland, Norway, and Sweden

Economy

Overview: This modern economy features high-tech agriculture, up-to-date small-scale and corporate industry, extensive government welfare measures, comfortable living standards, and high dependence on foreign trade. Growth in output, however, has been sluggish in 1987-89, and unemployment in early 1989 stood at 9.6% of the labor force. The government is trying to revitalize growth in preparation for the economic integration of Europe in 1992.
GDP: $73.7 billion, per capita $14,300; real growth rate 1.4% (1989 est.)

Denmark (continued)

Inflation rate (consumer prices): 4.25% (1989 est.)
Unemployment rate: 9.6% (1989)
Budget: revenues $34 billion; expenditures $34 billion, including capital expenditures of $19 billion (1988)
Exports: $27.7 billion (f.o.b., 1989 est.); *commodities*—meat and meat products, dairy products, transport equipment, fish, chemicals, industrial machinery; *partners*—US 6.0%, FRG, Norway, Sweden, UK, other EC, Japan
Imports: $26.4 billion (c.i.f., 1989 est.); *commodities*—petroleum, machinery and equipment, chemicals, grain and foodstuffs, textiles, paper; *partners*—US 7.0%, FRG, Netherlands, Sweden, UK, other EC
External debt: $41.1 billion (1989 est.)
Industrial production: growth rate 0.9% (1988)
Electricity: 11,215,000 kW capacity; 30,910 million kWh produced, 6,030 kWh per capita (1989)
Industries: food processing, machinery and equipment, textiles and clothing, chemical products, electronics, construction, furniture, and other wood products
Agriculture: accounts for 7% of GNP and employs 1.8% of labor force (includes fishing); farm products account for nearly 16% of export revenues; principal products—meat, dairy, grain, potatoes, rape, sugar beets, fish; self-sufficient in food production
Aid: donor—ODA and OOF commitments (1970-87) $4.8 billion
Currency: Danish krone (plural—kroner); 1 Danish krone (DKr) = 100 øre
Exchange rates: Danish kroner (DKr) per US$1—6.560 (January 1990), 7.310 (1989), 6.732 (1988), 6.840 (1987), 8.091 (1986), 10.596 (1985)
Fiscal year: calendar year

Communications

Railroads: 2,675 km 1.435-meter standard gauge; Danish State Railways (DSB) operate 2,025 km (1,999 km rail line and 121 km rail ferry services); 188 km electrified, 730 km double tracked; 650 km of standard-gauge lines are privately owned and operated
Highways: 66,482 km total; 64,551 km concrete, bitumen, or stone block; 1,931 km gravel, crushed stone, improved earth
Inland waterways: 417 km
Pipelines: crude oil, 110 km; refined products, 578 km; natural gas, 700 km
Ports: Ålborg, Århus, Copenhagen, Esbjerg, Fredericia; numerous secondary and minor ports
Merchant marine: 252 ships (1,000 GRT or over) totaling 4,498,611 GRT/ 6,711,011 DWT; includes 12 short-sea passenger, 82 cargo, 15 refrigerated cargo, 28 container, 36 roll-on/roll-off cargo, 1 railcar carrier, 37 petroleum, oils, and lubricants (POL) tanker, 13 chemical tanker, 12 liquefied gas, 4 livestock carrier, 12 bulk; note—Denmark has created a captive register called the Danish International Ship Register (DIS) as its own internal register; DIS ships do not have to meet Danish manning regulations, and they amount to a flag of convenience within the Danish register; by the end of 1990, most Danish flag ships will belong to the DIS
Civil air: 58 major transport aircraft
Airports: 130 total, 114 usable; 27 with permanent-surface runways; none with runways over 3,659 m; 9 with runways 2,440-3,659 m; 6 with runways 1,220-2,439 m
Telecommunications: excellent telephone, telegraph, and broadcast services; 4,237,000 telephones; stations—2 AM, 15 (39 repeaters) FM, 27 (25 repeaters) TV stations; 7 submarine coaxial cables; 1 satellite earth station operating in INTELSAT, 4 Atlantic Ocean, EUTELSAT, and domestic systems

---

Defense Forces

Branches: Royal Danish Army, Royal Danish Navy, Royal Danish Air Force
Military manpower: males 15-49, 1,368,013; 1,180,865 fit for military service; 37,228 reach military age (20) annually
Defense expenditures: 2.1% of GDP, or $1.5 billion (1989 est.)

Djibouti

50 km

See regional map VII

Geography

Total area: 22,000 km²; land area: 21,980 km²
Comparative area: slightly larger than Massachusetts
Land boundaries: 517 km total; Ethiopia 459 km, Somalia 58 km
Coastline: 314 km
Maritime claims:
Contiguous zone: 24 nm
Extended economic zone: 200 nm
Territorial sea: 12 nm
Disputes: possible claim by Somalia based on unification of ethnic Somalis
Climate: desert; torrid, dry
Terrain: coastal plain and plateau separated by central mountains
Natural resources: geothermal areas
Land use: 0% arable land; 0% permanent crops; 9% meadows and pastures; NEGL% forest and woodland; 91% other
Environment: vast wasteland
Note: strategic location near world's busiest shipping lanes and close to Arabian oilfields; terminus of rail traffic into Ethiopia

---

People

Population: 337,386 (July 1990), growth rate 2.6% (1990)
Birth rate: 43 births/1,000 population (1990)
Death rate: 17 deaths/1,000 population (1990)
Net migration rate: 0 migrants/1,000 population (1990)
Infant mortality rate: 119 deaths/1,000 live births (1990)
Life expectancy at birth: 46 years male, 49 years female (1990)
Total fertility rate: 6.4 children born/ woman (1990)
Nationality: noun—Djiboutian(s); adjective—Djiboutian

Ethnic divisions: 60% Somali (Issa); 35% Afar, 5% French, Arab, Ethiopian, and Italian

Religion: 94% Muslim, 6% Christian

Language: French (official); Arabic, Somali, and Afar widely used

Literacy: 20%

Labor force: NA, but a small number of semiskilled laborers at the port and 3,000 railway workers; 52% of population of working age (1983)

Organized labor: 3,000 railway workers

Government

Long-form name: Republic of Djibouti

Type: republic

Capital: Djibouti

Administrative divisions: 5 districts (cercles, singular—cercle); 'Ali Sahîh, Dikhil, Djibouti, Obock, Tadjoura

Independence: 27 June 1977 (from France; formerly French Territory of the Afars and Issas)

Constitution: partial constitution ratified January 1981 by the Chamber of Deputies

Legal system: based on French civil law system, traditional practices, and Islamic law

National holiday: Independence Day, 27 June (1977)

Executive branch: president, prime minister, Council of Ministers

Legislative branch: Chamber of Deputies (Chambre des Députés)

Judicial branch: Supreme Court (Cour Suprême)

Leaders: *Chief of State*—President Hassan GOULED Aptidon (since 24 June 1977);

Head of Government—Prime Minister Barkat GOURAD Hamadou (since 30 September 1978)

Political parties and leaders: only party—People's Progress Assembly (RPP), Hassan Gouled Aptidon

Suffrage: universal adult at age NA

Elections: *President*—last held 24 April 1987 (next to be held April 1993); results—President Hassan Gouled Aptidon was reelected without opposition; *Chamber of Deputies*—last held 24 April 1987 (next to be held April 1992); results—RPP is the only party; seats—(65 total) RPP 65

Communists: NA

Member of: ACP, AfDB, Arab League, FAO, G-77, IBRD, ICAO, IDA, IDB—Islamic Development Bank, IFAD, IFC, ILO, IMF, IMO, INTERPOL, ITU, NAM, OAU, OIC, UN, UPU, WFTU, WHO, WMO

Diplomatic representation: Ambassador Roble OLHAYE; Chancery (temporary) at the Djiboutian Permanent Mission to the UN; 866 United Nations Plaza, Suite 4011, New York, NY 10017; telephone (212) 753-3163; *US*—Ambassador Robert S. BARRETT IV; Embassy at Villa Plateau du Serpent Boulevard, Marechal Joffre, Djibouti (mailing address is B. P. 185, Djibouti); telephone [253] 35-38-49 or 35-39-95, 35-29-16, 35-29-17

Flag: two equal horizontal bands of light blue (top) and light green with a white isosceles triangle based on the hoist side bearing a red five-pointed star in the center

---

Economy

Overview: The economy is based on service activities connected with the country's strategic location and status as a free trade zone. Djibouti provides services as both a transit port for the region and an international transshipment and refueling center. It has few natural resources and little industry. The nation is, therefore, heavily dependent on foreign assistance to help support its balance of payments and to finance development projects. An unemployment rate of over 50% continues to be a major problem.

GNP: $333 million, $1,070 per capita; real growth rate −0.7% (1986)

Inflation rate (consumer prices): 8.0% (1987)

Unemployment rate: over 50% (1987)

Budget: revenues $117 million; expenditures $163 billion, including capital expenditures of $52 million (1987 est.)

Exports: $128 million (f.o.b., 1986); *commodities*—hides and skins, coffee (in transit); *partners*—Middle East 50%, Africa 43%, Western Europe 7%

Imports: $198 million (f.o.b., 1986); *commodities*—foods, beverages, transport equipment, chemicals, petroleum products; *partners*—EC 36%, Africa 21%, Bahrain 14%, Asia 12%, US 2%

External debt: $250 million (December 1988)

Industrial production: growth rate −1.6% (1986)

Electricity: 110,000 kW capacity; 190 million kWh produced, 580 kWh per capita (1989)

Industries: limited to a few small-scale enterprises, such as dairy products and mineral-water bottling

Agriculture: accounts for 30% of GDP; scanty rainfall limits crop production to mostly fruit and vegetables; half of population pastoral nomads herding goats, sheep, and camels; imports bulk of food needs

Aid: US commitments, including Ex-Im (FY78-88), $36 million; Western (non-US) countries, including ODA and OOF bilateral commitments (1970-87), $962 million; OPEC bilateral aid (1979-89), $149 million; Communist countries (1970-88), $35 million

Currency: Djiboutian franc (plural—francs); 1 Djiboutian franc (DF) = 100 centimes

Exchange rates: Djiboutian francs (DF) per US$1—177.721 (fixed rate since 1973)

Fiscal year: calendar year

Communications

Railroads: the Ethiopian-Djibouti railroad extends for 97 km through Djibouti

Highways: 2,900 km total; 280 km bituminous surface, 2,620 km improved or unimproved earth (1982)

Ports: Djibouti

Civil air: 2 major transport aircraft

Airports: 12 total, 9 usable; none with runways over 3,659 m; 1 with permanent-surface runways; 1 with runways 2,440-3,659 m; 4 with runways 1,220-2,439 m

Telecommunications: fair system of urban facilities in Djibouti and radio relay stations at outlying places; 7,300 telephones; stations—2 AM, 1 FM, 2 TV; 1 Indian Ocean INTELSAT earth station and 1 ARABSAT; 1 submarine cable to Saudi Arabia

---

Defense Forces

Branches: Army, Navy, Air Force; paramilitary National Security Force

Military manpower: males 15-49, 88,132; 51,260 fit for military service

Defense expenditures: $29.9 million, 23% of central government budget (1986)

Dominica

See regional map III

Geography

Total area: 750 km²; land area: 750 km²
Comparative area: slightly more than four times the size of Washington, DC
Land boundaries: none
Coastline: 148 km
Maritime claims:
Contiguous zone: 24 nm
Extended economic zone: 200 nm
Territorial sea: 12 nm
Climate: tropical; moderated by northeast trade winds; heavy rainfall
Terrain: rugged mountains of volcanic origin
Natural resources: timber
Land use: 9% arable land; 13% permanent crops; 3% meadows and pastures; 41% forest and woodland; 34% other
Environment: flash floods a constant hazard; occasional hurricanes
Note: located 550 km southeast of Puerto Rico in the Caribbean Sea

People

Population: 84,854 (July 1990), growth rate 1.7% (1990)
Birth rate: 26 births/1,000 population (1990)
Death rate: 5 deaths/1,000 population (1990)
Net migration rate: −4 migrants/1,000 population (1990)
Infant mortality rate: 13 deaths/1,000 live births (1990)
Life expectancy at birth: 73 years male, 79 years female (1990)
Total fertility rate: 2.6 children born/woman (1990)
Nationality: noun—Dominican(s); adjective—Dominican
Ethnic divisions: mostly black; some Carib indians
Religion: 80% Roman Catholic; Anglican, Methodist

Language: English (official); French patois widely spoken
Literacy: 80% (est.)
Labor force: 25,000; 40% agriculture, 32% industry and commerce, 28% services (1984)
Organized labor: 25% of labor force

Government

Long-form name: Commonwealth of Dominica
Type: parliamentary democracy
Capital: Roseau
Administrative divisions: 10 parishes; Saint Andrew, Saint David, Saint George, Saint John, Saint Joseph, Saint Luke, Saint Mark, Saint Patrick, Saint Paul, Saint Peter
Independence: 3 November 1978 (from UK)
Constitution: 3 November 1978
Legal system: based on English common law
National holiday: Independence Day, 3 November (1978)
Executive branch: president, prime minister, Cabinet
Legislative branch: unicameral House of Assembly (includes 9 appointed senators and 21 elected representatives)
Judicial branch: Eastern Caribbean Supreme Court
Leaders: *Chief of State*—President Sir Clarence Augustus SEIGNORET (since 19 December 1983);
Head of Government—Prime Minister (Mary) Eugenia CHARLES (since 21 July 1980)
Political parties and leaders: Dominica Freedom Party (DFP), (Mary) Eugenia Charles; Labor Party of Dominica (LPD, a leftist-dominated coalition), Michael Douglas; United Workers Party (UWP), Edison James
Suffrage: universal at age 18
Elections: *President*—last held 20 December 1988 (next to be held December 1993); the president is elected by the House of Assembly;
House of Assembly—last held 1 July 1985 (next to be held July 1990); results—percent of vote by party NA; seats—(21 total) DFP 17, LPD 4
Communists: negligible
Other political or pressure groups: Dominica Liberation Movement (DLM), a small leftist group
Member of: ACP, CARICOM, Commonwealth, FAO, GATT (de facto), G-77, IBRD, IDA, IFAD, IFC, ILO, IMF, IMO, INTERPOL, OAS, OECS, UN, UNESCO, UPU, WHO, WMO
Diplomatic representation: there is no Chancery in the US; *US*—no official pres-

ence since the Ambassador resides in Bridgetown (Barbados), but travels frequently to Dominica
Flag: green with a centered cross of three equal bands—the vertical part is yellow (hoist side), black, and white—the horizontal part is yellow (top), black, and white; superimposed in the center of the cross is a red disk bearing a sisserou parrot encircled by 10 green five-pointed stars edged in yellow; the 10 stars represent the 10 administrative divisions (parishes)

Economy

Overview: The economy is dependent on agriculture and thus is highly vulnerable to climatic conditions. Agriculture accounts for about 30% of GDP and employs 40% of the labor force. Principal products include bananas, coconuts, citrus, and root crops. In 1988 the economy achieved a 5.6% growth in real GDP on the strength of a boost in construction, higher agricultural production, and growth of the small manufacturing sector based on soap and garment industries. The tourist industry remains undeveloped because of a rugged coastline and the lack of an international-class airport.
GDP: $137 million, per capita $1,408; real growth rate 5.6% (1988 est.)
Inflation rate (consumer prices): 4.9% (1987)
Unemployment rate: 10% (1989 est.)
Budget: revenues $60 million; expenditures $52 million, including capital expenditures of $18 million (FY88)
Exports: $46 million (f.o.b., 1987); *commodities*—bananas, coconuts, grapefruit, soap, galvanized sheets; *partners*—UK 72%, Jamaica 10%, OECS 6%, US 3%, other 9%
Imports: $66.0 million (c.i.f., 1987); *commodities*—food, oils and fats, chemicals, fuels and lubricants, manufactured goods, machinery and equipment; *partners*—US 23%, UK 18%, CARICOM 15%, OECS 15%, Japan 5%, Canada 3%, other 21%
External debt: $63.6 million (December 1987)
Industrial production: growth rate 5.9% in manufacturing (1987)
Electricity: 7,000 kW capacity; 16 million kWh produced, 190 kWh per capita (1989)
Industries: agricultural processing, tourism, soap and other coconut-based products, cigars, pumice mining
Agriculture: accounts for 30% of GDP; principal crops—bananas, citrus fruit, coconuts, root crops; bananas provide the bulk of export earnings; forestry and fisheries potential not exploited

Dominican Republic

See regional map III

See regional map III

Aid: Western (non-US) countries, ODA and OOF bilateral commitments (1970-87), $109 million
Currency: East Caribbean dollar (plural—dollars); 1 EC dollar (EC$) = 100 cents
Exchange rates: East Caribbean dollars (EC$) per US$1—2.70 (fixed rate since 1976)
Fiscal year: 1 July-30 June

Communications

Highways: 750 km total; 370 km paved, 380 km gravel and earth
Ports: Roseau, Portsmouth
Civil air: NA
Airports: 2 total, 2 usable; 2 with permanent-surface runways; none with runways over 2,439 m; 1 with runways 1,220-2,439 m
Telecommunications: 4,600 telephones in fully automatic network; VHF and UHF link to St. Lucia; new SHF links to Martinique and Guadeloupe; stations—3 AM, 2 FM, 1 cable TV

Defense Forces

Branches: Commonwealth of Dominica Police Force
Military manpower: NA
Defense expenditures: NA

Geography

Total area: 48,730 km²; land area: 48,380 km²
Comparative area: slightly more than twice the size of New Hampshire
Land boundary 275 km with Haiti
Coastline: 1,288 km
Maritime claims:
Contiguous zone: 24 nm
Continental shelf: outer edge of continental margin or 200 nm
Extended economic zone: 200 nm
Territorial sea: 6 nm
Climate: tropical maritime; little seasonal temperature variation
Terrain: rugged highlands and mountains with fertile valleys interspersed
Natural resources: nickel, bauxite, gold, silver
Land use: 23% arable land; 7% permanent crops; 43% meadows and pastures; 13% forest and woodland; 14% other; includes 4% irrigated
Environment: subject to occasional hurricanes (July to October); deforestation
Note: shares island of Hispaniola with Haiti (western one-third is Haiti, eastern two-thirds is the Dominican Republic)

People

Population: 7,240,793 (July 1990), growth rate 2.0% (1990)
Birth rate: 28 births/1,000 population (1990)
Death rate: 7 deaths/1,000 population (1990)
Net migration rate: −1 migrant/1,000 population (1990)
Infant mortality rate: 62 deaths/1,000 live births (1990)
Life expectancy at birth: 65 years male, 69 years female (1990)
Total fertility rate: 3.2 children born/woman (1990)

Nationality: noun—Dominican(s); adjective—Dominican
Ethnic divisions: 73% mixed, 16% white, 11% black
Religion: 95% Roman Catholic
Language: Spanish
Literacy: 74%
Labor force: 2,300,000-2,600,000; 49% agriculture, 33% services, 18% industry (1986)
Organized labor: 12% of labor force (1989 est.)

Government

Long-form name: Dominican Republic (no short-form name)
Type: republic
Capital: Santo Domingo
Administrative divisions: 29 provinces (provincias, singular—provincia) and 1 district* (distrito); Azua, Baoruco, Barahona, Dajabón, Distrito Nacional*, Duarte, Elías Piña, El Seibo, Espaillat, Hato Mayor, Independencia, La Altagracia, La Romana, La Vega, María Trinidad Sánchez, Monseñor Nouel, Monte Cristi, Monte Plata, Pedernales, Peravia, Puerto Plata, Salcedo, Samaná, Sánchez Ramírez, San Cristóbal, San Juan, San Pedro De Macorís, Santiago, Santiago Rodríguez, Valverde
Independence: 27 February 1844 (from Haiti)
Constitution: 28 November 1966
Legal system: based on French civil codes
National holiday: Independence Day, 27 February (1844)
Executive branch: president, vice president, Cabinet
Legislative branch: bicameral National Congress (Congreso Nacional) consists of an upper chamber or Senate (Senado) and lower chamber or Chamber of Deputies (Cámara de Diputados)
Judicial branch: Supreme Court (Corte Suprema)
Leaders: *Chief of State and Head of Government*—President Joaquín BALAGUER Ricardo (since 16 August 1986); Vice President Carlos A. MORALES Troncoso (since 16 August 1986)
Political parties and leaders:
Major parties—Social Christian Reformist Party (PRSC), Joaquín Balaguer Ricardo; Dominican Revolutionary Party (PRD), which fractured in May 1989 with the understanding that leading rivals Jacobo Majluta and José Francisco Peña Gómez would run separately for president at the head of the Independent Revolutionary Party (PRI) and the Social Democratic Institutional Bloc (BIS), respectively, and try to reconstitute the PRD after the election; Dominican Liberation Party (PLD), Juan Bosch Gaviño;

Dominican Republic *(continued)*

Minor parties—National Veterans and Civilian Party (PNVC), Juan Rene Beauchanps Javier; The Structure (LE), Andres Van Der Horst; Democratic Quisqueyan Party (PQD), Elías Wessín Chavez; Constitutional Action Party (PAC), Luis Arzeno Rodríguez; National Progressive Force (FNP), Marino Vinicio Castillo; Popular Christian Party (PPC), Rogelio Delgado Bogaert; Dominican Communist Party (PCD), Narciso Isa Conde; Anti-Imperialist Patriotic Union (UPA), Iván Rodríguez; in 1983 several leftist parties, including the PCD, joined to form the Dominican Leftist Front (FID); however, they still retain individual party structures
Suffrage: universal and compulsory at age 18 or if married; members of the armed forces and police cannot vote
Elections: *President*—last held 16 May 1986 (next to be held May 1990); results—Joaquín Balaguer (PRSC) 41.8%, Jacobo Majluta (PRD) 39.7%, Juan Bosch Gaviño (PLD) 18.5%; *Senate*—last held 16 May 1986 (next to be held May 1990); results—percent of vote by party NA; seats—(30 total) PRSC 21, PRD 7, PLD 2; *Chamber of Deputies*—last held 16 May 1986 (next to be held May 1990); results—PRSC 40.6%, PRD 33.5%, PLD 18.3%, LE 5.3%, other 2.3%; seats—(120 total) PRSC 56, PRD 48, PLD 16
Communists: an estimated 8,000 to 10,000 members in several legal and illegal factions; effectiveness limited by ideological differences and organizational inadequacies
Member of: FAO, G-77, GATT, IADB, IAEA, IBA, IBRD, ICAO, ICO, IDA, IDB—Inter-American Development Bank, IFAD, IFC, IHO, ILO, IMF, IMO, INTELSAT, INTERPOL, IOOC, IRC, ISO, ITU, OAS, PAHO, SELA, UN, UNESCO, UPU, WFTU, WHO, WMO, WTO
Diplomatic representation: Ambassador Carlos A. MORALES Troncoso (serves concurrently as Vice President); Chancery at 1715 22nd Street NW, Washington DC 20008; telephone (202) 332-6280; there are Dominican Consulates General in Boston, Chicago, Los Angeles, Mayaguez (Puerto Rico), Miami, New Orleans, New York, Philadelphia, San Juan (Puerto Rico), and Consulates in Charlotte Amalie (Virgin Islands), Detroit, Houston, Jacksonville, Minneapolis, Mobile, Ponce (Puerto Rico), and San Francisco; *US*—Ambassador Paul D. TAYLOR; Embassy at the corner of Calle César Nicolás Penson and Calle Leopoldo Navarro, Santo Domingo (mailing address is APO Miami 34041-0008); telephone [809] 541-2171
Flag: a centered white cross that extends to the edges, divides the flag into four

rectangles—the top ones are blue (hoist side) and red, the bottom ones are red (hoist side) and blue; a small coat of arms is at the center of the cross

---

Economy

Overview: The economy is largely dependent on the agricultural sector, which employs 50% of the labor force and provides about half of export revenues. The principal commercial crop is sugarcane, followed by coffee, cocoa, and tobacco. Industry is based on the processing of agricultural products, durable consumer goods, minerals, and chemicals. Rapid growth of free trade zones has established a significant expansion of manufacturing for export, especially wearing apparel. Over the past decade tourism has also increased in importance and is a significant earner of foreign exchange and a source of new jobs. Unemployment is officially reported at about 25%, but underemployment may be much higher.
GDP: $5.1 billion, per capita $790; real growth rate 0.5% (1988)
Inflation rate (consumer prices): 57.6% (1988)
Unemployment rate: 25% (1988)
Budget: revenues $413 million; expenditures $522 million, including capital expenditures of $218 million (1988)
Exports: $711 million (f.o.b., 1988); *commodities*—sugar, coffee, cocoa, gold, ferronickel; *partners*—US, including Puerto Rico, 74%
Imports: $1.8 billion (c.i.f., 1988); *commodities*—foodstuffs, petroleum, cotton and fabrics, chemicals and pharmaceuticals; *partners*—US, including Puerto Rico, 37% (1985)
External debt: $3.6 billion (1989) est.
Industrial production: growth rate 30% (1987 est.)
Electricity: 1,376,000 kW capacity; 4,000 million kWh produced, 560 kWh per capita (1989)
Industries: tourism, sugar processing, ferronickel and gold mining, textiles, cement, tobacco
Agriculture: accounts for 18% of GDP and employs 49% of labor force; sugarcane most important commercial crop, followed by coffee, cotton, and cocoa; food crops—rice, beans, potatoes, corn, bananas; animal output—cattle, hogs, dairy products, meat, eggs; not self-sufficient in food
Aid: US commitments, including Ex-Im (FY70-88), $1.1 billion; Western (non-US) countries, ODA and OOF bilateral commitments (1970-87), $529 million
Currency: Dominican peso (plural—pesos); 1 Dominican peso (RD$) = 100 centavos
Exchange rates: Dominican pesos per US$1—6.3400 (January 1990), 6.3400

(1989), 6.1125 (1988), 3.8448 (1987), 2.9043 (1986), 3.1126 (1985)
Fiscal year: calendar year

Communications

Railroads: 1,655 km total in numerous segments; 4 different gauges from 0.558 m to 1.435 m
Highways: 12,000 km total; 5,800 km paved, 5,600 km gravel and improved earth, 600 km unimproved
Pipelines: crude oil, 96 km; refined products, 8 km
Ports: Santo Domingo, Haina, San Pedro de Macoris, Puerto Plata
Merchant marine: 4 cargo ships (1,000 GRT or over) totaling 23,335 GRT/40,297 DWT
Civil air: 14 major transport aircraft
Airports: 44 total, 30 usable; 14 with permanent-surface runways; none with runways over 3,659 m; 3 with runways 2,440-3,659 m; 9 with runways 1,220-2,439 m
Telecommunications: relatively efficient domestic system based on islandwide radio relay network; 190,000 telephones; stations—120 AM, no FM, 18 TV, 6 shortwave; 1 coaxial submarine cable; 1 Atlantic Ocean INTELSAT earth station

---

Defense Forces

Branches: Army, Navy, Air Force
Military manpower: males 15-49, 1,912,101; 1,210,172 fit for military service; 80,290 reach military age (18) annually
Defense expenditures: 1.2% of GDP, or $61 million (1989 est.)

Ecuador

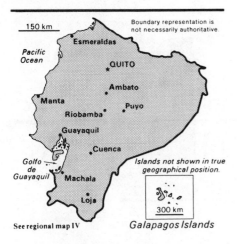

150 km

Boundary representation is not necessarily authoritative.

Pacific Ocean

Esmeraldas

★ QUITO

Ambato

Manta

Riobamba • Puyo

Guayaquil

Cuenca

Golfo de Guayaquil

Machala

Loja

Islands not shown in true geographical position.

300 km

See regional map IV

Galapagos Islands

Geography

Total area: 283,560 km²; land area: 276,840 km²; includes Galapagos Islands
Comparative area: slightly smaller than Nevada
Land boundaries: 2,010 km total; Colombia 590 km, Peru 1,420 km
Coastline: 2,237 km
Maritime claims:
Continental shelf: 200 m
Territorial sea: 200 nm
Disputes: two sections of the boundary with Peru are in dispute
Climate: tropical along coast becoming cooler inland
Terrain: coastal plain (Costa), inter-Andean central highlands (Sierra), and flat to rolling eastern jungle (Oriente)
Natural resources: petroleum, fish, timber
Land use: 6% arable land; 3% permanent crops; 17% meadows and pastures; 51% forest and woodland; 23% other; includes 2% irrigated
Environment: subject to frequent earthquakes, landslides, volcanic activity; deforestation; desertification; soil erosion; periodic droughts
Note: Cotopaxi in Andes is highest active volcano in world

People

Population: 10,506,668 (July 1990), growth rate 2.3% (1990)
Birth rate: 30 births/1,000 population (1990)
Death rate: 7 deaths/1,000 population (1990)
Net migration rate: 0 migrants/1,000 population (1990)
Infant mortality rate: 61 deaths/1,000 live births (1990)
Life expectancy at birth: 64 years male, 68 years female (1990)
Total fertility rate: 3.8 children born/woman (1990)

Nationality: noun—Ecuadorian(s); adjective—Ecuadorian
Ethnic divisions: 55% mestizo (mixed Indian and Spanish), 25% Indian, 10% Spanish, 10% black
Religion: 95% Roman Catholic
Language: Spanish (official); Indian languages, especially Quechua
Literacy: 85% (1981)
Labor force: 2,800,000; 35% agriculture, 21% manufacturing, 16% commerce, 28% services and other activities (1982)
Organized labor: less than 15% of labor force

Government

Long-form name: Republic of Ecuador
Type: republic
Capital: Quito
Administrative divisions: 21 provinces (provincias, singular—provincia); Azuay, Bolívar, Cañar, Carchi, Chimborazo, Cotopaxi, El Oro, Esmeraldas, Galápagos, Guayas, Imbabura, Loja, Los Ríos, Manabí, Morona-Santiago, Napo, Pastaza, Pichincha, Sucúmbios, Tungurahua, Zamora-Chinchipe
Independence: 24 May 1822 (from Spain; Battle of Pichincha)
Constitution: 10 August 1979
Legal system: based on civil law system; has not accepted compulsory ICJ jurisdiction
National holiday: Independence Day, 10 August (1809, independence of Quito)
Executive branch: president, vice president, Cabinet
Legislative branch: unicameral Chamber of Representatives (Cámara de Representantes)
Judicial branch: Supreme Court (Corte Suprema)
Leaders: *Chief of State and Head of Government*—President Rodrigo BORJA Cevallos (since 10 August 1988); Vice President Luis PARODI Valverde (since 10 August 1988)
Political parties and leaders: *Right to center parties*—Social Christian Party (PSC), Camilio Ponce, president; Conservative Party (PC), José Terán Varea, director; Radical Liberal Party (PLR), Blasco Peñaherrera, director;
Centrist parties—Concentration of Popular Forces (CFP), Averroes Bucaram Saxida, director; Radical Alfarist Front (FRA), Cecilia Calderón de Castro, leader; People, Change, and Democracy (PCD), Aquiles Rigaíl Santisteván, director; Revolutionary Nationalist Party (PNR), Carlos Julio Arosemena Monroy, leader;
Center-left parties—Democratic Left (ID), President Rodrigo Borja, leader; Roldosist Party of Ecuador (PRE), Abdala Buca-

ram, director; Popular Democracy (DP), Vladimiro Alvarez, leader; Christian Democratic (CD), Julio César Trujillo; Democratic Party (PD), Francisco Huerta Montalvo, leader;
Far-left parties—Broad Leftist Front (FADI), René Maugé Mosquera, director; Socialist Party (PSE), Víctor Granda Aguilar, secretary general; Democratic Popular Movement (MPD), Jaime Hurtado González, leader; Ecuadorian National Liberation (LN), Alfredo Castillo; Popular Revolutionary Action Party (APRE), Lt. Gen. Frank Vargas Pazzos, leader
Suffrage: universal at age 18; compulsory for literate persons ages 18-65, optional for other eligible voters
Elections: *President*—first round held 31 January 1988 and second round on 8 May 1988 (next first round to be held January 1992 and second round May 1992); results—Rodrigo Borja Cevallos (ID) 54%, Abdalá Bucaram Ortiz (PRE) 46%;
Chamber of Representatives—last held 31 January 1988 (next to be held June 1990); results—ID 42%, PSC 11%, PRE 11%, DP 9%, others 27%; seats—(71 total) ID 30, PRE 8, PSC 8, DP 7, CFP 6, PSE 4, FADI 2, MPD 2, FRA 2, PCE 1, PLR 1; note—with the addition of the new province of Sucúmbios there will be 72 seats in the August 1990 election
Communists: Communist Party of Ecuador (PCE, pro-Moscow), René Maugé Mosquera, secretary general, 5,000 members; Communist Party of Ecuador/Marxist Leninist (PCMLE, Maoist), 3,000 members; Socialist Party of Ecuador (PSE, pro-Cuba), 5,000 members (est.); National Liberation Party (PLN, Communist), 5,000 members (est.)
Member of: Andean Pact, ECOSOC, FAO, G-77, IADB, IAEA, IBRD, ICAO, ICO, IDA, IDB—Inter-American Development Bank, IFAD, IFC, IHO, ILO, IMF, IMO, INTELSAT, INTERPOL, IRC, ITU, LAIA, NAM, OAS, OPEC, PAHO, SELA, UN, UNESCO, UPEB, UPU, WFTU, WHO, WMO, WTO
Diplomatic representation: Ambassador Jaime MONCAYO; Chancery at 2535 15th Street NW, Washington DC 20009; telephone (202) 234-7200; there are Ecuadorian Consulates General in Chicago, Houston, Los Angeles, Miami, New Orleans, New York, and San Francisco, and a Consulate in San Diego; *US*—Ambassador-designate Paul C. LAMBERT; Embassy at Avenida Patria 120, on the corner of Avenida 12 de Octubre, Quito (mailing address is P. O. Box 538, Quito, or APO Miami 34039); telephone [593] (2) 562-890; there is a US Consulate General in Guayaquil

Ecuador (continued)

Flag: three horizontal bands of yellow (top, double width), blue, and red with the coat of arms superimposed at the center of the flag; similar to the flag of Colombia which is shorter and does not bear a coat of arms

Economy

Overview: Ecuador continues to recover from a 1986 drop in international oil prices and a major earthquake in 1987 that interrupted oil exports for six months and forced Ecuador to suspend foreign debt payments. In 1988-89 oil exports recovered—accounting for nearly half of Ecuador's total export revenues—and Quito resumed full interest payments on its official debt, and partial payments on its commercial debt. The Borja administration has pursued austere economic policies that have helped reduce inflation and restore international reserves. Ecuador was granted an IMF standby agreement worth $135 million in 1989, and Quito will seek to reschedule its foreign commercial debt in 1990.
GDP: $9.8 billion, per capita $935; real growth rate 0.5% (1989)
Inflation rate (consumer prices): 54% (1989)
Unemployment rate: 14.3% (1988)
Budget: revenues $2.2 billion; expenditures $2.7 billion, including capital expenditures of $601 million (1988 est.)
Exports: $2.2 billion (f.o.b., 1988); *commodities*—petroleum 47%, coffee, bananas, cocoa products, shrimp, fish products; *partners*—US 58%, Latin America, Caribbean, EC countries
Imports: $1.6 billion (f.o.b., 1988); *commodities*—transport equipment, vehicles, machinery, chemical, petroleum; *partners*—US 28%, Latin America, Caribbean, EC, Japan
External debt: $10.9 billion (1989)
Industrial production: growth rate 0.7% (1988)
Electricity: 1,953,000 kW capacity; 5,725 million kWh produced, 560 kWh per capita (1989)
Industries: food processing, textiles, chemicals, fishing, timber, petroleum
Agriculture: accounts for 18% of GDP and 35% of labor force (including fishing and forestry); leading producer and exporter of bananas and balsawood; other exports—coffee, cocoa, fish, shrimp; crop production—rice, potatoes, manioc, plantains, sugarcane; livestock sector—cattle, sheep, hogs, beef, pork, dairy products; net importer of foodgrain, dairy products, and sugar
Illicit drugs: relatively small producer of coca following the successful eradication campaign of 1985-87; significant transit country, however, for derivatives of coca originating in Colombia, Bolivia, and Peru
Aid: US commitments, including Ex-Im (FY70-88), $457 million; Western (non-US) countries, ODA and OOF bilateral commitments (1970-87), $1.4 billion; Communist countries (1970-88), $64 million
Currency: sucre (plural—sucres); 1 sucre (S/) = 100 centavos
Exchange rates: sucres (S/) per US$1— 526.35 (1989), 301.61 (1988), 170.46 (1987), 122.78 (1986), 69.56 (1985)
Fiscal year: calendar year

Communications

Railroads: 965 km total; all 1.067-meter-gauge single track
Highways: 28,000 km total; 3,600 km paved, 17,400 km gravel and improved earth, 7,000 km unimproved earth
Inland waterways: 1,500 km
Pipelines: crude oil, 800 km; refined products, 1,358 km
Ports: Guayaquil, Manta, Puerto Bolivar, Esmeraldas
Merchant marine: 47 ships (1,000 GRT or over) totaling 340,446 GRT/492,670 DWT; includes 1 passenger, 7 cargo, 17 refrigerated cargo, 2 container, 1 roll-on/ roll-off cargo, 16 petroleum, oils, and lubricants (POL) tanker, 1 chemical tanker, 1 liquefied gas, 1 bulk
Civil air: 44 major transport aircraft
Airports: 179 total, 178 usable; 43 with permanent-surface runways; 1 with runways over 3,659 m; 6 with runways 2,440-3,659 m; 20 with runways 1,220-2,439 m
Telecommunications: domestic facilities generally adequate; 318,000 telephones; stations—272 AM, no FM, 33 TV, 39 shortwave; 1 Atlantic Ocean INTELSAT earth station

Defense Forces

Branches: Ecuadorean Army (Ejercito Ecuatoriano), Ecuadorean Air Force (Fuerza Aerea Ecuatoriana), Ecuadorean Navy (Armada Ecuatoriana)
Military manpower: males 15-49, 2,635,543; 1,786,068 fit for military service; 114,976 reach military age (20) annually
Defense expenditures: 1% of GDP, or $100 million (1988 est.)

Egypt

See regional map VI and VII

Boundary representation is not necessarily authoritative.

Geography

Total area: 1,001,450 km²; land area: 995,450 km²
Comparative area: slightly more than three times the size of New Mexico
Land boundaries: 2,689 km total; Gaza Strip 11, Israel 255 km, Libya 1,150 km, Sudan 1,273 km
Coastline: 2,450 km
Maritime claims:
Contiguous zone: 24 nm
Continental shelf: 200 meters or to depth of exploitation
Extended economic zone: undefined
Territorial sea: 12 nm
Disputes: Administrative Boundary and international boundary with Sudan
Climate: desert; hot, dry summers with moderate winters
Terrain: vast desert plateau interrupted by Nile valley and delta
Natural resources: crude oil, natural gas, iron ore, phosphates, manganese, limestone, gypsum, talc, asbestos, lead, zinc
Land use: 3% arable land; 2% permanent crops; 0% meadows and pastures; NEGL% forest and woodland; 95% other; includes 5% irrigated
Environment: Nile is only perennial water source; increasing soil salinization below Aswan High Dam; hot, driving windstorm called khamsin occurs in spring; water pollution; desertification
Note: controls Sinai Peninsula, only land bridge between Africa and remainder of Eastern Hemisphere; controls Suez Canal, shortest sea link between Indian Ocean and Mediterranean; size and juxtaposition to Israel establish its major role in Middle Eastern geopolitics

People

Population: 54,705,746 (July 1990), growth rate 2.5% (1990)

Birth rate: 34 births/1,000 population (1990)
Death rate: 10 deaths/1,000 population (1990)
Net migration rate: NEGL migrants/ 1,000 population (1990)
Infant mortality rate: 90 deaths/1,000 live births (1990)
Life expectancy at birth: 60 years male, 61 years female (1990)
Total fertility rate: 4.7 children born/ woman (1990)
Nationality: noun—Egyptian(s); adjective—Egyptian
Ethnic divisions: 90% Eastern Hamitic stock; 10% Greek, Italian, Syro-Lebanese
Religion: (official estimate) 94% Muslim (mostly Sunni), 6% Coptic Christian and other
Language: Arabic (official); English and French widely understood by educated classes
Literacy: 45%
Labor force: 15,000,000 (1989 est.); 36% government, public sector enterprises, and armed forces; 34% agriculture; 20% privately owned service and manufacturing enterprises (1984); shortage of skilled labor; 2,500,000 Egyptians work abroad, mostly in Iraq and the Gulf Arab states (1988 est.)
Organized labor: 2,500,000 (est.)

Government

Long-form name: Arab Republic of Egypt
Type: republic
Capital: Cairo
Administrative divisions: 26 governorates (muḥāfaẓat, singular—muḥāfaẓah); Ad Daqahlīyah, Al Baḥr al Aḥmar, Al Buḥayrah, Al Fayyūm, Al Gharbīyah, Al Iskandarīyah, Al Ismā'īlīyah, Al Jīzah, Al Minūfiyah, Al Minyā, Al Qāhirah, Al Qalyūbīyah, Al Wādī al Jadīd, Ash Sharqīyah, As Suways, Aswān, Asyūṭ, Banī Suwayf, Būr Sa'īd, Dumyāṭ, Janūb Sīnā', Kafr ash Shaykh, Maṭrūḥ, Qinā, Shamal Sīnā', Sūhāj
Independence: 28 February 1922 (from UK); formerly United Arab Republic
Constitution: 11 September 1971
Legal system: based on English common law, Islamic law, and Napoleonic codes; judicial review by Supreme Court and Council of State (oversees validity of administrative decisions); accepts compulsory ICJ jurisdiction, with reservations
National holiday: Anniversary of the Revolution, 23 July (1952)
Executive branch: president, prime minister, Cabinet
Legislative branch: unicameral People's Assembly (Majlis al-Sha'ab); note—there is an Advisory Council (Majlis al-Shura) that functions in a consultative role

Judicial branch: Supreme Constitutional Court
Leaders: *Chief of State*—President Mohammed Hosni MUBARAK (was made acting President on 6 October 1981 upon the assassination of President Sadat and sworn in as President on 14 October 1981);
Head of Government—Prime Minister Atef Mohammed Najib SEDKY (since 12 November 1986)
Political parties and leaders: formation of political parties must be approved by government; National Democratic Party (NDP), President Mohammed Hosni Mubarak, leader, is the dominant party; legal opposition parties are Socialist Liberal Party (SLP), Kamal Murad; Socialist Labor Party, Ibrahim Shukri; National Progressive Unionist Grouping, Khalid Muhyi-al-Din; Umma Party, Ahmad al-Sabahi; and New Wafd Party (NWP), Fu'ad Siraj al-Din
Suffrage: universal and compulsory at age 18
Elections: *President*—last held 5 October 1987 (next to be held October 1993); results—President Hosni Mubarek was re-elected;
People's Assembly—last held 6 April 1987 (next to be held April 1992); results—NDP 69.3%, Socialist Labor Party Coalition 17%, NWP 10.9%; seats—(458 total, 448 elected)—NDP 346, Socialist Labor Party Coalition 60, Labor-Liberal-Muslim Brotherhood Alliance 60 (37 belong to the Muslim Brotherhood), NWP 36, independents 7;
Advisory Council (Majlis al-Shura)—last held October 1986 (next to be held October 1992); results—percent of vote by party NA; seats—(210 total, 140 elected)
Communists: about 500 party members
Other political or pressure groups: Islamic groups are illegal, but the largest one, the Muslim Brotherhood, is tolerated by the government and recently gained a sizable presence in the new People's Assembly; trade unions and professional associations are officially sanctioned
Member of: ACC, AfDB, Arab League, CCC, FAO, G-77, GATT, IAEA, IBRD, ICAC, ICAO, IDA, IDB—Islamic Development Bank, IFAD, IFC, IHO, ILO, IMF, IMO, INTELSAT, INTERPOL, IOOC, IPU, IRC, ITU, IWC—International Wheat Council, NAM, OAPEC, OAU, OIC, UN, UNESCO, UPU, WHO, WIPO, WMO, WSG, WTO; Egypt was suspended from Arab League and OAPEC in April 1979 and readmitted in May 1989
Diplomatic representation: Ambassador El Sayed Abdel Raouf EL REEDY; Chancery at 2310 Decatur Place NW, Washington DC 20008; telephone (202) 232-

5400; there are Egyptian Consulates General in Chicago, Houston, New York, and San Francisco; *US*—Ambassador Frank G. WISNER; Embassy at 5 Sharia Latin America, Garden City, Cairo (mailing address is FPO New York 09527); telephone [20] [2] 355-7371; there is a US Consulate General in Alexandria
Flag: three equal horizontal bands of red (top), white, and black with the national emblem (a shield superimposed on a golden eagle facing the hoist side above a scroll bearing the name of the country in Arabic) centered in the white band; similar to the flags of the YAR which has one star, Syria which has two stars, and Iraq which has three stars—all green and five-pointed in a horizontal line centered in the white band

Economy

Overview: Egypt has one of the largest public sectors of all the Third World economies, most industrial plants being owned by the government. Overregulation holds back technical modernization and foreign investment. Even so, the economy grew rapidly during the late 1970s and early 1980s, but in 1986 the collapse of world oil prices and an increasingly heavy burden of debt servicing led Egypt to begin negotiations with the IMF for balance-of-payments support. As part of the 1987 agreement with the IMF, the government agreed to institute a reform program to reduce inflation, promote economic growth, and improve its external position. The reforms have been slow in coming, however, and the economy has been largely stagnant for the past three years. With 1 million people being added every eight months to Egypt's population, urban growth exerts enormous pressure on the 5% of the total land area available for agriculture.
GDP: $38.3 billion, per capita $700; real growth rate 1.0% (1989 est.)
Inflation rate (consumer prices): 25% (1989 est.)
Unemployment rate: 15% (1989 est.)
Budget: revenues $7 billion; expenditures $11.5 billion, including capital expenditures of $4 billion (FY89 est.)
Exports: $2.55 billion (f.o.b., 1989); *commodities*—raw cotton, crude and refined petroleum, cotton yarn, textiles; *partners*—US, EC, Japan, Eastern Europe
Imports: $10.1 billion (c.i.f., 1988); *commodities*—foods, machinery and equipment, fertilizers, wood products, durable consumer goods, capital goods; *partners*—US, EC, Japan, Eastern Europe
External debt: $45 billion (December 1989)

Egypt (continued)

Industrial production: growth rate 2-4% (1989 est.)
Electricity: 11,273,000 kW capacity; 42,500 million kWh produced, 780 kWh per capita (1989)
Industries: textiles, food processing, tourism, chemicals, petroleum, construction, cement, metals
Agriculture: accounts for 20% of GNP and employs more than one-third of labor force; dependent on irrigation water from the Nile; world's fifth-largest cotton exporter; other crops produced include rice, corn, wheat, beans, fruit, vegetables; not self-sufficient in food; livestock—cattle, water buffalo, sheep, and goats; annual fish catch about 140,000 metric tons
Aid: US commitments, including Ex-Im (FY70-88), $14.7 billion; Western (non-US) countries, ODA and OOF bilateral commitments (1970-87), $7.8 billion; OPEC bilateral aid (1979-89), $2.9 billion; Communist countries (1970-88), $2.4 billion
Currency: Egyptian pound (plural—pounds); 1 Egyptian pound (Ė) = 100 piasters
Exchange rates: Egyptian pounds (Ė) per US$1—2.5790 (January 1990), 2.5171 (1989), 2.2128 (1988), 1.5015 (1987), 1.3503 (1986), 1.3010 (1985)
Fiscal year: 1 July-30 June

Communications

Railroads: 5,110 km total; 4,763 km 1,435-meter standard gauge, 347 km 0.750-meter gauge; 951 km double track; 25 km electrified
Highways: 51,925 km total; 17,900 km paved, 2,500 km gravel, 13,500 km improved earth, 18,025 km unimproved earth
Inland waterways: 3,500 km (including the Nile, Lake Nasser, Alexandria-Cairo Waterway, and numerous smaller canals in the delta); Suez Canal, 193.5 km long (including approaches), used by oceangoing vessels drawing up to 16.1 meters of water
Pipelines: crude oil, 1,171 km; refined products, 596 km; natural gas, 460 km
Ports: Alexandria, Port Said, Suez, Bur Safajah, Damietta
Merchant marine: 142 ships (1,000 GRT or over) totaling 1,141,799 GRT/ 1,754,181 DWT; includes 1 passenger, 7 short-sea passenger, 2 passenger-cargo, 88 cargo, 2 refrigerated cargo, 13 roll-on/ roll-off cargo, 14 petroleum, oils, and lubricants (POL) tanker, 15 bulk
Civil air: 43 major transport aircraft
Airports: 97 total, 87 usable; 67 with permanent-surface runways; 2 with runways over 3,659 m; 46 with runways 2,440-3,659 m; 21 with runways 1,220-2,439 m

Telecommunications: system is large but still inadequate for needs; principal centers are Alexandria, Cairo, Al Manşūrah, Ismailia, and Ţanţā; intercity connections by coaxial cable and microwave; extensive upgrading in progress; 600,000 telephones (est.); stations—25 AM, 5 FM, 47 TV; satellite earth stations—1 Atlantic Ocean INTELSAT, 1 Indian Ocean INTELSAT, 1 INMARSAT; 4 submarine coaxial cables; tropospheric scatter to Sudan; radio relay to Libya (may not be operational); new radio relay to Jordan

Defense Forces

Branches: Army, Navy, Air Force, Air Defense Command
Military manpower: males 15-49, 13,271,942; 8,642,075 fit for military service; 547,084 reach military age (20) annually
Defense expenditures: 7.2% of GDP, or $2.8 billion (FY90 est.)

El Salvador

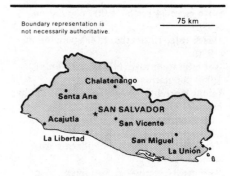

Boundary representation is not necessarily authoritative.

75 km

North Pacific Ocean

See regional map III

Geography

Total area: 21,040 km²; land area: 20,720 km²
Comparative area: slightly smaller than Massachusetts
Land boundaries: 545 km total; Guatemala 203 km, Honduras 342 km
Coastline: 307 km
Maritime claims:
 Territorial sea: 200 nm (overflight and navigation permitted beyond 12 nm)
Disputes: several sections of the boundary with Honduras are in dispute
Climate: tropical; rainy season (May to October); dry season (November to April)
Terrain: mostly mountains with narrow coastal belt and central plateau
Natural resources: hydropower and geothermal power, crude oil
Land use: 27% arable land; 8% permanent crops; 29% meadows and pastures; 6% forest and woodland; 30% other; includes 5% irrigated
Environment: The Land of Volcanoes; subject to frequent and sometimes very destructive earthquakes; deforestation; soil erosion; water pollution
Note: smallest Central American country and only one without a coastline on Caribbean Sea

People

Population: 5,309,865 (July 1990), growth rate 2.0% (1990)
Birth rate: 34 births/1,000 population (1990)
Death rate: 7 deaths/1,000 population (1990)
Net migration rate: −7 migrants/1,000 population (1990)
Infant mortality rate: 49 deaths/1,000 live births (1990)
Life expectancy at birth: 62 years male, 68 years female (1990)

Total fertility rate: 4.1 children born/woman (1990)

Nationality: noun—Salvadoran(s); adjective—Salvadoran

Ethnic divisions: 89% mestizo, 10% Indian, 1% white

Religion: about 97% Roman Catholic, with activity by Protestant groups throughout the country

Language: Spanish, Nahua (among some Indians)

Literacy: 65%

Labor force: 1,700,000 (1982 est.); 40% agriculture, 16% commerce, 15% manufacturing, 13% government, 9% financial services, 6% transportation; shortage of skilled labor and a large pool of unskilled labor, but manpower training programs improving situation (1984 est.)

Organized labor: 15% total labor force; 10% agricultural labor force; 7% urban labor force (1987 est.)

Government

Long-form name: Republic of El Salvador

Type: republic

Capital: San Salvador

Administrative divisions: 14 departments (departamentos, singular—departamento); Ahuachapán, Cabañas, Chalatenango, Cuscatlán, La Libertad, La Paz, La Unión, Morazán, San Miguel, San Salvador, Santa Ana, San Vicente, Sonsonate, Usulután

Independence: 15 September 1821 (from Spain)

Constitution: 20 December 1983

Legal system: based on civil and Roman law, with traces of common law; judicial review of legislative acts in the Supreme Court; accepts compulsory ICJ jurisdiction, with reservations

National holiday: Independence Day, 15 September (1821)

Executive branch: president, vice president, Council of Ministers (cabinet)

Legislative branch: unicameral Legislative Assembly (Asamblea Legislativa)

Judicial branch: Supreme Court (Corte Suprema)

Leaders: *Chief of State and Head of Government*—President Alfredo CRISTIANI (since 1 June 1989); Vice President José Francisco MERINO (since 1 June 1989)

Political parties and leaders: National Republican Alliance (ARENA), Armando Calderon Sol; Christian Democratic Party (PDC), José Antonio Morales Erlich; National Conciliation Party (PCN), Ciro Cruz Zepeda; Democratic Action (AD), Ricardo González Camacho; Salvadoran Authentic Institutional Party (PAISA), Roberto Escobar García; Patria Libre (PL), Hugo Barrera; Authentic Christian Movement (MAC), Julio Rey Prendes;

Salvadoran Popular Party (PPS), Francisco Quiñónez; Democratic Convergence (CD), a coalition composed of the Social Democratic Party (PSD), Mario René Roldan; the National Revolutionary Movement (MNR), Guillermo Ungo; and the Popular Social Christian Movement (MPSC), Ruben Zamora

Suffrage: universal at age 18

Elections: *President*—last held 19 March 1989 (next to be held March 1994); results—Alfredo Cristiani (ARENA) 53.8%, Fidel Chavez Mena (PDC) 36.6%, other 9.6%;

Legislative Assembly—last held 20 March 1988 (next to be held March 1991); results—percent of vote by party NA; seats—(60 total) ARENA 32, MAC 13, PDC 9, PCN 6

Other political or pressure groups:

Leftist revolutionary movement—Farabundo Martí National Liberation Front (FMLN), leadership body of the insurgency; Popular Liberation Forces (FPL), Armed Forces of National Resistance (FARN), People's Revolutionary Army (ERP), Salvadoran Communist Party/Armed Forces of Liberation (PCES/FAL), and Central American Workers' Revolutionary Party (PRTC)/Popular Liberation Revolutionary Armed Forces (FARLP);

Militant front organizations—Revolutionary Coordinator of Masses (CRM; alliance of front groups), Popular Revolutionary Bloc (BPR), Unified Popular Action Front (FAPU), Popular Leagues of 28 February (LP-28), National Democratic Union (UDN), and Popular Liberation Movement (MLP); Revolutionary Democratic Front (FDR), coalition of CRM and Democratic Front (FD); FD consists of moderate leftist groups—Independent Movement of Professionals and Technicians of El Salvador (MIPTES), National Revolutionary Movement (MNR), and Popular Social Christian Movement (MPSC);

Extreme rightist vigilante organizations—Anti-Communist Army (ESA); Maximiliano Hernández Brigade; Organization for Liberation From Communism (OLC);

Labor organizations—Federation of Construction and Transport Workers Unions (FESINCONSTRANS), independent; Salvadoran Communal Union (UCS), peasant association; Unitary Federation of Salvadoran Unions (FUSS), leftist; National Federation of Salvadoran Workers (FENASTRAS), leftist; Democratic Workers Central (CTD), moderate; General Confederation of Workers (CGT), moderate; Popular Democratic Unity (UPD), moderate labor coalition which includes FESINCONSTRANS, and other democratic labor organizations; National Unity of Salvadoran Workers (UNTS), leftist; Na-

tional Union of Workers and Peasants (UNOC), moderate labor coalition of democratic labor organizations;

Business organizations—National Association of Private Enterprise (ANEP), conservative; Productive Alliance (AP), conservative; National Federation of Salvadoran Small Businessmen (FENAPES), conservative

Member of: CACM, FAO, G-77, IADB, IAEA, IBRD, ICAC, ICAO, ICO, IDA, IDB—Inter-American Development Bank, IFAD, IFC, ILO, IMF, IMO, INTELSAT, INTERPOL, ITU, IWC—International Wheat Council, OAS, ODECA, PAHO, SELA, UN, UNESCO, UPU, WFTU, WHO, WIPO, WMO, WTO

Diplomatic representation: Ambassador Miguel Angel SALAVERRIA; Chancery at 2308 California Street NW, Washington DC 20008; telephone (202) 265-3480 through 3482; there are Salvadoran Consulates General in Houston, Los Angeles, Miami, New Orleans, New York, and San Francisco, *US*—Ambassador William G. WALKER; Embassy at 25 Avenida Norte No. 1230, San Salvador (mailing address is APO Miami 34023); telephone [503] 26-7100

Flag: three equal horizontal bands of blue (top), white, and blue with the national coat of arms centered in the white band; the coat of arms features a round emblem encircled by the words *REPUBLICA DE EL SALVADOR EN LA AMERICA CENTRAL*; similar to the flag of Nicaragua which has a different coat of arms centered in the white band—it features a triangle encircled by the words *REPUBLICA DE NICARAGUA* on top and *AMERICA CENTRAL* on the bottom; also similar to the flag of Honduras which has five blue stars arranged in an *X* pattern centered in the white band

---

Economy

Overview: The economy experienced a modest recovery during the period 1983-86, after a sharp decline in the early 1980s. Real GDP grew by 1.5% a year on the strength of value added by the manufacturing and service sectors. In 1987 the economy expanded by 2.5% as agricultural output recovered from the 1986 drought. The agricultural sector accounts for 25% of GDP, employs about 40% of the labor force, and contributes about 66% to total exports. Coffee is the major commercial crop, contributing 60% to export earnings. The manufacturing sector, based largely on food and beverage processing, accounts for 17% of GDP and 16% of employment. Economic losses due to guerrilla sabotage total more than $2.0

El Salvador (continued)

billion since 1979. The costs of maintaining a large military seriously constrain the government's ability to provide essential social services.
GDP: $5.5 billion, per capita $1,020 (1988); real growth rate 0.9% (1989 est.)
Inflation rate (consumer prices): 16.8% (September 1989)
Unemployment rate: 10% (1989)
Budget: revenues $688 million; expenditures $725 million, including capital expenditures of $112 million (1988)
Exports: $497 million (f.o.b., 1989); *commodities*—coffee 60%, sugar, cotton, shrimp; *partners*—US 49%, FRG 24%, Guatemala 7%, Costa Rica 4%, Japan 4%
Imports: $1.1 billion (c.i.f., 1989); *commodities*—petroleum products, consumer goods, foodstuffs, machinery, construction materials, fertilizer; partners—US 40%, Guatemala 12%, Venezuela 7%, Mexico 7%, FRG 5%, Japan 4%
External debt: $1.7 billion (December 1989)
Industrial production: growth rate 2.9% (1989)
Electricity: 669,000 kW capacity; 1,813 million kWh produced, 350 kWh per capita (1989)
Industries: food processing, textiles, clothing, petroleum products, cement
Agriculture: accounts for 25% of GDP and 40% of labor force (including fishing and forestry); coffee most important commercial crop; other products—sugarcane, corn, rice, beans, oilseeds, beef, dairy products, shrimp; not self-sufficient in food
Aid: US commitments, including Ex-Im (FY70-88), $2.4 billion; Western (non-US) countries, ODA and OOF bilateral commitments (1970-87), $353 million
Currency: Salvadoran colón (plural—colones); 1 Salvadoran colón (C) = 100 centavos
Exchange rates: Salvadoran colones (C) per US$1—5.0000 (fixed rate since 1986)
Fiscal year: calendar year

Communications

Railroads: 602 km 0.914-meter gauge, single track
Highways: 10,000 km total; 1,500 km paved, 4,100 km gravel, 4,400 km improved and unimproved earth
Inland waterways: Río Lempa partially navigable
Ports: Acajutla, Cutuco
Civil air: 7 major transport aircraft
Airports: 125 total, 84 usable; 6 with permanent-surface runways; none with runways over 3,659 m; 1 with runways 2,440-3,659 m; 5 with runways 1,220-2,439 m

Telecommunications: nationwide trunk radio relay system; connection into Central American Microwave System; 116,000 telephones; stations—77 AM, no FM, 5 TV, 2 shortwave; 1 Atlantic Ocean INTELSAT earth station

Defense Forces

Branches: Army, Navy, Air Force, National Guard, National Police, Treasury Police
Military manpower: males 15-49, 1,180,751; 754,350 fit for military service; 68,805 reach military age (18) annually
Defense expenditures: 4% of GDP, or $220 million (1990 est.)

Equatorial Guinea

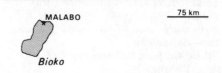

See regional map VII

Geography

Total area: 28,050 km²; land area: 28,050 km²
Comparative area: slightly larger than Maryland
Land boundaries: 539 km total; Cameroon 189 km, Gabon 350 km
Coastline: 296 km
Maritime claims:
  Exclusive economic zone: 200 nm
  Territorial sea: 12 nm
Disputes: maritime boundary dispute with Gabon
Climate: tropical; always hot, humid
Terrain: coastal plains rise to interior hills; islands are volcanic
Natural resources: timber, crude oil, small unexploited deposits of gold, manganese, uranium
Land use: 8% arable land; 4% permanent crops; 4% meadows and pastures; 51% forest and woodland; 33% other
Environment: subject to violent windstorms
Note: insular and continental regions rather widely separated

People

Population: 368,935 (July 1990), growth rate 2.6% (1990)
Birth rate: 43 births/1,000 population (1990)
Death rate: 16 deaths/1,000 population (1990)
Net migration rate: 0 migrants/1,000 population (1990)
Infant mortality rate: 118 deaths/1,000 live births (1990)
Life expectancy at birth: 48 years male, 52 years female (1990)
Total fertility rate: 5.5 children born/woman (1990)
Nationality: noun—Equatorial Guinean(s) or Equatoguinean(s); adjective—Equatorial Guinean or Equatoguinean

Ethnic divisions: indigenous population of Bioko, primarily Bubi, some Fernandinos; Rio Muni, primarily Fang; less than 1,000 Europeans, mostly Spanish

Religion: natives all nominally Christian and predominantly Roman Catholic; some pagan practices retained

Language: Spanish (official), pidgin English, Fang, Bubi, Ibo

Literacy: 40%

Labor force: 172,000 (1986 est.); 66% agriculture, 23% services, 11% industry (1980); labor shortages on plantations; 58% of population of working age (1985)

Organized labor: no formal trade unions

Government

Long-form name: Republic of Equatorial Guinea

Type: republic

Capital: Malabo

Administrative divisions: 2 provinces (provincias, singular—provincia); Bioko, Rio Muni; note—there may now be 6 provinces named Bioko Norte, Bioko Sur, Centro Sur, Kié-Ntem, Litoral, Wele Nzas

Independence: 12 October 1968 (from Spain; formerly Spanish Guinea)

Constitution: 15 August 1982

Legal system: in transition; partly based on Spanish civil law and tribal custom

National holiday: Independence Day, 12 October (1968)

Executive branch: president, prime minister, deputy prime minister, Council of Ministers (cabinet)

Legislative branch: unicameral Chamber of People's Representatives (Cámara de Representantes del Pueblo)

Judicial branch: Supreme Tribunal

Leaders: *Chief of State*—President Brig. Gen. Teodoro OBIANG NGUEMA MBASOGO (since 3 August 1979); *Head of Government*—Prime Minister Cristino SERICHE Bioko Malabo (since 15 August 1982); Deputy Prime Minister Isidoro Eyi Monsuy Andeme (since 15 August 1989)

Political parties and leaders: only party—Democratic Party for Equatorial Guinea (PDEG), Obiang Nguema Mbasogo, party leader

Suffrage: universal adult at age NA

Elections: *President*—last held 25 June 1989 (next to be held 25 June 1996); results—President Brig. Gen. Obiang Nguema Mbasogo was reelected without opposition; *Chamber of Deputies*—last held 10 July 1988 (next to be held 10 July 1993); results—PDEG is the only party; seats—(41 total) PDEG 41

Communists: no significant number but some sympathizers

Member of: ACP, AfDB, Conference of East and Central African States, ECA, FAO, G-77, GATT (de facto), IBRD, ICAO, ICO, IDA, IFAD, IFC, ILO, IMF, IMO, INTERPOL, IPU, ITU, NAM, OAU, UN, UNESCO, UPU, WHO

Diplomatic representation: Ambassador Damaso OBIANG NDONG; Chancery at 801 Second Avenue, Suite 1403, New York, NY 10017; telephone (212) 599-1523; *US*—Ambassador Chester E. NORRIS, Jr.; Embassy at Calle de Los Ministros, Malabo (mailing address is P. O. Box 597, Malabo); telephone 2406 or 2507

Flag: three equal horizontal bands of green (top), white, and red with a blue isosceles triangle based on the hoist side and the coat of arms centered in the white band; the coat of arms has six yellow six-pointed stars (representing the mainland and five offshore islands) above a gray shield bearing a silk-cotton tree and below which is a scroll with the motto *UNIDAD, PAZ, JUSTICIA* (Unity, Peace, Justice)

Economy

Overview: The economy, destroyed during the regime of former President Macías Nguema, is now based on agriculture, forestry, and fishing, which account for about 60% of GNP and nearly all exports. Subsistence agriculture predominates, with cocoa, coffee, and wood products providing income, foreign exchange, and government revenues. There is little industry. Commerce accounts for about 10% of GNP, and the construction, public works, and service sectors for about 34%. Undeveloped natural resources include titanium, iron ore, manganese, uranium, and alluvial gold. Oil exploration is taking place under concessions offered to US, French, and Spanish firms.

GNP: $103 million, per capita $293; real growth rate NA% (1987)

Inflation rate (consumer prices): −6.0% (1988 est.)

Unemployment rate: NA%

Budget: revenues $23 million; expenditures $31 million, including capital expenditures of NA (1988)

Exports: $30 million (f.o.b., 1988 est.); *commodities*—coffee, timber, cocoa beans; partners—Spain 44%, FRG 19%, Italy 12%, Netherlands 11% (1987)

Imports: $50 million (c.i.f., 1988 est.); *commodities*—petroleum, food, beverages, clothing, machinery; *partners*—Spain 34%, Italy 16%, France 14%, Netherlands 8% (1987)

External debt: $191 million (December 1988)

Industrial production: growth rate NA%

Electricity: 23,000 kW capacity; 60 million kWh produced, 170 kWh per capita (1989)

Industries: fishing, sawmilling

Agriculture: cash crops—timber and coffee from Rio Muni, cocoa from Bioko; food crops—rice, yams, cassava, bananas, oil palm nuts, manioc, livestock

Aid: US commitments, including Ex-Im (FY81-88), $11 million; Western (non-US) countries, ODA and OOF bilateral commitments (1970-87), $100 million; Communist countries (1970-88), $55 million

Currency: Communauté Financière Africaine franc (plural—francs); 1 CFA franc (CFAF) = 100 centimes

Exchange rates: Communauté Financière Africaine francs (CFAF) per US$1—287.99 (January 1990), 319.01 (1989), 297.85 (1988), 300.54 (1987), 346.30 (1986), 449.26 (1985)

Fiscal year: 1 April-31 March

Communications

Highways: Rio Muni—1,024 km; Bioko—216 km

Ports: Malabo, Bata

Merchant marine: 2 ships (1,000 GRT or over) totaling 6,413 GRT/6,699 DWT; includes 1 cargo and 1 passenger-cargo

Civil air: 1 major transport aircraft

Airports: 4 total, 3 usable; 2 with permanent-surface runways; none with runways over 3,659 m; 1 with runways 2,440-3,659 m; 1 with runways 1,220-2,439 m

Telecommunications: poor system with adequate government services; international communications from Bata and Malabo to African and European countries; 2,000 telephones; stations—2 AM, no FM, 1 TV; 1 Indian Ocean INTELSAT earth station

Defense Forces

Branches: Army, Navy, and possibly Air Force

Military manpower: males 15-49, 77,363; 39,174 fit for military service

Defense expenditures: 11% of GNP (FY81 est.)

Ethiopia

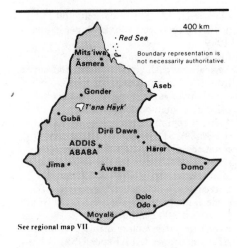

400 km

Boundary representation is not necessarily authoritative.

See regional map VII

Geography

Total area: 1,221,900 km²; land area: 1,101,000 km²
Comparative area: slightly less than twice the size of Texas
Land boundaries: 5,141 km total; Djibouti 459 km, Kenya 861 km, Somalia 1,600 km, Sudan 2,221 km
Coastline: 1,094 km
Maritime claims:
   Territorial sea: 12 nm
Disputes: southern half of the boundary with Somalia is a Provisional Administrative Line; possible claim by Somalia based on unification of ethnic Somalis; territorial dispute with Somalia over the Ogaden; separatist movement in Eritrea; antigovernment insurgencies in Tigray and other areas
Climate: tropical monsoon with wide topographic-induced variation; prone to extended droughts
Terrain: high plateau with central mountain range divided by Great Rift Valley
Natural resources: small reserves of gold, platinum, copper, potash
Land use: 12% arable land; 1% permanent crops; 41% meadows and pastures; 24% forest and woodland; 22% other; includes NEGL% irrigated
Environment: geologically active Great Rift Valley susceptible to earthquakes, volcanic eruptions; deforestation; overgrazing; soil erosion; desertification; frequent droughts; famine
Note: strategic geopolitical position along world's busiest shipping lanes and close to Arabian oilfields; major resettlement project ongoing in rural areas will significantly alter population distribution and settlement patterns over the next several decades

People

Population: 51,666,622 (July 1990), growth rate 3.5% (1990)
Birth rate: 45 births/1,000 population (1990)
Death rate: 15 deaths/1,000 population (1990)
Net migration rate: 5 migrants/1,000 population (1990)
Infant mortality rate: 116 deaths/1,000 live births (1990)
Life expectancy at birth: 49 years male, 52 years female (1990)
Total fertility rate: 7.0 children born/woman (1990)
Nationality: noun—Ethiopian(s); adjective—Ethiopian
Ethnic divisions: 40% Oromo, 32% Amhara and Tigrean, 9% Sidamo, 6% Shankella, 6% Somali, 4% Afar, 2% Gurage, 1% other
Religion: 40-45% Muslim, 35-40% Ethiopian Orthodox, 15-20% animist, 5% other
Language: Amharic (official), Tigrinya, Orominga, Arabic, English (major foreign language taught in schools)
Literacy: 55.2%
Labor force: 18,000,000; 80% agriculture and animal husbandry, 12% government and services, 8% industry and construction (1985)
Organized labor: All Ethiopian Trade Union formed by the government in January 1977 to represent 273,000 registered trade union members

Government

Long-form name: People's Democratic Republic of Ethiopia
Type: Communist state
Capital: Addis Ababa
Administrative divisions: 14 administrative regions (plural—NA, singular—kifle hāger); Ārsī, Balē, Eritrea, Gamo Gofa, Gojam, Gonder, Hārergē, Ilubabor, Kefa, Shewa, Sīdamo, Tigray, Welega, Welo; note—the administrative structure may be changing to 25 administrative regions (astedader akababiwach, singular—astedader akababee) and 5 autonomous regions* (rasgez akababiwach, singular—rasgez akababee); Addis Ababa, Ārsī, Āseb*, Asosa, Balē, Borena, Dirē Dawa*, East Gojam, East Hārergē, Eritrea*, Gambela, Gamo Gofa, Ilubabor, Kefa, Metekel, Nazaret, North Gonder, North Shewa, North Welo, Ogādēn*, Omo, Sīdamo, South Gonder, South Shewa, South Welo, Tigray*, Welega, West Gojam, West Hārergē, West Shewa
Independence: oldest independent country in Africa and one of the oldest in the world—at least 2,000 years
Constitution: 12 September 1987

Legal system: complex structure with civil, Islamic, common, and customary law influences; has not accepted compulsory ICJ jurisdiction
National holiday: National Revolution Day, 12 September (1974)
Executive branch: president, vice president, Council of State prime minister, five deputy prime ministers, Council of Ministers
Legislative branch: unicameral National Assembly (Shengo)
Judicial branch: Supreme Court
Leaders: *Chief of State*—President MENGISTU Haile-Mariam (Chairman from 11 September 1977 until becoming President on 10 September 1987); Vice President FISSEHA Desta (since 10 September 1987);
Head of Government—Prime Minister (Acting) and Deputy Prime Minister HAILU Yimenu (since 7 November 1989; Deputy Prime Minister WOLLE Chekol (since 21 November 1989); Deputy Prime Minister ALEMU Abebe (since 10 September 1987); Deputy Prime Minister TESFAYE Dinka (since 10 September 1987); Deputy Prime Minister ASHAGRE Yigletu (since 21 November 1989)
Political parties and leaders: only party—Workers' Party of Ethiopia (WPE), Mengistu Haile-Mariam, secretary general
Suffrage: universal at age 18
Elections: *President*—last held 10 September 1987 (next to be held September 1992); results—National Assembly elected President Mengistu Haile-Mariam; *National Assembly*—last held 14 June 1987 (next to be held June 1992); results—WPE is the only party; seats—(835 total) WPE 835
Other political or pressure groups: important dissident groups include Eritrean People's Liberation Front (EPLF) in Eritrea; Tigrean People's Liberation Front (TPLF) and Ethiopian Peoples Democratic Movement in Tigray, Welo, and border regions; Oromo Liberation Front in Welega and Hārergē regions
Member of: ACP, AfDB, CCC, ECA, FAO, G-77, IAEA, IBRD, ICO, ICAO, IDA, IFAD, IFC, ILO, IMF, IMO, INTELSAT, INTERPOL, IPU, ITU, NAM, OAU, UN, UNESCO, UPU, WFTU, WHO, WMO, WTO
Diplomatic representation: Counselor, Chargé d'Affaires ad interim GIRMA Amare; Chancery at 2134 Kalorama Road NW, Washington DC 20008; telephone (202) 234-2281 or 2282; *US*—Chargé d'Affaires Robert G. HOUDEK; Embassy at Entoto Street, Addis Ababa (mailing address is P.O. Box 1014, Addis Ababa); telephone 254-233-4141

Flag: three equal horizontal bands of green (top), yellow, and red; Ethiopia is the oldest independent country in Africa and the colors of her flag were so often adopted by other African countries upon independence that they became known as the pan-African colors

Economy

Overview: Ethiopia is one of the poorest and least developed countries in Africa. Its economy is based on subsistence agriculture, which accounts for about 45% of GDP, 90% of exports, and 80% of total employment; coffee generates over 60% of export earnings. The manufacturing sector is heavily dependent on inputs from the agricultural sector. The economy is centrally planned, and over 90% of large-scale industry is state run. Favorable agricultural weather largely explains the 4.5% growth in output in FY89.
GDP: $6.6 billion, per capita $130, real growth rate 4.5% (FY89 est.)
Inflation rate (consumer prices): 9.6% (FY89)
Unemployment rate: NA; shortage of skilled manpower
Budget: revenues $1.4 billion; expenditures $1.9 billion, including capital expenditures of $0.7 billion (FY87)
Exports: $418 million (f.o.b., FY88); *commodities*—coffee 60%, hides; *partners*—US, FRG, Djibouti, Japan, PDRY, France, Italy
Imports: $1.1 billion (c.i.f., FY88), *commodities*—food, fuels, capital goods; *partners*—USSR, Italy, FRG, Japan, UK, US, France
External debt: $2.6 billion (1988)
Industrial production: growth rate −0.2% (FY88 est.)
Electricity: 330,000 kW capacity; 700 million kWh produced, 14 kWh per capita (1989)
Industries: cement, textiles, food processing, oil refinery
Agriculture: accounts for 45% of GDP and is the most important sector of the economy even though frequent droughts, poor cultivation practices, and state economic policies keep farm output low; famines not uncommon; export crops of coffee and oilseeds grown partly on state farms; estimated 50% of agricultural production at subsistence level; principal crops and livestock—cereals, pulses, coffee, oilseeds, potatoes, sugarcane, vegetables, hides and skins, cattle, sheep, goats
Aid: US commitments, including Ex-Im (FY70-88), $471 million; Western (non-US) countries, ODA and OOF bilateral commitments (1970-87), $2.6 billion;

OPEC bilateral aid (1979-89), $8 million; Communist countries (1970-88), $2.0 billion
Currency: birr (plural—birr); 1 birr (Br) = 100 cents
Exchange rates: birr (Br) per US$1— 2.0700 (fixed rate)
Fiscal year: 8 July-7 July

Communications

Railroads: 988 km total; 681 km 1.000-meter gauge; 307 km 0.950-meter gauge (nonoperational)
Highways: 44,300 km total; 3,650 km bituminous, 9,650 km gravel, 3,000 km improved earth, 28,000 km unimproved earth
Ports: Aseb, Mitsiwa
Merchant marine: 14 ships (1,000 GRT or over) totaling 71,837 GRT/92,067 DWT; includes 10 cargo, 1 roll-on/roll off cargo, 1 livestock carrier, 2 petroleum, oils, and lubricants (POL) tanker
Civil air: 21 major transport aircraft
Airports: 152 total, 111 usable; 9 with permanent-surface runways; 2 with runways over 3,659 m; 10 with runways 2,440-3,659 m; 51 with runways 1,220-2,439 m
Telecommunications: open-wire and radio relay system adequate for government use; open-wire to Sudan and Djibouti; radio relay to Kenya and Djibouti; stations—4 AM, no FM, 1 TV; 45,000 TV sets; 3,300,000 radios; 1 Atlantic Ocean INTELSAT earth station

Defense Forces

Branches: Army, Navy, Air Force, Air Defense
Military manpower: males 15-49, 11,438,616; 5,922,555 fit for military service; 589,231 reach military age (18) annually
Defense expenditures: 8.5% of GDP (1988)

Europa Island
(French possession)

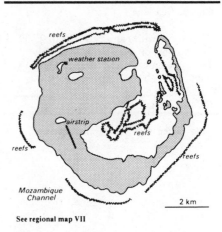

See regional map VII

Geography

Total area: 28 km²; land area: 28 km²
Comparative area: about 0.2 times the size of Washington, DC
Land boundaries: none
Coastline: 22.2 km
Maritime claims:
  Contiguous zone: 12 nm
  Continental shelf: 200 meters or to depth of exploitation
  Extended economic zone: 200 nm
  Territorial sea: 12 nm
Disputes: claimed by Madagascar
Climate: tropical
Terrain: NA
Natural resources: negligible
Land use: NA% arable land; NA% permanent crops; NA% meadows and pastures; NA% forest and woodland; NA% other; heavily wooded
Environment: wildlife sanctuary
Note: located in the Mozambique Channel 340 km west of Madagascar

People

Population: uninhabited

Government

Long-form name: none
Type: French possession administered by Commissioner of the Republic Daniel CONSTANTIN, resident in Reunion

Economy

Overview: no economic activity

Europa Island (continued)

Communications

Airports: 1 with runway 1,220 to 2,439 m
Ports: none; offshore anchorage only
Telecommunications: 1 meteorological station

Defense Forces

Note: defense is the responsibility of France

Falkland Islands
(Islas Malvinas)
(dependent territory of the UK)

Administered by U.K.,
claimed by Argentina

See regional map IV

Geography

Total area: 12,170 km²; land area: 12,170 km²; includes the two main islands of East and West Falkland and about 200 small islands
Comparative area: slightly smaller than Connecticut
Land boundaries: none
Coastline: 1,288 km
Maritime claims:
  Continental shelf: 100 meter depth
  Exclusive fishing zone: 150 nm
  Territorial sea: 12 nm
Disputes: administered by the UK, claimed by Argentina
Climate: cold marine; strong westerly winds, cloudy, humid; rain occurs on more than half of days in year; occasional snow all year, except in January and February, but does not accumulate
Terrain: rocky, hilly, mountainous with some boggy, undulating plains
Natural resources: fish and wildlife
Land use: 0% arable land; 0% permanent crops; 99% meadows and pastures; 0% forest and woodland; 1% other
Environment: poor soil fertility and a short growing season
Note: deeply indented coast provides good natural harbors

People

Population: 1,958 (July 1990), growth rate 0.5% (1990)
Birth rate: NA births/1,000 population (1990)
Death rate: NA deaths/1,000 population (1990)
Net migration rate: NA migrants/1,000 population (1990)
Infant mortality rate: NA deaths/1,000 live births (1990)
Life expectancy at birth: NA years male, NA years female (1990)

Total fertility rate: NA children born/woman (1990)
Nationality: noun—Falkland Islander(s); adjective—Falkland Island
Ethnic divisions: almost totally British
Religion: primarily Anglican, Roman Catholic, and United Free Church; Evangelist Church, Jehovah's Witnesses, Lutheran, Seventh-Day Adventist
Language: English
Literacy: NA%, but compulsory education up to age 15
Labor force: 1,100 (est.); about 95% in agriculture, mostly sheepherding
Organized labor: Falkland Islands General Employees Union, 400 members

Government

Long-form name: Colony of the Falkland Islands
Type: dependent territory of the UK
Capital: Stanley
Administrative divisions: none (dependent territory of the UK)
Independence: none (dependent territory of the UK)
Constitution: 3 October 1985
Legal system: English common law
National holiday: Liberation Day, 14 June (1982)
Executive branch: British monarch, governor, Executive Council
Legislative branch: unicameral Legislative Council
Judicial branch: Supreme Court
Leaders: *Chief of State*—Queen ELIZABETH II (since 6 February 1952);
Head of Government—Governor William Hugh FULLERTON (since NA 1988)
Political parties: NA
Suffrage: universal at age 18
Elections: *Legislative Council*—last held 3 October 1985 (next to be held October 1990); results—percent of vote by party NA; seats—(10 total, 8 elected) number of seats by party NA
Diplomatic representation: none (dependent territory of the UK)
Flag: blue with the flag of the UK in the upper hoist-side quadrant and the Falkland Island coat of arms in a white disk centered on the outer half of the flag; the coat of arms contains a white ram (sheep raising is the major economic activity) above the sailing ship Desire (whose crew discovered the islands) with a scroll at the bottom bearing the motto *DESIRE THE RIGHT*

Economy

Overview: The economy is based on sheep farming, which directly or indirectly employs most of the work force. A few dairy herds are kept to meet domestic consumption of milk and milk products, and crops grown are primarily those for providing winter fodder. Major sources of income are from the export of high-grade wool to the UK and the sale of stamps and coins. Rich stocks of fish in the surrounding waters are not presently exploited by the islanders, but development plans called for the islands to have six trawlers by 1989. In 1987 the government began to sell fishing licenses to foreign trawlers operating within the Falklands exclusive fishing zone. These license fees amount to more than $25 million per year. To encourage tourism, the Falkland Islands Development Corporation has built three lodges for visitors who are attracted by the abundant wildlife and trout fishing.

GNP: $NA, per capita $NA; real growth rate NA%

Inflation rate (consumer prices): NA%

Unemployment rate: 0%

Budget: revenues $11 million; expenditures $11.8 million, including capital expenditures of $1.2 million (FY87)

Exports: at least $14.7 million; *commodities*—wool, hides and skins, and other; *partners*—UK, Netherlands, Japan (1987 est.)

Imports: at least $13.9 million; *commodities*—food, clothing, fuels, and machinery; *partners*—UK, Netherlands Antilles (Curaçao), Japan (1987 est.)

External debt: $NA

Industrial production: growth rate NA%

Electricity: 9,200 kW capacity; 17 million kWh produced, 8,700 kWh per capita (1989)

Industries: wool processing

Agriculture: predominantly sheep farming; small dairy herds and fodder crops

Aid: Western (non-US) countries, ODA and OOF bilateral commitments (1970-87), $102 million

Currency: Falkland pound (plural—pounds); 1 Falkland pound (£F) = 100 pence

Exchange rates: Falkland pound (£F) per US$1—0.6055 (January 1990), 0.6099 (1989), 0.5614 (1988), 0.6102 (1987), 0.6817 (1986), 0.7714 (1985); note—the Falkland pound is at par with the British pound

Fiscal year: 1 April-31 March

Communications

Highways: 510 km total; 30 km paved, 80 km gravel, and 400 km unimproved earth

Ports: Port Stanley

Civil air: no major transport aircraft

Airports: 5 total, 5 usable; 2 with permanent-surface runways; none with runways over 3,659 m; 1 with runways 2,440-3,659 m; none with runways 1,220 to 2,439 m

Telecommunications: government-operated radiotelephone and private VHF/CB radio networks provide effective service to almost all points on both islands; 590 telephones; stations—2 AM, 3 FM, no TV; 1 Atlantic Ocean INTELSAT earth station with links through London to other countries

Defense Forces

Note: defense is the responsibility of the UK

Faroe Islands
(part of the Danish realm)

See regional map V

Geography

Total area: 1,400 km²; land area: 1,400 km²

Comparative area: slightly less than eight times the size of Washington, DC

Land boundaries: none

Coastline: 764 km

Maritime claims:
Contiguous zone: 4 nm
Continental shelf: 200 meters or to depth of exploitation
Exclusive fishing zone: 200 nm
Territorial sea: 3 nm

Climate: mild winters, cool summers; usually overcast; foggy, windy

Terrain: rugged, rocky, some low peaks; cliffs along most of coast

Natural resources: fish

Land use: 2% arable land; 0% permanent crops; 0% meadows and pastures; 0% forest and woodland; 98% other

Environment: precipitous terrain limits habitation to small coastal lowlands; archipelago of 18 inhabited islands and a few uninhabited islets

Note: strategically located along important sea lanes in northeastern Atlantic about midway between Iceland and Shetland Islands

People

Population: 47,715 (July 1990), growth rate 0.9% (1990)

Birth rate: 17 births/1,000 population (1990)

Death rate: 8 deaths/1,000 population (1990)

Net migration rate: 0 migrants/1,000 population (1990)

Infant mortality rate: 9 deaths/1,000 live births (1990)

Life expectancy at birth: 74 years male, 81 years female (1990)

Total fertility rate: 2.2 children born/woman (1990)

97

Faroe Islands (continued)

Nationality: noun—Faroese (sing., pl.); adjective—Faroese
Ethnic divisions: homogeneous Scandinavian population
Religion: Evangelical Lutheran
Language: Faroese (derived from Old Norse), Danish
Literacy: 99%
Labor force: 17,585; largely engaged in fishing, manufacturing, transportation, and commerce
Organized labor: NA

Government

Long-form name: none
Type: part of the Danish realm; self-governing overseas administrative division of Denmark
Capital: Tórshavn
Administrative divisions: none (self-governing overseas administrative division of Denmark)
Independence: part of the Danish realm; self-governing overseas administrative division of Denmark
Constitution: Danish
Legal system: Danish
National holiday: Birthday of the Queen, 16 April (1940)
Executive branch: Danish monarch, high commissioner, prime minister, deputy prime minister, Cabinet (Landsstýri)
Legislative branch: unicameral Parliament (Løgting)
Judicial branch: none
Leaders: *Chief of State*—Queen MARGRETHE II (since 14 January 1972), represented by High Commissioner Bent KLINTE (since NA);
Head of Government—Prime Minister Jógvan SUNDSTEIN (since 17 January 1989)
Political parties and leaders: *four-party ruling coalition*—People's Party, Jógvan Sundstein; Republican Party, Signer Hansen; Progressive and Fishing Industry Party combined with the Christian People's Party (CPP-PFIP); Home Rule Party, Hilmar Kass; *opposition*—Social Democratic Party, Atli P. Dam; Cooperation Coalition Party, Pauli Ellefsen; Progress Party
Suffrage: universal at age 20
Elections: *Parliament*—last held 8 November 1988 (next to be held November 1992); results—percent of vote by party NA; seats—(32 total) three-party coalition 21 (People's Party 8, Cooperation Coalition Party 7, Republican Party 6); Social Democrat 7, CPP-PFIP 2, Home Rule 2
Communists: insignificant number
Member of: Nordic Council
Diplomatic representation: none (self-governing overseas administrative division of Denmark)

Flag: white with a red cross outlined in blue that extends to the edges of the flag; the vertical part of the cross is shifted to the hoist side in the style of the *Dannebrog* (Danish flag)

Economy

Overview: The Faroese enjoy the high standard of living characteristic of the Danish and other Scandinavian economies. Fishing is the dominant economic activity. It employs over 25% of the labor force, accounts for about 25% of GDP, and contributes over 80% to export revenues. A handicraft industry employs about 20% of the labor force. Because of cool summers agricultural activities are limited to raising sheep and to potato and vegetable cultivation. There is a labor shortage, and immigrant workers accounted for 5% of the work force in 1989. Denmark annually subsidizes the economy, perhaps on the order of 15% of GDP.
GDP: $662 million, per capita $14,000; real growth rate 3% (1989 est.)
Inflation rate (consumer prices): 2.0% (1988)
Unemployment rate: labor shortage
Budget: revenues $176 million; expenditures $176 million, including capital expenditures of NA (FY86)
Exports: $267 million (f.o.b., 1986); *commodities*—fish and fish products 86%, animal feedstuffs, transport equipment; *partners*—Denmark 18%, US 14%, FRG, France, UK, Canada
Imports: $363 million (c.i.f., 1986); *commodities*—machinery and transport equipment 38%, food and livestock 11%, fuels 10%, manufactures 10%, chemicals 5%; *partners:* Denmark 46%, FRG, Norway, Japan, UK
External debt: $NA
Industrial production: growth rate NA%
Electricity: 80,000 kW capacity; 280 million kWh produced, 5,910 kWh per capita (1989)
Industries: fishing, shipbuilding, handicrafts
Agriculture: accounts for 27% of GDP and employs 27% of labor force; principal crops—potatoes and vegetables; livestock—sheep; annual fish catch about 360,000 metric tons
Aid: none
Currency: Danish krone (plural—kroner); 1 Danish krone (DKr) = 100 øre
Exchange rates: Danish kroner (DKr) per US$1—6.560 (January 1990), 7.310 (1989), 6.732 (1988), 6.840 (1987), 8.091 (1986), 10.596 (1985)
Fiscal year: 1 April-31 March

Communications

Highways: 200 km
Ports: Torshavn, Tvoroyri; 8 minor
Merchant marine: 7 ships (1,000 GRT or over) totaling 17,249 GRT/11,887 DWT; includes 1 short-sea passenger, 2 cargo, 2 roll-on/roll-off cargo, 2 refrigerated cargo; note—a subset of the Danish register
Airports: 1 with permanent-surface runway 1,220-2,439 m
Telecommunications: good international communications; fair domestic facilities; 27,900 telephones; stations—1 AM, 3 (10 repeaters) FM, 3 (29 repeaters) TV; 3 coaxial submarine cables

Defense Forces

Note: defense is the responsibility of Denmark

Fiji

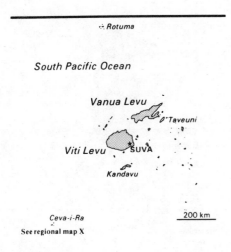

South Pacific Ocean

Vanua Levu
Taveuni
Viti Levu SUVA
Kandavu

Ceva-i-Ra
200 km
See regional map X

Geography

Total area: 18,270 km²; land area: 18,270 km²
Comparative area: slightly smaller than New Jersey
Land boundaries: none
Coastline: 1,129 km
Maritime claims: (measured from claimed archipelagic baselines)
  Continental shelf: 200 meters or to depth of exploitation
  Extended economic zone: 200 nm
  Territorial sea: 12 nm
Climate: tropical marine; only slight seasonal temperature variation
Terrain: mostly mountains of volcanic origin
Natural resources: timber, fish, gold, copper; offshore oil potential
Land use: 8% arable land; 5% permanent crops; 3% meadows and pastures; 65% forest and woodland; 19% other; includes NEGL% irrigated
Environment: subject to hurricanes from November to January; includes 332 islands of which approximately 110 are inhabited
Note: located 2,500 km north of New Zealand in the South Pacific Ocean

People

Population: 759,567 (July 1990), growth rate 1.5% (1990)
Birth rate: 28 births/1,000 population (1990)
Death rate: 6 deaths/1,000 population (1990)
Net migration rate: −7 migrants/1,000 population (1990)
Infant mortality rate: 22 deaths/1,000 live births (1990)
Life expectancy at birth: 66 years male, 70 years female (1990)
Total fertility rate: 3.3 children born/woman (1990)

Nationality: noun—Fijian(s); adjective—Fijian
Ethnic divisions: 49% Indian, 46% Fijian, 5% European, other Pacific Islanders, overseas Chinese, and others
Religion: Fijians are mainly Christian, Indians are Hindu with a Muslim minority
Language: English (official); Fijian; Hindustani
Literacy: 80%
Labor force: 176,000; 60% subsistence agriculture, 40% wage earners (1979)
Organized labor: about 45,000 employees belong to some 46 trade unions, which are organized along lines of work and ethnic origin (1983)

Government

Long-form name: Republic of Fiji
Type: military coup leader Major General Sitiveni Rabuka formally declared Fiji a republic on 6 October 1987
Capital: Suva
Administrative divisions: 4 divisions and 1 dependency*; Central, Eastern, Northern, Rotuma*, Western
Independence: 10 October 1970 (from UK)
Constitution: 10 October 1970 (suspended 1 October 1987); note—a new constitution was proposed on 23 September 1988 and awaits final approval
Legal system: based on British system
National holiday: Independence Day, 10 October (1970)
Executive branch: president, prime minister, Cabinet
Legislative branch: the bicameral Parliament, consisting of an upper house or Senate and a lower house or House of Representatives, was dissolved following the coup of 14 May 1987; the proposed constitution of NA September 1988 provides for a bicameral Parliament
Judicial branch: Supreme Court
Leaders: *Chief of State*—President Ratu Sir Penaia Kanatabatu GANILAU (since 5 December 1987);
Head of Government—Prime Minister Ratu Sir Kamisese MARA (since 5 December 1987); note—Ratu Sir Kamisese Mara served as prime minister from 10 October 1970 until the 5-11 April 1987 election; after a second coup led by Major General Sitiveni Rabuka on 25 September 1987, Ratu Mara was reappointed as prime minister
Political parties and leaders: Alliance, primarily Fijian, Ratu Mara; National Federation, primarily Indian, Siddiq Koya; Western United Front, Fijian, Ratu Osea Gavidi; Fiji Labor Party, Adi Kuini Bavadra; coalition of the National Federation Party and the Fiji Labor Party, Adi Kuini Vuikaba Bavadra

Suffrage: none
Elections: none
Communists: some
Member of: ACP, ADB, Colombo Plan, EC (associate), ESCAP, FAO, G-77, GATT (de facto), IBRD, ICAO, IDA, IFAD, IFC, ILO, IMF, IMO, INTELSAT, INTERPOL, ISO, ITU, SPF, UN, UNESCO, UPU, WFTU, WHO, WIPO, WMO
Diplomatic representation: Counselor (Commercial), Vice Consul, Chargé d'Affaires ad interim Abdul H. YUSUF; Chancery at Suite 240, 2233 Wisconsin Avenue NW, Washington, DC 20007; telephone (202) 337-8320; there is a Fijian Consulate in New York; *US*—Ambassador Leonard ROCHWARGER; Embassy at 31 Loftus Street, Suva (mailing address is P. O. Box 218, Suva); telephone [679] 314-466 or 314-069
Flag: light blue with the flag of the UK in the upper hoist-side quadrant and the Fijian shield centered on the outer half of the flag; the shield depicts a yellow lion above a white field quartered by the cross of St. George featuring stalks of sugarcane, a palm tree, bananas, and a white dove

Economy

Overview: Fiji's economy is primarily agricultural, with a large subsistence sector. Sugar exports are a major source of foreign exchange and sugar processing accounts for one-third of industrial output. Industry, including sugar milling, contributes 10% to GDP. Fiji traditionally earned considerable sums of hard currency from the 250,000 tourists who visited each year. In 1987, however, after two military coups, the economy went into decline. GDP dropped by 7.8% in 1987 and by another 2.5% in 1988; political uncertainty created a drop in tourism, and the worst drought of the century caused sugar production to fall sharply. In contrast, sugar and tourism turned in strong performances in 1989, and the economy rebounded vigorously.
GDP: $1.32 billion, per capita $1,750; real growth rate 12.5% (1989 est.)
Inflation rate (consumer prices): 11.8% (1988)
Unemployment rate: 11% (1988)
Budget: revenues $260 million; expenditures $233 million, including capital expenditures of $47 million (1988)
Exports: $312 million (f.o.b., 1988); *commodities*—sugar 49%, copra, processed fish, lumber; *partners*—UK 45%, Australia 21%, US 4.7%
Imports: $454 million (c.i.f., 1988); *commodities*—food 15%, petroleum products,

Fiji *(continued)*

machinery, consumer goods; *partners*—
US 4.8%, NZ, Australia, Japan
External debt: $398 million (December
1989 est.)
Industrial production: growth rate −15%
(1988 est.)
Electricity: 215,000 kW capacity; 330 million kWh produced, 440 kWh per capita
(1989)
Industries: sugar, copra, tourism, gold,
silver, fishing, clothing, lumber, small cot-
tage industries
Agriculture: principal cash crop is sugarcane; coconuts, cassava, rice, sweet potatoes, and bananas; small livestock sector
includes cattle, pigs, horses, and goats
Aid: Western (non-US) countries, ODA
and OOF bilateral commitments (1980-
87), $677 million
Currency: Fijian dollar (plural—dollars); 1
Fijian dollar (F$) = 100 cents
Exchange rates: Fijian dollars (F$) per
US$1—1.4950 (January 1990), 1.4833
(1989), 1.4303 (1988), 1.2439 (1987),
1.1329 (1986), 1.1536 (1985)
Fiscal year: calendar year

Communications

Railroads: 644 km 0.610-meter narrow
gauge, belonging to the government-owned
Fiji Sugar Corporation
Highways: 3,300 km total (1984)—390 km
paved; 1,200 km bituminous-surface treatment; 1,290 km gravel, crushed stone, or
stabilized soil surface; 420 unimproved
earth
Inland waterways: 203 km; 122 km navigable by motorized craft and 200-metric-
ton barges
Ports: Lambasa, Lautoka, Savusavu, Suva
Merchant marine: 9 ships (1,000 GRT or
over) totaling 42,872 GRT/49,795 DWT;
includes 1 cargo, 2 roll-on/roll-off cargo,
2 container, 2 liquefied gas, 1 petroleum,
oils, and lubricants (POL) tanker, 1 chemical tanker
Civil air: 1 DC-3 and 1 light aircraft
Airports: 26 total, 24 usable; 2 with
permanent-surface runways; none with
runways over 3,659 m; 1 with runways
2,440-3,659 m; 2 with runways
1,220-2,439 m
Telecommunications: modern local, interisland, and international (wire/radio integrated) public and special-purpose telephone, telegraph, and teleprinter facilities;
regional radio center; important COM-
PAC cable link between US-Canada and
New Zealand-Australia; 53,228
telephones; stations—7 AM, 1 FM, no
TV; 1 Pacific Ocean INTELSAT earth
station

Defense Forces

Branches: integrated ground and naval
forces
Military manpower: males 15-49, 194,433;
107,317 fit for military service; 7,864
reach military age (18) annually
Defense expenditures: 2.5% of GDP (1988)

Finland

Geography

Total area: 337,030 km²; land area:
305,470 km²
Comparative area: slightly smaller than
Montana
Land boundaries: 2,578 km total; Norway
729 km, Sweden 536 km, USSR 1,313 km
Coastline: 1,126 km excluding islands and
coastal indentations
Maritime claims:
  Contiguous zone: 6 nm
  Continental shelf: 200 meters or to
  depth of exploitation
  Exclusive fishing zone: 12 nm
  Territorial sea: 4 nm
Climate: cold temperate; potentially subarctic, but comparatively mild because of
moderating influence of the North Atlantic Current, Baltic Sea, and more than
60,000 lakes
Terrain: mostly low, flat to rolling plains
interspersed with lakes and low hills
Natural resources: timber, copper, zinc,
iron ore, silver
Land use: 8% arable land; 0% permanent
crops; NEGL% meadows and pastures;
76% forest and woodland; 16% other; includes NEGL% irrigated
Environment: permanently wet ground
covers about 30% of land; population concentrated on small southwestern coastal
plain
Note: long boundary with USSR; Helsinki
is northernmost national capital on European continent

People

Population: 4,977,325 (July 1990), growth
rate 0.3% (1990)
Birth rate: 13 births/1,000 population
(1990)
Death rate: 10 deaths/1,000 population
(1990)
Net migration rate: NEGL migrants/
1,000 population (1990)

Infant mortality rate: 6 deaths/1,000 live births (1990)
Life expectancy at birth: 71 years male, 80 years female (1990)
Total fertility rate: 1.7 children born/ woman (1990)
Nationality: noun—Finn(s); adjective— Finnish
Ethnic divisions: Finn, Swede, Lapp, Gypsy, Tatar
Religion: 97% Evangelical Lutheran, 1.2% Eastern Orthodox, 1.8% other
Language: 93.5% Finnish, 6.3% Swedish (both official); small Lapp- and Russian-speaking minorities
Literacy: almost 100%
Labor force: 2,556,000; 33.1% services, 22.9% mining and manufacturing, 13.8% commerce, 10.3% agriculture, forestry, and fishing, 7.2% construction, 7.1% transportation and communications (1989 est.)
Organized labor: 80% of labor force

Government

Long-form name: Republic of Finland
Type: republic
Capital: Helsinki
Administrative divisions: 12 provinces (läänit, singular—lääni); Ahvenanmaa, Häme, Keski-Suomi, Kuopio, Kymi, Lappi, Mikkeli, Oulu, Pohjois-Karjala, Turku ja Pori, Uusimaa, Vaasa
Independence: 6 December 1917 (from Soviet Union)
Constitution: 17 July 1919
Legal system: civil law system based on Swedish law; Supreme Court may request legislation interpreting or modifying laws; accepts compulsory ICJ jurisdiction, with reservations
National holiday: Independence Day, 6 December (1917)
Executive branch: president, prime minister, deputy prime minister, Council of State (Valtioneuvosto)
Legislative branch: unicameral Parliament (Eduskunta)
Judicial branch: Supreme Court (Korkein Oikeus)
Leaders: *Chief of State*—President Mauno KOIVISTO (since 27 January 1982);
Head of Government—Prime Minister Harri HOLKERI (since 30 April 1987); Deputy Prime Minister Pertti PAASIO (since NA January 1989)
Political parties and leaders: Social Democratic Party, Pertti Paasio; Center Party, Paavo Väyrynen; People's Democratic League (majority Communist front), Reijo Kakela; National Coalition (Conservative) Party, Ilkka Suominen; Liberal People's

Party, Kyösti Lallukka; Swedish People's Party, Christoffer Taxell; Rural Party, leader NA
Suffrage: universal at age 18
Elections: *President*—last held 31 January-1 February and 15 February 1988 (next to be held January 1994); results—Mauno Koivisto 48%, Paavo Väyrynen 20%, Harri Holkeri 18%; *Parliament*—last held 15-16 March 1987 (next to be held March 1991); results— Social Democratic 24.3%, National Coalition (Conservative) 23.9%, Center-Liberal People's 18.6%, People's Democratic League 9.4%, Rural 6.3%, Swedish People's 5.3%, Democratic Alternative 4.3%, Green League 4.0%, Finnish Christian League 2.6%, Finnish Pensioners 1.2%, Constitutional Rightist 0.1%; seats—(200 total) Social Democratic 56, National Coalition (Conservative) 53, Center-Liberal People's 40, People's Democratic League 16, Swedish People's 13, Rural 9, Finnish Christian League 5; Democratic Alternative 4, Green League 4
Communists: 28,000 registered members; an additional 45,000 persons belong to People's Democratic League
Other political or pressure groups: Finnish Communist Party (majority Communist faction), Jarmo Wahlström; Finnish Communist Party-Unity (minority faction), Esko-Juhani Tennila; Democratic Alternative (minority Communist front), Kristiina Halkola; Finnish Christian League, Esko Almgren; Constitutional Rightist Party; Finnish Pensioners Party; Green League, Heidi Hautala; Communist Workers Party, Timo Lahdenmaki
Member of: ADB, CCC, CEMA (special cooperation agreement), DAC, EC (free trade agreement), EFTA, ESA (associate), FAO, GATT, IAEA, IBRD, ICAC, ICAO, ICES, ICO, IDA, IDB—Inter-American Development Bank, IFAD, IFC, IHO, ILO, ILZSG, IMF, IMO, INTELSAT, INTERPOL, IPU, ITU, IWC—International Wheat Council, Nordic Council, OECD, UN, UNESCO, UPU, WHO, WIPO, WMO, WSG
Diplomatic representation: Ambassador Jukka VALTASAARI; Chancery at 3216 New Mexico Avenue NW, Washington DC 20016; telephone (202) 363-2430; there are Finnish Consulates General in Los Angeles and New York, and Consulates in Chicago and Houston; *US*—Ambassador John G. WEINMANN; Embassy at Itainen Puistotie 14ASF-00140, Helsinki (mailing address is APO New York 09664); telephone [358] (0) 171931
Flag: white with a blue cross that extends to the edges of the flag; the vertical part of the cross is shifted to the hoist side in the style of the *Dannebrog* (Danish flag)

Economy

Overview: Finland has a highly industrialized, largely free market economy, with per capita output nearly three-fourths the US figure. Its main economic force is the manufacturing sector—principally the wood, metals, and engineering industries. Trade is important, with the export of goods representing about 25% of GNP. Except for timber and several minerals, Finland depends on imported raw materials, energy, and some components of manufactured goods. Because of the climate, agricultural development is limited to maintaining self-sufficiency in basic commodities. Economic prospects are generally bright, the main shadow being the increasing pressures on wages and prices.
GDP: $74.4 billion, per capita $15,000; real growth rate 4.6% (1989 est.)
Inflation rate (consumer prices): 6.5% (1989)
Unemployment rate: 3.4% (1989)
Budget: revenues $28.3 billion; expenditures $28.1 billion, including capital expenditures of $NA billion (1988 est.)
Exports: $22.2 billion (f.o.b., 1988); *commodities*—timber, paper and pulp, ships, machinery, clothing and footwear; *partners*—EC 44.2% (UK 13.0%, FRG 10.8%), USSR 14.9%, Sweden 14.1%, US 5.8%
Imports: $22.0 billion (c.i.f., 1988); *commodities*—foodstuffs, petroleum and petroleum products, chemicals, transport equipment, iron and steel, machinery, textile yarn and fabrics, fodder grains; *partners*—EC 43.5% (FRG 16.9%, UK 6.8%), Sweden 13.3%, USSR 12.1%, US 6.3%
External debt: $5.3 billion (1989)
Industrial production: growth rate 4.3% (1989)
Electricity: 13,324,000 kW capacity; 49,330 million kWh produced, 9,940 kWh per capita (1989)
Industries: metal manufacturing and shipbuilding, forestry and wood processing (pulp, paper), copper refining, foodstuffs, textiles, clothing
Agriculture: accounts for 8% of GNP (including forestry); livestock production, especially dairy cattle, predominates; forestry is an important export earner and a secondary occupation for the rural population; main crops—cereals, sugar beets, potatoes; 85% self-sufficient, but short of food and fodder grains; annual fish catch about 160,000 metric tons
Aid: donor—ODA and OOF commitments (1970-87), $1.7 billion
Currency: markka (plural—markkaa); 1 markka (FMk) or Finmark = 100 penniä
Exchange rates: markkaa (FMk) per US$1—4.0022 (January 1990), 4.2912

Finland (continued)

(1989), 4.1828 (1988), 4.3956 (1987),
5.0695 (1986), 6.1979 (1985)
Fiscal year: calendar year

Communications

Railroads: 5,924 km total; Finnish State
Railways (VR) operate a total of 5,863 km
1.524-meter gauge, of which 480 km are
multiple track and 1,445 km are electrified
Highways: about 103,000 km total, including 35,000 km paved (bituminous,
concrete, bituminous-treated surface) and
38,000 km unpaved (stabilized gravel,
gravel, earth); additional 30,000 km of
private (state-subsidized) roads
Inland waterways: 6,675 km total
(including Saimaa Canal); 3,700 km suitable for steamers
Pipelines: natural gas, 580 km
Ports: Helsinki, Oulu, Pori, Rauma,
Turku; 6 secondary, numerous minor ports
Merchant marine: 82 ships (1,000 GRT or
over) totaling 737,811 GRT/764,695
DWT; includes 1 passenger, 11 short-sea
passenger, 18 cargo, 1 refrigerated cargo,
24 roll-on/roll-off cargo, 12 petroleum,
oils, and lubricants (POL) tanker, 5 chemical tanker, 2 liquefied gas, 7 bulk, 1 combination bulk
Civil air: 39 major transport
Airports: 160 total, 157 usable; 56 with
permanent-surface runways; none with
runways over 3,659 m; 23 with runways
2,440-3,659 m; 22 with runways 1,220-
2,439 m
Telecommunications: good service from
cable and radio relay network; 3,140,000
telephones; stations—4 AM, 42 (101 relays) FM, 79 (195 relays) TV; 2 submarine
cables; satellite service via Swedish earth
stations; satellite earth stations—2 Atlantic Ocean INTELSAT and 1 EUTELSAT

Defense Forces

Branches: Army, Navy, Air Force
Military manpower: males 15-49,
1,312,941; 1,091,416 fit for military service; 32,288 reach military age (17) annually
Defense expenditures: 1.5% of GDP (1989
est.)

France

English Channel
300 km
Lille
PARIS ★
Brest
Nancy
Strasbourg
Orléans
Nantes
Dijon
*Bay of
Biscay*
Limoges
Lyon
Bordeaux
Grenoble
Toulouse
Nice
Perpignan
Marseille
Corsica
*Mediterranean
Sea*
See regional map V

Geography

Total area: 547,030 km²; land area:
545,630 km²; includes Corsica and the
rest of metropolitan France, but excludes
the overseas administrative divisions
Comparative area: slightly more than
twice the size of Colorado
Land boundaries: 2,892.4 km total; An-
dorra 60 km, Belgium 620 km, FRG 451
km, Italy 488 km, Luxembourg 73 km,
Monaco 4.4 km, Spain 623 km, Switzerland 573 km
Coastline: 3,427 km (includes Corsica, 644
km)
Maritime claims:
  Contiguous zone: 12-24 nm
  Extended economic zone: 200 nm
  Territorial sea: 12 nm
Disputes: maritime boundary dispute with
Canada (St. Pierre and Miquelon); Mada-
gascar claims Bassas da India, Europa
Island, Glorioso Islands, Juan de Nova
Island, and Tromelin Island; Comoros
claims Mayotte; Mauritius claims Trome-
lin Island; Seychelles claims Tromelin Is-
land; Suriname claims part of French Gui-
ana; territorial claim in Antarctica
(Adélie Land)
Climate: generally cool winters and mild
summers, but mild winters and hot summers along the Mediterranean
Terrain: mostly flat plains or gently rolling
hills in north and west; remainder is
mountainous, especially Pyrenees in south,
Alps in east
Natural resources: coal, iron ore, bauxite,
fish, timber, zinc, potash
Land use: 32% arable land; 2% permanent
crops; 23% meadows and pastures; 27%
forest and woodland; 16% other; includes
2% irrigated
Environment: most of large urban areas
and industrial centers in Rhône, Garonne,
Seine, or Loire River basins; occasional
warm tropical wind known as mistral
Note: largest West European nation

People

Population: 56,358,331 (July 1990),
growth rate 0.4% (1990)
Birth rate: 14 births/1,000 population
(1990)
Death rate: 9 deaths/1,000 population
(1990)
Net migration rate: 0 migrants/1,000 pop-
ulation (1990)
Infant mortality rate: 6 deaths/1,000 live
births (1990)
Life expectancy at birth: 73 years male,
82 years female (1990)
Total fertility rate: 1.8 children born/
woman (1990)
Nationality: noun—Frenchman(men),
Frenchwoman(women); adjective—French
Ethnic divisions: Celtic and Latin with
Teutonic, Slavic, North African, Indochi-
nese, and Basque minorities
Religion: 90% Roman Catholic, 2% Prot-
estant, 1% Jewish, 1% Muslim (North Af-
rican workers), 6% unaffiliated
Language: French (100% of population);
rapidly declining regional dialects (Pro-
vençal, Breton, Alsatian, Corsican, Cata-
lan, Basque, Flemish)
Literacy: 99%
Labor force: 24,170,000; 61.5% services,
31.3% industry, 7.3% agriculture (1987)
Organized labor: 20% of labor force (est.)

Government

Long-form name: French Republic
Type: republic
Capital: Paris
Administrative divisions: metropolitan
France—22 regions (régions, singular—
région); Alsace, Aquitaine, Auvergne,
Basse-Normandie, Bourgogne, Bretagne,
Centre, Champagne-Ardenne, Corse,
Franche-Comté, Haute-Normandie, Île-
de-France, Languedoc-Roussillon, Limou-
sin, Lorraine, Midi-Pyrénées, Nord-Pas-
de-Calais, Pays de la Loire, Picardie,
Poitou-Charentes, Provence-Alpes-Côte
d'Azur, Rhône-Alpes; note—the 22 re-
gions are subdivided into 96 departments;
see separate entries for the overseas de-
partments (French Guiana, Guadeloupe,
Martinique, Reunion) and the territorial
collectivities (Mayotte, St. Pierre and Miquelon)
Dependent areas: Bassas da India, Clipperton Island, Europa Island, French
Polynesia, French Southern and Antarctic
Lands, Glorioso Islands, Juan de Nova
Island, New Caledonia, Tromelin Island,
Wallis and Futuna
Independence: unified by Clovis in 486,
First Republic proclaimed in 1792
Constitution: 28 September 1958,
amended concerning election of president
in 1962

Legal system: civil law system with indigenous concepts; review of administrative but not legislative acts

National holiday: Taking of the Bastille, 14 July (1789)

Executive branch: president, prime minister, Council of Ministers (cabinet)

Legislative branch: bicameral Parliament (Parlement) consists of an upper house or Senate (Sénat) and a lower house or National Assembly (Assemblée Nationale)

Judicial branch: Court of Cassation (Cour de Cassation)

Leaders: *Chief of State*—President François MITTERRAND (since 21 May 1981);

Head of Government—Prime Minister Michel ROCARD (since 10 March 1988)

Political parties and leaders: Rally for the Republic (RPR, formerly UDR), Jacques Chirac; Union for French Democracy (UDF, federation of PR, CDS, and RAD), Valéry Giscard d'Estaing; Republicans (PR), François Léotard; Center for Social Democrats (CDS), Pierre Méhaignerie; Radical (RAD), Yves Gallard; Socialist Party (PS), Pierre Mauroy; Left Radical Movement (MRG), Yves Collin; Communist Party (PCF), Georges Marchais; National Front (FN), Jean-Marie Le Pen

Suffrage: universal at age 18

Elections: *President*—last held 8 May 1988 (next to be held May 1995); results—Second Ballot François Mitterrand 54%, Jacques Chirac 46%; *Senate*—last held 24 September 1989 (next to be held September 1992); results—percent of vote by party NA; seats—(321 total; 296 metropolitan France, 13 for overseas departments and territories, and 12 for French nationals abroad) RPR 93, UDF 143 (PR 53, CDS 65, RAD 25), PS 64, PCF 16, independents 2, unknown 3; *National Assembly*—last held 5 and 12 June 1988 (next to be held June 1993); results—Second Ballot PS-MRG 48.7%, RPR 23.1%, UDF 21%, PCF 3.4%, other 3.8%; seats—(577 total) PS 275, RPR 132, UDF 90, UDC 40, PCF 25, independents 15

Communists: 700,000 claimed but probably closer to 150,000; Communist voters, 2.8 million in 1988 election

Other political or pressure groups: Communist-controlled labor union (Confédération Générale du Travail) nearly 2.4 million members (claimed); Socialist-leaning labor union (Confédération Française Démocratique du Travail or CFDT) about 800,000 members est.; independent labor union (Force Ouvrière) about 1,000,000 members est.; independent white-collar union (Confédération Générale des Cadres) 340,000 members (claimed); National Council of French Employers (Conseil National du Patronat Français—CNPF or Patronat)

Member of: ADB, CCC, Council of Europe, DAC, EC, EIB, EMA, EMS, ESA, ESCAP, FAO, GATT, IAEA, IATP, IBRD, ICAC, ICAO, ICES, ICO, IDA, IDB—Inter-American Development Bank, IFAD, IFC, IHO, ILO, ILZSG, IMF, IMO, INTELSAT, INTERPOL, IOOC, IPU, IRC, ISO, ITC, ITU, IWC—International Whaling Commission, NATO (signatory), OAS (observer), OECD, SPC, UN, UNESCO, UPU, WEU, WFTU, WHO, WIPO, WMO, WSG, WTO

Diplomatic representation: Ambassador Jacques ANDREANI; Chancery at 4101 Reservoir Road NW, Washington DC 20007; telephone (202) 944-6000; there are French Consulates General in Boston, Chicago, Detroit, Houston, Los Angeles, New Orleans, Miami, New York, San Francisco, and San Juan (Puerto Rico); *US*—Ambassador Walter J. P. CURLEY; Embassy at 2 Avenue Gabriel, 75382 Paris Cedex 08 (mailing address is APO New York 09777); telephone [33] (1) 42-96-12-02 or 42-61-80-75; there are US Consulates General in Bordeaux, Lyon, Marseille, and Strasbourg

Flag: three equal vertical bands of blue (hoist side), white, and red; known as the French *Tricouleur* (Tricolor); the design and colors have been the basis for a number of other flags, including those of Belgium, Chad, Ireland, Ivory Coast, and Luxembourg; the official flag for all French dependent areas

Economy

Overview: One of the world's most developed economies, France has substantial agricultural resources and a highly diversified modern industrial sector. Large tracts of fertile land, the application of modern technology, and subsidies have combined to make it the leading agricultural producer in Western Europe. France is largely self-sufficient in agricultural products and is a major exporter of wheat and dairy products. The industrial sector generates about one-third of GDP and employs about one-third of the work force. During the period 1982-86 economic growth was sluggish, averaging only 1.4% annually. This trend was reversed by late 1987, however, with a strong expansion of consumer demand, followed by a surge in investment. The economy has had difficulty generating enough jobs for new entrants into the labor force, resulting in a high unemployment rate, but the upward trend in growth recently pushed the jobless rate below 10%. The steadily advancing economic integration within the European Community is a major force affecting the fortunes of the various economic sectors.

GDP: $819.6 billion, per capita $14,600; real growth rate 3.4% (1989 est.)

Inflation rate (consumer prices): 3.5% (1989 est.)

Unemployment rate: 9.7% (1989 est.)

Budget: revenues $197.0 billion; expenditures $213.4 billion, including capital expenditures of $NA (1989 est.)

Exports: $183.1 billion (f.o.b., 1989 est.); *commodities*—machinery and transportation equipment, chemicals, foodstuffs, agricultural products, iron and steel products, textiles and clothing; *partners*—FRG 15.8%, Italy 12.2%, UK 9.8%, Belgium-Luxembourg 8.9%, Netherlands 8.7%, US 6.7%, Spain 5.6%, Japan 1.8%, USSR 1.3% (1989 est.)

Imports: $194.5 billion (c.i.f., 1989 est.); *commodities*—crude oil, machinery and equipment, agricultural products, chemicals, iron and steel products; *partners*—FRG 19.4%, Italy 11.5%, Belgium-Luxembourg 9.2%, US 7.7%, UK 7.2%, Netherlands 5.2%, Spain 4.4%, Japan 4.1%, USSR 2.1% (1989 est.)

External debt: $59.3 billion (December 1987)

Industrial production: growth rate 4.4% (1989 est.)

Electricity: 109,972,000 kW capacity; 403,570 million kWh produced, 7,210 kWh per capita (1989)

Industries: steel, machinery, chemicals, automobiles, metallurgy, aircraft, electronics, mining, textiles, food processing, and tourism

Agriculture: accounts for 4% of GNP (including fishing and forestry); one of the world's top five wheat producers; other principal products—beef, dairy products, cereals, sugar beets, potatoes, wine grapes; self-sufficient for most temperate-zone foods; shortages include fats and oils and tropical produce, but overall net exporter of farm products; fish catch of 850,000 metric tons ranks among world's top 20 countries and is all used domestically

Aid: donor—ODA and OOF commitments (1970-87), $59.8 billion

Currency: French franc (plural—francs); 1 French franc (F) = 100 centimes

Exchange rates: French francs (F) per US$1—5.7598 (January 1990), 6.3801 (1989), 5.9569 (1988), 6.0107 (1987), 6.9261 (1986), 8.9852 (1985)

Fiscal year: calendar year

France (continued)

Communications

Railroads: French National Railways (SNCF) operates 34,568 km 1.435-meter standard gauge; 11,674 km electrified, 15,132 km double or multiple track; 2,138 km of various gauges (1.000-meter to 1.440-meter), privately owned and operated

Highways: 1,551,400 km total; 33,400 km national highway; 347,000 km departmental highway; 421,000 km community roads; 750,000 km rural roads; 5,401 km of controlled-access divided autoroutes; about 803,000 km paved

Inland waterways: 14,932 km; 6,969 km heavily traveled

Pipelines: crude oil, 3,059 km; refined products, 4,487 km; natural gas, 24,746 km

Ports: maritime—Bordeaux, Boulogne, Brest, Cherbourg, Dunkerque, Fos-Sur-Mer, Le Havre, Marseille, Nantes, Rouen, Sete, Toulon; inland—42

Merchant marine: 153 ships (1,000 GRT or over) totaling 3,671,645 GRT/ 5,950,785 DWT; includes 10 short-sea passenger, 19 cargo, 19 container, 1 multifunction large-load carrier, 30 roll-on/ roll-off cargo, 37 petroleum, oils, and lubricants (POL) tanker, 9 chemical tanker, 6 liquefied gas, 4 specialized tanker, 17 bulk, 1 combination bulk; note—France also maintains a captive register for French-owned ships in the Kerguelen Islands (French Southern and Antarctic Lands) and French Polynesia

Civil air: 355 major transport aircraft (1982)

Airports: 470 total, 460 usable; 204 with permanent-surface runways; 3 with runways over 3,659 m; 34 with runways 2,440-3,659 m; 133 with runways 1,220-2,439 m

Telecommunications: highly developed system provides satisfactory telephone, telegraph, radio and TV broadcast services; 39,110,000 telephones; stations—42 AM, 138 (777 relays) FM, 215 TV (8,900 relays); 25 submarine coaxial cables; communication satellite earth stations operating in INTELSAT, 3 Atlantic Ocean and 2 Indian Ocean, EUTELSAT, MARISAT, and domestic systems

Defense Forces

Branches: Army, Navy, Air Force, National Gendarmerie

Military manpower: males 15-49, 14,285,904; 12,042,731 fit for military service; 409,544 reach military age (18) annually

Defense expenditures: 3.8% of GDP, or $31.1 billion (1989 est.)

French Guiana
(overseas department of France)

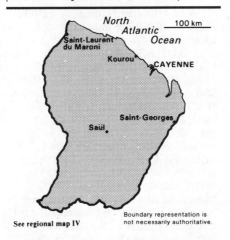

North Atlantic Ocean
100 km
Saint-Laurent du Maroni
Kourou
CAYENNE
Saint-Georges
Saül

See regional map IV

Boundary representation is not necessarily authoritative.

Geography

Total area: 91,000 km²; land area: 89,150 km²

Comparative area: slightly smaller than Indiana

Land boundaries: 1,183 km total; Brazil 673 km, Suriname 510 km

Coastline: 378 km

Maritime claims:
Extended economic zone: 200 nm
Territorial sea: 12 nm

Disputes: Suriname claims area between Rivière Litani and Rivière Marouini (both headwaters of the Lawa)

Climate: tropical; hot, humid; little seasonal temperature variation

Terrain: low-lying coastal plains rising to hills and small mountains

Natural resources: bauxite, timber, gold (widely scattered), cinnabar, kaolin, fish

Land use: NEGL% arable land; NEGL% permanent crops; NEGL% meadows and pastures; 82% forest and woodland; 18% other

Environment: mostly an unsettled wilderness

People

Population: 97,781 (July 1990), growth rate 3.4% (1990)

Birth rate: 29 births/1,000 population (1990)

Death rate: 5 deaths/1,000 population (1990)

Net migration rate: 10 migrants/1,000 population (1990)

Infant mortality rate: 19 deaths/1,000 live births (1990)

Life expectancy at birth: 68 years male, 76 years female (1990)

Total fertility rate: 3.8 children born/ woman (1990)

Nationality: noun—French Guianese (sing., pl.); adjective—French Guiana

Ethnic divisions: 66% black or mulatto; 12% Caucasian; 12% East Indian, Chinese, Amerindian; 10% other

Religion: predominantly Roman Catholic

Language: French

Literacy: 73%

Labor force: 23,265; 60.6% services, government, and commerce, 21.2% industry, 18.2% agriculture (1980)

Organized labor: 7% of labor force

Government

Long-form name: Department of Guiana

Type: overseas department of France

Capital: Cayenne

Administrative divisions: none (overseas department of France)

Independence: none (overseas department of France)

Constitution: 28 September 1958 (French Constitution)

Legal system: French legal system

National holiday: Taking of the Bastille, 14 July (1789)

Executive branch: French president, commissioner of the republic

Legislative branch: unicameral General Council and a unicameral Regional Council

Judicial branch: highest local court is the Court of Appeals based in Martinique with jurisdiction over Martinique, Guadeloupe, and French Guiana

Leaders: *Chief of State*—President François MITTERRAND (since 21 May 1981);

Head of Government—Commissioner of the Republic Jean-Pierre LACROIX (since NA August 1988)

Political parties and leaders: Guianese Socialist Party (PSG), Gérard Holder; Rally for the Republic (RPR), Paulin Bruné; Guyanese Democratic Action (ADG), André Lecante; Union for French Democracy (UDF), Claude Ho A Chuck; National Front, Guy Malon; Popular and National Party of Guiana (PNPG), Claude Robo; National Anti-Colonist Guianese Party (PANGA), Michel Kapel

Suffrage: universal at age 18

Elections: *Regional Council*—last held 16 March 1986 (next to be held March 1991); results—PSG 43%, RPR 27.7%, ADG 12.2%, UDF 8.9%, FN 3.7%, PNPG 1.4%, others 3.1%; seats—(31 total) PSG 15, RPR 9, ADG 4, UDF 3;

French Senate—last held 24 September 1989 (next to be held September 1992); results—percent of vote by party NA; seats—(1 total) PSG 1;

French National Assembly—last held 24 September 1989 (next to be held September 1992); results—percent of vote by party NA; seats—(2 total) PSG 1, RPR 1

Communists: Communist party membership negligible
Member of: WFTU
Diplomatic representation: as an overseas department of France the interests of French Guiana are represented in the US by France
Flag: the flag of France is used

Economy

Overview: The economy is tied closely to that of France through subsidies and imports. Besides the French space center at Kourou, fishing and forestry are the most important economic activities, with exports of fish and fish products (mostly shrimp) accounting for about two-thirds of total revenue in 1985. The large reserves of tropical hardwoods, not fully exploited, support an expanding sawmill industry that provides sawn logs for export. Cultivation of crops—rice, cassava, bananas, and sugarcane—are limited to the coastal area, where the population is largely concentrated. French Guiana is heavily dependent on imports of food and energy. Unemployment is a serious problem, particularly among younger workers, with an unemployment rate of 15%.
GDP: $210 million, per capita $3,230; real growth rate NA% (1982)
Inflation rate (consumer prices): 4.1% (1987)
Unemployment rate: 15% (1987)
Budget: revenues $735 million; expenditures $735 million, including capital expenditures of NA (1987)
Exports: $37.0 million (f.o.b., 1986); *commodities*—shrimp, timber, rum, rosewood essence; *partners*—US 41%, Japan 18%, France 9% (1984)
Imports: $297.7 million (c.i.f., 1986); *commodities*—food (grains, processed meat), other consumer goods, producer goods, petroleum; *partners*—France 55%, Trinidad and Tobago 13%, US 3% (1984)
External debt: $1.2 billion (1988)
Industrial production: growth rate NA%
Electricity: 92,000 kW capacity; 185 million kWh produced, 1,950 kWh per capita (1989)
Industries: construction, shrimp processing, forestry products, rum, gold mining
Agriculture: some vegetables for local consumption; rice, corn, manioc, cocoa, bananas, sugar
Aid: Western (non-US) countries, ODA and OOF bilateral commitments (1970-87), $1.1 billion
Currency: French franc (plural—francs); 1 French franc (F) = 100 centimes
Exchange rates: French francs (F) per US$1—5.7598 (January 1990), 6.3801 (1989), 5.9569 (1988), 6.0107 (1987), 6.9261 (1986), 8.9852 (1985)

Fiscal year: calendar year

Communications

Highways: 680 km total; 510 km paved, 170 km improved and unimproved earth
Inland waterways: 460 km, navigable by small oceangoing vessels and river and coastal steamers; 3,300 km possibly navigable by native craft
Ports: Cayenne
Civil air: no major transport aircraft
Airports: 11 total, 11 usable; 5 with permanent-surface runways; none with runways over 3,659 m; 1 with runways 2,440-3,659 m; 1 with runways 1,220-2,439 m
Telecommunications: fair open wire and radio relay system; 18,100 telephones; stations—5 AM, 7 FM, 9 TV; 1 Atlantic Ocean INTELSAT earth station

---

Defense Forces

Military manpower: males 15-49 27,866; 18,430 fit for military service
Note: defense is the responsibility of France

French Polynesia
(overseas territory of France)

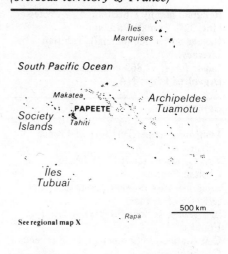

See regional map X

Geography

Total area: 3,941 km²; land area: 3,660 km²
Comparative area: slightly less than one-third the size of Connecticut
Land boundaries: none
Coastline: 2,525 km
Maritime claims:
  Extended economic zone: 200 nm
  Territorial sea: 12 nm
Climate: tropical, but moderate
Terrain: mixture of rugged high islands and low islands with reefs
Natural resources: timber, fish, cobalt
Land use: 1% arable land; 19% permanent crops; 5% meadows and pastures; 31% forest and woodland; 44% other
Environment: occasional cyclonic storm in January; includes five archipelagoes
Note: Makatea is one of three great phosphate rock islands in the Pacific (others are Banaba or Ocean Island in Kiribati and Nauru)

People

Population: 190,181 (July 1990), growth rate 2.5% (1990)
Birth rate: 31 births/1,000 population (1990)
Death rate: 6 deaths/1,000 population (1990)
Net migration rate: 0 migrants/1,000 population (1990)
Infant mortality rate: 23 deaths/1,000 live births (1990)
Life expectancy at birth: 66 years male, 71 years female (1990)
Total fertility rate: 3.9 children born/woman (1990)
Nationality: noun—French Polynesian(s); adjective—French Polynesian
Ethnic divisions: 78% Polynesian, 12% Chinese, 6% local French, 4% metropolitan French

French Polynesia (continued)

Religion: mainly Christian; 55% Protestant, 32% Roman Catholic
Language: French (official), Tahitian
Literacy: NA%
Labor force: 57,863 employed (1983)
Organized labor: NA

Government

Long-form name: Territory of French Polynesia
Type: overseas territory of France
Capital: Papeete
Administrative divisions: none (overseas territory of France)
Independence: none (overseas territory of France)
Constitution: 28 September 1958 (French Constitution)
Legal system: based on French system
National holiday: Taking of the Bastille, 14 July (1789)
Executive branch: French president, high commissioner of the republic, president of the Council of Ministers, vice president of the Council of Ministers, Council of Ministers
Legislative branch: unicameral Territorial Assembly
Judicial branch: Court of Appeal
Leaders: *Chief of State*—President François MITTERRAND (since 21 May 1981); High Commissioner of the Republic Jean MONTPEZAT (since NA November 1987);
Head of Government—President of the Council of Ministers Alexandre LEONTIEFF (since 9 December 1987); Vice President of the Council of Ministers Georges KELLY (since 9 December 1987)
Political parties and leaders: Tahoeraa Huiraatira (Gaullist), Gaston Flosse; Pupu Here Ai'a, Jean Juventin; Front de Libération, Oscar Temaru; Ai'a Api, Emile Vernaudon; Ia Mana Te Nunaa, Jacques Drollet; Pupu Taina, Michel Law; Toatiraa Polynesia, Arthur Chung; Te E'a Api, Francis Sanford
Suffrage: universal at age 18
Elections: *Territorial Assembly*—last held 16 March 1986 (next to be held March 1991); results—percent of vote by party NA; seats—(41 total) Tahoeraa Huiraatira 24, Amuitahiraa Mo Porinesia 6, Pupu Here Ai'a 4, Ia Mana 3, Front de Libération 2, other 2;
French Senate—last held 24 September 1989 (next to be held September 1992); results—percent of vote by party NA; seats—(1 total) Democrats for Progress 1;
French National Assembly last held 5 and 12 June 1988 (next to be held June 1993); results—percent of vote by party NA; seats—(2 total) Rally for the Republic 1, Ai'a Api 1

Diplomatic representation: as an overseas territory of France, French Polynesian interests are represented in the US by France
Flag: the flag of France is used

Economy

Overview: Since 1962, when France stationed military personnel in the region, French Polynesia has changed from a subsistence economy to one in which a high proportion of the work force is either employed by the military or supports the tourist industry. Tourism accounts for about 20% of GDP and is a primary source of hard currency earnings.
GDP: $2.24 billion, per capita $6,400; real growth rate NA% (1986)
Inflation rate (consumer prices): 1.2% (1987)
Unemployment rate: 8% (1986 est.)
Budget: revenues $431; expenditures $418, including capital expenditures of $NA (1986)
Exports: $75 million (f.o.b., 1987); *commodities*—coconut products 79%, mother-of-pearl 14%, vanilla, shark meat; *partners*—France 44%, US 21%
Imports: $767 million (c.i.f., 1986); *commodities*—fuels, foodstuffs, equipment; *partners*—France 50%, US 16%, New Zealand 6%
External debt: $NA
Industrial production: growth rate NA%
Electricity: 72,000 kW capacity; 265 million kWh produced, 1,350 kWh per capita (1989)
Industries: tourism, pearls, agricultural processing, handicrafts
Agriculture: coconut and vanilla plantations; vegetables and fruit; poultry, beef, dairy products
Aid: Western (non-US) countries, ODA and OOF bilateral commitments (1970-87), $3.6 billion
Currency: Comptoirs Français du Pacifique franc (plural—francs); 1 CFP franc (CFPF) = 100 centimes
Exchange rates: Comptoirs Français du Pacifique francs (CFPF) per US$1— 104.71 (January 1990), 115.99 (1989), 108.30 (1988), 109.27 (1987), 125.92 (1986), 163.35 (1985); note—linked at the rate of 18.18 to the French franc
Fiscal year: calendar year

Communications

Highways: 600 km (1982)
Ports: Papeete, Bora-bora
Merchant marine: 2 ships (1,000 GRT or over) totaling 2,732 GRT/4,191 DWT; includes 1 cargo, 1 refrigerated cargo; note—a subset of the French register
Civil air: about 6 major transport aircraft
Airports: 43 total, 41 usable; 23 with permanent-surface runways; none with runways over 3,659 m; 2 with runways 2,440-3,659 m; 12 with runways 1,220-2,439 m
Telecommunications: 33,200 telephones; 84,000 radio receivers; 26,400 TV sets; stations—5 AM, 2 FM, 6 TV; 1 Pacific Ocean INTELSAT earth station

Defense Forces

Note: defense is responsibility of France

French Southern and Antarctic Lands
(overseas territory of France)

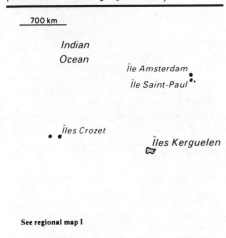

700 km

Indian
Ocean

Île Amsterdam
Île Saint-Paul

Îles Crozet

Îles Kerguelen

See regional map I

Geography

Total area: 7,781 km²; land area: 7,781 km²; includes Île Amsterdam, Île Saint-Paul, Îles Kerguelen, and Îles Crozet; excludes claim not recognized by the US of about 500,000 km² in Antarctica known as Terre Adélie
Comparative area: slightly less than 1.5 times the size of Delaware
Land boundaries: none
Coastline: 1,232 km
Maritime claims:
Contiguous zone: 12 nm
Continental shelf: 200 meters or to depth of exploration
Extended economic zone: 200 nm
Territorial sea: 12 nm
Disputes: claim in Antarctica (Terre Adélie) not recognized by the US
Climate: antarctic
Terrain: volcanic
Natural resources: fish, crayfish
Land use: 0% arable land; 0% permanent crops; 0% meadows and pastures; 0% forest and woodland; 100% other
Environment: Île Amsterdam and Île Saint-Paul are extinct volcanoes
Note: located in the southern Indian Ocean about equidistant between Africa, Antarctica, and Australia

People

Population: 210 (July 1990), growth rate 0.00% (1990); mostly researchers

Government

Long-form name: Territory of the French Southern and Antarctic Lands
Type: overseas territory of France governed by High Administrator Claude CORBIER (since NA 1988)
Flag: the flag of France is used

Economy

Overview: Economic activity is limited to servicing meteorological and geophysical research stations and French and other fishing fleets. The fishing catches landed on Îles Kerguelen by foreign ships are exported to France and Reunion.

Communications

Ports: none; offshore anchorage only
Merchant marine: 10 ships (1,000 GRT or over) totaling 217,203 GRT/348,632 DWT; includes 2 cargo, 3 refrigerated cargo, 1 petroleum, oils, and lubricants (POL) tanker, 2 liquefied gas, 2 bulk; note—a subset of the French register
Telecommunications: NA

Defense Forces

Note: defense is the responsibility of France

Gabon

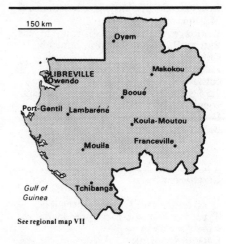

150 km

Oyem

LIBREVILLE
Owendo

Makokou

Booué

Port-Gentil Lambaréné

Koula-Moutou

Mouila

Franceville

Gulf of
Guinea

Tchibanga

See regional map VII

Geography

Total area: 267,670 km²; land area: 257,670 km²
Comparative area: slightly smaller than Colorado
Land boundaries: 2,551 km total; Cameroon 298 km, Congo 1,903 km, Equatorial Guinea 350 km
Coastline: 885 km
Maritime claims:
Contiguous zone: 24 nm
Exclusive fishing zone: 200 nm
Territorial sea: 12 nm
Disputes: maritime boundary with Equatorial Guinea
Climate: tropical; always hot, humid
Terrain: narrow coastal plain; hilly interior; savanna in east and south
Natural resources: crude oil, manganese, uranium, gold, timber, iron ore
Land use: 1% arable land; 1% permanent crops; 18% meadows and pastures; 78% forest and woodland; 2% other
Environment: deforestation

People

Population: 1,068,240 (July 1990), growth rate 0.8% (1990)
Birth rate: 28 births/1,000 population (1990)
Death rate: 15 deaths/1,000 population (1990)
Net migration rate: −6 migrants/1,000 population (1990)
Infant mortality rate: 106 deaths/1,000 live births (1990)
Life expectancy at birth: 50 years male, 56 years female (1990)
Total fertility rate: 4.0 children born/woman (1990)
Nationality: noun—Gabonese (sing., pl.); adjective—Gabonese
Ethnic divisions: about 40 Bantu tribes, including four major tribal groupings (Fang, Eshira, Bapounou, Bateke); about 100,000 expatriate Africans and Europeans, including 27,000 French

Gabon (continued)

Religion: 55-75% Christian, less than 1% Muslim, remainder animist
Language: French (official), Fang, Myene, Bateke, Bapounou/Eschira, Bandjabi
Literacy: 61.6%
Labor force: 120,000 salaried; 65.0% agriculture, 30.0% industry and commerce, 2.5% services, 2.5% government; 58% of population of working age (1983)
Organized labor: there are 38,000 members of the national trade union, the Gabonese Trade Union Confederation (COSYGA)

Government

Long-form name: Gabonese Republic
Type: republic; one-party presidential regime since 1964
Capital: Libreville
Administrative divisions: 9 provinces; Estuaire, Haut-Ogooué, Moyen-Ogooué, Ngounié, Nyanga, Ogooué-Ivindo, Ogooué-Lolo, Ogooué-Maritime, Woleu-Ntem
Independence: 17 August 1960 (from France)
Constitution: 21 February 1961, revised 15 April 1975
Legal system: based on French civil law system and customary law; judicial review of legislative acts in Constitutional Chamber of the Supreme Court; compulsory ICJ jurisdiction not accepted
National holiday: Renovation Day (Gabonese Democratic Party established), 12 March (1968)
Executive branch: president, prime minister, Cabinet
Legislative branch: unicameral National Assembly (Assemblé Nationale)
Judicial branch: Supreme Court (Cour Suprême)
Leaders: *Chief of State*—President El Hadj Omar BONGO (since 2 December 1967);
Head of Government—Prime Minister Léon MEBIAME (since 16 April 1975)
Political parties and leaders: only party—Gabonese Social Democratic Rally (RSDG), El Hadj Omar Bongo, president; formerly Gabonese Democratic Party (PDG), which was dissolved in February 1990
Suffrage: universal at age 21
Elections: *President*—last held on 9 November 1986 (next to be held November 1993); results—President Omar BONGO was reelected without opposition;
National Assembly—last held on 17 February 1985 (next to be held by February 1992); results—PDG was the only party; seats—(120 total, 111 elected) PDG 111
Communists: no organized party; probably some Communist sympathizers
Member of: ACP, AfDB, CCC, Conference of East and Central African States, EAMA, EIB (associate), FAO, G-77, GATT, IAEA, IBRD, ICAO, ICCO, ICO, IDA, IDB—Islamic Development Bank, IFAD, IFC, ILO, IMF, IMO, INTELSAT, INTERPOL, IPU, ITU,

NAM, OAU, OIC, OPEC, UDEAC, UN, UNESCO, UPU, WHO, WIPO, WMO, WTO
Diplomatic representation: Ambassador Jean Robert ODZAGA; Chancery at 2034 20th Street NW, Washington DC 20009; telephone (202) 797-1000; *US*—Ambassador Keith L. WAUCHOPE; Embassy at Boulevard de la Mer, Libreville (mailing address is B. P. 4000, Libreville); telephone 762003 or 762004, 761337, 721348, 740248
Flag: three equal horizontal bands of green (top), yellow, and blue

Economy

Overview: The economy, dependent on timber and manganese until the early 1970s, is now dominated by the oil sector. During the period 1981-85 oil accounted for about 46% of GDP, 83% of export earnings, and 65% of government revenues on average. The high oil prices of the early 1980s contributed to a substantial increase in per capita income, stimulated domestic demand, reinforced migration from rural to urban areas, and raised the level of real wages to among the highest in Sub-Saharan Africa. The three-year slide of Gabon's economy, which began with falling oil prices in 1985, stabilized in 1989 because of a near doubling of oil prices over their 1988 lows. The agricultural and industrial sectors are relatively underdeveloped, accounting for only 8% and 10%, respectively, of GDP in 1986.
GDP: $3.2 billion, per capita $3,200; real growth rate 0% (1989)
Inflation rate (consumer prices): 3% (1989)
Unemployment rate: NA%
Budget: revenues $927 million; expenditures $1.2 billion, including capital expenditures of $33 million (1988)
Exports: $1.14 billion (f.o.b., 1989 est.); *commodities*—crude oil 70%, manganese 11%, wood 12%, uranium 6%; *partners*—France 53%, US 22%, FRG, Japan
Imports: $0.76 billion (c.i.f., 1989); *commodities*—foodstuffs, chemical products, petroleum products, construction materials, manufactures, machinery; *partners*—France 48%, US 2.6%, FRG, Japan, UK
External debt: $2.0 billion (October 1989)
Industrial production: growth rate 1.7% (1986)
Electricity: 310,000 kW capacity; 980 million kWh produced, 920 kWh per capita (1989)
Industries: sawmills, petroleum, food and beverages; mining of increasing importance (especially manganese and uranium)
Agriculture: accounts for 8% of GDP (including fishing and forestry); cash crops—cocoa, coffee, palm oil; livestock not developed; importer of food; small fishing operations provide a catch of about 20,000 metric tons; okoume (a tropical softwood) is the most important timber product
Aid: US commitments, including Ex-Im (FY70-88), $64 million; Western (non-US) countries, ODA and OOF bilateral com-

mitments (1970-87), $1.7 billion; Communist countries (1970-88), $27 million
Currency: Communauté Financière Africaine franc (plural—francs); 1 CFA franc (CFAF) = 100 centimes
Exchange rates: Communauté Financière Africaine francs (CFAF) per US$1—287.99 (January 1990), 319.01 (1989), 297.85 (1988), 300.54 (1987), 346.30 (1986), 449.26 (1985)
Fiscal year: calendar year

Communications

Railroads: 649 km 1.437-meter standard-gauge single track (Transgabonese Railroad)
Highways: 7,500 km total; 560 km paved, 960 km laterite, 5,980 km earth
Inland waterways: 1,600 km perennially navigable
Pipelines: crude oil, 270 km; refined products, 14 km
Ports: Owendo, Port-Gentil, Libreville
Merchant marine: 2 cargo ships (1,000 GRT or over) totaling 18,563 GRT/25,330 DWT
Civil air: 11 major transport aircraft
Airports: 79 total, 68 usable; 10 with permanent-surface runways; none with runways over 3,659 m; 2 with runways 2,440-3,659 m; 21 with runways 1,220-2,439 m
Telecommunications: adequate system of open-wire, radio relay, tropospheric scatter links and radiocommunication stations; 13,800 telephones; stations—6 AM, 6 FM, 8 TV; satellite earth stations—2 Atlantic Ocean INTELSAT and 12 domestic satellite

Defense Forces

Branches: Army, Navy, Air Force, paramilitary Gendarmerie
Military manpower: males 15-49, 266,110; 133,158 fit for military service; 9,282 reach military age (20) annually
Defense expenditures: 3.2% of GDP, or $102 million (1990 est.)

The Gambia

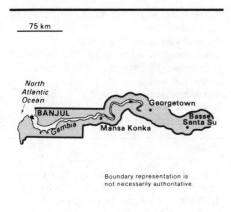

75 km

North
Atlantic
Ocean

BANJUL
Gambia
Mansa Konka
Georgetown
Basse
Santa Su

Boundary representation is
not necessarily authoritative.

See regional map VII

Geography

Total area: 11,300 km²; land area: 10,000 km²
Comparative area: slightly more than twice the size of Delaware
Land boundary: 740 km with Senegal
Coastline: 80 km
Maritime claims:
  Contiguous zone: 18 nm
  Continental shelf: not specific
  Exclusive fishing zone: 200 nm
  Territorial sea: 12 nm
Disputes: short section of boundary with Senegal is indefinite
Climate: tropical; hot, rainy season (June to November); cooler, dry season (November to May)
Terrain: flood plain of the Gambia River flanked by some low hills
Natural resources: fish
Land use: 16% arable land; 0% permanent crops; 9% meadows and pastures; 20% forest and woodland; 55% other; includes 3% irrigated
Environment: deforestation
Note: almost an enclave of Senegal; smallest country on the continent of Africa

People

Population: 848,147 (July 1990), growth rate 3.1% (1990)
Birth rate: 48 births/1,000 population (1990)
Death rate: 18 deaths/1,000 population (1990)
Net migration rate: 0 migrants/1,000 population (1990)
Infant mortality rate: 140 deaths/1,000 live births (1990)
Life expectancy at birth: 46 years male, 50 years female (1990)
Total fertility rate: 6.5 children born/woman (1990)
Nationality: noun—Gambian(s); adjective—Gambian

Ethnic divisions: 99% African (42% Mandinka, 18% Fula, 16% Wolof, 10% Jola, 9% Serahuli, 4% other); 1% non-Gambian
Religion: 90% Muslim, 9% Christian, 1% indigenous beliefs
Language: English (official); Mandinka, Wolof, Fula, other indigenous vernaculars
Literacy: 25.1%
Labor force: 400,000 (1986 est.); 75.0% agriculture, 18.9% industry, commerce, and services, 6.1% government; 55% population of working age (1983)
Organized labor: 25-30% of wage labor force

Government

Long-form name: Republic of The Gambia
Type: republic
Capital: Banjul
Administrative divisions: 5 divisions and 1 city*; Banjul*, Lower River, MacCarthy Island, North Bank, Upper River, Western
Independence: 18 February 1965 (from UK); The Gambia and Senegal signed an agreement on 12 December 1981 (effective 1 February 1982) that called for the creation of a loose confederation to be known as Senegambia, but the agreement was dissolved on 30 September 1989
Constitution: 24 April 1970
Legal system: based on a composite of English common law, Koranic law, and customary law; accepts compulsory ICJ jurisdiction, with reservations
National holiday: Independence Day, 18 February (1965)
Executive branch: president, vice president, Cabinet
Legislative branch: unicameral House of Representatives
Judicial branch: Supreme Court
Leaders: *Chief of State and Head of Government*—President Alhaji Sir Dawda Kairaba JAWARA (since 24 April 1970); Vice President Bakary Bunja DARBO (since 12 May 1982)
Political parties and leaders: People's Progressive Party (PPP), Dawda K. Jawara, secretary general; National Convention Party (NCP), Sheriff Dibba; Gambian People's Party (GPP), Assan Musa Camara; United Party (UP); People's Democratic Organization of Independence and Socialism (PDOIS)
Suffrage: universal at age 21
Elections: *President*—last held on 11 March 1987 (next to be held March 1992); results—Sir Dawda Jawara (PPP) 61.1%, Sherif Mustapha Dibba (NCP) 25.2%, Assan Musa Camara (GPP) 13.7%; *House of Representatives*—last held on 11 March 1987 (next to be held by March 1992); results—PPP 56.6%, NCP 27.6%, GPP 14.7%, PDOIS 1%; seats—(43 total, 36 elected) PPP 31, NCP 5
Communists: no Communist party
Member of: ACP, AfDB, APC, Commonwealth, ECA, ECOWAS, FAO, G-77, GATT, IBRD, ICAO, IDA, IDB—Inter-American Development Bank, IFAD,

IFC, IMF, IMO, IRC, ITU, NAM, OAU, OIC, UN, UNESCO, UPU, WFTU, WHO, WMO, WTO
Diplomatic representation: Ambassador Ousman A. SALLAH; Chancery at Suite 720, 1030 15th Street NW, Washington DC 20005; telephone (202) 842-1356 or 842-1359; *US*—Ambassador (vacant); Embassy at Pipeline Road (Kairaba Avenue), Fajara, Banjul (mailing address is P. M. B. No. 19, Banjul); telephone Serrekunda [220] 92856 or 92858, 91970, 91971
Flag: three equal horizontal bands of red (top), blue with white edges, and green

Economy

Overview: The Gambia has no important mineral or other natural resources and has a limited agricultural base. It is one of the world's poorest countries with a per capita income of about $250. About 75% of the population is engaged in crop production and livestock raising, which contributes about 30% to GDP. Small-scale manufacturing activity—processing peanuts, fish, and hides—accounts for less than 10% of GDP. Tourism is a growing industry. The Gambia imports about 33% of its food, all fuel, and most manufactured goods. Exports are concentrated on peanut products (over 75% of total value).
GDP: $195 million, per capita $250; real growth rate 4.6% (FY89 est.)
Inflation rate (consumer prices): 8.0% (FY89 est.)
Unemployment rate: NA%
Budget: revenues $75 million; expenditures $67 million, including capital expenditures of $21 million (FY89)
Exports: $133 million (f.o.b., FY89); *commodities*—peanuts and peanut products, fish, cotton lint, palm kernels; *partners*—Ghana 49%, Europe 27%, Japan 12%, US 1% (1986)
Imports: $105 million (c.i.f., FY89); *commodities*—foodstuffs, manufactures, raw materials, fuel, machinery and transport equipment; *partners*—Europe 55% (EC 39%, other 16%), Asia 20%, US 11%, Senegal 4% (1986)
External debt: $330 million (December 1989 est.)
Industrial production: growth rate 7.3% (FY88)
Electricity: 29,000 kW capacity; 64 million kWh produced, 80 kWh per capita (1989)
Industries: peanut processing, tourism, beverages, agricultural machinery assembly, woodworking, metalworking, clothing
Agriculture: accounts for 30% of GDP and employs about 75% of the population; imports one-third of food requirements; major export crop is peanuts; the principal crops—millet, sorghum, rice, corn, cassava, palm kernels; livestock—cattle, sheep, and goats; forestry and fishing resources not fully exploited
Aid: US commitments, including Ex-Im (FY70-88), $84 million; Western (non-US) countries, ODA and OOF bilateral com-

The Gambia (continued)

mitments (1970-87), $422 million; Communist countries (1970-88), $39 million
Currency: dalasi (plural—dalasi); 1 dalasi (D) = 100 bututs
Exchange rates: dalasi (D) per US$1— 8.3232 (December 1989), 7.5846 (1989), 6.7086 (1988), 7.0744 (1987), 6.9380 (1986), 3.8939 (1985)
Fiscal year: 1 July-30 June

Communications

Highways: 3,083 km total; 431 km paved, 501 km gravel/laterite, and 2,151 km unimproved earth
Inland waterways: 400 km
Ports: Banjul
Civil air: 2 major transport aircraft
Airports: 1 with permanent-surface runway 2,440-3,659 m
Telecommunications: adequate network of radio relay and wire; 3,500 telephones; stations—3 AM, 2 FM, 1 TV; 1 Atlantic Ocean INTELSAT earth station

Defense Forces

Branches: Army, paramilitary Gendarmerie
Military manpower: males 15-49, 182,308; 92,001 fit for military service
Defense expenditures: NA

Gaza Strip

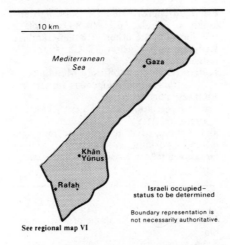

10 km

Mediterranean Sea

Gaza

Khān Yūnus

Rafah

Israeli occupied- status to be determined

Boundary representation is not necessarily authoritative.

See regional map VI

Note: The war between Israel and the Arab states in June 1967 ended with Israel in control of the West Bank and the Gaza Strip, the Sinai, and the Golan Heights. As stated in the 1978 Camp David Accords and reaffirmed by President Reagan's 1 September 1982 peace initiative, the final status of the West Bank and the Gaza Strip, their relationship with their neighbors, and a peace treaty between Israel and Jordan are to be negotiated among the concerned parties. Camp David further specifies that these negotiations will resolve the respective boundaries. Pending the completion of this process, it is US policy that the final status of the West Bank and the Gaza Strip has yet to be determined. In the view of the US, the term West Bank describes all of the area west of the Jordan under Jordanian administration before the 1967 Arab-Israeli war. With respect to negotiations envisaged in the framework agreement, however, it is US policy that a distinction must be made between Jerusalem and the rest of the West Bank because of the city's special status and circumstances. Therefore, a negotiated solution for the final status of Jerusalem could be different in character from that of the rest of the West Bank.

Geography

Total area: 380km^2; land area: 380 km^2
Comparative area: slightly more than twice the size of Washington, DC
Land boundaries: 62 km total; Egypt 11 km, Israel 51 km
Coastline: 40 km
Maritime claims: Israeli occupied with status to be determined
Disputes: Israeli occupied with status to be determined
Climate: temperate, mild winters, dry and warm to hot summers

Terrain: flat to rolling, sand and dune covered coastal plain
Natural resources: negligible
Land use: 13% arable land, 32% permanent crops, 0% meadows and pastures, 0% forest and woodland, 55% other
Environment: desertification
Note: there are 18 Jewish settlements in the Gaza Strip

People

Population: 615,575 (July 1990), growth rate 3.2% (1990); in addition, there are 2,500 Jewish settlers in the Gaza Strip
Birth rate: 47 births/1,000 population (1990)
Death rate: 7 deaths/1,000 population (1990)
Net migration rate: −7 migrants/1,000 population (1990)
Infant mortality rate: 55 deaths/1,000 live births (1990)
Life expectancy at birth: 63 years male, 66 years female (1990)
Total fertility rate: 7.0 children born/ woman (1990)
Nationality: NA
Ethnic divisions: 99.8% Palestinian Arab and other, 0.2% Jewish
Religion: 99% Muslim (predominantly Sunni), 0.7% Christian, 0.3% Jewish
Language: Arabic, Israeli settlers speak Hebrew, English widely understood
Literacy: NA%
Labor force: (excluding Israeli Jewish settlers) 32.0% small industry, commerce and business, 24.4% construction, 25.5% service and other, and 18.1% agriculture (1984)
Organized labor: NA

Government

Long-form name: none
Note: The Gaza Strip is currently governed by Israeli military authorities and Israeli civil administration. It is US policy that the final status of the Gaza Strip will be determined by negotiations among the concerned parties. These negotiations will determine how this area is to be governed.

Economy

Overview: Nearly half of the labor force of the Gaza Strip is employed across the border by Israeli industrial, construction, and agricultural enterprises, with worker transfer funds accounting for 40% of GNP in 1989. The once dominant agricultural sector now contributes only 13% to GNP, about the same as that of the construction sector, and industry accounts for 7%. Gaza depends upon Israel for 90% of its imports and as a market for 80% of its

110

exports. Unrest in the territory in 1988-89 (*intifadah*) has raised unemployment and substantially lowered the incomes of the population.

GNP: $380 million, per capita $650; real growth rate NA% (1988)

Inflation rate (consumer prices): NA%

Unemployment rate: NA%

Budget: revenues $36.6 million; expenditures $32.0 million, including capital expenditures of NA (1986)

Exports: $88 million; *commodities*—citrus; *partners*—Israel, Egypt (1989 est.)

Imports: $260 million; *commodities*—food, consumer goods, construction materials; *partners*—Israel, Egypt (1989 est.)

External debt: $NA

Industrial production: growth rate NA%

Electricity: power supplied by Israel

Industries: generally small family businesses that produce cement, textiles, soap, olive-wood carvings, and mother-of-pearl souvenirs; the Israelis have established some small-scale modern industries in an industrial center

Agriculture: olives, citrus and other fruits, vegetables, beef, dairy products

Aid: none

Currency: new Israeli shekel (plural—shekels); 1 new Israeli shekel (NIS) = 100 new agorot

Exchange rates: new Israeli shekels (NIS) per US$1—1.9450 (January 1990), 1.9164 (1989), 1.5989 (1988), 1.5946 (1987), 1.4878 (1986), 1.1788 (1985)

Fiscal year: 1 April-March 31

Communications

Railroads: one line, abandoned and in disrepair, but trackage remains

Highways: small, poorly developed indigenous road network

Ports: facilities for small boats to service Gaza

Airports: 1 with permanent-surface runway less than 1,220 m

Telecommunications: stations--no AM, no FM, no TV

Defense Forces

Branches: NA

Military manpower: NA

Defense expenditures: NA

German Democratic Republic (East Germany)*

The final borders of Germany have not been established.

100 km

See regional map V

Geography

Total area: 108,330 km²; land area: 105,980 km²

Comparative area: slightly smaller than Tennessee

Land boundaries: 2,296 km total; Czechoslovakia 459 km, Poland 456 km, FRG 1,381 km

Coastline: 901 km

Maritime claims:
   Continental shelf: 200 meters or to depth of exploitation
   Exclusive fishing zone: 200 nm
   Territorial sea: 12 nm

Disputes: it is US policy that the final borders of Germany have not been established; the US is seeking to settle the property claims of US nationals against the GDR

Climate: temperate; cloudy, cold winters with frequent rain and snow; cool, wet summers

Terrain: mostly flat plain with hills and mountains in south

Natural resources: lignite, potash, uranium, copper, natural gas, salt, nickel

Land use: 45% arable land; 3% permanent crops; 12% meadows and pastures; 28% forest and woodland; 12% other; includes 2% irrigated

Environment: significant deforestation in mountains caused by air pollution and acid rain

Note: strategic location on North European Plain and near the entrance to the Baltic Sea; West Berlin is an enclave (about 116 km by air or 176 km by road from FRG)

People

Population: 16,307,170 (July 1990), growth rate −0.6% (1990)

Birth rate: 12 births/1,000 population (1990)

Death rate: 12 deaths/1,000 population (1990)

Net migration rate: −6 migrants/1,000 population (1990)

Infant mortality rate: 7 deaths/1,000 live births (1990)

Life expectancy at birth: 71 years male, 77 years female (1990)

Total fertility rate: 1.7 children born/woman (1990)

Nationality: noun—German(s); adjective—German

Ethnic divisions: 99.7% German, 0.3% Slavic and other

Religion: 47% Protestant, 7% Roman Catholic, 46% unaffiliated or other; less than 5% of Protestants and about 25% of Roman Catholics active participants

Language: German

Literacy: 99%

Labor force: 8,960,000; 37.5% industry, 21.1% services, 10.8% agriculture and forestry, 10.3% commerce, 7.4% transport and communications, 6.6% construction, 3.1% handicrafts, 3.2% other (1987)

Organized labor: 87.7% of labor force

Government*

Long-form name: German Democratic Republic; abbreviated GDR

Type: Communist state

Capital: East Berlin (not officially recognized by France, UK, and US, which together with the USSR have special rights and responsibilities in Berlin)

Administrative divisions: 14 districts (bezirke, singular—bezirk); Cottbus, Dresden, Erfurt, Frankfurt, Gera, Halle, Karl-Marx-Stadt, Leipzig, Magdeburg, Neubrandenburg, Potsdam, Rostock, Schwerin, Suhl

Independence: self-government proclaimed 7 October 1949, with permission of the Soviet authorities

Constitution: 9 April 1968, amended 7 October 1974

Legal system: civil law system modified by Communist legal theory; no judicial review of legislative acts; has not accepted compulsory ICJ jurisdiction

National holiday: Foundation of the German Democratic Republic, 7 October (1949)

Executive branch: Council of State abolished on 5 April 1990, post of president to be created; chairman of the Council of Ministers, Council of Ministers (cabinet)

Legislative branch: unicameral People's Chamber (Volkskammer)

Judicial branch: Supreme Court

Leaders: *Chief of State*—Acting President of the People's Chamber Sabine BERGMANN-POHL (since 5 April 1990);

*Update note: At September 1, 1990, reunification of the two German states was scheduled for October 3, 1990.

111

German Democratic Republic
(East Germany) *(continued)*

Head of Government—Chairman of the Council of Ministers Lothar DE MAIZIERE (since 12 April 1990); Deputy Chairman Peter-Michael DIESTEL (since 16 April 1990)

Political parties and leaders: *Alliance for Germany*—Christian Democratic Union (CDU), Lothar de Maiziere, chairman; German Social Union (DSU), Hans-Wilhelm Ebeling, chairman; and Democratic Awakening (DA), Rainer Eppelmann, chairman; Social Democratic Party of Germany (SPD), Markus Meckel, acting chairman; Party for Democratic Socialism (PDS, former Communist), Gregor Gysi, chairman; *League of Free Democrats (BFD)*—Liberals, Rainer Ortleb, chairman; Free Democratic Party (FDP), Bruno Menzel, chairman; and German Forum Party (DFP), Juergen Schmieder, chairman; *Alliance '90*—New Forum, Baerbel Bohley, Jens Reich, Sebastian Pflugbeil, spokespersons; Democracy Now, Konrad Weiss, spokesperson; and United Left, Herbert Misslitz, spokesperson; Greens Party (GP), Vera Wollenberger, spokesperson; Democratic Peasants' Party (DBD), Guenther Maleuda, chairman

Suffrage: universal at age 18

Elections: *People's Chamber*—last held on 18 March 1990 (next to be held March NA); results—Alliance for Germany—CDU 40.9%, DSU 6.3%, DA 0.9%; SPD 21.8; BFD 5.3%; SPD 21.8%; PDS 16.3%; Alliance 90 2.9%; DBD 2.2%; GP 2.0%; NDPD 0.4%; others 1.0%; seats—(400 total, including 66 from East Berlin) Alliance for Germany—CDU 164, DSU 25, DA 4; SPD 87; BFD 21; PDS 65; Alliance 90 12, DBD 9; GP 8; NDPD 2; others 3

Communists: 500,000 to 700,000 party members (1990)

Member of: CEMA, IAEA, IBEC, ICES, ILO, IMO, IPU, ITU, UN, UNESCO, UPU, Warsaw Pact, WFTU, WHO, WIPO, WMO, WTO

Diplomatic representation: Ambassador Dr. Gerhard HERDER; Chancery at 1717 Massachusetts Avenue NW, Washington DC 20036; telephone (202) 232-3134; *US*—Ambassador Richard C. BARKLEY; Embassy at 1080 Berlin, Neustaedtische Kirchstrasse 4-5, East Berlin (mailing address is Box E, APO New York 09742); telephone [37] (2) 220-2741

Flag: three equal horizontal bands of black (top), red, and yellow with the coat of arms centered; the coat of arms contains, in yellow, a hammer and compass encircled by a wreath of grain with a black, red, and gold ribbon at the bottom; similar to the flag of the FRG which does not have a coat of arms

---

Economy

Overview: The GDR is moving rapidly away from its centrally planned economy. As the 1990s begin, economic integration with West Germany appears inevitable, beginning with the establishment of a common currency. The opening of the border with the FRG in late 1989 and the continuing emigration of hundreds of thousands of skilled workers had brought growth to a standstill by yearend 1989. Features of the old economic regime that will quickly change: (a) the collectivization of 95% of East German farms; (b) state ownership of nearly all transportation facilities, industrial plants, foreign trade organizations, and financial institutions; (c) the 65% share in trade of the USSR and other CEMA countries; and (d) the detailed control over economic details exercised by Party and state. Once integrated into the thriving West German economy, the area will have to stem the outflow of workers and renovate the obsolescent industrial base. After an initial readjustment period, living standards and quality of output will steadily rise toward West German levels.

GNP: $159.5 billion, per capita $9,679; real growth rate 1.2% (1989 est.)

Inflation rate (consumer prices): NA

Unemployment rate: NA%

Budget: revenues $123.5 billion; expenditures $123.2 billion, including capital expenditures of $33 billion (1986)

Exports: $30.7 billion (f.o.b., 1988); *commodities*—machinery and transport equipment 47%, fuels and metals 16%, consumer goods 16%, chemical products and building materials 13%, semimanufactured goods and processed foodstuffs 8%; *partners*—USSR, Czechoslovakia, Poland, FRG, Hungary, Bulgaria, Switzerland, Romania

Imports: $31.0 billion (f.o.b., 1988); *commodities*—fuels and metals 40%, machinery and transport equipment 29%, chemical products and building materials 9%; *partners*—CEMA countries 65%, non-Communist 33%, other 2%

External debt: $20.6 billion (1989)

Industrial production: growth rate 2.7% (1989 est.)

Electricity: (including East Berlin) 24,585,000 kW capacity; 122,500 million kWh produced, 7,390 kWh per capita (1989)

Industries: metal fabrication, chemicals, brown coal, shipbuilding, machine building, food and beverages, textiles, petroleum

Agriculture: accounts for about 10% of GNP (including fishing and forestry); principal crops—wheat, rye, barley, potatoes, sugar beets, fruit; livestock products include pork, beef, chicken, milk, hides and skins; net importer of food; fish catch of 193,600 metric tons in 1987

Aid: donor—$4.0 billion extended bilaterally to non-Communist less developed countries (1956-88)

Currency: GDR mark (plural—marks); 1 GDR mark (M) = 100 pfennige

Exchange rates: GDR marks (M) per US$1—3.01 (1988), 3.00 (1987), 3.30 (1986), 3.70 (1985), 3.64 (1984)

Fiscal year: calendar year

Communications

Railroads: 14,005 km total; 13,730 km 1.435-meter standard gauge, 275 km 1.000-meter or other narrow gauge, 3,830 (est.) km 1.435-meter double-track standard gauge; 2,754 km overhead electrified (1986)

Highways: 124,615 km total; 47,214 km concrete, asphalt, stone block, of which 1,913 km are autobahn and limited access roads, 11,261 are trunk roads, and 34,040 are regional roads; 77,401 municipal roads (1985)

Inland waterways: 2,319 km (1986)

Pipelines: crude oil, 1,301 km; refined products, 500 km; natural gas, 2,150 km (1988)

Ports: Rostock, Wismar, Stralsund, Sassnitz; river ports are East Berlin, Riesa, Magdeburg, and Eisenhuttenstadt on the Elbe or Oder Rivers and connecting canals

Merchant marine: 145 ships (1,000 GRT or over) totaling 1,349,537 GRT/ 1,733,089 DWT; includes 1 passenger, 89 cargo, 10 refrigerated cargo, 6 roll-on/ roll-off cargo, 16 container, 1 multifunction large-load carrier, 2 railcar carrier, 1 petroleum, oils, and lubricants (POL) tanker, 2 chemical tanker, 1 liquefied gas tanker, 16 bulk

Civil air: 45 major transport aircraft

Airports: 190 total, 190 usable; 70 with permanent-surface runways; 1 with runway over 3,659 m; 45 with runways 2,440-3,659 m; 40 with runways 1,220-2,439 m

Telecommunications: stations—23 AM, 17 FM, 21 TV; 15 Soviet TV relays; 6,181,860 TV sets; 6,700,000 radio receivers; at least 1 satellite earth station

---

Defense Forces

Branches: National People's Army, Border Troops, Air and Air Defense Command, People's Navy

Military manpower: eligible 15-49, 7,944,305; of the 4,045,396 males 15-49, 3,243,970 are fit for military service; 91,579 reach military age (18) annually; of the 3,898,909 females 15-49, 3,117,847 are fit for military service; 85,892 reach military age (18) annually

Defense expenditures: 16.2 billion marks, 5.4% of total budget (1989); note—conversion of the military budget into US dollars using the official administratively set exchange rate would produce misleading results

Germany, Federal Republic of (West Germany)*

200 km
North Sea
Kiel Bay
Kiel
Hamburg
Bremen
Hannover
Berlin
The final borders of Germany have not been established.
Cologne
*BONN
Frankfurt
Nurnberg
Stuttgart
Munich
Freiburg

See regional map V

Geography

Total area: 248,580 km^2; land area: 244,280 km^2; includes West Berlin
Comparative area: slightly smaller than Oregon
Land boundaries: 4,256 km total; Austria 784 km, Belgium 167 km, Czechoslovakia 356 km, Denmark 68 km, France 451 km, GDR 1,381 km; Luxembourg 138 km, Netherlands 577 km, Switzerland 334 km
Coastline: 1,488 km
Maritime claims:
Continental shelf: 200 meters or to depth of exploitation
Exclusive fishing zone: 200 nm
Territorial sea: 3 nm (extends, at one point, to 16 nm in the Helgoländer Bucht)
Disputes: it is US policy that the final borders of Germany have not been established
Climate: temperate and marine; cool, cloudy, wet winters and summers; occasional warm, tropical foehn wind; high relative humidity
Terrain: lowlands in north, uplands in center, Bavarian Alps in south
Natural resources: iron ore, coal, potash, timber
Land use: 30% arable land; 1% permanent crops; 19% meadows and pastures; 30% forest and woodland; 20% other; includes 1% irrigated
Environment: air and water pollution
Note: West Berlin is an exclave (about 116 km by air or 176 km by road from FRG)

People

Population: 62,168,200 (July 1990), growth rate 0.5% (1990)
Birth rate: 11 births/1,000 population (1990)
Death rate: 11 deaths/1,000 population (1990)

Net migration rate: 5 migrants/1,000 population (1990)
Infant mortality rate: 6 deaths/1,000 live births (1990)
Life expectancy at birth: 73 years male, 81 years female (1990)
Total fertility rate: 1.4 children born/woman (1990)
Nationality: noun—German(s); adjective—German
Ethnic divisions: primarily German; Danish minority
Religion: 45% Roman Catholic, 44% Protestant, 11% other
Language: German
Literacy: 99%
Labor force: 27,790,000; 41.6% industry, 35.4% services and other, 18.2% trade and transport, 4.8% agriculture (1987)
Organized labor: 9,300,000 total; 7,760,000 in German Trade Union Federation (DGB); union membership constitutes about 40% of union-eligible labor force, 34% of total labor force, and 35% of wage and salary earners (1986)

Government*

Long-form name: Federal Republic of Germany; abbreviated FRG
Type: federal republic
Capital: Bonn
Administrative divisions: 10 states (länder, singular—land); Baden-Württemberg, Bayern, Bremen, Hamburg, Hessen, Niedersachsen, Nordrhein-Westfalen, Rheinland-Pfalz, Saarland, Schleswig-Holstein
Constitution: 23 May 1949, provisional constitution known as Basic Law
Legal system: civil law system with indigenous concepts; judicial review of legislative acts in the Federal Constitutional Court; has not accepted compulsory ICJ jurisdiction
National holiday: NA
Executive branch: president, chancellor, Cabinet
Legislative branch: bicameral Parliament (Parlament) consists of an upper chamber or Federal Assembly (Bundesrat) and a lower chamber or National Assembly (Bundestag)
Judicial branch: Federal Constitutional Court (Bundesverfassungsgericht)
Leaders: *Chief of State*—President Dr. Richard von WEIZSÄCKER (since 1 July 1984);
Head of Government—Chancellor Dr. Helmut KOHL (since 4 October 1982)
Political parties and leaders: Christian Democratic Union (CDU), Helmut Kohl; Christian Social Union (CSU), Theo Waigel; Free Democratic Party (FDP), Otto Lambsdorff; Social Democratic Party (SPD), Hans-Jochen Vogel; National

Democratic Party (NPD), Martin Mussgnug; Republikaner, Franz Schoerhuber; Communist Party (DKP), Herbert Mies; Green Party—Realos faction, Joschka Fischer; Green Party—Fundis faction, Jutta Ditfurth
Suffrage: universal at age 18
Elections: *National Assembly*—last held 25 January 1987 (next to be held by 18 January 1991); results—SPD 37.0%, CDU 34.5%, CSU 9.8%, FDP 9.1%, Green Party 8.2%, others 1.4%; seats—(497 total, 22 are elected by the West Berlin House of Representatives and have limited voting rights) SPD 186, CDU 174, CSU 49, FDP 46, Green Party 42
Communists: about 40,000 members and supporters
Other political or pressure groups: expellee, refugee, and veterans groups
Member of: ADB, CCC, Council of Europe, DAC, EC, EIB, EMS, ESA, FAO, GATT, IAEA, IBRD, ICAC, ICAO, ICES, ICO, IDA, IDB—Inter-American Development Bank, IFAD, IEA, IFC, IHO, ILO, ILZSG, IMF, IMO, INTELSAT, INTERPOL, IPU, ITC, ITU, NATO, OAS (observer), OECD, UN, UNESCO, UPU, WEU, WHO, WIPO, WMO, WSG, WTO
Diplomatic representation: Ambassador Jeurgen RUHFUS; Chancery at 4645 Reservoir Road NW, Washington DC 20007; telephone (202) 298-4000; there are FRG Consulates General in Atlanta, Boston, Chicago, Detroit, Houston, Los Angeles, San Francisco, Seattle, and New York, and Consulates in Miami and New Orleans; *US*—Ambassador Vernon WALTERS; Embassy at Deichmanns Avenue, 5300 Bonn 2 (mailing address is APO New York 09080); telephone 49 (228) 3391; there are US Consulates General in Frankfurt, Hamburg, Munich, and Stuttgart
Flag: three equal horizontal bands of black (top), red, and yellow; similar to the flag of the GDR which has a coat of arms in the center

Economy

Overview: West Germany, a major economic power and a leading exporter, has a highly urbanized and skilled population that enjoys excellent living standards and comprehensive social welfare benefits. The FRG is poor in natural resources, coal being the most important mineral. The FRG's comparative advantage lies in the technologically advanced production stages. Thus manufacturing and services dominate economic activity, and raw materials and semimanufactures constitute a large proportion of imports. In 1988 manufacturing accounted for 35% of GDP,

*Update note: At September 1, 1990, reunification of the two German states was scheduled for October 3, 1990.

113

Germany, Federal Republic of
(West Germany) (continued)

with other sectors contributing lesser amounts. The major economic problem in 1989 is persistent unemployment of over 8%. The FRG is well poised to take advantage of the increasing economic integration of the European Community. The dramatic opening of the boundary with East Germany in late 1989 poses new economic challenges that could tax even this powerful economy.

GDP: $945.7 billion, per capita $15,300; real growth rate 4.3% (1989 est.)

Inflation rate (consumer prices): 3.0% (1989)

Unemployment rate: 8.4% (1989)

Budget: revenues $539 billion; expenditures $563 billion, including capital expenditures of $11.5 billion (1988)

Exports: $323.4 billion (f.o.b., 1988); *commodities*—manufactures 86.6% (including machines and machine tools, chemicals, motor vehicles, iron and steel products), agricultural products 4.9%, raw materials 2.3%, fuels 1.3%; *partners*—EC 52.7% (France 12%, Netherlands 9%, Italy 9%, UK 9%, Belgium-Luxembourg 7%), other West Europe 18%, US 10%, Eastern Europe 4%, OPEC 3% (1987)

Imports: $250.6 billion (f.o.b., 1988); *commodities*—manufactures 68.5%, agricultural products 12.0%, fuels 9.7%, raw materials 7.1%; *partners*—EC 52.7% (France 12%, Netherlands 11%, Italy 10%, UK 7%, Belgium-Luxembourg 7%), other West Europe 15%, US 6%, Japan 6%, Eastern Europe 5%, OPEC 3% (1987)

External debt: $500 million (June 1988)

Industrial production: growth rate 3.3% (1988)

Electricity: (including West Berlin) 110,075,000 kW capacity; 452,390 million kWh produced, 7,420 kWh per capita (1989)

Industries: among world's largest producers of iron, steel, coal, cement, chemicals, machinery, ships, vehicles, and machine tools; electronics, food and beverages

Agriculture: accounts for about 2% of GDP (including fishing and forestry); diversified crop and livestock farming; principal crops and livestock include potatoes, wheat, barley, sugar beets, fruit, cabbage, cattle, pigs, poultry; net importer of food; fish catch of 202,000 metric tons in 1987

Aid: donor—ODA and OOF commitments (1970-87), $60.0 billion

Currency: deutsche mark (plural—marks); 1 deutsche mark (DM) = 100 pfennige

Exchange rates: deutsche marks (DM) per US$1—1.6918 (January 1990), 1.8800 (1989), 1.7562 (1988), 1.7974 (1987), 2.1715 (1986), 2.9440 (1985)

Fiscal year: calendar year

Communications

Railroads: 31,443 km total; 27,421 km government owned, 1.435-meter standard gauge (12,491 km double track, 11,501 km electrified); 4,022 km nongovernment owned, including 3,598 km 1.435-meter standard gauge (214 km electrified) and 424 km 1.000-meter gauge (186 km electrified)

Highways: 466,305 km total; 169,568 km primary, includes 6,435 km autobahn, 32,460 km national highways (Bundesstrassen), 65,425 km state highways (Landesstrassen), 65,248 km county roads (Kreisstrassen); 296,737 km of secondary communal roads (Gemeindestrassen)

Inland waterways: 5,222 km, of which almost 70% are usable by craft of 1,000-metric ton capacity or larger; major rivers include the Rhine and Elbe; Kiel Canal is an important connection between the Baltic Sea and the North Sea

Pipelines: crude oil, 2,343 km; refined products, 3,446 km; natural gas, 95,414 km

Ports: maritime—Bremerhaven, Brunsbuttel, Cuxhaven, Emden, Bremen, Hamburg, Kiel, Lübeck, Wilhelmshaven; inland—27 major

Merchant marine: 422 ships (1,000 GRT or over) totaling 3,436,568 GRT/4,297,520 DWT; includes 2 passenger, 7 short-sea passenger, 218 cargo, 4 refrigerated cargo, 95 container, 20 roll-on/roll-off cargo, 2 railcar carrier, 7 barge carrier, 2 multifunction large-load carrier, 12 petroleum, oils, and lubricants (POL) tanker, 21 chemical tanker, 15 liquefied gas, 5 combination ore/oil, 13 combination bulk

Civil air: 194 major transport aircraft

Airports: 466 total, 457 usable; 240 with permanent-surface runways; 3 with runways over 3,659 m; 41 with runways 2,440-3,659 m; 55 with runways 1,220-2,439 m

Telecommunications: highly developed, modern telecommunication service to all parts of the country; fully adequate in all respects; 40,300,000 telephones; stations—87 AM, 205 (376 relays) FM, 300 (6,400 relays) TV; 6 submarine coaxial cables; satellite earth stations operating in INTELSAT (12 Atlantic Ocean, 2 Indian Ocean), EUTELSAT, and domestic systems

Defense Forces

Branches: Army, Navy, Air Force

Military manpower: males 15-49, 16,006,352; 13,883,536 fit for military service; 326,666 reach military age (18) annually

Defense expenditures: 2.9% of GDP (1989 est.)

Ghana

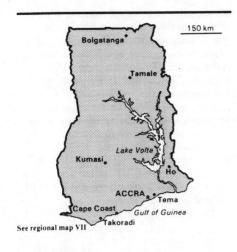

150 km

Bolgatanga

Tamale

Kumasi

Lake Volta

Ho

ACCRA

Tema

Cape Coast

Gulf of Guinea

Takoradi

See regional map VII

Geography

Total area: 238,540 km²; land area: 230,020 km²
Comparative area: slightly smaller than Oregon
Land boundaries: 2,093 km total; Burkina 548 km, Ivory Coast 668 km, Togo 877 km
Coastline: 539 km
Maritime claims:
  Contiguous zone: 24 nm
  Continental shelf: 200 nm
  Exclusive economic zone: 200 nm
  Territorial sea: 12 nm
Climate: tropical; warm and comparatively dry along southeast coast; hot and humid in southwest; hot and dry in north
Terrain: mostly low plains with dissected plateau in south-central area
Natural resources: gold, timber, industrial diamonds, bauxite, manganese, fish, rubber
Land use: 5% arable land; 7% permanent crops; 15% meadows and pastures; 37% forest and woodland; 36% other; includes NEGL% irrigated
Environment: recent drought in north severely affecting marginal agricultural activities; deforestation; overgrazing; soil erosion; dry, northeasterly harmattan wind (January to March)
Note: Lake Volta is world's largest artificial lake

People

Population: 15,165,243 (July 1990), growth rate 3.2% (1990)
Birth rate: 46 births/1,000 population (1990)
Death rate: 13 deaths/1,000 population (1990)
Net migration rate: −1 migrant/1,000 population (1990)
Infant mortality rate: 89 deaths/1,000 live births (1990)
Life expectancy at birth: 52 years male, 56 years female (1990)
Total fertility rate: 6.4 children born/woman (1990)
Nationality: noun—Ghanaian(s); adjective—Ghanaian
Ethnic divisions: 99.8% black African (major tribes—44% Akan, 16% Moshi-Dagomba, 13% Ewe, 8% Ga), 0.2% European and other
Religion: 38% indigenous beliefs, 30% Muslim, 24% Christian, 8% other
Language: English (official); African languages include Akan, Moshi-Dagomba, Ewe, and Ga
Literacy: 53.2%
Labor force: 3,700,000; 54.7% agriculture and fishing, 18.7% industry, 15.2% sales and clerical, 7.7% services, transportation, and communications, 3.7% professional; 48% of population of working age (1983)
Organized labor: 467,000 (about 13% of labor force)

Government

Long-form name: Republic of Ghana
Type: military
Capital: Accra
Administrative divisions: 10 regions; Ashanti, Brong-Ahafo, Central, Eastern, Greater Accra, Northern, Upper East, Upper West, Volta, Western
Independence: 6 March 1957 (from UK, formerly Gold Coast)
Constitution: 24 September 1979; suspended 31 December 1981
Legal system: based on English common law and customary law; has not accepted compulsory ICJ jurisdiction
National holiday: Independence Day, 6 March (1957)
Executive branch: chairman of the Provisional National Defense Council (PNDC), PNDC, Cabinet
Legislative branch: unicameral National Assembly dissolved after 31 December 1981 coup, and legislative powers were assumed by the Provisional National Defense Council
Judicial branch: Supreme Court
Leaders: *Chief of State and Head of Government*—Chairman of the Provisional National Defense Council Flt. Lt. (Ret.) Jerry John RAWLINGS (since 31 December 1981)
Political parties and leaders: none; political parties outlawed after 31 December 1981 coup
Suffrage: none
Elections: none
Communists: a small number of Communists and sympathizers
Member of: ACP, AfDB, CCC, Commonwealth, ECA, ECOWAS, FAO, G-77, GATT, IAEA, IBA, IBRD, ICAO, ICO, IDA, IFAD, IFC, ILO, IMF, IMO, INTELSAT, INTERPOL, IRC, ISO, ITU, NAM, OAU, UN, UNESCO, UPU, WCL, WHO, WIPO, WMO, WTO

Diplomatic representation: Ambassador Eric K. OTOO; Chancery at 2460 16th Street NW, Washington DC 20009; telephone (202) 462-0761; there is a Ghanaian Consulate General in New York; US—Ambassador Raymond C. EWING; Embassy at Ring Road East, East of Danquah Circle, Accra (mailing address is P. O. Box 194, Accra); telephone 775347 through 775349
Flag: three equal horizontal bands of red (top), yellow, and green with a large black five-pointed star centered in the gold band; uses the popular pan-African colors of Ethiopia; similar to the flag of Bolivia which has a coat of arms centered in the yellow band

Economy

Overview: Supported by substantial international assistance, Ghana has been implementing a steady economic rebuilding program since 1983. Good harvests in 1988 featured the 6% growth in GNP. Moves toward privatization and relaxation of government controls continued in 1988-89, although at a slower-than-expected pace. In 1988 service on the $2.8 billion debt was equivalent to 75% of export earnings. As Ghana obtains concessional loans and pays off high-interest debt, however, debt service is expected to fall below 30% of export earnings in the early 1990s. The economic rebuilding program has both helped and harmed the manufacturing sector, for example, by improving the supply of raw materials and by increasing competition from imports. The long-term outlook is favorable provided that the political structure can endure the slow pace at which living standards are improving and can manage the problems stemming from excessive population growth.
GNP: $5.2 billion, per capita $400; real growth rate 6% (1988)
Inflation rate (consumer prices): 32.7% (1988)
Unemployment rate: 26% (April 1987)
Budget: revenues $769 million; expenditures $749 million, including capital expenditures of $179 million (1988 est.)
Exports: $977 million (f.o.b., 1987); *commodities*—cocoa 60%, timber, gold, tuna, bauxite, and aluminum; *partners*—US 23%, UK, other EC
Imports: $988 million (c.i.f., 1987); *commodities*—petroleum 16%, consumer goods, foods, intermediate goods, capital equipment; *partners*—US 10%, UK, FRG, France, Japan, South Korea, GDR
External debt: $3.0 billion (December 1989 est.)
Industrial production: growth rate 0.5% in manufacturing (1987)
Electricity: 1,172,000 kW capacity; 4,110 million kWh produced, 280 kWh per capita (1989)

Ghana (continued)

Industries: mining, lumbering, light manufacturing, fishing, aluminum, food processing

Agriculture: accounts for more than 50% of GDP (including fishing and forestry); the major cash crop is cocoa; other principal crops—rice, coffee, cassava, peanuts, corn, shea nuts, timber; normally self-sufficient in food

Illicit drugs: illicit producer of cannabis for the international drug trade

Aid: US commitments, including Ex-Im (FY70-88), $424 million; Western (non-US) countries, ODA and OOF bilateral commitments (1970-87), $1.9 billion; OPEC bilateral aid (1979-89), $78 million; Communist countries (1970-88), $84 million

Currency: cedi (plural—cedis); 1 cedi (C) = 100 pesewas

Exchange rates: cedis (C) per US$1—301.68 (December 1989), 270.00 (1989), 202.35 (1988), 153.73 (1987), 89.20 (1986), 54.37 (1985)

Fiscal year: calendar year

Communications

Railroads: 953 km, all 1.067-meter gauge; 32 km double track; railroads undergoing major renovation

Highways: 28,300 km total; 6,000 km concrete or bituminous surface, 22,300 km gravel, laterite, and improved earth surfaces

Inland waterways: Volta, Ankobra, and Tano Rivers provide 155 km of perennial navigation for launches and lighters; Lake Volta provides 1,125 km of arterial and feeder waterways

Pipelines: none

Ports: Tema, Takoradi

Merchant marine: 4 cargo ships (1,000 GRT or over) totaling 52,016 GRT/66,627 DWT

Civil air: 6 major transport aircraft

Airports: 10 total, 9 usable; 5 with permanent-surface runways; none with runways over 3,659 m; 1 with runways 2,440-3,659 m; 7 with runways 1,220-2,439 m

Telecommunications: poor to fair system of open-wire and cable, radio relay links; 38,000 telephones; stations—6 AM, no FM, 9 TV; 1 Atlantic Ocean INTELSAT earth station

---

Defense Forces

Branches: Army, Navy, Air Force, paramilitary Palace Guard, paramilitary People's Militia

Military manpower: males 15-49, 3,437,300; 1,927,817 fit for military service; 167,778 reach military age (18) annually

Defense expenditures: 0.9% of GNP (1987)

Gibraltar
(dependent territory of the UK)

See regional map V

Geography

Total area: 6.5 km²; land area: 6.5 km²

Comparative area: about 11 times the size of The Mall in Washington, DC

Land boundaries: 1.2 km with Spain

Coastline: 12 km

Maritime claims:
  Continental shelf: 200 meters or to depth of exploitation
  Exclusive fishing zone: 3 nm
  Territorial sea: 3 nm

Disputes: source of occasional friction between Spain and the UK

Climate: Mediterranean with mild winters and warm summers

Terrain: a narrow coastal lowland borders The Rock

Natural resources: negligible

Land use: 0% arable land; 0% permanent crops; 0% meadows and pastures; 0% forest and woodland; 100% other

Environment: natural freshwater sources are meager so large water catchments (concrete or natural rock) collect rain water

Note: strategic location on Strait of Gibraltar that links the North Atlantic Ocean and Mediterranean Sea

---

People

Population: 29,572 (July 1990), growth rate 0.1% (1990)

Birth rate: 18 births/1,000 population (1990)

Death rate: 8 deaths/1,000 population (1990)

Net migration rate: −8 migrants/1,000 population (1990)

Infant mortality rate: 6 deaths/1,000 live births (1990)

Life expectancy at birth: 72 years male, 78 years female (1990)

Total fertility rate: 2.4 children born/woman (1990)

Nationality: noun—Gibraltarian; adjective—Gibraltar

Ethnic divisions: mostly Italian, English, Maltese, Portuguese, and Spanish descent

Religion: 75% Roman Catholic, 8% Church of England, 2.25% Jewish

Language: English and Spanish are primary languages; Italian, Portuguese, and Russian also spoken; English used in the schools and for official purposes

Literacy: 99% (est.)

Labor force: about 14,800 (including non-Gibraltar laborers); UK military establishments and civil government employ nearly 50% of the labor force

Organized labor: over 6,000

Government

Long-form name: none

Type: dependent territory of the UK

Capital: Gibraltar

Administrative divisions: none (colony of the UK)

Independence: none (colony of the UK)

Constitution: 30 May 1969

Legal system: English law

National holiday: Commonwealth Day (second Monday of March), 12 March 1990

Executive branch: British monarch, governor, chief minister, Gibraltar Council, Council of Ministers (cabinet)

Legislative branch: unicameral House of Assembly

Judicial branch: Supreme Court, Court of Appeal

Leaders: *Chief of State*—Queen ELIZABETH II (since 6 February 1952), represented by Governor and Commander in Chief Air Chief Marshal Sir Peter TERRY (since NA 1985);
Head of Government—Chief Minister Joe BOSSANO (since NA March 1988)

Political parties and leaders: Socialist Labor Party (SL), Joe Bossano; Gibraltar Labor Party/Association for the Advancement of Civil Rights (GCL/AACR), Adolfo Canepa; Independent Democratic Party, Joe Pitaluga

Suffrage: universal at age 18, plus other UK subjects resident six months or more

Elections: *House of Assembly:* last held on 24 March 1988 (next to be held March 1992); results—percent of vote by party NA; seats—(18 total, 15 elected) SL 8, GCL/AACR 7

Communists: negligible

Other political or pressure groups: Housewives Association, Chamber of Commerce, Gibraltar Representatives Organization

Diplomatic representation: none (colony of the UK)

Flag: two horizontal bands of white (top, double-width) and red with a three-towered red castle in the center of the white band; hanging from the castle gate is a gold key centered in the red band

Economy

Overview: The economy depends heavily on British defense expenditures, revenue from tourists, fees for services to shipping, and revenues from banking and finance activities. Because more than 70% of the economy is in the public sector, changes in government spending have a major impact on the level of employment. Construction workers are particularly affected when government expenditures are cut.
GNP: $129 million, per capita $4,450; real growth rate NA% (FY85)
Inflation rate (consumer prices): 4.4% (1986)
Unemployment rate: NA%
Budget: revenues $105 million; expenditures $104 million, including capital expenditures of NA (FY87)
Exports: $62.2 million (1985); *commodities*—(principally reexports) petroleum 75%, beverages and tobacco 12%, manufactured goods 8%; *partners*—UK, Morocco, Portugal, Netherlands, Spain, US, FRG
Imports: $147 million (1985); *commodities*—manufactured goods, fuels, and foodstuffs; *partners*—UK, Morocco, Portugal, Netherlands, Spain, US, FRG
External debt: $NA
Industrial production: growth rate NA%
Electricity: 46,000 kW capacity; 200 million kWh produced, 6,770 kWh per capita (1989)
Industries: tourism, banking and finance, construction, commerce; support to large UK naval and air bases; transit trade and supply depot in the port; light manufacturing of tobacco, roasted coffee, ice, mineral waters, candy, beer, and canned fish
Agriculture: NA
Aid: US commitments, including Ex-Im (FY70-87), $0.8 million; Western (non-US) countries, ODA and OOF bilateral commitments (1970-87), $162.5 million
Currency: Gibraltar pound (plural—pounds); 1 Gibraltar pound (£G) = 100 pence
Exchange rates: Gibraltar pounds (£G) per US$1—0.6055 (January 1990), 0.6099 (1989), 0.5614 (1988), 0.6102 (1987), 0.6817 (1986), 0.7714 (1985); note—the Gibraltar pound is at par with the British pound
Fiscal year: 1 July-30 June

Communications

Railroads: 1.000-meter-gauge system in dockyard area only
Highways: 50 km, mostly good bitumen and concrete
Ports: Gibraltar
Merchant marine: 45 ships (1,000 GRT or over) totaling 2,126,060 GRT/4,189,948 DWT; includes 10 cargo, 2 refrigerated cargo, 1 container, 16 petroleum, oils, and lubricants (POL) tanker, 1 chemical tanker 1 combination oil/ore, 1 liquefied gas, 13 bulk; note—a flag of convenience registry
Civil air: 1 major transport aircraft
Airports: 1 with permanent-surface runway 1,220-2,439 m
Telecommunications: adequate international radiocommunication facilities; automatic telephone system with 10,500 telephones; stations—1 AM, 6 FM, 4 TV; 1 Atlantic Ocean INTELSAT earth station

Defense Forces

Note: defense is the responsibility of the UK

Glorioso Islands
(French possession)

See regional map VII

Geography

Total area: 5 km²; land area: 5 km²; includes Île Glorieuse, Île du Lys, Verte Rocks, Wreck Rock, and South Rock
Comparative area: about 8.5 times the size of The Mall in Washington, DC
Land boundaries: none
Coastline: 35.2 km
Maritime claims:
Contiguous zone: 12 nm
Continental shelf: 200 meters or to depth of exploitation
Extended economic zone: 200 nm
Territorial sea: 12 nm
Disputes: claimed by Madagascar
Climate: tropical
Terrain: undetermined
Natural resources: guano, coconuts
Land use: 0% arable land; 0% permanent crops; 0% meadows and pastures; 0% forest and woodland; 100% other—lush vegetation and coconut palms
Environment: subject to periodic cyclones
Note: located in the Indian Ocean just north of the Mozambique Channel between Africa and Madagascar

People

Population: uninhabited

Government

Long-form name: none
Type: French possession administered by Commissioner of the Republic Daniel CONSTANTIN, resident in Reunion

Glorioso Islands *(continued)*

Economy

Overview: no economic activity

Communications

Airports: 1 with runway 1,220-2,439 m
Ports: none; offshore anchorage only

Defense Forces

Note: defense is the responsibility of France

Greece

See regional map V

Geography

Total area: 131,940 km²; land area: 130,800 km²
Comparative area: slightly smaller than Alabama
Land boundaries: 1,228 km total; Albania 282 km, Bulgaria 494 km, Turkey 206 km, Yugoslavia 246 km
Coastline: 13,676 km
Maritime claims:
  Continental shelf: 200 meters or to depth of exploitation
  Territorial sea: 6 nm
Disputes: complex maritime and air (but not territorial) disputes with Turkey in Aegean Sea; Cyprus question; Macedonia question with Bulgaria and Yugoslavia; Northern Epirus question with Albania
Climate: temperate; mild, wet winters; hot, dry summers
Terrain: mostly mountains with ranges extending into sea as peninsulas or chains of islands
Natural resources: bauxite, lignite, magnesite, crude oil, marble
Land use: 23% arable land; 8% permanent crops; 40% meadows and pastures; 20% forest and woodland; 9% other; includes 7% irrigated
Environment: subject to severe earthquakes; air pollution; archipelago of 2,000 islands
Note: strategic location dominating the Aegean Sea and southern approach to Turkish Straits

People

Population: 10,028,171 (July 1990), growth rate 0.2% (1990)
Birth rate: 11 births/1,000 population (1990)
Death rate: 9 deaths/1,000 population (1990)
Net migration rate: 0 migrants/1,000 population (1990)

Infant mortality rate: 10 deaths/1,000 live births (1990)
Life expectancy at birth: 75 years male, 80 years female (1990)
Total fertility rate: 1.5 children born/woman (1990)
Nationality: noun—Greek(s); adjective—Greek
Ethnic divisions: Greek 98%, others 2%; note—the Greek Government states there are no ethnic divisions in Greece
Religion: 98% Greek Orthodox, 1.3% Muslim, 0.7% other
Language: Greek (official); English and French widely understood
Literacy: 95%
Labor force: 3,860,000; 43% services, 27% agriculture, 20% manufacturing and mining, 7% construction (1985)
Organized labor: 10-15% of total labor force, 20-25% of urban labor force

Government

Long-form name: Hellenic Republic
Type: presidential parliamentary government; monarchy rejected by referendum 8 December 1974
Capital: Athens
Administrative divisions: 51 departments (nomoi, singular—nomós); Aitolía kai Akarnanía, Akhaïa, Argolís, Arkadhía, Arta, Attikí, Dhodhekánisos, Dráma, Evritanía, Evros, Evvoia, Flórina, Fokís, Fthiótis, Grevená, Ilía, Imathía, Ioánnina, Iráklion, Kardhítsa, Kastoría, Kavála, Kefallinía, Kérkira, Khalkidhikí, Khaniá, Khíos, Kikládhes, Kilkís, Korinthía, Kozáni, Lakonía, Lárisa, Lasíthi, Lésvos, Levkás, Magnisía, Messinía, Pélla, Piería, Préveza, Rethímni, Rodhópi, Sámos, Sérrai, Thesprotía, Thessaloníki, Tríkala, Voiotía, Xánthi, Zákinthos
Independence: 1827 (from the Ottoman Empire)
Constitution: 11 June 1975
Legal system: NA
National holiday: Independence Day (proclamation of the war of independence), 25 March (1821)
Executive branch: president, prime minister, Cabinet
Legislative branch: unicameral Parliament (Vouli)
Judicial branch: Supreme Court
Leaders: *Chief of State*—President Christos SARTZETAKIS (since 30 March 1985);
Head of Government—Prime Minister Constantin MITSOTAKIS (since 11 April 1990)
Political parties and leaders: New Democracy (ND; conservative), Constantine Mitsotakis; Panhellenic Socialist Movement

(PASOK), Andreas Papandreou; Democratic Renewal (DR), Constantine Stefanopoulos; Communist Party (KKE), Grigorios Farakos; Greek Left Party (EAR), Leonidas Kyrkos; KKE and EAR have joined in the Left Alliance, Harilaos Florakis, president

Suffrage: universal and compulsory at age 18

Elections: *President*—last held 30 March 1985 (next to be held after 8 April 1990 parliamentary election); results—Christos Sartzetakis was elected by Parliament; *Parliament:*—last held on 8 April 1990 (next to be held April 1994); results—New Democracy 46.89%, Panhellenic Socialist Movement 38.62%, Left Alliance 10.27%, PASOK-Left Alliance Cooperation 1.02%, Ecologist-Alternative 0.77%, Democratic Renewal 0.67%, Muslim 0.5%; seats— (300 total) New Democracy 150, Panhellenic Socialist Movement 123, Left Alliance 19, PASOK-Left Alliance Cooperation 4, Muslim independent 2, Democratic Renewal 1, Ecologist-Alternative 1

Communists: an estimated 60,000 members and sympathizers

Member of: CCC, EC, EIB (associate), FAO, GATT, IAEA, IBRD, ICAO, IDA, IFAD, IFC, IHO, ILO, IMF, IMO, INTELSAT, INTERPOL, IOOC, ITU, IWC—International Wheat Council, NATO, OECD, UN, UNESCO, UPU, WHO, WIPO, WMO, WSG, WTO

Diplomatic representation: Ambassador Christos ZACHARAKIS; Chancery at 2221 Massachusetts Avenue NW, Washington DC 20008; telephone (202) 667-3168; there are Greek Consulates General in Atlanta, Chicago, Los Angeles, New York, and San Francisco, and Consulates in Boston and New Orleans; *US*—Ambassador Michael G. SOTIRHOS; Embassy at 91 Vasilissis Sophias Boulevard, 10160 Athens (mailing address is APO New York 09253); telephone [30] (1) 721-2951 or 721-8401; there is a US Consulate General in Thessaloniki

Flag: nine equal horizontal stripes of blue (top and bottom) alternating with white; there is a blue square in the upper hoist-side corner bearing a white cross; the cross symbolizes Christianity, the established religion of the country

Economy

Overview: Greece has a mixed capitalistic economy with the basic entrepreneurial system overlaid in 1981-89 by a socialist-left-government that enlarged the public sector and became the nation's largest employer. Like many other Western economies, Greece suffered severely from the global oil price hikes of the 1970s, annual GDP growth plunging from 8% to 2% in the 1980s, and inflation, unemployment, and budget deficits rising sharply. The fall of the socialist government in 1989 and the inability of the conservative opposition to muster a clear majority have led to business uncertainty and the continued prospects for lackluster economic performance. Once the political situation is sorted out, Greece will have to face the challenges posed by the steadily increasing integration of the European Community, including the progressive lowering of tariff barriers. Tourism continues as a major industry, providing a vital offset to the sizable commodity trade deficit.

GDP: $56.3 billion, per capita $5,605; real growth rate 2.3% (1989 est.)

Inflation rate (consumer prices): 14.8% (December 1989)

Unemployment rate: 7.7% (1988)

Budget: revenues $15.5 billion; expenditures $23.9 billion, including capital expenditures of $2.5 billion (1988)

Exports: $5.9 billion (f.o.b., 1988); *commodities*—manufactured goods, food and live animals, fuels and lubricants, raw materials; *partners*—FRG 24%, Italy 14%, nonoil developing countries 11.8%, France 9.5%, US 7.1%, UK 6.8%

Imports: $13.5 billion (c.i.f., 1988); *commodities*—machinery and transport equipment, light manufactures, fuels and lubricants, foodstuffs, chemicals; *partners*—FRG 22%, nonoil developing countries 14%, oil exporting countries 13%, Italy 12%, France 8%, US 3.2%

External debt: $20.0 billion (December 1988)

Industrial production: growth rate 1.6% (1989 est.)

Electricity: 10,500,000 kW capacity; 36,420 million kWh produced, 3,630 kWh per capita (1989)

Industries: food and tobacco processing, textiles, chemicals, metal products, tourism, mining, petroleum

Agriculture: including fishing and forestry, accounts for 14% of GNP and 27% of the labor force; principal products—wheat, corn, barley, sugar beets, olives, tomatoes, wine, tobacco, potatoes, beef, mutton, pork, dairy products; self-sufficient in food; fish catch of 135,000 metric tons in 1987

Aid: US commitments, including Ex-Im (FY70-81), $525 million; Western (non-US) countries, ODA and OOF bilateral commitments (1970-87), $1.3 billion

Currency: drachma (plural—drachmas); 1 drachma (Dr) = 100 lepta

Exchange rates: drachma (Dr) per US$1—158.03 (January 1990), 162.42 (1989), 141.86 (1988), 135.43 (1987), 139.98 (1986), 138.12 (1985)

Fiscal year: calendar year

Communications

Railroads: 2,479 km total; 1,565 km 1.435-meter standard gauge, of which 36 km electrified and 100 km double track, 892 km 1.000-meter gauge; 22 km 0.750-meter narrow gauge; all government owned

Highways: 38,938 km total; 16,090 km paved, 13,676 km crushed stone and gravel, 5,632 km improved earth, 3,540 km unimproved earth

Inland waterways: 80 km; system consists of three coastal canals and three unconnected rivers

Pipelines: crude oil, 26 km; refined products, 547 km

Ports: Piraeus, Thessaloniki

Merchant marine: 954 ships (1,000 GRT or over) totaling 20,544,516 GRT/ 36,858,545 DWT; includes 15 passenger, 58 short-sea passenger, 2 passenger-cargo, 164 cargo, 18 container, 20 roll-on/roll-off cargo, 27 refrigerated cargo, 182 petroleum, oils, and lubricants (POL) tanker, 10 chemical tanker, 10 liquefied gas, 20 combination ore/oil, 6 specialized tanker, 407 bulk, 15 specialized bulk; note—ethnic Greeks also own large numbers of ships under the registry of Liberia, Panama, Cyprus, and Lebanon

Civil air: 39 major transport aircraft

Airports: 79 total, 77 usable; 60 with permanent-surface runways; none with runways over 3,659 m; 20 with runways 2,440-3,659 m; 22 with runways 1,220-2,439 m

Telecommunications: adequate, modern networks reach all areas; 4,079,000 telephones; stations—30 AM, 17 (20 repeaters) FM, 39 (560 repeaters) TV; 8 submarine cables; satellite earth stations operating in INTELSAT (1 Atlantic Ocean and 1 Indian Ocean), EUTELSAT, and MARISAT systems

Defense Forces

Branches: Hellenic Army, Hellenic Navy, Hellenic Air Force

Military manpower: males 15-49, 2,418,754; 1,861,141 fit for military service; about 73,809 reach military age (21) annually

Defense expenditures: 6.0% of GDP, or $3.4 billion (1989 est.)

Greenland
(part of the Danish realm)

See regional map II

Geography

Total area: 2,175,600 km²; land area: 341,700 km² (ice free)
Comparative area: slightly more than three times the size of Texas
Land boundaries: none
Coastline: 44,087 km
Maritime claims:
Contiguous zone: 4 nm
Continental shelf: 200 meters or to depth of exploitation
Exclusive fishing zone: 200 nm
Territorial sea: 3 nm
Disputes: Denmark has challenged Norway's maritime claims between Greenland and Jan Mayen
Climate: arctic to subarctic; cool summers, cold winters
Terrain: flat to gradually sloping icecap covers all but a narrow, mountainous, barren, rocky coast
Natural resources: zinc, lead, iron ore, coal, molybdenum, cryolite, uranium, fish
Land use: 0% arable land; 0% permanent crops; 1% meadows and pastures; NEGL% forest and woodland; 99% other
Environment: sparse population confined to small settlements along coast; continuous permafrost over northern two-thirds of the island
Note: dominates North Atlantic Ocean between North America and Europe

People

Population: 56,078 (July 1990), growth rate 1.2% (1990)
Birth rate: 20 births/1,000 population (1990)
Death rate: 8 deaths/1,000 population (1990)
Net migration rate: 0 migrants/1,000 population (1990)
Infant mortality rate: 28 deaths/1,000 live births (1990)

Life expectancy at birth: 62 years male, 68 years female (1990)
Total fertility rate: 2.2 children born/woman (1990)
Nationality: noun—Greenlander(s); adjective—Greenlandic
Ethnic divisions: 86% Greenlander (Eskimos and Greenland-born Caucasians), 14% Danish
Religion: Evangelical Lutheran
Language: Eskimo dialects, Danish
Literacy: 99%
Labor force: 22,800; largely engaged in fishing, hunting, sheep breeding
Organized labor: NA

Government

Long-form name: none
Type: part of the Danish realm; self-governing overseas administrative division
Capital: Nuuk (Godthåb)
Administrative divisions: 3 municipalities (kommuner, singular—kommun); Nordgrønland, Østgrønland, Vestgrønland
Independence: part of the Danish realm; self-governing overseas administrative division
Constitution: Danish
Legal system: Danish
National holiday: Birthday of the Queen, 16 April (1940)
Executive branch: Danish monarch, high commissioner, home rule chairman, prime minister, Cabinet (Landsstyre)
Legislative branch: unicameral Parliament (Landsting)
Judicial branch: High Court (Landsret)
Leaders: *Chief of State*—Queen MARGRETHE II (since 14 January 1972), represented by High Commissioner Bent KLINTE (since NA);
Head of Government—Home Rule Chairman Jonathan MOTZFELDT (since NA May 1979)
Political parties: Siumut (moderate socialist, advocates more distinct Greenlandic identity and greater autonomy from Denmark); Atassut Party (more conservative, favors continuing close relations with Denmark); Inuit Ataqatigiit (Marxist-Leninist party that favors complete independence from Denmark rather than home rule); Polar Party (Conservative-Greenland Nationalist)
Suffrage: universal at age 18
Elections: *Parliament*—last held on 27 May 1987 (next to be held by 27 May 1991); results—Siumut 39.8%, Atassut Party 40.1%, Inuit Ataqatigiit 15.3%, Polar Party 4.5%; seats—(27 total) Siumut 11, Atassut Party 11, Inuit Ataqatigiit 4, Polar Party 1;
Danish Parliament—last held on 10 May 1988 (next to be held by 10 May 1992);

Greenland elects two representatives to the Danish Parliament; results—(percent of vote by party NA; seats—(2 total) number of seats by party NA
Diplomatic representation: none (self-governing overseas administrative division of Denmark)
Flag: the flag of Denmark is used

Economy

Overview: Over the past 25 years, the economy has changed from one based on subsistence whaling, hunting, and fishing to one dependent on foreign trade. Fishing is still the most important industry, accounting for over two-thirds of exports and about 25% of the population's income. Exploitation of mineral resources is limited to lead and zinc. Maintenance of a social welfare system similar to Denmark's has given the public sector a dominant role in the economy. Greenland is heavily dependent on an annual subsidy of about $400 million from the Danish Government.
GNP: $500 million, per capita $9,000; real growth rate 5% (1988)
Inflation rate (consumer prices): 2.9% (1987)
Unemployment rate: 10%
Budget: revenues $380 million; expenditures $380 million, including capital expenditures of $NA (1985)
Exports: $386.2 million (f.o.b., 1988); *commodities*—fish and fish products, metallic ores and concentrates; *partners*—Denmark 76%, FRG 7%, Sweden 5%
Imports: $445.6 million (c.i.f., 1988); *commodities*—petroleum and petroleum products, machinery and transport equipment, food products; *partners*—Denmark 66%, Norway 5%, Sweden 4%, FRG 4%, Japan 4% US 3%
External debt: $445 million (1988)
Industrial production: growth rate NA%
Electricity: 84,000 kW capacity; 176 million kWh produced, 3,180 kWh per capita (1989)
Industries: fish processing, lead and zinc mining, handicrafts
Agriculture: sector dominated by fishing and sheep raising; crops limited to forage and small garden vegetables; 1987 fish catch of 101,000 metric tons
Aid: none
Currency: Danish krone (plural—kroner); 1 Danish krone (DKr) = 100 øre
Exchange rates: Danish kroner (DKr) per US$1—6.560 (January 1990), 7.310 (1989), 6.732 (1988), 6.840 (1987), 8.091 (1986), 10.596 (1985)
Fiscal year: calendar year

Grenada

Communications

Highways: 80 km
Ports: Kangerluarsoruseq (Faeringehavn), Paamiut (Frederikshaab), Nuuk (Godthaab), Sisimiut (Holsteinsborg), Julianehaab, Maarmorilik, North Star Bay, and at least 10 minor ports
Merchant marine: 1 refrigerated cargo (1,000 GRT or over) totaling 1,021 GRT/1,778 DWT; note—operates under the registry of Denmark
Civil air: 2 major transport aircraft
Airports: 11 total, 8 usable; 5 with permanent-surface runways; none with runways over 3,659 m; 2 with runways 2,440-3,659 m; 2 with runways 1,220-2,439 m
Telecommunications: adequate domestic and international service provided by cables and radio relay; 17,900 telephones; stations—5 AM, 7 (35 relays) FM, 4 (9 relays) TV; 2 coaxial submarine cables; 1 Atlantic Ocean INTELSAT earth station

Defense Forces

Note: defense is responsibility of Denmark

See regional map III

Geography

Total area: 340 km²; land area: 340 km²
Comparative area: slightly less than twice the size of Washington, DC
Land boundaries: none
Coastline: 121 km
Maritime claims:
  Extended economic zone: 200 nm
  Territorial sea: 12 nm
Climate: tropical; tempered by northeast trade winds
Terrain: volcanic in origin with central mountains
Natural resources: timber, tropical fruit, deepwater harbors
Land use: 15% arable land; 26% permanent crops; 3% meadows and pastures; 9% forest and woodland; 47% other
Environment: lies on edge of hurricane belt; hurricane season lasts from June to November
Note: islands of the Grenadines group are divided politically with St. Vincent and the Grenadines

People

Population: 84,135 (July 1990), growth rate −0.4% (1990)
Birth rate: 36 births/1,000 population (1990)
Death rate: 7 deaths/1,000 population (1990)
Net migration rate: −33 migrants/1,000 population (1990)
Infant mortality rate: 30 deaths/1,000 live births (1990)
Life expectancy at birth: 69 years male, 74 years female (1990)
Total fertility rate: 4.9 children born/woman (1990)
Nationality: noun—Grenadian(s); adjective—Grenadian
Ethnic divisions: mainly of black African descent

Religion: largely Roman Catholic; Anglican; other Protestant sects
Language: English (official); some French patois
Literacy: 85%
Labor force: 36,000; 31% services, 24% agriculture, 8% construction, 5% manufacturing, 32% other (1985)
Organized labor: 20% of labor force

Government

Long-form name: none
Type: parliamentary democracy
Capital: Saint George's
Administrative divisions: 6 parishes and 1 dependency*; Carriacou and Little Martinique*, Saint Andrew, Saint David, Saint George, Saint John, Saint Mark, Saint Patrick
Independence: 7 February 1974 (from UK)
Constitution: 19 December 1973
Legal system: based on English common law
National holiday: Independence Day, 7 February (1974)
Executive branch: British monarch, governor general, prime minister, Ministers of Government (cabinet)
Legislative branch: bicameral Parliament consists of an upper house or Senate and a lower house or House of Representatives
Judicial branch: Supreme Court
Leaders: *Chief of State*—Queen ELIZABETH II (since 6 February 1952), represented by Governor General Sir Paul SCOON (since 30 September 1978);
Head of Government—Prime Minister Nicholas BRATHWAITE (since 13 March 1990)
Political parties and leaders: National Democratic Congress (NDC), Nicholas Brathwaite; Grenada United Labor Party (GULP), Sir Eric Gairy; The National Party (TNP), Ben Jones; New National Party (NNP), Keith Mitchell; Maurice Bishop Patriotic Movement (MBPM), Terrence Merryshow; New Jewel Movement (NJM), Bernard Coard
Suffrage: universal at age 18
Elections: *House of Representatives*—last held on 13 March 1990 (next to be held by March 1996); results—percent of vote by party NA; seats—(15 total) NDC 8, GULP 3, TNP 2, NNP 2
Communists: about 450 members of the New Jewel Movement (pro-Soviet) and the Maurice Bishop Patriotic Movement (pro-Cuban)
Member of: ACP, CARICOM, FAO, G-77, GATT (de facto), IBRD, ICAO, IDA, IFAD, IFC, ILO, IMF, ITU, NAM, OAS, OECS, PAHO, SELA, UN, UNESCO, UPU, WHO

Grenada (continued)

Diplomatic representation: Ambassador Albert O. XAVIER; Chancery at 1701 New Hampshire Avenue NW, Washington DC 20009; telephone (202) 265-2561; there is a Grenadian Consulate General in New York; *US*—Chargé d'Affaires James F. COOPER; Embassy at Ross Point Inn, Saint George's (mailing address is P. O. Box 54, Saint George's); telephone [440] 1731 or 1734

Flag: a rectangle divided diagonally into yellow triangles (top and bottom) and green triangles (hoist side and outer side) with a red border around the flag; there are seven yellow five-pointed stars with three centered in the top red border, three centered in the bottom red border, and one on a red disk superimposed at the center of the flag; there is also a symbolic nutmeg pod on the hoist-side triangle (Grenada is the world's second-largest producer of nutmeg, after Indonesia); the seven stars represent the seven administrative divisions

Economy

Overview: The economy is essentially agricultural and centers on the traditional production of spices and tropical plants. Agriculture accounts for about 20% of GDP and 90% of exports and employs 24% of the labor force. Tourism is the leading foreign exchange earner, followed by agricultural exports. Manufacturing remains relatively undeveloped, but with a more favorable private investment climate since 1983, it is expected to grow. Despite an impressive average annual growth rate for the economy of 5.5% during the period 1984-88, unemployment remains high at about 26%.

GDP: $129.7 million, per capita $1,535; real growth rate 5% (1988)

Inflation rate (consumer prices): 5.0% (1989 est.)

Unemployment rate: 26% (1988)

Budget: revenues $74.2 million; expenditures $82.3 million, including capital expenditures of $27.8 million (1989 est.)

Exports: $31.8 million (f.o.b., 1988 est.); *commodities*—nutmeg 35%, cocoa beans 15%, bananas 13%, mace 7%, textiles; *partners*—US 4%, UK, FRG, Netherlands, Trinidad and Tobago

Imports: $92.6 million (c.i.f., 1988 est.); *commodities*—machinery 24%, food 22%, manufactured goods 19%, petroleum 8%; *partners*—US 32%, UK, Trinidad and Tobago, Japan, Canada

External debt: $108 million (1989 est.)

Industrial production: growth rate 5.8% (1989 est.)

Electricity: 11,400 kW capacity; 24 million kWh produced, 280 kWh per capita (1989)

Industries: food and beverage, textile, light assembly operations, tourism, construction

Agriculture: accounts for 20% of GDP and 90% of exports; bananas, cocoa, nutmeg, and mace account for two-thirds of total crop production; world's second-largest producer and fourth-largest exporter of nutmeg and mace; small-size farms predominate, growing a variety of citrus fruits, avocados, root crops, sugarcane, corn, and vegetables

Aid: US commitments, including Ex-Im (FY84-88), $60 million; Western (non-US) countries, ODA and OOF bilateral commitments (1970-87), $61 million; Communist countries (1970-88), $32 million

Currency: East Caribbean dollar (plural—dollars); 1 EC dollar (EC$) = 100 cents

Exchange rates: East Caribbean dollars (EC$) per US$1—2.70 (fixed rate since 1976)

Fiscal year: calendar year

Communications

Highways: 1,000 km total; 600 km paved, 300 km otherwise improved; 100 km unimproved

Ports: Saint George's

Civil air: no major transport aircraft

Airports: 3 total, 3 usable; 2 with permanent-surface runways; none with runways over 3,659 m; 1 with runways 2,440-3,659 m; 1 with runways 1,220-2,439 m

Telecommunications: automatic, island-wide telephone system with 5,650 telephones; new SHF links to Trinidad and Tobago and St. Vincent; VHF and UHF links to Trinidad and Carriacou; stations—1 AM, no FM, 1 TV

Defense Forces

Branches: Royal Grenada Police Force

Military manpower: NA

Defense expenditures: NA

Guadeloupe
(overseas department of France)

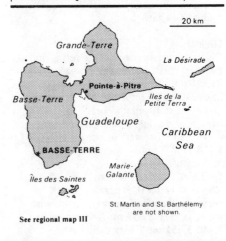

See regional map III

Geography

Total area: 1,780 km²; land area: 1,760 km²

Comparative area: 10 times the size of Washington, DC

Land boundaries: 14 km with Netherlands Antilles

Coastline: 306 km

Maritime claims:
Continental shelf: 200 meters or to depth of exploitation
Extended economic zone: 200 nm
Territorial sea: 12 nm

Climate: subtropical tempered by trade winds; relatively high humidity

Terrain: Basse-Terre is volcanic in origin with interior mountains; Grand-Terre is low limestone formation

Natural resources: cultivable land, beaches, and climate that foster tourism

Land use: 18% arable land; 5% permanent crops; 13% meadows and pastures; 40% forest and woodland; 24% other; includes 1% irrigated

Environment: subject to hurricanes (June to October); La Soufrière is an active volcano

Note: located 500 km southeast of Puerto Rico in the Caribbean Sea

People

Population: 342,175 (July 1990), growth rate 0.8% (1990)

Birth rate: 20 births/1,000 population (1990)

Death rate: 7 deaths/1,000 population (1990)

Net migration rate: −6 migrants/1,000 population (1990)

Infant mortality rate: 17 deaths/1,000 live births (1990)

Life expectancy at birth: 70 years male, 77 years female (1990)

Total fertility rate: 2.1 children born/woman (1990)

Nationality: noun—Guadeloupian(s); adjective—Guadeloupe
Ethnic divisions: 90% black or mulatto; 5% white; less than 5% East Indian, Lebanese, Chinese
Religion: 95% Roman Catholic, 5% Hindu and pagan African
Language: French, creole patois
Literacy: over 70%
Labor force: 120,000; 53.0% services, government, and commerce, 25.8% industry, 21.2% agriculture
Organized labor: 11% of labor force

Government

Long-form name: Department of Guadeloupe
Type: overseas department of France
Capital: Basse-Terre
Administrative divisions: none (overseas department of France)
Independence: none (overseas department of France)
Constitution: 28 September 1958 (French Constitution)
Legal system: French legal system
National holiday: Taking of the Bastille, 14 July (1789)
Executive branch: government commissioner
Legislative branch: unicameral General Council and unicameral Regional Council
Judicial branch: Court of Appeal (Cour d'Appel) with jurisdiction over Guadeloupe, French Guiana, and Martinique
Leaders: *Chief of State*—President François MITTERRAND (since 21 May 1981);
Head of Government—Commissioner of the Republic Jean-Paul PROUST (since November 1989)
Political parties and leaders: Rally for the Republic (RPR), Marlène Captant; Communist Party of Guadeloupe (PCG), Christian Medard Celeste; Socialist Party (PSG), Dominique Larifla; Independent Republicans; Union for French Democracy (UDF); Union for a New Majority (UNM)
Suffrage: universal at age 18
Elections: *General Council* —last held NA 1986 (next to be held by NA 1992); results—percent of vote by party NA; seats—(42 total) number of seats by party NA;
Regional Council—last held on 16 March 1986 (next to be held by 16 March 1992); results—RPR 33.1%, PS 28.7%, PCG 23.8%, UDF 10.7%, others 3.8%; seats—(41 total) RPR 15, PS 12, PCG 10, UDF 4;
French Senate—last held on 5 and 12 June 1988 (next to be held June 1994); Guadeloupe elects two representatives;

results—percent of vote by party NA; seats—(2 total) PCG 1, PS 1;
French National Assembly—last held on 5 and 12 June 1988 (next to be held June 1994); Guadeloupe elects four representatives; results—percent of vote by party NA; seats—(4 total) PS 2 seats, RPR 1 seat, PCG 1 seat
Communists: 3,000 est.
Other political or pressure groups: Popular Union for the Liberation of Guadeloupe (UPLG); Popular Movement for Independent Guadeloupe (MPGI); General Union of Guadeloupe Workers (UGTG); General Federation of Guadeloupe Workers (CGT-G); Christian Movement for the Liberation of Guadeloupe (KLPG)
Member of: WFTU
Diplomatic representation: as an overseas department of France, the interests of Guadeloupe are represented in the US by France
Flag: the flag of France is used

Economy

Overview: The economy depends on agriculture, tourism, light industry, and services. It is also dependent upon France for large subsidies and income and social transfers. Tourism is a key industry, with most tourists from the US. In addition, an increasingly large number of cruise ships visit the islands. The traditionally important sugarcane crop is slowly being replaced by other crops, such as bananas (which now supply about 50% of export earnings), eggplant, and flowers. Other vegetables and root crops are cultivated for local consumption, although Guadeloupe is still dependent on imported food, which comes mainly from France. Light industry consists mostly of sugar and rum production. Most manufactured goods and fuel are imported. Unemployment is especially high among the young.
GDP: $1.1 billion, per capita $3,300; real growth rate NA% (1987)
Inflation rate (consumer prices): 3.0% (1987)
Unemployment rate: 25% (1983)
Budget: revenues $251 million; expenditures $251 million, including capital expenditures of NA (1985)
Exports: $109 million (f.o.b., 1986); *commodities*—bananas, sugar, rum; *partners*—France 72%, Martinique 16% (1984)
Imports: $792 million (c.i.f., 1986); *commodities*—vehicles, foodstuffs, clothing and other consumer goods, construction materials, petroleum products; *partners*—France 59% (1984)
External debt: $NA
Industrial production: growth rate NA%

Electricity: 103,000 kW capacity; 315 million kWh produced, 920 kWh per capita (1989)
Industries: construction, cement, rum, sugar, tourism
Agriculture: cash crops—bananas and sugarcane; other products include tropical fruits and vegetables; livestock—cattle, pigs, and goats; not self-sufficient in food
Aid: US commitments, including Ex-Im (FY70-87), $4 million; Western (non-US) countries, ODA and OOF bilateral commitments (1970-87), $7.7 billion
Currency: French franc (plural—francs); 1 French franc (F) = 100 centimes
Exchange rates: French francs (F) per US$1—5.7598 (January 1990), 6.3801 (1989), 5.9569 (1988), 6.0107 (1987), 6.9261 (1986), 8.9852 (1985)
Fiscal year: calendar year

Communications

Railroads: privately owned, narrow-gauge plantation lines
Highways: 1,940 km total; 1,600 km paved, 340 km gravel and earth
Ports: Pointe-a-Pitre, Basse-Terre
Civil air: 2 major transport aircraft
Airports: 9 total, 9 usable, 8 with permanent-surface runways; none with runways over 3,659 m; 1 with runways 2,440-3,659 m; 1 with runways 1,220-2,439 m
Telecommunications: domestic facilities inadequate; 57,300 telephones; interisland radio relay to Antigua and Barbuda, Dominica, and Martinique; stations—2 AM, 8 FM (30 private stations licensed to broadcast FM), 9 TV; 1 Atlantic Ocean INTELSAT ground station

Defense Forces

Note: defense is responsibility of France

Guam
(territory of the US)

10 km

reefs

reefs

Cabras
Island
Apra
Harbor

AGANA

*North
Pacific
Ocean*

reefs

Cocos
Island

See regional map X

Geography

Total area: 541 km²; land area: 541 km²
Comparative area: slightly more than three times the size of Washington, DC
Land boundaries: none
Coastline: 125.5 km
Maritime claims:
Contiguous zone: 12 nm
Continental shelf: 200 m
Extended economic zone: 200 nm
Territorial sea: 12 nm
Climate: tropical marine; generally warm and humid, moderated by northeast trade winds; dry season from January to June, rainy season from July to December; little seasonal temperature variation
Terrain: volcanic origin, surrounded by coral reefs; relatively flat coraline limestone plateau (source of most fresh water) with steep coastal cliffs and narrow coastal plains in north, low-rising hills in center, mountains in south
Natural resources: fishing (largely undeveloped), tourism (especially from Japan)
Land use: 11% arable land; 11% permanent crops; 15% meadows and pastures; 18% forest and woodland; 45% other
Environment: frequent squalls during rainy season; subject to relatively rare, but potentially very destructive typhoons (especially in August)
Note: largest and southernmost island in the Mariana Islands archipelago; strategic location in western North Pacific Ocean 5,955 km west-southwest of Honolulu about three-quarters of the way between Hawaii and the Philippines

People

Population: 141,039 (July 1990), growth rate 2.8% (1990)
Birth rate: 26 births/1,000 population (1990)
Death rate: 4 deaths/1,000 population (1990)

Net migration rate: 5 migrants/1,000 population (1990)
Infant mortality rate: 12 deaths/1,000 live births (1990)
Life expectancy at birth: 70 years male, 75 years female (1990)
Total fertility rate: 3.0 children born/woman (1990)
Nationality: noun—Guamanian(s); adjective—Guamanian
Ethnic divisions: 47% Chamorro, 25% Filipino, 10% Caucasian, 18% Chinese, Japanese, Korean, and other
Religion: 98% Roman Catholic, 2% other
Language: English and Chamorro, most residents bilingual; Japanese also widely spoken
Literacy: 90%
Labor force: 54,000; 42% government, 58% private (1988)
Organized labor: 13% of labor force

Government

Long-form name: Territory of Guam
Type: organized, unincorporated territory of the US
Capital: Agana
Administrative divisions: none (territory of the US)
Independence: none (territory of the US)
Constitution: Organic Act of 1 August 1950
Legal system: NA
National holiday: Guam Discovery Day (first Monday in March), 6 March 1989
Executive branch: US president, governor, lieutenant governor, Cabinet
Legislative branch: unicameral Legislature
Judicial branch: Superior Court of Guam (Federal District Court)
Leaders: *Chief of State*—President George BUSH (since 20 January 1989); *Head of Government*—Governor Joseph A. ADA (since NA November 1986)
Political parties and leaders: Democratic Party (controls the legislature); Republican Party (party of the Governor)
Suffrage: universal at age 18; US citizens, but do not vote in US presidential elections
Elections: *Governor*—last held on NA November 1986 (next to be held November 1990);
Legislature—last held on 8 November 1988 (next to be held November 1990); results—percent of vote by party NA; seats—(21 total) Democratic 13, Republican 8;
US House of Representatives—last held 8 November 1988 (next to be held November 1990); Guam elects one nonvoting delegate; results—percent of vote by party NA; seats—(1 total) Republican 1
Communists: none

Note: relations between Guam and the US are under the jurisdiction of the Office of Territorial and International Affairs, US Department of the Interior
Diplomatic representation: none (territory of the US)
Flag: dark blue with a narrow red border on all four sides; centered is a red-bordered, pointed, vertical ellipse containing a beach scene, outrigger canoe with sail, and a palm tree with the word *GUAM* superimposed in bold red letters

Economy

Overview: The economy is based on US military spending and on revenues from tourism. Over the past 20 years the tourist industry has grown rapidly, creating a construction boom for new hotels and the expansion of older ones. Visitors numbered about 800,000 in 1989. The small manufacturing sector includes textile and clothing, beverage, food, and watch production. About 58% of the labor force works for the private sector and the rest for government. Most food and industrial goods are imported, with about 75% from the US. In 1989 the unemployment rate was about 3%, down from 10% in 1983.
GNP: $1.0 billion, per capita $7,675; real growth rate 20% (1988 est.)
Inflation rate (consumer prices): 5.9% (1988)
Unemployment rate: 3% (1989 est.)
Budget: revenues $208.0 million; expenditures $175 million, including capital expenditures of $17 million (1987 est.)
Exports: $39 million (f.o.b., 1983); *commodities*—mostly transshipments of refined petroleum products, copra, fish; *partners*—US 25%, others 75%
Imports: $611 million (c.i.f., 1983); *commodities*—mostly crude petroleum and petroleum products, food, manufactured goods; *partners*—US 77%, others 23%
External debt: $NA
Industrial production: growth rate NA%
Electricity: 500,000 kW capacity; 2,300 million kWh produced, 16,660 kWh per capita (1989)
Industries: US military, tourism, petroleum refining, construction, concrete products, printing and publishing, food processing, textiles
Agriculture: relatively undeveloped with most food imported; fruits, vegetables, eggs, pork, poultry, beef, copra
Aid: NA
Currency: US currency is used
Exchange rates: US currency is used
Fiscal year: 1 October-30 September

Guatemala

Communications

Highways: 674 km all-weather roads
Ports: Apra Harbor
Airports: 5 total, 4 usable; 3 with permanent-surface runways; none with runways over 3,659 m; 3 with runways 2,440-3,659 m; none with runways 1,220-2,439 m
Telecommunications: 26,317 telephones (1989); stations—3 AM, 3 FM, 3 TV; 2 Pacific Ocean INTELSAT ground stations

Defense Forces

Note: defense is the responsibility of the US

See regional map III

Geography

Total area: 108,890 km²; land area: 108,430 km²
Comparative area: slightly smaller than Tennessee
Land boundaries: 1,687 km total; Belize 266 km, El Salvador 203 km, Honduras 256 km, Mexico 962 km
Coastline: 400 km
Maritime claims:
  Continental shelf: not specific
  Extended economic zone: 200 nm
  Territorial sea: 12 nm
Disputes: claims Belize, but boundary negotiations are under way
Climate: tropical; hot, humid in lowlands; cooler in highlands
Terrain: mostly mountains with narrow coastal plains and rolling limestone plateau (Petén)
Natural resources: crude oil, nickel, rare woods, fish, chicle
Land use: 12% arable land; 4% permanent crops; 12% meadows and pastures; 40% forest and woodland; 32% other; includes 1% irrigated
Environment: numerous volcanoes in mountains, with frequent violent earthquakes; Caribbean coast subject to hurricanes and other tropical storms; deforestation; soil erosion; water pollution
Note: no natural harbors on west coast

People

Population: 9,097,636 (July 1990), growth rate 2.6% (1990)
Birth rate: 37 births/1,000 population (1990)
Death rate: 9 deaths/1,000 population (1990)
Net migration rate: −3 migrants/1,000 population (1990)
Infant mortality rate: 61 deaths/1,000 live births (1990)

Life expectancy at birth: 60 years male, 65 years female (1990)
Total fertility rate: 5.1 children born/woman (1990)
Nationality: noun—Guatemalan(s); adjective—Guatemalan
Ethnic divisions: 56% Ladino (mestizo—mixed Indian and European ancestry), 44% Indian
Religion: predominantly Roman Catholic; also Protestant, traditional Mayan
Language: Spanish, but over 40% of the population speaks an Indian language as a primary tongue (18 Indian dialects, including Quiche, Cakchiquel, Kekchi)
Literacy: 50%
Labor force: 2,500,000; 57.0% agriculture, 14.0% manufacturing, 13.0% services, 7.0% commerce, 4.0% construction, 3.0% transport, 0.8% utilities, 0.4% mining (1985)
Organized labor: 8% of labor force (1988 est.)

Government

Long-form name: Republic of Guatemala
Type: republic
Capital: Guatemala
Administrative divisions: 22 departments (departamentos, singular—departamento); Alta Verapaz, Baja Verapaz, Chimaltenango, Chiquimula, El Progreso, Escuintla, Guatemala, Huehuetenango, Izabal, Jalapa, Jutiapa, Petén, Quezaltenango, Quiché, Retalhuleu, Sacatepéquez, San Marcos, Santa Rosa, Sololá, Suchitepéquez, Totonicapán, Zacapa
Independence: 15 September 1821 (from Spain)
Constitution: 31 May 1985, effective 14 January 1986
Legal system: civil law system; judicial review of legislative acts; has not accepted compulsory ICJ jurisdiction
National holiday: Independence Day, 15 September (1821)
Executive branch: president, vice president, Council of Ministers (cabinet)
Legislative branch: unicameral National Congress (Congreso Nacional)
Judicial branch: Supreme Court of Justice (Corte Suprema de Justicia)
Leaders: *Chief of State and Head of Government*—President Mario Vinicio CEREZO Arévalo (since 14 January 1986); Vice President Roberto CARPIO Nicolle (since 14 January 1986)
Political parties and leaders: Christian Democratic Party (DCG), Marco Vinicio Cerezo Arévalo; National Centrist Union (UCN), Jorge Carpio Nicolle; National Liberation Movement (MLN), Mario Sandoval Alarcón; Social Action Movement (MAS), Jorge Serrano Elías; Revolutionary Party (PR) in coalition with National

Renewal Party (PNR), Alejandro Maldonado Aguirre; Social Democratic Party (PSD), Mario Solarzano Martínez; National Authentic Center (CAN), Mario David García; United Anti-Communist Party (PUA), Leonel Sisniega; Emerging Movement for Harmony (MEC), Louis Gordillo; Democratic Party of National Cooperation (PDCN), Adan Fletes; Democratic Institutional Party (PID), Oscar Rivas; Nationalist United Front (FUN), Gabriel Giron
Suffrage: universal at age 18, compulsory for literates, voluntary for illiterates
Elections: *President*—last held on 3 December 1985 (next to be held 3 November 1990); results—Mario Vinicio Cerezo Arévalo (DCG) 38.7%, Jorge Carpio Nicolle (UCN) 20.2%, Jorge Serrano Elías (PDCN/PR) 14.8%;
National Congress—last held on 3 November 1985 (next to be held 3 November 1990); results—DCG 38.7%, UCN 20.2%, PDCN/PR 13.8%, MLN/PID 12.6%, CAN 6.3%, PSD 3.4%, PNR 3.2%, PUA/FUN/MEC 1.9%; seats—(100 total) DCG 51, UCN 22, MLN 12, PDCN/PR 11, PSD 2, PNR 1, CAN 1
Communists: Guatemalan Labor Party (PGT); main radical left guerrilla groups—Guerrilla Army of the Poor (EGP), Revolutionary Organization of the People in Arms (ORPA), Rebel Armed Forces (FAR), and PGT dissidents
Other political or pressure groups: Federated Chambers of Commerce and Industry (CACIF), Mutual Support Group (GAM), Unity for Popular and Labor Action (UASP), Agrarian Owners Group (UNAGRO), Committee for Campesino Unity (CUC)
Member of: CACM, CCC, FAO, G-77, IADB, IAEA, IBRD, ICAC, ICAO, ICO, IDA, IDB—Inter-American Development Bank, IFAD, IFC, IHO, ILO, IMF, IMO, INTELSAT, INTERPOL, IRC, ISO, ITU, IWC—International Wheat Council, OAS, ODECA, PAHO, SELA, UN, UNESCO, UPEB, UPU, WFTU, WHO, WMO
Diplomatic representation: Ambassador Rodolfo ROHRMOSER V; Chancery at 2220 R Street NW, Washington DC 20008; telephone (202) 745-4952 through 4954; there are Guatemalan Consulates General in Chicago, Houston, Los Angeles, Miami, New Orleans, New York, and San Francisco; *US*—Ambassador Thomas F. STROOCK; Embassy at 7-01 Avenida de la Reforma, Zone 10, Guatemala City (mailing address is APO Miami 34024); telephone [502] (2) 31-15-41
Flag: three equal vertical bands of light blue (hoist side), white, and light blue with the coat of arms centered in the white band; the coat of arms includes a green and red quetzal (the national bird) and a scroll bearing the inscription *LIBERTAD 15 DE SEPTIEMBRE DE 1821* (the original date of independence from Spain) all superimposed on a pair of crossed rifles and a pair of crossed swords and framed by a wreath

Economy

Overview: The economy is based on agriculture, which accounts for 25% of GDP, employs about 60% of the labor force, and supplies two-thirds of exports. Industry accounts for about 20% of GDP and 15% of the labor force. The economy has reentered a slow-growth phase, but is hampered by political uncertainty. In 1988 the economy grew by 3.7%, the third consecutive year of mild growth. Government economic reforms introduced since 1986 have stabilized exchange rates and have helped to stem inflationary pressures. The inflation rate has dropped from 36.9% in 1986 to 15% in 1989.
GDP: $10.8 billion, per capita $1,185; real growth rate 1.3% (1989 est.)
Inflation rate (consumer prices): 15% (1989)
Unemployment rate: 13%, with 30-40% underemployment (1988 est.)
Budget: revenues $771 million; expenditures $957 million, including capital expenditures of $188 million (1988)
Exports: $1.02 billion (f.o.b., 1988); *commodities*—coffee 38%, bananas 7%, sugar 7%, cardamom 4%; *partners*—US 29%, El Salvador, FRG, Costa Rica, Italy
Imports: $1.5 billion (c.i.f., 1988); *commodities*—fuel and petroleum products, machinery, grain, fertilizers, motor vehicles; *partners*—US 38%, Mexico, FRG, Japan, El Salvador
External debt: $3.0 billion (December 1989 est.)
Industrial production: growth rate 3.5% (1988 est.)
Electricity: 807,000 kW capacity; 2,540 million kWh produced, 280 kWh per capita (1989)
Industries: sugar, textiles and clothing, furniture, chemicals, petroleum, metals, rubber, tourism
Agriculture: accounts for 25% of GDP; most important sector of economy and contributes two-thirds to export earnings; principal crops—sugarcane, corn, bananas, coffee, beans, cardamom; livestock—cattle, sheep, pigs, chickens; food importer
Illicit drugs: illicit producer of opium poppy and cannabis for the international drug trade; the government has engaged in aerial eradication of opium poppy; transit country for cocaine shipments

Aid: US commitments, including Ex-Im (FY70-88), $869 million; Western (non-US) countries, ODA and OOF bilateral commitments (1970-87), $7.7 billion
Currency: quetzal (plural—quetzales); 1 quetzal (Q) = 100 centavos
Exchange rates: free market quetzales (Q) per US$1—3.3913 (January 1990), 2.8261 (1989), 2.6196 (1988), 2.500 (1987), 1.875 (1986), 1.000 (1985); note—black-market rate 2.800 (May 1989)
Fiscal year: calendar year

Communications

Railroads: 870 km 0.914-meter gauge, single track; 780 km government owned, 90 km privately owned
Highways: 26,429 km total; 2,868 km paved, 11,421 km gravel, and 12,140 unimproved
Inland waterways: 260 km navigable year round; additional 730 km navigable during high-water season
Pipelines: crude oil, 275 km
Ports: Puerto Barrios, Puerto Quetzal, Santo Tomas de Castilla
Merchant marine: 1 cargo ship (1,000 GRT or over) totaling 4,129 GRT/6,450 DWT
Civil air: 10 major transport aircraft
Airports: 451 total, 391 usable; 11 with permanent-surface runways; none with runways over 3,659 m; 3 with runways 2,440-3,659 m; 19 with runways 1,220-2,439 m
Telecommunications: fairly modern network centered in Guatemala [city]; 97,670 telephones; stations—91 AM, no FM, 25 TV, 15 shortwave; connection into Central American Microwave System; 1 Atlantic Ocean INTELSAT earth station

Defense Forces

Branches: Army, Navy, Air Force
Military manpower: males 15-49, 2,028,875; 1,327,374 fit for military service; 107,251 reach military age (18) annually
Defense expenditures: 1% of GDP, or $115 million (1990 est.)

Guernsey
(British crown dependency)

English Channel

See regional map V

Geography

Total area: 194 km²; land area: 194 km²; includes Alderney, Guernsey, Herm, Sark, and some other smaller islands
Comparative area: slightly larger than Washington, DC
Land boundaries: none
Coastline: 50 km
Maritime claims:
Continental shelf: 200 meters or to depth of exploitation
Exclusive fishing zone: 200 nm
Territorial sea: 3 nm
Climate: temperate with mild winters and cool summers; about 50% of days are overcast
Terrain: mostly level with low hills in southwest
Natural resources: cropland
Land use: NA% arable land; NA% permanent crops; NA% meadows and pastures; NA% forest and woodland; NA% other; about 50% cultivated
Environment: large, deepwater harbor at St. Peter Port
Note: 52 km west of France

People

Population: 57,227 (July 1990), growth rate 0.7% (1990)
Birth rate: 12 births/1,000 population (1990)
Death rate: 11 deaths/1,000 population (1990)
Net migration rate: 6 migrants/1,000 population (1990)
Infant mortality rate: 6 deaths/1,000 live births (1990)
Life expectancy at birth: 72 years male, 78 years female (1990)
Total fertility rate: 1.6 children born/woman (1990)
Nationality: noun—Channel Islander(s); adjective—Channel Islander

Ethnic divisions: UK and Norman-French descent
Religion: Anglican, Roman Catholic, Presbyterian, Baptist, Congregational, Methodist
Language: English, French; Norman-French dialect spoken in country districts
Literacy: NA%, but universal education
Labor force: NA
Organized labor: NA

Government

Long-form name: Bailiwick of Guernsey
Type: British crown dependency
Capital: St. Peter Port
Administrative divisions: none (British crown dependency)
Independence: none (British crown dependency)
Constitution: unwritten; partly statutes, partly common law and practice
Legal system: English law and local statute; justice is administered by the Royal Court
National holiday: Liberation Day, 9 May (1945)
Executive branch: British monarch, lieutenant governor, bailiff, deputy bailiff
Legislative branch: States of Deliberation
Judicial branch: Royal Court
Leaders: *Chief of State*—Queen ELIZABETH II (since 6 February 1952); *Head of Government*—Lieutenant Governor Lt. Gen. Sir Alexander BOSWELL (since 1985); Bailiff Sir Charles FROSSARD (since 1982)
Political parties and leaders: none; all independents
Suffrage: universal at age 18
Elections: *States of Deliberation*—last held NA (next to be held NA); results—percent of vote NA; seats—(60 total, 33 elected), all independents
Communists: none
Diplomatic representation: none (British crown dependency)
Flag: white with the red cross of St. George (patron saint of England) extending to the edges of the flag

Economy

Overview: Tourism is a major source of revenue. Other economic activity includes financial services, breeding the world-famous Guernsey cattle, and growing tomatoes and flowers for export.
GDP: $NA, per capita $NA; real growth rate 9% (1987)
Inflation rate (consumer prices): 7% (1988)
Unemployment rate: NA%

Budget: revenues $145.0 million; expenditures $117.2 million, including capital expenditures of NA (1985)
Exports: $NA; *commodities*—tomatoes, flowers and ferns, sweet peppers, eggplant, other vegetables; *partners*—UK (regarded as internal trade)
Imports: $NA; *commodities*—coal, gasoline and oil; *partners*—UK (regarded as internal trade)
External debt: $NA
Industrial production: growth rate NA%
Electricity: 173,000 kW capacity; 525 million kWh produced, 9,340 kWh per capita (1989)
Industries: tourism, banking
Agriculture: tomatoes, flowers (mostly grown in greenhouses), sweet peppers, eggplant, other vegetables and fruit; Guernsey cattle
Aid: none
Currency: Guernsey pound (plural—pounds); 1 Guernsey (£G) pound = 100 pence
Exchange rates: Guernsey pounds (£G) per US$1—0.6055 (January 1990), 0.6099 (1989), 0.5614 (1988), 0.6102 (1987), 0.6817 (1986), 0.7714 (1985); note—the Guernsey pound is at par with the British pound
Fiscal year: calendar year

Communications

Ports: St. Peter Port, St. Sampson
Airport: 1 with permanent-surface runway 1,220-2,439 m (La Villiaze)
Telecommunications: stations—1 AM, no FM, 1 TV; 41,900 telephones; 1 submarine cable

Defense Forces

Note: defense is the responsibility of the UK

Guinea

200 km

North
Atlantic
Ocean

See regional map VII

Geography

Total area: 245,860 km²; land area: 245,860 km²
Comparative area: slightly smaller than Oregon
Land boundaries: 3,399 km total; Guinea-Bissau 386 km, Ivory Coast 610 km, Liberia 563 km, Mali 858 km, Senegal 330 km, Sierra Leone 652 km
Coastline: 320 km
Maritime claims:
Extended economic zone: 200 nm
Territorial sea: 12 nm
Climate: generally hot and humid; monsoonal-type rainy season (June to November) with southwesterly winds; dry season (December to May) with northeasterly harmattan winds
Terrain: generally flat coastal plain, hilly to mountainous interior
Natural resources: bauxite, iron ore, diamonds, gold, uranium, hydropower, fish
Land use: 6% arable land; NEGL% permanent crops; 12% meadows and pastures; 42% forest and woodland; 40% other; includes NEGL% irrigated
Environment: hot, dry, dusty harmattan haze may reduce visibility during dry season; deforestation

People

Population: 7,269,240 (July 1990), growth rate 2.6% (1990)
Birth rate: 47 births/1,000 population (1990)
Death rate: 22 deaths/1,000 population (1990)
Net migration rate: 0 migrants/1,000 population (1990)
Infant mortality rate: 147 deaths/1,000 live births (1990)
Life expectancy at birth: 40 years male, 44 years female (1990)
Total fertility rate: 6.1 children born/woman (1990)

Nationality: noun—Guinean(s); adjective—Guinean
Ethnic divisions: Fulani, Malinke, Sousou, 15 smaller tribes
Religion: 85% Muslim, 5% indigenous beliefs, 1.5% Christian
Language: French (official); each tribe has its own language
Literacy: 20% in French; 48% in local languages
Labor force: 2,400,000 (1983); 82.0% agriculture, 11.0% industry and commerce, 5.4% services; 88,112 civil servants (1987); 52% of population of working age (1985)
Organized labor: virtually 100% of wage earners loosely affiliated with the National Confederation of Guinean Workers

Government

Long-form name: Republic of Guinea
Type: republic
Capital: Conakry
Administrative divisions: 29 administrative regions (régions administratives, singular—région administrative); Beyla, Boffa, Boke, Conakry, Dabola, Dalaba, Dinguiraye, Dubreka, Faranah, Forecariah, Fria, Gaoual, Gueckedou, Kankan, Kerouane, Kindia, Kissidougou, Koundara, Kouroussa, Labe, Macenta, Mali, Mamou, Nzerekore, Pita, Siguiri, Telimele, Tougue, Yomou
Independence: 2 October 1958 (from France; formerly French Guinea)
Constitution: 14 May 1982, suspended after coup of 3 April 1984
Legal system: based on French civil law system, customary law, and decree; legal codes currently being revised; has not accepted compulsory ICJ jurisdiction
National holiday: Anniversary of the Second Republic, 3 April (1984)
Executive branch: president, Military Committee for National Recovery (Comité Militaire de Redressement National or CMRN), Council of Ministers (cabinet)
Legislative branch: People's National Assembly (Assemblée Nationale Populaire) was dissolved after the 3 April 1984 coup
Judicial branch: Court of Appeal (Cour d'Appel)
Leaders: *Chief of State and Head of Government*—Gen. Lansana CONTE (since 5 April 1984)
Political parties and leaders: none; following the 3 April 1984 coup all political activity was banned
Suffrage: none
Elections: none
Communists: no Communist party, although there are some sympathizers
Member of: ACP, AfDB, ECA, ECOWAS, FAO, G-77, IBA, IBRD, ICAO, ICO, IDA, IDB—Islamic Development Bank, IFAD, ILO, IMF, IMO,

INTELSAT, INTERPOL, ITU, Mano River Union, Niger River Commission, NAM, OAU, OIC, UN, UNESCO, UPU, WHO, WMO
Diplomatic representation: Ambassador Kekoura CAMARA; Chancery at 2112 Leroy Place NW, Washington DC 20008; telephone (202) 483-9420; *US*—Ambassador Samuel E. LUPO; Embassy at 2nd Boulevard and 9th Avenue, Conakry (mailing address is B. P. 603, Conakry); telephone 44-15-20 through 24
Flag: three equal vertical bands of red (hoist side), yellow, and green; uses the popular pan-African colors of Ethiopia; similar to the flag of Rwanda which has a large black letter *R* centered in the yellow band

Economy

Overview: Although possessing many natural resources and considerable potential for agricultural development, Guinea is one of the poorest countries in the world. The agricultural sector contributes about 40% to GDP and employs more than 80% of the work force, while industry accounts for about 25% of GDP. Guinea possesses over 25% of the world's bauxite reserves; exports of bauxite and alumina accounted for more than 80% of total exports in 1986.
GDP: $2.5 billion, per capita $350; real growth rate 5.0% (1988)
Inflation rate (consumer prices): 27.0% (1988)
Unemployment rate: NA%
Budget: revenues $357 million; expenditures $480 million, including capital expenditures of $229 million (1988 est.)
Exports: $553 million (f.o.b., 1988 est.); *commodities*—alumina, bauxite, diamonds, coffee, pineapples, bananas, palm kernels; *partners*—US 33%, EC 33%, USSR and Eastern Europe 20%, Canada
Imports: $509 million (c.i.f., 1988 est.); *commodities*—petroleum products, metals, machinery, transport equipment, foodstuffs, textiles and other grain; *partners*—US 16%, France, Brazil
External debt: $1.6 billion (December 1988)
Industrial production: growth rate NA%
Electricity: 113,000 kW capacity; 300 million kWh produced, 40 kWh per capita (1989)
Industries: bauxite mining, alumina, diamond mining, light manufacturing and agricultural processing industries
Agriculture: accounts for 40% of GDP (includes fishing and forestry); mostly subsistence farming; principal products—rice, coffee, pineapples, palm kernels, cassava,

Guinea-Bissau

bananas, sweet potatoes, timber; livestock—cattle, sheep and goats; not self-sufficient in food grains
Aid: US commitments, including Ex-Im (FY70-88), $203 million; Western (non-US) countries, ODA and OOF bilateral commitments (1970-87), $882 million; OPEC bilateral aid (1979-89), $120 million; Communist countries (1970-88), $446 million
Currency: Guinean franc (plural—francs); 1 Guinean franc (FG) = 100 centimes
Exchange rates: Guinean francs (FG) per US$1—505.00 (October 1988), 440.00 (January 1988), 440.00 (1987), 235.63 (1986), 22.47 (1985)
Fiscal year: calendar year

Communications

Railroads: 1,045 km; 806 km 1.000-meter gauge, 239 km 1.435-meter standard gauge
Highways: 30,100 km total; 1,145 km paved, 12,955 km gravel or laterite (of which barely 4,500 km are currently all-weather roads), 16,000 km unimproved earth (1987)
Inland waterways: 1,295 km navigable by shallow-draft native craft
Ports: Conakry, Kamsar
Civil air: 2 major transport aircraft
Airports: 16 total, 16 usable; 5 with permanent-surface runways; none with runways over 3,659 m; 3 with runways 2,440-3,659 m; 9 with runways 1,220-2,439 m
Telecommunications: fair system of open-wire lines, small radiocommunication stations, and new radio relay system; 10,000 telephones; stations—3 AM, 1 FM, 1 TV; 12,000 TV sets; 125,000 radio receivers; 1 Atlantic Ocean INTELSAT earth station

Defense Forces

Branches: Army (ground forces), Navy (acts primarily as a coast guard), Air Force, paramilitary National Gendarmerie
Military manpower: males 15-49, 1,657,787; 834,777 fit for military service
Defense expenditures: 3.1% of GDP (1984)

North Atlantic Ocean

See regional map VII

Geography

Total area: 36,120 km²; land area: 28,000 km²
Comparative area: slightly less than three times the size of Connecticut
Land boundaries: 724 km total; Guinea 386, Senegal 338 km
Coastline: 350 km
Maritime claims:
  Extended economic zone: 200 nm
  Territorial sea: 12 nm
Disputes: the International Court of Justice (ICJ) has rendered its decision on the Guinea-Bissau/Senegal maritime boundary (in favor of Senegal)—that decision has been rejected by Guinea-Bissau
Climate: tropical; generally hot and humid; monsoon-type rainy season (June to November) with southwesterly winds; dry season (December to May) with northeasterly harmattan winds
Terrain: mostly low coastal plain rising to savanna in east
Natural resources: unexploited deposits of petroleum, bauxite, phosphates; fish, timber
Land use: 11% arable land; 1% permanent crops; 43% meadows and pastures; 38% forest and woodland; 7% other
Environment: hot, dry, dusty harmattan haze may reduce visibility during dry season

People

Population: 998,963 (July 1990), growth rate 2.5% (1990)
Birth rate: 43 births/1,000 population (1990)
Death rate: 19 deaths/1,000 population (1990)
Net migration rate: 0 migrants/1,000 population (1990)
Infant mortality rate: 127 deaths/1,000 live births (1990)

Life expectancy at birth: 44 years male, 48 years female (1990)
Total fertility rate: 5.9 children born/woman (1990)
Nationality: noun—Guinea-Bissauan(s); adjective—Guinea-Bissauan
Ethnic divisions: about 99% African (30% Balanta, 20% Fula, 14% Manjaca, 13% Mandinga, 7% Papel); less than 1% European and mulatto
Religion: 65% indigenous beliefs, 30% Muslim, 5% Christian
Language: Portuguese (official); Criolo and numerous African languages
Literacy: 34% (1986)
Labor force: 403,000 (est.); 90% agriculture, 5% industry, services, and commerce, 5% government; 53% of population of working age (1983)
Organized labor: only one trade union—the National Union of Workers of Guinea-Bissau (UNTG)

Government

Long-form name: Republic of Guinea-Bissau
Type: republic; highly centralized one-party regime since September 1974
Capital: Bissau
Administrative divisions: 9 regions (regiões, singular—região); Bafatá, Biombo, Bissau, Bolama, Cacheu, Gabú, Oio, Quinara, Tombali
Independence: 24 September 1973 (from Portugal; formerly Portuguese Guinea)
Constitution: 16 May 1984
Legal system: NA
National holiday: Independence Day, 24 September (1973)
Executive branch: president of the Council of State, vice presidents of the Council of State, Council of State, Council of Ministers (cabinet)
Legislative branch: unicameral National People's Assembly (Assembléia Nacional Popular)
Judicial branch: none; there is a Ministry of Justice in the Council of Ministers
Leaders: *Chief of State and Head of Government*—President of the Council of State Brig. Gen. João Bernardo VIEIRA (assumed power 14 November 1980 and elected President of Council of State on 16 May 1984); First Vice President Col. Iafai CAMARA (since 7 November 1985); Second Vice President Vasco CABRAL (since 21 June 1989)
Political parties and leaders: only party—African Party for the Independence of Guinea-Bissau and Cape Verde (PAIGC), President João Bernardo Vieira, leader;

the party decided to retain the binational title despite its formal break with Cape Verde

Suffrage: universal at age 15

Elections: *President of Council of State*—last held 19 June 1989 (next to be held 19 June 1994); results—Brig. Gen. João Bernardo Vieira was reelected without opposition by the National People's Assembly; *National People's Assembly*—last held 15 June 1989 (next to be held 15 June 1994); results—PAIGC is the only party; seats—(150 total) PAIGC 150, appointed by Regional Councils; *Regional Councils*—last held 1 June 1989 (next to be held 1 June 1994); results—PAIGC is the only party; seats—(473 total) PAIGC 473, by public plebiscite

Communists: a few Communists, some sympathizers

Member of: ACP, AfDB, ECA, ECOWAS, FAO, G-77, GATT (de facto), IBRD, ICAO, IDA, IDB—Islamic Development Bank, IFAD, IFC, ILO, IMF, IMO, IRC, ITU, NAM, OAU, OIC, UN, UNESCO, UPU, WFTU, WHO, WMO

Diplomatic representation: Ambassador Alfredo Lopes CABRAL; Chancery (temporary) at the Guinea-Bissauan Permanent Mission to the UN, Suite 604, 211 East 43rd Street, New York, NY 10017; telephone (212) 661-3977; *US*—Ambassador William L. JACOBSEN; Embassy at 17 Avenida Domingos Ramos, Bissau (mailing address is C. P. 297, Bissau); telephone [245] 212816, 21817, 213674

Flag: two equal horizontal bands of yellow (top) and green with a vertical red band on the hoist side; there is a black five-pointed star centered in the red band; uses the popular pan-African colors of Ethiopia; similar to the flag of Cape Verde which has the black star raised above the center of the red band and is framed by two corn stalks and a yellow clam shell

Economy

Overview: Guinea-Bissau ranks among the poorest countries in the world, with a per capita GDP below $200. Agriculture and fishing are the main economic activities, with cashew nuts, peanuts, and palm kernels the primary exports. Exploitation of known mineral deposits is unlikely at present because of a weak infrastructure and the high cost of development. The government's four-year plan (1988-91) has targeted agricultural development as the top priority.

GDP: $152 million, per capita $160 (1988); real growth rate 5.6% (1987)

Inflation rate (consumer prices): NA%

Unemployment rate: NA%

Budget: revenues $20 million; expenditures $25 million, including capital expenditures of $NA (1987)

Exports: $15 million (f.o.b., 1987); *commodities*—cashews, fish, peanuts, palm kernels; *partners*—Portugal, Spain, Switzerland, Cape Verde, China

Imports: $49 million (f.o.b., 1987); *commodities*—capital equipment, consumer goods, semiprocessed goods, foods, petroleum; *partners*—Portugal, USSR, EC countries, other Europe, Senegal, US

External debt: $465 million (December 1989 est.)

Industrial production: growth rate −1.7% (1986 est.)

Electricity: 22,000 kW capacity; 28 million kWh produced, 30 kWh per capita (1989)

Industries: agricultural processing, beer, soft drinks

Agriculture: accounts for over 50% of GDP, nearly 100% of exports, and 80% of employment; rice is the staple food; other crops include corn, beans, cassava, cashew nuts, peanuts, palm kernels, and cotton; not self-sufficient in food; fishing and forestry potential not fully exploited

Aid: US commitments, including Ex-Im (FY70-88), $46 million; Western (non-US) countries, ODA and OOF bilateral commitments (1970-87), $519 million; OPEC bilateral aid (1979-89), $41 million; Communist countries (1970-88), $68 million

Currency: Guinea-Bissauan peso (plural—pesos); 1 Guinea-Bissauan peso (PG) = 100 centavos

Exchange rates: Guinea-Bissauan pesos (PG) per US$1—650 pesos (December 1989), NA (1988), 851.65 (1987), 238.98 (1986), 173.61 (1985)

Fiscal year: calendar year

Communications

Highways: 3,218 km; 2,698 km bituminous, remainder earth

Inland waterways: scattered stretches are important to coastal commerce

Ports: Bissau

Civil air: 2 major transport aircraft

Airports: 37 total, 18 usable; 5 with permanent-surface runways; none with runways over 3,659 m; 1 with runways 2,440-3,659 m; 5 with runways 1,220-2,439 m

Telecommunications: poor system of radio relay, open-wire lines, and radiocommunications; 3,000 telephones; stations—1 AM, 2 FM, 1 TV; 1 Atlantic Ocean INTELSAT earth station

Defense Forces

Branches: People's Revolutionary Armed Force (FARP); Army, Navy, and Air Force are separate components

Military manpower: males 15-49, 215,552; 122,824 fit for military service

Defense expenditures: 3.2% of GDP (1987)

Guyana

200 km

Mabaruma

North Atlantic Ocean

GEORGETOWN

New Amsterdam

Boundary representation is not necessarily authoritative

Lethem

See regional map IV

Geography

Total area: 214,970 km²; land area: 196,850 km²
Comparative area: slightly smaller than Idaho
Land boundaries: 2,462 km total; Brazil 1,119 km, Suriname 600 km, Venezuela 743 km
Coastline: 459 km
Maritime claims:
Continental shelf: outer edge of continental margin or 200 nm
Exclusive fishing zone: 200 nm
Territorial sea: 12 nm
Disputes: Essequibo area claimed by Venezuela; Suriname claims area between New (Upper Courantyne) and Courantyne/Kutari Rivers (all headwaters of the Courantyne)
Climate: tropical; hot, humid, moderated by northeast trade winds; two rainy seasons (May to mid-August, mid-November to mid-January)
Terrain: mostly rolling highlands; low coastal plain; savanna in south
Natural resources: bauxite, gold, diamonds, hardwood timber, shrimp, fish
Land use: 3% arable land; NEGL% permanent crops; 6% meadows and pastures; 83% forest and woodland; 8% other; includes 1% irrigated
Environment: flash floods a constant threat during rainy seasons; water pollution

People

Population: 764,649 (July 1990), growth rate −0.1% (1990)
Birth rate: 24 births/1,000 population (1990)
Death rate: 6 deaths/1,000 population (1990)
Net migration rate: −19 migrants/1,000 population (1990)
Infant mortality rate: 40 deaths/1,000 live births (1990)
Life expectancy at birth: 65 years male, 70 years female (1990)
Total fertility rate: 2.7 children born/woman (1990)
Nationality: noun—Guyanese (sing., pl.); adjective—Guyanese
Ethnic divisions: 51% East Indian, 43% black and mixed, 4% Amerindian, 2% European and Chinese
Religion: 57% Christian, 33% Hindu, 9% Muslim, 1% other
Language: English, Amerindian dialects
Literacy: 85%
Labor force: 268,000; 44.5% industry and commerce, 33.8% agriculture, 21.7% services; public-sector employment amounts to 60-80% of the total labor force (1985)
Organized labor: 34% of labor force

Government

Long-form name: Co-operative Republic of Guyana
Type: republic
Capital: Georgetown
Administrative divisions: 10 regions; Barima-Waini, Cuyuni-Mazaruni, Demerara-Mahaica, East Berbice-Corentyne, Essequibo Islands-West Demerara, Mahaica-Berbice, Pomeroon-Supenaam, Potaro-Siparuni, Upper Demerara-Berbice, Upper Takutu-Upper Essequibo
Independence: 26 May 1966 (from UK; formerly British Guiana)
Constitution: 6 October 1980
Legal system: based on English common law with certain admixtures of Roman-Dutch law; has not accepted compulsory ICJ jurisdiction
National holiday: Republic Day, 23 February (1970)
Executive branch: executive president, first vice president, prime minister, first deputy prime minister, Cabinet
Legislative branch: unicameral National Assembly
Judicial branch: Supreme Court of Judicature
Leaders: *Chief of State*—President Hugh Desmond HOYTE (since 6 August 1985); First Vice President Hamilton GREEN (since 6 August 1985);
Head of Government—Prime Minister Hamilton GREEN (since 6 August 1985)
Political parties and leaders: People's National Congress (PNC), Hugh Desmond Hoyte; People's Progressive Party (PPP), Cheddi Jagan; Working People's Alliance (WPA), Eusi Kwayana, Rupert Roopnarine, Moses Bhagwan; Democratic Labor Movement (DLM), Paul Tennassee; People's Democratic Movement (PDM), Llewellyn John; National Democratic Front (NDF), Joseph Bacchus; United Force (UF), Marcellus Feilden Singh; Vanguard

for Liberation and Democracy (VLD, also known as Liberator Party), Gunraj Kumar, J. K. Makepeace Richmond
Suffrage: universal at age 18
Elections: *Executive President*—last held on 9 December 1985 (next to be held late 1990); Hugh Desmond Hoyte was elected president (the leader of the party with the most votes in the National Assembly elections—PNC 78%);
National Assembly—last held on 9 December 1985 (next to be held by 9 December 1990); results—PNC 78%, PPP 16%, UF 4%, WPA 2%; seats—(65 total, 53 elected) PNC 42, PPP 8, UF 2, WPA 1
Communists: 100 (est.) hardcore within PPP; top echelons of PPP and PYO (Progressive Youth Organization, militant wing of the PPP) include many Communists; small but unknown number of orthodox Marxist-Leninists within PNC, some of whom formerly belonged to the PPP
Other political or pressure groups: Trades Union Congress (TUC); Guyana Council of Indian Organizations (GCIO); Civil Liberties Action Committee (CLAC); the latter two organizations are small but active but not well organized
Member of: ACP, CARICOM, CCC, CDB, FAO, G-77, GATT, IADB, IBA, IBRD, ICAO, ICJ, IDA, IDB—Inter-American Development Bank, IFAD, IFC, ILO, IMF, IMO, INTERPOL, IRC, ISO, ITU, NAM, OAS (observer), PAHO, SELA, UN, UNESCO, UPU, WFTU, WHO, WMO
Diplomatic representation: Ambassador Dr. Cedric Hilburn GRANT; Chancery at 2490 Tracy Place NW, Washington DC 20008; telephone (202) 265-6900; there is a Guyanese Consulate General in New York; *US*—Ambassador Theresa A. TULL; Embassy at 31 Main Street, Georgetown; telephone [592] (02) 54900 through 54909
Flag: green with a red isosceles triangle (based on the hoist side) superimposed on a long yellow arrowhead; there is a narrow black border between the red and yellow, and a narrow white border between the yellow and the green

Economy

Overview: After growing on average at less than 1% a year in 1984-87, GDP dropped by 3% in 1988, the result of bad weather, labor trouble in the canefields, and flooding and equipment problems in the bauxite industry. Consumer prices rose about 35%, and the current account deficit widened substantially as sugar and bauxite exports fell. Moreover, electric power is in short supply and constitutes a major barrier to future gains in national output. The government, in association with inter-

Guyana (continued)

national financial agencies, seeks to reduce its payment arrears and to raise new funds. The government's stabilization program—aimed at establishing realistic exchange rates, reasonable price stability, and a resumption of growth—requires considerable public administrative abilities and continued patience by consumers during a long incubation period.
GDP: $323 million, per capita $420; real growth rate −3.0% (1988 est.)
Inflation rate (consumer prices): 35% (1988 est.)
Unemployment rate: NA%
Budget: revenues $173 million; expenditures $414 million, including capital expenditures of $75 million (1988 est.)
Exports: $215 million (f.o.b., 1988 est.) *commodities*—bauxite, sugar, rice, shrimp, gold, molasses, timber, rum; *partners*—UK 37%, US 12%, Canada 10.6%, CARICOM 4.8% (1986)
Imports: $216 million (c.i.f., 1988 est.); *commodities*—manufactures machinery, food, petroleum; *partners*—CARICOM 41%, US 18%, UK 9%, Canada 3% (1984)
External debt: $1.8 billion, including arrears (December 1988)
Industrial production: growth rate −5.0% (1988 est.)
Electricity: 221,000 kW capacity; 583 million kWh produced, 760 kWh per capita (1989)
Industries: bauxite mining, sugar, rice milling, timber, fishing (shrimp), textiles, gold mining
Agriculture: most important sector, accounting for 25% of GDP and over 50% of exports; sugar and rice are key crops; development potential exists for fishing and forestry; not self-sufficient in food, especially wheat, vegetable oils, and animal products
Aid: US commitments, including Ex-Im (FY70-88), $109 million; Western (non-US) countries, ODA and OOF bilateral commitments (1970-87), $234 million; Communist countries (1970-88), $242 million
Currency: Guyanese dollar (plural—dollars); 1 Guyanese dollar (G$) = 100 cents
Exchange rates: Guyanese dollars (G$) per US$1—33.0000 (January 1990), 27.159 (1989), 10.000 (1988), 9.756 (1987), 4.272 (1986), 4.252 (1985)
Fiscal year: calendar year

Communications

Railroads: 187 km total, all single track 0.914-meter gauge
Highways: 7,665 km total; 550 km paved, 5,000 km gravel, 1,525 km earth, 590 km unimproved
Inland waterways: 6,000 km total of navigable waterways; Berbice, Demerara, and Essequibo Rivers are navigable by ocean-going vessels for 150 km, 100 km, and 80 km, respectively
Ports: Georgetown
Civil air: 5 major transport aircraft
Airports: 66 total, 63 usable; 5 with permanent-surface runways; none with runways over 2,439 m; 12 with runways 1,220-2,439 m
Telecommunications: fair system with radio relay network; over 27,000 telephones; tropospheric scatter link to Trinidad; stations—4 AM, 3 FM, no TV, 1 shortwave; 1 Atlantic Ocean INTELSAT earth station

Defense Forces

Branches: Guyana Defense Force (including Maritime Corps and Air Corps), Guyana Police Force, Guyana People's Militia, Guyana National Service
Military manpower: males 15-49, 201,104; 152,958 fit for military service
Defense expenditures: 4.3% of GDP, or $13.8 million (1988 est.)

Haiti

See regional map III

Geography

Total area: 27,750 km²; land area: 27,560 km²
Comparative area: slightly larger than Maryland
Land boundary: 275 km with the Dominican Republic
Coastline: 1,771 km
Maritime claims:
  Contiguous zone: 24 nm
  Continental shelf: to depth of exploitation
  Extended economic zone: 200 nm
  Territorial sea: 12 nm
Disputes: claims US-administered Navassa Island
Climate: tropical; semiarid where mountains in east cut off trade winds
Terrain: mostly rough and mountainous
Natural resources: bauxite
Land use: 20% arable land; 13% permanent crops; 18% meadows and pastures; 4% forest and woodland; 45% other; includes 3% irrigated
Environment: lies in the middle of the hurricane belt and subject to severe storms from June to October; occasional flooding and earthquakes; deforestation
Note: shares island of Hispaniola with Dominican Republic

People

Population: 6,142,141 (July 1990), growth rate 2.3% (1990)
Birth rate: 45 births/1,000 population (1990)
Death rate: 16 deaths/1,000 population (1990)
Net migration rate: −6 migrants/1,000 population (1990)
Infant mortality rate: 107 deaths/1,000 live births (1990)
Life expectancy at birth: 52 years male, 55 years female (1990)

Total fertility rate: 6.4 children born/woman (1990)

Nationality: noun—Haitian(s); adjective—Haitian

Ethnic divisions: 95% black, 5% mulatto and European

Religion: 75-80% Roman Catholic (of which an overwhelming majority also practice Voodoo), 10% Protestant

Language: French (official) spoken by only 10% of population; all speak Creole

Literacy: 23%

Labor force: 2,300,000; 66% agriculture, 25% services, 9% industry; shortage of skilled labor, unskilled labor abundant (1982)

Organized labor: NA

Government

Long-form name: Republic of Haiti

Type: republic

Capital: Port-au-Prince

Administrative divisions: 9 departments, (départements, singular—département); Artibonite, Centre, Grand'Anse, Nord, Nord-Est, Nord-Ouest, Ouest, Sud, Sud-Est

Independence: 1 January 1804 (from France)

Constitution: 27 August 1983, suspended February 1986; draft constitution approved March 1987, suspended June 1988, most articles reinstated March 1989

Legal system: based on Roman civil law system; accepts compulsory ICJ jurisdiction

National holiday: Independence Day, 1 January (1804)

Executive branch: president, Council of Ministers (cabinet)

Legislative branch: bicameral National Assembly (Assemblée Nationale) consisted of an upper house or Senate and a lower house or House of Representatives, but was dissolved on 20 June 1988 after the coup of 19 June 1988 (there was a subsequent coup on 18 September 1988); after naming a civilian as provisional president on 13 March 1990, it was announced that a Council of State was being formed

Judicial branch: Court of Appeal (Cour de Cassation)

Leaders: *Chief of State and Head of Government*—Provisional President Ertha PASCAL-TROUILLOT (since 13 March 1990)

Political parties and leaders: Haitian Christian Democratic Party (PDCH), Sylvio Claude; Haitian Social Christian Party (PSCH), Grégoire Eugéne; Movement for the Installation of Democracy in Haiti (MIDH), Marc Bazin; National Alliance Front (FNC), Gerard Gourgue; National Agricultural and Industrial Party (PAIN), Louis Dejoie; Congress of Democratic Movements (CONACOM), Victor Bono; National Progressive Revolutionary Party (PANPRA), Serge Gilles; National Patriotic Movement of November 28 (MNP-28), Dejean Belizaire; Movement for the Organization of the Country (MOP), Gesner Comeau; Mobilization for National Development (MDN), Hubert De Ronceray

Suffrage: none

Elections: *President*—last held 17 January 1988 (next to be held by mid-June 1990); on 13 March 1990 Ertha Pascal-Trouillot became provisional president after the resignation of President Lieut. Gen Prosper Avril;

Legislature—last held 17 January 1988, but dissolved on 20 June 1988; the government has promised an election by mid-June 1990

Communists: United Party of Haitian Communists (PUCH), René Théodore (roughly 2,000 members)

Other political or pressure groups: Democratic Unity Confederation (KID), Roman Catholic Church, Confederation of Haitian Workers (CTH), Federation of Workers Trade Unions (FOS), Autonomous Haitian Workers (CATH), National Popular Assembly (APN)

Member of: CCC, FAO, G-77, GATT, IADB, IAEA, IBA, IBRD, ICAO, ICO, IDA, IDB—Inter-American Development Bank, IFAD, IFC, ILO, IMF, IMO, INTELSAT, INTERPOL, IRC, ITU, OAS, PAHO, SELA, UN, UNESCO, UPU, WHO, WMO, WTO

Diplomatic representation: Ambassador (vacant), Chargé d'Affaires Fritz VOUGY; Chancery at 2311 Massachusetts Avenue NW, Washington DC 20008; telephone (202) 332-4090 through 4092; there are Haitian Consulates General in Boston, Chicago, Miami, New York, and San Juan (Puerto Rico); *US*—Ambassador Alvin ADAMS; Embassy at Harry Truman Boulevard, Port-au-Prince (mailing address is P. O. Box 1761, Port-au-Prince), telephone [509] (1) 20354 or 20368, 20200, 20612

Flag: two equal horizontal bands of blue (top) and red with a centered white rectangle bearing the coat of arms which contains a palm tree flanked by flags and two cannons above a scroll bearing the motto *L'UNION FAIT LA FORCE* (Union Makes Strength)

Economy

Overview: About 85% of the population live in absolute poverty. Agriculture is mainly small-scale subsistence farming and employs 65% of the work force. The majority of the population does not have ready access to safe drinking water, adequate medical care, or sufficient food. Few social assistance programs exist, and the lack of employment opportunities remains the most critical problem facing the economy.

GDP: $2.4 billion, per capita $380; real growth rate 0.3% (1988 est.)

Inflation rate (consumer prices): 5.8% (1988)

Unemployment rate: 50% (1988 est.)

Budget: revenues $252 million; expenditures $357 million, including capital expenditures of $NA million (1988)

Exports: $200 million (f.o.b., FY88); *commodities*—light manufactures 65%, coffee 17%, other agriculture 8%, other products 10%; *partners*—US 77%, France 5%, Italy 4%, FRG 3%, other industrial 9%, less developed countries 2% (FY86)

Imports: $344 million (c.i.f., FY88); *commodities*—machines and manufactures 36%, food and beverages 21%, petroleum products 11%, fats and oils 12%, chemicals 12%; *partners*—US 65%, Netherlands Antilles 6%, Japan 5%, France 4%, Canada 2%, Asia 2% (FY86)

External debt: $820 million (December 1988)

Industrial production: growth rate −2% (FY87)

Electricity: 230,000 kW capacity; 482 million kWh produced, 75 kWh per capita (1989)

Industries: sugar refining, textiles, flour milling, cement manufacturing, bauxite mining, tourism, light assembly industries based on imported parts

Agriculture: accounts for 32% of GDP and employs 65% of work force; mostly small-scale subsistence farms; commercial crops—coffee and sugarcane; staple crops—rice, corn, sorghum, mangoes; shortage of wheat flour

Aid: US commitments, including Ex-Im (FY70-88), $638 million; Western (non-US) countries, ODA and OOF bilateral commitments (1970-87), $627 million

Currency: gourde (plural—gourdes); 1 gourde (G) = 100 centimes

Exchange rates: gourdes (G) per US$1—5.0 (fixed rate)

Fiscal year: 1 October-30 September

Communications

Railroads: 40 km 0.760-meter narrow gauge, single-track, privately owned industrial line

Highways: 4,000 km total; 950 km paved, 900 km otherwise improved, 2,150 km unimproved

Inland waterways: negligible; less than 100 km navigable

Haiti (continued)

Ports: Port-au-Prince, Cap-Haitien
Civil air: 4 major transport aircraft
Airports: 15 total, 10 usable; 3 with permanent-surface runways; none with runways over 3,659 m; 1 with runways 2,440-3,659 m; 4 with runways 1,220-2,439 m
Telecommunications: domestic facilities barely adequate, international facilities slightly better; 36,000 telephones; stations—33 AM, no FM, 4 TV, 2 short-wave; 1 Atlantic Ocean earth station

Defense Forces

Branches: Army, Navy, Air Corps
Military manpower: males 15-49, 1,264,238; 679,209 fit for military service; 59,655 reach military age (18) annually
Defense expenditures: NA

Heard Island and McDonald Islands
(territory of Australia)

See regional map XII

Geography

Total area: 412 km^2; land area: 412 km^2
Comparative area: slightly less than 2.5 times the size of Washington, DC
Land boundaries: none
Coastline: 101.9 km
Maritime claims:
Contiguous zone: 12 nm
Continental shelf: 200 meters or to depth of exploration
Exclusive fishing zone: 200 nm *Territorial sea:* 3 nm
Climate: antarctic
Terrain: Heard Island—bleak and mountainous, with an extinct volcano; McDonald Islands—small and rocky
Land use: 0% arable land; 0% permanent crops; 0% meadows and pastures; 0% forest and woodland; 100% other
Environment: primarily used as research stations
Note: located 4,100 km southwest of Australia in the southern Indian Ocean

People

Population: uninhabited

Government

Long-form name: Territory of Heard Island and McDonald Islands
Type: territory of Australia administered by the Antarctic Division of the Department of Science in Canberra (Australia)

Economy

Overview: no economic activity

Communications

Ports: none; offshore anchorage only

Defense Forces

Note: defense is the responsibility of Australia

Honduras

150 km

Caribbean Sea

Swan Islands ··

See regional map III

Boundary representation is not necessarily authoritative.

Geography

Total area: 112,090 km²; land area: 111,890 km²
Comparative area: slightly larger than Tennessee
Land boundaries: 1,520 km total; Guatemala 256 km, El Salvador 342 km, Nicaragua 922 km
Coastline: 820 km
Maritime claims:
Contiguous zone: 24 nm
Continental shelf: 200 meters or to depth of exploitation
Extended economic zone: 200 nm
Territorial sea: 12 nm
Disputes: several sections of the boundary with El Salvador are in dispute
Climate: subtropical in lowlands, temperate in mountains
Terrain: mostly mountains in interior, narrow coastal plains
Natural resources: timber, gold, silver, copper, lead, zinc, iron ore, antimony, coal, fish
Land use: 14% arable land; 2% permanent crops; 30% meadows and pastures; 34% forest and woodland; 20% other; includes 1% irrigated
Environment: subject to frequent, but generally mild, earthquakes; damaging hurricanes along Caribbean coast; deforestation; soil erosion

People

Population: 5,259,699 (July 1990), growth rate 3.0% (1990)
Birth rate: 37 births/1,000 population (1990)
Death rate: 7 deaths/1,000 population (1990)
Net migration rate: 0 migrants/1,000 population (1990)
Infant mortality rate: 62 deaths/1,000 live births (1990)

Life expectancy at birth: 64 years male, 67 years female (1990)
Total fertility rate: 4.8 children born/woman (1990)
Nationality: noun—Honduran(s); adjective—Honduran
Ethnic divisions: 90% mestizo (mixed Indian and European), 7% Indian, 2% black, 1% white
Religion: about 97% Roman Catholic; small Protestant minority
Language: Spanish, Indian dialects
Literacy: 56%
Labor force: 1,300,000; 62% agriculture, 20% services, 9% manufacturing, 3% construction, 6% other (1985)
Organized labor: 40% of urban labor force, 20% of rural work force (1985)

Government

Long-form name: Republic of Honduras
Type: republic
Capital: Tegucigalpa
Administrative divisions: 18 departments (departamentos, singular—departamento); Atlántida, Choluteca, Colón, Comayagua, Copán, Cortés, El Paraíso, Francisco Morazán, Gracias a Dios, Intibucá, Islas de la Bahía, La Paz, Lempira, Ocotepeque, Olancho, Santa Bárbara, Valle, Yoro
Independence: 15 September 1821 (from Spain)
Constitution: 11 January 1982, effective 20 January 1982
Legal system: rooted in Roman and Spanish civil law; some influence of English common law; accepts ICJ jurisdiction, with reservations
National holiday: Independence Day, 15 September (1821)
Executive branch: president, Council of Ministers (cabinet)
Legislative branch: unicameral National Congress (Congreso Nacional)
Judicial branch: Supreme Court of Justice (Corte Suprema de Justica)
Leaders: *Chief of State and Head of Government*—Rafael Leonardo CALLEJAS Romero (since 26 January 1990)
Political parties and leaders: Liberal Party (PLH)—faction leaders, Carlos Flores Facusse (leader of Florista Liberal Movement), Carlos Montoya (Azconista subfaction), Ramon Villeda Bermudez and Jorge Arturo Reina (M-Líder faction); National Party (PNH), Ricardo Maduro, party president; PNH faction leaders—Oswaldo Ramos Soto and Rafael Leonardo Callejas (Monarca faction); National Innovation and Unity Party-Social Democrats (PINU-SD), Enrique Aguilar Cerrato Paz; Christian Democratic Party (PDCH), Jorge Illescas; Democratic Action (AD), Walter Lopez Reyes

Suffrage: universal and compulsory at age 18
Elections: *President*—last held on 26 November 1989 (next to be held November 1993); results—Leonardo Rafael Callejas (PNH) 51%, José Azcona Hoyo (PLH) 43.3%, others 5.7%;
National Congress—last held on 24 November 1985 (next to be held November 1993); results—PLH 51%, PNH 45%, PDCH 1.9%, PINU 1.5%, others 0.65; seats—(134 total) PLH 62, PNH 71, PINU 1
Communists: up to 1,500; Honduran leftist groups—Communist Party of Honduras (PCH), Party for the Transformation of Honduras (PTH), Morazanist Front for the Liberation of Honduras (FMLH), People's Revolutionary Union/Popular Liberation Movement (URP/MPL), Popular Revolutionary Forces-Lorenzo Zelaya (FPR/LZ), Socialist Party of Honduras Central American Workers Revolutionary Party (PASO/PRTC)
Other political or pressure groups: National Association of Honduran Campesinos (ANACH), Honduran Council of Private Enterprise (COHEP), Confederation of Honduran Workers (CTH), National Union of Campesinos (UNC), General Workers Confederation (CGT), United Federation of Honduran Workers (FUTH), Committee for the Defense of Human Rights in Honduras (CODEH), Coordinating Committee of Popular Organizations (CCOP)
Member of: CACM, FAO, G-77, IADB, IBRD, ICAO, ICO, IDA, IDB—Inter-American Development Bank, IFAD, IFC, ILO, IMF, IMO, INTELSAT, INTERPOL, ISO, ITU, OAS, PAHO, SELA, UN, UNESCO, UPEB, UPU, WFTU, WHO, WMO
Diplomatic representation: Ambassador Jorge Ramon HERNANDEZ Alcerro; Chancery at Suite 100, 4301 Connecticut Avenue NW, Washington DC 20008; telephone (202) 966-7700 through 7702; there are Honduran Consulates General in Chicago, Los Angeles, Miami, New Orleans, New York, and San Francisco, and Consulates in Baton Rouge, Boston, Detroit, Houston, and Jacksonville; *US*—Ambassador Crescencio ARCOS; Embassy at Avenida La Paz, Tegucigalpa (mailing address is APO Miami 34022); telephone [504] 32-3120
Flag: three equal horizontal bands of blue (top), white, and blue with five blue five-pointed stars arranged in an X pattern centered in the white band; the stars represent the members of the former Federal Republic of Central America—Costa Rica, El Salvador, Guatemala, Honduras, and Nicaragua; similar to the flag of El Salvador which features a round emblem

135

Honduras *(continued)*

encircled by the words *REPUBLICA DE EL SALVADOR EN LA AMERICA CENTRAL* centered in the white band; also similar to the flag of Nicaragua which features a triangle encircled by the words *REPUBLICA DE NICARAGUA* on top and *AMERICA CENTRAL* on the bottom, centered in the white band

Economy

Overview: Honduras is one of the poorest countries in the Western Hemisphere. Agriculture is the most important sector of the economy, accounting for nearly 30% of GDP, employing 62% of the labor force, and producing two-thirds of exports. Productivity remains low, however, leaving considerable room for improvement. Although industry is still in its early stages, it employs nearly 15% of the labor force, accounts for 23% of GDP, and generates 20% of exports. The service sectors, including public administration, account for 48% of GDP and employ nearly 20% of the labor force. Basic problems facing the economy include a high population growth rate, a high unemployment rate, a lack of basic services, a large and inefficient public sector, and an export sector dependent mostly on coffee and bananas, which are subject to sharp price fluctuations.
GDP: $4.4 billion, per capita $890; real growth rate 4.0% (1988)
Inflation rate (consumer prices): 11% (1989)
Unemployment rate: 12% unemployed, 30-40% underemployed (1988)
Budget: revenues $1,053 million; expenditures $949 million, including capital expenditures of $159 million (1989)
Exports: $1.0 billion (f.o.b., 1988); *commodities*—bananas, coffee, shrimp, lobster, minerals, lumber; *partners*—US 52%, FRG 11%, Japan, Italy, Belgium
Imports: $1.4 billion (c.i.f. 1988); *commodities*—machinery and transport equipment, chemical products, manufactured goods, fuel and oil, foodstuffs; *partners*—US 39%, Japan 9%, CACM, Venezuela, Mexico
External debt: $3.2 billion (December 1989)
Industrial production: growth rate 5% (1988)
Electricity: 655,000 kW capacity; 1,980 million kWh produced, 390 kWh per capita (1989)
Industries: agricultural processing (sugar and coffee), textiles, clothing, wood products
Agriculture: most important sector, accounting for nearly 30% of GDP, over 60% of the labor force, and two-thirds of exports; principal products include ba-

nanas, coffee, timber, beef, citrus fruit, shrimp; importer of wheat
Illicit drugs: illicit producer of cannabis, cultivated on small plots and used principally for local consumption; transshipment point for cocaine
Aid: US commitments, including Ex-Im (FY70-88), $1.3 billion; Western (non-US) countries, ODA and OOF bilateral commitments (1970-87), $776 million
Currency: lempira (plural—lempiras); 1 lempira (L) = 100 centavos
Exchange rates: lempiras (L) per US$1— 2.00 (fixed rate); 3.50 parallel exchange and black-market rate (October 1989)
Fiscal year: calendar year

Communications

Railroads: 785 km total; 508 km 1.067-meter gauge, 277 km 0.914-meter gauge
Highways: 8,950 km total; 1,700 km paved, 5,000 km otherwise improved, 2,250 km unimproved earth
Inland waterways: 465 km navigable by small craft
Ports: Puerto Castilla, Puerto Cortes, San Lorenzo
Merchant marine: 149 ships (1,000 GRT or over) totaling 438,495 GRT/660,990 DWT; includes 2 passenger-cargo, 87 cargo, 12 refrigerated cargo, 9 container, 1 roll-on/roll-off cargo, 17 petroleum, oils, and lubricants (POL) tanker, 2 liquefied gas, 1 specialized tanker, 1 vehicle carrier, 17 bulk; note—a flag of convenience registry
Civil air: 9 major transport aircraft
Airports: 180 total, 140 usable; 8 with permanent-surface runways; none with runways over 3,659 m; 4 with runways 2,440-3,659 m; 12 with runways 1,220-2,439 m
Telecommunications: improved, but still inadequate; connection into Central American Microwave System; 35,100 telephones; stations—176 AM, no FM, 28 TV, 7 shortwave; 2 Atlantic Ocean INTELSAT earth stations

Defense Forces

Branches: Armed Forces, Naval Forces, Air Force
Military manpower: males 15-49, 1,222,858; 727,851 fit for military service; 61,493 reach military age (18) annually
Defense expenditures: 1.9% of GDP, or $82.5 million (1990 est.)

Hong Kong
(colony of the UK)

Lema Channel

See regional map VIII

Geography

Total area: 1,040 km²; land area: 990 km²
Comparative area: slightly less than six times the size of Washington, DC
Land boundary: 30 km with China
Coastline: 733 km
Maritime claims:
  Continental shelf: 200 meters or to depth of exploitation
  Exclusive fishing zone: 3 nm
  Territorial sea: 3 nm
Disputes: scheduled to become a Special Administrative Region of China in 1997
Climate: tropical monsoon; cool and humid in winter, hot and rainy from spring through summer, warm and sunny in fall
Terrain: hilly to mountainous with steep slopes; lowlands in north
Natural resources: outstanding deepwater harbor, feldspar
Land use: 7% arable land; 1% permanent crops; 1% meadows and pastures; 12% forest and woodland; 79% other; includes 3% irrigated
Environment: more than 200 islands; occasional typhoons

People

Population: 5,759,990 (July 1990), growth rate 1.0% (1990)
Birth rate: 13 births/1,000 population (1990)
Death rate: 5 deaths/1,000 population (1990)
Net migration rate: 2 migrants/1,000 population (1990)
Infant mortality rate: 6 deaths/1,000 live births (1990)
Life expectancy at birth: 76 years male, 82 years female (1990)
Total fertility rate: 1.4 children born/woman (1990)
Nationality: adjective—Hong Kong
Ethnic divisions: 98% Chinese, 2% other

Religion: 90% eclectic mixture of local religions, 10% Christian
Language: Chinese (Cantonese), English
Literacy: 75%
Labor force: 2,640,000; 35.8% manufacturing; 22.7% wholesale and retail trade, restaurants and hotel, 17.1% services, 7.5% construction, 8.4% transport and communications, 6.1% financing, insurance, and real estate (1986)
Organized labor: 15% of labor force (1986)

Government

Long-form name: none; abbreviated HK
Type: colony of the UK; scheduled to revert to China in 1997
Capital: Victoria
Administrative divisions: none (colony of the UK)
Independence: none (colony of the UK); the UK signed an agreement with China on 19 December 1984 to return Hong Kong to China on 1 July 1997; in the joint declaration, China promises to respect Hong Kong's existing social and economic systems and lifestyle for 50 years after transition
Constitution: unwritten; partly statutes, partly common law and practice
Legal system: based on English common law
National holiday: Liberation Day, 29 August (1945)
Executive branch: British monarch, governor, chief secretary of the Executive Council
Legislative branch: Legislative Council
Judicial branch: Supreme Court
Leaders: *Chief of State*—Queen ELIZABETH II (since 6 February 1952); *Head of Government*—Governor Sir David Clive WILSON (since 9 April 1987); Chief Secretary Sir David Robert FORD (since NA February 1987)
Political parties: none
Suffrage: limited to about 71,000 professionals of electoral college and functional constituencies
Elections: *Legislative Council*—indirect elections last held 26 September 1985 (next to be held in September 1991) seats—(58 total; 26 elected, 32 appointed)
Communists: 5,000 (est.) cadres affiliated with Communist Party of China
Other political or pressure groups: Federation of Trade Unions (Communist controlled), Hong Kong and Kowloon Trade Union Council (Nationalist Chinese dominated), Hong Kong General Chamber of Commerce, Chinese General Chamber of Commerce (Communist controlled), Federation of Hong Kong Industries, Chinese Manufacturers' Association of Hong

Kong, Hong Kong Professional Teachers' Union, and several small pro-democracy groups.
Member of: ADB, ESCAP (associate member), GATT, IMO, INTERPOL, Multifiber Arrangement, WMO
Diplomatic representation: as a British colony, the interests of Hong Kong in the US are represented by the UK; *US*—Consul General Donald M. ANDERSON; Consulate General at 26 Garden Road, Hong Kong (mailing address is Box 30, Hong Kong, or FPO San Francisco 96659-0002); telephone [852] (5) 239011
Flag: blue with the flag of the UK in the upper hoist-side quadrant with the Hong Kong coat of arms on a white disk centered on the outer half of the flag; the coat of arms contains a shield (bearing two junks below a crown) held by a lion (representing the UK) and a dragon (representing China) with another lion above the shield and a banner bearing the words *HONG KONG* below the shield

Economy

Overview: Hong Kong has a free-market economy and is autonomous in financial affairs. Natural resources are limited and food and raw materials must be imported. Manufacturing is the backbone of the economy, accounting for more than 20% of GDP, employing 36% of the labor force, and exporting about 90% of output. Real GDP growth averaged a remakable 8% in 1987-88, then slowed to a respectable 3% in 1989. Unemployment, which has been declining since the mid-1980s, is now less than 2%. A shortage of labor continues to put upward pressure on prices and the cost of living. Short-term prospects remain solid so long as major trading partners continue to be prosperous. The crackdown in China in 1989 casts a long shadow over the longer term economic outlook.
GDP: $57 billion, per capita $10,000; real growth rate 3% (1989)
Inflation rate (consumer prices): 9.5% (1989)
Unemployment rate: 1.6% (1988)
Budget: $6.9 billion (FY89)
Exports: $63.2 billion (f.o.b., 1988), including reexports of $22.9 billion; *commodities*—clothing, textile yarn and fabric, footwear, electrical appliances, watches and clocks, toys; *partners*—US 31%, China 14%, FRG 8%, UK 6%, Japan 5%
Imports: $63.9 billion (c.i.f., 1988); *commodities*—foodstuffs, transport equipment, raw materials, semimanufactures, petroleum; *partners*—China 31%, Japan 20%, Taiwan 9%, US 8%

External debt: $9.6 billion (December 1988)
Industrial production: growth rate 7.0% (1988)
Electricity: 7,800,000 kW capacity; 23,000 million kWh produced, 4,030 kWh per capita (1989)
Industries: textiles, clothing, tourism, electronics, plastics, toys, watches, clocks
Agriculture: minor role in the economy; rice, vegetables, dairy products; less than 20% self-sufficient; shortages of rice, wheat, water
Aid: US commitments, including Ex-Im (FY70-87), $141.2 million; Western (non-US) countries, ODA and OOF bilateral commitments (1970-87), $899.8 million
Currency: Hong Kong dollar (plural—dollars); 1 Hong Kong dollar (HK$) = 100 cents
Exchange rates: Hong Kong dollars (HK$) per US$—7.800 (March 1989), 7.810 (1988), 7.760 (1987), 7.795 (1986), 7.811 (1985); note—linked to the US dollar at the rate of about 7.8 HK$ per 1 US$ since 1985
Fiscal year: 1 April-31 March

Communications

Railroads: 35 km 1.435-meter standard gauge, government owned
Highways: 1,100 km total; 794 km paved, 306 km gravel, crushed stone, or earth
Ports: Hong Kong
Merchant marine: 134 ships (1,000 GRT or over), totaling 4,391,102 GRT/ 7,430,337 DWT; includes 1 passenger, 1 short-sea passenger, 11 cargo, 10 refrigerated cargo, 13 container, 2 roll-on/roll-off cargo, 10 petroleum, oils, and lubricants (POL) tanker, 1 chemical tanker, 9 combination ore/oil, 7 liquefied gas, 69 bulk; note—a flag of convenience registry; ships registered in Hong Kong fly the UK flag and an estimated 500 Hong Kong-owned ships are registered elsewhere
Civil air: 16 major transport aircraft
Airports: 2 total; 2 usable; 2 with permanent-surface runways; none with runways over 3,659 m; 1 with runways 2,440-3,659 m; none with runways 1,220-2,439 m
Telecommunications: modern facilities provide excellent domestic and international services; 2,300,000 telephones; microwave transmission links and extensive optical fiber transmission network; stations—6 AM, 6 FM, 4 TV; 1 British Broadcasting Corporation (BBC) relay station and 1 British Forces Broadcasting Service relay station; 2,500,000 radio receivers; 1,312,000 TV sets (1,224,000 color TV sets); satellite earth stations—1 Pacific Ocean INTELSAT and 2 Indian Ocean INTELSAT; coaxial cable to Guangzhou,

Hong Kong (continued)

China; links to 5 international submarine cables providing access to ASEAN member nations, Japan, Taiwan, Australia, Middle East, and Western Europe

Defense Forces

Branches: Headquarters of British Forces, Gurkha Brigade, Royal Navy, Royal Air Force, Royal Hong Kong Auxiliary Air Force, Royal Hong Kong Police Force
Military manpower: males 15-49, 1,703,890; 1,320,914 fit for military service; 46,440 reach military age (18) annually
Defense expenditures: 0.5% of GDP, or $300 million (1989 est.); this represents one-fourth of the total cost of defending the colony, the remainder being paid by the UK
Note: defense is the responsibility of the UK

Howland Island
(territory of the US)

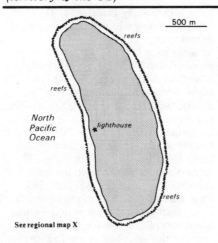

North Pacific Ocean

reefs

reefs

lighthouse

reefs

500 m

See regional map X

Geography

Total area: 1.6 km²; land area: 1.6 km²
Comparative area: about 2.7 times the size of The Mall in Washington, DC
Land boundaries: none
Coastline: 6.4 km
Maritime claims:
Contiguous zone: 12 nm
Continental shelf: 200 m
Extended economic zone: 200 nm
Territorial sea: 12 nm
Climate: equatorial; scant rainfall, constant wind, burning sun
Terrain: low-lying, nearly level, sandy, coral island surrounded by a narrow fringing reef; depressed central area
Natural resources: guano (deposits worked until late 1800s)
Land use: 0% arable land; 0% permanent crops; 0% meadows and pastures; 5% forest and woodland; 95% other
Environment: almost totally covered with grasses, prostrate vines, and low-growing shrubs; small area of trees in the center; lacks fresh water; primarily a nesting, roosting, and foraging habitat for seabirds, shorebirds, and marine wildlife; feral cats
Note: remote location 2,575 km southwest of Honolulu in the North Pacific Ocean, just north of the Equator, about halfway between Hawaii and Australia

People

Population: uninhabited
Note: American civilians evacuated in 1942 after Japanese air and naval attacks during World War II; occupied by US military during World War II, but abandoned after the war; public entry is by special-use permit only and generally restricted to scientists and educators

Government

Long-form name: none
Type: unincorporated territory of the US administered by the Fish and Wildlife Service of the US Department of the Interior as part of the National Wildlife Refuge System

Economy

Overview: no economic activity

Communications

Airports: airstrip constructed in 1937 for scheduled refueling stop on the round-the-world flight of Amelia Earhart and Fred Noonan—they left Lae, New Guinea, for Howland Island, but were never seen again; the airstrip is no longer serviceable
Ports: none; offshore anchorage only, one boat landing area along the middle of the west coast
Note: Earhart Light is a day beacon near the middle of the west coast that was partially destroyed during World War II, but has since been rebuilt in memory of famed aviatrix Amelia Earhart

Defense Forces

Note: defense is the responsibility of the US; visited annually by the US Coast Guard

Hungary

125 km

See regional map V

Geography

Total area: 93,030 km²; land area: 92,340 km²
Comparative area: slightly smaller than Indiana
Land boundaries: 2,251 km total; Austria 366 km, Czechoslovakia 676 km, Romania 443 km, USSR 135 km, Yugoslavia 631 km
Coastline: none—landlocked
Maritime claims: none—landlocked
Disputes: Transylvania question with Romania; Nagymaros Dam dispute with Czechoslovakia
Climate: temperate; cold, cloudy, humid winters; warm summers
Terrain: mostly flat to rolling plains
Natural resources: bauxite, coal, natural gas, fertile soils
Land use: 54% arable land; 3% permanent crops; 14% meadows and pastures; 18% forest and woodland; 11% other; includes 2% irrigated
Environment: levees are common along many streams, but flooding occurs almost every year
Note: landlocked; strategic location astride main land routes between Western Europe and Balkan Peninsula as well as between USSR and Mediterranean basin

People

Population: 10,568,686 (July 1990), growth rate −0.1% (1990)
Birth rate: 12 births/1,000 population (1990)
Death rate: 13 deaths/1,000 population (1990)
Net migration rate: 0 migrants/1,000 population (1990)
Infant mortality rate: 15 deaths/1,000 live births (1990)
Life expectancy at birth: 67 years male, 75 years female (1990)

Total fertility rate: 1.8 children born/woman (1990)
Nationality: noun—Hungarian(s); adjective—Hungarian
Ethnic divisions: 96.6% Hungarian, 1.6% German, 1.1% Slovak, 0.3% Southern Slav, 0.2% Romanian
Religion: 67.5% Roman Catholic, 20.0% Calvinist, 5.0% Lutheran, 7.5% atheist and other
Language: 98.2% Hungarian, 1.8% other
Literacy: 99%
Labor force: 4,860,000; 43.2% services, trade, government, and other, 30.9% industry, 18.8% agriculture, 7.1% construction (1988)
Organized labor: 96.5% of labor force; Central Council of Hungarian Trade Unions (SZOT) includes 19 affiliated unions, all controlled by the government; independent unions legal; may be as many as 12 small independent unions in operation

Government

Long-form name: Republic of Hungary
Type: republic
Capital: Budapest
Administrative divisions: 19 counties (megyék, singular—megye) and 1 capital city* (fováros); Bács-Kiskun, Baranya, Békés, Borsod-Abaúj-Zemplén, Budapest*, Csongrád, Fejér, Gyor-Sopron, Hajdú-Bihar, Heves, Komárom, Nógrád, Pest, Somogy, Szabolcs-Szatmár, Szolnok, Tolna, Vas, Veszprém, Zala
Independence: 1001, unification by King Stephen I
Constitution: 18 August 1949, effective 20 August 1949, revised 19 April 1972 and 18 October 1989
Legal system: based on Communist legal theory, with both civil law system (civil code of 1960) and common law elements; Supreme Court renders decisions of principle that sometimes have the effect of declaring legislative acts unconstitutional; has not accepted compulsory ICJ jurisdiction
National holiday: Anniversary of the Liberation, 4 April (1945)
Executive branch: president, premier, Council of Ministers
Legislative branch: unicameral National Assembly (Országgyülés)
Judicial branch: Supreme Court
Leaders: *Chief of State*—President-designate Arpad GONCZ (since 2 May 1990); *Head of Government*—Prime Minister-designate Jozsef ANTALL (since 2 May 1990)
Political parties and leaders: Democratic Forum, Jozsef Antall, chairman; Free Democrats, Janos Kis, chairman; Independent Smallholders, Istvan Prepeliczay,

president; Hungarian Socialist Party (MSP), Rezso Nyers, chairman; Young Democrats; Christian Democrats, Sandor Keresztes, president; note—the Hungarian Socialist (Communist) Workers' Party (MSZMP) renounced Communism and became the Hungarian Socialist Party (MSP) in October 1989
Suffrage: universal at age 18
Elections: *National Assembly*—last held on 25 March 1990 (first round, with the second round held 8 April 1990); results—percent of vote by party NA; seats—(394 total) Democratic Forum 165, Free Democrats 92, Independent Smallholders 43, Hungarian Socialist Party (MSP) 33, Young Democrats 21, Christian Democrats 21; independent candidates or jointly sponsored candidates 19; an additional 8 seats will be given to representatives of minority nationalities
Communists: fewer than 100,000 (December 1989)
Member of: CCC, CEMA, FAO, GATT, IAEA, IBRD, ICAC, ICAO, ILO, ILZSG, IMF, IMO, IPU, ISO, ITC, ITU, UN, UNESCO, UPU, Warsaw Pact, WFTU, WHO, WIPO, WMO
Diplomatic representation: Ambassador Dr. Peter VARKONYI; Chancery at 3910 Shoemaker Street NW, Washington DC 20008; telephone (202) 362-6730; there is a Hungarian Consulate General in New York; *US*—Ambassador-designate Charles THOMAS; Embassy at V. Szabadsag Ter 12, Budapest (mailing address is APO New York 09213); telephone [36] (1) 126-450
Flag: three equal horizontal bands of red (top), white, and green

Economy

Overview: Hungary's postwar Communist government spurred the movement from a predominantly agricultural to an industrialized economy. The share of the labor force in agriculture dropped from over 50% in 1950 to under 20% in 1989. Agriculture nevertheless remains an important sector, providing sizable export earnings and meeting domestic food needs. Industry accounts for about 40% of GNP and 30% of employment. Nearly three-fourths of foreign trade is with the USSR and Eastern Europe. Low rates of growth reflect the inability of the Soviet-style economy to modernize capital plant and motivate workers. GNP grew about 1% in 1988 and declined by 1% in 1989. Since 1985 external debt has more than doubled, to nearly $20 billion. In recent years Hungary has moved further than any other East European country in experimenting with decentralized and market-

Hungary (continued)

oriented enterprises. These experiments have failed to jump-start the economy because of: limitations on funds for privatization; continued subsidization of insolvent state enterprises; and the leadership's reluctance to implement sweeping market reforms that would cause additional social dislocations in the short term.

GNP: $64.6 billion, per capita $6,108; real growth rate −1.3% (1989 est.)

Inflation rate (consumer prices): 18% (1989 est.)

Unemployment rate: 0.4% (1989)

Budget: revenues $14.0 billion; expenditures $14.2 billion, including capital expenditures of $944 million (1988)

Exports: $19.1 billion (f.o.b. 1988); *commodities*—capital goods 36%, foods 24%, consumer goods 18%, fuels and minerals 11%, other 11%; *partners* USSR 48%, Eastern Europe 25%, developed countries 16%, less developed countries 8% (1987)

Imports: $18.3 billion (c.i.f., 1988); *commodities*—machinery and transport 28%, fuels 20%, chemical products 14%, manufactured consumer goods 16%, agriculture 6%, other 16%; *partners*—USSR 43%, Eastern Europe 28%, less developed countries 23%, US 3% (1987)

External debt: $19.6 billion (1989)

Industrial production: growth rate 0.6% (1988)

Electricity: 7,250,000 kW capacity; 30,300 million kWh produced, 2,870 kWh per capita (1989)

Industries: mining, metallurgy, engineering industries, processed foods, textiles, chemicals (especially pharmaceuticals)

Agriculture: including forestry, accounts for about 15% of GNP and 19% of employment; highly diversified crop-livestock farming; principal crops—wheat, corn, sunflowers, potatoes, sugar beets; livestock—hogs, cattle, poultry, dairy products; self-sufficient in food output

Aid: donor—$1.8 billion in bilateral aid to non-Communist less developed countries (1962-88)

Currency: forint (plural—forints); 1 forint (Ft) = 100 fillér

Exchange rates: forints (Ft) per US$1— 62.5 (January 1990), 59.2 (1989), 50.413 (1988), 46.971 (1987), 45.832 (1986), 50.119 (1985)

Fiscal year: calendar year

Communications

Railroads: 7,770 km total; 7,513 km 1.435-meter standard gauge, 222 km narrow gauge (mostly 0.760-meter), 35 km 1.524-meter broad gauge; 1,138 km double track, 2,088 km electrified; all government owned (1987)

Highways: 130,000 km total; 29,701 km national highway system—26,727 km asphalt and bitumen, 146 km concrete, 55 km stone and road brick, 2,345 km macadam, 428 km unpaved; 58,495 km country roads (66% unpaved), and 41,804 km (est.) other roads (70% unpaved) (1987)

Inland waterways: 1,622 km (1986)

Pipelines: crude oil, 1,204 km; refined products, 600 km; natural gas, 3,800 km (1986)

Ports: Budapest and Dunaujvaros are river ports on the Danube; maritime outlets are Rostock (GDR), Gdansk (Poland), Gdynia (Poland), Szczecin (Poland), Galati (Romania), and Braila (Romania)

Merchant marine: 16 cargo ships (1,000 GRT or over) totaling 77,141 GRT/ 103,189 DWT

Civil air: 22 major transport aircraft

Airports: 90 total, 90 usable; 20 with permanent-surface runways; 2 with runways over 3,659 m; 10 with runways 2,440-3,659 m; 15 with runways 1,220-2,439 m

Telecommunications: stations—13 AM, 11 FM, 21 TV; 8 Soviet TV relays; 3,500,000 TV sets; 5,500,000 receiver sets; at least 1 satellite earth station

Defense Forces

Branches: Hungarian People's Army, Frontier Guard, Air and Air Defense Command

Military manpower: males 15-49, 2,645,016; 2,112,651 fit for military service; 86,481 reach military age (18) annually

Defense expenditures: 43.7 billion forints, NA% of total budget (1989); note—conversion of the military budget into US dollars using the official administratively set exchange rate would produce misleading results

Iceland

125 km

Greenland Sea

See regional map V

Geography

Total area: 103,000 km^2; land area: 100,250 km^2

Comparative area: slightly smaller than Kentucky

Land boundaries: none

Coastline: 4,988 km

Maritime claims:
Continental shelf: edge of continental margin or 200 nm
Extended economic zone: 200 nm
Territorial sea: 12 nm

Disputes: Rockall continental shelf dispute involving Denmark, Ireland, and the UK (Ireland and the UK have signed a boundary agreement in the Rockall area)

Climate: temperate; moderated by North Atlantic Current; mild, windy winters; damp, cool summers

Terrain: mostly plateau interspersed with mountain peaks, icefields; coast deeply indented by bays and fiords

Natural resources: fish, hydroelectric and geothermal power, diatomite

Land use: NEGL% arable land; 0% permanent crops; 23% meadows and pastures; 1% forest and woodland; 76% other

Environment: subject to earthquakes and volcanic activity

Note: strategic location between Greenland and Europe; westernmost European country

People

Population: 257,023 (July 1990), growth rate 1.1% (1990)

Birth rate: 18 births/1,000 population (1990)

Death rate: 7 deaths/1,000 population (1990)

Net migration rate: 0 migrants/1,000 population (1990)

Infant mortality rate: 7 deaths/1,000 live births (1990)

Life expectancy at birth: 75 years male, 80 years female (1990)
Total fertility rate: 2.2 children born/woman (1990)
Nationality: noun—Icelander(s); adjective—Icelandic
Ethnic divisions: homogeneous mixture of descendants of Norwegians and Celts
Religion: 95% Evangelical Lutheran, 3% other Protestant and Roman Catholic, 2% no affiliation
Language: Icelandic
Literacy: 100%
Labor force: 134,429; 55.4% commerce, finance, and services, 14.3% other manufacturing, 5.8% agriculture, 7.9% fish processing, 5.0% fishing (1986)
Organized labor: 60% of labor force

Government

Long-form name: Republic of Iceland
Type: republic
Capital: Reykjavík
Administrative divisions: 23 counties (sýslar, singular—sýsla) and 14 independent towns* (kaupstadar, singular—kaupstadur); Akranes*, Akureyri*, Arnessýsla, Austur-Bardhastrandarsýsla, Austur-Húnavatnssýsla, Austur-Skaftafellssýsla, Borgarfjardharsýsla, Dalasýsla, Eyjafjardharsýsla, Gullbringusýsla, Hafnarfjördhur*, Húsavík*, Isafjördhur*, Keflavík*, Kjósarsýsla, Kópavogur*, Mýrasýsla, Neskaupstadhur*, Nordhur-Isafjardharsýsla, Nordhur-Múlasýsla, Nordhur-Thingeyjarsýsla, Olafsfjördhur*, Rangárvallasýsla, Reykjavík*, Saudhárkrókur*, Seydhisfjördhur*, Siglufjördhur*, Skagafjardharsýsla, Snaefellsnes-og Hanppadalssýsla, Strandasýsla, Sudhur-Múlasýsla, Sudhur-Thingeyjarsýsla, Vestmannaeyjar*, Vestur-Bardhastrandarsýsla, Vestur-Húnavatnssýsla, Vestur-Isafjardharsýsla, Vestur-Skaftafellssýsla
Independence: 17 June 1944 (from Denmark)
Constitution: 16 June 1944, effective 17 June 1944
Legal system: civil law system based on Danish law; does not accept compulsory ICJ jurisdiction
National holiday: Anniversary of the Establishment of the Republic, 17 June (1944)
Executive branch: president, prime minister, Cabinet
Legislative branch: unicameral Parliament (Althing) with an Upper House (Efri Deild) and a Lower House (Nedri Deild)
Judicial branch: Supreme Court (Haestiréttur)

Leaders: *Chief of State*—President Vigdís FINNBOGADOTTIR (since 1 August 1980);
Head of Government—Prime Minister Steingrimur HERMANNSSON (since 28 September 1988)
Political parties and leaders: Independence (conservative), Thorsteinn Pálsson; Progressive, Steingrímur Hermannsson; Social Democratic, Jon Baldvin Hannibalsson; People's Alliance (left socialist), Olafur Ragnar Grimsson; Citizens Party (conservative nationalist), Julius Solnes; Women's List
Suffrage: universal at age 20
Elections: *President*—last held on 29 June 1980 (next scheduled for June 1992); results—there were no elections in 1984 and 1988 as President Vigdís Finnbogadóttir was unopposed;
Parliament—last held on 25 April 1987 (next to be held by 25 April 1991); results—Independence 27.2%, Progressive 18.9%, Social Democratic 15.2%, People's Alliance 13.4%, Citizens Party 10.9%, Womens List 10.1%, other 4.3%; seats—(63 total) Independence 18, Progressive 13, Social Democratic 10, People's Alliance 8, Citizens Party 7, Womens List 6, Regional Equality Platform 1
Communists: less than 100 (est.), some of whom participate in the People's Alliance
Member of: CCC, Council of Europe, EC (free trade agreement pending resolution of fishing limits issue), EFTA, FAO, GATT, IAEA, IBRD, ICAO, ICES, IDA, IFC, IHO, ILO, IMF, IMO, INTELSAT, INTERPOL, IPU, ITU, IWC—International Whaling Commission, NATO, Nordic Council, OECD, UN, UNESCO, UPU, WHO, WMO, WSG
Diplomatic representation: Ambassador Ingvi S. INGVARSSON; Chancery at 2022 Connecticut Avenue NW, Washington DC 20008; telephone (202) 265-6653 through 6655; there is an Icelandic Consulate General in New York; *US*—Ambassador Charles E. COBB; Embassy at Laufasvegur 21, Reykjavik (mailing address is FPO New York 09571-0001); telephone [354] (1) 29100
Flag: blue with a red cross outlined in white that extends to the edges of the flag; the vertical part of the cross is shifted to the hoist side in the style of the *Dannebrog* (Danish flag)

Economy

Overview: Iceland's prosperous Scandinavian-type economy is basically capitalistic, but with extensive welfare measures, low unemployment, and comparatively even distribution of income. The economy is heavily dependent on the fishing industry, which provides nearly

75% of export earnings. In the absence of other natural resources, Iceland's economy is vulnerable to changing world fish prices. National output declined for the second consecutive year in 1989, and two of the largest fish farms filed for bankruptcy. Other economic activities include livestock raising and aluminum smelting. A fall in the fish catch is expected for 1990, resulting in a continuation of the recession.
GDP: $4.0 billion, per capita $16,200; real growth rate −1.8% (1989 est.)
Inflation rate (consumer prices): 17.4% (1989 est.)
Unemployment rate: 1.3% (1989 est.)
Budget: revenues $1.5 billion; expenditures $1.7 billion, including capital expenditures of $NA million (1988)
Exports: $1.4 billion (f.o.b., 1988); *commodities*—fish and fish products, animal products, aluminum, diatomite; *partners*—EC 58.9% (UK 23.3%, FRG 10.3%), US 13.6%, USSR 3.6%
Imports: $1.6 billion (c.i.f., 1988); *commodities*—machinery and transportation equipment, petroleum, foodstuffs, textiles; *partners*—EC 58% (FRG 16%, Denmark 10.4%, UK 9.2%), US 8.5%, USSR 3.9%
External debt: $1.8 billion (1988)
Industrial production: growth rate 4.7% (1987 est.)
Electricity: 1,063,000 kW capacity; 5,165 million kWh produced, 20,780 kWh per capita (1989)
Industries: fish processing, aluminum smelting, ferro-silicon production, hydropower
Agriculture: accounts for about 25% of GDP (including fishing); fishing is most important economic activity, contributing nearly 75% to export earnings; principal crops—potatoes and turnips; livestock—cattle, sheep; self-sufficient in crops; fish catch of about 1.6 million metric tons in 1987
Aid: US commitments, including Ex-Im (FY70-81), $19.1 million
Currency: króna (plural—krónur); 1 Icelandic króna (IKr) = 100 aurar
Exchange rates: Icelandic krónur (IKr) per US$1—60.751 (January 1990), 57.042 (1989), 43.014 (1988), 38.677 (1987), 41.104 (1986), 41.508 (1985)
Fiscal year: calendar year

Communications

Highways: 12,343 km total; 166 km bitumen and concrete; 1,284 km bituminous treated and gravel; 10,893 km earth
Ports: Reykjavik, Akureyri, Hafnarfjordhur, Keflavik, Seydhisfjordhur, Siglufjordur, Vestmannaeyjar; numerous minor ports

Iceland (continued)

Merchant marine: 18 ships (1,000 GRT or over) totaling 62,867 GRT/87,610 DWT; includes 9 cargo, 2 refrigerated cargo, 1 container, 2 roll-on/roll-off cargo, 1 petroleum, oils, and lubricants (POL) tanker, 1 chemical tanker, 2 bulk
Civil air: 20 major transport aircraft
Airports: 99 total, 92 usable; 4 with permanent-surface runways; none with runways over 3,659 m; 1 with runways 2,440-3,659 m; 14 with runways 1,220-2,439 m
Telecommunications: adequate domestic service, wire and radio communication system; 135,000 telephones; stations—10 AM, 17 (43 relays) FM, 14 (132 relays) TV; 2 submarine cables; 1 Atlantic Ocean INTELSAT earth station

Defense Forces

Branches: Police, Coast Guard
Military manpower: males 15-49, 68,688; 61,553 fit for military service; no conscription or compulsory military service
Defense expenditures: none

India

See regional map VIII

Geography

Total area: 3,287,590 km²; land area: 2,973,190 km²
Comparative area: slightly more than one-third the size of the US
Land boundaries: 14,103 km total; Bangladesh 4,053 km, Bhutan 605 km, Burma 1,463 km, China 3,380, Nepal 1,690 km, Pakistan 2,912 km
Coastline: 7,000 km
Maritime claims:
Contiguous zone: 24 nm
Continental shelf: edge of continental margin or 200 nm
Extended economic zone: 200 nm
Territorial sea: 12 nm
Disputes: boundaries with Bangladesh, China, and Pakistan; water sharing problems with downstream riparians, Bangladesh over the Ganges and Pakistan over the Indus
Climate: varies from tropical monsoon in south to temperate in north
Terrain: upland plain (Deccan Plateau) in south, flat to rolling plain along the Ganges, deserts in west, Himalayas in north
Natural resources: coal (fourth-largest reserves in the world), iron ore, manganese, mica, bauxite, titanium ore, chromite, natural gas, diamonds, crude oil, limestone
Land use: 55% arable land; 1% permanent crops; 4% meadows and pastures; 23% forest and woodland; 17% other; includes 13% irrigated
Environment: droughts, flash floods, severe thunderstorms common; deforestation; soil erosion; overgrazing; air and water pollution; desertification
Note: dominates South Asian subcontinent; near important Indian Ocean trade routes

People

Population: 849,746,001 (July 1990), growth rate 2.0% (1990)
Birth rate: 30 births/1,000 population (1990)
Death rate: 10 deaths/1,000 population (1990)
Net migration rate: 0 migrants/1,000 population (1990)
Infant mortality rate: 89 deaths/1,000 live births (1990)
Life expectancy at birth: 57 years male, 59 years female (1990)
Total fertility rate: 3.8 children born/woman (1990)
Nationality: noun—Indian(s); adjective—Indian
Ethnic divisions: 72% Indo-Aryan, 25% Dravidian, 3% Mongoloid and other
Religion: 82.6% Hindu, 11.4% Muslim, 2.4% Christian, 2.0% Sikh, 0.7% Buddhist, 0.5% Jains, 0.4% other
Language: Hindi, English, and 14 other official languages—Bengali, Telgu, Marathi, Tamil, Urdu, Gujarati, Malayalam, Kannada, Oriya, Punjabi, Assamese, Kashmiri, Sindhi, and Sanskrit; 24 languages spoken by a million or more persons each; numerous other languages and dialects, for the most part mutually unintelligible; Hindi is the national language and primary tongue of 30% of the people; English enjoys associate status but is the most important language for national, political, and commercial communication; Hindustani, a popular variant of Hindi/Urdu, is spoken widely throughout northern India
Literacy: 36%
Labor force: 284,400,000; 67% agriculture (FY85)
Organized labor: less than 5% of the labor force

Government

Long-form name: Republic of India
Type: federal republic
Capital: New Delhi
Administrative divisions: 24 states and 7 union territories*; Andaman and Nicobar Islands*, Andhra Pradesh, Arunāchal Pradesh, Assam, Bihār, Chandīgarh*, Dādra and Nagar Haveli*, Delhi*, Goa and Damān and Diu*, Gujarāt, Haryāna, Himāchal Pradesh, Jammu and Kashmīr, Karnātaka, Kerala, Lakshadweep*, Madhya Pradesh, Mahārāshtra, Manipur, Meghālaya, Mizoram, Nāgāland, Orissa, Pondicherry*, Punjab, Rājasthān, Sikkim, Tamil Nādu, Tripura, Uttar Pradesh, West Bengal; note—Goa may have become a state with Damān and Diu remaining a union territory
Independence: 15 August 1947 (from UK)

Constitution: 26 January 1950
Legal system: based on English common law; limited judicial review of legislative acts; accepts compulsory ICJ jurisdiction, with reservations
National holiday: Anniversary of the Proclamation of the Republic, 26 January (1950)
Executive branch: president, vice president, prime minister, Council of Ministers
Legislative branch: bicameral Parliament (Sansad) consists of an upper house or Government Assembly (Rajya Sabha) and a lower house or People's Assembly (Lok Sabha)
Judicial branch: Supreme Court
Leaders: *Chief of State*—President Ramaswamy Iyer VENKATARAMAN (since 25 July 1987); Vice President Dr. Shankar Dayal SHARMA (since 3 September 1987);
Head of Government—Prime Minister Vishwanath Pratap SINGH (since 2 December 1989)
Political parties and leaders: Janata Dal Party, Prime Minister V. P. Singh; Congress (I) Party, Rajiv Gandhi; Bharatiya Janata Party, L. K. Advani; Communist Party of India (CPI), C. Rajeswara Rao; Communist Party of India/Marxist (CPI/M), E. M. S. Namboodiripad; Communist Party of India/Marxist-Leninist (CPI/ML), Satyanarayan Singh; All-India Anna Dravida Munnetra Kazagham (AIADMK), a regional party in Tamil Nadu, Jayalalitha; Dravida Munnetra Kazagham, M. Karunanidhi; Akali Dal factions representing Sikh religious community in the Punjab; Telugu Desam, a regional party in Andhra Pradesh, N. T. Rama Rao; National Conference (NC), a regional party in Jammu and Kashmir, Farooq Abdullah; Asom Gana Parishad, a regional party in Assam, Prafulla Mahanta
Suffrage: universal at age 18
Elections: *People's Assembly*—last held 22, 24, 26 November 1989 (next to be held by November 1994, subject to postponement); results—percent of vote by party NA; seats—(544 total), 525 elected—Congress (I) Party 193, Janata Dal Party 141, Bharatiya Janata Party 86, Communist Party of India (Marxist) 32, independents 18, Communist Party of India 12, AIADMK 11, Akali Dal 6, Shiv Sena 4, RSP 4, Forward Bloc 3, BSP 3, Telugu Desam 2, Congress (S) Party 1, others 9
Communists: 466,000 members claimed by CPI, 361,000 members claimed by CPI/M; Communist extremist groups, about 15,000 members
Other political or pressure groups: various separatist groups seeking greater communal autonomy; numerous senas or militant/chauvinistic organizations, including Shiv Sena (in Bombay), Anand Marg, and Rashtriya Swayamsevak Sangh
Member of: ADB, AIOEC, ANRPC, CCC, Colombo Plan, Commonwealth, ESCAP, FAO, G-77, GATT, IAEA, IBRD, ICAC, ICAO, ICO, IDA, IFAD, IFC, IHO, ILO, ILZSG, IMF, IMO, INTELSAT, INTERPOL, IPU, IRC, ITC, ITU, IWC—International Wheat Council, NAM, SAARC, UN, UNESCO, UPU, WFTU, WHO, WIPO, WMO, WSG, WTO
Diplomatic representation: Ambassador-designate Abid HUSSEIN; Chancery at 2107 Massachusetts Avenue NW, Washington DC 20008; telephone (202) 939-7000; there are Indian Consulates General in Chicago, New York, and San Francisco; *US*—Ambassador William CLARK; Embassy at Shanti Path, Chanakyapuri 110021, New Delhi; telephone [91] (11) 600651; there are US Consulates General in Bombay, Calcutta, and Madras
Flag: three equal horizontal bands of orange (top), white, and green with a blue *chakra* (24-spoked wheel) centered in the white band; similar to the flag of Niger which has a small orange disk centered in the white band

Economy

Overview: India's Malthusian economy is a mixture of traditional village farming and handicrafts, modern agriculture, old and new branches of industry, and a multitude of support services. It presents both the entrepreneurial skills and drives of the capitalist system and widespread government intervention of the socialist mold. Growth of 4% to 5% annually in the 1980s has softened the impact of population growth on unemployment, social tranquility, and the environment. Agricultural output has continued to expand, reflecting the greater use of modern farming techniques and improved seed that have helped to make India self-sufficient in food grains and a net agricultural exporter. However, tens of millions of villagers, particularly in the south, have not benefited from the green revolution and live in abject poverty. Industry has benefited from a liberalization of controls. The growth rate of the service sector has also been strong.
GNP: $333 billion, per capita $400; real growth rate 5.0% (1989 est.)
Inflation rate (consumer prices): 9.5% (1989 est.)
Unemployment rate: 20% (1989 est.)
Budget: revenues $48 billion; expenditures $53 billion, including capital expenditures of $13.6 billion (1989)
Exports: $17.2 billion (f.o.b., 1989); *commodities*—tea, coffee, iron ore, fish products, manufactures; *partners*—EC 25%, USSR and Eastern Europe 17%, US 19%, Japan 10%
Imports: $24.7 billion (c.i.f., 1989); *commodities*—petroleum, edible oils, textiles, clothing, capital goods; *partners*—EC 33%, Middle East 19%, Japan 10%, US 9%, USSR and Eastern Europe 8%
External debt: $48.7 billion (1989)
Industrial production: growth rate 8.8% (1989)
Electricity: 59,000,000 kW capacity; 215,000 million kWh produced, 260 kWh per capita (1989)
Industries: textiles, food processing, steel, machinery, transportation equipment, cement, jute manufactures, mining, petroleum, power, chemicals, pharmaceuticals, electronics
Agriculture: accounts for about 33% of GNP and employs 67% of labor force; self-sufficient in food grains; principal crops—rice, wheat, oilseeds, cotton, jute, tea, sugarcane, potatoes; livestock—cattle, buffaloes, sheep, goats and poultry; fish catch of about 3 million metric tons ranks India in the world's top 10 fishing nations
Illicit drugs: licit producer of opium poppy for the pharmaceutical trade, but some opium is diverted to international drug markets; major transit country for illicit narcotics produced in neighboring countries
Aid: US commitments, including Ex-Im (FY70-88), $4.2 billion; Western (non-US) countries, ODA and OOF bilateral commitments (1980-87), $18.6 billion; OPEC bilateral aid (1979-89), $315 million; USSR (1970-88), $10.0 billion; Eastern Europe (1970-88), $105 million
Currency: Indian rupee (plural—rupees); 1 Indian rupee (Re) = 100 paise
Exchange rates: Indian rupees (Rs) per US$1—16.965 (January 1990), 16.226 (1989), 13.917 (1988), 12.962 (1987), 12.611 (1986), 12.369 (1985)
Fiscal year: 1 April-31 March

Communications

Railroads: 61,850 km total (1986); 33,553 km 1.676-meter broad gauge, 24,051 km 1.000-meter gauge, 4,246 km narrow gauge (0.762 meter and 0.610 meter); 12,617 km is double track; 6,500 km is electrified
Highways: 1,633,300 km total (1986); 515,300 km secondary and 1,118,000 km gravel, crushed stone, or earth
Inland waterways: 16,180 km; 3,631 km navigable by large vessels
Pipelines: crude oil, 3,497 km; refined products, 1,703 km; natural gas, 902 km (1989)

India (continued)

Ports: Bombay, Calcutta, Cochin, Kandla, Madras, New Mangalore, Port Blair (Andaman Islands)

Merchant marine: 296 ships (1,000 GRT or over) totaling 5,855,842 GRT/ 9,790,260 DWT; includes 1 short-sea passenger, 8 passenger-cargo, 95 cargo, 1 roll-on/ roll-off cargo, 8 container, 53 petroleum, oils, and lubricants (POL) tanker, 10 chemical tanker, 9 combination ore/ oil,109 bulk, 2 combination bulk

Civil air: 93 major transport aircraft

Airports: 345 total, 292 usable; 202 with permanent-surface runways; 2 with runways over 3,659 m; 57 with runways 2,440-3,659 m; 91 with runways 1,220-2,439 m

Telecommunications: poor domestic telephone service, international radio communications adequate; 3,200,000 telephones; stations—170 AM, no FM, 14 TV (government controlled); domestic satellite system for communications and TV; 3 Indian Ocean INTELSAT earth stations; submarine cables to Sri Lanka, Malaysia, and Pakistan

Defense Forces

Branches: Army, Navy, Air Force, Border Security Forces, Coast Guard, Paramilitary Forces

Military manpower: males 15-49, 227,436,282; 134,169,114 fit for military service; about 9,403,063 reach military age (17) annually

Defense expenditures: 2.6% of GNP, or $8.7 billion (FY90 est.)

Indian Ocean

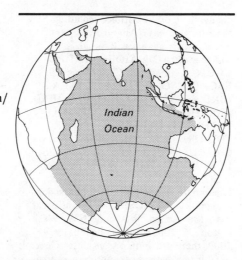

Geography

Total area: 73,600,000 km^2; Arabian Sea, Bass Strait, Bay of Bengal, Java Sea, Persian Gulf, Red Sea, Strait of Malacca, Timor Sea, and other tributary water bodies

Comparative area: slightly less than eight times the size of the US; third-largest ocean (after the Pacific Ocean and Atlantic Ocean, but larger than the Arctic Ocean)

Coastline: 66,526 km

Climate: northeast monsoon (December to April), southwest monsoon (June to October); tropical cyclones occur during May/ June and October/November in the north Indian Ocean and January/February in the south Indian Ocean

Terrain: surface dominated by counterclockwise gyre (broad, circular system of currents) in the south Indian Ocean; unique reversal of surface currents in the north Indian Ocean—low pressure over southwest Asia from hot, rising, summer air results in the southwest monsoon and southwest-to-northeast winds and currents, while high pressure over northern Asia from cold, falling, winter air results in the northeast monsoon and northeast-to-southwest winds and currents; ocean floor is dominated by the Mid-Indian Ocean Ridge and subdivided by the Southeast Indian Ocean Ridge, Southwest Indian Ocean Ridge, and Ninety East Ridge; maximum depth is 7,258 meters in the Java Trench

Natural resources: oil and gas fields, fish, shrimp, sand and gravel aggregates, placer deposits, polymetallic nodules

Environment: endangered marine species include the dugong, seals, turtles, and whales; oil pollution in the Arabian Sea, Persian Gulf, and Red Sea

Note: major choke points include Bab el Mandeb, Strait of Hormuz, Strait of Malacca, southern access to the Suez Canal,

and the Lombok Strait; ships subject to superstructure icing in extreme south near Antarctica from May to October

Economy

Overview: The Indian Ocean provides a major transportation highway for the movement of petroleum products from the Middle East to Europe and North and South American countries. Fish from the ocean are of growing economic importance to many of the bordering countries as a source of both food and exports. Fishing fleets from the USSR, Japan, Korea, and Taiwan also exploit the Indian Ocean for mostly shrimp and tuna. Large reserves of hydrocarbons are being tapped in the offshore areas of Saudi Arabia, Iran, India, and Western Australia. An estimated 40% of the world's offshore oil production comes from the Indian Ocean. Beach sands rich in heavy minerals and offshore placer deposits are actively exploited by bordering countries, particularly India, South Africa, Indonesia, Sri Lanka, and Thailand.

Industries: based on exploitation of natural resources, particularly marine life, minerals, oil and gas production, fishing, sand and gravel aggregates, placer deposits

Communications

Ports: Bombay (India), Calcutta (India), Madras (India), Colombo (Sri Lanka), Durban (South Africa), Fremantle (Australia), Jakarta (Indonesia), Melbourne (Australia), Richard's Bay (South Africa)

Telecommunications: no submarine cables

Indonesia

1200 km

Strait of Malacca

Medan

Sumatra

JAKARTA

Java

Borneo

Celebes

Timor

North Pacific Ocean

New Guinea

Indian Ocean

See regional map IX

Geography

Total area: 1,919,440 km²; land area: 1,826,440 km²
Comparative area: slightly less than three times the size of Texas
Land boundaries: 2,602 km total; Malaysia 1,782 km, Papua New Guinea 820 km
Coastline: 54,716 km
Maritime claims: (measured from claimed archipelagic baselines)
  Continental shelf: to depth of exploitation
  Extended economic zone: 200 nm *Territorial sea:* 12 nm
Disputes: East Timor question with Portugal
Climate: tropical; hot, humid; more moderate in highlands
Terrain: mostly coastal lowlands; larger islands have interior mountains
Natural resources: crude oil, tin, natural gas, nickel, timber, bauxite, copper, fertile soils, coal, gold, silver
Land use: 8% arable land; 3% permanent crops; 7% meadows and pastures; 67% forest and woodland; 15% other; includes 3% irrigated
Environment: archipelago of 13,500 islands (6,000 inhabited); occasional floods, severe droughts, and tsunamis; deforestation
Note: straddles Equator; strategic location astride or along major sea lanes from Indian Ocean to Pacific Ocean

People

Population: 190,136,221 (July 1990), growth rate 1.8% (1990)
Birth rate: 27 births/1,000 population (1990)
Death rate: 9 deaths/1,000 population (1990)
Net migration rate: 0 migrants/1,000 population (1990)
Infant mortality rate: 75 deaths/1,000 live births (1990)

Life expectancy at birth: 58 years male, 63 years female (1990)
Total fertility rate: 3.1 children born/woman (1990)
Nationality: noun—Indonesian(s); adjective—Indonesian
Ethnic divisions: majority of Malay stock comprising 45.0% Javanese, 14.0% Sundanese, 7.5% Madurese, 7.5% coastal Malays, 26.0% other
Religion: 88% Muslim, 6% Protestant, 3% Roman Catholic, 2% Hindu, 1% other
Language: Bahasa Indonesia (modified form of Malay; official); English and Dutch leading foreign languages; local dialects, the most widely spoken of which is Javanese
Literacy: 62%
Labor force: 67,000,000; 55% agriculture, 10% manufacturing, 4% construction, 3% transport and communications (1985 est.)
Organized labor: 3,000,000 members (claimed); about 5% of labor force

Government

Long-form name: Republic of Indonesia
Type: republic
Capital: Jakarta
Administrative divisions: 24 provinces (propinsi-propinsi, singular—propinsi), 2 special regions* (daerah-daerah istimewa, singular—daerah istimewa), and 1 special capital city district** (daerah khusus ibukota); Aceh*, Bali, Bengkulu, Irian Jaya, Jakarta Raya**, Jambi, Jawa Barat, Jawa Tengah, Jawa Timur, Kalimantan Barat, Kalimantan Selatan, Kalimantan Tengah, Kalimantan Timur, Lampung, Maluku, Nusa Tenggara Barat, Nusa Tenggara Timur, Riau, Sulawesi Selatan, Sulawesi Tengah, Sulawesi Tenggara, Sulawesi Utara, Sumatera Barat, Sumatera Selatan, Sumatera Utara, Timor Timur, Yogyakarta*
Independence: 17 August 1945 (from Netherlands; formerly Netherlands or Dutch East Indies)
Constitution: August 1945, abrogated by Federal Constitution of 1949 and Provisional Constitution of 1950, restored 5 July 1959
Legal system: based on Roman-Dutch law, substantially modified by indigenous concepts and by new criminal procedures code; has not accepted compulsory ICJ jurisdiction
National holiday: Independence Day, 17 August (1945)
Executive branch: president, vice president, Cabinet
Legislative branch: unicameral House of Representatives (Dewan Perwakilan Rakyat or DPR); note—the People's Consultative Assembly (Majelis Permusyawaratan Rakyat or MPR) includes the DPR plus

500 indirectly elected members who meet every five years to elect the president and vice president and, theoretically, to determine national policy
Judicial branch: Supreme Court (Mahkamah Agung)
Leaders: *Chief of State and Head of Government*—President Gen. (Ret.) SOEHARTO (since 27 March 1968); Vice President Lt. Gen. (Ret.) SUDHARMONO (since 11 March 1983)
Political parties and leaders: GOLKAR (quasi-official party based on functional groups), Lt. Gen. (Ret.) Wahono, general chairman; Indonesia Democracy Party (PDI—federation of former Nationalist and Christian Parties), Soeryadi, chairman; Development Unity Party (PPP, federation of former Islamic parties), Ismail Hasan Metareum, chairman
Suffrage: universal at age 17 and married persons regardless of age
Elections: *House of Representatives*—last held on 23 April 1987 (next to be held 23 April 1992); results—Golkar 73%, UDP 16%, PDI 11%; seats—(500 total—400 elected, 100 appointed) Golkar 299, UDP 61, PDI 40
Communists: Communist Party (PKI) was officially banned in March 1966; current strength about 1,000-3,000, with less than 10% engaged in organized activity; pre-October 1965 hardcore membership about 1.5 million
Member of: ADB, ANRPC, ASEAN, Association of Tin Producing Countries, CCC, CIPEC, ESCAP, FAO, G-77, GATT, IAEA, IBA, IBRD, ICAO, ICO, IDA, IDB—Islamic Development Bank, IFAD, IFC, IHO, ILO, IMF, IMO, INTELSAT, INTERPOL, IPU, IRC, ISO, ITC, ITU, NAM, OIC, OPEC, UN, UNESCO, UPU, WFTU, WHO, WIPO, WMO, WTO
Diplomatic representation: Ambassador Abdul Rachman RAMLY; Chancery at 2020 Massachusetts Avenue NW, Washington DC 20036; telephone (202) 775-5200; there are Indonesian Consulates General in Houston, New York, and Los Angeles, and Consulates in Chicago and San Francisco; *US*—Ambassador John C. MONJO; Embassy at Medan Merdeka Selatan 5, Jakarta (mailing address is APO San Francisco 96356); telephone [62] (21) 360-360; there are US Consulates in Medan and Surabaya
Flag: two equal horizontal bands of red (top) and white; similar to the flag of Monaco which is shorter; also similar to the flag of Poland which is white (top) and red

Indonesia (continued)

Economy

Overview: Indonesia is a mixed economy with many socialist institutions and central planning but with a recent emphasis on deregulation and private enterprise. Indonesia has extensive natural wealth but, with a large and rapidly increasing population, it remains a poor country. GNP growth in 1985-89 averaged about 4%, somewhat short of the 5% rate needed to absorb the 2.3 million workers annually entering the labor force. Agriculture, including forestry and fishing, is the most important sector, accounting for 21% of GDP and over 50% of the labor force. The staple crop is rice. Once the world's largest rice importer, Indonesia is now nearly self-sufficient. Plantation crops—rubber and palm oil—are being encouraged for both export and job generation. The diverse natural resources include crude oil, natural gas, timber, metals, and coal. Of these, the oil sector dominates the external economy, generating more than 20% of the government's revenues and 40% of export earnings in 1989. Japan is Indonesia's most important customer and supplier of aid.

GNP: $80 billion, per capita $430; real growth rate 5.7% (1989 est.)

Inflation rate (consumer prices): 5.5% (1989)

Unemployment rate: 3.1% (1989 est.)

Budget: revenues $20.9 billion; expenditures $20.9 billion, including capital expenditures of $7.5 billion (FY89)

Exports: $21.0 billion (f.o.b., 1989 est.); *commodities*—petroleum and liquefied natural gas 40%, timber 15%, textiles 7%, rubber 5%, coffee 3%; *partners*—Japan 42%, US 16%, Singapore 9%, EC 11% (1988)

Imports: $13.2 billion (f.o.b., 1989 est.); *commodities*—machinery 39%, chemical products 19%, manufactured goods 16%; *partners*—Japan 26%, EC 19%, US 13%, Singapore 7% (1988)

External debt: $55.0 billion, medium and long-term (1989 est.)

Industrial production: growth rate 4.8% (1988 est.)

Electricity: 11,600,000 kW capacity; 38,000 million kWh produced, 200 kWh per capita (1989)

Industries: petroleum, textiles, mining, cement, chemical fertilizer production, timber, food, rubber

Agriculture: subsistence food production; small-holder and plantation production for export; rice, cassava, peanuts, rubber, cocoa, coffee, copra, other tropical products

Illicit drugs: illicit producer of cannabis for the international drug trade, but not a major player; government actively eradicating plantings and prosecuting traffickers

Aid: US commitments, including Ex-Im (FY70-88), $4.2 billion; Western (non-US) countries, ODA and OOF bilateral commitments (1970-87), $19.8 billion; OPEC bilateral aid (1979-89), $213 million; Communist countries (1970-88), $175 million

Currency: Indonesian rupiah (plural—rupiahs); 1 Indonesian rupiah (Rp) = 100 sen (sen no longer used)

Exchange rates: Indonesian rupiahs (Rp) per US$1—1,804.9 (January 1990), 1,770.1 (1989), 1,685.7 (1988), 1,643.8 (1987), 1,282.6 (1986), 1,110.6 (1985)

Fiscal year: 1 April-31 March

Communications

Railroads: 6,964 km total; 6,389 km 1.067-meter gauge, 497 km 0.750-meter gauge, 78 km 0.600-meter gauge; 211 km double track; 101 km electrified; all government owned

Highways: 119,500 km total; 11,812 km state, 34,180 km provincial, and 73,508 km district roads

Inland waterways: 21,579 km total; Sumatra 5,471 km, Java and Madura 820 km, Kalimantan 10,460 km, Celebes 241 km, Irian Jaya 4,587 km

Pipelines: crude oil, 2,505 km; refined products, 456 km; natural gas, 1,703 km (1989)

Ports: Cilacap, Cirebon, Jakarta, Kupang, Palembang, Ujungpandang, Semarang, Surabaya

Merchant marine: 313 ships (1,000 GRT or over) totaling 1,480,912 GRT/ 2,245,233 DWT; includes 5 short-sea passenger, 13 passenger-cargo, 173 cargo, 6 container, 3 roll-on/roll-off cargo, 2 vehicle carrier, 77 petroleum, oils, and lubricants (POL) tanker, 1 chemical tanker, 2 liquefied gas, 6 specialized tanker, 1 livestock carrier, 24 bulk

Civil air: about 216 commercial transport aircraft

Airports: 468 total, 435 usable; 106 with permanent-surface runways; 1 with runways over 3,659 m; 12 with runways 2,440-3,659 m; 62 with runways 1,220-2,439 m

Telecommunications: interisland microwave system and HF police net; domestic service fair, international service good; radiobroadcast coverage good; 763,000 telephones (1986); stations—618 AM, 38 FM, 9 TV; satellite earth stations—1 Indian Ocean INTELSAT earth station and 1 Pacific Ocean INTELSAT earth station; and 1 domestic satellite communications system

Defense Forces

Branches: Army, Navy, Air Force, National Police

Military manpower: males 15-49, 49,283,496; 29,137,291 fit for military service; 2,098,169 reach military age (18) annually

Defense expenditures: 2.1% of GNP (1987)

Iran

See regional map VI

Geography

Total area: 1,648,000 km²; land area: 1,636,000 km²
Comparative area: slightly larger than Alaska
Land boundaries: 5,492 km total; Afghanistan 936 km, Iraq 1,458 km, Pakistan 909 km, Turkey 499 km, USSR 1,690 km
Coastline: 3,180 km
Maritime claims:
  Continental shelf: not specific
  Exclusive fishing zone: 50 nm in the Sea of Oman; median-line boundaries in the Persian Gulf
  Territorial sea: 12 nm
Disputes: Iran began formal UN peace negotiations with Iraq in August 1988 to end the war that began on 22 September 1980—troop withdrawal, freedom of navigation, sovereignty over the Shatt al Arab waterway and prisoner-of-war exchange are the major issues for negotiation; Kurdish question among Iran, Iraq, Syria, Turkey, and the USSR; occupies three islands in the Persian Gulf claimed by UAE (Jazīreh-ye Abū Mūsá or Abū Mūsá, Jazīreh-ye Tonb-e Bozorg or Greater Tunb, and Jazīreh-ye Tonb-e Kūchek or Lesser Tunb); periodic disputes with Afghanistan over Helmand water rights; Boluch question with Afghanistan and Pakistan
Climate: mostly arid or semiarid, subtropical along Caspian coast
Terrain: rugged, mountainous rim; high, central basin with deserts, mountains; small, discontinuous plains along both coasts
Natural resources: petroleum, natural gas, coal, chromium, copper, iron ore, lead, manganese, zinc, sulfur
Land use: 8% arable land; NEGL% permanent crops; 27% meadows and pastures; 11% forest and woodland; 54% other; includes 2% irrigated

Environment: deforestation; overgrazing; desertification

People

Population: 55,647,001 (July 1990), growth rate 3.1% (1990)
Birth rate: 45 births/1,000 population (1990)
Death rate: 10 deaths/1,000 population (1990)
Net migration rate: −5 migrants/1,000 population (1990)
Infant mortality rate: 91 deaths/1,000 live births (1990)
Life expectancy at birth: 62 years male, 63 years female (1990)
Total fertility rate: 6.3 children born/woman (1990)
Nationality: noun—Iranian(s); adjective—Iranian
Ethnic divisions: 51% Persian, 25% Azerbaijani, 9% Kurd, 8% Gilaki and Mazandarani, 2% Lur, 1% Baloch, 1% Arab, 3% other
Religion: 95% Shi'a Muslim, 4% Sunni Muslim, 2% Zoroastrian, Jewish, Christian, and Baha'i
Language: 58% Persian and Persian dialects, 26% Turkic and Turkic dialects, 9% Kurdish, 2% Luri, 1% Baloch, 1% Arabic, 1% Turkish, 2% other
Literacy: 48% (est.)
Labor force: 15,400,000; 33% agriculture, 21% manufacturing; shortage of skilled labor (1988 est.)
Organized labor: none

Government

Long-form name: Islamic Republic of Iran
Type: theocratic republic
Capital: Tehrān
Administrative divisions: 24 provinces (ostānha, singular—ostān); Āžarbāyjān-e Bākhtarī, Āžarbāyjān-e Khāvarī, Bākhtarān, Bushēhr, Chahār Maḥāll va Bakhtīārī, Esfahān, Fārs, Gīlān, Hamadān, Hormozgān, Īlām, Kermān, Khorāsān, Khūzestān, Kohkīlūyeh va Būyer Aḥmadī, Kordestān, Lorestān, Markazī, Māzandarān, Semnān, Sīstān va Balūchestān, Tehrān, Yazd, Zanjān
Independence: 1 April 1979, Islamic Republic of Iran proclaimed
Constitution: 2-3 December 1979; revised 1989 to expand powers of the presidency
Legal system: the new Constitution codifies Islamic principles of government
National holiday: Islamic Republic Day, 1 April (1979)
Executive branch: cleric (faqih), president, Council of Cabinet Ministers

Legislative branch: unicameral Islamic Consultative Assembly (Majlis-e-Shura-e-Islami)
Judicial branch: Supreme Court
Leaders: *Cleric and functional Chief of State*—Leader of the Islamic Revolution Ayatollah Ali Hoseini-KHAMENEI (since 3 June 1989);
Head of Government—President Ali Akbar RAFSANJANI (since 3 August 1989);
Political parties and leaders: there are at least seven licensed parties; the two most important are—Militant Clerics Association, Mehdi Mahdavi-Karubi and Mohammad Asqar Musavi-Khoinima; Fedaiyin Islam Organization, Sadeq Khalkhali
Suffrage: universal at age 15
Elections: *President*—last held NA July 1989 (next to be held April 1993); results—Ali Akbar Rafsanjani was elected with only token opposition;
Islamic Consultative Assembly—last held 8 April and 13 May 1988 (next to be held April 1992); results—percent of vote by party NA; seats—(270 seats total) number of seats by party NA
Communists: 1,000 to 2,000 est. hardcore; 15,000 to 20,000 est. sympathizers; crackdown in 1983 crippled the party; trials of captured leaders began in late 1983 and remain incomplete
Other political or pressure groups: groups that generally support the Islamic Republic include Hizballah, Hojjatiyeh Society, Mojahedin of the Islamic Revolution, Muslim Students Following the Line of the Imam, and Tehran Militant Clergy Association; Mojahedin Khalq Organization (MKO), People's Fedayeen, and Kurdish Democratic Party are armed political groups that have been almost completely repressed by the government
Member of: CCC, ESCAP, FAO, G-77, IAEA, IBRD, IDA, IDB, IFC, ILO, IMF, IMO, INTELSAT, IPU, OIC, OPEC, UN, UNESCO, UNICEF, UNIDO, WHO
Diplomatic representation: none; protecting power in the US is Algeria—Iranian Interests Section, 2209 Wisconsin Avenue NW, Washington DC 20007; telephone (202) 965-4990; *US*—protecting power in Iran is Switzerland
Flag: three equal horizontal bands of green (top), white, and red; the national emblem (a stylized representation of the word Allah) in red is centered in the white band; *Allah Akbar* (God is Great) in white Arabic script is repeated 11 times along the bottom edge of the green band and 11 times along the top edge of the red band

Economy

Overview: Since the 1979 revolution, the banks, petroleum industry, transportation, utilities, and mining have been nationalized, but the new five-year plan—the first since the revolution—passed in January 1990, calls for the transfer of many government-controlled enterprises to the private sector. War-related disruptions, massive corruption, mismanagement, demographic pressures, and ideological rigidities have kept economic growth at depressed levels. Oil accounts for 90% of export revenues. A combination of war damage and low oil prices brought a 2% drop in GNP in 1988. GNP probably rose slightly in 1989, considerably short of the 3.4% population growth rate in 1989. Heating oil and gasoline are rationed. Agriculture has suffered from the war, land reform, and shortages of equipment and materials. The five-year plan seeks to reinvigorate the economy by increasing the role of the private sector, boosting nonoil income, and securing foreign loans. The plan is overly ambitious but probably will generate some short-term relief.

GNP: $97.6 billion, per capita $1,800; real growth rate 0-1% (1989)

Inflation rate (consumer prices): 50-80% (1989)

Unemployment rate: 30% (1989)

Budget: revenues $NA; expenditures $55.1 billion, including capital expenditures of $11.5 billion (FY88 est.)

Exports: $12.3 billion (f.o.b., 1988); *commodities*—petroleum 90%, carpets, fruits, nuts, hides; *partners*—Japan, Turkey, Italy, Netherlands, Spain, France, FRG

Imports: $12.0 billion (c.i.f., 1988); *commodities*—machinery, military supplies, metal works, foodstuffs, pharmaceuticals, technical services, refined oil products; *partners*—FRG, Japan, Turkey, UK, Italy

External debt: $4-5 billion (1989)

Industrial production: growth rate NA%

Electricity: 14,579,000 kW capacity; 40,000 million kWh produced, 740 kWh per capita (1989)

Industries: petroleum, petrochemicals, textiles, cement and other building materials, food processing (particularly sugar refining and vegetable oil production), metal fabricating (steel and copper)

Agriculture: principal products—rice, other grains, sugar beets, fruits, nuts, cotton, dairy products, wool, caviar; not self-sufficient in food

Illicit drugs: illicit producer of opium poppy for the domestic and international drug trade

Aid: US commitments, including Ex-Im (FY70-80), $1.0 billion; Western (non-US) countries, ODA and OOF bilateral commitments (1970-87), $1.5 billion; Communist countries (1970-88), $976 million; note—aid fell sharply following the 1979 revolution

Currency: Iranian rial (plural—rials); 1 Iranian rial (IR) = 100 dinars; note—domestic figures are generally referred to in terms of the toman (plural—tomans), which equals 10 rials

Exchange rates: Iranian rials (IR) per US$1—70.019 (January 1990), 72.015 (1989), 68.683 (1988), 71.460 (1987), 78.760 (1986), 91.052 (1985)

Fiscal year: 21 March-20 March

Communications

Railroads: 4,601 km total; 4,509 km 1.432-meter gauge, 92 km 1.676-meter gauge; 730 km under construction from Bafq to Bandar Abbas

Highways: 140,072 km total; 46,866 km gravel and crushed stone; 49,440 km improved earth; 42,566 km bituminous and bituminous-treated surfaces; 1,200 km (est.) of rural road network

Inland waterways: 904 km; the Shatt al Arab is usually navigable by maritime traffic for about 130 km, but closed since September 1980 because of Iran-Iraq war

Pipelines: crude oil, 5,900 km; refined products, 3,900 km; natural gas, 3,300 km

Ports: Abadan (largely destroyed in fighting during 1980-88 war), Bandar Beheshtī, Bandar-e Abbas, Bandar-e Būshehr, Bandar-e Khomeyni, Bandar-e Shahīd Rāja'ī, Khorramshahr (largely destroyed in fighting during 1980-88 war)

Merchant marine: 133 ships (1,000 GRT or over) totaling 4,631,836 GRT/ 8,662,454 DWT; includes 36 cargo, 6 roll-on/roll-off cargo, 33 petroleum, oils, and lubricants (POL) tanker, 4 chemical tanker, 3 refrigerated cargo, 49 bulk, 2 combination bulk

Civil air: 42 major transport aircraft

Airports: 201 total, 175 usable; 82 with permanent-surface runways; 17 with runways over 3,659 m; 17 with runways 2,440-3,659 m; 68 with runways 1,220-2,439 m

Telecommunications: radio relay extends throughout country; system centered in Tehrān; 2,143,000 telephones; stations—62 AM, 30 FM, 250 TV; satellite earth stations—2 Atlantic Ocean INTELSAT and 1 Indian Ocean INTELSAT; HF and microwave to Turkey, Pakistan, Syria, Kuwait, and USSR

Defense Forces

Branches: Islamic Republic of Iran Ground Forces, Navy, Air Force, and Revolutionary Guard Corps (includes Basij militia and own ground, air, and naval forces), Gendarmerie

Military manpower: males 15-49, 12,302,967; 7,332,614 fit for military service; 569,647 reach military age (21) annually

Defense expenditures: 8% of GNP, or $7.8 billion (1989 est.)

Iraq

200 km

See regional map VI

Geography

Total area: 434,920 km²; land area: 433,970 km²
Comparative area: slightly more than twice the size of Idaho
Land boundaries: 3,454 km total; Iran 1,458 km, Iraq −Saudi Arabia Neutral Zone 191 km, Jordan 134 km, Kuwait 240 km, Saudi Arabia 495 km, Syria 605 km, Turkey 331 km
Coastline: 58 km
Maritime claims:
Continental shelf: not specific
Territorial sea: 12 nm
Disputes: Iraq began formal UN peace negotiations with Iran in August 1988 to end the war that began on 22 September 1980—sovereignty over the Shatt al Arab waterway, troop withdrawal, freedom of navigation, and prisoner of war exchange are the major issues for negotiation; Kurdish question among Iran, Iraq, Syria, Turkey, and the USSR; shares Neutral Zone with Saudi Arabia—in July 1975, Iraq and Saudi Arabia signed an agreement to divide the zone between them, but the agreement must be ratified before it becomes effective; disputes Kuwaiti ownership of Warbah and Būbiyān islands; periodic disputes with upstream riparian Syria over Euphrates water rights; potential dispute over water development plans by Turkey for the Tigris and Euphrates Rivers
Climate: desert; mild to cool winters with dry, hot, cloudless summers
Terrain: mostly broad plains; reedy marshes in southeast; mountains along borders with Iran and Turkey
Natural resources: crude oil, natural gas, phosphates, sulfur
Land use: 12% arable land; 1% permanent crops; 9% meadows and pastures; 3% forest and woodland; 75% other; includes 4% irrigated

Environment: development of Tigris-Euphrates river systems contingent upon agreements with upstream riparians (Syria, Turkey); air and water pollution; soil degradation (salinization) and erosion; desertification

People

Population: 18,781,770 (July 1990), growth rate 3.9% (1990)
Birth rate: 46 births/1,000 population (1990)
Death rate: 7 deaths/1,000 population (1990)
Net migration rate: 0 migrants/1,000 population (1990)
Infant mortality rate: 67 deaths/1,000 live births (1990)
Life expectancy at birth: 66 years male, 68 years female (1990)
Total fertility rate: 7.3 children born/woman (1990)
Nationality: noun—Iraqi(s); adjective—Iraqi
Ethnic divisions: 75-80% Arab, 15-20% Kurdish, 5% Turkoman, Assyrian or other
Religion: 97% Muslim (60-65% Shi'a, 32-37% Sunni), 3% Christian or other
Language: Arabic (official), Kurdish (official in Kurdish regions), Assyrian, Armenian
Literacy: 55-65% (1989 est.)
Labor force: 3,400,000 (1984); 39% services, 33% agriculture, 28% industry, severe labor shortage (1987); expatriate labor force about 1,000,000 (1989)
Organized labor: less than 10% of the labor force

Government

Long-form name: Republic of Iraq
Type: republic
Capital: Baghdād
Administrative divisions: 18 provinces (muḥāfaẓat, singular—muḥāfaẓah); Al Anbār, Al Baṣrah, Al Muthanná, Al Qādisīyah, An Najaf, Arbīl, As Sulaymānīyah, At Ta'mīm, Bābil, Baghdād, Dahūk, Dhī Qār, Diyālá, Karbalā', Maysān, Nīnawá, Ṣalāḥ ad Dīn, Wāsiṭ
Independence: 3 October 1932 (from League of Nations mandate under British administration)
Constitution: 22 September 1968, effective 16 July 1970 (interim Constitution); new constitution now in final stages of drafting
Legal system: based on Islamic law in special religious courts, civil law system elsewhere; has not accepted compulsory ICJ jurisdiction
National holiday: Anniversary of the Revolution, 17 July (1968)

Executive branch: president, vice president, chairman of the Revolutionary Command Council, vice chairman of the Revolutionary Command Council, prime minister, first deputy prime minister, Council of Ministers
Legislative branch: unicameral National Assembly (Majlis al 'Umma)
Judicial branch: Court of Cassation
Leaders: *Chief of State and Head of Government*—President Saddam HUSAYN (since 16 July 1979); Vice President Taha Muhyi al-Din MA'RUF (since 21 April 1974)
Political parties: National Progressive Front is a coalition of the Arab Ba'th Socialist Party, Kurdistan Democratic Party, and Kurdistan Revolutionary Party
Suffrage: universal adult at age 18
Elections: *National Assembly*—last held on 1 April 1989 (next to be held NA); results—Shi'a Arabs 30%, Kurds 15%, Sunni Arabs 53%, Christians 2% est.; seats—(250 total) number of seats by party NA
Communists: about 1,500 hardcore members
Other political or pressure groups: political parties and activity severely restricted; possibly some opposition to regime from disaffected members of the regime, Army officers, and religious and ethnic dissidents
Member of: ACC, Arab League, FAO, G-77, IAEA, IBRD, ICAO, IDA, IDB-Islamic Development Bank, IFAD, IFC, ILO, IMF, IMO, INTELSAT, INTERPOL, ITU, NAM, OAPEC, OIC, OPEC, UN, UNESCO, UPU, WFTU, WHO, WIPO, WMO, WSG, WTO
Diplomatic representation: Ambassador Dr. Mohamed Sadiq AL-MASHAT; Chancery at 1801 P Street NW, Washington DC 20036; telephone (202) 483-7500; *US*—Ambassador April C. GLASPIE; Embassy in Masbah Quarter (opposite the Foreign Ministry Club), Baghdad (mailing address is P. O. Box 2447 Alwiyah, Baghdad); telephone [964] (1) 719-6138 or 719-6139, 718-1840, 719-3791
Flag: three equal horizontal bands of red (top), white, and black with three green five-pointed stars in a horizontal line centered in the white band; similar to the flags of the YAR which has one star and Syria which has two stars (in a horizontal line centered in the white band)—all green and five-pointed; also similar to the flag of Egypt which has a symbolic eagle centered in the white band

Economy

Overview: The Ba'thist regime engages in extensive central planning and management of industrial production and foreign

149

Iraq (continued)

trade while leaving some small-scale industry and services and most agriculture to private enterprise. The economy is dominated by the oil sector, which provides about 95% of foreign exchange earnings. Since the early 1980s financial problems, caused by war expenditures and damage to oil export facilities by Iran, have led the government to implement austerity measures and to reschedule foreign debt payments. Oil exports have gradually increased with the construction of new pipelines. Agricultural development remains hampered by labor shortages, salinization, and dislocations caused by previous land reform and collectivization programs. The industrial sector, although accorded high priority by the government, is under financial constraints. New investment funds are generally allocated only to projects that result in import substitution or foreign exchange earnings.

GNP: $35 billion, per capita $1,940; real growth rate 5% (1989 est.)

Inflation rate (consumer prices): 30-40% (1989 est.)

Unemployment rate: less than 5% (1989 est.)

Budget: revenues $NA billion; expenditures $35 billion, including capital expenditures of NA (1989)

Exports: $12.5 billion (f.o.b., 1988); *commodities*—crude oil and refined products, machinery, chemicals, dates; *partners*—US, Brazil, USSR, Italy, Turkey, France, Japan, Yugoslavia (1988)

Imports: $10.2 billion (c.i.f., 1988); *commodities*—manufactures, food; *partners*—Turkey, US, FRG, UK, France, Japan, Romania, Yugoslavia, Brazil (1988)

External debt: $40 billion (1988 est.), excluding debt to Persian Gulf Arab states

Industrial production: NA%

Electricity: 9,902,000 kW capacity; 20,000 million kWh produced, 1,110 kWh per capita (1989)

Industries: petroleum, chemicals, textiles, construction materials, food processing

Agriculture: accounts for less than 10% of GNP but 33% of labor force; principal products—wheat, barley, rice, vegetables, dates, other fruit, cotton, wool; livestock—cattle, sheep; not self-sufficient in food output

Aid: US commitments, including Ex-Im (FY70-80), $3 million; Western (non-US) countries, ODA and OOF bilateral commitments (1970-87), $607 million; OPEC bilateral aid (1980-89), $37.2 billion; Communist countries (1970-88), $3.9 billion

Currency: Iraqi dinar (plural—dinars); 1 Iraqi dinar (ID) = 1,000 fils

Exchange rates: Iraqi dinars (ID) per US$1—0.3109 (fixed rate since 1982)

Fiscal year: calendar year

Communications

Railroads: 2,962 km total; 2,457 km 1.435-meter standard gauge, 505 km 1.000-meter gauge

Highways: 25,479 km total; 8,290 km paved, 5,534 km improved earth, 11,655 km unimproved earth

Inland waterways: 1,015 km; Shatt al Arab usually navigable by maritime traffic for about 130 km, but closed since September 1980 because of Iran-Iraq war; Tigris and Euphrates navigable by shallow-draft steamers (of little importance); Shatt al Baṣrah canal navigable in sections by shallow-draft vessels

Ports: Umm Qasr, Khawr az Zubayr

Merchant marine: 44 ships (1,000 GRT or over) totaling 947,721 GRT/1,703,988 DWT; includes 1 passenger, 1 passenger-cargo, 18 cargo, 1 refrigerated cargo, 3 roll-on/roll-off cargo, 19 petroleum, oils, and lubricants (POL) tanker, 1 chemical tanker

Pipelines: crude oil, 4,350 km; 725 km refined products; 1,360 km natural gas

Civil air: 64 major transport aircraft (including 30 IL-76s used by the Iraq Air Force)

Airports: 111 total, 101 usable; 72 with permanent-surface runways; 8 with runways over 3,659 m; 53 with runways 2,440-3,659 m; 14 with runways 1,220-2,439 m

Telecommunications: good network consists of coaxial cables, radio relay links, and radiocommunication stations; 632,000 telephones; stations—9 AM, 1 FM, 81 TV; satellite earth stations—1 Atlantic Ocean INTELSAT, 1 Indian Ocean INTELSAT, 1 GORIZONT Atlantic Ocean in the Intersputnik system; coaxial cable and radio relay to Kuwait, Jordan, Syria, and Turkey

Defense Forces

Branches: Army, Navy, Air Force, Border Guard Force, mobile police force, Republican Guard

Military manpower: males 15-49, 4,097,190; 2,284,417 fit for military service; 219,701 reach military age (18) annually

Defense expenditures: NA

Iraq-Saudi Arabia Neutral Zone

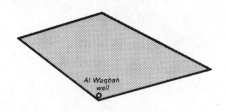

See regional map VI

Geography

Total area: 3,520 km²; land area: 3,520 km²

Comparative area: slightly larger than Rhode Island

Land boundaries: 389 km total; 191 km Iraq, 198 km Saudi Arabia

Coastline: none—landlocked

Maritime claims: none—landlocked

Climate: harsh, dry desert

Terrain: sandy desert

Natural resources: none

Land use: 0% arable land; 0% permanent crops; 0% meadows and pastures; 0% forest and woodland; 100% other (sandy desert)

Environment: harsh, inhospitable

Note: landlocked; located west of quadripoint with Iraq, Kuwait, and Saudi Arabia

People

Population: uninhabited

Government

Long-form name: none

Type: joint administration by Iraq and Saudi Arabia; in July 1975, Iraq and Saudi Arabia signed an agreement to divide the zone between them, but the agreement must be ratified, however, before it becomes effective

Economy

Overview: no economic activity

Communications

Highways: none; some secondary roads

Ireland

Defense Forces

Note: defense is the joint responsibility of Iraq and Saudi Arabia

See regional map V

Geography

Total area: 70,280 km^2; land area: 68,890 km^2
Comparative area: slightly larger than West Virginia
Land boundary: 360 km with UK
Coastline: 1,448 km
Maritime claims:
  Continental shelf: no precise definition
  Exclusive fishing zone: 200 nm
  Territorial sea: 12 nm
Disputes: maritime boundary with the UK; Northern Ireland question with the UK; Rockall continental shelf dispute involving Denmark, Iceland, and the UK (Ireland and the UK have signed a boundary agreement in the Rockall area)
Climate: temperate maritime; modified by North Atlantic Current; mild winters, cool summers; consistently humid; overcast about half the time
Terrain: mostly level to rolling interior plain surrounded by rugged hills and low mountains; sea cliffs on west coast
Natural resources: zinc, lead, natural gas, crude oil, barite, copper, gypsum, limestone, dolomite, peat, silver
Land use: 14% arable land; NEGL% permanent crops; 71% meadows and pastures; 5% forest and woodland; 10% other
Environment: deforestation

People

Population: 3,500,212 (July 1990), growth rate -0.4% (1990)
Birth rate: 15 births/1,000 population (1990)
Death rate: 9 deaths/1,000 population (1990)
Net migration rate: −10 migrants/1,000 population (1990)
Infant mortality rate: 6 deaths/1,000 live births (1990)
Life expectancy at birth: 72 years male, 78 years female (1990)

Total fertility rate: 2.1 children born/ woman (1990)
Nationality: noun—Irishman(men), Irish (collective pl.); adjective—Irish
Ethnic divisions: Celtic, with English minority
Religion: 94% Roman Catholic, 4% Anglican, 2% other
Language: Irish (Gaelic) and English; English is the language generally used, with Gaelic spoken in a few areas, mostly along the western seaboard
Literacy: 99%
Labor force: 1,310,000; 57.3% services, 19.1% manufacturing and construction, 14.8% agriculture, forestry, and fishing (1988)
Organized labor: 36% of labor force

Government

Long-form name: Republic of Ireland
Type: republic
Capital: Dublin
Administrative divisions: 26 counties; Carlow, Cavan, Clare, Cork, Donegal, Dublin, Galway, Kerry, Kildare, Kilkenny, Laois, Leitrim, Limerick, Longford, Louth, Mayo, Meath, Monaghan, Offaly, Roscommon, Sligo, Tipperary, Waterford, Westmeath, Wexford, Wicklow
Independence: 6 December 1921 (from UK)
Constitution: 29 December 1937; adopted 1937
Legal system: based on English common law, substantially modified by indigenous concepts; judicial review of legislative acts in Supreme Court; has not accepted compulsory ICJ jurisdiction
National holiday: St. Patrick's Day, 17 March
Executive branch: president, prime minister, deputy prime minister, Cabinet
Legislative branch: bicameral Parliament (Oireachtas) consists of an upper house or Senate (Seanad Eireann) and a lower house or House of Representatives (Dáil Eireann)
Judicial branch: Supreme Court
Leaders: *Chief of State*—President Dr. Patrick J. HILLERY (since 3 December 1976);
Head of Government—Prime Minister Charles J. HAUGHEY (since 12 July 1989, the fourth time elected as prime minister)
Political parties and leaders: Fianna Fail, Charles Haughey; Labor Party, Richard Spring; Fine Gael, Alan Dukes; Communist Party of Ireland, Michael O'Riordan; Workers' Party, Proinsias DeRossa; Sinn Fein, Gerry Adams; Progressive Democrats, Desmond O'Malley; note—Prime

Minister Haughey heads a coalition consisting of the Fianna Fail and the Progressive Democrats

Suffrage: universal at age 18

Elections: *President*—last held 21 October 1983 (next to be held October 1990); results—Dr. Patrick Hillery reelected; *Senate*—last held on 17 February 1987 (next to be held February 1992); results—percent of vote by party NA; seats—(60 total, 49 elected) Fianna Fail 30, Fine Gael 16, Labor 3, Independents 11; *House of Representatives*—last held on 12 July 1989 (next to be held NA June 1994); results—Fianna Fail 44.0%, Fine Gael 29.4%, Labor Party 9.3%, Progressive Democrats 5.4%, Workers' Party 4.9%, Sinn Fein 1.1%, independents 5.9%; seats—(166 total) Fianna Fail 77, Fine Gael 55, Labor Party 15, Workers' Party 7, Progressive Democrats 6, independents 6

Communists: under 500

Member of: CCC, Council of Europe, EC, EMS, ESA, FAO, GATT, IAEA, IBRD, ICAO, ICES, IDA, IEA, IFAD, IFC, ILO, IMF, IMO, INTELSAT, INTERPOL, IPU, ISO, ITC, ITU, IWC—International Wheat Council, OECD, UN, UNESCO, UPU, WHO, WIPO, WMO, WSG

Diplomatic representation: Ambassador Padraic N. MACKERNAN; Chancery at 2234 Massachusetts Avenue NW, Washington DC 20008; telephone (202) 462-3939; there are Irish Consulates General in Boston, Chicago, New York, and San Francisco; *US*—Ambassador Richard A. MOORE; Embassy at 42 Elgin Road, Ballsbridge, Dublin; telephone [353] (1) 688777

Flag: three equal vertical bands of green (hoist side), white, and orange; similar to the flag of the Ivory Coast which is shorter and has the colors reversed—orange (hoist side), white, and green; also similar to the flag of Italy which is shorter and has colors of green (hoist side), white, and red

Economy

Overview: The economy is small, open, and trade dependent. Agriculture, once the most important sector, is now dwarfed by industry, which accounts for 35% of GNP and about 80% of exports and employs 20% of the labor force. The government has successfully reduced the rate of inflation from double-digit figures in the late 1970s to about 4% in 1989. In 1987, after years of deficits, the balance of payments was brought into the black. Unemployment, however, is a serious problem. A 1989 unemployment rate of 17.7% placed Ireland along with Spain as the countries with the worst jobless records in Western Europe.

GDP: $31.4 billion, per capita $8,900; real growth rate 4.3% (1989 est.)

Inflation rate (consumer prices): 4.2% (1989)

Unemployment rate: 17.7% (1989)

Budget: revenues $10.9 billion; expenditures $11.2 billion, including capital expenditures of $1.5 billion (1989)

Exports: $20.3 billion (f.o.b., 1989); *commodities*—live animals, animal products, chemicals, data processing equipment, industrial machinery; *partners*—EC 74% (UK 35%, FRG 11%, France 9%), US 8%

Imports: $17.3 billion (c.i.f., 1989); *commodities*—food, animal feed, chemicals, petroleum and petroleum products, machinery, textiles, clothing; *partners*—EC 66% (UK 42%, FRG 9%, France 4%), US 16%

External debt: $16.1 billion (1988)

Industrial production: growth rate 9.5% (1989 est.)

Electricity: 4,957,000 kW capacity; 14,480 million kWh produced, 4,080 kWh per capita (1989)

Industries: food products, brewing, textiles, clothing, chemicals, pharmaceuticals, machinery, transportation equipment, glass and crystal

Agriculture: accounts for 11% of GNP and 14.8% of the labor force; principal crops—turnips, barley, potatoes, sugar beets, wheat; livestock—meat and dairy products; 85% self-sufficient in food; food shortages include bread grain, fruits, vegetables

Aid: NA

Currency: Irish pound (plural—pounds); 1 Irish pound (Ĭr) = 100 pence

Exchange rates: Irish pounds (Ĭr) per US$1—0.6399 (January 1990), 0.7047 (1989), 0.6553 (1988), 0.6720 (1987), 0.7454 (1986), 0.9384 (1985)

Fiscal year: calendar year

Communications

Railroads: Irish National Railways (CIE) operates 1,947 km 1.602-meter gauge, government owned; 485 km double track; 38 km electrified

Highways: 92,294 km total; 87,422 km surfaced, 4,872 km gravel or crushed stone

Inland waterways: limited for commercial traffic

Pipelines: natural gas, 225 km

Ports: Cork, Dublin, Shannon Estuary, Waterford

Merchant marine: 67 ships (1,000 GRT or over) totaling 113,569 GRT/139,681 DWT; includes 3 short-sea passenger, 29 cargo, 2 refrigerated cargo, 2 container, 23 petroleum, oils, and lubricants (POL) tanker, 1 specialized tanker, 2 chemical tanker, 5 bulk

Civil air: 23 major transport aircraft

Airports: 40 total, 37 usable; 18 with permanent-surface runways; none with runways over 3,659 m; 2 with runways 2,440-3,659 m; 5 with runways 1,220-2,439 m

Telecommunications: small, modern system using cable and radio relay circuits; 900,000 telephones; stations—45 AM, 16 (29 relays) FM, 18 (68 relays) TV; 5 coaxial submarine cables; 2 Atlantic Ocean INTELSAT earth stations

Defense Forces

Branches: Army, Naval Service, Army Air Corps

Military manpower: males 15-49, 870,161; 705,765 fit for military service; 33,259 reach military age (17) annually

Defense expenditures: 1.6% of GDP, or $500 million (1989 est.)

Israel (also see separate Gaza Strip and West Bank entries)

100 km

Haifa
Nazareth
Lake Tiberias
Mediterranean Sea
Tel Aviv-Yafo
Ashdod
Jerusalem
Dead Sea
Beersheba
Elat

Boundary representation is not necessarily authoritative.

See regional map VI

Note: The Arab territories occupied by Israel since the 1967 war are not included in the data below. As stated in the 1978 Camp David Accords and reaffirmed by President Reagan's 1 September 1982 peace initiative, the final status of the West Bank and Gaza Strip, their relationship with their neighbors, and a peace treaty between Israel and Jordan are to be negotiated among the concerned parties. The Camp David Accords further specify that these negotiations will resolve the location of the respective boundaries. Pending the completion of this process, it is US policy that the final status of the West Bank and Gaza Strip has yet to be determined (see West Bank and Gaza Strip entries). On 25 April 1982 Israel relinquished control of the Sinai to Egypt. Statistics for the Israeli-occupied Golan Heights are included in the Syria entry.

Geography

Total area: 20,770 km²; land area: 20,330 km²
Comparative area: slightly larger than New Jersey
Land boundaries: 1,006 km total; Egypt 255 km, Jordan 238 km, Lebanon 79 km, Syria 76 km, West Bank 307, Gaza Strip 51 km
Coastline: 273 km
Maritime claims:
Continental shelf: to depth of exploitation
Territorial sea: 6 nm
Disputes: separated from Lebanon, Syria, and the West Bank by the 1949 Armistice Line; differences with Jordan over the location of the 1949 Armistice Line which separates the two countries; West Bank and Gaza Strip are Israeli occupied with status to be determined; Golan Heights is Israeli occupied; Israeli troops in southern Lebanon since June 1982; water-sharing issues with Jordan

Climate: temperate; hot and dry in desert areas
Terrain: Negev desert in the south; low coastal plain; central mountains; Jordan Rift Valley
Natural resources: copper, phosphates, bromide, potash, clay, sand, sulfur, asphalt, manganese, small amounts of natural gas and crude oil
Land use: 17% arable land; 5% permanent crops; 40% meadows and pastures; 6% forest and woodland; 32% other; includes 11% irrigated
Environment: sandstorms may occur during spring and summer; limited arable land and natural water resources pose serious constraints; deforestation;
Note: there are 173 Jewish settlements in the West Bank, 35 in the Israeli-occupied Golan Heights, 18 in the Gaza Strip, and 14 Israeli-built Jewish neighborhoods in East Jerusalem

People

Population: 4,409,218 (July 1990), growth rate 1.5% (1989); includes 70,000 Jewish settlers in the West Bank, 10,500 in the Israeli-occupied Golan Heights, 2,500 in the Gaza Strip, and 110,000 in East Jerusalem (1989 est.)
Birth rate: 22 births/1,000 population (1990)
Death rate: 6 deaths/1,000 population (1990)
Net migration rate: 0 migrants/1,000 population (1990)
Infant mortality rate: 9 deaths/1,000 live births (July 1990)
Life expectancy at birth: 76 years male, 79 years female (July 1990)
Total fertility rate: 2.9 children born/woman (1990)
Nationality: noun—Israeli(s); adjective—Israeli
Ethnic divisions: 83% Jewish, 17% non-Jewish (mostly Arab)
Religion: 83% Judaism, 13.1% Islam (mostly Sunni Muslim), 2.3% Christian, 1.6% Druze
Language: Hebrew (official); Arabic used officially for Arab minority; English most commonly used foreign language
Literacy: 88% Jews, 70% Arabs
Labor force: 1,400,000 (1984 est.); 29.5% public services; 22.8% industry, mining, and manufacturing; 12.8% commerce; 9.5% finance and business; 6.8% transport, storage, and communications; 6.5% construction and public works; 5.5% agriculture, forestry, and fishing; 5.8% personal and other services; 1.0% electricity and water (1983)
Organized labor: 90% of labor force

Government

Long-form name: State of Israel
Type: republic
Capital: Israel proclaimed Jerusalem its capital in 1950, but the US, like nearly all other countries, maintains its Embassy in Tel Aviv
Administrative divisions: 6 districts (mehozot, singular—mehoz); Central, Haifa, Jerusalem, Northern, Southern, Tel Aviv
Independence: 14 May 1948 (from League of Nations mandate under British administration)
Constitution: no formal constitution; some of the functions of a constitution are filled by the Declaration of Establishment (1948), the basic laws of the Parliament (Knesset), and the Israeli citizenship law
Legal system: mixture of English common law, British Mandate regulations, and, in personal matters, Jewish, Christian, and Muslim legal systems; in December 1985 Israel informed the UN Secretariat that it would no longer accept compulsory ICJ jurisdiction
National holiday: Independence Day, 10 May 1989; Israel declared independence on 14 May 1948, but the Jewish calendar is lunar and the holiday may occur in April or May
Executive branch: president, prime minister, vice prime minister, Cabinet
Legislative branch: unicameral Knesset
Judicial branch: Supreme Court
Leaders: *Chief of State*—President Gen. Chaim HERZOG (since 5 May 1983); *Head of Government*—Prime Minister Yitzhak SHAMIR (since 20 October 1986); Vice Prime Minister Shimon PERES (Prime Minister from 13 September 1984 to 20 October 1986, when he rotated to Vice Prime Minister)
Political parties and leaders: Israel currently has a national unity government comprising five parties that hold 95 of the Knesset's 120 seats; *Members of the unity government*—Likud bloc, Prime Minister Yitzhak Shamir; Labor Party, Vice Prime Minister and Finance Minister Shimon Peres; Sephardic Torah Guardians (SHAS), Minister of Immigrant Absorption Yitzhak Peretz; National Religious Party, Minister of Religious Affairs Zevulun Hammer; Agudat Yisrael, Deputy Minister of Labor and Social Welfare Moshe Zeev Feldman;
Opposition parties—Tehiya Party, Yuval Ne'eman; Tzomet Party, Rafael Eytan; Moledet Party, Rehavam Ze'evi; Degel HaTorah, Avraham Ravitz; Citizens' Rights Movement, Shulamit Aloni; United Workers' Party (MAPAM), Yair Tzaban; Center Movement-Shinui,

Amnon Rubenstein; New Communist Party of Israel (RAKAH), Meir Wilner; Progressive List for Peace, Muhammad Mi'ari; Arab Democratic Party, 'Abd Al Wahab Darawshah
Suffrage: universal at age 18
Elections: *President*—last held 23 February 1988 (next to be held February 1994); results—Gen. Chaim Herzog reelected by Knesset;
Parliament—last held 1 November 1988 (next to be held by November 1992); seats—(120 total) Likud bloc 40, Labor Party 39, SHAS 6, National Religious Party 5, Agudat Yisrael 5, Citizens' Rights Movement 5, RAKAH 4, Tehiya Party 3, MAPAM 3, Tzomet Party 2, Moledet Party 2, Degel HaTorah 2, Center Movement-Shinui 2, Progressive List for Peace 1, Arab Democratic Party 1
Communists: Hadash (predominantly Arab but with Jews in its leadership) has some 1,500 members
Other political or pressure groups: Gush Emunim, Jewish nationalists advocating Jewish settlement on the West Bank and Gaza Strip; Peace Now, critical of government's West Bank/Gaza Strip and Lebanon policies
Member of: CCC, FAO, GATT, IAEA, IBRD, ICAC, ICAO, IDA, IDB—Inter-American Development Bank, IFAD, IFC, ILO, IMF, IMO, IOOC, INTELSAT, INTERPOL, IPU, ITU, IWC—International Wheat Council, OAS (observer), UN, UNESCO, UPU, WHO, WIPO, WMO, WSG, WTO
Diplomatic representation: Ambassador Moshe ARAD; Chancery at 3514 International Drive NW, Washington DC 20008; telephone (202) 364-5500; there are Israeli Consulates General in Atlanta, Boston, Chicago, Houston, Los Angeles, Miami, New York, Philadelphia, and San Francisco; *US*—Ambassador William A. BROWN; Embassy at 71 Hayarkon Street, Tel Aviv (mailing address is APO New York 09672); telephone [972] (3) 654338; there is a US Consulate General in Jerusalem
Flag: white with a blue hexagram (six-pointed linear star) known as the Magen David (Shield of David) centered between two equal horizontal blue bands near the top and bottom edges of the flag

Economy

Overview: Israel has a market economy with substantial government participation. It depends on imports for crude oil, food, grains, raw materials, and military equipment. Despite limited natural resources, Israel has developed its agriculture and industry sectors on an intensive scale over the past 20 years. Industry accounts for about 23% of the labor force, agriculture for 6%, and services for most of the balance. Diamonds, high-technology machinery, and agricultural products (fruits and vegetables) are the biggest export earners. The balance of payments has traditionally been negative, but is offset by large transfer payments and foreign loans. Nearly two-thirds of Israel's $16 billion external debt is owed to the US, which is its major source for economic and military aid. To earn needed foreign exchange, Israel must continue to exploit high-technology niches in the international market, such as medical scanning equipment. In 1987 the economy showed a 5.2% growth in real GNP, the best gain in nearly a decade; in 1988-89 the gain was only 1% annually, largely because of the economic impact of the Palestinian uprising (*intifadah*). Inflation dropped from an annual rate of over 400% in 1984 to about 16% in 1987-88 without any major increase in unemployment.
GNP: $38 billion, per capita $8,700; real growth rate 1% (1989)
Inflation rate (consumer prices): 20% (1989)
Unemployment rate: 9% (December 1989)
Budget: revenues $24.2 billion; expenditures $26.3 billion, including capital expenditures of $7 billion (FY89 est.)
Exports: $10.4 billion (f.o.b., 1989 est.); *commodities*—polished diamonds, citrus and other fruits, textiles and clothing, processed foods, fertilizer and chemical products, military hardware, electronics; *partners*—US, UK, FRG, France, Belgium, Luxembourg, Italy
Imports: $12.4 billion (c.i.f., 1989 est.); *commodities*—military equipment, rough diamonds, oil, chemicals, machinery, iron and steel, cereals, textiles, vehicles, ships, aircraft; *partners*—US, FRG, UK, Switzerland, Italy, Belgium, Luxembourg
External debt: $16.4 billion (March 1989)
Industrial production: growth rate −1.5% (1989)
Electricity: 4,392,000 kW capacity; 17,500 million kWh produced, 4,000 kWh per capita (1989)
Industries: food processing, diamond cutting and polishing, textiles, clothing, chemicals, metal products, military equipment, transport equipment, electrical equipment, miscellaneous machinery, potash mining, high-technology electronics, tourism
Agriculture: accounts for 5% of GNP; largely self-sufficient in food production, except for bread grains; principal products—citrus and other fruits, vegetables, cotton; livestock products—beef, dairy, and poultry
Aid: US commitments, including Ex-Im (FY70-88), $15.8 billion; Western (non-US) countries, ODA and OOF bilateral commitments (1970-87), $2.2 billion
Currency: new Israeli shekel (plural—shekels); 1 new Israeli shekel (NIS) = 100 new agorot
Exchange rates: new Israeli shekels (NIS) per US$1—1.9450 (January 1990), 1.9164 (1989), 1.5989 (1988), 1.5946 (1987), 1.4878 (1986), 1.1788 (1985)
Fiscal year: 1 April-31 March

Communications

Railroads: 594 km 1.435-meter gauge, single track; diesel operated
Highways: 4,500 km; majority is bituminous surfaced
Pipelines: crude oil, 708 km; refined products, 290 km; natural gas, 89 km
Ports: Ashdod, Haifa, Elat
Merchant marine: 31 ships (1,000 GRT or over) totaling 483,424 GRT/560,085 DWT; includes 9 cargo, 20 container, 2 roll-on/roll-off cargo
Civil air: 27 major transport aircraft
Airports: 55 total, 52 usable; 26 with permanent-surface runways; none with runways over 3,659 m; 6 with runways 2,440-3,659 m; 11 with runways 1,220-2,439 m
Telecommunications: most highly developed in the Middle East though not the largest; good system of coaxial cable and radio relay; 1,800,000 telephones; stations—11 AM, 24 FM, 54 TV; 2 submarine cables; satellite earth stations—2 Atlantic Ocean INTELSAT and 1 Indian Ocean INTELSAT

Defense Forces

Branches: Israel Defense Forces; historically there have been no separate Israeli military services; ground, air, and naval components are branches of Israel Defense Forces
Military manpower: eligible 15-49, 2,159,462; of the 1,089,346 males 15-49, 898,272 are fit for military service; of the 1,070,116 females 15-49, 878,954 are fit for military service; 43,644 males and 41,516 females reach military age (18) annually; both sexes are liable for military service
Defense expenditures: 8.5% of GNP, or $3.2 billion (1989 est.); note—does not include an estimated $1.8 billion in US military aid

Italy

300 km

See regional map V

Geography

Total area: 301,230 km²; land area: 294,020 km²; includes Sardinia and Sicily
Comparative area: slightly larger than Arizona
Land boundaries: 1,902.2 km total; Austria 430 km, France 488 km, San Marino 39 km, Switzerland 740 km, Vatican City 3.2 km, Yugoslavia 202 km
Coastline: 4,996 km
Maritime claims:
Continental shelf: 200 m or to depth of exploitation
Territorial sea: 12 nm
Disputes: South Tyrol question with Austria
Climate: predominantly Mediterranean; Alpine in far north; hot, dry in south
Terrain: mostly rugged and mountainous; some plains, coastal lowlands
Natural resources: mercury, potash, marble, sulfur, dwindling natural gas and crude oil reserves, fish, coal
Land use: 32% arable land; 10% permanent crops; 17% meadows and pastures; 22% forest and woodland; 19% other; includes 10% irrigated
Environment: regional risks include landslides, mudflows, snowslides, earthquakes, volcanic eruptions, flooding, pollution; land sinkage in Venice
Note: strategic location dominating central Mediterranean as well as southern sea and air approaches to Western Europe

People

Population: 57,664,405 (July 1990), growth rate 0.2% (1990)
Birth rate: 10 births/1,000 population (1990)
Death rate: 9 deaths/1,000 population (1990)
Net migration rate: 1 migrant/1,000 population (1990)

Infant mortality rate: 6 deaths/1,000 live births (1990)
Life expectancy at birth: 74 years male, 81 years female (1990)
Total fertility rate: 1.4 children born/woman (1990)
Nationality: noun—Italian(s); adjective—Italian
Ethnic divisions: primarily Italian but population includes small clusters of German-,French-, and Slovene-Italians in the north and Albanian-Italians in the south; Sicilians; Sardinians
Religion: almost 100% nominally Roman Catholic
Language: Italian; parts of Trentino-Alto Adige region are predominantly German speaking; significant French-speaking minority in Valle d'Aosta region; Slovene-speaking minority in the Trieste-Gorizia area
Literacy: 93%
Labor force: 23,670,000; 56.7% services, 37.9% industry, 5.4% agriculture (1987)
Organized labor: 40-45% of labor force (est.)

Government

Long-form name: Italian Republic
Type: republic
Capital: Rome
Administrative divisions: 20 regions (regioni, singular—regione); Abruzzi, Basilicata, Calabria, Campania, Emilia-Romagna, Friuli-Venezia Giulia, Lazio, Liguria, Lombardia, Marche, Molise, Piemonte, Puglia, Sardegna, Sicilia, Toscana, Trentino-Alto Adige, Umbria, Valle d'Aosta, Veneto
Independence: 17 March 1861, Kingdom of Italy proclaimed
Constitution: 1 January 1948
Legal system: based on civil law system, with ecclesiastical law influence; judicial review under certain conditions in Constitutional Court; has not accepted compulsory ICJ jurisdiction
National holiday: Anniversary of the Republic, 2 June (1946)
Executive branch: president, prime minister,
Legislative branch: bicameral Parliament (Parlamento) consists of an upper chamber or Senate (Senato) and a lower chamber or Chamber of Deputies (Camera dei Deputati)
Judicial branch: Constitutional Court (Corte Costituzionale)
Leaders: *Chief of State*—President Francesco COSSIGA (since 3 July 1985);
Head of Government—Prime Minister Giulio ANDREOTTI (since 22 July 1989, heads the government for the sixth time); Deputy Prime Minister Claudio MARTELLI (since 23 July 1989)

Political parties and leaders: Christian Democratic Party (DC), Arnaldo Forlani (general secretary), Ciriaco De Mita (president); Communist Party (PCI), Achille Occhetto (secretary general); Socialist Party (PSI), Bettino Craxi (party secretary); Social Democratic Party (PSDI), Antonio Cariglia (party secretary); Liberal Party (PLI), Renato Altissimo (secretary general); Italian Social Movement (MSI), Giuseppe (Pino) Rauti (national secretary); Republican Party (PRI), Giorgio La Malfa (political secretary); Italy's 49th postwar government was formed on 23 July 1989, with Prime Minister Andreotti, a Christian Democrat, presiding over a five-party coalition consisting of the Christian Democrats, Socialists, Social Democrats, Republicans, and Liberals
Suffrage: universal at age 18 (except in senatorial elections, where minimum age is 25)
Elections: *Senate*—last held 14-15 June 1987 (next to be held by June 1992); results—DC 33.9%, PCI 28.3%, PSI 10.7%, others 27.1%; seats—(320 total, 315 elected) DC 125, PCI 100, PSI 36, others 54;
Chamber of Deputies—last held 14-15 June 1987 (next to be held by June 1992); results—DC 34.3%, PCI 26.6%, PSI 14.3%, MSI 5.9%, PRI 3.7%, PSDI 3.0%, Radicals 2.6%, Greens 2.5%, PLI 2.1%, Proletarian Democrats 1.7%, others 3.3%; seats—(630 total) DC 234, PCI 177, PSI 94, MSI 35, PRI 21, PSDI 17, Radicals 13, Greens 13, PLI 11, Proletarian Democrats 8, others 7
Communists: 1,673,751 members (1983)
Other political or pressure groups: Vatican City; three major trade union confederations (CGIL—Communist dominated, CISL—Christian Democratic, and UIL—Social Democratic, Socialist, and Republican); Italian manufacturers association (Confindustria); organized farm groups (Confcoltivatori, Confagricoltura)
Member of: ADB, ASSIMER, CCC, Council of Europe, DAC, EC, ECOWAS, EIB, EMS, ESA, FAO, GATT, IAEA, IBRD, ICAC, ICAO, ICO, IDA, IDB—Inter-American Development Bank, IFAD, IEA, IFC, IHO, ILO, ILZSG, IMF, IMO, INTELSAT, INTERPOL, IOOC, IPU, IRC, ITC, ITU, NATO, OAS (observer), OECD, UN, UNESCO, UPU, WEU, WHO, WIPO, WMO, WSG
Diplomatic representation: Ambassador Rinaldo PETRIGNANI; Chancery at 1601 Fuller Street NW, Washington DC 20009; telephone (202) 328-5500; there are Italian Consulates General in Boston, Chicago, Houston, New Orleans, Los Angeles, Philadelphia, San Francisco, and Consulates in Detroit and Newark (New Jersey); *US*—Ambassador

Italy (continued)

Peter F. SECCHIA; Embassy at Via Veneto 119/A, 00187-Rome (mailing address is APO New York 09794); telephone [39] (6) 46741; there are US Consulates General in Florence, Genoa, Milan, Naples, and Palermo (Sicily)

Flag: three equal vertical bands of green (hoist side), white, and red; similar to the flag of Ireland which is longer and is green (hoist side), white, and orange; also similar to the flag of the Ivory Coast which has the colors reversed—orange (hoist side), white, and green

Economy

Overview: Since World War II the economy has changed from one based on agriculture into a ranking industrial economy, with approximately the same total and per capita output as France and the UK. The country is still divided into a developed industrial north, dominated by large private companies and state enterprises and an undeveloped agricultural south. Services account for 58% of GDP, industry 37%, and agriculture 5%. Most raw materials needed by industry and over 75% of energy requirements must be imported. The economic recovery that began in mid-1983 has continued through 1989, with the economy growing at an annual average rate of 3%. For the 1990s, Italy faces the problems of refurbishing a tottering communications system, curbing the increasing pollution in major industrial centers, and adjusting to the new competitive forces accompanying the ongoing economic integration of the European Community.

GDP: $803.3 billion, per capita $14,000; real growth rate 3.3% (1989 est.)

Inflation rate (consumer prices): 6.6% (1989 est.)

Unemployment rate: 11.9% (1989)

Budget: revenues $355 billion; expenditures $448 billion, including capital expenditures of $NA (1989)

Exports: $141.6 billion (f.o.b., 1989); *commodities*—textiles, wearing apparel, metals, transportation equipment, chemicals; *partners*—EC 57%, US 9%, OPEC 4%

Imports: $143.1 billion (f.o.b., 1989); *commodities*—petroleum, industrial machinery, chemicals, metals, food, agricultural products; *partners*—EC 57%, OPEC 6%, US 6%

External debt: NA

Industrial production: growth rate 2.9% (1989)

Electricity: 56,022,000 kW capacity; 201,400 million kWh produced, 3,500 kWh per capita (1989)

Industries: machinery and transportation equipment, iron and steel, chemicals, food processing, textiles, motor vehicles

Agriculture: accounts for about 5% of GNP and 5% of the work force; self-sufficient in foods other than meat and dairy products; principal crops—fruits, vegetables, grapes, potatoes, sugar beets, soybeans, grain, olives; fish catch of 554,000 metric tons in 1987

Aid: donor—ODA and OOF commitments (1970-87), $18.7 billion

Currency: Italian lira (plural—lire); 1 Italian lira (Lit) = 100 centesimi

Exchange rates: Italian lire (Lit) per US$1—1,262.5 (January 1990), 1,372.1 (1989), 1,301.6 (1988), 1,296.1 (1987), 1,490.8 (1986), 1,909.4 (1985)

Fiscal year: calendar year

Communications

Railroads: 20,011 km total; 16,066 km 1.435-meter government-owned standard gauge (8,999 km electrified); 3,945 km privately owned—2,100 km 1.435-meter standard gauge (1,155 km electrified) and 1,845 km 0.950-meter narrow gauge (380 km electrified)

Highways: 294,410 km total; autostrada 5,900 km, state highways 45,170 km, provincial highways 101,680 km, communal highways 141,660 km; 260,500 km concrete, bituminous, or stone block, 26,900 km gravel and crushed stone, 7,010 km earth

Inland waterways: 2,400 km for various types of commercial traffic, although of limited overall value

Pipelines: crude oil, 1,703 km; refined products, 2,148 km; natural gas, 19,400 km

Ports: Cagliari (Sardinia), Genoa, La Spezia, Livorno, Naples, Palermo (Sicily), Taranto, Trieste, Venice

Merchant marine: 547 ships (1,000 GRT or over) totaling 6,871,505 GRT/10,805,368 DWT; includes 6 passenger, 41 short-sea passenger, 100 cargo, 5 refrigerated cargo, 22 container, 72 roll-on/roll-off cargo, 4 vehicle carrier, 1 multifunction large-load carrier, 2 livestock carrier, 147 petroleum, oils, and lubricants (POL) tanker, 37 chemical tanker, 29 liquefied gas, 8 specialized tanker, 16 combination ore/oil, 55 bulk, 2 combination bulk

Civil air: 132 major transport aircraft

Airports: 143 total, 138 usable; 88 with permanent-surface runways; 2 with runways over 3,659 m; 35 with runways 2,440-3,659 m; 42 with runways 1,220-2,439 m

Telecommunications: well engineered, constructed, and operated; 28,000,000 telephones; stations—144 AM, 54 (over 1,800 repeaters) FM, 135 (over 1,300 repeaters) TV; 22 submarine cables; communication satellite earth stations operating in INTELSAT 3 Atlantic Ocean and 2 Indian Ocean, INMARSAT, and EUTELSAT systems

Defense Forces

Branches: Army, Navy, Air Force

Military manpower: males 15-49, 14,721,704; 12,855,022 fit for military service; 430,782 reach military age (18) annually

Defense expenditures: 2.4% of GDP, or $19 billion (1989 est.)

Ivory Coast
(also known as Côte d'Ivoire)

See regional map VII

Geography

Total area: 322,460 km²; land area: 318,000 km²

Comparative area: slightly larger than New Mexico

Land boundaries: 3,110 km total; Burkina 584 km, Ghana 668 km, Guinea 610 km, Liberia 716 km, Mali 532 km

Coastline: 515 km

Maritime claims:
Continental shelf: 200 m
Extended economic zone: 200 nm
Territorial sea: 12 nm

Climate: tropical along coast, semiarid in far north; three seasons—warm and dry (November to March), hot and dry (March to May), hot and wet (June to October)

Terrain: mostly flat to undulating plains; mountains in northwest

Natural resources: crude oil, diamonds, manganese, iron ore, cobalt, bauxite, copper

Land use: 9% arable land; 4% permanent crops; 9% meadows and pastures; 26% forest and woodland; 52% other; includes NEGL% irrigated

Environment: coast has heavy surf and no natural harbors; severe deforestation

People

Population: 12,478,024 (July 1990), growth rate 4.0% (1990)

Birth rate: 48 births/1,000 population (1990)

Death rate: 13 deaths/1,000 population (1990)

Net migration rate: 4 migrants/1,000 population (1990)

Infant mortality rate: 100 deaths/1,000 live births (1990)

Life expectancy at birth: 52 years male, 56 years female (1990)

Total fertility rate: 6.9 children born/woman (1990)

Nationality: noun—Ivorian(s); adjective—Ivorian

Ethnic divisions: over 60 ethnic groups; most important are the Baoule 23%, Bete 18%, Senoufou 15%, Malinke 11%, and Agni; about 2 million foreign Africans, mostly Burkinabe; about 130,000 to 330,000 non-Africans (30,000 French and 100,000 to 300,000 Lebanese)

Religion: 63% indigenous, 25% Muslim, 12% Christian

Language: French (official), over 60 native dialects; Dioula most widely spoken

Literacy: 42.7%

Labor force: 5,718,000; over 85% of population engaged in agriculture, forestry, livestock raising; about 11% of labor force are wage earners, nearly half in agriculture and the remainder in government, industry, commerce, and professions; 54% of population of working age (1985)

Organized labor: 20% of wage labor force

Government

Long-form name: Republic of the Ivory Coast; note—the local official name is République de Côte d'Ivoire

Type: republic; one-party presidential regime established 1960

Capital: Abidjan (capital city changed to Yamoussoukro in March 1983 but not recognized by US)

Administrative divisions: 49 departments (départements, singular—(département); Abengourou, Abidjan, Aboisso, Adzopé, Agboville, Bangolo, Béoumi, Biankouma, Bondoukou, Bongouanou, Bouaflé, Bouaké, Bouna, Boundiali, Dabakala, Daloa, Danané, Daoukro, Dimbokro, Divo, Duékoué, Ferkessédougou, Gagnoa, Grand-Lahou, Guiglo, Issia, Katiola, Korhogo, Lakota, Man, Mankono, Mbahiakro, Odienné, Oumé, Sakassou, San-Pédro, Sassandra, Séguéla, Sinfra, Soubré, Tabou, Tanda, Tengréla, Tiassalé, Touba, Toumodi, Vavoua, Yamoussoukro, Zuénoula

Independence: 7 August 1960 (from France)

Constitution: 3 November 1960

Legal system: based on French civil law system and customary law; judicial review in the Constitutional Chamber of the Supreme Court; has not accepted compulsory ICJ jurisdiction

National holiday: National Day, 7 December

Executive branch: president, Council of Ministers (cabinet)

Legislative branch: unicameral National Assembly (Assemblée Nationale)

Judicial branch: Supreme Court (Cour Suprême)

Leaders: *Chief of State and Head of Government*—President Dr. Félix HOUPHOUËT-BOIGNY (since 27 November 1960)

Political parties and leaders: only party—Democratic Party of the Ivory Coast (PDCI), Dr. Félix Houphouët-Boigny

Suffrage: universal at age 21

Elections: *President*—last held 27 October 1985 (next to be held October 1990); results—President Félix Houphouët-Boigny was reelected without opposition to his fifth consecutive five-year term; *National Assembly*—last held 10 November 1985 (next to be held 10 November 1990); results—PDCI is the only party; seats—(175 total) PDCI 175

Communists: no Communist party; possibly some sympathizers

Member of: ACP, AfDB, CCC, CEAO, EAMA, ECA, ECOWAS, EIB (associate), Entente, FAO, G-77, GATT, IAEA, IBRD, ICAO, ICO, IDA, IFAD, IFC, ILO, IMF, IMO, INTELSAT, INTERPOL, IPU, ITU, Niger River Commission, NAM, OAU, OCAM, UN, UNESCO, UPU, WHO, WIPO, WMO, WTO

Diplomatic representation: Ambassador Charles GOMIS; Chancery at 2424 Massachusetts Avenue NW, Washington DC 20008; telephone (202) 797-0300; *US*—Ambassador Kenneth BROWN; Embassy at 5 Rue Jesse Owens, Abidjan (mailing address is B. P. 1712, Abidjan 01); telephone [225] 32-09-79

Flag: three equal vertical bands of orange (hoist side), white, and green; similar to the flag of Ireland which is longer and has the colors reversed—green (hoist side), white, and orange; also similar to the flag of Italy which is green (hoist side), white, and red; design was based on the flag of France

Economy

Overview: The Ivory Coast is among the world's largest producers and exporters of coffee, cocoa beans, and palm-kernel oil. Consequently, the economy is highly sensitive to fluctuations in international prices for coffee and cocoa and to weather conditions. Despite attempts by the government to diversify, the economy is still largely dependent on agriculture and related industries. The agricultural sector accounts for over one-third of GDP and about 80% of export earnings and employs about 85% of the labor force. A collapse of world cocoa and coffee prices in 1986 threw the economy into a recession, from which the country had not recovered by 1989.

GDP: $10.0 billion, per capita $900; real growth rate −6.4% (1988)

Ivory Coast (continued)

Inflation rate (consumer prices): 7.5% (1988)
Unemployment rate: 14% (1985)
Budget: revenues $1.6 billion (1986); expenditures $2.3 billion, including capital expenditures of $504 million (1988 est.)
Exports: $2.2 billion (f.o.b., 1988); *commodities*—cocoa 30%, coffee 20%, tropical woods 11%, cotton, bananas, pineapples, palm oil, cotton; *partners*—France, FRG, Netherlands, US, Belgium, Spain (1985)
Imports: $1.3 billion (f.o.b., 1988); *commodities*—manufactured goods and semifinished products 50%, consumer goods 40%, raw materials and fuels 10%; *partners*—France, other EC, Nigeria, US, Japan (1985)
External debt: $14.7 billion (1989 est.)
Industrial production: growth rate 0% (1987)
Electricity: 1,081,000 kW capacity; 2,440 million kWh produced, 210 kWh per capita (1989)
Industries: foodstuffs, wood processing, oil refinery, automobile assembly, textiles, fertilizer, beverage
Agriculture: most important sector, contributing one-third to GDP and 80% to exports; cash crops include coffee, cocoa beans, timber, bananas, palm kernels, rubber; food crops—corn, rice, manioc, sweet potatoes; not selfsufficient in bread grain and dairy products
Illicit drugs: illicit producer of cannabis on a small scale for the international drug trade
Aid: US commitments, including Ex-Im (FY70-87), $344 million; Western (non-US) countries, ODA and OOF bilateral commitments (1970-87), $4.6 billion
Currency: Communauté Financière Africaine franc (plural—francs); 1 CFA franc (CFAF) = 100 centimes
Exchange rates: Communauté Financière Africaine francs (CFAF) per US$1— 287.99 (January 1990), 319.01 (1989), 297.85 (1988), 300.54 (1987), 346.30 (1986), 449.26 (1985)
Fiscal year: calendar year

Communications

Railroads: 660 km (Burkina border to Abidjan, 1.00-meter gauge, single track, except 25 km Abidjan-Anyama section is double track)
Highways: 46,600 km total; 3,600 km bituminous and bituminous-treated surface; 32,000 km gravel, crushed stone, laterite, and improved earth; 11,000 km unimproved
Inland waterways: 980 km navigable rivers, canals, and numerous coastal lagoons
Ports: Abidjan, San-Pedro
Merchant marine: 7 ships (1,000 GRT or over) totaling 71,945 GRT/ 90,684 DWT; includes 5 cargo, 1 petroleum, oils, and lubricants (POL) tanker, 1 chemical tanker
Civil air: 12 major transport aircraft, including multinationally owned Air Afrique fleet
Airports: 49 total, 42 usable; 7 with permanent-surface runways; none with runways over 3,659 m; 3 with runways 2,440-3,659 m; 16 with runways 1,220-2,439 m
Telecommunications: system above African average; consists of open-wire lines and radio relay links; 87,700 telephones; stations—3 AM, 17 FM, 11 TV; 2 Atlantic Ocean INTELSAT earth stations; 2 coaxial submarine cables

Defense Forces

Branches: Army, Navy, Air Force, paramilitary Gendarmerie
Military manpower: males 15-49, 2,874,925; 1,487,909 fit for military service; 141,193 males reach military age (18) annually
Defense expenditures: 1.9% of GDP (1987)

Jamaica

See regional map III

Geography

Total area: 10,990 km²; land area: 10,830 km²
Comparative area: slightly smaller than Connecticut
Land boundaries: none
Coastline: 1,022 km
Maritime claim:
Territorial sea: 12 nm
Climate: tropical; hot, humid; temperate interior
Terrain: mostly mountains with narrow, discontinuous coastal plain
Natural resources: bauxite, gypsum, limestone
Land use: 19% arable land; 6% permanent crops; 18% meadows and pastures; 28% forest and woodland; 29% other; includes 3% irrigated
Environment: subject to hurricanes (especially July to November); deforestation; water pollution
Note: strategic location between Cayman Trench and Jamaica Channel, the main sea lanes for Panama Canal

People

Population: 2,441,396 (July 1990), growth rate 0.6% (1990)
Birth rate: 21 births/1,000 population (1990)
Death rate: 5 deaths/1,000 population (1990)
Net migration rate: −10 migrants/1,000 population (1990)
Infant mortality rate: 16 deaths/1,000 live births (1990)
Life expectancy at birth: 75 years male, 79 years female (1990)
Total fertility rate: 2.3 children born/ woman (1990)
Nationality: noun—Jamaican(s); adjective—Jamaican
Ethnic divisions: 76.3% African, 15.1% Afro-European, 3.4% East Indian and

158

Afro-East Indian, 3.2% white, 1.2% Chinese and Afro-Chinese, 0.8% other
Religion: predominantly Protestant (including Anglican and Baptist), some Roman Catholic, some spiritualist cults
Language: English, Creole
Literacy: 74%
Labor force: 728,700; 32% agriculture, 28% industry and commerce, 27% services, 13% government; shortage of technical and managerial personnel (1984)
Organized labor: 25% of labor force (1989)

Government

Long-form name: none
Type: parliamentary democracy
Capital: Kingston
Administrative divisions: 14 parishes; Clarendon, Hanover, Kingston, Manchester, Portland, Saint Andrew, Saint Ann, Saint Catherine, Saint Elizabeth, Saint James, Saint Mary, Saint Thomas, Trelawny, Westmoreland
Independence: 6 August 1962 (from UK)
Constitution: 6 August 1962
Legal system: based on English common law; has not accepted compulsory ICJ jurisdiction
National holiday: Independence Day (first Monday in August), 6 August 1990
Executive branch: British monarch, governor general, prime minister, Cabinet
Legislative branch: bicameral Parliament consists of an upper house or Senate and a lower house or House of Representatives
Judicial branch: Supreme Court
Leaders: *Chief of State*—Queen ELIZABETH II (since 6 February 1952), represented by Governor General Sir Florizel A. GLASSPOLE (since 2 March 1973); *Head of Government*—Prime Minister Michael MANLEY (since 9 February 1989)
Political parties and leaders: People's National Party (PNP), Michael Manley; Jamaica Labor Party (JLP), Edward Seaga; Workers' Party of Jamaica (WPJ), Trevor Munroe
Suffrage: universal at age 18
Elections: *House of Representatives*—last held 9 February 1989 (next to be held by February 1994); results—PNP 57%, JLP 43%; seats—(60 total) PNP 45, JLP 15
Communists: Workers' Party of Jamaica (Marxist-Leninist)
Other political or pressure groups: Rastafarians (black religious/racial cultists, pan-Africanists)
Member of: ACP, CARICOM, CCC, Commonwealth, FAO, G-77, GATT, IADB, IAEA, IBA, IBRD, ICAO, ICO, IDB—Inter-American Development Bank, IFAD, IFC, ILO, IMF, IMO, INTELSAT, INTERPOL, ISO, ITU,

NAM, OAS, PAHO, SELA, UN, UNESCO, UPU, WFTU, WHO, WIPO, WMO, WTO
Diplomatic representation: Ambassador Keith JOHNSON; Chancery at Suite 355, 1850 K Street NW, Washington DC 20006; telephone (202) 452-0660; there are Jamaican Consulates General in Miami and New York; *US*—Ambassador Glen HOLDEN; Embassy at 3rd Floor, Jamaica Mutual Life Center, 2 Oxford Road, Kingston; telephone [809] 929-4850
Flag: diagonal yellow cross divides the flag into four triangles—green (top and bottom) and black (hoist side and fly side)

Economy

Overview: The economy is based on sugar, bauxite, and tourism. In 1985 it suffered a setback with the closure of some facilities in the bauxite and alumina industry, a major source of hard currency earnings. Since 1986 an economic recovery has been under way. In 1987 conditions began to improve for the bauxite and alumina industry because of increases in world metal prices. The recovery has also been supported by growth in the manufacturing and tourism sectors. In September 1988, Hurricane Gilbert inflicted severe damage on crops and the electric power system, a sharp but temporary setback to the economy. By October 1989 the economic recovery from the hurricane was largely complete and real growth was up about 3% for 1989.
GDP: $3.8 billion, per capita $1,529; real growth rate 3.0% (1989 est.)
Inflation rate (consumer prices): 15% (1989)
Unemployment rate: 18.7% (1988)
Budget: revenues $1.1 billion; expenditures $1.5 billion, including capital expenditures of $NA (FY88 est.)
Exports: $948 million (f.o.b., 1989 est.); *commodities*—bauxite, alumina, sugar, bananas; *partners*—US 40%, UK, Canada, Trinidad and Tobago, Norway
Imports: $1.6 billion (c.i.f., 1989 est.); *commodities*—petroleum, machinery, food, consumer goods, construction goods; *partners*—US 46%, UK, Venezuela, Canada, Japan, Trinidad and Tobago
External debt: $4.4 billion (1989 est.)
Industrial production: growth rate 3% (1989 est.)
Electricity: 1,437,000 kW capacity; 2,390 million kWh produced, 960 kWh per capita (1989)
Industries: tourism, bauxite mining, textiles, food processing, light manufactures
Agriculture: accounts for about 9% of GDP, one-third of work force, and 17% of exports; commercial crops—sugarcane, bananas, coffee, citrus, potatoes, and vege-

tables; livestock and livestock products include poultry, goats, milk; not self-sufficient in grain, meat, and dairy products
Illicit drugs: illicit cultivation of cannabis has decreased, with production shifting from large to small plots and nurseries to evade aerial detection and eradication
Aid: US commitments, including Ex-Im (FY70-88), $1.1 billion; Western (non-US) countries, ODA and OOF bilateral commitments (1970-87), $1.2 billion; OPEC bilateral aid (1979-89), $27 million; Communist countries (1974-88), $349 million
Currency: Jamaican dollar (plural—dollars); 1 Jamaican dollar (J$) = 100 cents
Exchange rates: Jamaican dollars (J$) per US$1—6.5013 (January 1990), 5.7446 (1989), 5.4886 (1988), 5.4867 (1987), 5.4778 (1986), 5.5586 (1985)
Fiscal year: 1 April-31 March

Communications

Railroads: 370 km, all 1.435-meter standard gauge, single track
Highways: 18,200 km total; 12,600 km paved, 3,200 km gravel, 2,400 km improved earth
Pipelines: refined products, 10 km
Ports: Kingston, Montego Bay
Merchant marine: 5 ships (1,000 GRT or over) totaling 13,048 GRT/21,412 DWT; includes 1 cargo, 1 container, 1 roll-on/roll-off cargo, 1 petroleum, oils, and lubricants (POL) tanker, 1 bulk
Civil air: 6 major transport aircraft
Airports: 41 total, 25 usable; 14 with permanent-surface runways; none with runways over 3,659 m; 2 with runways 2,440-3,659 m; 2 with runways 1,220-2,439 m
Telecommunications: fully automatic domestic telephone network; 127,000 telephones; stations—10 AM, 17 FM, 8 TV; 2 Atlantic Ocean INTELSAT earth stations; 3 coaxial submarine cables

Defense Forces

Branches: Jamaica Defense Force (includes Coast Guard and Air Wing)
Military manpower: males 15-49, 620,400; 440,967 fit for military service; no conscription; 27,014 reach minimum volunteer age (18) annually
Defense expenditures: 1.1% of GDP (1987)

Jan Mayen
(territory of Norway)

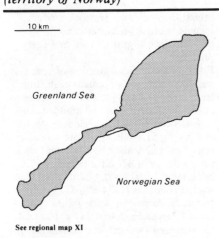

See regional map XI

Geography

Total area: 373 km²; land area: 373 km²
Comparative area: slightly more than twice the size of Washington, DC
Land boundaries: none
Coastline: 124.1 km
Maritime claims:
Contiguous zone: 10 nm
Continental shelf: 200 meters or to depth of exploitation
Exclusive fishing zone: 200 nm *Territorial sea:* 4 nm
Disputes: Denmark has challenged Norway's maritime claims beween Greenland and Jan Mayen
Climate: arctic maritime with frequent storms and persistent fog
Terrain: volcanic island, partly covered by glaciers; Beerenberg is the highest peak, with an elevation of 2,277 meters
Natural resources: none
Land use: 0% arable land; 0% permanent crops; 0% meadows and pastures; 0% forest and woodland; 100% other
Environment: barren volcanic island with some moss and grass; volcanic activity resumed in 1970
Note: located 590 km north-northwest of Iceland between the Greenland Sea and the Norwegian Sea north of the Arctic Circle

People

Population: no permanent inhabitants

Government

Long-form name: none
Type: territory of Norway
Note: administered by a governor (sysselmann) resident in Longyearbyen (Svalbard)

Economy

Overview: Jan Mayen is a volcanic island with no exploitable natural resources. Economic activity is limited to providing services for employees of Norway's radio and meteorological stations located on the island.
Electricity: 15,000 kW capacity; 40 million kWh produced, NA kWh per capita (1989)

Communications

Airports: 1 with runway 1,220 to 2,439 m
Ports: none; offshore anchorage only
Telecommunications: radio and meteorological station

Defense Forces

Note: defense is the responsibility of Norway

Japan

See regional map VIII

Geography

Total area: 377,835 km²; land area: 374,744 km²; includes Bonin Islands (Ogasawara-guntō), Daitō-shotō, Minamijima, Okinotori-shima, Ryukyu Islands (Nansei-shotō), and Volcano Islands (Kazan-rettō)
Comparative area: slightly smaller than California
Land boundaries: none
Coastline: 29,751 km
Maritime claims:
Exclusive fishing zone: 200 nm
Territorial sea: 12 nm (3 nm in international straits—La Perouse or Soya, Tsugaru, Osumi, and Eastern and Western channels of the Korea or Tsushima Strait)
Disputes: Habomai Islands, Etorofu, Kunashiri, and Shikotan Islands occupied by Soviet Union since 1945, claimed by Japan; Kuril Islands administered by Soviet Union; Liancourt Rocks disputed with South Korea; Senkaku-shotō (Senkaku Islands) claimed by China and Taiwan
Climate: varies from tropical in south to cool temperate in north
Terrain: mostly rugged and mountainous
Natural resources: negligible mineral resources, fish
Land use: 13% arable land; 1% permanent crops; 1% meadows and pastures; 67% forest and woodland; 18% other; includes 9% irrigated
Environment: many dormant and some active volcanoes; about 1,500 seismic occurrences (mostly tremors) every year; subject to tsunamis
Note: strategic location in northeast Asia

People

Population: 123,642,461 (July 1990), growth rate 0.4% (1990)
Birth rate: 11 births/1,000 population (1990)

Death rate: 7 deaths/1,000 population (1990)

Net migration rate: 0 migrants/1,000 population (1990)

Infant mortality rate: 5 deaths/1,000 live births (1990)

Life expectancy at birth: 76 years male, 82 years female (1990)

Total fertility rate: 1.6 children born/woman (1990)

Nationality: noun—Japanese (sing., pl.); adjective—Japanese

Ethnic divisions: 99.4% Japanese, 0.6% other (mostly Korean)

Religion: most Japanese observe both Shinto and Buddhist rites; about 16% belong to other faiths, including 0.8% Christian

Language: Japanese

Literacy: 99%

Labor force: 63,330,000; 54% trade and services; 33% manufacturing, mining, and construction; 7% agriculture, forestry, and fishing; 3% government (1988)

Organized labor: about 29% of employed workers; 76.4% public service, 57.9% transportation and telecommunications, 48.7% mining, 33.7% manufacturing, 18.2% services, 9.3% wholesale, retail, and restaurant

Government

Long-form name: none

Type: constitutional monarchy

Capital: Tokyo

Administrative divisions: 47 prefectures (fuken, singular and plural); Aichi, Akita, Aomori, Chiba, Ehime, Fukui, Fukuoka, Fukushima, Gifu, Gumma, Hiroshima, Hokkaidō, Hyōgo, Ibaraki, Ishikawa, Iwate, Kagawa, Kagoshima, Kanagawa, Kōchi, Kumamoto, Kyōto, Mie, Miyagi, Miyazaki, Nagano, Nagasaki, Nara, Niigata, Ōita, Okayama, Okinawa, Ōsaka, Saga, Saitama, Shiga, Shimane, Shizuoka, Tochigi, Tokushima, Tōkyō, Tottori, Toyama, Wakayama, Yamagata, Yamaguchi, Yamanashi

Independence: 660 BC, traditional founding by Emperor Jimmu; 3 May 1947, constitutional monarchy established

Constitution: 3 May 1947

Legal system: civil law system with English-American influence; judicial review of legislative acts in the Supreme Court; accepts compulsory ICJ jurisdiction, with reservations

National holiday: Birthday of the Emperor, 23 December (1933)

Executive branch: emperor, prime minister, Cabinet

Legislative branch: bicameral Diet (Kokkai) consists of an upper house or House of Councillors (Sangi-in) and a lower house or House of Representatives (Shūgi-in)

Judicial branch: Supreme Court

Leaders: *Chief of State*—Emperor AKIHITO (since 7 January 1989);
Head of Government—Prime Minister Toshiki KAIFU (since 9 August 1989)

Political parties and leaders: Liberal Democratic Party (LDP), Toshiki Kaifu, president; Japan Socialist Party (JSP), T. Doi, chairman; Democratic Socialist Party (DSP), Eiichi Nagasue, chairman; Japan Communist Party (JCP), K. Miyamoto, Presidium chairman; Komeito (Clean Government Party, CGP), Koshiro Ishida, chairman

Suffrage: universal at age 20

Elections: *House of Councillors*—last held on 23 July 1989 (next to be held 23 July 1992); results—percent of vote by party NA; seats—(252 total, 100 elected) LDP 109, JSP 67, CGP 21, JCP 14, others 33; *House of Representatives*—last held on 18 February 1990 (next to be held by February 1993); results—percent of vote by party NA; seats—(512 total) LDP 275, JSP 136, CGP 45, JCP 16, JDSP 14, other parties 5, independents 21; note—nine independents are expected to join the LDP, five the JSP

Communists: about 470,000 registered Communist party members

Member of: ADB, ASPAC, CCC, Colombo Plan, DAC, ESCAP, FAO, GATT, IAEA, IBRD, ICAC, ICAO, ICO, IDA, IDB—Inter-American Development Bank, IEA, IFAD, IFC, IHO, ILO, ILZSG, IMF, IMO, INTELSAT, INTERPOL, IPU, IRC, ISO, ITC, ITU, IWC—International Whaling Commission, IWC—International Wheat Council, OECD, UN, UNESCO, UPU, WFTU, WHO, WIPO, WMO, WSG

Diplomatic representation: Ambassador Nobuo MATSUNAGA; Chancery at 2520 Massachusetts Avenue NW, Washington DC 20008; telephone (202) 939-6700; there are Japanese Consulates General in Agana (Guam), Anchorage, Atlanta, Boston, Chicago, Honolulu, Houston, Kansas City (Missouri), Los Angeles, New Orleans, New York, San Francisco, Seattle, and Portland (Oregon), and a Consulate in Saipan (Northern Mariana Islands); *US*—Ambassador Michael H. ARMACOST; Embassy at 10-1, Akasaka 1-chome, Minato-ku (107), Tokyo (mailing address is APO San Francisco 96503); telephone [81] (3) 224-5000; there are US Consulates General in Naha, Osaka-Kobe, and Sapporo and a Consulate in Fukuoka

Flag: white with a large red disk (representing the sun without rays) in the center

Economy

Overview: Although Japan has few natural resources, since 1971 it has become the world's third-largest industrial economy, ranking behind only the US and the USSR. Government-industry cooperation, a strong work ethic, and a comparatively small defense allocation have helped Japan advance rapidly, notably in high-technology fields. Industry, the most important sector of the economy, is heavily dependent on imported raw materials and fuels. Self-suffcient in rice, Japan must import 50% of its requirements for other grain and fodder crops. Japan maintains one of the world's largest fishing fleets and accounts for nearly 15% of the total global catch. Overall economic growth has been spectacular: a 10% average in the 1960s, a 5% average in the 1970s and 1980s. In 1989 strong investment and consumption spending helped maintain growth at nearly 5%. Inflation remains low at 2.1% despite high oil prices and a somewhat weaker yen. Japan continues to run a huge trade surplus, $60 billion in 1989, which supports extensive investment in foreign properties.

GNP: $1,914.1 billion, per capita $15,600; real growth rate 4.8% (1989 est.)

Inflation rate (consumer prices): 2.1% (1989)

Unemployment rate: 2.3% (1989)

Budget: revenues $392 billion; expenditures $464 billion, including capital expenditures of $NA (FY89)

Exports: $270 billion (f.o.b., 1989); *commodities*—manufactures 97% (including machinery 38%, motor vehicles 17%, consumer electronics 10%); *partners*—US 34%, Southeast Asia 22%, Western Europe 21%, Communist countries 5%, Middle East 5%

Imports: $210 billion (c.i.f., 1989); *commodities*—manufactures 42%, fossil fuels 30%, foodstuffs 15%, nonfuel raw materials 13%; *partners*—Southeast Asia 23%, US 23%, Middle East 15%, Western Europe 16%, Communist countries 7%

External debt: $NA

Industrial production: growth rate 9.0% (1989)

Electricity: 191,000,000 kW capacity; 700,000 million kWh produced, 5,680 kWh per capita (1989)

Industries: metallurgy, engineering, electrical and electronic, textiles, chemicals, automobiles, fishing

Agriculture: accounts for 3% of GNP; highly subsidized and protected sector, with crop yields among highest in world; principal crops—rice, sugar beets, vegetables, fruit; animal products include pork, poultry, dairy and eggs; about 50% self-sufficient in food production; shortages of

Japan (continued)

wheat, corn, soybeans; world's largest fish catch of 11.8 million metric tons in 1987
Aid: donor—ODA and OOF commitments (1970-87), $57.5 billion
Currency: yen (plural—yen); 1 yen (¥) = 100 sen
Exchange rates: yen (¥) per US$1—145.09 (January 1990), 137.96 (1989), 128.15 (1988), 144.64 (1987), 168.52 (1986), 238.54 (1985)
Fiscal year: 1 April-31 March

Communications

Railroads: 27,327 km total; 2,012 km 1.435-meter standard gauge and 25,315 km predominantly 1.067-meter narrow gauge; 5,724 km doubletrack and multitrack sections, 9,038 km 1.067-meter narrow-gauge electrified, 2,012 km 1.435-meter standard-gauge electrified (1987)
Highways: 1,098,900 km total; 718,700 km paved, 380,200 km gravel, crushed stone, or unpaved; 3,900 km national expressways, 46,544 km national highways, 43,907 km principal local roads, 86,930 km prefectural roads, and 917,619 other (1987)
Inland waterways: about 1,770 km; seagoing craft ply all coastal inland seas
Pipelines: crude oil, 84 km; refined products, 322 km; natural gas, 1,800 km
Ports: Chiba, Muroran, Kitakyushu, Kobe, Tomakomai, Nagoya, Osaka, Tokyo, Yokkaichi, Yokohama, Kawasaki, Niigata, Fushiki-Toyama, Shimizu, Himeji, Wakayama-Shimozu, Shimonoseki, Tokuyama-Shimomatsu
Merchant marine: 1,088 ships (1,000 GRT or over) totaling 23,597,688 GRT/ 36,655,266 DWT; includes 7 passenger, 57 short-sea passenger, 4 passenger cargo, 108 cargo, 44 container, 27 roll-on/roll-off cargo, 135 refrigerated cargo, 117 vehicle carrier, 237 petroleum, oils, and lubricants (POL) tanker, 21 chemical tanker, 42 liquefied gas, 12 combination ore/oil, 3 specialized tanker, 272 bulk, 1 combination bulk, 1 multifunction large-load carrier
Civil air: 341 major transport aircraft
Airports: 165 total, 156 usable; 128 with permanent-surface runways; 2 with runways over 3,659 m; 27 with runways 2,440-3,659 m; 55 with runways 1,220-2,439 m
Telecommunications: excellent domestic and international service; 64,000,000 telephones; stations—318 AM, 58 FM, 12,350 TV (196 major—1 kw or greater); satellite earth stations—4 Pacific Ocean INTELSAT and 1 Indian Ocean INTELSAT; submarine cables to US (via Guam), Philippines, China, and USSR

Defense Forces

Branches: Japan Ground Self-Defense Force (army), Japan Maritime Self-Defense Force (navy), Japan Air Self-Defense Force (air force), Maritime Safety Agency (coast guard)
Military manpower: males 15-49, 32,181,866; 27,695,890 fit for military service; 1,004,052 reach military age (18) annually
Defense expenditures: 1% of GNP (1989 est.)

Jarvis Island
(territory of the US)

See regional map X

Geography

Total area: 4.5 km²; land area: 4.5 km²
Comparative area: about 7.5 times the size of The Mall in Washington, DC
Land boundaries: none
Coastline: 8 km
Maritime claims:
   Contiguous zone: 12 nm
   Continental shelf: 200 m
   Extended economic zone: 200 nm
   Territorial sea: 12 nm
Climate: tropical; scant rainfall, constant wind, burning sun
Terrain: sandy, coral island surrounded by a narrow fringing reef
Natural resources: guano (deposits worked until late 1800s)
Land use: 0% arable land; 0% permanent crops; 0% meadows and pastures; 0% forest and woodland; 100% other
Environment: sparse bunch grass, prostrate vines, and low-growing shrubs; lacks fresh water; primarily a nesting, roosting, and foraging habitat for seabirds, shorebirds, and marine wildlife; feral cats
Note: 2,090 km south of Honolulu in the South Pacific Ocean, just south of the Equator, about halfway between Hawaii and the Cook Islands

People

Population: uninhabited
Note: Millersville settlement on western side of island occasionally used as a weather station from 1935 until World War II, when it was abandoned; reoccupied in 1957 during the International Geophysical Year by scientists who left in 1958; public entry is by special-use permit only and generally restricted to scientists and educators

Government

Long-form name: none (territory of the US)
Type: unincorporated territory of the US administered by the Fish and Wildlife Service of the US Department of the Interior as part of the National Wildlife Refuge System

Economy

Overview: no economic activity

Communications

Ports: none; offshore anchorage only—one boat landing area in the middle of the west coast and another near the southwest corner of the island
Note: there is a day beacon near the middle of the west coast

Defense Forces

Note: defense is the responsibility of the US; visited annually by the US Coast Guard

---

Jersey
(British crown dependency)

English Channel

St. Aubin · Gorey · SAINT HELIER

English Channel

See regional map V

Geography

Total area: 117 km²; land area: 117 km²
Comparative area: about 0.7 times the size of Washington, DC
Land boundaries: none
Coastline: 70 km
Maritime claims:
  Continental shelf: 200 meters or to depth of exploitation
  Exclusive fishing zone: 200 nm
  Territorial sea: 3 nm
Climate: temperate; mild winters and cool summers
Terrain: gently rolling plain with low, rugged hills along north coast
Natural resources: agricultural land
Land use: NA% arable land; NA% permanent crops; NA% meadows and pastures; NA% forest and woodland; NA% other; about 58% of land under cultivation
Environment: about 30% of population concentrated in Saint Helier
Note: largest and southernmost of Channel Islands; 27 km from France

People

Population: 83,609 (July 1990), growth rate 0.9% (1990)
Birth rate: 12 births/1,000 population (1990)
Death rate: 10 deaths/1,000 population (1990)
Net migration rate: 7 migrants/1,000 population (1990)
Infant mortality rate: 6 deaths/1,000 live births (1990)
Life expectancy at birth: 72 years male, 78 years female (1990)
Total fertility rate: 1.3 children born/woman (1990)
Nationality: noun—Channel Islander(s); adjective—Channel Islander
Ethnic divisions: UK and Norman-French descent

Religion: Anglican, Roman Catholic, Baptist, Congregational New Church, Methodist, Presbyterian
Language: English and French (official), with the Norman-French dialect spoken in country districts
Literacy: NA%, but probably high
Labor force: NA
Organized labor: none

Government

Long-form name: Bailiwick of Jersey
Type: British crown dependency
Capital: Saint Helier
Administrative divisions: none (British crown dependency)
Independence: none (British crown dependency)
Constitution: unwritten; partly statutes, partly common law and practice
Legal system: English law and local statute
National holiday: Liberation Day, 9 May (1945)
Executive branch: British monarch, lieutenant governor, bailiff
Legislative branch: unicameral Assembly of the States
Judicial branch: Royal Court
Leaders: *Chief of State*—Queen ELIZABETH II (since 6 February 1952);
Head of Government—Lieutenant Governor Adm. Sir William PILLAR (since NA 1985); Bailiff Peter CRILL (since NA)
Political parties and leaders: none; all independents
Suffrage: universal adult at age NA
Elections: *Assembly of the States*—last held NA (next to be held NA); results—percent of vote NA; seats—(56 total, 52 elected) 52 independents
Communists: probably none
Diplomatic representation: none (British crown dependency)
Flag: white with the diagonal red cross of St. Patrick (patron saint of Ireland) extending to the corners of the flag

Economy

Overview: The economy is based largely on financial services, agriculture, and tourism. Potatoes, cauliflower, tomatoes, and especially flowers are important export crops, shipped mostly to the UK. The Jersey breed of dairy cattle is known worldwide and represents an important export earner. Milk products go to the UK and other EC countries. In 1986 the finance sector overtook tourism as the main contributor to GDP, accounting for 40% of the island's output. In recent years the

Jersey (continued)

electronics industry has developed alongside the traditional manufacturing of knitwear. All raw material and energy requirements are imported, as well as a large share of Jersey's food needs.
GDP: $NA, per capita $NA; real growth rate 8% (1987 est.)
Inflation rate (consumer prices): 8% (1988 est.)
Unemployment rate: NA%
Budget: revenues $308.0 million; expenditures $284.4 million, including capital expenditures of NA (1985)
Exports: $NA; *commodities*—light industrial and electrical goods, foodstuffs, textiles; *partners*—UK
Imports: $NA; *commodities*—machinery and transport equipment, manufactured goods, foodstuffs, mineral fuels, chemicals; *partners*—UK
External debt: $NA
Industrial production: growth rate NA%
Electricity: 50,000 kW standby capacity (1989); power supplied by France
Industries: tourism, banking and finance, dairy
Agriculture: potatoes, cauliflowers, tomatoes; dairy and cattle farming
Aid: none
Currency: Jersey pound (plural—pounds); 1 Jersey pound (£J) = 100 pence
Exchange rates: Jersey pounds (£J) per US$1—0.6055 (January 1990), 0.6099 (1989), 0.5614 (1988), 0.6102 (1987), 0.6817 (1986), 0.7714 (1985); the Jersey pound is at par with the British pound
Fiscal year: 1 April-31 March

Communications

Ports: Saint Helier, Gorey, St. Aubin
Airports: 1 with permanent-surface runway 1,220-2,439 m (St. Peter)
Telecommunications: 63,700 telephones; stations—1 AM, no FM, 1 TV; 3 submarine cables

Defense Forces

Note: defense is the responsibility of the UK

Johnston Atoll
(territory of the US)

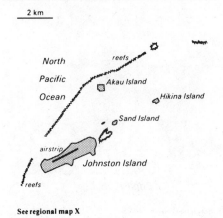

See regional map X

Geography

Total area: 2.8 km^2; land area: 2.8 km^2
Comparative area: about 4.7 times the size of The Mall in Washington, DC
Land boundaries: none
Coastline: 10 km
Maritime claims:
  Contiguous zone: 12 nm
  Continental shelf: 200 m
  Extended economic zone: 200 nm
  Territorial sea: 12 nm
Climate: tropical, but generally dry; consistent northeast trade winds with little seasonal temperature variation
Terrain: mostly flat with a maximum elevation of 4 meters
Natural resources: guano (deposits worked until about 1890)
Land use: 0% arable land; 0% permanent crops; 0% meadows and pastures; 0% forest and woodland; 100% other
Environment: some low-growing vegetation
Note: strategic location 1,328 km west-southwest of Honolulu in the North Pacific Ocean, about one-third of the way between Hawaii and the Marshall Islands; Johnston Island and Sand Island are natural islands; North Island (Akau) and East Island (Hikina) are manmade islands formed from coral dredging; closed to the public; former nuclear weapons test site

People

Population: 1,203 (December 1989); all US government personnel and contractors

Government

Long-form name: none (territory of the US)
Type: unincorporated territory of the US administered by the US Defense Nuclear Agency (DNA) and managed cooperatively by DNA and the Fish and Wildlife

Service of the US Department of the Interior as part of the National Wildlife Refuge system
Diplomatic representation: none (territory of the US)
Flag: the flag of the US is used

Economy

Overview: Economic activity is limited to providing services to US military personnel and contractors located on the island. All food and manufactured goods must be imported.

Communications

Ports: Johnston Island
Airports: 1 with permanent-surface runway 2,743 m
Telecommunications: excellent system including 60-channel submarine cable, Autodin/SRT terminal, digital telephone switch, Military Affiliated Radio System (MARS station), and a (receive only) commercial satellite television system
Note: US Coast Guard operates a LORAN transmitting station

Defense Forces

Note: defense is the responsibility of the US

Jordan
(see separate West Bank entry)

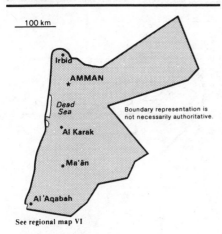

100 km

Irbid

AMMAN
★

Dead
Sea

Boundary representation is
not necessarily authoritative.

Al Karak

Ma'ān

Al 'Aqabah

See regional map VI

Note: The war between Israel and the Arab states in June 1967 ended with Israel in control of the West Bank. As stated in the 1978 Camp David Accords and reaffirmed by President Reagan's 1 September 1982 peace initiative, the final status of the West Bank and Gaza Strip, their relationship with their neighbors, and a peace treaty between Israel and Jordan are to be negotiated among the concerned parties. The Camp David Accords further specify that these negotiations will resolve the location of the respective boundaries. Pending the completion of this process, it is US policy that the final status of the West Bank and Gaza Strip has yet to be determined.

Geography

Total area: 91,880 km²; land area: 91,540 km²
Comparative area: slightly smaller than Indiana
Land boundaries: 1,586 km total; Iraq 134 km, Israel 238 km, Saudi Arabia 742 km, Syria 375 km, West Bank 97 km
Coastline: 26 km
Maritime claim:
Territorial sea: 3 nm
Disputes: differences with Israel over the location of the 1949 Armistice Line which separates the two countries
Climate: mostly arid desert; rainy season in west (November to April)
Terrain: mostly desert plateau in east, highland area in west; Great Rift Valley separates East and West Banks of the Jordan River
Natural resources: phosphates, potash, shale oil
Land use: 4% arable land; 0.5% permanent crops; 1% meadows and pastures; 0.5% forest and woodland; 94% other; includes 0.5% irrigated

Environment: lack of natural water resources; deforestation; overgrazing; soil erosion; desertification

People

Population: 3,064,508 (July 1990), growth rate 3.6% (1990)
Birth rate: 42 births/1,000 population (1990)
Death rate: 5 deaths/1,000 population (1990)
Net migration rate: 0 migrants/1,000 population (1990)
Infant mortality rate: 55 deaths/1,000 live births (1990)
Life expectancy at birth: 68 years male, 71 years female (1990)
Total fertility rate: 6.2 children born/woman (1990)
Nationality: noun—Jordanian(s); adjective—Jordanian
Ethnic divisions: 98% Arab, 1% Circassian, 1% Armenian
Religion: 92% Sunni Muslim, 8% Christian
Language: Arabic (official); English widely understood among upper and middle classes
Literacy: 71% (est.)
Labor force: 572,000 (1988); 20% agriculture, 20% manufacturing and mining (1987 est.)
Organized labor: about 10% of labor force
Note: 1.5-1.7 million Palestinians live on the East Bank (55-60% of the population), most are Jordanian citizens

Government

Long-form name: Hashemite Kingdom of Jordan
Type: constitutional monarchy
Capital: Amman
Administrative divisions: 8 governorates (muḥāfaẓat, singular—muḥāfaẓah); Al Balqā', Al Karak, Al Mafraq, 'Ammān, Aṭ Ṭafīlah, Az Zarqā', Irbid, Ma'ān
Independence: 25 May 1946 (from League of Nations mandate under British administration; formerly Trans-Jordan)
Constitution: 8 January 1952
Legal system: based on Islamic law and French codes; judicial review of legislative acts in a specially provided High Tribunal; has not accepted compulsory ICJ jurisdiction
National holiday: Independence Day, 25 May (1946)
Executive branch: monarch, prime minister, deputy prime minister, Cabinet
Legislative branch: bicameral National Assembly (Majlis al 'Umma) consists of an upper house or House of Notables (Majlis al-A'yaan) and a lower house or House of Representatives (Majlis

al-Nuwwab); note—the House of Representatives was dissolved by King Hussein on 30 July 1988 as part of Jordanian disengagement from the West Bank and in November 1989 the first parliamentary elections in 22 years were held, with no seats going to Palestinians on the West Bank
Judicial branch: Court of Cassation
Leaders: *Chief of State*—King HUSSEIN Ibn Talal I (since 11 August 1952); *Head of Government*—Prime Minister Mudar BADRAN (since 4 December 1989)
Political parties and leaders: none; after 1989 parliamentary elections, King Hussein promised to allow the formation of political parties
Suffrage: universal at age 20
Elections: *House of Representatives*—last held 8 November 1989 (next to be held NA); results—percent of vote NA; seats—(80 total) percent of vote NA
Communists: party actively repressed, membership less than 500 (est.)
Member of: ACC, Arab League, CCC, FAO, G-77, IAEA, IBRD, ICAO, IDA, IDB—Islamic Development Bank, IFAD, IFC, ILO, IMF, IMO, INTELSAT, INTERPOL, IPU, ITU, NAM, OIC, UN, UNESCO, UPU, WFTU, WHO, WIPO, WMO, WTO
Diplomatic representation: Ambassador Hussein A. HAMMAMI; Chancery at 3504 International Drive NW, Washington DC 20008; telephone (202) 966-2664; *US*—Ambassador Roscoe S. SUDDARTH; Embassy on Jebel Amman, Amman (mailing address is P. O. Box 354, Amman, or APO New York 09892); telephone [962] (6) 644371 through 644376
Flag: three equal horizontal bands of black (top), white, and green with a red isosceles triangle based on the hoist side bearing a small white seven-pointed star; the seven points on the star represent the seven fundamental laws of the Koran

Economy

Overview: Jordan was a secondary beneficiary of the oil boom of the late 1970s and early 1980s, when its GNP growth averaged 10-12%. Recent years, however, have witnessed a sharp reduction in cash aid from Arab oil-producing countries and in worker remittances, with growth averaging 1-2%. Imports—mainly oil, capital goods, consumer durables, and foodstuffs—have been outstripping exports by roughly $2 billion annually, the difference being made up by aid, remittances, and borrowing. In 1989 the government pursued policies to encourage private investment, curb imports of luxury goods,

Jordan *(continued)*

promote exports, reduce the budget deficit, and, in general, reinvigorate economic growth. Success will depend largely on exogenous forces, such as the absence of drought and a pickup in outside support. Down the road, the completion of the proposed Unity Dam on the Yarmuk is vital to meet rapidly growing requirements for water.
GNP: $5.2 billion, per capita $1,760; real growth rate 0% (1989)
Inflation rate (consumer prices): 35% (1989 est.)
Unemployment rate: 9-10% (December 1989 est.)
Budget: revenues $0.92 billion; expenditures $1.6 billion, including capital expenditures of $540 million (1989 est.)
Exports: $0.910 billion (f.o.b., 1989 est.); *commodities*—fruits and vegetables, phosphates, fertilizers; *partners*—Iraq, Saudi Arabia, India, Kuwait, Japan, China, Yugoslavia, Indonesia
Imports: $1.7 billion (c.i.f., 1989 est.); *commodities*—crude oil, textiles, capital goods, motor vehicles, foodstuffs; *partners*—EC, US, Saudi Arabia, Japan, Turkey, Romania, China, Taiwan
External debt: $8.3 billion (December 1989)
Industrial production: growth rate −7.8% (1988 est.)
Electricity: 981,000 kW capacity; 3,500 million kWh produced, 1,180 kWh per capita (1989)
Industries: phosphate mining, petroleum refining, cement, potash, light manufacturing
Agriculture: accounts for only 5% of GDP; principal products are wheat, barley, citrus fruit, tomatoes, melons, olives; livestock—sheep, goats, poultry; large net importer of food
Aid: US commitments, including Ex-Im (FY70-88), $1.7 billion; Western (non-US) countries, ODA and OOF bilateral commitments (1970-87), $1.2 billion; OPEC bilateral aid (1979-89), $9.5 billion; Communist countries (1970-88), $44 million
Currency: Jordanian dinar (plural—dinars); 1 Jordanian dinar (JD) = 1,000 fils
Exchange rates: Jordanian dinars (JD) per US$1—0.6557 (January 1990), 0.5704 (1989), 0.3715 (1988), 0.3387 (1987), 0.3499 (1986), 0.3940 (1985)
Fiscal year: calendar year

Communications

Railroads: 619 km 1.050-meter gauge, single track
Highways: 7,500 km; 5,500 km asphalt, 2,000 km gravel and crushed stone
Pipelines: crude oil, 209 km
Ports: Al Aqabah

Merchant marine: 3 ships (1,000 GRT or over) totaling 32,635 GRT/44,618 DWT; includes 1 short-sea passenger, 2 bulk cargo
Civil air: 19 major transport aircraft
Airports: 19 total, 16 usable; 14 with permanent-surface runways; 1 with runways over 3,659 m; 13 with runways 2,440-3,659 m; none with runways 1,220-2,439 m
Telecommunications: adequate system of radio relay, cable, and radio; 81,500 telephones; stations—4 AM, 3 FM, 24 TV; satellite earth stations—1 Atlantic Ocean INTELSAT, 1 Indian Ocean INTELSAT, 1 ARABSAT, 1 domestic TV receive-only; coaxial cable and radio relay to Iraq, Saudi Arabia, and Syria; radio relay to Lebanon is inactive; a microwave network linking Syria, Egypt, Libya, Tunisia, Algeria, Morocco and Jordan

Defense Forces

Branches: Jordan Arab Army, Royal Jordanian Air Force, Royal Jordanian Coast Guard
Military manpower: males 15-49, 726,736; 519,972 fit for military service; 38,730 reach military age (18) annually
Defense expenditures: 11% of GNP, or $570 million (1990 est.)

Juan de Nova Island
(French possession)

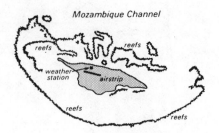

See regional map VII

Geography

Total area: 4.4 km²; land area: 4.4 km²
Comparative area: about 7.5 times the size of The Mall in Washington, DC
Land boundaries: none
Coastline: 24.1 km
Maritime claims:
Contiguous zone: 12 nm
Continental shelf: 200 meters or to depth of exploitation
Extended economic zone: 200 nm
Territorial sea: 12 nm
Disputes: claimed by Madagascar
Climate: tropical
Terrain: undetermined
Natural resources: guano deposits and other fertilizers
Land use: 0% arable land; 0% permanent crops; 0% meadows and pastures; 90% forest and woodland; 10% other
Environment: subject to periodic cyclones; wildlife sanctuary
Note: located in the central Mozambique Channel about halfway between Africa and Madagascar

People

Population: uninhabited

Government

Long-form name: none
Type: French possession administered by Commissioner of the Republic Daniel CONSTANTIN, resident in Reunion

Economy

Overview: no economic activity

Kenya

Communications

Railroads: short line going to a jetty
Airports: 1 with nonpermanent-surface runway less than 1,220 m
Ports: none; offshore anchorage only
Note: one weather station

Defense Forces

Note: defense is the responsibility of France

200 km

See regional map VII

Geography

Total area: 582,650 km²; land area: 569,250 km²
Comparative area: slightly more than twice the size of Nevada
Land boundaries: 3,477 km total; Ethiopia 861 km, Somalia 682 km, Sudan 232 km, Tanzania 769 km, Uganda 933 km
Coastline: 536 km
Maritime claims:
  Extended economic zone: 200 nm
  Territorial sea: 12 nm
Disputes: international boundary and Administrative Boundary with Sudan; possible claim by Somalia based on unification of ethnic Somalis
Climate: varies from tropical along coast to arid in interior
Terrain: low plains rise to central highlands bisected by Great Rift Valley; fertile plateau in west
Natural resources: gold, limestone, diotomite, salt barytes, magnesite, feldspar, sapphires, fluorspar, garnets, wildlife
Land use: 3% arable land; 1% permanent crops; 7% meadows and pastures; 4% forest and woodland; 85% other; includes NEGL% irrigated
Environment: unique physiography supports abundant and varied wildlife of scientific and economic value; deforestation; soil erosion; desertification; glaciers on Mt. Kenya
Note: Kenyan Highlands one of the most successful agricultural production regions in Africa

People

Population: 24,639,261 (July 1990), growth rate 3.8% (1990)
Birth rate: 45 births/1,000 population (1990)
Death rate: 7 deaths/1,000 population (1990)
Net migration rate: 0 migrants/1,000 population (1990)
Infant mortality rate: 60 deaths/1,000 live births (1990)
Life expectancy at birth: 62 years male, 67 years female (1990)
Total fertility rate: 6.5 children born/woman (1990)
Nationality: noun—Kenyan(s); adjective—Kenyan
Ethnic divisions: 21% Kikuyu, 14% Luhya, 13% Luo, 11% Kalenjin, 11% Kamba, 6% Kisii, 6% Meru, 1% Asian, European, and Arab
Religion: 38% Protestant, 28% Roman Catholic, 26% indigenous beliefs, 6% Muslim
Language: English and Swahili (official); numerous indigenous languages
Literacy: 59.2%
Labor force: 9,003,000; 78% agriculture, 22% nonagriculture (1987 est.)
Organized labor: 390,000 (est.)

Government

Long-form name: Republic of Kenya
Type: republic
Capital: Nairobi
Administrative divisions: 7 provinces and 1 area*; Central, Coast, Eastern, Nairobi Area*, North-Eastern, Nyanza, Rift Valley, Western
Independence: 12 December 1963 (from UK; formerly British East Africa)
Constitution: 12 December 1963, amended as a republic 1964; reissued with amendments 1979, 1983, 1986, and 1988
Legal system: based on English common law, tribal law, and Islamic law; judicial review in High Court; accepts compulsory ICJ jurisdiction, with reservations; constitutional amendment in 1982 made Kenya a de jure one-party state
National holiday: Independence Day, 12 December (1963)
Executive branch: president, vice president, Cabinet
Legislative branch: unicameral National Assembly
Judicial branch: Court of Appeal, High Court
Leaders: *Chief of State and Head of Government*—President Daniel Teroitich arap MOI (since 14 October 1978); Vice President George SAITOTI (since 10 May 1989)
Political parties and leaders: only party—Kenya African National Union (KANU), Daniel T. arap Moi, president
Suffrage: universal at age 18
Elections: *President*—last held on 21 March 1988 (next to be held February 1993); results—President Daniel T. arap Moi was reelected;

Kenya (continued)

National Assembly—last held on 21 March 1988 (next to be held March 1993); results—KANU is the only party; seats—(202 total, 188 elected) KANU 200
Communists: may be a few Communists and sympathizers
Other political or pressure groups: labor unions; exile opposition—Mwakenya and other groups
Member of: ACP, AfDB, CCC, Commonwealth, FAO, G-77, GATT, IAEA, IBRD, ICAO, ICO, IDA, IFAD, IFC, ILO, IMF, IMO, INTELSAT, INTERPOL, IRC, ISO, ITU, IWC—International Wheat Council, NAM, OAU, UN, UNDP, UNESCO, UPU, WHO, WIPO, WMO, WTO
Diplomatic representation: Ambassador Denis Daudi AFANDE; Chancery at 2249 R Street NW, Washington DC 20008; telephone (202) 387-6101; there are Kenyan Consulates General in Los Angeles and New York; *US*—Ambassador Smith HEMPSTONE; Embassy at the corner of Moi Avenue and Haile Selassie Avenue, Nairobi (mailing address is P. O. Box 30137, Nairobi or APO New York 09675); telephone [254] (2) 334141; there is a US Consulate in Mombasa
Flag: three equal horizontal bands of black (top), red, and green; the red band is edged in white; a large warrior's shield covering crossed spears is superimposed at the center

Economy

Overview: A serious underlying economic problem is Kenya's 3.8% annual population growth rate—one of the highest in the world. In the meantime, GDP growth in the near term has kept slightly ahead of population—annually averaging 5.2% in the 1986-88 period. Undependable weather conditions and a shortage of arable land hamper long-term growth in agriculture, the leading economic sector.
GDP: $8.5 billion, per capita $360; real growth rate 4.9% (1989 est.)
Inflation rate (consumer prices): 8.3% (1988)
Unemployment rate: NA%, but there is a high level of unemployment and underemployment
Budget: revenues $2.3 billion; expenditures $2.6 billion, including capital expenditures of $0.71 billion (FY87)
Exports: $1.0 billion (f.o.b., 1988); *commodities*—coffee 20%, tea 18%, manufactures 15%, petroleum products 10% (1987); *partners*—Western Europe 45%, Africa 22%, Far East 10%, US 4%, Middle East 3% (1987)
Imports: $1.8 billion (f.o.b., 1988); *commodities*—machinery and transportation equipment 36%, raw materials 33%, fuels

and lubricants 20%, food and consumer goods 11% (1987); *partners*—Western Europe 49%, Far East 20%, Middle East 19%, US 7% (1987)
External debt: $6.2 billion (December 1989 est.)
Industrial production: growth rate 4.8% (1987 est.)
Electricity: 587,000 kW capacity; 2,250 million kWh produced, 90 kWh per capita (1989)
Industries: small-scale consumer goods (plastic, furniture, batteries, textiles, soap, cigarettes, flour), agricultural processing, oil refining, cement, tourism
Agriculture: most important sector, accounting for 30% of GDP, about 80% of the work force, and over 50% of exports; cash crops—coffee, tea, sisal, pineapple; food products—corn, wheat, sugarcane, fruit, vegetables, dairy products; food output not keeping pace with population growth
Illicit drugs: illicit producer of cannabis used mostly for domestic consumption; widespread cultivation of cannabis and qat on small plots; transit country for heroin and methaqualone en route from Southwest Asia to West Africa, Western Europe, and the US
Aid: US commitments, including Ex-Im (FY70-88), $771 million; Western (non-US) countries, ODA and OOF bilateral commitments (1970-87), $6.0 billion; OPEC bilateral aid (1979-89), $74 million; Communist countries (1970-88), $83 million
Currency: Kenyan shilling (plural—shillings); 1 Kenyan shilling (KSh) = 100 cents
Exchange rates: Kenyan shillings (KSh) per US$1—21.749 (December 1989), 20.572 (1989), 17.747 (1988), 16.454 (1987), 16.226 (1986), 16.432 (1985)
Fiscal year: 1 July-30 June

Communications

Railroads: 2,040 km 1.000-meter gauge
Highways: 64,590 km total; 7,000 km paved, 4,150 km gravel, remainder improved earth
Inland waterways: part of Lake Victoria system is within boundaries of Kenya; principal inland port is at Kisumu
Pipelines: refined products, 483 km
Ports: Mombasa, Lamu
Civil air: 14 major transport aircraft
Airports: 247 total, 211 usable; 18 with permanent-surface runways; 2 with runways over 3,659 m; 1 with runways 2,440-3,659 m; 45 with runways 1,220-2,439 m
Telecommunications: in top group of African systems; consists of radio relay links, open-wire lines, and radiocommunication stations; 260,000 telephones; stations—11

AM, 4 FM, 4 TV; satellite earth stations—1 Atlantic Ocean INTELSAT and 1 Indian Ocean INTLESAT

Defense Forces

Branches: Kenya Army, Kenya Navy, Air Force; paramilitary General Service Unit
Military manpower: males 15-49, 5,240,551; 3,235,557 fit for military service; no conscription
Defense expenditures: 1.0% of GDP, or $100 million (1989 est.)

Kingman Reef
(territory of the US)

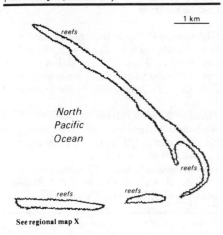

North
Pacific
Ocean

See regional map X

Geography

Total area: 1 km^2; land area: 1 km^2
Comparative area: about 1.7 times the size of The Mall in Washington, DC
Land boundaries: none
Coastline: 3 km
Maritime claims:
   Contiguous zone: 12 nm
   Continental shelf: 200 m
   Extended economic zone: 200 nm
   Territorial sea: 12 nm
Climate: tropical, but moderated by prevailing winds
Terrain: low and nearly level with a maximum elevation of about 1 meter
Natural resources: none
Land use: 0% arable land; 0% permanent crops; 0% meadows and pastures; 0% forest and woodland; 100% other
Environment: barren coral atoll with deep interior lagoon; wet or awash most of the time
Note: located 1,600 km south-southwest of Honolulu in the North Pacific Ocean, about halfway between Hawaii and American Samoa; maximum elevation of about 1 meter makes this a navigational hazard; closed to the public

People

Population: uninhabited

Government

Long-form name: none
Type: unincorporated territory of the US administered by the US Navy

Economy

Overview: no economic activity

Communications

Airports: lagoon was used as a halfway station between Hawaii and American Samoa by Pan American Airways for flying boats in 1937 and 1938
Ports: none; offshore anchorage only

Defense Forces

Note: defense is the responsibility of the US

Kiribati

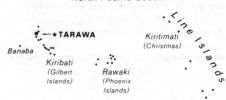

North Pacific Ocean

★ TARAWA
Banaba
Kiribati
(Gilbert
Islands)
Rawaki
(Phoenix
Islands)
Kiritimati
(Christmas)
Line Islands

South Pacific Ocean

See regional map X

Geography

Total area: 717 km^2; land area: 717 km^2; includes three island groups—Gilbert Islands, Line Islands, Phoenix Islands
Comparative area: slightly more than four times the size of Washington, DC
Land boundaries: none
Coastline: 1,143 km
Maritime claims:
   Exclusive fishing zone: 200 nm
   Territorial sea: 12 nm
Climate: tropical; marine, hot and humid, moderated by trade winds
Terrain: mostly low-lying coral atolls surrounded by extensive reefs
Natural resources: phosphate (production discontinued in 1979)
Land use: NEGL% arable land; 51% permanent crops; 0% meadows and pastures; 3% forest and woodland; 46% other
Environment: typhoons can occur any time, but usually November to March; 20 of the 33 islands are inhabited
Note: Banaba or Ocean Island is one of the three great phosphate rock islands in the Pacific (the others are Makatea in French Polynesia and Nauru)

People

Population: 70,012 (July 1990), growth rate 1.7% (1990)
Birth rate: 34 births/1,000 population (1990)
Death rate: 13 deaths/1,000 population (1990)
Net migration rate: −5 migrants/1,000 population (1990)
Infant mortality rate: 65 deaths/1,000 live births (1990)
Life expectancy at birth: 52 years male, 57 years female (1990)
Total fertility rate: 4.3 children born/woman (1990)
Nationality: noun—Kiribatian(s); adjective—Kiribati

169

Kiribati (continued)

Ethnic divisions: Micronesian
Religion: 48% Roman Catholic, 45% Protestant (Congregational), some Seventh-Day Adventist and Baha'i
Language: English (official), Gilbertese
Literacy: 90%
Labor force: 7,870 economically active (1985 est.)
Organized labor: Kiribati Trades Union Congress—2,500 members

Government

Long-form name: Republic of Kiribati
Type: republic
Capital: Tarawa
Administrative divisions: 3 units; Gilbert Islands, Line Islands, Phoenix Islands; note—a new administrative structure of 6 districts (Banaba, Central Gilberts, Line Islands, Northern Gilberts, Southern Gilberts, Tarawa) may have been changed to 20 island councils (one for each of the inhabited islands) named Abaiang, Abemama, Aranuka, Arorae, Banaba, Beru, Butaritari, Kiritimati, Kuria, Maiana, Makin, Marakei, Nikunau, Nonouti, Onotoa, Tabiteuea, Tabuaeran, Tamana, Tarawa, Teraina
Independence: 12 July 1979 (from UK; formerly Gilbert Islands)
Constitution: 12 July 1979
National holiday: Independence Day, 12 July (1979)
Executive branch: president, vice president, Cabinet
Legislative branch: unicameral House of Assembly (Maneaba Ni Maungatabu)
Judicial branch: Court of Appeal, High Court
Leaders: *Chief of State and Head of Government*—President Ieremia T. TABAI (since 12 July 1979); Vice President Teatao TEANNAKI (since 20 July 1979)
Political parties and leaders: Gilbertese National Party; Christian Democratic Party, Teburoro Tito, secretary; essentially not organized on basis of political parties
Suffrage: universal at age 18
Elections: *President*—last held on 12 May 1987 (next to be held May 1991); results—Ieremia T. Tabai 50.1%, Tebruroro Tito 42.7%, Tetao Tannaki 7.2%; *National Assembly*—last held on 19 March 1987 (next to be held March 1991); results—percent of vote by party NA; seats—(40 total; 39 elected) percent of seats by party NA
Member of: ACP, ADB, Commonwealth, ESCAP (associate member), GATT (de facto), ICAO, IMF, SPF, WHO
Diplomatic representation: Ambassador (vacant) lives in Tarawa (Kiribati); *US*—none

Flag: the upper half is red with a yellow frigate bird flying over a yellow rising sun and the lower half is blue with three horizontal wavy white stripes to represent the ocean

Economy

Overview: The country has few national resources. Phosphate deposits were exhausted at the time of independence in 1979. Copra and fish now represent the bulk of production and exports. The economy has fluctuated widely in recent years. Real GDP declined about 8% in 1987, as the fish catch fell sharply to only one-fourth the level of 1986 and copra production was hampered by repeated rains. Output rebounded strongly in 1988, with real GDP growing by 17%. The upturn in economic growth came from an increase in copra production and a good fish catch. Following the strong surge in output in 1988, GDP remained about the same in 1989.
GDP: $34 million, per capita $500; real growth rate 0% (1989)
Inflation rate (consumer prices): 3.1% (1988)
Unemployment rate: 2% (1985); considerable underemployment
Budget: revenues $22.0 million; expenditures $12.7 million, including capital expenditures of $9.7 million (1988)
Exports: $5.1 million (f.o.b., 1988); *commodities*—fish 55%, copra 42%; *partners*—EC 20%, Marshall Islands 12%, US 8%, American Samoa 4% (1985)
Imports: $21.5 million (c.i.f., 1988); *commodities*—foodstuffs, fuel, transportation equipment; *partners*—Australia 39%, Japan 21%, NZ 6%, UK 6%, US 3% (1985)
External debt: $2.0 million (December 1987 est.)
Industrial production: growth rate NA%
Electricity: 5,000 kW capacity; 13 million kWh produced, 190 kWh per capita (1989)
Industries: fishing, handicrafts
Agriculture: accounts for 30% of GDP (including fishing); copra and fish contribute 95% to exports; subsistence farming predominates; food crops—taro, breadfruit, sweet potatoes, vegetables; not self-sufficient in food
Aid: Western (non-US) countries, ODA and OOF bilateral commitments (1970-87), $245 million
Currency: Australian dollar (plural—dollars); 1 Australian dollar ($A) = 100 cents
Exchange rates: Australian dollars ($A) per US$1—1.2784 (January 1990), 1.2618 (1989), 1.2752 (1988), 1.4267 (1987), 1.4905 (1986), 1.4269 (1985)
Fiscal year: NA

Communications

Highways: 640 km of motorable roads
Inland waterways: small network of canals, totaling 5 km, in Line Islands
Ports: Banaba and Betio (Tarawa)
Civil air: 2 Trislanders; no major transport aircraft
Airports: 22 total; 21 usable; 4 with permanent-surface runways; none with runways over 2,439 m; 5 with runways 1,220-2,439 m
Telecommunications: 1,400 telephones; stations—1 AM, no FM, no TV; 1 Pacific Ocean INTELSAT earth station

Defense Forces

Branches: NA
Military manpower: NA
Defense expenditures: NA

Korea, North

150 km

Boundary representation is not necessarily authoritative.

Geography

Total area: 120,540 km²; land area: 120,410 km²
Comparative area: slightly smaller than Mississippi
Land boundaries: 1,671 km total; China 1,416 km, South Korea 238 km, USSR 17 km
Coastline: 2,495 km
Maritime claims:
Extended economic zone: 200 nm
Territorial sea: 12 nm
Military boundary line: 50 nm (all foreign vessels and aircraft without permission are banned)
Disputes: short section of boundary with China is indefinite; Demarcation Line with South Korea
Climate: temperate with rainfall concentrated in summer
Terrain: mostly hills and mountains separated by deep, narrow valleys; coastal plains wide in west, discontinuous in east
Natural resources: coal, lead, tungsten, zinc, graphite, magnesite, iron ore, copper, gold, pyrites, salt, fluorspar, hydropower
Land use: 18% arable land; 1% permanent crops; NEGL% meadows and pastures; 74% forest and woodland; 7% other; includes 9% irrigated
Environment: mountainous interior is isolated, nearly inaccessible, and sparsely populated; late spring droughts often followed by severe flooding
Note: strategic location bordering China, South Korea, and USSR

People

Population: 21,292,649 (July 1990), growth rate 1.7% (1990)
Birth rate: 22 births/1,000 population (1990)
Death rate: 5 deaths/1,000 population (1990)

Net migration rate: 0 migrants/1,000 population (1990)
Infant mortality rate: 27 deaths/1,000 live births (1990)
Life expectancy at birth: 69 years male, 75 years female (1990)
Total fertility rate: 2.1 children born/woman (1990)
Nationality: noun—Korean(s); adjective—Korean
Ethnic divisions: racially homogeneous
Religion: Buddhism and Confucianism; religious activities now almost nonexistent
Language: Korean
Literacy: 95% (est.)
Labor force: 9,615,000; 36% agricultural, 64% nonagricultural; shortage of skilled and unskilled labor (mid-1987 est.)
Organized labor: 1,600,000 members; single-trade union system coordinated by the General Federation of Trade Unions of Korea under the Central Committee

Government

Long-form name: Democratic People's Republic of Korea; abbreviated DPRK
Type: Communist state; one-man rule
Capital: P'yŏngyang
Administrative divisions: 9 provinces (do, singular and plural) and 3 special cities* (jikhalsi, singular and plural); Chagang-do, Hamgyŏng-namdo, Hamgyŏng-bukto, Hwanghae-namdo, Hwanghae-bukto, Kaesŏng-si*, Kangwŏn-do, Namp'o-si*, P'yŏngan-bukto, P'yŏngan-namdo, P'yŏngyang-si*, Yanggang-do
Independence: 9 September 1948
Constitution: adopted 1948, revised 27 December 1972
Legal system: based on German civil law system with Japanese influences and Communist legal theory; no judicial review of legislative acts; has not accepted compulsory ICJ jurisdiction
National holiday: Independence Day, 9 September (1948)
Executive branch: president, two vice presidents, premier, nine vice premiers, State Administration Council (cabinet)
Legislative branch: unicameral Supreme People's Assembly (Choe Ko In Min Hoe Ui)
Judicial branch: Central Court
Leaders: *Chief of State*—President KIM Il-sŏng (since 28 December 1972); Designated Successor KIM Chong-Il (son of President, born 16 February 1942); *Head of Government*—Premier YON Hyong-muk (since NA December 1988)
Political parties and leaders: only party—Korean Workers' Party (KWP); Kim Il-sŏng, General Secretary, and his son, Kim Chong-Il, Secretary, Central Committee
Suffrage: universal at age 17

Elections: *President*—last held 29 December 1986 (next to be held December 1990); results—President Kim Il Sŏng was reelected without opposition; *Supreme People's Assembly*—last held on 2 November 1986 (next to be held November 1990, but the constitutional provision for elections every four years is not always followed); results—KWP is the only party; seats—(655 total) KWP 655; the KWP approves a single list of candidates who are elected without opposition
Communists: KWP claims membership of about 2 million, or about one-tenth of population
Member of: ESCAP, FAO, G-77, IAEA, ICAO, IMO, IPU, ITU, NAM, UNCTAD, UNESCO, UPU, WFTU, WHO, WIPO, WTO, UNIDO, WMO; official observer status at UN
Diplomatic representation: none
Flag: three horizontal bands of blue (top), red (triple width), and blue; the red band is edged in white; on the hoist side of the red band is a white disk with a red five-pointed star

Economy

Overview: More than 90% of this command economy is socialized; agricultural land is collectivized; and state-owned industry produces 95% of manufactured goods. State control of economic affairs is unusually tight even for a Communist country because of the small size and homogeneity of the society and the strict one-man rule of Kim. Economic growth during the period 1984-89 has averaged approximately 3%. Abundant natural resources and hydropower form the basis of industrial development. Output of the extractive industries includes coal, iron ore, magnesite, graphite, copper, zinc, lead, and precious metals. Manufacturing emphasis is centered on heavy industry, with light industry lagging far behind. The use of high-yielding seed varieties, expansion of irrigation, and the heavy use of fertilizers have enabled North Korea to become largely self-sufficient in food production. North Korea, however, is far behind South Korea in economic development and living standards.
GNP: $28 billion, per capita $1,240; real growth rate 3% (1989)
Inflation rate (consumer prices): NA%
Unemployment rate: officially none
Budget: revenues $15.6 billion; expenditures $15.6 billion, including capital expenditures of $NA (1989)
Exports: $2.4 billion (f.o.b., 1988); *commodities*—minerals, metallurgical products, agricultural products, manufactures; *partners*—USSR, China, Japan, FRG, Hong Kong, Singapore

171

Korea, North *(continued)*

Imports: $3.1 billion (f.o.b., 1988); *commodities*—petroleum, machinery and equipment, coking coal, grain; *partners*—USSR, Japan, China, FRG, Hong Kong, Singapore

External debt: $2.5 billion hard currency (1989)

Industrial production: growth rate NA%

Electricity: 6,440,000 kW capacity; 40,250 million kWh produced, 1,740 kWh per capita (1989)

Industries: machine building, military products, electric power, chemicals, mining, metallurgy, textiles, food processing

Agriculture: accounts for about 25% of GNP and 36% of work force; principal crops—rice, corn, potatoes, soybeans, pulses; livestock and livestock products—cattle, hogs, pork, eggs; not self-sufficient in grain; fish catch estimated at 1.7 million metric tons in 1987

Aid: Communist countries (1970-88), $1.3 billion

Currency: North Korean won (plural—won); 1 North Korean won (Wn) = 100 chŏn

Exchange rates: North Korean won (Wn) per US$1—2.3 (December 1989), 2.13 (December 1988), 0.94 (March 1987), NA (1986), NA (1985)

Fiscal year: calendar year

Communications

Railroads: 4,535 km total operating in 1980; 3,870 km 1.435-meter standard gauge, 665 km 0.762-meter narrow gauge, 159 km double track; 3,175 km electrified; government owned

Highways: about 20,280 km (1980); 98.5% gravel, crushed stone, or earth surface; 1.5% concrete or bituminous

Inland waterways: 2,253 km; mostly navigable by small craft only

Pipelines: crude oil, 37 km

Ports: Ch'ŏngjin, Haeju, Hungnam, Namp'o, Wonsan, Songnim, Najin

Merchant marine: 65 ships (1,000 GRT and over) totaling 437,103 GRT/663,835 DWT; includes 1 passenger, 1 short-sea passenger, 1 passenger-cargo, 56 cargo, 2 petroleum, oils, and lubricants (POL) tanker, 3 bulk, 1 combination bulk

Airports: 50 total, 50 usable; about 30 with permanent-surface runways; fewer than 5 with runways over 3,659 m; 20 with runways 2,440-3,659 m; 30 with runways 1,220-2,439 m

Telecommunications: stations—18 AM, no FM, 11 TV; 200,000 TV sets; 3,500,000 radio receivers; 1 Indian Ocean INTELSAT earth station

Defense Forces

Branches: Ministry of People's Armed Forces (consists of the army, navy, and air force)

Military manpower: males 15-49, 6,054,774; 3,699,088 fit for military service; 223,087 reach military age (18) annually

Defense expenditures: 22% of GNP (1987)

Korea, South

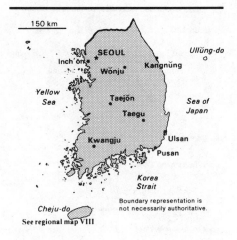

150 km

SEOUL
Inch'ŏn
Wŏnju
Kangnŭng
Ullŭng-do
Yellow Sea
Taejŏn
Sea of Japan
Taegu
Kwangju
Ulsan
Pusan
Korea Strait
Cheju-do
Boundary representation is not necessarily authoritative.

See regional map VIII

Geography

Total area: 98,480 km²; land area: 98,190 km²

Comparative area: slightly larger than Indiana

Land boundary: 238 km with North Korea

Coastline: 2,413 km

Maritime claims:
 Territorial sea: 12 nm (3 nm in the Korea Strait)

Disputes: Demarcation Line with North Korea; Liancourt Rocks claimed by Japan

Climate: temperate, with rainfall heavier in summer than winter

Terrain: mostly hills and mountains; wide coastal plains in west and south

Natural resources: coal, tungsten, graphite, molybdenum, lead, hydropower

Land use: 21% arable land; 1% permanent crops; 1% meadows and pastures; 67% forest and woodland; 10% other; includes 12% irrigated

Environment: occasional typhoons bring high winds and floods; earthquakes in southwest; air pollution in large cities

Notes: strategic location along the Korea Strait, Sea of Japan, and Yellow Sea

People

Population: 43,045,098 (July 1990), growth rate 0.8% (1990)

Birth rate: 20 births/1,000 population (1990)

Death rate: 6 deaths/1,000 population (1990)

Net migration rate: −1 migrants/1,000 population (1990)

Infant mortality rate: 23 deaths/1,000 live births (1990)

Life expectancy at birth: 66 years male, 73 years female (1990)

Total fertility rate: 1.6 children born/woman (1990)

Nationality: noun—Korean(s); adjective—Korean

Ethnic divisions: homogeneous; small Chinese minority (about 20,000)
Religion: strong Confucian tradition; vigorous Christian minority (28% of the total population); Buddhism; pervasive folk religion (Shamanism); Chondokyo (religion of the heavenly way), eclectic religion with nationalist overtones founded in 19th century, claims about 1.5 million adherents
Language: Korean; English widely taught in high school
Literacy: over 90%
Labor force: 16,900,000; 52% services and other; 27% mining and manufacturing; 21% agriculture, fishing, forestry (1987)
Organized labor: about 10% of nonagricultural labor force in government-sanctioned unions

Government

Long-form name: Republic of Korea; abbreviated ROK
Type: republic
Capital: Seoul
Administrative divisions: 9 provinces (do, singular and plural) and 6 special cities* (jikhalsi, singular and plural); Cheju-do, Chŏlla-bukto, Chŏlla-namdo, Ch'ungch'ŏng-bukto, Ch'ungch'ŏng-namdo, Inch'ŏn-jikhalsi*, Kangwŏn-do, Kwangju-jikhalsi*, Kyŏnggi-do, Kyŏngsang-bukto, Kyŏngsang-namdo, Pusan-jikhalsi*, Sŏul-t'ŭkpyŏlsi*, Taegu-jikhalsi*, Taejŏn-jikhalsi*
Independence: 15 August 1948
Constitution: 25 February 1988
Legal system: combines elements of continental European civil law systems, Anglo-American law, and Chinese classical thought; has not accepted compulsory ICJ jurisdiction
National holiday: Independence Day, 15 August (1948)
Executive branch: president, prime minister, deputy prime minister, State Council (cabinet)
Legislative branch: unicameral National Assembly
Judicial branch: Supreme Court
Leaders: *Chief of State*—President ROH Tae Woo (since 25 February 1988); *Head of Government*—Prime Minister KANG Young Hoon (since 5 December 1988); Deputy Prime Minister CHO Soon (since 5 December 1988)
Political parties and leaders: major party is government's Democratic Justice Party (DJP), Roh Tae Woo, president, and Park Tae Chun, chairman; opposition parties are Peace and Democracy Party (PPD), Kim Dae Jung; Korea Reunification Democratic Party (RPD), Kim Young Sam; New Democratic Republican Party (NDRP), Kim Jong Pil; several smaller parties

Suffrage: universal at age 20
Elections: *President*—last held on 16 December 1987 (next to be held December 1992); results—Roh Tae Woo (DJP) 35.9%, Kim Young Sam (RDP) 27.5%, Kim Dae Jung (PPD) 26.5%, other 10.1%; *National Assembly*—last held on 26 April 1988 (next to be held April 1992); results—DJP 34%, RPD 24%, PPD 19%, NDRP 15%, others 8%; seats—(299 total) DJP 125, PPD 71, RPD 59, NDRP 35, others 9
Communists: Communist party activity banned by government
Other political or pressure groups: Korean National Council of Churches; large, potentially volatile student population concentrated in Seoul; Federation of Korean Trade Unions; Korean Veterans' Association; Federation of Korean Industries; Korean Traders Association
Member of: ADB, AfDB, ASPAC, CCC, Colombo Plan, ESCAP, FAO, G-77, GATT, IAEA, IBRD, ICAC, ICAO, IDA, IFAD, IFC, IHO, IMF, IMO, INTELSAT, INTERPOL, IPU, IRC, ITU, IWC—International Whaling Commission, IWC—International Wheat Council, UNCTAD, UNDP, UNESCO, UNICEF, UNIDO, UN Special Fund, UPU, WHO, WIPO, WMO, WTO; official observer status at UN
Diplomatic representation: Ambassador Tong-Jin PARK; Chancery at 2320 Massachusetts Avenue NW, Washington DC 20008; telephone (202) 939-5600; there are Korean Consulates General in Agana (Guam), Anchorage, Atlanta, Chicago, Honolulu, Houston, Los Angeles, New York, San Francisco, and Seattle; *US*—Ambassador Donald GREGG; Embassy at 82 Sejong-Ro, Chongro-ku, Seoul (mailing address is APO San Francisco 96301); telephone [82] (2) 732-2601 through 2618; there is a US Consulate in Pusan
Flag: white with a red (top) and blue yin-yang symbol in the center; there is a different black trigram from the ancient *I Ching* (Book of Changes) in each corner of the white field

Economy

Overview: The driving force behind the economy's dynamic growth has been the planned development of an export-oriented economy in a vigorously entrepreneurial society. GNP increased almost 13% in both 1986 and 1987 and 12% in 1988 before slowing to 6.5% in 1989. Such a rapid rate of growth was achieved with an inflation rate of only 3% in the period 1986-87, rising to 7% in 1988 and 5% in 1989. Unemployment is also low, and some labor bottlenecks have appeared in

several processing industries. While the South Korean economy is expected to grow at more than 5% annually during the 1990s, labor unrest—which led to substantial wage hikes in 1987-89—threatens to undermine noninflationary growth.
GNP: $200 billion, per capita $4,600; real growth rate 6.5% (1989)
Inflation rate (consumer prices): 5% (1989)
Unemployment rate: 3% (1989)
Budget: revenues $33.6 billion; expenditures $33.6 billion, including capital expenditures of NA (1990)
Exports: $62.3 billion (f.o.b., 1989); *commodities*—textiles, clothing, electronic and electrical equipment, footwear, machinery, steel, automobiles, ships, fish; *partners*—US 33%, Japan 21%
Imports: $61.3 billion (c.i.f., 1989); *commodities*—machinery, electronics and electronic equipment, oil, steel, transport equipment, textiles, organic chemicals, grains; *partners*—Japan 28%, US 25% (1990)
External debt: $30.5 billion (September 1989)
Industrial production: growth rate 3.5% (1989)
Electricity: 20,500,000 kW capacity; 80,000 million kWh produced, 1,850 kWh per capita (1989)
Industries: textiles, clothing, footwear, food processing, chemicals, steel, electronics, automobile production, ship building
Agriculture: accounts for 11% of GNP and employs 21% of work force (including fishing and forestry); principal crops—rice, root crops, barley, vegetables, fruit; livestock and livestock products—cattle, hogs, chickens, milk, eggs; self-sufficient in food, except for wheat; fish catch of 2.9 million metric tons, seventh-largest in world
Aid: US commitments, including Ex-Im (FY70-85), $3.9 billion
Currency: South Korean won (plural—won); 1 South Korean won (W) = 100 chŏn (theoretical)
Exchange rates: South Korean won (W) per US$1—683.43 (January 1990), 671.46 (1989), 731.47 (1988), 822.57 (1987), 881.45 (1986), 870.02 (1985)
Fiscal year: calendar year

Communications

Railroads: 3,106 km operating in 1983; 3,059 km 1.435-meter standard gauge, 47 km 0.610-meter narrow gauge, 712 km double track, 418 km electrified; government owned
Highways: 62,936 km total (1982); 13,476 km national highway, 49,460 km provincial and local roads
Inland waterways: 1,609 km; use restricted to small native craft
Pipelines: 294 km refined products

Korea, South *(continued)*

Ports: Pusan, Inchon, Kunsan, Mokpo, Ulsan

Merchant marine: 423 ships (1,000 GRT or over) totaling 7,006,481 GRT/ 11,658,104 DWT; includes 2 short-sea passenger, 130 cargo, 41 container, 11 refrigerated cargo, 11 vehicle carrier, 49 petroleum, oils, and lubricants (POL) tanker, 8 chemical tanker, 10 liquefied gas, 10 combination ore/oil, 143 bulk, 7 combination bulk, 1 multifunction large-load carrier

Civil air: 93 major transport aircraft

Airports: 112 total, 105 usable; 61 with permanent-surface runways; none with runways over 3,659 m; with runways 2,440-3,659 m; 17 with runways 1,220-2,439 m

Telecommunications: adequate domestic and international services; 4,800,000 telephones; stations—79 AM, 46 FM, 256 TV (57 of 1 kW or greater); satellite earth stations—2 Pacific Ocean INTELSAT and 1 Indian Ocean INTELSAT

Defense Forces

Branches: Army, Navy, Air Force, Marine Corps

Military manpower: males 15-49, 12,792,426; 8,260,886 fit for military service; 445,320 reach military age (18) annually

Defense expenditures: 5% of GNP, or $10 billion (1989 est.)

Kuwait

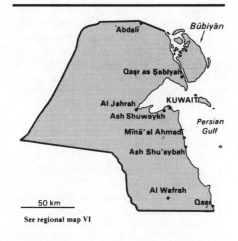

50 km

See regional map VI

Geography

Total area: 17,820 km²; land area: 17,820 km²

Comparative area: slightly smaller than New Jersey

Land boundaries: 462 km total; Iraq 240 km, Saudi Arabia 222 km

Coastline: 499 km

Maritime claims:
  Continental shelf: not specific
  Territorial sea: 12 nm

Disputes: ownership of Warbah and Būbiyān islands disputed by Iraq; ownership of Qaruh and Umm al Maradim Islands disputed by Saudi Arabia

Climate: dry desert; intensely hot summers; short, cool winters

Terrain: flat to slightly undulating desert plain

Natural resources: petroleum, fish, shrimp, natural gas

Land use: NEGL% arable land; 0% permanent crops; 8% meadows and pastures; NEGL% forest and woodland; 92% other; includes NEGL% irrigated

Environment: some of world's largest and most sophisticated desalination facilities provide most of water; air and water pollution; desertification

Note: strategic location at head of Persian Gulf

People

Population: 2,123,711 (July 1990), growth rate 3.8% (1990)

Birth rate: 29 births/1,000 population (1990)

Death rate: 2 deaths/1,000 population (1990)

Net migration rate: 11 migrants/1,000 population (1990)

Infant mortality rate: 15 deaths/1,000 live births (1990)

Life expectancy at birth: 72 years male, 76 years female (1990)

Total fertility rate: 3.7 children born/ woman (1990)

Nationality: noun—Kuwaiti(s); adjective— Kuwaiti

Ethnic divisions: 27.9% Kuwaiti, 39% other Arab, 9% South Asian, 4% Iranian, 20.1% other

Religion: 85% Muslim (30% Shi'a, 45% Sunni, 10% other), 15% Christian, Hindu, Parsi, and other

Language: Arabic (official); English widely spoken

Literacy: 71% (est.)

Labor force: 566,000 (1986); 45.0% services, 20.0% construction, 12.0% trade, 8.6% manufacturing, 2.6% finance and real estate, 1.9% agriculture, 1.7% power and water, 1.4% mining and quarrying; 70% of labor force is non-Kuwaiti

Organized labor: labor unions exist in oil industry and among government personnel

Government

Long-form name: State of Kuwait

Type: nominal constitutional monarchy

Capital: Kuwait

Administrative divisions: 4 governorates (muḥāfaẓat, singular—muḥāfaẓah); Al Aḥmadī, Al Jahrah, Al Kuwayt, Ḥawallī; note—there may be a new governorate of Farwaniyyah

Independence: 19 June 1961 (from UK)

Constitution: 16 November 1962 (some provisions suspended since 29 August 1962)

Legal system: civil law system with Islamic law significant in personal matters; has not accepted compulsory ICJ jurisdiction

National holiday: National Day, 25 February

Executive branch: amir, prime minister, deputy prime minister, Council of Ministers (cabinet)

Legislative branch: National Assembly (Majlis al 'Umma) dissolved 3 July 1986

Judicial branch: High Court of Appeal

Leaders: *Chief of State*—Amir Sheikh Jabir al-Ahmad al-Jabir Al SABAH (since 31 December 1977);

Head of Government—Prime Minister and Crown Prince Sa'd Abdallah al-Salim Al SABAH (since 8 February 1978)

Political parties and leaders: none

Suffrage: adult males who resided in Kuwait before 1920 and their male descendants at age 21; note—out of all citizens, only 8.3% are eligible to vote and only 3.5% actually vote

Elections: *National Assembly*—dissolved 3 July 1986 and no elections are planned

Communists: insignificant

Other political or pressure groups: large (350,000) Palestinian community; several

small, clandestine leftist and Shi'a funda-
mentalist groups are active
Member of: Arab League, FAO, G-77,
GATT, GCC, IAEA, IBRD, ICAO, IDA,
IDB—Islamic Development Bank, IFAD,
IFC, ILO, IMF, IMO, INTELSAT,
INTERPOL, IPU, ITU, NAM, OAPEC,
OIC, OPEC, UN, UNESCO, UPU,
WFTU, WHO, WMO, WTO
Diplomatic representation: Ambassador
Shaikh Saud Nasir AL-SABAH; Chan-
cery at 2940 Tilden Street NW, Washing-
ton DC 20008; telephone (202) 966-0702;
US—Ambassador W. Nathaniel
HOWELL; Embassy at Bneid al-Gar (op-
posite the Hilton Hotel), Kuwait City
(mailing address is P. O. Box 77 Safat,
13001 Safat, Kuwait City); telephone
[965] 242-4151 through 4159
Flag: three equal horizontal bands of
green (top), white, and red with a black
trapezoid based on the hoist side

Economy

Overview: The oil sector dominates the
economy. Of the countries in the Middle
East, Kuwait has oil reserves second only
to those of Saudi Arabia. Earnings from
hydrocarbons generate over 90% of both
export and government revenues and contribute about 40% to GDP. Most of the
nonoil sector is dependent upon oil-derived
government revenues to provide
infrastructure development and to promote limited industrial diversification. The
economy is heavily dependent upon foreign labor—Kuwaitis account for less
than 20% of the labor force. The early
years of the Iran-Iraq war pushed Kuwait's GDP well below its 1980 peak;
however, during the period 1986-88, GDP
increased each year, rising to 5% in 1988.
GDP: $20.5 billion, per capita $10,500;
real growth rate 5.0% (1988)
Inflation rate (consumer prices): 1.5%
(1988)
Unemployment rate: 0%
Budget: revenues $7.1 billion; expenditures
$10.5 billion, including capital expendi-
tures of $3.1 billion (FY88)
Exports: $7.1 billion (f.o.b., 1988); *com-
modities*—oil 90%; *partners*—Japan, Italy, FRG, US
Imports: $5.2 billion (f.o.b., 1988); *com-
modities*—food, construction material,
vehicles and parts, clothing; *partners*—
Japan, US, FRG, UK
External debt: $7.2 billion (December
1989 est.)
Industrial production: growth rate 3%
(1988)
Electricity: 8,287,000 kW capacity;
21,500 million kWh produced, 10,710
kWh per capita (1989)

Industries: petroleum, petrochemicals, desalination, food processing, salt, construction
Agriculture: virtually none; dependent on
imports for food; about 75% of potable
water must be distilled or imported
Aid: donor—pledged $18.3 billion in bilat-
eral aid to less developed countries (1979-
89)
Currency: Kuwaiti dinar (plural—dinars);
1 Kuwaiti dinar (KD) = 1,000 fils
Exchange rates: Kuwaiti dinars (KD) per
US$1—0.2915 (January 1990), 0.2937
(1989), 0.2790 (1988), 0.2786 (1987),
0.2919 (1986), 0.3007 (1985)
Fiscal year: 1 July-30 June

Communications

Highways: 3,000 km total; 2,500 km bitu-
minous; 500 km earth, sand, light gravel
Pipelines: crude oil, 877 km; refined products, 40 km; natural gas, 165 km
Ports: Ash Shuwaykh, Ash Shuaybah,
Mina al Ahmadi
Merchant marine: 51 ships (1,000 GRT or
over), totaling 1,862,010 GRT/2,935,007
DWT; includes 18 cargo, 5 container, 5
livestock carrier, 18 petroleum, oils, and
lubricants (POL) tanker, 5 liquefied gas
Civil air: 19 major transport aircraft
Airports: 8 total, 4 usable; 4 with
permanent-surface runways; none with
runways over 3,659 m; 4 with runways
2,440-3,659 m; none with runways 1,220-
2,439 m
Telecommunications: excellent international, adequate domestic facilities;
258,000 telephones; stations—3 AM, 2
FM, 3 TV; satellite earth stations—1 Indian Ocean INTELSAT, and 2 Atlantic
Ocean INTELSAT; 1 INMARSAT, 1
ARABSAT; coaxial cable and radio relay
to Iraq and Saudi Arabia

Defense Forces

Branches: Army, Navy, Air Force, National Police Force, National Guard
Military manpower: males 15-49, about
688,516; about 411,742 fit for military
service; 18,836 reach military age (18) annually
Defense expenditures: 5.8% of GDP, or
$1.2 billion (FY89)

Laos

See regional map IX

Geography

Total area: 236,800 km²; land area:
230,800 km²
Comparative area: slightly larger than
Utah
Land boundaries: 5,083 km total; Burma
235 km, Cambodia 541 km, China 423
km, Thailand 1,754 km, Vietnam 2,130
km
Coastline: none—landlocked
Maritime claims: none—landlocked
Disputes: boundary dispute with Thailand
Climate: tropical monsoon; rainy season
(May to November); dry season
(December to April)
Terrain: mostly rugged mountains; some
plains and plateaus
Natural resources: timber, hydropower,
gypsum, tin, gold, gemstones
Land use: 4% arable land; NEGL% per-
manent crops; 3% meadows and pastures;
58% forest and woodland; 35% other; in-
cludes 1% irrigated
Environment: deforestation; soil erosion;
subject to floods
Note: landlocked

People

Population: 4,023,726 (July 1990), growth
rate 2.2% (1990)
Birth rate: 37 births/1,000 population
(1990)
Death rate: 15 deaths/1,000 population
(1990)
Net migration rate: 0 migrants/1,000 pop-
ulation (1990)
Infant mortality rate: 126 deaths/1,000
live births (1990)
Life expectancy at birth: 48 years male,
51 years female (1990)
Total fertility rate: 5.1 children born/
woman (1990)
Nationality: noun—Lao (sing., Lao or
Laotian); adjective—Lao or Laotian

Laos (continued)

Ethnic divisions: 50% Lao, 15% Phoutheung (Kha), 20% tribal Thai, 15% Meo, Hmong, Yao, and other
Religion: 85% Buddhist, 15% animist and other
Language: Lao (official), French, and English
Literacy: 85%
Labor force: 1-1.5 million; 85-90% in agriculture (est.)
Organized labor: Lao Federation of Trade Unions is subordinate to the Communist party

Government

Long-form name: Lao People's Democratic Republic
Type: Communist state
Capital: Vientiane
Administrative divisions: 16 provinces (khouèng, singular and plural) and 1 municipality* (kampheng nakhon, singular and plural); Attapu, Bokeo, Bolikhamsai, Champasak, Houaphan, Khammouan, Louang Namtha, Louangphrabang, Oudômxai, Phôngsali, Saravan, Savannakhét, Sekong, Vientiane, Vientiane*, Xaignabouri, Xiangkhoang
Independence: 19 July 1949 (from France)
Constitution: draft constitution under discussion since 1976
Legal system: based on civil law system; has not accepted compulsory ICJ jurisdiction
National holiday: National Day (proclamation of the Lao People's Democratic Republic), 2 December (1975)
Executive branch: president, chairman and five vice chairmen of the Council of Ministers, Council of Ministers (cabinet)
Legislative branch: Supreme People's Assembly
Judicial branch: Central Supreme Court
Leaders: *Chief of State*—Acting President PHOUMI VONGVICHIT (since 29 October 1986);
Head of Government—Chairman of the Council of Ministers General KAYSONE PHOMVIHAN (since 2 December 1975)
Political parties and leaders: Lao People's Revolutionary Party (LPRP), Kaysone Phomvihan, party chairman; includes Lao Patriotic Front and Alliance Committee of Patriotic Neutralist Forces; other parties moribund
Suffrage: universal at age 18
Elections: *Supreme People's Assembly*— last held on 26 March 1989 (next to be held NA); results—percent of vote by party NA; seats—(79 total) number of seats by party NA
Other political or pressure groups: non-Communist political groups moribund; most leaders have fled the country

Member of: ADB, Colombo Plan, ESCAP, FAO, G-77, IBRD, ICAO, IDA, IFAD, ILO, IMF, INTERPOL, IPU, IRC, ITU, Mekong Committee, NAM, UN, UNCTAD, UNESCO, UPU, WFTU, WHO, WMO, WTO
Diplomatic representation: First Secretary, Chargé d'Affaires ad interim DONE SOMVORACHIT; Chancery at 2222 S Street NW, Washington DC 20008; telephone (202) 332-6416 or 6417; *US*— Chargé d'Affaires Charles B. SALMON; Embassy at Rue Bartholonie, Vientiane (mailing address is B. P. 114, Vientiane, or Box V, APO San Francisco 96346); telephone 2220, 2357, 2384
Flag: three horizontal bands of red (top), blue (double width), and red with a large white disk centered in the blue band

Economy

Overview: One of the world's poorest nations, Laos has had a Communist centrally planned economy with government ownership and control of productive enterprises of any size. Recently, however, the government has been decentralizing control and encouraging private enterprise. Laos is a landlocked country with a primitive infrastructure, that is, it has no railroads, a rudimentary road system, limited external and internal telecommunications, and electricity available in only a limited area. Subsistence agriculture is the main occupation, accounting for over 60% of GDP and providing about 85-90% of total employment. The predominant crop is rice. For the foreseeable future the economy will continue to depend for its survival on foreign aid—from CEMA, IMF, and other international sources.
GDP: $585 million, per capita $150; real growth rate 3% (1989 est.)
Inflation rate (consumer prices): 35% (1989 est.)
Unemployment rate: 15% (1989 est.)
Budget: revenues $71 million; expenditures $198 million, including capital expenditures of $132 million (1988 est.)
Exports: $57.5 million (f.o.b., 1989 est.); *commodities*— electricity, wood products, coffee, tin; *partners*—Thailand, Malaysia, Vietnam, USSR, US
Imports: $219 million (c.i.f., 1989 est.); *commodities*—food, fuel oil, consumer goods, manufactures; *partners*—Thailand, USSR, Japan, France, Vietnam
External debt: $964 million (1989 est.)
Industrial production: growth rate 8% (1989 est.)
Electricity: 176,000 kW capacity; 900 million kWh produced, 225 kWh per capita (1989)
Industries: tin mining, timber, electric power, agricultural processing

Agriculture: accounts for 60% of GDP and employs most of the work force; subsistence farming predominates; normally self-sufficient; principal crops—rice (80% of cultivated land), potatoes, vegetables, coffee, sugarcane, cotton
Illicit drugs: illicit producer of cannabis and opium poppy for the international drug trade; production of cannabis increased in 1989; marijuana and heroin are shipped to Western countries, including the US
Aid: US commitments, including Ex-Im (FY70-79), $276 million; Western (non-US) countries, ODA and OOF bilateral commitments (1970-87), $468 million; Communist countries (1970-88), $895 million
Currency: new kip (plural—kips); 1 new kip (NK) = 100 at
Exchange rates: new kips (NK) per US$1—700 (December 1989), 725 (1989), 350 (1988), 200 (1987), 108 (1986), 95 (1985)
Fiscal year: 1 July-30 June

Communications

Highways: about 27,527 km total; 1,856 km bituminous or bituminous treated; 7,451 km gravel, crushed stone, or improved earth; 18,220 km unimproved earth and often impassable during rainy season mid-May to mid-September
Inland waterways: about 4,587 km, primarily Mekong and tributaries; 2,897 additional kilometers are sectionally navigable by craft drawing less than 0.5 m
Pipelines: 136 km, refined products
Ports: none
Airports: 64 total, 50 usable; 9 with permanent-surface runways; none with runways over 3,659 m; 2 with runways 2,440-3,659 m; 12 with runways 1,220-2,439 m
Telecommunications: service to general public considered poor; radio network provides generally erratic service to government users; 7,390 telephones (1986); stations—10 AM, no FM, 1 TV; 1 satellite earth station

Defense Forces

Branches: Lao People's Army (LPA, which consists of an army with naval, aviation, and militia elements), Air Force, National Police Department
Military manpower: males 15-49, 967,047; 517,666 fit for military service; 44,176 reach military age (18) annually; conscription age NA
Defense expenditures: 3.8% of GDP (1987)

Lebanon

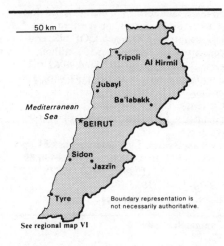

50 km

Mediterranean
Sea

Tripoli
Al Hirmil
Jubayl
Ba'labakk
*BEIRUT
Sidon
Jazzin
Tyre

Boundary representation is
not necessarily authoritative.

See regional map VI

Geography

Total area: 10,400 km²; land area: 10,230
km²
Comparative area: about 0.8 times the size
of Connecticut
Land boundaries: 454 km total; Israel 79
km, Syria 375 km
Coastline: 225 km
Maritime claim:
Territorial sea: 12 nm
Disputes: separated from Israel by the
1949 Armistice Line; Israeli troops in
southern Lebanon since June 1982; Syrian
troops in northern Lebanon since October
1976
Climate: Mediterranean; mild to cool, wet
winters with hot, dry summers
Terrain: narrow coastal plain; Al Biqā'
separates Lebanon and Anti-Lebanon
Mountains
Natural resources: limestone, iron ore,
salt; water-surplus state in a water-deficit
region
Land use: 21% arable land; 9% permanent
crops; 1% meadows and pastures; 8% forest and woodland; 61% other; includes 7%
irrigated
Environment: rugged terrain historically
helped isolate, protect, and develop numerous factional groups based on religion,
clan, ethnicity; deforestation; soil erosion;
air and water pollution; desertification
Note: Nahr al Līṭānī only major river in
Near East not crossing an international
boundary

People

Population: 3,339,331 (July 1990), growth
rate 1.3% (1990)
Birth rate: 28 births/1,000 population
(1990)
Death rate: 7 deaths/1,000 population
(1990)
Net migration rate: −8 migrants/1,000
population (1990)

Infant mortality rate: 49 deaths/1,000 live
births (1990)
Life expectancy at birth: 66 years male,
70 years female (1990)
Total fertility rate: 3.7 children born/
woman (1990)
Nationality: noun—Lebanese (sing., pl.);
adjective—Lebanese
Ethnic divisions: 93% Arab, 6% Armenian,
1% other
Religion: 75% Islam, 25% Christian,
NEGL% Judaism; 17 legally recognized
sects—4 Orthodox Christian (Armenian
Orthodox, Greek Orthodox, Nestorean,
Syriac Orthodox), 7 Uniate Christian (Armenian Catholic, Caldean, Greek Catholic, Maronite, Protestant, Roman Catholic, Syrian Catholic), 5 Islam (Alawite or
Nusayri, Druze, Isma'ilite, Shi'a, Sunni),
and 1 Jewish
Language: Arabic and French (both official); Armenian, English
Literacy: 75%
Labor force: 650,000; 79% industry, commerce, and services, 11% agriculture, 10%
goverment (1985)
Organized labor: 250,000 members (est.)

Government

Note: Between early 1975 and late 1976
Lebanon was torn by civil war between its
Christians—then aided by Syrian troops—
and its Muslims and their Palestinian al-
lies. The cease-fire established in October
1976 between the domestic political
groups generally held for about six years,
despite occasional fighting. Syrian troops
constituted as the Arab Deterrent Force
by the Arab League have remained in
Lebanon. Syria's move toward supporting
the Lebanese Muslims and the Palestinians and Israel's growing support for Lebanese Christians brought the two sides
into rough equilibrium, but no progress
was made toward national reconciliation
or political reforms—the original cause of
the war.
Continuing Israeli concern about the Palestinian presence in Lebanon led to the
Israeli invasion of Lebanon in June 1982.
Israeli forces occupied all of the southern
portion of the country and mounted a
summer-long siege of Beirut, which resulted in the evacuation of the PLO from
Beirut in September under the supervision
of a multinational force (MNF) made up
of US, French, and Italian troops.
Within days of the departure of the
MNF, Lebanon's newly elected president,
Bashir Gemayel, was assassinated. In the
wake of his death, Christian militiamen
massacred hundreds of Palestinian refugees in two Beirut camps. This prompted
the return of the MNF to ease the security burden on Lebanon's weak Army and

security forces. In late March 1984 the
last MNF units withdrew.
Lebanese Parliamentarians met in Ta'if,
Saudi Arabia in late 1989 and concluded
a national reconciliation pact that codified
a new power-sharing formula, specifiying
a Christian president but giving Muslims
more authority. Rene Muawad was subsequently elected president on 4 November
1989, ending a 13-month period during
which Lebanon had no president and rival
Muslim and Christian governments. Muawad was assassinated 17 days later, on 22
November; on 24 November Elias Harawi
was elected to succeed Muawad.
Progress toward lasting political compro-
mise in Lebanon has been stalled by opposition from Christian strongman Gen. Michel 'Awn. 'Awn—appointed acting Prime
Minister by outgoing president Amin Gemayel in September 1988—called the national reconciliation accord illegitimate
and has refused to recognize the new Lebanese Government.
Lebanon continues to be partially occupied by Syrian troops. Syria augmented
its troop presence during the weeks following Muawad's assassination. Troops are
deployed in West Beirut and its southern
suburbs, in Al Biqā', and in northern Lebanon. Iran also maintains a small contingent of revolutionary guards in Al Biqā',
from which it supports Lebanese Islamic
fundamentalist groups.
Israel withdrew the bulk of its forces from
the south in 1985, although it still retains
troops in a 10-km-deep security zone
north of its border with Lebanon. Israel
arms and trains the Army of South Lebanon (ASL), which also occupies the security zone and is Israel's first line of defense against attacks on its northern
border.
The following description is based on the
present constitutional and customary practices of the Lebanese system.
Long-form name: Republic of Lebanon;
note—may be changed to Lebanese Republic
Type: republic
Capital: Beirut
Administrative divisions: 5 governorates
(muḥāfaẓat, singular—muḥāfaẓah); Al
Biqā', Al Janūb, Ash Shamāl, Bayrūt,
Jabal Lubnān
Independence: 22 November 1943 (from
League of Nations mandate under French
administration)
Constitution: 26 May 1926 (amended)
Legal system: mixture of Ottoman law,
canon law, Napoleonic code, and civil law;
no judicial review of legislative acts; has
not accepted compulsory ICJ jurisdiction
National holiday: Independence Day, 22
November (1943)

Lebanon (continued)

Executive branch: president, prime minister, Cabinet; note—by custom, the president is a Maronite Christian, the prime minister is a Sunni Muslim, and the president of the legislature is a Shi'a Muslim
Legislative branch: unicameral National Assembly (Arabic—Majlis Alnuwab, French—Assemblée Nationale)
Judicial branch: four Courts of Cassation (three courts for civil and commercial cases and one court for criminal cases)
Leaders: *Chief of State*—Elias HARAWI (since 24 November 1989);
Head of Government—Prime Minister Salim AL-HUSS (since 24 November 1989)
Political parties and leaders: political party activity is organized along largely sectarian lines; numerous political groupings exist, consisting of individual political figures and followers motivated by religious, clan, and economic considerations; most parties have well-armed militias, which are still involved in occasional clashes
Suffrage: compulsory for all males at age 21; authorized for women at age 21 with elementary education
Elections: *National Assembly*—elections should be held every four years but security conditions have prevented elections since May 1972
Communists: the Lebanese Communist Party was legalized in 1970; members and sympathizers estimated at 2,000-3,000
Member of: Arab League, CCC, FAO, G-77, IAEA, IBRD, ICAO, IDA, IDB—Islamic Development Bank, IFAD, IFC, ILO, IMF, IMO, INTELSAT, INTERPOL, IPU, ITU, IWC—International Wheat Council, NAM, OIC, UN, UNESCO, UPU, WFTU, WHO, WMO, WSG, WTO
Diplomatic representation: Ambassador (vacant); Chargé d'Affaires Suleiman RASSI; note—the former Lebanese Ambassador, Dr. Abdallah Bouhabib, is loyal to Gen. 'Awn and has refused to abandon his residence or relinquish his post; Chancery at 2560 28th Street NW, Washington DC 20008; telephone (202) 939-6300; there are Lebanese Consulates General in Detroit, New York, and Los Angeles;
US—Ambassador John T. MCCARTHY; Embassy at Avenue de Paris, Beirut (mailing address is P. O. Box 70-840, Beirut); telephone [961] 417774 or 415802, 415803, 402200, 403300
Flag: three horizontal bands of red (top), white (double width), and red with a green and brown cedar tree centered in the white band

Economy

Overview: Severe factional infighting in 1989 has been destroying physical property, interrupting the established pattern of economic affairs, and practically ending chances of restoring Lebanon's position as a Middle Eastern entrepôt and banking hub. The ordinary Lebanese citizen struggles to keep afloat in an environment of physical danger, high unemployment, and growing shortages. The central government's ability to collect taxes has suffered greatly from militia control and taxation of local areas. As the civil strife persists, the US dollar has become more and more the medium of exchange. Transportation, communications, and other parts of the infrastructure continue to deteriorate. Family remittances, foreign political money going to the factions, international emergency aid, and a small volume of manufactured exports help prop up the battered economy. Prospects for 1990 are grim, with expected further declines in economic activity and living standards.
GDP: $2.3 billion, per capita $700; real growth rate NA% (1989 est.)
Inflation rate (consumer prices): 60% (1989 est.)
Unemployment rate: 33% (1987 est.)
Budget: revenues $50 million; expenditures $650 million, including capital expenditures of $NA (1988 est.)
Exports: $1.0 billion (f.o.b., 1987); *commodities*—agricultural products, chemicals, textiles, precious and semiprecious metals and jewelry, metals and metal products; *partners*—Saudi Arabia 16%, Switzerland 8%, Jordan 6%, Kuwait 6%, US 5%
Imports: $1.5 billion (c.i.f., 1987); *commodities*—NA; *partners*—Italy 14%, France 12%, US 6%, Turkey 5%, Saudi Arabia 3%
External debt: $935 million (December 1988)
Industrial production: growth rate NA%
Electricity: 1,381,000 kW capacity; 3,870 million kWh produced, 1,170 kWh per capita (1989)
Industries: banking, food processing, textiles, cement, oil refining, chemicals, jewelry, some metal fabricating
Agriculture: accounts for about one-third of GDP; principal products—citrus fruits, vegetables, potatoes, olives, tobacco, hemp (hashish), sheep, and goats; not self-sufficient in grain
Illicit drugs: illicit producer of opium poppy and cannabis for the international drug trade; opium poppy production in Al Biqā' is increasing; most hashish production is shipped to Western Europe

Aid: US commitments, including Ex-Im (FY70-88), $356 million; Western (non-US) countries, ODA and OOF bilateral commitments (1970-87), $509 million; OPEC bilateral aid (1979-89), $962 million; Communist countries (1970-86), $9 million
Currency: Lebanese pound (plural—pounds); 1 Lebanese pound (£L) = 100 piasters
Exchange rates: Lebanese pounds (£L) per US$1—474.21 (December 1989), 496.69 (1989), 409.23 (1988), 224.60 (1987), 38.37 (1986), 16.42 (1985)
Fiscal year: calendar year

Communications

Railroads: 378 km total; 296 km 1.435-meter standard gauge, 82 km 1.050-meter gauge; all single track; system almost entirely inoperable
Highways: 7,370 km total; 6,270 km paved, 450 km gravel and crushed stone, 650 km improved earth
Pipelines: crude oil, 72 km (none in operation)
Ports: Beirut, Tripoli, Ra's Sil'ātā, Jūniyah, Sidon, Az Zahrānī, Tyre, Shikkā (none are under the direct control of the Lebanese Government); northern ports are occupied by Syrian forces and southern ports are occupied or partially quarantined by Israeli forces; illegal ports scattered along the central coast are owned and operated by various Christian, Druze, and Shi'a militias
Merchant marine: 67 ships (1,000 GRT or over) totaling 325,361 GRT/494,319 DWT; includes 43 cargo, 1 refrigerated cargo, 2 vehicle carrier, 2 roll-on/roll-off cargo, 2 container, 7 livestock carrier, 1 petroleum, oils, and lubricants (POL) tanker, 1 chemical tanker, 1 specialized tanker, 6 bulk, 1 combination tanker
Civil air: 15 major transport aircraft
Airports: 9 total, 8 usable; 5 with permanent-surface runways; none with runways over 3,659 m; 3 with runways 2,440-3,659 m; 2 with runways 1,220-2,439 m; none under the direct control of the Lebanese Government
Telecommunications: rebuilding program disrupted; had fair system of radio relay, cable; 325,000 telephones; stations—5 AM, 3 FM, 15 TV; 1 inactive Indian Ocean INTELSAT satellite earth station; 3 submarine coaxial cables; radio relay to Jordan and Syria, inoperable

Lesotho

Defense Forces

Branches: Army, Navy, Air Force
Military manpower: males 15-49, 702,961; 434,591 fit for military service; about 44,625 reach military age (18) yearly
Defense expenditures: NA

50 km

Leribe

Mokhotlong

*MASERU

Thaba Tseka

Mafeteng

Qachas Nek

Mohales Hoek

Quthing

See regional map VII

Geography

Total area: 30,350 km²; land area: 30,350 km² **Comparative area:** slightly larger than Maryland
Land boundary: 909 km with South Africa
Coastline: none—landlocked
Maritime claims: none—landlocked
Climate: temperate; cool to cold, dry winters; hot, wet summers
Terrain: mostly highland with some plateaus, hills, and mountains
Natural resources: some diamonds and other minerals, water, agricultural and grazing land
Land use: 10% arable land; 0% permanent crops; 66% meadows and pastures; 0% forest and woodland; 24% other
Environment: population pressure forcing settlement in marginal areas results in overgrazing, severe soil erosion, soil exhaustion; desertification
Note: surrounded by South Africa; Highlands Water Project will control, store, and redirect water to South Africa

People

Population: 1,754,664 (July 1990), growth rate 2.6% (1990)
Birth rate: 37 births/1,000 population (1990)
Death rate: 10 deaths/1,000 population (1990)
Net migration rate: 0 migrants/1,000 population (1990)
Infant mortality rate: 80 deaths/1,000 live births (1990)
Life expectancy at birth: 59 years male, 62 years female (1990)
Total fertility rate: 4.9 children born/woman (1990)
Nationality: noun—Mosotho (sing.), Basotho (pl.); adjective—Basotho
Ethnic divisions: 99.7% Sotho; 1,600 Europeans, 800 Asians

Religion: 80% Christian, rest indigenous beliefs
Language: Sesotho (southern Sotho) and English (official); also Zulu and Xhosa
Literacy: 59% (1989)
Labor force: 689,000 economically active; 86.2% of resident population engaged in subsistence agriculture; roughly 60% of active male labor force works in South Africa
Organized labor: there are two trade union federations; the government favors formation of a single, umbrella trade union confederation

Government

Long-form name: Kingdom of Lesotho
Type: constitutional monarchy
Capital: Maseru
Administrative divisions: 10 districts; Berea, Butha-Buthe, Leribe, Mafeteng, Maseru, Mohales Hoek, Mokhotlong, Qachas Nek, Quthing, Thaba-Tseka
Independence: 4 October 1966 (from UK; formerly Basutoland)
Constitution: 4 October 1966, suspended January 1970
Legal system: based on English common law and Roman-Dutch law; judicial review of legislative acts in High Court and Court of Appeal; has not accepted compulsory ICJ jurisdiction
National holiday: Independence Day, 4 October (1966)
Executive branch: monarch, chairman of the Military Council, Military Council, Council of Ministers (cabinet)
Legislative branch: a bicameral Parliament consisting of an upper house or Senate and a lower house or National Assembly was dissolved in January 1970; following the military coup of 20 January 1986, legislative powers were vested in the monarch
Judicial branch: High Court, Court of Appeal
Leaders: *Chief of State*—King MOSHOESHOE II (Paramount Chief from 1960 until independence on 4 October 1966, when he became King); Heir Apparent Letsie David SEEISO (son of the King);
Head of Government—Chairman of the Military Council Maj. Gen. Justin Metsing LEKHANYA (since 24 January 1986)
Political parties and leaders: Basotho National Party (BNP), position vacant; Basutoland Congress Party (BCP), Ntsu Mokhehle; Basotho Democratic Alliance (BDA), A. S. Nqojane; National Independent Party (NIP), A. C. Manyeli; Marematlou Freedom Party (MFP), S. H. Mapheleba; United Democratic Party, C. D. Mofeli

Suffrage: universal at age 21
Elections: *National Assembly* —dissolved following the military coup in January 1986; no date set for national elections
Communists: small Lesotho Communist Party
Member of: ACP, AfDB, CCC, Commonwealth, FAO, G-77, GATT (de facto), IBRD, ICAO, IDA, IFAD, IFC, ILO, IMF, INTERPOL, ITU, NAM, OAU, Southern African Customs Union, SADCC, UN, UNESCO, UPU, WHO, WMO
Diplomatic representation: Ambassador W. T. VAN TONDER; Chancery at 2511 Massachusetts Avenue NW, Washington DC 20008; telephone (202) 797-5 534; *US*—Ambassador (vacant): Deputy Chief of Mission Howard F. JETER; Embassy at address NA, Maseru (mailing address is P. O. Box 333, Maseru 100); telephone [266] 312666
Flag: divided diagonally from the lower hoist side corner; the upper half is white bearing the brown silhouette of a large shield with crossed spear and club; the lower half is a diagonal blue band with a green triangle in the corner

Economy

Overview: Small, landlocked, and mountainous, Lesotho has no important natural resources other than water. Its economy is based on agriculture, light manufacturing, and remittances from laborers employed in South Africa. Subsistence farming is the principal occupation for about 86% of the domestic labor force and accounts for about 20% of GDP. Manufacturing depends largely on farm products to support the milling, canning, leather, and jute industries; other industries include textile, clothing, and light engineering. Industry's share of total GDP rose from 6% in 1982 to 10.5% in 1987. During the period 1985-87 real GDP growth averaged 2.9% per year, only slightly above the population growth rate. In FY89 per capita GDP was only $245 and nearly 25% of the labor force was unemployed.
GDP: $412 million, per capita $245; real growth rate 8.2% (FY89 est.)
Inflation rate (consumer prices): 15.0% (FY89 est.)
Unemployment rate: 23% (1988)

Budget: revenues $159 million; expenditures $224 million, including capital expenditures of $68 million (FY89 est.)
Exports: $55 million (f.o.b., FY89 est.); *commodities*—wool, mohair, wheat, cattle, peas, beans, corn, hides, skins, baskets; *partners*—South Africa 87%, EC 10%, (1985)
Imports: $526 million (f.o.b., FY89 est.); *commodities*—mainly corn, building materials, clothing, vehicles, machinery, medicines, petroleum, oil, and lubricants; *partners*—South Africa 95%, EC 2% (1985)
External debt: $235 million (December 1988)
Industrial production: growth rate 10.3% (1988 est.)
Electricity: power supplied by South Africa
Industries: tourism
Agriculture: exceedingly primitive, mostly subsistence farming and livestock; principal crops are corn, wheat, pulses, sorghum, barley
Aid: US commitments, including Ex-Im (FY70-88), $252 million; Western (non-US) countries, ODA and OOF bilateral commitments (1970-87), $714 million; OPEC bilateral aid (1979-89), $4 million; Communist countries (1970-88), $14 million
Currency: loti (plural—maloti); 1 loti (L) = 100 lisente
Exchange rates: maloti (M) per US$1— 2.5555 (January 1990), 2.6166 (1989), 2.2611 (1988), 2.0350 (1987), 2.2685 (1986), 2.1911 (1985); note—the Basotho loti is at par with the South African rand
Fiscal year: 1 April-31 March

Communications

Railroads: 1.6 km; owned, operated, and included in the statistics of South Africa
Highways: 5,167 km total; 508 km paved; 1,585 km crushed stone, gravel, or stabilized soil; 946 km improved earth, 2,128 km unimproved earth
Civil air: 2 major transport aircraft
Airports: 28 total, 28 usable; 2 with permanent surface runways; none with runways over 3,659 m; 1 with runways 2,440-3,659 m; 2 with runways 1,220-2,439 m
Telecommunications: modest system consisting of a few land lines, a small radio relay system, and minor radiocommunication stations; 5,920 telephones; stations—2 AM, 2 FM, 1 TV; 1 Atlantic Ocean INTELSAT earth station

Defense Forces

Branches: Army, Air Wing, Police Department
Military manpower: males 15-49, 381,015; 205,499 fit for military service
Defense expenditures: 8.6% of GDP, or $35 million (1989 est.)

Liberia

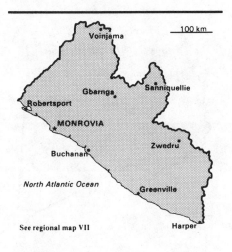

Monrovia
Voinjama
Gbarnga
Sanniquellie
Robertsport
Buchanan
Zwedru
Greenville
Harper
North Atlantic Ocean
See regional map VII
100 km

Geography

Total area: 111,370 km²; land area: 96,320 km²
Comparative area: slightly larger than Tennessee
Land boundaries: 1,585 km total; Guinea 563 km, Ivory Coast 716 km, Sierra Leone 306 km
Coastline: 579 km
Maritime claims:
Continental shelf: 200 meters or to depth of exploitation
Territorial sea: 200 nm
Climate: tropical; hot, humid; dry winters with hot days and cool to cold nights; wet, cloudy summers with frequent heavy showers
Terrain: mostly flat to rolling coastal plains rising to rolling plateau and low mountains in northeast
Natural resources: iron ore, timber, diamonds, gold
Land use: 1% arable land; 3% permanent crops; 2% meadows and pastures; 39% forest and woodland; 55% other; includes NEGL% irrigated
Environment: West Africa's largest tropical rain forest, subject to deforestation

People

Population: 2,639,809 (July 1990), growth rate 3.4% (1990)
Birth rate: 45 births/1,000 population (1990)
Death rate: 14 deaths/1,000 population (1990)
Net migration rate: 2 migrants/1,000 population (1990)
Infant mortality rate: 126 deaths/1,000 live births (1990)
Life expectancy at birth: 54 years male, 58 years female (1990)
Total fertility rate: 6.6 children born/woman (1990)

Nationality: noun—Liberian(s); adjective—Liberian
Ethnic divisions: 95% indigenous African tribes, including Kpelle, Bassa, Gio, Kru, Grebo, Mano, Krahn, Gola, Gbandi, Loma, Kissi, Vai, and Bella; 5% descendants of repatriated slaves known as Americo-Liberians
Religion: 70% traditional, 20% Muslim, 10% Christian
Language: English (official); more than 20 local languages of the Niger-Congo language group; English used by about 20%
Literacy: 35%
Labor force: 510,000, including 220,000 in the monetary economy; 70.5% agriculture, 10.8% services, 4.5% industry and commerce, 14.2% other; non-African foreigners hold about 95% of the top-level management and engineering jobs; 52% of population of working age
Organized labor: 2% of labor force

Government

Long-form name: Republic of Liberia
Type: republic
Capital: Monrovia
Administrative divisions: 13 counties; Bomi, Bong, Grand Bassa, Grand Cape Mount, Grand Jide, Grand Kru, Lofa, Margibi, Maryland, Montserrado, Nimba, Rivercess, Sino
Independence: 26 July 1847
Constitution: 6 January 1986
Legal system: dual system of statutory law based on Anglo-American common law for the modern sector and customary law based on unwritten tribal practices for indigenous sector
National holiday: Independence Day, 26 July (1847)
Executive branch: president, vice president, Cabinet
Legislative branch: bicameral National Assembly consists of an upper house or Senate and a lower house or House of Representatives
Judicial branch: People's Supreme Court
Leaders: *Chief of State and Head of Government*—President Gen. Dr. Samuel Kanyon DOE (since 12 April 1980); Vice President Harry F. MONIBA (since 6 January 1986)
Political parties and leaders: National Democratic Party of Liberia (NDPL), Augustus Caine, chairman; Liberian Action Party (LAP), Emmanuel Koromah, chairman; Unity Party (UP), Carlos Smith, chairman; United People's Party (UPP), Gabriel Baccus Matthews, chairman
Suffrage: universal at age 18
Elections: *President*—last held on 15 October 1985 (next to be held October 1991);

results—Samuel Kanyon Doe (NDPL) 50.9%, Jackson Doe (LAP) 26.4%, others 22.7%;
Senate—last held on 15 October 1985 (next to be held 15 October 1991); results—percent of vote by party NA; seats—(26 total) NDPL 21, LAP 3, UP 1, LUP 1;
House of Representatives—last held on 15 October 1985 (next to be held October 1991); results—percent of vote by party NA; seats—(64 total) NDPL 51, LAP 8, UP 3, LUP 2
Member of: ACP, AfDB, CCC, ECA, ECOWAS, FAO, G-77, IAEA, IBRD, ICAO, ICO, IDA, IFAD, IFC, ILO, IMF, IMO, INTERPOL, IPU, IRC, ITU, Mano River Union, NAM, OAU, UN, UNESCO, UPU, WHO, WMO
Diplomatic representation: Ambassador Eugenia A. WORDSWORTH-STEVENSON; Chancery at 5201 16th Street NW, Washington DC 20011; telephone (202) 723-0437 through 0440; there is a Liberian Consulate General in New York; *US*—Ambassador James K. BISHOP; Embassy at 111 United Nations Drive, Monrovia (mailing address is P. O. Box 98, Monrovia, or APO New York 09155); telephone [231] 222991 through 222994
Flag: 11 equal horizontal stripes of red (top and bottom) alternating with white; there is a white five-pointed star on a blue square in the upper hoist-side corner; the design was based on the US flag

Economy

Overview: In 1988 and 1989 the Liberian economy posted its best two years in a decade, thanks to a resurgence of the rubber industry and rapid growth in exports of forest products. Richly endowed with water, mineral resources, forests, and a climate favorable to agriculture, Liberia is a producer and exporter of basic products. Local manufacturing, mainly foreign owned, is small in scope. Liberia imports primarily machinery and parts, transportation equipment, petroleum products, and foodstuffs. Persistent budget deficits, the flight of capital, and deterioration of transport and other infrastructure continue to hold back economic progress.
GDP: $988 million, per capita $395; real growth rate 1.5% (1988)
Inflation rate (consumer prices): 12% (1989)
Unemployment rate: 43% urban (1988)
Budget: revenues $242.1 million; expenditures $435.4 million, including capital expenditures of $29.5 million (1989)

Liberia (continued)

Exports: $550 million (f.o.b., 1989); *commodities*—iron ore 61%, rubber 20%, timber 11%, coffee; *partners*—US, EC, Netherlands

Imports: $335 million (c.i.f., 1989); *commodities*—rice, mineral fuels, chemicals, machinery, transportation equipment, other foodstuffs; *partners*—US, EC, Japan, China, Netherlands, ECOWAS

External debt: $1.7 billion (December 1989 est.)

Industrial production: growth rate 1.5% in manufacturing (1987)

Electricity: 400,000 kW capacity; 730 million kWh produced, 290 kWh per capita (1989)

Industries: rubber processing, food processing, construction materials, furniture, palm oil processing, mining (iron ore, diamonds)

Agriculture: accounts for about 40% of GDP (including fishing and forestry); principal products—rubber, timber, coffee, cocoa, rice, cassava, palm oil, sugarcane, bananas, sheep, and goats; not self-sufficient in food, imports 25% of rice consumption

Aid: US commitments, including Ex-Im (FY70-88), $634 million; Western (non-US) countries, ODA and OOF bilateral commitments (1970-87), $793 million; OPEC bilateral aid (1979-89), $25 million; Communist countries (1970-88), $77 million

Currency: Liberian dollar (plural—dollars); 1 Liberian dollar (L$) = 100 cents

Exchange rates: Liberian dollars (L$) per US$1—1.00 (fixed rate since 1940); unofficial parallel exchange rate of L$2.5 = US$1, January 1989

Fiscal year: calendar year

Communications

Railroads: 480 km total; 328 km 1.435-meter standard gauge, 152 km 1.067-meter narrow gauge; all lines single track; rail systems owned and operated by foreign steel and financial interests in conjunction with Liberian Government

Highways: 10,087 km total; 603 km bituminous treated, 2,848 km all weather, 4,313 km dry weather; there are also 2,323 km of private, laterite-surfaced roads open to public use, owned by rubber and timber companies

Ports: Monrovia, Buchanan, Greenville, Harper (or Cape Palmas)

Merchant marine: 1,379 ships (1,000 GRT or over) totaling 48,655,666 DWT/ 90,005,898 DWT; includes 11 passenger, 148 cargo, 26 refrigerated cargo, 18 roll-on/roll-off cargo, 42 vehicle carrier, 42 container, 4 barge carrier, 436 petroleum, oils, and lubricants (POL) tanker, 100 chemical, 63 combination ore/oil, 41 liquefied gas, 6 specialized tanker, 413 bulk, 2 multifunction large-load carrier, 26 combination bulk; note—a flag of convenience registry; all ships are foreign owned; the top four owning flags are US 17%, Hong Kong 13%, Japan 10%, and Greece 10%; China owns at least 20 ships and Vietnam owns 1

Civil air: 3 major transport aircraft

Airports: 76 total, 60 usable; 2 with permanent-surface runways; none with runways over 3,659 m; 1 with runways 2,440-3,659 m; 4 with runways 1,220-2,439 m

Telecommunications: telephone and telegraph service via radio relay network; main center is Monrovia; 8,500 telephones; stations—3 AM, 4 FM, 5 TV; 2 Atlantic Ocean INTELSAT earth stations

Defense Forces

Branches: Armed Forces of Liberia, Liberia National Coast Guard

Military manpower: males 15-49, 627,519; 335,063 fit for military service; no conscription

Defense expenditures: 2.4% of GDP (1987)

Libya

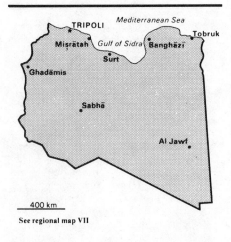

See regional map VII

Geography

Total area: 1,759,540 km²; land area: 1,759,540 km²

Comparative area: slightly larger than Alaska

Land boundaries: 4,383 km total; Algeria 982 km, Chad 1,055 km, Egypt 1,150 km, Niger 354 km, Sudan 383 km, Tunisia 459 km

Coastline: 1,770 km

Maritime claims:
  Territorial sea: 12 nm
  Gulf of Sidra closing line: 32° 30′ N

Disputes: claims and occupies a small portion of the Aozou Strip in northern Chad; maritime boundary dispute with Tunisia; Libya claims about 19,400 km² in northern Niger; Libya claims about 19,400 km² in southeastern Algeria

Climate: Mediterranean along coast; dry, extreme desert interior

Terrain: mostly barren, flat to undulating plains, plateaus, depressions

Natural resources: crude oil, natural gas, gypsum

Land use: 1% arable land; 0% permanent crops; 8% meadows and pastures; 0% forest and woodland; 91% other; includes NEGL% irrigated

Environment: hot, dry, dust-laden ghibli is a southern wind lasting one to four days in spring and fall; desertification; sparse natural surface-water resources

Note: the Great Manmade River Project, the largest water development scheme in the world, is being built to bring water from large aquifers under the Sahara to coastal cities

People

Population: 4,221,141 (July 1990), growth rate 3.1% (1990)

Birth rate: 37 births/1,000 population (1990)

Death rate: 7 deaths/1,000 population (1990)
Net migration rate: 0 migrants/1,000 population (1990)
Infant mortality rate: 64 deaths/1,000 live births (1990)
Life expectancy at birth: 65 years male, 70 years female (1990)
Total fertility rate: 5.2 children born/woman (1990)
Nationality: noun—Libyan(s); adjective—Libyan
Ethnic divisions: 97% Berber and Arab; some Greeks, Maltese, Italians, Egyptians, Pakistanis, Turks, Indians, and Tunisians
Religion: 97% Sunni Muslim
Language: Arabic; Italian and English widely understood in major cities
Literacy: 50-60%
Labor force: 1,000,000; includes about 280,000 resident foreigners; 31% industry, 27% services, 24% government, 18% agriculture
Organized labor: National Trade Unions' Federation, 275,000 members; General Union for Oil and Petrochemicals; Pan-Africa Federation of Petroleum Energy and Allied Workers

Government

Long-form name: Socialist People's Libyan Arab Jamahiriya
Type: Jamahiriya (a state of the masses); in theory, governed by the populace through local councils; in fact, a military dictatorship
Capital: Tripoli
Administrative divisions: 46 municipalities (baladīyat, singular—baladīyah); Ajdābiyā, Al Abyār, Al 'Azīzīyah, Al Bayḍā', Al Jufrah, Al Jumayl, Al Khums, Al Kufrah, Al Marj, Al Qarābūllī, Al Qubbah, Al 'Ujaylāt, Ash Shāṭi', Awbārī, Az Zahrā', Az Zāwiyah, Banghāzī, Banī Walīd, Bin Jawwād, Darnah, Ghadāmis, Gharyān, Ghāt, Jādū, Jālū, Janzūr, Masallātah, Miṣrātah, Mizdah, Murzuq, Nālūt, Qamīnis, Qaṣr Bin Ghashīr, Sabhā, Ṣabrātah, Shaḥḥāt, Ṣurmān, Surt, Tājūrā', Ṭarābulus, Tarhūnah, Ṭubruq, Tūkrah, Yafran, Zlītan, Zuwārah; note—the number of municipalities may have been reduced to 13 named Al Jabal al-Akhdar, Al Jabal al-Gharbi, Al Jabal al-Khums, Al Batnam, Al Kufrah, Al Marqab, Al Marzuq, Az Zāwiyah, Banghāzī, Khalij Surt, Sabhā, Tripoli, Wadi al-Hayat
Independence: 24 December 1951 (from Italy)
Constitution: 11 December 1969, amended 2 March 1977
Legal system: based on Italian civil law system and Islamic law; separate religious courts; no constitutional provision for judicial review of legislative acts; has not accepted compulsory ICJ jurisdiction
National holiday: Revolution Day, 1 September (1969)
Executive branch: revolutionary leader, chairman of the General People's Committee, General People's Committee (cabinet)
Legislative branch: unicameral General People's Congress
Judicial branch: Supreme Court
Leaders: *Chief of State*—Revolutionary Leader Col. Mu'ammar Abu Minyar al-QADHAFI (since 1 September 1969); *Head of Government*—Chairman of the General People's Committee (Premier) 'Umar Mustafa al-MUNTASIR (since 1 March 1987)
Political parties and leaders: none
Suffrage: universal and compulsory at age 18
Elections: national elections are indirect through a hierarchy of revolutionary committees
Flag: plain green; green is the traditional color of Islam (the state religion)

Economy

Overview: The socialist-oriented economy depends primarily upon revenues from the oil sector, which contributes virtually all export earnings and over 50% to GNP. Since 1980, however, the sharp drop in oil prices and resulting decline in export revenues has adversely affected economic development. In 1986 per capita GNP was the highest in Africa at $5,410, but it had been $2,000 higher in 1982. Severe cutbacks in imports over the past five years have led to shortages of basic goods and foodstuffs, although the reopening of the Libyan-Tunisian border in April 1988 and the Libyan-Egyptian border in December 1989 have somewhat eased shortages. Austerity budgets and a lack of trained technicians have undermined the government's ability to implement a number of planned infrastructure development projects. The nonoil industrial and construction sectors, which account for about 15% of GNP, have expanded from processing mostly agricultural products to include petrochemicals, iron, steel, and aluminum. Although agriculture accounts for less than 5% of GNP, it employs 20% of the labor force. Climatic conditions and poor soils severely limit farm output, requiring Libya to import about 75% of its food requirements.
GNP: $20 billion, per capita $5,410; real growth rate 0% (1988 est.)
Inflation rate (consumer prices): 20% (1988 est.)
Unemployment rate: 2% (1988 est.)

Budget: revenues $6.4 billion; expenditures $11.3 billion, including capital expenditures of $3.6 billion (1986 est.)
Exports: $6.1 billion (f.o.b., 1988 est.); *commodities*—petroleum, peanuts, hides; *partners*—Italy, USSR, FRG, Spain, France, Belgium/Luxembourg, Turkey
Imports: $5.0 billion (f.o.b., 1988 est.); *commodities*—machinery, transport equipment, food, manufactured goods; *partners*—Italy, USSR, FRG, UK, Japan
External debt: $2.1 billion, excluding military debt (December 1988)
Industrial production: growth rate NA%
Electricity: 4,580,000 kW capacity; 13,360 million kWh produced, 3,270 kWh per capita (1989)
Industries: petroleum, food processing, textiles, handicrafts, cement
Agriculture: 5% of GNP; cash crops—wheat, barley, olives, dates, citrus fruits, peanuts; 75% of food is imported
Aid: Western (non-US) countries, ODA and OOF bilateral commitments (1970-87), $242 million
Currency: Libyan dinar (plural—dinars); 1 Libyan dinar (LD) = 1,000 dirhams
Exchange rates: Libyan dinars (LD) per US$1—0.2896 (January 1990), 0.2922 (1989), 0.2853 (1988), 0.2706 (1987), 0.3139 (1986), 0.2961 (1985)
Fiscal year: calendar year

Communications

Highways: 32,500 km total; 24,000 km bituminous and bituminous treated, 8,500 km gravel, crushed stone and earth
Pipelines: crude oil 4,383 km; natural gas 1,947 km; refined products 443 km (includes 256 km liquid petroleum gas)
Ports: Tobruk, Tripoli, Banghazi, Misratah, Marsa el Brega
Merchant marine: 30 ships (1,000 GRT or over) totaling 816,546 GRT/1,454,874 DWT; includes 3 short-sea passenger, 11 cargo, 4 roll-on/roll-off cargo, 11 petroleum, oils, and lubricants (POL) tanker, 1 chemical tanker
Civil air: 59 major transport aircraft
Airports: 130 total, 122 usable; 53 with permanent-surface runways; 7 with runways over 3,659 m; 30 with runways 2,440-3,659 m; 44 with runways 1,220-2,439 m
Telecommunications: modern telecommunications system using radio relay, coaxial cable, tropospheric scatter, and domestic satellite stations; 370,000 telephones; stations—18 AM, 3 FM, 13 TV; satellite earth stations— 1 Atlantic Ocean INTELSAT, 1 Indian Ocean INTELSAT, and 14 domestic; submarine cables to France and Italy; radio relay to

Libya (continued)

Tunisia; tropospheric scatter to Greece; planned ARABSAT and Intersputnik satellite stations

Defense Forces

Branches: Armed Forces of the Libyan Arab Jamahariya includes People's Defense (Army), Arab Air Force and Air Defense Command, Arab Navy
Military manpower: males 15-49, 991,368; 584,512 fit for military service; 50,379 reach military age (17) annually; conscription now being implemented
Defense expenditures: 11.1% of GNP (1987)

Liechtenstein

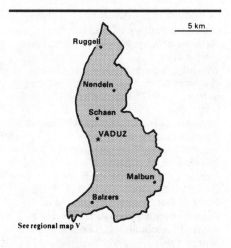

See regional map V

Geography

Total area: 160 km^2; land area: 160 km^2
Comparative area: about 0.9 times the size of Washington, DC
Land boundaries: 78 km total; Austria 37 km, Switzerland 41 km
Coastline: none—landlocked
Maritime claims: none—landlocked
Climate: continental; cold, cloudy winters with frequent snow or rain; cool to moderately warm, cloudy, humid summers
Terrain: mostly mountainous (Alps) with Rhine Valley in western third
Natural resources: hydroelectric potential
Land use: 25% arable land; 0% permanent crops; 38% meadows and pastures; 19% forest and woodland; 18% other
Environment: variety of microclimatic variations based on elevation
Note: landlocked

People

Population: 28,292 (July 1990), growth rate 0.7% (1990)
Birth rate: 13 births/1,000 population (1990)
Death rate: 7 deaths/1,000 population (1990)
Net migration rate: 1 migrant/1,000 population (1990)
Infant mortality rate: 5 deaths/1,000 live births (1990)
Life expectancy at birth: 73 years male, 81 years female (1990)
Total fertility rate: 1.5 children born/woman (1990)
Nationality: noun—Liechtensteiner(s); adjective—Liechtenstein
Ethnic divisions: 95% Alemannic, 5% Italian and other
Religion: 82.7% Roman Catholic, 7.1% Protestant, 10.2% other
Language: German (official), Alemannic dialect
Literacy: 100%

Labor force: 12,258; 5,078 foreign workers (mostly from Switzerland and Austria); 54.4% industry, trade, and building; 41.6% services; 4.0% agriculture, fishing, forestry, and horticulture
Organized labor: NA

Government

Long-form name: Principality of Liechtenstein
Type: hereditary constitutional monarchy
Capital: Vaduz
Administrative divisions: 11 communes (gemeinden, singular—gemeinde); Balzers, Eschen, Gamprin, Mauren, Planken, Ruggell, Schaan, Schellenberg, Triesen, Triesenberg, Vaduz
Independence: 23 January 1719, Imperial Principality of Liechtenstein established
Constitution: 5 October 1921
Legal system: local civil and penal codes; accepts compulsory ICJ jurisdiction, with reservations
National holiday: St. Joseph's Day, 19 March
Executive branch: reigning prince, hereditary prince, prime minister, deputy prime minister
Legislative branch: unicameral Diet (Landtag)
Judicial branch: Supreme Court (Oberster Gerichtshof) for criminal cases and Superior Court (Obergericht) for civil cases
Leaders: *Chief of State*—Prince HANS ADAM von und zu Liechtenstein (since 13 November 1989; assumed executive powers 26 August 1984);
Head of Government—Prime Minister Hans BRUNHART (since 26 April 1978); Deputy Prime Minister Dr. Herbert WILLE (since 2 February 1986)
Political parties and leaders: Fatherland Union (VU), Dr. Otto Hasler; Progressive Citizens' Party (FBP), Dr. Herbert Batliner; Christian Social Party, Fritz Kaiser
Suffrage: universal at age 18
Elections: *Diet*—last held on 5 March 1989 (next to be held by March 1993); results—percent of vote by party NA; seats—(25 total) VU 13, FBP 12
Communists: none
Member of: Council of Europe, EFTA, IAEA, INTELSAT, INTERPOL, ITU, UNCTAD, UNIDO, UNICEF, UPU, WIPO; considering UN membership; has consultative status in the EC
Diplomatic representation: in routine diplomatic matters, Liechtenstein is represented in the US by the Swiss Embassy; *US*—the US has no diplomatic or consular mission in Liechtenstein, but the US Consul General at Zurich (Switzerland) has consular accreditation at Vaduz

Flag: two equal horizontal bands of blue (top) and red with a gold crown on the hoist side of the blue band

Economy

Overview: The prosperous economy is based primarily on small-scale light industry and some farming. Industry accounts for 54% of total employment, the service sector 42% (mostly based on tourism), and agriculture and forestry 4%. The sale of postage stamps to collectors is estimated at $10 million annually and accounts for 10% of revenues. Low business taxes (the maximum tax rate is 20%) and easy incorporation rules have induced about 25,000 holding or so-called letter box companies to establish nominal offices in Liechtenstein. Such companies, incorporated solely for tax purposes, provide an additional 30% of state revenues. The economy is tied closely to that of Switzerland in a customs union, and incomes and living standards parallel those of the more prosperous Swiss groups.
GNP: $NA, per capita $NA; real growth rate NA%
Inflation rate (consumer prices): 1.5% (1987 est.)
Unemployment rate: 0.1% (December 1986)
Budget: revenues $171 million; expenditures $189 million, including capital expenditures of NA (1986)
Exports: $807 million; *commodities*—small specialty machinery, dental products, stamps, hardware, pottery; *partners*—EC 40%, EFTA 26% (Switzerland 19%) (1986)
Imports: $NA; *commodities*—machinery, metal goods, textiles, foodstuffs, motor vehicles; *partners*—NA
External debt: $NA
Industrial production: growth rate NA%
Electricity: 23,000 kW capacity; 150 million kWh produced, 5,340 kWh per capita (1989)
Industries: electronics, metal manufacturing, textiles, ceramics, pharmaceuticals, food products, precision instruments, tourism
Agriculture: livestock, vegetables, corn, wheat, potatoes, grapes
Aid: none
Currency: Swiss franc, franken, or franco (plural—francs, franken, or franchi); 1 Swiss franc, franken, or franco (SwF) = 100 centimes, rappen, or centesimi
Exchange rates: Swiss francs, franken, or franchi (SwF) per US$1—1.5150 (January 1990), 1.6359 (1989), 1.4633 (1988), 1.4912 (1987), 1.7989 (1986), 2.4571 (1985)
Fiscal year: calendar year

Communications

Railroads: 18.5 km 1.435-meter standard gauge, electrified; owned, operated, and included in statistics of Austrian Federal Railways
Highways: 130.66 km main roads, 192.27 km byroads
Civil air: no transport aircraft
Airports: none
Telecommunications: automatic telephone system; 25,400 telephones; stations—no AM, no FM, no TV

Defense Forces

Note: defense is responsibility of Switzerland

Luxembourg

See regional map V

Geography

Total area: 2,586 km²; land area: 2,586 km²
Comparative area: slightly smaller than Rhode Island
Land boundaries: 359 km total; Belgium 148 km, France 73 km, FRG 138 km
Coastline: none—landlocked
Maritime claims: none—landlocked
Climate: modified continental with mild winters, cool summers
Terrain: mostly gently rolling uplands with broad, shallow valleys; uplands to slightly mountainous in the north; steep slope down to Moselle floodplain in the southeast
Natural resources: iron ore (no longer exploited)
Land use: 24% arable land; 1% permanent crops; 20% meadows and pastures; 21% forest and woodland; 34% other
Environment: deforestation
Note: landlocked

People

Population: 383,813 (July 1990), growth rate 1.1% (1989)
Birth rate: 12 births/1,000 population (1990)
Death rate: 10 deaths/1,000 population (1990)
Net migration rate: 9 migrants/1,000 population (1990)
Infant mortality rate: 7 deaths/1,000 live births (1990)
Life expectancy at birth: 72 years male, 80 years female (1990)
Total fertility rate: 1.5 children born/woman (1990)
Nationality: noun—Luxembourger(s); adjective—Luxembourg
Ethnic divisions: Celtic base, with French and German blend; also guest and worker residents from Portugal, Italy, and European countries

Religion: 97% Roman Catholic, 3% Protestant and Jewish
Language: Luxembourgish, German, French; many also speak English
Literacy: 100%
Labor force: 161,000; one-third of labor force is foreign workers, mostly from Portugal, Italy, France, Belgium, and FRG; 48.9% services, 24.7% industry, 13.2% government, 8.8% construction, 4.4% agriculture (1984)
Organized labor: 100,000 (est.) members of four confederated trade unions

Government

Long-form name: Grand Duchy of Luxembourg
Type: constitutional monarchy
Capital: Luxembourg
Administrative divisions: 3 districts; Diekirch, Grevenmacher, Luxembourg
Independence: 1839
Constitution: 17 October 1868, occasional revisions
Legal system: based on civil law system; accepts compulsory ICJ jurisdiction
National holiday: National Day (public celebration of the Grand Duke's birthday), 23 June (1921)
Executive branch: grand duke, prime minister, vice prime minister, Council of Ministers (cabinet)
Legislative branch: unicameral Chamber of Deputies (Chambre des Députés); note—the Council of State (Conseil d'Etat) is an advisory body whose views are considered by the Chamber of Deputies
Judicial branch: Superior Court of Justice (Cour Supérieure de de Justice)
Leaders: *Chief of State*—Grand Duke JEAN (since 12 November 1964); Heir Apparent Prince HENRI (son of Grand Duke Jean, born 16 April 1955);
Head of Government—Prime Minister Jacques SANTER (since 21 July 1984); Deputy Prime Minister Jacques F. POOS (since 21 July 1984)
Political parties and leaders: Christian Social Party (CSV), Jacques Santer; Socialist Workers Party (LSAP), Jacques Poos; Liberal (DP), Colette Flesch; Communist (KPL), René Urbany; Green Alternative (GAP), Jean Huss
Suffrage: universal and compulsory at age 18
Elections: *Chamber of Deputies*—last held on 18 June 1989 (next to be held by June 1994); results—CSV 31.7%, LSAP 27.2%, DP 16.2%, Greens 8.4%, PAC 7.3%, KPL 5.1%, others 4%; seats—(60 total) CSV 22, LSAP 18, DP 11, Greens 4, PAC 4, KPL 1, others 4
Communists: 500 party members (1982)
Other political or pressure groups: group of steel industries representing iron and steel industry, Centrale Paysanne representing agricultural producers; Christian and Socialist labor unions; Federation of Industrialists; Artisans and Shopkeepers Federation
Member of: Benelux, BLEU, CCC, Council of Europe, EC, EIB, EMS, FAO, GATT, IAEA, IBRD, ICAO, IDA, IEA, IFAD, IFC, ILO, IMF, INTELSAT, INTERPOL, IOOC, IPU, ITU, NATO, OECD, UN, UNESCO, UPU, WEU, WHO, WIPO, WMO
Diplomatic representation: Ambassador André PHILIPPE; Chancery at 2200 Massachusetts Avenue NW, Washington DC 20008; telephone (202) 265-4171; there are Luxembourg Consulates General in New York and San Francisco; *US*—Ambassador Jean B. S. GERARD; Embassy at 22 Boulevard Emmanuel-Servais, 2535 Luxembourg City (mailing address is APO New York 09132); telephone [352] 460123
Flag: three equal horizontal bands of red (top), white, and light blue; similar to the flag of the Netherlands which uses a darker blue and is shorter; design was based on the flag of France

Economy

Overview: The stable economy features moderate growth, low inflation, and negligible unemployment. Agriculture is based on small but highly productive family-owned farms. The industrial sector, until recently dominated by steel, has become increasingly more diversified, particularly toward high-technology firms. During the past decade growth in the financial sector has more than compensated for the decline in steel. Services, especially banking, account for a growing proportion of the economy. Luxembourg participates in an economic union with Belgium on trade and most financial matters and is also closely connected economically with the Netherlands.
GDP: $6.3 billion, per capita $17,200; real growth rate 4% (1989 est.)
Inflation rate (consumer prices): 3.0% (1989 est.)
Unemployment rate: 1.6% (1989 est.)
Budget: revenues $2.5 billion; expenditures $2.3 billion, including capital expenditures of NA (1988)
Exports: $4.7 billion (f.o.b., 1988); *commodities*—finished steel products, chemicals, rubber products, glass, aluminum, other industrial products; *partners*—EC 75%, US 6%
Imports: $5.9 billion (c.i.f., 1988 est.); *commodities*—minerals, metals, foodstuffs, quality consumer goods; *partners*—FRG 40%, Belgium 35%, France 15%, US 3%

External debt: $131.6 million (1989 est.)
Industrial production: growth rate 5% (1989 est.)
Electricity: 1,500,000 kW capacity; 1,163 million kWh produced, 3,170 kWh per capita (1989)
Industries: banking, iron and steel, food processing, chemicals, metal products, engineering, tires, glass, aluminum
Agriculture: accounts for less than 3% of GDP (including forestry); principal products—barley, oats, potatoes, wheat, fruits, wine grapes; cattle raising widespread
Aid: none
Currency: Luxembourg franc (plural—francs); 1 Luxembourg franc (LuxF) = 100 centimes
Exchange rates: Luxembourg francs (LuxF) per US$1—35.468 (January 1990), 39.404 (1989), 36.768 (1988), 37.334 (1987), 44.672 (1986), 59.378 (1985); note—the Luxembourg franc is at par with the Belgian franc, which circulates freely in Luxembourg
Fiscal year: calendar year

Communications

Railroads: Luxembourg National Railways (CFL) operates 270 km 1.435-meter standard gauge; 162 km double track; 162 km electrified
Highways: 5,108 km total; 4,995 km paved, 57 km gravel, 56 km earth; about 80 km limited access divided highway
Inland waterways: 37 km; Moselle River
Pipelines: refined products, 48 km
Ports: Mertert (river port)
Merchant marine: 4 ships (1,000 GRT or over) totaling 6,138 GRT/9,373 DWT; includes 2 petroleum, oils, and lubricants (POL) tanker, 2 chemical tanker
Civil air: 13 major transport aircraft
Airports: 2 total, 2 usable; 1 with permanent-surface runways; 1 with runways less than 1,220 m; 1 with runways over 3,659 m
Telecommunications: adequate and efficient system, mainly buried cables; 230,000 telephones; stations—2 AM, 4 FM, 6 TV; 2 communication satellite earth stations operating in EUTELSAT and domestic systems

Defense Forces

Branches: Army
Military manpower: males 15-49, 99,734; 83,237 fit for military service; 2,368 reach military age (19) annually
Defense expenditures: 1.2% of GDP, or $76 million (1989 est.)

Macau
(overseas territory of Portugal)

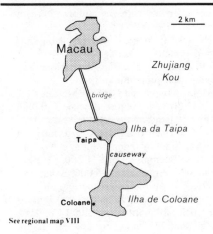

Macau

Zhujiang Kou

bridge

Taipa · Ilha da Taipa

causeway

Coloane · Ilha de Coloane

See regional map VIII

Geography

Total area: 16 km²; land area: 16 km²
Comparative area: about 0.1 times the size of Washington, DC
Land boundary: 0.34 km with China
Coastline: 40 km
Maritime claims:
  Exclusive fishing zone: 12 nm
  Territorial sea: 6 nm
Disputes: scheduled to become a Special Administrative Region of China in 1999
Climate: subtropical; marine with cool winters, warm summers
Terrain: generally flat
Natural resources: negligible
Land use: 0% arable land; 0% permanent crops; 0% meadows and pastures; 0% forest and woodland; 100% other
Environment: essentially urban; one causeway and one bridge connect the two islands to the peninsula on mainland
Note: 27 km west southwest of Hong Kong on the southeast coast of China

People

Population: 441,691 (July 1990), growth rate 1.1% (1990)
Birth rate: 16 births/1,000 population (1990)
Death rate: 5 deaths/1,000 population (1990)
Net migration rate: 0 migrants/1,000 population (1990)
Infant mortality rate: 7 deaths/1,000 live births (1990)
Life expectancy at birth: 75 years male, 79 years female (1990)
Total fertility rate: 2.2 children born/woman (1990)
Nationality: noun—Macanese (sing. and pl.); adjective—Macau
Ethnic divisions: 95% Chinese, 3% Portuguese, 2% other

Religion: mainly Buddhist; 17,000 Roman Catholics, of whom about half are Chinese
Language: Portuguese (official); Cantonese is the language of commerce
Literacy: almost 100% among Portuguese and Macanese; no data on Chinese population
Labor force: 180,000 (1986)
Organized labor: none

Government

Long-form name: none
Type: overseas territory of Portugal; scheduled to revert to China in 1999
Capital: Macau
Administrative divisions: 2 districts (concelhos, singular—concelho); Ilhas, Macau
Independence: none (territory of Portugal); Portugal signed an agreement with China on 13 April 1987 to return Macau to China on 20 December 1999; in the joint declaration, China promises to respect Macau's existing social and economic systems and lifestyle for 50 years after transition
Constitution: 17 February 1976, Organic Law of Macau
Legal system: Portuguese civil law system
National holiday: Day of Portugal, 10 June
Executive branch: president of Portugal, governor, Consultative Council, (cabinet)
Legislative branch: Legislative Assembly
Judicial branch: Supreme Court
Leaders: *Chief of State*—President (of Portugal) Mário Alberto SOARES (since 9 March 1986);
Head of Government—Governor Carlos MELANCIA (since 3 July 1987)
Political parties and leaders: Association to Defend the Interests of Macau; Macau Democratic Center; Group to Study the Development of Macau; Macau Independent Group
Suffrage: universal at age 18
Elections: *Legislative Assembly*—last held on 9 November 1988 (next to be held November 1991); results—percent of vote by party NA; seats—(17 total; 6 elected by universal suffrage, 6 by indirect suffrage) number of seats by party NA
Other political or pressure groups: wealthy Macanese and Chinese representing local interests, wealthy pro-Communist merchants representing China's interests; in January 1967 the Macau Government acceded to Chinese demands that gave China veto power over administration
Member of: Multifiber Agreement
Diplomatic representation: as Chinese territory under Portuguese administration, Macanese interests in the US are represented by Portugal; *US*—the US has no

offices in Macau and US interests are monitored by the US Consulate General in Hong Kong
Flag: the flag of Portugal is used

Economy

Overview: The economy is based largely on tourism (including gambling), and textile and fireworks manufacturing. Efforts to diversify have spawned other small industries—toys, artificial flowers, and electronics. The tourist sector has accounted for roughly 25% of GDP, and the clothing industry has provided about two-thirds of export earnings. Macau depends on China for most of its food, fresh water, and energy imports. Japan and Hong Kong are the main suppliers of raw materials and capital goods.
GDP: $2.7 billion, per capita $6,300; real growth rate 5% (1989 est.)
Inflation rate (consumer prices): 9.5% (1989)
Unemployment rate: 2% (1989 est.)
Budget: revenues $305 million; expenditures $298 million, including capital expenditures of $NA (1989)
Exports: $1.7 billion (1989 est.); *commodities*—textiles, clothing, toys; *partners*—US 33%, Hong Kong 15%, FRG 12%, France 10% (1987)
Imports: $1.6 billion (1989 est.); *commodities*—raw materials, foodstuffs, capital goods; *partners*—Hong Kong 39%, China 21%, Japan 10% (1987)
External debt: $91 million (1985)
Industrial production: NA
Electricity: 179,000 kW capacity; 485 million kWh produced, 1,110 kWh per capita (1989)
Industries: clothing, textiles, toys, plastic products, furniture, tourism
Agriculture: rice, vegetables; food shortages—rice, vegetables, meat; depends mostly on imports for food requirements
Aid: none
Currency: pataca (plural—patacas); 1 pataca (P) = 100 avos
Exchange rates: patacas (P) per US$1—8.03 (1989), 8.044 (1988), 7.993 (1987), 8.029 (1986), 8.045 (1985); note—linked to the Hong Kong dollar at the rate of 1.03 patacas per Hong Kong dollar
Fiscal year: calendar year

Communications

Highways: 42 km paved
Ports: Macau
Civil air: no major transport aircraft
Airports: none; 1 seaplane station
Telecommunications: fairly modern communication facilities maintained for domestic and international services; 52,000 telephones; stations—4 AM, 3 FM, no

Macau (continued)

TV; 75,000 radio receivers (est.); international high-frequency radio communication facility; access to international communications carriers provided via Hong Kong and China; 1 Indian Ocean INTELSAT earth station

Defense Forces

Military manpower: males 15-49, 166,956; 93,221 fit for military service
Note: defense is responsibility of Portugal

Madagascar

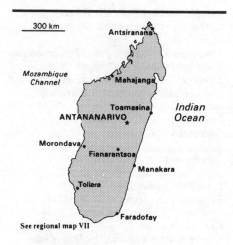

300 km

Mozambique Channel

Antsiranana

Mahajanga

Toamasina

ANTANANARIVO

Indian Ocean

Morondava

Fianarantsoa

Manakara

Toliara

Faradofay

See regional map VII

Geography

Total area: 587,040 km²; land area: 581,540 km²
Comparative area: slightly less than twice the size of Arizona
Land boundaries: none
Coastline: 4,828 km
Maritime claims:
  Exclusive fishing zone: 150 nm
  Extended economic zone: 200 nm
  Territorial sea: 12 nm
Disputes: claims Bassas da India, Europa Island, Glorioso Islands, Juan de Nova Island, and Tromelin Island (all administered by France)
Climate: tropical along coast, temperate inland, arid in south
Terrain: narrow coastal plain, high plateau and mountains in center
Natural resources: graphite, chromite, coal, bauxite, salt, quartz, tar sands, semiprecious stones, mica, fish
Land use: 4% arable land; 1% permanent crops; 58% meadows and pastures; 26% forest and woodland; 11% other; includes 2% irrigated
Environment: subject to periodic cyclones; deforestation; overgrazing; soil erosion; desertification
Note: world's fourth-largest island; strategic location along Mozambique Channel

People

Population: 11,800,524 (July 1990), growth rate 3.2% (1990)
Birth rate: 47 births/1,000 population (1990)
Death rate: 15 deaths/1,000 population (1990)
Net migration rate: 0 migrants/1,000 population (1990)
Infant mortality rate: 97 deaths/1,000 live births (1990)
Life expectancy at birth: 50 years male, 54 years female (1990)

Total fertility rate: 6.9 children born/woman (1990)
Nationality: noun—Malagasy (sing. and pl.); adjective—Malagasy
Ethnic divisions: basic split between highlanders of predominantly Malayo-Indonesian origin (Merina 1,643,000 and related Betsileo 760,000) on the one hand and coastal tribes, collectively termed the Côtiers, with mixed African, Malayo-Indonesian, and Arab ancestry (Betsimisaraka 941,000, Tsimihety 442,000, Antaisaka 415,000, Sakalava 375,000), on the other; there are also 11,000 European French, 5,000 Indians of French nationality, and 5,000 Creoles
Religion: 52% indigenous beliefs; about 41% Christian, 7% Muslim
Language: French and Malagasy (official)
Literacy: 67.5%
Labor force: 4,900,000; 90% nonsalaried family workers engaged in subsistence agriculture; 175,000 wage earners—26% agriculture, 17% domestic service, 15% industry, 14% commerce, 11% construction, 9% services, 6% transportation, 2% other; 51% of population of working age (1985)
Organized labor: 4% of labor force

Government

Long-form name: Democratic Republic of Madagascar
Type: republic
Capital: Antananarivo
Administrative divisions: 6 provinces (plural—NA, singular—faritanin'); Antananarivo, Antsiranana, Fianarantsoa, Mahajanga, Toamasina, Toliara
Independence: 26 June 1960 (from France; formerly Malagasy Republic)
Constitution: 21 December 1975
Legal system: based on French civil law system and traditional Malagasy law; has not accepted compulsory ICJ jurisdiction
National holiday: Independence Day, 26 June (1960)
Executive branch: president, Supreme Council of the Revolution, prime minister, Council of Ministers
Legislative branch: unicameral Popular National Assembly (Assemblée Nationale Populaire)
Judicial branch: Supreme Court (Cour Suprême), High Constitutional Court (Haute Cour Constitutionnelle)
Leaders: *Chief of State*—President Adm. Didier RATSIRAKA (since 15 June 1975);
Head of Government—Prime Minister Lt. Col. Victor RAMAHATRA (since 12 February 1988)
Political parties and leaders: seven parties are now allowed limited political activity under the national front and are repre-

sented on the Supreme Revolutionary Council: Advance Guard of the Malagasy Revolution (AREMA), Didier Ratsiraka; Congress Party for Malagasy Independence (AKFM); Congress Party for Malagasy Independence-Revival (AKFM-R), Pastor Richard Andriamanjato; Movement for National Unity (VONJY), Dr. Marojama Razanabahiny; Malagasy Christian Democratic Union (UDECMA), Norbert Andriamorasata; Militants for the Establishment of a Proletarian Regime (MFM), Manandafy Rakotonirina; National Movement for the Independence of Madagascar (MONIMA), Monja Jaona; Socialist Organization Monima (VSM, an offshoot of MONIMA), Tsihozony Maharanga
Suffrage: universal at age 18
Elections: *President*—last held on 12 March 1989 (next to be held March 1996); results—Didier Ratsiraka (AREMA) 62%, Manandafy Rakotonirina (MFM/MFT) 20%, Dr. Jérôme Marojama Razanabahiny (VONJY) 15%, Monja Jaona (MONIMA) 3%;
People's National Assembly—last held on 28 May 1989 (next to be held May 1994); results—AREMA 88.2%, MFM 5.1%, AKFM 3.7%, VONJY 2.2%, others 0.8%; seats—(137 total) AREMA 120, MFM 7, AKFM 5, VONJY 4, MONIMA 1, independent 1
Communists: Communist party of virtually no importance; small and vocal group of Communists has gained strong position in leadership of AKFM, the rank and file of which is non-Communist
Member of: ACP, AfDB, CCC, EAMA, FAO, G-77, GATT, IAEA, IBRD, ICAO, ICO, IDA, IFAD, IFC, ILO, IMF, IMO, INTELSAT, INTERPOL, IRC, ISO, ITU, NAM, OAU, OCAM, UN, UNESCO, UPU, WFTU, WHO, WMO, WTO
Diplomatic representation: Ambassador Pierrot Jocelyn RAJAONARIVELO; Chancery at 2374 Massachusetts Avenue NW, Washington DC 20008; telephone (202) 265-5525 or 5526; there is a Malagasy Consulate General in New York; *US*—Ambassador Howard K. WALKER; Embassy at 14 and 16 Rue Rainitovo, Antsahavola, Antananarivo (mailing address is B. P. 620, Antananarivo); telephone 212-57, 209-56, 200-89, 207-18
Flag: two equal horizontal bands of red (top) and green with a vertical white band of the same width on hoist side

Economy

Overview: Madagascar is one of the poorest countries in the world. During the period 1980-85 it had a population growth of 3% a year and a −0.4% GDP growth rate. Agriculture, including fishing and forestry, is the mainstay of the economy, accounting for over 40% of GDP, employing about 85% of the labor force, and contributing more than 70% to export earnings. Industry is confined to the processing of agricultural products and textile manufacturing; in 1988 it contributed only 16% to GDP and employed 3% of the labor force. Industrial development has been hampered by government policies that have restricted imports of equipment and spare parts and put strict controls on foreign-owned enterprises. In 1986 the government introduced a five-year development plan that stresses self-sufficiency in food (mainly rice) by 1990, increased production for exports, and reduced energy imports.
GDP: $1.7 billion, per capita $155; real growth rate 2.2% (1988)
Inflation rate (consumer prices): 17.0% (1988)
Unemployment rate: NA%
Budget: revenues $337 million; expenditures $245 million, including capital expenditures of $163 million (1988)
Exports: $284 million (f.o.b., 1988); *commodities*—coffee 45%, vanilla 15%, cloves 11%, sugar, petroleum products; *partners*—France, Japan, Italy, FRG, US
Imports: $319 million (f.o.b., 1988); *commodities*—intermediate manufactures 30%, capital goods 28%, petroleum 15%, consumer goods 14%, food 13%; *partners*—France, FRG, UK, other EC, US
External debt: $3.6 billion (1989)
Industrial production: growth rate −3.9 % (1988)
Electricity: 119,000 kW capacity; 430 million kWh produced, 40 kWh per capita (1989)
Industries: agricultural processing (meat canneries, soap factories, brewery, tanneries, sugar refining), light consumer goods industries (textiles, glassware), cement, automobile assembly plant, paper, petroleum
Agriculture: accounts for 40% of GDP; cash crops—coffee, vanilla, sugarcane, cloves, cocoa; food crops—rice, cassava, beans, bananas, peanuts; cattle raising widespread; not self-sufficient in rice and wheat flour
Illicit drugs: illicit producer of cannabis (cultivated and wild varieties) used mostly for domestic consumption
Aid: US commitments, including Ex-Im (FY70-88), $118 million; Western (non-US) countries, ODA and OOF bilateral commitments (1970-87), $2.6 billion; Communist countries (1970-88), $491 million

Currency: Malagasy franc (plural—francs); 1 Malagasy franc (FMG) = 100 centimes
Exchange rates: Malagasy francs (FMG) per US$1—1,531.0 (January 1990), 1603.4 (1989), 1,407.1 (1988), 1,069.2 (1987), 676.3 (1986), 662.5 (1985)
Fiscal year: calendar year

Communications

Railroads: 1,020 km 1.000-meter gauge
Highways: 40,000 km total; 4,694 km paved, 811 km crushed stone, gravel, or stabilized soil, 34,495 km improved and unimproved earth (est.)
Inland waterways: of local importance only; isolated streams and small portions of Canal des Pangalanes
Ports: Toamasina, Antsiranana, Mahajanga, Toliara
Merchant marine: 13 ships (1,000 GRT or over) totaling 58,126 GRT/79,420 DWT; includes 8 cargo, 2 roll-on/roll-off cargo, 1 petroleum, oils, and lubricants (POL) tanker, 1 chemical tanker, 1 liquefied gas
Civil air: 5 major transport aircraft
Airports: 147 total, 115 usable; 30 with permanent-surface runways; none with runways over 3,659 m; 3 with runways 2,440-3,659 m; 43 with runways 1,220-2,439 m
Telecommunications: above average system includes open-wire lines, coaxial cables, radio relay, and troposcatter links; submarine cable to Bahrain; satellite earth stations—1 Indian Ocean INTELSAT and 1 Atlantic Ocean INTELSAT; over 38,200 telephones; stations—14 AM, 1 FM, 7 (30 repeaters) TV

Defense Forces

Branches: Popular Army, Aeronaval Forces (includes Navy and Air Force), paramilitary Gendarmerie
Military manpower: males 15-49, 2,550,775; 1,519,084 fit for military service; 116,438 reach military age (20) annually
Defense expenditures: 2.2% of GDP, or $37 million (1989 est.)

Malawi

200 km

Lake Nyasa

Mzuzu

Chisamula Island
Likoma Island

LILONGWE

Zomba

Blantyre

See regional map VII

Geography

Total area: 118,480 km²; land area: 94,080 km²
Comparative area: slightly larger than Pennsylvania
Land boundaries: 2,881 km total; Mozambique 1,569 km, Tanzania 475 km, Zambia 837 km
Coastline: none—landlocked
Maritime claims: none—landlocked
Disputes: dispute with Tanzania over the boundary in Lake Nyasa (Lake Malawi)
Climate: tropical; rainy season (November to May); dry season (May to November)
Terrain: narrow elongated plateau with rolling plains, rounded hills, some mountains
Natural resources: limestone; unexploited deposits of uranium, coal, and bauxite
Land use: 25% arable land; NEGL% permanent crops; 20% meadows and pastures; 50% forest and woodland; 5% other; includes NEGL% irrigated
Environment: deforestation
Note: landlocked

People

Population: 9,157,528 (July 1990), growth rate 1.8% (1990)
Birth rate: 52 births/1,000 population (1990)
Death rate: 18 deaths/1,000 population (1990)
Net migration rate: −16 migrants/1,000 population (1990)
Infant mortality rate: 130 deaths/1,000 live births (1990)
Life expectancy at birth: 48 years male, 50 years female (1990)
Total fertility rate: 7.7 children born/woman (1990)
Nationality: noun—Malawian(s); adjective—Malawian

Ethnic divisions: Chewa, Nyanja, Tumbuko, Yao, Lomwe, Sena, Tonga, Ngoni, Ngonde, Asian, European
Religion: 55% Protestant, 20% Roman Catholic, 20% Muslim; traditional indigenous beliefs are also practiced
Language: English and Chichewa (official); other languages important regionally
Literacy: 41.2%
Labor force: 428,000 wage earners; 43% agriculture, 16% manufacturing, 15% personal services, 9% commerce, 7% construction, 4% miscellaneous services, 6% other permanently employed (1986)
Organized labor: small minority of wage earners are unionized
Note: there are 800,000 Mozambican refugees in Malawi (1989 est.)

Government

Long-form name: Republic of Malawi
Type: one-party state
Capital: Lilongwe
Administrative divisions: 24 districts; Blantyre, Chikwawa, Chiradzulu, Chitipa, Dedza, Dowa, Karonga, Kasungu, Kasupe, Lilongwe, Mangochi, Mchinji, Mulanje, Mwanza, Mzimba, Ncheu, Nkhata Bay, Nkhota Kota, Nsanje, Ntchisi, Rumphi, Salima, Thyolo, Zomba
Independence: 6 July 1964 (from UK; formerly Nyasaland)
Constitution: 6 July 1964; republished as amended January 1974
Legal system: based on English common law and customary law; judicial review of legislative acts in the Supreme Court of Appeal; has not accepted compulsory ICJ jurisdiction
National holiday: Independence Day, 6 July (1964)
Executive branch: president, Cabinet
Legislative branch: unicameral National Assembly
Judicial branch: High Court, Supreme Court of Appeal
Leaders: *Chief of State and Head of Government*—President Dr. Hastings Kamuzu BANDA (since 6 July 1966; sworn in as President for Life 6 July 1971)
Political parties and leaders: only party—Malawi Congress Party (MCP), Maxwell Pashane, administrative secretary; John Tembo, treasurer general; top party position of secretary general vacant since 1983
Suffrage: universal at age 21
Elections: *President*—President Banda sworn in as President for Life on 6 July 1971;
National Assembly—last held 27-28 May 1987 (next to be held by May 1992); results—MCP is the only party; seats—(133 total, 112 elected) MCP 133
Communists: no Communist party

Member of: ACP, AfDB, CCC, Commonwealth, EC (associated member), FAO, G-77, GATT, IBRD, ICAO, IDA, IFAD, IFC, ILO, IMF, INTELSAT, INTERPOL, IPU, ISO, ITU, NAM, OAU, SADCC, UN, UNESCO, UPU, WHO, WIPO, WMO, WTO
Diplomatic representation: Ambassador Robert B. MBAYA; Chancery at 2408 Massachusetts Avenue NW, Washington DC 20008; telephone (202) 797-1007; *US*—Ambassador George A. TRAIL, III; Embassy in new capital city development area, address NA (mailing address is P. O. Box 30016, Lilongwe); telephone 730-166
Flag: three equal horizontal bands of black (top), red, and green with a radiant, rising, red sun centered in the black band; similar to the flag of Afghanistan which is longer and has the national coat of arms superimposed on the hoist side of the black and red bands

Economy

Overview: A landlocked country, Malawi ranks among the world's least developed with a per capita GDP of $180. The economy is predominately agricultural and operates under a relatively free enterprise environment, with about 90% of the population living in rural areas. Agriculture accounts for 40% of GDP and 90% of export revenues. After two years of weak performance, economic growth improved significantly in 1988 as a result of good weather and a broadly based economic adjustment effort by the government. The closure of traditional trade routes through Mozambique continues to be a constraint on the economy.
GDP: $1.4 billion, per capita $180; growth rate 3.6% (1988)
Inflation rate (consumer prices): 31.5% (1988)
Unemployment rate: NA%
Budget: revenues $246 million; expenditures $390 million, including capital expenditures of $97 million (FY88 est.)
Exports: $292 million (f.o.b., 1988); *commodities*—tobacco, tea, sugar, coffee, peanuts; *partners*—US, UK, Zambia, South Africa, FRG
Imports: $402 million (c.i.f., 1988); *commodities*—food, petroleum, semimanufactures, consumer goods, transportation equipment; *partners*—South Africa, Japan, US, UK, Zimbabwe
External debt: $1.4 billion (December 1989 est.)
Industrial production: growth rate 6.4% (1988)
Electricity: 181,000 kW capacity; 535 million kWh produced, 60 kWh per capita (1989)

Malaysia

Industries: agricultural processing (tea, tobacco, sugar), sawmilling, cement, consumer goods
Agriculture: accounts for 40% of GDP; cash crops—tobacco, sugarcane, cotton, tea, and corn; subsistence crops—potatoes, cassava, sorghum, pulses; livestock—cattle and goats
Aid: US commitments, including Ex-Im (FY70-88), $182 million; Western (non-US) countries, ODA and OOF bilateral commitments (1970-87), $1.8 billion
Currency: Malawian kwacha (plural—kwacha); 1 Malawian kwacha (MK) = 100 tambala
Exchange rates: Malawian kwacha (MK) per US$1—2.6793 (January 1990), 2.7595 (1989), 2.5613 (1988), 2.2087 (1987), 1.8611 (1986), 1.7191 (1985)
Fiscal year: 1 April-31 March

Communications

Railroads: 789 km 1.067-meter gauge
Highways: 13,135 km total; 2,364 km paved; 251 km crushed stone, gravel, or stabilized soil; 10,520 km earth and improved earth
Inland waterways: Lake Nyasa (Lake Malawi); Shire River, 144 km
Ports: Chipoka, Monkey Bay, Nkhata Bay, and Nkotakota—all on Lake Nyasa (Lake Malawi)
Civil air: 3 major transport aircraft
Airports: 48 total, 47 usable; 6 with permanent-surface runways; none with runways over 3,659 m; 1 with runways 2,440-3,659 m; 9 with runways 1,220-2,439 m
Telecommunications: fair system of openwire lines, radio relay links, and radio communication stations; 36,800 telephones; stations—8 AM, 4 FM, no TV; satellite earth stations—1 Indian Ocean INTELSAT and 1 Atlantic Ocean INTELSAT
Note: a majority of exports would normally go through Mozambique on the Beira or Nacala railroads, but now most go through South Africa because of insurgent activity and damage to rail lines

Defense Forces

Branches: Army, Army Air Wing, Army Naval Detachment, paramilitary Police Mobile Force Unit, paramilitary Young Pioneers
Military manpower: males 15-49, 1,904,445; 967,032 fit for military service
Defense expenditures: 1.6% of GDP, or $22 million (1989 est.)

See regional map IX

Geography

Total area: 329,750 km^2; land area: 328,550 km^2
Comparative area: slightly larger than New Mexico
Land boundaries: 2,669 km total; Brunei 381 km, Indonesia 1,782, Thailand 506 km
Coastline: 4,675 km total (2,068 km Peninsular Malaysia, 2,607 km East Malaysia)
Maritime claims:
Continental shelf: 200 meters or to depth of exploitation; specified boundary in the South China Sea
Exclusive fishing zone: 200 nm
Extended economic zone: 200 nm
Territorial sea: 12 nm
Disputes: involved in a complex dispute over the Spratly Islands with China, Philippines, Taiwan, and Vietnam; state of Sabah claimed by the Philippines; Brunei may wish to purchase the Malaysian salient that divides Brunei into two parts
Climate: tropical; annual southwest (April to October) and northeast (October to February) monsoons
Terrain: coastal plains rising to hills and mountains
Natural resources: tin, crude oil, timber, copper, iron ore, natural gas, bauxite
Land use: 3% arable land; 10% permanent crops; NEGL% meadows and pastures; 63% forest and woodland; 24% other; includes 1% irrigated
Environment: subject to flooding; air and water pollution
Note: strategic location along Strait of Malacca and southern South China Sea

People

Population: 17,510,546 (July 1990), growth rate 2.3% (1990)
Birth rate: 29 births/1,000 population (1990)

Death rate: 6 deaths/1,000 population (1990)
Net migration rate: 0 migrants/1,000 population (1990)
Infant mortality rate: 30 deaths/1,000 live births (1990)
Life expectancy at birth: 65 years male, 71 years female (1990)
Total fertility rate: 3.5 children born/woman (1990)
Nationality: noun—Malaysian(s); adjective—Malaysian
Ethnic divisions: 59% Malay and other indigenous, 32% Chinese, 9% Indian
Religion: Peninsular Malaysia—Malays nearly all Muslim, Chinese predominantly Buddhists, Indians predominantly Hindu; Sabah—38% Muslim, 17% Christian, 45% other; Sarawak—35% tribal religion, 24% Buddhist and Confucianist, 20% Muslim, 16% Christian, 5% other
Language: Peninsular Malaysia—Malay (official); English, Chinese dialects, Tamil; Sabah—English, Malay, numerous tribal dialects, Mandarin and Hakka dialects predominate among Chinese; Sarawak—English, Malay, Mandarin, numerous tribal languages
Literacy: 65.0% overall, age 20 and up; Peninsular Malaysia—80%; Sabah—60%; Sarawak—60%
Labor force: 6,800,000; 30.8% agriculture, 17% manufacturing, 13.6% government, 5.8% construction, 4.3% finance, 3.4% business services, transport and communications, 0.6% mining, 24.5% other (1989 est.)
Organized labor: 660,000, 10% of total labor force (1988)

Government

Long-form name: none
Type: Federation of Malaysia formed 9 July 1963; constitutional monarchy nominally headed by the paramount ruler (king) and a bicameral Parliament composed of a 58-member Senate and a 177-member House of Representatives; Peninsular Malaysian states—hereditary rulers in all but Penang and Melaka, where governors are appointed by Malaysian Government; powers of state governments are limited by federal Constitution; Sabah—self-governing state, holds 20 seats in House of Representatives, with foreign affairs, defense, internal security, and other powers delegated to federal government; Sarawak—self-governing state within Malaysia, holds 24 seats in House of Representatives, with foreign affairs, defense, internal security, and other powers delegated to federal government
Capital: Kuala Lumpur
Administrative divisions: 13 states (negeri-negeri, singular—negeri) and 2 federal

territories* (wilayah-wilayah persekutuan, singular—wilayah persekutuan); Johor, Kedah, Kelantan, Labuan*, Melaka, Negeri Sembilan, Pahang, Perak, Perlis, Pulau Pinang, Sabah, Sarawak, Selangor, Terengganu, Wilayah Persekutuan*

Independence: 31 August 1957 (from UK)

Constitution: 31 August 1957, amended 16 September 1963 when Federation of Malaya became Federation of Malaysia

Legal system: based on English common law; judicial review of legislative acts in the Supreme Court at request of supreme head of the federation; has not accepted compulsory ICJ jurisdiction

National holiday: National Day, 31 August (1957)

Executive branch: paramount ruler, deputy paramount ruler, prime minister, deputy prime minister, Cabinet

Legislative branch: bicameral Parliament (Parlimen) consists of an upper house or Senate (Dewan Negara) and a lower house or House of Representatives (Dewan Rakyat)

Judicial branch: Supreme Court

Leaders: *Chief of State*—Paramount Ruler AZLAN Muhibbuddin Shah ibni Sultan Yusof Izzudin (since 26 April 1989); Deputy Paramount Ruler JA'A-FAR ibni Abdul Rahman (since 26 April 1989);

Head of Government—Prime Minister Dr. MAHATHIR bin Mohamad (since 16 July 1981); Deputy Prime Minister Abdul GHAFAR Baba (since 7 May 1986)

Political parties and leaders: *Peninsular Malaysia*—National Front, a confederation of 14 political parties dominated by United Malays National Organization Baru (UMNO Baru), Mahathir bin Mohamad; Malaysian Chinese Association (MCA), Ling Liong Sik; Gerakan Rakyat Malaysia, Datuk Lim Keng Yaik; Malaysian Indian Congress (MIC), Datuk Samy Vellu;

Sabah—Berjaya Party, Datuk Haji Mohamed Noor Mansoor; Bersatu Sabah (PBS), Joseph Pairin Kitingan; United Sabah National Organizaton (USNO), Tun Datuk Mustapha;

Sarawak—coalition Sarawak National Front composed of the Party Pesaka Bumiputra Bersatu (PBB), Datuk Patinggi Tan Sri Haji Abdul Taib Mahmud; Sarawak United People's Party (SUPP), Datuk Amar Stephen Yong Kuat Tze; Sarawak National Party (SNAP), Datuk James Wong; Parti Bansa Dayak Sarawak (PBDS), Datuk Leo Moggie; major opposition parties are Democratic Action Party (DAP), Lim Kit Siang and Pan-Malaysian Islamic Party (PAS), Fadzil Noor

Suffrage: universal at age 21

Elections: *House of Representatives*—last held 2-3 August 1986 (next to be held by August 1991); results—National Front 57.4%, DAP 20.8%, PAS 15.6%, independents 3.3%, others 2.9%; note—within the National Front, UMNO got 35% and MCA got 14% of the vote; seats—(177 total) National Front 148, DAP 24, PAS 1, independents 4; note—within the National Front, UMNO got 83 seats and MCA got 17 seats

Communists: Peninsular Malaysia—about 1,000 armed insurgents on Thailand side of international boundary and about 200 full time inside Malaysia surrendered on 2 December 1989; only about 100 Communist insurgents remain in North Kalimantan and Sabah

Member of: ADB, ANRPC, ASEAN, Association of Tin Producing Countries, CCC, Colombo Plan, Commonwealth, ESCAP, FAO, G-77, GATT, IAEA, IBRD, ICAO, IDA, IDB—Islamic Development Bank, IFC, ILO, IMF, IMO, INTELSAT, INTERPOL, IPU, IRC, ITC, ITU, NAM, OIC, UN, UNESCO, UPU, WHO, WMO, WTO

Diplomatic representation: Ambassador Albert S. TALALLA; Chancery at 2401 Massachusetts Avenue NW, Washington DC 20008; telephone (202) 328-2700; there are Malaysian Consulates General in Los Angeles and New York; *US*—Ambassador Paul M. CLEVELAND; Embassy at 376 Jalan Tun Razak, 50400 Kuala Lumpur (mailing address is P. O. Box No. 10035, 50700 Kuala Lumpur); telephone [6] (03) 248-9011

Flag: fourteen equal horizontal stripes of red (top) alternating with white (bottom); there is a blue rectangle in the upper hoist-side corner bearing a yellow crescent and a yellow fourteen-pointed star; the crescent and the star are traditional symbols of Islam; the design was based on the flag of the US

Economy

Overview: In 1988-89 booming exports helped Malaysia continue to recover from the severe 1985-86 recession. Real output grew by 8.7% in 1988 and about 7.7% in 1989, helped by vigorous growth in manufacturing output and further increases in foreign direct investment, particularly from Japanese and Taiwanese firms facing higher costs at home. Malaysia has become the world's third-largest producer of semiconductor devices (after the US and Japan) and the world's largest exporter of semiconductor devices. Inflation remained low as unemployment stood at about 8% of the labor force and as the government followed prudent fiscal/monetary policies. The country is not self-sufficient in food, and a majority of the rural population subsists at the poverty level. Malaysia's high export dependence (merchandise exports are 63% of GDP) leaves it vulnerable to a recession in the OECD countries or a fall in world commodity prices.

GDP: $37.9 billion, per capita $2,270; real growth rate 7.7% (1989 est.)

Inflation rate (consumer prices): 3.6% (1989 est.)

Unemployment rate: 7.9% (1989 est.)

Budget: revenues $8.8 billion; expenditures $11.2 billion, including capital expenditures of $2.5 billion (1989 est.)

Exports: $24 billion (f.o.b., 1989 est.); *commodities*—natural rubber, palm oil, tin, timber, petroleum, electronics, light manufactures; *partners*—Singapore, Japan, USSR, EC, Australia, US

Imports: $20 billion (f.o.b., 1989 est.); *commodities*—food, crude oil, consumer goods, intermediate goods, capital equipment, chemicals; *partners*—Japan, Singapore, FRG, UK, Thailand, China, Australia, US

External debt: $16.3 billion (1989 est.)

Industrial production: growth rate 13.6% (1988)

Electricity: 5,600,000 kW capacity; 16,500 million kWh produced, 990 kWh per capita (1989)

Industries: Peninsular Malaysia—rubber and oil palm processing and manufacturing, light manufacturing industry, electronics, tin mining and smelting, logging and processing timber; Sabah—logging, petroleum production; Sarawak—agriculture processing, petroleum production and refining, logging

Agriculture: Peninsular Malaysia—natural rubber, palm oil, rice; Sabah—mainly subsistence; main crops—rubber, timber, coconut, rice; Sarawak—main crops—rubber, timber, pepper; there is a deficit of rice in all areas; fish catch of 608,000 metric tons in 1987

Aid: US commitments, including Ex-Im (FY70-84), $170 million; Western (non-US) countries, ODA and OOF bilateral commitments (1970-87), $3.8 billion; OPEC bilateral aid (1979-89), $42 million

Currency: ringgit (plural—ringgits); 1 ringgit (M$) = 100 sen

Exchange rates: ringgits (M$) per US$1—2.7038 (January 1990), 2.7087 (1989), 2.6188 (1988), 2.5196 (1987), 2.5814 (1986), 2.4830 (1985)

Fiscal year: calendar year

Communications

Railroads: Peninsular Malaysia—1,665 km 1.04-meter gauge; 13 km double track, government owned; Sabah—136 km 1.000-meter gauge

Highways: Peninsular Malaysia—23,600 km (19,352 km hard surfaced, mostly

Maldives

bituminous-surface treatment, and 4,248 km unpaved); Sabah—3,782 km; Sarawak—1,644 km

Inland waterways: Peninsular Malaysia—3,209 km; Sabah—1,569 km; Sarawak—2,518 km

Ports: Tanjong, Kidurong, Kota Kinabalu, Kuching, Pasir Gudang, Penang, Port Kelang, Sandakan, Tawau

Merchant marine: 159 ships (1,000 GRT or over) totaling 1,525,635 GRT/2,216,215 DWT; includes 2 short-sea passenger, 71 cargo, 21 container, 2 vehicle carrier, 2 roll-on/roll-off cargo, 1 livestock carrier, 28 petroleum, oils, and lubricants (POL) tanker, 1 chemical tanker, 6 liquefied gas, 1 specialized tanker, 1 passenger-cargo, 22 bulk, 1 passenger

Civil air: 53 major transport aircraft

Pipelines: crude oil, 1,307 km; natural gas, 379 km

Airports: 126 total, 121 usable; 32 with permanent-surface runways; none with runways over 3,659 m; 8 with runways 2,440-3,659 m; 19 with runways 1,220-2,439 m

Telecommunications: good intercity service provided to peninsular Malaysia mainly by microwave relay, adequate intercity radio relay network between Sabah and Sarawak via Brunei; international service good; good coverage by radio and television broadcasts; 994,860 telephones (1984); stations—28 AM, 3 FM, 33 TV; submarine cables extend to India and Sarawak; SEACOM submarine cable links to Hong Kong and Singapore; satellite earth stations—1 Indian Ocean INTELSAT and 1 Pacific Ocean INTELSAT, and 2 domestic

---

Defense Forces

Branches: Royal Malaysian Army, Royal Malaysian Navy, Royal Malaysian Air Force, Royal Malaysian Police Force

Military manpower: males 15-49, 4,499,495; 2,744,743 fit for military service; 178,923 reach military age (21) annually

Defense expenditures: 3.8% of GDP, or $1.4 billion (1990 est.)

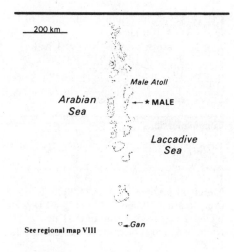

200 km

Arabian Sea

Male Atoll

★ MALE

Laccadive Sea

Gan

See regional map VIII

Geography

Total area: 300 km²; land area: 300 km²

Comparative area: slightly more than 1.5 times the size of Washington, DC

Land boundaries: none

Coastline: 644 km

Maritime claims:

Exclusive fishing zone: about 100 nm (defined by geographic coordinates)

Extended economic zone: 37-310 nm (segment of zone coincides with maritime boundary with India)

Territorial sea: 12 nm

Climate: tropical; hot, humid; dry, northeast monsoon (November to March); rainy, southwest monsoon (June to August)

Terrain: flat with elevations only as high as 2.5 meters

Natural resources: fish

Land use: 10% arable land; 0% permanent crops; 3% meadows and pastures; 3% forest and woodland; 84% other

Environment: 1,200 coral islands grouped into 19 atolls

Note: archipelago of strategic location astride and along major sea lanes in Indian Ocean

---

People

Population: 217,945 (July 1990), growth rate 3.7% (1990)

Birth rate: 46 births/1,000 population (1990)

Death rate: 9 deaths/1,000 population (1990)

Net migration rate: 0 migrants/1,000 population (1990)

Infant mortality rate: 76 deaths/1,000 live births (1990)

Life expectancy at birth: 60 years male, 65 years female (1990)

Total fertility rate: 6.6 children born/woman (1990)

Nationality: noun—Maldivian(s); adjective—Maldivian

Ethnic divisions: admixtures of Sinhalese, Dravidian, Arab, and black

Religion: Sunni Muslim

Language: Divehi (dialect of Sinhala; script derived from Arabic); English spoken by most government officials

Literacy: 36%

Labor force: 66,000 (est.); 80% engaged in fishing industry

Organized labor: none

Government

Long-form name: Republic of Maldives

Type: republic

Capital: Male

Administrative divisions: 19 district (atolls); Aliff, Baa, Daalu, Faafu, Gaafu Aliff, Gaafu Daalu, Haa Aliff, Haa Daalu, Kaafu, Laamu, Laviyani, Meemu, Naviyani, Noonu, Raa, Seenu, Shaviyani, Thaa, Waavu

Independence: 26 July 1965 (from UK)

Constitution: 4 June 1964

Legal system: based on Islamic law with admixtures of English common law primarily in commercial matters; has not accepted compulsory ICJ jurisdiction

National holiday: Independence Day, 26 July (1965)

Executive branch: president, Cabinet

Legislative branch: unicameral Citizens' Council (Majlis)

Judicial branch: High Court

Leaders: *Chief of State and Head of Government*—President Maumoon Abdul GAYOOM (since since 11 November 1978)

Political parties and leaders: no organized political parties; country governed by the Didi clan for the past eight centuries

Suffrage: universal at age 21

Elections: *President*—last held 23 September 1988 (next to be held September 1994); results—President Maumoon Abdul Gayoom reelected;

Citizens' Council—last held on 7 December 1984 (next to be held 7 December 1989); results—percent of vote NA; seats—(48 total, 40 elected)

Communists: negligible

Member of: ADB, Colombo Plan, Commonwealth (special member), ESCAP, FAO, G-77, GATT (de facto), IBRD, ICAO, IDA, IDB—Islamic Development Bank, IFAD, IFC, IMF, IMO, ITU, NAM, OIC, SAARC, UN, UNESCO, UPU, WHO, WMO

Diplomatic representation: Maldives does not maintain an embassy in the US, but does have a UN mission in New York; *US*—the US Ambassador to Sri Lanka is accredited to Maldives and makes periodic

Maldives *(continued)*

visits there; US Consular Agency, Mahduedu	age, Violet Magu, Henveru, Male; telephone 2581

Flag: red with a large green rectangle in the center bearing a vertical white crescent; the closed side of the crescent is on the hoist side of the flag

---

Economy

Overview: The economy is based on fishing, tourism, and shipping. Agriculture is limited to the production of a few subsistence crops that provide only 10% of food requirements. Fishing is the largest industry, employing 80% of the work force and accounting for over 60% of exports; it is also an important source of government revenue. During the 1980s tourism has become one of the most important and highest growth sectors of the economy. In 1988 industry accounted for about 14% of GDP. Real GDP is officially estimated to have increased by about 10% annually during the period 1974-86, and GDP estimates for 1988 show a further growth of 9% on the strength of a record fish catch and an improved tourist season.

GDP: $136 million, per capita $670; real growth rate 9.2% (1988)

Inflation rate (consumer prices): 14% (1988 est.)

Unemployment rate: NA%

Budget: revenues $51 million; expenditures $50 million, including capital expenditures of $25 million (1988 est.)

Exports: $47.0 million (f.o.b., 1988 est.); *commodities*—fish 57%, clothing 39%; *partners*—Thailand, Western Europe, Sri Lanka

Imports: $90.0 million (c.i.f., 1988 est.); *commodities*— intermediate and capital goods 47%, consumer goods 42%, petroleum products 11%; *partners*—Japan, Western Europe, Thailand

External debt: $70 million (December 1988)

Industrial production: growth rate 3.9% (1988 est.)

Electricity: 5,000 kW capacity; 10 million kWh produced, 50 kWh per capita (1989)

Industries: fishing and fish processing, tourism, shipping, boat building, some coconut processing, garments, woven mats, coir (rope), handicrafts

Agriculture: accounts for almost 30% of GDP (including fishing); fishing more important than farming; limited production of coconuts, corn, sweet potatoes; most staple foods must be imported

Aid: US commitments, including Ex-Im (FY70-88), $28 million; Western (non-US) countries, ODA and OOF bilateral commitments (1970-87), $84 million; OPEC bilateral aid (1979-89), $14 million

Currency: rufiyaa (plural—rufiyaa); 1 rufiyaa (Rf) = 100 laaris

Exchange rates: rufiyaa (Rf) per US$1— 9.3043 (January 1990), 9.0408 (1989), 8.7846 (1988), 9.2230 (1987), 7.1507 (1986), 7.0981 (1985)

Fiscal year: calendar year

Communications

Highways: Male has 9.6 km of coral highways within the city

Ports: Male, Gan

Merchant marine: 16 ships (1,000 GRT or over) totaling 70,066 GRT/112,480 DWT; includes 12 cargo, 1 container, 1 petroleum, oils, and lubricants (POL) tanker, 2 bulk

Civil air: 1 major transport aircraft

Airports: 2 with permanent-surface runways 2,440-3,659 m

Telecommunications: minimal domestic and international facilities; 2,325 telephones; stations—2 AM, 1 FM, 1 TV; 1 Indian Ocean INTELSAT earth station

---

Defense Forces

Branches: no military force

Military manpower: males 15-49, 49,261; 27,519 fit for military service

Defense expenditures: $1.8 million (1984 est.)

Mali

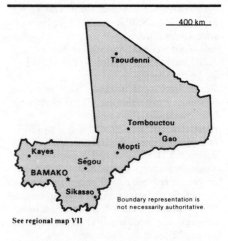

See regional map VII

Boundary representation is not necessarily authoritative.

Geography

Total area: 1,240,000 km^2; land area: 1,220,000 km^2

Comparative area: slightly less than twice the size of Texas

Land boundaries: 7,243 km total; Algeria 1,376 km, Burkina 1,000 km, Guinea 858 km, Ivory Coast 532 km, Mauritania 2,237 km, Niger 821 km, Senegal 419 km

Coastline: none—landlocked

Maritime claims: none—landlocked

Disputes: the disputed international boundary between Burkina and Mali was submitted to the International Court of Justice (ICJ) in October 1983 and the ICJ issued its final ruling in December 1986, which both sides agreed to accept; Burkina and Mali are proceeding with boundary demarcation, including the tripoint with Niger

Climate: subtropical to arid; hot and dry February to June; rainy, humid, and mild June to November; cool and dry November to February

Terrain: mostly flat to rolling northern plains covered by sand; savanna in south, rugged hills in northeast

Natural resources: gold, phosphates, kaolin, salt, limestone, uranium; bauxite, iron ore, manganese, tin, and copper deposits are known but not exploited

Land use: 2% arable land; NEGL% permanent crops; 25% meadows and pastures; 7% forest and woodland; 66% other; includes NEGL% irrigated

Environment: hot, dust-laden harmattan haze common during dry seasons; desertification

Note: landlocked

People

Population: 8,142,373 (July 1990), growth rate 2.3% (1990)

Birth rate: 51 births/1,000 population (1990)

Death rate: 21 deaths/1,000 population (1990)

Net migration rate: −7 migrants/1,000 population (1990)

Infant mortality rate: 116 deaths/1,000 live births (1990)

Life expectancy at birth: 45 years male, 47 years female (1990)

Total fertility rate: 7.1 children born/woman (1990)

Nationality: noun—Malian(s); adjective—Malian

Ethnic divisions: 50% Mande (Bambara, Malinke, Sarakole), 17% Peul, 12% Voltaic, 6% Songhai, 5% Tuareg and Moor, 10% other

Religion: 90% Muslim, 9% indigenous beliefs, 1% Christian

Language: French (official); Bambara spoken by about 80% of the population; numerous African languages

Literacy: 18%

Labor force: 2,666,000 (1986 est.); 80% agriculture, 19% services, 1% industry and commerce (1981); 50% of population of working age (1985)

Organized labor: National Union of Malian Workers (UNTM) is umbrella organization for over 13 national unions

Government

Long-form name: Republic of Mali

Type: republic; single-party constitutional government

Capital: Bamako

Administrative divisions: 7 regions (régions, singular—région); Gao, Kayes, Koulikoro, Mopti, Ségou, Sikasso, Tombouctou; note—there may be a new capital district of Bamako

Independence: 22 September 1960 (from France; formerly French Sudan)

Constitution: 2 June 1974, effective 19 June 1979; amended September 1981 and March 1985

Legal system: based on French civil law system and customary law; judicial review of legislative acts in Constitutional Section of Court of State; has not accepted compulsory ICJ jurisdiction

National holiday: Anniversary of the Proclamation of the Republic, 22 September (1960)

Executive branch: president, Council of Ministers (cabinet)

Legislative branch: unicameral National Assembly (Assemblé Nationale)

Judicial branch: Supreme Court (Cour Suprême)

Leaders: *Chief of State and Head of Government*—President Gen. Moussa TRAORE (since 6 December 1968)

Political parties and leaders: only party—Democratic Union of Malian People (UDPM)

Suffrage: universal at age 21

Elections: *President*—last held on 9 June 1985 (next to be held June 1991); results—General Moussa Traoré was re-elected without opposition; *National Assembly*—last held on 26 June 1988 (next to be held June 1991); results—UDPM is the only party; seats—(82 total) UDPM 82

Communists: a few Communists and some sympathizers (no legal Communist party)

Member of: ACP, AfDB, CEAO, ECA, ECOWAS, FAO, G-77, GATT (de facto), IAEA, IBRD, ICAO, IDA, IDB—Islamic Development Bank, IFAD, IFC, ILO, IMF, INTELSAT, INTERPOL, IPU, IRC, ITU, NAM, Niger River Commission, OAU, OIC, OMVS (Organization for the Development of the Senegal River Valley), UN, UNESCO, UPU, WHO, WMO, WTO,

Diplomatic representation: Ambassador Alhousseyni TOURE; Chancery at 2130 R Street NW, Washington DC 20008; telephone (202) 332-2249 or 939-8950; *US*—Ambassador Robert M. PRINGLE; Embassy at Rue Testard and Rue Mohamed V., Bamako (mailing address is B. P. 34, Bamako); telephone 225834

Flag: three equal vertical bands of green (hoist side), yellow, and red; uses the popular pan-African colors of Ethiopia

Economy

Overview: Mali is among the poorest countries in the world, with about 80% of its land area desert or semidesert. Economic activity is largely confined to the riverine area irrigated by the Niger. About 10% of the population lives as nomads and some 80% of the labor force is engaged in agriculture and fishing. Industrial activity is concentrated on processing farm commodities.

GDP: $1.94 billion, per capita $220; real growth rate −0.9% (1988 est.)

Inflation rate (consumer prices): NA% (1987)

Unemployment rate: NA%

Budget: revenues $338 million; expenditures $559 million, including capital expenditures of $NA (1987)

Exports: $260 million (f.o.b., 1987); *commodities*—livestock, peanuts, dried fish, cotton, skins; *partners*—mostly franc zone and Western Europe

Imports: $493 million (f.o.b., 1987); *commodities*—textiles, vehicles, petroleum products, machinery, sugar, cereals; *partners*—mostly franc zone and Western Europe

External debt: $2.1 billion (December 1988 est.)

Industrial production: growth rate NA%

Electricity: 92,000 kW capacity; 165 million kWh produced, 20 kWh per capita (1989)

Industries: small local consumer goods and processing, construction, phosphate, gold, fishing

Agriculture: accounts for 50% of GDP; most production based on small subsistence farms; cotton and livestock products account for over 70% of exports; other crops—millet, rice, corn, vegetables, peanuts; livestock—cattle, sheep, and goats

Aid: US commitments, including Ex-Im (FY70-88), $313 million; Western (non-US) countries, ODA and OOF bilateral commitments (1970-87), $2.4 billion; OPEC bilateral aid (1979-89), $92 million; Communist countries (1970-88), $190 million

Currency: Communauté Financière Africaine franc (plural—francs); 1 CFA franc (CFAF) = 100 centimes

Exchange rates: Communauté Financière Africaine francs (CFAF) per US$1—287.99 (January 1990), 319.01 (1989), 297.85 (1988), 300.54 (1987), 346.30 (1986), 449.26 (1985)

Fiscal year: calendar year

Communications

Railroads: 642 km 1,000-meter gauge; linked to Senegal's rail system through Kayes

Highways: about 15,700 km total; 1,670 km bituminous, 3,670 km gravel and improved earth, 10,360 km unimproved earth

Inland waterways: 1,815 km navigable

Civil air: no major transport aircraft

Airports: 37 total, 29 usable; 8 with permanent-surface runways; none with runways over 3,659 m; 7 with runways 2,440-3,659 m; 9 with runways 1,220-2,439 m

Telecommunications: domestic system poor but improving; provides only minimal service with radio relay, wire, and radio communications stations; expansion of radio relay in progress; 11,000 telephones; stations—2 AM, 2 FM, 2 TV; satellite earth stations—1 Atlantic Ocean INTELSAT and 1 Indian Ocean INTELSAT

Defense Forces

Branches: Army, Air Force; paramilitary, Gendarmerie, Republican Guard, National Guard

Military manpower: males 15-49, 1,585,878; 913,000 fit for military service; no conscription

Defense expenditures: 2.5% of GDP (1987)

Malta

See regional map V

Geography

Total area: 320 km²; land area: 320 km²
Comparative area: slightly less than twice the size of Washington, DC
Land boundaries: none
Coastline: 140 km
Maritime claims:
Contiguous zone: 24 nm
Continental shelf: 200 meters or to depth of exploitation
Exclusive fishing zone: 25 nm
Territorial sea: 12 nm
Climate: Mediterranean with mild, rainy winters and hot, dry summers
Terrain: mostly low, rocky, flat to dissected plains; many coastal cliffs
Natural resources: limestone, salt
Land use: 38% arable land; 3% permanent crops; 0% meadows and pastures; 0% forest and woodland; 59% other; includes 3% irrigated
Environment: numerous bays provide good harbors; fresh water very scarce—increasing reliance on desalination
Note: strategic location in central Mediterranean, 93 km south of Sicily, 290 km north of Libya

People

Population: 353,465 (July 1990), growth rate 0.9% (1990)
Birth rate: 15 births/1,000 population (1990)
Death rate: 8 deaths/1,000 population (1990)
Net migration rate: 1 migrant/1,000 population (1990)
Infant mortality rate: 8 deaths/1,000 live births (1990)
Life expectancy at birth: 74 years male, 78 years female (1990)
Total fertility rate: 2.0 children born/woman (1990)
Nationality: noun—Maltese (sing. and pl.); adjective—Maltese

Ethnic divisions: mixture of Arab, Sicilian, Norman, Spanish, Italian, English
Religion: 98% Roman Catholic
Language: Maltese and English (official)
Literacy: 83%
Labor force: 125,674; 30% services, 24% manufacturing, 21% government (except job corps), 8% construction, 5% utilities and drydocks, 4% agriculture (1987)
Organized labor: about 40% of labor force

Government

Long-form name: Republic of Malta
Type: parliamentary democracy
Capital: Valletta
Administrative divisions: none (administration directly from Valletta)
Independence: 21 September 1964 (from UK)
Constitution: 26 April 1974, effective 2 June 1974
Legal system: based on English common law and Roman civil law; has accepted compulsory ICJ jurisdiction, with reservations
National holiday: Freedom Day, 31 March
Executive branch: president, prime minister, deputy prime minister, Cabinet
Legislative branch: unicameral House of Representatives
Judicial branch: Constitutional Court and Court of Appeal
Leaders: *Chief of State*—President Vincent (Censu) TABONE (since 4 April 1989);
Head of Government—Prime Minister Dr. Edward (Eddie) FENECH ADAMI (since 12 May 1987); Deputy Prime Minister Dr. Guido DE MARCO (since 14 May 1987)
Political parties and leaders: Nationalist Party, Edward Fenech Adami; Malta Labor Party, Karmenu Mifsud Bonnici
Suffrage: universal at age 18
Elections: *House of Representatives*—last held on 9 May 1987 (next to be held by May 1992); results—NP 51.1%, MLP 48.9%; seats—(usually 65 total, but additional seats are given to the party with the largest popular vote to ensure a legislative majority; current total 69) MLP 34, NP 31 before popular vote adjustment; MLP 34, NP 35 after adjustment
Communists: fewer than 100 (est.)
Member of: CCC, Commonwealth, Council of Europe, FAO, G-77, GATT, IBRD, ICAO, IFAD, ILO, IMF, IMO, INTERPOL, ITU, IWC—International Wheat Council, NAM, UN, UNDP, UNESCO, UNICEF, UPU, WHO, WIPO, WMO
Diplomatic representation: Ambassador Salvatore J. STELLINI; Chancery at 2017 Connecticut Avenue NW, Washington DC 20008; telephone (202) 462-3611 or 3612; there is a Maltese Consulate

General in New York; *US*—Ambassador Sally J. NOVETZKE; Embassy at 2nd Floor, Development House, St. Anne Street, Floriana, Valletta (mailing address is P. O. Box 535, Valletta); telephone [356] 623653 or 620424, 623216
Flag: two equal vertical bands of white (hoist side) and red; in the upper hoist-side corner is a representation of the George Cross, edged in red

Economy

Overview: Significant resources are limestone, a favorable geographic location, and a productive labor force. Malta produces only about 20% of its food needs, has limited freshwater supplies, and has no domestic energy sources. Consequently, the economy is highly dependent on foreign trade and services. Manufacturing and tourism are the largest contributors to the economy. Manufacturing accounts for about 30% of GDP, with the textile and clothing industry a major contributor. In 1988 inflation was held to a low 0.9%. Per capita GDP at $5,100 places Malta in the middle-income range of the world's nations.
GDP: $1.9 billion, per capita $5,100; real growth rate 7.1% (1988)
Inflation rate (consumer prices): 0.9% (1988)
Unemployment rate: 4.4% (1987)
Budget: revenues $844 million; expenditures $938 million, including capital expenditures of $226 million (1989 est.)
Exports: $710 million (f.o.b., 1988); *commodities*—clothing, textiles, footwear, ships; *partners*—FRG 31%, UK 14%, Italy 14%
Imports: $1,360 million (c.i.f., 1988); *commodities*—food, petroleum, nonfood raw materials; *partners*—FRG 19%, UK 17%, Italy 17%, US 11%
External debt: $90 million, medium and long-term (December 1987)
Industrial production: growth rate 6.2% (1987)
Electricity: 328,000 kW capacity; 1,110 million kWh produced, 2,990 kWh per capita (1989)
Industries: tourism, ship repair yard, clothing, construction, food manufacturing, textiles, footwear, clothing, beverages, tobacco
Agriculture: overall, 20% self-sufficient; main products—potatoes, cauliflower, grapes, wheat, barley, tomatoes, citrus, cut flowers, green peppers, hogs, poultry, eggs; generally adequate supplies of vegetables, poultry, milk, pork products; seasonal or periodic shortages in grain, animal fodder, fruits, other basic foodstuffs

Aid: US commitments, including Ex-Im (FY70-81), $172 million; Western (non-US) countries, ODA and OOF bilateral commitments (1970-87), $332 million; OPEC bilateral aid (1979-89), $76 million; Communist countries (1970-88), $48 million

Currency: Maltese lira (plural—liri); 1 Maltese lira (LM) = 100 cents

Exchange rates: Maltese liri (LM) per US$1—0.3332 (January 1990), 0.3483 (1989), 0.3306 (1988), 0.3451 (1987), 0.3924 (1986), 0.4676 (1985)

Fiscal year: 1 April-31 March

Communications

Highways: 1,291 km total; 1,179 km paved (asphalt), 77 km crushed stone or gravel, 35 km improved and unimproved earth

Ports: Valletta, Marsaxlokk

Merchant marine: 314 ships (1,000 GRT or over) totaling 3,677,797 GRT/ 6,357,733 DWT; includes 3 passenger, 4 short-sea passenger, 127 cargo, 2 container, 1 passenger-cargo, 13 roll-on/ roll-off cargo, 2 vehicle carrier, 6 refrigerated cargo, 7 chemical tanker, 4 combination ore/oil, 1 specialized tanker, 61 petroleum, oils, and lubricants (POL) tanker, 72 bulk, 11 combination bulk; note—a flag of convenience registry; China owns 1 ship, Cuba owns 8, and Vietnam owns 1

Civil air: 8 major transport aircraft

Airports: 1 with permanent-surface runways 2,440-3,659 m

Telecommunications: modern automatic system centered in Valletta; 153,000 telephones; stations—9 AM, 3 FM, 2 TV; 1 submarine cable; 1 Atlantic Ocean INTELSAT earth station

Defense Forces

Branches: Armed Forces, Police, Paramilitary Dejima Force

Military manpower: males 15-49, 92,610; 74,256 fit for military service

Defense expenditures: 1.3% of GDP, or $25 million (1989 est.)

10 km

Irish Sea

Ramsey

Peel

DOUGLAS

Irish Sea

Castletown

See regional map V

Geography

Total area: 588 km^2; land area: 588 km^2

Comparative area: slightly less than 3.5 times the size of Washington, DC

Land boundaries: none

Coastline: 113 km

Maritime claims:

Continental shelf: 200 meters or to depth of exploitation

Exclusive fishing zone: 200 nm

Territorial sea: 3 nm

Climate: cool summers and mild winters; humid; overcast about half the time

Terrain: hills in north and south bisected by central valley

Natural resources: lead, iron ore

Land use: NA% arable land; NA% permanent crops; NA% meadows and pastures; NA% forest and woodland; NA% other; extensive arable land and forests

Environment: strong westerly winds prevail

Note: located in Irish Sea equidistant from England, Scotland, and Ireland

People

Population: 64,859 (July 1990), growth rate 0.2% (1990)

Birth rate: 11 births/1,000 population (1990)

Death rate: 15 deaths/1,000 population (1990)

Net migration rate: 5 migrants/1,000 population (1990)

Infant mortality rate: 9 deaths/1,000 live births (1990)

Life expectancy at birth: 72 years male, 78 years female (1990)

Total fertility rate: 1.8 children born/ woman (1990)

Nationality: noun—Manxman, Manxwoman, adjective—Manx

Ethnic divisions: native Manx of Norse-Celtic descent; British

Religion: Anglican, Roman Catholic, Methodist, Baptist, Presbyterian, Society of Friends

Language: English, Manx Gaelic

Literacy: NA%, but compulsory education between ages of 5 and 15

Labor force: 25,864 (1981)

Organized labor: 22 labor unions patterned along British lines

Government

Long-form name: none

Type: British crown dependency

Capital: Douglas

Administrative divisions: none (British crown dependency)

Independence: none (British crown dependency)

Constitution: 1961, Isle of Man Constitution Act

Legal system: English law and local statute

National holiday: Tynwald Day, 5 July

Executive branch: British monarch, lieutenant governor, prime minister, Executive Council (cabinet)

Legislative branch: bicameral Parliament (Tynwald) consists of an upper house or Legislative Council and a lower house or House of Keys

Judicial branch: High Court of Justice

Leaders: *Chief of State*—Lord of Mann Queen ELIZABETH II (since 6 February 1952), represented by Lieutenant Governor Maj. Gen. Laurence NEW (since 1985);

Head of Government—President of the Legislative Council J. C. NIVISON (since 1985)

Political parties and leaders: there is no party system and members sit as independents

Suffrage: universal at age 21

Elections: *House of Keys*—last held in 1986 (next to be held 1991); results—percent of vote NA; seats—(24 total) independents 24

Communists: probably none

Diplomatic representation: none (British crown dependency)

Flag: red with the Three Legs of Man emblem (*Trinacria*), in the center; the three legs are joined at the thigh and bent at the knee; in order to have the toes pointing clockwise on both sides of the flag, a two-sided emblem is used

Economy

Overview: Offshore banking, manufacturing, and tourism are key sectors of the economy. The government's policy of offering incentives to high-technology companies and financial institutions to locate on the island has paid off in expanding

Man, Isle of (continued)

employment opportunities in high-income industries. As a result, agriculture and fishing, once the mainstays of the economy, have declined in their shares of GNP. Banking now contributes over 20% to GNP and manufacturing about 15%. Trade is mostly with the UK.

GNP: $490 million, per capita $7,573; real growth rate NA% (1988)
Inflation rate (consumer prices): NA%
Unemployment rate: 1.5% (1988)
Budget: revenues $130.4 million; expenditures $114.4 million, including capital expenditures of $18.1 million (FY85 est.)
Exports: $NA; *commodities*—tweeds, herring, processed shellfish meat; *partners*—UK
Imports: $NA; *commodities*—timber, fertilizers, fish; *partners*—UK
External debt: $NA
Industrial production: growth rate NA%
Electricity: 61,000 kW capacity; 190 million kWh produced, 2,930 kWh per capita (1989)
Industries: an important offshore financial center; financial services, light manufacturing, tourism
Agriculture: cereals and vegetables; cattle, sheep, pigs, poultry
Aid: NA
Currency: Manx pound (plural—pounds); 1 Manx pound (£M) = 100 pence
Exchange rates: Manx pounds (£M) per US$1—0.6055 (January 1990), 0.6099 (1989), 0.5614 (1988), 0.6102 (1987), 0.6817 (1986), 0.7714 (1985); the Manx pound is at par with the British pound
Fiscal year: 1 April-31 March

Communications

Railroads: 36 km electric track, 24 km steam track
Highways: 640 km motorable roads
Ports: Douglas, Ramsey, Peel
Merchant marine: 77 ships (1,000 GRT or over) totaling 1,656,216 GRT/2,984,047 DWT; includes 1 short-sea passenger, 8 cargo, 5 container, 6 roll-on/roll-off cargo, 32 petroleum, oils, and lubricants (POL) tanker, 5 chemical tanker, 2 combination ore/oil, 6 liquefied gas, 12 bulk; note—a captive register of the United Kingdom, although not all ships on the register are British-owned
Airports: 2 total; 1 usable with permanent-surface runways 1,220-2,439 m
Telecommunications: 24,435 telephones; stations—1 AM, 4 FM, 4 TV

Defense Forces

Note: defense is the responsibility of the UK

Marshall Islands

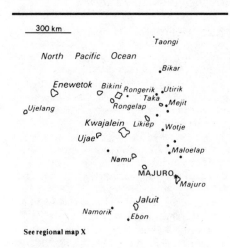

300 km

North Pacific Ocean

Taongi
Bikar
Enewetok   Bikini   Rongerik   Utirik
Taka   Mejit
Rongelap
Ujelang
Kwajalein   Likiep   Wotje
Ujae
Maloelap
Namu
MAJURO
Majuro
Jaluit
Namorik
Ebon

See regional map X

Geography

Total area: 181.3 km²; land area: 181.3 km²; includes the atolls of Bikini, Eniwetak, and Kwajalein
Comparative area: slightly larger than Washington, DC
Land boundaries: none
Coastline: 370.4 km
Maritime claims:
  Contiguous zone: 24 nm
  Extended economic zone: 200 nm
  Territorial sea: 12 nm
Disputes: claims US-administered Wake Island
Climate: wet season May to November; hot and humid; islands border typhoon belt
Terrain: low coral limestone and sand islands
Natural resources: phosphate deposits, marine products, deep seabed minerals
Land use: 0% arable land; 60% permanent crops; 0% meadows and pastures; 0% forest and woodland; 40% other
Environment: occasionally subject to typhoons; two archipelagic island chains of 30 atolls and 1,152 islands
Note: located 3,825 km southwest of Honolulu in the North Pacific Ocean, about two-thirds of the way between Hawaii and Papua New Guinea; Bikini and Eniwetak are former US nuclear test sites; Kwajalein, the famous World War II battleground, is now used as a US missile test range

People

Population: 43,417 (July 1990), growth rate 3.2% (1990)
Birth rate: 39 births/1,000 population (1990)
Death rate: 5 deaths/1,000 population (1990)
Net migration rate: −1 migrant/1,000 population (1990)

Infant mortality rate: 43 deaths/1,000 live births (1990)
Life expectancy at birth: 70 years male, 75 years female (1990)
Total fertility rate: 5.9 children born/woman (1990)
Nationality: noun—Marshallese; adjective—Marshallese
Ethnic divisions: almost entirely Micronesian
Religion: predominantly Christian, mostly Protestant
Language: English universally spoken and is the official language; two major Marshallese dialects from Malayo-Polynesian family; Japanese
Literacy: 90%
Labor force: 4,800 (1986)
Organized labor: none

Government

Long-form name: Republic of the Marshall Islands
Type: constitutional government in free association with the US; the Compact of Free Association entered into force 21 October 1986
Capital: Majuro
Administrative divisions: none
Independence: 21 October 1986 (from the US-administered UN trusteeship; formerly the Marshall Islands District of the Trust Territory of the Pacific Islands)
Constitution: 1 May 1979
Legal system: based on adapted Trust Territory laws, acts of the legislature, municipal, common, and customary laws
National holiday: Proclamation of the Republic of the Marshall Islands, 1 May (1979)
Executive branch: president, Cabinet
Legislative branch: unicameral Parliament (Nitijela)
Judicial branch: Supreme Court
Leaders: *Chief of State and Head of Government*—President Amata KABUA (since 1979)
Political parties and leaders: no formal parties; President Kabua is chief political (and traditional) leader
Suffrage: universal at age 18
Elections: *President*—last held NA November 1987 (next to be held November 1991); results—President Amata Kabua was reelected;
Parliament—last held NA November 1987 (next to be held November 1991); results—percent of vote NA; seats—(33 total)
Communists: none
Member of: SPF, ESCAP (associate)
Diplomatic representation: Representative Wilfred I. KENDALL; Representative Office at Suite 1004, 1901 Pennsylvania Avenue NW, Washington DC 20006; tele-

Flag: blue with two stripes radiating from the lower hoist-side corner—orange (top) and white; there is a white star with four large rays and 20 small rays on the hoist side above the two stripes

Economy

Overview: Agriculture and tourism are the mainstays of the economy. Agricultural production is concentrated on small farms, and the most important commercial crops are coconuts, tomatoes, melons, and breadfruit. A few cattle ranches supply the domestic meat market. Small-scale industry is limited to handicrafts, fish processing, and copra. The tourist industry is the primary source of foreign exchange and employs about 10% of the labor force. The islands have few natural resources, and imports far exceed exports. In 1987 the US Government provided grants of $40 million out of the Marshallese budget of $55 million.

GDP: $63 million, per capita $1,500; real growth rate NA% (1989 est.)

Inflation rate (consumer prices): 5.6% (1981)

Unemployment rate: NA%

Budget: revenues $55 million; expenditures NA, including capital expenditures of NA (1987 est.)

Exports: $2.5 million (f.o.b., 1985); *commodities*—copra, copra oil, agricultural products, handicrafts; *partners*—NA

Imports: $29.2 million (c.i.f., 1985); *commodities*—foodstuffs, beverages, building materials; *partners*—NA

External debt: $NA

Industrial production: growth rate NA%

Electricity: 12,000 kW capacity; 10 million kWh produced, 240 kWh per capita (1989)

Industries: copra, fish, tourism; craft items from shell, wood, and pearl; offshore banking (embryonic)

Agriculture: coconuts, cacao, taro, breadfruit, fruits, copra; pigs, chickens

Aid: under the terms of the Compact of Free Association, the US is to provide approximately $40 million in aid annually

Currency: US currency is used

Exchange rates: US currency is used

Fiscal year: 1 October-30 September

Communications

Highways: macadam and concrete roads on major islands (Majuro, Kwajalein), otherwise stone-, coral-, or laterite-surfaced roads and tracks

Ports: Majuro

Merchant marine: 3 ships (1,000 GRT or over) totaling 475,968 GRT/949,888 DWT; includes 2 petroleum, oils, and lubricants (POL) tanker, 1 bulk carrier; note—a flag of convenience registry

Airports: 5 total, 5 usable; 4 with permanent-surface runways; 5 with runways 1,220-2,439 m

Telecommunications: telephone network—570 lines (Majuro) and 186 (Ebeye); telex services; islands interconnected by shortwave radio (used mostly for government purposes); stations—1 AM, 2 FM, 1 TV, 1 shortwave; 2 Pacific Ocean INTELSAT earth stations; US Government satellite communications system on Kwajalein

Defense Forces

Note: defense is the responsibility of the US

Martinique
(overseas department of France)

See regional map III

Geography

Total area: 1,100 km^2; land area: 1,060 km^2

Comparative area: slightly more than six times the size of Washington, DC

Land boundaries: none

Coastline: 290 km

Maritime claims:
Continental shelf: 200 meters or to depth of exploitation
Extended economic zone: 200 nm
Territorial sea: 12 nm

Climate: tropical; moderated by trade winds; rainy season (June to October)

Terrain: mountainous with indented coastline; dormant volcano

Natural resources: coastal scenery and beaches, cultivable land

Land use: 10% arable land; 8% permanent crops; 30% meadows and pastures; 26% forest and woodland; 26% other; includes 5% irrigated

Environment: subject to hurricanes, flooding, and volcanic activity that result in an average of one major natural disaster every five years

Note: located 625 km southeast of Puerto Rico in the Caribbean Sea

People

Population: 340,381 (July 1990), growth rate 0.9% (1990)

Birth rate: 19 births/1,000 population (1990)

Death rate: 7 deaths/1,000 population (1990)

Net migration rate: −3 migrants/1,000 population (1990)

Infant mortality rate: 11 deaths/1,000 live births (1990)

Life expectancy at birth: 71 years male, 77 years female (1990)

Total fertility rate: 2.1 children born/woman (1990)

Martinique (continued)

Nationality: noun—Martiniquais (sing. and pl.); adjective—Martiniquais
Ethnic divisions: 90% African and African-Caucasian-Indian mixture, 5% Caucasian, less than 5% East Indian, Lebanese, Chinese
Religion: 95% Roman Catholic, 5% Hindu and pagan African
Language: French, Creole patois
Literacy: over 70%
Labor force: 100,000; 31.7% service industry, 29.4% construction and public works, 13.1% agriculture, 7.3% industry, 2.2% fisheries, 16.3% other
Organized labor: 11% of labor force

Government

Long-form name: Department of Martinique
Type: overseas department of France
Capital: Fort-de-France
Administrative divisions: none (overseas department of France)
Independence: none (overseas department of France)
Constitution: 28 September 1958 (French Constitution)
Legal system: French legal system
National holiday: Taking of the Bastille, 14 July (1789)
Executive branch: government commissioner
Legislative branch: unicameral General Council and unicameral Regional Council
Judicial branch: Supreme Court
Leaders: *Chief of State*—President François MITTERRAND (since 21 May 1981);
Head of Government—Government Commissioner Jean Claude ROURE (since 5 May 1989); President of the General Council Emile MAURICE (since NA 1988)
Political parties: Rally for the Republic (RPR), Stephen Bago; Union of the Left composed of the Progressive Party of Martinique (PPM), Aimé Césaire; Socialist Federation of Martinique, Michael Yoyo; and the Communist Party of Martinique (PCM), Armand Nicolas; Union for French Democracy (UDF), Jean Maran
Suffrage: universal at age 18
Elections: *General Council*—last held on NA October 1988 (next to be held by March 1991); results—percent of vote by party NA; seats—(44 total) number of seats by party NA;
Regional Assembly—last held on 16 March 1986 (next to be held by March 1992); results—UDF/RPR coalition 49.8%, PPM/FSM/PCM coalition 41.3%, others 8.9%; seats—(41 total) PPM/FSM/PCM coalition 21, UDF/RPR coalition 20;

French Senate—last held 24 September 1989 (next to be held September 1992); results—percent of vote by party NA; seats—(2 total) UDF 1, PPM 1;
French National Assembly—last held on 5 and 12 June 1988 (next to be held June 1993); results—percent of vote by party NA; seats—(4 total) PPM 1, FSM 1, RPR 1, UDF 1
Communists: 1,000 (est.)
Other political or pressure groups: Proletarian Action Group (GAP); Alhed Marie-Jeanne Socialist Revolution Group (GRS), Martinique Independence Movement (MIM), Caribbean Revolutionary Alliance (ARC), Central Union for Martinique Workers (CSTM), Marc Pulvar; Frantz Fanon Circle; League of Workers and Peasants
Member of: WFTU
Diplomatic representation: as an overseas department of France, Martiniquais interests are represented in the US by France; *US*—Consul General Ray ROBINSON; Consulate General at 14 Rue Blenac, Fort-de-France (mailing address is B. P. 561, Fort-de-France); telephone [596] 63-13-03
Flag: the flag of France is used

Economy

Overview: The economy is based on sugarcane, bananas, tourism, and light industry. Agriculture accounts for about 7% of GDP and the small industrial sector for 10%. Sugar production has declined, with most of the sugarcane now used for the production of rum. Banana exports are increasing, however, going mostly to France. The bulk of meat, vegetable, and grain requirements must be imported, contributing to a chronic trade deficit that requires large annual transfers of aid from France. Tourism has become more important than agricultural exports as a source of foreign exchange. The majority of the work force is employed in the service sector and in administration. In 1984 the annual per capita income was relatively high at $3,650. During 1985 the unemployment rate was between 25% and 30% and was particularly severe among younger workers.
GDP: $1.3 billion, per capita $3,650; real growth rate NA% (1984)
Inflation rate (consumer prices): 3.4% (1986)
Unemployment rate: 25-30% (1985)
Budget: revenues $223 million; expenditures $223 million, including capital expenditures of $NA (1987 est.)
Exports: $209 million (f.o.b., 1986); *commodities*—refined petroleum products, bananas, rum, pineapples; *partners*—France 65%, Guadeloupe 26% (1986)

Imports: $879 million (c.i.f., 1986); *commodities*—petroleum products, foodstuffs, construction materials, vehicles, clothing and other consumer goods; *partners*—France 64% (1986)
External debt: $NA
Industrial production: growth rate NA%
Electricity: 108,000 kW capacity; 330 million kWh produced, 990 kWh per capita (1989)
Industries: construction, rum, cement, oil refining, sugar, tourism
Agriculture: accounts for about 7% of GDP; principal crops—pineapples, avocados, bananas, flowers, vegetables, and sugarcane for rum; dependent on imported food, particularly meat and vegetables
Aid: Western (non-US) countries, ODA and OOF bilateral commitments (1970-87), $9.8 billion
Currency: French franc (plural—francs); 1 French franc (F) = 100 centimes
Exchange rates: French francs (F) per US$1—5.7598 (January 1990), 6.3801 (1989), 5.9569 (1988), 6.0107 (1987), 6.9261 (1986), 8.9852 (1985)
Fiscal year: calendar year

Communications

Highways: 1,680 km total; 1,300 km paved, 380 km gravel and earth
Ports: Fort-de-France
Civil air: no major transport aircraft
Airports: 2 total; 2 usable; 1 with permanent-surface runways; 1 with runways 2,440-3,659 m; 1 with runways less than 2,439 m
Telecommunications: domestic facilities are adequate; 68,900 telephones; interisland radio relay links to Guadeloupe, Dominica, and St. Lucia; stations—1 AM, 6 FM, 10 TV; 2 Atlantic Ocean INTELSAT earth stations

Defense Forces

Note: defense is the responsibility of France

Mauritania

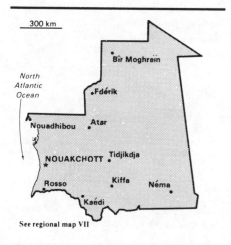

300 km

North Atlantic Ocean

Bîr Moghreïn
• Fdérik
Nouadhibou • Atar
NOUAKCHOTT • Tidjikdja
Rosso • Kiffa • Néma
Kaédi

See regional map VII

Geography

Total area: 1,030,700 km²; land area: 1,030,400 km²
Comparative area: slightly larger than three times the size of New Mexico
Land boundaries: 5,074 km total; Algeria 463 km, Mali 2,237 km, Senegal 813 km, Western Sahara 1,561 km
Coastline: 754 km
Maritime claims:
  Continental shelf: edge of continental margin or 200 nm
  Extended economic zone: 200 nm
  Territorial sea: 12 nm
Disputes: armed conflict in Western Sahara; boundary with Senegal
Climate: desert; constantly hot, dry, dusty
Terrain: mostly barren, flat plains of the Sahara; some central hills
Natural resources: iron ore, gypsum, fish, copper, phosphate
Land use: 1% arable land; NEGL% permanent crops; 38% meadows and pastures; 5% forest and woodland; 56% other; includes NEGL% irrigated
Environment: hot, dry, dust/sand-laden sirocco wind blows primarily in March and April; desertification; only perennial river is the Senegal

People

Population: 1,934,549 (July 1990), growth rate 3.1% (1990)
Birth rate: 49 births/1,000 population (1990)
Death rate: 18 deaths/1,000 population (1990)
Net migration rate: 0 migrants/1,000 population (1990)
Infant mortality rate: 96 deaths/1,000 live births (1990)
Life expectancy at birth: 44 years male, 49 years female (1990)
Total fertility rate: 7.3 children born/woman (1990)

Nationality: noun—Mauritanian(s); adjective—Mauritanian
Ethnic divisions: 40% mixed Maur/black, 30% Maur, 30% black
Religion: nearly 100% Muslim
Language: Hasaniya Arabic (national); French (official); Toucouleur, Fula, Sarakole, Wolof
Literacy: 17%
Labor force: 465,000 (1981 est.); 45,000 wage earners (1980); 47% agriculture, 29% services, 14% industry and commerce, 10% government; 53% of population of working age (1985)
Organized labor: 30,000 members claimed by single union, Mauritanian Workers' Union

Government

Long-form name: Islamic Republic of Mauritania
Type: republic; military first seized power in bloodless coup 10 July 1978; a palace coup that took place on 24 December 1984 brought President Taya to power
Capital: Nouakchott
Administrative divisions: 12 regions (régions, singular—région); Adrar, Brakna, Dakhlet Nouadhibou, El 'Açâba, Gorgol, Guidimaka, Hodh Ech Chargui, Hodh El Gharbi, Inchiri, Tagant, Tiris Zemmour, Trarza; note—there may be a new capital district of Nouakchott
Independence: 28 November 1960 (from France)
Constitution: 20 May 1961, abrogated after coup of 10 July 1978; provisional constitution published 17 December 1980 but abandoned in 1981; new constitutional charter published 27 February 1985
Legal system: based on Islamic law
National holiday: Independence Day, 28 November (1960)
Executive branch: president, Military Committee for National Salvation (CMSN), Council of Ministers (cabinet)
Legislative branch: unicameral National Assembly (Assemblée Nationale), dissolved after 10 July 1978 coup; legislative power resides with the CMSN
Judicial branch: Supreme Court (Cour Suprême)
Leaders: *Chief of State and Head of Government*—President Col. Maaouiya Ould Sid'Ahmed TAYA (since 12 December 1984)
Political parties and leaders: suspended
Suffrage: none
Elections: none; last presidential election August 1976; National Assembly dissolved 10 July 1978; no national elections are scheduled
Communists: no Communist party, but there is a scattering of Maoist sympathizers

Member of: ACP, AfDB, AIOEC, Arab League, CCC, CEAO, CIPEC (associate), EAMA, EIB (associate), FAO, G-77, GATT, IBRD, ICAO, IDA, IDB—Islamic Development Bank, IFAD, IFC, ILO, IMF, IMO, INTELSAT, INTERPOL, IPU, ITU, NAM, OAU, OIC, OMVS (Organization for the Development of the Senegal River Valley), UN, UNESCO, UPU, WHO, WIPO, WMO
Diplomatic representation: Ambassador Abdellah OULD DADDAH; Chancery at 2129 Leroy Place NW, Washington DC 20008; telephone (202) 232-5700; *US*—Ambassador William H. TWADDELL; Embassy at address NA, Nouakchott (mailing address is B. P. 222, Nouakchott); telephone [2222] 52660 or 52663
Flag: green with a yellow five-pointed star above a yellow, horizontal crescent; the closed side of the crescent is down; the crescent, star, and color green are traditional symbols of Islam

Economy

Overview: A majority of the population still depends on agriculture and livestock for a livelihood, even though most of the nomads and many subsistence farmers were forced into the cities by recurrent drought in 1983. Mauritania has extensive deposits of iron ore that account for almost 50% of total exports. The decline in world demand for this ore, however, has led to cutbacks in production in recent years. The nation's coastal waters are among the richest fishing areas in the world, but overexploitation by foreigners threatens this key source of revenue. The country's first deepwater port opened near Nouakchott in 1986.
GDP: $1.0 billion, per capita $520; real growth rate 3.6% (1988)
Inflation rate (consumer prices): 1.4% (1988 est.)
Unemployment rate: 50% (1988 est.)
Budget: revenues $358 million; expenditures $334 million, including capital expenditures of $79 million (1988 est.)
Exports: $424 million (f.o.b., 1988); *commodities*—iron ore, processed fish, small amounts of gum arabic and gypsum, unrecorded but numerically significant cattle exports to Senegal; *partners*—EC 57%, Japan 39%, Ivory Coast 2%
Imports: $365 million (c.i.f., 1988); *commodities*—foodstuffs, consumer goods, petroleum products, capital goods; *partners*—EC 79%, Africa 5%, US 4%, Japan 2%
External debt: $2.3 billion (December 1989)
Industrial production: growth rate 4.4% (1988 est.)

Mauritania *(continued)*

Electricity: 189,000 kW capacity; 136 million kWh produced, 70 kWh per capita (1989)
Industries: fishing, fish processing, mining of iron ore and gypsum
Agriculture: accounts for 29% of GDP (including fishing); largely subsistence farming and nomadic cattle and sheep herding except in Senegal river valley; crops—dates, millet, sorghum, root crops; fish products number-one export; large food deficit in years of drought
Aid: US commitments, including Ex-Im (FY70-88), $160 million; Western (non-US) countries, ODA and OOF bilateral commitments (1970-87), $1.1 billion; OPEC bilateral aid (1979-89), $490 million; Communist countries (1970-88), $277 million
Currency: ouguiya (plural—ouguiya); 1 ouguiya (UM) = 5 khoums
Exchange rates: ouguiya (UM) per US$1—83.838 (January 1990), 83.051 (1989), 75.261 (1988), 73.878 (1987), 74.375 (1986), 77.085 (1985)
Fiscal year: calendar year

Communications

Railroads: 670 km 1.435-meter standard gauge, single track, owned and operated by government mining company
Highways: 7,525 km total; 1,685 km paved; 1,040 km gravel, crushed stone, or otherwise improved; 4,800 km unimproved roads, trails, tracks
Inland waterways: mostly ferry traffic on the Senegal River
Ports: Nouadhibou, Nouakchott
Merchant marine: 1 cargo ship (1,000 GRT or over) totaling 1,272 GRT/ 1,840 DWT
Civil air: 2 major transport aircraft
Airports: 30 total, 29 usable; 9 with permanent-surface runways; none with runways over 3,659 m; 4 with runways 2,440-3,659 m; 17 with runways 1,220-2,439 m
Telecommunications: poor system of cable and open-wire lines, minor radio relay links, and radio communications stations; 5,200 telephones; stations—2 AM, no FM, 1 TV; satellite earth stations—1 Atlantic Ocean INTELSAT and 2 ARABSAT, with a third planned

Defense Forces

Branches: Army, Navy, Air Force, paramilitary Gendarmerie, paramilitary National Guard, paramilitary National Police, paramilitary Presidential Guard, paramilitary Nomad Security Guards
Military manpower: males 15-49, 410,153; 200,212 fit for military service; conscription law not implemented
Defense expenditures: 4.2% of GDP (1987)

Mauritius

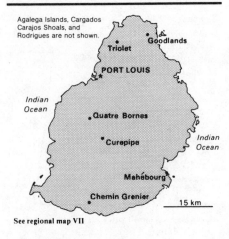

Agalega Islands, Cargados Carajos Shoals, and Rodrigues are not shown.

See regional map VII

Geography

Total area: 1,860 km²; land area: 1,850 km²; includes Agalega Islands, Cargados Carajos Shoals (St. Brandon) and Rodrigues
Comparative area: slightly less than 10.5 times the size of Washington, DC
Land boundaries: none
Coastline: 177 km
Maritime claims:
Continental shelf: edge of continental margin or 200 nm
Extended economic zone: 200 nm
Territorial sea: 12 nm
Disputes: claims Chagos Archipelago, which includes the island of Diego Garcia in UK-administered British Indian Ocean Territory; claims French-administered Tromelin Island
Climate: tropical modified by southeast trade winds; warm, dry winter (May to November); hot, wet, humid summer (November to May)
Terrain: small coastal plain rising to discontinuous mountains encircling central plateau
Natural resources: arable land, fish
Land use: 54% arable land; 4% permanent crops; 4% meadows and pastures; 31% forest and woodland; 7% other; includes 9% irrigated
Environment: subject to cyclones (November to April); almost completely surrounded by reefs
Note: located 900 km east of Madagascar in the Indian Ocean

People

Population: 1,070,005 (July 1990), growth rate 1.8% (1990)
Birth rate: 21 births/1,000 population (1990)
Death rate: 6 deaths/1,000 population (1990)

Net migration rate: 4 migrants/1,000 population (1990)
Infant mortality rate: 20 deaths/1,000 live births (1990)
Life expectancy at birth: 66 years male, 73 years female (1990)
Total fertility rate: 2.0 children born/woman (1990)
Nationality: noun—Mauritian(s); adjective—Mauritian
Ethnic divisions: 68% Indo-Mauritian, 27% Creole, 3% Sino-Mauritian, 2% Franco-Mauritian
Religion: 51% Hindu, 30% Christian (mostly Roman Catholic with a few Anglicans), 17% Muslim, 2% other
Language: English (official), Creole, French, Hindi, Urdu, Hakka, Bojpoori
Literacy: 82.8%
Labor force: 335,000; 29% government services, 27% agriculture and fishing, 22% manufacturing, 22% other; 43% of population of working age (1985)
Organized labor: 35% of labor force in more than 270 unions

Government

Long-form name: none
Type: parliamentary democracy
Capital: Port Louis
Administrative divisions: 5 urban councils and 3 district councils*; Beau Bassin-Rose Hill, Curepipe, Moka-Flacq*, North*, Port Louis, Quatre Bornes, South*, Vacoas-Phoenix; note—there may now be 4 urban councils and 9 district councils* named Beau Bassin-Rose Hill, Black River*, Curepipe, Flacq*, Grand Port*, Moka*, Pamplemousses*, Plaine Wilhems*, Port Louis*, Quartre Bornes, Rivière du Rempart*, Savanne*, and Vacoas-Phoenix
Independence: 12 March 1968 (from UK)
Constitution: 12 March 1968
Legal system: based on French civil law system with elements of English common law in certain areas
National holiday: Independence Day, 12 March (1968)
Executive branch: British monarch, governor general, prime minister, deputy prime minister, Council of Ministers (cabinet)
Legislative branch: unicameral Legislative Assembly
Judicial branch: Supreme Court
Leaders: *Chief of State*—Queen ELIZABETH II (since 6 February 1952), represented by Governor General Sir Veerasamy RINGADOO (since 17 January 1986);
Head of Government—Prime Minister Anerood JUGNAUTH (since 12 June 1982); Deputy Prime Minister Sir Satcam BOOLELL (since 15 August 1988)
Political parties and leaders: the government is currently controlled by a coalition composed of the Militant Socialist Movement (MSM), A. Jugnauth, and the Mauritian Labor Party (MLP), S. Boolell; the

main opposition union consists of the Mauritian Militant Movement (MMM), Prem Nababsing; Socialist Workers Front, Sylvio Michel; Democratic Labor Movement, Anil Baichoo; Mauritian Social Democratic Party (PMSD), G. Duval
Suffrage: universal at age 18
Elections: *Legislative Assembly*—last held on 30 August 1987 (next to be held 30 August 1992); results—percent of vote by party NA; seats—(70 total, 62 elected) MSM 24, MMM 21, MLP 10, PMSD 5, others 10
Communists: may be 2,000 sympathizers; several Communist organizations; Mauritius Lenin Youth Organization, Mauritius Women's Committee, Mauritius Communist Party, Mauritius People's Progressive Party, Mauritius Young Communist League, Mauritius Liberation Front, Chinese Middle School Friendly Association, Mauritius/USSR Friendship Society
Other political or pressure groups: various labor unions
Member of: ACP, AfDB, CCC, Commonwealth, FAO, G-77, GATT, IAEA, IBRD, ICAO, IDA, IFAD, IFC, ILO, IMF, IMO, INTELSAT, INTERPOL, ISO, ITU, IWC—International Wheat Council, NAM, OAU, OCAM, UN, UNESCO, UPU, WFTU, WHO, WIPO, WMO, WTO
Diplomatic representation: Ambassador Chitmansing JESSERAMSING; Chancery at Suite 134, 4301 Connecticut Avenue NW, Washington DC 20008; telephone (202) 244-1491 or 1492; *US*—Ambassador Penne KORTH; Embassy at 4th Floor, Rogers Building, John Kennedy Street, Port Louis; telephone 082347
Flag: four equal horizontal bands of red (top), blue, yellow, and green

Economy

Overview: The economy is based on sugar, manufacturing (mainly textiles), and tourism. Despite significant expansion in other sectors over the past decade, sugarcane remains dominant and is grown on about 90% of the cultivated land area, accounting for 40% of export earnings. The government's development strategy is centered on industrialization (with a view to exports), agricultural diversification, and tourism. Economic performance in 1988 was impressive, with 6.3% real growth rate and low unemployment.
GDP: $1.9 billion, per capita $1,910; real growth rate 6.3% (1988)
Inflation rate (consumer prices): 9.2% (1988)
Unemployment rate: 3.6% (1988)
Budget: revenues $351 million; expenditures $414 million, including capital expenditures of $76 million (FY87 est.)
Exports: $1.0 billion (f.o.b., 1988); *commodities*—textiles 44%, sugar 40%, light manufactures 10%; *partners*—EC and US have preferential treatment, EC 77%, US 15%
Imports: $1.3 billion (c.i.f., 1988); *commodities*—manufactured goods 50%, capi-

tal equipment 17%, foodstuffs 13%, petroleum products 8%, chemicals 7%; *partners*—EC, US, South Africa, Japan
External debt: $670 million (December 1989)
Industrial production: growth rate 12.9% (FY87)
Electricity: 233,000 kW capacity; 420 million kWh produced, 375 kWh per capita (1989)
Industries: food processing (largely sugar milling), textiles, wearing apparel, chemical and chemical products, metal products, transport equipment, nonelectrical machinery, tourism
Agriculture: accounts for 14% of GDP; about 90% of cultivated land in sugarcane; other products—tea, corn, potatoes, bananas, pulses, cattle, goats, fish; net food importer, especially rice and fish
Illicit drugs: illicit producer of cannabis for the international drug trade
Aid: US commitments, including Ex-Im (FY70-88), $72 million; Western (non-US) countries (1970-87), $538 million; Communist countries (1970-88), $54 million
Currency: Mauritian rupee (plural—rupees); 1 Mauritian rupee (MauR) = 100 cents
Exchange rates: Mauritian rupees (MauRs) per US$1—15.033 (January 1990), 15.250 (1989), 13.438 (1988), 12.878 (1987), 13.466 (1986), 15.442 (1985)
Fiscal year: 1 July-30 June

Communications

Highways: 1,800 km total; 1,640 km paved, 160 km earth
Ports: Port Louis
Merchant marine: 9 ships (1,000 GRT or over) totaling 143,029 GRT/ 248,754 DWT; includes 1 passenger-cargo, 3 cargo, 1 petroleum, oils, and lubricants (POL) tanker, 1 liquefied gas, 3 bulk
Civil air: 4 major transport aircraft
Airports: 5 total, 4 usable; 2 with permanent-surface runways; none with runways over 3,659 m; 1 with runways 2,440-3,659 m
Telecommunications: small system with good service; new microwave link to Reunion; high-frequency radio links to several countries; 48,000 telephones; stations—2 AM, no FM, 4 TV; 1 Indian Ocean INTELSAT earth station

Defense Forces

Branches: paramilitary Special Mobile Force, Special Support Units, regular Police Force
Military manpower: males 15-49, 297,975; 153,130 fit for military service
Defense expenditures: NA

Mayotte

(territorial collectivity of France)

Île M'Zambourou

10 km

Administered by France,
claimed by Comoros.

DZAOUDZI

Mayotte

Île
Pamanzi

Sada

Bandrélé

See regional map VII   *Mozambique Channel*

Geography

Total area: 375 km²; land area: 375 km²
Comparative area: slightly more than twice the size of Washington, DC
Land boundaries: none
Coastline: 185.2 km
Maritime claims:
Continental shelf: 200 meters or to depth of exploitation
Extended economic zone: 200 nm
Territorial sea: 12 nm
Disputes: claimed by Comoros
Climate: tropical; marine; hot, humid, rainy season during northeastern monsoon (November to May); dry season is cooler (May to November)
Terrain: generally undulating with ancient volcanic peaks, deep ravines
Natural resources: negligible
Land use: NA% arable land; NA% permanent crops; NA% meadows and pastures; NA% forest and woodland; NA% other
Environment: subject to cyclones during rainy season
Note: part of Comoro Archipelago; located in the Mozambique Channel about halfway between Africa and Madagascar

People

Population: 72,186 (July 1990), growth rate 3.9% (1990)
Birth rate: 51 births/1,000 population (1990)
Death rate: 12 deaths/1,000 population (1990)
Net migration rate: 0 migrants/1,000 population (1990)
Infant mortality rate: 89 deaths/1,000 live births (1990)
Life expectancy at birth: 54 years male, 58 years female (1990)
Total fertility rate: 6.8 children born/woman (1990)
Nationality: noun—Mahorais (sing., pl.); adjective—Mahoran

Religion: 99% Muslim; remainder Christian, mostly Roman Catholic
Language: Mahorian (a Swahili dialect), French
Literacy: NA%, but probably high
Labor force: NA
Organized labor: NA

Government

Long-form name: Territorial Collectivity of Mayotte
Type: territorial collectivity of France
Capital: Dzaoudzi
Administrative divisions: none (territorial collectivity of France)
Independence: none (territorial collectivity of France)
Constitution: 28 September 1958 (French Constitution)
Legal system: French law
National holiday: Taking of the Bastille, 14 July (1789)
Executive branch: government commissioner
Legislative branch: unicameral General Council (Conseil Général)
Judicial branch: Supreme Court (Tribunal Supérieur d'Appel)
Leaders: *Chief of State* President François MITTERRAND (since 21 May 1981); *Head of Government* Government Commissioner Akli KHIDER (since 1983); President of the General Council Youssouf BAMANA (since 1976)
Political parties and leaders: Mahoran Popular Movement (MPM), Zńa M'Oere; Party for the Mahoran Democratic Rally (PRDM), Daroueche Maoulida; Mahoran Rally for the Republic (RMPR), Abdoul Anizizi; Union of the Center (UDC)
Suffrage: universal at age 18
Elections: *General Council*—last held NA June 1988 (next to be held June 1993); results—percent of vote by party NA; seats—(17 total) MPM 9, RPR 6, others 2;
French Senate—last held on 24 September 1989 (next to be held September 1992); results—percent of vote by party NA; seats—(1 total) MPM 1;
French National Assembly—last held 5 and 12 June 1988 (next to be held June 1993); results—percent of vote by party NA; seats—(1 total) UDC 1
Communists: probably none
Diplomatic representation: as a territorial collectivity of France, Mahoran interests are represented in the US by France
Flag: the flag of France is used

Economy

Overview: Economic activity is based primarily on the agricultural sector, including fishing and livestock raising. Mayotte

is not self-sufficient and must import a large portion of its food requirements, mainly from France. The economy and future development of the island is heavily dependent on French financial assistance.
GDP: NA
Inflation rate (consumer prices): NA%
Unemployment rate: NA%
Budget: revenues NA; expenditures $37.3 million, including capital expenditures of NA (1985)
Exports: $4.0 million (f.o.b., 1984); *commodities*—ylang-ylang, vanilla; *partners*—France 79%, Comoros 10%, Reunion 9%
Imports: $21.8 million (f.o.b., 1984); *commodities*—building materials, transportation equipment, rice, clothing, flour; *partners*—France 57%, Kenya 16%, South Africa 11%, Pakistan 8%
External debt: $NA
Industrial production: growth rate NA%
Electricity: NA kW capacity; NA million kWh produced, NA kWh per capita
Industries: newly created lobster and shrimp industry
Agriculture: most important sector; provides all export earnings; crops—vanilla, ylang-ylang, coffee, copra; imports major share of food needs
Aid: Western (non-US) countries, ODA and OOF bilateral commitments (1970-87), $287.8 million
Currency: French franc (plural—francs); 1 French franc (F) = 100 centimes
Exchange rates: French francs (F) per US$1—5.7598 (January 1990), 6.3801 (1989), 5.9569 (1988), 6.0107 (1987), 6.9261 (1986), 8.9852 (1985)
Fiscal year: calendar year

Communications

Highways: 42 km total; 18 km bituminous
Civil air: no major transport aircraft
Airports: 1 with permanent-surface runway 1,220-2,439 m
Ports: Dzaoudzi
Telecommunications: small system administered by French Department of Posts and Telecommunications; includes radio relay and high-frequency radio communications for links with Comoros and international communications; 450 telephones; stations—1 AM, no FM, no TV

Defense Forces

Note: defense is the responsibility of France

Mexico

1000 km

North
Pacific
Ocean

See regional map II

Geography

Total area: 1,972,550 km²; land area: 1,923,040 km²
Comparative area: slightly less than three times the size of Texas
Land boundaries: 4,538 km total; Belize 250 km, Guatemala 962 km, US 3,326 km
Coastline: 9,330 km
Maritime claims:
Contiguous zone: 24 nm
Continental shelf: natural prolongation of continental margin or 200 nm
Extended economic zone: 200 nm
Territorial sea: 12 nm
Climate: varies from tropical to desert
Terrain: high, rugged mountains, low coastal plains, high plateaus, and desert
Natural resources: crude oil, silver, copper, gold, lead, zinc, natural gas, timber
Land use: 12% arable land; 1% permanent crops; 39% meadows and pastures; 24% forest and woodland; 24% other; includes 3% irrigated
Environment: subject to tsunamis along the Pacific coast and destructive earthquakes in the center and south; natural water resources scarce and polluted in north, inaccessible and poor quality in center and extreme southeast; deforestation; erosion widespread; desertification; serious air pollution in Mexico City and urban centers along US-Mexico border
Note: strategic location on southern border of US

People

Population: 87,870,154 (July 1990), growth rate 2.2% (1990)
Birth rate: 29 births/1,000 population (1990)
Death rate: 5 deaths/1,000 population (1990)
Net migration rate: −2 migrants/1,000 population (1990)

Infant mortality rate: 33 deaths/1,000 live births (1990)
Life expectancy at birth: 68 years male, 76 years female (1990)
Total fertility rate: 3.4 children born/woman (1990)
Nationality: noun—Mexican(s); adjective—Mexican
Ethnic divisions: 60% mestizo (Indian-Spanish), 30% Amerindian or predominantly Amerindian, 9% white or predominantly white, 1% other
Religion: 97% nominally Roman Catholic, 3% Protestant
Language: Spanish
Literacy: 88%
Labor force: 26,100,000 (1988); 31.4% services; 26% agriculture, forestry, hunting, and fishing, 13.9% commerce, 12.8% manufacturing, 9.5% construction, 4.8% transportation, 1.3% mining and quarrying, 0.3% electricity, (1986)
Organized labor: 35% of labor force

Government

Long-form name: United Mexican States
Type: federal republic operating under a centralized government
Capital: Mexico
Administrative divisions: 31 states (estados, singular—estado) and 1 federal district* (distrito federal); Aguascalientes, Baja California Norte, Baja California Sur, Campeche, Chiapas, Chihuahua, Coahuila, Colima, Distrito Federal*, Durango, Guanajuato, Guerrero, Hidalgo, Jalisco, México, Michoacán, Morelos, Nayarit, Nuevo León, Oaxaca, Puebla, Querétaro, Quintana Roo, San Luis Potosí, Sinaloa, Sonora, Tabasco, Tamaulipas, Tlaxcala, Veracruz, Yucatán, Zacatecas
Independence: 16 September 1810 (from Spain)
Constitution: 5 February 1917
Legal system: mixture of US constitutional theory and civil law system; judicial review of legislative acts; accepts compulsory ICJ jurisdiction, with reservations
National holiday: Independence Day, 16 September (1810)
Executive branch: president, Cabinet
Legislative branch: bicameral National Congress (Congreso de la Unión) consists of an upper chamber or Senate (Cámara de Senadores) and a lower chamber or Chamber of Deputies (Cámara de Diputados)
Judicial branch: Supreme Court of Justice (Suprema Corte de Justicia)
Leaders: *Chief of State and Head of Government*—President Carlos SALINAS de Gortari (since 1 December 1988)
Political parties and leaders: (recognized parties) Institutional Revolutionary Party

(PRI), Luís Donaldo Colosio Murrieta; National Action Party (PAN), Luis Alvarez; Popular Socialist Party (PPS), Indalecio Sayago Herrera; Democratic Revolutionary Party (PRD), Cuauhtemoc Cardenas; Cardenist Front for the National Reconstruction Party (PFCRN), Rafael Aguilar Talamantes; Authentic Party of the Mexican Revolution (PARM), Carlos Enrique Cantu Rosas
Suffrage: universal and compulsory (but not enforced) at age 18
Elections: *President*—last held on 6 July 1988 (next to be held September 1994); results—Carlos Salinas de Gortari (PRI) 50.74%, Cuauhtémoc Cárdenas Solórzano (FDN) 31.06%, Manuel Clouthier (PAN) 16.81%; others 1.39%; note—several of the smaller parties ran a common candidate under a coalition called the National Democratic Front (FDN)
Senate—last held on 6 July 1988 (next to be held September 1991); results—PRI 94%, FDN (now PRD) 6%; seats—(64 total) number of seats by party NA;
Chamber of Deputies—last held on 6 July 1988 (next to be held September 1991); results—PRI 53%, PAN 20%, PFCRN 10%, PPS 6%, PARM 7%, PMS (now part of PRD) 4%; seats—(500 total) number of seats by party NA
Other political or pressure groups: Roman Catholic Church, Confederation of Mexican Workers (CTM), Confederation of Industrial Chambers (CONCAMIN), Confederation of National Chambers of Commerce (CONCANACO), National Peasant Confederation (CNC), National Confederation of Popular Organizations (CNOP), Revolutionary Workers Party (PRT), Mexican Democratic Party (PDM), Revolutionary Confederation of Workers and Peasants (CROC), Regional Confederation of Mexican Workers (CROM), Confederation of Employers of the Mexican Republic (COPARMEX), National Chamber of Transformation Industries (CANACINTRA), Business Coordination Council (CCE)
Member of: FAO, G-77, GATT, Group of Eight, IADB, IAEA, IBRD, ICAC, ICAO, ICO, IDA, IDB—Inter-American Development Bank, IFAD, IFC, ILO, ILZSG, IMF, IMO, INTELSAT, INTERPOL, IRC, ISO, ITU, IWC—International Whaling Commission, LAIA, OAS, PAHO, SELA, UN, UNESCO, UPU, WHO, WIPO, WMO, WSG, WTO
Diplomatic representation: Ambassador Gustavo PETRICIOLI Iturbide; Chancery at 1911 Pennsylvania Avenue NW, Washington DC 20006; telephone (202) 728-1600; there are Mexican Consulates General in Chicago, Dallas, Denver, El

Mexico (continued)

Paso, Houston, Los Angeles, New Orleans, New York, San Francisco, San Antonio, San Diego, and Consulates in Albuquerque, Atlanta, Austin, Boston, Brownsville (Texas), Calexico (California), Corpus Christi, Del Rio (Texas), Detroit, Douglas (Arizona), Eagle Pass (Texas), Fresno (California), Kansas City (Missouri), Laredo, McAllen (Texas), Miami, Nogales (Arizona), Oxnard (California), Philadelphia, Phoenix, Presidio (Texas), Sacramento, St. Louis, St. Paul (Minneapolis), Salt Lake City, San Bernardino, San Jose, San Juan (Puerto Rico), and Seattle; *US*—Ambassador John D. NEGROPONTE, Jr.; Embassy at Paseo de la Reforma 305, Mexico 5, D.F. (mailing address is P. O. Box 3087, Laredo, TX 78044); telephone [52] (5) 211-0042; there are US Consulates General in Ciudad Juarez, Guadalajara, Monterrey, and Tijuana, and Consulates in Hermosillo, Matamoros, Mazatlan, Merida, and Nuevo Laredo
Flag: three equal vertical bands of green (hoist side), white, and red; the coat of arms (an eagle perched on a cactus with a snake is its beak) is centered in the white band

Economy

Overview: Mexico's economy is a mixture of state-owned industrial plants (notably oil), private manufacturing and services, and both large-scale and traditional agriculture. In the 1980s Mexico experienced severe economic difficulties: the nation accumulated large external debts as world petroleum prices fell; rapid population growth outstripped the domestic food supply; and inflation, unemployment, and pressures to emigrate became more acute. Growth in national output dropped from 8% in 1980 to 1.1% in 1988 and 2.5% in 1989. The US is Mexico's major trading partner, accounting for two-thirds of its exports and imports. After petroleum, border assembly plants and tourism are the largest earners of foreign exchange. The government, in consultation with international economic agencies, is implementing programs to stabilize the economy and foster growth.
GDP: $187.0 billion, per capita $2,165; real growth rate 2.5% (1989)
Inflation rate (consumer prices): 20% (1989)
Unemployment rate: 20% (1989 est.)
Budget: revenues $36.1 billion; expenditures $56.1 billion, including capital expenditures of $7.7 biilion (1988)
Exports: $23.1 billion (f.o.b., 1989); *commodities*—crude oil, oil products, coffee, shrimp, engines, cotton; *partners*—US 66%, EC 16%, Japan 11%

Imports: $23.3 billion (c.i.f., 1989); *commodities*—grain, metal manufactures, agricultural machinery, electrical equipment; *partners*—US 62%, EC 18%, Japan 10%
External debt: $95.1 billion (1989)
Industrial production: growth rate 1.3% (1988)
Electricity: 26,900,000 kW capacity; 103,670 million kWh produced, 1,200 kWh per capita (1989)
Industries: food and beverages, tobacco, chemicals, iron and steel, petroleum, mining, textiles, clothing, transportation equipment, tourism
Agriculture: accounts for 9% of GDP and over 25% of work force; large number of small farms at subsistence level; major food crops—corn, wheat, rice, beans; cash crops—cotton, coffee, fruit, tomatoes; fish catch of 1.4 million metric tons among top 20 nations (1987)
Illicit drugs: illicit cultivation of opium poppy and cannabis continues in spite of government eradication efforts; major link in chain of countries used to smuggle cocaine from South American dealers to US markets
Aid: US commitments, including Ex-Im (FY70-88), $3.0 billion; Western (non-US) countries, ODA and OOF bilateral commitments (1970-87), $6.8 billion; Communist countries (1970-88), $110 million
Currency: Mexican peso (plural—pesos); 1 Mexican peso (Mex$) = 100 centavos
Exchange rates: market rate of Mexican pesos (Mex$) per US$1—2,660.3 (January 1990), 2,461.3 (1989), 2,273.1 (1988), 1,378.2 (1987), 611.8 (1986), 256.9 (1985)
Fiscal year: calendar year

Communications

Railroads: 20,680 km total; 19,950 km 1.435-meter standard gauge; 730 km 0.914-meter narrow gauge
Highways: 210,000 km total; 65,000 km paved, 30,000 km semipaved or cobblestone, 60,000 km rural roads (improved earth) or roads under construction, 55,000 km unimproved earth roads
Inland waterways: 2,900 km navigable rivers and coastal canals
Pipelines: crude oil, 4,381 km; refined products, 8,345 km; natural gas, 13,254 km
Ports: Acapulco, Coatzacoalcos, Ensenada, Guaymas, Manzanillo, Mazatlan, Progreso, Puerto Vallarta, Salina Cruz, Tampico, Veracruz
Merchant marine: 68 ships (1,000 GRT or over) totaling 1,041,229 GRT/1,552,478 DWT; includes 5 short-sea passenger, 10 cargo, 2 refrigerated cargo, 2 roll-on/roll-off cargo, 31 petroleum, oils, and lubricants (POL) tanker, 3 chemical tanker, 7 liquefied gas, 4 bulk, 4 combination bulk

Civil air: 174 major transport aircraft
Airports: 1,785 total, 1,484 usable; 190 with permanent-surface runways; 2 with runways over 3,659 m; 31 with runways 2,440-3,659 m; 259 with runways 1,220-2,439 m
Telecommunications: highly developed system with extensive radio relay links; connection into Central American Microwave System; 6.41 million telephones; stations—679 AM, no FM, 238 TV, 22 shortwave; 120 domestic satellite terminals; satellite earth stations—4 Atlantic Ocean INTELSAT and 1 Pacific Ocean INTELSAT

Defense Forces

Branches: Army, Air Force, Navy, Marine Corps
Military manpower: males 15-49, 21,575,525; 15,803,322 fit for military service; 1,118,046 reach military age (18) annually
Defense expenditures: 0.5% of GDP

Micronesia, Federated States of

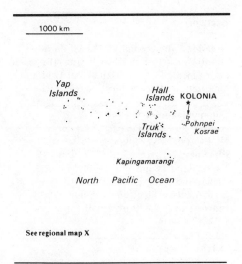

1000 km

Yap Islands
Hall Islands KOLONIA
Truk Islands
Pohnpei
Kosrae

Kapingamarangi

North Pacific Ocean

See regional map X

Geography

Total area: 702 km²; land area: 702 km²; includes Pohnpei, Truk, Yap, and Kosrae
Comparative area: slightly less than four times the size of Washington, DC
Land boundaries: none
Coastline: 6,112 km
Maritime claims:
Extended economic zone: 200 nm
Territorial sea: 12 nm
Climate: tropical; heavy year-round rainfall, especially in the eastern islands; located on southern edge of the typhoon belt with occasional severe damage
Terrain: islands vary geologically from high mountainous islands to low, coral atolls; volcanic outcroppings on Pohnpei, Kosrae, and Truk
Natural resources: forests, marine products, deep-seabed minerals
Land use: NA% arable land; NA% permanent crops; NA% meadows and pastures; NA% forest and woodland; NA% other
Environment: subject to typhoons from June to December; four major island groups totaling 607 islands
Note: located 5,150 km west-southwest of Honolulu in the North Pacific Ocean, about three-quarters of the way between Hawaii and Indonesia

People

Population: 104,937 (July 1990), growth rate 2.6% (1990)
Birth rate: 34 births/1,000 population (1990)
Death rate: 5 deaths/1,000 population (1990)
Net migration rate: −2 migrants/1,000 population (1990)
Infant mortality rate: 26 deaths/1,000 live births (1990)
Life expectancy at birth: 68 years male, 73 years female (1990)
Total fertility rate: 5.0 children born/woman (1990)
Nationality: noun—Micronesian(s); adjective—Micronesian; Kosrae(s), Pohnpeian(s), Trukese, Yapese
Ethnic divisions: nine ethnic Micronesian and Polynesian groups
Religion: predominantly Christian, divided between Roman Catholic and Protestant; other churches include Assembly of God, Jehovah's Witnesses, Seventh-Day Adventist, Latter Day Saints, and the Bahá'í Faith
Language: English is the official and common language; most indigenous languages fall within the Austronesian language family, the exceptions are the Polynesian languages; major indigenous languages are Trukese, Pohnpeian, Yapese, and Kosrean
Literacy: NA%, but education compulsory through eight grades
Labor force: NA; two-thirds are government employees; 45,000 people are between the ages of 15 and 65
Organized labor: NA

Government

Long-form name: Federated States of Micronesia (no short-form name)
Type: constitutional government in free association with the US; the Compact of Free Association entered into force 3 November 1986
Capital: Kolonia (on the island of Pohnpei); note—a new capital is being built about 10 km southwest in the Palikir valley
Administrative divisions: 4 states; Kosrae, Pohnpei, Truk, Yap
Independence: 3 November 1986 (from the US-administered UN Trusteeship; formerly the Kosrae, Pohnpei, Truk, and Yap districts of the Trust Territory of the Pacific Islands)
Constitution: 10 May 1979
Legal system: based on adapted Trust Territory laws, acts of the legislature, municipal, common, and customary laws
National holiday: Proclamation of the Federated States of Micronesia, 10 May (1979)
Executive branch: president, vice president, Cabinet
Legislative branch: unicameral House of Representatives
Judicial branch: Supreme Court
Leaders: *Chief of State and Head of Government*—President John R. HAGLELGAM (since 11 May 1987); Vice President Hiroshi H. ISMAEL (since 11 May 1987)
Political parties and leaders: no formal parties
Suffrage: universal at age 18
Elections: *President*—last held 11 May 1987 (next to be held May 1991); results—John R. Haglelgam was elected; *House of Representatives*—last held on NA (next to be held NA); results—percent of vote NA; seats—(NA total)
Communists: none
Member of: SPF, ESCAP (associate)
Diplomatic representation: Deputy Representative Jesse B. MAREHALAN; Representative Office at 706 G Street SE, Washington DC 20003; telephone (202) 544-2640; *US*—Representative Michael G. WYGANT; US Office at address NA, Kolonia (mailing address is P. O. Box 1286, Pohnpei, Federated States of Micronesia 96941); telephone 691-320-2187
Flag: light blue with four white five-pointed stars centered; the stars are arranged in a diamond pattern

Economy

Overview: Financial assistance from the US is the primary source of revenue, with the US pledged to spend $1 billion in the islands in the 1990s. Micronesia also earns about $4 million a year in fees from foreign commercial fishing concerns. Economic activity consists primarily of subsistence farming and fishing. The islands have few mineral deposits worth exploiting, except for high-grade phosphate. The potential for a tourist industry exists, but the remoteness of the location and a lack of adequate facilities hinder development; note—GNP numbers reflect US spending.
GNP: $150 million, per capita $1,500; real growth rate NA% (1989 est.)
Inflation rate (consumer prices): NA%
Unemployment rate: 80%
Budget: revenues $110.8 million; expenditures NA, including capital expenditures of NA (1987 est.)
Exports: $1.6 million (f.o.b., 1983); *commodities*—copra; *partners*—NA
Imports: $48.9 million (c.i.f., 1983); *commodities*—NA; *partners*—NA
External debt: $NA
Industrial production: growth rate NA%
Electricity: 15,000 kW capacity; 35 million kWh produced, 340 kWh per capita (1989)
Industries: tourism, craft items from shell, wood, and pearl
Agriculture: mainly a subsistence economy; copra, black pepper; tropical fruits and vegetables, coconuts, cassava, sweet potatoes, pigs, chickens
Aid: under terms of the Compact of Free Association, the US will provide $1.3 billion in grant aid during the period 1986-2001
Currency: US currency is used
Exchange rates: US currency is used

Micronesia, Federated States of
(continued)
Fiscal year: 1 October-30 September

Communications

Highways: 39 km of paved macadam and concrete roads on major islands, otherwise 187 km stone-, coral-, or laterite-surfaced roads
Ports: Colonia (Yap), Truk (Kosrae), Okat (Kosrae)
Airports: 11 total, 10 usable; 7 with permanent-surface runways; 6 with runways 1,220-2,439
Telecommunications: 16,000 radio receivers, 1,125 TV sets (est. 1987); telephone network—960 telephone lines at both Kolonia and Truk; islands interconnected by shortwave radio (used mostly for government purposes); stations—5 AM, 1 FM, 6 TV, 1 shortwave; 4 Pacific Ocean INTELSAT earth stations

Defense Forces

Note: defense is the responsibility of the US

Midway Islands
(territory of the US)

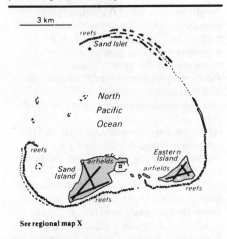

See regional map X

Geography

Total area: 5.2 km²; land area: 5.2 km²; includes Eastern Island and Sand Island
Comparative area: about nine times the size of The Mall in Washington, DC
Land boundaries: none
Coastline: 15 km
Maritime claims:
  Contiguous zone: 12 nm
  Continental shelf: 200 m
  Extended economic zone: 200 nm
  Territorial sea: 12 nm
Climate: tropical, but moderated by prevailing easterly winds
Terrain: low, nearly level
Natural resources: fish and wildlife
Land use: 0% arable land; 0% permanent crops; 0% meadows and pastures; 0% forest and woodland; 100% other
Environment: coral atoll
Note: located 2,350 km west-northwest of Honolulu at the western end of Hawaiian Islands group, about one-third of the way between Honolulu and Tokyo; closed to the public

People

Population: 453 US military personnel (1989)

Government

Long-form name: none
Type: unincorporated territory of the US administered by the US Navy, under command of the Barbers Point Naval Air Station in Hawaii and managed cooperatively by the US Navy and the Fish and Wildlife Service of the US Department of the Interior as part of the National Wildlife Refuge System
Diplomatic representation: none (territory of the US)
Flag: the US flag is used

Economy

Overview: The economy is based on providing support services for US naval operations located on the islands. All food and manufactured goods must be imported.

Communications

Highways: 32 km total
Pipelines: 7.8 km
Ports: Sand Island
Airports: 3 total; 2 usable; 1 with permanent-surface runways; none with runways over 2,439 m; 2 with runways 1,220-2,439 m

Defense Forces

Note: defense is the responsibility of the US

Monaco

1 km

Monte Carlo Casino

Mediterranean Sea

Palace

See regional map V

Geography

Total area: 1.9 km²; land area: 1.9 km²
Comparative area: about three times the size of The Mall in Washington, DC
Land boundary: 4.4 km with France
Coastline: 4.1 km
Maritime claim:
Territorial sea: 12 nm
Climate: Mediterranean with mild, wet winters and hot, dry summers
Terrain: hilly, rugged, rocky
Natural resources: none
Land use: 0% arable land; 0% permanent crops; 0% meadows and pastures; 0% forest and woodland; 100% other
Environment: almost entirely urban
Note: second-smallest independent state in world (after Vatican City)

People

Population: 29,453 (July 1990), growth rate 0.9% (1990)
Birth rate: 7 births/1,000 population (1990)
Death rate: 7 deaths/1,000 population (1990)
Net migration rate: 9 migrants/1,000 population (1990)
Infant mortality rate: 9 deaths/1,000 live births (1990)
Life expectancy at birth: 72 years male, 80 years female (1990)
Total fertility rate: 1.2 children born/woman (1990)
Nationality: noun—Monacan(s) or Monegasque(s); adjective—Monacan or Monegasque
Ethnic divisions: 47% French, 16% Monegasque, 16% Italian, 21% other
Religion: 95% Roman Catholic
Language: French (official), English, Italian, Monegasque
Literacy: 99%
Labor force: NA

Organized labor: 4,000 members in 35 unions

Government

Long-form name: Principality of Monaco
Type: constitutional monarchy
Capital: Monaco
Administrative divisions: 4 quarters (quartiers, singular—quartier); Fontvieille, La Condamine, Monaco-Ville, Monte-Carlo
Independence: 1419, rule by the House of Grimaldi
Constitution: 17 December 1962
Legal system: based on French law; has not accepted compulsory ICJ jurisdiction
National holiday: National Day, 19 November
Executive branch: prince, minister of state, Council of Government (cabinet)
Legislative branch: National Council (Conseil National)
Judicial branch: Supreme Tribunal (Tribunal Suprême)
Leaders: *Chief of State*—Prince RAINIER III (since November 1949); Heir Apparent Prince ALBERT Alexandre Louis Pierre (born 14 March 1958);
Head of Government Minister of State Jean AUSSEIL (since 10 September 1985)
Political parties and leaders: National and Democratic Union (UND), Democratic Union Movement (MUD), Monaco Action, Monegasque Socialist Party (PSM)
Suffrage: universal adult at age 25
Elections: *National Council*—last held on 24 January 1988 (next to be held 24 January 1993); results—percent of vote by party NA; seats—(18 total) UND 18
Member of: IAEA, ICAO, IHO, INTELSAT, INTERPOL, IPU, ITU, UN (permanent observer), UNESCO, UPU, WHO, WIPO
Diplomatic representation: Monaco maintains honorary consulates general in Boston, Chicago, Los Angeles, New Orleans, New York, and San Francisco, and honorary consulates in Dallas, Honolulu, Palm Beach, Philadelphia, and Washington; *US*—no mission in Monaco, but the US Consul General in Marseille, France, is accredited to Monaco; Consul General R. Susan WOOD; Consulate General at 12 Boulevard Paul Peytral, 13286 Marseille Cedex (mailing address APO NY 09777); telephone [33] (91) 549-200
Flag: two equal horizontal bands of red (top) and white; similar to the flag of Indonesia which is longer and the flag of Poland which is white (top) and red

Economy

Overview: No data are published on the economy. Monaco, situated on the French

Mediterranean coast, is a popular resort, attracting tourists to its casino and pleasant climate. The Principality has successfully sought to diversify into services and small, high-value-added, non-polluting industries. The state has no income tax and low business taxes and thrives as a tax haven both for individuals who have established residence and for foreign companies that have set up businesses and offices. About 50% of Monaco's annual revenue comes from value-added taxes on hotels, banks, and the industrial sector; about 25% of revenue comes from tourism. Living standards are high, that is, roughly comparable to those in prosperous French metropolitan suburbs.
GNP: NA
Inflation rate (consumer prices): NA%
Unemployment rate: full employment (1989)
Budget: revenues $386 million; expenditures $NA, including capital expenditures of $NA (1988 est.)
Exports: $NA; full customs integration with France, which collects and rebates Monacan trade duties; also participates in EC market system through customs union with France
Imports: $NA; full customs integration with France, which collects and rebates Monacan trade duties; also participates in EC market system through customs union with France
External debt: $NA
Industrial production: growth rate NA%
Electricity: 10,000 kW standby capacity (1988); power supplied by France
Industries: pharmaceuticals, food processing, precision instruments, glassmaking, printing, tourism
Agriculture: NA
Aid: NA
Currency: French franc (plural—francs); 1 French franc (F) = 100 centimes
Exchange rates: French francs (F) per US$1—5.7598 (January 1990), 6.3801 (1989), 5.9569 (1988), 6.0107 (1987), 6.9261 (1986), 8.9852 (1985)
Fiscal year: calendar year

Communications

Railroads: 1.6 km 1.435-meter gauge
Highways: none; city streets
Ports: Monaco
Merchant marine: 1 tanker (1,000 GRT or over) totaling 3,268 GRT/4,959 DWT
Civil air: no major transport aircraft
Airports: 1 usable airfield with permanent-surface runways
Telecommunications: served by the French communications system; automatic telephone system; 38,200 telephones; stations—3 AM, 4 FM, 5 TV; no communication satellite stations

Monaco (continued)

Defense Forces

Note: defense is the responsibility of France

Mongolia

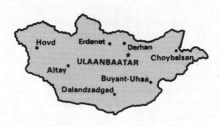

500 km

See regional map VIII

Geography

Total area: 1,565,000 km²; land area: 1,565,000 km²
Comparative area: slightly larger than Alaska
Land boundaries: 8,114 km total; China 4,673 km, USSR 3,441 km
Coastline: none—landlocked
Maritime claims: none—landlocked
Climate: desert; continental (large daily and seasonal temperature ranges)
Terrain: vast semidesert and desert plains; mountains in west and southwest; Gobi Desert in southeast
Natural resources: coal, copper, molybdenum, tungsten, phosphates, tin, nickel, zinc, wolfram, fluorspar, gold
Land use: 1% arable land; 0% permanent crops; 79% meadows and pastures; 10% forest and woodland; 10% other; includes NEGL% irrigated
Environment: harsh and rugged
Note: landlocked; strategic location between China and Soviet Union

People

Population: 2,187,275 (July 1990), growth rate 2.7% (1990)
Birth rate: 35 births/1,000 population (1990)
Death rate: 8 deaths/1,000 population (1990)
Net migration rate: 0 migrants/1,000 population (1990)
Infant mortality rate: 50 deaths/1,000 live births (1990)
Life expectancy at birth: 62 years male, 67 years female (1990)
Total fertility rate: 4.7 children born/woman (1990)
Nationality: noun—Mongolian(s); adjective—Mongolian
Ethnic divisions: 90% Mongol, 4% Kazakh, 2% Chinese, 2% Russian, 2% other

Religion: predominantly Tibetan Buddhist, about 4% Muslim, limited religious activity because of Communist regime
Language: Khalkha Mongol used by over 90% of population; minor languages include Turkic, Russian, and Chinese
Literacy: 80% (est.); 100% claimed (1985)
Labor force: NA, but primarily agricultural; over half the adult population is in the labor force, including a large percentage of women; shortage of skilled labor
Organized labor: 425,000 members of the Central Council of Mongolian Trade Unions (CCMTU) controlled by the government (1984)

Government

Long-form name: Mongolian People's Republic; abbreviated MPR
Type: Communist state
Capital: Ulaanbaatar
Administrative divisions: 18 provinces (aymguud, singular—aymag) and 3 municipalities* (hotuud, singular—hot); Arhangay, Bayanhongor, Bayan-Ölgiy, Bulgan, Darhan*, Dornod, Dornogovi, Dundgovi, Dzavhan, Erdenet*, Govi-Altay, Hentiy, Hovd, Hövsgöl, Ömnögovi, Övörhangay, Selenge, Süh-baatar, Töv, Ulaanbaatar*, Uvs
Independence: 13 March 1921 (from China; formerly Outer Mongolia)
Constitution: 6 July 1960
Legal system: blend of Russian, Chinese, and Turkish systems of law; no constitutional provision for judicial review of legislative acts; has not accepted compulsory ICJ jurisdiction
National holiday: People's Revolution Day, 11 July (1921)
Executive branch: chairman and deputy chairman of the Presidium of the People's Great Hural, Presidium of the People's Great Hural, chairman of the Council of Ministers, Council of Ministers (cabinet)
Legislative branch: unicameral People's Great Hural
Judicial branch: Supreme Court
Leaders: *Chief of State*—Chairman of the Presidium of the People's Great Hural Punsalmaagiyn OCHIRBAT (since 21 March 1990);
Head of Government—Chairman of the Council of Ministers Sharabyn GUNGAADORJ (since 21 March 1990);
Political parties and leaders: only party—Mongolian People's Revolutionary Party (MPRP), Gombojabin Ochirbat, General Secretary
Suffrage: universal at age 18
Elections: *President*—last held 21 March 1990 (next to be held July 1991); results—Punsalmaagiyn Ochirbat elected by the People's Great Hural;

People's Great Hural—last held on 22 June 1986 (next to be held June 1990); results—MPRP was the only party; seats—(370 total) MPRP 370
Communists: MPRP membership 88,150 (1986 est.)
Member of: CEMA, ESCAP, FAO, IAEA, ILO, IPU, ITU, UN, UNESCO, UPU, WFTU, WHO, WIPO, WMO
Diplomatic representation: Ambassador Gendengiin NYAMDOO; *US*—Ambassador Richard L. WILLIAMS
Flag: three equal, vertical bands of red (hoist side), blue, and red; centered on the hoist-side red band in yellow is a five-pointed star above the national emblem (*soyombo*—a columnar arrangement of abstract and geometric representations for fire, sun, moon, earth, water, and the yin-yang symbol)

Economy

Overview: Economic activity traditionally has been based on agriculture and the breeding of livestock—Mongolia has the highest number of livestock per person in the world. In recent years extensive mineral resources have been developed with Soviet support. The mining and processing of coal, copper, molybdenum, tin, tungsten, and gold account for a large part of industrial production.
GDP: $1.7 billion, per capita $880 (1985 est.); average real growth rate 3.6% (1976-85 est.)
Inflation rate (consumer prices): NA%
Unemployment rate: NA%
Budget: revenues $2.2 billion; expenditures $2.19 billion, including capital expenditures of $0.9 billion (1987 est.)
Exports: $388 million (f.o.b., 1985); *commodities*—livestock, animal products, wool, hides, fluorspar, nonferrous metals, minerals; *partners*—nearly all trade with Communist countries (about 80% with USSR)
Imports: $1.0 billion (c.i.f., 1985); *commodities*—machinery and equipment, fuels, food products, industrial consumer goods, chemicals, building materials, sugar, tea; *partners*—nearly all trade with Communist countries (about 80% with USSR)
External debt: $NA
Industrial production: growth rate 10.9% (1985)
Electricity: 657,000 kW capacity; 29,500 million kWh produced, 1,340 kWh per capita (1989)
Industries: processing of animal products, building materials, food and beverage, mining (particularly coal)
Agriculture: accounts for 90% of exports and provides livelihood for about 50% of the population; livestock raising predomi-

nates (sheep, goats, horses); crops—wheat, barley, potatoes, forage
Aid: about $500-$700 million annually from USSR
Currency: tughrik (plural—tughriks); 1 tughrik (Tug) = 100 mongos
Exchange rates: tughriks (Tug) per US$1—3.355 (1986-1988), 3.600 (1985)
Fiscal year: calendar year

Communications

Railroads: 1,750 km 1.524-meter broad gauge (1986)
Highways: 46,700 km total; 1,000 km hard surface; 45,700 km other surfaces (1986)
Inland waterways: 397 km of principal routes (1986)
Civil air: 22 major transport aircraft
Airports: 80 total, 30 usable; 10 with permanent-surface runways; fewer than 5 with runways over 3,659 m; fewer than 20 with runways 2,440-3,659 m; 10 with runways 1,220-2,439 m
Telecommunications: stations—13 AM, 1 FM, 1 TV (with 18 provincial relays); relay of Soviet TV; 60,000 TV sets; 186,000 radio receivers; at least 1 satellite earth station

Defense Forces

Branches: Mongolian People's Army, Air Force (negligible)
Military manpower: males 15-49, 518,482; 338,652 fit for military service; 24,783 reach military age (18) annually
Defense expenditures: NA

Montserrat
(dependent territory of the UK)

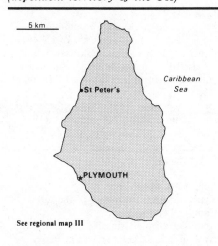

5 km

St Peter's

Caribbean Sea

★PLYMOUTH

See regional map III

Geography

Total area: 100 km²; land area: 100 km²
Comparative area: about 0.6 times the size of Washington, DC
Land boundaries: none
Coastline: 40 km
Maritime claims:
  Exclusive fishing zone: 200 nm
  Territorial sea: 3 nm
Climate: tropical; little daily or seasonal temperature variation
Terrain: volcanic islands, mostly mountainous, with small coastal lowland
Natural resources: negligible
Land use: 20% arable land; 0% permanent crops; 10% meadows and pastures; 40% forest and woodland; 30% other
Environment: subject to severe hurricanes from June to November
Note: located 400 km southeast of Puerto Rico in the Caribbean Sea

People

Population: 12,467 (July 1990), growth rate 0.3% (1990)
Birth rate: 16 births/1,000 population (1990)
Death rate: 10 deaths/1,000 population (1990)
Net migration rate: −4 migrant/1,000 population (1990)
Infant mortality rate: 9 deaths/1,000 live births (1990)
Life expectancy at birth: 74 years male, 80 years female (1990)
Total fertility rate: 2.2 children born/woman (1990)
Nationality: noun—Montserratian(s); adjective—Montserratian
Ethnic divisions: mostly black with a few Europeans
Religion: Anglican, Methodist, Roman Catholic, Pentecostal, Seventh-Day Adventist, other Christian denominations
Language: English

Montserrat (continued)

Literacy: 77%
Labor force: 5,100; 40.5% community, social, and personal services, 13.5% construction, 12.3% trade, restaurants, and hotels, 10.5% manufacturing, 8.8% agriculture, forestry, and fishing, 14.4% other (1983 est.)
Organized labor: 30% of labor force, three trade unions with 1,500 members (1984 est.)

Government

Long-form name: none
Type: dependent territory of the UK
Capital: Plymouth
Administrative divisions: 3 parishes; Saint Anthony, Saint Georges, Saint Peter
Independence: none (colony of the UK)
Constitution: 1 January 1960
Legal system: English common law and statute law
National holiday: Celebration of the Birthday of the Queen (second Saturday of June)
Executive branch: monarch, governor, Executive Council (cabinet), chief minister
Legislative branch: unicameral Legislative Council
Judicial branch: Supreme Court
Leaders: *Chief of State*—Queen ELIZABETH II (since 6 February 1952), represented by Governor Christopher J. TURNER (since 1987);
Head of Government—Chief Minister John A. OSBORNE (since 1978)
Political parties and leaders: People's Liberation Movement (PLM), John Osborne; Progressive Democratic Party (PDP), Howell Bramble; United National Front (UNF), Dr. George Irish; National Development Party (NDP), Bertrand Osborne
Suffrage: universal at age 18
Elections: *Legislative Council*—last held on 25 August 1987 (next to be held NA 1992); results—percent of vote by party NA; seats—(11 total, 7 elected) PLM 4, NDP 2, PDP 1
Communists: probably none
Diplomatic representation: none (colony of the UK)
Flag: blue with the flag of the UK in the upper hoist-side quadrant and the Montserratian coat of arms centered in the outer half of the flag; the coat of arms features a woman standing beside a yellow harp with her arm around a black cross

Economy

Overview: The economy is small and open with economic activity centered on tourism and construction. Tourism is the most important sector and accounted for 20% of GDP in 1986. Agriculture accounted for about 4% of GDP and industry 9%.

The economy is heavily dependent on imports, making it vulnerable to fluctuations in world prices. Exports consist mainly of electronic parts sold to the US.
GDP: $45.4 million, per capita $3,780; real growth rate 12% (1988 est.)
Inflation rate (consumer prices): 3.7% (1987)
Unemployment rate: 3.0% (1987)
Budget: revenues $10.0 million; expenditures $9.4 million, including capital expenditures of $3.2 million (1987)
Exports: $3.0 million (f.o.b., 1987); *commodities*—plastic bags, electronic parts, apparel, hot peppers, live plants, cattle; *partners*—NA
Imports: $25.3 million (c.i.f., 1987); *commodities*—machinery and transportation equipment, foodstuffs, manufactured goods, fuels, lubricants, and related materials; *partners*—NA
External debt: $3.7 million (1985)
Industrial production: growth rate 8.1% (1986)
Electricity: 5,000 kW capacity; 12 million kWh produced, 930 kWh per capita (1989)
Industries: tourism; light manufacturing—rum, textiles, electronic appliances
Agriculture: accounts for 4% of GDP; small-scale farming; food crops—tomatoes, onions, peppers; not self-sufficient in food, especially livestock products
Aid: NA
Currency: East Caribbean dollar (plural—dollars); 1 EC dollar (EC$) = 100 cents
Exchange rates: East Caribbean dollars (EC$) per US$1—2.70 (fixed rate since 1976)
Fiscal year: 1 April-31 March

Communications

Highways: 280 km total; about 200 km paved, 80 km gravel and earth
Ports: Plymouth
Airports: 1 with permanent-surface runway 1,036 m
Telecommunications: 3,000 telephones; stations—8 AM, 4 FM, 1 TV

Defense Forces

Note: defense is the responsibility of the UK

Morocco

See regional map VII

Geography

Total area: 446,550 km^2; land area: 446,300 km^2
Comparative area: slightly larger than California
Land boundaries: 2,002 km total; Algeria 1,559 km, Western Sahara 443 km
Coastline: 1,835 km
Maritime claims:
Contiguous zone: 24 nm
Continental shelf: 200 meters or to depth of exploitation
Extended economic zone: 200 nm
Territorial sea: 12 nm
Disputes: claims and administers Western Sahara, but sovereignty is unresolved; armed conflict in Western Sahara; Spain controls two coastal presidios or places of sovereignty (Ceuta, Melilla)
Climate: Mediterranean, becoming more extreme in the interior
Terrain: mostly mountains with rich coastal plains
Natural resources: phosphates, iron ore, manganese, lead, zinc, fish, salt
Land use: 18% arable land; 1% permanent crops; 28% meadows and pastures; 12% forest and woodland; 41% other; includes 1% irrigated
Environment: northern mountains geologically unstable and subject to earthquakes; desertification
Note: strategic location along Strait of Gibraltar

People

Population: 25,648,241 (July 1990), growth rate 2.2% (1990)
Birth rate: 31 births/1,000 population (1990)
Death rate: 8 deaths/1,000 population (1990)
Net migration rate: −1 migrants/1,000 population (1990)

Infant mortality rate: 78 deaths/1,000 live births (1990)

Life expectancy at birth: 63 years male, 66 years female (1990)

Total fertility rate: 4.0 children born/woman (1990)

Nationality: noun—Moroccan(s); adjective—Moroccan

Ethnic divisions: 99.1% Arab-Berber, 0.7% non-Moroccan, 0.2% Jewish

Religion: 98.7% Muslim, 1.1% Christian, 0.2% Jewish

Language: Arabic (official); several Berber dialects; French is language of business, government, diplomacy, and postprimary education

Literacy: 28%

Labor force: 7,400,000; 50% agriculture, 26% services, 15% industry, 9% other (1985)

Organized labor: about 5% of the labor force, mainly in the Union of Moroccan Workers (UMT) and the Democratic Confederation of Labor (CDT)

Government

Long-form name: Kingdom of Morocco

Type: constitutional monarchy

Capital: Rabat

Administrative divisions: 36 provinces (provinces, singular—province) and 2 municipalities* (wilayas, singular—wilaya); Agadir, Al Hoceïma, Azilal, Beni Mellal, Ben Slimane, Boulemane, Casablanca*, Chaouen, El Jadida, El Kelaa des Srarhna, Er Rachidia, Essaouira, Fès, Figuig, Guelmim, Ifrane, Kenitra, Khemisset, Khenifra, Khouribga, Laâyoune, Marrakech, Meknès, Nador, Ouarzazate, Oujda, Rabat-Salé*, Safi, Settat, Sidi Kacem, Tanger, Tan-Tan, Taounate, Taroudannt, Tata, Taza, Tétouan, Tiznit

Independence: 2 March 1956 (from France)

Constitution: 10 March 1972

Legal system: based on Islamic law and French and Spanish civil law system; judicial review of legislative acts in Constitutional Chamber of Supreme Court

National holiday: National Day (anniversary of King Hassan II's accession to the throne), 3 March (1961)

Executive branch: monarch, prime minister, Council of Ministers (cabinet)

Legislative branch: unicameral Chamber of Representatives (Majlis al Nuwab)

Judicial branch: Supreme Court

Leaders: *Chief of State*—King HASSAN II (since 3 March 1961);
Head of Government—Prime Minister Dr. Azzedine LARAKI (since 30 September 1986)

Political parties and leaders: Morocco has 15 political parties; the major ones are Istiqlal Party, M'Hamed Boucetta; Social-ist Union of Popular Forces (USFP), Abderrahim Bouabid; Popular Movement (MP), Secretariat General; National Assembly of Independents (RNI), Ahmed Osman; National Democratic Party (PND), Mohamed Arsalane El-Jadidi; Party for Progress and Socialism (PPS), Ali Yata; Constitutional Union (UC), Maati Bouabid

Suffrage: universal at age 21

Elections: *Chamber of Representatives*—last held on 14 September 1984 (were scheduled for September 1990, but postponed until NA 1992); results—percent of vote by party NA; seats—(306 total, 206 elected) CU 83, RNI 61, MP 47, Istiqlal 41, USFP 36, PND 24, others 14

Communists: about 2,000

Member of: AfDB, Arab League, CCC, EC (associate), FAO, G-77, GATT, IAEA, IBRD, ICAO, IDA, IDB—Islamic Development Bank, IFAD, IFC, ILO, ILZSG, IMF, IMO, INTELSAT, INTERPOL, IOOC, IPU, ITU, NAM, OIC, UN, UNESCO, UPU, WHO, WIPO, WMO, WTO

Diplomatic representation: Ambassador Ali BENGELLOUN; Chancery at 1601 21st Street NW, Washington DC 20009; telephone (202) 462-7979; there is a Moroccan Consulate General in New York; *US*—Ambassador Michael USSERY; Embassy at 2 Avenue de Marrakech, Rabat (mailing address is P. O. Box 120, Rabat, or APO New York 09284); telephone [212] (7) 622-65; there are US Consulates General in Casablanca and Tangier

Flag: red with a green pentacle (five-pointed, linear star) known as Solomon's seal in the center of the flag; green is the traditional color of Islam

---

Economy

Overview: After registering a robust 10% growth in 1988, the economy slowed in 1989 because of higher prices for food and oil imports, lower worker remittances, and a trade dispute with India over phosphoric acid prices that cost Rabat $500 million. To meet the foreign payments shortfall, Rabat has been drawing down foreign exchange reserves. Servicing the $22 billion foreign debt, high unemployment, and Morocco's vulnerability to external forces remain severe problems for the 1990s.

GDP: $21.9 billion, per capita $880 (1988); real growth rate 4.5% (1989 est.)

Inflation rate (consumer prices): 6% (1989)

Unemployment rate: 15% (1988)

Budget: revenues $5.1 billion; expenditures $6.0 billion, including capital expenditures of $1.4 billion (1988)

Exports: $3.1 billion (f.o.b., 1989); *commodities*—food and beverages 30%, semiprocessed goods 23%, consumer goods 21%, phosphates 17%; *partners*—EC 58%, India 7%, Japan 5%, USSR 3%, US 2%

Imports: $5.1 billion (f.o.b., 1989); *commodities*—capital goods 24%, semiprocessed goods 22%, raw materials 16%, fuel and lubricants 16%, food and beverages 13%, consumer goods 10%; *partners*—EC 53%, US 11%, Canada 4%, Iraq 3%, USSR 3%, Japan 2%

External debt: $22.2 billion (1989)

Industrial production: growth rate 4% (1989 est.)

Electricity: 2,140,000 kW capacity; 7,760 million kWh produced, 300 kWh per capita (1989)

Industries: phosphate rock mining and processing, food processing, leather goods, textiles, construction, tourism

Agriculture: 50% of employment and 30% of export value; not self-sufficient in food; cereal farming and livestock raising predominate; barley, wheat, citrus fruit, wine, vegetables, olives; fishing catch of 491,000 metric tons in 1987

Illicit drugs: illicit producer of cannabis; trafficking on the increase for both domestic and international drug markets; shipments of cannabis mostly directed to Western Europe; occasional transit point for cocaine from South America destined for Western Europe.

Aid: US commitments, including Ex-Im (FY70-88), $1.2 billion; Western (non-US) countries, ODA and OOF bilateral commitments (1970-87), $6.3 billion; OPEC bilateral aid (1979-89), $4.8 billion; Communist countries (1970-88), $2.3 billion

Currency: Moroccan dirham (plural—dirhams); 1 Moroccan dirham (DH) = 100 centimes

Exchange rates: Moroccan dirhams (DH) per US$1—8.093 (January 1990), 8.488 (1989), 8.209 (1988), 8.359 (1987), 9.104 (1986), 10.062 (1985)

Fiscal year: calendar year

Communications

Railroads: 1,893 km 1.435-meter standard gauge (246 km double track, 974 km electrified)

Highways: 59,198 km total; 27,740 km bituminous treated, 31,458 km gravel, crushed stone, improved earth, and unimproved earth

Pipelines: 362 km crude oil; 491 km (abandoned) refined products; 241 km natural gas

Ports: Agadir, Casablanca, El Jorf Lasfar, Kenitra, Mohammedia, Nador, Safi, Tangier; also Spanish-controlled Ceuta and Melilla

Merchant marine: 54 ships (1,000 GRT or over) totaling 334,931 GRT/513,762 DWT; includes 11 cargo, 2 container, 14 refrigerated cargo, 5 roll-on/roll-off cargo,

Morocco (continued)

3 petroleum, oils, and lubricants (POL) tanker, 12 chemical tanker, 4 bulk, 3 short-sea passenger
Civil air: 23 major transport aircraft
Airports: 75 total, 68 usable; 26 with permanent-surface runways; 2 with runways over 3,659 m; 14 with runways 2,440-3,659 m; 27 with runways 1,220-2,439 m
Telecommunications: good system composed of wire lines, cables, and radio relay links; principal centers are Casablanca and Rabat, secondary centers are Fès, Marrakech, Oujda, Tangier, and Tétouan; 280,000 telephones; stations—14 AM, 6 FM, 47 TV; 5 submarine cables; satellite earth stations—2 Atlantic Ocean INTELSAT and 1 ARABSAT; radio relay to Gibraltar, Spain, and Western Sahara; coaxial cable to Algeria; microwave network linking Syria, Jordan, Egypt, Libya, Tunisia, Algeria and Morocco

Defense Forces

Branches: Royal Moroccan Army, Royal Moroccan Navy, Royal Moroccan Air Force, Royal Gendarmerie
Military manpower: males 15-49, 6,203,759; 3,946,408 fit for military service; 293,893 reach military age (18) annually; limited conscription
Defense expenditures: 7.1% of GDP (1987)

Mozambique

See regional map VII

Geography

Total area: 801,590 km²; land area: 784,090 km²
Comparative area: slightly less than twice the size of California
Land boundaries: 4,571 km total; Malawi 1,569 km, South Africa 491 km, Swaziland 105 km, Tanzania 756 km, Zambia 419 km, Zimbabwe 1,231 km
Coastline: 2,470 km
Maritime claims:
Extended economic zone: 200 nm
Territorial sea: 12 nm
Climate: tropical to subtropical
Terrain: mostly coastal lowlands, uplands in center, high plateaus in northwest, mountains in west
Natural resources: coal, titanium
Land use: 4% arable land; NEGL% permanent crops; 56% meadows and pastures; 20% forest and woodland; 20% other; includes NEGL% irrigated
Environment: severe drought and floods occur in south; desertification

People

Population: 14,565,656 (July 1990), growth rate 2.6% (1990)
Birth rate: 47 births/1,000 population (1990)
Death rate: 18 deaths/1,000 population (1990)
Net migration rate: −3 migrants/1,000 population (1990)
Infant mortality rate: 138 deaths/1,000 live births (1990)
Life expectancy at birth: 45 years male, 49 years female (1990)
Total fertility rate: 6.5 children born/woman (1990)
Nationality: noun—Mozambican(s); adjective—Mozambican
Ethnic divisions: majority from indigenous tribal groups; about 10,000 Europeans, 35,000 Euro-Africans, 15,000 Indians

Religion: 60% indigenous beliefs, 30% Christian, 10% Muslim
Language: Portuguese (official); many indigenous dialects
Literacy: 38%
Labor force: NA, but 90% engaged in agriculture
Organized labor: 225,000 workers belong to a single union, the Mozambique Workers' Organization (OTM)
Note: there are 800,000 Mozambican refugees in Malawi (1989 est.)

Government

Long-form name: People's Republic of Mozambique
Type: people's republic
Capital: Maputo
Administrative divisions: 10 provinces (províncias, singular—província); Cabo Delgado, Gaza, Inhambane, Manica, Maputo, Nampula, Niassa, Sofala, Tete, Zambézia
Independence: 25 June 1975 (from Portugal)
Constitution: 25 June 1975
Legal system: based on Portuguese civil law system and customary law
National holiday: Independence Day, 25 June (1975)
Executive branch: president, prime minister, Cabinet
Legislative branch: unicameral People's Assembly (Assembléia Popular)
Judicial branch: People's Courts at all levels
Leaders: *Chief of State*—President Joaquím Alberto CHISSANO (since 6 November 1986);
Head of Government—Prime Minister Mário da Graça MACHUNGO (since 17 July 1986)
Political parties and leaders: Front for the Liberation of Mozambique (FRELIMO) is the only legal party and is a Marxist organization with close ties to the USSR
Suffrage: universal adult at age 18
Elections: national elections are indirect and based on mass meetings throughout the country
Communists: about 60,000 FRELIMO members
Member of: ACP, AfDB, CCC, FAO, G-77, GATT (de facto), IBRD, ICAO, IFAD, ILO, IMF, IMO, ITU, NAM, OAU, SADCC, UN, UNESCO, UPU, WHO, WMO
Diplomatic representation: Ambassador Valeriano FERRAO; Chancery at Suite 570, 1990 M Street NW, Washington DC 20036; telephone (202) 293-7146; *US*—Ambassador Melissa F. WELLS; Embassy at 3rd Floor, 35 Rua Da Mesquita, Maputo (mailing address is P. O. Box 783, Maputo); telephone 743167 or 744163

Flag: three equal horizontal bands of green (top), black, and yellow with a red isosceles triangle based on the hoist side; the black band is edged in white; centered in the triangle is a yellow five-pointed star bearing a crossed rifle and hoe in black superimposed on an open white book

Economy

Overview: One of Africa's poorest countries, with a per capita GDP of little more than $100, Mozambique has failed to exploit the economic potential of its sizable agricultural, hydropower, and transportation resources. Indeed, national output, consumption, and investment declined throughout the first half of the 1980s because of internal disorders, lack of government administrative control, and a growing foreign debt. A sharp increase in foreign aid, attracted by an economic reform policy, has resulted in successive years of economic growth since 1985. Agricultural output, nevertheless, is only at about 75% of its 1981 level, and grain has to be imported. Industry operates at only 20-40% of capacity. The economy depends heavily on foreign assistance to keep afloat.

GDP: $1.6 billion, per capita less than $110; real growth rate 5.0% (1988)

Inflation rate (consumer prices): 81.1% (1988)

Unemployment rate: 40.0 (1988)

Budget: revenues $186 million; expenditures $239 million, including capital expenditures of $208 million (1988 est.)

Exports: $100 million (f.o.b., 1988); *commodities*—shrimp 48%, cashews 21%, sugar 10%, copra 3%, citrus 3%; *partners*—US, Western Europe, GDR, Japan

Imports: $764 million (c.i.f., 1988), including aid; *commodities*—food, clothing, farm equipment, petroleum; *partners*—US, Western Europe, USSR

External debt: $4.4 billion (1988)

Industrial production: growth rate 7% (1989 est.)

Electricity: 2,265,000 kW capacity; 1,740 million kWh produced, 120 kWh per capita (1989)

Industries: food, beverages, chemicals (fertilizer, soap, paints), petroleum products, textiles, nonmetallic mineral products (cement, glass, asbestos), tobacco

Agriculture: accounts for 50% of GDP, over 80% of labor force, and about 90% of exports; cash crops—cotton, cashew nuts, sugarcane, tea, shrimp; other crops—cassava, corn, rice, tropical fruits; not self-sufficient in food

Aid: US commitments, including Ex-Im (FY70-88), $282 million; Western (non-US) countries, ODA and OOF bilateral commitments (1970-87), $3.1 billion; OPEC bilateral aid (1979-89), $37 million; Communist countries (1970-88), $887 million

Currency: metical (plural—meticais); 1 metical (Mt) = 100 centavos

Exchange rates: meticais (Mt) per US$1—800 (September 1989), 528.60 (1988), 289.44 (1987), 40.43 (1986), 43.18 (1985)

Fiscal year: calendar year

Communications

Railroads: 3,288 km total; 3,140 km 1.067-meter gauge; 148 km 0.762-meter narrow gauge; Malawi-Nacala, Malawi-Beira, and Zimbabwe-Maputo lines are subject to closure because of insurgency

Highways: 26,498 km total; 4,593 km paved; 829 km gravel, crushed stone, stabilized soil; 21,076 km unimproved earth

Inland waterways: about 3,750 km of navigable routes

Pipelines: 306 km crude oil (not operating); 289 km refined products

Ports: Maputo, Beira, Nacala

Merchant marine: 5 cargo ships (1,000 GRT or over) totaling 7,806 GRT/12,873 DWT

Civil air: 5 major transport aircraft

Airports: 203 total, 153 usable; 27 with permanent-surface runways; none with runways over 3,659 m; 6 with runways 2,440-3,659 m; 29 with runways 1,220-2,439 m

Telecommunications: fair system of troposcatter, open-wire lines, and radio relay; 57,400 telephones; stations—15 AM, 3 FM, 1 TV; satellite earth stations—1 Atlantic Ocean INTELSAT and 3 domestic

Defense Forces

Branches: Mozambique Armed Forces (including Army, Border Guard, Naval Command, Air Defense Forces)

Military manpower: males 15-49, 3,295,067; 1,892,699 fit for military service

Defense expenditures: 8.4% of GDP (1987)

Namibia

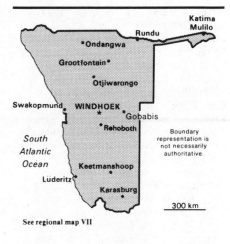

See regional map VII

Geography

Total area: 824,290 km²; land area: 823,290 km²

Comparative area: slightly more than half the size of Alaska

Land boundaries: 3,935 km total; Angola 1,376 km, Botswana 1,360 km, South Africa 966 km, Zambia 233 km

Coastline: 1,489 km

Maritime claims:

Exclusive fishing zone: 12 nm

Territorial sea: 6 nm

Disputes: short section of boundary with Botswana is indefinite; quadripoint with Botswana, Zambia, and Zimbabwe is in disagreement; possible future claim to South Africa's Walvis Bay

Climate: desert; hot, dry; rainfall sparse and erratic

Terrain: mostly high plateau; Namib Desert along coast; Kalahari Desert in east

Natural resources: diamonds, copper, uranium, gold, lead, tin, zinc, salt, vanadium, natural gas, fish; suspected deposits of coal and iron ore

Land use: 1% arable land; NEGL% permanent crops; 64% meadows and pastures; 22% forest and woodland; 13% other; includes NEGL% irrigated

Environment: inhospitable with very limited natural water resources; desertification

Note: Walvis Bay area is an exclave of South Africa in Namibia

People

Population: 1,452,951 (July 1990), growth rate 5.6% (1990)

Birth rate: 46 births/1,000 population (1990)

Death rate: 10 deaths/1,000 population (1990)

Net migration rate: 20 migrants/1,000 population (1990)

Namibia (continued)

Infant mortality rate: 71 deaths/1,000 live births (1990)
Life expectancy at birth: 57 years male, 63 years female (1990)
Total fertility rate: 6.6 children born/woman (1990)
Nationality: noun—Namibian(s); adjective—Namibian
Ethnic divisions: 86% black, 6.5% white, 7.5% mixed; about 50% of the population belong to the Ovambo tribe and 9% from the Kavangos tribe
Religion: predominantly Christian
Language: Afrikaans principal language of about 60% of white population, German of 33%, and English of 7% (all official); several indigenous languages
Literacy: 100% whites, 16% nonwhites
Labor force: 500,000; 60% agriculture, 19% industry and commerce, 8% services, 7% government, 6% mining (1981 est.)
Organized labor: 15 trade unions—largest is the mineworkers' union which has a sizable black membership

Government

Long-form name: Republic of Namibia
Type: republic as of 21 March 1990
Capital: Windhoek
Administrative divisions: 26 districts; Bethanien, Boesmanland, Caprivi Oos, Damaraland, Gobabis, Grootfontein, Hereroland Oos, Hereroland Wes, Kaokoland, Karasburg, Karibib, Kavango, Keetmanshoop, Lüderitz, Maltahöhe, Mariental, Namaland, Okahandja, Omaruru, Otjiwarongo, Outjo, Owambo, Rehoboth, Swakopmund, Tsumeb, Windhoek
Independence: 21 March 1990
Constitution: ratified 9 February 1990
Legal system: based on Roman-Dutch law and customary law
National holiday: Settlers' Day, 10 December
Executive branch: president, Cabinet, Constitutional Council
Legislative branch: bicameral National Assembly
Judicial branch: Supreme Court
Leaders: *Chief of State and Head of Government* President Sam NUJOMA (since 21 March 1990)
Political parties and leaders: South-West Africa People's Organization (SWAPO), Sam Nujoma; Democratic Turnhalle Alliance (DTA), Dirk Mudge; United Democratic Front (UDF), Justus Garoeb; Action Christian National (ACN), Kosie Pretorius; National Patriotic Front (NPF), Moses Katjiuongua; Federal Convention of Namibia (FCN), Hans Diergaardt; Namibia National Front (NNF), Vekuii Rukoro
Suffrage: universal at age 18

Elections: *National Assembly*—last held on 7-11 November 1989 (next to be held NA); results—percent of vote by party NA; seats—(72 total) SWAPO 41, DTA 21, UDF 4, ACN 3, NNF 1, FCN 1, NPF 1
Communists: no Communist party
Other political or pressure groups: NA
Member of: FAO, IAEA, ILO, UNESCO, WHO
Diplomatic representation: NA
Flag: a large blue triangle with a yellow sunburst fills the upper left section, and an equal green triangle (solid) fills the lower right section; the triangles are separated by a red stripe which is contrasted by two narrow white edge borders

Economy

Overview: The economy is heavily dependent on the mining industry to extract and process minerals for export. Mining accounts for almost 35% of GDP, agriculture and fisheries 10-15%, and manufacturing about 5%. Namibia is the fourth-largest exporter of nonfuel minerals in Africa and the world's fifth-largest producer of uranium. Alluvial diamond deposits are among the richest in the world, making Namibia a primary source for gem-quality diamonds. Namibia also produces large quantities of lead, zinc, tin, silver, and tungsten, and it has substantial resources of coal.
GNP: $1.54 billion, per capita $1,245; real growth rate 2.9% (1987)
Inflation rate (consumer prices): 15.1% (1989)
Unemployment rate: over 30% (1988)
Budget: revenues $781 million; expenditures $932 million, including capital expenditures of $NA (FY88)
Exports: $935 million (f.o.b., 1988); *commodities*—diamonds, uranium, zinc, copper, meat, processed fish, karakul skins; *partners*—South Africa
Imports: $856 million (f.o.b., 1988); *commodities*—foodstuffs, manufactured consumer goods, machinery and equipment; *partners*—South Africa, FRG, UK, US
External debt: about $27 million at independence; under a 1971 International Court of Justice (ICJ) ruling, Namibia may not be liable for debt incurred during its colonial period
Industrial production: growth rate NA%
Electricity: 486,000 kW capacity; 1,280 million kWh produced, 930 kWh per capita (1989)
Industries: meatpacking, fish processing, dairy products, mining (copper, lead, zinc, diamond, uranium)
Agriculture: accounts for 10% of GDP (including fishing); mostly subsistence farming; livestock raising major source of cash

income; crops—millet, sorghum, peanuts; fish catch potential of over 1 million metric tons not being fulfilled, 1987 catch reaching only 520,000 metric tons; not self-sufficient in food
Aid: Western (non-US) countries, ODA and OOF bilateral commitments (1970-87), $47.2 million
Currency: South African rand (plural—rand); 1 South African rand (R) = 100 cents
Exchange rates: South African rand (R) per US$1—2.5555 (January 1990), 2.6166 (1989), 2.2611 (1988), 2.0350 (1987), 2.2685 (1986), 2.1911 (1985)
Fiscal year: 1 April-31 March

Communications

Railroads: 2,341 km 1.067-meter gauge, single track
Highways: 54,500 km; 4,079 km paved, 2,540 km gravel, 47,881 km earth roads and tracks
Ports: Luderitz; primary maritime outlet is Walvis Bay (South Africa)
Civil air: 2 major transport aircraft
Airports: 143 total, 123 usable; 21 with permanent-surface runways; 1 with runways over 3,659 m; 5 with runways 2,440-3,659 m; 63 with runways 1,220-2,439 m
Telecommunications: good urban, fair rural services; radio relay connects major towns, wires extend to other population centers; 62,800 telephones; stations—2 AM, 40 FM, 3 TV

Defense Forces

Branches: NA
Military manpower: males 15-49, 298,249; 176,660 fit for military service
Defense expenditures: 4.9% of GNP (1986)
Note: the South-West Africa Territorial Force, established in 1980, was demobilized in June 1989; a new national defense force will probably be formed by the new government

Nauru

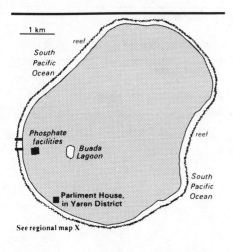

Geography

Total area: 21 km²; land area: 21 km²
Comparative area: about 0.1 times the size of Washington, DC
Land boundaries: none
Coastline: 30 km
Maritime claims:
Exclusive fishing zone: 200 nm
Territorial sea: 12 nm .
Climate: tropical; monsoonal; rainy season (November to February)
Terrain: sandy beach rises to fertile ring around raised coral reefs with phosphate plateau in center
Natural resources: phosphates
Land use: 0% arable land; 0% permanent crops; 0% meadows and pastures; 0% forest and woodland; 100% other
Environment: only 53 km south of Equator
Note: one of three great phosphate rock islands in the Pacific (others are Banaba or Ocean Island in Kiribati and Makatea in French Polynesia)

People

Population: 9,202 (July 1990), growth rate 1.5% (1990)
Birth rate: 20 births/1,000 population (1990)
Death rate: 5 deaths/1,000 population (1990)
Net migration rate: NEGL migrants/1,000 population (1990)
Infant mortality rate: 41 deaths/1,000 live births (1990)
Life expectancy at birth: 64 years male, 69 years female (1990)
Total fertility rate: 2.3 children born/woman (1990)
Nationality: noun—Nauruan(s); adjective—Nauruan
Ethnic divisions: 58% Nauruan, 26% other Pacific Islander, 8% Chinese, 8% European

Religion: Christian (two-thirds Protestant, one-third Roman Catholic)
Language: Nauruan, a distinct Pacific Island language (official); English widely understood, spoken, and used for most government and commercial purposes
Literacy: 99%
Labor force: NA
Organized labor: NA

Government

Long-form name: Republic of Nauru
Type: republic
Capital: no capital city as such; government offices in Yaren District
Administrative divisions: 14 districts; Aiwo, Anabar, Anetan, Anibare, Baiti, Boe, Buada, Denigomodu, Ewa, Ijuw, Meneng, Nibok, Uaboe, Yaren
Independence: 31 January 1968 (from UN trusteeship under Australia, New Zealand, and UK); formerly Pleasant Island
Constitution: 29 January 1968
Legal system: own Acts of Parliament and British common law
National holiday: Independence Day, 31 January (1968)
Executive branch: president, Cabinet
Legislative branch: unicameral Parliament
Judicial branch: Supreme Court
Leaders: *Chief of State and Head of Government*—President Bernard DOWIYOGO (since 12 December 1989)
Political parties and leaders: none
Suffrage: universal and compulsory at age 20
Elections: *President*—last held 9 December 1989 (next to be held December 1992); results—Bernard Dowiyogo elected by Parliament;
Parliament—last held on 9 December 1989 (next to be held December 1992); results—percent of vote NA; seats—(18 total) independents 18
Member of: Commonwealth (special member), ESCAP, ICAO, INTERPOL, ITU, SPC, SPF, UPU
Diplomatic representation: Ambassador T. W. STAR resides in Melbourne (Australia); there is a Nauruan Consulate in Agana (Guam); *US*—the US Ambassador to Australia is accredited to Nauru
Flag: blue with a narrow, horizontal, yellow stripe across the center and a large white 12-pointed star below the stripe on the hoist side; the star indicates the country's location in relation to the Equator (the yellow stripe) and the 12 points symbolize the 12 original tribes of Nauru

Economy

Overview: Revenues come from the export of phosphates, the reserves of which are expected to be exhausted by the year

2000. Phosphates have given Nauruans one of the highest per capita incomes in the Third World—$10,000 annually. Few other resources exist so most necessities must be imported, including fresh water from Australia. The rehabilitation of mined land and the replacement of income from phosphates constitute serious long-term problems. Substantial investment in trust funds, out of phosphate income, will help cushion the transition.
GNP: over $90 million, per capita $10,000; real growth rate NA% (1989)
Inflation rate (consumer prices): NA%
Unemployment rate: 0%
Budget: revenues $69.7 million; expenditures $51.5 million, including capital expenditures of $NA (FY86 est.)
Exports: $93 million (f.o.b., 1984); *commodities*—phosphates; *partners*—Australia, NZ
Imports: $73 million (c.i.f., 1984); *commodities*—food, fuel, manufactures, building materials, machinery; *partners*—Australia, UK, NZ, Japan
External debt: $33.3 million
Industrial production: growth rate NA%
Electricity: 13,250 kW capacity; 48 million kWh produced, 5,300 kWh per capita (1989)
Industries: phosphate mining, financial services, coconuts
Agriculture: negligible; almost completely dependent on imports for food and water
Aid: none
Currency: Australian dollar (plural—dollars); 1 Australian dollar ($A) = 100 cents
Exchange rates: Australian dollars ($A) per US$1—1.2784 (January 1990), 1.2618 (1989), 1.2752 (1988), 1.4267 (1987), 1.4905 (1986), 1.4269 (1985)
Fiscal year: 1 July-30 June

Communications

Railroads: 3.9 km; used to haul phosphates from the center of the island to processing facilities on the southwest coast
Highways: about 27 km total; 21 km paved, 6 km improved earth
Ports: Nauru
Merchant marine: 4 ships (1,000 GRT or over) totaling 39,597 GRT/50,729 DWT; includes 1 passenger-cargo, 1 cargo, 2 bulk
Civil air: 3 major transport aircraft, one on order
Airports: 1 with permanent-surface runway 1,220-2,439 m
Telecommunications: adequate intraisland and international radio communications provided via Australian facilities; 1,600 telephones; 4,000 radio receivers; stations—1 AM, no FM, no TV; 1 Pacific Ocean INTELSAT earth station

Nauru *(continued)*

Defense Forces

Branches: no regular armed forces
Military manpower: males 15-49, 298,249; 176,660 fit for military service; 100 reach age 18 annually
Defense expenditures: no formal defense structure

Navassa Island
(territory of the US)

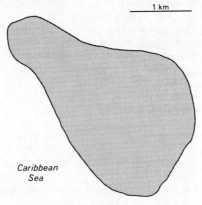

Caribbean
Sea

See regional map III

Geography

Total area: 5.2 km^2; land area: 5.2 km^2
Comparative area: about nine times the size of The Mall in Washington, DC
Land boundaries: none
Coastline: 8 km
Maritime claims:
  Contiguous zone: 12 nm
  Continental shelf: 200 m
  Extended economic zone: 200 nm
  Territorial sea: 12 nm
Disputes: claimed by Haiti
Climate: marine, tropical
Terrain: raised coral and limestone plateau, flat to undulating; ringed by vertical white cliffs (9 to 15 meters high)
Natural resources: guano
Land use: 0% arable land; 0% permanent crops; 10% meadows and pastures; 0% forest and woodland; 90% other
Environment: mostly exposed rock, but enough grassland to support goat herds; dense stands of fig-like trees, scattered cactus
Note: strategic location between Cuba, Haiti, and Jamaica in the Caribbean Sea; 160 km south of the US Naval Base at Guantánamo, Cuba

People

Population: uninhabited; transient Haitian fishermen and others camp on the island

Government

Long-form name: none (territory of the US)
Type: unincorporated territory of the US administered by the US Coast Guard

Economy

Overview: no economic activity

Communications

Ports: none; offshore anchorage only

Defense Forces

Note: defense is the responsibility of the US

Nepal

200 km

See regional map VIII

Geography

Total area: 140,800 km²; land area: 136,800 km²

Comparative area: slightly larger than Arkansas

Land boundaries: 2,926 km total; China 1,236 km, India 1,690 km

Coastline: none—landlocked

Maritime claims: none—landlocked

Climate: varies from cool summers and severe winters in north to subtropical summers and mild winter in south

Terrain: Tarai or flat river plain of the Ganges in south, central hill region, rugged Himalayas in north

Natural resources: quartz, water, timber, hydroelectric potential, scenic beauty; small deposits of lignite, copper, cobalt, iron ore

Land use: 17% arable land; NEGL% permanent crops; 13% meadows and pastures; 33% forest and woodland; 37% other; includes 2% irrigated

Environment: contains eight of world's 10 highest peaks; deforestation; soil erosion; water pollution

Note: landlocked; strategic location between China and India

People

Population: 19,145,800 (July 1990), growth rate 2.4% (1990)

Birth rate: 39 births/1,000 population (1990)

Death rate: 15 deaths/1,000 population (1990)

Net migration rate: 0 migrants/1,000 population (1990)

Infant mortality rate: 99 deaths/1,000 live births (1990)

Life expectancy at birth: 50 years male, 50 years female (1990)

Total fertility rate: 5.6 children born/woman (1990)

Nationality: noun—Nepalese (sing. and pl.); adjective—Nepalese

Ethnic divisions: Newars, Indians, Tibetans, Gurungs, Magars, Tamangs, Bhotias, Rais, Limbus, Sherpas, as well as many smaller groups

Religion: only official Hindu state in world, although no sharp distinction between many Hindu (about 88% of population) and Buddhist groups; small groups of Muslims and Christians

Language: Nepali (official); 20 languages divided into numerous dialects

Literacy: 20%

Labor force: 4,100,000; 93% agriculture, 5% services, 2% industry; severe lack of skilled labor

Organized labor: Teachers' Union, not officially recognized

Government

Long-form name: Kingdom of Nepal

Type: constitutional monarchy, but King Birendra exercises control over multitiered system of government

Capital: Kathmandu

Administrative divisions: 14 zones (anchal, singular and plural); Bāgmatī, Bherī, Dhawalāgiri, Gandakī, Janakpur, Karnālī, Kosī, Lumbinī, Mahākālī, Mechī, Nārāyanī, Rāptī, Sagarmāthā, Setī

Independence: 1768, unified by Prithyi Narayan Shah

Constitution: 16 December 1962

Legal system: based on Hindu legal concepts and English common law; has not accepted compulsory ICJ jurisdiction

National holiday: Birthday of His Majesty the King, 28 December (1945)

Executive branch: monarch, chairman of the Council of State, Council of State, prime minister

Legislative branch: unicameral National Assembly (Rashtriya Panchayat)

Judicial branch: Supreme Court (Sarbochha Adalat)

Leaders: *Chief of State*—King BIRENDRA Bir Bikram Shah Dev (since 31 January 1972, crowned King 24 February 1985); Heir Apparent Crown Prince DIPENDRA Bir Bikram Shah Dev, son of the King (born 21 June 1971);

Head of Government—Prime Minister Marich Man Singh SHRESTHA (since 15 July 1986)

Political parties and leaders: all political parties outlawed but operate more or less openly; Nepali Congress Party (NCP), Ganesh Man Singh, K. P. Bhattarai, G. P. Koirala

Suffrage: universal at age 21

Elections: *National Assembly*—last held on 12 May 1986 (next to be held May 1991); results—all independents since political parties are officially banned; seats—(140 total, 112 elected) independents 112

Communists: Communist Party of Nepal (CPN); factions include V. B. Manandhar, Man Mohan Adhikari/Sahana Pradhan, Bharat Raj Joshi, Rai Majhi, Tulsi Lal, Krishna Raj Burma

Other political or pressure groups: numerous small, left-leaning student groups in the capital; Indian merchants in Tarai and capital; several small, radical Nepalese antimonarchist groups operating from north India

Member of: ADB, CCC, Colombo Plan, ESCAP, FAO, G-77, IBRD, ICAO, IDA, IFAD, IFC, ILO, IMF, IMO, INTERPOL, IPU, IRC, ITU, NAM, SAARC, UN, UNESCO, UPU, WHO, WMO, WTO

Diplomatic representation: Ambassador Mohan Man SAINJU; Chancery at 2131 Leroy Place NW, Washington DC 20008; telephone (202) 667-4550; there is a Nepalese Consulate General in New York; *US*—Ambassador Julia Chang BLOCH; Embassy at Pani Pokhari, Kathmandu; telephone [977] 411179 or 412718, 411601

Flag: red with a blue border around the unique shape of two overlapping right triangles; the smaller, upper triangle bears a white stylized moon and the larger, lower triangle bears a white 12-pointed sun

Economy

Overview: Nepal is among the poorest and least developed countries in the world with a per capita income of only $158. Real growth averaged 4% in the 1980s until FY89, when it plunged to 1.5% because of the ongoing trade/transit dispute with India. Agriculture is the mainstay of the economy, providing a livelihood for over 90% of the population and accounting for 60% of GDP and about 75% of exports. Industrial activity is limited, and what there is involves the processing of agricultural produce (jute, sugarcane, tobacco, and grain). Apart from agricultural land and forests, the only other exploitable natural resources are mica, hydropower, and tourism. Despite considerable investment in the agricultural sector, production in the 1980s has not kept pace with the population growth of 2.7%, which has led to a reduction in exportable surpluses and balance-of-payments difficulties. Economic prospects for the 1990s remain grim.

GDP: $2.9 billion, per capita $158; real growth rate 1.5% (FY89)

Inflation rate (consumer prices): 8.1% (FY89 est.)

Unemployment rate: 5%; underemployment estimated at 25-40% (1987)

Nepal (continued)

Budget: revenues $296 million; expenditures $635 million, including capital expenditures of $394 million (FY89 est.)

Exports: $374 million (f.o.b., FY89 est.), but does not include unrecorded border trade with India; *commodities*—clothing, carpets, leather goods, grain; *partners*—India 38%, US 23%, UK 6%, other Europe 9% (FY88)

Imports: $724 million (c.i.f., FY89 est.); *commodities*—petroleum products 20%, fertilizer 11%, machinery 10%; *partners*—India 36%, Japan 13%, Europe 4%, US 1% (FY88)

External debt: $1.3 billion (December 1989 est.)

Industrial production: growth rate −4.5% (FY89 est.)

Electricity: 205,000 kW capacity; 535 million kWh produced, 30 kWh per capita (1989)

Industries: small rice, jute, sugar, and oilseed mills; cigarette, textiles, cement, brick; tourism

Agriculture: accounts for 60% of GDP and 90% of work force; farm products—rice, corn, wheat, sugarcane, root crops, milk, buffalo meat; not self-sufficient in food, particularly in drought years

Illicit drugs: illicit producer of cannabis for the domestic and international drug markets

Aid: US commitments, including Ex-Im (FY70-88), $285 million; Western (non-US) countries, ODA and OOF bilateral commitments (1980-87), $1.8 billion; OPEC bilateral aid (1979-89), $30 million; Communist countries (1970-88), $273 million

Currency: Nepalese rupee (plural—rupees); 1 Nepalese rupee (NR) = 100 paisa

Exchange rates: Nepalese rupees (NRs) per US$1—28.559 (January 1990), 27.189 (1989), 23.289 (1988), 21.819 (1987), 21.230 (1986), 18.246 (1985)

Fiscal year: 16 July-15 July

Communications

Railroads: 52 km (1985), all 0.762-meter narrow gauge; all in Tarai close to Indian border; 10 km from Raxaul to Bīrganj is government owned

Highways: 5,958 km total (1986); 2,645 km paved, 815 km gravel or crushed stone, 2,257 km improved and unimproved earth; also 241 km of seasonally motorable tracks

Civil air: 5 major and 11 minor transport aircraft

Airports: 38 total, 38 usable; 5 with permanent-surface runways; none with runways over 3,659 m; 1 with runways 2,440-3,659 m; 9 with runways 1,220-2,439 m

Telecommunications: poor telephone and telegraph service; fair radio communication and broadcast service; international radio communication service is poor; 30,000 telephones (1987); stations—4 AM, no FM, 1 TV; 1 Indian Ocean INTELSAT earth station

Defense Forces

Branches: Royal Nepalese Army, Royal Nepalese Army Air Service, Nepalese Police Force

Military manpower: males 15-49, 4,531,660; 2,347,412 fit for military service; 225,349 reach military age (17) annually

Defense expenditures: 2% of GDP, or $58 million (1989 est.)

Netherlands

See regional map V

Geography

Total area: 37,290 km²; land area: 33,940 km²

Comparative area: slightly less than twice the size of New Jersey

Land boundaries: 1,027 km total; Belgium 450 km, FRG 577 km

Coastline: 451 km

Maritime claims:
Exclusive fishing zone: 200 nm
Territorial sea: 12 nm

Climate: temperate; marine; cool summers and mild winters

Terrain: mostly coastal lowland and reclaimed land (polders); some hills in southeast

Natural resources: natural gas, crude oil, fertile soil

Land use: 25% arable land; 1% permanent crops; 34% meadows and pastures; 9% forest and woodland; 31% other; includes 15% irrigated

Environment: 27% of the land area is below sea level and protected from the North Sea by dikes

Note: located at mouths of three major European rivers (Rhine, Maas or Meuse, Schelde)

People

Population: 14,936,032 (July 1990), growth rate 0.6% (1990)

Birth rate: 13 births/1,000 population (1990)

Death rate: 8 deaths/1,000 population (1990)

Net migration rate: 2 migrants/1,000 population (1990)

Infant mortality rate: 7 deaths/1,000 live births (1990)

Life expectancy at birth: 74 years male, 81 years female (1990)

Total fertility rate: 1.6 children born/woman (1990)

Nationality: noun—Dutchman(men), Dutchwoman(women); adjective—Dutch
Ethnic divisions: 96% Dutch, 4% Moroccans, Turks, and others (1988)
Religion: 36% Roman Catholic, 27% Protestant, 4% other, 33% unaffiliated (1986)
Language: Dutch
Literacy: 99%
Labor force: 5,300,000; 50.1% services, 28.2% manufacturing and construction, 15.9% government, 5.8% agriculture (1986)
Organized labor: 29% of labor force

Government

Long-form name: Kingdom of the Netherlands
Type: constitutional monarchy
Capital: Amsterdam, but government resides at The Hague
Administrative divisions: 12 provinces (provinciën, singular—provincie); Drenthe, Flevoland, Friesland, Gelderland, Groningen, Limburg, Noord-Brabant, Noord-Holland, Overijssel, Utrecht, Zeeland, Zuid-Holland
Dependent areas: Aruba, Netherlands Antilles
Independence: 1579 (from Spain)
Constitution: 17 February 1983
Legal system: civil law system incorporating French penal theory; judicial review in the Supreme Court of legislation of lower order rather than Acts of Parliament; accepts compulsory ICJ jurisdiction, with reservations
National holiday: Queen's Day, 30 April (1938)
Executive branch: monarch, prime minister, vice prime minister, Cabinet, Cabinet of Ministers
Legislative branch: bicameral States General (Staten Generaal) consists of an upper chamber or First Chamber (Eerste Kamer) and a lower chamber or Second Chamber (Tweede Kamer)
Judicial branch: Supreme Court (De Hoge Raad)
Leaders: *Chief of State*—Queen BEATRIX Wilhelmina Armgard (since 30 April 1980); Heir Apparent WILLEM-ALEXANDER, Prince of Orange, son of Queen Beatrix (born 27 April 1967);
Head of Government—Prime Minister Ruud (Rudolph) F. M. LUBBERS (since 4 November 1982); Deputy Prime Minister Wim KOK (since 2 November 1989)
Political parties and leaders: Christian Democratic Appeal (CDA), Willem van Velzen; Labor (PvdA), Wim Kok; Liberal (VVD), Joris Voorhoeve; Democrats '66 (D'66), Hans van Mierio; Communist (CPN), Henk Hoekstra; a host of minor parties

Suffrage: universal at age 18
Elections: *First Chamber*—last held on 9 June 1987 (next to be held 9 June 1991); results—elected by the country's 12 provincial councils; seats—(75 total) percent of seats by party NA;
Second Chamber—last held on 6 September 1989 (next to be held by September 1993); results—CDA 35.3%, PvdA 31.9%, VVD 14.6%, D'66 7.9%, others 10.3%; seats—(150 total) CDA 54, PvdA 49, VVD 22, D'66 12, others 13
Communists: about 6,000
Other political or pressure groups: large multinational firms; Federation of Netherlands Trade Union Movement (comprising Socialist and Catholic trade unions) and a Protestant trade union; Federation of Catholic and Protestant Employers Associations; the nondenominational Federation of Netherlands Enterprises; and IKV—Interchurch Peace Council
Member of: ADB, Benelux, CCC, Council of Europe, DAC, EC, ECE, EIB, EMS, ESA, ESCAP, FAO, GATT, IAEA, IBRD, ICAC, ICAO, ICES, ICO, IDA, IDB—Inter-American Development Bank, IEA, IFAD, IFC, IHO, ILO, ILZSG, IMF, IMO, INRO, INTELSAT, INTERPOL, IPU, IRC, ITC, ITU, IWC—International Wheat Council (with respect to interests of the Netherlands Antilles and Suriname), NATO, OAS (observer), OECD, UN, UNESCO, UPU, WEU, WHO,
Diplomatic representation: Ambassador Richard H. FEIN; Chancery at 4200 Linnean Avenue NW, Washington DC 20008; telephone (202) 244-5300; there are Dutch Consulates General in Chicago, Houston, Los Angeles, New York, and San Francisco; *US*—Ambassador C. Howard WILKINS; Embassy at Lange Voorhout 102, 2514 EJ The Hague (mailing address APO New York 09159); telephone [31] (70) 62-49-11; there is a US Consulate General in Amsterdam
Flag: three equal horizontal bands of red (top), white, and blue; similar to the flag of Luxembourg which uses a lighter blue and is longer

Economy

Overview: This highly developed and affluent economy is based on private enterprise. The government makes its presence felt, however, through many regulations, permit requirements, and welfare programs affecting most aspects of economic activity. The trade and financial

services sector contributes over 50% of GDP. Industrial activity, including construction, provides about 25% of GDP, and is led by the food-processing, oil-refining, and metal-working industries. The highly mechanized agricultural sector employs only 6% of the labor force, but provides large surpluses for export and the domestic food-processing industry. An unemployment rate of over 8.6% and a sizable budget deficit are currently the most serious economic problems.
GDP: $205.9 billion, per capita $13,900; real growth rate 4.2% (1989 est.)
Inflation rate (consumer prices): 1.5% (1989 est.)
Unemployment rate: 8.6% (1989 est.)
Budget: revenues $71 billion; expenditures $82 billion, including capital expenditures of $NA billion (1989)
Exports: $110.3 billion (f.o.b., 1989); *commodities*—agricultural products, processed foods and tobacco, natural gas, chemicals, metal products, textiles, clothing; *partners*—EC 74.9% (FRG 28.3%, Belgium-Luxembourg 14.2%, France 10.7%, UK 10.2%), US 4.7% (1988)
Imports: $100.9 billion (c.i.f., 1989); *commodities*—raw materials and semifinished products, consumer goods, transportation equipment, crude oil, food products; *partners*—EC 63.8% (FRG 26.5%, Belgium-Luxembourg 23.1%, UK 8.1%), US 7.9% (1988)
External debt: none
Industrial production: growth rate 4.8% (1989 est.)
Electricity: 22,216,000 kW capacity; 63,570 million kWh produced, 4,300 kWh per capita (1989)
Industries: agroindustries, metal and engineering products, electrical machinery and equipment, chemicals, petroleum, fishing, construction, microelectronics
Agriculture: accounts for 4% of GDP; animal production predominates; crops—grains, potatoes, sugar beets, fruits, vegetables; shortages of grain, fats, and oils
Aid: donor—ODA and OOF commitments (1970-87), $15.8 billion
Currency: Netherlands guilder, gulden, or florin (plural—guilders, gulden, or florins); 1 Netherlands guilder, gulden, or florin (f.) = 100 cents
Exchange rates: Netherlands guilders, gulden, or florins (f.) per US$1—2.2906 (January 1990), 2.1207 (1989), 1.9766 (1988), 2.0257 (1987), 2.4500 (1986), 3.3214 (1985)
Fiscal year: calendar year

Netherlands (continued)

Communications

Railroads: 3,037 km track (includes 1,871 km electrified and 1,800 km double track; 2,871 km 1.435-meter standard gauge operated by Netherlands Railways (NS); 166 km privately owned

Highways: 108,360 km total; 92,525 km paved (including 2,185 km of limited access, divided highways); 15,835 km gravel, crushed stone

Inland waterways: 6,340 km, of which 35% is usable by craft of 1,000 metric ton capacity or larger

Pipelines: 418 km crude oil; 965 km refined products; 10,230 km natural gas

Ports: maritime—Amsterdam, Delfzijl, Den Helder, Dordrecht, Eemshaven, Ijmuiden, Rotterdam, Scheveningen, Terneuzen, Vlissingen; inland—29 ports

Merchant marine: 345 ships (1,000 GRT or over) totaling 2,661,822 GRT/3,732,282 DWT; includes 2 short-sea passenger, 187 cargo, 42 refrigerated cargo, 23 container, 9 roll-on/roll-off cargo, 3 livestock carrier, 12 multifunction large-load carrier, 15 petroleum, oils, and lubricants (POL) tanker, 27 chemical tanker, 11 liquefied gas, 2 specialized tanker, 1 combination ore/oil, 9 bulk, 2 combination bulk; note—many Dutch-owned ships are also registered in the captive Netherlands Antilles register

Civil air: 98 major transport aircraft

Airports: 28 total, 28 usable; 19 with permanent-surface runways; none with runways over 3,659 m; 12 with runways 2,440-3,659 m; 3 with runways 1,220-2,439 m

Telecommunications: highly developed, well maintained, and integrated; extensive system of multiconductor cables, supplemented by radio relay links; 9,418,000 telephones; stations—6 AM, 20 (32 repeaters) FM, 21 (8 repeaters) TV; 5 submarine cables; communication satellite earth stations operating in INTELSAT (1 Indian Ocean and 2 Atlantic Ocean) and EUTELSAT systems

Defense Forces

Branches: Royal Netherlands Army, Royal Netherlands Navy/Marine Corps, Royal Netherlands Air Force

Military manpower: males 15-49, 4,134,006; 3,660,048 fit for military service; 111,948 reach military age (20) annually

Defense expenditures: 2.9% of GDP, or $6.0 billion (1989 est.)

Netherlands Antilles
(part of the Dutch realm)

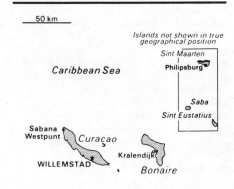

See regional map III

Geography

Total area: 960 km²; land area: 960 km²; includes Bonaire, Curaçao, Saba, Sint Eustatius, and Sint Maarten (Dutch part of the island of Saint Martin)

Comparative area: slightly less than 5.5 times the size of Washington, DC

Land boundaries: 14 km with Guadeloupe

Coastline: 364 km

Maritime claims:
  Exclusive fishing zone: 12 nm
  Territorial sea: 12 nm

Climate: tropical; modified by northeast trade winds

Terrain: generally hilly, volcanic interiors

Natural resources: phosphates (Curaçao only), salt (Bonaire only)

Land use: 8% arable land; 0% permanent crops; 0% meadows and pastures; 0% forest and woodland; 92% other

Environment: Curaçao and Bonaire are south of Caribbean hurricane belt, so rarely threatened; Sint Maarten, Saba, and Sint Eustatius are subject to hurricanes from July to October

Note: consists of two island groups—Curaçao and Bonaire are located off the coast of Venezuela, and Sint Maarten, Saba, and Sint Eustatius lie 800 km to the north

People

Population: 183,503 (July 1990), growth rate 0.2% (1990)

Birth rate: 18 births/1,000 population (1990)

Death rate: 5 deaths/1,000 population (1990)

Net migration rate: −11 migrants/1,000 population (1990)

Infant mortality rate: 9 deaths/1,000 live births (1990)

Life expectancy at birth: 74 years male, 79 years female (1990)

Total fertility rate: 2.0 children born/woman (1990)
Nationality: noun—Netherlands Antillean(s); adjective—Netherlands Antillean
Ethnic divisions: 85% mixed African; remainder Carib Indian, European, Latin, and Oriental
Religion: predominantly Roman Catholic; Protestant, Jewish, Seventh-Day Adventist
Language: Dutch (official); Papiamento, a Spanish-Portuguese-Dutch-English dialect predominates; English widely spoken; Spanish
Literacy: 95%
Labor force: 89,000; 65% government, 28% industry and commerce (1983)
Organized labor: 60-70% of labor force

Government

Long-form name: none
Type: part of the Dutch realm—full autonomy in internal affairs granted in 1954
Capital: Willemstad
Administrative divisions: none (part of the Dutch realm)
Independence: none (part of the Dutch realm)
Constitution: 29 December 1954, Statute of the Realm of the Netherlands, as amended
Legal system: based on Dutch civil law system, with some English common law influence
National holiday: Queen's Day, 30 April (1938)
Executive branch: Dutch monarch, governor, prime minister, vice prime minister, Council of Ministers (cabinet)
Legislative branch: Parliament (Staten)
Judicial branch: Joint High Court of Justice
Leaders: *Chief of State*—Queen BEATRIX Wilhelmina Armgard (since 30 April 1980), represented by Governor General Jaime SALEH (since October 1989);
Head of Government—Prime Minister Maria LIBERIA-PETERS (since 17 May 1988, previously served from September 1984 to November 1985)
Political parties and leaders: political parties are indigenous to each island: *Curaçao*—National People's Party (NVP), Maria Liberia-Peters; New Antilles Movement (MAN), Domenico Felip Martina; Democratic Party of Curaçao (DP), Augustus Diaz; Workers' Liberation Front (FOL), Wilson (Papa) Godett; Socialist Independent (SI), George Hueck and Nelson Monte;
Bonaire—New Force, Rudy Ellis; Democratic Party of Bonaire (PDB), John Evert (Jopie) Abraham;

Sint Maarten—Democratic Party of Sint Maarten, Claude Wathey; Patriotic Movement of Sint Maarten, Romeo Paplophlet;
Sint Eustatius—Democratic Party of Sint Eustatius, Albert K. Van Putten; Windward Islands People's Movement (WIPM), Eric Henriquez;
Saba—Windward Islands People's Movement (WIPM Saba), Will Johnston; Saba Democratic Labor Movement, Vernon Hassell; Saba Unity Party, Carmen Simmonds
Suffrage: universal at age 18
Elections: *Parliament*—last held on 22 November 1985 (next to be held November 1989); results—percent of vote by party NA; seats—(22 total) PNP 6, MAN 4, DP-Curaçao 3, DP-St. Maarten 3, DP-Bonaire 2, DP-St. Eustatius 1, FOL 1, UPB 1, WIPM 1; note—the government of Prime Minister Maria Liberia-Peters is a coalition of several parties
Communists: small leftist groups
Member of: EC (associate), INTERPOL; associated with UN through the Netherlands; UPU, WMO
Diplomatic representation: as an autonomous part of the Netherlands, Netherlands Antillean interests in the US are represented by the Netherlands; *US*—Consul General Sharon P. WILKINSON; Consulate General at St. Anna Boulevard 19, Willemstad, Curaçao (mailing address P. O. Box 158, Willemstad, Curaçao); telephone [599] (9) 613066
Flag: white with a horizontal blue stripe in the center superimposed on a vertical red band also centered; five white five-pointed stars are arranged in an oval pattern in the center of the blue band; the five stars represent the five main islands of Bonaire, Curaçao, Saba, Sint Eustatius, and Sint Maarten

Economy

Overview: Tourism, petroleum refining, and offshore finance are the mainstays of the economy. The islands enjoy a comparatively high per capita income and a well-developed infrastructure compared with other countries in the region. Unlike many Latin American countries, the Netherlands Antilles has avoided large international debt. Almost all consumer and capital goods are imported, with the US being the major supplier. The economy has suffered somewhat in recent years because of the depressed state of the world oil market and declining tax revenues. In 1983 the drop in oil prices led to the devaluation of the Venezuelan bolivar, which ended a substantial flow of Venezuelan tourists to the islands. As a result of a decline in tax

revenues, the government has been seeking financial support from the Netherlands.
GDP: $1.0 billion, per capita $5,500; real growth rate 3% (1988 est.)
Inflation rate (consumer prices): 2.0% (1988)
Unemployment rate: 26.0% (1988)
Budget: revenues $180 million; expenditures $289 million, including capital expenditures of $NA (1987 est.)
Exports: $1.3 billion (f.o.b., 1988); *commodities*—petroleum products 98%; *partners*—US 55%, UK 7%, Jamaica 5%
Imports: $1.5 billion (c.i.f., 1988); *commodities*—crude petroleum 64%, food, manufactures; *partners*—Venezuela 52%, Nigeria 15%, US 12%
External debt: $701.2 million (December 1987)
Industrial production: growth rate NA%
Electricity: 125,000 kW capacity; 365 million kWh produced, 1,990 kWh per capita (1989)
Industries: tourism (Curaçao and Sint Maarten), petroleum refining (Curaçao), petroleum transshipment facilities (Curaçao and Bonaire), light manufacturing (Curaçao)
Agriculture: hampered by poor soils and scarcity of water; chief products—aloes, sorghum, peanuts, fresh vegetables, tropical fruit; not self-sufficient in food
Aid: Western (non-US) countries, ODA and OOF bilateral commitments (1970-79), $353 million
Currency: Netherlands Antillean guilder, gulden, or florin (plural—guilders, gulden, or florins); 1 Netherlands Antillean guilder, gulden, or florin (NAf.) = 100 cents
Exchange rates: Netherlands Antillean guilders, gulden, or florins (NAf.) per US$1—1.80 (fixed rate since 1971)
Fiscal year: calendar year

Communications

Highways: 950 km total; 300 km paved, 650 km gravel and earth
Ports: Willemstad, Philipsburg, Kralendijk
Merchant marine: 52 ships (1,000 GRT or over) totaling 418,206 GRT/414,325 DWT; includes 4 passenger, 19 cargo, 5 refrigerated cargo, 7 container, 4 roll-on/roll-off cargo, 6 multifunction large-load carrier, 1 petroleum, oils, and lubricants (POL) tanker, 2 chemical tanker, 2 liquefied gas, 2 bulk; note—all but a few are foreign owned

Netherlands Antilles (continued)

Civil air: 5 major transport aircraft
Airports: 7 total, 7 usable; 7 with permanent-surface runways; none with runways over 3,659 m; 2 with runways 2,440-3,659 m; 2 with runways 1,220-2,439 m
Telecommunications: generally adequate facilities; extensive interisland radio relay links; stations—9 AM, 4 FM, 1 TV; 2 submarine cables; 2 Atlantic Ocean INTELSAT earth stations

Defense Forces

Military Manpower: males 15-49 49,299; 27,888 fit for military service; 1,678 reach military age (20) annually
Note: defense is responsibility of the Netherlands

New Caledonia
(overseas territory of France)

150 km

Coral Sea

Kone · Poindimie · Îles · Loyauté

We

New Caledonia

La

Foa

NOUMEA

Coral Sea · South Pacific Ocean · Île des Pins

Islands of Huon and Chesterfield are not shown.

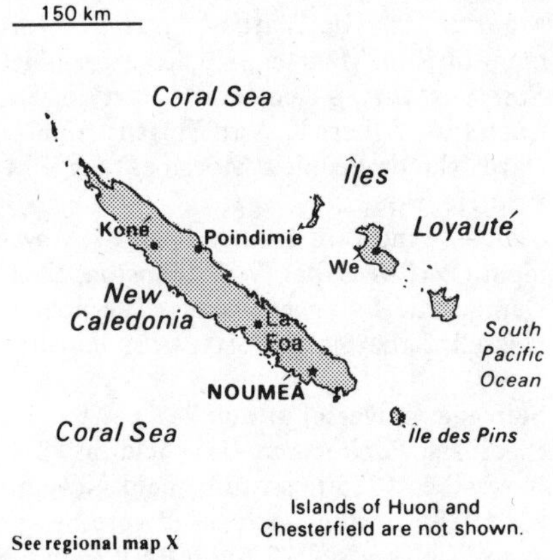

See regional map X

Geography

Total area: 19,060 km^2; land area: 18,760 km^2
Comparative area: slightly smaller than New Jersey
Land boundaries: none
Coastline: 2,254 km
Maritime claims:
Continental shelf: 200 meters or to depth of exploitation
Extended economic zone: 200 nm
Territorial sea: 12 nm
Climate: tropical; modified by southeast trade winds; hot, humid
Terrain: coastal plains with interior mountains
Natural resources: nickel, chrome, iron, cobalt, manganese, silver, gold, lead, copper
Land use: NEGL% arable land; NEGL% permanent crops; 14% meadows and pastures; 51% forest and woodland; 35% other
Environment: typhoons most frequent from November to March
Note: located 1,750 km east of Australia in the South Pacific Ocean

People

Population: 153,215 (July 1990), growth rate 1.1% (1990)
Birth rate: 24 births/1,000 population (1990)
Death rate: 7 deaths/1,000 population (1990)
Net migration rate: −7 migrants/1,000 population (1990)
Infant mortality rate: 39 deaths/1,000 live births (1990)
Life expectancy at birth: 64 years male, 71 years female (1990)
Total fertility rate: 3.0 children born/woman (1990)
Nationality: noun—New Caledonian(s); adjective—New Caledonian

Ethnic divisions: Melanesian 42.5%, European 37.1%, Wallisian 8.4%, Polynesian 3.8%, Indonesian 3.6%, Vietnamese 1.6%, other 3.0%
Religion: over 60% Roman Catholic, 30% Protestant, 10% other
Language: French; Melanesian-Polynesian dialects
Labor force: 50,469; foreign workers for plantations and mines from Wallis and Futuna, Vanuatu, and French Polynesia (1980 est.)
Organized labor: NA

Government

Long-form name: Territory of New Caledonia and Dependencies
Type: overseas territory of France
Capital: Nouméa
Administrative divisions: none (overseas territory of France)
Independence: none (overseas territory of France); note—a referendum on independence will be held in 1998 (there will be a review of the issue in 1992)
Constitution: 28 September 1958 (French Constitution)
Legal system: the 1988 Matignon Accords grant substantial autonomy to the islands; formerly under French law
National holiday: Taking of the Bastille, 14 July (1789)
Executive branch: high commissioner, Consultative Committee (cabinet)
Legislative branch: unicameral Territorial Assembly
Judicial branch: Court of Appeal
Leaders: *Chief of State*—President François MITTERRAND (since 21 May 1981);
Head of Government High Commissioner and President of the Council of Government Bernard GRASSET (since 15 July 1988)
Political parties: white-dominated Rassemblement pour la Calédonie dans la République (RPCR), conservative; Melanesian proindependence Kanak Socialist National Liberation Front (FLNKS); Melanesian moderate Kanak Socialist Liberation (LKS); National Front (FN), extreme right; Caledonian Separatist Front, extreme left
Suffrage: universal adult at age NA
Elections: *Territorial Congress*—last held NA June 1989 (next to be held NA 1993); results—percent of vote by party NA; seats—(54 total) RPCR 27, FLNKS 19, FN 3, others 5;
French Senate—last held 24 September 1989 (next to be held September 1992); results—percent of vote by party NA; seats—(1 total) RPCR 1;

French National Assembly—last held 5 and 12 June 1988 (next to be held June 1993); results—percent of vote by party NA; seats—(2 total) RPCR 2

Communists: number unknown; Palita extreme left party; some politically active Communists deported during 1950s; small number of North Vietnamese

Member of: EIB (associate), WFTU, WMO

Diplomatic representation: as an overseas territory of France, New Caledonian interests are represented in the US by France

Flag: the flag of France is used

Economy

Overview: New Caledonia has more than 40% of the world's known nickel resources. In recent years the economy has suffered because of depressed international demand for nickel, the principal source of export earnings. Only a negligible amount of the land is suitable for cultivation, and food accounts for about 25% of imports.

GNP: $860 million, per capita $5,810; real growth rate 2.4%. (1989 est.)

Inflation rate (consumer prices): 1.5% (1986)

Unemployment rate: 6.2% (1983)

Budget: revenues $110.5 million; expenditures $110.5 million, including capital expenditures of NA (1981)

Exports: $75 million (f.o.b., 1986); commodities—nickel metal 87%, nickel ore; partners—France 56.3%, Japan

Imports: $180 million (c.i.f., 1986); commodities—foods, fuels, minerals, machines, electrical equipment; partners—France 50.3%, Australia

External debt: $NA

Industrial production: growth rate NA%

Electricity: 400,000 kW capacity; 2,200 million kWh produced, 14,440 kWh per capita (1989)

Industries: nickel mining

Agriculture: large areas devoted to cattle grazing; coffee, corn, wheat, vegetables; 60% self-sufficient in beef

Aid: Western (non-US) countries, ODA and OOF bilateral commitments (1970-87), $3.6 billion

Currency: Comptoirs Français du Pacifique franc (plural—francs); 1 CFP franc (CFPF) = 100 centimes

Exchange rates: Comptoirs Français du Pacifique francs (CFPF) per US$1—104.71 (January 1990), 115.99 (1989), 108.30 (1988), 105.27 (1987), 125.92 (1986), 163.35 (1985); note—linked at the rate of 18.18 to the French franc

Fiscal year: calendar year

Communications

Highways: 5,448 km total; 558 km paved, 2,251 km improved earth, 2,639 km unimproved earth

Ports: Noumea, Nepoui, Poro, Thio

Civil air: no major transport aircraft

Airports: 29 total, 27 usable; 5 with permanent-surface runways; none with runways over 3,659 m; 1 with runways 2,440-3,659 m; 1 with runways 1,220-2,439 m

Telecommunications: 32,578 telephones (1987); stations—5 AM, 3 FM, 7 TV; 1 Pacific Ocean INTELSAT earth station

Defense Forces

Note: defense is the responsibility of France

New Zealand

Geography

Total area: 268,680 km^2; land area: 268,670 km^2; includes Antipodes Islands, Auckland Islands, Bounty Islands, Campbell Island, Chatham Islands, and Kermadec Islands

Comparative area: about the size of Colorado

Land boundaries: none

Coastline: 15,134 km

Maritime claims:
   Continental shelf: edge of continental margin or 200 nm
   Extended economic zone: 200 nm
   Territorial sea: 12 nm

Disputes: territorial claim in Antarctica (Ross Dependency)

Climate: temperate with sharp regional contrasts

Terrain: predominately mountainous with some large coastal plains

Natural resources: natural gas, iron ore, sand, coal, timber, hydropower, gold, limestone

Land use: 2% arable land; 0% permanent crops; 53% meadows and pastures; 38% forest and woodland; 7% other; includes 1% irrigated

Environment: earthquakes are common, though usually not severe

People

Population: 3,295,866 (July 1990), growth rate 0.4% (1990)

Birth rate: 16 births/1,000 population (1990)

Death rate: 8 deaths/1,000 population (1990)

Net migration rate: −3 migrant/1,000 population (1990)

Infant mortality rate: 10 deaths/1,000 live births (1990)

Life expectancy at birth: 72 years male, 78 years female (1990)

New Zealand (continued)

Total fertility rate: 2.0 children born/woman (1990)
Nationality: noun—New Zealander(s); adjective—New Zealand
Ethnic divisions: 88% European, 8.9% Maori, 2.9% Pacific Islander, 0.2% other
Religion: 81% Christian, 18% none or unspecified, 1% Hindu, Confucian, and other
Language: English (official), Maori
Literacy: 99%
Labor force: 1,591,900; 67.4% services, 19.8% manufacturing, 9.3% primary production (1987)
Organized labor: 681,000 members; 43% of labor force (1986)

Government

Long-form name: none; abbreviated NZ
Type: parliamentary democracy
Capital: Wellington
Administrative divisions: 93 counties, 9 districts*, and 3 town districts**; Akaroa, Amuri, Ashburton, Bay of Islands, Bruce, Buller, Chatham Islands, Cheviot, Clifton, Clutha, Cook, Dannevirke, Egmont, Eketahuna, Ellesmere, Eltham, Eyre, Featherston, Franklin, Golden Bay, Great Barrier Island, Grey, Hauraki Plains, Hawera*, Hawke's Bay, Heathcote, Hikurangi**, Hobson, Hokianga, Horowhenua, Hurunui, Hutt, Inangahua, Inglewood, Kaikoura, Kairanga, Kiwitea, Lake, Mackenzie, Malvern, Manaia**, Manawatu, Mangonui, Maniototo, Marlborough, Masterton, Matamata, Mount Herbert, Ohinemuri, Opotiki, Oroua, Otamatea, Otorohanga*, Oxford, Pahiatua, Paparua, Patea, Piako, Pohangina, Raglan, Rangiora*, Rangitikei, Rodney, Rotorua*, Runanga, Saint Kilda, Silverpeaks, Southland, Stewart Island, Stratford, Strathallan, Taranaki, Taumarunui, Taupo, Tauranga, Thames-Coromandel*, Tuapeka, Vincent, Waiapu, Waiheke, Waihemo, Waikato, Waikohu, Waimairi, Waimarino, Waimate, Waimate West, Waimea, Waipa, Waipawa*, Waipukurau*, Wairarapa South, Wairewa, Wairoa, Waitaki, Waitomo*, Waitotara, Wallace, Wanganui, Waverley**, Westland, Whakatane*, Whangarei, Whangaroa, Woodville
Dependent areas: Cook Islands, Niue, Tokelau
Independence: 26 September 1907 (from UK)
Constitution: no formal, written constitution; consists of various documents, including certain acts of the UK and New Zealand Parliaments; Constitution Act 1986 was to have come into force 1 January 1987, but has not been enacted
Legal system: based on English law, with special land legislation and land courts for Maoris; accepts compulsory ICJ jurisdiction, with reservations

National holiday: Waitangi Day (Treaty of Waitangi established British sovereignty), 6 February (1840)
Executive branch: British monarch, governor general, prime minister, deputy prime minister, Cabinet
Legislative branch: unicameral House of Representatives (commonly called Parliament)
Judicial branch: High Court, Court of Appeal
Leaders: *Chief of State*—Queen ELIZABETH II (since 6 February 1952), represented by Governor General The Most Rev. Sir Paul REEVES (since 20 November 1985);
Head of Government—Prime Minister Geoffrey PALMER (since 8 August 1989); Deputy Prime Minister Helen CLARK (since 8 August 1989)
Political parties and leaders: New Zealand Labor Party (NZLP; government), Geoffrey Palmer; National Party (NP; opposition), Jim Bolger; Democratic Party, Neil Morrison; Socialist Unity Party (SUP; pro-Soviet), Ken Douglas
Suffrage: universal at age 18
Elections: *House of Representatives*—last held on 15 August 1987 (next to be held by August 1990); results—LP 47%, NP 45%, DP 6%; seats—(97 total) LP 58, NP 39
Communists: SUP about 140, other groups, about 200
Member of: ADB, ANZUS, ASPAC, CCC, Colombo Plan, Commonwealth, DAC, ESCAP, FAO, GATT, IAEA, IBRD, ICAO, ICO, IDA, IEA, IFAD, IFC, IHO, ILO, IMF, IMO, INTELSAT, INTERPOL, IPU, ISO, ITU, OECD, SPF, UN, UNESCO, UPU, WHO, WMO, WSG
Diplomatic representation: Ambassador Harold Huyton FRANCIS; Chancery at 37 Observatory Circle NW, Washington DC 20008; telephone (202) 328-4800; there are New Zealand Consulates General in Los Angeles and New York; *US*—Ambassador Della NEWMAN; Embassy at 29 Fitzherbert Terrace, Thorndon, Wellington (mailing address is Private Bag, Wellington, or FPO San Francisco 96690-0001); telephone [64] (4) 722-068; there is a US Consulate General in Auckland
Flag: blue with the flag of the UK in the upper hoist-side quadrant with four red five-pointed stars edged in white centered in the outer half of the flag; the stars represent the Southern Cross constellation

---

Economy

Overview: Since 1984 the government has been reorienting an agrarian economy dependent on a guaranteed British market to an open free market economy that can compete on the global scene. The government has hoped that dynamic growth would boost real incomes, reduce inflationary pressures, and permit the expansion of welfare benefits. The results have been mixed: inflation is down from double-digit levels but growth has been sluggish and unemployment, always a highly sensitive issue, has been at a record high 7.4%. In 1988 GDP fell by 1% and in 1989 grew by a moderate 2.4%.
GDP: $39.1 billion, per capita $11,600; real growth rate 2.4% (1989 est.)
Inflation rate (consumer prices): 5% (1989)
Unemployment rate: 7.4% (1989)
Budget: revenues $18.6 billion; expenditures $19.1 billion, including capital expenditures of $NA (FY90 est.)
Exports: $8.9 billion (f.o.b., FY89); *commodities*—wool, lamb, mutton, beef, fruit, fish, cheese, manufactures, chemicals, foresty products; *partners*—EC 18.3%, Japan 17.9%, Australia 17.5%, US 13.5%, China 3.6%, South Korea 3.1%
Imports: $7.5 billion (c.i.f., FY89); *commodities*—petroleum, consumer goods, motor vehicles, industrial equipment; *partners*—Australia 19.7%, Japan 16.9%, EC 16.9%, US 15.3%, Taiwan 3.0%
External debt: $17.0 billion (1989)
Industrial production: growth rate −1.6% (FY88)
Electricity: 7,800,000 kW capacity; 27,600 million kWh produced, 8,190 kWh per capita (1989)
Industries: food processing, wood and paper products, textiles, machinery, transportation equipment, banking and insurance, tourism, mining
Agriculture: accounts for about 9% of GNP and 10% of the work force; livestock predominates—wool, meat, dairy products all export earners; crops—wheat, barley, potatoes, pulses, fruits, and vegetables; surplus producer of farm products; fish catch reached a record 431,000 metric tons in 1987
Aid: donor—ODA and OOF commitments (1970-87), $448 million
Currency: New Zealand dollar (plural—dollars); 1 New Zealand dollar (NZ$) = 100 cents
Exchange rates: New Zealand dollars (NZ$) per US$1—1.6581 (January 1990), 1.6708 (1989), 1.5244 (1988), 1.6886 (1987), 1.9088 (1986), 2.0064 (1985)
Fiscal year: 1 July-30 June

Communications

Railroads: 4,716 km total; all 1.067-meter gauge; 274 km double track; 113 km electrified; over 99% government owned
Highways: 92,648 km total; 49,547 km paved, 43,101 km gravel or crushed stone

Nicaragua

Inland waterways: 1,609 km; of little importance to transportation
Pipelines: 1,000 km natural gas; 160 km refined products; 150 km condensate
Ports: Auckland, Christchurch, Dunedin, Wellington, Tauranga
Merchant marine: 18 ships (1,000 GRT or over) totaling 190,553 GRT/257,782 DWT; includes 1 cargo, 2 container, 4 roll-on/roll-off cargo, 1 railcar carrier, 4 petroleum, oils, and lubricants (POL) tanker, 1 liquefied gas, 5 bulk
Civil air: about 40 major transport aircraft
Airports: 157 total, 157 usable; 33 with permanent-surface runways; none with runways over 3,659 m; 2 with runways 2,440-3,659 m; 47 with runways 1,220-2,439 m
Telecommunications: excellent international and domestic systems; 2,110,000 telephones; stations 64 AM, 2 FM, 14 TV; submarine cables extend to Australia and Fiji; 2 Pacific Ocean INTELSAT earth stations

Defense Forces

Branches: Royal New Zealand Navy, New Zealand Army, Royal New Zealand Air Force
Military manpower: males 15-49, 872,336; 740,207 fit for military service; 29,532 reach military age (20) annually
Defense expenditures: 2.1% of GDP, or $820 million (1989 est.)

See regional map III

Geography

Total area: 129,494 km^2; land area: 120,254 km^2
Comparative area: slightly larger than New York State
Land boundaries: 1,231 km total; Costa Rica 309 km, Honduras 922 km
Coastline: 910 km
Maritime claims:
Contiguous zone: 25 nm security zone (status of claim uncertain)
Continental shelf: not specified
Territorial sea: 200 nm
Disputes: territorial disputes with Colombia over the Archipelago de San Andres y Providencia and Quita Sueno Bank
Climate: tropical in lowlands, cooler in highlands
Terrain: extensive Atlantic coastal plains rising to central interior mountains; narrow Pacific coastal plain interrupted by volcanoes
Natural resources: gold, silver, copper, tungsten, lead, zinc, timber, fish
Land use: 9% arable land; 1% permanent crops; 43% meadows and pastures; 35% forest and woodland; 12% other; including 1% irrigated
Environment: subject to destructive earthquakes, volcanoes, landslides, and occasional severe hurricanes; deforestation; soil erosion; water pollution

People

Population: 3,722,683 (July 1990), growth rate 2.8% (1990)
Birth rate: 40 births/1,000 population (1990)
Death rate: 9 deaths/1,000 population (1990)
Net migration rate: −3 migrants/1,000 population (1990)
Infant mortality rate: 68 deaths/1,000 live births (1990)

Life expectancy at birth: 61 years male, 62 years female (1990)
Total fertility rate: 5.0 children born/woman (1990)
Nationality: noun—Nicaraguan(s); adjective—Nicaraguan
Ethnic divisions: 69% mestizo, 17% white, 9% black, 5% Indian
Religion: 95% Roman Catholic, 5% Protestant
Language: Spanish (official); English- and Indian-speaking minorities on Atlantic coast
Literacy: 88% (1981)
Labor force: 1,086,000; 43% service, 44% agriculture, 13% industry (1986)
Organized labor: 35% of labor force

Government

Long-form name: Republic of Nicaragua
Type: republic
Capital: Managua
Administrative divisions: 9 administrative regions encompassing 17 departments (departamentos, singular—departamento); North, Atlantic Coast, South, Atlantic Coast, Boaco, Carazo, Chinandega, Chontales, Estelí, Granada, Jinotega, León, Madriz, Managua, Masaya, Matagalpa, Nueva Segovia, Río San Juan, Rivas
Independence: 15 September 1821 (from Spain)
Constitution: January 1987
Legal system: civil law system; Supreme Court may review administrative acts
National holiday: Independence Day, 15 September (1821)
Executive branch: president, vice president, Cabinet
Legislative branch: National Assembly (Asamblea Nacional)
Judicial branch: Supreme Court (Corte Suprema) and municipal courts
Leaders: *Chief of State and Head of Government*—President-Elect Violeta Barios de CHAMORRO (since 25 February 1990; takes office 25 April 1990); Vice President-elect Virgilio GODOY (since 25 February 1990; takes office 25 April 1990)
Political parties and leaders:
Ruling coalition: National Opposition Union (UNO)—14 party alliance: National Conservative Party (PNC), Silviano Matamoros; Conservative Popular Alliance Party (PAPC), Miriam Arguello; National Conservative Action Party (PANC), Hernaldo Zuniga; National Democratic Confidence Party (PDCN), Augustin Jarquin; Independent Liberal Party (PLI), Virgilio Godoy; Neo-Liberal Party (PALI), Andres Zuniga; Liberal Constitutionalist Party (PLC), Jose Ernesto Somarriba; National Action Party (PAN), Eduardo Rivas; Nicaraguan Socialist Party (PSN), Gustavo Tablada; Commu-

nist Party of Nicaragua (PCdeN), Eli Altimirano; Popular Social Christian Party (PPSC), Luis Humberto; Nicaraguan Democratic Movement (MDN), Roberto Urroz; Social Democratic Party (PSD), Guillermo Potoy; Central American Integrationist Party (PIAC), Alejandro Perez; *Opposition parties:* Sandinista National Liberation Front (FSLN), Daniel Ortega; Central American Unionist Party (PUCA), Blanca Rojas; Democratic Conservative Party of Nicaragua (PCDN), Jose Brenes; Liberal Party of National Unity (PLUIN), Eduardo Coronado; Movement of Revolutionary Unity (MUR), Francisco Samper; Social Christian Party (PSC), Erick Ramirez; Revolutionary Workers' Party (PRT), Bonifacio Miranda; Social Conservative Party (PSOC), Fernando Aguerro; Popular Action Movement—Marxist-Leninist (MAP-ML), Isidro Tellez; Popular Social Christian Party (PPSC), Mauricio Diaz

Suffrage: universal at age 16

Elections: *President*—last held on 25 February 1990 (next to be held February 1996); results—Violeta Barrios de Chamorro (UNO) 54.7%, Daniel Ortega Saavedra (FSLN) 40.8%, others 4.5%; *National Constituent Assembly*—last held on 25 February 1990 (next to be held February 1996); results—UNO 53.9%, FSLN 40.8%, PSC 1.6%, MUR 1.0%; seats—(92 total) UNO 51, FSLN 39, PSC 1, MUR 1

Communists: FSLN—35,000; other Communists—15,000-20,000

Other political or pressure groups: Permanent Congress of Workers (CPT), Confederation of Labor Unification (CUS), Autonomous Nicaraguan Workers' Central (CTN-A), Independent General Confederation of Workers (CTG-I), Communist Labor Action and Unity Central (CAUS), Nicaraguan Workers' Central (CST); Superior Council of Private Enterprise (COSEP) is an umbrella group of 11 different business groups, including the Chamber of Commerce, the Chamber of Industry, and the Nicaraguan Development Institute (INDE)

Member of: CACM, CEMA (observer), FAO, G-77, GATT, IADB, IAEA, IBRD, ICAC, ICAO, ICO, IDA, IDB—Inter-American Development Bank, IFAD, IFC, ILO, IMF, IMO, INTELSAT, INTERPOL, IPU, IRC, ISO, ITU, NAM, OAS, ODECA, PAHO, SELA, UN, UNESCO, UPEB, UPU, WFTU, WHO, WMO, WTO

Diplomatic representation: Chargé d'Affaires Leonor Arguello de HUPER; Chancery at 1627 New Hampshire Avenue NW, Washington DC 20009; telephone (202) 387-4371 or 4372; *US*—Chargé d'Affaires John P. LEONARD; Embassy

at Kilometer 4.5 Carretera Sur, Managua (mailing address is APO Miami 34021); telephone [505] (2) 66010 or 66013, 66015 through 66018, 66026, 66027, 66032 through 66034; note—Nicaragua expelled the US Ambassador on 11 July 1988, and the US expelled the Nicaraguan Ambassador on 12 July 1988

Flag: three equal horizontal bands of blue (top), white, and blue with the national coat of arms centered in the white band; the coat of arms features a triangle encircled by the words *REPUBLICA DE NICARAGUA* on the top and *AMERICA CENTRAL* on the bottom; similar to the flag of El Salvador which features a round emblem encircled by the words *REPUBLICA DE EL SALVADOR EN LA AMERICA CENTRAL* centered in the white band; also similar to the flag of Honduras, which has five blue stars arranged in an *X* pattern centered in the white band

Economy

Overview: Government control of the economy historically has been extensive, although the new government has pledged to reduce it. The financial system is directly controlled by the state, which also regulates wholesale purchasing, production, sales, foreign trade, and distribution of most goods. Over 50% of the agricultural and industrial firms are state owned. Sandinista economic policies and the war have produced a severe economic crisis. The foundation of the economy continues to be the export of agricultural commodities, largely coffee and cotton. Farm production fell by roughly 7% in 1989, the fifth successive year of decline. The agricultural sector employs 44% of the work force and accounts for 23% of GDP and 86% of export earnings. Industry, which employs 13% of the work force and contributes 26% to GDP, showed a sharp drop of −23% in 1988 and remains below pre-1979 levels. External debt is one of the highest in the world on a per capita basis. In 1989 the annual inflation rate was 1,700%, down from a record 16,000% in 1988. Shortages of basic consumer goods are widespread.

GDP: $1.7 billion, per capita $470; real growth rate −5.0% (1989 est.)

Inflation rate (consumer prices): 1,700% (1989)

Unemployment rate: 25% (1989)

Budget: revenues $0.9 billion; expenditures $1.4 billion, including capital expenditures of $0.15 billion (1987)

Exports: $250 million (f.o.b., 1989 est.); *commodities*—coffee, cotton, sugar, ba-

nanas, seafood, meat, chemicals; *partners*—CEMA 15%, OECD 75%, others 10%

Imports: $550 million (c.i.f., 1989 est.); *commodities*—petroleum, food, chemicals, machinery, clothing; *partners*—CEMA 55%, EC 20%, Latin America 10%, others 10%

External debt: $8 billion (year end 1988)

Industrial production: growth rate −23% (1988 est.)

Electricity: 415,000 kW capacity; 1,340 million kWh produced, 380 kWh per capita (1989)

Industries: food processing, chemicals, metal products, textiles, clothing, petroleum refining and distribution, beverages, footwear

Agriculture: accounts for 23% of GDP and 44% of work force; cash crops—coffee, bananas, sugarcane, cotton; food crops—rice, corn, cassava, citrus fruit, beans; variety of animal products—beef, veal, pork, poultry, dairy; while normally self-sufficient in food, war-induced shortages now exist

Aid: US commitments, including Ex-Im (FY70-82), $290 million; Western (non-US) countries, ODA and OOF bilateral commitments (1970-87), $981 million; Communist countries (1970-88), $3.3 billion

Currency: córdoba (plural—córdobas); 1 córdoba (C$) = 100 centavos

Exchange rates: córdobas (C$) per US$1—65,000 (February 1990) is the free market rate; official rate is 46,000 (February 1990), 270 (1988), 0.103 (1987), 0.097 (1986), 0.039 (1985)

Fiscal year: calendar year

Communications

Railroads: 373 km 1.067-meter gauge, government owned; majority of system not operating; 3 km 1.435-meter gauge line at Puerto Cabezas (does not connect with mainline)

Highways: 25,930 km total; 4,000 km paved (includes all 2,170 km gravel or crushed stone, 5,425 km earth or graded earth, 14,335 km unimproved, 368.5 km of the Pan-American highway)

Inland waterways: 2,220 km, including 2 large lakes

Pipelines: crude oil, 56 km

Ports: Corinto, El Bluff, Puerto Cabezas, Puerto Sandino, Rama

Merchant marine: 2 cargo ships (1,000 GRT or over) totaling 2,161 GRT/2,500 DWT

Civil air: 12 major transport aircraft

Airports: 261 total, 169 usable; 9 with permanent-surface runways; none with

Niger

runways over 3,659 m; 2 with runways 2,440-3,659 m; 12 with runways 1,220-2,439 m

Telecommunications: low-capacity radio relay and wire system being expanded; connection into Central American Microwave System; 60,000 telephones; stations—45 AM, no FM, 7 TV, 3 shortwave; satellite earth stations—1 Intersputnik and 1 Atlantic Ocean INTELSAT

Defense Forces

Branches: Sandinista Popular Army, Sandinista Navy, Sandinista Air Force/Air Defense, Sandinista People's Militia
Military manpower: males 15-49, 747,144; 459,333 fit for military service; 44,213 reach military age (18) annually
Defense expenditures: NA

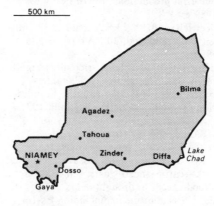

500 km

See regional map VII

Geography

Total area: 1,267,000 km²; land area: 1,266,700 km²
Comparative area: slightly less than twice the size of Texas
Land boundaries: 5,697 km total; Algeria 956 km, Benin 266 km, Burkina 628 km, Chad 1,175 km, Libya 354 km, Mali 821 km, Nigeria 1,497 km
Coastline: none—landlocked
Maritime claims: none—landlocked
Disputes: Libya claims about 19,400 km² in northern Niger; exact locations of the Chad-Niger-Nigeria and Cameroon-Chad-Nigeria tripoints in Lake Chad have not been determined, so the boundary has not been demarcated and border incidents have resulted; Burkina and Mali are proceeding with boundary demarcation, including the tripoint with Niger
Climate: desert; mostly hot, dry, dusty; tropical in extreme south
Terrain: predominately desert plains and sand dunes; flat to rolling plains in south; hills in north
Natural resources: uranium, coal, iron ore, tin, phosphates
Land use: 3% arable land; 0% permanent crops; 7% meadows and pastures; 2% forest and woodland; 88% other; includes NEGL% irrigated
Environment: recurrent drought and desertification severely affecting marginal agricultural activities; overgrazing; soil erosion
Note: landlocked

People

Population: 7,969,309 (July 1990), growth rate 3.6% (1990)
Birth rate: 52 births/1,000 population (1990)
Death rate: 17 deaths/1,000 population (1990)
Net migration rate: 0 migrants/1,000 population (1990)

Infant mortality rate: 131 deaths/1,000 live births (1990)
Life expectancy at birth: 48 years male, 53 years female (1990)
Total fertility rate: 7.4 children born/woman (1990)
Nationality: noun—Nigerien(s) adjective—Nigerien
Ethnic divisions: 56% Hausa; 22% Djerma; 8.5% Fula; 8% Tuareg; 4.3% Beri Beri (Kanouri); 1.2% Arab, Toubou, and Gourmantche; about 4,000 French expatriates
Religion: 80% Muslim, remainder indigenous beliefs and Christians
Language: French (official); Hausa, Djerma
Literacy: 13.9%
Labor force: 2,500,000 wage earners (1982); 90% agriculture, 6% industry and commerce, 4% government; 51% of population of working age (1985)
Organized labor: negligible

Government

Long-form name: Republic of Niger
Type: republic; presidential system in which military officers hold key offices
Capital: Niamey
Administrative divisions: 7 departments (départements, singular—département); Agadez, Diffa, Dosso, Maradi, Niamey, Tahoua, Zinder
Independence: 3 August 1960 (from France)
Constitution: adopted NA December 1989 after 15 years of military rule
Legal system: based on French civil law system and customary law; has not accepted compulsory ICJ jurisdiction
National holidays: Republic Day, 18 December (1958)
Executive branch: president, prime minister, Council of Ministers (cabinet)
Legislative branch: National Development Council
Judicial branch: State Court (Cour d'Etat), Court of Appeal (Cour d'Apel)
Leaders: *Chief of State*—President Brig. Gen. Ali SAIBOU (since 14 November 1987);
Head of Government—Prime Minister ALIOU MAHAMIDA (since 2 March 1990)
Political parties and leaders: only party—National Movement for the Development Society (MNSD), leader NA
Suffrage: universal adult at age 18
Elections: *President*—last held December 1989 (next to be held NA 1996); results—President Ali Saibou was reelected without opposition;
National Development Council—last held December 1989 (next to be held NA

Niger *(continued)*

1994); results—MNSD is the only party; seats—(150 total) MNSD 150 (indirectly elected)

Communists: no Communist party; some sympathizers in outlawed Sawaba party

Member of: ACP, AfDB, APC, CCC, CEAO, EAMA, ECA, ECOWAS, Entente, FAO, G-77, GATT, IAEA, IBRD, ICAO, IDA, IDB—Islamic Development Bank, IFAD, IFC, ILO, IMF, INTELSAT, INTERPOL, IPU, ITU, Lake Chad Basin Commission, Niger River Commission, NAM, OAU, OCAM, OIC, UN, UNESCO, UPU, WHO, WIPO, WMO

Diplomatic representation: Ambassador Moumouni Adamou DJERMAKOYE; Chancery at 2204 R Street NW, Washington DC 20008; telephone (202) 483-4224 through 4227; *US*—Ambassador Carl C. CUNDIFF; Embassy at Avenue des Ambassadeurs, Niamey (mailing address is B. P. 11201, Niamey); telephone [227] 72-26-61 through 64 and 72-26-70

Flag: three equal horizontal bands of orange (top), white, and green with a small orange disk (representing the sun) centered in the white band; similar to the flag of India which has a blue, spoked wheel centered in the white band

Economy

Overview: About 90% of the population is engaged in farming and stock rearing, activities which generate almost half of the national income. The economy also depends heavily on exploitation of large uranium deposits. Uranium production grew rapidly in the mid-1970s, but tapered off in the early 1980s, when world prices declined. France is a major customer, while FRG, Japan, and Spain also make regular purchases. The depressed demand for uranium has contributed to an overall sluggishness in the economy, a severe trade imbalance, and a mounting external debt.

GDP: $2.4 billion, per capita $330; real growth rate 7.1% (1988 est.)

Inflation rate (consumer prices): −1.4% (1988)

Unemployment rate: NA%

Budget: revenues $254 million; expenditures $510 million, including capital expenditures of $239 million (1988 est.)

Exports: $371 million (f.o.b., 1988 est.); *commodities*—uranium 76%, livestock, cowpeas, onions, hides, skins; *partners*—NA

Imports: $441 million (c.i.f., 1988 est.); *commodities*—petroleum products, primary materials, machinery, vehicles and parts, electronic equipment, pharmaceuticals, chemical products, cereals, foodstuffs

External debt: $1.8 billion (December 1989 est.)

Industrial production: growth rate 4.7% (1989 est.)

Electricity: 102,000 kW capacity; 225 million kWh produced, 30 kWh per capita (1989)

Industries: cement, brick, rice mills, small cotton gins, oilseed presses, slaughterhouses, and a few other small light industries; uranium production began in 1971

Agriculture: accounts for roughly 40% of GDP and 90% of labor force; cash crops—cowpeas, cotton, peanuts; food crops—millet, sorghum, cassava, rice; livestock—cattle, sheep, goats; self-sufficient in food except in drought years

Aid: US commitments, including Ex-Im (FY70-88), $349 million; Western (non-US) countries, ODA and OOF bilateral commitments (1970-87), $2.8 billion; OPEC bilateral aid (1979-89), $504 million; Communist countries (1970-88), $61 million

Currency: Communauté Financière Africaine franc (plural—francs); 1 CFA franc (CFAF) = 100 centimes

Exchange rates: Communauté Financière Africaine francs (CFAF) per US$1—287.99 (January 1990), 319.01 (1989), 297.85 (1988), 300.54 (1987), 346.30 (1986), 449.26 (1985)

Fiscal year: 1 October-30 September

Communications

Highways: 39,970 km total; 3,170 km bituminous, 10,330 km gravel and laterite, 3,470 km earthen, 23,000 km tracks

Inland waterways: Niger river is navigable 300 km from Niamey to Gaya on the Benin frontier from mid-December through March

Civil air: no major transport aircraft

Airports: 31 total, 29 usable; 7 with permanent-surface runways; 1 with runways over 3,659 m; 1 with runways 2,440-3,659 m; 11 with runways 1,220-2,439 m

Telecommunications: small system of wire, radiocommunications, and radio relay links concentrated in southwestern area; 11,900 telephones; stations—15 AM, 5 FM, 16 TV; satellite earth stations—1 Atlantic Ocean INTELSAT, 1 Indian Ocean INTELSAT, and 4 domestic

Defense Forces

Branches: Army, Air Force, paramilitary Gendarmerie, paramilitary Republican Guard, paramilitary Presidential Guard, paramilitary National Police

Military manpower: males 15-49, 1,656,466; 894,095 fit for military service; 87,478 reach military age (18) annually

Defense expenditures: $20.6 million (1988)

Nigeria

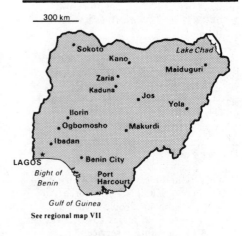

300 km

See regional map VII

Geography

Total area: 923,770 km²; land area: 910,770 km²

Comparative area: slightly more than twice the size of California

Land boundaries: 4,047 km total; Benin 773 km, Cameroon 1,690 km, Chad 87 km, Niger 1,497 km

Coastline: 853 km

Maritime claims:
Continental shelf: 200 meters or to depth of exploitation
Extended economic zone: 200 nm
Territorial sea: 30 nm

Disputes: exact locations of the Chad-Niger-Nigeria and Cameroon-Chad-Nigeria tripoints in Lake Chad have not been determined, so the boundary has not been demarcated and border incidents have resulted; Nigerian proposals to reopen maritime boundary negotiations and redemarcate the entire land boundary have been rejected by Cameroon

Climate: varies—equatorial in south, tropical in center, arid in north

Terrain: southern lowlands merge into central hills and plateaus; mountains in southeast, plains in north

Natural resources: crude oil, tin, columbite, iron ore, coal, limestone, lead, zinc, natural gas

Land use: 31% arable land; 3% permanent crops; 23% meadows and pastures; 15% forest and woodland; 28% other; includes NEGL% irrigated

Environment: recent droughts in north severely affecting marginal agricultural activities; desertification; soil degradation, rapid deforestation

People

Population: 118,819,377 (July 1990), growth rate 3.0% (1990)

Birth rate: 46 births/1,000 population (1990)

Death rate: 17 deaths/1,000 population (1990)

Net migration rate: 1 migrant/1,000 population (1990)

Infant mortality rate: 119 deaths/1,000 live births (1990)

Life expectancy at birth: 48 years male, 49 years female (1990)

Total fertility rate: 6.5 children born/woman (1990)

Nationality: noun—Nigerian(s); adjective—Nigerian

Ethnic divisions: more than 250 tribal groups; Hausa and Fulani of the north, Yoruba of the southwest, and Ibos of the southeast make up 65% of the population; about 27,000 non-Africans

Religion: 50% Muslim, 40% Christian, 10% indigenous beliefs

Language: English (official); Hausa, Yoruba, Ibo, Fulani, and several other languages also widely used

Literacy: 42.4%

Labor force: 42,844,000; 54% agriculture, 19% industry, commerce, and services, 15% government; 49% of population of working age (1985)

Organized labor: 3,520,000 wage earners belong to 42 recognized trade unions, which come under a single national labor federation—the Nigerian Labor Congress (NLC)

Government

Long-form name: Federal Republic of Nigeria

Type: military government since 31 December 1983

Capital: Lagos

Administrative divisions: 21 states and 1 territory*; Abuja Capital Territory*, Akwa Ibom, Anambra, Bauchi, Bendel, Benue, Borno, Cross River, Gongola, Imo, Kaduna, Kano, Katsina, Kwara, Lagos, Niger, Ogun, Ondo, Oyo, Plateau, Rivers, Sokoto

Independence: 1 October 1960 (from UK)

Constitution: 1 October 1979, amended 9 February 1984, revised 1989

Legal system: based on English common law, Islamic, and tribal law

National holiday: Independence Day, 1 October (1960)

Executive branch: president of the Armed Forces Ruling Council, Armed Forces Ruling Council, National Council of State, Council of Ministers (cabinet)

Legislative branch: National Assembly was dissolved after the military coup of 31 December 1983

Judicial branch: Supreme Court, Federal Court of Appeal

Leaders: *Chief of State and Head of Government*—President and Commander in Chief of Armed Forces Gen. Ibrahim BABANGIDA (since 27 August 1985)

Political parties and leaders: two political parties established by the government in 1989—Social Democratic Party (SDP) and National Republican Convention (NRC)

Suffrage: universal at age 21

Elections: *President*—scheduled for 1 October 1992

Communists: the pro-Communist underground consists of a small fraction of the Nigerian left; leftist leaders are prominent in the country's central labor organization but have little influence on government

Member of: ACP, AfDB, APC, CCC, Commonwealth, ECA, ECOWAS, FAO, G-77, GATT, IAEA, IBRD, ICAO, ICO, IDA, IFAD, IFC, ILO, IMO, IMF, INTELSAT, INTERPOL, IRC, ISO, ITC, ITU, IWC—International Wheat Council, Lake Chad Basin Commission, Niger River Commission, NAM, OAU, OPEC, UN, UNESCO, UPU, WHO, WMO, WTO

Diplomatic representation: Ambassador Hamzat AHMADU; Chancery at 2201 M Street NW, Washington DC 20037; telephone (202) 822-1500; there are Nigerian Consulates General in Atlanta, New York and San Francisco; *US*—Ambassador Lannon WALKER; Embassy at 2 Eleke Crescent, Victoria Island, Lagos (mailing address is P. O. Box 554, Lagos); telephone [234] (1) 610097; there is a US Consulate General in Kaduna

Flag: three equal vertical bands of green (hoist side), white, and green

Economy

Overview: In 1989, despite rising oil prices, the economic performance failed to meet government expectations because of higher inflationary pressures fueled by a relatively poor agricultural performance. Agricultural production was up only 4% following a 10% decline in 1988, and manufacturing remained below the 1985 level with only a 6% increase. The government is continuing an economic adjustment program to reduce Nigeria's dependence on oil and to help create a basis for sustainable noninflationary growth.

GNP: $30.0 billion, per capita $270; real growth rate 4% (1989)

Inflation rate (consumer prices): 47.5% (1989)

Unemployment rate: 7.5% (1988 est.)

Budget: revenues $6.5 billion; expenditures $7.4 billion, including capital expenditures of $1.9 billion (1988 est.)

Exports: $8.4 billion (f.o.b., 1989 est.); *commodities*—oil 95%, cocoa, palm kernels, rubber; *partners*—EC 51%, US 32%

Imports: $5.7 billion (c.i.f., 1989 est.); *commodities*—consumer goods, capital equipment, chemicals, raw materials; *partners*—EC, US

External debt: $32 billion, medium and long-term (December 1989 est.)

Industrial production: growth rate 5% (1987 est.)

Electricity: 4,737,000 kW capacity; 11,270 million kWh produced, 100 kWh per capita (1989)

Industries: mining—crude oil, natural gas, coal, tin, columbite; primary processing industries—palm oil, peanut, cotton, rubber, petroleum, wood, hides and skins; manufacturing industries—textiles, cement, building materials, food products, footwear, chemical, printing, ceramics, steel

Agriculture: accounts for 28% of GNP and half of labor force; inefficient small-scale farming dominates; once a large net exporter of food and now an importer; cash crops—cocoa, peanuts, palm oil, rubber; food crops—corn, rice, sorghum, millet, cassava, yams; livestock—cattle, sheep, goats, pigs; fishing and forestry resources extensively exploited

Illicit drugs: illicit heroin and some cocaine trafficking; marijuana cultivation for domestic consumption and export; major transit country for heroin en route from Southwest Asia via Africa to Western Europe and the US; growing transit route for cocaine from South America via West Africa to Western Europe and the US

Aid: US commitments, including Ex-Im (FY70-88), $662 million; Western (non-US) countries, ODA and OOF bilateral commitments (1970-87), $1.9 billion; Communist countries (1970-88), $2.2 billion

Currency: naira (plural—naira); 1 naira (₦) = 100 kobo

Exchange rates: naira (₦) per US$1—7.6221 (December 1989), 7.3647 (1989), 4.5370 (1988), 4.0160 (1987), 1.7545 (1986), 0.8938 (1985)

Fiscal year: calendar year

Communications

Railroads: 3,505 km 1.067-meter gauge

Highways: 107,990 km total 30,019 km paved (mostly bituminous-surface treatment); 25,411 km laterite, gravel, crushed stone, improved earth; 52,560 km unimproved

Inland waterways: 8,575 km consisting of Niger and Benue Rivers and smaller rivers and creeks

Pipelines: 2,042 km crude oil; 500 km natural gas; 3,000 km refined products

Ports: Lagos, Port Harcourt, Calabar, Warri, Onne, Sapele

Nigeria *(continued)*

Merchant marine: 28 ships (1,000 GRT or over) totaling 428,116 GRT/680,343 DWT; includes 19 cargo, 1 refrigerated, 1 roll-on/roll-off cargo, 5 petroleum, oils, and lubricants (POL) tanker, 1 chemical tanker, 1 bulk

Civil air: 76 major transport aircraft

Airports: 84 total, 72 usable; 32 with permanent-surface runways; 1 with runways over 3,659 m; 13 with runways 2,440-3,659 m; 22 with runways 1,220-2,439 m

Telecommunications: above-average system limited by poor maintenance; major expansion in progress; radio relay and cable routes; 155,000 telephones; stations—37 AM, 19 FM, 38 TV; 2 Atlantic Ocean INTELSAT, 1 Indian Ocean INTELSAT, domestic, with 19 stations; 1 coaxial submarine cable

Defense Forces

Branches: Army, Navy, Air Force, paramilitary Police Force

Military manpower: males 15-49, 27,282,248; 15,587,485 fit for military service; 1,263,883 reach military age (18) annually

Defense expenditures: 1% of GNP, or $300 million (1990 est.)

Niue
(free association with New Zealand)

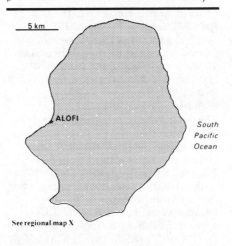

See regional map X

Geography

Total area: 260 km²; land area: 260 km²

Comparative area: slightly less than 1.5 times the size of Washington, DC

Land boundaries: none

Coastline: 64 km

Maritime claims:

Extended economic zone: 200 nm

Territorial sea: 12 nm

Climate: tropical; modified by southeast trade winds

Terrain: steep limestone cliffs along coast, central plateau

Natural resources: fish, arable land

Land use: 61% arable land; 4% permanent crops; 4% meadows and pastures; 19% forest and woodland; 12% other

Environment: subject to typhoons

Note: one of world's largest coral islands; located about 460 km east of Tonga

---

People

Population: 2,019 (July 1990), growth rate NA (1990)

Birth rate: NA births/1,000 population (1990)

Death rate: NA deaths/1,000 population (1990)

Net migration rate: NA migrants/1,000 population (1990)

Infant mortality rate: NA deaths/1,000 live births (1990)

Life expectancy at birth: NA years male, NA years female (1990)

Total fertility rate: NA children born/woman (1990)

Nationality: noun—Niuean(s); adjective—Niuean

Ethnic divisions: Polynesian, with some 200 Europeans, Samoans, and Tongans

Religion: 75% Ekalesia Nieue (Niuean Church)—a Protestant church closely related to the London Missionary Society, 10% Mormon, 5% Roman Catholic, Jehovah's Witnesses, Seventh-Day Adventist

---

Language: Polynesian tongue closely related to Tongan and Samoan; English

Literacy: NA%, but education compulsory between 5 and 14 years of age

Labor force: 1,000 (1981 est.); most work on family plantations; paid work exists only in government service, small industry, and the Niue Development Board

Organized labor: NA

Government

Long-form name: none

Type: self-governing territory in free association with New Zealand

Capital: Alofi

Administrative divisions: none

Independence: none (self-governing territory in free association with New Zealand)

Constitution: no formal, written constitution

Legal system: English common law

National holiday: Waitangi Day (Treaty of Waitangi established British sovereignty), 6 February (1840)

Executive branch: British monarch, premier, Cabinet

Legislative branch: Legislative Assembly

Judicial branch: Appeal Court of New Zealand, High Court

Leaders: *Chief of State*—Queen ELIZABETH II (since 6 February 1952), represented by New Zealand Representative John SPRINGFORD (since 1974);

Head of Government—Premier Sir Robert R. REX (since NA October 1974)

Suffrage: universal adult at age 18

Political parties and leaders: Niue People's Action Party, leader NA

Elections: *Legislative Assembly*—last held on 28 March 1987 (next to be held NA 1990); results—percent of vote NA; seats—(20 total, 6 elected) independents 5, Niue People's Action Party 1

Member of: ESCAP (associate member), SPF

Diplomatic representation: none (self-governing territory in free association with New Zealand)

Flag: yellow with the flag of the UK in the upper hoist-side quadrant; the flag of the UK bears five yellow five-pointed stars—a large one on a blue disk in the center and a smaller one on each arm of the bold red cross

---

Economy

Overview: The economy is heavily dependent on aid from New Zealand. Government expenditures regularly exceed revenues, with the shortfall made up by grants from New Zealand—the grants are used to pay wages to the 80% or more of the work force employed in public service.

The agricultural sector consists mainly of subsistence gardening, although some cash crops are grown for export. Industry consists primarily of small factories to process passion fruit, lime oil, honey, and coconut cream. The sale of postage stamps to foreign collectors is an important source of revenue. The island in recent years has suffered a serious loss of population because of migration of Niueans to New Zealand.

GNP: $2.1 million, per capita $1,000; real growth rate NA% (1989 est.)

Inflation rate (consumer prices): 9.6% (1984)

Unemployment rate: NA%

Budget: revenues $5.5 million; expenditures $6.3 million, including capital expenditures of NA (FY85 est.)

Exports: $175,274 (f.o.b., 1985); *commodities*—canned coconut cream, copra, honey, passion fruit products, pawpaw, root crops, limes, footballs, stamps, handicrafts; *partners*—NZ 89%, Fiji, Cook Islands, Australia

Imports: $3.8 million (c.i.f., 1985); *commodities*—food, live animals, manufactured goods, machinery, fuels, lubricants, chemicals, drugs; *partners*—NZ 59%, Fiji 20%, Japan 13%, Western Samoa, Australia, US

External debt: $NA

Industrial production: growth rate NA%

Electricity: 1,500 kW capacity; 3 million kWh produced, 1,420 kWh per capita (1989)

Industries: tourist, handicrafts

Agriculture: copra, coconuts, passion fruit, honey, limes; subsistence crops—taro, yams, cassava (tapioca), sweet potatoes; pigs, poultry, beef cattle

Aid: Western (non-US) countries, ODA and OOF bilateral commitments (1970-87), $58 million

Currency: New Zealand dollar (plural—dollars); 1 New Zealand dollar (NZ$) = 100 cents

Exchange rates: New Zealand dollars (NZ$) per US$1—1.6581 (January 1990), 1.6708 (1989), 1.5244 (1988), 1.6886 (1987), 1.9088 (1986), 2.0064 (1985)

Fiscal year: 1 April-31 March

Communications

Highways: 123 km all-weather roads, 106 km access and plantation roads

Ports: none; offshore anchorage only

Airports: 1 with permanent-surface runway of 1,650 m

Telecommunications: single-line telephone system connects all villages on island; 383 telephones; 1,000 radio receivers (1987 est.); stations—1 AM, 1 FM, no TV

Defense Forces

Note: defense is the responsibility of New Zealand

Norfolk Island
(territory of Australia)

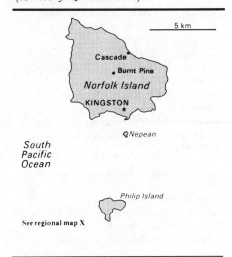

South Pacific Ocean

See regional map X

Geography

Total area: 34.6 km²; land area: 34.6 km²

Comparative area: about 0.2 times the size of Washington, DC

Land boundaries: none

Coastline: 32 km

Maritime claims:
Contiguous zone: 12 nm
Continental shelf: 200 meters or to depth of exploitation
Exclusive fishing zone: 200 nm
Territorial sea: 3 nm

Climate: subtropical, mild, little seasonal temperature variation

Terrain: volcanic formation with mostly rolling plains

Natural resources: fish

Land use: 0% arable land; 0% permanent crops; 25% meadows and pastures; 0% forest and woodland; 75% other

Environment: subject to typhoons (especially May to July)

Note: located 1,575 km east of Australia in the South Pacific Ocean

People

Population: 2,533 (July 1990), growth rate 1.7% (1990)

Birth rate: NA births/1,000 population (1990)

Death rate: NA deaths/1,000 population (1990)

Net migration rate: NA migrants/1,000 population (1990)

Infant mortality rate: NA deaths/1,000 live births (1990)

Life expectancy at birth: NA years male, NA years female (1990)

Total fertility rate: NA children born/woman (1990)

Nationality: noun—Norfolk Islander(s); adjective—Norfolk Islander(s)

Ethnic divisions: descendants of the Bounty mutiny; more recently, Australian and New Zealand settlers

Norfolk Island (continued)

Religion: Anglican, Roman Catholic, Uniting Church in Australia, and Seventh-Day Adventist
Language: English (official) and Norfolk—a mixture of 18th century English and ancient Tahitian
Literacy: NA%, but probably high
Labor force: NA
Organized labor: NA

Government

Long-form name: Territory of Norfolk Island
Type: territory of Australia
Capital: Kingston (administrative center), Burnt Pine (commercial center)
Administrative divisions: none (territory of Australia)
Independence: none (territory of Australia)
Constitution: Norfolk Island Act of 1957
Legal system: wide legislative and executive responsibility under the Norfolk Island Act of 1979; Supreme Court
National holiday: Pitcairners Arrival Day Anniversary, 8 June (1856)
Executive branch: British monarch, governor general of Australia, administrator, Executive Council (cabinet)
Legislative branch: unicameral Legislative Assembly
Judicial branch: Supreme Court
Leaders: *Chief of State*—Queen ELIZABETH II (since 6 February 1952), represented by Administrator H. B. MACDONALD (since NA 1989), who is appointed by the Governor General of Australia;
Head of Government—Assembly President and Chief Minister John Terence BROWN (since NA)
Political parties and leaders: NA
Suffrage: universal at age 18
Elections: *Legislative Assembly*—last held NA (next to be held NA); results—percent of vote by party NA; seats—(9 total) percent of seats by party NA
Diplomatic representation: none (territory of Australia)
Flag: three vertical bands of green (hoist side), white, and green with a large green Norfolk Island pine tree centered in the slightly wider white band

Economy

Overview: The primary economic activity is tourism, which has brought a level of prosperity unusual among inhabitants of the Pacific Islands. The number of visitors has increased steadily over the years and reached almost 30,000 in 1986. Revenues from tourism have given the island a favorable balance of trade and helped the agricultural sector to become self-sufficient in the production of beef, poultry, and eggs.
GNP: NA
Inflation rate (consumer prices): NA%
Unemployment rate: NA%
Budget: revenues $3.4 million; expenditures $3.4 million, including capital expenditures of NA (FY88)
Exports: $1.8 million (f.o.b., FY85); *commodities*—postage stamps, seeds of the Norfolk Island pine and Kentia Palm, small quantities of avocados; *partners*—Australia, Pacific Islands, NZ, Asia, Europe
Imports: $16.3 million (c.i.f., FY85); *commodities*—NA; *partners*—Australia, Pacific Islands, NZ, Asia, Europe
External debt: NA
Industrial production: growth rate NA%
Electricity: 7,000 kW capacity; 8 million kWh produced, 3,210 kWh per capita (1989)
Industries: tourism
Agriculture: Norfolk Island pine seed, Kentia palm seed, cereals, vegetables, fruit, cattle, poultry
Aid: none
Currency: Australian dollar (plural—dollars); 1 Australian dollar ($A) = 100 cents
Exchange rates: Australian dollars ($A) per US$1—1.2784 (January 1990), 1.2618 (1989), 1.2752 (1988), 1.4267 (1987), 1.4905 (1986), 1.4269 (1985)
Fiscal year: 1 July-30 June

Communications

Highways: 80 km of roads, including 53 km of sealed roads; remainder are earth formed or coral surfaced
Ports: none; loading jetties at Kingston and Cascade
Airports: 1 with permanent-surface runways 1,220-2,439 m (Australian owned)
Telecommunications: 1,500 radio receivers (1982); radio link service with Sydney; 987 telephones (1983); stations—1 AM, no FM, no TV

Defense Forces

Note: defense is the responsibility of Australia

Northern Mariana Islands
(commonwealth associated with the US)

See regional map X

Geography

Total area: 477 km²; land area: 477 km²; includes Saipan, Rota, and Tinian
Comparative area: slightly more than 2.5 times the size of Washington, DC
Land boundaries: none
Coastline: 1,482 km
Maritime claims:
  Contiguous zone: 12 nm
  Continental shelf: 200 m
  Extended economic zone: 200 nm
  Territorial sea: 3 nm
Climate: tropical marine; moderated by northeast trade winds, little seasonal temperature variation; dry season December to July, rainy season July to October
Terrain: southern islands are limestone with level terraces and fringing coral reefs; northern islands are volcanic; highest elevation is 471 meters (Mt. Tagpochu on Saipan)
Natural resources: arable land, fish
Land use: 1% arable land; NA% permanent crops; 19% meadows and pastures; NA% forest and woodland; NA% other
Environment: Mt. Pagan is an active volcano (last erupted in October 1988); subject to typhoons during the rainy season
Note: strategic location 5,635 km west-southwest of Honolulu in the North Pacific Ocean, about three-quarters of the way between Hawaii and the Philippines

People

Population: 22,719 (July 1990), growth rate 3.4% (1990)
Birth rate: 43 births/1,000 population (1990)
Death rate: 6 deaths/1,000 population (1990)
Net migration rate: −3 migrants/1,000 population (1990)
Infant mortality rate: 17 deaths/1,000 live births (1990)

Life expectancy at birth: 65 years male, 70 years female (1990)
Total fertility rate: 5.8 children born/woman (1990)
Nationality: undetermined
Ethnic divisions: Chamorro majority; Carolinians and other Micronesians; Spanish, German, Japanese admixtures
Religion: Christian with a Roman Catholic majority, although traditional beliefs and taboos may still be found
Language: English, but Chamorro and Carolinian are also spoken in the home and taught in school
Literacy: NA%
Labor force: 17,533, including 10,000 foreign workers (1988 est.)
Organized labor: NA

Government

Long-form name: Commonwealth of the Northern Mariana Islands
Type: commonwealth associated with the US and administered by the Office of Territorial and International Affairs, US Department of the Interior
Capital: Saipan
Administrative divisions: none
Independence: none (commonwealth associated with the US)
Constitution: Covenant Agreement effective 3 November 1986
Legal system: NA
National holiday: Commonwealth Day, 8 January (1978)
Executive branch: governor, lieutenant governor
Legislative branch: bicameral Legislature consists of an upper house or Senate and a lower house or House of Representatives
Judicial branch: Supreme Court
Leaders: *Chief of State*—President George BUSH (since 20 January 1989); Vice President Dan QUAYLE (since 20 January 1989);
Head of Government—Governor Pedro P. TENORIO (since 1978); Lieutenant Governor Pedro A. TENORIO (since NA)
Political parties and leaders: Democratic Party, Antonio S. Guerrero; Republican Party, Alonso Igisomar
Suffrage: universal at age 18; indigenous inhabitants are US citizens but do not vote in US presidential elections
Elections: *Governor*—last held on NA (next to be held NA); results—Pedro P. TENORIO (Democratic Party) was elected;
Senate—last held on NA (next to be held NA); results—percent of vote by party NA; seats—(9 total) number of seats by party NA;

House of Representatives—last held on NA (next to be held NA); results—percent of vote by party NA; seats—(14 total) number of seats by party NA;
US House of Representatives—last held NA (next to be held NA); results—percent of vote by party NA; seats—(1 total) party of nonvoting delegate NA
Diplomatic representation: none
Flag: blue with a white five-pointed star superimposed on the gray silhouette of a latte stone (a traditional foundation stone used in building) in the center

Economy

Overview: The economy benefits substantially from financial assistance from the US. An agreement for the years 1986 to 1992 entitles the islands to $228 million for capital development, government operations, and special programs. Another major source of income is the tourist industry, which employs about 10% of the work force. The agricultural sector is made up of cattle ranches and small farms producing coconuts, breadfruit, tomatoes, and melons. Industry is small scale in nature—mostly handicrafts and fish processing.
GNP: $165 million, per capita $9,170; real growth rate NA% (1982)
Inflation rate (consumer prices): NA%
Unemployment rate: NA%
Budget: revenues $NA; expenditures $70.6 million, including capital expenditures of $NA (1987)
Exports: $NA; *commodities*—vegetables, beef, pork; *partners*—NA
Imports: $NA; *commodities*—NA; *partners*—NA
External debt: $NA
Industrial production: growth rate NA%
Electricity: 25,000 kW capacity; 35 million kWh produced, 1,640 kWh per capita (1989)
Industries: tourism, construction, light industry, handicrafts
Agriculture: coffee, coconuts, fruits, tobacco, cattle
Aid: none
Currency: US currency is used
Exchange rates: US currency is used
Fiscal year: 1 October-30 September

Communications

Highways: 300 km total (53 km primary, 55 km secondary, 192 km local)
Ports: Saipan, Rota, Tinian
Airports: 6 total, 4 usable; 3 with permanent-surface runways; none with runways over 3,659 m; 1 with runways 2,440-3,659 m; 2 with runways 1,220-2,439 m
Telecommunications: stations—2 AM, no FM, 1 TV; 2 Pacific Ocean INTELSAT earth stations

Defense Forces

Note: defense is the responsibility of the US

Norway

400 km

See regional maps V and XI

Geography

Total area: 324,220 km²; land area: 307,860 km²
Comparative area: slightly larger than New Mexico
Land boundaries: 2,582 km total; Finland 729 km, Sweden 1,657, USSR 196 km
Coastline: 21,925 km (3,419 km mainland; 2,413 km large islands; 16,093 km long fjords, numerous small islands, and minor indentations)
Maritime claims:
Contiguous zone: 10 nm
Continental shelf: 200 meters or to depth of exploitation
Extended economic zone: 200 nm
Territorial sea: 4 nm
Disputes: maritime boundary dispute with USSR; territorial claim in Antarctica (Queen Maud Land); Denmark has challenged Norway's maritime claims beween Greenland and Jan Mayen
Climate: temperate along coast, modified by North Atlantic Current; colder interior; rainy year-round on west coast
Terrain: glaciated; mostly high plateaus and rugged mountains broken by fertile valleys; small, scattered plains; coastline deeply indented by fjords; arctic tundra in north
Natural resources: crude oil, copper, natural gas, pyrites, nickel, iron ore, zinc, lead, fish, timber, hydropower
Land use: 3% arable land; 0% permanent crops; NEGL% meadows and pastures; 27% forest and woodland; 70% other; includes NEGL% irrigated
Environment: air and water pollution; acid rain
Note: strategic location adjacent to sea lanes and air routes in North Atlantic; one of most rugged and longest coastlines in world; Norway and Turkey only NATO members having a land boundary with the USSR

People

Population: 4,252,806 (July 1990), growth rate 0.5% (1990)
Birth rate: 14 births/1,000 population (1990)
Death rate: 11 deaths/1,000 population (1990)
Net migration rate: 2 migrants/1,000 population (1990)
Infant mortality rate: 7 deaths/1,000 live births (1990)
Life expectancy at birth: 73 years male, 81 years female (1990)
Total fertility rate: 1.8 children born/woman (1990)
Nationality: noun—Norwegian(s); adjective—Norwegian
Ethnic divisions: Germanic (Nordic, Alpine, Baltic) and racial-cultural minority of 20,000 Lapps
Religion: 94% Evangelical Lutheran (state church), 4% other Protestant and Roman Catholic, 2% other
Language: Norwegian (official); small Lapp- and Finnish-speaking minorities
Literacy: 100%
Labor force: 2,164,000; 33.6% services, 17.4% commerce, 16.6% mining and manufacturing, 8.4% transportation, 7.8% construction, 6.8% banking and financial services, 6.5% agriculture, forestry, and fishing (1986)
Organized labor: 66% of labor force (1985)

Government

Long-form name: Kingdom of Norway
Type: constitutional monarchy
Capital: Oslo
Administrative divisions: 19 provinces (fylker, singular—fylke); Akershus, Aust-Agder, Buskerud, Finnmark, Hedmark, Hordaland, Møre og Romsdal, Nordland, Nord-Trøndelag, Oppland, Oslo, Østfold, Rogaland, Sogn og Fjordane, Sør-Trøndelag, Telemark, Troms, Vest-Agder, Vestfold
Independence: 26 October 1905 (from Sweden)
Constitution: 17 May 1814, modified in 1884
Dependent areas: Bouvet Island, Jan Mayen, Svalbard
Legal system: mixture of customary law, civil law system, and common law traditions; Supreme Court renders advisory opinions to legislature when asked; accepts compulsory ICJ jurisdiction, with reservations
National holiday: Constitution Day, 17 May (1814)
Executive branch: monarch, prime minister, State Council (cabinet)

Legislative branch: unicameral Parliament (Storting or Stortinget) with an Upper Chamber (Lagting) and a Lower Chamber (Odelsting)
Judicial branch: Supreme Court (Hoiesterett)
Leaders: *Chief of State*—King OLAV V (since 21 September 1957); Heir Apparent Crown Prince HARALD (born 21 February 1937);
Head of Government—Prime Minister Jan P. SYSE (since 16 October 1989)
Political parties and leaders: Labor, Gro Harlem Brundtland; Conservative, Jan P. Syse; Center, Johan J. Jakobsen; Christian People's, Kjell Magne Bondevik; Socialist Left, Eric Solheim; Norwegian Communist, Hans I. Kleven; Progress, Carl I. Hagen; Liberal, Arne Fjortoft; Finnmark List, leader NA
Suffrage: universal at age 18
Elections: *Parliament*—last held on 11 September 1989 (next to be held 6 September 1993); results—Labor 34.3%, Conservative 22.2%, Progress 13.0%, Socialist Left 10.1%, Christian People's 8.5%, Center 6.6%, Finnmark List 0.3%, others 5%; seats—(165 total) Labor 63, Conservative 37, Progress 22, Socialist Left 17, Christian People's 14, Center 11, Finnmark List 1
Communists: 15,500 est.; 5,500 Norwegian Communist Party (NKP); 10,000 Workers Communist Party Marxist-Leninist (AKP-ML, pro-Chinese)
Member of: ADB, CCC, Council of Europe, DAC, EFTA, ESA, FAO, GATT, IAEA, IBRD, ICAC, ICAO, ICES, ICO, IDA, IEA (associate member), IFAD, IFC, IHO, ILO, ILZSG, IMF, IMO, INTELSAT, INTERPOL, IPU, ITU, IWC—International Whaling Commission, IWC—International Wheat Council, NATO, Nordic Council, OECD, UN, UNESCO, UPU, WHO, WIPO, WMO, WSG
Diplomatic representation: Ambassador Kjeld VIBE; Chancery at 2720 34th Street NW, Washington DC 20008; telephone (202) 333-6000; there are Norwegian Consulates General in Houston, Los Angeles, Minneapolis, New York, and San Francisco, and Consulates in Miami and New Orleans; *US*—Ambassador Loret Miller RUPPE; Embassy at Drammensveien 18, Oslo 2 (mailing address is APO New York 09085); telephone [47] (2) 44-85-50
Flag: red with a blue cross outlined in white that extends to the edges of the flag; the vertical part of the cross is shifted to the hoist side in the style of the *Dannebrog* (Danish flag)

Economy

Overview: Norway is a prosperous capitalist nation with the resources to finance extensive welfare measures. Since 1975 exploitation of large crude oil and natural gas reserves has helped achieve an average annual growth of roughly 4%, the third-highest among OECD countries. Growth slackened in 1987-88 because of the sharp drop in world oil prices and a slowdown in consumer spending, but picked up again in 1989. Future economic issues involve the aging of the population, the increased economic integration of Europe, and the balance between private and public influence in economic decisions.
GDP: $75.8 billion, per capita $17,900; real growth rate 5.7% (1989 est.)
Inflation rate (consumer prices): 4.5% (1989)
Unemployment rate: 3.9% (1989 est., excluding people in job-training programs)
Budget: revenues $40.6 billion; expenditures $41.3 billion, including capital expenditures of $NA (1989)
Exports: $22.2 billion (f.o.b., 1989); *commodities*—petroleum and petroleum products 25%, natural gas 11%, fish 7%, aluminum 6%, ships 3.5%, pulp and paper; *partners*—UK 26%, EFTA 16.3%, less developed countries 14%, Sweden 12%, FRG 12%, US 6%, Denmark 5% (1988)
Imports: $18.7 billion (c.i.f., 1989); *commodities*—machinery, fuels and lubricants, transportation equipment, chemicals, foodstuffs, clothing, ships; *partners*—Sweden 18%, less developed countries 18%, FRG 14%, Denmark 8%, UK 7%, US 7%, Japan 5% (1988)
External debt: $18.3 billion (December 1989)
Industrial production: growth rate 15.8% (1989)
Electricity: 26,735,000 kW capacity; 121,685 million kWh produced, 28,950 kWh per capita (1989)
Industries: petroleum and gas, food processing, shipbuilding, pulp and paper products, metals, chemicals, timber, mining, textiles, fishing
Agriculture: accounts for 3.1% of GNP and 6.5% of labor force; among world's top 10 fishing nations; livestock output exceeds value of crops; over half of food needs imported; fish catch of 1.9 million metric tons in 1987
Aid: donor—ODA and OOF commitments (1970-87), $3.7 billion
Currency: Norwegian krone (plural—kroner); 1 Norwegian krone (NKr) = 100 øre
Exchange rates: Norwegian kroner (NKr) per US$1—6.5405 (January 1990), 6.9045 (1989), 6.5170 (1988), 6.7375 (1987), 7.3947 (1986), 8.5972 (1985)
Fiscal year: calendar year

Communications

Railroads: 4,223 km 1.435-meter standard gauge; Norwegian State Railways (NSB) operates 4,219 km (2,450 km electrified and 96 km double track); 4 km other
Highways: 79,540 km total; 18,600 km concrete, bituminous, stone block; 19,980 km bituminous treated; 40,960 km gravel, crushed stone, and earth
Inland waterways: 1,577 km along west coast; 1.5-2.4 m draft vessels maximum
Pipelines: refined products, 53 km
Ports: Oslo, Bergen, Fredrikstad, Kristiansand, Stavanger, Trondheim
Merchant marine: 660 ships (1,000 GRT or over) totaling 16,702,254 GRT/28,722,304 DWT; includes 11 passenger, 19 short-sea passenger, 104 cargo, 3 passenger-cargo, 19 refrigerated cargo, 6 container, 40 roll-on/roll-off cargo, 6 vehicle carrier, 1 railcar carrier, 128 petroleum, oils, and lubricants (POL) tanker, 86 chemical tanker, 62 liquefied gas, 26 combination ore/oil, 142 bulk, 7 combination bulk; note—the government has created a captive register, the Norwegian International Ship Register (NIS), as a subset of the Norwegian register; ships on the NIS enjoy many benefits of flags of convenience and do not have to be crewed by Norwegians; the majority of ships under the Norwegian flag are now registered with the NIS
Civil air: 76 major transport aircraft
Airports: 104 total, 104 usable; 64 with permanent-surface runways; none with runways over 3,659 m; 12 with runways 2,440-3,659 m; 16 with runways 1,220-2,439 m
Telecommunications: high-quality domestic and international telephone, telegraph, and telex services; 3,102,000 telephones; stations—8 AM, 46 (1,400 relays) FM, 55 (2,100 relays) TV; 4 coaxial submarine cables; communications satellite earth stations operating in the EUTELSAT, INTELSAT (1 Atlantic Ocean), MARISAT, and domestic systems

Defense Forces

Branches: Royal Norwegian Army, Royal Norwegian Navy, Royal Norwegian Air Force
Military manpower: males 15-49, 1,115,620; 937,555 fit for military service; 32,748 reach military age (20) annually
Defense expenditures: 3.3% of GDP, or $2.5 billion (1989 est.)

Oman

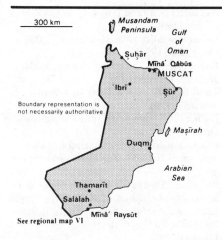

See regional map VI

Geography

Total area: 212,460 km²; land area: 212,460 km²
Comparative area: slightly smaller than Kansas
Land boundaries: 1,374 km total; Saudi Arabia 676 km, UAE 410 km, PDRY 288 km
Coastline: 2,092 km
Maritime claims:
  Continental shelf: to be defined
  Extended economic zone: 200 nm
  Territorial sea: 12 nm
Disputes: Administrative Line with PDRY; no defined boundary with most of UAE, Administrative Line in far north
Climate: dry desert; hot, humid along coast; hot, dry interior; strong southwest summer monsoon (May to September) in far south
Terrain: vast central desert plain, rugged mountains in north and south
Natural resources: crude oil, copper, asbestos, some marble, limestone, chromium, gypsum, natural gas
Land use: NEGL% arable land; NEGL% permanent crops; 5% meadows and pastures; 0% forest and woodland; 95% other; includes NEGL% irrigated
Environment: summer winds often raise large sandstorms and duststorms in interior; sparse natural freshwater resources
Note: strategic location with small foothold on Musandam Peninsula controlling Strait of Hormuz (17% of world's oil production transits this point going from Persian Gulf to Arabian Sea)

People

Population: 1,457,064 (July 1990), growth rate 3.1% (1990)
Birth rate: 43 births/1,000 population (1990)
Death rate: 12 deaths/1,000 population (1990)

Net migration rate: 0 migrants/1,000 population (1990)
Infant mortality rate: 105 deaths/1,000 live births (1990)
Life expectancy at birth: 56 years male, 58 years female (1990)
Total fertility rate: 6.8 children born/woman (1990)
Nationality: noun—Omani(s); adjective—Omani
Ethnic divisions: almost entirely Arab, with small Balochi, Zanzibari, and Indian groups
Religion: 75% Ibadhi Muslim; remainder Sunni Muslim, Shi'a Muslim, some Hindu
Language: Arabic (official); English, Balochi, Urdu, Indian dialects
Literacy: 20%
Labor force: 430,000; 60% agriculture (est.); 58% are non-Omani
Organized labor: trade unions are illegal

Government

Long-form name: Sultanate of Oman
Type: absolute monarchy; independent, with residual UK influence
Capital: Muscat
Administrative divisions: none
Independence: 1650, expulsion of the Portuguese
Constitution: none
Legal system: based on English common law and Islamic law; ultimate appeal to the sultan; has not accepted compulsory ICJ jurisdiction
Executive branch: sultan, Cabinet, State Consultative Assembly
Legislative branch: none
Judicial branch: none; traditional Islamic judges and a nascent civil court system
National holiday: National Day, 18 November
Leaders: *Chief of State and Head of Government*—Sultan and Prime Minister QABOOS bin Sa'id Al Said (since 23 July 1970)
Political parties: none
Suffrage: none
Elections: none
Other political or pressure groups: outlawed Popular Front for the Liberation of Oman (PFLO), based in South Yemen; small, clandestine Shi'a fundamentalist groups are active
Member of: Arab League, FAO, G-77, GCC, IBRD, ICAO, IDA, IDB—Islamic Development Bank, IFAD, IFC, IMF, IMO, INTELSAT, INTERPOL, ITU, NAM, OIC, UN, UNESCO, UPU, WFTU, WHO, WMO
Diplomatic representation: Ambassador Awadh Bader AL-SHANFARI; Chancery at 2342 Massachusetts Avenue NW, Washington DC 20008; telephone (202) 387-1980 through 1982; *US*—Ambassador

Richard BOEHM; Embassy at address NA, Muscat (mailing address is P. O. Box 966, Muscat); telephone 738-231 or 738-006
Flag: three horizontal bands of white (top, double width), red, and green (double width) with a broad, vertical, red band on the hoist side; the national emblem (a *khanjar* dagger in its sheath superimposed on two crossed swords in scabbards) in white is centered at the top of the vertical band

Economy

Overview: Economic performance is closely tied to the fortunes of the oil industry. Petroleum accounts for nearly all export earnings, about 70% of government revenues, and more than 50% of GDP. Oman has proved oil reserves of 4 billion barrels, equivalent to about 20 years' supply at the current rate of extraction. Although agriculture employs a majority of the population, urban centers depend on imported food.
GDP: $7.8 billion, per capita $6,006; real growth rate −3.0% (1987 est.)
Inflation rate (consumer prices): 2.0% (1988 est.)
Unemployment rate: NA%
Budget: revenues $3.1 billion; expenditures $4.2 billion, including capital expenditures of $1.0 billion (1989 est.)
Exports: $3.6 billion (f.o.b., 1988 est.); *commodities*—petroleum, reexports, processed copper, dates, nuts, fish; *partners*—Japan, South Korea, Thailand
Imports: $1.9 billion (f.o.b., 1988 est.); *commodities*—machinery, transportation equipment, manufactured goods, food, livestock, lubricants; *partners*—Japan, UAE, UK, FRG, US
External debt: $3.1 billion (December 1989 est.)
Industrial production: growth rate 5.0% (1986)
Electricity: 1,130,000 kW capacity; 3,600 million kWh produced, 2,760 kWh per capita (1989)
Industries: crude oil production and refining, natural gas production, construction, cement, copper
Agriculture: accounts for 3.4% of GDP and 60% of the labor force (including fishing); less than 2% of land cultivated; largely subsistence farming (dates, limes, bananas, alfalfa, vegetables, camels, cattle); not self-sufficient in food; annual fish catch averages 100,000 metric tons
Aid: US commitments, including Ex-Im (FY70-88), $122 million; Western (non-US) countries, ODA and OOF bilateral commitments (1970-87), $92 million; OPEC bilateral aid (1979-89), $797 million

Currency: Omani rial (plural—rials); 1 Omani rial (RO) = 1,000 baiza
Exchange rates: Omani rials (RO) per US$1—0.3845 (fixed rate since 1986)
Fiscal year: calendar year

Communications

Highways: 22,800 km total; 3,800 km bituminous surface, 19,000 km motorable track
Pipelines: crude oil 1,300 km; natural gas 1,030 km
Ports: Mīnā' Qābūs, Mīnā' Raysūt
Civil air: 4 major transport aircraft
Airports: 128 total, 119 usable; 6 with permanent-surface runways; 1 with runways over 3,659 m; 6 with runways 2,440-3,659 m; 63 with runways 1,220-2,439 m
Telecommunications: fair system of openwire, radio relay, and radio communications stations; 50,000 telephones; stations—3 AM, 3 FM, 11 TV; satellite earth stations—2 Indian Ocean INTELSAT, 1 ARABSAT and 8 domestic

Defense Forces

Branches: Army, Navy, Air Force, Royal Oman Police
Military manpower: males 15-49, 350,173; 198,149 fit for military service
Defense expenditures: 16.5% of GDP, or $1.3 billion (1990 est.)

Pacific Islands, Trust Territory of the (Palau)

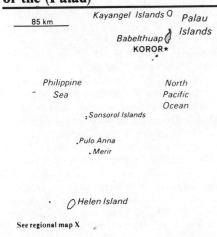

See regional map X

Geography

Total area: 458 km²; land area: 458 km²
Comparative area: slightly more than 2.5 times the size of Washington, DC
Land boundaries: none
Coastline: 1,519 km
Maritime claims:
  Contiguous zone: 12 nm
  Continental shelf: 200 m
  Extended economic zone: 200 nm
  Territorial sea: 3 nm
Climate: wet season May to November; hot and humid
Terrain: islands vary geologically from the high mountainous main island of Babelthuap to low, coral islands usually fringed by large barrier reefs
Natural resources: forests, minerals (especially gold), marine products; deep-seabed minerals
Land use: NA% arable land; NA% permanent crops; NA% meadows and pastures; NA% forest and woodland; NA% other
Environment: subject to typhoons from June to December; archipelago of six island groups totaling over 200 islands in the Caroline chain
Note: important location 850 km southeast of the Philippines; includes World War II battleground of Peleliu and world-famous rock islands

People

Population: 14,310 (July 1990), growth rate 0.7% (1990)
Birth rate: 25 births/1,000 population (1990)
Death rate: 6 deaths/1,000 population (1990)
Net migration rate: −12 migrants/1,000 population (1990)
Infant mortality rate: 26 deaths/1,000 live births (1990)
Life expectancy at birth: 68 years male, 74 years female (1990)
Total fertility rate: 3.3 children born/woman (1990)
Nationality: noun—Palauan(s); adjective—Palauan
Ethnic divisions: Palauans are a composite of Polynesian, Malayan, and Melanesian races
Religion: predominantly Christian, mainly Roman Catholic
Language: Palauan is the official language, though English is commonplace; inhabitants of the isolated southwestern islands speak a dialect of Trukese
Literacy: NA%, but education compulsory through eight grades
Labor force: NA
Organized labor: NA

Government

Long-form name: Trust Territory of the Pacific Islands (no short-form name); may change to Republic of Palau after independence; note—Belau, the native form of Palau, is sometimes used
Type: UN trusteeship administered by the US; constitutional government signed a Compact of Free Association with the US on 10 January 1986, after approval in a series of UN-observed plebiscites; until the UN trusteeship is terminated with entry into force of the Compact, Palau remains under US administration as the Palau District of the Trust Territory of the Pacific Islands
Capital: Koror; a new capital is being built about 20 km northeast in eastern Babelthuap
Administrative divisions: none
Independence: still part of the US-administered UN trusteeship (the last polity remaining under the trusteeship; the Republic of the Marshall Islands, Federated States of Micronesia, and Commonwealth of the Northern Marianas have left); administered by the Office of Territorial and International Affairs, US Department of Interior
Constitution: 11 January 1981
Legal system: based on Trust Territory laws, acts of the legislature, municipal, common, and customary laws
National holiday: Constitution Day, 9 July (1979)
Executive branch: US president, US vice president, national president, national vice president
Legislative branch: bicameral Parliament (Olbiil Era Kelulau or OEK) consists of an upper house or Senate and a lower house or House of Delegates
Judicial branch: Supreme Court
Leaders: *Chief of State*—President George BUSH (since 20 January 1989), represented by High Commissioner Janet MCCOY (since NA);

Head of Government—President Ngiratkel ETPISON (since 2 November 1988)
Political parties: no formal parties
Suffrage: universal at age 18
Elections: *President*—last held on 2 November 1988 (next to be held November 1992); Ngiratkel Etpison 26.3%, Roman Tmetuchl 25.9%, Thomas Remengesau 19.5%, others 28.3%;
Senate—last held 2 November 1988 (next to be held November 1992); results—percent of vote NA; seats—(18 total);
House of Delegates—last held 2 November 1988 (next to be held November 1992); results—percent of vote NA; seats—(16 total)
Diplomatic representation: none; *US*—US Liaison Officer Steven R. PRUETT; US Liaison Office at Top Side, Neeriyas, Koror (mailing address: P. O. Box 6028, Koror, Republic of Palau 96940); telephone 160-680-920 or 990
Flag: light blue with a large yellow disk (representing the moon) shifted slightly to the hoist side

Economy

Overview: The economy consists primarily of subsistence agriculture and fishing. Tourism provides some foreign exchange, although the remote location of Palau and a shortage of suitable facilities has hindered development. The government is the major employer of the work force, relying heavily on financial assistance from the US.
GDP: $31.6 million, per capita $2,260; real growth rate NA% (1986)
Inflation rate (consumer prices): NA%
Unemployment rate: 20% (1986)
Budget: revenues $6.0 million; expenditures NA, including capital expenditures of NA (1986)
Exports: $0.5 million (f.o.b., 1986); *commodities*—NA; *partners*—US, Japan
Imports: $27.2 million (c.i.f., 1986); *commodities*—NA; *partners*—US
External debt: $NA
Industrial production: growth rate NA%
Electricity: 16,000 kW capacity; 22 million kWh produced, 1,550 kWh per capita (1989)
Industries: tourism, craft items (shell, wood, pearl), some commercial fishing and agriculture
Agriculture: subsistence-level production of coconut, copra, cassava, sweet potatoes
Aid: US commitments, including Ex-Im (FY70-87), $2 billion; Western (non-US) countries, ODA and OOF bilateral commitments (1970-87), $62.6 million
Currency: US currency is used
Exchange rates: US currency is used
Fiscal year: 1 October-30 September

239

Pacific Islands, Trust Territory of the (Palau) *(continued)*

Communications

Highways: 25.7 km paved macadam and concrete roads, otherwise stone-, coral-, or laterite-surfaced roads (1986)
Ports: Koror
Airports: 2 with permanent-surface runways 1,220-2,439 m
Telecommunications: stations—1 AM, 1 FM, 1 TV; 1 Pacific Ocean INTELSAT earth station

Defense Forces

Note: defense is the responsibility of the US and that will not change when the UN trusteeship terminates

Pacific Ocean

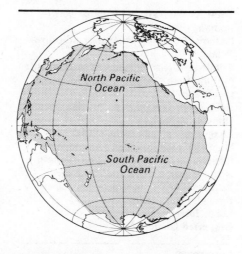

Geography

Total area: 165,384,000 km^2; includes Arafura Sea, Banda Sea, Bellingshausen Sea, Bering Sea, Bering Strait, Coral Sea, East China Sea, Gulf of Alaska, Makassar Strait, Philippine Sea, Ross Sea, Sea of Japan, Sea of Okhotsk, South China Sea, Tasman Sea, and other tributary water bodies
Comparative area: slightly less than 18 times the size of the US; the largest ocean (followed by the Atlantic Ocean, Indian Ocean, and Arctic Ocean); covers about one-third of the global surface; larger than the total land area of the world
Coastline: 135,663 km
Climate: the western Pacific is monsoonal—a rainy season occurs during the summer months, when moisture-laden winds blow from the ocean over the land, and a dry season during the winter months, when dry winds blow from the Asian land mass back to the ocean
Terrain: surface in the northern Pacific dominated by a clockwise, warm water gyre (broad, circular system of currents) and in the southern Pacific by a counterclockwise, cool water gyre; sea ice occurs in the Bering Sea and Sea of Okhotsk during winter and reaches maximum northern extent from Antarctica in October; the ocean floor in the eastern Pacific is dominated by the East Pacific Rise, while the western Pacific is dissected by deep trenches; the world's greatest depth is 10,924 meters in the Marianas Trench
Natural resources: oil and gas fields, polymetallic nodules, sand and gravel aggregates, placer deposits, fish

Environment: endangered marine species include the dugong, sea lion, sea otter, seals, turtles, and whales; oil pollution in Philippine Sea and South China Sea; dotted with low coral islands and rugged volcanic islands in the southwestern Pacific Ocean; subject to tropical cyclones (typhoons) in southeast and east Asia from May to December (most frequent from July to October); tropical cyclones (hurricanes) may form south of Mexico and strike Central America and Mexico from June to October (most common in August and September); southern shipping lanes subject to icebergs from Antarctica; occasional El Niño phenomenon occurs off the coast of Peru when the trade winds slacken and the warm Equatorial Countercurrent moves south, which kills the plankton that is the primary food source for anchovies; consequently, the anchovies move to better feeding grounds, causing resident marine birds to starve by the thousands because of their lost food source
Note: the major choke points are the Bering Strait, Panama Canal, Luzon Strait, and the Singapore Strait; the Equator divides the Pacific Ocean into the North Pacific Ocean and the South Pacific Ocean; ships subject to superstructure icing in extreme north from October to May and in extreme south from May to October; persistent fog in the northern Pacific from June to December is a hazard to shipping; surrounded by a zone of violent volcanic and earthquake activity sometimes referred to as the Pacific Ring of Fire

Economy

Overview: The Pacific Ocean is a major contributor to the world economy and particularly to those nations its waters directly touch. It provides cheap sea transportation between East and West, extensive fishing grounds, offshore oil and gas fields, minerals, and sand and gravel for the construction industry. In 1985 over half (54%) of the world's total fish catch came from the Pacific Ocean, which is the only ocean where the fish catch has increased every year since 1978. Exploitation of offshore oil and gas reserves is playing an ever increasing role in the energy supplies of Australia, New Zealand, China, US, and Peru. The high cost of recovering offshore oil and gas, combined with the lower world prices for oil since 1985, has slowed but not stopped new drillings.
Industries: fishing, oil and gas production

Pakistan

Communications

Ports: Bangkok (Thailand), Hong Kong, Los Angeles (US), Manila (Philippines), Pusan (South Korea), San Francisco (US), Seattle (US), Shanghai (China), Singapore, Sydney (Australia), Vladivostok (USSR), Wellington (NZ), Yokohama (Japan)

Telecommunications: several submarine cables with network focused on Guam and Hawaii

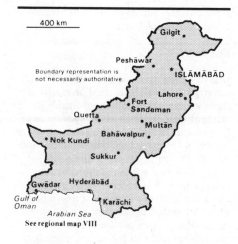

Boundary representation is not necessarily authoritative

Gulf of Oman
Arabian Sea
See regional map VIII

Geography

Total area: 803,940 km²; land area: 778,720 km²

Comparative area: slightly less than twice the size of California

Land boundaries: 6,774 km total; Afghanistan 2,430 km, China 523 km, India 2,912 km, Iran 909 km

Coastline: 1,046 km

Maritime claims:

Contiguous zone: 24 nm

Continental shelf: edge of continental margin or 200 nm

Extended economic zone: 200 nm

Territorial sea: 12 nm

Disputes: boundary with India; Pashtun question with Afghanistan; Baloch question with Afghanistan and Iran; water sharing problems with upstream riparian India over the Indus

Climate: mostly hot, dry desert; temperate in northwest; arctic in north

Terrain: flat Indus plain in east; mountains in north and northwest; Balochistan plateau in west

Natural resources: land, extensive natural gas reserves, limited crude oil, poor quality coal, iron ore, copper, salt, limestone

Land use: 26% arable land; NEGL% permanent crops; 6% meadows and pastures; 4% forest and woodland; 64% other; includes 19% irrigated

Environment: frequent earthquakes, occasionally severe especially in north and west; flooding along the Indus after heavy rains (July and August); deforestation; soil erosion; desertification; water logging

Note: controls Khyber Pass and Malakand Pass, traditional invasion routes between Central Asia and the Indian Subcontinent

People

Population: 114,649,406 (July 1990), growth rate 2.2% (1990)

Birth rate: 43 births/1,000 population (1990)

Death rate: 14 deaths/1,000 population (1990)

Net migration rate: −6 migrants/1,000 population (1990)

Infant mortality rate: 110 deaths/1,000 live births (1990)

Life expectancy at birth: 56 years male, 57 years female (1990)

Total fertility rate: 6.7 children born/woman (1990)

Nationality: noun—Pakistani(s); adjective—Pakistani

Ethnic divisions: Punjabi, Sindhi, Pashtun (Pathan), Baloch, Muhajir (immigrants from India and their descendents)

Religion: 97% Muslim (77% Sunni, 20% Shi'a), 3% Christian, Hindu, and other

Language: Urdu and English (official); total spoken languages—64% Punjabi, 12% Sindhi, 8% Pashtu, 7% Urdu, 9% Balochi and other; English is lingua franca of Pakistani elite and most government ministries, but official policies are promoting its gradual replacement by Urdu

Literacy: 26%

Labor force: 28,900,000; 54% agriculture, 13% mining and manufacturing, 33% services; extensive export of labor (1987 est.)

Organized labor: about 10% of industrial work force

Government

Long-form name: Islamic Republic of Pakistan

Type: parliamentary with strong executive, federal republic

Capital: Islāmābād

Administrative divisions: 4 provinces, 1 tribal area*, and 1 territory**; Balochistān, Federally Administered Tribal Areas*, Islāmābād Capital Territory**, North-West Frontier, Punjab, Sindh; note—the Pakistani-administered portion of the disputed Jammu and Kashmir region includes Azad Kashmir and the Northern Areas

Independence: 15 August 1947 (from UK; formerly West Pakistan)

Constitution: 10 April 1973, suspended 5 July 1977, restored 30 December 1985

Legal system: based on English common law with provisions to accommodate Pakistan's stature as an Islamic state; accepts compulsory ICJ jurisdiction, with reservations

National holiday: Pakistan Day (proclamation of the republic), 23 March (1956)

Executive branch: president, prime minister, Cabinet

Legislative branch: bicameral Federal Legislature (Mijlis-e-Shoora) consists of

an upper house or Senate and a lower house or National Assembly
Judicial branch: Supreme Court, Federal Islamic (Shari'at) Court
Leaders: *Chief of State*—President GHULAM ISHAQ Khan (since 13 December 1988);
Head of Government—Prime Minister Benazir BHUTTO (since 2 December 1988)
Political parties and leaders: Pakistan People's Party (PPP), Prime Minister Benazir Bhutto; Pakistan Muslim League (PML), former Prime Minister Mohammed Khan Junejo; PML is the main party in the anti-PPP Islamic Democratic Alliance (IDA); Muhajir Quami Movement, Altaf Hussain; Jamiat-ul-Ulema-i-Islam (JUI), Fazlur Rahman; Jamaat-i-Islami (JI), Qazi Hussain Ahmed; Awami National Party (ANP), Khan Abdul Wali Khan
Suffrage: universal at age 21
Elections: *President*—last held on 12 December 1988 (next to be held December 1993); results—Ghulam Ishaq Khan was elected by the Federal Legislature; *Senate*—last held March 1988 (next to be held March 1990); results—elected by provincial assemblies; seats—(87 total) PML 84, PPP 2, independent 1; *National Assembly*—last held on 16 November 1988 (next to be held November 1993); results—percent of vote by party NA; seats—(237 total) PPP 109, IJI 65, MQM 14, JUI 8, PAI 3, ANP 3, BNA 3, others 3, independents 29
Communists: the Communist party is no longer outlawed and operates openly
Other political or pressure groups: military remains dominant political force; ulema (clergy), industrialists, and small merchants also influential
Member of: ADB, CCC, Colombo Plan, ESCAP, FAO, G-77, GATT, IAEA, IBRD, ICAC, ICAO, IDA, IDB—Islamic Development Bank, IFAD, IFC, IHO, ILO, IMF, IMO, INTELSAT, INTERPOL, IPU, IRC, ITU, IWC—International Wheat Council, NAM, OIC, SAARC, UN, UNESCO, UPU, WHO, WFTU, WIPO, WMO, WSG, WTO
Diplomatic representation: Ambassador Zulfikar ALI KHAN; Chancery at 2315 Massachusetts Avenue NW, Washington DC 20008; telephone (202) 939-6200; there is a Pakistani Consulate General in New York; *US*—Ambassador Robert B. OAKLEY; Embassy at Diplomatic Enclave, Ramna 5, Islāmābād (mailing address is P. O. Box 1048, Islāmābād); telephone [92] (51) 8261-61 through 79; there are US Consulates General in Karachi and Lahore, and a Consulate in Peshāwar
Flag: green with a vertical white band on the hoist side; a large white crescent and star are centered in the green field; the crescent, star, and color green are traditional symbols of Islam

Economy

Overview: Pakistan is a poor Third World country faced with the usual problems of rapidly increasing population, sizable government deficits, and heavy dependence on foreign aid. In addition, the economy must support a large military establishment and provide for the needs of 4 million Afghan refugees. A real economic growth rate averaging 5-6% in recent years has enabled the country to cope with these problems. Almost all agriculture and small-scale industry is in private hands, and the government seeks to privatize a portion of the large-scale industrial enterprises now publicly owned. In December 1988, Pakistan signed a three-year economic reform agreement with the IMF, which provides for a reduction in the government deficit and a liberalization of trade in return for further IMF financial support. The so-called Islamization of the economy has affected mainly the financial sector; for example, a prohibition on certain types of interest payments. Pakistan almost certainly will make little headway against its population problem; at the current rate of growth, population would double in 32 years.
GNP: $43.2 billion, per capita $409; real growth rate 5.1% (FY89)
Inflation rate (consumer prices): 11% (FY89)
Unemployment rate: 4% (FY89 est.)
Budget: revenues $7.5 billion; expenditures $10.3 billion, including capital expenditures of $2.3 billion (FY89 est.)
Exports: $4.5 billion (f.o.b., FY89); *commodities*—rice, cotton, textiles, clothing; *partners*—EC 31%, US 11%, Japan 11% (FY88)
Imports: $7.2 billion (f.o.b., FY89); *commodities*—petroleum, petroleum products, machinery, transportation, equipment, vegetable oils, animal fats, chemicals; *partners*—EC 26%, Japan 15%, US 11% (FY88)
External debt: $17.4 billion (1989)
Industrial production: growth rate 3% (FY89)
Electricity: 7,575,000 kW capacity; 29,300 million kWh produced, 270 kWh per capita (1989)
Industries: textiles, food processing, beverages, petroleum products, construction materials, clothing, paper products, international finance, shrimp
Agriculture: 24% of GNP, over 50% of labor force; world's largest contiguous irrigation system; major crops—cotton, wheat, rice, sugarcane, fruits, and vegetables; livestock products—milk, beef, mutton, eggs; self-sufficient in food grain
Illicit drugs: illicit producer of opium poppy and cannabis for the international drug trade; government eradication efforts on poppy cultivation of limited success; 1988 output of opium and hashish each estimated at about 200 metric tons
Aid: (including Bangladesh before 1972) US commitments, including Ex-Im (FY70-88), $4.2 billion authorized (excluding what is now Bangladesh); Western (non-US) countries, ODA and OOF bilateral commitments (1980-87), $7.5 billion; OPEC bilateral aid (1979-89), $2.3 billion; Communist countries (1970-88), $2.9 billion
Currency: Pakistani rupee (plural—rupees); 1 Pakistani rupee (PRe) = 100 paisa
Exchange rates: Pakistani rupees (PRs) per US$1—21.420 (January 1990), 20.541 (1989), 18.003 (1988), 17.399 (1987), 16.648 (1986), 15.928 (1985)
Fiscal year: 1 July-30 June

Communications

Railroads: 8,773 km total; 7,718 km broad gauge, 445 km meter gauge, and 610 km narrow gauge; 1,037 km broad-gauge double track; 286 km electrified; all government owned (1985)
Highways: 101,315 km total (1987); 40,155 km paved, 23,000 km gravel, 29,000 km improved earth, and 9,160 km unimproved earth or sand tracks (1985)
Pipelines: 250 km crude oil; 4,044 km natural gas; 885 km refined products (1987)
Ports: Gwadar, Karachi, Port Muhammad bin Qasim
Merchant marine: 29 ships (1,000 GRT or over) totaling 338,173 GRT/508,107 DWT; includes 4 passenger-cargo, 24 cargo, 1 petroleum, oils, and lubricants (POL) tanker
Civil air: 30 major transport aircraft
Airports: 115 total, 102 usable; 70 with permanent-surface runways; 1 with runways over 3,659 m; 30 with runways 2,440-3,659 m; 42 with runways 1,220-2,439 m
Telecommunications: good international radiocommunication service over microwave and INTELSAT satellite; domestic radio communications poor; broadcast service good; 564,500 telephones (1987); stations—16 AM, 8 FM, 16; satellite eath station—1 Atlantic Ocean INTELSAT and 2 Indian Ocean INTELSAT

Palmyra Atoll
(territory of the US)

Defense Forces

Branches: Army, Air Force, Navy, Civil Armed Forces, National Guard
Military manpower: males 15-49, 26,215,898; 16,080,545 fit for military service; 1,282,294 reach military age (17) annually
Defense expenditures: 5.6% of GNP, or $2.4 billion (1989 est.)

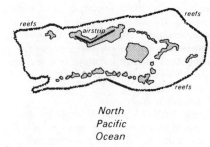

2 km

reefs

airstrip

reefs

reefs

North Pacific Ocean

See regional map X

Communications

Ports: none; offshore anchorage in West Lagoon
Airports: 1 with permanent-surface runway 1,220-2,439 m

Defense Forces

Note: defense is the responsibility of the US

Geography

Total area: 11.9 km^2; land area: 11.9 km^2
Comparative area: about 20 times the size of The Mall in Washington, DC
Land boundaries: none
Coastline: 14.5 km
Maritime claims:
   Contiguous zone: 12 nm
   Continental shelf: 200 m
   Extended economic zone: 200 nm
   Territorial sea: 12 nm
Climate: equatorial, hot, and very rainy
Terrain: low, with maximum elevations of about 2 meters
Natural resources: none
Land use: 0% arable land; 0% permanent crops; 0% meadows and pastures; 100% forest and woodland; 0% other
Environment: about 50 islets covered with dense vegetation, coconut trees, and balsa-like trees up to 30 meters tall
Note: located 1,600 km south-southwest of Honolulu in the North Pacific Ocean, almost halfway between Hawaii and American Samoa

People

Population: uninhabited

Government

Long-form name: none
Type: unincorporated territory of the US; privately owned, but administered by the Office of Territorial and International Affairs, US Department of the Interior

Economy

Overview: no economic activity

Panama

150 km

Caribbean Sea

Bocas del Toro · Colón · Panama Canal
PANAMA
David · Santiago · Gulf of Panama · La Palma
Chitré

North Pacific Ocean

See regional map III

Geography

Total area: 78,200 km²; land area: 75,990 km²
Comparative area: slightly smaller than South Carolina
Land boundaries: 555 km total; Colombia 225 km, Costa Rica 330 km
Coastline: 2,490 km
Maritime claims:
Territorial sea: 200 nm
Climate: tropical; hot, humid, cloudy; prolonged rainy season (May to January), short dry season (January to May)
Terrain: interior mostly steep, rugged mountains and dissected, upland plains; coastal areas largely plains and rolling hills
Natural resources: copper, mahogany forests, shrimp
Land use: 6% arable land; 2% permanent crops; 15% meadows and pastures; 54% forest and woodland; 23% other; includes NEGL% irrigated
Environment: dense tropical forest in east and northwest
Note: strategic location on eastern end of isthmus forming land bridge connecting North and South America; controls Panama Canal that links North Atlantic Ocean via Caribbean Sea with North Pacific Ocean

People

Population: 2,425,400 (July 1990), growth rate 2.1% (1990)
Birth rate: 26 births/1,000 population (1990)
Death rate: 5 deaths/1,000 population (1990)
Net migration rate: NEGL migrants/1,000 population (1990)
Infant mortality rate: 22 deaths/1,000 live births (1990)
Life expectancy at birth: 72 years male, 76 years female (1990)
Total fertility rate: 3.1 children born/woman (1990)
Nationality: noun—Panamanian(s); adjective—Panamanian
Ethnic divisions: 70% mestizo (mixed Indian and European ancestry), 14% West Indian, 10% white, 6% Indian
Religion: over 93% Roman Catholic, 6% Protestant
Language: Spanish (official); 14% speak English as native tongue; many Panamanians bilingual
Literacy: 90%
Labor force: 770,472 (1987); 27.9% government and community services; 26.2% agriculture, hunting, and fishing; 16% commerce, restaurants, and hotels; 10.5% manufacturing and mining; 5.3% construction; 5.3% transportation and communications; 4.2% finance, insurance, and real estate; 2.4% Canal Zone; shortage of skilled labor, but an oversupply of unskilled labor
Organized labor: 17% of labor force (1986)

Government

Long-form name: Republic of Panama
Type: centralized republic
Capital: Panama
Administrative divisions: 9 provinces (provincias, singular—provincia) and 1 territory* (comarca); Bocas del Toro, Chiriquí, Coclé, Colón, Darién, Herrera, Los Santos, Panamá, San Blas*, Veraguas
Independence: 3 November 1903 (from Colombia; became independent from Spain 28 November 1821)
Constitution: 11 October 1972; major reforms adopted April 1983
Legal system: based on civil law system; judicial review of legislative acts in the Supreme Court of Justice; accepts compulsory ICJ jurisdiction, with reservations
National holiday: Independence Day, 3 November (1903)
Executive branch: president, two vice presidents, Cabinet
Legislative branch: unicameral Legislative Assembly (Asamblea Legislativa)
Judicial branch: Supreme Court of Justice (Corte Suprema de Justica) currently being reorganized
Leaders: *Chief of State and Head of Government*—President Guillermo ENDARA (since 20 December 1989, elected 7 May 1989); First Vice President Ricardo Arias CALDERON (since 20 December 1989, elected 7 May 1989); Second Vice President Guillermo FORD (since 20 December 1989, elected 7 May 1989)
Political parties and leaders: Government alliance—Authentic Liberal Party (PLA); faction of Authentic Panamenista Party (PPA), Guillermo Endara; Christian Democrat Party (PDC), Ricardo Arias Calderon; Nationalist Republican Liberal Movement (MOLIRENA), Alfredo Ramirez; former Noriegist parties—Democratic Revolutionary Party (PRD, ex-official government party), Carlos Duque; Labor Party (PALA), Ramon Sieiro Murgas; People's Party (PdP, Soviet-oriented Communist party), Ruben Dario Sousa Batista; Democratic Workers Party; National Action Party (PAN);
other opposition parties—Popular Nationalist Party (PNP), Olimpo A. Saez Maruci; factions of the former Liberal and Republican parties; Popular Action Party (PAP), Carlos Iván Zuniga; Socialist Workers Party (PST, leftist), José Cambra; Revolutionary Workers Party (PRT, leftist), Graciela Dixon
Suffrage: universal and compulsory at age 18
Elections: *President*—last held on 7 May 1989, annulled but later upheld (next to be held May 1994); results—anti-Noriega coalition believed to have won about 75% of the total votes cast;
Legislative Assembly—last held on 7 May 1989, annulled but later upheld; in process of reorganization (next to be held May 1994); results—percent of vote by party NA; seats—(67 total) the Electoral Tribunal has confirmed 58 of the 67 seats—PDC 27, MOLIRENA 15, PLA 6, Noriegist PRD 7, PPA 3; legitimate holders of the other 9 seats cannot be determined and a special election will be held
Communists: People's Party (PdP), pro-Noriega regime mainline Communist party, did not obtain the necessary 3% of the total vote in the 1984 election to retain its legal status; about 3,000 members
Other political or pressure groups: National Council of Organized Workers (CONATO); National Council of Private Enterprise (CONEP); Panamanian Association of Business Executives (APEDE)
Member of: FAO, G-77, IADB, IAEA, IBRD, ICAO, ICO, IDA, IFAD, IDB—Inter-American Development Bank, IFC, ILO, IMF, IMO, INTELSAT, INTERPOL, IRC, ITU, IWC—International Whaling Commission, IWC—International Wheat Council, NAM, OAS, PAHO, SELA, UN, UNESCO, UPEB, UPU, WFTU, WHO, WMO, WTO
Diplomatic representation: Ambassador Eduardo VALLARINO; Chancery at 2862 McGill Terrace NW, Washington DC 20008; telephone (202) 483-1407; the status of the Consulates General and Consulates has not yet been determined;
US—Ambassador Deane R. HINTON; Embassy at Avenida Balboa and Calle 38, Apartado 6959, Panama City 5 (mailing address is Box E, APO Miami 34002); telephone [507] 27-1777

Flag: divided into four, equal rectangles; the top quadrants are white with a blue five-pointed star in the center (hoist side) and plain red, the bottom quadrants are plain blue (hoist side) and white with a red five-pointed star in the center

Economy

Overview: The GDP contracted an estimated 7.5% in 1989, following a drop of 20% in 1988. Political instability, lack of credit, and the erosion of business confidence prompted declines of 20-70% in the financial, agricultural, commercial, manufacturing, and construction sectors between 1987 and 1989. Transits through the Panama Canal were off slightly, as were toll revenues. Unemployment remained about 23% during 1989. Imports of foodstuffs and crude oil increased during 1989, but capital goods imports continued their slide. Exports were widely promoted by Noriega trade delegations, but sales abroad remained stagnant.
GDP: $3.9 billion, per capita $1,648; real growth rate −7.5% (1989 est.)
Inflation rate (consumer prices): −0.1% (1989 est.)
Unemployment rate: 23% (1989 est.)
Budget: revenues $598 million; expenditures $750 million, including capital expenditures of $NA (1989 est.)
Exports: $220 million (f.o.b., 1989 est.); *commodities*—bananas 40%, shrimp 27%, coffee 4%, sugar, petroleum products; *partners*—US 90%, Central America and Caribbean, EC (1989 est.)
Imports: $830 million (f.o.b., 1989 est.); *commodities*—foodstuffs 16%, capital goods 9%, crude oil 16%, consumer goods, chemicals; *partners*—US 35%, Central America and Caribbean, EC, Mexico, Venezuela (1989 est.)
External debt: $5.2 billion (November 1989 est.)
Industrial production: growth rate −4.1% (1989 est.)
Electricity: 1,113,000 kW capacity; 3,270 million kWh produced, 1,380 kWh per capita (1989)
Industries: manufacturing and construction activities, petroleum refining, brewing, cement and other construction material, sugar mills, paper products
Agriculture: accounts for 10% of GDP (1989 est.), 26% of labor force (1987); crops—bananas, rice, corn, coffee, sugarcane; livestock; fishing; importer of food grain, vegetables, milk products
Aid: US commitments, including Ex-Im (FY70-88), $515 million; Western (non-US) countries, ODA and OOF bilateral commitments (1970-87), $568 million; Communist countries (1970-88), $4 million

Currency: balboa (plural—balboas); 1 balboa (B) = 100 centésimos
Exchange rates: balboas (B) per US$1—1.000 (fixed rate)
Fiscal year: calendar year

Communications

Railroads: 238 km total; 78 km 1.524-meter gauge, 160 km 0.914-meter gauge
Highways: 8,530 km total; 2,745 km paved, 3,270 km gravel or crushed stone, 2,515 km improved and unimproved earth
Inland waterways: 800 km navigable by shallow draft vessels; 82 km Panama Canal
Pipelines: crude oil, 130 km
Ports: Cristobal, Balboa, Puerto de La Bahía de Las Minas
Merchant marine: 3,187 ships (1,000 GRT or over) totaling 46,502,092 GRT/72,961,250 DWT; includes 34 passenger, 22 short-sea passenger, 3 passenger-cargo, 1,087 cargo, 179 refrigerated cargo, 186 container, 71 roll-on/roll-off cargo, 136 vehicle carrier, 7 livestock carrier, 9 multifunction large-load carrier, 315 petroleum, oils, and lubricants (POL) tanker, 184 chemical tanker, 30 combination ore/oil, 91 liquefied gas, 8 specialized tanker, 767 bulk, 58 combination bulk; note—all but 5 are foreign owned and operated; the top 4 foreign owners are Japan 41%, Greece 9%, Hong Kong 9%, and the US 7% (China owns at least 144 ships, Yugoslavia 12, Cuba 6, and Vietnam 9)
Civil air: 16 major transport aircraft
Airports: 123 total, 112 usable; 42 with permanent-surface runways; none with runways over 3,659 m; 2 with runways 2,440-3,659 m; 15 with runways 1,220-2,439 m
Telecommunications: domestic and international facilities well developed; connection into Central American Microwave System; 2 Atlantic Ocean satellite antennas; 220,000 telephones; stations—91 AM, no FM, 23 TV; 1 coaxial submarine cable

Defense Forces

Branches: the Panamanian Defense Forces (PDF) ceased to exist as a military institution shortly after the United States invaded Panama on 20 December 1989; President Endara is attempting to restructure the forces, with more civilian control, under the new name of Panamanian Public Forces (PPF)
Military manpower: males 15-49, 628,327; 433,352 fit for military service; no conscription
Defense expenditures: 2.0% of GDP (1987)

Papua New Guinea

500 km

South Pacific Ocean

New Ireland

Wewak
Madang
Lae
Daru
New Britain
Bougainville

PORT MORESBY

Coral Sea

See regional map X

Geography

Total area: 461,690 km²; land area: 451,710 km²
Comparative area: slightly larger than California
Land boundary: 820 km with Indonesia
Coastline: 5,152 km
Maritime claims: (measured from claimed archipelagic baselines)
  Continental shelf: 200 meters or to depth of exploitation
  Extended economic zone: 200 nm
  Territorial sea: 3 nm
Climate: tropical; northwest monsoon (December to March), southeast monsoon (May to October); slight seasonal temperature variation
Terrain: mostly mountains with coastal lowlands and rolling foothills
Natural resources: gold, copper, silver, natural gas, timber, oil potential
Land use: NEGL% arable land; 1% permanent crops; NEGL% meadows and pastures; 71% forest and woodland; 28% other
Environment: one of world's largest swamps along southwest coast; some active volcanos; frequent earthquakes
Note: shares island of New Guinea with Indonesia

People

Population: 3,822,875 (July 1990), growth rate 2.3% (1990)
Birth rate: 34 births/1,000 population (1990)
Death rate: 11 deaths/1,000 population (1990)
Net migration rate: 0 migrants/1,000 population (1990)
Infant mortality rate: 68 deaths/1,000 live births (1990)
Life expectancy at birth: 54 years male, 56 years female (1990)

Total fertility rate: 5.0 children born/woman (1990)
Nationality: noun—Papua New Guinean(s); adjective—Papua New Guinean
Ethnic divisions: predominantly Melanesian and Papuan; some Negrito, Micronesian, and Polynesian
Religion: over half of population nominally Christian (490,000 Roman Catholic, 320,000 Lutheran, other Protestant sects); remainder indigenous beliefs
Language: 715 indigenous languages; English spoken by 1-2%, pidgin English widespread, Motu spoken in Papua region
Literacy: 32%
Labor force: 1,660,000; 732,806 in salaried employment; 54% agriculture, 25% government, 9% industry and commerce, 8% services (1980)
Organized labor: more than 50 trade unions, some with fewer than 20 members

---

Government

Long-form name: Independent State of Papua New Guinea
Type: parliamentary democracy
Capital: Port Moresby
Administrative divisions: 20 provinces; Central, Chimbu, Eastern Highlands, East New Britain, East Sepik, Enga, Gulf, Madang, Manus, Milne Bay, Morobe, National Capital, New Ireland, Northern, North Solomons, Sandaun, Southern Highlands, Western, Western Highlands, West New Britain
Independence: 16 September 1975 (from UN trusteeship under Australian administration)
Constitution: 16 September 1975
Legal system: based on English common law
National holiday: Independence Day, 16 September (1975)
Executive branch: British monarch, governor general, prime minister, deputy prime minister, National Executive Council (cabinet)
Legislative branch: unicameral National Parliament (sometimes referred to as the House of Assembly)
Judicial branch: Supreme Court
Leaders: *Chief of State*—Queen Elizabeth II (since 6 February 1952), represented by Governor General Vincent ERI (since 18 January 1990);
Head of Government—Prime Minister Rabbie NAMALIU (since 4 July 1988); Deputy Prime Minister Akoko DOI (since 7 July 1988)
Political parties: Pangu Party, People's Progress Party, United Party, Papua Besena, National Party, Melanesian Alliance
Suffrage: universal at age 18

Elections: *National Parliament*—last held 13 June-4 July 1987 (next to be held 4 July 1992); results—PP 14.7%, PDM 10.8%, PPP 6.1%, MA 5.6%, NP 5.1%, PAP 3.2%, independents 42.9%, others 11.6%; seats—(109 total) PP 26, PDM 17, NP 12, MA 7, PAP 6, PPP 5, independents 22, others 14
Communists: no significant strength
Member of: ACP, ADB, ANRPC, CIPEC (associate), Commonwealth, ESCAP, FAO, G-77, GATT (de facto), IBRD, ICAO, IDA, IFAD, IFC, ILO, IMF, IMO, INTELSAT, INTERPOL, ITU, SPC, SPF, UN, UNESCO, UPU, WHO, WMO
Diplomatic representation: Ambassador Margaret TAYLOR; Chancery at Suite 350, 1330 Connecticut Avenue NW, Washington DC 20036; telephone (202) 659-0856; *US*—Ambassador-designate William FERRAND; Embassy at Armit Street, Port Moresby (mailing address is P. O. Box 1492, Port Moresby); telephone [675] 211-455 or 594, 654
Flag: divided diagonally from upper hoist-side corner; the upper triangle is red with a soaring yellow bird of paradise centered; the lower triangle is black with five white five-pointed stars of the Southern Cross constellation centered

---

Economy

Overview: Papua New Guinea is richly endowed with natural resources, but exploitation has been hampered by the rugged terrain and the high cost of developing an infrastructure. Agriculture provides a subsistence livelihood for more than half of the population. Mining of numerous deposits, including copper and gold, accounts for about 60% of export earnings. Budgetary support from Australia and development aid under World Bank auspices help sustain the economy.
GDP: $3.26 billion, per capita $890; real growth rate 1.2% (1988 est.)
Inflation rate (consumer prices): 5% (1988 est.)
Unemployment rate: 5% (1988)
Budget: revenues $962 million; expenditures $998 million, including capital expenditures of $169 million (1988)
Exports: $1.4 billion (f.o.b., 1988); *commodities*—gold, copper ore, coffee, copra, palm oil, timber, lobster; *partners*—FRG, Japan, Australia, UK, Spain, US
Imports: $1.2 billion (f.o.b., 1988); *commodities*—machinery and transport equipment, fuels, food, chemicals, consumer goods; *partners*—Australia, Singapore, Japan, US, New Zealand, UK
External debt: $2.5 billion (December 1988)
Industrial production: growth rate NA%

Electricity: 397,000 kW capacity; 1,510 million kWh produced, 400 kWh per capita (1989)
Industries: copra crushing, oil palm processing, plywood processing, wood chip production, gold, silver, copper, construction, tourism
Agriculture: one-third of GDP; livelihood for 85% of population; fertile soils and favorable climate permits cultivating a wide variety of crops; cash crops—coffee, cocoa, coconuts, palm kernels; other products—tea, rubber, sweet potatoes, fruit, vegetables, poultry, pork; net importer of food for urban centers
Aid: US commitments, including Ex-Im (FY70-87), $38.8 million; Western (non-US) countries, ODA and OOF bilateral commitments (1970-87), $5.8 billion; OPEC bilateral aid (1979-89), $17 million
Currency: kina (plural—kina); 1 kina (K) = 100 toea
Exchange rates: kina (K) per US$1—1.1592 (December 1989), 1.1685 (1989), 1.1538 (1988), 1.1012 (1987), 1.0296 (1986), 1.0000 (1985)
Fiscal year: calendar year

Communications

Highways: 19,200 km total; 640 km paved, 10,960 km gravel, crushed stone, or stabilized-soil surface, 7,600 km unimproved earth
Inland waterways: 10,940 km
Ports: Anewa Bay, Lae, Madang, Port Moresby, Rabaul
Merchant marine: 11 ships (1,000 GRT or over) totaling 18,675 GRT/27,954 DWT; includes 6 cargo, 2 roll-on/roll-off cargo, 1 combination ore/oil, 2 bulk
Civil air: about 15 major transport aircraft
Airports: 575 total, 455 usable; 19 with permanent-surface runways; none with runways over 3,659 m; 1 with runways 2,440-3,659 m; 38 with runways 1,220-2,439 m
Telecommunications: services are adequate and being improved; facilities provide radiobroadcast, radiotelephone and telegraph, coastal radio, aeronautical radio, and international radiocommunication services; submarine cables extend to Australia and Guam; 51,700 telephones (1985); stations—31 AM, 2 FM, 2 TV (1987); 1 Pacific Ocean INTELSAT earth station

---

Defense Forces

Branches: Papua New Guinea Defense Force
Military manpower: males 15-49, 952,454; 529,570 fit for military service
Defense expenditures: 1.3% of GDP, or $42 million (1989 est.)

Paracel Islands

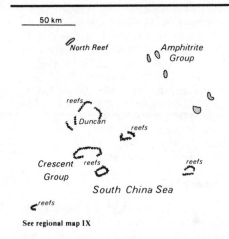

See regional map IX

Geography

Total area: undetermined
Comparative area: undetermined
Land boundaries: none
Coastline: 518 km
Maritime claims: undetermined
Disputes: occupied by China, but claimed by Taiwan and Vietnam
Climate: tropical
Terrain: undetermined
Natural resources: none
Land use: 0% arable land; 0% permanent crops; 0% meadows and pastures; 0% forest and woodland; 100% other
Environment: subject to typhoons
Note: located 400 km east of Vietnam in the South China Sea about one-third of the way between Vietnam and the Philippines

People

Population: no permanent inhabitants

Government

Long-form name: none

Economy

Overview: no economic activity

Communications

Ports: none; offshore anchorage only

Defense Forces

Note: occupied by China

Paraguay

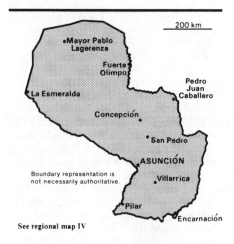

Boundary representation is not necessarily authoritative.

See regional map IV

Geography

Total area: 406,750 km²; land area: 397,300 km²
Comparative area: slightly smaller than California
Land boundaries: 3,920 km total; Argentina 1,880 km, Bolivia 750 km, Brazil 1,290 km
Coastline: none—landlocked
Maritime claims: none—landlocked
Disputes: short section of the boundary with Brazil (just west of Guaíra Falls on the Rio Paraná) is in dispute
Climate: varies from temperate in east to semiarid in far west
Terrain: grassy plains and wooded hills east of Río Paraguay; Gran Chaco region west of Río Paraguay mostly low, marshy plain near the river, and dry forest and thorny scrub elsewhere
Natural resources: iron ore, manganese, limestone, hydropower, timber
Land use: 20% arable land; 1% permanent crops; 39% meadows and pastures; 35% forest and woodland; 5% other; includes NEGL% irrigated
Environment: local flooding in southeast (early September to June); poorly drained plains may become boggy (early October to June)
Note: landlocked; buffer between Argentina and Brazil

People

Population: 4,660,270 (July 1990), growth rate 3.0% (1990)
Birth rate: 36 births/1,000 population (1990)
Death rate: 6 deaths/1,000 population (1990)
Net migration rate: NEGL migrants/1,000 population (1990)
Infant mortality rate: 48 deaths/1,000 live births (1990)

Life expectancy at birth: 67 years male, 72 years female (1990)
Total fertility rate: 4.8 children born/woman (1990)
Nationality: noun—Paraguayan(s); adjective—Paraguayan
Ethnic divisions: 95% mestizo (Spanish and Indian), 5% white and Indian
Religion: 90% Roman Catholic; Mennonite and other Protestant denominations
Language: Spanish (official) and Guarani
Literacy: 81%
Labor force: 1,300,000; 44% agriculture, 34% industry and commerce, 18% services, 4% government (1986)
Organized labor: about 2% of labor force

Government

Long-form name: Republic of Paraguay
Type: republic
Capital: Asunción
Administrative divisions: 19 departments (departamentos, singular—departamento); Alto Paraguay, Alto Paraná, Amambay, Boquerón, Caaguazú, Caazapá, Canendiyú, Central, Chaco, Concepción, Cordillera, Guairá, Itapúa, Misiones, Ñeembucú, Nueva Asunción, Paraguarí, Presidente Hayes, San Pedro
Independence: 14 May 1811 (from Spain)
Constitution 25 August 1967
Legal system: based on Argentine codes, Roman law, and French codes; judicial review of legislative acts in Supreme Court of Justice; does not accept compulsory ICJ jurisdiction
National holiday: Independence Days, 14-15 May (1811)
Executive branch: president, Council of Ministers (cabinet), Council of State
Legislative branch: bicameral National Congress (Congreso Nacional) consists of an upper chamber or Senate and a lower chamber or Chamber of Deputies
Judicial branch: Supreme Court of Justice (Corte Suprema de Justicia)
Leaders: *Chief of State and Head of Government*—President Gen. Andrés RODRIGUEZ Pedotti (since 15 May 1989)
Political parties and leaders: Colorado Party, Juan Ramon Chaves; Authentic Radical Liberal Party (PLRA), Domingo Laino; Christian Democratic Party (PDC), Jorge Dario Cristaldo; Febrerista Revolutionary Party (PRF), Euclides Acevedo; Liberal Party (PL), Reinaldo Odone; Popular Colorado Movement (MOPOCO), Miguel Angel Gonzalez Casabianca; Radical Liberal Party (PLR), Emilio Forestieri; Popular Democratic Movement (MDP)
Suffrage: universal and compulsory at age 18 and up to age 60

Paraguay (continued)

Elections: *President*—last held 1 May 1989 (next to be held February 1993); results—Gen. Rodríguez 75.8%, Domingo Laino 19.4%;
Senate—last held 1 May 1989 (next to be held by May 1993); results—percent of vote by party NA; seats—(36 total) Colorado Party 24, PLRA 10, PLR 1, PRF 1;
Chamber of Deputies—last held on 1 May 1989 (next to be held by May 1994); results—percent of vote by party NA; seats—(72 total) Colorado Party 48, PLRA 19, PRF 2, PDC 1, PL 1, PLR 1

Communists: Oscar Creydt faction and Miguel Angel Soler faction (both illegal); 3,000 to 4,000 (est.) party members and sympathizers in Paraguay, very few are hard core; party beginning to return from exile is small and deeply divided

Other political or pressure groups: Febrerista; Authentic Radical Liberal; Christian Democratic Parties; Confederation of Workers (CUT); Roman Catholic Church

Member of: CCC, FAO, G-77, IADB, IAEA, IBRD, ICAO, ICO, IDA, IDB—Inter-American Development Bank, IFAD, IFC, ILO, IMF, INTELSAT, INTERPOL, IPU, IRC, ITU, LAIA, OAS, SELA, UN, UNESCO, UPU, WHO, WMO, WSG

Diplomatic representation: Ambassador Marcos MARTINEZ MENDIETA; Chancery at 2400 Massachusetts Avenue NW, Washington DC 20008; telephone (202) 483-6960 through 6962; there are Paraguayan Consulates General in New Orleans and New York, and a Consulate in Houston; *US*—Ambassador Timothy L. TOWELL; Embassy at 1776 Avenida Mariscal Lopez, Asunción (mailing address is C. P. 402, Asunción, or APO Miami 34036-0001); telephone [595] (21) 201-041 or 049

Flag: three equal, horizontal bands of red (top), white, and blue with an emblem centered in the white band; unusual flag in that the emblem is different on each side; the obverse (hoist side at the left) bears the national coat of arms (a yellow five-pointed star within a green wreath capped by the words *REPUBLICA DEL PARAGUAY*, all within two circles); the reverse (hoist side at the right) bears the seal of the treasury (a yellow lion below a red Cap of Liberty and the words *Paz y Justica* (Peace and Justice) capped by the words *REPUBLICA DEL PARAGUAY*, all within two circles)

Economy

Overview: The economy is predominantly agricultural. Agriculture, including forestry, accounts for about 25% of GNP, employs about 45% of the labor force, and provides the bulk of exports. Paraguay has no known significant mineral or petroleum resources, but does have a large hydropower potential. Since 1981 economic performance has declined compared with the boom period of 1976-81, when real GDP grew at an average annual rate of nearly 11%. During 1982-86 real GDP fell three out of five years, inflation jumped to an annual rate of 32%, and foreign debt rose. Factors responsible for the erratic behavior of the economy were the completion of the Itaipu hydroelectric dam, bad weather for crops, and weak international commodity prices for agricultural exports. In 1987 the economy experienced a modest recovery because of improved weather conditions and stronger international prices for key agricultural exports. The recovery continued through 1988, with a bumper soybean crop and record cotton production. The government, however, must follow through on promises of reforms needed to deal with large fiscal deficits, growing debt arrearages, and falling reserves.

GDP: $8.9 billion, per capita $1,970; real growth rate 5.2% (1989 est.)

Inflation rate (consumer prices): 30% (1989 est.)

Unemployment rate: 12% (1989 est.)

Budget: revenues $609 million; expenditures $909 million, including capital expenditures of $401 million (1988)

Exports: $1,020 million (registered f.o.b., 1989 est.); *commodities*—cotton, soybean, timber, vegetable oils, coffee, tung oil, meat products; *partners*—EC 37%, Brazil 25%, Argentina 10%, Chile 6%, US 6%

Imports: $1,010 million (registered c.i.f., 1989 est.); *commodities*—capital goods 35%, consumer goods 20%, fuels and lubricants 19%, raw materials 16%, foodstuffs, beverages, and tobacco 10%; *partners*—Brazil 30%, EC 20%, US 18%, Argentina 8%, Japan 7%

External debt: $2.9 billion (1989 est.)

Industrial production: growth rate 2% (1987)

Electricity: 5,169,000 kW capacity; 15,140 million kWh produced, 3,350 kWh per capita (1989)

Industries: meat packing, oilseed crushing, milling, brewing, textiles, other light consumer goods, cement, construction

Agriculture: accounts for 25% of GDP and 50% of labor force; cash crops—cotton, sugarcane; other crops—corn, wheat, tobacco, soybeans, cassava, fruits, and vegetables; animal products—beef, pork, eggs, milk; surplus producer of timber; self-sufficient in most foods

Illicit drugs: illicit producer of cannabis for the international drug trade with an estimated 300 hectares cultivated in 1988; important transshipment point for Bolivian cocaine headed for the US and Europe

Aid: US commitments, including Ex-Im (FY70-88), $168 million; Western (non-US) countries, ODA and OOF bilateral commitments (1970-87), $994 million

Currency: guaraní (plural—guaraníes); 1 guaraní (₲) = 100 céntimos

Exchange rates: guaraníes (₲) per US$1—1,200.20 (November 1989; floated in February 1989), 550.00 (fixed rate 1986-February 1989), 339.17 (1986), 306.67 (1985)

Fiscal year: calendar year

Communications

Railroads: 970 km total; 440 km 1.435-meter standard gauge, 60 km 1.000-meter gauge, 470 km various narrow gauge (privately owned)

Highways: 21,960 km total; 1,788 km paved, 474 km gravel, and 19,698 km earth

Inland waterways: 3,100 km

Ports: Asuncion

Merchant marine: 15 ships (1,000 GRT or over) totaling 20,735 GRT/26,043 DWT; includes 13 cargo, 2 petroleum, oils, and lubricants (POL) tanker; note—1 naval cargo ship is sometimes used commercially

Civil air: 4 major transport aircraft

Airports: 873 total, 753 usable; 6 with permanent-surface runways; 1 with runways over 3,659 m; 2 with runways 2,440-3,659 m; 52 with runways 1,220-2,439 m

Telecommunications: principal center in Asunción; fair intercity microwave net; 78,300 telephones; stations—40 AM, no FM, 5 TV, 7 shortwave; 1 Atlantic Ocean INTELSAT earth station

Defense Forces

Branches: Paraguayan Army, Paraguayan Navy, Paraguayan Air Force

Military manpower: males 15-49, 1,096,227; 798,750 fit for military service; 49,791 reach military age (17) annually

Defense expenditures: NA

Peru

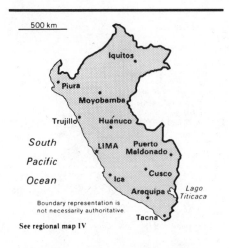

500 km

South Pacific Ocean

Boundary representation is not necessarily authoritative

See regional map IV

Geography

Total area: 1,285,220 km²; land area: 1,280,000 km²
Comparative area: slightly smaller than Alaska
Land boundaries: 6,940 km total; Bolivia 900 km, Brazil 1,560 km, Chile 160 km, Colombia 2,900 km, Ecuador 1,420 km
Coastline: 2,414 km
Maritime claims:
Territorial sea: 200 nm
Disputes: two sections of the boundary with Ecuador are in dispute
Climate: varies from tropical in east to dry desert in west
Terrain: western coastal plain (costa), high and rugged Andes in center (sierra), eastern lowland jungle of Amazon Basin (selva)
Natural resources: copper, silver, gold, petroleum, timber, fish, iron ore, coal, phosphate, potash
Land use: 3% arable land; NEGL% permanent crops; 21% meadows and pastures; 55% forest and woodland; 21% other; includes 1% irrigated
Environment: subject to earthquakes, tsunamis, landslides, mild volcanic activity; deforestation; overgrazing; soil erosion; desertification; air pollution in Lima
Note: shares control of Lago Titicaca, world's highest navigable lake, with Bolivia

People

Population: 21,905,605 (July 1990), growth rate 2.1% (1990)
Birth rate: 28 births/1,000 population (1990)
Death rate: 8 deaths/1,000 population (1990)
Net migration rate: 0 migrants/1,000 population (1990)
Infant mortality rate: 67 deaths/1,000 live births (1990)

Life expectancy at birth: 62 years male, 66 years female (1990)
Total fertility rate: 3.6 children born/woman (1990)
Nationality: noun—Peruvian(s); adjective—Peruvian
Ethnic divisions: 45% Indian; 37% mestizo (mixed Indian and European ancestry); 15% white; 3% black, Japanese, Chinese, and other
Religion: predominantly Roman Catholic
Language: Spanish and Quechua (official), Aymara
Literacy: 80% (est.)
Labor force: 6,800,000 (1986); 44% government and other services, 37% agriculture, 19% industry (1988 est.)
Organized labor: about 40% of salaried workers (1983 est.)

Government

Long-form name: Republic of Peru
Type: republic
Capital: Lima
Administrative divisions: 24 departments (departamentos, singular—departamento) and 1 constitutional province* (provincia constitucional); Amazonas, Ancash, Apurímac, Arequipa, Ayacucho, Cajamarca, Callao*, Cusco, Huancavelica, Huánuco, Ica, Junín, La Libertad, Lambayeque, Lima, Loreto, Madre de Dios, Moquegua, Pasco, Piura, Puno, San Martín, Tacna, Tumbes, Ucayali
Independence: 28 July 1821 (from Spain)
Constitution: 28 July 1980 (often referred to as the 1979 Constitution because constituent assembly met in 1979, but Constitution actually took effect the following year); reestablished civilian government with a popularly elected president and bicameral legislature
Legal system: based on civil law system; has not accepted compulsory ICJ jurisdiction
National holiday: Independence Day, 28 July (1821)
Executive branch: president, two vice presidents, prime minister, Council of Ministers (cabinet)
Legislative branch: bicameral Congress (Congreso) consists of an upper chamber or Senate (Senado) and a lower chamber or Chamber of Deputies (Cámara de Diputados)
Judicial branch: Supreme Court of Justice (Corte Suprema de Justicia)
Leaders: *Chief of State*—President Alán GARCIA Pérez (since 28 July 1985); First Vice President Luis Alberto SANCHEZ Sánchez (since 28 July 1985); Second Vice President Luis Juan ALVA Castro (since 28 July 1985);

Head of Government—Prime Minister Guillermo LARCO Cox (since 3 October 1989)
Political parties and leaders: American Popular Revolutionary Alliance (APRA), Alán García Pérez; United Left (IU), run by committee; Democratic Front (FREDEMO), headed by Maria Vargas Llosa of the Liberty Movement (ML), coalition also includes the Popular Christian Party (PPC), Luis Bedoya Reyes and the Popular Action Party (AP), Fernando Belaúnde Terry; Socialist Left (ISO), Alfonso Barrantes Lingan
Suffrage: universal at age 18
Elections: *President*—last held on 14 April 1985 (next to be held 8 April 1990); results—Alán García Pérez (APRA) 46%, Alfonso Barrantes Lingan (IU) 22%, others 32%;
Senate—last held on 14 April 1985 (next to be held April 1990); results—percent of vote by party NA; seats—(60 total) APRA 32, IU 15, AP 5, others 8;
Chamber of Deputies—last held 14 April 1985 (next to be held April 1990); results—percent of vote by party NA; seats—(180 total) APRA 107, IU 48, AP 10, others 15
Communists: Peruvian Communist Party-Unity (PCP-U), pro-Soviet, 2,000; other minor Communist parties
Other political or pressure groups: NA
Member of: Andean Pact, AIOEC, ASSIMER, CCC, CIPEC, FAO, G-77, GATT, Group of Eight, IADB, IAEA, IATP, IBRD, ICAO, ICO, IDA, IDB—Inter-American Development Bank, IFAD, IFC, ILO, ILZSG, INTERPOL, IMF, IMO, INTELSAT, ISO, ITU, IWC—International Wheat Council, LAIA, NAM, OAS, PAHO, SELA, UN, UNESCO, UPU, WFTU, WHO, WMO, WSG, WTO
Diplomatic representation: Ambassador Cesar G. ATALA; Chancery at 1700 Massachusetts Avenue NW, Washington DC 20036; telephone (202) 833-9860 through 9869); Peruvian Consulates General are located in Chicago, Houston, Los Angeles, Miami, New York, Paterson (New Jersey), San Francisco, and San Juan (Puerto Rico); *US*—Ambassador Anthony QUAINTON; Embassy at the corner of Avenida Inca Garcilaso de la Vega and Avenida Espana, Lima (mailing address is P. O. Box 1995, Lima 1010, or APO Miami 34031); telephone [51] (14) 338-000
Flag: three equal, vertical bands of red (hoist side), white, and red with the coat of arms centered in the white band; the coat of arms features a shield bearing a llama, cinchona tree (the source of quinine), and a yellow cornucopia spilling out gold coins, all framed by a green wreath

Peru *(continued)*

Economy

Overview: The economy is verging on hyperinflation and economic activity is contracting rapidly. Deficit spending is at the root of domestic economic problems, but poor relations with international lenders—the result of curtailing debt payments since 1985—are preventing an inflow of funds to generate a recovery. Reduced standards of living have increased labor tensions, and strikes, particularly in the key mining sector, have cut production and exports. Foreign exchange shortages have forced reductions in vital consumer imports such as food and industrial inputs. Peru is the world's leading producer of coca, from which the drug cocaine is produced.
GDP: $18.9 billion, per capita $880; real growth rate −12.2% (1989 est.)
Inflation rate (consumer prices): 2,775% (1989)
Unemployment rate: 15.0%; underemployment estimated at 60% (1989)
Budget: revenues $3.2 billion; expenditures $3.7 billion, including capital expenditures of $796 million (1986)
Exports: $3.55 billion (f.o.b., 1989); *commodities*—fishmeal, cotton, sugar, coffee, copper, iron ore, refined silver, lead, zinc, crude petroleum and byproducts; *partners*—EC 22%, US 20%, Japan 11%, Latin America 8%, USSR 4%
Imports: $2.50 billion (f.o.b., 1989); *commodities*—foodstuffs, machinery, transport equipment, iron and steel semimanufactures, chemicals, pharmaceuticals; *partners*—US 23%, Latin America 16%, EC 12%, Japan 7%, Switzerland 3%
External debt: $17.7 billion (December 1989)
Industrial production: growth rate −25.0% (1988 est.)
Electricity: 4,867,000 kW capacity; 15,540 million kWh produced, 725 kWh per capita (1989)
Industries: mining of metals, petroleum, fishing, textiles, clothing, food processing, cement, auto assembly, steel, shipbuilding, metal fabrication
Agriculture: accounts for 12% of GDP, 37% of labor force; commercial crops—coffee, cotton, sugarcane; other crops—rice, wheat, potatoes, plantains, coca; animal products—poultry, red meats, dairy, wool; not self-sufficient in grain or vegetable oil; fish catch of 4.6 million metric tons (1987), world's fifth-largest
Illicit drugs: world's largest coca producer and source of supply for coca paste and cocaine base; about 85% of cultivation is for illicit production; most of coca base is shipped to Colombian drug dealers for processing into cocaine for the international drug market

Aid: US commitments, including Ex-Im (FY70-88), $1.6 billion; Western (non-US) countries, ODA and OOF bilateral commitments (1970-87), $3.7 billion; Communist countries (1970-88), $577 million
Currency: inti (plural—intis); 1 inti (I/) = 1,000 soles
Exchange rates: intis (I/) per US$1—5,261.40 (December 1989), 128.83 (1988), 16.84 (1987), 13.95 (1986), 10.97 (1985)
Fiscal year: calendar year

Communications

Railroads: 1,876 km total; 1,576 km 1.435-meter standard gauge, 300 km 0.914-meter gauge
Highways: 56,645 km total; 6,030 km paved, 11,865 km gravel, 14,610 km improved earth, 24,140 km unimproved earth
Inland waterways: 8,600 km of navigable tributaries of Amazon system and 208 km Lago Titicaca
Pipelines: crude oil, 800 km; natural gas and natural gas liquids, 64 km
Ports: Callao, Ilo, Iquitos, Matarani, Talara
Merchant marine: 32 ships (1,000 GRT or over) totaling 341,213 GRT/535,215 DWT; includes 18 cargo, 1 refrigerated cargo, 1 roll-on/roll-off cargo, 3 petroleum, oils, and lubricants (POL) tanker, 1 chemical tanker, 8 bulk; note—in addition, 7 naval tankers and 1 naval cargo are sometimes used commercially
Civil air: 27 major transport aircraft
Airports: 242 total, 226 usable; 35 with permanent-surface runways; 2 with runways over 3,659 m; 24 with runways 2,440-3,659 m; 39 with runways 1,220-2,439 m
Telecommunications: fairly adequate for most requirements; nationwide radio relay system; 544,000 telephones; stations—273 AM, no FM, 140 TV, 144 shortwave; 2 Atlantic Ocean INTELSAT earth stations, 12 domestic antennas

Defense Forces

Branches: Peruvian Army (Ejercito Peruano), Peruvian Navy (Marina de Guerra del Peru), Peruvian Air Force (Fuerza Aerea del Peru)
Military manpower: males 15-49, 5,543,166; 3,751,077 fit for military service; 236,814 reach military age (20) annually
Defense expenditures: 4.9% of GNP (1987)

Philippines

500 km

Aparri
Baguio
Angeles
MANILA
Luzon
Quezon
Legaspi
Mindoro
Panay
Palawan
Negros
Sulu Sea
Zamboanga
Cebu
Samar
Davao
Mindanao
Celebes Sea
South China Sea
Philippine Sea

See regional map IX

Geography

Total area: 300,000 km²; land area: 298,170 km²
Comparative area: slightly larger than Arizona
Land boundaries: none
Coastline: 36,289 km
Maritime claims: (measured from claimed archipelagic baselines)
Continental shelf: to depth of exploitation
Extended economic zone: 200 nm
Territorial sea: irregular polygon extending up to 100 nm from coastline as defined by 1898 treaty; since late 1970s has also claimed polygonal-shaped area in South China Sea up to 285 nm in breadth
Disputes: involved in a complex dispute over the Spratly Islands with China, Malaysia, Taiwan, and Vietnam; claims Malaysian state of Sabah
Climate: tropical marine; northeast monsoon (November to April); southwest monsoon (May to October)
Terrain: mostly mountains with narrow to extensive coastal lowlands
Natural resources: timber, crude oil, nickel, cobalt, silver, gold, salt, copper
Land use: 26% arable land; 11% permanent crops; 4% meadows and pastures; 40% forest and woodland; 19% other; includes 5% irrigated
Environment: astride typhoon belt, usually affected by 15 and struck by five to six cyclonic storms per year; subject to landslides, active volcanoes, destructive earthquakes, tsunami; deforestation; soil erosion; water pollution

People

Population: 66,117,284 (July 1990), growth rate 2.5% (1990)
Birth rate: 32 births/1,000 population (1990)

Death rate: 7 deaths/1,000 population (1990)
Net migration rate: −1 migrant/1,000 population (1990)
Infant mortality rate: 48 deaths/1,000 live births (1990)
Life expectancy at birth: 63 years male, 69 years female (1990)
Total fertility rate: 4.3 children born/woman (1990)
Nationality: noun—Filipino(s); adjective—Philippine
Ethnic divisions: 91.5% Christian Malay, 4% Muslim Malay, 1.5% Chinese, 3% other
Religion: 83% Roman Catholic, 9% Protestant, 5% Muslim, 3% Buddhist and other
Language: Pilipino (based on Tagalog) and English; both official
Literacy: 88% (est.)
Labor force: 22,889,000; 47% agriculture, 20% industry and commerce, 13.5% services, 10% government, 9.5% other (1987)
Organized labor: 2,064 registered unions; total membership 4.8 million (includes 2.7 million members of the National Congress of Farmers Organizations)

Government

Long-form name: Republic of the Philippines
Type: republic
Capital: Manila
Administrative divisions: 73 provinces and 61 chartered cities*; Abra, Agusan del Norte, Agusan del Sur, Aklan, Albay, Angeles*, Antique, Aurora, Bacolod*, Bago*, Baguio*, Bais*, Basilan, Basilan City*, Bataan, Batanes, Batangas, Batangas City*, Benguet, Bohol, Bukidnon, Bulacan, Butuan*, Cabanatuan*, Cadiz*, Cagayan, Cagayan de Oro*, Calbayog*, Caloocan*, Camarines Norte, Camarines Sur, Camiguin, Canlaon*, Capiz, Catanduanes, Cavite, Cavite City*, Cebu, Cebu City*, Cotabato*, Dagupan*, Danao*, Dapitan*, Davao City* Davao, Davao del Sur, Davao Oriental, Dipolog*, Dumaguete*, Eastern Samar, General Santos*, Gingoog*, Ifugao, Iligan*, Ilocos Norte, Ilocos Sur, Iloilo, Iloilo City*, Iriga*, Isabela, Kalinga-Apayao, La Carlota*, Laguna, Lanao del Norte, Lanao del Sur, Laoag*, Lapu-Lapu*, La Union, Legaspi*, Leyte, Lipa*, Lucena*, Maguindanao, Mandaue*, Manila*, Marawi*, Marinduque, Masbate, Mindoro Occidental, Mindoro Oriental, Misamis Occidental, Misamis Oriental, Mountain, Naga*, Negros Occidental, Negros Oriental, North Cotabato, Northern Samar, Nueva Ecija, Nueva Vizcaya, Olongapo*, Ormoc*, Oroquieta*, Ozamis*, Pagadian*, Palawan, Palayan*,

Pampanga, Pangasinan, Pasay*, Puerto Princesa*, Quezon, Quezon City*, Quirino, Rizal, Romblon, Roxas*, Samar, San Carlos* (in Negros Occidental), San Carlos* (in Pangasinan), San Jose*, San Pablo*, Silay*, Siquijor, Sorsogon, South Cotabato, Southern Leyte, Sultan Kudarat, Sulu, Surigao*, Surigao del Norte, Surigao del Sur, Tacloban*, Tagaytay*, Tagbilaran*, Tangub*, Tarlac, Tawitawi, Toledo*, Trece Martires*, Zambales, Zamboanga*, Zamboanga del Norte, Zamboanga del Sur
Independence: 4 July 1946 (from US)
Constitution: 2 February 1987, effective 11 February 1987
Legal system: based on Spanish and Anglo-American law; accepts compulsory ICJ jurisdiction, with reservations
National holiday: Independence Day (from Spain), 12 June (1898)
Executive branch: president, vice president, Cabinet
Legislative branch: bicameral Congress consists of an upper house or Senate and a lower house or House of Representatives
Judicial branch: Supreme Court
Leaders: *Chief of State and Head of Government*—President Corazon C. AQUINO (since 25 February 1986); Vice President Salvador H. LAUREL (since 25 February 1986)
Political parties and leaders: PDP-Laban, Aquilino Pimentel; Struggle of Philippine Democrats (LDP), Neptali Gonzales; Nationalista Party, Salvador Laurel, Juan Ponce Enrile; Liberal Party, Jovito Salonga
Suffrage: universal at age 15
Elections: *President*—last held 7 February 1986 (next election to be held May 1992); results—Corazon C. Aquino elected after the fall of the Marcos regime; *Senate*—last held 11 May 1987 (next to be held May 1993); results—*Pro-Aquino* LDP 63%, *Liberals* LDP and PDP-Laban (Pimentel wing) 25%, *Opposition* Nationalista Party 4%, independents 8%; seats—(24 total) *Pro-Aquino* LDP 15, *Liberals* LDP-Laban (Pimentel wing) 6, *Opposition* 1, independents 2; *House of Representatives*—last held on 11 May 1987 (next to be held May 1992); results—*Pro-Aquino* LDP 73%, *Liberals* LDP and PDP-Laban (Pimentel wing) 10%, *Opposition* Nationalista Party 17%; seats—(250 total, 180 elected) number of seats by party NA
Communists: the Communist Party of the Philippines (CPP) controls about 18,000-23,000 full-time insurgents and is not recognized as a legal party; a second Communist party, the pro-Soviet Philippine Communist Party (PKP), has quasi-legal status

Member of: ADB, ASEAN, ASPAC, CCC, Colombo Plan, ESCAP, FAO, G-77, GATT, IAEA, IBRD, ICAO, IDA, IFAD, IFC, IHO, ILO, IMF, IMO, INTELSAT, INTERPOL, IPU, IRC, ISO, ITU, UN, UNESCO, UPU, WFTU, WHO, WIPO, WMO, WTO
Diplomatic representation: Ambassador Emmanuel PELAEZ; Chancery at 1617 Massachusetts Avenue NW, Washington DC 20036; telephone (202) 483-1414; there are Philippine Consulates General in Agana (Guam), Chicago, Honolulu, Houston, Los Angeles, New York, San Francisco, and Seattle; *US*—Ambassador Nicholas PLATT; Embassy at 1201 Roxas Boulevard, Manila (mailing address is APO San Francisco 96528); telephone [63] (2) 521-7116; there is a US Consulate in Cebu
Flag: two equal horizontal bands of blue (top) and red with a white equilateral triangle based on the hoist side; in the center of the triangle is a yellow sun with eight primary rays (each containing three individual rays) and in each corner of the triangle is a small yellow five-pointed star

Economy

Overview: The economy continues to recover from the political turmoil following the ouster of former President Marcos and several coup attempts. After two consecutive years of economic contraction (1984 and 1985), the economy has since 1986 had positive growth. The agricultural sector, together with forestry and fishing, plays an important role in the economy, employing about 50% of the work force and providing almost 30% of GDP. The Philippines is the world's largest exporter of coconuts and coconut products. Manufacturing contributed about 25% of GDP. Major industries include food processing, chemicals, and textiles.
GNP: $40.5 billion, per capita $625; real growth rate 5.2% (1989)
Inflation rate (consumer prices): 10.6% (1989)
Unemployment rate: 8.7% (1989)
Budget: $7.2 billion; expenditures $8.12 billion, including capital expenditures of $0.97 billion (1989 est.)
Exports: revenues $8.1 billion (f.o.b., 1989); *commodities*—electrical equipment 19%, textiles 16%, minerals and ores 11%, farm products 10%, coconut 10%, chemicals 5%, fish 5%, forest products 4%; *partners*—US 36%, EC 19%, Japan 18%, ESCAP 9%, ASEAN 7%
Imports: $10.5 billion (c.i.f., 1989); *commodities*—raw materials 53%, capital goods 17%, petroleum products 17%; *partners*—US 25%, Japan 17%, ESCAP 13%, EC 11%, ASEAN 10%, Middle East 10%

251

Philippines (continued)

External debt: $27.8 billion (1988)
Industrial production: growth rate 7.3% (1989)
Electricity: 6,700,000 kW capacity; 25,000 million kWh produced, 385 kWh per capita (1989)
Industries: textiles, pharmaceuticals, chemicals, wood products, food processing, electronics assembly, petroleum refining, fishing
Agriculture: accounts for about one-third of GNP and 50% of labor force; major crops—rice, coconut, corn, sugarcane, bananas, pineapple, mango; animal products—pork, eggs, beef; net exporter of farm products; fish catch of 2 million metric tons annually
Illicit drugs: illicit producer of cannabis for the international drug trade; growers are producing more and better quality cannabis despite government eradication efforts
Aid: US commitments, including Ex-Im (FY70-88), $3.2 billion; Western (non-US) countries, ODA and OOF bilateral commitments (1970-87), $6.4 billion; OPEC bilateral aid (1979-89), $5 million; Communist countries (1975-88), $123 million
Currency: Philippine peso (plural—pesos); 1 Philippine peso (₱) = 100 centavos
Exchange rates: Philippine pesos (₱) per US$1—22.464 (January 1990), 21.737 (1989), 21.095 (1988), 20.568 (1987), 20.386 (1986), 18.607 (1985)
Fiscal year: calendar year

Communications

Railroads: 378 km operable on Luzon, 34% government owned (1982)
Highways: 156,000 km total (1984); 29,000 km paved; 77,000 km gravel, crushed-stone, or stabilized-soil surface; 50,000 km unimproved earth
Inland waterways: 3,219 km; limited to shallow-draft (less than 1.5 m) vessels
Pipelines: refined products, 357 km
Ports: Cagayan de Oro, Cebu, Davao, Guimaras, Iloilo, Legaspi, Manila, Subic Bay
Merchant marine: 595 ships (1,000 GRT or over) totaling 9,134,924 GRT/ 15,171,692 DWT; includes 1 passenger, 10 short-sea passenger, 16 passenger-cargo, 166 cargo, 17 refrigerated cargo, 30 vehicle carrier, 8 livestock carrier, 7 roll-on/roll-off cargo, 6 container, 36 petroleum, oils, and lubricants (POL) tanker, 2 chemical tanker, 6 liquefied gas, 3 combination ore/oil, 282 bulk, 5 combination bulk; note—many Philippine flag ships are foreign owned and are on the register for the purpose of long-term bare-boat charter back to their original owners who are principally in Japan and FRG

Civil air: 53 major transport aircraft
Airports: 301 total, 237 usable; 70 with permanent-surface runways; none with runways over 3,659 m; 9 with runways 2,440-3,659 m; 49 with runways 1,220-2,439 m
Telecommunications: good international radio and submarine cable services; domestic and interisland service adequate; 872,900 telephones; stations—267 AM (including 6 US), 55 FM, 33 TV (including 4 US); submarine cables extended to Hong Kong, Guam, Singapore, Taiwan, and Japan; satellite earth stations—1 Indian Ocean INTELSAT, 2 Pacific Ocean INTELSAT, and 11 domestic

Defense Forces

Branches: Army, Navy, Marine Corps, Air Force, Constabulary—Integrated National Police
Military manpower: males 15-49, 16,160,543; 11,417,451 fit for military service; 684,976 reach military age (20) annually
Defense expenditures: 2.1% of GNP, or $850 million (1990 est.)

Pitcairn Islands
(dependent territory of the UK)

Geography

Total area: 47 km²; land area: 47 km²
Comparative area: about 0.3 times the size of Washington, DC
Land boundaries: none
Coastline: 51 km
Maritime claims:
 Exclusive fishing zone: 200 nm
 Territorial sea: 3 nm
Climate: tropical, hot, humid, modified by southeast trade winds; rainy season (November to March)
Terrain: rugged volcanic formation; rocky coastline with cliffs
Natural resources: miro trees (used for handicrafts), fish
Land use: NA% arable land; NA% permanent crops; NA% meadows and pastures; NA% forest and woodland; NA% other
Environment: subject to typhoons (especially November to March)
Note: located in the South Pacific Ocean about halfway between Peru and New Zealand

---

People

Population: 56 (July 1990), growth rate 0.0% (1990)
Birth rate: NA births/1,000 population (1990)
Death rate: NA deaths/1,000 population (1990)
Net migration rate: NA migrants/1,000 population (1990)
Infant mortality rate: NA deaths/1,000 live births (1990)
Life expectancy at birth: NA years male, NA years female (1990)
Total fertility rate: NA children born/ woman (1990)
Nationality: noun—Pitcairn Islander(s); adjective—Pitcairn Islander
Ethnic divisions: descendants of Bounty mutineers
Religion: 100% Seventh-Day Adventist

Language: English (official); also a Tahitian/English dialect
Literacy: NA%, but probably high
Labor force: NA; no business community in the usual sense; some public works; subsistence farming and fishing
Organized labor: NA

Government

Long-form name: Pitcairn, Henderson, Ducie, and Oeno Islands
Type: dependent territory of the UK
Capital: Adamstown
Administrative divisions: none (dependent territory of the UK)
Independence: none (dependent territory of the UK)
Constitution: Local Government Ordinance of 1964
Legal system: local island by-laws
National holiday: Celebration of the Birthday of the Queen (second Saturday in June), 10 June 1989
Executive branch: British monarch, governor, island magistrate
Legislative branch: unicameral Island Council
Judicial branch: Island Court
Leaders: *Chief of State*—Queen ELIZABETH II (since 6 February 1952), represented by the Governor and UK High Commissioner to New Zealand Robin A. C. BYATT (since NA 1988);
Head of Government—Island Magistrate and Chairman of the Island Council Brian YOUNG (since NA 1985)
Political parties and leaders: NA
Suffrage: universal at age 18 with three years residency
Elections: *Island Council*—last held NA (next to be held NA); results—percent of vote by party NA; seats—(11 total, 5 elected) number of seats by party NA
Communists: none
Other political or pressure groups: NA
Diplomatic representation: none (dependent territory of the UK)
Flag: blue with the flag of the UK in the upper hoist-side quadrant and the Pitcairn Islander coat of arms centered on the outer half of the flag; the coat of arms is yellow, green, and light blue with a shield featuring a yellow anchor

---

Economy

Overview: The inhabitants exist on fishing and subsistence farming. The fertile soil of the valleys produces a wide variety of fruits and vegetables, including citrus, sugarcane, watermelons, bananas, yams, and beans. Bartering is an important part of the economy. The major sources of revenue are the sale of postage stamps to collectors and the sale of handicrafts to passing ships.
GNP: NA
Inflation rate (consumer prices): NA%
Unemployment rate: NA%
Budget: revenues $430,440; expenditures $429,983, including capital expenditures of $NA (FY87 est.)
Exports: $NA; *commodities*—fruits, vegetables, curios; *partners*—NA
Imports: $NA; *commodities*—fuel oil, machinery, building materials, flour, sugar, other foodstuffs; *partners*—NA
External debt: $NA
Industrial production: growth rate NA%
Electricity: 110 kW capacity; 0.30 million kWh produced, 4,410 kWh per capita (1989)
Industries: postage stamp sales, handicrafts
Agriculture: based on subsistence fishing and farming; wide variety of fruits and vegetables grown; must import grain products
Aid: none
Currency: New Zealand dollar (plural—dollars); 1 New Zealand dollar (NZ$) = 100 cents
Exchange rates: New Zealand dollars (NZ$) per US$1—1.6581 (January 1990), 1.6708 (1989), 1.5244 (1988), 1.6866 (1987), 1.9088 (1986), 2.0064 (1985)
Fiscal year: 1 April-31 March

Communications

Railroads: none
Highways: 6.4 km dirt roads
Ports: Bounty Bay
Airports: none
Telecommunications: 24 telephones; party line telephone service on the island; stations—1 AM, no FM, no TV; diesel generator provides electricity

---

Defense Forces

Note: defense is the responsibility of the UK

Poland

Baltic Sea · Gdynia · Gdańsk · Szczecin · Bydgoszcz · Białystok · Poznań · WARSAW · Łódź · Wrocław · Lublin · Katowice · Rzeszów · Kraków
150 km

See regional map V

Boundary representation is not necessarily authoritative.

Geography

Total area: 312,680 km²; land area: 304,510 km²
Comparative area: slightly smaller than New Mexico
Land boundaries: 2,980 km total; Czechoslovakia 1,309 km, GDR 456 km, USSR 1,215 km
Coastline: 491 km
Maritime claims:
Territorial sea: 12 nm
Climate: temperate with cold, cloudy, moderately severe winters with frequent precipitation; mild summers with frequent showers and thundershowers
Terrain: mostly flat plain, mountains along southern border
Natural resources: coal, sulfur, copper, natural gas, silver, lead, salt
Land use: 46% arable land; 1% permanent crops; 13% meadows and pastures; 28% forest and woodland; 12% other; includes NEGL% irrigated
Environment: plain crossed by a few north-flowing, meandering streams; severe air and water pollution in south
Note: historically, an area of conflict because of flat terrain and the lack of natural barriers on the North European Plain

---

People

Population: 37,776,725 (July 1990), growth rate NEGL (1990)
Birth rate: 14 births/1,000 population (1990)
Death rate: 9 deaths/1,000 population (1990)
Net migration rate: −5 migrants/1,000 population (1990)
Infant mortality rate: 13 deaths/1,000 live births (1990)
Life expectancy at birth: 68 years male, 77 years female (1990)
Total fertility rate: 2.1 children born/woman (1990)

Poland *(continued)*

Nationality: noun—Pole(s); adjective—Polish
Ethnic divisions: 98.7% Polish, 0.6% Ukrainian, 0.5% Byelorussian, less than 0.05% Jewish
Religion: 95% Roman Catholic (about 75% practicing), 5% Russian Orthodox, Protestant, and other
Language: Polish
Literacy: 98%
Labor force: 17,128,000 (1988); 36.5% industry and construction; 28.5% agriculture; 14.7% trade, transport, and communications; 20.3% government and other
Organized labor: trade union pluralism

Government

Long-form name: Republic of Poland
Type: democratic state
Capital: Warsaw
Administrative divisions: 49 provinces (województwa, singular—województwo); Biała Podlaska, Białystok, Bielsko-Biała, Bydgoszcz, Chełm, Ciechanów, Częstochowa, Elbląg, Gdańsk, Gorzów Wielkopolski, Jelenia Góra, Kalisz, Katowice, Kielce, Konin, Koszalin, Kraków, Krosno, Legnica, Leszno, Łódź, Łomza, Lublin, Nowy Sącz, Olsztyn, Opole, Ostrołęka, Piła, Piotrków, Płock, Poznań, Przemyśl, Radom, Rzeszów, Siedlce, Sieradz, Skierniewice, Słupsk, Suwałki, Szczecin, Tarnobrzeg, Tarnów, Toruń, Wałbrzych, Warszawa, Włocławek, Wrocław, Zamość, Zielona Góra
Independence: 11 November 1918, independent republic proclaimed
Constitution: the Communist-imposed Constitution of 22 July 1952 will be replaced by a democratic Constitution before May 1991
Legal system: mixture of Continental (Napoleonic) civil law and Communist legal theory; no judicial review of legislative acts; has not accepted compulsory ICJ jurisdiction
National holiday: National Liberation Day, 22 July (1952) will probably be replaced by Constitution Day, 3 May (1794)
Executive branch: president, prime minister, Council of Ministers (cabinet)
Legislative branch: bicameral Parliament (Parlament) consists of an upper house or Senate (Senat) and a lower house or National Assembly (Sejm)
Judicial branch: Supreme Court
Leaders: *Chief of State*—President Gen. Wojciech JARUZELSKI (since 19 July 1989, Chairman of Council of State since 6 November 1985);
Head of Government—Premier Tadeusz MAZOWIECKI (since 24 August 1989)
Political parties and leaders: *Center-right agrarian parties*—Polish Peasant Party (PSL, known unofficially as PSL-Wilanowska), Gen. Franciszek Kaminski, chairman; Polish Peasant Party-Solidarity, Josef Slisz, chairman; Polish Peasant Party-Rebirth (formerly the United Peasant Party), Kazimirrz Olrsiak, chairman;
Other center-right parties—National Party, Bronislaw Ekert, chairman; Christian National Union, Urrslaw Chnzanowski, chairman; Christian Democratic Labor Party, Wladyslaw Sila Nowicki, chairman; Democratic Party, Jerzy Jozwiak, chairman;
Center-left parties—Polish Socialist Party, Jan Jozef Lipski, chairman;
Left-wing parties—Polish Socialist Party-Democratic Revolution;
Other—Social Democracy of the Republic of Poland (formerly the Communist Party or Polish United Workers' Party/PZPR), Aleksander Kwasnuewski, chairman; Union of the Social Democracy of the Republic of Poland (breakaway faction of the PZPR), Tadrusz Fiszbach, chairman
Suffrage: universal at age 18
Elections: *Senate*—last held 4 and 18 June 1989 (next to be held June 1993); results—percent of vote by party NA; seats—(100 total) Solidarity 99, independent 1;
National Assembly—last held 4 and 18 June 1989 (next to be held June 1993); results—percent of vote by party NA; seats—(460 total) Communists 173, Solidarity 161, Polish Peasant Party 76, Democratic Party 27, Christian National Union 23; note—rules governing the election limited Solidarity's share of the vote to 35% of the seats; future elections are to be freely contested
Communists: 70,000 members in the Communist successor party (1990)
Other political or pressure groups: powerful Roman Catholic Church; Confederation for an Independent Poland (KPN), a nationalist group; Solidarity (trade union); All Poland Trade Union Alliance (OPZZ), populist program; Clubs of Catholic Intellectuals (KIKs); Freedom and Peace (WiP), a pacifist group; Independent Student Union (NZS)
Member of: CCC, CEMA, Council of Europe, FAO, GATT, IAEA, ICAO, ICES, IHO, ILO, ILZSG, IMO, IPU, ISO, ITC, ITU, UN, UNESCO, UPU, WFTU, WHO, Warsaw Pact, WIPO, WMO
Diplomatic representation: Ambassador Jan KINAST; Chancery at 2640 16th Street NW, Washington DC 20009; telephone (202) 234-3800 through 3802; there are Polish Consulates General in Chicago and New York; *US*—Ambassador John R. DAVIS, Jr.; Embassy at Aleje Ujazdowskie 29/31, Warsaw (mailing address is APO New York 09213); telephone [48] 283041 through 283049; there is a US Consulate General in Krakow and a Consulate in Poznan
Flag: two equal horizontal bands of white (top) and red—a crowned eagle is to be added; similar to the flags of Indonesia and Monaco which are red (top) and white

---

Economy

Overview: The economy, except for the agricultural sector, had followed the Soviet model of state ownership and control of the country's productive assets. About 75% of agricultural production had come from the private sector and the rest from state farms. The economy has presented a picture of moderate but slowing growth against a background of underlying weaknesses in technology and worker motivation. GNP increased between 3% and 6% annually during the period 1983-1986, but grew only 2.5% and 2.1% in 1987 and 1988, respectively. Output dropped by 1.5% in 1989. The inflation rate, after falling sharply from the 1982 peak of 100% to 22% in 1986, rose to a galloping rate of 640% in 1989. Shortages of consumer goods and some food items worsened in 1988-89. Agricultural products and coal have remained the biggest hard currency earners, but manufactures are increasing in importance. Poland, with its hard currency debt of approximately $40 billion, is severely limited in its ability to import much-needed hard currency goods. The sweeping political changes of 1989 disrupted normal economic channels and exacerbated shortages. In January 1990, the new Solidarity-led government adopted a cold turkey program for transforming Poland to a market economy. The government moved to eliminate subsidies, end artificially low prices, make the złoty convertible, and, in general, halt the hyperinflation. These financial measures are accompanied by plans to privatize the economy in stages. Substantial outside aid will be needed if Poland is to make a successful transition in the 1990s.
GNP: $172.4 billion, per capita $4,565; real growth rate −1.6% (1989 est.)
Inflation rate (consumer prices): 640% (1989 est.)
Unemployment rate: NA%; 215,000 (official number, mid-March 1990)
Budget: revenues $23 billion; expenditures $24 billion, including capital expenditures of $3.5 billion (1988)
Exports: $24.7 billion (f.o.b., 1987 est.); *commodities*—machinery and equipment 63%; fuels, minerals, and metals 14%; manufactured consumer goods 14%; agricultural and forestry products 5% (1987

est.); *partners*—USSR 25%, FRG 12%, Czechoslovakia 6% (1988)

Imports: $22.8 billion (f.o.b., 1987 est.); *commodities*—machinery and equipment 36%; fuels, minerals, and metals 35%; manufactured consumer goods 9%; agricultural and forestry products 12%; *partners*—USSR 23%, FRG 13%, Czechoslovakia 6% (1988)

External debt: $40 billion (1989 est.)

Industrial production: growth rate −2.0% (1988)

Electricity: 31,390,000 kW capacity; 125,000 million kWh produced, 3,260 kWh per capita (1989)

Industries: machine building, iron and steel, extractive industries, chemicals, shipbuilding, food processing, glass, beverages, textiles

Agriculture: accounts for 15% of GNP and 28% of labor force; 75% of output from private farms, 25% from state farms; productivity remains low by European standards; leading European producer of rye, rapeseed, and potatoes; wide variety of other crops and livestock; major exporter of pork products; normally self-sufficient in food

Aid: donor—bilateral aid to non-Communist less developed countries, $2.1 billion (1954-88)

Currency: złoty (plural—złotych); 1 złoty (Zł) = 100 groszy

Exchange rates: złotych (Zł) per US$1—9,500.00 (January 1990), 1,439.18 (1989), 430.55 (1988), 265.08 (1987), 175.29 (1986), 147.14 (1985)

Fiscal year: calendar year

Communications

Railroads: 27,245 km total; 24,333 km 1.435-meter standard gauge, 397 km 1.524-meter broad gauge, 2,515 km narrow gauge; 8,986 km double track; 10,000 km electrified; government owned (1986)

Highways: 299,887 km total; 130,000 km improved hard surface (concrete, asphalt, stone block); 24,000 km unimproved hard surface (crushed stone, gravel); 100,000 km earth; 45,887 km other urban roads (1985)

Inland waterways: 3,997 km navigable rivers and canals (1988)

Pipelines: 4,500 km for natural gas; 1,986 km for crude oil; 360 km for refined products (1987)

Ports: Gdańsk, Gdynia, Szczecin, Świnoujście; principal inland ports are Gliwice on Kanał Gliwice, Wrocław on the Oder, and Warsaw on the Vistula

Merchant marine: 234 ships (1,000 GRT or over) totaling 2,957,534 GRT/4,164,665 DWT; includes 5 short-sea passenger, 93 cargo, 3 refrigerated cargo, 12 roll-on/roll-off cargo, 9 container, 3 petro-leum, oils, and lubricants (POL) tanker, 4 chemical tanker, 105 bulk

Civil air: 42 major transport aircraft

Airports: 160 total, 160 usable; 85 with permanent-surface runways; 1 with runway over 3,659 m; 35 with runways 2,440-3,659 m; 65 with runways 1,220-2,439 m

Telecommunications: stations—30 AM, 28 FM, 41 TV; 4 Soviet TV relays; 9,691,075 TV sets; 9,290,000 radio receivers; at least 1 Atlantic Ocean INTELSAT earth station

Defense Forces

Branches: Ground Forces, National Air Defense Forces, Air Force Command, Navy

Military manpower: males 15-49, 9,501,088; 7,503,477 fit for military service; 292,769 reach military age (19) annually

Defense expenditures: 954 billion złotych, NA% of total budget (1989); note—conversion of the military budget into US dollars using the official administratively set exchange rate would produce misleading results

Portugal

125 km

North Atlantic Ocean

Braga
Porto
Covilhã
Coimbra
Portalegre
LISBON
Beja
Faro

Azores and Madeira Islands are not shown

See regional map V and VII

Geography

Total area: 92,080 km²; land area: 91,640 km²; includes Azores and Madeira Islands

Comparative area: slightly smaller than Indiana

Land boundary: 1,214 km with Spain

Coastline: 1,793 km

Maritime claims:
Continental shelf: 200 meters or to depth of exploitation
Extended economic zone: 200 nm
Territorial sea: 12 nm

Disputes: Macau is scheduled to become a Special Administrative Region of China in 1999; East Timor question with Indonesia

Climate: maritime temperate; cool and rainy in north, warmer and drier in south

Terrain: mountainous north of the Tagus, rolling plains in south

Natural resources: fish, forests (cork), tungsten, iron ore, uranium ore, marble

Land use: 32% arable land; 6% permanent crops; 6% meadows and pastures; 40% forest and woodland; 16% other; includes 7% irrigated

Environment: Azores subject to severe earthquakes

Note: Azores and Madeira Islands occupy strategic locations along western sea approaches to Strait of Gibraltar

People

Population: 10,354,497 (July 1990), growth rate 0.3% (1990)

Birth rate: 12 births/1,000 population (1990)

Death rate: 10 deaths/1,000 population (1990)

Net migration rate: 1 migrants/1,000 population (1990)

Infant mortality rate: 14 deaths/1,000 live births (1990)

Life expectancy at birth: 71 years male, 78 years female (1990)

Portugal (continued)

Total fertility rate: 1.5 children born/ woman (1990)
Nationality: noun—Portuguese (sing. and pl.); adjective—Portuguese
Ethnic divisions: homogeneous Mediterranean stock in mainland, Azores, Madeira Islands; citizens of black African descent who immigrated to mainland during decolonization number less than 100,000
Religion: 97% Roman Catholic, 1% Protestant denominations, 2% other
Language: Portuguese
Literacy: 83%
Labor force: 4,605,700; 45% services, 35% industry, 20% agriculture (1988)
Organized labor: about 55% of the labor force; the Communist-dominated General Confederation of Portuguese Workers—Intersindical (CGTP-IN) represents more than half of the unionized labor force; its main competition, the General Workers Union (UGT), is organized by the Socialists and Social Democrats and represents less than half of unionized labor

Government

Long-form name: Portuguese Republic
Type: republic
Capital: Lisbon
Administrative divisions: 18 districts (distritos, singular—distrito) and 2 autonomous regions* (regiões autónomas, singular—região autónoma); Açores*, Aveiro, Beja, Braga, Bragança, Castelo Branco, Coimbra, Evora, Faro, Guarda, Leiria, Lisboa, Madeira*, Portalegre, Porto, Santarém, Setúbal, Viana do Castelo, Vila Real, Viseu
Dependent area: Macau (scheduled to become a Special Administrative Region of China in 1999)
Independence: 1140; independent republic proclaimed 5 October 1910
Constitution: 25 April 1976, revised 30 October 1982; new discussions on constitutional revision began October 1987
Legal system: civil law system; the Constitutional Tribunal reviews the constitutionality of legislation; accepts compulsory ICJ jurisdiction, with reservations
National holiday: Day of Portugal, 10 June
Executive branch: president, Council of State, prime minister, deputy prime minister, Council of Ministers (cabinet)
Legislative branch: unicameral Assembly of the Republic (Assembléia da República)
Judicial branch: Supreme Tribunal of Justice (Supremo Tribunal de Justiça)
Leaders: *Chief of State*—President Dr. Mário Alberto Nobre Lopes SOARES (since 9 March 1986);

Head of Government—Prime Minister Aníbal CAVAÇO SILVA (since 6 November 1985); Deputy Prime Minister (vacant)
Political parties and leaders: Social Democratic Party (PSD), Aníbal Cavaço Silva; Portuguese Socialist Party (PS), Jorge Sampaio; Party of Democratic Renewal (PRD), Hermínio Martinho; Portuguese Communist Party (PCP), Alvaro Cunhal; Social Democratic Center (CDS), Diogo Freitas do Amaral
Suffrage: universal at age 18
Elections: *President*—last held 16 February 1986 (next to be held January 1991); results—Dr. Mário Lopes Soares 51.3%, Prof. Diogo Freitas do Amal 48.7%; *Assembly of the Republic*—last held 19 July 1987 (next to be held July 1991); results—Social Democrats 59.2%, Socialists 24.0%, Communists (in a front coalition) 12.4%, Democratic Renewal 2.8%, Center Democrats 1.6%; seats—(250 total) Social Democrats 148, Socialists 60, Communists (in a front coalition) 31 seats, Democratic Renewal 7, Center Democrats 4
Communists: Portuguese Communist Party claims membership of 200,753 (December 1983)
Member of: CCC, Council of Europe, EC, EFTA, FAO, GATT, IAEA, IATP, IBRD, ICAC, ICAO, ICES, ICO, IDB—Inter-American Development Bank, IEA, IFAD, IFC, IHO, ILO, IMF, IMO, INTELSAT, INTERPOL, IOOC, IRC, ISO, ITU, IWC—International Wheat Council, NATO, OECD, UN, UNESCO, UPU, WEU, WHO, WIPO, WMO, WSG
Diplomatic representation: Ambassador Joao Eduardo M. PEREIRA BASTOS; Chancery at 2125 Kalorama Road NW, Washington DC 20008; telephone (202) 328-8610; there are Portuguese Consulates General in Boston, New York, and San Francisco, and Consulates in Los Angeles, Newark (New Jersey), New Bedford (Massachusetts), and Providence (Rhode Island); *US*—Ambassador Edward M. ROWELL; Embassy at Avenida das Forcas Armadas, 1600 Lisbon (mailing address is APO New York 09678-0002); telephone [351] (1) 726-6600 or 6659, 8670, 8880; there are US Consulates in Oporto and Ponta Delgada (Azores)
Flag: two vertical bands of green (hoist side, two-fifths) and red (three-fifths) with the Portuguese coat of arms centered on the dividing line

Economy

Overview: During the past four years, the economy has made a sustained recovery from the severe recession of 1983-85. The economy grew by 4.7% in 1987, 4.1% in 1988, and 3.5% in 1989, largely because

of strong domestic consumption and investment spending. Unemployment has declined for the third consecutive year, but inflation continues to be about three times the European Community average. The government is pushing economic restructuring and privatization measures in anticipation of the 1992 European Community timetable to form a single large market in Europe.
GDP: $72.1 billion, per capita $6,900; real growth rate 3.5% (1989 est.)
Inflation rate (consumer prices): 11.8% (1989 est.)
Unemployment rate: 5.9% (1989 est.)
Budget: revenues $19.0 billion; expenditures $22.2 billion, including capital expenditures of $3.1 billion (1989 est.)
Exports: $11.0 billion (f.o.b., 1988); *commodities*—cotton textiles, cork and cork products, canned fish, wine, timber and timber products, resin, machinery, appliances; *partners*—EC 72%, other developed countries 13%, US 6%
Imports: $17.7 billion (c.i.f., 1988); *commodities*—petroleum, cotton, foodgrains, industrial machinery, iron and steel, chemicals; *partners*—EC 67%, other developed countries 13%, less developed countries 15%, US 4%
External debt: $17.2 billion (1988)
Industrial production: growth rate 5.5% (1988)
Electricity: 6,729,000 kW capacity; 16,000 million kWh produced, 1,530 kWh per capita (1989)
Industries: textiles and footwear; wood pulp, paper, and cork; metalworking; oil refining; chemicals; fish canning; wine; tourism
Agriculture: accounts for 9% of GDP and 20% of labor force; small inefficient farms; imports more than half of food needs; major crops—grain, potatoes, olives, grapes; livestock sector—sheep, cattle, goats, poultry, meat, dairy products
Aid: US commitments, including Ex-Im (FY70-88), $1.8 billion; Western (non-US) countries, ODA and OOF bilateral commitments (1970-87), $998 million
Currency: Portuguese escudo (plural—escudos); 1 Portuguese escudo (Esc) = 100 centavos
Exchange rates: Portuguese escudos (Esc) per US$1—149.15 (January 1990), 157.46 (1989), 143.95 (1988), 140.88 (1987), 149.59 (1986), 170.39 (1985)
Fiscal year: calendar year

Communications

Railroads: 3,613 km total; state-owned Portuguese Railroad Co. (CP) operates 2,858 km 1.665-meter gauge (434 km electrified and 426 km double track), 755 km 1.000-meter gauge; 12 km

(1.435-meter gauge) electrified, double track, privately owned

Highways: 73,661 km total; 61,599 km paved (bituminous, gravel, and crushed stone), including 140 km of limited-access divided highway; 7,962 km improved earth; 4,100 km unimproved earth (motorable tracks)

Inland waterways: 820 km navigable; relatively unimportant to national economy, used by shallow-draft craft limited to 300-metric-ton cargo capacity

Pipelines: crude oil, 11 km; refined products, 58 km

Ports: Leixões, Lisbon, Porto, Ponta Delgada (Azores), Velas (Azores), Setúbal, Sines

Merchant marine: 50 ships (1,000 GRT or over) totaling 576,654 GRT/1,005,740 DWT; includes 1 short-sea passenger, 21 cargo, 2 refrigerated cargo, 1 container, 1 roll-on/roll-off cargo, 10 petroleum, oils, and lubricants (POL) tanker, 2 chemical tanker, 1 liquefied gas, 10 bulk, 1 combination bulk; note—Portugal has created a captive register on Madeira (MAR) for Portuguese-owned ships that will have the taxation and crewing benefits of a flag of convenience; although only one ship is currently known to fly the Portuguese flag on the MAR register, it is likely that a majority of Portuguese flag ships will transfer to this subregister in a few years

Airports: 69 total, 64 usable; 37 with permanent-surface runways; 1 with runways over 3,659 m; 11 with runways 2,440-3,659 m; 8 with runways 1,220-2,439 m

Telecommunications: facilities are generally adequate; 2,250,000 telephones; stations—44 AM, 66 (22 relays) FM, 25 (23 relays) TV; 7 submarine cables; communication satellite ground stations operating in the INTELSAT (2 Atlantic Ocean and 1 Indian Ocean), EUTELSAT, and domestic systems (mainland and Azores)

Defense Forces

Branches: Army, Navy, Air Force
Military manpower: males 15-49, 2,583,782; 2,102,835 fit for military service; 88,384 reach military age (20) annually
Defense expenditures: $1.3 billion (1989 est.)

Puerto Rico
(commonwealth associated with the US)

40 km

North Atlantic Ocean

SAN JUAN
Arecibo
Isla de Culebra
Puerto Rico
Mayagüez
Ponce
Isla de Vieques

Caribbean Sea

See regional map III

Isla Desecheo and Isla Mona are not shown.

Geography

Total area: 9,104 km²; land area: 8,959 km²
Comparative area: slightly less than three times the size of Rhode Island
Land boundaries: none
Coastline: 501 km
Maritime claims:
　Contiguous zone: 12 nm
　Continental shelf: 200 m
　Extended economic zone: 200 nm
　Territorial sea: 12 nm
Climate: tropical marine, mild, little seasonal temperature variation
Terrain: mostly mountains with coastal plain belt in north; mountains precipitous to sea on west coast
Natural resources: some copper and nickel; potential for onshore and offshore crude oil
Land use: 8% arable land; 9% permanent crops; 51% meadows and pastures; 25% forest and woodland; 7% other
Environment: many small rivers and high central mountains ensure land is well watered; south coast relatively dry; fertile coastal plain belt in north
Note: important location between the Dominican Republic and the Virgin Islands group along the Mona Passage—a key shipping lane to the Panama Canal; San Juan is one of the biggest and best natural harbors in the Caribbean

---

People

Population: 3,291,207 (July 1990), growth rate 0.1% (1990)
Birth rate: 19 births/1,000 population (1990)
Death rate: 8 deaths/1,000 population (1990)
Net migration rate: −11 migrants/1,000 population (1990)
Infant mortality rate: 17 deaths/1,000 live births (1990)

Life expectancy at birth: 68 years male, 76 years female (1990)
Total fertility rate: 2.2 children born/woman (1990)
Nationality: noun—Puerto Rican(s); adjective—Puerto Rican
Ethnic divisions: almost entirely Hispanic
Religion: mostly Christian, 85% Roman Catholic, 15% Protestant denominations and other
Language: Spanish (official); English is widely understood
Literacy: 89%
Labor force: 1,062,000; 23% government, 20% trade, 18% manufacturing, 4% agriculture, 35% other (1988)
Organized labor: 115,000 members in 4 unions; the largest is the General Confederation of Puerto Rican Workers with 35,000 members (1983)

Government

Long-form name: Commonwealth of Puerto Rico
Type: commonwealth associated with the US
Capital: San Juan
Administrative divisions: none (commonwealth associated with the US)
Independence: none (commonwealth associated with the US)
Constitution: ratified 3 March 1952; approved by US Congress 3 July 1952; effective 25 July 1952
National holiday: Constitution Day, 25 July (1952)
Legal system: based on English common law
Executive branch: US president, US vice president, governor
Legislative branch: bicameral Legislative Assembly consists of an upper house or Senate and a lower house or House of Representatives
Judicial branch: Supreme Court
Leaders: *Chief of State*—President George BUSH (since 20 January 1989); Vice President Dan QUAYLE (since 20 January 1989);
Head of Government Governor Rafael HERNANDEZ Colón (since 2 January 1989)
Political parties and leaders: Popular Democratic Party (PPD), Rafael Hernández Colón; New Progressive Party (PNP), Baltasar Corrado del Rio; Puerto Rican Socialist Party (PSP), Juan Mari Bras and Carlos Gallisa; Puerto Rican Independence Party (PIP), Rubén Berríos Martínez; Puerto Rican Communist Party (PCP), leader(s) unknown
Suffrage: universal at age 18; indigenous inhabitants are US citizens, but do not vote in US presidential elections

Puerto Rico (continued)

Elections: *Governor*—last held 8 November 1988 (next to be held November 1992); results—Rafael Hernández Colón (PPD) 48.7%, Baltasar Corrada Del Rio (PNP) 45.8%, Rubén Barríos Martínez (PIP) 5.5%;
Senate—last held 8 November 1988 (next to be held November 1992); results—percent of vote by party NA; seats—(27 total) PPD 18, PNP 8, PIP 1;
House of Representatives—last held 8 November 1988 (next to be held November 1992); results—percent of vote by party NA; seats—(53 total) PPD 36, PNP 15, PIP 2
Other political or pressure groups: all have engaged in terrorist activities—Armed Forces for National Liberation (FALN), Volunteers of the Puerto Rican Revolution, Boricua Popular Army (also known as the Macheteros), Armed Forces of Popular Resistance
Diplomatic representation: none (commonwealth associated with the US)
Flag: five equal horizontal bands of red (top and bottom) alternating with white; a blue isosceles triangle based on the hoist side bears a large white five-pointed star in the center; design based on the US flag

Economy

Overview: Puerto Rico has one of the most dynamic economies in the Caribbean region. Industry has surpassed agriculture as the primary sector of economic activity and income. Encouraged by duty-free access to the US and by tax incentives, US firms have invested heavily in Puerto Rico since the 1970s. Important new industries include pharmaceuticals, electronics, textiles, petrochemicals, and processed foods. Sugar production has lost out to dairy production and other livestock products as the main source of income in the agricultural sector. Tourism has traditionally been an important source of income for the island.
GNP: $18.4 billion, per capita $5,574; real growth rate 4.9% (FY88)
Inflation rate (consumer prices): 33% (December 1987-88)
Unemployment rate: 12.8% (December 1988)
Budget: revenues $4.9 million; expenditures $4.9 million, including capital expenditures of $NA (FY88)
Exports: $13.2 billion (f.o.b., FY88); *commodities*—sugar, coffee, petroleum products, chemical, metal products, textiles, electronic equipment; *partners*—US 87%
Imports: $11.8 billion (c.i.f., FY88); *commodities*—chemicals, clothing, food, fish products, crude oil; *partners*—US 60%
External debt: $NA

Industrial production: growth rate 5.8% (FY87)
Electricity: 4,149,000 kW capacity; 14,050 million kWh produced, 4,260 kWh per capita (1989)
Industries: tourism, manufacturing, pharmaceuticals, chemicals, food processing, petroleum refining
Agriculture: accounts for 4% of labor force; crops—sugarcane, coffee, pineapples, tobacco, bananas; livestock—cattle, chickens; imports a large share of food needs
Aid: none
Currency: US currency is used
Exchange rates: US currency is used
Fiscal year: 1 July-30 June

Communications

Railroads: 100 km rural narrow-gauge system for hauling sugarcane; no passenger railroads
Highways: 13,762 km paved
Ports: San Juan, Ponce, Mayaguez, Arecibo
Airports: 33 total; 23 usable; 19 with permanent-surface runways; none with runways over 3,659 m; 3 with runways 2,440-3,659 m; 4 with runways 1,220-2,439 m
Telecommunications: 2,000,000 radio receivers; 810,000 TV receivers; 769,140 telephones; stations—69 AM, 42 FM, 24 TV (1984)

Defense Forces

Note: defense is the responsibility of the US; paramilitary National Guard; police force of 10,050 men and women (1984)

Qatar

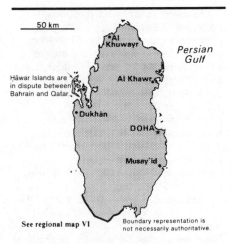

See regional map VI Boundary representation is not necessarily authoritative.

Geography

Total area: 11,000 km²; land area: 11,000 km²
Comparative area: slightly smaller than Connecticut
Land boundaries: 60 km total; Saudi Arabia 40 km, UAE 20 km
Coastline: 563 km
Maritime claims:
Continental shelf: not specific
Exclusive fishing zone: as delimited with neighboring states, or to limit of shelf, or to median line
Extended economic zone: to median line
Territorial sea: 3 nm
Disputes: boundary with UAE is in dispute; territorial dispute with Bahrain over the Ḩawār Islands
Climate: desert; hot, dry; humid and sultry in summer
Terrain: mostly flat and barren desert covered with loose sand and gravel
Natural resources: crude oil, natural gas, fish
Land use: NEGL% arable land; 0% permanent crops; 5% meadows and pastures; 0% forest and woodland; 95% other
Environment: haze, duststorms, sandstorms common; limited freshwater resources mean increasing dependence on large-scale desalination facilities
Note: strategic location in central Persian Gulf near major crude oil sources

People

Population: 490,897 (July 1990), growth rate 5.7% (1990)
Birth rate: 22 births/1,000 population (1990)
Death rate: 3 deaths/1,000 population (1990)
Net migration rate: 38 migrants/1,000 population (1990)

Infant mortality rate: 25 deaths/1,000 live births (1990)
Life expectancy at birth: 69 years male, 73 years female (1990)
Total fertility rate: 4.2 children born/woman (1990)
Nationality: noun—Qatari(s); adjective—Qatari
Ethnic divisions: 40% Arab, 18% Pakistani, 18% Indian, 10% Iranian, 14% other
Religion: 95% Muslim
Language: Arabic (official); English is commonly used as second language
Literacy: 40%
Labor force: 104,000; 85% non-Qatari in private sector (1983)
Organized labor: trade unions are illegal

Government

Long-form name: State of Qatar
Type: traditional monarchy
Capital: Doha
Administrative divisions: none
Independence: 3 September 1971 (from UK)
Constitution: provisional constitution enacted 2 April 1970
Legal system: discretionary system of law controlled by the amir, although civil codes are being implemented; Islamic law is significant in personal matters
National holiday: Independence Day, 3 September (1971)
Executive branch: amir, Council of Ministers (cabinet)
Legislative branch: unicameral Advisory Council (Majlis al-Shura)
Judicial branch: Court of Appeal
Leaders: *Chief of State and Head of Government*—Amir and Prime Minister Khalifa bin Hamad Al THANI (since 22 February 1972); Heir Apparent Hamad bin Khalifa AL THANI (appointed 31 May 1977; son of Amir)
Political parties and leaders: none
Suffrage: none
Elections: *Advisory Council*—constitution calls for elections for part of this consultative body, but no elections have been held; seats—(30 total)
Member of: Arab League, FAO, G-77, GATT (de facto), GCC, IBRD, ICAO, IDB—Islamic Development Bank, IFAD, ILO, IMF, IMO, INTELSAT, INTERPOL, ITU, NAM, OAPEC, OIC, OPEC, UN, UNESCO, UPU, WHO, WIPO, WMO
Diplomatic representation: Ambassador Hamad 'Abd al-'Aziz AL-KAWARI, Chancery at Suite 1180, 600 New Hampshire Avenue NW, Washington DC 20037; telephone (202) 338-0111; *US*—Ambassador Mark G. HAMBLEY; Embassy at Fariq Bin Omran (opposite the television station), Doha (mailing address is P. O. Box 2399, Doha); telephone [974] 864701 through 864703
Flag: maroon with a broad white serrated band (nine white points) on the hoist side

Economy

Overview: Oil is the backbone of the economy and accounts for 90% of export earnings and more than 80% of government revenues. Proved oil reserves of 3.3 billion barrels should ensure continued output at current levels for about 25 years. Oil has given Qatar a per capita GDP of about $17,000, among the highest in the world.
GDP: $5.4 billion, per capita $17,070; real growth rate 9.0% (1987)
Inflation rate (consumer prices): 1.6% (1987)
Unemployment rate: NA%
Budget: revenues $1.7 billion; expenditures $3.4 billion, including capital expenditures of $NA (FY88 est.)
Exports: $2.2 billion (f.o.b., 1988 est.); *commodities*—petroleum products 90%, steel, fertilizers; *partners*—France, FRG, Italy, Japan, Spain
Imports: $1.0 billion (f.o.b., 1988 est.), excluding military equipment; *commodities*—foodstuffs, beverages, animal and vegetable oils, chemicals, machinery and equipment; *partners*—EC, Japan, Arab countries, US, Australia
External debt: $1.1 billion (December 1989 est.)
Industrial production: growth rate 0.6% (1987)
Electricity: 1,514,000 kW capacity; 4,000 million kWh produced, 8,540 kWh per capita (1989)
Industries: crude oil production and refining, fertilizers, petrochemicals, steel, cement
Agriculture: farming and grazing on small scale, less than 2% of GDP; commercial fishing increasing in importance; most food imported
Aid: donor—pledged $2.7 billion in ODA to less developed countries (1979- 88)
Currency: Qatari riyal (plural—riyals); 1 Qatari riyal (QR) = 100 dirhams
Exchange rates: Qatari riyals (QR) per US$1—3.6400 riyals (fixed rate)
Fiscal year: 1 April-31 March

Communications

Highways: 1,500 km total; 1,000 km bituminous, 500 km gravel or natural surface (est.)
Pipelines: crude oil, 235 km; natural gas, 400 km
Ports: Doha, Musayid, Halul Island
Merchant marine: 12 ships (1,000 GRT or over) totaling 273,318 GRT/420,227 DWT; includes 7 cargo, 3 container, 2 petroleum, oils, and lubricants (POL) tanker
Civil air: 3 major transport aircraft
Airports: 4 total, 4 usable; 1 with permanent-surface runways; 1 with runways over 3,659 m; none with runways 2,440-3,659 m; 2 with runways 1,220-2,439 m
Telecommunications: modern system centered in Doha; 110,000 telephones; tropospheric scatter to Bahrain; radio relay to Saudi Arabia; submarine cable to Bahrain and UAE; stations—2 AM, 1 FM, 3 TV; satellite earth stations—1 Atlantic Ocean INTELSAT, 1 Indian Ocean INTELSAT, 1 ARABSAT

Defense Forces

Branches: Army, Navy, Air Force, Police Department
Military manpower: males 15-49, 255,474; 120,614 fit for military service; 3,982 reach military age (18) annually
Defense expenditures: NA

259

Reunion
(overseas department of France)

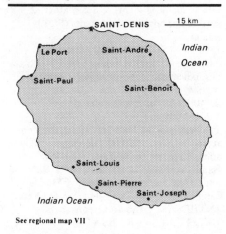

SAINT-DENIS

15 km

Indian Ocean

Le Port

Saint-André

Saint-Paul

Saint-Benoit

Saint-Louis

Saint-Pierre

Saint-Joseph

Indian Ocean

See regional map VII

Geography

Total area: 2,510 km²; land area: 2,500 km²
Comparative area: slightly smaller than Rhode Island
Land boundaries: none
Coastline: 201 km
Maritime claims:
  Continental shelf: 200 meters or to depth of exploitation
  Extended economic zone: 200 nm
  Territorial sea: 12 nm
Climate: tropical, but moderates with elevation; cool and dry from May to November, hot and rainy from November to April
Terrain: mostly rugged and mountainous; fertile lowlands along coast
Natural resources: fish, arable land
Land use: 20% arable land; 2% permanent crops; 4% meadows and pastures; 35% forest and woodland; 39% other; includes 2% irrigated
Environment: periodic devastating cyclones
Note: located 750 km east of Madagascar in the Indian Ocean

People

Population: 595,583 (July 1990), growth rate 1.9% (1990)
Birth rate: 24 births/1,000 population (1990)
Death rate: 5 deaths/1,000 population (1990)
Net migration rate: 0 migrants/1,000 population (1990)
Infant mortality rate: 9 deaths/1,000 live births (1990)
Life expectancy at birth: 70 years male, 76 years female (1990)
Total fertility rate: 2.6 children born/woman (1990)
Nationality: noun—Reunionese (sing. and pl.); adjective—Reunionese

Ethnic divisions: most of the population is of intermixed French, African, Malagasy, Chinese, Pakistani, and Indian ancestry
Religion: 94% Roman Catholic
Language: French (official); Creole widely used
Literacy: NA%, but over 80% among younger generation
Labor force: NA; 30% agriculture, 21% industry, 49% services (1981); 63% of population of working age (1983)
Organized labor: General Confederation of Workers of Reunion (CGTR)

Government

Long-form name: Department of Reunion
Type: overseas department of France
Capital: Saint-Denis
Administrative divisions: none (overseas department of France)
Independence: none (overseas department of France)
Constitution: 28 September 1958 (French Constitution)
Legal system: French law
National holiday: Taking of the Bastille, 14 July (1789)
Executive branch: French president, Commissioner of the Republic
Legislative branch: unicameral General Council, unicameral Regional Council
Judicial branch: Court of Appeals (Cour d'appel)
Leaders: *Chief of State*—President François MITTERRAND (since 21 May 1981);
Head of Government—Commissioner of the Republic Daniel CONSTANTIN (since September 1989)
Political parties and leaders: Rally for the Republic (RPR), François Mas; Union for French Democracy (UDF), Gilbert Gerard; Communist Party of Reunion (PCR); France-Reunion Future (FRA), André Thien Ah Koon; Socialist Party (PS), Jean-Claude Fruteau; Social Democrats (CDS), other small parties
Suffrage: universal at age 18
Elections: *Regional Council*—last held 16 March 1986 (next to be held March 1991); results—RPR/UDF 36.8%, PCR 28.2%, FRA and other right wing 17.3%, PS 14.1%, other 3.6%; seats—(45 total) RPR/UDF 18, PCR 13, FRA and other right wing 8, PS 6;
French Senate—last held 24 September 1989 (next to be held September 1992); results—percent of vote by party NA; seats—(3 total) RPR-UDF 1, PS 1, independent 1;
French National Assembly—last held 5 and 12 June 1988 (next to be held June 1993); results—percent of vote by party NA; seats—(5 total) PCR 2, RPR 1, UDF-CDS 1, FRA 1

Communists: Communist party small but has support among sugarcane cutters, the minuscule Popular Movement for the Liberation of Reunion (MPLR), and in the district of Le Port
Member of: WFTU
Diplomatic representation: as an overseas department of France, Reunionese interests are represented in the US by France
Flag: the flag of France is used

Economy

Overview: The economy has traditionally been based on agriculture. Sugarcane has been the primary crop for more than a century, and in some years it accounts for 85% of exports. The government is pushing the development of a tourist industry to relieve a high unemployment rate that was over 30% in 1986. The economic well-being of Reunion depends heavily on continued financial assistance from France.
GDP: $2.4 billion, per capita $4,290 (1985); real growth rate 9% (1987 est.)
Inflation rate (consumer prices): 2.8% (1987)
Unemployment rate: 32.0%; high seasonal unemployment (1986)
Budget: revenues $358 million; expenditures $914 million, including capital expenditures of $NA (1986)
Exports: $136 million (f.o.b., 1986); *commodities*—sugar 75%, rum and molasses 4%, perfume essences 4%, vanilla and tea 1%; *partners*—France, Mauritius, Bahrain, S. Africa, Italy
Imports: $1.1 million (c.i.f., 1986); *commodities*—manufactured goods, food, beverages, tobacco, machinery and transportation equipment, raw materials, and petroleum products; *partners*—France, Mauritius, Bahrain, South Africa, Italy
External debt: NA
Industrial production: growth rate NA%
Electricity: 245,000 kW capacity; 546 million kWh produced, 965 kWh per capita (1989)
Industries: sugar, rum, cigarettes, several small shops producing handicraft items
Agriculture: accounts for 30% of labor force; dominant sector of economy; cash crops—sugarcane, vanilla, tobacco; food crops—tropical fruits, vegetables, corn; imports large share of food needs
Aid: Western (non-US) countries, ODA and OOF bilateral commitments (1970-87), $13.5 billion
Currency: French franc (plural—francs); 1 French franc (F) = 100 centimes
Exchange rates: French francs (F) per US$1—5.7598 (January 1990), 6.3801 (1989), 5.9569 (1988), 6.0107 (1987), 6.9261 (1986), 8.9852 (1985)
Fiscal year: calendar year

260

Romania

Communications

Highways: 2,800 km total; 2,200 km paved, 600 km gravel, crushed stone, or stabilized earth
Ports: Pointe des Galets
Civil air: 1 major transport aircraft
Airports: 2 total, 2 usable; 2 with permanent-surface runways; none with runways over 3,659 m; 1 with runways 2,440-3,659 m; 1 with runways 1,220-2,439 m
Telecommunications: adequate system for needs; modern open-wire line and radio relay network; principal center Saint-Denis; radiocommunication to Comoros, France, Madagascar; new radio relay route to Mauritius; 85,900 telephones; stations—3 AM, 13 FM, 1 (18 relays) TV; 1 Indian Ocean INTELSAT earth station

Defense Forces

Military manpower: males 15-49, 158,812; 82,400 fit for military service; 6,075 reach military age (18) annually
Note: defense is the responsibility of France

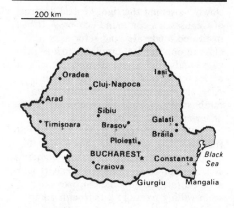

See regional map V

Geography

Total area: 237,500 km^2; land area: 230,340 km^2
Comparative area: slightly smaller than Oregon
Land boundaries: 2,904 km total; Bulgaria 608 km, Hungary 443 km, USSR 1,307 km, Yugoslavia 546 km
Coastline: 225 km
Maritime claims:
  Continental shelf: 200 meters or to depth of exploitation
  Extended economic zone: 200 nm
  Territorial sea: 12 nm
Disputes: Transylvania question with Hungary; Bessarabia question with USSR
Climate: temperate; cold, cloudy winters with frequent snow and fog; sunny summers with frequent showers and thunderstorms
Terrain: central Transylvanian Basin is separated from the plain of Moldavia on the east by the Carpathian Mountains and separated from the Walachian Plain on the south by the Transylvanian Alps
Natural resources: crude oil (reserves being exhausted), timber, natural gas, coal, iron ore, salt
Land use: 43% arable land; 3% permanent crops; 19% meadows and pastures; 28% forest and woodland; 7% other; includes 11% irrigated
Environment: frequent earthquakes most severe in south and southwest; geologic structure and climate promote landslides, air pollution in south
Note: controls most easily traversable land route between the Balkans and western USSR

People

Population: 23,273,285 (July 1990), growth rate 0.5% (1990)
Birth rate: 16 births/1,000 population (1990)

Death rate: 10 deaths/1,000 population (1990)
Net migration rate: −1 migrants/1,000 population (1990)
Infant mortality rate: 19 deaths/1,000 live births (1990)
Life expectancy at birth: 69 years male, 75 years female (1990)
Total fertility rate: 2.2 children born/ woman (1990)
Nationality: noun—Romanian(s); adjective—Romanian
Ethnic divisions: 89.1% Romanian; 7.8% Hungarian; 1.5% German; 1.6% Ukrainian, Serb, Croat, Russian, Turk, and Gypsy
Religion: 80% Romanian Orthodox; 6% Roman Catholic; 4% Calvinist, Lutheran, Jewish, Baptist
Language: Romanian, Hungarian, German
Literacy: 98%
Labor force: 10,690,000; 34% industry, 28% agriculture, 38% other (1987)
Organized labor: until December 1989, a single trade union system organized by the General Confederation of Romanian Trade Unions (UGSR) under control of the Communist Party; since Ceauşescu's overthrow, newly-created trade and professional trade unions are joining two rival umbrella organizations—Organization of Free Trade Unions and Fratia (Brotherhood)

Government

Long-form name: none
Type: former Communist state; current multiparty provisional government has scheduled a general democratic election for 20 May 1990
Capital: Bucharest
Administrative divisions: 40 counties (judeţe, singular—judeţ) and 1 municipality* (municipiu); Alba, Arad, Argeş, Bacău, Bihor, Bistriţa-Năsăud, Botoşani, Brăila, Braşov, Bucureşti*, Buzău, Călăraşi, Caraş-Severin, Cluj, Constanţa, Covasna, Dîmboviţa, Dolj, Galaţi, Gorj, Giurgiu, Harghita, Hunedoara, Ialomiţa, Iaşi, Maramureş, Mehedinţi, Mureş, Neamţ, Olt, Prahova, Sălaj, Satu Mare, Sibiu, Suceava, Teleorman, Timiş, Tulcea, Vaslui, Vîlcea, Vrancea
Independence: 1881 (from Turkey); republic proclaimed 30 December 1947
Constitution: 21 August 1965; new constitution being drafted
Legal system: former mixture of civil law system and Communist legal theory that increasingly reflected Romanian traditions is being revised; Communist regime had not accepted compulsory ICJ jurisdiction; Provisional Council of National Unity will probably accept ICJ jurisdiction

National holiday: Liberation Day, 23 August (1944); new national day to commemorate popular anti-Ceauşescu uprising under discussion

Executive branch: president, vice president, prime minister, and Council of Ministers (cabinet) appointed by provisional government

Legislative branch: bicameral Parliament consists of an upper house or Senate (Senat) and a lower house or House of Deputies (Adunarea Deputaţilor)

Judicial branch: Supreme Court of Justice

Leaders: *Chief of State*—President of Provisional Council of National Unity Ion ILIESCU (since 23 December 1989); *Head of Government*—Prime Minister of Council of Ministers Petre ROMAN (since 23 December 1989)

Political parties and leaders: Social Democratic Party, Sergiu Cunescu; National Liberal Party, Radu Cimpeanu; National Christian Peasants Party, Corneliu Coposu; Free Democratic Social Justice Party, Gheorghe Susana; several others being formed; Communist Party has ceased to exist; formation of left-wing parties is uncertain

Suffrage: universal at age 18

Elections: *Senate*—elections for the new upper house to be held 20 May 1990; *House of Deputies*—elections for the new lower house to be held 20 May 1990

Communists: 3,400,000 (November 1984); Communist Party has ceased to exist

Member of: CCC, CEMA, FAO, G-77, GATT, IAEA, IBRD, ICAO, IFAD, ILO, IMF, IMO, INTERPOL, IPU, ITC, ITU, UN, UNESCO, UPU, Warsaw Pact, WFTU, WHO, WIPO, WMO, WTO

Diplomatic representation: Ambassador Virgil CONSTANTINESCU; Chancery at 1607 23rd Street NW, Washington DC 20008; telephone (202) 232-4747; *US*—Ambassador Alan GREEN, Jr.; Embassy at Strada Tudor Arghezi 7-9, Bucharest (mailing address is APO New York 09213); telephone [40] (0) 10-40-40

Flag: three equal vertical bands of blue (hoist side), yellow, and red; the national coat of arms that used to be centered in the yellow band, has been removed; now similar to the flags of Andorra and Chad

Economy

Overview: Industry, which accounts for one-third of the labor force and generates over half the GNP, suffers from an aging capital plant and persistent shortages of energy. In recent years the agricultural sector has had to contend with drought, mismanagement, and shortages of inputs. Favorable weather in 1989 helped produce a good harvest, although far below government claims. The new government is slowly loosening the tight central controls of Ceauşescu's command economy. It has instituted moderate land reforms, with close to one-third of cropland now in private hands, and it has allowed changes in prices for private agricultural output. Also, the new regime is permitting the establishment of private enterprises of 20 or fewer employees in services, handicrafts, and small-scale industry. Furthermore, the government has halted the old policy of diverting food from domestic consumption to hard currency export markets. So far, the government does not seem willing to adopt a thorough-going market system.

GNP: $79.8 billion, per capita $3,445; real growth rate –1.5% (1989 est.)

Inflation rate (consumer prices): 0% (1987)

Unemployment rate: NA%

Budget: revenues $26 billion; expenditures $21.6 billion, including capital expenditures of $13.6 billion (1987)

Exports: $11.5 billion (f.o.b., 1988); *commodities*—machinery and equipment 34.7%, fuels, minerals and metals 24.7%, manufactured consumer goods 16.9%, agricultural materials and forestry products 11.9%, other 11.6% (1986); *partners*—USSR 27%, Eastern Europe 23%, EC 15%, US 5%, China 4% (1987)

Imports: $8.75 billion (f.o.b., 1988); *commodities*—fuels, minerals, and metals 51.0%, machinery and equipment 26.7%, agricultural and forestry products 11.0%, manufactured consumer goods 4.2% (1986); *partners*—Communist countries 60%, non-Communist countries 40% (1987)

External debt: none (mid-1989)

Industrial production: growth rate 3.6% (1988)

Electricity: 22,640,000 kW capacity; 80,000 million kWh produced, 3,440 kWh per capita (1989)

Industries: mining, timber, construction materials, metallurgy, chemicals, machine building, food processing, petroleum

Agriculture: accounts for 15% of GNP and 28% of labor force; major wheat and corn producer; other products—sugar beets, sunflower seed, potatoes, milk, eggs, meat, grapes

Aid: donor—$4.3 billion in bilateral aid to non-Communist less developed countries (1956-88)

Currency: leu (plural—lei); 1 leu (L) = 100 bani

Exchange rates: lei (L) per US$1—20.96 (February 1990), 14.922 (1989), 14.277 (1988), 14.557 (1987), 16.153 (1986), 17.141 (1985)

Fiscal year: calendar year

Communications

Railroads: 11,221 km total; 10,755 km 1.435-meter standard gauge, 421 km narrow gauge, 45 km broad gauge; 3,328 km electrified, 3,060 km double track; government owned (1986)

Highways: 72,799 km total; 15,762 km concrete, asphalt, stone block; 20,208 km asphalt treated; 27,729 km gravel, crushed stone, and other paved surfaces; 9,100 km unpaved roads (1985)

Inland waterways: 1,724 km (1984)

Pipelines: 2,800 km crude oil; 1,429 km refined products; 6,400 km natural gas

Ports: Constanta, Galati, Braila, Mangalia; inland ports are Giurgiu, Drobeta-Turnu Severin, Orsova

Merchant marine: 282 ships (1,000 GRT or over) totaling 3,313,320 GRT/5,134,335 DWT; includes 1 passenger-cargo, 184 cargo, 1 container, 1 rail-car carrier, 14 roll-on/roll-off cargo, 2 livestock carrier, 10 petroleum, oils, and lubricants (POL) tanker, 69 bulk

Civil air: 70 major transport aircraft

Airports: 165 total, 165 usable; 25 with permanent-surface runways; 15 with runways 2,440-3,659 m; 15 with runways 1,220-2,439 m

Telecommunications: stations—39 AM, 30 FM, 38 TV; 3,910,000 TV sets; 3,225,000 radio receivers; satellite earth stations—1 Indian Ocean INTELSAT and 1 Atlantic Ocean INTELSAT

Defense Forces

Branches: Romanian Army, Security Troops, Air and Air Defense Forces, Romanian Navy

Military manpower: males 15-49, 5,736,783; 4,860,427 fit for military service; 193,537 reach military age (20) annually

Defense expenditures: 11.8 billion lei, 2.8% of total budget (1989); note—conversion of the military budget into US dollars using the official administratively set exchange rate would produce misleading results

Rwanda

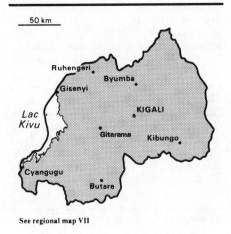

50 km

See regional map VII

Geography

Total area: 26,340 km²; land area: 24,950 km²
Comparative area: slightly smaller than Maryland
Land boundaries: 893 km total; Burundi 290 km, Tanzania 217 km, Uganda 169 km, Zaire 217 km
Coastline: none—landlocked
Maritime claims: none—landlocked
Climate: temperate; two rainy seasons (February to April, November to January); mild in mountains with frost and snow possible
Terrain: mostly grassy uplands and hills; mountains in west
Natural resources: gold, cassiterite (tin ore), wolframite (tungsten ore), natural gas, hydropower
Land use: 29% arable land; 11% permanent crops; 18% meadows and pastures; 10% forest and woodland; 32% other; includes NEGL% irrigated
Environment: deforestation; overgrazing; soil exhaustion; soil erosion; periodic droughts
Note: landlocked

People

Population: 7,609,119 (July 1990), growth rate 3.8% (1990)
Birth rate: 53 births/1,000 population (1990)
Death rate: 15 deaths/1,000 population (1990)
Net migration rate: 0 migrants/1,000 population (1990)
Infant mortality rate: 113 deaths/1,000 live births (1990)
Life expectancy at birth: 50 years male, 54 years female (1990)
Total fertility rate: 8.5 children born/woman (1990)
Nationality: noun and adjective—Rwandan(s)

Ethnic divisions: Hutu 90%, Tutsi 9%, Twa (Pygmoid) 1%
Religion: Roman Catholic 65%, Protestant 9%, Muslim 1%, indigenous beliefs and other 25%
Language: Kinyarwanda, French (official); Kiswahili used in commercial centers
Literacy: 46.6%
Labor force: 3,600,000; 93% agriculture, 5% government and services, 2% industry and commerce; 49% of population of working age (1985)
Organized labor: NA

Government

Long-form name: Republic of Rwanda
Type: republic; presidential system in which military leaders hold key offices
Capital: Kigali
Administrative divisions: 10 prefectures (préfectures, singular—préfecture in French; plural—NA, singular—prefegitura in Kinyarwanda); Butare, Byumba, Cyangugu, Gikongoro, Gisenyi, Gitarama, Kibungo, Kibuye, Rigali, Ruhengeri
Constitution: 17 December 1978
Independence: 1 July 1962 (from UN trusteeship under Belgian administration)
Legal system: based on German and Belgian civil law systems and customary law; judicial review of legislative acts in the Supreme Court; has not accepted compulsory ICJ jurisdiction
National holiday: Independence Day, 1 July (1962)
Executive branch: president, Council of Ministers (cabinet)
Legislative branch: unicameral National Development Council (Conseil pour le Développement National)
Judicial branch: Constitutional Court (consists of the Court of Cassation and the Council of State in joint session)
Leaders: *Chief of State and Head of Government*—President Maj. Gen. Juvénal HABYARIMANA (since 5 July 1973)
Political parties and leaders: only party—National Revolutionary Movement for Development (MRND), Maj. Gen. Juvénal Habyarimana (officially a development movement, not a party)
Suffrage: universal adult, exact age NA
Elections: *President*—last held 19 December 1988 (next to be held December 1993); results—President Maj. Gen. Juvénal Habyarimana reelected;
National Development Council—last held 19 December 1988 (next to be held December 1993); results—MRND is the only party; seats—(70 total); MRND 70
Communists: no Communist party
Member of: ACP, AfDB, EAMA, CCC, FAO, G-77, GATT, IBRD, ICAO, ICO, IDA, IFAD, IFC, ILO, IMF, INTELSAT, INTERPOL, IPU, ITU, NAM, OAU, OCAM, UN, UNESCO, UPU, WHO, WMO, WTO
Diplomatic representation: Ambassador Aloys UWIMANA; Chancery at 1714 New Hampshire Avenue NW, Washington DC 20009; telephone (202) 232-2882; *US*—Ambassador Leonard H. O. SPEARMAN, Sr.; Embassy at Boulevard de la Revolution, Kigali (mailing address is B. P. 28, Kigali); telephone [205] 75601 through 75603 or 72126 through 72128
Flag: three equal vertical bands of red (hoist side), yellow, and green with a large black letter *R* centered in the yellow band; uses the popular pan-African colors of Ethiopia; similar to the flag of Guinea, which has a plain yellow band

Economy

Overview: About 40% of GDP comes from the agricultural sector; coffee and tea make up 80-90% of total exports. The amount of fertile land is limited, however, and deforestation and soil erosion have created problems. The industrial sector in Rwanda is small, contributing less than 20% to GDP. Manufacturing focuses mainly on the processing of agricultural products. The Rwandan economy remains dependent on coffee exports and foreign aid, with no relief in sight. Weak international prices since 1986 have caused the economy to contract and per capita GDP to decline.
GDP: $2.3 billion, per capita $325; real growth rate −2.5% (1988 est.)
Inflation rate (consumer prices): 3% (1988)
Unemployment rate: NA%
Budget: revenues $413 million; expenditures $522 million, including capital expenditures of $230 million (1988 est.)
Exports: $118 million (f.o.b., 1988); *commodities*—coffee 85%, tea, tin, cassiterite, wolframite, pyrethrum; *partners*—FRG, Belgium, Italy, Uganda, UK, France, US
Imports: $278 million (f.o.b., 1988); *commodities*—textiles, foodstuffs, machines and equipment, capital goods, steel, petroleum products, cement and construction material; *partners*—US, Belgium, FRG, Kenya, Japan
External debt: $645 million (December 1989 est.)
Industrial production: growth rate 1.2% (1988)
Electricity: 26,000 kW capacity; 112 million kWh produced, 15 kWh per capita (1989)
Industries: mining of cassiterite (tin ore) and wolframite (tungsten ore), tin, cement, agricultural processing, small-scale beverage production, soap, furniture, shoes, plastic goods, textiles, cigarettes
Agriculture: cash crops—coffee, tea, pyrethrum (insecticide made from

Rwanda (continued)

chrysanthemums); main food crops—bananas, beans, sorghum, potatoes; stock raising; self-sufficiency declining; country imports foodstuffs as farm production fails to keep up with a 3.8% annual growth in population

Aid: US commitments, including Ex-Im (FY70-88), $118 million; Western (non-US) countries, ODA and OOF bilateral commitments (1970-87), $1.7 billion; OPEC bilateral aid (1979-89), $45 million; Communist countries (1970-88), $58 million

Currency: Rwandan franc (plural—francs); 1 Rwandan franc (RF) = 100 centimes

Exchange rates: Rwandan francs (RF) per US$1—78.99 (December 1989), 79.98 (1989), 76.45 (1988), 79.67 (1987), 87.64 (1986), 101.26 (1985)

Fiscal year: calendar year

Communications

Highways: 4,885 km total; 460 km paved, 1,725 km gravel and/or improved earth, 2,700 km unimproved

Inland waterways: Lac Kivu navigable by shallow-draft barges and native craft

Civil air: 1 major transport aircraft

Airports: 8 total, 8 usable; 2 with permanent-surface runways; none with runways over 3,659 m; 1 with runways 2,440-3,659 m; 2 with runways 1,220-2,439 m

Telecommunications: fair system with low-capacity radio relay system centered on Kigali; 6,600 telephones; stations—2 AM, 5 FM, no TV; satellite earth stations—1 Indian Ocean INTELSAT and 1 SYMPHONIE

Defense Forces

Branches: Army, paramilitary, Gendarmerie

Military manpower: males 15-49, 1,586,989; 810,560 fit for military service; no conscription

Defense expenditures: 2.1% of GDP (1987)

St. Helena
(dependent territory of the UK)

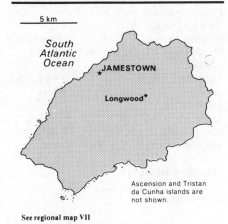

South Atlantic Ocean
★JAMESTOWN
Longwood ·

Ascension and Tristan da Cunha islands are not shown.

See regional map VII

Geography

Total area: 410 km²; land area: 410 km²; includes Ascension, Gough Island, Inaccessible Island, Nightingale Island, and Tristan da Cunha

Comparative area: slightly more than 2.3 times the size of Washington, DC

Land boundaries: none

Coastline: 60 km

Maritime claims:
Exclusive fishing zone: 200 nm
Territorial sea: 12 nm

Climate: tropical; marine; mild, tempered by trade winds

Terrain: rugged, volcanic; small scattered plateaus and plains

Natural resources: fish; Ascension is a breeding ground for sea turtles and sooty terns; no minerals

Land use: 7% arable land; 0% permanent crops; 7% meadows and pastures; 3% forest and woodland; 83% other

Environment: very few perennial streams

Note: Napoleon Bonaparte's place of exile and burial; the remains were taken to Paris in 1840

People

Population: 6,657 (July 1990), growth rate 0.6% (1990)

Birth rate: 13 births/1,000 population (1990)

Death rate: 8 deaths/1,000 population (1990)

Net migration rate: NEGl migrants/1,000 population (1990)

Infant mortality rate: 46 deaths/1,000 live births (1990)

Life expectancy at birth: 70 years male, 75 years female (1990)

Total fertility rate: 1.4 children born/woman (1990)

Nationality: noun—St. Helenian(s); adjective—St. Helenian

Ethnic divisions: NA

Religion: Anglican majority; also Baptist, Seventh-Day Adventist, and Roman Catholic

Language: English

Literacy: NA%, but probably high

Labor force: NA

Organized labor: St. Helena General Workers' Union, 472 members; 17% crafts, 10% professional and technical, 10% service, 9% management and clerical, 9% farming and fishing, 6% transport, 5% sales, 1% security, and 33% other

Government

Long-form name: none

Type: dependent territory of the UK

Capital: Jamestown

Administrative divisions: 2 dependencies and 1 administrative area*; Ascension*, Saint Helena, Tristan da Cunha

Independence: none (dependent territory of the UK)

Constitution: 1 January 1967

Legal system: NA

National holiday: Celebration of the Birthday of the Queen (second Saturday in June), 10 June 1989

Executive branch: British monarch, governor, Executive Council (cabinet)

Legislative branch: unicameral Legislative Council

Judicial branch: Supreme Court

Leaders: *Chief of State*—Queen ELIZABETH II (since 6 February 1952);
Head of Government—Governor and Commander in Chief Robert F. STIMSON (since 1987)

Political parties and leaders: St. Helena Labor Party, G. A. O. Thornton; St. Helena Progressive Party, leader unknown; note—both political parties inactive since 1976

Suffrage: NA

Elections: *Legislative Council*—last held October 1984 (next to be held NA); results—percent of vote by party NA; seats—(15 total, 12 elected) number of seats by party NA

Communists: probably none

Diplomatic representation: none (dependent territory of the UK)

Flag: blue with the flag of the UK in the upper hoist-side quadrant and the St. Helenian shield centered on the outer half of the flag; the shield features a rocky coastline and three-masted sailing ship

Economy

Overview: The economy depends primarily on financial assistance from the UK. The local population earns some income from fishing, the rearing of livestock, and sales of handicrafts. Because there are few jobs, a large proportion of the work force have left to seek employment overseas.
GDP: $NA, per capita $NA; real growth rate NA%
Inflation rate (consumer prices): −1.1% (1986)
Unemployment rate: NA%
Budget: revenues $3.2 million; expenditures $2.9 million, including capital expenditures of NA (1984)
Exports: $23.9 thousand (f.o.b., 1984); *commodities*—fish (frozen skipjack, tuna, salt-dried skipjack), handicrafts; *partners*—South Africa, UK
Imports: $2.4 million (c.i.f., 1984); *commodities*—food, beverages, tobacco, fuel oils, animal feed, building materials, motor vehicles and parts, machinery and parts; *partners*—UK, South Africa
External debt: $NA
Industrial production: growth rate NA%
Electricity: 9,800 kW capacity; 10 million kWh produced, 1,390 kWh per capita (1989)
Industries: crafts (furniture, lacework, fancy woodwork), fish
Agriculture: maize, potatoes, vegetables; timber production being developed; crawfishing on Tristan da Cunha
Aid: Western (non-US) countries, ODA and OOF bilateral commitments (1970-87), $168 million
Currency: St. Helenian pound (plural—pounds); 1 St. Helenian pound (£S) = 100 pence
Exchange rates: St. Helenian pounds (£S) per US$1—0.6055 (January 1990), 0.6099 (1989), 0.5614 (1988), 0.6102 (1987), 0.6817 (1986), 0.7714 (1985); note—the St. Helenian pound is at par with the British pound
Fiscal year: 1 April-31 March

Communications

Highways: 87 km bitumen-sealed roads, 20 km earth roads on St. Helena; 80 km bitumen-sealed on Ascension; 2.7 km bitumen-sealed on Tristan da Cunha
Ports: Jamestown (St. Helena), Georgetown (Ascension)

Merchant marine: 1 passenger-cargo ship totaling 3,150 GRT/2,264 DWT
Airports: 1 with permanent-surface runway 2,440-3,659 m on Ascension
Telecommunications: 1,500 radio receivers; stations—1 AM, no FM, no TV; 550 telephones in automatic network; HF radio links to Ascension, then into worldwide submarine cable and satellite networks; major coaxial cable relay point between South Africa, Portugal, and UK at Ascension; 2 Atlantic Ocean INTELSAT earth stations

Defense Forces

Note: defense is the responsibility of the UK

St. Kitts and Nevis

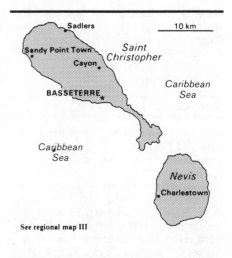

See regional map III

Geography

Total area: 360 km²; land area: 360 km²
Comparative area: slightly more than twice the size of Washington, DC
Land boundaries: none
Coastline: 135 km
Maritime claims:
  Contiguous zone: 24 nm
  Extended economic zone: 200 nm
  Territorial sea: 12 nm
Climate: subtropical tempered by constant sea breezes; little seasonal temperature variation; rainy season (May to November)
Terrain: volcanic with mountainous interiors
Natural resources: negligible
Land use: 22% arable land; 17% permanent crops; 3% meadows and pastures; 17% forest and woodland; 41% other
Environment: subject to hurricanes (July to October)
Note: located 320 km southeast of Puerto Rico

People

Population: 40,157 (July 1990), growth rate 0.3% (1990)
Birth rate: 24 births/1,000 population (1990)
Death rate: 10 deaths/1,000 population (1990)
Net migration rate: −11 migrants/1,000 population (1990)
Infant mortality rate: 40 deaths/1,000 live births (1990)
Life expectancy at birth: 64 years male, 71 years female (1990)
Total fertility rate: 2.7 children born/woman (1990)
Ethnic divisions: mainly of black African descent
Nationality: noun—Kittsian(s), Nevisian(s); adjective—Kittsian, Nevisian

St. Kitts and Nevis (continued)

Religion: Anglican, other Protestant sects, Roman Catholic
Language: English
Literacy: 80%
Labor force: 20,000 (1981)
Organized labor: 6,700

Government

Long-form name: Federation of Saint Kitts and Nevis
Type: constitutional monarchy
Capital: Basseterre
Administrative divisions: 14 parishs; Christ Church Nichola Town, Saint Anne Sandy Point, Saint George Basseterre, Saint George Gingerland, Saint James Windward, Saint John Capisterre, Saint John Figtree, Saint Mary Cayon, Saint Paul Capisterre, Saint Paul Charlestown, Saint Peter Basseterre, Saint Thomas Lowland, Saint Thomas Middle Island, Trinity Palmetto Point
Independence: 19 September 1983 (from UK)
Constitution: 19 September 1983
Legal system: based on English common law
National holiday: Independence Day, 19 September (1983)
Executive branch: British monarch, governor general, prime minister, deputy prime minister, Cabinet
Legislative branch: unicameral House of Assembly (sometimes referred to as the National Assembly)
Judicial branch: Eastern Caribbean Supreme Court
Leaders: *Chief of State*—Queen ELIZABETH II (since 6 February 1952), represented by Governor General Sir Clement Athelston ARRINDELL (since 19 September 1983, previously Governor General of the Associated State since November 1981);
Head of Government—Prime Minister Dr. Kennedy Alphonse SIMMONDS (since 19 September 1983, previously Premier of the Associated State since February 1980); Deputy Prime Minister Michael Oliver POWELL (since NA)
Political parties and leaders: People's Action Movement (PAM), Kennedy Simmonds; St. Kitts and Nevis Labor Party (SKNLP), Lee Moore; Nevis Reformation Party (NRP), Simeon Daniel; Concerned Citizens Movement (CCM), Vance Amory
Suffrage: universal adult at age NA
Elections: *House of Assembly*—last held 21 March 1989 (next to be held by 21 March 1994); seats—(14 total, 11 elected) PAM 6, SKNLP 2, NRP 2, CCM 1
Communists: none known
Member of: ACP, CARICOM, Commonwealth, FAO, IBRD, IMF, ISO, OAS, OECS, UN

Diplomatic representation:
Minister-Counselor (Deputy Chief of Mission), Chargé d'Affaires ad interim Erstein M. EDWARDS; Chancery at Suite 540, 2501 M Street NW, Washington DC 20037; telephone (202) 833-3550; *US*—none
Flag: divided diagonally from the lower hoist side by a broad black band bearing two white five-pointed stars; the black band is edged in yellow; the upper triangle is green, the lower triangle is red

---

Economy

Overview: The economy has historically depended on the growing and processing of sugarcane and on remittances from overseas workers. In recent years, tourism and export-oriented manufacturing have assumed larger roles.
GDP: $119 million, per capita $3,240; real growth rate 6% (1988 est.)
Inflation rate (consumer prices): 0.9% (1987)
Unemployment rate: 20-25% (1987)
Budget: revenues $38.5 million; expenditures $45.0 million, including capital expenditures of $15.8 million (1988)
Exports: $30.3 million (f.o.b., 1988); *commodities*—sugar, manufactures, postage stamps; *partners*—US 44%, UK 30%, Trinidad and Tobago 12% (1987)
Imports: $94.7 million (c.i.f., 1988); *commodities*—foodstuffs, intermediate manufactures, machinery, fuels; *partners*—US 35%, UK 18%, Trinidad and Tobago 10%, Canada 6%, Japan 4% (1987)
External debt: $27.6 million (1988)
Industrial production: growth rate 5.8% (1986)
Electricity: 15,800 kW capacity; 45 million kWh produced, 1,120 kWh per capita (1989)
Industries: sugar processing, tourism, cotton, salt, copra, clothing, footwear, beverages
Agriculture: accounts for 10% of GDP; cash crop—sugarcane; subsistence crops—rice, yams, bananas; fishing potential not fully exploited; most food imported
Aid: US commitments, including Ex-Im (FY70-87), $13.6 million; Western (non-US) countries, ODA and OOF bilateral commitments (1970-87), $46 million
Currency: East Caribbean dollar (plural—dollars); 1 EC dollar (EC$) = 100 cents
Exchange rates: East Caribbean dollars (EC$) per US$1—2.70 (fixed rate since 1976)
Fiscal year: calendar year

Communications

Railroads: 58 km 0.760-meter narrow gauge on St. Kitts for sugarcane

Highways: 300 km total; 125 km paved, 125 km otherwise improved, 50 km unimproved earth
Ports: Basseterre (St. Kitts), Charlestown (Nevis)
Civil air: no major transport aircraft
Airports: 2 total, 2 usable; 2 with permanent-surface runways; none with runways over 3,659 m; 1 with runways 2,440-3,659 m; none with runways 1,220-2,439 m
Telecommunications: good interisland VHF/UHF/SHF radio connections and international link via Antigua and Barbuda and St. Martin; 2,400 telephones; stations—2 AM, no FM, 4 TV

Defense Forces

Branches: Royal St. Kitts and Nevis Police Force
Military manpower: NA
Defense expenditures: NA

St. Lucia

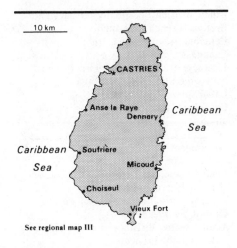

See regional map III

Geography

Total area: 620 km²; land area: 610 km²
Comparative area: slightly less than 3.5 times the size of Washington, DC
Land boundaries: none
Coastline: 158 km
Maritime claims:
Contiguous zone: 24 nm
Extended economic zone: 200 nm
Territorial sea: 12 nm
Climate: tropical, moderated by northeast trade winds; dry season from January to April, rainy season from May to August
Terrain: volcanic and mountainous with some broad, fertile valleys
Natural resources: forests, sandy beaches, minerals (pumice), mineral springs, geothermal potential
Land use: 8% arable land; 20% permanent crops; 5% meadows and pastures; 13% forest and woodland; 54% other; includes 2% irrigated
Environment: subject to hurricanes and volcanic activity; deforestation; soil erosion
Note: located 700 km southeast of Puerto Rico

People

Population: 153,196 (July 1990), growth rate 2.6% (1990)
Birth rate: 33 births/1,000 population (1990)
Death rate: 5 deaths/1,000 population (1990)
Net migration rate: −2 migrants/1,000 population (1990)
Infant mortality rate: 18 deaths/1,000 live births (1990)
Life expectancy at birth: 69 years male, 74 years female (1990)
Total fertility rate: 3.8 children born/ woman (1990)
Nationality: noun—St. Lucian(s); adjective—St. Lucian

Ethnic divisions: 90.3% African descent, 5.5% mixed, 3.2% East Indian, 0.8% Caucasian
Religion: 90% Roman Catholic, 7% Protestant, 3% Anglican
Language: English (official), French patois
Literacy: 78%
Labor force: 43,800; 43.4% agriculture, 38.9% services, 17.7% industry and commerce (1983 est.)
Organized labor: 20% of labor force

Government

Long-form name: none
Type: parliamentary democracy
Capital: Castries
Administrative divisions: 11 parishes; Anse-la-Raye, Castries, Choiseul, Dauphin, Dennery, Gros-Islet, Laborie, Micoud, Praslin, Soufrière, Vieux-Fort
Independence: 22 February 1979 (from UK)
Constitution: 22 February 1979
Legal system: based on English common law
National holiday: Independence Day, 22 February (1979)
Executive branch: British monarch, governor general, prime minister, Cabinet
Legislative branch: bicameral Parliament consists of an upper house or Senate and a lower house or House of Assembly
Judicial branch: Eastern Caribbean Supreme Court
Leaders: *Chief of State*—Queen ELIZABETH II (since 6 February 1952), represented by Governor General Stanislaus Anthony JAMES (since 10 October 1988); *Head of Government*—Prime Minister John George Melvin COMPTON (since 3 May 1982)
Political parties and leaders: United Workers' Party (UWP), John Compton; St. Lucia Labor Party (SLP), Julian Hunte; Progressive Labor Party (PLP), George Odlum
Suffrage: universal at age 18
Elections: *House of Assembly*—last held 6 April 1987 (next to be held April 1992); results—percent of vote by party NA; seats—(17 total) UWP 10, SLP 7
Communists: negligible
Member of: ACP, CARICOM, FAO, G-77, GATT (de facto), IBRD, ICAO, IDA, IFAD, IFC, ILO, IMF, IMO, NAM, OAS, OECS, PAHO, UN, UNESCO, UPU, WFTU, WHO, WMO
Diplomatic representation: Ambassador Dr. Joseph Edsel EDMUNDS; Chancery at Suite 309, 2100 M Street NW, Washington DC 30037; telephone (202) 463-7378 or 7379; there is a St. Lucian Consulate General in New York; *US*—none

Flag: blue with a gold isosceles triangle below a black arrowhead; the upper edges of the arrowhead have a white border

Economy

Overview: Since 1983 the economy has shown an impressive average annual growth rate of almost 5% because of strong agricultural and tourist industry sectors. There is also an expanding industrial base supported by foreign investment in manufacturing and other activities, such as in data processing. The economy, however, remains vulnerable because the important agricultural sector is dominated by banana production. St. Lucia is subject to periodic droughts and/or tropical storms, and its protected market agreement with the UK for bananas may end in 1992.
GDP: $172 million, per capita $1,258; real growth rate 6.8% (1988 est.)
Inflation rate (consumer prices): 7.0% (1987)
Unemployment rate: 18.6% (1986)
Budget: revenues $71.7 million; expenditures $79.3 million, including capital expenditures of $19.6 million (1987)
Exports: $76.8 million (f.o.b., 1987); *commodities*—bananas 67%, cocoa, vegetables, fruits, coconut oil, clothing; *partners*—UK 55%, CARICOM 21%, US 18%, other 6%
Imports: $178.1 million (c.i.f., 1987); *commodities*—manufactured goods 22%, machinery and transportation equipment 21%, food and live animals 20%, mineral fuels, foodstuffs, machinery and equipment, fertilizers, petroleum products; *partners*—US 33%, UK 16%, CARICOM 14.8%, Japan 6.5%, other 29.7%
External debt: $39.5 million (December 1987)
Industrial production: growth rate 2.4% (1987)
Electricity: 20,000 kW capacity; 80 million kWh produced, 530 kWh per capita (1989)
Industries: clothing, assembly of electronic components, beverages, corrugated boxes, tourism, lime processing, coconut processing
Agriculture: accounts for 15% of GDP and 43% of labor force; crops—bananas, coconuts, vegetables, citrus fruit, root crops, cocoa; imports food for the tourist industry
Aid: US commitments, including Ex-Im (FY70-87), $4 million; Western (non-US) countries, ODA and OOF bilateral commitments (1970-87), $93 million
Currency: East Caribbean dollar (plural—dollars); 1 EC dollar (EC$) = 100 cents

St. Lucia (continued)

Exchange rates: East Caribbean dollars (EC$) per US$1—2.70 (fixed rate since 1976)
Fiscal Year: 1 April-31 March

Communications

Highways: 760 km total; 500 km paved; 260 km otherwise improved
Ports: Castries
Civil air: 2 major transport aircraft
Airports: 2 total, 2 usable; 2 with permanent-surface runways; none with runways over 3,659 m; 1 with runways 2,440-3,659 m; 1 with runways 1,220-2,439
Telecommunications: fully automatic telephone system; 9,500 telephones; direct radio relay link with Martinique and St. Vincent and the Grenadines; interisland troposcatter link to Barbados; stations—4 AM, 1 FM, 1 TV (cable)

Defense Forces

Branches: Royal St. Lucia Police Force
Military manpower: NA
Defense expenditures: NA

St. Pierre and Miquelon
(territorial collectivity of France)

See regional map II

Geography

Total area: 242 km²; land area: 242 km²; includes eight small islands in the St. Pierre and the Miquelon groups
Comparative area: slightly less than 1.5 times the size of Washington, DC
Land boundaries: none
Coastline: 120 km
Maritime claims:
  Contiguous zone: 12 nm
  Continental shelf: 200 meters or to depth of exploitation
  Extended economic zone: 200 nm
  Territorial sea: 12 nm
Disputes: focus of maritime boundary dispute between Canada and France
Climate: cold and wet, with much mist and fog; spring and autumn are windy
Terrain: mostly barren rock
Natural resources: fish, deep-water ports
Land use: 13% arable land; 0% permanent crops; 0% meadows and pastures; 4% forest and woodland; 83% other
Environment: vegetation scanty
Note: located 25 km south of Newfoundland, Canada, in the North Atlantic Ocean

---

People

Population: 6,330 (July 1990), growth rate 0.4% (1990)
Birth rate: 17 births/1,000 population (1990)
Death rate: 7 deaths/1,000 population (1990)
Net migration rate: −6 migrants/1,000 population (1990)
Infant mortality rate: 9 deaths/1,000 live births (1990)
Life expectancy at birth: 72 years male, 79 years female (1990)
Total fertility rate: 2.2 children born/woman (1990)
Nationality: noun—Frenchman(men), Frenchwoman(women); adjective—French

Ethnic divisions: originally Basques and Bretons (French fishermen)
Religion: 98% Roman Catholic
Language: French
Literacy: NA%, but compulsory education between 6 and 16 years of age
Labor force: 2,510 (1982)
Organized labor: Workers' Force trade union

Government

Long-form name: Territorial Collectivity of Saint Pierre and Miquelon
Type: territorial collectivity of France
Capital: St. Pierre
Administrative divisions: none (territorial collectivity of France)
Independence: none (territorial collectivity of France)
Constitution: 28 September 1958 (French Constitution)
Legal system: French law
National holiday: National Day, 14 July
Executive branch: commissioner of the Republic
Legislative branch: unicameral General Council
Judicial branch: Superior Tribunal of Appeals (Tribunal Supérieur d'Appel)
Leaders: *Chief of State*—President François MITTERRAND (since 21 May 1981);
Head of Government—Commissioner of the Republic Jean-Pierre MARQUIE (since February 1989); President of the General Council Marc PLANTEGENEST (since NA)
Political parties and leaders: Socialist Party (PS); Union for French Democracy (UDF/CDS), Gerard Grignon
Suffrage: universal at age 18
Elections: *General Council*—last held September-October 1988 (next to be held September 1994); results—percent of vote by party NA; seats—(19 total) Socialist and other left-wing parties 13, UDF and right-wing parties 6;
French President—last held 8 May 1988 (next to be held May 1995); results—(second ballot) Jacques Chirac 56%, François Mitterrand 44%;
French Senate—last held 24 September 1989 (next to be held September 1992); results—percent of vote by party NA; seats—(1 total) PS 1;
French National Assembly—last held 5 and 12 June 1988 (next to be held June 1993); results—percent of vote by party NA; seats—(1 total) UDF/CDS 1
Diplomatic representation: as a territorial collectivity of France, local interests are represented in the US by France
Flag: the flag of France is used

Economy

Overview: The inhabitants have traditionally earned their livelihood by fishing and by servicing fishing fleets operating off the coast of Newfoundland. The economy has been declining, however, because the number of ships stopping at St. Pierre has steadily dropped over the years. In March 1989, an agreement between France and Canada set fish quotas for St. Pierre's trawlers fishing in Canadian and Canadian-claimed waters for three years. The agreement settles a longstanding dispute that had virtually brought fish exports to a halt. The islands are heavily subsidized by France. Imports come primarily from Canada.

GDP: $NA, per capita $2,495 (1984); real growth rate NA%

Inflation rate (consumer prices): NA%

Unemployment rate: 13.3% (1987)

Budget: revenues $NA million; expenditures $13.9 million, including capital expenditures of $NA (1988)

Exports: $23.3 million (f.o.b., 1986); *commodities*—fish and fish products, fox and mink pelts; *partners*—US 58%, France 17%, UK 11%, Canada, Portugal

Imports: $50.3 million (c.i.f., 1986); *commodities*—meat, clothing, fuel, electrical equipment, machinery, building materials; *partners*—Canada, France, US, Netherlands, UK

External debt: $NA

Industrial production: growth rate NA%

Electricity: 10,000 kW capacity; 25 million kWh produced, 3,970 kWh per capita (1989)

Industries: fishing and supply base for fishing fleets; tourism

Agriculture: vegetables, cattle, sheep and pigs for local consumption; fish catch, 14,750 metric tons (1986)

Aid: Western (non-US) countries, ODA and OOF bilateral commitments (1970-87), $477 million

Currency: French franc (plural—francs); 1 French franc (F) = 100 centimes

Exchange rates: French francs (F) per US$1—5.7598 (January 1990), 6.3801 (1989), 5.9569 (1988), 6.0107 (1987), 6.9261 (1986), 8.9852 (1985)

Fiscal year: calendar year

Communications

Highways: 120 km total; 60 kM paved (1985)

Ports: St. Pierre

Civil air: Air Saint-Pierre

Airports: 2 total, 2 usable; 2 with permanent-surface runways, none with runways over 2,439 m; 1 with runway 1,220-2,439 m

Telecommunications: 3,601 telephones; stations—1 AM, 3 FM, no TV; radiotelecommunication with most countries in the world; 1 satellite earth station in French domestic system

Defense Forces

Note: defense is the responsibility of France

St. Vincent and the Grenadines

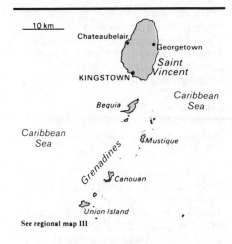

See regional map III

Geography

Total area: 340 km²; land area: 340 km²

Comparative area: slightly less than twice the size of Washington, DC

Land boundaries: none

Coastline: 84 km

Maritime claims:

Contiguous zone: 24 nm

Extended economic zone: 200 nm

Territorial sea: 12 nm

Climate: tropical; little seasonal temperature variation; rainy season (May to November)

Terrain: volcanic, mountainous; Soufrière volcano on the island of St. Vincent

Natural resources: negligible

Land use: 38% arable land; 12% permanent crops; 6% meadows and pastures; 41% forest and woodland; 3% other; includes 3% irrigated

Environment: subject to hurricanes; Soufrière volcano is a constant threat

Note: some islands of the Grenadines group are administered by Grenada

People

Population: 112,646 (July 1990), growth rate 1.4% (1990)

Birth rate: 27 births/1,000 population (1990)

Death rate: 6 deaths/1,000 population (1990)

Net migration rate: −8 migrants/1,000 population (1990)

Infant mortality rate: 32 deaths/1,000 live births (1990)

Life expectancy at birth: 68 years male, 72 years female (1990)

Total fertility rate: 2.9 children born/woman (1990)

Nationality: noun—St. Vincentian(s) or Vincentian(s); adjectives—St. Vincentian or Vincentian

St. Vincent and the Grenadines

(continued)

Ethnic divisions: mainly of black African descent; remainder mixed, with some white, East Indian, Carib Indian
Religion: Anglican, Methodist, Roman Catholic, Seventh-Day Adventist
Language: English, some French patois
Literacy: 82%
Labor force: 67,000 (1984 est.)
Organized labor: 10% of labor force

Government

Long-form name: none
Type: constitutional monarchy
Capital: Kingstown
Administrative divisions: 6 parishes; Charlotte, Grenadines, Saint Andrew, Saint David, Saint George, Saint Patrick
Independence: 27 October 1979 (from UK)
Constitution: 27 October 1979
Legal system: based on English common law
National holiday: Independence Day, 27 October (1979)
Executive branch: British monarch, governor general, prime minister, Cabinet
Legislative branch: unicameral House of Assembly (includes 15 elected representatives and six appointed senators)
Judicial branch: Eastern Caribbean Supreme Court
Leaders: *Chief of State*—Queen ELIZABETH II (since 6 February 1952), represented by Governor General David JACK (since 29 September 1989);
Head of Government—Prime Minister James F. MITCHELL (since 30 July 1984)
Political parties and leaders: New Democratic Party (NDP), James (Son) Mitchell; St. Vincent Labor Party (SVLP), Vincent Beach; United People's Movement (UPM), Adrian Saunders; Movement for National Unity (MNU), Ralph Gonsalves; National Reform Party (NRP), Joel Miguel
Suffrage: universal at age 18
Elections: *House of Assembly*—last held 16 May 1989 (next to be held July 1994); results—percent of vote by party NA; seats—(15 total) NDP 15
Member of: ACP, CARICOM, FAO, G-77, GATT (de facto), IBRD, ICAO, IDA, IFAD, IMF, IMO, OAS, OECS, UN, UNESCO, UPU, WFTU, WHO
Diplomatic representation: none
Flag: three vertical bands of blue (hoist side), gold (double width), and green; the gold band bears three green diamonds arranged in a *V* pattern

---

Economy

Overview: Agriculture, dominated by banana production, is the most important sector of the economy, providing employment for over 60% of the labor force and contributing about 20% to GDP. The services sector is next in importance, based mostly on a growing tourist industry. The economy continues to have a high unemployment rate of 30% because of an overdependence on the weather-plagued banana crop as a major export earner. Government progress toward diversifying into new industries has been relatively unsuccessful.
GDP: $136 million, per capita $1,305; real growth rate 8.4% (1988)
Inflation rate (consumer prices): 2.0% (1988)
Unemployment rate: 30% (1989 est.)
Budget: revenues $42.7 million; expenditures $67.5 million, including capital expenditures of $25.8 (FY88)
Exports: $63.8 million (f.o.b., 1986); *commodities*—bananas, eddoes and dasheen (taro), arrowroot starch, copra; *partners*—CARICOM 60%, UK 27%, US 10%
Imports: $87.3 million (c.i.f., 1986); *commodities*—foodstuffs, machinery and equipment, chemicals and fertilizers, minerals and fuels; *partners*—US 37%, CARICOM 18%, UK 13%
External debt: $35 million (July 1987)
Industrial production: growth rate -1.2% (1986)
Electricity: 16,600 kW capacity; 64 million kWh produced, 610 kWh per capita (1989)
Industries: food processing (sugar, flour), cement, furniture, rum, starch, sheet metal, beverage
Agriculture: accounts for 20% of GDP and 60% of labor force; provides bulk of exports; products—bananas, arrowroot (world's largest producer), coconuts, sweet potatoes, spices; small numbers of cattle, sheep, hogs, goats; small fish catch used locally
Aid: US commitments, including Ex-Im (FY70-87), $11 million; Western (non-US) countries, ODA and OOF bilateral commitments (1970-87), $71 million
Currency: East Caribbean dollar (plural—dollars); 1 EC dollar (EC$) = 100 cents
Exchange rates: East Caribbean dollars (EC$) per US$1—2.70 (fixed rate since 1976)
Fiscal year: 1 July-30 June

Communications

Highways: about 1,000 km total; 300 km paved; 400 km improved; 300 km unimproved
Ports: Kingstown
Merchant marine: 175 ships (1,000 GRT or over) totaling 1,305,945 GRT/2,029,935 DWT; includes 2 passenger, 1 passenger cargo, 103 cargo, 10 container, 8 roll-on/roll-off cargo, 4 refrigerated cargo, 9 petroleum, oils, and lubricants (POL) tanker, 4 chemical tanker, 2 liquefied gas, 28 bulk, 4 combination bulk; note—a flag of convenience registry
Civil air: no major transport aircraft
Airports: 6 total, 6 usable; 4 with permanent-surface runways; none with runways over 2,439 m; 1 with runways 1,220-2,439 m
Telecommunications: islandwide fully automatic telephone system; 6,500 telephones; VHF/UHF interisland links to Barbados and the Grenadines; new SHF links to Grenada and St. Lucia; stations—2 AM, no FM, 1 TV (cable)

Defense Forces

Branches: Royal St. Vincent and the Grenadines Police Force
Military manpower: NA
Defense expenditures: NA

San Marino

2 km

See regional map V

Geography

Total area: 60 km²; land area: 60 km²
Comparative area: about 0.3 times the size of Washington, DC
Land boundary: 39 km with Italy
Coastline: none—landlocked
Maritime claims: none—landlocked
Climate: Mediterranean; mild to cool winters; warm, sunny summers
Terrain: rugged mountains
Natural resources: building stones
Land use: 17% arable land; 0% permanent crops; 0% meadows and pastures; 0% forest and woodland; 83% other
Environment: dominated by the Appenines
Note: landlocked; world's smallest republic; enclave of Italy

People

Population: 23,123 (July 1990), growth rate 0.6% (1990)
Birth rate: 8 births/1,000 population (1990)
Death rate: 7 deaths/1,000 population (1990)
Net migration rate: 5 migrants/1,000 population (1990)
Infant mortality rate: 9 deaths/1,000 live births (1990)
Life expectancy at birth: 74 years male, 79 years female (1990)
Total fertility rate: 1.3 children born/woman (1990)
Nationality: noun—Sanmarinese (sing. and pl.); adjective—Sanmarinese
Ethnic divisions: Sanmarinese, Italian
Religion: Roman Catholic
Language: Italian
Literacy: 97%
Labor force: about 4,300
Organized labor: Democratic Federation of Sanmarinese Workers (affiliated with ICFTU) has about 1,800 members; Communist-dominated General Federation of Labor, 1,400 members

Government

Long-form name: Republic of San Marino
Type: republic
Capital: San Marino
Administrative divisions: 9 municipalities (castelli, singular—castello); Acquaviva, Borgo Maggiore, Chiesanuova, Domagnano, Faetano, Fiorentino, Monte Giardino, San Marino, Serravalle
Independence: 301 (by tradition)
Constitution: 8 October 1600; electoral law of 1926 serves some of the functions of a constitution
Legal system: based on civil law system with Italian law influences; has not accepted compulsory ICJ jurisdiction
National holiday: Anniversary of the Foundation of the Republic, 3 September
Executive branch: two captains regent, Congress of State (cabinet); real executive power is wielded by the secretary of state for foreign affairs and the secretary of state for internal affairs
Legislative branch: unicameral Grand and General Council (Consiglio Grande e Generale)
Judicial branch: Council of Twelve (Consiglio dei XII)
Leaders: *Co-Chiefs of State and Co-Heads of Government*—Captain Regent Salvatori REVES (since April 1989) and Captain Regent Luciano CARDELLI (since April 1989); Captains Regent are elected for six-month terms
Political parties and leaders: Christian Democratic Party (DCS), Gabriele Gatti; Communist Party (PCS), Gilberto Ghiotti; Socialist Unity Party (PSU), Emilio Della Balda and Patrizia Busignani; San Marino Socialist Party (PSS), Antonio Volpinari; San Marino Social Democratic Party (PSDS), Augusto Casali; San Marino Republican Party (PRS), Cristoforo Buscarini
Suffrage: universal at age 18
Elections: *Grand and General Council*—last held 29 May 1988 (next to be held by May 1993); results—percent of vote by party NA; seats—(60 total) DCS 27, PCS 18, PSU 8, PSS 7
Communists: about 300 members; the PCS, in conjunction with the PSS, PSU, and PSDS, has led the government since 1978
Other political parties or pressure groups: political parties influenced by policies of their counterparts in Italy
Member of: ICJ, ITU, IRC, UNESCO, UPU, WFTU, WHO, WTO; observer status in NAM
Diplomatic representation: San Marino maintains honorary Consulates General in Washington and New York, and an honorary Consulate in Detroit; *US*—no mission in San Marino, but the Consul General in Florence (Italy) is accredited to San Marino; Consulate General at 38 Lungarno Amerigo Vespucci, Florence, Italy (mailing address is APO NY 09019); telephone [39] (55) 298-276
Flag: two equal horizontal bands of white (top) and light blue with the national coat of arms superimposed in the center; the coat of arms has a shield (featuring three towers on three peaks) flanked by a wreath, below a crown and above a scroll bearing the word *LIBERTAS* (Liberty)

Economy

Overview: The economy relies heavily on the tourist industry as a source of revenue. More than 2 million tourists visit each year, contributing about 60% to GDP. The sale of postage stamps to foreign collectors is another important income producer. The manufacturing sector employs nearly 40% of the labor force and agriculture less than 4%. The per capita level of output and standard of living are comparable to northern Italy.
GDP: $NA, per capita $NA; real growth rate NA%
Inflation rate (consumer prices): 6.4% (1986)
Unemployment rate: 6.5% (1985)
Budget: revenues $99.2 million; expenditures $NA, including capital expenditures of $NA (1983)
Exports: trade data are included with the statistics for Italy; commodity trade consists primarily of exchanging building stone, lime, wood, chestnuts, wheat, wine, baked goods, hides, and ceramics for a wide variety of consumer manufactures
Imports: see **Exports**
External debt: $NA
Industrial production: growth rate NA%
Electricity: supplied by Italy
Industries: wine, olive oil, cement, leather, textile, tourist
Agriculture: employs less than 4% of labor force; products—wheat, grapes, corn, olives, meat, cheese, hides; small numbers of cattle, pigs, horses; depends on Italy for food imports
Aid: NA
Currency: Italian lira (plural—lire); 1 Italian lira (Lit) = 100 centesimi; also mints its own coins
Exchange rates: Italian lire (Lit) per US$1—1,262.5 (January 1990), 1,372.1 (1989), 1,301.6 (1988), 1,296.1 (1987), 1,490.8 (1986), 1,909.4 (1985)
Fiscal year: calendar year

San Marino (continued)

Communications

Highways: 104 km
Telecommunications: automatic telephone system; 11,700 telephones; stations—no AM, 20 FM, no TV; radio relay and cable links into Italian networks; no communication satellite facilities

Defense Forces

Branches: public security or police force of less than 50 people
Military manpower: all fit men ages 16-60 constitute a militia that can serve as an army
Defense expenditures: NA

Sao Tome and Principe

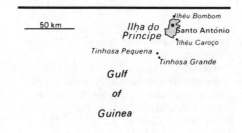

Geography

Total area: 960 km²; land area: 960 km²
Comparative area: slightly less than 5.5 times the size of Washington, DC
Land boundaries: none
Coastline: 209 km
Maritime claims: (measured from claimed archipelagic baselines)
  Extended economic zone: 200 nm
  Territorial sea: 12 nm
Climate: tropical; hot, humid; one rainy season (October to May)
Terrain: volcanic, mountainous
Natural resources: fish
Land use: 1% arable land; 20% permanent crops; 1% meadows and pastures; 75% forest and woodland; 3% other
Environment: deforestation; soil erosion
Note: located south of Nigeria and west of Gabon near the Equator in the North Atlantic Ocean

People

Population: 124,765 (July 1990), growth rate 3.0% (1990)
Birth rate: 38 births/1,000 population (1990)
Death rate: 8 deaths/1,000 population (1990)
Net migration rate: 0 migrants/1,000 population (1990)
Infant mortality rate: 61 deaths/1,000 live births (1990)
Life expectancy at birth: 64 years male, 67 years female (1990)
Total fertility rate: 5.4 children born/woman (1990)
Nationality: noun—Sao Tomean(s); adjective—Sao Tomean
Ethnic divisions: mestiço, angolares (descendents of Angolan slaves), forros (descendents of freed slaves), servicais (contract laborers from Angola, Mozambique, and Cape Verde), tongas (children of ser-

vicais born on the islands), and Europeans (primarily Portuguese)
Religion: Roman Catholic, Evangelical Protestant, Seventh-Day Adventist
Language: Portuguese (official)
Literacy: 50% (est.)
Labor force: 21,096 (1981); most of population engaged in subsistence agriculture and fishing; labor shortages on plantations and of skilled workers; 56% of population of working age (1983)
Organized labor: NA

Government

Long-form name: Democratic Republic of Sao Tome and Principe
Type: republic
Capital: São Tomé
Administrative divisions: 2 districts (concelhos, singular—concelho); Príncipe, São Tomé
Independence: 12 July 1975 (from Portugal)
Constitution: 5 November 1975, approved 15 December 1982
Legal system: based on Portuguese law system and customary law; has not accepted compulsory ICJ jurisdiction
National holiday: Independence Day, 12 July (1975)
Executive branch: president, prime minister, Council of Ministers (cabinet)
Legislative branch: unicameral National People's Assembly, sometimes referred to as the National Popular Assembly (Assembléia Popular Nacional)
Judicial branch: Supreme Court
Leaders: *Chief of State*—President Dr. Manuel Pinto da COSTA (since 12 July 1975);
Head of Government—Prime Minister Celestino Rocha da COSTA (since 8 January 1988)
Political parties and leaders: only party—Movement for the Liberation of Sao Tome and Principe (MLSTP), Dr. Manuel Pinto da Costa
Suffrage: universal at age 18
Elections: *President*—last held 30 September 1985 (next to be held September 1990); results—President Dr. Manuel Pinto da Costa was reelected without opposition by the National People's Assembly;
National People's Assembly—last held 30 September 1985 (next to be held September 1990); results—MLSTP is the only party; seats—(40 total) MLSTP 40 (indirectly elected)
Member of: ACP, AfDB, FAO, G-77, GATT (de facto), IBRD, ICAO, IDA, IFAD, IFC, ILO, IMF, ITU, NAM, OAU, UN, UNESCO, UPU, WHO, WMO

Diplomatic representation: Ambassador Joaquim Rafael BRANCO; Chancery (temporary) at 801 Second Avenue, Suite 1504, New York, NY 10017; telephone (212) 697-4211; *US*—the US Ambassador in Gabon is accredited to Sao Tome and Principe on a nonresident basis and makes periodic visits to the islands

Flag: three horizontal bands of green (top), yellow (double width), and green with two black five-pointed stars placed side by side in the center of the yellow band and a red isosceles triangle based on the hoist side; uses the popular pan-African colors of Ethiopia

Economy

Overview: The economy has remained dependent on cocoa since the gained independence nearly 15 years ago. Since then, however, cocoa production has gradually deteriorated because of drought and mismanagement, so that by 1987 output had fallen to less than 50% of its former levels. As a result, a shortage of cocoa for export has created a serious balance-of-payments problem. Production of less important crops, such as coffee, copra, and palm kernels, has also declined. The value of imports generally exceeds that of exports by a ratio of 4 to 1. The emphasis on cocoa production at the expense of other food crops has meant that Sao Tome has to import 90% of food needs. It also has to import all fuels and most manufactured goods. Over the years, Sao Tome has been unable to service its external debt, which amounts to roughly 80% of export earnings. Considerable potential exists for development of a tourist industry, and the government has taken steps to expand facilities in recent years. The government also implemented a Five-Year Plan covering 1986-90 to restructure the economy and reschedule external debt service payments in cooperation with the International Development Association and Western lenders.

GDP: $37.9 million, per capita $340; real growth rate 1.8% (1986)

Inflation rate (consumer prices): 4.2% (1986)

Unemployment rate: NA%

Budget: revenues $19.2 million; expenditures $25.1 million, including capital expenditures of $19.9 million (1987)

Exports: $9.1 million (f.o.b., 1988 est.); *commodities*—cocoa 90%, copra, coffee, palm oil; *partners*—FRG, GDR, Netherlands, China

Imports: $17.3 million (c.i.f., 1988 est.); *commodities*—machinery and electrical equipment 59%, food products 32%, fuels 9%; *partners*—Portugal, GDR, Angola, China

External debt: $95 million (1988)

Industrial production: growth rate 7.1% (1986)

Electricity: 6,000 kW capacity; 12 million kWh produced, 100 kWh per capita (1989)

Industries: light construction, shirts, soap, beer, fisheries, shrimp processing

Agriculture: dominant sector of economy, primary source of exports; cash crops—cocoa (90%), coconuts, palm kernels, coffee; food products—bananas, papaya, beans, poultry, fish; not self-sufficient in food grain and meat

Aid: US commitments, including Ex-Im (FY70-87), $7 million; Western (non-US) countries, ODA and OOF bilateral commitments (1970-87), 41.9 million

Currency: dobra (plural—dobras); 1 dobra (Db) = 100 céntimos

Exchange rates: dobras (Db) per US$1—122.48 (December 1988), 72.827 (1987), 36.993 (1986), 41.195 (1985)

Fiscal year: calendar year

Communications

Highways: 300 km (two-thirds are paved); roads on Príncipe are mostly unpaved and in need of repair

Ports: São Tomé, Santo António

Civil air: 8 major transport aircraft

Airports: 2 total, 2 usable; 2 with permanent-surface runways 1,220-2,439 m

Telecommunications: minimal system; 2,200 telephones; stations—1 AM, 2 FM, no TV; 1 Atlantic Ocean INTELSAT earth station

Defense Forces

Branches: Army, Navy

Military manpower: males 15-49, 27,805; 14,662 fit for military service

Defense expenditures: 1.6% of GDP (1980)

Saudi Arabia

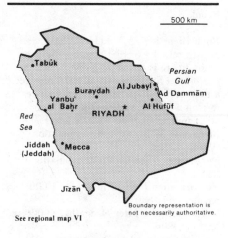

See regional map VI

Boundary representation is not necessarily authoritative.

Geography

Total area: 2,149,690 km²; land area: 2,149,690 km²

Comparative area: slightly less than one-fourth the size of US

Land boundaries: 4,410 km total; Iraq 488 km, Iraq-Saudi Arabia Neutral Zone 198 km, Jordan 742 km, Kuwait 222 km, Oman 676 km, Qatar 40 km, UAE 586 km, PDRY 830 km, YAR 628 km

Coastline: 2,510 km

Maritime claims:

Contiguous zone: 18 nm

Continental shelf: not specific

Exclusive fishing zone: not specific

Territorial sea: 12 nm

Disputes: no defined boundaries with PDRY, UAE, and YAR; shares Neutral Zone with Iraq—in July 1975, Iraq and Saudi Arabia signed an agreement to divide the zone between them, but the agreement must be ratified, however, before it becomes effective; Kuwaiti ownership of Qaruh and Umm al Maradim Islands is disputed by Saudi Arabia

Climate: harsh, dry desert with great extremes of temperature

Terrain: mostly uninhabited, sandy desert

Natural resources: crude oil, natural gas, iron ore, gold, copper

Land use: 1% arable land; NEGL% permanent crops; 39% meadows and pastures; 1% forest and woodland; 59% other; includes NEGL% irrigated

Environment: no perennial rivers or permanent water bodies; developing extensive coastal seawater desalination facilities; desertification

Note: extensive coastlines on Persian Gulf and Red Sea provide great leverage on shipping (especially crude oil) through Persian Gulf and Suez Canal

Saudi Arabia *(continued)*

People

Population: 17,115,728 (July 1990),
growth rate 4.4% (1990); note—the population figure is based on growth since the
last official Saudi census of 1974 reported
a total of 7 million persons and includes
foreign workers, while estimates from
other sources may be 15-30% lower
Birth rate: 37 births/1,000 population
(1990)
Death rate: 7 deaths/1,000 population
(1990)
Net migration rate: 13 migrants/1,000
population (1990)
Infant mortality rate: 71 deaths/1,000 live
births (1990)
Life expectancy at birth: 64 years male,
67 years female (1990)
Total fertility rate: 6.8 children born/
woman (1990)
Nationality: noun—Saudi(s); adjective—
Saudi or Saudi Arabian
Ethnic divisions: 90% Arab, 10% Afro-
Asian
Religion: 100% Muslim
Language: Arabic
Literacy: 52%
Labor force: 4,200,000; about 60% are
foreign workers; 34% government, 28%
industry and oil, 22% services, and 16%
agriculture
Organized labor: trade unions are illegal

Government

Long-form name: Kingdom of Saudi Ara-
bia
Type: monarchy
Capital: Riyadh
Administrative divisions: 14 emirates
(imārāt, singular—imārah); Al Bāḥah, Al
Ḥudūd ash Shamālīyah, Al Jawf, Al
Madīnah, Al Qaṣīm, Al Qurayyāt, Ar
Riyāḍ, Ash Sharqīyah, 'Asīr, Ḥā'il, Jīzān,
Makkah, Najrān, Tabūk
Independence: 23 September 1932 (unifi-
cation)
Constitution: none; governed according to
Shari'a (Islamic law)
Legal system: based on Islamic law, sev-
eral secular codes have been introduced;
commercial disputes handled by special
committees; has not accepted compulsory
ICJ jurisdiction
National holiday: Unification of the King-
dom, 23 September (1932)
Executive branch: monarch and prime
minister, crown prince and deputy prime
minister, Council of Ministers
Legislative branch: none
Judicial branch: Supreme Council of Jus-
tice
Leaders: *Chief of State and Head of Government*—King and Prime Minister
FAHD bin 'Abd al-'Aziz Al Sa'ud (since

13 June 1982); Crown Prince and Deputy
Prime Minister 'ABDALLAH bin 'Abd
al-'Aziz Al Sa'ud (half-brother to the
King, appointed heir to the throne 13
June 1982)
Suffrage: none
Elections: none
Communists: negligible
Member of: Arab League, CCC, FAO,
G-77, GCC, IAEA, IBRD, ICAO, IDA,
IDB—Islamic Development Bank, IFAD,
IFC, ILO, IMF, IMO, INTELSAT,
INTERPOL, ITU, IWC—International
Wheat Council, NAM, OAPEC, OIC,
OPEC, UN, UNESCO, UPU, WHO,
WMO
Diplomatic representation: Ambassador
BANDAR Bin Sultan; Chancery at 601
New Hampshire Avenue NW, Washing-
ton DC 20037; telephone (202) 342-3800;
there are Saudi Arabian Consulates Gen-
eral in Houston, Los Angeles, and New
York; *US*—Ambassador Charles W.
FREEMAN; Embassy at Collector Road
M, Diplomatic Quarter, Riyadh (mailing
address is P. O. Box 9041, Riyadh 11143,
or APO New York 09038); telephone
[966] (1) 488-3800; there are US Consulates General in Dhahran and Jiddah
(Jeddah)
Flag: green with large white Arabic script
(that may be translated as There is no
God but God; Muhammad is the Messen-
ger of God) above a white horizontal saber
(the tip points to the hoist side); green is
the traditional color of Islam

Economy

Overview: By far the most important economic activity is the production of petroleum and petroleum products. The petroleum sector accounts for about 85% of
budget revenues, 80% of GDP, and almost
all export earnings. Saudi Arabia has the
largest reserves of petroleum in the world,
is the largest exporter of petroleum, and
plays a leading role in OPEC. Oil wealth
has provided a per capita GDP that is
comparable to most industrialized countries. Saudi Arabia is one of the few countries where consumer prices have been
dropping or showing little change in recent years.
GDP: $73 billion, per capita $4,720; real
growth rate 3.2% (1988)
Inflation rate (consumer prices): 1.5%
(1989 est.)
Unemployment rate: 0% (1989 est.)
Budget: revenues $31.5 billion; expendi-
tures $38.1 billion, including capital ex-
penditures of $NA (1990)
Exports: $24.5 billion (f.o.b., 1989 est.);
commodities—petroleum and petroleum
products 89%; *partners*—Japan 26%, US
26%, France 6%, Bahrain 6%

Imports: $21.8 billion (f.o.b., 1989 est.);
commodities—manufactured goods, transportation equipment, construction materials, processed food products; *partners*—
US 20%, Japan 18%, UK 16%, Italy 11%
External debt: $18.9 billion (December
1989 est.)
Industrial production: growth rate 6.1%
(1980-86)
Electricity: 25,066,000 kW capacity;
50,000 million kWh produced, 3,100 kWh
per capita (1989)
Industries: crude oil production, petroleum
refining, basic petrochemicals, cement,
small steel-rolling mill, construction, fertilizer, plastic
Agriculture: accounts for about 10% of
GDP, 16% of labor force; fastest growing
economic sector; subsidized by government; products—wheat, barley, tomatoes,
melons, dates, citrus fruit, mutton, chickens, eggs, milk; approaching self-sufficiency in food
Aid: donor—pledged $64.7 billion in bilat-
eral aid (1979-89)
Currency: Saudi riyal (plural—riyals); 1
Saudi riyal (SR) = 100 halalas
Exchange rates: Saudi riyals (SR) per
US$1—3.7450 (fixed rate since late 1986),
3.7033 (1986), 3.6221 (1985)
Fiscal year: calendar year

Communications

Railroads: 886 km 1.435-meter standard
gauge
Highways: 74,000 km total; 35,000 km
bituminous, 39,000 km gravel and improved earth
Pipelines: 6,400 km crude oil; 150 km refined products; 2,200 km natural gas, includes 1,600 km of natural gas liquids
Ports: Jiddah, Ad Dammam, Ras Tanura,
Jizan, Al Jubayl, Yanbu al Bahr, Yanbu
al Sinaiyah
Merchant marine: 94 ships (1,000 GRT or
over) totaling 1,988,322 GRT/3,474,788
DWT; includes 1 passenger, 6 short-sea
passenger, 1 passenger-cargo, 15 cargo, 12
roll-on/roll-off cargo, 3 container, 6 refrigerated cargo, 4 livestock carrier, 32
petroleum, oils, and lubricants (POL)
tanker, 8 chemical tanker, 1 liquefied gas,
1 combination ore/oil, 1 specialized
tanker, 3 bulk
Civil air: 182 major transport aircraft
available
Airports: 204 total, 179 usable; 66 with
permanent-surface runways; 13 with runways over 3,659 m; 33 with runways
2,440-3,659 m; 98 with runways 1,220-
2,439 m
Telecommunications: good system with
extensive microwave and coaxial cable

Senegal

systems; 1,624,000 telephones; stations—21 AM, 16 FM, 97 TV; radio relay to Bahrain, Jordan, Kuwait, Qatar, UAE, YAR, and Sudan; coaxial cable to Kuwait; submarine cable to Djibouti and Egypt; satellite earth stations—3 Atlantic Ocean INTELSAT, 2 Indian Ocean INTELSAT, 1 ARABSAT, 1 INMARSAT, 1 ARABSAT

Defense Forces

Branches: Saudi Arabian Land Forces, Royal Saudi Naval Forces, Royal Saudi Air Force, Royal Saudi Air Defense Force, Saudi Arabian National Guard, Coast Guard and Frontier Forces, Special Security Force, Public Security Force, Special Emergency Force
Military manpower: males 15-49, 6,437,039; 3,606,344 fit for military service; 159,186 reach military age (18) annually
Defense expenditures: 16.9% of GDP, or $12.3 billion (1990 est.)

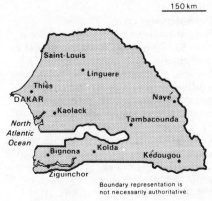

150 km

Boundary representation is not necessarily authoritative.

See regional map VII

Geography

Total area: 196,190 km^2; land area: 192,000 km^2
Comparative area: slightly smaller than South Dakota
Land boundaries: 2,640 km total; The Gambia 740 km, Guinea 330 km, Guinea-Bissau 338 km, Mali 419 km, Mauritania 813 km
Coastline: 531 km
Maritime claims:
  Contiguous zone: 24 nm
  Continental shelf: edge of continental margin or 200 nm
  Exclusive fishing zone: 200 nm
  Territorial sea: 12 nm
Disputes: short section of the boundary with The Gambia is indefinite; the International Court of Justice (ICJ) rendered its decision on the Guinea-Bissau/Senegal maritime boundary in favor of Senegal—that decision has been rejected by Guinea-Bissau; boundary with Mauritania
Climate: tropical; hot, humid; rainy season (December to April) has strong southeast winds; dry season (May to November) dominated by hot, dry harmattan wind
Terrain: generally low, rolling, plains rising to foothills in southeast
Natural resources: fish, phosphates, iron ore
Land use: 27% arable land; 0% permanent crops; 30% meadows and pastures; 31% forest and woodland; 12% other; includes 1% irrigated
Environment: lowlands seasonally flooded; deforestation; overgrazing; soil erosion; desertification
Note: The Gambia is almost an enclave

People

Population: 7,713,851 (July 1990), growth rate 3.0% (1990)
Birth rate: 44 births/1,000 population (1990)

Death rate: 14 deaths/1,000 population (1990)
Net migration rate: 0 migrants/1,000 population (1990)
Infant mortality rate: 87 deaths/1,000 live births (1990)
Life expectancy at birth: 53 years male, 56 years female (1990)
Total fertility rate: 6.3 children born/woman (1990)
Nationality: noun—Senegalese (sing. and pl.); adjective—Senegalese
Ethnic divisions: 36% Wolof, 17% Fulani, 17% Serer, 9% Toucouleur, 9% Diola, 9% Mandingo, 1% European and Lebanese, 2% other
Religion: 92% Muslim, 6% indigenous beliefs, 2% Christian (mostly Roman Catholic)
Language: French (official); Wolof, Pulaar, Diola, Mandingo
Literacy: 28.1%
Labor force: 2,509,000; 77% subsistence agricultural workers; 175,000 wage earners—40% private sector, 60% government and parapublic; 52% of population of working age (1985)
Organized labor: majority of wage-labor force represented by unions; however, dues-paying membership very limited; major confederation is National Confederation of Senegalese Labor (CNTS), an affiliate of governing party

Government

Long-form name: Republic of Senegal
Type: republic under multiparty democratic rule
Capital: Dakar
Administrative divisions: 10 regions (régions, singular—région); Dakar, Diourbel, Fatick, Kaolack, Kolda, Louga, Saint-Louis, Tambacounda, Thiès, Ziguinchor
Independence: 4 April 1960 (from France); The Gambia and Senegal signed an agreement on 12 December 1981 (effective 1 February 1982) that called for the creation of a loose confederation to be known as Senegambia, but the agreement was dissolved on 30 September 1989
Constitution: 3 March 1963, last revised in 1984
Legal system: based on French civil law system; judicial review of legislative acts in Supreme Court, which also audits the government's accounting office; has not accepted compulsory ICJ jurisdiction
National holiday: Independence Day, 4 April (1960)
Executive branch: president, Council of Ministers (cabinet)
Legislative branch: unicameral National Assembly (Assemblée Nationale)
Judicial branch: Supreme Court (Cour Suprême)

275

Leaders: *Chief of State and Head of Government*—President Abdou DIOUF (since 1 January 1981)
Political parties and leaders: Socialist Party (PS), Abdou Diouf; Senegalese Democratic Party (PDS), Abdoulaye Wade; 13 other small uninfluential parties
Suffrage: universal at age 21
Elections: *President*—last held 28 February 1988 (next to be held February 1993); results—Abdou Diouf (PS) 73%, Abdoulaye Wade (PDS) 26%, others 1%; *National Assembly*—last held 28 February 1988 (next to be held February 1993); results—PS 71%, PDS 25%, others 4%; seats—(120 total) PS 103, PDS 17
Communists: small number of Communists and sympathizers
Other political or pressure groups: students, teachers, labor, Muslim Brotherhoods
Member of: ACP, AfDB, APC, CCC, CEAO, EAMA, ECA, ECOWAS, EIB (associate), FAO, G-77, GATT, IAEA, IBRD, ICAO, IDA, IDB—Islamic Development Bank, IFAD, IFC, ILO, IMF, IMO, INTELSAT, INTERPOL, ITU, NAM, OAU, OCAM, OIC, OMVS (Organization for the Development of the Senegal River Valley), UN, UNESCO, UPU, WFTU, WHO, WIPO, WMO, WTO
Diplomatic representation: Ambassador Ibra Deguene KA; Chancery at 2112 Wyoming Avenue NW, Washington DC 20008; telephone (202) 234-0540 or 0541; *US*—Ambassador George E. MOOSE; Embassy on Avenue Jean XXIII at the corner of Avenue Kleber, Dakar (mailing address is B. P. 49, Dakar); telephone [221] 21-42-96
Flag: three equal vertical bands of green (hoist side), yellow, and red with a small green five-pointed star centered in the yellow band; uses the popular pan-African colors of Ethiopia

Economy

Overview: The agricultural sector accounts for about 20% of GDP and provides employment for about 75% of the labor force. About 40% of the total cultivated land is used to grow peanuts, an important export crop. The principal economic resource is fishing, which brought in about $200 million or about 25% of total foreign exchange earnings in 1987. Mining is dominated by the extraction of phosphate, but production has faltered because of reduced worldwide demand for fertilizers in recent years. Over the past 10 years tourism has become increasingly more important to the economy.
GDP: $5.0 billion, per capita $680; real growth rate 5.1% (1988 est.)

Inflation rate (consumer prices): −1.8% (1988 est.)
Unemployment rate: 3.5% (1987)
Budget: revenues $921 million; expenditures $1,024 million; including capital expenditures of $14 million (FY89 est.)
Exports: $761 million (f.o.b., 1988); *commodities*—manufactures 30%, fish products 27%, peanuts 11%, petroleum products 11%, phosphates 10%; *partners*—US, France, other EC, Ivory Coast, India
Imports: $1.1 billion (c.i.f., 1988); *commodities*—semimanufactures 30%, food 27%, durable consumer goods 17%, petroleum 12%, capital goods 14%; *partners*—US, France, other EC, Nigeria, Algeria, China, Japan
External debt: $3.8 billion (1988)
Industrial production: growth rate 4.9% (1986)
Electricity: 210,000 kW capacity; 760 million kWh produced, 100 kWh per capita (1989)
Industries: fishing, agricultural processing, phosphate mining, petroleum refining, building materials
Agriculture: including fishing, accounts for 20% of GDP and 75% of labor force; major products—peanuts (cash crop), millet, corn, sorghum, rice, cotton, tomatoes, green vegetables; estimated two-thirds self-sufficient in food; fish catch of 299,000 metric tons in 1987
Aid: US commitments, including Ex-Im (FY70-88), $492 million; Western (non-US) countries, ODA and OOF bilateral commitments (1970-87), $4.4 billion; OPEC bilateral aid (1979-89), $589 million; Communist countries (1970-88), $295 million
Currency: Communauté Financière Africaine franc (plural—francs); 1 CFA franc (CFAF) = 100 centimes
Exchange rates: Communauté Financière Africaine francs (CFAF) per US$1—287.99 (January 1990), 319.01 (1989), 297.85 (1988), 300.54 (1987), 346.30 (1986), 449.26 (1985)
Fiscal year: 1 July-30 June

Communications

Railroads: 1,034 km 1.000-meter gauge; all single track except 70 km double track Dakar to Thies
Highways: 14,000 km total; 3,770 km paved, 10,230 km laterite or improved earth
Inland waterways: 900 km total; 785 km on the Sénégal, 115 km on the Saloum
Ports: Dakar, Kaolack
Merchant marine: 3 ships (1,000 GRT and over) totaling 9,263 GRT/15,167 DWT; includes 2 cargo, 1 bulk
Civil air: 2 major transport aircraft

Airports: 25 total, 20 usable; 10 with permanent-surface runways; none with runways over 3,659 m; 1 with runways 2,440-3,659 m; 15 with runways 1,220-2,439 m
Telecommunications: above-average urban system, using radio relay and cable; 40,200 telephones; stations—8 AM, no FM, 1 TV; 3 submarine cables; 1 Atlantic Ocean INTELSAT earth station

Defense Forces

Branches: Army, Navy, Air Force, paramilitary Gendarmerie
Military manpower: males 15-49, 1,682,786; 878,812 fit for military service; 88,940 reach military age (18) annually
Defense expenditures: 2% of GDP, or $100 million (1989 est.)

Seychelles

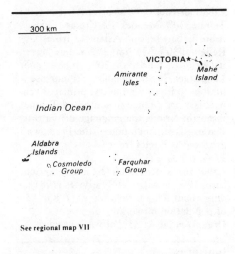

300 km

VICTORIA★

Amirante
Isles

Mahé
Island

Indian Ocean

Aldabra
Islands

Cosmoledo
Group

Farquhar
Group

See regional map VII

Geography

Total area: 455 km²; land area: 455 km²
Comparative area: slightly more than 2.5 times the size of Washington, DC
Land boundaries: none
Coastline: 491 km
Maritime claims:
Continental shelf: edge of continental margin or 200 nm
Extended economic zone: 200 nm
Territorial sea: 12 nm
Disputes: claims Tromelin Island
Climate: tropical marine; humid; cooler season during southeast monsoon (late May to September); warmer season during northwest monsoon (March to May)
Terrain: Mahé Group is granitic, narrow coastal strip, rocky, hilly; others are coral, flat, elevated reefs
Natural resources: fish, copra, cinnamon trees
Land use: 4% arable land; 18% permanent crops; 0% meadows and pastures; 18% forest and woodland; 60% other
Environment: lies outside the cyclone belt, so severe storms are rare; short droughts possible; no fresh water, catchements collect rain; 40 granitic and about 50 coral-line islands
Note: located north-northeast of Madagascar in the Indian Ocean

People

Population: 68,336 (July 1990), growth rate 0.9% (1990)
Birth rate: 24 births/1,000 population (1990)
Death rate: 7 deaths/1,000 population (1990)
Net migration rate: −8 migrants/1,000 population (1990)
Infant mortality rate: 15 deaths/1,000 live births (1990)
Life expectancy at birth: 65 years male, 75 years female (1990)
Total fertility rate: 2.6 children born/woman (1990)
Nationality: noun—Seychellois (sing. and pl.); adjective—Seychelles
Ethnic divisions: Seychellois (mixture of Asians, Africans, Europeans)
Religion: 90% Roman Catholic, 8% Anglican, 2% other
Language: English and French (official); Creole
Literacy: 60%
Labor force: 27,700; 31% industry and commerce, 21% services, 20% government, 12% agriculture, forestry, and fishing, 16% other (1985); 57% of population of working age (1983)
Organized labor: three major trade unions

Government

Long-form name: Republic of Seychelles
Type: republic; member of the Commonwealth
Capital: Victoria
Administrative divisions: none; note—there may be 21 administrative districts named Anse Boileau, Anse Etoile, Anse Louis, Anse Royale, Baie Lazare, Baie St. Anne, Beau Vallon, Bel Air, Bel Ombre, Cascade, Glacis, Grand Anse (on Mahé Island), Grand Anse (on Praslin Island), La Digue, Mont Fleuri, Plaisance, Pointe Larue, Port-Glaud, Riviere Anglaise, St. Louis, Takamaka
Independence: 29 June 1976 (from UK)
Constitution: 5 June 1979
Legal system: based on English common law, French civil law, and customary law
National holiday: Liberation Day (anniversary of coup), 5 June (1977)
Executive branch: president, Council of Ministers
Legislative branch: unicameral National Assembly (Assemblée Nationale)
Judicial branch: Court of Appeal, Supreme Court
Leaders: *Chief of State and Head of Government*—President France Albert RENE (since 5 June 1977)
Political parties and leaders: only party—Seychelles People's Progressive Front (SPPF), France Albert René
Suffrage: universal at age 17
Elections: *President*—last held 9-11 June 1989 (next to be held June 1994); results—President France Albert René reelected without opposition;
National Assembly—last held 5 December 1987 (next to be held December 1992); results—SPPF is the only party; seats—(25 total, 23 elected) SPPF 23
Communists: negligible, although some Cabinet ministers espouse pro-Soviet line
Other political or pressure groups: trade unions, Roman Catholic Church
Member of: ACP, AfDB, FAO, G-77, GATT (de facto), IBRD, ICAO, IFAD, IFC, ILO, IMF, IMO, INTERPOL, NAM, OAU, UN, UNESCO, UPU, WHO, WMO
Diplomatic representation: Second Secretary, Chargé d'Affaires ad interim Marc R. MARENGO; Chancery (temporary) at 820 Second Avenue, Suite 201, New York, NY 10017; telephone (212) 687-9766; *US*—Ambassador James MORAN; Embassy at 4th Floor, Victoria House, Victoria (mailing address is Box 148, Victoria, or APO New York 09030); telephone 23921 or 23922
Flag: three horizontal bands of red (top), white (wavy), and green; the white band is the thinnest, the red band is the thickest

Economy

Overview: In this small, open tropical island economy, the tourist industry employs about 30% of the labor force and provides the main source of hard currency earnings. In recent years the government has encouraged foreign investment in order to upgrade hotels and other services. At the same time, the government has moved to reduce the high dependence on tourism by promoting the development of farming, fishing, and small-scale manufacturing.
GDP: $255 million, per capita $3,720; real growth rate 6.2%; (1988 est.)
Inflation rate (consumer prices): 2.3% (1988)
Unemployment rate: 15% (1986)
Budget: revenues $106 million; expenditures $130 million, including capital expenditures of $21 million (1987)
Exports: $17 million (f.o.b., 1988 est.); *commodities*—fish, copra, cinnamon bark, petroleum products (reexports); *partners*—France 63%, Pakistan 12%, Reunion 10%, UK 7% (1987)
Imports: $116 million (f.o.b., 1988 est.); *commodities*—manufactured goods, food, tobacco, beverages, machinery and transportation equipment, petroleum products; *partners*—UK 20%, France 14%, South Africa 13%, PDRY 13%, Singapore 8%, Japan 6% (1987)
External debt: $178 million (December 1988)
Industrial production: growth rate 7% (1987)
Electricity: 25,000 kW capacity; 67 million kWh produced, 960 kWh per capita (1989)
Industries: tourism, processing of coconut and vanilla, fishing, coir rope factory, boat building, printing, furniture, beverage
Agriculture: accounts for 7% of GDP, mostly subsistence farming; cash crops—coconuts, cinnamon, vanilla; other prod-

Seychelles *(continued)*

ucts—sweet potatoes, cassava, bananas; broiler chickens; large share of food needs imported; expansion of tuna fishing under way
Aid: US commitments, including Ex-Im (FY78-88), $23 million; Western (non-US) countries, ODA and OOF bilateral commitments (1978-87), $297 million; OPEC bilateral aid (1979-89), $5 million; Communist countries (1970-88), $56 million
Currency: Seychelles rupee (plural—rupees); 1 Seychelles rupee (SRe) = 100 cents
Exchange rates: Seychelles rupees (SR) per US$1—5.4884 (January 1990), 5.6457 (1989), 5.3836 (1988), 5.6000 (1987), 6.1768 (1986), 7.1343 (1985)
Fiscal year: calendar year

Communications

Highways: 260 km total; 160 km bituminous, 100 km crushed stone or earth
Ports: Victoria
Merchant marine: 1 refrigerated cargo (1,000 GRT or over) totaling 1,827 GRT/2,170 DWT
Civil air: 3 major transport aircraft
Airports: 14 total, 14 usable; 8 with permanent-surface runways; none with runways over 3,659 m; 1 with runways 2,440-3,659 m; 1 with runways 1,220-2,439 m
Telecommunications: direct radio communications with adjacent islands and African coastal countries; 13,000 telephones; stations—2 AM, no FM, 1 TV; 1 Indian Ocean INTELSAT earth station; USAF tracking station

Defense Forces

Branches: Army, Navy, Air Force, Militia
Military manpower: males 15-49, 17,073; 8,776 fit for military service
Defense expenditures: 6% of GDP, or $12 million (1990 est.)

Sierra Leone

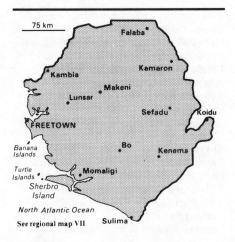

75 km

Falaba

Kamaron

Kambia

Makeni

Lunsar

Sefadu

Koidu

FREETOWN

Banana Islands

Bo

Kenema

Turtle Islands

Momaligi

Sherbro Island

North Atlantic Ocean

Sulima

See regional map VII

Geography

Total area: 71,740 km^2; land area: 71,620 km^2
Comparative area: slightly smaller than South Carolina
Land boundaries: 958 km total; Guinea 652 km, Liberia 306 km
Coastline: 402 km
Maritime claims:
  Territorial sea: 200 nm
Climate: tropical; hot, humid; summer rainy season (May to December); winter dry season (December to April)
Terrain: coastal belt of mangrove swamps, wooded hill country, upland plateau, mountains in east
Natural resources: diamonds, titanium ore, bauxite, iron ore, gold, chromite
Land use: 25% arable land; 2% permanent crops; 31% meadows and pastures; 29% forest and woodland; 13% other; includes NEGL% irrigated
Environment: extensive mangrove swamps hinder access to sea; deforestation; soil degradation

People

Population: 4,165,953 (July 1990), growth rate 2.6% (1990)
Birth rate: 47 births/1,000 population (1990)
Death rate: 21 deaths/1,000 population (1990)
Net migration rate: 0 migrants/1,000 population (1990)
Infant mortality rate: 154 deaths/1,000 live births (1990)
Life expectancy at birth: 42 years male, 47 years female (1990)
Total fertility rate: 6.2 children born/woman (1990)
Nationality: noun—Sierra Leonean(s); adjective—Sierra Leonean

Ethnic divisions: 99% native African (30% Temne, 30% Mende); 1% Creole, European, Lebanese, and Asian; 13 tribes
Religion: 30% Muslim, 30% indigenous beliefs, 10% Christian, 30% other or none
Language: English (official); regular use limited to literate minority; principal vernaculars are Mende in south and Temne in north; Krio is the language of the resettled ex-slave population of the Freetown area and is lingua franca
Literacy: 31% (1986)
Labor force: 1,369,000 (est.); 65% agriculture, 19% industry, 16% services (1981); only about 65,000 earn wages (1985); 55% of population of working age
Organized labor: 35% of wage earners

Government

Long-form name: Republic of Sierra Leone
Type: republic under presidential regime
Capital: Freetown
Administrative divisions: 4 provinces; Eastern, Northern, Southern, Western
Independence: 27 April 1961 (from UK)
Constitution: 14 June 1978
Legal system: based on English law and customary laws indigenous to local tribes; has not accepted compulsory ICJ jurisdiction
National holiday: Republic Day, 27 April (1961)
Executive branch: president, two vice presidents, Cabinet
Legislative branch: unicameral House of Representatives
Judicial branch: Supreme Court
Leaders: *Chief of State and Head of Government*—President Gen. Joseph Saidu MOMOH (since 28 November 1985); First Vice President Abu Bakar KAMARA (since 4 April 1987); Second Vice President Salia JUSU-SHERIFF (since 4 April 1987)
Political parties and leaders: only party—All People's Congress (APC), Gen. Joseph Saidu Momoh
Suffrage: universal at age 21
Elections: *President*—last held 1 October 1985 (next to be held October 1992); results—Gen. Joseph Saidu Momoh was elected without opposition;
House of Representatives—last held 30 May 1986 (next to be held May 1991); results—APC is the only party; seats—(127 total, 105 elected) APC 105
Communists: no party, although there are a few Communists and a slightly larger number of sympathizers
Member of: ACP, AfDB, Commonwealth, ECA, ECOWAS, FAO, G-77, GATT, IAEA, IBA, IBRD, ICAO, ICO, IDA, IDB—Islamic Development Bank, IFAD, IFC, ILO, IMF, IMO, INTERPOL, IPU,

IRC, ITU, Mano River Union, NAM, OAU, OIC, UN, UNESCO, UPU, WHO, WMO, WTO
Diplomatic representation: Ambassador George CAREW; Chancery at 1701 19th Street NW, Washington DC 20009; telephone (202) 939-9261; *US*—Ambassador Johnny YOUNG; Embassy at the corner of Walpole and Siaka Stevens Street, Freetown; telephone 26481
Flag: three equal horizontal bands of light green (top), white, and light blue

---

Economy

Overview: The economic and social infrastructure is not well developed. Subsistence agriculture dominates the economy, generating about one-third of GDP and employing about two-thirds of the working population. Manufacturing accounts for less than 10% of GDP, consisting mainly of the processing of raw materials and of light manufacturing for the domestic market. Diamond mining provides an important source of hard currency. The economy suffers from high unemployment, rising inflation, large trade deficits, and a growing dependency on foreign assistance.
GDP: $965 million, per capita $250; real growth rate 1.8% (FY87)
Inflation rate (consumer prices): 42% (September 1988)
Unemployment rate: NA%
Budget: revenues $86 million; expenditures $128 million, including capital expenditures of $NA (FY90 est.)
Exports: $106 million (f.o.b., 1988); *commodities*—rutile 50%, bauxite 17%, cocoa 11%, diamonds 3%, coffee 3%; *partners*—US, UK, Belgium, FRG, other Western Europe
Imports: $167 million (c.i.f., 1988); *commodities*—capital goods 40%, food 32%, petroleum 12%, consumer goods 7%, light industrial goods; *partners*—US, EC, Japan, China, Nigeria
External debt: $805 million (1989 est.)
Industrial production: growth rate −19% (FY88 est.)
Electricity: 83,000 kW capacity; 180 million kWh produced, 45 kWh per capita (1989)
Industries: mining (diamonds, bauxite, rutile), small-scale manufacturing (beverages, textiles, cigarettes, footwear), petroleum refinery
Agriculture: accounts for over 30% of GDP and two-thirds of the labor force; largely subsistence farming; cash crops—coffee, cocoa, palm kernels; harvests of food staple rice meets 80% of domestic needs; annual fish catch averages 53,000 metric tons
Aid: US commitments, including Ex-Im (FY70-88), $149 million; Western (non-US) countries, ODA and OOF bilateral commitments (1970-87), $698 million; OPEC bilateral aid (1979-89), $18 million; Communist countries (1970-88), $101 million
Currency: leone (plural—leones); 1 leone (Le) = 100 cents
Exchange rates: leones per US$1—87.7193 (January 1990), 58.1395 (1989), 31.2500 (1988), 30.7692 (1987), 8.3963 (1986), 4.7304 (1985)
Fiscal year: 1 July-30 June

Communications

Railroads: 84 km 1.067-meter narrow-gauge mineral line is used on a limited basis because the mine at Marampa is closed
Highways: 7,400 km total; 1,150 km bituminous, 490 km laterite (some gravel), remainder improved earth
Inland waterways: 800 km; 600 km navigable year round
Ports: Freetown, Pepel
Civil air: no major transport aircraft
Airports: 12 total, 8 usable; 5 with permanent-surface runways; none with runways over 3,659 m; 1 with runways 2,440-3,659 m; 3 with runways 1,220-2,439 m
Telecommunications: marginal telephone and telegraph service; national microwave radio relay system unserviceable at present; 23,650 telephones; stations—1 AM, 1 FM, 1 TV; 1 Atlantic Ocean INTELSAT earth station

---

Defense Forces

Branches: Army, Navy
Military manpower: males 15-49, 918,078; 433,350 fit for military service; no conscription
Defense expenditures: 1% of GDP (1986)

Singapore

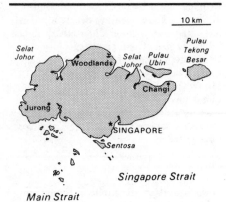

See regional map IX

Geography

Total area: 632.6 km²; land area: 622.6 km²
Comparative area: slightly less than 3.5 times the size of Washington, DC
Land boundaries: none
Coastline: 193 km
Maritime claims:
Exclusive fishing zone: not specific
Territorial sea: 3 nm
Climate: tropical; hot, humid, rainy; no pronounced rainy or dry seasons; thunderstorms occur on 40% of all days (67% of days in April)
Terrain: lowland; gently undulating central plateau contains water catchment area and nature preserve
Natural resources: fish, deepwater ports
Land use: 4% arable land; 7% permanent crops; 0% meadows and pastures; 5% forest and woodland; 84% other
Environment: mostly urban and industrialized
Note: focal point for Southeast Asian sea routes

People

Population: 2,720,915 (July 1990), growth rate 1.3% (1990)
Birth rate: 18 births/1,000 population (1990)
Death rate: 5 deaths/1,000 population (1990)
Net migration rate: 0 migrants/1,000 population (1990)
Infant mortality rate: 8 deaths/1,000 live births (1990)
Life expectancy at birth: 72 years male, 77 years female (1990)
Total fertility rate: 2.0 children born/woman (1990)
Nationality: noun—Singaporean(s), adjective—Singapore
Ethnic divisions: 76.4% Chinese, 14.9% Malay, 6.4% Indian, 2.3% other

Singapore (continued)

Religion: majority of Chinese are Buddhists or atheists; Malays nearly all Muslim (minorities include Christians, Hindus, Sikhs, Taoists, Confucianists)
Language: Chinese, Malay, Tamil, and English (official); Malay (national)
Literacy: 86.8% (1987)
Labor force: 1,280,000; 34.4% industry, 1.2% agriculture, 61.7% services (1988)
Organized labor: 211,200; 16.5% of labor force (1988)

Government

Long-form name: Republic of Singapore
Type: republic within Commonwealth
Capital: Singapore
Administrative divisions: none
Independence: 9 August 1965 (from Malaysia)
Constitution: 3 June 1959, amended 1965; based on preindependence State of Singapore Constitution
Legal system: based on English common law; has not accepted compulsory ICJ jurisdiction
National holiday: National Day, 9 August (1965)
Executive branch: president, prime minister, two deputy prime ministers, Cabinet
Legislative branch: unicameral Parliament
Judicial branch: Supreme Court
Leaders: *Chief of State*—President WEE Kim Wee (since 3 September 1985); *Head of Government*—Prime Minister LEE Kuan Yew (since 5 June 1959); First Deputy Prime Minister GOH Chok Tong (since 2 January 1985); Second Deputy Prime Minister ONG Teng Cheong (since 2 January 1985)
Political parties and leaders: government—People's Action Party (PAP), Lee Kuan Yew; opposition—Workers' Party (WP), J. B. Jeyaretnam; Singapore Democratic Party (SDP), Chiam See Tong; National Solidarity Party (NSP), Soon Kia Seng; United People's Front (UPF), Harbans Singh; Barisan Sosialis (BS); Communist party illegal
Suffrage: universal and compulsory at age 20
Elections: *President*—last held 31 August 1989 (next to be held NA August 1993); results—President Wee Kim Wee was reelected by Parliament without opposition; *Parliament*—last held 3 September 1988 (next to be held NA September 1993); results—PAP 61.8%, WP 18.4%, SDP 11.5%, NSP 3.7%, UPF 1.3%, others 3.3%; seats—(81 total) PAP 80, SDP 1; note—BS has 1 nonvoting seat
Communists: 200-500; Barisan Sosialis infiltrated by Communists
Member of: ADB, ANRPC, ASEAN, CCC, Colombo Plan, Commonwealth, ESCAP, G-77, GATT, IAEA, IBRD, ICAO, IFC, IHO, ILO, IMF, IMO, INTELSAT, INTERPOL, IPU, ISO, ITU, NAM, UN, UNESCO, UPU, WHO, WMO, WTO
Diplomatic representation: Ambassador Tommy KOH Tong Bee; Chancery at 1824 R Street NW, Washington DC 20009; telephone (202) 667-7555; *US*—Ambassador Robert D. ORR; Embassy at 30 Hill Street, Singapore 0617 (mailing address is FPO San Francisco 96699); telephone [65] 338-0251
Flag: two equal horizontal bands of red (top) and white; near the hoist side of the red band, there is a vertical, white crescent (closed portion is toward the hoist side) partially enclosing five white five-pointed stars arranged in a circle

Economy

Overview: Singapore has an open entrepreneurial economy with strong service and manufacturing sectors and excellent international trading links derived from its entrepôt history. During the 1970s and early 1980s, the economy expanded rapidly, achieving an average annual growth rate of 9%. Per capita GDP is among the highest in Asia. In 1985 the economy registered its first drop in 20 years and achieved less than a 2% increase in 1986. Recovery was strong. Estimates for 1989 suggest a 9.2% growth rate based on rising demand for Singapore's products in OECD countries, a strong Japanese yen, and improved competitiveness of domestic manufactures.
GDP: $27.5 billion, per capita $10,300; real growth rate 9.2% (1989 est.)
Inflation rate (consumer prices): 3.5% (1989 est.)
Unemployment rate: 2% (1989 est.)
Budget: revenues $6.6 billion; expenditures $5.9 billion, including capital expenditures of $2.2 billion (FY88)
Exports: $46 billion (f.o.b., 1989 est.); *commodities*—includes transshipments to Malaysia—petroleum products, rubber, electronics, manufactured goods; *partners*—US 24%, Malaysia 14%, Japan 9%, Thailand 6%, Hong Kong 5%, Australia 3%, FRG 3%
Imports: $53 billion (c.i.f., 1989 est.); *commodities*—includes transshipments from Malaysia—capital equipment, petroleum, chemicals, manufactured goods, foodstuffs; *partners*—Japan 22%, US 16%, Malaysia 15%, EC 12%, Kuwait 1%
External debt: $5.2 billion (December 1988)
Industrial production: growth rate 9% (1989 est.)

Electricity: 4,000,000 kW capacity; 12,000 million kWh produced, 4,490 kWh per capita (1989)
Industries: petroleum refining, electronics, oil drilling equipment, rubber processing and rubber products, processed food and beverages, ship repair, entrepôt trade, financial services, biotechnology
Agriculture: occupies a position of minor importance in the economy; self-sufficient in poultry and eggs; must import much of other food; major crops—rubber, copra, fruit, vegetables
Aid: US commitments, including Ex-Im (FY70-83), $590 million; Western (non-US) countries, ODA and OOF bilateral commitments (1970-87), $882 million
Currency: Singapore dollar (plural—dollars); 1 Singapore dollar (S$) = 100 cents
Exchange rates: Singapore dollars per US$1—1.8895 (January 1990), 1.9503 (1989), 2.0124 (1988), 2.1060 (1987), 2.1774 (1986), 2.2002 (1985)
Fiscal year: 1 April-31 March

Communications

Railroads: 38 km of 1.000-meter gauge
Highways: 2,597 km total (1984)
Ports: Singapore
Merchant marine: 407 ships (1,000 GRT or over) totaling 7,286,824 GRT/ 11,921,610 DWT; includes 126 cargo, 52 container, 5 roll-on/roll-off cargo, 11 refrigerated cargo, 13 vehicle carrier, 1 livestock carrier, 103 petroleum, oils, and lubricants (POL) tanker, 5 chemical tanker, 4 combination ore/oil, 1 specialized tanker, 15 liquefied gas, 68 bulk, 3 combination bulk; note—many Singapore flag ships are foreign owned
Civil air: 38 major transport aircraft (est.)
Airports: 6 total, 6 usable; 6 with permanent-surface runways; 2 with runways over 3,659 m; 2 with runways 2,440-3,659 m; 1 with runways 1,220-2,439 m
Telecommunications: good domestic facilities; good international service; good radio and television broadcast coverage; 1,110,000 telephones; stations—13 AM, 4 FM, 2 TV; submarine cables extend to Malaysia (Sabah and peninsular Malaysia), Indonesia, and the Philippines; satellite earth stations—1 Indian Ocean INTELSAT and 1 Pacific Ocean INTELSAT

Defense Forces

Branches: Army, Navy, Air Force, Army Reserve
Military manpower: males 15-49, 834,720; 621,497 fit for military service
Defense expenditures: 5% of GDP, or $1.4 billion (1989 est.)

Solomon Islands

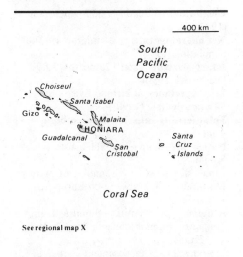

South Pacific Ocean

Choiseul
Santa Isabel
Gizo
Malaita
HONIARA
Guadalcanal
San Cristobal
Santa Cruz Islands

Coral Sea

See regional map X

Geography

Total area: 28,450 km²; land area: 27,540 km²
Comparative area: slightly larger than Maryland
Land boundaries: none
Coastline: 5,313 km
Maritime claims: (measured from claimed archipelagic baselines)
Extended economic zone: 200 nm
Territorial sea: 12 nm
Climate: tropical monsoon; few extremes of temperature and weather
Terrain: mostly rugged mountains with some low coral atolls
Natural resources: fish, forests, gold, bauxite, phosphates
Land use: 1% arable land; 1% permanent crops; 1% meadows and pastures; 93% forest and woodland; 4% other
Environment: subject to typhoons, which are rarely destructive; geologically active region with frequent earth tremors
Note: located just east of Papua New Guinea in the South Pacific Ocean

People

Population: 335,082 (July 1990), growth rate 3.5% (1990)
Birth rate: 41 births/1,000 population (1990)
Death rate: 5 deaths/1,000 population (1990)
Net migration rate: 0 migrants/1,000 population (1990)
Infant mortality rate: 40 deaths/1,000 live births (1990)
Life expectancy at birth: 67 years male, 72 years female (1990)
Total fertility rate: 6.3 children born/woman (1990)
Nationality: noun—Solomon Islander(s); adjective—Solomon Islander
Ethnic divisions: 93.0% Melanesian, 4.0% Polynesian, 1.5% Micronesian, 0.8% European, 0.3% Chinese, 0.4% other

Religion: almost all at least nominally Christian; Anglican, Seventh-Day Adventist, and Roman Catholic Churches dominant
Language: 120 indigenous languages; Melanesian pidgin in much of the country is lingua franca; English spoken by 1-2% of population
Literacy: 60%
Labor force: 23,448 economically active; 32.4% agriculture, forestry, and fishing; 25% services, 7.0% construction, manufacturing, and mining; 4.7% commerce, transport, and finance (1984)
Organized labor: NA, but most of the cash-economy workers have trade union representation

Government

Long-form name: none
Type: independent parliamentary state within Commonwealth
Capital: Honiara
Administrative divisions: 7 provinces and 1 town*; Central, Guadalcanal, Honiara*, Isabel, Makira, Malaita, Temotu, Western
Independence: 7 July 1978 (from UK; formerly British Solomon Islands)
Constitution: 7 July 1978
Legal system: common law
National holiday: Independence Day, 7 July (1978)
Executive branch: British monarch, governor general, prime minister, Cabinet
Legislative branch: unicameral National Parliament
Judicial branch: High Court
Leaders: *Chief of State*—Queen ELIZABETH II (since 6 February 1952), represented by Governor General George LEPPING (since 27 June 1989, previously acted as governor general since 7 July 1988);
Head of Government—Prime Minister Solomon MAMALONI (since 28 March 1989); Deputy Prime Minister Danny PHILIP (since 31 March 1989)
Political parties and leaders: People's Alliance Party (PAP), Solomon Mamaloni; United Party (UP), Sir Peter Kenilorea; Solomon Islands Liberal Party (SILP), Bartholemew Ulufa'alu; Nationalist Front for Progress (NFP), Andrew Nori; Labor Party (LP), Joses Tuhanuku
Suffrage: universal at age 21
Elections: *National Parliament*—last held 22 February 1989 (next to be held February 1993); results—percent of vote by party NA; seats—(38 total) PAP 13, UP 6, NFP 4, SILP 4, LP 2, independents 9
Member of: ACP, ADB, Commonwealth, ESCAP, G-77, GATT (de facto), IBRD, IDA, IFAD, IFC, ILO, IMF, SPF, UN, UPU, WHO

Diplomatic representation: Ambassador (vacant) resides in Honiara (Solomon Islands); *US*—the ambassador in Papua New Guinea is accredited to the Solomon Islands; Embassy at Mud Alley, Honiara (mailing address is American Embassy, P. O. Box 561, Honiara); telephone (677) 23488
Flag: divided diagonally by a thin yellow stripe from the lower hoist-side corner; the upper triangle (hoist side) is blue with five white five-pointed stars arranged in an *X* pattern; the lower triangle is green

Economy

Overview: About 90% of the population depend on subsistence agriculture, fishing, and forestry for at least part of their livelihood. Agriculture, fishing, and forestry contribute about 75% to GDP, with the fishing and forestry sectors being important export earners. The service sector contributes about 25% to GDP. Manufacturing activity is negligible. Most manufactured goods and petroleum products must be imported. The islands are rich in undeveloped mineral resources such as lead, zinc, nickel, and gold. The economy suffered from a severe cyclone in mid-1986 which caused widespread damage to the infrastructure.
GDP: $156 million, per capita $500; real growth rate 4.3% (1988)
Inflation rate (consumer prices): 11.2% (1988)
Unemployment rate: NA%
Budget: revenues $139.0 million; expenditures $154.4 million, including capital expenditures of $113.4 million (1987)
Exports: $80.1 million (f.o.b., 1988); *commodities*—fish 46%, timber 31%, copra 5%, palm oil 5%; *partners*—Japan 51%, UK 12%, Thailand 9%, Netherlands 8%, Australia 2%, US 2% (1985)
Imports: $101.7 million (f.o.b., 1988); *commodities*—plant and machinery 30%, fuel 19%, food 16%; *partners*—Japan 36%, US 23%, Singapore 9%, UK 9%, NZ 9%, Australia 4%, Hong Kong 4%, China 3% (1985)
External debt: $128 million (1988 est.)
Industrial production: growth rate 0% (1987)
Electricity: 15,000 kW capacity; 30 million kWh produced, 90 kWh per capita (1989)
Industries: copra, fish (tuna)
Agriculture: including fishing and forestry, accounts for about 75% of GDP; mostly subsistence farming; cash crops—cocoa, beans, coconuts, palm kernels, timber; other products—rice, potatoes, vegetables, fruit, cattle, pigs; not self-sufficient in food grains; 90% of the total fish catch of 44,500 metric tons was exported (1988)

Solomon Islands (continued)

Aid: Western (non-US) countries, ODA and OOF bilateral commitments (1985), $16.1 million
Currency: Solomon Islands dollar (plural—dollars); 1 Solomon Islands dollar (SI$) = 100 cents
Exchange rates: Solomon Islands dollars (SI$) per US$1—2.4067 (January 1990), 2.3090 (1989), 2.0825 (1988), 2.0033 (1987), 1.7415 (1986), 1.4808 (1985)
Fiscal year: calendar year

Communications

Highways: about 2,100 km total (1982); 30 km sealed, 290 km gravel, 980 km earth, 800 private logging and plantation roads of varied construction
Ports: Honiara, Ringi Cove
Civil air: no major transport aircraft
Airports: 29 total, 27 usable; 2 with permanent-surface runways; none with runways over 2,439 m; 5 with runways 1,220-2,439 m
Telecommunications: 3,000 telephones; stations—4 AM, no FM, no TV; 1 Pacific Ocean INTELSAT earth station

Defense Forces

Branches: NA
Military manpower: NA
Defense expenditures: NA

Somalia

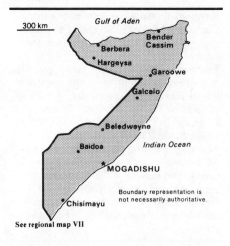

300 km
Gulf of Aden
Bender Cassim
Berbera
Hargeysa
Garoowe
Galcaio
Beledweyne
Indian Ocean
Baidoa
MOGADISHU
Chisimayu
Boundary representation is not necessarily authoritative.
See regional map VII

Geography

Total area: 637,660 km²; land area: 627,340 km²
Comparative area: slightly smaller than Texas
Land boundaries: 2,340 km total; Djibouti 58 km, Ethiopia 1,600 km, Kenya 682 km
Coastline: 3,025 km
Maritime claims:
  Territorial sea: 200 nm
Disputes: southern half of boundary with Ethiopia is a Provisional Administrative Line; territorial dispute with Ethiopia over the Ogaden; possible claims to Djibouti, Ethiopia, and Kenya based on unification of ethnic Somalis
Climate: desert; northeast monsoon (December to February), cooler southwest monsoon (May to October); irregular rainfall; hot, humid periods (tangambili) between monsoons
Terrain: mostly flat to undulating plateau rising to hills in north
Natural resources: uranium, and largely unexploited reserves of iron ore, tin, gypsum, bauxite, copper, salt
Land use: 2% arable land; NEGL% permanent crops; 46% meadows and pastures; 14% forest and woodland; 38% other; includes 3% irrigated
Environment: recurring droughts; frequent dust storms over eastern plains in summer; deforestation; overgrazing; soil erosion; desertification
Note: strategic location on Horn of Africa along southern approaches to Bab el Mandeb and route through Red Sea and Suez Canal

People

Population: 8,424,269 (July 1990), growth rate 0.8% (1990)
Birth rate: 47 births/1,000 population (1990)

Death rate: 15 deaths/1,000 population (1990)
Net migration rate: −24 migrants/1,000 population (1990)
Infant mortality rate: 125 deaths/1,000 live births (1990)
Life expectancy at birth: 53 years male, 54 years female (1990)
Total fertility rate: 7.3 children born/ woman (1990)
Nationality: noun—Somali(s); adjective— Somali
Ethnic divisions: 85% Somali, rest mainly Bantu; 30,000 Arabs, 3,000 Europeans, 800 Asians
Religion: almost entirely Sunni Muslim
Language: Somali (official); Arabic, Italian, English
Literacy: 11.6% (government est.)
Labor force: 2,200,000; very few are skilled laborers; 70% pastoral nomad, 30% agriculture, government, trading, fishing, handicrafts, and other; 53% of population of working age (1985)
Organized labor: General Federation of Somali Trade Unions is controlled by the government

Government

Long-form name: Somali Democratic Republic
Type: republic
Capital: Mogadishu
Administrative divisions: 16 regions (plural—NA, singular—gobolka); Bakool, Banaadir, Bari, Bay, Galguduud, Gedo, Hiiraan, Jubbada Dhexe, Jubbada Hoose, Mudug, Nugaal, Sanaag, Shabeellaha Dhexe, Shabeellaha Hoose, Togdheer, Woqooyi Galbeed
Independence: 1 July 1960 (from a merger of British Somaliland, which became independent from the UK on 26 June 1960, and Italian Somaliland, which became independent from the Italian-administered UN trusteeship on 1 July 1960, to form the Somali Republic)
Constitution: 25 August 1979, presidential approval 23 September 1979
National holiday: Anniversary of the Revolution, 21 October (1969)
Executive branch: president, two vice presidents, prime minister, Council of Ministers (cabinet)
Legislative branch: unicameral People's Assembly
Judicial branch: Supreme Court
Leaders: *Chief of State*—President and Commander in Chief of the Army Maj. Gen. Mohamed SIAD Barre (since 21 October 1969);
Head of Government—Prime Minister Lt. Gen. Mohamed Ali SAMANTAR (since 1 February 1987)

Political parties and leaders: only party—Somali Revolutionary Socialist Party (SRSP), Maj. Gen. Mohamed Siad Barre, general secretary
Suffrage: universal at age 18
Elections: *President*—last held 23 December 1986 (next to be held December 1993); results—President Siad was reelected without opposition; *People's Assembly*—last held 31 December 1984 (next scheduled for December 1989 was postponed); results—SRSP is the only party; seats—(177 total, 171 elected) SRSP 171
Communists: probably some Communist sympathizers in the government hierarchy
Member of: ACP, AfDB, Arab League, EAMA, FAO, G-77, IBRD, ICAO, IDA, IDB—Islamic Development Bank, IFAD, IFC, ILO, IMF, IMO, INTELSAT, INTERPOL, ITU, NAM, OAU, OIC, UN, UNESCO, UPU, WFTU, WHO, WMO
Diplomatic representation: Ambassador ABDIKARIM Ali Omar; Chancery at Suite 710, 600 New Hampshire Avenue NW, Washington DC 20037; telephone (202) 342-1575; there is a Somali Consulate General in New York; *US*—Ambassador T. Frank CRIGLER; Embassy at Corso Primo Luglio, Mogadishu (mailing address is P. O. Box 574, Mogadishu); telephone [252] (01) 20811
Flag: light blue with a large white five-pointed star in the center; design based on the flag of the UN (Italian Somaliland was a UN trust territory)

Economy

Overview: One of the world's least developed countries, Somalia has few resources. In 1988 per capita GDP was $210. Agriculture is the most important sector of the economy, with the livestock sector accounting for about 40% of GDP and about 65% of export earnings. Nomads and seminomads who are dependent upon livestock for their livelihoods make up about 50% of the population. Crop production generates only 10% of GDP and employs about 20% of the work force. The main export crop is bananas; sugar, sorghum, and corn are grown for the domestic market. The small industrial sector is based on the processing of agricultural products and accounts for less than 10% of GDP. At the end of 1988 serious economic problems facing the nation were the external debt of $2.8 billion and double-digit inflation.
GDP: $1.7 billion, per capita $210; real growth rate −1.4% (1988)
Inflation rate (consumer prices): 81.7% (1988 est.)
Unemployment rate: NA%

Budget: revenues $273 million; expenditures $405 million, including capital expenditures of $219 million (1987)
Exports: $58.0 million (f.o.b., 1988); *commodities*—livestock, hides, skins, bananas, fish; *partners*—US 0.5%, Saudi Arabia, Italy, FRG (1986)
Imports: $354.0 million (c.i.f., 1988); *commodities*—textiles, petroleum products, foodstuffs, construction materials; *partners*—US 13%, Italy, FRG, Kenya, UK, Saudi Arabia (1986)
External debt: $2.8 billion (1989 est.)
Industrial production: growth rate NA%
Electricity: 71,000 kW capacity; 65 million kWh produced, 8 kWh per capita (1989)
Industries: a few small industries, including sugar refining, textiles, petroleum refining
Agriculture: dominant sector, led by livestock raising (cattle, sheep, goats); crops—bananas, sorghum, corn, mangoes, sugarcane; not self-sufficient in food; fishing potential largely unexploited
Aid: US commitments, including Ex-Im (FY70-88), $618 million; Western (non-US) countries, ODA and OOF bilateral commitments (1970-87), $2.8 billion; OPEC bilateral aid (1979-89), $1.1 billion; Communist countries (1970-88), $336 million
Currency: Somali shilling (plural—shillings); 1 Somali shilling (So.Sh.) = 100 centesimi
Exchange rates: Somali shillings (So. Sh.) per US$1—643.92 (December 1989), 170.45 (1988), 105.18 (1987), 72.00 (1986), 39.49 (1985)
Fiscal year: calendar year

Communications

Highways: 15,215 km total; including 2,335 km bituminous surface, 2,880 km gravel, and 10,000 km improved earth or stabilized soil (1983)
Pipelines: 15 km crude oil
Ports: Mogadishu, Berbera, Chisimayu
Merchant marine: 3 cargo ships (1,000 GRT or over) totaling 6,563 GRT/9,512 DWT; includes 2 cargo, 1 refrigerated cargo
Civil air: 2 major transport aircraft
Airports: 60 total, 45 usable; 8 with permanent-surface runways; 2 with runways over 3,659 m; 5 with runways 2,440-3,659 m; 20 with runways 1,220-2,439 m
Telecommunications: minimal telephone and telegraph service; radio relay and troposcatter system centered on Mogadishu connects a few towns; 6,000 telephones; stations—2 AM, no FM, 1 TV; 1 Indian Ocean INTELSAT earth station; scheduled to receive an ARABSAT station

Defense Forces

Branches: Somali National Army (including Navy, Air Force, and Air Defense Force), National Police Force
Military manpower: males 15-49, 1,878,939; 1,052,644 fit for military service
Defense expenditures: NA

South Africa

400 km

Walvis Bay
Messina
Pietersburg
PRETORIA
Johannesburg
Upington
Kimberley
Ladysmith
Bloemfontein
Durban
De Aar
South Atlantic Ocean
East London
Cape Town
Port Elizabeth
Mosselbaai
Indian Ocean

See regional map VII

Geography

Total area: 1,221,040 km²; land area: 1,221,040 km²; includes Walvis Bay, Marion Island, and Prince Edward Island
Comparative area: slightly less than twice the size of Texas
Land boundaries: 4,973 km total; Botswana 1,840 km, Lesotho 909 km, Mozambique 491 km, Namibia 1,078 km, Swaziland 430 km, Zimbabwe 225 km
Coastline: 2,881 km
Maritime claims:
Continental shelf: 200 meters or to depth of exploitation
Exclusive fishing zone: 200 nm
Territorial sea: 12 nm
Disputes: South Africa administered Namibia until independence was achieved on 21 March 1990; possible future claim to Walvis Bay by Namibia
Climate: mostly semiarid; subtropical along coast; sunny days, cool nights
Terrain: vast interior plateau rimmed by rugged hills and narrow coastal plain
Natural resources: gold, chromium, antimony, coal, iron ore, manganese, nickel, phosphates, tin, uranium, gem diamonds, platinum, copper, vanadium, salt, natural gas
Land use: 10% arable land; 1% permanent crops; 65% meadows and pastures; 3% forest and woodland; 21% other; includes 1% irrigated
Environment: lack of important arterial rivers or lakes requires extensive water conservation and control measures
Note: Walvis Bay is an exclave of South Africa in Namibia; completely surrounds Lesotho; almost completely surrounds Swaziland

People

Population: 39,549,941 (July 1990), growth rate 2.67%; includes the 10 so-called homelands, which are not recognized by the US
four independent homelands—Bophuthatswana 2,352,296, growth rate 2.80%; Ciskei 1,025,873, growth rate 2.93%; Transkei 4,367,648, growth rate 4.19%; Venda 665,197, growth rate 3.86%
six other homelands—Gazankulu 742,361, growth rate 3.99%; Kangwane 556,009, growth rate 3.64%; KwaNdebele 348,655, growth rate 3.35%; KwaZulu 5,349,247, growth rate 3.62%; Lebowa 2,704,641, growth rate 3.92%; Qwagwa 268,138, growth rate 3.59%
Birth rate: 35 births/1,000 population (1990)
Death rate: 8 deaths/1,000 population (1990)
Net migration rate: NEGL migrants/1,000 population (1990)
Infant mortality rate: 52 deaths/1,000 live births (1990)
Life expectancy at birth: 61 years male, 67 years female (1990)
Total fertility rate: 4.5 children born/woman (1990)
Nationality: noun—South African(s); adjective—South African
Ethnic divisions: 73.8% black, 14.3% white, 9.1% Colored, 2.8% Indian
Religion: most whites and Coloreds and roughly 60% of blacks are Christian; roughly 60% of Indians are Hindu, 20% Muslim
Language: Afrikaans, English (official); many vernacular languages, including Zulu, Xhosa, North and South Sotho, Tswana
Literacy: almost all white population literate; government estimates 50% of blacks literate
Labor force: 11,000,000 economically active; 34% services, 30% agriculture, 29% industry and commerce, 7% mining (1985)
Organized labor: about 17% of total labor force is unionized; African unions represent 15% of black labor force

Government

Long-form name: Republic of South Africa; abbreviated RSA
Type: republic
Capital: administrative, Pretoria; legislative, Cape Town; judicial, Bloemfontein
Administrative divisions: 4 provinces; Cape, Natal, Orange Free State, Transvaal; there are 10 homelands not recognized by the US—4 independent (Bophuthatswana, Ciskei, Transkei, Venda) and 6 other (Gazankulu, Kangwane, KwaNdebele, KwaZulu, Lebowa, Qwaqwa)

Independence: 31 May 1910 (from UK)
Constitution: 3 September 1984
Legal system: based on Roman-Dutch law and English common law; accepts compulsory ICJ jurisdiction, with reservations
National holiday: Republic Day, 31 May (1910)
Executive branch: state president, cabinet, Executive Council (cabinet) Ministers' Councils (from the three houses of Parliament)
Legislative branch: tricameral Parliament consists of the House of Assembly (whites), House of Representatives (Coloreds), and House of Delegates (Indians)
Judicial branch: Supreme Court
Leaders: *Chief of State and Head of Government*—State President Frederik W. DE KLERK (since 13 September 1989)
Political parties and leaders: *white political parties and leaders*—National Party (NP), Frederik W. de Klerk (majority party); Conservative Party (CP), Dr. Andries P. Treurnicht (official opposition party); Herstigte National Party (HNP), Jaap Marais; Democratic Party (DP), Zach De Beer, Wynand Malan, and Denis Worrall;
Colored political parties and leaders—Labor Party (LP), Allan Hendrickse (majority party); Democratic Reform Party (DRP), Carter Ebrahim; United Democratic Party (UDP), Jac Rabie; Freedom Party;
Indian political parties and leaders—Solidarity, J. N. Reddy (majority party); National People's Party (NPP), Amichand Rajbansi; Merit People's Party
Suffrage: universal at age 18, but voting rights are racially based
Elections: *House of Assembly (whites)*—last held 6 September 1989 (next to be held by September 1994); results—NP 58%, CP 23%, DP 19%; seats—(178 total, 166 elected) NP 103, CP 41, DP 34;
House of Representatives (Coloreds)—last held 6 September 1989 (next to be held by September 1994); results—percent of vote by party NA; seats—(85 total, 80 elected) LP 69, DRP 5, UDP 3, Freedom Party 1, independents 2;
House of Delegates (Indians)—last held 6 September 1989 (next to be held by September 1994); results—percent of vote by party NA; seats—(45 total, 40 elected) Solidarity 16, NPP 9, Merit People's Party 3, United Party 2, Democratic Party 2, People's Party 1, National Federal Party 1, independents 6
Communists: small Communist party illegal since 1950; party in exile maintains headquarters in London, Daniel Tloome (Chairman) and Joe Slovo (General Secretary)
Other political groups: *insurgent groups in exile*—African National Congress (ANC),

Oliver Tambo; Pan-Africanist Congress (PAC), Zephania Mothopeng; *internal antiapartheid groups—* Pan-Africanist Movement (PAM), Clarence Makwetu; United Democratic Front (UDF), Albertina Sisulu and Archibald Gumede
Member of: CCC, GATT, IAEA, IBRD, ICAO, IDA, IFC, IHO, ILZSG, IMF, INTELSAT, ISO, ITU, IWC—International Whaling Commission, IWC—International Wheat Council, Southern African Customs Union, UN, UPU, WFTU, WHO, WIPO, WMO, WSG (membership rights in IAEA, ICAO, ITU, WHO, WIPO, and WMO suspended or restricted)
Diplomatic representation: Ambassador Piet G. J. KOORNHOF; Chancery at 3051 Massachusetts Avenue NW, Washington DC 20008; telephone (202) 232-4400; there are South African Consulates General in Beverly Hills (California), Chicago, Houston, and New York; *US—*Ambassador William L. SWING; Embassy at Thibault House, 225 Pretorius Street, Pretoria; telephone [27] (12) 28-4266; there are US Consulates General in Cape Town, Durban, and Johannesburg
Flag: actually four flags in one—three miniature flags reproduced in the center of the white band of the former flag of the Netherlands which has three equal horizontal bands of orange (top), white, and blue; the miniature flags are a vertically hanging flag of the old Orange Free State with a horizontal flag of the UK adjoining on the hoist side and a horizontal flag of the old Transvaal Republic adjoining on the other side

---

Economy

Overview: Many of the white one-seventh of the South African population enjoy incomes, material comforts, and health and educational standards equal to those of Western Europe. In contrast, most of the remaining population suffers from the poverty patterns of the Third World, including unemployment, lack of job skills, and barriers to movement into higher-paying fields. Inputs and outputs thus do not move smoothly into the most productive employments, and the effectiveness of the market is further lowered by international constraints on dealings with South Africa. The main strength of the economy lies in its rich mineral resources, which provide two-thirds of exports. Average growth of 2% in output in recent years falls far short of the level needed to cut into the high unemployment level.
GDP: $83.5 billion, per capita $2,380; real growth rate 3.2% (1988)

Inflation rate (consumer prices): 14.67% (1989)
Unemployment rate: 22% (1988); blacks 25-30%, up to 50% in homelands (1988 est.)
Budget: revenues $24.3 billion; expenditures $27.3 billion, including capital expenditures of $NA billion (FY91)
Exports: $21.5 billion (f.o.b., 1988 est.); *commodities*—gold 40%, minerals and metals 23%, food 6%, chemicals 3%; *partners*—FRG, Japan, UK, US, other EC, Hong Kong
Imports: $18.5 billion (c.i.f., 1989 est.); *commodities*—machinery 27%, chemicals 11%, vehicles and aircraft 11%, textiles, scientific instruments, base metals; *partners*—US, FRG, Japan, UK, France, Italy, Switzerland
External debt: $21.2 billion (1988 est.)
Industrial production: growth rate 5.6% (1988)
Electricity: 34,941,000 kW capacity; 158,000 million kWh produced, 4,100 kWh per capita (1989)
Industries: mining (world's largest producer of diamonds, gold, chrome), automobile assembly, metalworking, machinery, textile, iron and steel, chemical, fertilizer, foodstuffs
Agriculture: accounts for 6% of GDP and 30% of labor force; diversified agriculture, with emphasis on livestock; products—cattle, poultry, sheep, wool, milk, beef, corn, wheat; sugarcane, fruits, vegetables; self-sufficient in food
Aid: NA
Currency: rand (plural—rand); 1 rand (R) = 100 cents
Exchange rates: rand (R) per US$1—2.5555 (January 1990), 2.6166 (1989), 2.2611 (1988), 2.0350 (1987), 2.2685 (1986), 2.1911 (1985)
Fiscal year: 1 April-31 March

Communications

Railroads: 20,638 km route distance total; 35,079 km of 1.067-meter gauge trackage (counts double and multiple tracking as single track); 314 km of 610 mm gauge
Highways: 188,309 km total; 54,013 km paved, 134,296 km crushed stone, gravel, or improved earth
Pipelines: 931 km crude oil; 1,748 km refined products; 322 km natural gas
Ports: Durban, Cape Town, Port Elizabeth, Richard's Bay, Saldanha, Mosselbaai, Walvis Bay
Merchant marine: 9 ships (1,000 GRT or over) totaling 275,684 GRT/273,973 DWT; includes 7 container, 1 vehicle carrier, 1 petroleum, oils, and lubricants (POL) tanker
Civil air: 81 major transport aircraft

Airports: 931 total, 793 usable; 124 with permanent-surface runways; 4 with runways over 3,659 m; 10 with runways 2,440-3,659 m; 213 with runways 1,220-2,439 m
Telecommunications: the system is the best developed, most modern, and has the highest capacity in Africa; it consists of carrier-equipped open-wire lines, coaxial cables, radio relay links, fiber optic cable, and radiocommunication stations; key centers are Bloemfontein, Cape Town, Durban, Johannesburg, Port Elizabeth, and Pretoria; 4,500,000 telephones; stations—14 AM, 286 FM, 67 TV; 1 submarine cable; satellite earth stations—1 Indian Ocean INTELSAT and 2 Atlantic Ocean INTELSAT

Defense Forces

Branches: Army, Navy, Air Force, Medical Services
Military manpower: males 15-49, 9,544,357; 5,828,167 fit for military service; 419,815 reach military age (18) annually; obligation for service in Citizen Force or Commandos begins at 18; volunteers for service in permanent force must be 17; national service obligation is two years; figures include the so-called homelands not recognized by the US
Defense expenditures: 5% of GDP, or $4 billion (1989 est.)

South Georgia and the South Sandwich Islands
(dependent territory of the UK)

South Sandwich Islands, Shag, and Clerke Rocks are not shown

50 km

South Atlantic Ocean

Grytviken

Scotia Sea

Administered by U.K., claimed by Argentina

See regional map IV

Geography

Total area: 4,066 km²; land area: 4,066 km²; includes Shag and Clerke Rocks
Comparative area: slightly larger than Rhode Island
Land boundaries: none
Coastline: undetermined
Maritime claims:
  Continental shelf: 200 meters or to depth of exploitation
  Exclusive fishing zone: 200 nm
  Territorial sea: 12 nm
Disputes: administered by the UK, claimed by Argentina
Climate: variable, with mostly westerly winds throughout the year, interspersed with periods of calm; nearly all precipitation falls as snow
Terrain: most of the islands, rising steeply from the sea, are rugged and mountainous; South Georgia is largely barren and has steep, glacier-covered mountains; the South Sandwich Islands are of volcanic origin with some active volcanoes
Natural resources: fish
Land use: 0% arable land; 0% permanent crops; 0% meadows and pastures; 0% forest and woodland; 100% other; largely covered by permanent ice and snow with some sparse vegetation consisting of grass, moss, and lichen
Environment: reindeer, introduced early in this century, live on South Georgia; weather conditions generally make it difficult to approach the South Sandwich Islands; the South Sandwich Islands are subject to active volcanism
Note: the north coast of South Georgia has several large bays, which provide good anchorage

People

Population: no permanent population; there is a small military garrison on South Georgia and the British Antarctic Survey has a biological station on Bird Island; the South Sandwich islands are uninhabited

Government

Long-form name: South Georgia and the South Sandwich Islands (no short-form name)
Type: dependent territory of the UK
Capital: Grytviken Harbour on South Georgia is the chief town
Administrative divisions: none (dependent territory of the UK)
Independence: none (dependent territory of the UK)
Constitution: 3 October 1985
Legal system: English common law
National holiday: Liberation Day, 14 June (1982)
Executive branch: British monarch, commissioner
Legislative branch: none
Judicial branch: none
Leaders: *Chief of State*—Queen ELIZABETH II (since 6 February 1952), represented by Commissioner William Hugh FULLERTON (since 1988; resident at Stanley, Falkland Islands)

Economy

Overview: Some fishing takes place in adjacent waters. There is a potential source of income from harvesting fin fish and krill. The islands receive income from postage stamps produced in the UK.
Budget: revenues $291,777; expenditures $451,011, including capital expenditures of $NA (FY88 est.)
Electricity: 900 kW capacity; 2 million kWh produced, NA kWh per capita (1989)

Communications

Highways: NA
Ports: Grytviken Harbour on South Georgia
Airports: none
Telecommunications: coastal radio station at Grytviken; no broadcast stations

Defense Forces

Note: defense is the responsibility of the UK

Soviet Union

2000 km

Arctic Ocean

Barents Sea
Murmansk
Baltic Sea
Bering Sea
Leningrad
Magadan
Black Sea
MOSCOW
Kiev
Sverdlovsk
Yakutsk
Sea of Okhotsk
Novosibirsk
Baku
Caspian Sea
Tashkent
Vladivostok

The United States Government has not recognized the incorporation of Estonia, Latvia, and Lithuania into the Soviet Union. Other boundary representation is not necessarily authoritative.

See regional maps VIII and XI

Geography

Total area: 22,402,200 km²; land area: 22,272,000 km²
Comparative area: slightly less than 2.5 times the size of US
Land boundaries: 19,933 km total; Afghanistan 2,384 km, Czechoslovakia 98 km, China 7,520 km, Finland 1,313 km, Hungary 135 km, Iran 1,690 km, North Korea 17 km, Mongolia 3,441 km, Norway 196 km, Poland 1,215 km, Romania 1,307 km, Turkey 617 km
Coastline: 42,777 km
Maritime claims:
  Continental shelf: 200 meters or to depth of exploitation
  Extended economic zone: 200 nm
  Territorial sea: 12 nm
Disputes: bilateral negotiations are under way to resolve four disputed sections of the boundary with China (Pamir, Argun, Amur, and Khabarovsk areas); US Government has not recognized the incorporation of Estonia, Latvia, and Lithuania into the Soviet Union; Habomai Islands, Etorofu, Kunashiri, and Shikotan islands occupied by Soviet Union since 1945, claimed by Japan; Kuril Islands administered by Soviet Union; maritime dispute with Norway over portion of Barents Sea; has made no territorial claim in Antarctica (but has reserved the right to do so) and does not recognize the claims of any other nation; Bessarabia question with Romania; Kurdish question among Iran, Iraq, Syria, Turkey, and the USSR
Climate: mostly temperate to arctic continental; winters vary from cool along Black Sea to frigid in Siberia; summers vary from hot in southern deserts to cool along Arctic coast
Terrain: broad plain with low hills west of Urals; vast coniferous forest and tundra in Siberia, deserts in Central Asia, mountains in south

Natural resources: self-sufficient in oil, natural gas, coal, and strategic minerals (except bauxite, alumina, tantalum, tin, tungsten, fluorspar, and molybdenum), timber, gold, manganese, lead, zinc, nickel, mercury, potash, phosphates

Land use: 10% arable land; NEGL% permanent crops; 17% meadows and pastures; 41% forest and woodland; 32% other; includes 1% irrigated

Environment: despite size and diversity, small percentage of land is arable and much is too far north; some of most fertile land is water deficient or has insufficient growing season; many better climates have poor soils; hot, dry, desiccating sukhovey wind affects south; desertification; continuous permafrost over much of Siberia is a major impediment to development

Note: largest country in world, but unfavorably located in relation to major sea lanes of world

---

People

Population: 290,938,469 (July 1990), growth rate 0.7% (1990)

Birth rate: 18 births/1,000 population (1990)

Death rate: 10 deaths/1,000 population (1990)

Net migration rate: 0 migrants/1,000 population (1990)

Infant mortality rate: 24 deaths/1,000 live births (1990)

Life expectancy at birth: 65 years male, 74 years female (1990)

Total fertility rate: 2.4 children born/woman (1990)

Nationality: noun—Soviet(s); adjective—Soviet

Ethnic divisions: Russian 50.78%, Ukrainian 15.45%, Uzbek 5.84%, Byelorussian 3.51%, Kazakh 2.85%, Azerbaijan 2.38%, Armenian 1.62%, Tajik 1.48%, Georgian 1.39%, Moldavian 1.17%, Lithuanian 1.07%, Turkmen 0.95%, Kirghiz 0.89%, Latvian 0.51%, Estonian 0.36%, others 9.75%

Religion: 20% Russian Orthodox; 10% Muslim; 7% Protestant, Georgian Orthodox, Armenian Orthodox, and Roman Catholic; less than 1% Jewish; 60% atheist (est.)

Language: Russian (official); more than 200 languages and dialects (at least 18 with more than 1 million speakers); 75% Slavic group, 8% other Indo-European, 12% Altaic, 3% Uralian, 2% Caucasian

Literacy: 99%

Labor force: 152,300,000 civilians; 80% industry and other nonagricultural fields, 20% agriculture; shortage of skilled labor (1989)

Organized labor: 98% of workers are union members; all trade unions are organized within the All-Union Central Council of Trade Unions (AUCCTU) and conduct their work under guidance of the Communist party

---

Government

Long-form name: Union of Soviet Socialist Republics; abbreviated USSR

Type: Communist state

Capital: Moscow

Administrative divisions: 1 soviet federative socialist republic* (sovetskaya federativnaya sotsialistcheskaya respublika) and 14 soviet socialist republics (sovetskiye sotsialisticheskiye respubliki, singular—sovetskaya sotsialisticheskaya respublika); Armenian Soviet Socialist Republic, Azerbaijan Soviet Socialist Republic, Byelorussian Soviet Socialist Republic, Estonian Soviet Socialist Republic, Georgian Soviet Socialist Republic, Kazakh Soviet Socialist Republic, Kirghiz Soviet Socialist Republic, Latvian Soviet Socialist Republic, Lithuanian Soviet Socialist Republic, Moldavian Soviet Socialist Republic, Russian Soviet Federative Socialist Republic*, Tajik Soviet Socialist Republic, Turkmen Soviet Socialist Republic, Ukrainian Soviet Socialist Republic, Uzbek Soviet Socialist Republic; note—the Russian Soviet Federative Socialist Republic is often abbreviated RSFSR and Soviet Socialist Republic is often abbreviated SSR

Independence: 1721 (Russian Empire proclaimed)

Constitution: 7 October 1977

Legal system: civil law system as modified by Communist legal theory; no judicial review of legislative acts; has not accepted compulsory ICJ jurisdiction

National holiday: Great October Socialist Revolution, 7-8 November (1917)

Executive branch: president

Legislative branch: the Congress of People's Deputies is the supreme organ of USSR state power and selects the bicameral USSR Supreme Soviet (Verkhovnyy Sovyet) which consists of two coequal houses—Council of the Union (Sovet Soyuza) and Council of Nationalities (Sovet Natsionalnostey)

Judicial branch: Supreme Court of the USSR

Leaders: *Chief of State*—President Mikhail Sergeyevich GORBACHEV (since 14 March 1990; General Secretary of the Central Committee of the Communist Party since 11 March 1985);

Head of Government—Chairman of the USSR Council of Ministers Nikolay Ivanovich RYZHKOV (since 28 September 1985)

Political parties and leaders: only party—Communist Party of the Soviet Union (CPSU), President Mikhail Sergeyevich Gorbachev, general secretary of the Central Committee of the CPSU; note—the CPSU is the only party, but others are forming

Suffrage: universal at age 18

Elections: *President*—last held 14 March 1990 (next to be held NA 1995); results—Mikhail Sergeyevich Gorbachev was elected by the Congress of People's Deputies;

Congress of People's Deputies—last held 12 March 1990 (next to be held NA); results—CPSU is the only party; seats—(2,250 total) CPSU 1,931, non-CPSU 319;

USSR Supreme Soviet—last held NA June 1989 (next to be held NA); results—CPSU is the only party; seats—(542 total) CPSU 475, non-CPSU 67;

Council of the Union—last held Spring 1989 (next to be held NA); results—CPSU is the only party; seats—(271 total) CPSU 239, non-CPSU 32;

Council of Nationalities—last held Spring 1989 (next to be held NA); results—CPSU is the only party; seats—(271 total) CPSU 236, non-CPSU 35

Communists: about 19 million party members

Other political or pressure groups: Komsomol, trade unions, and other organizations that facilitate Communist control; regional popular fronts, informal organizations, and nascent parties with varying attitudes toward the Communist Party establishment

Member of: CEMA, ESCAP, IAEA, IBEC, ICAC, ICAO, ICCO, ICES, ILO, ILZSG, IMO, INRO, INTERPOL, IPU, ISO, ITC, ITU, International Whaling Commission, IWC—International Wheat Council, UN, UNCTAD, UNESCO, UPU, Warsaw Pact, WFTU, WHO, WIPO, WMO, WTO

Diplomatic representation: Ambassador-designate Aleksandr BESSMERTNYKH; Chancery at 1125 16th Street NW, Washington DC 20036; telephone (202) 628-7551 or 8548; there is a Soviet Consulate General in San Francisco; *US*—Ambassador Jack F. MATLOCK, Jr.; Embassy at Ulitsa Chaykovskogo 19/21/23, Moscow (mailing address is APO New York 09862); telephone [7] (096) 252-24-51 through 59; there is a US Consulate General in Leningrad

Flag: red with the yellow silhouette of a crossed hammer and sickle below a yellow-edged five-pointed red star in the upper hoist-side corner

---

Economy

Overview: The first five years of perestroyka (economic restructuring) have undermined the institutions and processes

287

of the Soviet command economy without replacing them with efficiently functioning markets. The initial reforms featured greater authority for enterprise managers over prices, wages, product mix, investment, sources of supply, and customers. But in the absence of effective market discipline, the result was the disappearance of low-price goods, excessive wage increases, an even larger volume of unfinished construction projects, and, in general, continued economic stagnation. The Gorbachev regime has made at least four serious errors in economic policy in these five years: the unpopular and short-lived anti-alcohol campaign; the initial cutback in imports of consumer goods; the failure to act decisively for the privatization of agriculture; and the buildup of a massive overhang of unspent rubles in the hands of households and enterprises. In October 1989, a top economic adviser, Leonid Abalkin presented an ambitious but reasonable timetable for the conversion to a partially privatized market system in the 1990s. In December 1989, however, Premier Ryzhkov's conservative approach prevailed, namely, the contention that a period of retrenchment was necessary to provide a stable financial and legislative base for launching further reforms. Accordingly, the new strategy was to put the reform process on hold in 1990-92 by recentralizing economic authority and to placate the rank-and-file through sharp increases in consumer goods output. In still another policy twist, the leadership in early 1990 was considering a marked speedup in the marketization process. Because the economy is caught in between two systems, there was in 1989 an even greater mismatch between what was produced and what would serve the best interests of enterprises and households. Meanwhile, the seething nationality problems have been dislocating regional patterns of economic specialization and pose a further major threat to growth prospects over the next few years.

GNP: $2,659.5 billion, per capita $9,211; real growth rate 1.4% (1989 est. based on Soviet statistics; cutbacks in Soviet reporting on products included in sample make the estimate subject to greater uncertainty than in earlier years)

Inflation rate (consumer prices): 6% (1989 est.)

Unemployment rate: officially, no unemployment

Budget: revenues $622 billion; expenditures $781 billion, including capital expenditures of $119 billion (1989 est.)

Exports: $110.7 billion (f.o.b., 1988); *commodities*—petroleum and petroleum products, natural gas, metals, wood, agricultural products, and a wide variety of manufactured goods (primarily capital goods and arms); *partners*—Eastern Europe 49%, EC 14%, Cuba 5%, US, Afghanistan (1988)

Imports: $107.3 billion (c.i.f., 1988); *commodities*—grain and other agricultural products, machinery and equipment, steel products (including large-diameter pipe), consumer manufactures; *partners*—Eastern Europe 54%, EC 11%, Cuba, China, US (1988)

External debt: $27.3 billion (1988)

Industrial production: growth rate 0.2% (1989 est.)

Electricity: 355,000,000 kW capacity; 1,790,000 million kWh produced, 6,150 kWh per capita (1989)

Industries: diversified, highly developed capital goods and defense industries; consumer goods industries comparatively less developed

Agriculture: accounts for roughly 20% of GNP and labor force; production based on large collective and state farms; inefficiently managed; wide range of temperate crops and livestock produced; world's second-largest grain producer after the US; shortages of grain, oilseeds, and meat; world's leading producer of sawnwood and roundwood; annual fish catch among the world's largest—11.2 million metric tons (1987)

Illicit drugs: illegal producer of cannabis and opium poppy, mostly for domestic consumption; government has begun eradication program to control cultivation; used as a transshipment country

Aid: donor—extended to non-Communist less developed countries (1954-88), $47.4 billion; extended to other Communist countries (1954-88), $147.6 billion

Currency: ruble (plural—rubles); 1 ruble (R) = 100 kopeks

Exchange rates: rubles (R) per US$1—0.600 (February 1990), 0.629 (1989), 0.629 (1988), 0.633 (1987), 0.704 (1986), 0.838 (1985); note—the exchange rate is administratively set and should not be used indiscriminately to convert domestic rubles to dollars; on 1 November 1989 the USSR began using a rate of 6.26 rubles to the dollar for Western tourists buying rubles and for Soviets traveling abroad, but retained the official exchange rate for most trade transactions

Fiscal year: calendar year

Communications

Railroads: 146,100 km total; 51,700 km electrified; does not include industrial lines (1987)

Highways: 1,609,900 km total; 1,196,000 km hard-surfaced (asphalt, concrete, stone block, asphalt treated, gravel, crushed stone); 413,900 km earth (1987)

Inland waterways: 122,500 km navigable, exclusive of Caspian Sea (1987)

Pipelines: 81,500 km crude oil and refined products; 195,000 km natural gas (1987)

Ports: Leningrad, Riga, Tallinn, Kaliningrad, Liepaja, Ventspils, Murmansk, Arkhangel'sk, Odessa, Novorossiysk, Il'ichevsk, Nikolayev, Sevastopol', Vladivostok, Nakhodka; inland ports are Astrakhan', Baku, Gor'kiy, Kazan', Khabarovsk, Krasnoyarsk, Kuybyshev, Moscow, Rostov, Volgograd, Kiev

Merchant marine: 1,646 ships (1,000 GRT or over) totaling 16,436,063 GRT/22,732,215 DWT; includes 53 passenger, 937 cargo, 52 container, 11 barge carrier, 5 roll-on/float off cargo, 5 railcar carrier, 108 roll-on/roll-off cargo, 251 petroleum, oils, and lubricants (POL) tanker, 11 liquefied gas, 21 combination ore/oil, 4 specialized liquid carrier, 17 chemical tanker, 171 bulk; note—639 merchant ships are based in Black Sea, 383 in Baltic Sea, 408 in Soviet Far East, and 216 in Barents Sea and White Sea; the Soviet Ministry of Merchant Marine is beginning to use foreign registries for its merchant ships to increase the economic competitiveness of the fleet in the international market—the first reregistered ships have gone to the Cypriot flag

Civil air: 4,500 major transport aircraft

Airports: 6,950 total, 4,530 usable; 1,050 with permanent-surface runways; 30 with runways over 3,659 m; 490 with runways 2,440-3,659 m; 660 with runways 1,220-2,439 m

Telecommunications: extensive network of AM-FM stations broadcasting both Moscow and regional programs; main TV centers in Moscow and Leningrad plus 11 more in the Soviet republics; hundreds of TV stations; 85,000,000 TV sets; 162,000,000 radio receivers; many satellite earth stations and extensive satellite networks (including 2 Atlantic Ocean INTELSAT and 1 Indian Ocean INTELSAT earth stations)

Defense Forces

Branches: Ground Forces, Navy, Air Defense Forces, Air Forces, Strategic Rocket Forces

Military manpower: males 15-49, 69,634,893; 55,588,743 fit for military service; 2,300,127 million reach military age (18) annually (down somewhat from 2,500,000 a decade ago)

Defense expenditures: NA

Spain

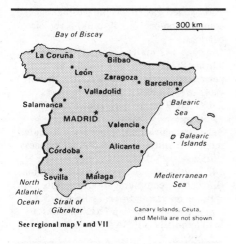

Bay of Biscay
La Coruña • Bilbao
• León • Zaragoza
Valladolid • Barcelona
Salamanca •
MADRID • Valencia
• Córdoba • Alicante
Sevilla • Málaga

Balearic Sea
Balearic Islands
Mediterranean Sea
North Atlantic Ocean
Strait of Gibraltar
300 km
Canary Islands, Ceuta, and Melilla are not shown

See regional map V and VII

Geography

Total area: 504,750 km²; land area: 499,400 km²; includes Balaeric Islands, Canary Islands, Ceuta, Mellila, Islas Chafarinas, Peñón de Alhucemas, and Peñón de Vélez de la Gomera
Comparative area: slightly more than twice the size of Oregon
Land boundaries: 1,903.2 km total; Andorra 65 km, France 623 km, Gibraltar 1.2 km, Portugal 1,214 km
Coastline: 4,964 km
Maritime claims:
 Extended economic zone: 200 nm
 Territorial sea: 12 nm
Disputes: Gibraltar question with UK; controls two presidios or places of sovereignty (Ceuta and Melilla) on the north coast of Morocco
Climate: temperate; clear, hot summers in interior, more moderate and cloudy along coast; cloudy, cold winters in interior, partly cloudy and cool along coast
Terrain: large, flat to dissected plateau surrounded by rugged hills; Pyrenees in north
Natural resources: coal, lignite, iron ore, uranium, mercury, pyrites, fluorspar, gypsum, zinc, lead, tungsten, copper, kaolin, potash, hydropower
Land use: 31% arable land; 10% permanent crops; 21% meadows and pastures; 31% forest and woodland; 7% other; includes 6% irrigated
Environment: deforestation; air pollution
Note: strategic location along approaches to Strait of Gibraltar

People

Population: 39,268,715 (July 1990), growth rate 0.3% (1990)
Birth rate: 11 births/1,000 population (1990)
Death rate: 8 deaths/1,000 population (1990)

Net migration rate: 0 migrants/1,000 population (1990)
Infant mortality rate: 6 deaths/1,000 live births (1990)
Life expectancy at birth: 75 years male, 82 years female (1990)
Total fertility rate: 1.4 children born/woman (1990)
Nationality: noun—Spaniard(s); adjective—Spanish
Ethnic divisions: composite of Mediterranean and Nordic types
Religion: 99% Roman Catholic, 1% other sects
Language: Castilian Spanish; second languages include 17% Catalan, 7% Galician, and 2% Basque
Literacy: 97%
Labor force: 14,621,000; 53% services, 24% industry, 14% agriculture, 9% construction (1988)
Organized labor: less 10% of labor force (1988)

Government

Long-form name: Kingdom of Spain
Type: parliamentary monarchy
Capital: Madrid
Administrative divisions: 17 autonomous communities (comunidades autónomas, singular—comunidad autónoma); Andalucía, Aragón, Asturias, Canarias, Cantabria, Castilla-La Mancha, Castilla y León, Cataluña, Extremadura, Galicia, Islas Baleares, La Rioja, Madrid, Murcia, Navarra, Pais Vasco, Valenciana
Independence: 1492 (expulsion of the Moors and unification)
Constitution: 6 December 1978, effective 29 December 1978
Legal system: civil law system, with regional applications; does not accept compulsory ICJ jurisdiction
National holiday: National Day, 12 October
Executive branch: monarch, president of the government (prime minister), deputy prime minister, Council of Ministers (cabinet), Council of State
Legislative branch: bicameral The General Courts or National Assembly (Las Cortes Generales) consists of an upper house or Senate (Senado) and a lower house or Congress of Deputies (Congreso de los Diputados)
Judicial branch: Supreme Court (Tribunal Supremo)
Leaders: *Chief of State*—King JUAN CARLOS I (since 22 November 1975); *Head of Government*—Prime Minister Felipe GONZALEZ Márquez (since 2 December 1982); Deputy Prime Minister Alfonso GUERRA González (since 2 December 1982)

Political parties and leaders: principal national parties, from right to left—Popular Party (PP), José Maria Aznar; Popular Democratic Party (PDP), Luis de Grandes; Social Democratic Center (CDS), Adolfo Suárez González; Spanish Socialist Workers Party (PSOE), Felipe González Márquez; Spanish Communist Party (PCE), Julio Anguita; chief regional parties—Convergence and Unity (CiU), Jordi Pujol Saley, in Catalonia; Basque Nationalist Party (PNV), Xabier Arzallus; Basque Solidarity (EA), Carlos Garaicoetxea Urizza; Basque Popular Unity (HB), Jon Idigoras; Basque Left (EE), Juan Maria Bandries Molet; Andalusian Party (PA); Independent Canary Group (AIC); Aragon Regional Party (PAR); Valencian Union (UV)
Suffrage: universal at age 18
Elections: *The Courts General*—last held 29 October 1989 (next to be held October 1993); results—PSOE 39.6%, PP 25.8%, CDS 9%, Communist-led coalition (IU) 9%, CiU 5%, Basque Nationalist Party 1.2%, HB 1%, Andalusian Party 1%, others 8.4%; seats—(350 total, 18 vacant pending new elections caused by voting irregularities) PSOE 176, PP 106, CiU 18, IU 17, CDS 14, PNV 5, HB 4, others 10
Communists: PCE membership declined from a possible high of 160,000 in 1977 to roughly 60,000 in 1987; the party gained almost 1 million voters and 10 deputies in the 1989 election; voters came mostly from the disgruntled socialist left; remaining strength is in labor, where it dominates the Workers Commissions trade union (one of the country's two major labor centrals), which claims a membership of about 1 million; experienced a modest recovery in 1986 national election, nearly doubling the share of the vote it received in 1982
Other political or pressure groups: on the extreme left, the Basque Fatherland and Liberty (ETA) and the First of October Antifascist Resistance Group (GRAPO) use terrorism to oppose the government; free labor unions (authorized in April 1977) include the Communist-dominated Workers Commissions (CCOO); the Socialist General Union of Workers (UGT), and the smaller independent Workers Syndical Union (USO); the Catholic Church; business and landowning interests; Opus Dei; university students
Member of: Andean Pact (observer), ASSIMER, CCC, Council of Europe, EC, ESA, FAO, GATT, IAEA, IBRD, ICAC, ICAO, ICES, ICO, IDA, IDB—Inter-American Development Bank, IEA, IFAD, IFC, IHO, ILO, ILZSG, IMF, IMO, INTELSAT, INTERPOL, IOOC, IPU, ITC, ITU, IWC—International

Spain (continued)

Wheat Council, NATO, OAS (observer), OECD, UN, UNESCO, UPU, WEU, WHO, WIPO, WMO, WSG, WTO
Diplomatic representation: Ambassador Julian SANTAMARIA; Chancery at 2700 15th Street NW, Washington DC 20009; telephone (202) 265-0190 or 0191; there are Spanish Consulates General in Boston, Chicago, Houston, Los Angeles, Miami, New Orleans, New York, San Francisco, and San Juan (Puerto Rico); *US*—Ambassador Joseph ZAPPALA; Embassy at Serrano 75, Madrid 6 (mailing address is APO New York 09285); telephone [34] (1) 276-3400 or 3600; there is a US Consulate General in Barcelona and a Consulate in Bilbao
Flag: three horizontal bands of red (top), yellow (double width), and red with the national coat of arms on the hoist side of the yellow band; the coat of arms includes the royal seal framed by the Pillars of Hercules which are the two promontories (Gibraltar and Ceuta) on either side of the eastern end of the Strait of Gibraltar

Economy

Overview: This Western capitalistic economy has done well since Spain joined the European Economic Community in 1986. With increases in real GNP of 5.5% in 1987 and about 5% in 1988 and 1989, Spain has been the fastest growing member of the EC. Increased investment—both domestic and foreign—has been the most important factor pushing the economic expansion. Inflation moderated to 4.8% in 1988, but an overheated economy caused inflation to reach an estimated 7% in 1989. Another economic problem facing Spain is an unemployment rate of 16.5%, the highest in Europe.
GNP: $398.7 billion, per capita $10,100; real growth rate 4.8% (1989 est.)
Inflation rate (consumer prices): 7.0% (1989 est.)
Unemployment rate: 16.5% (1989 est.)
Budget: revenues $57.8 billion; expenditures $66.7 billion, including capital expenditures of $10.4 billion (1987)
Exports: $40.2 billion (f.o.b., 1988); *commodities*—foodstuffs, live animals, wood, footwear, machinery, chemicals; *partners*—EC 66%, US 8%, other developed countries 9%
Imports: $60.4 billion (c.i.f., 1988); *commodities*—petroleum, footwear, machinery, chemicals, grain, soybeans, coffee, tobacco, iron and steel, timber, cotton, transport equipment; *partners*—EC 57%, US 9%, other developed countries 13%, Middle East 3%
External debt: $32.7 billion (1988)
Industrial production: growth rate 3.0% (1988)

Electricity: 46,589,000 kW capacity; 157,040 million kWh produced, 3,980 kWh per capita (1989)
Industries: textiles and apparel (including footwear), food and beverages, metals and metal manufactures, chemicals, shipbuilding, automobiles, machine tools
Agriculture: accounts for 5% of GNP and 14% of labor force; major products—grain, vegetables, olives, wine grapes, sugar beets, citrus fruit, beef, pork, poultry, dairy; largely self-sufficient in food; fish catch of 1.4 million metric tons among top 20 nations
Aid: US commitments, including Ex-Im (FY70-87), $1.9 billion; Western (non-US) countries, ODA and OOF bilateral commitments (1970-79), $545.0 million
Currency: peseta (plural—pesetas); 1 peseta (Pta) = 100 céntimos
Exchange rates: pesetas (Ptas) per US$1—109.69 (January 1990), 118.38 (1989), 116.49 (1988), 123.48 (1987), 140.05 (1986), 170.04 (1985)
Fiscal year: calendar year

Communications

Railroads: 15,430 km total; Spanish National Railways (RENFE) operates 12,691 km 1.668-meter gauge, 6,184 km electrified, and 2,295 km double track; FEVE (government-owned narrow-gauge railways) operates 1,821 km of predominantly 1.000-meter gauge and 441 km electrified; privately owned railways operate 918 km of predominantly 1.000-meter gauge, 512 km electrified, and 56 km double track
Highways: 150,839 km total; 82,513 km national (includes 2,433 km limited-access divided highway, 63,042 km bituminous treated, 17,038 km intermediate bituminous, concrete, or stone block) and 68,326 km provincial or local roads (bituminous treated, intermediate bituminous, or stone block)
Inland waterways: 1,045 km, but of minor economic importance
Pipelines: 265 km crude oil; 1,794 km refined products; 1,666 km natural gas
Ports: Algeciras, Alicante, Almería, Barcelona, Bilbao, Cádiz, Cartagena, Castellón de la Plana, Ceuta, El Ferrol del Caudillo, Puerto de Gijón, Huelva, La Coruña, Las Palmas (Canary Islands), Mahón, Málaga, Melilla, Rota, Santa Cruz de Tenerife, Sagunto, Tarragona, Valencia, Vigo, and 175 minor ports
Merchant marine: 324 ships (1,000 GRT or over) totaling 3,492,563 GRT/6,128,190 DWT; includes 2 passenger, 9 short-sea passenger, 121 cargo, 19 refrigerated cargo, 17 container, 23 roll-on/roll-off cargo, 51 petroleum, oils, and lubricants (POL) tanker, 16 chemical tanker,

10 liquefied gas, 1 specialized tanker, 1 combination ore/oil, 49 bulk, 5 vehicle carrier
Civil air: 142 major transport aircraft
Airports: 110 total, 103 usable; 62 with permanent-surface runways; 4 with runways over 3,659 m; 20 with runways 2,440-3,659 m; 29 with runways 1,220-2,439 m
Telecommunications: generally adequate, modern facilities; 15,310,000 telephones; stations—196 AM, 404 (134 relays) FM, 143 (1,297 relays) TV; 17 coaxial submarine cables; communications satellite earth stations operating in INTELSAT (5 Atlantic Ocean, 1 Indian Ocean), MARISAT, and ENTELSAT systems

Defense Forces

Branches: Army, Navy, Air Force
Military manpower: males 15-49, 10,032,649; 8,141,384 fit for military service; 338,582 reach military age (20) annually
Defense expenditures: 2.1% of GDP, or $8.4 billion (1989 est.)

Spratly Islands

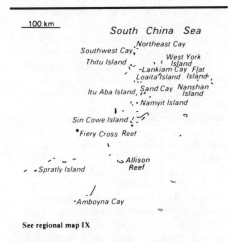

See regional map IX

Geography

Total area: less than 5 km²; land area: less than 5 km²; includes 100 or so islets, coral reefs, and sea mounts scattered over the South China Sea
Comparative area: undetermined
Land boundaries: none
Coastline: 926 km
Maritime claims: undetermined
Disputes: China, Malaysia, the Philippines, Taiwan, and Vietnam claim all or part of the Spratly Islands
Climate: tropical
Terrain: flat
Natural resources: fish, guano; oil and natural gas potential
Land use: 0% arable land; 0% permanent crops; 0% meadows and pastures; 0% forest and woodland; 100% other
Environment: subject to typhoons; includes numerous small islands, atolls, shoals, and coral reefs
Note: strategically located near several primary shipping lanes in the central South China Sea; serious navigational hazard

People

Population: no permanent inhabitants; garrisons

Government

Long-form name: none

Economy

Overview: Economic activity is limited to commercial fishing and phosphate mining. Geological surveys carried out several years ago suggest that substantial reserves of oil and natural gas may lie beneath the islands; commercial exploitation has yet to be developed.
Industries: some guano mining

Communications

Airports: 3 total, 2 usable; none with runways over 2,439 m; 1 with runways 1,220-2,439 m
Ports: none; offshore anchorage only

Defense Forces

Note: approximately 50 small islands or reefs are occupied by China, Malaysia, the Philippines, Taiwan, and Vietnam

Sri Lanka

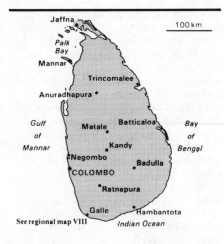

See regional map VIII

Geography

Total area: 65,610 km²; land area: 64,740 km²
Comparative area: slightly larger than West Virginia
Land boundaries: none
Coastline: 1,340 km
Maritime claims:
  Contiguous zone: 24 nm
  Continental shelf: edge of continental margin or 200 nm
  Extended economic zone: 200 nm
  Territorial sea: 12 nm
Climate: tropical; monsoonal; northeast monsoon (December to March); southwest monsoon (June to October)
Terrain: mostly low, flat to rolling plain; mountains in south-central interior
Natural resources: limestone, graphite, mineral sands, gems, phosphates, clay
Land use: 16% arable land; 17% permanent crops; 7% meadows and pastures; 37% forest and woodland; 23% other; includes 8% irrigated
Environment: occasional cyclones, tornados; deforestation; soil erosion
Note: only 29 km from India across the Palk Strait; near major Indian Ocean sea lanes

People

Population: 17,196,436 (July 1990), growth rate 1.5% (1990)
Birth rate: 21 births/1,000 population (1990)
Death rate: 6 deaths/1,000 population (1990)
Net migration rate: NEGL migrants/1,000 population (1990)
Infant mortality rate: 31 deaths/1,000 live births (1990)
Life expectancy at birth: 68 years male, 72 years female (1990)
Total fertility rate: 2.3 children born/woman (1990)

291

Sri Lanka (continued)

Nationality: noun—Sri Lankan(s); adjective—Sri Lankan
Ethnic divisions: 74% Sinhalese; 18% Tamil; 7% Moor; 1% Burgher, Malay, and Veddha
Religion: 69% Buddhist, 15% Hindu, 8% Christian, 8% Muslim
Language: Sinhala (official); Sinhala and Tamil listed as national languages; Sinhala spoken by about 74% of population, Tamil spoken by about 18%; English commonly used in government and spoken by about 10% of the population
Literacy: 87%
Labor force: 6,600,000; 45.9% agriculture, 13.3% mining and manufacturing, 12.4% trade and transport, 28.4% services and other (1985 est.)
Organized labor: about 33% of labor force, over 50% of which are employed on tea, rubber, and coconut estates

---

Government

Long-form name: Democratic Socialist Republic of Sri Lanka
Type: republic
Capital: Colombo
Administrative divisions: 24 districts; Amparai, Anuradhapura, Badulla, Batticaloa, Colombo, Galle, Gampaha, Hambantota, Jaffna, Kalutara, Kandy, Kegalla, Kurunegala, Mannar, Matale, Matara, Moneragala, Mullativu, Nuwara Eliya, Polonnaruwa, Puttalam, Ratnapura, Trincomalee, Vavuniya; note—the administrative structure may now include 8 provinces (Central, North Central, North Eastern, North Western, Sabaragamuwa, Southern, Uva, and Western) and 25 districts (with Kilinochchi added to the existing districts)
Independence: 4 February 1948 (from UK; formerly Ceylon)
Constitution: 31 August 1978
Legal system: a highly complex mixture of English common law, Roman-Dutch, Muslim, and customary law; has not accepted compulsory ICJ jurisdiction
National holiday: Independence and National Day, 4 February (1948)
Executive branch: president, prime minister, Cabinet
Legislative branch: unicameral Parliament
Judicial branch: Supreme Court
Leaders: *Chief of State*—President Ranasinghe PREMADASA (since 2 January 1989);
Head of Government—Prime Minister Dingiri Banda WIJETUNGE (since 6 March 1989)
Political parties and leaders: United National Party (UNP), Ranasinghe Premadasa; Sri Lanka Freedom Party (SLFP), Sirimavo Bandaranaike; Sri Lanka Muslim Congress (SLMC), Mhm. Ashraff; All

Ceylon Tamil Congress (ACTC), Kumar Ponnambalam; Mahajana Eksath Peramuna (MEP, or People's United Front), Dinesh Gundawardene; Sri Lanka Mahajana Party (SLMP, or Sri Lanka People's Party), Chandrika Baudaranaike Kumaranatunga; Lanka Sama Samaja Party (LSSP, Lanka Socialist Party/Trotskyite), Colin R. de Silva; Nava Sama Samaja Party (NSSP, or New Socialist Party), Vasudeva Nanayakkara; Tamil United Liberation Front (TULF), leader NA; Communist Party/Moscow (CP/M), K. P. Silva; Communist Party/Beijing (CP/B), N. Shanmugathasan
Suffrage: universal at age 18
Elections: *President*—last held 19 December 1988 (next to be held December 1994); results—Ranasinghe Premadasa (UNP) 50%, Sirimavo Bandaranaike (SLFP) 45%, others 5%;
Parliament—last held 15 February 1989 (next to be held by February 1995); results—percent of vote by party NA; seats—(225 total) UNP 125, SLFP 67, others 33
Other political or pressure groups: Liberation Tigers of Tamil Eelam (LTTE) and other smaller Tamil separatist groups; Janatha Vimukthi Peramuna (JVP or People's Liberation Front); Buddhist clergy; Sinhalese Buddhist lay groups; labor unions
Member of: ADB, ANRPC, CCC, Colombo Plan, Commonwealth, ESCAP, FAO, G-77, GATT, IAEA, IBRD, ICAO, IDA, IFAD, IFC, ILO, IMF, IMO, INTELSAT, INTERPOL, IPU, IRC, ITU, NAM, SAARC, UN, UNESCO, UPU, WFTU, WHO, WIPO, WMO, WTO
Diplomatic representation: Ambassador W. Susanta De ALWIS; Chancery at 2148 Wyoming Avenue NW, Washington DC 20008; telephone (202) 483-4025 through 4028; there is a Sri Lankan Consulate in New York; *US*—Ambassador Marion V. CREEKMORE; Embassy at 210 Galle Road, Colombo 3 (mailing address is P. O. Box 106, Colombo); telephone [94] (1) 548007
Flag: yellow with two panels; the smaller hoist-side panel has two equal vertical bands of green (hoist side) and orange; the other panel is a large dark red rectangle with a yellow lion holding a sword and there is a yellow bo leaf in each corner; the yellow field appears as a border that goes around the entire flag and extends between the two panels

---

Economy

Overview: Agriculture, forestry, and fishing dominate the economy, employing about half of the labor force and account-

ing for about 25% of GDP. The plantation crops of tea, rubber, and coconuts provide about 50% of export earnings and almost 20% of budgetary revenues. The economy has been plagued by high rates of unemployment since the late 1970s.
GDP: $6.1 billion, per capita $370; real growth rate 2.7% (1988)
Inflation rate (consumer prices): 15% (1988)
Unemployment rate: 20% (1988 est.)
Budget: revenues $1.5 billion; expenditures $2.3 billion, including capital expenditures of $0.7 billion (1989)
Exports: $1.5 billion (f.o.b., 1988); *commodities*—tea, textiles and garments, petroleum products, coconut, rubber, agricultural products, gems and jewelry, marine products; *partners*—US 26%, Egypt, Iraq, UK, FRG, Singapore, Japan
Imports: $2.3 billion (c.i.f., 1988); *commodities*—petroleum, machinery and equipment, textiles and textile materials, wheat, transportation equipment, electrical machinery, sugar, rice; *partners*—Japan, Saudi Arabia, US 5.6%, India, Singapore, FRG, UK, Iran
External debt: $5.6 billion (1989)
Industrial production: growth rate 5% (1988)
Electricity: 1,300,000 kW capacity; 4,200 million kWh produced, 250 kWh per capita (1989)
Industries: processing of rubber, tea, coconuts, and other agricultural commodities; cement, petroleum refining, textiles, tobacco, clothing
Agriculture: accounts for 25% of GDP and nearly half of labor force; most important staple crop is paddy rice; other field crops—sugarcane, grains, pulses, oilseeds, roots, spices; cash crops—tea, rubber, coconuts; animal products—milk, eggs, hides, meat; not self-sufficient in rice production
Aid: US commitments, including Ex-Im (FY70-88), $932 million; Western (non-US) countries, ODA and OOF bilateral commitments (1980-87), $4.3 billion; OPEC bilateral aid (1979-89), $169 million; Communist countries (1970-88), $369 million
Currency: Sri Lankan rupee (plural—rupees); 1 Sri Lankan rupee (SLRe) = 100 cents
Exchange rates: Sri Lankan rupees (SLRs) per US$1—40.000 (January 1990), 36.047 (1989), 31.807 (1988), 29.445 (1987), 28.017 (1986), 27.163 (1985)
Fiscal year: calendar year

Sudan

Communications

Railroads: 1,868 km total (1985); all 1.868-meter broad gauge; 102 km double track; no electrification; government owned

Highways: 66,176 km total (1985); 24,300 km paved (mostly bituminous treated), 28,916 km crushed stone or gravel, 12,960 km improved earth' or unimproved earth; several thousand km of mostly unmotorable tracks

Inland waterways: 430 km; navigable by shallow-draft craft

Pipelines: crude and refined products, 62 km (1987)

Ports: Colombo, Trincomalee

Merchant marine: 40 ships (1,000 GRT or over) totaling 258,923 GRT/334,702 DWT; includes 22 cargo, 8 refrigerated cargo, 4 container, 1 livestock carrier, 2 petroleum, oils, and lubricants (POL) tanker, 3 bulk

Civil air: 8 major transport (including 1 leased)

Airports: 14 total, 13 usable; 12 with permanent-surface runways; none with runways over 3,659 m; 1 with runways 2,440-3,659 m; 7 with runways 1,220-2,439 m

Telecommunications: good international service; 109,900 telephones (1982); stations—12 AM, 5 FM, 1 TV; submarine cables extend to Indonesia, Djibouti, India; 2 Indian Ocean INTELSAT earth stations

Defense Forces

Branches: Army, Air Force, Navy, Police Force, Special Police Task Force, National Auxiliary Force

Military manpower: males 15-49, 4,568,648; 3,574,637 fit for military service; 177,610 reach military age (18) annually

Defense expenditures: 5% of GDP, or $300 million (1989 est.)

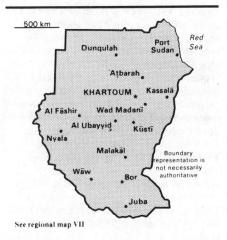

500 km

Red Sea

Dunqulah

Port Sudan

Aṭbarah

KHARTOUM

Kassalā

Al Fāshir

Wad Madanī

Al Ubayyiḍ

Küstï

Nyala

Malakāl

Boundary representation is not necessarily authoritative

Wāw

Bor

Juba

See regional map VII

Geography

Total area: 2,505,810 km²; land area: 2,376,000 km²

Comparative area: slightly more than one quarter the size of US

Land boundaries: 7,697 km total; Central African Republic 1,165 km, Chad 1,360 km, Egypt 1,273 km, Ethiopia 2,221 km, Kenya 232 km, Libya 383 km, Uganda 435 km, Zaire 628 km

Coastline: 853 km

Maritime claims:

Contiguous zone: 18 nm

Continental shelf: 200 meters or to depth of exploitation

Territorial sea: 12 nm

Disputes: international boundary and Administrative Boundary with Kenya; international boundary and Administrative Boundary with Egypt

Climate: tropical in south; arid desert in north; rainy season (April to October)

Terrain: generally flat, featureless plain; mountains in east and west

Natural resources: modest reserves of crude oil, iron ore, copper, chromium ore, zinc, tungsten, mica, silver, crude oil

Land use: 5% arable land; NEGL% permanent crops; 24% meadows and pastures; 20% forest and woodland; 51% other; includes 1% irrigated

Environment: dominated by the Nile and its tributaries; dust storms; desertification

Note: largest country in Africa

People

Population: 24,971,806 (July 1990), growth rate 2.9% (1990)

Birth rate: 44 births/1,000 population (1990)

Death rate: 14 deaths/1,000 population (1990)

Net migration rate: −2 migrants/1,000 population (1990)

Infant mortality rate: 107 deaths/1,000 live births (1990)

Life expectancy at birth: 51 years male, 55 years female (1990)

Total fertility rate: 6.5 children born/woman (1990)

Nationality: noun—Sudanese (sing. and pl.); adjective—Sudanese

Ethnic divisions: 52% black, 39% Arab, 6% Beja, 2% foreigners, 1% other

Religion: 70% Sunni Muslim (in north), 20% indigenous beliefs, 5% Christian (mostly in south and Khartoum)

Language: Arabic (official), Nubian, Ta Bedawie, diverse dialects of Nilotic, Nilo-Hamitic, and Sudanic languages, English; program of Arabization in process

Literacy: 31% (1986)

Labor force: 6,500,000; 80% agriculture, 10% industry and commerce, 6% government; labor shortages for almost all categories of skilled employment (1983 est.); 52% of population of working age (1985)

Organized labor: trade unions suspended following 30 June 1989 coup; now in process of being legalized anew

Government

Long-form name: Republic of the Sudan

Type: military; civilian government suspended and martial law imposed after 30 June 1989 coup

Capital: Khartoum

Administrative divisions: 9 regions (aqalīm, singular—iqlīm); A'ālī an Nīl, Al Awsaṭ, Al Istiwā'ī, Al Kharṭūm, Ash Shamālī, Ash Sharqī, Baḥr al Ghazāl, Dārfūr, Kurdufān

Independence: 1 January 1956 (from Egypt and UK; formerly Anglo-Egyptian Sudan)

Constitution: 12 April 1973, suspended following coup of 6 April 1985; interim constitution of 10 October 1985 suspended following coup of 30 June 1989

Legal system: based on English common law and Islamic law; in September 1983 then President Nimeiri declared the penal code would conform to Islamic law; some separate religious courts; accepts compulsory ICJ jurisdiction, with reservations

National holiday: Independence Day, 1 January (1956)

Executive branch: executive and legislative authority vested in a 15-member Revolutionary Command Council (RCC); chairman of the RCC acts as prime minister; in July 1989 RCC appointed a predominately civilian 22-member cabinet to function as advisers

Legislative branch: none

Judicial branch: Supreme Court, Special Revolutionary Courts

Sudan (continued)

Leaders: *Chief of State and Head of Government*—Revolutionary Command Council Chairman and Prime Minister Brig. Gen. Umar Hasan Ahmad al-BASHIR (since 30 June 1989); Deputy Chairman of the Command Council and Deputy Prime Minister Brig. Gen. al-Zubayr Muhammad SALIH (since 9 July 1989)

Political parties and leaders: none; banned following 30 June 1989 coup

Suffrage: none

Elections: none

Member of: ACP, AfDB, APC, Arab League, CCC, FAO, G-77, IAEA, IBRD, ICAC, ICAO, IDA, IDB—Islamic Development Bank, IFAD, IFC, ILO, IMF, IMO, INTELSAT, INTERPOL, ITU, NAM, OAU, OIC, UN, UNESCO, UPU, WFTU, WHO, WIPO, WMO, WTO

Diplomatic representation: Ambassador 'Abdallah Ahmad 'ABDALLAH; Chancery at 2210 Massachusetts Avenue NW, Washington DC 20008; telephone (202) 338-8565 through 8570; there is a Sudanese Consulate General in New York; *US*—Ambassador James CHEEK; Embassy at Shar'ia Ali Abdul Latif, Khartoum (mailing address is P. O. Box 699, Khartoum, or APO New York 09668); telephone 74700 or 75680, 74611

Flag: three equal horizontal bands of red (top), white, and black with a green isosceles triangle based on the hoist side

Economy

Overview: Sudan, one of the world's poorest countries, is buffeted by civil war, chronic political instability, adverse weather, and counterproductive economic policies. The economy is dominated by governmental entities that account for more than 70% of new investment. The private sector's main areas of activity are agriculture and trading, with most private industrial investment predating 1980. The economy's base is agriculture, which employs 80% of the work force. Industry mainly processes agricultural items. A high foreign debt and arrearages of about $13 billion continue to cause difficulties. Since 1979 the International Monetary Fund has provided assistance and has forced Sudan to make economic reforms aimed at improving the performance of the economy.

GDP: $8.5 billion, per capita $340 (FY87); real growth rate 7.0% (FY89 est.)

Inflation rate (consumer prices): 70% (FY89)

Unemployment rate: NA

Budget: revenues $514 million; expenditures $1.3 billion, including capital expenditures of $183 million (FY89 est.)

Exports: $550 million (f.o.b., FY89 est.); *commodities*—cotton 43%, sesame, gum arabic, peanuts; *partners*—Western Europe 46%, Saudi Arabia 14%, Eastern Europe 9%, Japan 9%, US 3% (FY88)

Imports: $1.2 billion (c.i.f., FY89 est.); *commodities*—petroleum products, manufactured goods, machinery and equipment, medicines and chemicals; *partners*—Western Europe 32%, Africa and Asia 15%, US 13%, Eastern Europe 3% (FY88)

External debt: $11.6 billion (December 1989 est.)

Industrial production: growth rate −1.7% (FY89 est.)

Electricity: 606,000 kW capacity; 900 million kWh produced, 37 kWh per capita (1989)

Industries: cotton ginning, textiles, cement, edible oils, sugar, soap distilling, shoes, petroleum refining

Agriculture: accounts for 35% of GNP and 80% of labor force; untapped potential for higher farm production; two-thirds of land area suitable for raising crops and livestock; major products—cotton, oilseeds, sorghum, millet, wheat, gum arabic, sheep; marginally self-sufficient in most foods

Aid: US commitments, including Ex-Im (FY70-88), $1.4 billion; Western (non-US) countries, ODA and OOF bilateral commitments (1970-87), $4.4 billion; OPEC bilateral aid (1979-89), $3.1 billion; Communist countries (1970-88), $588 million

Currency: Sudanese pound (plural—pounds); 1 Sudanese pound (£Sd) = 100 piasters

Exchange rates: official rate—Sudanese pounds (£Sd) per US$1—4.5004 (fixed rate since 1987), 2.8121 (1987), 2.5000 (1986), 2.2883 (1985); note—commercial exchange rate is set daily, 12.2 (March 1990)

Fiscal year: 1 July-30 June

Communications

Railroads: 5,500 km total; 4,784 km 1.067-meter gauge, 716 km 1.6096-meter-gauge plantation line

Highways: 20,000 km total; 1,600 km bituminous treated, 3,700 km gravel, 2,301 km improved earth, 12,399 km unimproved earth and track

Inland waterways: 5,310 km navigable

Pipelines: refined products, 815 km

Ports: Port Sudan, Suakin

Merchant marine: 10 ships (1,000 GRT or over) totaling 91,107 GRT/122,222 DWT; includes 8 cargo, 2 roll-on/roll-off cargo

Civil air: 14 major transport aircraft

Airports: 78 total, 68 usable; 8 with permanent-surface runways; none with runways over 3,659 m; 4 with runways 2,440-3,659 m; 31 with runways 1,220-2,439 m

Telecommunications: large, well-equipped system by African standards, but barely adequate and poorly maintained; consists of radio relay, cables, radio communications, and troposcatter; domestic satellite system with 14 stations; 73,400 telephones; stations—4 AM, 1 FM, 2 TV; satellite earth stations—1 Atlantic Ocean INTELSAT and 1 ARABSAT

Defense Forces

Branches: Army, Navy, Air Force, Air Defense Force

Military manpower: males 15-49, 5,621,469; 3,437,004 fit for military service; 273,011 reach military age (18) annually

Defense expenditures: 7.2% of GDP, or $610 million (1989 est)

Suriname

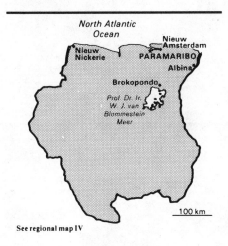

North Atlantic Ocean

Nieuw Nickerie · PARAMARIBO · Nieuw Amsterdam · Albina · Brokopondo · Prof. Dr. Ir. W. J. van Blommestein Meer

100 km

See regional map IV

Geography

Total area: 163,270 km²; land area: 161,470 km²
Comparative area: slightly larger than Georgia
Land boundaries: 1,707 km total; Brazil 597 km, French Guiana 510 km, Guyana 600 km
Coastline: 386 km
Maritime claims:
Extended economic zone: 200 nm
Territorial sea: 12 nm
Disputes: claims area in French Guiana between Litani Rivier and Rivière Marouini (both headwaters of the Lawa); claims area in Guyana between New (Upper Courantyne) and Courantyne/Kutari Rivers (all headwaters of the Courantyne)
Climate: tropical; moderated by trade winds
Terrain: mostly rolling hills; narrow coastal plain with swamps
Natural resources: timber, hydropower potential, fish, shrimp, bauxite, iron ore, and modest amounts of nickel, copper, platinum, gold
Land use: NEGL% arable land; NEGL% permanent crops; NEGL% meadows and pastures; 97% forest and woodland; 3% other; includes NEGL% irrigated
Environment: mostly tropical rain forest

People

Population: 396,813 (July 1990), growth rate 1.4% (1990)
Birth rate: 27 births/1,000 population (1990)
Death rate: 6 deaths/1,000 population (1990)
Net migration rate: −7 migrants/1,000 population (1990)
Infant mortality rate: 40 deaths/1,000 live births (1990)

Life expectancy at birth: 66 years male, 71 years female (1990)
Total fertility rate: 2.9 children born/woman (1990)
Nationality: noun—Surinamer(s); adjective—Surinamese
Ethnic divisions: 37.0% Hindustani (East Indian), 31.0% Creole (black and mixed), 15.3% Javanese, 10.3% Bush black, 2.6% Amerindian, 1.7% Chinese, 1.0% Europeans, 1.1% other
Religion: 27.4% Hindu, 19.6% Muslim, 22.8% Roman Catholic, 25.2% Protestant (predominantly Moravian), about 5% indigenous beliefs
Language: Dutch (official); English widely spoken; Sranan Tongo (Surinamese, sometimes called Taki-Taki) is native language of Creoles and much of the younger population and is lingua franca among others; also Hindi Suriname Hindustani (a variant of Bhoqpuri), and Javanese
Literacy: 65%
Labor force: 104,000 (1984)
Organized labor: 49,000 members of labor force

Government

Long-form name: Republic of Suriname
Type: republic
Capital: Paramaribo
Administrative divisions: 10 districts (distrikten, singular—distrikt); Brokopondo, Commewijne, Coronie, Marowijne, Nickerie, Para, Paramaribo, Saramacca, Sipaliwini, Wanica
Independence: 25 November 1975 (from Netherlands; formerly Netherlands Guiana or Dutch Guiana)
Constitution: ratified 30 September 1987
Legal system: NA
National holiday: Independence Day, 25 November (1975)
Executive branch: president, vice president and prime minister, Cabinet of Ministers, Council of State; note—commander in chief of the National Army maintains significant power
Legislative branch: unicameral National Assembly
Judicial branch: Supreme Court
Leaders: *Chief of State and Head of Government*—President Ramsewak SHANKAR (since 25 January 1988); Vice President and Prime Minister Henck Alfonsus Eugene ARRON (since 25 January 1988)
Political parties and leaders: 25 February Movement established by Lt. Col. Desire Bouterse in November 1983, but much of its activity taken over by New Democratic Party (NDP) in May 1987; leftists (all small groups)—Revolutionary People's Party (RVP), Michael Naarendorp; Progressive Workers and Farmers (PALU),

Iwan Krolis; traditional parties—Progressive Reform Party (VHP), Jaggernath Lachmon; National Party of Suriname (NPS), Henck Arron; Indonesian Peasants Party (KTPI), Willy Soemita; the VHP, NPS, and KTPI formed a coalition known as The Front in July 1987 that overwhelmingly defeated the NDP in the November 1987 elections
Suffrage: universal at age 18
Elections: *National Assembly*—last held 25 November 1987 (next to be held November 1992); results—The Front 80%, others 20%; seats—(51 total) The Front 40, NDP 3, PALU 4, Pendawa Llwa 4
Member of: ACP, ECLA, FAO, GATT, G-77, IBA, IBRD, ICAO, IDB—Inter-American Development Bank, IFAD, ILO, IMF, IMO, INTERPOL, ITU, NAM, OAS, PAHO, SELA, UN, UNESCO, UPU, WHO, WIPO, WMO
Diplomatic representation: Ambassador Willem A. UDENHOUT; Chancery at Suite 108, 4301 Connecticut Avenue NW, Washington DC 20008; telephone (202) 244-7488 or 7490 through 7492; there is a Surinamese Consulate General in Miami; *US*—Ambassador Richard HOWLAND; Embassy at Dr. Sophie Redmonstraat 129, Paramaribo (mailing address is P. O. Box 1821, Paramaribo); telephone [597] 72900 or 76459
Flag: five horizontal bands of green (top, double width), white, red (quadruple width), white, and green (double width); there is a large yellow five-pointed star centered in the red band

Economy

Overview: The economy is dominated by the bauxite industry, which accounts for about 80% of export earnings and 40% of tax revenues. The economy has been in trouble since the Dutch ended development aid in 1982. A drop in world bauxite prices that started in the late 1970s and continued until late 1986, was followed by the outbreak of a guerrilla insurgency in the interior. The guerrillas targeted the economic infrastructure, crippling the important bauxite sector and shutting down other export industries. These problems have created both high inflation and high unemployment. A small gain in economic growth of 3.6% was registered in 1988 due to reduced guerrilla activity and improved international markets for bauxite.
GDP: $1.27 billion, per capita $3,215; real growth rate 3.6% (1988 est.)
Inflation rate (consumer prices): 50% (1988 est.)
Unemployment rate: 27% (1988)
Budget: revenues $466 million; expenditures $716 million, including capital expenditures of $123 million (1989 est.)

Suriname (continued)

Exports: $425 million (f.o.b., 1988 est.); *commodities*—alumina, bauxite, aluminum, rice, wood and wood products, shrimp and fish, bananas; *partners*—Netherlands 28%, US 22%, Norway 18%, Japan 11%, Brazil 10%, UK 4%

Imports: $365 million (f.o.b., 1988 est.); *commodities*—capital equipment, petroleum, foodstuffs, cotton, consumer goods; *partners*—US 34%, Netherlands 20%, Trinidad and Tobago 8%, Brazil 5%, UK 3%

External debt: $65 million (1989 est.)

Industrial production: growth rate −3.1% (1986)

Electricity: 458,000 kW capacity; 2,018 million kWh produced, 5,030 kWh per capita (1989)

Industries: bauxite mining, alumina and aluminum production, lumbering, food processing, fishing

Agriculture: accounts for 11% of both GDP and labor force; paddy rice planted on 85% of arable land and represents 60% of total farm output; other products—bananas, palm kernels, coconuts, plantains, peanuts, beef, chicken; shrimp and forestry products of increasing importance; self-sufficient in most foods

Aid: US commitments, including Ex-Im (FY70-83), $2.5 million; Western (non-US) countries, ODA and OOF bilateral commitments (1970-87), $1.4 billion

Currency: Surinamese guilder, gulden, or florin (plural—guilders, gulden, or florins); 1 Surinamese guilder, gulden, or florin (Sf.) = 100 cents

Exchange rates: Surinamese guilders, gulden, or florins (Sf.) per US$1—1.7850 (fixed rate)

Fiscal year: calendar year

Communications

Railroads: 166 km total; 86 km 1.000-meter gauge, government owned, and 80 km 1.435-meter standard gauge; all single track

Highways: 8,300 km total; 500 km paved; 5,400 km bauxite gravel, crushed stone, or improved earth; 2,400 km sand or clay

Inland waterways: 1,200 km; most important means of transport; oceangoing vessels with drafts ranging from 4.2 m to 7 m can navigate many of the principal waterways

Ports: Paramaribo, Moengo

Merchant marine: 3 ships (1,000 GRT or over) totaling 6,472 GRT/8,914 DWT; includes 2 cargo, 1 container

Civil air: 2 major transport aircraft

Airports: 47 total, 43 usable; 6 with permanent-surface runways; none with runways over 3,659 m; 1 with runways 2,440-3,659 m; 1 with runways 1,220-2,439 m

Telecommunications: international facilities good; domestic radio relay system; 27,500 telephones; stations—5 AM, 14 FM, 6 TV, 1 shortwave; 2 Atlantic Ocean INTELSAT earth stations

Defense Forces

Branches: National Army (including Support Battalion, Infantry Battalion, Mechanized Cavalry Unit, Military Police Brigade, Navy which is company-size, small Air Force element)

Military manpower: males 15-49, 105,328; 62,896 fit for military service

Defense expenditures: 7.2% of GDP, or $91 million (1990 est.)

Svalbard
(territory of Norway)

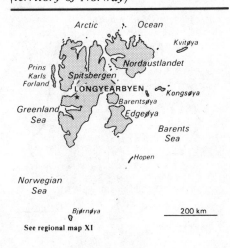

See regional map XI

Geography

Total area: 62,049 km²; land area: 62,049 km²; includes Spitsbergen and Bjørnøya (Bear Island)

Comparative area: slightly smaller than West Virginia

Land boundaries: none

Coastline: 3,587 km

Maritime claims:

Contiguous zone: 10 nm

Continental shelf: 200 meters or to depth of exploitation

Extended economic zone: 200 nm unilaterally claimed by Norway, not recognized by USSR

Territorial sea: 4 nm

Disputes: focus of maritime boundary dispute between Norway and USSR

Climate: arctic, tempered by warm North Atlantic Current; cool summers, cold winters; North Atlantic Current flows along west and north coasts of Spitsbergen, keeping water open and navigable most of the year

Terrain: wild, rugged mountains; much of high land ice covered; west coast clear of ice about half the year; fjords along west and north coasts

Natural resources: coal, copper, iron ore, phosphate, zinc, wildlife, fish

Land use: 0% arable land; 0% permanent crops; 0% meadows and pastures; 0% forest and woodland; 100% other; there are no trees and the only bushes are crowberry and cloudberry

Environment: great calving glaciers descend to the sea

Note: located 445 km north of Norway where the Arctic Ocean, Barents Sea, Greenland Sea, and Norwegian Sea meet

People

Population: 3,942 (July 1990), growth rate NA% (1990); about one-third of the population resides in the Norwegian areas

(Longyearbyen and Svea on Vestspitsbergen) and two-thirds in the Soviet areas (Barentsburg and Pyramiden on Vestspitsbergen); about 9 persons live at the Polish research station
Birth rate: NA births/1,000 population (1990)
Death rate: NA deaths/1,000 population (1990)
Net migration rate: NA migrants/1,000 population (1990)
Infant mortality rate: NA deaths/1,000 live births (1990)
Life expectancy at birth: NA years male, NA years female (1990)
Total fertility rate: NA children born/woman (1990)
Ethnic divisions: 64% Russian, 35% Norwegian, 1% other (1981)
Language: Russian, Norwegian
Literacy: NA%
Labor force: NA
Organized labor: none

Government

Long-form name: none
Type: territory of Norway administered by the Ministry of Industry, Oslo, through a governor (sysselmann) residing in Longyearbyen, Spitsbergen; by treaty (9 February 1920) sovereignty was given to Norway
Capital: Longyearbyen
Leaders: *Chief of State*—King OLAV V (since 21 September 1957);
Head of Government Governor Leif ELDRING (since NA)
Flag: the flag of Norway is used

Economy

Overview: Coal mining is the major economic activity on Svalbard. By treaty (9 February 1920), the nationals of the treaty powers have equal rights to exploit mineral deposits, subject to Norwegian regulation. Although US, UK, Dutch, and Swedish coal companies have mined in the past, the only companies still mining are Norwegian and Soviet. Each company mines about half a million tons of coal annually. The settlements on Svalbard are essentially company towns. The Norwegian state-owned coal company employs nearly 60% of the Norwegian population on the island, runs many of the local services, and provides most of the local infrastructure. There is also some trapping of seal, polar bear, fox, and walrus.
Electricity: 21,000 kW capacity; 45 million kWh produced, 11,420 kWh per capita (1989)
Currency: Norwegian krone (plural—kroner); 1 Norwegian krone (NKr) = 100 øre

Exchange rates: Norwegian kroner (NKr) per US$1—6.5405 (January 1990), 6.9045 (1989), 6.5170 (1988), 6.7375 (1987), 7.3947 (1986), 8.5972 (1985)

Communications

Ports: limited facilities—Ny-Alesund, Advent Bay
Airports: 4 total, 4 usable; 1 with permanent-surface runways; none with runways over 2,439 m; 1 with runways 1,220-2,439 m
Telecommunications: 5 meteorological/radio stations; stations—1 AM, 1 (2 relays) FM, 1 TV

Defense Forces

Note: demilitarized by treaty (9 February 1920)

Swaziland

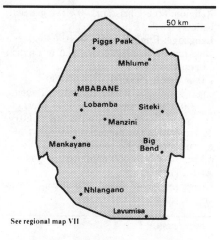

See regional map VII

Geography

Total area: 17,360 km²; land area: 17,200 km²
Comparative area: slightly smaller than New Jersey
Land boundaries: 535 km total; Mozambique 105 km, South Africa 430 km
Coastline: none—landlocked
Maritime claims: none—landlocked
Climate: varies from tropical to near temperate
Terrain: mostly mountains and hills; some moderately sloping plains
Natural resources: asbestos, coal, clay, tin, hydroelelectric power, forests, and small gold and diamond deposits
Land use: 8% arable land; NEGL% permanent crops; 67% meadows and pastures; 6% forest and woodland; 19% other; includes 2% irrigated
Environment: overgrazing; soil degradation; soil erosion
Note: landlocked; almost completely surrounded by South Africa

People

Population: 778,525 (July 1990), growth rate 3.1% (1990)
Birth rate: 46 births/1,000 population (1990)
Death rate: 15 deaths/1,000 population (1990)
Net migration rate: 0 migrants/1,000 population (1990)
Infant mortality rate: 126 deaths/1,000 live births (1990)
Life expectancy at birth: 48 years male, 55 years female (1990)
Total fertility rate: 6.0 children born/woman (1990)
Nationality: noun—Swazi(s); adjective—Swazi
Ethnic divisions: 97% African, 3% European

Swaziland (continued)

Religion: 60% Christian, 40% indigenous beliefs

Language: English and siSwati (official); government business conducted in English

Literacy: 67.9%

Labor force: 195,000; over 60,000 engaged in subsistence agriculture; about 92,000 wage earners (many only intermittently), with 36% agriculture and forestry, 20% community and social services, 14% manufacturing, 9% construction, 21% other; 24,000-29,000 employed in South Africa (1987)

Organized labor: about 10% of wage earners

Government

Long-form name: Kingdom of Swaziland

Type: monarchy; independent member of Commonwealth

Capital: Mbabane (administrative); Lobamba (legislative)

Administrative divisions: 4 districts; Hhohho, Lubombo, Manzini, Shiselweni

Independence: 6 September 1968 (from UK)

Constitution: none; constitution of 6 September 1968 was suspended on 12 April 1973; a new constitution was promulgated 13 October 1978, but has not been formally presented to the people

Legal system: based on South African Roman-Dutch law in statutory courts, Swazi traditional law and custom in traditional courts; has not accepted compulsory ICJ jurisdiction

National holiday: Somhlolo (Independence) Day, 6 September (1968)

Executive branch: monarch, prime minister, Cabinet

Legislative branch: bicameral Parliament (Libandla) is advisory and consists of an upper house or Senate and a lower house or House of Assembly

Judicial branch: High Court, Court of Appeal

Leaders: *Chief of State*—King MSWATI III (since 25 April 1986);
Head of Government—Prime Minister Obed MFANYANA (since 12 July 1989)

Political parties: none; banned by the Constitution promulgated on 13 October 1978

Suffrage: none

Elections: no direct elections

Communists: no Communist party

Member of: ACP, AfDB, CCC, FAO, G-77, GATT (de facto), IBRD, ICAO, IDA, IFAD, IFC, ILO, IMF, INTERPOL, ISO, ITU, NAM, OAU, Southern African Customs Union, SADCC, UN, UNESCO, UPU, WHO

Diplomatic representation: Ambassador Absalom Vusani MAMBA; Chancery at 4301 Connecticut Avenue NW, Washington DC 20008; telephone (202) 362-6683; *US*—Ambassador (vacant), Deputy Chief of Mission Armajane KARAER; Embassy at Central Bank Building, Warner Street, Mbabane (mailing address is P. O. Box 199, Mbabane); telephone 22281 through 22285

Flag: three horizontal bands of blue (top), red (triple width), and blue; the red band is edged in yellow; centered in the red band is a large black and white shield covering two spears and a staff decorated with feather tassels, all placed horizontally

Economy

Overview: The economy is based on subsistence agriculture, which occupies much of the labor force and contributes about 25% to GDP. Manufacturing, which includes a number of agroprocessing factories, accounts for another 25% of GDP. Mining has declined in importance in recent years; high-grade iron ore deposits were depleted in 1978, and health concerns cut world demand for asbestos. Exports of sugar and forestry products are the main earners of hard currency. Surrounded by South Africa, except for a short border with Mozambique, Swaziland is heavily dependent on South Africa, from which it receives 90% of its imports and to which it sends about one-third of its exports.

GNP: $539 million, per capita $750; real growth rate 5.7% (1989 est.)

Inflation rate (consumer prices): 17% (1989 est.)

Unemployment rate: NA%

Budget: revenues $255 million; expenditures $253 million, including capital expenditures of $NA million (FY91 est.)

Exports: $394 million (f.o.b., 1988); *commodities*—sugar, asbestos, wood pulp, citrus, canned fruit, soft drink concentrates; *partners*—South Africa, UK, US

Imports: $386 million (f.o.b., 1988); *commodities*—motor vehicles, machinery, transport equipment, chemicals, petroleum products, foodstuffs; *partners*—South Africa, US, UK

External debt: $275 million (December 1987)

Industrial production: growth rate 24% (1986)

Electricity: 50,000 kW capacity; 130 million kWh produced, 170 kWh per capita (1989)

Industries: mining (coal and asbestos), wood pulp, sugar

Agriculture: accounts for 25% of GDP and over 60% of labor force; mostly subsistence agriculture; cash crops—sugarcane, citrus fruit, cotton, pineapples; other crops and livestock—corn, sorghum, peanuts, cattle, goats, sheep; not self-sufficient in grain

Aid: US commitments, including Ex-Im (FY70-88), $132 million; Western (non-US) countries, ODA and OOF bilateral commitments (1970-87), $468 million

Currency: lilangeni (plural—emalangeni); 1 lilangeni (E) = 100 cents

Exchange rates: emalangeni (E) per US$1—2.5555 (January 1990), 2.6166 (1989), 2.2611 (1988), 2.0350 (1987), 2.2685 (1986), 2.1911 (1985); note—the Swazi emalangeni is at par with the South African rand

Fiscal year: 1 April-31 March

Communications

Railroads: 297 km plus 71 km disused, 1.067-meter gauge, single track

Highways: 2,853 km total; 510 km paved, 1,230 km crushed stone, gravel, or stabilized soil, and 1,113 km improved earth

Civil air: 1 major transport aircraft

Airports: 23 total, 22 usable; 1 with permanent-surfaced runways; none with runways over 3,659 m; 1 with runways 2,440-3,659 m; none with runways 1,220-2,439 m

Telecommunications: system consists of carrier-equipped open-wire lines and low-capacity radio relay links; 15,400 telephones; stations—6 AM, 6 FM, 10 TV; 1 Atlantic Ocean INTELSAT earth station

Defense Forces

Branches: Umbutfo Swaziland Defense Force, Royal Swaziland Police Force

Military manpower: males 15-49, 166,537; 96,239 fit for military service

Defense expenditures: NA

Sweden

400 km

Kiruna
Tärnaby • Luleå
Umeå
Gulf
of
Bothnia
Sundsvall
Gävle
Uppsala
Karlstad
★STOCKHOLM
Göteborg Jönköping
Gotland
Kattegat
Öland Baltic Sea
Malmö Karlskrona
See regional map V

Geography

Total area: 449,960 km^2; land area: 411,620 km^2
Comparative area: slightly larger than California
Land boundaries: 2,193 km total; Finland 536 km, Norway 1,657 km
Coastline: 3,218 km
Maritime claims:
  Continental shelf: 200 meters or to depth of exploitation
  Exclusive fishing zone: 200 nm
  Territorial sea: 12 nm
Climate: temperate in south with cold, cloudy winters and cool, partly cloudy summers; subarctic in north
Terrain: mostly flat or gently rolling lowlands; mountains in west
Natural resources: zinc, iron ore, lead, copper, silver, timber, uranium, hydropower potential
Land use: 7% arable land; 0% permanent crops; 2% meadows and pastures; 64% forest and woodland; 27% other; includes NEGL% irrigated
Environment: water pollution; acid rain
Note: strategic location along Danish Straits linking Baltic and North Seas

People

Population: 8,526,452 (July 1990), growth rate 0.5% (1990)
Birth rate: 13 births/1,000 population (1990)
Death rate: 11 deaths/1,000 population (1990)
Net migration rate: 3 migrants/1,000 population (1990)
Infant mortality rate: 6 deaths/1,000 live births (1990)
Life expectancy at birth: 75 years male, 81 years female (1990)
Total fertility rate: 1.9 children born/ woman (1990)

Nationality: noun—Swede(s); adjective— Swedish
Ethnic divisions: homogeneous white population; small Lappish minority; about 12% foreign born or first-generation immigrants (Finns, Yugoslavs, Danes, Norwegians, Greeks, Turks)
Religion: 93.5% Evangelical Lutheran, 1.0% Roman Catholic, 5.5% other
Language: Swedish, small Lapp- and Finnish-speaking minorities; immigrants speak native languages
Literacy: 99%
Labor force: 4,531,000 (1988); 32.8% private services, 30.0% government services, 22.0% mining and manufacturing, 5.9% construction, 5.0% agriculture, forestry, and fishing, 0.9% electricity, gas, and waterworks (1986)
Organized labor: 90% of labor force (1985 est.)

Government

Long-form name: Kingdom of Sweden
Type: constitutional monarchy
Capital: Stockholm
Administrative divisions: 24 provinces (län, singular and plural); Älvsborgs Län, Blekinge Län, Gävleborgs Län, Göteborgs och Bohus Län, Gotlands Län, Hallands Län, Jämtlands Län, Jönköpings Län, Kalmar Län, Kopparbergs Län, Kristianstads Län, Kronobergs Län, Malmöhus Län, Norrbottens Län, Örebro Län, Östergötlands Län, Skaraborgs Län, Södermanlands Län, Stockholms Län, Uppsala Län, Värmlands Län, Västerbottens Län, Västernorrlands Län, Västmanlands Län
Independence: 6 June 1809, constitutional monarchy established
Constitution: 1 January 1975
Legal system: civil law system influenced by customary law; accepts compulsory ICJ jurisdiction, with reservations
National holiday: Day of the Swedish Flag, 6 June
Executive branch: monarch, prime minister, Cabinet
Legislative branch: unicameral Parliament (Riksdag)
Judicial branch: Supreme Court (Högsta Domstolen)
Leaders: *Chief of State*—King CARL XVI Gustaf (since 19 September 1973); Heir Apparent Princess VICTORIA Ingrid Alice Désirée, daughter of the King (born 14 July 1977);
Head of Government—Prime Minister Ingvar CARLSSON (since 12 March 1986); Deputy Prime Minister Kjell-Olof FELDT (since NA March 1986)
Political parties and leaders: Moderate (conservative), Carl Bildt; Center, Olof Johansson; Liberal People's Party, Bengt

Westerberg; Social Democratic, Ingvar Carlsson; Left Party-Communist (VPK), Lars Werner; Swedish Communist Party (SKP), Rune Pettersson; Communist Workers' Party, Rolf Hagel; Green Party, no formal leader
Suffrage: universal at age 18
Elections: *Parliament*—last held 18 September 1988 (next to be held September 1991); results—percent of vote by party NA; seats—(349 total) Social Democratic 156, Moderate (conservative) 66, Liberals 44, Center 42, Communists 21, Greens 20
Communists: VPK and SKP; VPK, the major Communist party, is reported to have roughly 17,800 members; in the 1988 election, the VPK attracted 5.8% of the vote
Member of: ADB, CCC, Council of Europe, DAC, EFTA, ESA, FAO, GATT, IAEA, IBRD, ICAC, ICAO, ICES, ICO, IDA, IDB—Inter-American Development Bank, IEA, IFAD, IFC, IHO, ILO, ILZSG, IMF, IMO, INTERPOL, INTELSAT, IPU, ISO, ITU, IWC—International, Whaling Commission, IWC—International Wheat Council, Nordic Council, OECD, UN, UNESCO, UPU, WHO, WIPO, WMO, WSG
Diplomatic representation: Ambassador Anders THUNBORG; Chancery at Suite 1200, 600 New Hampshire Avenue NW, Washington DC 20037; telephone (202) 944-5600; there are Swedish Consulates General in Chicago, Los Angeles, Minneapolis, and New York; *US*—Ambassador Charles E. REDMAN; Embassy at Strandvagen 101, S-115 27 Stockholm; telephone [46] (8) 7835300
Flag: blue with a yellow cross that extends to the edges of the flag; the vertical part of the cross is shifted to the hoist side in the style of the *Dannebrog* (Danish flag)

Economy

Overview: Aided by a long period of peace and neutrality during World War I through World War II, Sweden has achieved an enviable standard of living under a mixed system of high-tech capitalism and extensive welfare benefits. It has essentially full employment, a modern distribution system, excellent internal and external communications, and a skilled and intelligent labor force. Timber, hydropower, and iron ore constitute the resource base of an economy that is heavily oriented toward foreign trade. Privately owned firms account for about 90% of industrial output, of which the engineering sector accounts for 50% of output and exports. As the 1990s open, however, Sweden faces serious economic problems: long waits for adequate housing, the decay of the work ethic, and a loss of competitive edge in international markets.

GDP: $132.7 billion, per capita $15,700; real growth rate 2.1% (1989 est.)

Inflation rate (consumer prices): 5.7% (September 1989)

Unemployment rate: 1.5% (1989)

Budget: revenues $58.0 billion; expenditures $57.9 billion, including capital expenditures of $NA (FY89)

Exports: $52.2 billion (f.o.b., 1989 est.); *commodities*—machinery, motor vehicles, paper products, pulp and wood, iron and steel products, chemicals, petroleum and petroleum products; *partners*—EC 52.1%, (FRG 12.1%, UK 11.2%, Denmark 6.8%), US 9.8%, Norway 9.3%

Imports: $48.5 billion (c.i.f., 1989 est.); *commodities*—machinery, petroleum and petroleum products, chemicals, motor vehicles, foodstuffs, iron and steel, clothing; *partners*—EC 55.8% (FRG 21.2%, UK 8.6%, Denmark 6.6%), US 7.5%, Norway 6.0%

External debt: $17.9 billion (1988)

Industrial production: growth rate 3.3% (1989)

Electricity: 39,716,000 kW capacity; 200,315 million kWh produced, 23,840 kWh per capita (1989)

Industries: iron and steel, precision equipment (bearings, radio and telephone parts, armaments), wood pulp and paper products, processed foods, motor vehicles

Agriculture: animal husbandry predominates, with milk and dairy products accounting for 37% of farm income; main crops—grains, sugar beets, potatoes; 100% self-sufficient in grains and potatoes, 85% self-sufficient in sugar beets

Aid: donor—ODA and OOF commitments (1970-87), $7.9 billion

Currency: Swedish krona (plural—kronor); 1 Swedish krona (SKr) = 100 öre

Exchange rates: Swedish kronor (SKr) per US$1—6.1798 (January 1990), 6.4469 (1989), 6.1272 (1988), 6.3404 (1987), 7.1236 (1986), 8.6039 (1985)

Fiscal year: 1 July-30 June

Communications

Railroads: 12,000 km total; Swedish State Railways (SJ)—10,819 km 1.435-meter standard gauge, 6,955 km electrified and 1,152 km double track; 182 km 0.891-meter gauge; 117 km rail ferry service; privately owned railways—511 km 1.435-meter standard gauge (332 km electrified); 371 km 0.891-meter gauge (all electrified)

Highways: 97,400 km (51,899 km paved, 20,659 km gravel, 24,842 km unimproved earth)

Inland waterways: 2,052 km navigable for small steamers and barges

Pipelines: 84 km natural gas

Ports: Gävle, Göteborg, Halmstad, Helsingborg, Kalmar, Malmö, Stockholm; numerous secondary and minor ports

Merchant marine: 173 ships (1,000 GRT or over) totaling 1,856,217 GRT/2,215,659 DWT; includes 9 short-sea passenger, 29 cargo, 3 container, 42 roll-on/roll-off cargo, 11 vehicle carrier, 2 railcar carrier, 27 petroleum, oils, and lubricants (POL) tanker, 25 chemical tanker, 1 liquefied gas, 5 combination ore/oil, 6 specialized tanker, 12 bulk, 1 combination bulk

Civil air: 65 major transports

Airports: 259 total, 256 usable; 138 with permanent-surface runways; none with runways over 3,659 m; 11 with runways 2,440-3,659 m; 91 with runways 1,220-2,439 m

Telecommunications: excellent domestic and international facilities; 8,200,000 telephones; stations—4 AM, 56 (320 relays) FM, 110 (925 relays) TV; 5 submarine coaxial cables; communication satellite earth stations operating in the INTELSAT (1 Atlantic Ocean) and EUTELSAT systems

Defense Forces

Branches: Royal Swedish Army, Royal Swedish Air Force, Royal Swedish Navy

Military manpower: males 15-49, 2,133,101; 1,865,526 fit for military service; 56,632 reach military age (19) annually

Defense expenditures: 4.5% billion (1989 est.)

100 km

See regional map V

Geography

Total area: 41,290 km^2; land area: 39,770 km^2

Comparative area: slightly more than twice the size of New Jersey

Land boundaries: 1,852 km total; Austria 164 km, France 573 km, Italy 740 km, Liechtenstein 41 km, FRG 334 km

Coastline: none—landlocked

Maritime claims: none—landlocked

Climate: temperate, but varies with altitude; cold, cloudy, rainy/snowy winters; cool to warm, cloudy, humid summers with occasional showers

Terrain: mostly mountains (Alps in south, Jura in northwest) with a central plateau of rolling hills, plains, and large lakes

Natural resources: hydropower potential, timber, salt

Land use: 10% arable land; 1% permanent crops; 40% meadows and pastures; 26% forest and woodland; 23% other; includes 1% irrigated

Environment: dominated by Alps

Note: landlocked; crossroads of northern and southern Europe

People

Population: 6,742,461 (July 1990), growth rate 0.6% (1990)

Birth rate: 12 births/1,000 population (1990)

Death rate: 9 deaths/1,000 population (1990)

Net migration rate: 3 migrants/1,000 population (1990)

Infant mortality rate: 5 deaths/1,000 live births (1990)

Life expectancy at birth: 75 years male, 83 years female (1990)

Total fertility rate: 1.6 children born/woman (1990)

Nationality: noun—Swiss (sing. & pl.); adjective—Swiss

Ethnic divisions: total population—65% German, 18% French, 10% Italian, 1% Romansch, 6% other; Swiss nationals—74% German, 20% French, 4% Italian, 1% Romansch, 1% other

Religion: 49% Roman Catholic, 48% Protestant, 0.3% Jewish

Language: total population—65% German, 18% French, 12% Italian, 1% Romansch, 4% other; Swiss nationals—74% German, 20% French, 4% Italian, 1% Romansch, 1% other

Literacy: 99%

Labor force: 3,220,000; 841,000 foreign workers, mostly Italian; 42% services, 39% industry and crafts, 11% government, 7% agriculture and forestry, 1% other (1988)

Organized labor: 20% of labor force

Government

Long-form name: Swiss Confederation

Type: federal republic

Capital: Bern

Administrative divisions: 26 cantons (cantons, singular—canton in French; cantoni, singular—cantone in Italian; kantone, singular—kanton in German); Aargau, Ausser-Rhoden, Basel-Landschaft, Basel-Stadt, Bern, Fribourg, Genève, Glarus, Graubünden, Inner-Rhoden, Jura, Luzern, Neuchâtel, Nidwalden, Obwalden, Sankt Gallen, Schaffhausen, Schwyz, Solothurn, Thurgau, Ticino, Uri, Valais, Vaud, Zug, Zürich

Independence: 1 August 1291

Constitution: 29 May 1874

Legal system: civil law system influenced by customary law; judicial review of legislative acts, except with respect to federal decrees of general obligatory character; accepts compulsory ICJ jurisdiction, with reservations

National holiday: Anniversary of the Founding of the Swiss Confederation, 1 August (1291)

Executive branch: president, vice president, Federal Council (German—Bundesrat, French—Conseil Fédéral)

Legislative branch: bicameral Federal Assembly (German—Bundesversammlung, French—Assemblée Fédérale) consists of an upper council or Council of States (German—Ständerat, French—Conseil des Etats) and and a lower council or National Council (German—Nationalrat, French—Conseil National)

Judicial branch: Federal Supreme Court

Leaders: *Chief of State and Head of Government*—President Arnold KOLLER (1990 calendar year; presidency rotates annually); Vice President Flavio COTTI (term runs concurrently with that of president)

Political parties and leaders: Social Democratic Party (SPS), Helmut Hubacher, chairman; Radical Democratic Party (FDP), Bruno Hunziker, president; Christian Democratic People's Party (CVP), Eva Segmüller-Weber, president; Swiss People's Party (SVP), Hans Uhlmann, president; Workers' Party (PdA), Armand Magnin, secretary general; National Action Party (NA), Hans Zwicky, chairman; Independents' Party (LdU), Dr. Franz Jaeger, president; Republican Movement (Rep), Dr. James Schworzenboch, Franz Baumgartner, leaders; Liberal Party (LPS), Gilbert Coutau, president; Evangelical People's Party (EVP), Max Dünki, president; Progressive Organizations of Switzerland (POCH), Georg Degen, secretary; Federation of Ecology Parties (GP), Laurent Rebeaud, president; Autonomous Socialist Party (PSA), Werner Carobbio, secretary

Suffrage: universal at age 20

Elections: *Council of State*—last held throughout 1987 (next to be held NA); results—percent of vote by party NA; seats—(46 total) CVP 19, FDP 14, SPS 5, SVP 4, others 4;
National Council—last held 18 October 1987 (next to be held October 1991); results—FDP 22.9%, CVP 20.0%, SPS 18.4%, SVP 11.0%, GP 4.8%, others 22.9%; seats—(200 total) FDP 51, CVP 42, SPS 41, SVP 25, GP 9, others 32

Communists: 4,500 members (est.)

Member of: ADB, CCC, Council of Europe, DAC, EFTA, ESA, FAO, GATT, IAEA, ICAC, ICAO, ICO, IDB—Inter-American Development Bank, IEA, IFAD, ILO, IMO, INTELSAT, INTERPOL, IPU, ITU, IWC—International Wheat Council, OECD, UNESCO, UPU, WCL, WFTU, WHO, WIPO, WMO, WSG, WTO; permanent observer status at the UN

Diplomatic representation: Ambassador Edouard BRUNNER; Chancery at 2900 Cathedral Avenue NW, Washington DC 20008; telephone (202) 745-7900; there are Swiss Consulates General in Atlanta, Chicago, Houston, Los Angeles, New York, and San Francisco; US—Ambassador Joseph B. GUILDENHORN; Embassy at Jubilaeumstrasse 93, 3005 Bern; telephone [41] (31) 437011; there is a Branch Office of the Embassy in Geneva and a Consulate General in Zurich

Flag: red square with a bold, equilateral white cross in the center that does not extend to the edges of the flag

Economy

Overview: Switzerland's economic success is matched in few, if any, other nations. Per capita output, general living standards, education and science, health care, and diet are unsurpassed in Europe. Inflation remains low because of sound government policy and harmonious labor-management relations. Unemployment is negligible, a marked contrast to the larger economies of Western Europe. This economic stability helps promote the important banking and tourist sectors. Since World War II, Switzerland's economy has adjusted smoothly to the great changes in output and trade patterns in Europe and presumably can adjust to the challenges of the 1990s, in particular, the further economic integration of Western Europe and the amazingly rapid changes in East European political/economic prospects.

GDP: $119.5 billion, per capita $17,800; real growth rate 3.0% (1989 est.)

Inflation rate (consumer prices): 2.8% (1989 est.)

Unemployment rate: 0.5% (1989 est.)

Budget: revenues $17.0 billion; expenditures $16.8 billion, including capital expenditures of $NA (1988)

Exports: $51.2 billion (f.o.b., 1988); *commodities*—machinery and equipment, precision instruments, metal products, foodstuffs, textiles and clothing; *partners*—Europe 64% (EC 56%, other 8%), US 9%, Japan 4%

Imports: $57.2 billion (c.i.f., 1988); *commodities*—agricultural products, machinery and transportation equipment, chemicals, textiles, construction materials; *partners*—Europe 79% (EC 72%, other 7%), US 5%

External debt: $NA

Industrial production: growth rate 7.0% (1988)

Electricity: 17,710,000 kW capacity; 59,070 million kWh produced, 8,930 kWh per capita (1989)

Industries: machinery, chemicals, watches, textiles, precision instruments

Agriculture: dairy farming predominates; less than 50% self-sufficient; food shortages—fish, refined sugar, fats and oils (other than butter), grains, eggs, fruits, vegetables, meat

Aid: donor—ODA and OOF commitments (1970-87), $2.5 billion

Currency: Swiss franc, franken, or franco (plural—francs, franken, or franchi); 1 Swiss franc, franken, or franco (SwF) = 100 centimes, rappen, or centesimi

Exchange rates: Swiss francs, franken, or franchi (SwF) per US$1—1.5150 (January 1990), 1.6359 (1989), 1.4633 (1988), 1.4912 (1987), 1.7989 (1986), 2.4571 (1985)

Fiscal year: calendar year

Communications

Railroads: 5,174 km total; 2,971 km are government owned and 2,203 km are nongovernment owned; the government

301

Switzerland (continued)

network consists of 2,897 km 1.435-meter standard gauge and 74 km 1.000-meter narrow gauge track; 1,432 km double track, 99% electrified; the nongovernment network consists of 710 km 1.435-meter standard gauge, 1,418 km 1.000-meter gauge, and 75 km 0.790-meter gauge track, 100% electrified

Highways: 62,145 km total (all paved), of which 18,620 km are canton and 1,057 km are national highways (740 km autobahn); 42,468 km are communal roads

Pipelines: 314 km crude oil; 1,506 km natural gas

Inland waterways: 65 km; Rhine (Basel to Rheinfelden, Schaffhausen to Bodensee); 12 navigable lakes

Ports: Basel (river port)

Merchant marine: 20 ships (1,000 GRT or over) totaling 215,851 GRT/365,131 DWT; includes 4 cargo, 2 roll-on/roll-off cargo, 3 chemical tanker, 3 specialized liquid cargo, 8 bulk

Civil air: 89 major transport aircraft

Airports: 72 total, 70 usable; 42 with permanent-surface runways; 2 with runways over 3,659 m; 6 with runways 2,440-3,659 m; 17 with runways 1,220-2,439 m

Telecommunications: excellent domestic, international, and broadcast services; 5,808,000 telephones; stations—6 AM, 36 (400 relays) FM, 145 (1,250 relays) TV; communications satellite earth stations operating in the INTELSAT (4 Atlantic Ocean and 1 Indian Ocean) and EUTELSAT systems

Defense Forces

Branches: Army, Air Force

Military manpower: males 15-49, 1,800,211; 1,550,662 fit for military service; 44,154 reach military age (20) annually

Defense expenditures: $1.2 billion (1989 est.)

Syria

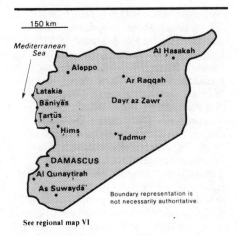

150 km

Mediterranean Sea

Al Hasakah
Aleppo
Ar Raqqah
Latakia
Baniyas
Dayr az Zawr
Tartus
Hims
Tadmur
DAMASCUS
Al Qunaytirah
As Suwayda

Boundary representation is not necessarily authoritative.

See regional map VI

Geography

Total area: 185,180 km²; land area: 184,050 km² (including 1,295 km² of Israeli-occupied territory)

Comparative area: slightly larger than North Dakota

Land boundaries: 2,253 km total; Iraq 605 km, Israel 76 km, Jordan 375 km, Lebanon 375 km, Turkey 822 km

Coastline: 193 km

Maritime claims:

Contiguous zone: 6 nm beyond territorial sea limit

Territorial sea: 35 nm

Disputes: separated from Israel by the 1949 Armistice Line; Golan Heights is Israeli occupied; Hatay question with Turkey; periodic disputes with Iraq over Euphrates water rights; ongoing dispute over water development plans by Turkey for the Tigris and Euphrates Rivers; Kurdish question among Iran, Iraq, Syria, Turkey, and the USSR

Climate: mostly desert; hot, dry, sunny summers (June to August) and mild, rainy winters (December to February) along coast

Terrain: primarily semiarid and desert plateau; narrow coastal plain; mountains in west

Natural resources: crude oil, phosphates, chrome and manganese ores, asphalt, iron ore, rock salt, marble, gypsum

Land use: 28% arable land; 3% permanent crops; 46% meadows and pastures; 3% forest and woodland; 20% other; includes 3% irrigated

Environment: deforestation; overgrazing; soil erosion; desertification

Note: there are 35 Jewish settlements in the Israeli-occupied Golan Heights

People

Population: 12,483,440 (July 1990), growth rate 3.8% (1990); in addition, there

are 13,500 Druze and 10,500 Jewish settlers in the Israeli-occupied Golan Heights

Birth rate: 44 births/1,000 population (1990)

Death rate: 6 deaths/1,000 population (1990)

Net migration rate: 0 migrants/1,000 population (1990)

Infant mortality rate: 38 deaths/1,000 live births (1990)

Life expectancy at birth: 68 years male, 70 years female (1990)

Total fertility rate: 6.7 children born/woman (1990)

Nationality: noun—Syrian(s); adjective—Syrian

Ethnic divisions: 90.3% Arab; 9.7% Kurds, Armenians, and other

Religion: 74% Sunni Muslim; 16% Alawite, Druze, and other Muslim sects; 10% Christian (various sects); tiny Jewish communities in Damascus, Al Qamishli, and Aleppo

Language: Arabic (official), Kurdish, Armenian, Aramaic, Circassian; French widely understood

Literacy: 49%

Labor force: 2,400,000; 36% miscellaneous and government services, 32% agriculture, 32% industry and construction); majority unskilled; shortage of skilled labor (1984)

Organized labor: 5% of labor force

Government

Long-form name: Syrian Arab Republic

Type: republic; under leftwing military regime since March 1963

Capital: Damascus

Administrative divisions: 14 provinces (muḥāfaẓat, singular—muḥāfaẓah); Al Ḥasakah, Al Lādhiqīyah, Al Qunayṭirah, Ar Raqqah, As Suwaydᵃ, Darᶜā, Dayr az Zawr, Dimashq, Ḥalab, Ḥamāh, Ḥimṣ, Idlib, Madīnat Dimashq, Ṭarṭūs

Independence: 17 April 1946 (from League of Nations mandate under French administration); formerly United Arab Republic

Constitution: 13 March 1973

Legal system: based on Islamic law and civil law system; special religious courts; has not accepted compulsory ICJ jurisdiction

National holiday: National Day, 17 April (1946)

Executive branch: president, three vice presidents, prime minister, three deputy prime ministers, Council of Ministers (cabinet)

Legislative branch: unicameral People's Council (Majlis ash Sha'ab)

Judicial branch: Supreme Constitutional Court, High Judicial Council, Court of Cassation, State Security Courts

Leaders: *Chief of State*—President Lt. Gen. Hafiz al-ASSAD (since 22 February

1971); Vice Presidents 'Abd al-Halim KHADDAM, Dr. Rif'at al-ASSAD, and Muhammad Zuhayr MASHARIQA (since 11 March 1984);

Head of Government—Prime Minister Mahmud ZU'BI (since 1 November 1987); Deputy Prime Minister Lt. Gen. Mustafa TALAS (since 11 March 1984)

Political parties and leaders: ruling party is the Arab Socialist Resurrectionist (Ba'th) Party; the Progressive National Front is dominated by Ba'thists but includes independents and members of the Syrian Arab Socialist Party (ASP), Arab Socialist Union (ASU), Socialist Unionist Movement, and Syrian Communist Party (SCP)

Suffrage: universal at age 18

Elections: *President*—last held 10-11 February 1985 (next to be held February 1992); results—President Hafiz al-Assad was reelected without opposition; *People's Council*—last held 10-11 February 1986 (next to be held 22 May 1990); results—Ba'th 66%, ASU 5%, SCP 5%, Socialist Unionist Movement 4%, ASP 2%, independents 18%; seats—(195 total) Ba'th 129, Communist 9, ASU 9, Socialist Unionist Movement 8, ASP 5, independents 35; the People's Council will have 250 seats total in the 22 May 1990 election

Communists: mostly sympathizers, numbering about 5,000

Other political or pressure groups: non-Ba'th parties have little effective political influence; Communist party ineffective; greatest threat to Assad regime lies in factionalism in the military; conservative religious leaders; Muslim Brotherhood

Member of: Arab League, CCC, FAO, G-77, IAEA, IBRD, ICAO, IDA, IDB—Islamic Development Bank, IFAD, IFC, ILO, IMF, IMO, INTELSAT, INTERPOL, IOOC, IPU, ITU, IWC—International Wheat Council, NAM, OAPEC, OIC, UN, UNESCO, UPU, WFTU, WHO, WMO, WSG, WTO

Diplomatic representation: Minister-Counselor, Chargé d'Affaires ad interim Bushra KANAFANI; Chancery at 2215 Wyoming Avenue NW, Washington DC 20008; telephone (202) 232-6313; *US*—Ambassador Edward P. DJEREJIAN; Embassy at Abu Rumaneh, Al Mansur Street No.2, Damascus (mailing address is P. O. Box 29, Damascus); telephone [963] (11) 333052 or 332557, 330416, 332814, 332315

Flag: three equal horizontal bands of red (top), white, and black with two small green five-pointed stars in a horizontal line centered in the white band; similar to the flags of the YAR which has one star and Iraq which has three stars (in a horizontal line centered in the white band)—

all green and five-pointed; also similar to the flag of Egypt which has a symbolic eagle centered in the white band

---

Economy

Overview: Syria's rigidly structured Ba'thist economy is turning out roughly the same amount of goods in 1989 as in 1983, when the population was 20% smaller. Economic difficulties are attributable, in part, to severe drought in several recent years, costly but unsuccessful attempts to match Israel's military strength, a falloff in Arab aid, and insufficient foreign exchange earnings to buy needed inputs for industry and agriculture. Socialist policy, embodied in a thicket of bureaucratic regulations, in many instances has driven away or pushed underground the mercantile and entrepreneurial spirit for which Syrian businessmen have long been famous. Two bright spots: a sizable number of villagers have benefited from land redistribution, electrification, and other rural development programs; and a recent find of light crude oil has enabled Syria to cut back its substantial imports of light crude. A long-term concern is the additional drain of upstream Euphrates water by Turkey when its vast dam and irrigation projects are completed toward the end of the 1990s.

GDP: $18.5 billion, per capita $1,540; real growth rate −2% (1989 est.)

Inflation rate (consumer prices): 70% (1989 est.)

Unemployment rate: NA%

Budget: revenues $NA; expenditures $3.2 billion, including capital expenditures of $1.92 billion (1989)

Exports: $1.3 billion (f.o.b., 1988 est.); *commodities*—petroleum, textiles, fruits and vegetables, phosphates; *partners*—Italy, Romania, USSR, US, Iran, France

Imports: $1.9 billion (f.o.b., 1988 est.); *commodities*—petroleum, machinery, base metals, foodstuffs and beverages; *partners*—Iran, FRG, USSR, France, GDR, Libya, US

External debt: $5.3 billion in hard currency (1989 est.)

Industrial production: growth rate NA%

Electricity: 2,867,000 kW capacity; 6,000 million kWh produced, 500 kWh per capita (1989)

Industries: textiles, food processing, beverages, tobacco, phosphate rock mining, petroleum

Agriculture: accounts for 27% of GDP and one-third of labor force; all major crops (wheat, barley, cotton, lentils, chickpeas) grown on rainfed land causing wide swings in yields; animal products—beef,

lamb, eggs, poultry, milk; not self-sufficient in grain or livestock products

Aid: US commitments, including Ex-Im (FY70-81), $538 million; Western (non-US) ODA and OOF bilateral commitments (1970-87), $1.0 billion; OPEC bilateral aid (1979-89), $12.3 billion; Communist countries (1970-88), $3.3 billion

Currency: Syrian pound (plural—pounds); 1 Syrian pound (£S) = 100 piasters

Exchange rates: Syrian pounds (£S) per US$1—11.2250 (fixed rate since 1987), 3.9250 (fixed rate 1976-87)

Fiscal year: calendar year

Communications

Railroads: 2,241 km total; 1,930 km standard gauge, 311 km 1.050-meter narrow gauge; note—the Tartus-Latakia line is nearly complete

Highways: 27,000 km total; 21,000 km paved, 3,000 km gravel or crushed stone, 3,000 km improved earth

Inland waterways: 672 km; of little economic importance

Pipelines: 1,304 km crude oil; 515 km refined products

Ports: Tartus, Latakia, Baniyas

Merchant marine: 19 ships (1,000 GRT or over) totaling 53,938 GRT/72,220 DWT; includes 16 cargo, 2 roll-on/roll-off cargo, 1 bulk

Civil air: 35 major transport aircraft

Airports: 97 total, 94 usable; 24 with permanent-surface runways; none with runways over 3,659 m; 21 with runways 2,440-3,659 m; 5 with runways 1,220-2,439 m

Telecommunications: fair system currently undergoing significant improvement; 512,600 telephones; stations—9 AM, 1 FM, 40 TV; satellite earth stations—1 Indian Ocean INTELSAT earth station, with 1 Intersputnik station under construction; 1 submarine cable; coaxial cable and radio relay to Iraq, Jordan, Turkey, and Lebanon (inactive)

Defense Forces

Branches: Syrian Arab Army, Syrian Arab Air Force, Syrian Arab Navy

Military manpower: males 15-49, 2,712,360; 1,520,798 fit for military service; 144,791 reach military age (19) annually

Defense expenditures: NA

Tanzania

See regional map VII

Geography

Total area: 945,090 km²; land area: 886,040 km²

Comparative area: slightly larger than twice the size of California

Land boundaries: 3,402 km total; Burundi 451 km, Kenya 769 km, Malawi 475 km, Mozambique 756 km, Rwanda 217 km, Uganda 396 km, Zambia 338 km

Coastline: 1,424 km

Maritime claim:

Extended economic zone: 200 nm

Territorial sea: 12 nm

Disputes: boundary dispute with Malawi in Lake Nyasa; Tanzania-Zaire-Zambia tripoint in Lake Tanganyika may no longer be indefinite since it is reported that the indefinite section of the Zaire-Zambia boundary has been settled

Climate: varies from tropical along coast to temperate in highlands

Terrain: plains along coast; central plateau; highlands in north, south

Natural resources: hydropower potential, tin, phosphates, iron ore, coal, diamonds, gemstones, gold, natural gas, nickel

Land use: 5% arable land; 1% permanent crops; 40% meadows and pastures; 47% forest and woodland; 7% other; includes NEGL% irrigated

Environment: lack of water and tsetse fly limit agriculture; recent droughts affected marginal agriculture; Kilimanjaro is highest point in Africa

People

Population: 25,970,843 (July 1990), growth rate 3.4% (1990)

Birth rate: 50 births/1,000 population (1990)

Death rate: 16 deaths/1,000 population (1990)

Net migration rate: NEGL migrants/ 1,000 population (1990)

Infant mortality rate: 107 deaths/1,000 live births (1990)

Life expectancy at birth: 49 years male, 54 years female (1990)

Total fertility rate: 7.1 children born/ woman (1990)

Nationality: noun—Tanzanian(s); adjective—Tanzanian

Ethnic divisions: mainland—99% native African consisting of well over 100 tribes; 1% Asian, European, and Arab

Religion: mainland—33% Christian, 33% Muslim, 33% indigenous beliefs; Zanzibar—almost all Muslim

Language: Swahili and English (official); English primary language of commerce, administration, and higher education; Swahili widely understood and generally used for communication between ethnic groups; first language of most people is one of the local languages; primary education is generally in Swahili

Literacy: 79%

Labor force: 732,200 wage earners; 90% agriculture, 10% industry and commerce (1986 est.)

Organized labor: 15% of labor force

Government

Long-form name: United Republic of Tanzania

Type: republic

Capital: Dar es Salaam; some government offices have been transferred to Dodoma, which is planned as the new national capital in the 1990s

Administrative divisions: 25 regions; Arusha, Dar es Salaam, Dodoma, Iringa, Kigoma, Kilimanjaro, Lindi, Mara, Mbeya, Morogoro, Mtwara, Mwanza, Pemba North, Pemba South, Pwani, Rukwa, Ruvuma, Shinyanga, Singida, Tabora, Tanga, Zanzibar Central/South, Zanzibar North, Zanzibar Urban/West, Ziwa Magharibi

Independence: Tanganyika became independent 9 December 1961 (from UN trusteeship under British administration); Zanzibar became independent 19 December 1963 (from UK); Tanganyika united with Zanzibar 26 April 1964 to form the United Republic of Tanganyika and Zanzibar; renamed United Republic of Tanzania 29 October 1964

Constitution: 15 March 1984 (Zanzibar has its own Constitution but remains subject to provisions of the union Constitution)

Legal system: based on English common law; judicial review of legislative acts limited to matters of interpretation; has not accepted compulsory ICJ jurisdiction

National holiday: Union Day, 26 April (1964)

Executive branch: president, first vice president and prime minister of the union, second vice president and president of Zanzibar, Cabinet

Legislative branch: unicameral National Assembly (Bunge)

Judicial branch: Court of Appeal, High Court

Leaders: *Chief of State*—President Ali Hassan MWINYI (since 5 November 1985);

Head of Government—First Vice President and Prime Minister Joseph Sinde WARIOBA (since 6 November 1985)

Political parties and leaders: only party—Chama Cha Mapinduzi (CCM or Revolutionary Party), Julius Nyerere, party chairman

Suffrage: universal at age 18

Elections: *President*—last held 27 October 1985 (next to be held October 1990); results—Ali Hassan Mwinyi was elected without opposition;

National Assembly—last held 27 October 1985 (next to be held October 1990); results—CCM is the only party; seats—(244 total, 168 elected) CCM 168

Communists: no Communist party; a few Communist sympathizers

Member of: ACP, AfDB, CCC, Commonwealth, FAO, G-77, GATT, IAEA, IBRD, ICAC, ICAO, ICO, IDA, IFAD, IFC, ILO, IMF, IMO, INTELSAT, INTERPOL, ITU, NAM, OAU, SADCC, UN, UNESCO, UPU, WHO, WMO, WTO

Diplomatic representation: Ambassador-designate Charles Musama NYIRABU; Chancery at 2139 R Street NW, Washington DC 20008; telephone (202) 939-6125; *US*—Ambassador Edmond DE JARNETTE; Embassy at 36 Laibon Road (off Bagamoyo Road), Dar es Salaam (mailing address is P. O. Box 9123, Dar es Salaam); telephone [255] (51) 37501 through 37504

Flag: divided diagonally by a yellow-edged black band from the lower hoist-side corner; the upper triangle (hoist side) is green and the lower triangle is blue

Economy

Overview: Tanzania is one of the poorest countries in the world. The economy is heavily dependent on agriculture, which accounts for about 40% of GDP, provides 85% of exports, and employs 90% of the work force. Industry accounts for about 10% of GDP and is mainly limited to processing agricultural products and light consumer goods. The economic recovery program announced in mid-1986 has generated notable increases in agricultural production and financial support for the program by bilateral donors. The World

Bank and the International Monetary Fund have increased the availability of imports and provided funds to rehabilitate Tanzania's deteriorated economic infrastructure.

GDP: $5.92 billion, per capita $235; real growth rate 4.5% (1989 est.)

Inflation rate (consumer prices): 29% (1989)

Unemployment rate: NA%

Budget: revenues $568 million; expenditures $835 million, including capital expenditures of $230 million (FY89)

Exports: $394 million (f.o.b., FY89); *commodities*—coffee, cotton, sisal, cashew nuts, meat, tobacco, tea, diamonds, coconut products, pyrethrum, cloves (Zanzibar); *partners*—FRG, UK, US, Netherlands, Japan

Imports: $1.3 billion (c.i.f., FY89); *commodities*—manufactured goods, machinery and transportation equipment, cotton piece goods, crude oil, foodstuffs; *partners*—FRG, UK, US, Iran, Japan, Italy

External debt: $4.5 billion (December 1989 est.)

Industrial production: growth rate 6% (1988 est.)

Electricity: 401,000 kW capacity; 895 million kWh produced, 35 kWh per capita (1989)

Industries: primarily agricultural processing (sugar, beer, cigarettes, sisal twine), diamond mine, oil refinery, shoes, cement, textiles, wood products, fertilizer

Agriculture: accounts for over 40% of GDP; topography and climatic conditions limit cultivated crops to only 5% of land area; cash crops—coffee, sisal, tea, cotton, pyrethrum (insecticide made from chrysanthemums), cashews, tobacco, cloves (Zanzibar); food crops—corn, wheat, cassava, bananas, fruits, and vegetables; small numbers of cattle, sheep, and goats; not self-sufficient in food grain production

Aid: US commitments, including Ex-Im (FY70-88), $387 million; Western (non-US) countries, ODA and OOF bilateral commitments (1970-87), $8.5 billion; OPEC bilateral aid (1979-89), $44 million; Communist countries (1970-88), $607 million

Currency: Tanzanian shilling (plural—shillings); 1 Tanzanian shilling (TSh) = 100 cents

Exchange rates: Tanzanian shillings (TSh) per US$1—192.901 (January 1990), 143.377 (1989), 99.292 (1988), 64.260 (1987), 32.698 (1986), 17.472 (1985)

Fiscal year: 1 July-30 June

Communications

Railroads: 3,555 km total; 960 km 1.067-meter gauge; 2,595 km 1.000-meter gauge, 6.4 km double track, 962 km Tazara Railroad 1.067-meter gauge; 115 km 1.000-meter gauge planned by end of decade

Highways: total 81,900 km, 3,600 km paved; 5,600 km gravel or crushed stone; remainder improved and unimproved earth

Pipelines: 982 km crude oil

Inland waterways: Lake Tanganyika, Lake Victoria, Lake Nyasa

Ports: Dar es Salaam, Mtwara, Tanga, and Zanzibar are ocean ports; Mwanza on Lake Victoria and Kigoma on Lake Tanganyika are inland ports

Merchant marine: 7 ships (1,000 GRT or over) totaling 29,174 GRT/39,186 DWT; includes 2 passenger-cargo, 3 cargo, 1 roll-on/roll-off cargo, 1 petroleum, oils, and lubricants (POL) tanker

Civil air: 6 major transport aircraft

Airports: 103 total, 92 usable; 13 with permanent-surface runways; none with runways over 3,659 m; 3 with runways 2,440-3,659 m; 44 with runways 1,220-2,439 m

Telecommunications: fair system of open wire, radio relay, and troposcatter; 103,800 telephones; stations—12 AM, 4 FM, 2 TV; 1 Indian Ocean INTELSAT earth station

---

Defense Forces

Branches: Tanzanian People's Defense Force includes Army, Navy, and Air Force; paramilitary Police Field Force Unit; Militia

Military manpower: males 15-49, 5,351,192; 3,087,501 fit for military service

Defense expenditures: 3.3% of GDP (1985)

Thailand

See regional map IX

Geography

Total area: 514,000 km^2; land area: 511,770 km^2

Comparative area: slightly more than twice the size of Wyoming

Land boundaries: 4,863 km total; Burma 1,800 km, Cambodia 803 km, Laos 1,754 km, Malaysia 506 km

Coastline: 3,219 km

Maritime claims:
Continental shelf: not specific
Extended economic zone: 200 nm
Territorial sea: 12 nm

Disputes: boundary dispute with Laos

Climate: tropical; rainy, warm, cloudy southwest monsoon (mid-May to September); dry, cool northeast monsoon (November to mid-March); southern isthmus always hot and humid

Terrain: central plain; eastern plateau (Khorat); mountains elsewhere

Natural resources: tin, rubber, natural gas, tungsten, tantalum, timber, lead, fish, gypsum, lignite, fluorite

Land use: 34% arable land; 4% permanent crops; 1% meadows and pastures; 30% forest and woodland; 31% other; includes 7% irrigated

Environment: air and water pollution; land subsidence in Bangkok area

Note: controls only land route from Asia to Malaysia and Singapore

---

People

Population: 55,115,683 (July 1990), growth rate 1.3% (1990)

Birth rate: 20 births/1,000 population (1990)

Death rate: 7 deaths/1,000 population (1990)

Net migration rate: 0 migrants/1,000 population (1990)

Infant mortality rate: 34 deaths/1,000 live births (1990)

Thailand (continued)

Life expectancy at birth: 64 years male, 70 years female (1990)
Total fertility rate: 2.1 children born/woman (1990)
Nationality: noun—Thai (sing. and pl.); adjective—Thai
Ethnic divisions: 75% Thai, 14% Chinese, 11% other
Religion: 95.5% Buddhist, 4% Muslim, 0.5% other
Language: Thai; English is the secondary language of the elite; ethnic and regional dialects
Literacy: 82%
Labor force: 26,000,000; 73% agriculture, 11% industry and commerce, 10% services, 6% government (1984)
Organized labor: 300,000 union members (1986)

Government

Long-form name: Kingdom of Thailand
Type: constitutional monarchy
Capital: Bangkok
Administrative divisions: 73 provinces (changwat, singular and plural); Ang Thong, Buriram, Chachoengsao, Chai Nat, Chaiyaphum, Chanthaburi, Chiang Mai, Chiang Rai, Chon Buri, Chumphon, Kalasin, Kamphaeng Phet, Kanchanaburi, Khon Kaen, Krabi, Krung Thep Mahanakhon, Lampang, Lamphun, Loei, Lop Buri, Mae Hong Son, Maha Sarakham, Nakhon Nayok, Nakhon Pathom, Nakhon Phanom, Nakhon Ratchasima, Nakhon Sawan, Nakhon Si Thammarat, Nan, Narathiwat, Nong Khai, Nonthaburi, Pathum Thani, Pattani, Phangnga, Phatthalung, Phayao, Phetchabun, Phetchaburi, Phichit, Phitsanulok, Phra Nakhon Si Ayutthaya, Phrae, Phuket, Prachin Buri, Prachuap Khiri Khan, Ranong, Ratchaburi, Rayong, Roi Et, Sakon Nakhon, Samut Prakan, Samut Sakhon, Samut Songkhram, Sara Buri, Satun, Sing Buri, Sisaket, Songkhla, Sukhothai, Suphan Buri, Surat Thani, Surin, Tak, Trang, Trat, Ubon Ratchathani, Udon Thani, Uthai Thani, Uttaradit, Yala, Yasothon
Independence: 1238 (traditional founding date); never colonized
Constitution: 22 December 1978
Legal system: based on civil law system, with influences of common law; has not accepted compulsory ICJ jurisdiction
National holiday: Birthday of His Majesty the King, 5 December (1927)
Executive branch: monarch, prime minister, three deputy prime ministers, Council of Ministers (cabinet), Privy Council
Legislative branch: bicameral National Assembly (Ratha Satha) consists of an upper house or Senate (Woothi Satha) and a lower house or House of Representatives (Satha Poothan)

Judicial branch: Supreme Court (Sarn Dika)
Leaders: *Chief of State*—King BHUMIBOL ADULYADEJ (since 9 June 1946); Heir Apparent Crown Prince VAJIRALONGKORN (born 28 July 1952); *Head of Government* Prime Minister Maj. Gen. CHATCHAI CHUNHAWAN (since 9 August 1988); Deputy Prime Minister CHUAN LIKPHAI
Political parties and leaders: Democrat Party (DP), Social Action Party (SAP), Thai Nation Party (TNP), People's Party (Ratsadon), People's Party (Prachachon), Thai Citizens Party (TCP), United Democracy Party, Solidarity Party, Thai People's Party, Mass Party, Force of Truth Party (Phalang Dharma)
Suffrage: universal at age 21
Elections: *House of Representatives*—last held 24 July 1988 (next to be held within 90 days of July 1992); results—TNP 27%, SAP 15%, DP 13%, TCP 9%, others 36%; seats—(357 total) TNP 96, Solidarity 62, SAP 54, DP 48, TCP 31, People's Party (Ratsadon) 21, People's Party (Prachachon) 17, Force of Truth Party (Phalang Dharma) 14, United Democracy Party 5, Mass Party 5, others 4
Communists: illegal Communist party has 500 to 1,000 members (est.); armed Communist insurgents throughout Thailand total 300 to 500 (est.)
Member of: ADB, ANRPC, ASEAN, ASPAC, Association of Tin Producing Countries, CCC, Colombo Plan, GATT, ESCAP, FAO, G-77, IAEA, IBRD, ICAO, IDA, IFAD, IFC, IHO, ILO, IMF, IMO, INRO, INTELSAT, INTERPOL, IPU, IRC, ITC, ITU, UN, UNESCO, UPU, WHO, WMO, WTO
Diplomatic representation: Ambassador VITTHYA VEJJAJIVA; Embassy at 2300 Kalorama Road NW, Washington DC 20008; telephone (202) 483-7200; there are Thai Consulates General in Chicago, Los Angeles, and New York; *US*—Ambassador Daniel O'DONAHUE; Embassy at 95 Wireless Road, Bangkok (mailing address is APO San Francisco 96346); telephone [66] (2) 252-5040; there is a US Consulate General in Chiang Mai and Consulates in Songkhla and Udorn
Flag: five horizontal bands of red (top), white, blue (double width), white, and red

Economy

Overview: Thailand, one of the more advanced developing countries in Asia, enjoyed its second straight exceptionally prosperous year in 1989. Real output again rose about 11%. The increasingly sophisticated manufacturing sector benefited from export-oriented investment, and agriculture grew by 4.0% because of im-

proved weather. The trade deficit of $5.2 billion was more than offset by earnings from tourism ($3.9 billion), remittances, and net capital inflows. The government has followed a fairly sound fiscal and monetary policy, aided by increased tax receipts from the fast-moving economy. In 1989 the government approved new projects—roads, ports, electric power, communications—needed to refurbish the now overtaxed infrastructure. Although growth in 1990-91 must necessarily fall below the 1988-89 pace, Thailand's immediate economic outlook is good, assuming the continuation of prudent government policies in the context of a private-sector-oriented development strategy.
GNP: $64.5 billion, per capita $1,160; real growth rate 10.8% (1989 est.)
Inflation rate (consumer prices): 5.4% (1989)
Unemployment rate: 6% (1989 est.)
Budget: revenues $12.1 billion; expenditures $9.7 billion, including capital expenditures of NA (FY89)
Exports: $19.9 billion (f.o.b., 1989); *commodities*—textiles 12%, fishery products 12%, rice 8%, tapioca 8%, jewelry 6%, manufactured gas, corn, tin; *partners*—US 18%, Japan 14%, Singapore 9%, Netherlands, Malaysia, Hong Kong, China (1988)
Imports: $25.1 billion (c.i.f., 1989); *commodities*—machinery and parts 23%, petroleum products 13%, chemicals 11%, iron and steel, electrical appliances; *partners*—Japan 26%, US 14%, Singapore 7%, FRG, Malaysia, UK (1987)
External debt: $18.5 billion (December 1989 est.)
Industrial production: growth rate 12.5% (1989)
Electricity: 7,100,000 kW capacity; 28,000 million kWh produced, 500 kWh per capita (1989)
Industries: tourism is the largest source of foreign exchange; textiles and garments, agricultural processing, beverages, tobacco, cement, other light manufacturing, such as jewelry; electric appliances and components, integrated circuits, furniture, plastics; world's second-largest tungsten producer and third-largest tin producer
Agriculture: accounts for 16% of GNP and 73% of labor force; leading producer and exporter of rice and cassava (tapioca); other crops—rubber, corn, sugarcane, coconuts, soybeans; except for wheat, self-sufficient in food; fish catch of 2.2 million tons (1987)
Illicit drugs: a minor producer, major illicit trafficker of heroin, particularly from Burma and Laos, and cannabis for the international drug market; eradication efforts have reduced the area of cannabis

cultivation and shifted some production to neighboring countries; opium poppy cultivation has been affected by eradication efforts, but unusually good weather boosted output in 1989

Aid: US commitments, including Ex-Im (FY70-88), $828 million; Western (non-US) countries, ODA and OOF bilateral commitments (1970-87), $7.0 billion; OPEC bilateral aid (1979-89), $19 million
Currency: baht (plural—baht); 1 baht (B) = 100 satang
Exchange rates: baht (B) per US$1— 25.726 (January 1990), 25.699 (1989), 25.294 (1988), 25.723 (1987), 26.299 (1986), 27.159 (1985)
Fiscal year: 1 October-30 September

Communications

Railroads: 3,940 km 1.000-meter gauge, 99 km double track
Highways: 44,534 km total; 28,016 km paved, 5,132 km earth surface, 11,386 km under development
Inland waterways: 3,999 km principal waterways; 3,701 km with navigable depths of 0.9 m or more throughout the year; numerous minor waterways navigable by shallow-draft native craft
Pipelines: natural gas, 350 km; refined products, 67 km
Ports: Bangkok, Pattani, Phuket, Sattahip, Si Racha
Merchant marine: 122 ships (1,000 GRT or over) totaling 483,688 GRT/730,750 DWT; includes 2 short-sea passenger, 70 cargo, 8 container, 27 petroleum, oils, and lubricants (POL) tanker, 8 liquefied gas, 1 chemical tanker, 3 bulk, 1 refrigerated cargo, 1 roll-on/roll-off, 1 combination bulk
Civil air: 41 (plus 2 leased) major transport aircraft
Airports: 127 total, 103 usable; 56 with permanent-surface runways; 1 with runways over 3,659 m; 13 with runways 2,440-3,659 m; 26 with runways 1,220-2,439 m
Telecommunications: service to general public adequate; bulk of service to government activities provided by multichannel cable and radio relay network; 739,500 telephones (1987); stations—over 200 AM, 100 FM, and 11 TV in government-controlled networks; satellite earth stations—1 Indian Ocean INTELSAT and 1 Pacific Ocean INTELSAT; domestic satellite system being developed

Defense Forces

Branches: Royal Thai Army, Royal Thai Navy (includes Royal Thai Marine Corps), Royal Thai Air Force; paramilitary forces include Border Patrol Police, Thahan Phran (irregular soldiers), Village Defense Forces
Military manpower: males 15-49, 15,617,486; 9,543,119 fit for military service; 610,410 reach military age (18) annually
Defense expenditures: 2.9% of GNP, or $1.9 billion (1989 est.)

Togo

See regional map VII · Bight of Benin

Geography

Total area: 56,790 km²; land area: 54,390 km²
Comparative area: slightly smaller than West Virginia
Land boundaries: 1,647 km total; Benin 644 km, Burkina 126 km, Ghana 877 km
Coastline: 56 km
Maritime claims:
Extended economic zone: 200 nm
Territorial sea: 30 nm
Climate: tropical; hot, humid in south; semiarid in north
Terrain: gently rolling savanna in north; central hills; southern plateau; low coastal plain with extensive lagoons and marshes
Natural resources: phosphates, limestone, marble
Land use: 25% arable land; 1% permanent crops; 4% meadows and pastures; 28% forest and woodland; 42% other; includes NEGL% irrigated
Environment: hot, dry harmattan wind can reduce visibility in north during winter; recent droughts affecting agriculture; deforestation

People

Population: 3,674,355 (July 1990), growth rate 3.7% (1990)
Birth rate: 50 births/1,000 population (1990)
Death rate: 14 deaths/1,000 population (1990)
Net migration rate: 0 migrants/1,000 population (1990)
Infant mortality rate: 112 deaths/1,000 live births (1990)
Life expectancy at birth: 53 years male, 57 years female (1990)
Total fertility rate: 7.2 children born/woman (1990)
Nationality: noun—Togolese (sing. and pl.); adjective—Togolese

307

Togo (continued)

Ethnic divisions: 37 tribes; largest and most important are Ewe, Mina, and Kabyè; under 1% European and Syrian-Lebanese
Religion: about 70% indigenous beliefs, 20% Christian, 10% Muslim
Language: French, both official and language of commerce; major African languages are Ewe and Mina in the south and Dagomba and Kabyè in the north
Literacy: 40.7%
Labor force: NA; 78% agriculture, 22% industry; about 88,600 wage earners, evenly divided between public and private sectors; 50% of population of working age (1985)
Organized labor: one national union, the National Federation of Togolese Workers

Government

Long-form name: Republic of Togo
Type: republic; one-party presidential regime
Capital: Lomé
Administrative divisions: 21 circumscriptions (circonscriptions, singular—circonscription); Amlamé (Amou), Aného (Lacs), Atakpamé (Ogou), Badou (Wawa), Bafilo (Assoli), Bassar (Bassari), Dapaong (Tôné), Kanté (Kéran), Klouto (Kloto), Kpagouda (Binah), Lama-Kara (Kozah), Lomé (Golfe), Mango (Oti), Niamtougou (Doufelgou), Notsé (Haho), Sotouboua, Tabligbo (Yoto), Tchamba, Tchaoudjo, Tsévié (Zio), Vogan (Vo); note—the 21 units may now be called prefectures (préfectures, singular—préfecture) and reported name changes for individual units are included in parenthesis
Independence: 27 April 1960 (from UN trusteeship under French administration, formerly French Togo)
Constitution: 30 December 1979, effective 13 January 1980
Legal system: French-based court system
National holiday: Liberation Day (anniversary of coup), 13 January (1967)
Executive branch: president, Council of Ministers (cabinet)
Legislative branch: unicameral National Assembly (Assemblée Nationale)
Judicial branch: Court of Appeal (Cour d'Appel), Supreme Court (Cour Suprême)
Leaders: *Chief of State and Head of Government* —President Gen. Gnassingbé EYADEMA (since 14 April 1967)
Political parties and leaders: only party—Rally of the Togolese People (RPT), President Eyadéma
Suffrage: universal adult at age NA
Elections: *President*—last held 21 December 1986 (next to be held December 1993); results—Gen. Eyadéma was reelected without opposition;

National Assembly—last held 4 March 1990 (next to be held March 1995); results—RPT is the only party; seats—(77 total) RPT 77
Communists: no Communist party
Member of: ACP, AfDB, CEAO (observer), EAMA, ECA, ECOWAS, ENTENTE, FAO, G-77, GATT, IBRD, ICAO, ICO, IDA, IFAD, IFC, ILO, IMF, IMO, INTELSAT, INTERPOL, ITU, NAM, OAU, OCAM, UN, UNESCO, UPU, WHO, WIPO, WMO, WTO
Diplomatic representation: Ambassador Ellom-Kodjo SCHUPPIUS; Chancery at 2208 Massachusetts Avenue NW, Washington DC 20008; telephone (202) 234-4212 or 4213; *US*—Ambassador Rush W. TAYLOR, Jr.; Embassy at Rue Pelletier Caventou and Rue Vauban, Lomé (mailing address is B. P. 852, Lomé); telephone [228] 21-29-91 through 94 and 21-36-09
Flag: five equal horizontal bands of green (top and bottom) alternating with yellow; there is a white five-pointed star on a red square in the upper hoist-side corner; uses the popular pan-African colors of Ethiopia

Economy

Overview: Togo is one of the least developed countries in the world with a per capita GDP of about $400. The economy is heavily dependent on subsistence agriculture, which accounts for about 35% of GDP and provides employment for 80% of the labor force. Primary agricultural exports are cocoa, coffee, and cotton, which together account for about 30% of total export earnings. Togo is self-sufficient in basic foodstuffs when harvests are normal. In the industrial sector phosphate mining is by far the most important activity, with phosphate exports accounting for about 40% of total foreign exchange earnings.
GDP: $1.35 billion, per capita $405; real growth rate 4.1% (1988 est.)
Inflation rate (consumer prices): 2.5% (1987 est.)
Unemployment rate: 2.0% (1987)
Budget: revenues $354 million; expenditures $399 million, including capital expenditures of $102 million (1988 est.)
Exports: $344 million (f.o.b., 1988); *commodities*—phosphates, cocoa, coffee, cotton, manufactures, palm kernels; *partners*—EC 70%, Africa 9%, US 2%, other 19% (1985)
Imports: $369 million (f.o.b., 1988); *commodities*—food, fuels, durable consumer goods, other intermediate goods, capital goods; *partners*—EC 69%, Africa 10%, Japan 7%, US 4%, other 10% (1985)
External debt: $1.3 billion (December 1988)

Industrial production: growth rate 4.9% (1987 est.)
Electricity: 117,000 kW capacity; 155 million kWh produced, 45 kWh per capita (1989)
Industries: phosphate mining, agricultural processing, cement, handicrafts, textiles, beverages
Agriculture: cash crops—coffee, cocoa, cotton; food crops—yams, cassava, corn, beans, rice, millet, sorghum, fish
Aid: US commitments, including Ex-Im (FY70-88), $121 million; Western (non-US) countries, ODA and OOF bilateral commitments (1970-87), $1.6 billion; OPEC bilateral aid (1979-89), $35 million; Communist countries (1970-88), $46 million
Currency: Communauté Financière Africaine franc (plural—francs); 1 CFA franc (CFAF) = 100 centimes
Exchange rates: Communauté Financière Africaine francs (CFAF) per US$1—287.99 (January 1990), 319.01 (1989), 297.85 (1988), 300.54 (1987), 346.30 (1986), 449.26 (1985)
Fiscal year: calendar year

Communications

Railroads: 515 km 1.000-meter gauge, single track
Highways: 6,462 km total; 1,762 km paved; 4,700 km unimproved roads
Inland waterways: none
Ports: Lomé, Kpeme (phosphate port)
Merchant marine: 7 ships (1,000 GRT or over) totaling 41,809 GRT/72,289 DWT; includes 4 roll-on/roll-off cargo, 3 multi-function large-load carrier
Civil air: 3 major transport aircraft
Airports: 9 total, 9 usable; 2 with permanent-surface runways; none with runways over 3,659 m; 2 with runways 2,440-3,659 m none with runways 1,220-2,439 m
Telecommunications: fair system based on network of open-wire lines supplemented by radio relay routes; 12,000 telephones; stations—2 AM, no FM, 3 (2 relays) TV; satellite earth stations—1 Atlantic Ocean INTELSAT and 1 SYMPHONIE

Defense Forces

Branches: Army, Navy, Air Force, paramilitary Gendarmerie
Military manpower: males 15-49, 767,949; 403,546 fit for military service; no conscription
Defense expenditures: 3.3% of GDP (1987)

Tokelau
(territory of New Zealand)

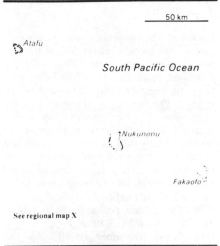

50 km

Atafu

South Pacific Ocean

Nukunonu

Fakaofo

See regional map X

Geography

Total area: 10 km²; land area: 10 km²
Comparative area: about 17 times the size of The Mall in Washington, DC
Land boundaries: none
Coastline: 101 km
Maritime claims:
Extended economic zone: 200 nm
Territorial sea: 12 nm
Climate: tropical; moderated by trade winds (April to November)
Terrain: coral atolls enclosing large lagoons
Natural resources: negligible
Land use: 0% arable land; 0% permanent crops; 0% meadows and pastures; 0% forest and woodland; 100% other
Environment: lies in Pacific typhoon belt
Note: located 3,750 km southwest of Honolulu in the South Pacific Ocean, about halfway between Hawaii and New Zealand

People

Population: 1,700 (July 1990), growth rate 0.0% (1990)
Birth rate: NA births/1,000 population (1990)
Death rate: NA deaths/1,000 population (1990)
Net migration rate: NA migrants/1,000 population (1990)
Infant mortality rate: NA deaths/1,000 live births (1990)
Life expectancy at birth: NA years male, NA years female (1990)
Total fertility rate: NA children born/woman (1990)
Nationality: noun—Tokelauan(s); adjective—Tokelauan
Ethnic divisions: all Polynesian, with cultural ties to Western Samoa
Religion: 70% Congregational Christian Church, 30% Roman Catholic; on Atafu, all Congregational Christian Church of Samoa; on Nukunonu, all Roman Catholic; on Fakaofo, both denominations, with the Congregational Christian Church predominant
Language: Tokelauan (a Polynesian language) and English
Literacy: NA%, but probably high
Labor force: NA
Organized labor: NA

Government

Long-form name: none
Type: territory of New Zealand
Capital: none, each atoll has its own administrative center
Administrative divisions: none (territory of New Zealand)
Independence: none (territory of New Zealand)
Constitution: administered under the Tokelau Islands Act of 1948, as amended in 1970
Legal system: British and local statutes
National holiday: Waitangi Day (Treaty of Waitangi established British sovereignty over New Zealand), 6 February (1840)
Executive branch: administrator (appointed by the Minister of Foreign Affairs in New Zealand), official secretary
Legislative branch: Council of Elders (Taupulega) on each atoll
Judicial branch: High Court in Niue, Supreme Court in New Zealand
Leaders: *Chief of State*—Queen ELIZABETH II (since 6 February 1952);
Head of Government—Administrator Neil WALTER; Official Secretary M. NORRISH, Office of Tokelau Affairs
Suffrage: NA
Elections: NA
Communists: probably none
Diplomatic representation: none (territory of New Zealand)
Flag: the flag of New Zealand is used

Economy

Overview: Tokelau's small size, isolation, and lack of resources greatly restrain economic development and confine agriculture to the subsistence level. The people must rely on aid from New Zealand to maintain public services, annual aid being substantially greater than GDP. The principal sources of revenue come from sales of copra, postage stamps, souvenir coins, and handicrafts. Money is also remitted to families from relatives in New Zealand.
GDP: $1.4 million, per capita $800; real growth rate NA% (1988 est.)
Inflation rate (consumer prices): NA%
Unemployment rate: NA%
Budget: revenues $430,830; expenditures $2.8 million, including capital expenditures of $37,300 (FY87)
Exports: $98,000 (f.o.b., 1983); *commodities*—stamps, copra, handicrafts; *partners*—NZ
Imports: $323,400 (c.i.f., 1983); *commodities*—foodstuffs, building materials, fuel; *partners*—NZ
External debt: none
Industrial production: growth rate NA%
Electricity: 200 kW capacity; 0.30 million kWh produced, 175 kWh per capita (1989)
Industries: small-scale enterprises for copra production, wood work, plaited craft goods; stamps, coins; fishing
Agriculture: coconuts, copra; basic subsistence crops—breadfruit, papaya, bananas; pigs, poultry, goats
Aid: Western (non-US) countries, ODA and OOF bilateral commitments (1970-87), $21 million
Currency: New Zealand dollar (plural—dollars); 1 New Zealand dollar (NZ$) = 100 cents
Exchange rates: New Zealand dollars (NZ$) per US$1—1.6581 (January 1990), 1.6708 (1989), 1.5244 (1988), 1.6886 (1987), 1.9088 (1986), 2.0064 (1985)
Fiscal year: 1 April-31 March

Communications

Ports: none; offshore anchorage only
Airports: none; lagoon landings by amphibious aircraft from Western Samoa
Telecommunications: telephone service between islands and to Western Samoa

Defense Forces

Note: defense is the responsibility of New Zealand

Tonga

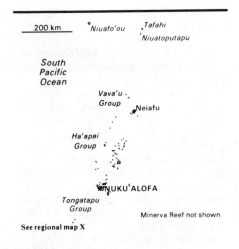

```
200 km
        °Niuafo'ou    .Tafahi
                       Niuatoputapu
South
Pacific
Ocean
        Vava'u .
        Group
              °Neiafu

Ha'apai
Group

       NUKU'ALOFA
Tongatapu
Group
                Minerva Reef not shown
See regional map X
```

Geography

Total area: 748 km²; land area: 718 km²
Comparative area: slightly more than four times the size of Washington, DC
Land boundaries: none
Coastline: 419 km
Maritime claims:
  Continental shelf: no specific limits
  Extended economic zone: 200 nm
  Territorial sea: 12 nm
Climate: tropical; modified by trade winds; warm season (December to May), cool season (May to December)
Terrain: most islands have limestone base formed from uplifted coral formation; others have limestone overlying volcanic base
Natural resources: fish, fertile soil
Land use: 25% arable land; 55% permanent crops; 6% meadows and pastures; 12% forest and woodland; 2% other
Environment: archipelago of 170 islands (36 inhabited); subject to cyclones (October to April); deforestation
Note: located about 2,250 km north-northwest of New Zealand, about two-thirds of the way between Hawaii and New Zealand

People

Population: 101,313 (July 1990), growth rate 0.9% (1990)
Birth rate: 27 births/1,000 population (1990)
Death rate: 7 deaths/1,000 population (1990)
Net migration rate: −11 migrants/1,000 population (1990)
Infant mortality rate: 24 deaths/1,000 live births (1990)
Life expectancy at birth: 65 years male, 70 years female (1990)
Total fertility rate: 3.9 children born/woman (1990)

Nationality: noun—Tongan(s); adjective—Tongan
Ethnic divisions: Polynesian; about 300 Europeans
Religion: Christian; Free Wesleyan Church claims over 30,000 adherents
Language: Tongan, English
Literacy: 90-95%; compulsory education for children ages 6 to 14
Labor force: NA; 70% agriculture; 600 engaged in mining
Organized labor: none

Government

Long-form name: Kingdom of Tonga
Type: hereditary constitutional monarchy
Capital: Nuku'alofa
Administrative divisions: three island groups; Ha'apai, Tongatapu, Vava'u
Independence: 4 June 1970 (from UK; formerly Friendly Islands)
Constitution: 4 November 1875, revised 1 January 1967
Legal system: based on English law
National holiday: Emancipation Day, 4 June (1970)
Executive branch: monarch, prime minister, deputy prime minister, Council of Ministers (cabinet), Privy Council
Legislative branch: unicameral Legislative Assembly
Judicial branch: Supreme Court
Leaders: *Chief of State*—King Taufa'ahau TUPOU IV (since 16 December 1965); *Head of Government*—Prime Minister Prince Fatafehi TU'IPELEHAKE (since 16 December 1965)
Political parties and leaders: none
Suffrage: all literate, tax-paying males and all literate females over 21
Elections: *Legislative Assembly*—last held 14-15 February 1990 (next to be held NA February 1993); results—percent of vote NA; seats—(29 total, 9 elected) 6 proreform, 3 traditionalist
Communists: none known
Member of: ACP, ADB, Commonwealth, FAO, ESCAP, GATT (de facto), IFAD, ITU, SPF, UNESCO, UPU, WHO
Diplomatic representation: Ambassador Siosaia Ma'Ulupekotofa TUITA resides in London; *US*—the US has no offices in Tonga; the Ambassador to Fiji is accredited to Tonga and makes periodic visits
Flag: red with a bold red cross on a white rectangle in the upper hoist-side corner

Economy

Overview: The economy's base is agriculture, which employs about 70% of the labor force and contributes 50% to GDP. Coconuts, bananas, and vanilla beans are the main crops and make up two-thirds of exports. The country must import a high proportion of its food, mainly from New Zealand. The manufacturing sector accounts for only 10% of GDP. Tourism is the primary source of hard currency earnings, but the island remains dependent on sizable external aid and remittances to sustain its trade deficit.
GDP: $86 million, per capita $850; real growth rate 3.6% (FY89 est.)
Inflation rate (consumer prices): 8.2% (FY87)
Unemployment rate: NA%
Budget: revenues $54.8 million; expenditures $56.2 million, including capital expenditures of $16.9 million (FY88 est.)
Exports: $9.1 million (f.o.b., FY88 est.); *commodities*—coconut oil, desiccated coconut, copra, bananas, taro, vanilla beans, fruits, vegetables, fish; *partners*—NZ 54%, Australia 30%, US 8%, Fiji 5% (FY87)
Imports: $60.1 million (c.i.f., FY88 est.); *commodities*—food products, beverages and tobacco, fuels, machinery and transport equipment, chemicals, building materials; *partners*—NZ 39%, Australia 25%, Japan 9%, US 6%, EC 5% (FY87)
External debt: $31.8 million (1987)
Industrial production: growth rate 15% (FY86)
Electricity: 5,000 kW capacity; 8 million kWh produced, 80 kWh per capita (1989)
Industries: tourism, fishing
Agriculture: dominated by coconut, copra, and banana production; vanilla beans, cocoa, coffee, ginger, black pepper
Aid: US commitments, including Ex-Im (FY70-87), $15 million; Western (non-US) countries, ODA and OOF bilateral commitments (1970-87), $220 million
Currency: pa'anga (plural—pa'anga); 1 pa'anga (T$) = 100 seniti
Exchange rates: pa'anga (T$) per US$1—1.23 (FY89 est.), 1.37 (FY88), 1.51 (FY87), 1.43 (FY86), 1.30 (FY85)
Fiscal year: 1 July-30 June

Trinidad and Tobago

Communications

Highways: 198 km sealed road (Tongatapu); 74 km (Vava'u); 94 km unsealed roads usable only in dry weather
Ports: Nukualofa, Neiafu, Pangai
Merchant marine: 6 ships (1,000 GRT or over) totaling 37,249 GRT/50,116 DWT; includes 2 cargo, 1 roll-on/roll-off cargo, 2 container, 1 liquefied gas
Civil air: no major transport aircraft
Airports: 6 total, 6 usable; 1 with permanent-surface runways; none with runways over 3,659 m; 1 with runways 2,440-3,659; 1 with runways 1,220-2,439 m
Telecommunications: 3,529 telephones; 66,000 radio receivers; no TV sets; stations—1 AM, no FM, no TV; 1 Pacific Ocean INTELSAT earth station

Defense Forces

Branches: Land Force, Maritime Force
Military manpower: NA
Defense expenditures: NA

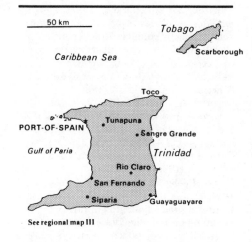

See regional map III

Geography

Total area: 5,130 km²; land area: 5,130 km²
Comparative area: slightly smaller than Delaware
Land boundaries: none
Coastline: 362 km
Maritime claims:
Continental shelf: 200 meters or to depth of exploitation
Exclusive fishing zone: 200 nm
Extended economic zone: 200 nm
Territorial sea: 12 nm
Disputes: maritime boundary with Venezuela in the Gulf of Paria
Climate: tropical; rainy season (June to December)
Terrain: mostly plains with some hills and low mountains
Natural resources: crude oil, natural gas, asphalt
Land use: 14% arable land; 17% permanent crops; 2% meadows and pastures; 44% forest and woodland; 23% other; includes 4% irrigated
Environment: outside usual path of hurricanes and other tropical storms
Note: located 11 km from Venezuela

People

Population: 1,344,639 (July 1990), growth rate 2.2% (1990)
Birth rate: 28 births/1,000 population (1990)
Death rate: 6 deaths/1,000 population (1990)
Net migration rate: 0 migrants/1,000 population (1990)
Infant mortality rate: 10 deaths/1,000 live births (1990)
Life expectancy at birth: 69 years male, 74 years female (1990)
Total fertility rate: 3.3 children born/woman (1990)

Nationality: noun—Trinidadian(s), Tobagonian(s); adjective—Trinidadian, Tobagonian
Ethnic divisions: 43% black, 40% East Indian, 14% mixed, 1% white, 1% Chinese, 1% other
Religion: 36.2% Roman Catholic, 23.0% Hindu, 13.1% Protestant, 6.0% Muslim, 21.7% unknown
Language: English (official), Hindi, French, Spanish
Literacy: 98%
Labor force: 463,900; 18.1% construction and utilities; 14.8% manufacturing, mining, and quarrying; 10.9% agriculture; 56.2% other (1985 est.)
Organized labor: 22% of labor force (1988)

Government

Long-form name: Republic of Trinidad and Tobago
Type: parliamentary democracy
Capital: Port-of-Spain
Administrative divisions: 8 counties, 3 municipalities*, and 1 ward**; Arima*, Caroni, Mayaro, Nariva, Port-of-Spain*, Saint Andrew, Saint David, Saint George, Saint Patrick, San Fernando*, Tobago**, Victoria
Independence: 31 August 1962 (from UK)
Constitution: 31 August 1976
Legal system: based on English common law; judicial review of legislative acts in the Supreme Court; has not accepted compulsory ICJ jurisdiction
National holiday: Independence Day, 31 August (1962)
Executive branch: president, prime minister, Cabinet
Legislative branch: bicameral Parliament consists of an upper house or Senate and a lower house or House of Representatives
Judicial branch: Court of Appeal, Supreme Court
Leaders: *Chief of State*—President Noor Mohammed HASSANALI (since 18 March 1987);
Head of Government—Prime Minister Arthur Napoleon Raymond ROBINSON (since 18 December 1986)
Political parties and leaders: National Alliance for Reconstruction (NAR), A. N. R. Robinson; People's National Movement (PNM), Patrick Manning; United National Congress, Basdeo Panday; Movement for Social Transformation (MOTION), David Abdullah
Suffrage: universal at age 18
Elections: *House of Representatives*—last held 15 December 1986 (next to be held by December 1991); results—NAR 66%, PNM 32%, others 2%; seats—(36 total) NAR 33, PNM 3

Communists: Communist Party of Trinidad and Tobago; Trinidad and Tobago Peace Council, James Millette

Other political pressure groups: National Joint Action Committee (NJAC), radical antigovernment black-identity organization; Trinidad and Tobago Peace Council, leftist organization affiliated with the World Peace Council; Trinidad and Tobago Chamber of Industry and Commerce; Trinidad and Tobago Labor Congress, moderate labor federation; Council of Progressive Trade Unions, radical labor federation

Member of: ACP, CARICOM, CCC, Commonwealth, FAO, G-77, GATT, IADB, IBRD, ICAO, ICO, IDA, IDB— Inter-American Development Bank, IFC, ILO, IMF, IMO, INTELSAT, INTERPOL, ISO, ITU, IWC—International Wheat Council, NAM, OAS, PAHO, SELA, UN, UNESCO, UPU, WFTU, WHO, WMO, WTO

Diplomatic representation: Ambassador Angus Albert KHAN; Chancery at 1708 Massachusetts Avenue NW, Washington DC 20036; telephone (202) 467-6490; Trinidad and Tobago has a Consulate General in New York; *US*—Ambassador Charles A. GARGANO; Embassy at 15 Queen's Park West, Port-of-Spain (mailing address is P. O. Box 752, Port-of-Spain); telephone [809] 622-6372 or 6376, 6176

Flag: red with a white-edged black diagonal band from the upper hoist side

Economy

Overview: Trinidad and Tobago's petroleum-based economy has been in decline since 1982. During the first half of the 1980s, the petroleum sector accounted for nearly 80% of export earnings, 40% of government revenues, and almost 25% of GDP. In recent years, however, the economy has suffered because of the sharp fall in the price of oil. The government, in response to the revenue loss, pursued a series of austerity measures that pushed the unemployment rate to 22% in 1988. Agriculture employs only about 11% of the labor force and produces less than 3% of GDP. Since this sector is small, it has been unable to absorb the large numbers of the unemployed. The government currently seeks to diversify its export base.

GDP: $3.75 billion, per capita $3,070; real growth rate −2.0% (1988 est.)

Inflation rate (consumer prices): 15.0% (1989 est.)

Unemployment rate: 22% (1988)

Budget: revenues $1.4 billion; expenditures $2.1 billion, including capital expenditures of $430 million (1988 est.)

Exports: $1.4 billion (f.o.b., 1987); *commodities*—includes reexports—petroleum and petroleum products 70%, fertilizer, chemicals 15%, steel products, sugar, cocoa, coffee, citrus (1987); *partners*—US 61%, EC 15%, CARICOM 9%, Latin America 7%, Canada 3% (1986)

Imports: $1.2 billion (c.i.f., 1987); *commodities*—raw materials 41%, capital goods 30%, consumer goods 29% (1986); *partners*—US 42%, EC 21%, Japan 10%, Canada 6%, Latin America 6%, CARICOM 4% (1986)

External debt: $2.02 billion (December 1987)

Industrial production: growth rate 5.2%, excluding oil refining (1986)

Electricity: 1,176,000 kW capacity; 3,350 million kWh produced, 2,700 kWh per capita (1989)

Industries: petroleum, chemicals, tourism, food processing, cement, beverage, cotton textiles

Agriculture: accounts for about 3% of GDP and 4% of labor force; highly subsidized sector; major crops—cocoa and sugarcane; sugarcane acreage is being shifted into rice, citrus, coffee, vegetables; must import large share of food needs

Aid: US commitments, including Ex-Im (FY70-85), $370 million; Western (non-US) countries, ODA and OOF bilateral commitments (1970-87), $437 million

Currency: Trinidad and Tobago dollar (plural—dollars); 1 Trinidad and Tobago dollar (TT$) = 100 cents

Exchange rates: Trinidad and Tobago dollars (TT$) per US$1—4.2500 (January 1990), 4.2500 (1989), 3.8438 (1988), 3.6000 (1987), 3.6000 (1986), 2.4500 (1985)

Fiscal year: calendar year

Communications

Railroads: minimal agricultural system near San Fernando

Highways: 8,000 km total; 4,000 km paved, 1,000 km improved earth, 3,000 km unimproved earth

Pipelines: 1,032 km crude oil; 19 km refined products; 904 km natural gas

Ports: Port-of-Spain, Point Lisas, Pointe-a-Pierre

Civil air: 14 major transport aircraft

Airports: 6 total, 5 usable; 3 with permanent-surface runways; none with runways over 3,659 m; 1 with runways 2,440-3,659 m; 3 with runways 1,220-2,439 m

Telecommunications: excellent international service via tropospheric scatter links to Barbados and Guyana; good local service; 109,000 telephones; stations—2 AM, 4 FM, 5 TV; 1 Atlantic Ocean INTELSAT earth station

Defense Forces

Branches: Trinidad and Tobago Defense Force, Trinidad and Tobago Police Service

Military manpower: males 15-49, 343,292; 248,674 fit for military service

Defense expenditures: 1.6% of GDP, or $59 million (1989 est.)

Tromelin Island
(French possession)

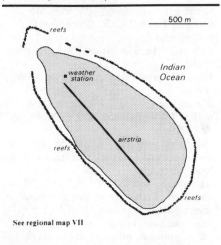

See regional map VII

Geography

Total area: 1 km²; land area: 1 km²
Comparative area: about 1.7 times the size of The Mall in Washington, DC
Land boundaries: none
Coastline: 3.7 km
Maritime claims:
Contiguous zone: 12 nm
Continental shelf: 200 meters or to depth of exploitation
Extended economic zone: 200 nm
Territorial sea: 12 nm
Disputes: claimed by Madagascar, Mauritius, and Seychelles
Climate: tropical
Terrain: sandy
Natural resources: fish
Land use: 0% arable land; 0% permanent crops; 0% meadows and pastures; 0% forest and woodland; 100% other—scattered bushes
Environment: wildlife sanctuary
Note: located 350 km east of Madagascar and 600 km north of Reunion in the Indian Ocean; climatologically important location for forecasting cyclones

People

Population: uninhabited

Government

Long-form name: none
Type: French possession administered by Commissioner of the Republic Daniel CONSTANTIN, resident in Reunion

Economy

Overview: no economic activity

Communications

Airports: 1 with runway less than 1,220 m
Ports: none; offshore anchorage only
Telecommunications: important meteorological station

Defense Forces

Note: defense is the responsibility of France

Tunisia

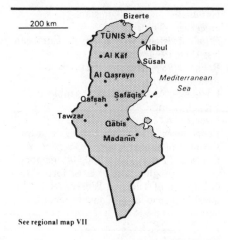

See regional map VII

Geography

Total area: 163,610 km²; land area: 155,360 km²
Comparative area: slightly larger than Georgia
Land boundaries: 1,424 km total; Algeria 965 km, Libya 459 km
Coastline: 1,148 km
Maritime claims:
Territorial sea: 12 nm
Disputes: maritime boundary dispute with Libya
Climate: temperate in north with mild, rainy winters and hot, dry summers; desert in south
Terrain: mountains in north; hot, dry central plain; semiarid south merges into the Sahara
Natural resources: crude oil, phosphates, iron ore, lead, zinc, salt
Land use: 20% arable land; 10% permanent crops; 19% meadows and pastures; 4% forest and woodland; 47% other; includes 1% irrigated
Environment: deforestation; overgrazing; soil erosion; desertification
Note: strategic location in central Mediterranean; only 144 km from Italy across the Strait of Sicily; borders Libya on east

People

Population: 8,095,492 (July 1990), growth rate 2.2% (1990)
Birth rate: 28 births/1,000 population (1990)
Death rate: 6 deaths/1,000 population (1990)
Net migration rate: 0 migrants/1,000 population (1990)
Infant mortality rate: 40 deaths/1,000 live births (1990)
Life expectancy at birth: 68 years male, 70 years female (1990)
Total fertility rate: 4.0 children born/woman (1990)

313

Tunisia (continued)

Nationality: noun—Tunisian(s); adjective—Tunisian
Ethnic divisions: 98% Arab, 1% European, less than 1% Jewish
Religion: 98% Muslim, 1% Christian, less than 1% Jewish
Language: Arabic (official); Arabic and French (commerce)
Literacy: 62% (est.)
Labor force: 2,250,000; 32% agriculture; shortage of skilled labor
Organized labor: about 360,000 members claimed, roughly 20% of labor force; General Union of Tunisian Workers (UGTT), quasi-independent of Constitutional Democratic Party

Government

Long-form name: Republic of Tunisia; note—may be changed to Tunisian Republic
Type: republic
Capital: Tūnis
Administrative divisions: 23 governorates (wilāyāt, singular—wilāyah); Al Kāf, Al Mahdīyah, Al Munastīr, Al Qaşrayn, Al Qayrawān, Aryānah, Bājah, Banzart, Bin 'Arūs, Jundūbah, Madanīn, Nābul, Qābis, Qafşah, Qibilī, Şafāqis, Sīdī Bū Zayd, Silyānah, Sūsah, Taţāwīn, Tawzar, Tūnis, Zaghwān
Independence: 20 March 1956 (from France)
Constitution: 1 June 1959
Legal system: based on French civil law system and Islamic law; some judicial review of legislative acts in the Supreme Court in joint session
National holiday: National Day, 20 March (1956)
Executive branch: president, prime minister, Cabinet
Legislative branch: unicameral National Assembly (Assemblée Nationale)
Judicial branch: Court of Cassation (Cour de Cassation)
Leaders: *Chief of State*—President Gen. Zine el Abidine BEN ALI (since 7 November 1987);
Head of Government—Prime Minister Hamed KAROUI (since 26 September 1989)
Political parties and leaders: Constitutional Democratic Rally Party (RCD), President Ben Ali (official ruling party); Movement of Democratic Socialists (MDS), Ahmed Mestiri; five other political parties are legal, including the Communist Party
Suffrage: universal at age 20
Elections: *President*—last held 2 April 1989 (next to be held April 1994); results—Gen. Zine el Abidine Ben Aliwas reelected without opposition;
National Assembly—last held 2 April 1989 (next to be held April 1994); results—RCD 80.7%, independents/ Islamists 13.7%, MDS 3.2%, others 2.4% seats—(141 total) RCD 141
Communists: a small number of nominal Communists, mostly students
Member of: AfDB, Arab League, AIOEC, CCC, FAO, G-77, GATT (de facto), IAEA, IBRD, ICAO, IDA, IDB—Islamic Development Bank, IFAD, IFC, ILO, ILZSG, IMF, IMO, INTELSAT, INTERPOL, IOOC, ITU, IWC—International Wheat Council, NAM, OAPEC, OAU, OIC, UN, UNESCO, UPU, WHO, WIPO, WMO, WTO
Diplomatic representation: Ambassador Abdelaziz HAMZAOUI; Chancery at 1515 Massachusetts Avenue NW, Washington DC 20005; telephone (202) 862-1850; *US*—Ambassador Robert H. PELLETREAU, Jr.; Embassy at 144 Avenue de la Liberte, 1002 Tunis-Belvedere; telephone [216] (1) 782-566
Flag: red with a white disk in the center bearing a red crescent nearly encircling a red five-pointed star; the crescent and star are traditional symbols of Islam

Economy

Overview: The economy depends primarily on petroleum, phosphates, and tourism for continued growth. Two successive drought-induced crop failures have strained the government's budget and increased unemployment. The current account fell from a $23 million surplus in 1988 to a $390 million deficit in 1989. Despite its foreign payments problems, Tunis appears committed to its IMF-supported structural adjustment program. Nonetheless, the government may have to slow its implementation to head off labor unrest. The increasing foreign debt—$7.6 billion at yearend 1989—is also a key problem. Tunis probably will seek debt relief in 1990.
GDP: $8.7 billion, per capita $1,105; real growth rate 3.1% (1989 est.)
Inflation rate (consumer prices): 10% (1989)
Unemployment rate: 25% (1989)
Budget: revenues $2.9 billion; expenditures $3.2 billion, including capital expenditures of $0.8 billion (1989 est.)
Exports: $3.1 billion (f.o.b., 1989); *commodities*—hydrocarbons, agricultural products, phosphates and chemicals; *partners*—EC 73%, Middle East 9%, US 1%, Turkey, USSR
Imports: $4.4 billion (f.o.b., 1989); *commodities*—industrial goods and equipment 57%, hydrocarbons 13%, food 12%, consumer goods; *partners*—EC 68%, US 7%, Canada, Japan, USSR, China, Saudi Arabia, Algeria
External debt: $7.6 billion (December 1989)
Industrial production: growth rate 3.5% (1988)
Electricity: 1,493,000 kW capacity; 4,210 million kWh produced, 530 kWh per capita (1989)
Industries: petroleum, mining (particularly phosphate and iron ore), textiles, footwear, food, beverages
Agriculture: accounts for 16% of GDP and one-third of labor force; output subject to severe fluctuations because of frequent droughts; export crops—olives, dates, oranges, almonds; other products—grain, sugar beets, wine grapes, poultry, beef, dairy; not self-sufficient in food; fish catch of 99,200 metric tons (1986)
Aid: US commitments, including Ex-Im (FY70-88), $694 million; Western (non-US) countries, ODA and OOF bilateral commitments (1970-87), $4.6 billion; OPEC bilateral aid (1979-89), $684 million; Communist countries (1970-88), $410 million
Currency: Tunisian dinar (plural—dinars); 1 Tunisian dinar (TD) = 1,000 millimes
Exchange rates: Tunisian dinars (TD) per US$1—0.9055 (January 1990), 0.9493 (1989), 0.8578 (1988), 0.8287 (1987), 0.7940 (1986), 0.8345 (1985)
Fiscal year: calendar year

Communications

Railroads: 2,154 km total; 465 km 1.435-meter standard gauge; 1,689 km 1.000-meter gauge
Highways: 17,700 km total; 9,100 km bituminous; 8,600 km improved and unimproved earth
Pipelines: 797 km crude oil; 86 km refined products; 742 km natural gas
Ports: Bizerte, Gabes, Sfax, Sousse, Tunis, La Goulette, Zarzis
Merchant marine: 21 ships (1,000 GRT or over) totaling 160,172 GRT/218,970 DWT; includes 1 short-sea passenger, 4 cargo, 2 roll-on/roll-off cargo, 2 petroleum, oils, and lubricants (POL) tanker, 6 chemical tanker, 1 liquefied gas, 5 bulk
Civil air: 13 major transport aircraft
Airports: 30 total, 28 usable; 13 with permanent-surface runways; none with runways over 3,659 m; 7 with runways 2,440-3,659 m; 7 with runways 1,220-2,439 m
Telecommunications: the system is above the African average; facilities consist of open-wire lines, multiconductor cable, and radio relay; key centers are Şafāqis, Sūsah, Bizerte, and Tūnis; 233,000 telephones; stations—18 AM, 4 FM, 14 TV;

Turkey

400 km

Black Sea

İstanbul · Samsun

ANKARA · Sivas · Trabzon
★
Bursa · Kayseri · Erzurum
İzmir · Konya · Diyarbakır
Antalya · Adana · Van

*Mediterranean
Sea*

See regional map VI

4 submarine cables; satellite earth stations—1 Atlantic Ocean INTELSAT and 1 ARABSAT with back-up control station; coaxial cable to Algeria; radio relay to Algeria, Libya, and Italy

Defense Forces

Branches: Army, Navy, Air Force
Military manpower: males 15-49, 1,997,197; 1,149,141 fit for military service; 88,368 reach military age (20) annually
Defense expenditures: 2.7% of GDP, or $235 million (1989 est.)

Geography

Total area: 780,580 km^2; land area: 770,760 km^2
Comparative area: slightly larger than Texas
Land boundaries: 2,715 km total; Bulgaria 240 km, Greece 206 km, Iran 499 km, Iraq 331 km, Syria 822 km, USSR 617 km
Coastline: 7,200 km
Maritime claims:
Extended economic zone: in Black Sea only—to the maritime boundary agreed upon with the USSR
Territorial sea: 6 nm (12 nm in Black Sea and Mediterranean Sea)
Disputes: complex maritime and air (but not territorial) disputes with Greece in Aegean Sea; Cyprus question; Hatay question with Syria; ongoing dispute with downstream riparians (Syria and Iraq) over water development plans for the Tigris and Euphrates rivers; Kurdish question among Iran, Iraq, Syria, Turkey, and the USSR
Climate: temperate; hot, dry summers with mild, wet winters; harsher in interior
Terrain: mostly mountains; narrow coastal plain; high central plateau (Anatolia)
Natural resources: antimony, coal, chromium, mercury, copper, borate, sulphur, iron ore
Land use: 30% arable land; 4% permanent crops; 12% meadows and pastures; 26% forest and woodland; 28% other; includes 3% irrigated
Environment: subject to severe earthquakes, especially along major river valleys in west; air pollution; desertification
Note: strategic location controlling the Turkish straits (Bosporus, Sea of Marmara, Dardanelles) that link Black and Aegean Seas; Turkey and Norway only NATO members having a land boundary with the USSR

People

Population: 56,704,327 (July 1990), growth rate 2.2% (1990)
Birth rate: 29 births/1,000 population (1990)
Death rate: 8 deaths/1,000 population (1990)
Net migration rate: 0 migrants/1,000 population (1990)
Infant mortality rate: 74 deaths/1,000 live births (1990)
Life expectancy at birth: 64 years male, 67 years female (1990)
Total fertility rate: 3.6 children born/woman (1990)
Nationality: noun—Turk(s); adjective—Turkish
Ethnic divisions: 85% Turkish, 12% Kurd, 3% other
Religion: 98% Muslim (mostly Sunni), 2% other (mostly Christian and Jewish)
Language: Turkish (official), Kurdish, Arabic
Literacy: 70%
Labor force: 18,800,000; 56% agriculture, 30% services, 14% industry; about 1,000,000 Turks work abroad (1987)
Organized labor: 10-15% of labor force

Government

Long-form name: Republic of Turkey
Type: republican parliamentary democracy
Capital: Ankara
Administrative divisions: 67 provinces (iller, singular—il); Adana, Adiyaman, Afyon, Ağri, Amasya, Ankara, Antalya, Artvin, Aydin, Balikesir, Bilecik, Bingöl, Bitlis, Bolu, Burdur, Bursa, Çanakkale, Çankiri, Çorum, Denizli, Diyarbakir, Edirne, Elaziğ, Erzincan, Erzurum, Eskişehir, Gaziantep, Giresun, Gümüşhane, Hakkâri, Hatay, İçel, Isparta, İstanbul, İzmir, Kahraman Maraş, Kars, Kastamonu, Kayseri, Kirklareli, Kirşehir, Kocaeli, Konya, Kütahya, Malatya, Manisa, Mardin, Muğla, Muş, Nevşehir, Niğde, Ordu, Rize, Sakarya, Samsun, Siirt, Sinop, Sivas, Tekirdağ, Tokat, Trabzon, Tunceli, Urfa, Uşak, Van, Yozgat, Zonguldak; note—there may be four new provinces named Aksaray, Bayburt, Karaman, and Kirikkale
Independence: 29 October 1923 (successor state to the Ottoman Empire)
Constitution: 7 November 1982
Legal system: derived from various continental legal systems; accepts compulsory ICJ jurisdiction, with reservations
National holiday: Anniversary of the Declaration of the Republic, 29 October (1923)

Executive branch: president, Presidential Council, prime minister, deputy prime minister, Cabinet
Legislative branch: unicameral Grand National Assembly (Büyük Millet Meclisi)
Judicial branch: Court of Cassation
Leaders: *Chief of State*—President Turgut ÖZAL (since 9 November 1989); *Head of Government*—Prime Minister Yildirim AKBULUT (since 9 November 1989); Deputy Prime Minister Ali BOZER (since 31 March 1989)
Political parties and leaders: Motherland Party (ANAP), Yildirim Akbulut; Social Democratic Populist Party (SHP), Erdal İnönü; Correct Way Party (CWP), Süleyman Demirel; Democratic Left Party (DLP), Bülent Ecevit; Prosperity Party (RP), Necmettin Erbakan; National Work Party (MCP), Alpaslan Türkeş; Reform Democratic Party (IDP), Aykut Edibali
Suffrage: universal at age 21
Elections: *Grand National Assembly*—last held 29 November 1987 (next to be held November 1992); results—ANAP 36%, SHP 25%, CWP 19%, others 20%; seats—(450 total) ANAP 283, SHP 81, CWP 56, independents 26, vacant 4
Communists: strength and support negligible
Member of: ASSIMER, CCC, Council of Europe, EC (associate member), ECOSOC, FAO, GATT, IAEA, IBRD, ICAC, ICAO, IDA, IDB—Islamic Development Bank, IEA, IFAD, IFC, IHO, ILO, IMF, IMO, INTELSAT, INTERPOL, IOOC, IPU, ITC, ITU, NATO, OECD, OIC, UN, UNESCO, UPU, WHO, WIPO, WMO, WSG, WTO
Diplomatic representation: Ambassador Nuzhet KANDEMIR; Chancery at 1606 23rd Street NW, Washington DC 20008; telephone (202) 387-3200; there are Turkish Consulates General in Chicago, Houston, Los Angeles, and New York; *US*—Ambassador Morton ABRAMOWITZ; Embassy at 110 Ataturk Boulevard, Ankara (mailing address is APO New York 09254—0001); telephone [90] (4) 126 54 70; there are US Consulates General in İstanbul and İzmir, and a Consulate in Adana
Flag: red with a vertical white crescent (the closed portion is toward the hoist side) and white five-pointed star centered on the hoist side

Economy

Overview: The economic reforms that Turkey launched in 1980 continue to bring an impressive stream of benefits. The economy has grown steadily since the early 1980s, with real growth in per capita GDP increasing more than 6% annually. Agriculture remains the most important economic sector, employing about 60% of the labor force, accounting for almost 20% of GDP, and contributing about 25% to exports. Impressive growth in recent years has not solved all of the economic problems facing Turkey. Inflation and interest rates remain high, and a large budget deficit will continue to provide difficulties for a country undergoing a substantial transformation from a centrally controlled to a free market economy. The government has launched a multimillion-dollar development program in the southeastern region, which includes the building of a dozen dams on the Tigris and Euphrates rivers to generate electric power and irrigate large tracts of farmland. The planned tapping of huge quantities of Euphrates water has raised serious concern in the downstream riparian nations of Syria and Iraq.
GDP: $75 billion, per capita $1,350; real growth rate 1.8% (1989 est.)
Inflation rate (consumer prices): 68.8% (1989)
Unemployment rate: 15.8% (1988)
Budget: revenues $12.1 billion; expenditures $14.5 billion, including capital expenditures of $2.08 billion (FY88 est.)
Exports: $11.7 billion (f.o.b., 1988); *commodities*—industrial products 70%, crops and livestock products 25%; *partners*—FRG 18.4%, Iraq 8.5%, Italy 8.2%, US 6.5%, UK 4.9%, Iran 4.7%
Imports: $14.3 billion (c.i.f., 1988); *commodities*—crude oil, machinery, transport equipment, metals, pharmaceuticals, dyes, plastics, rubber, mineral fuels, fertilizers, chemicals; *partners*—FRG 14.3%, US 10.6%, Iraq 10.0%, Italy 7.0%, France 5.8%, UK 5.2%
External debt: $36.3 billion (November 1989)
Industrial production: growth rate 7.4% (1988)
Electricity: 14,064,000 kW capacity; 40,000 million kWh produced, 720 kWh per capita (1989)
Industries: textiles, food processing, mining (coal, chromite, copper, boron minerals), steel, petroleum, construction, lumber, paper
Agriculture: accounts for 20% of GDP and employs majority of population; products—tobacco, cotton, grain, olives, sugar beets, pulses, citrus fruit, variety of animal products; self-sufficient in food most years
Illicit drugs: one of the world's major suppliers of licit opiate products; government maintains strict controls over areas of opium poppy cultivation and output of poppy straw concentrate
Aid: US commitments, including Ex-Im (FY70-88), $2.2 billion; Western (non-US) countries, ODA and OOF bilateral commitments (1970-87), $7.9 billion; OPEC bilateral aid (1979-89), $665 million; Communist countries (1970-88), $4.5 billion
Currency: Turkish lira (plural—liras); 1 Turkish lira (TL) = 100 kuruş
Exchange rates: Turkish liras (TL) per US$1—2,314.7 (November 1989), 1,422.3 (1988), 857.2 (1987), 674.5 (1986), 522.0 (1985)
Fiscal year: calendar year

Communications

Railroads: 8,401 km 1.435-meter standard gauge; 479 km electrified
Highways: 49,615 km total; 26,915 km bituminous; 16,500 km gravel or crushed stone; 4,000 km improved earth; 2,200 km unimproved earth (1985)
Inland waterways: about 1,200 km
Pipelines: 1,738 km crude oil; 2,321 km refined products; 708 km natural gas
Ports: İskenderun, İstanbul, Mersin, İzmir
Merchant marine: 327 ships (1,000 GRT or over) totaling 2,972,465 GRT/ 5,087,620 DWT; includes 6 short-sea passenger, 1 passenger, 1 passenger-cargo, 193 cargo, 1 container, 4 roll-on/roll-off cargo, 3 refrigerated cargo, 1 livestock carrier, 35 petroleum, oils, and lubricants (POL) tanker, 15 chemical tanker, 2 liquefied gas, 4 combination ore/oil, 1 specialized tanker, 55 bulk, 4 combination bulk, 1 specialized liquid cargo
Civil air: 30 major transport aircraft (1985)
Airports: 119 total, 112 usable; 69 with permanent-surface runways; 3 with runways over 3,659 m; 30 with runways 2,440-3,659 m; 28 with runways 1,220-2,439 m
Telecommunications: fair domestic and international systems; trunk radio relay network; 3,100,000 telephones; stations—15 AM; 45 (60 repeaters) FM; 61 (476 repeaters) TV; communications satellite earth stations operating in the INTELSAT (1 Atlantic Ocean) and EUTELSAT systems; 1 submarine telephone cable

Defense Forces

Branches: Land Forces, Navy, Air Force, Gendarmerie, Coast Guard
Military manpower: males 15-49, 14,413,944; 8,813,430 fit for military service; 597,547 reach military age (20) annually
Defense expenditures: 3.9% of GDP, or $2.9 billion (1989 est.)

Turks and Caicos Islands
(dependent territory of the UK)

North Atlantic Ocean

50 km

North Caicos

Middle Caicos

East Caicos

Providenciales

West Caicos

Cockburn Harbour

GRAND TURK (Cockburn Town)

Salt Cay

Turks Islands

North Atlantic Ocean

See regional map III

Geography

Total area: 430 km²; land area: 430 km²
Comparative area: slightly less than 2.5 times the size of Washington, DC
Land boundaries: none
Coastline: 389 km
Maritime claims:
Exclusive fishing zone: 200 nm
Territorial sea: 12 nm
Climate: tropical; marine; moderated by trade winds; sunny and relatively dry
Terrain: low, flat limestone; extensive marshes and mangrove swamps
Natural resources: spiny lobster, conch
Land use: 2% arable land; 0% permanent crops; 0% meadows and pastures; 0% forest and woodland; 98% other
Environment: 30 islands (eight inhabited); subject to frequent hurricanes
Note: located 190 km north of the Dominican Republic in the North Atlantic Ocean

People

Population: 9,761 (July 1990), growth rate 2.3% (1990)
Birth rate: 25 births/1,000 population (1990)
Death rate: 5 deaths/1,000 population (1990)
Net migration rate: 4 migrants/1,000 population (1990)
Infant mortality rate: 14 deaths/1,000 live births (1990)
Life expectancy at birth: 72 years male, 78 years female (1990)
Total fertility rate: 3.8 children born/woman (1990)
Nationality: no noun or adjectival forms
Ethnic divisions: majority of African descent
Religion: Anglican, Roman Catholic, Baptist, Methodist, Church of God, Seventh-Day Adventist
Language: English (official)

Literacy: 99% (est.)
Labor force: NA; majority engaged in fishing and tourist industries; some subsistence agriculture
Organized labor: St. George's Industrial Trade Union

Government

Long-form name: none
Type: dependent territory of the UK
Capital: Grand Turk (Cockburn Town)
Administrative divisions: none (dependent territory of the UK)
Independence: none (dependent territory of the UK)
Constitution: introduced 30 August 1976, suspended in 1986, and a Constitutional Commission is currently reviewing its contents
Legal system: based on laws of England and Wales with a small number adopted from Jamaica and The Bahamas
National holiday: Constitution Day, 30 August (1976)
Executive branch: British monarch, governor, Executive Council
Legislative branch: unicameral Legislative Council
Judicial branch: Supreme Court
Leaders: *Chief of State*—Queen ELIZABETH II (since 6 February 1953), represented by Governor Michael J. BRADLEY (since 1987);
Head of Government—Chief Minister Oswald O. SKIPPINGS (since 3 March 1988)
Political parties and leaders: People's Democratic Movement (PDM), Oswald Skippings; Progressive National Party (PNP), Dan Malcolm and Norman Saunders; National Democratic Alliance (NDA), Ariel Missick
Suffrage: universal at age 18
Elections: *Legislative Council*—last held on 3 March 1988 (next to be held NA); results—PDM 60%, PNP 30%, others 10%; seats—(20 total, 13 elected) PDM 11, PNP 2
Communists: none
Diplomatic representation: as a dependent territory of the UK, the interests of the Turks and Caicos Islands are represented in the US by the UK; *US*—none
Flag: blue with the flag of the UK in the upper hoist-side quadrant and the colonial shield centered on the outer half of the flag; the shield is yellow and contains a conch shell, lobster, and cactus

Economy

Overview: The economy is based on fishing, tourism, and offshore banking. Subsistence farming—corn and beans—

exists only on the Caicos Islands, so that most foods, as well as nonfood products, must be imported.
GDP: $44.9 million, per capita $5,000; real growth rate NA% (1986)
Inflation rate (consumer prices): NA%
Unemployment rate: 12% (1989)
Budget: revenues $12.4 million; expenditures $15.8 million, including capital expenditures of $2.6 million (FY87)
Exports: $2.9 million (f.o.b., FY84); *commodities*—lobster, dried and fresh conch, conch shells; *partners*—US, UK
Imports: $26.3 million (c.i.f., FY84); *commodities*—foodstuffs, drink, tobacco, clothing; *partners*—US, UK
External debt: $NA
Industrial production: growth rate NA%
Electricity: 9,050 kW capacity; 11 million kWh produced, 1,160 kWh per capita (1989)
Industries: fishing, tourism, offshore financial services
Agriculture: subsistence farming prevails, based on corn and beans; fishing more important than farming; not self-sufficient in food
Aid: Western (non-US) countries, ODA and OOF bilateral commitments (1970-87), $92.8 million
Currency: US currency is used
Exchange rates: US currency is used
Fiscal year: calendar year

Communications

Highways: 121 km, including 24 km tarmac
Ports: Grand Turk, Salt Cay, Providenciales, Cockburn Harbour
Civil air: Air Turks and Caicos (passenger service) and Turks Air Ltd. (cargo service)
Airports: 7 total, 7 usable; 4 with permanent-surface runways; none with runways over 2,439 m; 4 with runways 1,220-2,439 m
Telecommunications: fair cable and radio services; 1,446 telephones; stations—3 AM, no FM, several TV; 2 submarine cables; 1 Atlantic Ocean INTELSAT earth station

Defense Forces

Note: defense is the responsibility of the UK

Tuvalu

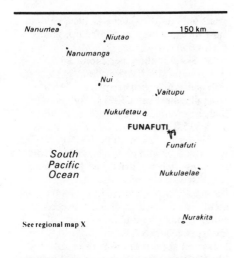

Nanumea
Niutao
Nanumanga
150 km
Nui
Vaitupu
Nukufetau
FUNAFUTI
Funafuti
South Pacific Ocean
Nukulaelae
Nurakita

See regional map X

Geography

Total area: 26 km²; land area: 26 km²
Comparative area: about 0.1 times the size of Washington, DC
Land boundaries: none
Coastline: 24 km
Maritime claims:
   Extended economic zone: 200 nm
   Territorial sea: 12 nm
Climate: tropical; moderated by easterly trade winds (March to November); westerly gales and heavy rain (November to March)
Terrain: very low-lying and narrow coral atolls
Natural resources: fish
Land use: 0% arable land; 0% permanent crops; 0% meadows and pastures; 0% forest and woodland; 100% other
Environment: severe tropical storms are rare
Note: located 3,000 km east of Papua New Guinea in the South Pacific Ocean

People

Population: 9,136 (July 1990), growth rate 2.0% (1990)
Birth rate: 30 births/1,000 population (1990)
Death rate: 10 deaths/1,000 population (1990)
Net migration rate: 0 migrants/1,000 population (1990)
Infant mortality rate: 33 deaths/1,000 live births (1990)
Life expectancy at birth: 60 years male, 63 years female (1990)
Total fertility rate: 3.1 children born/woman (1990)
Nationality: noun—Tuvaluans(s); adjective—Tuvaluan
Ethnic divisions: 96% Polynesian
Religion: Christian, predominantly Protestant
Language: Tuvaluan, English

Literacy: less than 50%
Labor force: NA
Organized labor: none

Government

Long-form name: none
Type: democracy
Capital: Funafuti
Administrative divisions: none
Independence: 1 October 1978 (from UK; formerly Ellice Islands)
Constitution: 1 October 1978
National holiday: Independence Day, 1 October (1978)
Executive branch: British monarch, governor general, prime minister, deputy prime minister, Cabinet
Legislative branch: unicameral Parliament
Judicial branch: High Court
Leaders: *Chief of State*—Queen ELIZABETH II (since 6 February 1952), represented by Governor General Tupua LEUPENA (since 1 March 1986);
Head of Government—Prime Minister Bikenibeu PAENIU (since 16 October 1989); Deputy Prime Minister Dr. Alesana SELUKA (since October 1989)
Political parties and leaders: none
Suffrage: universal at age 18
Elections: *Parliament*—last held 28 September 1989 (next to be held by September 1993); results—percent of vote NA; seats—(12 total)
Member of: ACP, ESCAP (associate member), GATT (de facto), SPF, SPC, UPU
Diplomatic representation: Ambassador (vacant); *US*—none
Flag: light blue with the flag of the UK in the upper hoist-side quadrant; the outer half of the flag represents a map of the country with nine yellow five-pointed stars symbolizing the nine islands

Economy

Overview: Tuvalu consists of a scattered group of nine coral atolls with poor-quality soil. The country has a small economy, no known mineral resources, and few exports. Subsistence farming and fishing are the primary economic activities. The islands are too small and too remote for development of a tourist industry. Government revenues largely come from the sale of stamps and coins and worker remittances. Substantial income is received annually from an international trust fund established in 1987 by Australia, New Zealand, and the UK and supported also by Japan and South Korea.
GNP: $4.6 million, per capita $530; real growth rate NA% (1989 est.)
Inflation rate (consumer prices): 3.9% (1984)

Unemployment rate: NA%
Budget: revenues $2.59 million; expenditures $3.6 million, including capital expenditures of NA (1983 est.)
Exports: $1.0 million (f.o.b., 1983 est.); *commodities*—copra; *partners*—Fiji, Australia, NZ
Imports: $2.8 million (c.i.f., 1983 est.); *commodities*—food, animals, mineral fuels, machinery, manufactured goods; *partners*—Fiji, Australia, NZ
External debt: $NA
Industrial production: growth rate NA
Electricity: 2,600 kW capacity; 3 million kWh produced, 350 kWh per capita (1989)
Industries: fishing, tourism, copra
Agriculture: coconuts, copra
Aid: US commitments, including Ex-Im (FY70-87), $1 million; Western (non-US) countries, ODA and OOF bilateral commitments (1970-87), $84 million
Currency: Tuvaluan dollar and Australian dollar (plural—dollars); 1 Tuvaluan dollar ($T) or 1 Australian dollar ($A) = 100 cents
Exchange rates: Tuvaluan dollars ($T) or Australian dollars ($A) per US$1—1.2784 (January 1990), 1.2618 (1989), 1.2752 (1988), 1.4267 (1987), 1.4905 (1986), 1.4269 (1985)
Fiscal year: NA

Communications

Highways: 8 km gravel
Ports: Funafuti, Nukufetau
Merchant marine: 1 passenger-cargo (1,000 GRT or over) totaling 1,043 GRT/450 DWT
Civil air: no major transport aircraft
Airports: 1 with runway 1,220-2,439 m
Telecommunications: stations—1 AM, no FM, no TV; 300 radiotelephones; 4,000 radio receivers; 108 telephones

Defense Forces

Branches: NA
Military manpower: NA
Defense expenditures: NA

Uganda

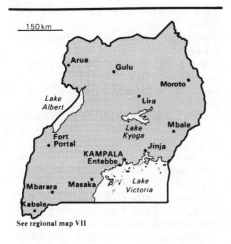

150 km

See regional map VII

Geography

Total area: 236,040 km²; land area: 199,710 km²
Comparative area: slightly smaller than Oregon
Land boundaries: 2,698 km total; Kenya 933 km, Rwanda 169 km, Sudan 435 km, Tanzania 396 km, Zaire 765 km
Coastline: none—landlocked
Maritime claims: none—landlocked
Climate: tropical; generally rainy with two dry seasons (December to February, June to August); semiarid in northeast
Terrain: mostly plateau with rim of mountains
Natural resources: copper, cobalt, limestone, salt
Land use: 23% arable land; 9% permanent crops; 25% meadows and pastures; 30% forest and woodland; 13% other; includes NEGL% irrigated
Environment: straddles Equator; deforestation; overgrazing; soil erosion
Note: landlocked

People

Population: 17,960,262 (July 1990), growth rate 3.5% (1990)
Birth rate: 52 births/1,000 population (1990)
Death rate: 17 deaths/1,000 population (1990)
Net migration rate: 0 migrants/1,000 population (1990)
Infant mortality rate: 107 deaths/1,000 live births (1990)
Life expectancy at birth: 48 years male, 50 years female (1990)
Total fertility rate: 7.4 children born/woman (1990)
Nationality: noun—Ugandan(s); adjective—Ugandan
Ethnic divisions: 99% African, 1% European, Asian, Arab

Religion: 33% Roman Catholic, 33% Protestant, 16% Muslim, rest indigenous beliefs
Language: English (official); Luganda and Swahili widely used; other Bantu and Nilotic languages
Literacy: 57.3%
Labor force: 4,500,000 (est.); 94% subsistence activities, 6% wage earners (est.); 50% of population of working age (1983)
Organized labor: 125,000 union members

Government

Long-form name: Republic of Uganda
Type: republic
Capital: Kampala
Administrative divisions: 10 provinces; Busoga, Central, Eastern, Karamoja, Nile, North Buganda, Northern, South Buganda, Southern, Western
Independence: 9 October 1962 (from UK)
Constitution: 8 September 1967, suspended following coup of 27 July 1985; in process of constitutional revision
Legal system: government plans to restore system based on English common law and customary law and reinstitute a normal judicial system; accepts compulsory ICJ jurisdiction, with reservations
National holiday: Independence Day, 9 October (1962)
Executive branch: president, prime minister, three deputy prime ministers, Cabinet
Legislative branch: unicameral National Resistance Council
Judicial branch: Court of Appeal, High Court
Leaders: *Chief of State*—President Lt. Gen. Yoweri Kaguta MUSEVENI (since 29 January 1986);
Head of Government—Prime Minister Samson Babi Mululu KISEKKA (since 30 January 1986); First Deputy Prime Minister Eriya KATEGAYA (since NA)
Political parties and leaders: only party—National Resistance Movement (NRM); note—the Uganda Patriotic Movement (UPM), Ugandan People's Congress (UPC), Democratic Party (DP), and Conservative Party (CP) are all proscribed from conducting public political activities
Suffrage: universal at age 18
Elections: *National Resistance Council*—last held 11-28 February 1989 (next to be held after January 1995); results—NRM is the only party; seats—(278 total, 210 indirectly elected) NRM 210
Other political parties or pressure groups: Uganda People's Democratic Movement (UPDM), Uganda People's Front (UPF), Uganda Freedom Movement (UFM), Holy Spirit Movement (HSM)
Communists: possibly a few sympathizers
Member of: ACP, AfDB, CCC, Commonwealth, FAO, G-77, GATT, IAEA,

IBRD, ICAC, ICAO, ICO, IDA, IDB—Islamic Development Bank, IFAD, IFC, ILO, IMF, INTELSAT, INTERPOL, ISO, ITU, NAM, OAU, OIC, UN, UNESCO, UPU, WHO, WIPO, WMO, WTO
Diplomatic representation: Ambassador Stephen Kapimpina KATENTA-APULI; 5909 16th Street NW, Washington DC 20011; telephone (202) 726-7100 through 7102; *US*—Ambassador John A. BURROUGHS, Jr.; Embassy at British High Commission Building, Obote Avenue, Kampala (mailing address is P. O. Box 7007, Kampala); telephone [256] (41) 259791
Flag: six equal horizonal bands of black (top), yellow, red, black, yellow, and red; a white disk is superimposed at the center and depicts a red-crested crane (the national symbol) facing the staff side

Economy

Overview: Uganda has substantial natural resources, including fertile soils, regular rainfall, and sizable mineral deposits of copper and cobalt. For most of the past 15 years the economy has been devastated by political instability, mismanagement, and civil war, keeping Uganda poor with a per capita income of about $300. (GDP remains below the levels of the early 1970s, as does industrial production.) Agriculture is the most important sector of the economy, employing over 80% of the work force. Coffee is the major export crop and accounted for 97% of export revenues in 1988. Since 1986 the government has acted to rehabilitate and stabilize the economy by undertaking currency reform, raising producer prices on export crops, increasing petroleum prices, and improving civil service wages. The policy changes are especially aimed at dampening inflation, which was running at over 300% in 1987, and boosting production and export earnings.
GDP: $4.9 billion, per capita $300 (1988); real growth rate 6.1% (1989 est.)
Inflation rate (consumer prices): 72% (FY89)
Unemployment rate: NA%
Budget: revenues $365 million; expenditures $545 million, including capital expenditures of $165 million (FY89 est.)
Exports: $272 million (f.o.b., 1988); *commodities*—coffee 97%, cotton, tea; *partners*—US 25%, UK 18%, France 11%, Spain 10%
Imports: $626 million (c.i.f., 1988); *commodities*—petroleum products, machinery, cotton piece goods, metals, transportation equipment, food; *partners*—Kenya 25%, UK 14%, Italy 13%
External debt: $1.4 billion (1989 est.)

Uganda (continued)

Industrial production: growth rate 25.1% (1988)
Electricity: 173,000 kW capacity; 312 million kWh produced, 18 kWh per capita (1989)
Industries: sugar, brewing, tobacco, cotton textiles, cement
Agriculture: accounts for 57% of GDP and 83% of labor force; cash crops—coffee, tea, cotton, tobacco; food crops—cassava, potatoes, corn, millet, pulses; livestock products—beef, goat meat, milk, poultry; self-sufficient in food
Aid: US commitments, including Ex-Im (1970-88), $123 million; Western (non-US) countries, ODA and OOF bilateral commitments (1970-87), $1.0 billion; OPEC bilateral aid (1979-89), $60 million; Communist countries (1970-88), $140 million
Currency: Ugandan shilling (plural—shillings); 1 Ugandan shilling (USh) = 100 cents
Exchange rates: Ugandan shillings (USh) per US$1—370 (December 1989), 223.09 (1989), 106.14 (1988), 42.84 (1987), 14.00 (1986), 6.72 (1985)
Fiscal year: 1 July-30 June

Communications

Railroads: 1,300 km, 1.000-meter-gauge single track
Highways: 26,200 km total; 1,970 km paved; 5,849 km crushed stone, gravel, and laterite; remainder earth roads and tracks
Inland waterways: Lake Victoria, Lake Albert, Lake Kyoga, Lake George, Lake Edward; Victoria Nile, Albert Nile; principal inland water ports are at Jinja and Port Bell, both on Lake Victoria
Merchant marine: 1 roll-on/roll-off cargo (1,000 GRT or over) totaling 1,697 GRT
Civil air: 4 major transport aircraft
Airports: 39 total, 30 usable; 5 with permanent-surface runways; 1 with runways over 3,659 m; 3 with runways 2,440-3,659 m; 10 with runways 1,220-2,439 m
Telecommunications: fair system with radio relay and radio communications stations; 61,600 telephones; stations—10 AM, no FM, 9 TV; satellite earth stations—1 Atlantic Ocean INTELSAT and 1 Indian Ocean INTELSAT

Defense Forces

Branches: National Resistance Army (NRA)
Military manpower: males 15-49, about 3,836,921; about 2,084,813 fit for military service
Defense expenditures: 1.4% of GDP (1985)

United Arab Emirates

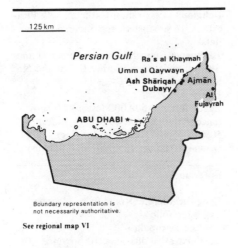

Boundary representation is not necessarily authoritative.

See regional map VI

Geography

Total area: 83,600 km²; land area: 83,600 km²
Comparative area: slightly smaller than Maine
Land boundaries: 1,016 km total; Oman 410 km, Saudi Arabia 586 km, Qatar 20 km
Coastline: 1,448 km
Maritime claims:
Continental shelf: defined by bilateral boundaries or equidistant line
Extended economic zone: 200 nm
Territorial sea: 3 nm
Disputes: boundary with Qatar is in dispute; no defined boundary with Saudi Arabia; no defined boundary with most of Oman, but Administrative Line in far north; claims three islands in the Persian Gulf occupied by Iran (Jazīreh-ye Abū Mūsá or Abū Mūsá, Jazīreh-ye Tonb-e Bozorg or Greater Tunb, and Jazīreh-ye Tonb-e Kūchek or Lesser Tunb)
Climate: desert; cooler in eastern mountains
Terrain: flat, barren coastal plain merging into rolling sand dunes of vast desert wasteland; mountains in east
Natural resources: crude oil and natural gas
Land use: NEGL% arable land; NEGL% permanent crops; 2% meadows and pastures; NEGL% forest and woodland; 98% other; includes NEGL% irrigated
Environment: frequent dust and sand storms; lack of natural freshwater resources being overcome by desalination plants; desertification
Note: strategic location along southern approaches to Strait of Hormuz, a vital transit point for world crude oil

People

Population: 2,253,624 (July 1990), growth rate 6.0% (1990)

Birth rate: 31 births/1,000 population (1990)
Death rate: 3 deaths/1,000 population (1990)
Net migration rate: 33 migrants/1,000 population (1990)
Infant mortality rate: 24 deaths/1,000 live births (1990)
Life expectancy at birth: 69 years male, 73 years female (1990)
Total fertility rate: 4.9 children born/ woman (1990)
Nationality: noun—Emirian(s), adjective—Emirian
Ethnic divisions: 19% Emirian, 23% other Arab, 50% South Asian (fluctuating), 8% other expatriates (includes Westerners and East Asians); less than 20% of the population are UAE citizens (1982)
Religion: 96% Muslim (16% Shi'a); 4% Christian, Hindu, and other
Language: Arabic (official); Farsi and English widely spoken in major cities; Hindi, Urdu
Literacy: 68%
Labor force: 580,000 (1986 est.); 85% industry and commerce, 5% agriculture, 5% services, 5% government; 80% of labor force is foreign
Organized labor: trade unions are illegal

Government

Long-form name: United Arab Emirates (no short-form name); abbreviated UAE
Type: federation with specified powers delegated to the UAE central government and other powers reserved to member shaykhdoms
Capital: Abu Dhabi
Administrative divisions: 7 emirates (imārāt, singular—imārah); Abū Ẓaby, 'Ajmān, Al Fujayrah, Ash Shāriqah, Dubayy, Ra's al Khaymah, Umm al Qaywayn
Independence: 2 December 1971 (from UK; formerly Trucial States)
Constitution: 2 December 1971 (provisional)
Legal system: secular codes are being introduced by the UAE Government and in several member shaykhdoms; Islamic law remains influential
National holiday: National Day, 2 December (1971)
Executive branch: president, vice president, Supreme Council of Rulers, prime minister, Council of Ministers
Legislative branch: unicameral Federal National Council
Judicial branch: Union Supreme Court
Leaders: *Chief of State*—President Shaykh Zayid bin Sultan Al NUHAY-YAN of Abu Dhabi (since 2 December

1971); Vice President Shaykh Rashid bin Sa'id Al MAKTUM of Dubayy (since 2 December 1971;
Head of Government—Prime Minister Shaykh Rashid bin Sa'id Al MAKTUM of Dubayy (Prime Minister since 30 April 1979); Deputy Prime Minister Maktum bin Rashid al MAKTUM (since 2 December 1971)
Political parties and leaders: none
Suffrage: none
Elections: none
Communists: NA
Other political or pressure groups: a few small clandestine groups are active
Member of: Arab League, CCC, FAO, G-77, GATT (de facto), GCC, IAEA, IBRD, ICAO, IDA, IDB—Islamic Development Bank, IFAD, IFC, ILO, IMF, IMO, INTELSAT, INTERPOL, ITU, NAM, OAPEC, OIC, OPEC, UN, UNESCO, UPU, WHO, WIPO, WTO
Diplomatic representation: Ambassador Abdullah bin Zayed AL-NAHAYYAN; Chancery at Suite 740, 600 New Hampshire Avenue NW, Washington DC 20037; telephone (202) 338-6500; *US*—Ambassador Edward S. WALKER, Jr.; Embassy at Al-Sudan Street, Abu Dhabi (mailing address is P. O. Box 4009, Abu Dhabi); telephone [971] (2) 336691; there is a US Consulate General in Dubai
Flag: three equal horizontal bands of green (top), white, and black with a thicker vertical red band on the hoist side

Economy

Overview: The UAE has an open economy with one of the world's higher levels of income per capita. This wealth is based on oil and gas, and the fortunes of the economy fluctuate with the prices of those commodities. Since 1973, when petroleum prices shot up, the UAE has undergone a profound transformation from an impoverished region of small desert principalities to a modern state with a high standard of living. At present levels of production, crude oil reserves should last for over 100 years.
GNP: $23.3 billion, per capita $11,680; real growth rate −2.1% (1988)
Inflation rate (consumer prices): 5-6% (1988 est.)
Unemployment rate: NEGL (1988)
Budget: revenues $3.5 billion; expenditures $4.0 billion, including capital expenditures of $NA (1989 est.)
Exports: $10.6 billion (f.o.b., 1988 est.); *commodities*—crude oil 75%, natural gas, reexports, dried fish, dates; *partners*—US, EC, Japan
Imports: $8.5 billion (c.i.f., 1988 est.); *commodities*—food, consumer and capital goods; *partners*—EC, Japan, US

External debt: $11.0 billion (December 1989 est.)
Industrial production: growth rate −9.3% (1986)
Electricity: 5,590,000 kW capacity; 15,000 million kWh produced, 7,090 kWh per capita (1989)
Industries: petroleum, fishing, petrochemicals, construction materials, some boat building, handicrafts, pearling
Agriculture: accounts for 1% of GNP and 5% of labor force; cash crop—dates; food products—vegetables, watermelons, poultry, eggs, dairy, fish; only 25% self-sufficient in food
Aid: donor—pledged $9.1 billion in bilateral aid to less developed countries (1979-89)
Currency: Emirian dirham (plural—dirhams); 1 Emirian dirham (Dh) = 100 fils
Exchange rates: Emirian dirhams (Dh) per US$1—3.6710 (fixed rate)
Fiscal year: calendar year

Communications

Highways: 2,000 km total; 1,800 km bituminous, 200 km gravel and graded earth
Pipelines: 830 km crude oil; 870 km natural gas, including natural gas liquids
Ports: Al Fujayrah, Khawr Fakkān, Mīnā' Jabal 'Alī, Mīnā' Khālid, Mīnā' Rāshid, Mīnā' Şaqr, Mīnā' Zāyid
Merchant marine: 47 ships (1,000 GRT or over) totaling 728,332 GRT/1,181,566 DWT; includes 14 cargo, 7 container, 2 roll-on/roll-off cargo, 20 petroleum, oils, and lubricants (POL) tanker, 4 bulk
Civil air: 8 major transport aircraft
Airports: 40 total, 34 usable; 19 with permanent-surface runways; 8 with runways over 3,659 m; 5 with runways 2,440-3,659 m; 4 with runways 1,220-2,439 m
Telecommunications: adequate system of radio relay and coaxial cable; key centers are Abu Dhabi and Dubayy; 386,600 telephones; stations—8 AM, 3 FM, 12 TV; satellite earth stations—1 Atlantic Ocean INTELSAT, 2 Indian Ocean INTELSAT and 1 ARABSAT; submarine cables to Qatar, Bahrain, India, and Pakistan; tropospheric scatter to Bahrain; radio relay to Saudi Arabia

Defense Forces

Branches: Army, Navy, Air Force, Central Military Command, Federal Police Force
Military manpower: males 15-49, 904,690; 498,082 fit for military service
Defense expenditures: $1.59 billion (1987)

United Kingdom

300 km

Shetland Islands
Orkney Islands
Hebrides
North Atlantic Ocean
Aberdeen
North Sea
Edinburgh
Belfast
Newcastle upon Tyne
Irish Sea
Liverpool
LONDON
Cardiff
English Channel

See regional map V

Geography

Total area: 244,820 km²; land area: 241,590 km²; includes Rockall and Shetland Islands
Comparative area: slightly smaller than Oregon
Land boundary: Ireland 360 km
Coastline: 12,429 km
Maritime claims:
Continental shelf: 200 meters or to depth of exploitation or in accordance with agreed upon boundaries
Exclusive fishing zone: 200 nm
Territorial sea: 12 nm
Disputes: maritime boundary with Ireland; Northern Ireland question with Ireland; Gibraltar question with Spain; Argentina claims Falkland Islands (Islas Malvinas); Argentina claims South Georgia and the South Sandwich Islands; Mauritius claims island of Diego Garcia in British Indian Ocean Territory; Hong Kong is scheduled to become a Special Administrative Region of China in 1997; Rockall continental shelf dispute involving Denmark, Iceland, and Ireland (Ireland and the UK have signed a boundary agreement in the Rockall area); territorial claim in Antarctica (British Antarctic Territory)
Climate: temperate; moderated by prevailing southwest winds over the North Atlantic Current; more than half of the days are overcast
Terrain: mostly rugged hills and low mountains; level to rolling plains in east and southeast
Natural resources: coal, crude oil, natural gas, tin, limestone, iron ore, salt, clay, chalk, gypsum, lead, silica
Land use: 29% arable land; NEGL% permanent crops; 48% meadows and pastures; 9% forest and woodland; 14% other; includes 1% irrigated
Environment: pollution control measures improving air, water quality; because of

United Kingdom (continued)

heavily indented coastline, no location is more than 125 km from tidal waters
Note: lies near vital North Atlantic sea lanes; only 35 km from France

People

Population: 57,365,665 (July 1990), growth rate 0.3% (1990)
Birth rate: 14 births/1,000 population (1990)
Death rate: 11 deaths/1,000 population (1990)
Net migration rate: 0 migrants/1,000 population (1990)
Infant mortality rate: 7 deaths/1,000 live births (1990)
Life expectancy at birth: 73 years male, 79 years female (1990)
Total fertility rate: 1.8 children born/woman (1990)
Nationality: noun—Briton(s), British (collective pl.); adjective—British
Ethnic divisions: 81.5% English, 9.6% Scottish, 2.4% Irish, 1.9% Welsh, 1.8% Ulster, 2.8% West Indian, Indian, Pakistani, and other
Religion: 27.0 million Anglican, 5.3 million Roman Catholic, 2.0 million Presbyterian, 760,000 Methodist, 410,000 Jewish
Language: English, Welsh (about 26% of population of Wales), Scottish form of Gaelic (about 60,000 in Scotland)
Literacy: 99%
Labor force: 28,120,000; 53.3% services, 23.6% manufacturing and construction, 10.8% self-employed, 6.8% government, 1.0% agriculture (1988)
Organized labor: 37% of labor force (1987)

Government

Long-form name: United Kingdom of Great Britain and Northern Ireland; abbreviated UK
Type: constitutional monarchy
Capital: London
Administrative divisions: 47 counties, 7 metropolitan counties, 26 districts, 9 regions, and 3 islands areas
England—39 counties, 7 metropolitan counties*; Avon, Bedford, Berkshire, Buckingham, Cambridge, Cheshire, Cleveland, Cornwall, Cumbria, Derby, Devon, Dorset, Durham, East Sussex, Essex, Gloucester, Greater London*, Greater Manchester*, Hampshire, Hereford and Worcester, Hertford, Humberside, Isle of Wight, Kent, Lancashire, Leicester, Lincoln, Merseyside*, Norfolk, Northampton, Northumberland, North Yorkshire, Nottingham, Oxford, Shropshire, Somerset, South Yorkshire*, Stafford, Suffolk, Surrey, Tyne and Wear*, Warwick, West Midlands*, West Sussex, West Yorkshire*, Wiltshire

Northern Ireland—26 districts; Antrim, Ards, Armagh, Ballymena, Ballymoney, Banbridge, Belfast, Carrickfergus, Castlereagh, Coleraine, Cookstown, Craigavon, Down, Dungannon, Fermanagh, Larne, Limavady, Lisburn, Londonderry, Magherafelt, Moyle, Newry and Mourne, Newtownabbey, North Down, Omagh, Strabane
Scotland—9 regions, 3 islands areas*; Borders, Central, Dumfries and Galloway, Fife, Grampian, Highland, Lothian, Orkney*, Shetland*, Strathclyde, Tayside, Western Isles*
Wales—8 counties; Clwyd, Dyfed, Gwent, Gwynedd, Mid Glamorgan, Powys, South Glamorgan, West Glamorgan
Independence: 1 January 1801, United Kingdom established
Constitution: unwritten; partly statutes, partly common law and practice
Dependent areas: Anguilla, Bermuda, British Indian Ocean Territory, British Virgin Islands, Cayman Islands, Falkland Islands, Gibraltar, Guernsey, Hong Kong (scheduled to become a Special Administrative Region of China in 1997), Jersey, Isle of Man, Montserrat, Pitcairn Islands, St. Helena, South Georgia and the South Sandwich Islands, Turks and Caicos Islands
Legal system: common law tradition with early Roman and modern continental influences; no judicial review of Acts of Parliament; accepts compulsory ICJ jurisdiction, with reservations
National holiday: Celebration of the Birthday of the Queen (second Saturday in June), 10 June 1989
Executive branch: monarch, prime minister, Cabinet
Legislative branch: bicameral Parliament consists of an upper house or House of Lords and a lower house or House of Commons
Judicial branch: House of Lords
Leaders: *Chief of State*—Queen ELIZABETH II (since 6 February 1952); Heir Apparent Prince CHARLES (son of the Queen, born 14 November 1948);
Head of Government—Prime Minister Margaret THATCHER (since 4 May 1979); Deputy Prime Minister Geoffrey HOWE (since 24 July 1989)
Political parties and leaders: Conservative, Margaret Thatcher; Labour, Neil Kinnock; Social Democratic, David Owen; Social and Liberal Democratic Party, Jeremy (Paddy) Ashdown; Communist, Gordon McLennan; Scottish National, Gordon Wilson; Plaid Cymru, Dafydd Thomas; Ulster Unionist, James Molyneaux; Democratic Unionist, Ian Paisley; Social Democratic and Labour, John Hume; Provisional Sinn Fein, Gerry Adams; Alliance/Northern Ireland

Suffrage: universal at age 18
Elections: *House of Commons*—last held 11 June 1987 (next to be held by June 1992); results—Conservative 43%, Labour 32%, Social and Liberal Democratic Party 23%, others 2%; seats—(650 total) Conservative 376, Labour 228, Social and Liberal Democratic Party 18, Ulster (Official) Unionist (Northern Ireland) 9, Social Democratic Party 4, Scottish National Party 4, Plaid Cymru (Welsh Nationalist) 3, Ulster Democratic Unionist (Northern Ireland) 3, Social Democratic and Labour (Northern Ireland) 3, Ulster Popular Unionist (Northern Ireland) 1, Sinn Fein (Northern Ireland) 1
Communists: 15,961
Other political or pressure groups: Trades Union Congress, Confederation of British Industry, National Farmers' Union, Campaign for Nuclear Disarmament
Member of: ADB, CCC, Colombo Plan, Council of Europe, DAC, EC, ESCAP, ESA, FAO, GATT, IAEA, IBRD, ICAC, ICAO, ICES, ICO, IDA, IDB—Inter-American Development Bank, IEA, IFAD, IFC, IHO, ILO, ILZSG, IMF, IMO, INTELSAT, INTERPOL, IOOC, IPU, IRC, ISO, ITC, ITU, IWC—International Whaling Commission, IWC—International Wheat Council, NATO, OECD, UN, UPU, WEU, WHO, WIPO, WMO, WSG
Diplomatic representation: Ambassador Sir Antony ACLAND; Chancery at 3100 Massachusetts Avenue NW, Washington DC 20008; telephone (202) 462-1340; there are British Consulates General in Atlanta, Boston, Chicago, Cleveland, Houston, Los Angeles, New York, and San Francisco, and Consulates in Dallas, Miami, and Seattle; *US*—Ambassador Henry E. CATTO; Embassy at 24/31 Grosvenor Square, London, W.1A1AE, (mailing address is Box 40, FPO New York 09509); telephone [44] (01) 499-9000; there are US Consulates General in Belfast and Edinburgh
Flag: blue with the red cross of St. George (patron saint of England) edged in white superimposed on the diagonal red cross of St. Patrick (patron saint of Ireland) which is superimposed on the diagonal white cross of St. Andrew (patron saint of Scotland); known as the Union Flag or Union Jack; the design and colors (especially the Blue Ensign) have been the basis for a number of other flags including dependencies, Commonwealth countries, and others

Economy

Overview: The UK is one of the world's great trading powers and financial centers, and its economy ranks among the four largest in Europe. The economy is essentially capitalistic with a generous admixture of social welfare programs and government ownership. Over the last decade the Thatcher government has halted the expansion of welfare measures and has promoted extensive reprivatization of the government economic sector. Agriculture is intensive, highly mechanized, and efficient by European standards, producing about 60% of food needs with only 1% of the labor force. Industry is a mixture of public and private enterprises, employing about 24% of the work force and generating 22% of GDP. The UK is an energy-rich nation with large coal, natural gas, and oil reserves; primary energy production accounts for 12% of GDP, one of the highest shares of any industrial nation. Following the recession of 1979-81, the economy has enjoyed the longest period of continuous economic growth it has had during the last 30 years. During the period 1982-89 real GDP grew by about 25%, while the inflation rate of 14% was nearly halved. Between 1986 and 1989 unemployment fell from 11% to about 6%. As a major trading nation, the UK will continue to be greatly affected by: world boom or recession; swings in the international oil market; productivity trends in domestic industry; and the terms on which the economic integration of Europe proceeds.

GDP: $818.0 billion, per capita $14,300; real growth rate 2.3% (1989 est.)

Inflation rate (consumer prices): 7.8% (1989)

Unemployment rate: 6.4% (1989)

Budget: revenues $348.7 billion; expenditures $327.8 billion, including capital expenditures of $42.0 billion (FY89)

Exports: $151.0 billion (f.o.b., 1989); *commodities*—manufactured goods, machinery, fuels, chemicals, semifinished goods, transport equipment; *partners*—EC 50.4% (FRG 11.7%, France 10.2%, Netherlands 6.8%), US 13.0%, Communist countries 2.3%

Imports: $189.2 billion (c.i.f., 1989); *commodities*—manufactured goods, machinery, semifinished goods, foodstuffs, consumer goods; *partners*—EC 52.5% (FRG 16.6%, France 8.8%, Netherlands 7.8%), US 10.2%, Communist countries 2.1%

External debt: $15.7 billion (1988)

Industrial production: growth rate 0.9% (1989)

Electricity: 98,000,000 kW capacity; 361,990 million kWh produced, 6,350 kWh per capita (1989)

Industries: machinery and transportation equipment, metals, food processing, paper and paper products, textiles, chemicals, clothing, other consumer goods, motor vehicles, aircraft, shipbuilding, petroleum, coal

Agriculture: accounts for only 1.5% of GNP and 1% of labor force; highly mechanized and efficient farms; wide variety of crops and livestock products produced; about 60% self-sufficient in food and feed needs; fish catch of 665,000 metric tons (1987)

Aid: donor—ODA and OOF commitments (1970-87), $18.9 billion

Currency: British pound or pound sterling (plural—pounds); 1 British pound (£) = 100 pence

Exchange rates: British pounds (£) per US$1—0.6055 (January 1990), 0.6099 (1989) 0.5614 (1988), 0.6102 (1987), 0.6817 (1986), 0.7714 (1985)

Fiscal year: 1 April-31 March

Communications

Railroads: Great Britain—16,629 km total; British Railways (BR) operates 16,629 km 1.435-meter standard gauge (4,205 km electrified and 12,591 km double or multiple track); several additional small standard-gauge and narrow-gauge lines are privately owned and operated; Northern Ireland Railways (NIR) operates 332 km 1.600-meter gauge, 190 km double track

Highways: UK, 362,982 km total; Great Britain, 339,483 km paved (including 2,573 km limited-access divided highway); Northern Ireland, 23,499 km (22,907 paved, 592 km gravel)

Inland waterways: 2,291 total; British Waterways Board, 606 km; Port Authorities, 706 km; other, 979 km

Pipelines: 933 km crude oil, almost all insignificant; 2,993 km refined products; 12,800 km natural gas

Ports: London, Liverpool, Felixstowe, Tees and Hartlepool, Dover, Sullom Voe, Southampton

Merchant marine: 285 ships (1,000 GRT or over) totaling 6,174,142GRT/9,024,090 DWT; includes 7 passenger, 22 short-sea passenger, 44 cargo, 44 container, 21 roll-on/roll-off cargo, 9 refrigerated cargo, 1 vehicle carrier, 1 railcar carrier, 78 petroleum, oils, and lubricants (POL) tanker, 4 chemical tanker, 5 liquefied gas, 2 combination ore/oil, 1 specialized tanker, 45 bulk, 1 combination bulk

Civil air: 618 major transport aircraft

Airports: 522 total, 379 usable; 245 with permanent-surface runways; 1 with runways over 3,659 m; 37 with runways 2,440-3,659 m; 132 with runways 1,220-2,439 m

Telecommunications: modern, efficient domestic and international system; 30,200,000 telephones; excellent country-wide broadcast systems; stations—223 AM, 165 (396 relays) FM, 205 (3,210 relays) TV; 38 coaxial submarine cables;

communication satellite earth stations operating in INTELSAT (7 Atlantic Ocean and 3 Indian Ocean), MARISAT, and EUTELSAT systems

---

Defense Forces

Branches: Royal Navy (includes Royal Marines), Army, Royal Air Force

Military manpower: males 15-49, 14,462,993; 12,180,580 fit for military service; no conscription

Defense expenditures: 4.3% of GDP, or $35 billion (1989 est.)

United States

2000 km

Anchorage

North Pacific Ocean.

North Atlantic Ocean

Great Lakes

Seattle

WASHINGTON, D.C.

New York

Los Angeles

Hawaiian Islands

Houston

Miami

Gulf of Mexico

See regional map II

Geography

Total area: 9,372,610 km²; land area: 9,166,600 km²; includes only the 50 states and District of Colombia
Comparative area: about four-tenths the size of USSR; about one-third the size of Africa; about one-half the size of South America (or slightly larger than Brazil); slightly smaller than China; about two and one-half times the size of Western Europe
Land boundaries: 12,248.1 km total; Canada 8,893 km (including 2,477 km with Alaska), Mexico 3,326 km, Cuba (US naval base at Guantánamo) 29.1 km
Coastline: 19,924 km
Maritime claims:
Contiguous zone: 12 nm
Continental shelf: not specified
Extended economic zone: 200 nm
Territorial sea: 12 nm
Disputes: maritime boundary disputes with Canada; US Naval Base at Guantánamo is leased from Cuba and only mutual agreement or US abandonment of the area can terminate the lease; Haiti claims Navassa Island; has made no territorial claim in Antarctica (but has reserved the right to do so) and does not recognize the claims of any other nation
Climate: mostly temperate, but varies from tropical (Hawaii) to arctic (Alaska); arid to semiarid in west with occasional warm, dry chinook wind
Terrain: vast central plain, mountains in west, hills and low mountains in east; rugged mountains and broad river valleys in Alaska; rugged, volcanic topography in Hawaii
Natural resources: coal, copper, lead, molybdenum, phosphates, uranium, bauxite, gold, iron, mercury, nickel, potash, silver, tungsten, zinc, crude oil, natural gas, timber

Land use: 20% arable land; NEGL% permanent crops; 26% meadows and pastures; 29% forest and woodland; 25% other; includes 2% irrigated
Environment: pollution control measures improving air and water quality; acid rain; agricultural fertilizer and pesticide pollution; management of sparse natural water resources in west; desertification; tsunamis, volcanoes, and earthquake activity around Pacific Basin; continuous permafrost in northern Alaska is a major impediment to development
Note: world's fourth-largest country (after USSR, Canada, and China)

People

Population: 250,410,000 (July 1990), growth rate 0.9% (1990)
Birth rate: 15 births/1,000 population (1990)
Death rate: 9 deaths/1,000 population (1990)
Net migration rate: 2 migrants/1,000 population (1990)
Infant mortality rate: 10 deaths/1,000 live births (1990)
Life expectancy at birth: 73 years male, 80 years female (1990)
Total fertility rate: 1.9 children born/woman (1990)
Nationality: noun—American(s); adjective—American
Ethnic divisions: 85% white, 12% black, 3% other (1985)
Religion: Protestant 61% (Baptist 21%, Methodist 12%, Lutheran 8%, Presbyterian 4%, Episcopalian 3%, other Protestant 13%), Roman Catholic 25%, Jewish 2%, other 5%; none 7%
Language: predominantly English; sizable Spanish-speaking minority
Literacy: 99%
Labor force: 125,557,000 (includes armed forces and unemployed); civilian labor force 123,869,000 (1989)
Organized labor: 16,960,000 members; 16.4% of labor force (1989)

Government

Long-form name: United States of America; abbreviated US or USA
Type: federal republic; strong democratic tradition
Capital: Washington, DC
Administrative divisions: 50 states and 1 district*; Alabama, Alaska, Arizona, Arkansas, California, Colorado, Connecticut, Delaware, District of Columbia*, Florida, Georgia, Hawaii, Idaho, Illinois, Indiana, Iowa, Kansas, Kentucky, Louisiana, Maine, Maryland, Massachusetts, Michigan, Minnesota, Mississippi, Missouri, Montana, Nebraska, Nevada, New

Hampshire, New Jersey, New Mexico, New York, North Carolina, North Dakota, Ohio, Oklahoma, Oregon, Pennysivania, Rhode Island, South Carolina, South Dakota, Tennessee, Texas, Utah, Vermont, Virginia, Washington, West Virginia, Wisconsin, Wyoming
Independence: 4 July 1776 (from England)
Constitution: 17 September 1787, effective 4 June 1789
Dependent areas: American Samoa, Baker Island, Guam, Howland Island; Jarvis Island, Johnston Atoll, Kingman Reef, Midway Islands, Navassa Island, Palmyra Atoll, Puerto Rico, Virgin Islands, Wake Island. Since 18 July 1947, the US has administered the Trust Territory of the Pacific Islands, but recently entered into a new political relationship with three of the four political units. The Northern Mariana Islands is a Commonwealth associated with the US (effective 3 November 1986). Palau concluded a Compact of Free Association with the US that was approved by the US Congress but to date the Compact process has not been completed in Palau, which continues to be administered by the US as the Trust Territory of the Pacific Islands. The Federated States of Micronesia signed a Compact of Free Association with the US (effective 3 November 1986). The Republic of the Marshall Islands signed a Compact of Free Association with the US (effective 21 October 1986).
Legal system: based on English common law; judicial review of legislative acts; accepts compulsory ICJ jurisdiction, with reservations
National holiday: Independence Day, 4 July (1776)
Executive branch: president, vice president, Cabinet
Legislative branch: bicameral Congress consists of an upper house or Senate and a lower house or House of Representatives
Judicial branch: Supreme Court
Leaders: *Chief of State and Head of Government*—President George BUSH (since 20 January 1989); Vice President Dan QUAYLE (since 20 January 1989)
Political parties and leaders: Republican Party, Lee Atwater, national committee chairman and Jeanie Austin, co-chairman; Democratic Party, Ronald H. Brown, national committee chairman; several other groups or parties of minor political significance
Suffrage: universal at age 18
Elections: *President*—last held 8 November 1988 (next to be held 3 November 1992); results—George Bush (Republican Party) 53.37%, Michael Dukakis (Democratic Party) 45.67%, others 0.96%;
Senate—last held 8 November 1988 (next to be held 6 November 1990); results—

Democratic Party 52.1%, Republican Party 46.2%, others 1.7%; seats—(100 total) Democratic Party 55, Republican Party 45;

House of Representatives—last held 8 November 1988 (next to be held 6 November 1990); results—Democratic Party 53.2%, Republican Party 45.3%, others 1.5%; seats—(435 total) Democratic Party 259, Republican Party 174, vacant 2

Communists: Communist Party (claimed 15,000-20,000 members), Gus Hall, general secretary; Socialist Workers Party (claimed 1,800 members), Jack Barnes, national secretary

Member of: ADB, ANZUS, CCC, Colombo Plan, DAC, FAO, ESCAP, GATT, IADB, IAEA, IBRD, ICAC, ICAO, ICEM, ICES, ICO, IDA, IDB—Inter-American Development Bank, IEA, IFAD, IFC, IHO, ILO, ILZSG, IMF, IMO, INTELSAT, INTERPOL, IPU, IRC, ITC, ITU, IWC—International Whaling Commission, IWC—International Wheat Council, NATO, OAS, OECD, PAHO, SPC, UN, UPU, WHO, WIPO, WMO, WSG, WTO

Diplomatic representation: US Representative to the UN, Ambassador Thomas R. PICKERING; Mission at 799 United Nations Plaza, New York, NY 10017; telephone (212) 415-4444

Flag: thirteen equal horizontal stripes of red (top and bottom) alternating with white; there is a blue rectangle in the upper hoist-side corner bearing 50 small white five-pointed stars arranged in nine offset horizontal rows of six stars (top and bottom) alternating with rows of five stars; the 50 stars represent the 50 states, the 13 stripes represent the 13 original colonies; known as Old Glory; the design and colors have been the basis for a number of other flags including Chile, Liberia, Malaysia, and Puerto Rico

Economy

Overview: The US has the most powerful and diversified economy in the world, with a per capita GNP of over $21,000, the largest among the major industrial nations. In 1989 the economy entered its eighth successive year of growth, the longest in peacetime history. The expansion has featured continued moderation in wage and consumer price increases, an unemployment rate of 5.2%, (the lowest in 10 years), and an inflation rate of 4.8%. On the negative side, the US enters the 1990s with massive budget and trade deficits, huge and rapidly rising medical costs, and inadequate investment in industrial capacity and economic infrastructure.

GNP: $5,233.3 billion, per capita $21,082; real growth rate 2.9% (1989)

Inflation rate (consumer prices): 4.8% (1989)

Unemployment rate: 5.2% (1989)

Budget: revenues $976 billion; expenditures $1,137 billion, including capital expenditures of NA (FY89 est.)

Exports: $322.3 billion (f.o.b., 1988); *commodities*—capital goods, automobiles, industrial supplies and raw materials, consumer goods, agricultural products; *partners*—Canada 22.9%, Japan 11.8% (1988)

Imports: $440.9 billion (c.i.f., 1988); *commodities*—crude and partly refined petroleum, machinery, automobiles, consumer goods, industrial raw materials, food and beverages; *partners*—Japan 19.6% , Canada 19.1% (1988)

External debt: $532 billion (December 1988)

Industrial production: growth rate 3.3% (1989)

Electricity: 776,550,000 kW capacity; 2,958,300 million kWh produced, 11,920 kWh per capita (1989)

Industries: leading industrial power in the world, highly diversified; petroleum, steel, motor vehicles, aerospace, telecommunications, chemicals, electronics, food processing, consumer goods, fishing, lumber, mining

Agriculture: accounts for 2% of GNP and 2.8% of labor force; favorable climate and soils support a wide variety of crops and livestock production; world's second-largest producer and number-one exporter of grain; surplus food producer; fish catch of 5.7 million metric tons (1987)

Illicit drugs: illicit producer of cannabis for domestic consumption with 1987 production estimated at 3,500 metric tons or about 25% of the available marijuana; ongoing eradication program aimed at small plots and greenhouses has not reduced production

Aid: donor—commitments, including Ex-Im (FY80-88), $90.5 billion

Currency: United States dollar (plural—dollars); 1 United States dollar (US$) = 100 cents

Exchange rates: *British pounds* (£) per US$—0.6055 (January 1990), 0.6099 (1989), 0.5614 (1988), 0.6102 (1987), 0.6817 (1986), 0.7714 (1985); *Canadian dollars* (Can$) per US$—1.1885 (February 1990), 1.2307 (1988), 1.3260 (1987), 1.3895 (1986); *French francs* (F) per US$—5.695 (February 1990), 5.9569 (1988), 6.0107 (1987), 6.9261 (1986), 8.9852 (1985); *Italian lire* (Lit) per US$—1,244.8 (February 1990), 1,301.6 (1988), 1,296.1 (1987), 1,490.8 (1986), 1,909.4 (1985); *Japanese yen* (¥) per US$—145.55 (February 1990), 128.15 (1988), 144.64 (1987), 168.52 (1986), 238.54 (1985);

FRG deutsche marks (DM) per US$—1.6775 (February 1990), 1.7562 (1988), 1.7974 (1987), 2.1715 (1986), 2.9440 (1985)

Fiscal year: 1 October-30 September

Communications

Railroads: 270,312 km

Highways: 6,365,590 km, including 88,641 km expressways

Inland waterways: 41,009 km of navigable inland channels, exclusive of the Great Lakes (est.)

Pipelines: 275,800 km petroleum, 305,300 km natural gas (1985)

Ports: Anchorage, Baltimore, Beaumont, Boston, Charleston, Cleveland, Duluth, Freeport, Galveston, Hampton Roads, Honolulu, Houston, Jacksonville, Long Beach, Los Angeles, Milwaukee, Mobile, New Orleans, New York, Philadelphia, Portland (Oregon), Richmond (California), San Francisco, Savannah, Seattle, Tampa, Wilmington

Merchant marine: 373 ships (1,000 GRT or over) totaling GRT/NA DWT); includes 2 passenger-cargo, 37 cargo, 22 bulk, 165 tanker, 13 tanker tug-barge, 10 liquefied gas, 124 intermodal; in addition there are 248 government-owned vessels

Civil air: 3,297 commercial multiengine transport aircraft, including 2,989 jet, 231 turboprop, 77 piston (1985)

Airports: 15,422 in operation (1981)

Telecommunications: 182,558,000 telephones; stations—4,892 AM, 5,200 FM (including 3,915 commercial and 1,285 public broadcasting), 7,296 TV (including 796 commercial, 300 public broadcasting, and 6,200 commercial cable); 495,000,000 radio receivers (1982); 150,000,000 TV sets (1982); satellite earth stations—45 Atlantic Ocean INTELSAT and 16 Pacific Ocean INTELSAT

Defense Forces

Branches: Department of the Army, Department of the Navy (including Marine Corps), Department of the Air Force

Military manpower: 2,247,000 total; 781,000 Army; 599,000 Air Force; 793,000 Navy (includes 200,000 Marine Corps) (1988)

Defense expenditures: 5.8% of GNP, or $302.8 billion (1989)

Uruguay

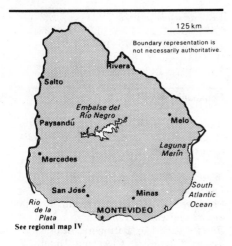

Boundary representation is not necessarily authoritative.

See regional map IV

Geography

Total area: 176,220 km²; land area: 173,620 km²
Comparative area: slightly smaller than Washington State
Land boundaries: 1,564 km total; Argentina 579 km, Brazil 985 km
Coastline: 660 km
Maritime claims:
Continental shelf: 200 meters or to depth of exploitation
Territorial sea: 200 nm (overflight and navigation permitted beyond 12 nm)
Disputes: short section of boundary with Argentina is in dispute; two short sections of the boundary with Brazil are in dispute (Arroyo de la Invernada area of the Rio Quarai and the islands at the confluence of the Rio Quarai and the Uruguay)
Climate: warm temperate; freezing temperatures almost unknown
Terrain: mostly rolling plains and low hills; fertile coastal lowland
Natural resources: soil, hydropower potential, minor minerals
Land use: 8% arable land; NEGL% permanent crops; 78% meadows and pastures; 4% forest and woodland; 10% other; includes 1% irrigated
Environment: subject to seasonally high winds, droughts, floods

People

Population: 3,036,660 (July 1990), growth rate 0.6% (1990)
Birth rate: 17 births/1,000 population (1990)
Death rate: 10 deaths/1,000 population (1990)
Net migration rate: −2 migrants/1,000 population (1990)
Infant mortality rate: 22 deaths/1,000 live births (1990)
Life expectancy at birth: 70 years male, 76 years female (1990)

Total fertility rate: 2.4 children born/woman (1990)
Nationality: noun—Uruguayan(s); adjective—Uruguayan
Ethnic divisions: 88% white, 8% mestizo, 4% black
Religion: 66% Roman Catholic (less than half adult population attends church regularly), 2% Protestant, 2% Jewish, 30% nonprofessing or other
Language: Spanish
Literacy: 94%
Labor force: 1,300,000; 25% government, 19% manufacturing, 11% agriculture, 12% commerce, 12% utilities, construction, transport, and communications, 21% other services (1988 est.)
Organized labor: Interunion Workers' Assembly/National Workers' Confederation (PIT/CNT) Labor Federation

Government

Long-form name: Oriental Republic of Uruguay
Type: republic
Capital: Montevideo
Administrative divisions: 19 departments (departamentos, singular—departamento); Artigas, Canelones, Cerro Largo, Colonia, Durazno, Flores, Florida, Lavalleja, Maldonado, Montevideo, Paysandú, Río Negro, Rivera, Rocha, Salto, San José, Soriano, Tacuarembó, Treinta y Tres
Independence: 25 August 1828 (from Brazil)
Constitution: 27 November 1966, effective February 1967, suspended 27 June 1973, new constitution rejected by referendum 30 November 1980
Legal system: based on Spanish civil law system; accepts compulsory ICJ jurisdiction
National holiday: Independence Day, 25 August (1828)
Executive branch: president, vice president, Council of Ministers (cabinet)
Legislative branch: bicameral Congress (Congreso) consists of an upper chamber or Senate (Senado) and a lower chamber or Chamber of Deputies (Camera del Diputados)
Judicial branch: Supreme Court
Leaders: *Chief of State and Head of Government*—President Luis Alberto LACALLE (since 1 March 1990); Vice President Gonzalo AGUIRRE (since 1 March 1990)
Political parties and leaders: National (Blanco) Party, Roberto Rubio; Colorado Party; Broad Front Coalition, Liber Seregni includes Communist Party led by Jaime Perez and National Liberation Movement (MLN) or Tupamaros led by Eleuterio Fernandez Huidobro; New Space Coalition consists of the Party of

the Government of the People (PGP) led by Hugo Batalla, Christian Democratic Party (PDC), and Civic Union led by Humberto Ciganda
Suffrage: universal and compulsory at age 18
Elections: *President*—last held 26 November 1989 (next to be held November 1994); results—Luis Lacalle (Blanco) 37%, Jorge Batlle (Colorado) 29%, Liber Seregni (Broad Front) 20%;
Senate—last held 26 November 1989 (next to be held November 1994); results—Blanco 40%, Colorado 30%, Broad Front 23% New Space 7%; seats—(30 total) Blanco 12, Colorado 9, Broad Front 7, New Space 2;
Chamber of Deputies—last held NA November 1989 (next to be held November 1994); results—Blanco 39%, Colorado 30%, Broad Front 22%, New Space 8%, others 1%; seats—(99 total) number of seats by party NA
Communists: 50,000
Member of: CCC, FAO, G-77, GATT, Group of Eight, IADB, IAEA, IBRD, ICAO, IDB—Inter-American Development Bank, IFAD, IFC, ILO, IMF, IMO, INTELSAT, INTERPOL, IRC, ITU, LAIA, OAS, PAHO, SELA, UN, UNESCO, UPU, WHO, WIPO, WMO, WSG
Diplomatic representation: Ambassador Juan Podesta PINON; Chancery at 1918 F Street NW, Washington DC 20006; telephone (202) 331-1313 through 1316; there are Uruguayan Consulates General in Los Angeles, Miami, and New York, and a Consulate in New Orleans; *US*—Ambassador Malcolm R. WILKEY; Embassy at Lauro Muller 1776, Montevideo (mailing address is APO Miami 34035); telephone [598] (2) 40-90-51
Flag: nine equal horizontal stripes of white (top and bottom) alternating with blue; there is a white square in the upper hoist-side corner with a yellow sun bearing a human face known as the Sun of May and 16 rays alternately triangular and wavy

Economy

Overview: The economy is slowly recovering from the deep recession of 1981-84. In 1986 real GDP grew by 6.6% and in 1987 by 4.9%. The recovery was led by growth in the agriculture and fishing sectors, agriculture alone contributing 20% to GDP, employing about 11% of the labor force, and generating a large proportion of export earnings. Raising livestock, particularly cattle and sheep, is the major agricultural activity. In 1988, despite healthy exports and an improved current account, domestic growth slowed because of government concentration on the external sector, adverse weather conditions, and prolonged strikes. High inflation rates of about 80%, a large domestic debt, and frequent strikes remain major economic problems for the government.

GDP: $8.8 billion, per capita $2,950; real growth rate 1% (1989 est.)
Inflation rate (consumer prices): 80% (1989 est.)
Unemployment rate: 9.0% (1989 est.)
Budget: revenues $1.2 billion; expenditures $1.4 billion, including capital expenditures of $165 million (1988)
Exports: $1.5 billion (f.o.b., 1989 est.); *commodities*—hides and leather goods 17%, beef 10%, wool 9%, fish 7%, rice 4%; *partners*—Brazil 17%, US 15%, FRG 10%, Argentina 10% (1987)
Imports: $1.1 billion (f.o.b., 1989 est.); *commodities*—fuels and lubricants 15%, metals, machinery, transportation equipment, industrial chemicals; *partners*—Brazil 24%, Argentina 14%, US 8%, FRG 8% (1987)
External debt: $6 billion (1988)
Industrial production: growth rate −2.9% (1988 est.)
Electricity: 1,950,000 kW capacity; 4,330 million kWh produced, 1,450 kWh per capita (1989)
Industries: meat processing, wool and hides, sugar, textiles, footwear, leather apparel, tires, cement, fishing, petroleum refining, wine
Agriculture: large areas devoted to extensive livestock grazing; wheat, rice, corn, sorghum; self-sufficient in most basic foodstuffs
Aid: US commitments, including Ex-Im (FY70-88), $105 million; Western (non-US) countries, ODA and OOF bilateral commitments (1970-87), $263 million; Communist countries (1970-88), $69 million
Currency: new Uruguayan peso (plural—pesos); 1 new Uruguayan peso (N$Ur) = 100 centésimos
Exchange rates: new Uruguayan pesos (N$Ur) per US$1—832.62 (January 1990), 605.62 (1989), 359.44 (1988), 226.67 (1987), 151.99 (1986), 101.43 (1985)
Fiscal year: calendar year

Communications

Railroads: 3,000 km, all 1.435-meter standard gauge and government owned
Highways: 49,900 km total; 6,700 km paved, 3,000 km gravel, 40,200 km earth
Inland waterways: 1,600 km; used by coastal and shallow-draft river craft
Ports: Montevideo, Punta del Este
Merchant marine: 4 ships (1,000 GRT or over) totaling 65,212 GRT/116,613 DWT; includes 2 cargo, 1 petroleum, oils, and lubricants (POL) tanker, 1 container
Civil air: 14 major transport aircraft
Airports: 92 total, 87 usable; 16 with permanent-surface runways; none with runways over 3,659 m; 2 with runways 2,440-3,659 m; 17 with runways 1,220-2,439 m
Telecommunications: most modern facilities concentrated in Montevideo; new nationwide radio relay network; 337,000 telephones; stations—99 AM, no FM, 26 TV, 9 shortwave; 2 Atlantic Ocean INTELSAT earth stations

Defense Forces

Branches: Army, Navy, Air Force
Military manpower: males 15-49, 711,700; 580,898 fit for military service; no conscription
Defense expenditures: 2.5% of GDP (1986)

Vanuatu

See regional map X

Geography

Total area: 14,760 km²; land area: 14,760 km²; includes more than 80 islands
Comparative area: slightly larger than Connecticut
Land boundary: none
Coastline: 2,528 km
Maritime claims: (measured from claimed archipelagic baselines)
Contiguous zone: 24 nm
Continental shelf: edge of continental margin or 200 nm
Extended economic zone: 200 nm
Territorial sea: 12 nm
Climate: tropical; moderated by southeast trade winds
Terrain: mostly mountains of volcanic origin; narrow coastal plains
Natural resources: manganese, hardwood forests, fish
Land use: 1% arable land; 5% permanent crops; 2% meadows and pastures; 1% forest and woodland; 91% other
Environment: subject to tropical cyclones or typhoons (January to April); volcanism causes minor earthquakes
Note: located 5,750 km southwest of Honolulu in the South Pacific Ocean about three-quarters of the way between Hawaii and Australia

People

Population: 165,006 (July 1990), growth rate 3.2% (1990)
Birth rate: 37 births/1,000 population (1990)
Death rate: 5 deaths/1,000 population (1990)
Net migration rate: 0 migrants/1,000 population (1990)
Infant mortality rate: 36 deaths/1,000 live births (1990)
Life expectancy at birth: 67 years male, 72 years female (1990)

Vanuatu (continued)

Total fertility rate: 5.5 children born/woman (1990)
Nationality: noun—Vanuatuan(s); adjective—Vanuatuan
Ethnic divisions: 94% indigenous Melanesian, 4% French, remainder Vietnamese, Chinese, and various Pacific Islanders
Religion: most at least nominally Christian
Language: English and French (official); pidgin (known as Bislama or Bichelama)
Literacy: 10-20% (est.)
Labor force: NA
Organized labor: 7 registered trade unions—largest include Oil and Gas Workers' Union, Vanuatu Airline Workers' Union

Government

Long-form name: Republic of Vanuatu
Type: republic
Capital: Port-Vila
Administrative divisions: 11 island councils; Ambrym, Aoba/Maéwo, Banks/Torres, Efaté, Epi, Malakula, Paama, Pentecôte, Santo/Malo, Shepherd, Taféa
Independence: 30 July 1980 (from France and UK; formerly New Hebrides)
Constitution: 30 July 1980
Legal system: unified system being created from former dual French and British systems
National holiday: Independence Day, 30 July (1980)
Executive branch: president, prime minister, Council of Ministers (cabinet)
Legislative branch: unicameral Parliament; note—the National Council of Chiefs advises on matters of custom and land
Judicial branch: Supreme Court
Leaders: *Chief of State*—President Frederick TIMAKATA (since 30 January 1989);
Head of Government—Prime Minister Father Walter Hadye LINI (since 30 July 1980); Deputy Prime Minister (vacant)
Political parties and leaders: National Party (Vanua'aku Pati), Walter Lini; Union of Moderate Parties, Maxine Carlot; Melanesian Progressive Party, Barak Sope
Suffrage: universal at age 18
Elections: *Parliament*—last held 30 November 1987 (next to be held NA); byelections were held NA December 1988 to fill vacancies resulting from the expulsion of opposition members for boycotting sessions; results—percent of vote by party NA; seats—(46 total) National Party 26, Union of Moderate Parties 19, independent 1
Member of: ACP, ADB, Commonwealth, ESCAP, FAO, G-77, IBRD, ICAO, IDA, IFC, IMF, ITU, NAM, SPF, UN, WHO, WMO

Diplomatic representation: Vanuatu does not have a mission in Washington; *US*—the ambassador in Papua New Guinea is accredited to Vanuatu
Flag: two equal horizontal bands of red (top) and green (bottom) with a black isosceles triangle (based on the hoist side) all separated by a black-edged yellow stripe in the shape of a horizontal *Y* (the two points of the *Y* face the hoist side and enclose the triangle); centered in the triangle is a boar's tusk encircling two crossed *namele* leaves, all in yellow

Economy

Overview: The economy is based primarily on subsistence farming that provides a living for about 80% of the population. Fishing and tourism are the other mainstays of the economy. Mineral deposits are negligible; the country has no known petroleum deposits. A small light-industry sector caters to the local market. Tax revenues come mainly from import duties.
GDP: $120 million, per capita $820; real growth rate 0.7% (1987 est.)
Inflation rate (consumer prices): 8.0% (1988 est.)
Unemployment rate: NA%
Budget: revenues $80.1 million; expenditures $86.6 million, including capital expenditures of $27.1 million (1988 est.)
Exports: $16 million (f.o.b., 1988 est.); *commodities*—copra 37%, cocoa 11%, meat 9%, fish 8%, timber 4%; *partners*—Netherlands 34%, France 27%, Japan 17%, Belgium 4%, New Caledonia 3%, Singapore 2% (1987)
Imports: $58 million (f.o.b., 1988 est.); *commodities*—machines and vehicles 25%, food and beverages 23%, basic manufactures 18%, raw materials and fuels 11%, chemicals 6%; *partners*—Australia 36%, Japan 13%, NZ 10%, France 8%, Fiji 5% (1987)
External debt: $57 million (1988)
Industrial production: growth rate NA%
Electricity: 10,000 kW capacity; 20 million kWh produced, 125 kWh per capita (1989)
Industries: food and fish freezing, forestry processing, meat canning
Agriculture: export crops—copra, cocoa, coffee, and fish; subsistence crops—copra, taro, yams, coconuts, fruits, and vegetables
Aid: Western (non-US) countries, ODA and OOF bilateral commitments (1970-87), $541 million
Currency: vatu (plural—vatu); 1 vatu (VT) = 100 centimes
Exchange rates: vatu (VT) per US$1—107.17 (January 1990), 116.04 (1989), 104.43 (1988), 109.85 (1987), 106.08 (1986), 106.03 (1985)
Fiscal year: calendar year

Communications

Railroads: none
Highways: 1,027 km total; at least 240 km sealed or all-weather roads
Ports: Port-Vila, Luganville, Palikoulo, Santu
Merchant marine: 65 ships (1,000 GRT or over) totaling 885,668 GRT/1,473,443 DWT; includes 26 cargo, 4 refrigerated cargo, 5 container, 2 roll-on/roll-off cargo, 1 vehicle carrier, 3 petroleum, oils, and lubricants (POL) tanker, 2 liquefied gas, 21 bulk, 1 combination bulk; note—a flag of convenience registry
Civil air: no major transport aircraft
Airports: 33 total, 28 usable; 2 with permanent-surface runways; none with runways over 2,439 m; 2 with runways 1,220-2,439 m
Telecommunications: stations—2 AM, no FM, no TV; 3,000 telephones; 1 Pacific Ocean INTELSAT earth station

Defense Forces

Branches: a paramilitary force is responsible for internal and external security; no military forces
Military manpower: NA
Defense expenditures: NA

Vatican City

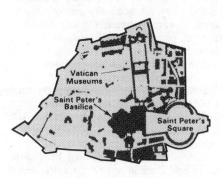

250 meters

Vatican Museums
Saint Peter's Basilica
Saint Peter's Square

See regional map V

Geography

Total area: 0.438 km^2; land area: 0.438 km^2
Comparative area: about 0.7 times the size of The Mall in Washington, DC
Land boundary: 3.2 km with Italy
Coastline: none—landlocked
Maritime claims: none—landlocked
Climate: temperate; mild, rainy winters (September to mid-May) with hot, dry summers (May to September)
Terrain: low hill
Natural resources: none
Land use: 0% arable land; 0% permanent crops; 0% meadows and pastures; 0% forest and woodland; 100% other
Environment: urban
Note: landlocked; enclave of Rome, Italy; world's smallest state; outside the Vatican City, 13 buildings in Rome and Castel Gandolfo (the pope's summer residence) enjoy extraterritorial rights

People

Population: 774 (July 1990), growth rate 0.5% (1990)
Nationality: no noun or adjectival forms
Ethnic divisions: primarily Italians but also many other nationalities
Religion: Roman Catholic
Language: Italian, Latin, and various other languages
Literacy: 100%
Labor force: about 1,500; Vatican City employees divided into three categories—executives, office workers, and salaried employees
Organized labor: Association of Vatican Lay Workers, 1,800 members (1987)

Government

Long-form name: State of the Vatican City; note—the Vatican City is the physi-cal seat of the Holy See which is the central government of the Roman Catholic Church
Type: monarchical-sacerdotal state
Capital: Vatican City
Independence: 11 February 1929 (from Italy)
Constitution: Apostolic Constitution of 1967 (effective 1 March 1968)
National holiday: Installation Day of the Pope (John Paul II), 22 October (1978); note—Pope John Paul II was elected on 16 October 1978
Executive branch: pope
Legislative branch: unicameral Pontifical Commission
Judicial branch: none; normally handled by Italy
Leaders: *Chief of State and Head of Government*—Pope JOHN PAUL II (Karol WOJTYŁA; since 16 October 1978)
Political parties and leaders: none
Suffrage: limited to cardinals less than 80 years old
Elections: *Pope*—last held 16 October 1978 (next to be held after the death of the current pope); results—Karol Wojtyła was elected for life by the College of Cardinals
Communists: NA
Other political or pressure groups: none (exclusive of influence exercised by church officers)
Member: IAEA, INTELSAT, ITU, IWC—International Wheat Council, UPU, WIPO, WTO; permanent observer status at FAO, OAS, UN, and UNESCO
Diplomatic representation: Apostolic Pro-Nuncio Archbishop Pio LAGHI; 3339 Massachusetts Avenue NW, Washington DC 20008; telephone (202) 333-7121; *US*—Ambassador Thomas P. MELADY; Embassy at Villino Pacelli, Via Aurelia 294, 00165 Rome (mailing address is APO New York 09794); telephone [396] 639-0558
Flag: two vertical bands of yellow (hoist side) and white with the crossed keys of St. Peter and the papal tiara centered in the white band

Economy

Overview: The economy is supported financially by contributions (known as Peter's pence) from Roman Catholics throughout the world, the sale of postage stamps, tourist mementos, fees for admission to museums, and the sale of publications.
Budget: revenues $57 million; expenditures $113.7 million, including capital expenditures of $NA (1986)
Electricity: 5,000 kW standby capacity (1989); power supplied by Italy
Industries: printing and production of a small amount of mosaics and staff uniforms; worldwide banking and financial activities
Currency: Vatican lira (plural—lire); 1 Vatican lira (VLit) = 100 centesimi
Exchange rates: Vatican lire (VLit) per US$1—1,262.5 (January 1990), 1,372.1 (1989), 1,301.6 (1988), 1,296.1 (1987), 1,490.8 (1986), 1,909.4 (1985); note—the Vatican lira is at par with the Italian lira which circulates freely
Fiscal year: calendar year

Communications

Railroads: 850 m, 750 mm gauge (links with Italian network near the Rome station of St. Peter's)
Highways: none; all city streets
Telecommunications: stations—3 AM, 4 FM, no TV; 2,000-line automatic telephone exchange; no communications satellite systems

Defense Forces

Note: defense is the responsibility of Italy; Swiss Papal Guards are posted at entrances to the Vatican City

Venezuela

400 km

Caribbean Sea

Maracaibo
CARACAS
Cumaná
Ciudad
Guayana
San Cristóbal
San Fernando
Puerto Ayacucho

Boundary representation is
not necessarily authoritative.

See regional map IV

Geography

Total area: 912,050 km²; land area:
882,050 km²
Comparative area: slightly more than
twice the size of California
Land boundaries: 4,993 km total; Brazil
2,200 km, Colombia 2,050 km, Guyana
743 km
Coastline: 2,800 km
Maritime claims:
Contiguous zone: 15 nm
Continental shelf: 200 meters or to
depth of exploitation
Extended economic zone: 200 nm
Territorial sea: 12 nm
Disputes: claims Essequibo area of Gu-
yana; maritime boundary disputes with
Colombia in the Gulf of Venezuela and
with Trinidad and Tobago in the Gulf of
Paria
Climate: tropical; hot, humid; more mod-
erate in highlands
Terrain: Andes mountains and Maracaibo
lowlands in northwest; central plains
(llanos); Guyana highlands in southeast
Natural resources: crude oil, natural gas,
iron ore, gold, bauxite, other minerals,
hydropower, diamonds
Land use: 3% arable land; 1% permanent
crops; 20% meadows and pastures; 39%
forest and woodland; 37% other; includes
NEGL% irrigated
Environment: subject to floods, rockslides,
mudslides; periodic droughts; increasing
industrial pollution in Caracas and Maracaibo
Note: on major sea and air routes linking
North and South America

People

Population: 19,698,104 (July 1990),
growth rate 2.5% (1990)
Birth rate: 28 births/1,000 population
(1990)

Death rate: 4 deaths/1,000 population
(1990)
Net migration rate: 1 migrant/1,000 population (1990)
Infant mortality rate: 27 deaths/1,000 live
births (1990)
Life expectancy at birth: 71 years male,
77 years female (1990)
Total fertility rate: 3.4 children born/
woman (1990)
Nationality: noun—Venezuelan(s); adjective—Venezuelan
Ethnic divisions: 67% mestizo, 21% white,
10% black, 2% Indian
Religion: 96% nominally Roman Catholic,
2% Protestant
Language: Spanish (official); Indian dialects spoken by about 200,000 Amerin-
dians in the remote interior
Literacy: 85.6%
Labor force: 5,800,000; 56% services, 28%
industry, 16% agriculture (1985)
Organized labor: 32% of labor force

Government

Long-form name: Republic of Venezuela
Type: republic
Capital: Caracas
Administrative divisions: 20 states (estados,
singular—estado), 2 territories* (territo-
rios, singular—territorio), 1 federal
district** (distrito federal), and 1 federal
dependence*** (dependencia federal);
Amazonas*, Anzoátegui, Apure, Aragua,
Barinas, Bolívar, Carabobo, Cojedes,
Delta Amacuro*, Dependencias
Federales***, Distrito Federal**, Falcón,
Guárico, Lara, Mérida, Miranda, Mo-
nagas, Nueva Esparta, Portuguesa, Sucre,
Táchira, Trujillo, Yaracuy, Zulia; note—
the federal dependence consists of 11 fed-
erally controlled island groups with a total
of 72 individual islands
Independence: 5 July 1811 (from Spain)
Constitution: 23 January 1961
Legal system: based on Napoleonic code;
judicial review of legislative acts in Cassa-
tion Court only; has not accepted compul-
sory ICJ jurisdiction
National holiday: Independence Day, 5
July (1811)
Executive branch: president, Council of
Ministers (cabinet)
Legislative branch: bicameral National
Congress (Congreso Nacional) consists of
an upper chamber or Senate (Senado) and
a lower chamber or Chamber of Deputies
(Cámara de Diputados)
Judicial branch: Supreme Court of Justice
(Corte Suprema de Justica)
Leaders: *Chief of State and Head of Gov-
ernment*—President Carlos Andrés
PEREZ (since 2 February 1989)
Political parties and leaders: Social Chris-
tian Party (COPEI), Eduardo Fernández,

secretary general; Democratic Action
(AD), Gonzalo Barrios, president, and
Humberto Celli, secretary general; Movement Toward Socialism (MAS), Teodoro
Petkoff, president, and Freddy Muñoz,
secretary general
Suffrage: universal and compulsory at age
18, though poorly enforced
Elections: *President*—last held 4 December 1988 (next to be held December
1993); results—Carlos Andrés Pérez (AD)
53%, Eduardo Fernández (COPEI) 40%,
others 7%;
Senate—last held 4 December 1988 (next
to be held December 1993); results—percent of vote by party NA; seats—(49 total) AD 23, COPEI 22, others 4;
Chamber of Deputies—last held 4 December 1988 (next to be held December
1993); results—AD 43.7%, COPEI 31.4%,
MAS 10.3%, others 14.6%; seats—(201
total) AD 97, COPEI 67, MAS 18, others
19
Communists: 10,000 members (est.)
Other political or pressure groups: FEDE-
CAMARAS, a conservative business
group; Venezuelan Confederation of
Workers, the Democratic Action-
dominated labor organization
Member of: Andean Pact, AIOEC, FAO,
G-77, Group of Eight, IADB, IAEA,
IBRD, ICAO, ICO, IDB—Inter-Ameri-
can Development Bank, IFAD, IFC, IHO,
ILO, IMF, IMO, INTELSAT,
INTERPOL, IPU, IRC, ITU, IWC—
International Wheat Council, LAIA,
NAM, OAS, OPEC, PAHO, SELA,
WFTU, UN, UNESCO, UPU, WHO,
WMO, WTO
Diplomatic representation: Ambassador
Simón Alberto CONSALVI Bottaro;
Chancery at 2445 Massachusetts Avenue
NW, Washington DC 20008; telephone
(202) 797-3800; there are Venezuelan
Consulates General in Baltimore, Boston,
Chicago, Houston, Miami, New Orleans,
New York, Philadelphia, San Francisco,
and San Juan (Puerto Rico); *US*—
Ambassador-designate Eric JAVITS; Em-
bassy at Avenida Francisco de Miranda
and Avenida Principal de la Floresta, Ca-
racas (mailing address is P. O. Box 62291,
Caracas 1060-A, or APO Miami 34037);
telephone [58] (2) 284-6111 or 7111; there
is a US Consulate in Maracaibo
Flag: three equal horizontal bands of yellow (top), blue, and red with the coat of
arms on the hoist side of the yellow band
and an arc of seven white five-pointed
stars centered in the blue band

Economy

Overview: Petroleum is the cornerstone of
the economy and accounted for 17% of
GDP, 52% of central government reve-

nues, and 81% of export earnings in 1988. President Pérez introduced an economic readjustment program when he assumed office in February 1989. Lower tariffs and price supports, a free market exchange rate, and market-linked interest rates have thrown the economy into confusion, causing about an 8% decline in GDP.

GDP: $52.0 billion, per capita $2,700; real growth rate −8.1% (1989 est.)

Inflation rate (consumer prices): 80.7% (1989)

Unemployment rate: 7.0% (1988)

Budget: revenues $8.4 billion; expenditures $8.6 billion, including capital expenditures of $5.9 billion (1989)

Exports: $10.4 billion (f.o.b., 1988); *commodities*—petroleum 81%, bauxite and aluminum, iron ore, agricultural products, basic manufactures; *partners*—US 50.3%, FRG 5.3%, Japan 4.1% (1988)

Imports: $10.9 billion (f.o.b., 1988); *commodities*—foodstuffs, chemicals, manufactures, machinery and transport equipment; *partners*—US 44%, FRG 8.5%, Japan 6%, Italy 5%, Brazil 4.4% (1987)

External debt: $33.6 billion (1988)

Industrial production: growth rate 3.7%, excluding oil (1988)

Electricity: 19,110,000 kW capacity; 54,516 million kWh produced, 2,830 kWh per capita (1989)

Industries: petroleum, iron-ore mining, construction materials, food processing, textiles, steel, aluminum, motor vehicle assembly

Agriculture: accounts for 6% of GDP and 15% of labor force; products—corn, sorghum, sugarcane, rice, bananas, vegetables, coffee, beef, pork, milk, eggs, fish; not self-sufficient in food other than meat

Illicit drugs: illicit producer of cannabis and coca for the international drug trade on a small scale; however, large quantities of cocaine and marijuana do transit the country

Aid: US commitments, including Ex-Im (FY70-86), $488 million; Communist countries (1970-88), $10 million

Currency: bolívar (plural—bolívares); 1 bolívar (Bs) = 100 céntimos

Exchange rates: bolívares (Bs) per US$1—43.42 (January 1990), 34.6815 (1989), 14.5000 (fixed rate 1987-88), 8.0833 (1986), 7.5000 (1985)

Fiscal year: calendar year

Communications

Railroads: 542 km total; 363 km 1.435-meter standard gauge all single track, government owned; 179 km 1.435-meter gauge, privately owned

Highways: 77,785 km total; 22,780 km paved, 24,720 km gravel, 14,450 km earth roads, and 15,835 km unimproved earth

Inland waterways: 7,100 km; Río Orinoco and Lago de Maracaibo accept oceangoing vessels

Pipelines: 6,370 km crude oil; 480 km refined products; 4,010 km natural gas

Ports: Amuay Bay, Bajo Grande, El Tablazo, La Guaira, Puerto Cabello, Puerto Ordaz

Merchant marine: 70 ships (1,000 GRT or over) totaling 997,458 GRT/1,615,155 DWT; includes 1 short-sea passenger, 1 passenger cargo, 28 cargo, 2 container, 3 roll-on/roll-off cargo, 17 petroleum, oils, and lubricants (POL) tanker, 2 chemical tanker, 2 liquefied gas, 11 bulk, 1 vehicle carrier, 1 combination bulk, 1 combination ore/oil

Civil air: 58 major transport aircraft

Airports: 306 total, 278 usable; 134 with permanent-surface runways; none with runways over 3,659 m; 12 with runways 2,440-3,659 m; 92 with runways 1,220-2,439 m

Telecommunications: modern and expanding; 1,440,000 telephones; stations—181 AM, no FM, 59 TV, 26 shortwave; 3 submarine coaxial cables; satellite earth stations—1 Atlantic Ocean INTELSAT and 3 domestic

Defense Forces

Branches: Ground Forces (Army), Naval Forces (Navy, Marines, Coast Guard), Air Forces, Armed Forces of Cooperation (National Guard)

Military manpower: males 15-49, 5,073,913; 3,680,176 fit for military service; 211,269 reach military age (18) annually

Defense expenditures: 1.1% of GDP, or $570 million (1990 est.)

Vietnam

Boundary representation is not necessarily authoritative

See regional map IX

Geography

Total area: 329,560 km²; land area: 325,360

Comparative area: slightly larger than New Mexico

Land boundaries: 3,818 km total; Cambodia 982 km, China 1,281 km, Laos 1,555 km

Coastline: 3,444 km (excluding islands)

Maritime claims:

  Contiguous zone: 24 nm

  Continental shelf: edge of continental margin or 200 nm

  Extended economic zone: 200 nm

  Territorial sea: 12 nm

Disputes: offshore islands and three sections of the boundary with Cambodia are in dispute; occupied Cambodia on 25 December 1978; sporadic border clashes with China; involved in a complex dispute over the Spratly Islands with China, Malaysia, Philippines, and Taiwan; maritime boundary dispute with China in the Gulf of Tonkin; Paracel Islands occupied by China but claimed by Vietnam and Taiwan

Climate: tropical in south; monsoonal in north with hot, rainy season (mid-May to mid-September) and warm, dry season (mid-October to mid-March)

Terrain: low, flat delta in south and north; central highlands; hilly, mountainous in far north and northwest

Natural resources: phosphates, coal, manganese, bauxite, chromate, offshore oil deposits, forests

Land use: 22% arable land; 2% permanent crops; 1% meadows and pastures; 40% forest and woodland; 35% other; includes 5% irrigated

Environment: occasional typhoons (May to January) with extensive flooding

Vietnam (continued)

People

Population: 66,170,889 (July 1990), growth rate 2.1% (1990)
Birth rate: 30 births/1,000 population (1990)
Death rate: 8 deaths/1,000 population (1990)
Net migration rate: −1 migrants/1,000 population (1990)
Infant mortality rate: 50 deaths/1,000 live births (1990)
Life expectancy at birth: 62 years male, 66 years female (1990)
Total fertility rate: 3.8 children born/woman (1990)
Nationality: noun—Vietnamese (sing. and pl.); adjective—Vietnamese
Ethnic divisions: 85-90% predominantly Vietnamese; 3% Chinese; ethnic minorities include Muong, Thai, Meo, Khmer, Man, Cham; other mountain tribes
Religion: Buddhist, Confucian, Taoist, Roman Catholic, indigenous beliefs, Islamic, Protestant
Language: Vietnamese (official), French, Chinese, English, Khmer, tribal languages (Mon-Khmer and Malayo-Polynesian)
Literacy: 78%
Labor force: 35,000,000 (1989 est.)
Organized labor: reportedly over 90% of wage and salary earners are members of the Vietnam Federation of Trade Unions (VFTU)

Government

Long-form name: Socialist Republic of Vietnam; abbreviated SRV
Type: Communist state
Capital: Hanoi
Administrative divisions: 37 provinces (tinh, singular and plural), 3 municipalities* (thành phô, singular and plural); An Giang, Bac Thai, Ben Tre, Binh Tri Thien, Cao Bang, Cuu Long, Dac Lac, Dong Nai, Dong Thap, Gia Lai-Cong Tum, Ha Bac, Hai Hung, Hai Phong*, Ha Nam Ninh, Ha Noi*, Ha Son Binh, Ha Tuyen, Hau Giang, Hoang Lien Son, Ho Chi Minh*, Kien Giang, Lai Chau, Lam Dong, Lang Son, Long An, Minh Hai, Nghe Tinh, Nghia Binh, Phu Khanh, Quang Nam-Da Nang, Quang Ninh, Song Be, Son La, Tay Ninh, Thai Binh, Thanh Hoa, Thuan Hai, Tien Giang, Vinh Pu, Vung Tau-Con Dao; note—diacritical marks are not included; the number of provinces may have been changed with the elimination of Binh Tri Thien, Nghia Binh, and Phu Khanh and the addition of Binh Dinh, Khanh Hoa, Phu Yen, Quang Binh, Quang Ngai, Quang Tri, and Thua Thien
Independence: 2 September 1945 (from France)

Constitution: 18 December 1980
Legal system: based on Communist legal theory and French civil law system
National holiday: Independence Day, 2 September (1945)
Executive branch: chairman of the Council of State, Council of State, chairman of the Council of Ministers, Council of Ministers
Legislative branch: unicameral National Assembly (Quoc Hoi)
Judicial branch: Supreme People's Court
Leaders: *Chief of State*—Chairman of the Council of State Vo Chi CONG (since 18 June 1987);
Head of Government—Chairman of the Council of Ministers (Premier) Do MUOI (since 22 June 1988)
Political parties and leaders: only party—Vietnam Communist Party (VCP), Nguyen Van Linh
Suffrage: universal at age 18
Elections: *National Assembly*—last held 19 April 1987 (next to be held April 1992); results—VCP is the only party; seats—(496 total) VCP or VCP-approved 496
Communists: nearly 2 million
Member of: ADB, CEMA, Colombo Plan, ESCAP, FAO, G-77, IAEA, IBRD, ICAO, IDA, IFAD, IFC, ILO, IMF, INTELSAT, IRC, ITU, Mekong Committee, NAM, UN, UNDP, UNESCO, UNICEF, UPU, WFTU, WHO, WIPO, WMO, WTO
Diplomatic representation: none
Flag: red with a large yellow five-pointed star in the center

Economy

Overview: This is a centrally planned, developing economy with extensive government ownership and control of productive facilities. The economy is primarily agricultural, employing about 65% of the labor force and accounting for almost half of GNP. Rice is the staple crop; substantial amounts of maize, sorghum, cassava, and sweet potatoes are also grown. The government permits sale of surplus grain on the open market. Most of the mineral resources are located in the north, including coal, which is an important export item. Following the end of the war in 1975, heavy handed government measures undermined efforts at an efficient merger of the agricultural resources of the south and the industrial resources of the north. The economy remains heavily dependent on foreign aid and has received assistance from Communist countries, Sweden, and UN agencies. Inflation, although down from recent triple-digit levels, is still a major weakness, and per capita output is among the world's lowest. Since early

1989 the government has sponsored a broad reform program that seeks to turn more economic activity over to the private sector.
GNP: $14.2 billion, per capita $215; real growth rate 8% (1989 est.)
Inflation rate (consumer prices): 40% (1989 est.)
Unemployment rate: 25% (1989 est.)
Budget: revenues $3.2 billion; expenditures $4.3 billion, including capital expenditures of $528 million (1987 est.)
Exports: $1.1 billion (f.o.b., 1988); *commodities*—agricultural and handicraft products, coal, minerals, ores; *partners*—USSR, Eastern Europe, Japan, Singapore
Imports: $2.5 billion (c.i.f., 1988); *commodities*—petroleum, steel products, railroad equipment, chemicals, medicines, raw cotton, fertilizer, grain; *partners*—USSR, Eastern Europe, Japan, Singapore
External debt: $16 billion (1989)
Industrial production: growth rate 10% (1989)
Electricity: 2,465,000 kW capacity; 6,730 million kWh produced, 100 kWh per capita (1989)
Industries: food processing, textiles, machine building, mining, cement, chemical fertilizer, glass, tires, oil, fishing
Agriculture: accounts for half of GNP; paddy rice, corn, potatoes make up 50% of farm output; commercial crops (rubber, soybeans, coffee, tea, bananas) and animal products other 50%; not self-sufficient in food staple rice; fish catch of 900,000 metric tons (1988 est.)
Aid: US commitments, including Ex-Im (FY70-74), $3.1 billion; Western (non-US) countries, ODA and OOF bilateral commitments (1970-87), $2.7 billion; OPEC bilateral aid (1979-89), $61 million; Communist countries (1970-88), $10.9 million
Currency: new dong (plural—new dong); 1 new dong (D) = 100 xu
Exchange rates: new dong (D) per US$1—4,000 (March 1990), 900 (1988), 225 (1987), 18 (1986), 12 (1985); note—1985-89 figures are end of year
Fiscal year: calendar year

Communications

Railroads: 3,059 km total; 2,454 1.000-meter gauge, 151 km 1.435-meter standard gauge, 230 km dual gauge (three rails), and 224 km not restored to service
Highways: about 85,000 km total; 9,400 km bituminous, 48,700 km gravel or improved earth, 26,900 km unimproved earth
Pipelines: 150 km, refined products
Inland waterways: about 17,702 km navigable; more than 5,149 km navigable at all times by vessels up to 1.8 meter draft

Ports: Da Nang, Haiphong, Ho Chi Minh City

Merchant marine: 71 ships (1,000 GRT or over) totaling 290,123 GRT/432,152 DWT; includes 1 short-sea passenger, 55 cargo, 4 refrigerated cargo, 1 roll-on/roll-off cargo, 1 vehicle carrier, 8 petroleum, oils, and lubricants (POL) tanker, 1 bulk; note—Vietnam owns 10 cargo ships (1,000 GRT or over) totaling 111,028 DWT under the registry of Panama and Malta

Civil air: controlled by military

Airports: 100 total, 100 usable; 50 with permanent-surface runways; 10 with runways 2,440-3,659 m; 20 with runways 1,220-2,439 m

Telecommunications: 35,000 telephones in Ho Chi Minh City (1984); stations—16 AM, 1 FM, 2 TV; 2,300,000 TV sets; 6,000,000 radio receivers; at least 2 satellite earth stations, including 1 Indian Ocean INTELSAT

Defense Forces

Branches: Army, Navy, Air Force

Military manpower: males 15-49, 15,707,629; 10,030,563 fit for military service; 787,444 reach military age (17) annually

Defense expenditures: 19.4% of GNP (1986 est.)

Virgin Islands
(territory of the US)

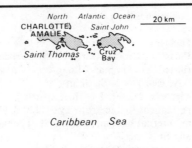

See regional map III

Geography

Total area: 352 km²; land area: 349 km²

Comparative area: slightly less than twice the size of Washington, DC

Land boundaries: none

Coastline: 188 km

Maritime claims:

Contiguous zone: 12 nm

Continental shelf: 200 m

Extended economic zone: 200 nm

Territorial sea: 12 nm

Climate: subtropical, tempered by easterly tradewinds, relatively low humidity, little seasonal temperature variation; rainy season May to November

Terrain: mostly hilly to rugged and mountainous with little level land

Natural resources: sun, sand, sea, surf

Land use: 15% arable land; 6% permanent crops; 26% meadows and pastures; 6% forest and woodland; 47% other

Environment: rarely affected by hurricanes; subject to frequent severe droughts, floods, earthquakes; lack of natural freshwater resources

Note: important location 1,770 km southeast of Miami and 65 km east of Puerto Rico, along the Anegada Passage—a key shipping lane for the Panama Canal; St. Thomas has one of the best natural, deepwater harbors in the Caribbean

People

Population: 99,200 (July 1990), growth rate −0.3% (1990)

Birth rate: 22 births/1,000 population (1990)

Death rate: 5 deaths/1,000 population (1990)

Net migration rate: −20 migrants/1,000 population (1990)

Infant mortality rate: 19 deaths/1,000 live births (1990)

Life expectancy at birth: 70 years male, 76 years female (1990)

Total fertility rate: 2.7 children born/ woman (1990)

Nationality: noun—Virgin Islander(s); adjective—Virgin Islander

Ethnic divisions: 74% West Indian (45% born in the Virgin Islands and 29% born elsewhere in the West Indies), 13% US mainland, 5% Puerto Rican, 8% other; 80% black, 15% white, 5% other; 14% of Hispanic origin

Religion: 42% Baptist, 34% Roman Catholic, 17% Episcopalian, 7% other

Language: English (official), but Spanish and Creole are widely spoken

Literacy: 90%

Labor force: 45,000 (1987)

Organized labor: 90% of the government labor force

Government

Long-form name: Virgin Islands of the United States

Type: organized, unincorporated territory of the US administered by the Office of Territorial and International Affairs, US Department of the Interior

Capital: Charlotte Amalie

Administrative divisions: none (territory of the US)

Independence: none (territory of the US)

Constitution: Revised Organic Act of 22 July 1954 serves as the constitution

Legal system: based on US

National holiday: Transfer Day (from Denmark to US), 31 March (1917)

Executive branch: US president, governor, lieutenant governor

Legislative branch: unicameral Senate

Judicial branch: US District Court handles civil matters over $50,000, felonies (persons 15 years of age and over), and federal cases; Territorial Court handles civil matters up to $50,000 small claims, juvenile, domestic, misdemeanors, and traffic cases

Leaders: *Chief of State and Head of Government*—President George BUSH (since 20 January 1989), represented by Governor Alexander FARRELLY (since 5 January 1987); Lieutenant Governor Derek HODGE (since 5 January 1987)

Political parties and leaders: Democratic Party, Marilyn Stapleton; Independent Citizens' Movement (ICM), Virdin Brown; Republican Party, Charlotte-Poole Davis

Suffrage: universal at age 18; indigenous inhabitants are US citizens, but do not vote in US presidential elections

Elections: *Governor*—last held NA 1986 (next to be held NA 1990); results—Alexander Farrelly (Democratic Party) defeated Adelbert Bryan (ICM);

Virgin Islands *(continued)*

Senate—last held 8 November 1988 (next to be held NA); results—percent of vote by party NA; seats—(15 total) number of seats by party NA;
US House of Representatives—last held 8 November 1988 (next to be held 6 November 1990); results—the Virgin Islands elects one nonvoting representative
Diplomatic representation: none (territory of the US)
Flag: white with a modified US coat of arms in the center between the large blue initials *V* and *I*; the coat of arms shows an eagle holding an olive branch in one talon and three arrows in the other with a superimposed shield of vertical red and white stripes below a blue panel

Economy

Overview: Tourism is the primary economic activity, accounting for more than 70% of GDP and 70% of employment. The manufacturing sector consists of textile, electronics, pharmaceutical, and watch assembly plants. The agricultural sector is small with most food imported. International business and financial services are a small but growing component of the economy. The world's largest petroleum refinery is at St. Croix.
GDP: $1.03 billion, per capita $9,030; real growth rate NA% (1985)
Inflation rate (consumer prices): NA%
Unemployment rate: 3.5% (1987)
Budget: revenues $315 million; expenditures $322 million, including capital expenditures of NA (FY88)
Exports: $3.4 billion (f.o.b., 1985); *commodities*—refined petroleum products; *partners*—US, Puerto Rico
Imports: $3.7 billion (c.i.f., 1985); *commodities*—crude oil, foodstuffs, consumer goods, building materials; *partners*—US, Puerto Rico
External debt: $NA
Industrial production: growth rate 12%
Electricity: 341,000 kW capacity; 507 million kWh produced, 4,650 kWh per capita (1989)
Industries: tourism, government service, petroleum refining, watch assembly, rum distilling, construction, pharmaceuticals, textiles, electronics
Agriculture: truck gardens, food crops (small scale), fruit, sorghum, Senepol cattle
Aid: Western (non-US) countries, ODA and OOF bilateral commitments (1970-87), $33.5 million
Currency: US currency is used
Exchange rates: US currency is used
Fiscal year: 1 October-30 September

Communications

Highways: 856 km total
Ports: St. Croix—Christiansted, Frederiksted; St. Thomas—Long Bay, Crown Bay, Red Hook; St. John—Cruz Bay
Airports: 2 total, 2 usable; 2 with permanent-surface runways 1,220-2,439 m; international airports on St. Thomas and St. Croix
Telecommunications: 44,280 telephones; stations—4 AM, 6 FM, 3 TV; modern system using fiber optic cable, submarine cable, microwave radio, and satellite facilities; 90,000 radio receivers; 56,000 television sets

Defense Forces

Note: defense is the responsibility of the US

Wake Island
(territory of the US)

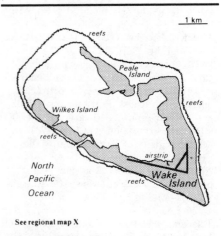

See regional map X

Geography

Total area: 6.5 km²; land area: 6.5 km²
Comparative area: about 11 times the size of The Mall in Washington, DC
Land boundaries: none
Coastline: 19.3 km
Maritime claims:
  Contiguous zone: 12 nm
  Continental shelf: 200 m
  Extended economic zone: 200 nm
  Territorial sea: 12 nm
Disputes: claimed by the Republic of the Marshall Islands
Climate: tropical
Terrain: atoll of three coral islands built up on an underwater volcano; central lagoon is former crater, islands are part of the rim; average elevation less than four meters
Natural resources: none
Land use: 0% arable land; 0% permanent crops; 0% meadows and pastures; 0% forest and woodland; 100% other
Environment: subject to occasional typhoons
Note: strategic location 3,700 km west of Honolulu in the North Pacific Ocean, about two-thirds of the way between Hawaii and the Northern Mariana Islands; emergency landing location for transpacific flights

People

Population: 195 (January 1990); no indigenous inhabitants; temporary population consists of 11 US Air Force personnel, 27 US civilians, and 151 Thai contractors
Note: population peaked about 1970 with over 1,600 persons during the Vietnam conflict

Government

Long-form name: none

Type: unincorporated territory of the US administered by the US Air Force (under an agreement with the US Department of Interior) since 24 June 1972
Flag: the US flag is used

Economy

Overview: Economic activity is limited to providing services to US military personnel and contractors located on the island. All food and manufactured goods must be imported.

Communications

Ports: none; because of the reefs, there are only two offshore anchorages for large ships
Airports: 1 with permanent-surface runways 2,987 m
Telecommunications: underwater cables to Guam and through Midway to Honolulu; AFRTS radio and television service provided by satellite; stations—1 AM, no FM, no TV
Note: formerly an important commercial aviation base, now used only by US military and some commercial cargo planes

Defense Forces

Note: defense is the responsibility of the US

Wallis and Futuna
(overseas territory of France)

```
  50 km


                        MATA-UTU
                         Île Uvéa

        South Pacific Ocean


Île Futuna
   Leava

    Île Alofi


See regional map X
```

Geography

Total area: 274 km^2; land area: 274 km^2
Comparative area: slightly larger than Washington, DC
Land boundaries: none
Coastline: 129 km
Maritime claims:
  Continental shelf: 200 meters or to depth of exploitation
  Extended economic zone: 200 nm
  Territorial sea: 12 nm
Climate: tropical; hot, rainy season (November to April); cool, dry season (May to October)
Terrain: volcanic origin; low hills
Natural resources: negligible
Land use: 5% arable land; 20% permanent crops; 0% meadows and pastures; 0% forest and woodland; 75% other
Environment: both island groups have fringing reefs
Note: located 4,600 km southwest of Honolulu in the South Pacific Ocean about two-thirds of the way from Hawaii to New Zealand

People

Population: 14,910 (July 1990), growth rate 3.0% (1990)
Birth rate: 28 births/1,000 population (1990)
Death rate: 6 deaths/1,000 population (1990)
Net migration rate: 8 migrants/1,000 population (1990)
Infant mortality rate: 32 deaths/1,000 population (1990)
Life expectancy at birth: 69 years male, 70 years female (1990)
Total fertility rate: 3.8 children born/woman (1990)
Nationality: noun—Wallisian(s), Futunan(s), or Wallis and Futuna Islanders; adjective—Wallisian, Futunan, or Wallis and Futuna Islander

Ethnic divisions: almost entirely Polynesian
Religion: largely Roman Catholic
Language: French, Wallisian (indigenous Polynesian language)
Literacy: NA%
Labor force: NA
Organized labor: NA

Government

Long-form name: Territory of the Wallis and Futuna Islands
Type: overseas territory of France
Capital: Mata-Utu
Administrative divisions: none (overseas territory of France)
Independence: none (overseas territory of France)
Constitution: 28 September 1958 (French Constitution)
Legal system: French
National holiday: Taking of the Bastille, 14 July (1789)
Executive branch: French president, high administrator; note—there are three traditional kings with limited powers
Legislative branch: unicameral Territorial Assembly (Assemblée Territoriale)
Judicial branch: none; justice generally administered under French law by the chief administrator, but the three traditional kings administer customary law and there is a magistrate in Mata-Utu
Leaders: *Chief of State*—President François MITTERRAND (since 21 May 1981);
Head of Government—Chief Administrator Roger DUMEC (since 15 July 1988)
Political parties and leaders: Rally for the Republic (RPR); Union Populaire Locale (UPL); Union Pour la Démocratie Française (UDF)
Suffrage: universal adult at age NA
Elections: *Territorial Assembly*—last held 15 March 1987 (next to be held March 1992); results—percent of vote by party NA; seats—(20 total) RPR 7, UDF coalition 7, UPL 6;
French Senate—last held NA (next to be held NA); results—percent of vote by party NA; seats—(1 total) party of the representative is NA;
French National Assembly—last held NA (next to be held NA); results—percent of vote by party NA; seats—(1 total) RPR 1
Diplomatic representation: as an overseas territory of France, local interests are represented in the US by France
Flag: the flag of France is used

Economy

Overview: The economy is limited to subsistence agriculture. The majority of the labor force earns its livelihood from agri-

Wallis and Futuna (continued)

culture, raising livestock, and fishing, with the rest employed by the government sector. Exports are negligible. The Territory has to import food, fuel, and construction materials, and is dependent on budgetary support from France to meet recurring expenses. The economy also benefits from cash remittances from expatriate workers.
GDP: $6.7 million, per capita $484; real growth rate NA% (est. 1985)
Inflation rate (consumer prices): NA%
Unemployment rate: NA%
Budget: revenues $NA; expenditures $NA, including capital expenditures of $NA
Exports: $NA; *commodities*—copra; *partners*—NA
Imports: $3.4 million (c.i.f., 1977); *commodities*—largely foodstuffs and some equipment associated with development programs; *partners*—France, Australia, New Zealand
External debt: $NA
Industrial production: growth rate NA%
Electricity: 1,200 kW capacity; 1 million kWh produced, 70 kWh per capita (1989)
Industries: copra, handicrafts, fishing, lumber
Agriculture: dominated by coconut production, with subsistence crops of yams, taro, bananas
Aid: Western (non-US) countries, ODA and OOF bilateral commitments (1970-87), $118 million
Currency: Comptoirs Français du Pacifique franc (plural—francs); 1 CFP franc (CFPF) = 100 centimes
Exchange rates: Comptoirs Français du Pacifique francs (CFPF) per US$1—104.71 (January 1990), 115.99 (1989), 108.30 (1988), 109.27 (1987), 125.92 (1986), 163.35 (1985); note—linked at the rate of 18.18 to the French franc
Fiscal year: NA

Communications

Highways: 100 km on Île Uvéa (Wallis Island), 16 km sealed; 20 km earth surface on Île Futuna (Futuna Island)
Inland waterways: none
Ports: Mata-Utu, Leava
Airports: 2 total; 2 usable; 1 with permanent-surface runways; none with runways over 2,439 m; 1 with runways 1,220-2,439 m
Telecommunications: 225 telephones; stations—1 AM, no FM, no TV

Defense Forces

Note: defense is the responsibility of France

West Bank

50 km

Nābulus

Israeli occupied-
status to be
determined

Jerusalem

Bethlehem

Dead
Sea

Hebron

Boundary representation is
not necessarily authoritative.

See regional map VI

Note: The war between Israel and the Arab states in June 1967 ended with Israel in control of the West Bank and the Gaza Strip, the Sinai, and the Golan Heights. As stated in the 1978 Camp David Accords and reaffirmed by President Reagan's 1 September 1982 peace initiative, the final status of the West Bank and the Gaza Strip, their relationship with their neighbors, and a peace treaty between Israel and Jordan are to be negotiated among the concerned parties. Camp David further specifies that these negotiations will resolve the respective boundaries. Pending the completion of this process, it is US policy that the final status of the West Bank and the Gaza Strip has yet to be determined. In the view of the US, the term West Bank describes all of the area west of the Jordan River under Jordanian administration before the 1967 Arab-Israeli war. However, with respect to negotiations envisaged in the framework agreement, it is US policy that a distinction must be made between Jerusalem and the rest of the West Bank because of the city's special status and circumstances. Therefore, a negotiated solution for the final status of Jerusalem could be different in character from that of the rest of the West Bank.

Geography

Total area: 5,860 km²; land area: 5,640 km²; includes West Bank, East Jerusalem, Latrun Salient, Jerusalem No Man's Land, and the northwest quarter of the Dead Sea, but excludes Mt. Scopus
Comparative area: slightly larger than Delaware
Land boundaries: 404 km total; Israel 307 km, Jordan 97 km;
Coastline: none—landlocked
Maritime claims: none—landlocked
Disputes: Israeli occupied with status to be determined

Climate: temperate, temperature and precipitation vary with altitude, warm to hot summers, cool to mild winters
Terrain: mostly rugged dissected upland, some vegetation in west, but barren in east
Natural resources: negligible
Land use: 27% arable land, 0% permanent crops, 32% meadows and pastures, 1% forest and woodland, 40% other
Environment: highlands are main recharge area for Israel's coastal aquifers
Note: landlocked; there are 173 Jewish settlements in the West Bank and 14 Israeli-built Jewish neighborhoods in East Jerusalem

People

Population: 1,058,122 (July 1990), growth rate 2.6% (1990); in addition, there are 70,000 Jewish settlers in the West Bank and 110,000 in East Jerusalem (1989 est.)
Birth rate: 37 births/1,000 population (1990)
Death rate: 6 deaths/1,000 population (1990)
Net migration rate: −5 migrants/1,000 population (1990)
Infant mortality rate: 48 deaths/1,000 live births (1990)
Life expectancy at birth: 65 years male, 68 years female (1990)
Total fertility rate: 5.0 children born/woman (1990)
Nationality: NA
Ethnic divisions: 88% Palestinian Arab and other, 12% Jewish
Religion: 80% Muslim (predominantly Sunni), 12% Jewish, 8% Christian and other
Language: Arabic, Israeli settlers speak Hebrew, English widely understood
Literacy: NA%
Labor force: NA; excluding Israeli Jewish settlers—29.8% small industry, commerce, and business, 24.2% construction, 22.4% agriculture, 23.6% service and other (1984)
Organized labor: NA

Government

Long-form name: none
Note: The West Bank is currently governed by Israeli military authorities and Israeli civil administration. It is US policy that the final status of the West Bank will be determined by negotiations among the concerned parties. These negotiations will determine how the area is to be governed.

Economy

Overview: Economic progress in the West Bank has been hampered by Israeli military occupation and the effects of the Palestinian uprising. Industries using advanced technology or requiring sizable financial resources have been discouraged by a lack of financial resources and Israeli policy. Capital investment has largely gone into residential housing, not into productive assets that could compete with Israeli industry. A major share of GNP is derived from remittances of workers employed in Israel and neighboring Gulf states. Israeli reprisals against Palestinian unrest in the West Bank since 1987 have pushed unemployment up and lowered living standards.
GNP: $1.0 billion, per capita $1,000; real growth rate —15% (1988 est.)
Inflation rate (consumer prices): NA%
Unemployment rate: NA%
Budget: revenues $47.4 million; expenditures $45.7 million, including capital expenditures of NA (FY86)
Exports: $150 million (f.o.b., 1988 est.); *commodities*—NA; *partners*—Jordan, Israel
Imports: $410 million (c.i.f., 1988 est.); *commodities*—NA; *partners*—Jordan, Israel
External debt: $NA
Industrial production: growth rate NA%
Electricity: power supplied by Israel
Industries: generally small family businesses that produce cement, textiles, soap, olive-wood carvings, and mother-of-pearl souvenirs; the Israelis have established some small-scale modern industries in the settlements and industrial centers
Agriculture: olives, citrus and other fruits, vegetables, beef, and dairy products
Aid: none
Currency: new Israeli shekel (plural—shekels) and Jordanian dinar (plural—dinars); 1 new Israeli shekel (NIS) = 100 new agorot and 1 Jordanian dinar (JD) = 1,000 fils
Exchange rates: new Israeli shekels (NIS) per US$1—1.9450 (January 1990), 1.9164 (1989), 1.5992 (1988), 1.5946 (1987), 1.4878 (1986), 1.1788 (1985); Jordanian dinars (JD) per US$1—0.6557 (January 1990), 0.5704 (1989), 0.3715 (1988), 0.3387 (1987), 0.3499 (1986), 0.3940 (1985)
Fiscal year: 1 April-31 March

Communications

Highways: small indigenous road network, Israelis developing east-west axial highways
Airports: 2 total, 2 usable; 2 with permanent-surface runways; none with runways over 2,439 m; 1 with runways 1,220-2,439 m
Telecommunications: open-wire telephone system currently being upgraded; stations—no AM, no FM, no TV

Defense Forces

Branches: NA
Military manpower: NA
Defense expenditures: NA

Western Sahara

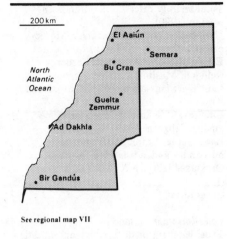

See regional map VII

Geography

Total area: 266,000 km^2; land area: 266,000 km^2
Comparative area: slightly smaller than Colorado
Land boundaries: 2,046 km total; Algeria 42 km, Mauritania 1,561 km, Morocco 443 km
Coastline: 1,110 km
Maritime claims: contingent upon resolution of sovereignty issue
Disputes: claimed and administered by Morocco, but sovereignty is unresolved and guerrilla fighting continues in the area
Climate: hot, dry desert; rain is rare; cold offshore currents produce fog and heavy dew
Terrain: mostly low, flat desert with large areas of rocky or sandy surfaces rising to small mountains in south and northeast
Natural resources: phosphates, iron ore
Land use: NEGL% arable land; 0% permanent crops; 19% meadows and pastures; 0% forest and woodland; 81% other
Environment: hot, dry, dust/sand-laden sirocco wind can occur during winter and spring; widespread harmattan haze exists 60% of time, often severely restricting visibility; sparse water and arable land

People

Population: 191,707 (July 1990), growth rate 2.7% (1990)
Birth rate: 48 births/1,000 population (1990)
Death rate: 23 deaths/1,000 population (1990)
Net migration rate: 2 migrants/1,000 population (1990)
Infant mortality rate: 177 deaths/1,000 live births (1990)
Life expectancy at birth: 39 years male, 41 years female (1990)

Western Sahara (continued)

Total fertility rate: 7.3 children born/woman (1990)
Nationality: noun—Saharan(s), Moroccan(s); adjective—Saharan, Moroccan
Ethnic divisions: Arab and Berber
Religion: Muslim
Language: Hassaniya Arabic, Moroccan Arabic
Literacy: 20% among Moroccans, 5% among Saharans (est.)
Labor force: 12,000; 50% animal husbandry and subsistence farming
Organized labor: NA

Government

Long-form name: none
Type: legal status of territory and question of sovereignty unresolved; territory contested by Morocco and Polisario Front (Popular Front for the Liberation of the Saguia el Hamra and Rio de Oro); territory partitioned between Morocco and Mauritania in April 1976, with Morocco acquiring northern two-thirds; Mauritania, under pressure from Polisario guerrillas, abandoned all claims to its portion in August 1979; Morocco moved to occupy that sector shortly thereafter and has since asserted administrative control; the Polisario's government in exile was seated as an OAU member in 1984; guerrilla activities continue to the present
Capital: none
Administrative divisions: none (under de facto control of Morocco)
Leaders: none
Diplomatic representation: none

Economy

Overview: Western Sahara, a territory poor in natural resources and having little rainfall, has a per capita GDP of just a few hundred dollars. Fishing and phosphate mining are the principal industries and sources of income. Most of the food for the urban population must be imported. All trade and other economic activities are controlled by the Moroccan Government.
GDP: $NA, per capita $NA; real growth rate NA%
Inflation rate (consumer prices): NA%
Unemployment rate: NA%
Budget: revenues $NA; expenditures $NA, including capital expenditures of $NA
Exports: $8 million (f.o.b., 1982 est.); *commodities*—phosphates 62%; *partners*—Morocco claims and administers Western Sahara, so trade partners are included in overall Moroccan accounts
Imports: $30 million (c.i.f., 1982 est.); *commodities*—fuel for fishing fleet, foodstuffs; *partners*—Morocco claims and ad-

ministers Western Sahara, so trade partners are included in overall Moroccan accounts
External debt: $NA
Industrial production: growth rate NA%
Electricity: 60,000 kW capacity; 79 million kWh produced, 425 kWh per capita (1989)
Industries: phosphate, fishing, handicrafts
Agriculture: practically none; some barley is grown in nondrought years; fruit and vegetables are grown in the few oases; food imports are essential; camels, sheep, and goats are kept by the nomadic natives; cash economy exists largely for the garrison forces
Aid: NA
Currency: Moroccan dirham (plural—dirhams); 1 Moroccan dirham (DH) = 100 centimes
Exchange rates: Moroccan dirhams (DH) per US$1—8.093 (January 1990), 8.488 (1989), 8.209 (1988), 8.359 (1987), 9.104 (1986), 10.062 (1985)
Fiscal year: NA

Communications

Highways: 6,100 km total; 1,350 km surfaced, 4,750 km improved and unimproved earth roads and tracks
Ports: El Aaiun, Ad Dakhla
Airports: 16 total, 14 usable; 3 with permanent-surface runways; none with runways over 3,659 m; 3 with runways 2,440-3,659 m; 6 with runways 1,220-2,439 m
Telecommunications: sparse and limited system; tied into Morocco's system by radio relay, tropospheric scatter, and 2 Atlantic Ocean INTELSAT earth stations linked to Rabat, Morocco; 2,000 telephones; stations—2 AM, no FM, 2 TV

Defense Forces

Branches: NA
Military manpower: NA
Defense expenditures: NA

Western Samoa

50 km

Savai'i

South Pacific Ocean

Apolima
APIA
Manono
Upolu

South Pacific Ocean

See regional map X

Geography

Total area: 2,860 km²; land area: 2,850 km²
Comparative area: slightly smaller than Rhode Island
Land boundaries: none
Coastline: 403 km
Maritime claims:
  Extended economic zone: 200 nm
  Territorial sea: 12 nm
Climate: tropical; rainy season (October to March), dry season (May to October)
Terrain: narrow coastal plain with volcanic, rocky, rugged mountains in interior
Natural resources: hardwood forests, fish
Land use: 19% arable land; 24% permanent crops; NEGL% meadows and pastures; 47% forest and woodland; 10% other
Environment: subject to occasional typhoons; active volcanism
Note: located 4,300 km southwest of Honolulu in the South Pacific Ocean about halfway between Hawaii and New Zealand

People

Population: 186,031 (July 1990), growth rate 2.3% (1990)
Birth rate: 34 births/1,000 population (1990)
Death rate: 7 deaths/1,000 population (1990)
Net migration rate: −5 migrants/1,000 population (1990)
Infant mortality rate: 48 deaths/1,000 live births (1990)
Life expectancy at birth: 64 years male, 69 years female (1990)
Total fertility rate: 4.6 children born/woman (1990)
Nationality: noun—Western Samoan(s); adjective—Western Samoan

Ethnic divisions: Samoan; about 7% Euronesians (persons of European and Polynesian blood), 0.4% Europeans
Religion: 99.7% Christian (about half of population associated with the London Missionary Society; includes Congregational, Roman Catholic, Methodist, Latter Day Saints, Seventh-Day Adventist)
Language: Samoan (Polynesian), English
Literacy: 90%
Labor force: 37,000; 22,000 employed in agriculture (1983 est.)
Organized labor: Public Service Association (PSA)

Government

Long-form name: Independent State of Western Samoa
Type: constitutional monarchy under native chief
Capital: Apia
Administrative divisions: 11 districts; A'ana, Aiga-i-le-Tai, Atua, Fa'asaleleaga, Gaga'emauga, Gagaifomauga, Palauli, Satupa'itea, Tuamasaga, Va'a-o-Fonoti, Vaisigano
Independence: 1 January 1962 (from UN trusteeship administered by New Zealand)
Constitution: 1 January 1962
Legal system: based on English common law and local customs; judicial review of legislative acts with respect to fundamental rights of the citizen; has not accepted compulsory ICJ jurisdiction
National holiday: National Day, 1 June
Executive branch: monarch, Executive Council, prime minister, Cabinet
Legislative branch: unicameral Legislative Assembly (Fono)
Judicial branch: Supreme Court, Court of Appeal
Leaders: *Chief of State*—Susuga Malietoa TANUMAFILI II (Co-Chief of State from 1 January 1962 until becoming sole Chief of State on 5 April 1963);
Head of Government—Prime Minister TOFILAU Eti Alesana (since 7 April 1988)
Political parties and leaders: Human Rights Protection Party (HRPP), Tofilau Eti, chairman; Samoan National Development Party (SNDP), Tupua Tamasese Efi, chairman
Suffrage: there are two electoral rolls—the matai (head of family) roll and the individuals roll; about 12,000 persons are on the matai roll, hold matai titles, and elect 45 members of the Legislative Assembly; about 1,600 persons are on the individuals roll, lack traditional matai ties, and elect two members of the Legislative Assembly by universal adult suffrage at the age of NA
Elections: *Legislative Assembly*—last held 26 February 1988 (next to be held by

February 1991); results—percent of vote by party NA; seats—(47 total) HRPP 25, SNDP 22
Member of: ACP, ADB, Commonwealth, ESCAP, FAO, G-77, IBRD, IDA, IFAD, IFC, IMF, SPC, SPF, UN, UNESCO, WHO
Diplomatic representation: Ambassador Fili (Felix) Tuaopepe WENDT; Chancery (temporary) at the Western Samoan Mission to the UN, 820 2nd Avenue, New York, NY 10017 (212) 599-6196; *US*—the ambassador to New Zealand is accredited to Western Samoa
Flag: red with a blue rectangle in the upper hoist-side quadrant bearing five white five-pointed stars representing the Southern Cross constellation

Economy

Overview: Agriculture employs two-thirds of the labor force, contributes 50% to GDP, and is the source of 90% of exports. The bulk of export earnings comes from the sale of coconut oil and copra. The economy depends on emigrant remittances and foreign aid to support a level of imports about five times export earnings. Tourism has become the most important growth industry, and construction of the first international hotel is under way.
GDP: $112 million, per capita $615; real growth rate 0.2% (1989 est.)
Inflation rate (consumer prices): 8.5% (1988)
Unemployment rate: NA%; shortage of skilled labor
Budget: revenues $54 million; expenditures $54 million, including capital expenditures of $28 million (1988)
Exports: $9.9 million (f.o.b., 1988); *commodities*—coconut oil and cream 42%, taro 19%, cocoa 14%, copra, timber; *partners*—NZ 30%, EC 24%, Australia 21%, American Samoa 7%, US 9% (1987)
Imports: $51.8 million (c.i.f., 1988); *commodities*—intermediate goods 58%, food 17%, capital goods 12%; *partners*—New Zealand 31%, Australia 20%, Japan 15%, Fiji 15%, US 5%, EC 4% (1987)
External debt: $75 million (December 1988 est.)
Industrial production: growth rate −4.0% (1987)
Electricity: 23,000 kW capacity; 35 million kWh produced, 190 kWh per capita (1989)
Industries: timber, tourism, food processing, fishing
Agriculture: coconuts, fruit (including bananas, taro, yams)
Aid: US commitments, including Ex-Im (FY70-88), $16 million; Western (non-US) countries, ODA and OOF bilateral com-

mitments (1970-87), $261 million; OPEC bilateral aid (1979-89), $4 million
Currency: tala (plural—tala); 1 tala (WS$) = 100 sene
Exchange rates: tala (WS$) per US$1—2.2857 (January 1990), 2.2686 (1989), 2.0790 (1988), 2.1204 (1987), 2.2351 (1986), 2.2437 (1985)
Fiscal year: calendar year

Communications

Highways: 2,042 km total; 375 km sealed; remainder mostly gravel, crushed stone, or earth
Ports: Apia
Merchant marine: 3 ships (1,000 GRT or over) totaling 24,930 GRT/34,135 DWT; includes 2 container, 1 roll-on/roll-off cargo
Civil air: 3 major transport aircraft
Airports: 4 total, 4 usable; 1 with permanent-surface runways; none with runways over 3,659 m; 1 with runways 2,440-3,659 m; none with runways 1,220-2,439 m
Telecommunications: 7,500 telephones; 70,000 radio receivers; stations—1 AM, no FM, no TV; 1 Pacific Ocean INTELSAT station

Defense Forces

Branches: NA
Military manpower: NA
Defense expenditures: NA

World

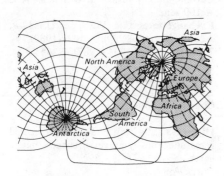

See regional map I

Geography

Total area: 510,072,000 km²; 361,132,000 km² (70.8%) is water and 148,940,000 km² (29.2%) is land
Comparative area: land area about 16 times the size of the US
Land boundaries: 442,000 km
Coastline: 359,000 km
Maritime claims:
Contiguous zone: generally 24 nm, but varies from 4 nm to 24 nm
Continental shelf: generally 200 nm, but some are 200 meters in depth
Exclusive fishing zone: most are 200 nm, but varies from 12 nm to 200 nm
Extended economic zone: 200 nm, only Madagascar claims 150 nm
Territorial sea: generally 12 nm, but varies from 3 nm to 200 nm
Disputes: 13 international land boundary disputes—Argentina-Uruguay, Bangladesh-India, Brazil-Paraguay, Brazil-Uruguay, Cambodia-Vietnam, China-India, China-USSR, Ecuador-Peru, El Salvador-Honduras, French Guiana-Suriname, Guyana-Suriname, Guyana-Venezuela, Qatar-UAE
Climate: two large areas of polar climates separated by two rather narrow temperate zones from a wide equatorial band of tropical to subtropical climates
Terrain: highest elevation is Mt. Everest at 8,848 meters and lowest elevation is the Dead Sea at 392 meters below sea level; greatest ocean depth is the Marianas Trench at 10,924 meters
Natural resources: the oceans represent the last major frontier for the discovery and development of natural resources
Land use: 10% arable land; 1% permanent crops; 24% meadows and pastures; 31% forest and woodland; 34% other; includes 1.6% irrigated
Environment: large areas subject to severe weather (tropical cyclones), natural disasters (earthquakes, landslides, tsunamis, volcanic eruptions), industrial disasters, pollution (air, water, acid rain, toxic substances), loss of vegetation (overgrazing, deforestation, desertification), loss of wildlife resources, soil degradation, soil depletion, erosion

People

Population: 5,316,644,000 (July 1990), growth rate 1.7% (1990)
Birth rate: 27 births/1,000 population (1990)
Death rate: 9 deaths/1,000 population (1990)
Infant mortality rate: 70 deaths/1,000 live births (1990)
Life expectancy at birth: 60 years male, 64 years female (1990)
Total fertility rate: 3.4 children born/woman (1990)
Literacy: 77% men; 66% women (1980)
Labor force: 1,939,000,000 (1984)
Organized labor: NA

Government

Administrative divisions: 248 nations, dependent areas, and other entities
Legal system: varies among each of the entities; 162 are parties to the United Nations International Court of Justice (ICJ) or World Court
Diplomatic representation: there are 159 members of the UN

Economy

Overview: In 1989 the World economy grew at an estimated 3.0%, somewhat lower than the estimated 3.4% for 1988. The technologically advanced areas—North America, Japan, and Western Europe—together account for 65% of the gross world product (GWP) of $20.3 trillion; these developed areas grew in the aggregate at 3.5%. In contrast, the Communist (Second World) countries typically grew at between 0% and 2%, accounting for 23% of GWP. Experience in the developing countries continued mixed, with the newly industrializing countries generally maintaining their rapid growth, and many others struggling with debt, inflation, and inadequate investment. The year 1989 ended with remarkable political upheavals in the Communist countries, which presumably will dislocate economic production still further. The addition of nearly 100 million people a year to an already overcrowded globe will exacerbate the problems of pollution, desertification, underemployment, and poverty throughout the 1990s.

GWP (gross world product): $20.3 trillion, per capita $3,870; real growth rate 3.0% (1989 est.)
Inflation rate (consumer prices): 5%, developed countries; 100%, developing countries with wide variations (1989 est.)
Unemployment rate: NA%
Exports: $2,694 billion (f.o.b., 1988); *commodities*—NA; *partners*—in value, about 70% of exports from industrial countries
Imports: $2,750 billion (c.i.f., 1988); *commodities*—NA; *partners*—in value, about 75% of imports by the industrial countries
External debt: $1,008 billion for less developed countries (1988 est.)
Industrial production: growth rate 5% (1989 est.)
Electricity: 2,838,680,000 kW capacity; 11,222,029 million kWh produced, 2,140 kWh per capita (1989)
Industries: chemicals, energy, machinery, electronics, metals, mining, textiles, food processing
Agriculture: cereals (wheat, maize, rice), sugar, livestock products, tropical crops, fruit, vegetables, fish
Aid: NA

Communications

Ports: Mina al Ahmadi (Kuwait), Chiba, Houston, Kawasaki, Kobe, Marseille, New Orleans, New York, Rotterdam, Yokohama

Defense Forces

Branches: ground, maritime, and air forces at all levels of technology
Military manpower: 29.15 million persons in the defense forces of the World (1987)
Defense expenditures: 5.4% of GWP, or $1.1 trillion (1989 est.)

Yemen Arab Republic
[Yemen (Sanaa) or North Yemen]

125 km

Ṣaʻdah
Maydi
SANAA
Harīb
Red Sea
Al Hudaydah
Taʻizz
Mocha

Boundary representation is not necessarily authoritative.

See regional map VI

Geography

Total area: 195,000 km²; land area: 195,000 km²
Comparative area: slightly smaller than South Dakota
Land boundaries: 1,209 km total; Saudi Arabia 628 km, PDRY 581 km
Coastline: 523 km
Maritime claims:
  Contiguous zone: 18 nm
  Continental shelf: 200 meters
  Territorial sea: 12 nm
Disputes: sections of the boundary with PDRY are indefinite or undefined; undefined section of boundary with Saudi Arabia
Climate: desert; hot and humid along coast; temperate in central mountains; harsh desert in east
Terrain: narrow coastal plain (Tihama); western mountains; flat dissected plain in center sloping into desert interior of Arabian Peninsula
Natural resources: crude oil, rock salt, marble; small deposits of coal, nickel, and copper; fertile soil
Land use: 14% arable land; NEGL% permanent crops; 36% meadows and pastures; 8% forest and woodland; 42% other; includes 1% irrigated
Environment: subject to sand and dust storms in summer; overgrazing; soil erosion; desertification
Note: controls northern approaches to Bab el Mandeb linking Red Sea and Gulf of Aden, one of world's most active shipping lanes

People

Population: 7,160,981 (July 1990), growth rate 3.1% (1990)
Birth rate: 52 births/1,000 population (1990)
Death rate: 17 deaths/1,000 population (1990)
Net migration rate: −4 migrants/1,000 population (1990)
Infant mortality rate: 129 deaths/1,000 live births (1990)
Life expectancy at birth: 48 years male, 49 years female (1990)
Total fertility rate: 7.6 children born/woman (1990)
Nationality: noun—Yemeni(s); adjective—Yemeni
Ethnic divisions: 90% Arab, 10% Afro-Arab (mixed)
Religion: 100% Muslim (Sunni and Shiʻa)
Language: Arabic
Literacy: 15% (est.)
Labor force: NA; 70% agriculture and herding, 30% expatriate laborers (est.)

Government

Long-form name: Yemen Arab Republic; abbreviated YAR
Type: republic; military regime assumed power in June 1974
Capital: Sanaa
Administrative divisions: 11 governorates (muḥāfaẓat, singular—muḥāfaẓah); Al Baydāʼ, Al Ḥudaydah, Al Jawf, Al Maḥwīt, Dhamār, Ḥajjah, Ibb, Maʼrib, Ṣaʻdah, Ṣanʻāʼ, Taʻizz
Independence: November 1918 (from Ottoman Empire)
Constitution: 28 December 1970, suspended 19 June 1974
Legal system: based on Turkish law, Islamic law, and local customary law; has not accepted compulsory ICJ jurisdiction
National holiday: Proclamation of the Republic, 26 September (1962)
Executive branch: president, vice president, prime minister, four deputy prime ministers, Council of Ministers (cabinet)
Legislative branch: unicameral Consultative Assembly (Majlis ash-Shura)
Judicial branch: State Security Court
Leaders: *Chief of State*—President Col. ʻAli ʻAbdallah SALIH (since 18 July 1978); Vice President (vacant);
Head of Government—Prime Minister ʻAbd al-ʻAziz ʻABD AL-GHANI (since 12 November 1983, previously prime minister from 1975-1980 and co-Vice President from October 1980 to November 1983)
Political parties and leaders: no legal political parties; in 1983 President Salih started the General People's Congress, which is designed to function as the country's sole political party
Suffrage: universal at age 18
Elections: *Consultative Assembly*—last held 5 July 1988 (next to be held NA); results—percent of vote NA; seats—(159 total, 128 elected)
Communists: small number

Other political or pressure groups: conservative tribal groups, Muslim Brotherhood, leftist factions—pro-Iraqi Baʻthists, Nasirists, National Democratic Front (NDF) supported by the PDRY
Member of: ACC, Arab League, FAO, G-77, IBRD, ICAO, IDA, IDB—Islamic Development Bank, IFAD, IFC, ILO, IMF, IMO, INTELSAT, INTERPOL, ITU, NAM, OIC, UN, UNESCO, UPU, WFTU, WHO, WIPO, WMO
Diplomatic representation: Ambassador Mohsin A. al-AINI; Chancery at Suite 840, 600 New Hampshire Avenue NW, Washington DC 20037; telephone (202) 965-4760 or 4761; there is a Yemeni Consulate General in Detroit and a Consulate in San Francisco; *US*—Ambassador Charles F. DUNBAR; Embassy at address NA, Sanaa (mailing address is P. O. Box 1088, Sanaa); telephone [967] (2) 271950 through 271958
Flag: three equal horizontal bands of red (top), white, and black with a large green five-pointed star centered in the white band; similar to the flags of Iraq, which has three stars, and Syria, which has two stars—all green and five-pointed in a horizontal line centered in the white band; also similar to the flag of Egypt, which has a symbolic eagle centered in the white band

Economy

Overview: The low level of domestic industry and agriculture make North Yemen dependent on imports for virtually all of its essential needs. Large trade deficits are made up for by remittances from Yemenis working abroad and foreign aid. Once self-sufficient in food production, the YAR is now a major importer. Land once used for export crops—cotton, fruit, and vegetables—has been turned over to growing qat, a mildly narcotic shrub chewed by Yemenis that has no significant export market. Oil export revenues started flowing in late 1987 and boosted 1988 earnings by about $800 million.
GDP: $5.5 billion, per capita $820; real growth rate 19.7% (1988 est.)
Inflation rate (consumer prices): 16.9% (1988)
Unemployment rate: 13% (1986)
Budget: revenues $1.32 billion; expenditures $2.18 billion, including capital expenditures of $588 million (1988 est.)
Exports: $853 million (f.o.b., 1988); *commodities*—crude oil, cotton, coffee, hides, vegetables; *partners*—US 41%, PDRY 14%, Japan 12%
Imports: $1.3 billion (f.o.b., 1988); *commodities*—textiles and other manufactured consumer goods, petroleum products, sugar, grain, flour, other foodstuffs,

Yemen Arab Republic *(continued)*

and cement; *partners*—Italy 10%, Saudi Arabia 9%, US 9.3%, Japan 9%, UK 8% (1985)

External debt: $3.5 billion (December 1989 est.)

Industrial production: growth rate 2% in manufacturing (1988)

Electricity: 415,000 kW capacity; 500 million kWh produced, 70 kWh per capita (1989)

Industries: crude oil production, small-scale production of cotton textiles and leather goods; food processing; handicrafts; fishing; small aluminum products factory; cement

Agriculture: accounts for 50% of GDP and 70% of labor force; farm products—grain, fruits, vegetables, qat (mildly narcotic shrub), coffee, cotton, dairy, poultry, meat, goat meat; not self-sufficient in grain

Aid: US commitments, including Ex-Im (1970-88), $354 million; Western (non-US) countries, ODA and OOF bilateral commitments (1970-87), $1.4 billion; OPEC bilateral aid (1979-89), $2.9 billion; Communist countries (1970-88), $248 million

Currency: Yemeni riyal (plural—riyals); 1 Yemeni riyal (YR) = 100 fils

Exchange rates: Yemeni riyals (YR) per US$1—9.7600 (January 1990), 9.7600 (1989), 9.7717 (1988), 10.3417 (1987), 9.6392 (1986), 7.3633 (1985)

Fiscal year: calendar year

Communications

Highways: 4,500 km; 2,000 km bituminous, 500 km crushed stone and gravel, 2,000 km earth, sand, and light gravel (est.)

Pipelines: crude oil, 424 km

Ports: Al Hudaydah, Al Mukhā, Ṣalīf, Ra's al Katib

Merchant marine: 1 petroleum, oils, and lubricants (POL) tanker (1,000 GRT or over) totaling 192,679 GRT/40,640 DWT

Civil air: 7 major transport aircraft

Airports: 19 total, 14 usable; 3 with permanent-surface runways; none with runways over 3,659 m; 9 with runways 2,440-3,659 m; 3 with runways 1,220-2,439 m

Telecommunications: system poor but improving; new radio relay and cable networks; 50,000 telephones; stations—3 AM, no FM, 17 TV; satellite earth stations—1 Indian Ocean INTELSAT, 1 Atlantic Ocean INTELSAT, 1 ARABSAT; tropospheric scatter to PDRY; radio relay to PDRY, Saudi Arabia, and Djibouti

Defense Forces

Branches: Army, Navy, Air Force, Police

Military manpower: males 15-49, 1,289,217; 734,403 fit for military service; 79,609 reach military age (18) annually

Defense expenditures: $358 million (1987)

Yemen, People's Democratic Republic of
[Yemen (Aden) or South Yemen]

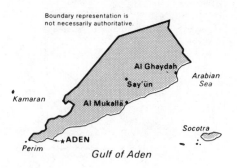

See regional map VI

Geography

Total area: 332,970 km²; land area: 332,970 km²; includes Perim, Socotra

Comparative area: slightly larger than New Mexico

Land boundaries: 1,699 km total; Oman 288 km, Saudi Arabia 830 km, YAR 581 km

Coastline: 1,383 km

Maritime claims:

Contiguous zone: 24 nm

Continental shelf: edge of continental margin or 200 nm

Extended economic zone: 200 nm

Territorial sea: 12 nm

Disputes: sections of boundary with YAR indefinite or undefined; Administrative Line with Oman; no defined boundary with Saudi Arabia

Climate: desert; extraordinarily hot and dry

Terrain: mostly upland desert plains; narrow, flat, sandy coastal plain backed by flat-topped hills and rugged mountains

Natural resources: fish, oil, minerals (gold, copper, lead)

Land use: 1% arable land; NEGL% permanent crops; 27% meadows and pastures; 7% forest and woodland; 65% other; includes NEGL% irrigated

Environment: scarcity of natural freshwater resources; overgrazing; soil erosion; desertification

Note: controls southern approaches to Bab el Mandeb linking Red Sea to Gulf of Aden, one of world's most active shipping lanes

People

Population: 2,585,484 (July 1990), growth rate 3.2% (1990)

Birth rate: 48 births/1,000 population (1990)

Death rate: 14 deaths/1,000 population (1990)

Net migration rate: −2 migrants/1,000 population (1990)

Infant mortality rate: 110 deaths/1,000 live births (1990)

Life expectancy at birth: 50 years male, 54 years female (1990)

Total fertility rate: 7.0 children born/ woman (1990)

Nationality: noun—Yemeni(s); adjective— Yemeni

Ethnic divisions: almost all Arabs; a few Indians, Somalis, and Europeans

Religion: Sunni Muslim, some Christian and Hindu

Language: Arabic

Literacy: 25%

Labor force: 477,000; 45.2% agriculture, 21.2% services, 13.4% construction, 10.6% industry, 9.6% commerce and other (1983)

Organized labor: 348,200; the General Confederation of Workers of the People's Democratic Republic of Yemen has 35,000 members

Government

Long-form name: People's Democratic Republic of Yemen; abbreviated PDRY

Type: republic

Capital: Aden

Administrative divisions: 6 governorates (muḥāfaẓat, singular—muḥāfaẓah); Abyan, 'Adan, Al Mahrah, Ḥaḍramawt, Laḥij, Shabwah

Independence: 30 November 1967 (from UK)

Constitution: 31 October 1978

Legal system: based on Islamic law (for personal matters) and English common law (for commercial matters)

National holiday: National Day, 14 October

Executive branch: president, prime minister, two deputy prime ministers, Council of Ministers

Legislative branch: unicameral Supreme People's Council

Judicial branch: Federal High Court

Leaders: *Chief of State*—President Haydar Abu Bakr al-'ATTAS (since 8 February 1986);

Head of Government—Chairman of the Council of Ministers (Prime Minister) Dr. Yasin Sa'id NU'MAN (since 8 February 1986); Deputy Prime Minister Salih Abu Bakr bin HUSAYNUN (since 8 February 1986); Deputy Prime Minister Salih Munassir al-SIYAYLI (since 8 February 1986)

Political parties and leaders: only party— Yemeni Socialist Party (YSP) is a coalition of National Front, Ba'th, and Communist Parties

Suffrage: universal at age 18

Elections: *Supreme People's Council*—last held 28-30 October 1986 (next to be held

NA); results—YSP is the only party; seats—(111 total) YSP or YSP approved 111

Communists: NA

Other political or pressure groups: NA

Member of: Arab League, FAO, G-77, GATT (de facto), IBRD, ICAO, IDA, IDB—Islamic Development Bank, IFAD, ILO, IMF, IMO, ITU, NAM, OIC, UN, UNESCO, UPU, WFTU, WHO, WMO, WTO

Diplomatic representation: none; the UK acts as the protecting power for the US in the PDRY

Flag: three equal horizontal bands of red (top), white, and black with a light blue, isosceles triangle based on the hoist side bearing a red five-pointed star

Economy

Overview: The PDRY is one of the poorest Arab countries, with a per capita GNP of about $500. A shortage of natural resources, a widely dispersed population, and an arid climate make economic development difficult. The economy has grown at an average annual rate of only 2-3% since the mid-1970s. The economy is organized along socialist lines, dominated by the public sector. Economic growth has been constrained by a lack of incentives, partly stemming from centralized control over production decisions, investment allocation, and import choices.

GNP: $1.2 billion, per capita $495; real growth rate 5.2% (1988 est.)

Inflation rate (consumer prices): 2.8% (1987)

Unemployment rate: NA%

Budget: revenues $429 million; expenditures $976 million, including capital expenditures of $402 million (1988 est.)

Exports: $82.2 million (f.o.b., 1988 est.); *commodities*—cotton, hides, skins, dried and salted fish; *partners*—Japan, YAR, Singapore

Imports: $598.0 million (f.o.b., 1988 est.); *commodities*—grain, consumer goods, crude oil, machinery, chemicals; *partners*—USSR, Australia, UK

External debt: $2.25 billion (December 1989 est.)

Industrial production: growth rate NA%

Electricity: 245,000 kW capacity; 600 million kWh produced, 240 kWh per capita (1989)

Industries: petroleum refinery (operates on imported crude oil); fish

Agriculture: accounts for 13% of GNP and 45% of labor force; products—grain, qat (mildly narcotic shrub), coffee, fish, livestock; fish and honey major exports; most food imported

Aid: US commitments, including Ex-Im (FY70-80), $4.5 million; Western (non-US)

countries, ODA and OOF bilateral commitments (1970-87), $241 million; OPEC bilateral aid (1979-89), $279 million; Communist countries (1970-88), $2.2 billion

Currency: Yemeni dinar (plural—dinars); 1 Yemeni dinar (YD) = 1,000 fils

Exchange rates: Yemeni dinars (YD) per US$1—0.3454 (fixed rate)

Fiscal year: calendar year

Communications

Highways: 11,000 km; 2,000 km bituminous, 9,000 km natural surface (est.)

Pipelines: refined products, 32 km

Ports: Aden, Al Khalf, Nishtūn

Merchant marine: 3 ships (1,000 GRT or over) totaling 4,309 GRT/6,568 DWT; includes 2 cargo, 1 petroleum, oils, and lubricants (POL) tanker

Civil air: 8 major transport aircraft

Airports: 42 total, 29 usable; 7 with permanent-surface runways; none with runways over 3,659 m; 11 with runways 2,440-3,659 m; 10 with runways 1,220-2,439 m

Telecommunications: small system of open-wire, radio relay, multiconductor cable, and radio communications stations; 15,000 telephones (est.); stations—1 AM, no FM, 5 TV; satellite earth stations—1 Indian Ocean INTELSAT, 1 Intersputnik, 1 ARABSAT; radio relay and tropospheric scatter to YAR

Defense Forces

Branches: Army, Navy, Air Force, People's Militia, People's Police

Military manpower: males 15-49, 544,190; 307,005 fit for military service

Defense expenditures: NA

Yugoslavia

150 km

Adriatic Sea

See regional map V

Geography

Total area: 255,800 km²; land area: 255,400 km²
Comparative area: slightly larger than Wyoming
Land boundaries: 2,961 km total; Albania 486 km, Austria 311 km, Bulgaria 539 km, Greece 246 km, Hungary 631 km, Italy 202 km, Romania 546 km
Coastline: 3,935 km (including 2,414 km offshore islands)
Maritime claims:
  Continental shelf: 200 meters or to depth of exploitation
  Territorial sea: 12 nm
Disputes: Kosovo question with Albania; Macedonia question with Bulgaria and Greece
Climate: temperate; hot, relatively dry summers with mild, rainy winters along coast; warm summer with cold winters inland
Terrain: mostly mountains with large areas of karst topography; plain in north
Natural resources: coal, copper, bauxite, timber, iron ore, antimony, chromium, lead, zinc, asbestos, mercury, crude oil, natural gas, nickel, uranium
Land use: 28% arable land; 3% permanent crops; 25% meadows and pastures; 36% forest and woodland; 8% other; includes 1% irrigated
Environment: subject to frequent and destructive earthquakes
Note: controls the most important land routes from central and western Europe to Aegean Sea and Turkish straits

People

Population: 23,841,608 (July 1990), growth rate 0.6% (1990)
Birth rate: 15 births/1,000 population (1990)
Death rate: 9 deaths/1,000 population (1990)

Net migration rate: 0 migrants/1,000 population (1990)
Infant mortality rate: 22 deaths/1,000 live births (1990)
Life expectancy at birth: 70 years male, 76 years female (1990)
Total fertility rate: 1.9 children born/woman (1990)
Nationality: noun—Yugoslav(s); adjective—Yugoslav
Ethnic divisions: 36.3% Serb, 19.7% Croat, 8.9% Muslim, 7.8% Slovene, 7.7% Albanian, 5.9% Macedonian, 5.4% Yugoslav, 2.5% Montenegrin, 1.9% Hungarian, 3.9% other (1981 census)
Religion: 50% Eastern Orthodox, 30% Roman Catholic, 9% Muslim, 1% Protestant, 10% other
Language: Serbo-Croatian, Slovene, Macedonian (all official); Albanian, Hungarian
Literacy: 90.5%
Labor force: 9,600,000; 22% agriculture, 27% mining and manufacturing; about 5% of labor force are guest workers in Western Europe (1986)
Organized labor: 6,200,000 members in the Confederation of Trade Unions of Yugoslavia (SSJ)

Government

Long-form name: Socialist Federal Republic of Yugoslavia; abbreviated SFRY
Type: Communist state, federal republic in form
Capital: Belgrade
Administrative divisions: 6 socialist republics (socijalističke republike, singular—socijalistička republika); Bosna I Hercegovina, Crna Gora, Hrvatska, Makedonija, Slovenija, Srbija; note—there are two autonomous provinces (autonomne pokajine, singular—autonomna pokajina) named Kosovo and Vojvodina within Srbija
Independence: 1 December 1918; independent monarchy established from the Kingdoms of Serbia and Montenegro, parts of the Turkish Empire, and the Austro-Hungarian Empire; SFRY proclaimed 29 November 1945
Constitution: 21 February 1974
Legal system: mixture of civil law system and Communist legal theory; has not accepted compulsory ICJ jurisdiction
National holiday: Proclamation of the Socialist Federal Republic of Yugoslavia, 29 November (1945)
Executive branch: president of the Collective State Presidency, vice president of the Collective State Presidency, Collective State Presidency, president of the Federal Executive Council, two vice presidents of the Federal Executive Council, Federal Executive Council

Legislative branch: bicameral Federal Assembly (Savezna Skupština) consists of an upper chamber or Chamber of Republics and Provinces and a lower chamber or Federal Chamber
Judicial branch: Federal Court (Savezna Sud), Constitutional Court
Leaders: *Chief of State* President of the Collective State Presidency Janez DRNOVSEK (from Slovenija; one-year term expires 15 May 1990); Vice President of the Collective State Presidency—Borisav JOVIC (from Srbija; one-year term expires 15 May 1990); note—the offices of president and vice president rotate annually among members of the Collective State Presidency with the current vice president assuming the presidency and a new vice president selected from area which has gone the longest without filling the position (the current sequence is Hrvatska, Crna Gora, Vojvodina, Kosovo, Makedonija, Bosna i Hercegovina, Slovenija, and Srbija);
Head of Government President of the Federal Executive Council Ante MARKOVIC (since 16 March 1989); Vice President of the Federal Executive Council Aleksandar MITROVIC (since 16 March 1989); Vice President of the Federal Executive Council Zivko PREGL (since 16 March 1989)
Political parties and leaders: there are about 90 political parties operating country-wide including the League of Communists of Yugoslavia (LCY)
Suffrage: at age 16 if employed, universal at age 18
Elections: direct national elections probably will be held in late 1990
Communists: 2,079,013 party members (1988)
Other political or pressure groups: Socialist Alliance of Working People of Yugoslavia (SAWPY), the major mass front organization; Confederation of Trade Unions of Yugoslavia (CTUY), League of Socialist Youth of Yugoslavia, Federation of Veterans' Associations of Yugoslavia (SUBNOR)
Member of: ASSIMER, CCC, CEMA (observer but participates in certain commissions), FAO, G-77, GATT, IAEA, IBA, IBRD, ICAC, ICAO, IDA, IDB—Inter-American Development Bank, IFAD, IFC, IHO, ILO, ILZSG, IMF, IMO, INTELSAT, INTERPOL, IPU, ITC, ITU, NAM, OECD (participant in some activities), UN, UNESCO, UPU, WHO, WIPO, WMO, WTO
Diplomatic representation: Ambassador Dzevad MUJEZINOVIC; Chancery at 2410 California Street NW, Washington DC 20008; telephone (202) 462-6566; there are Yugoslav Consulates General in Chicago, Cleveland, New York,

344

Pittsburgh, and San Francisco; *US*—Ambassador Warren ZIMMERMAN; Embassy at Kneza Milosa 50, Belgrade; telephone [38] (11) 645-655; there is a US Consulate General in Zagreb

Flag: three equal horizontal bands of blue (top), white, and red with a large red five-pointed star edged in yellow superimposed in the center over all three bands

Economy

Overview: Tito's reform programs 20 years ago changed the Stalinist command economy to a decentralized semimarket system but a system that the rigid, ethnically divided political structure ultimately could not accommodate. A prominent feature of the reforms was the establishment of workers' self-management councils in all large plants, which were to select managers, stimulate production, and divide the proceeds. The general result of these reforms has been rampant wage-price inflation, substantial rundown of capital plant, consumer shortages, and a still larger income gap between the poorer southern regions and the relatively affluent northern provinces of Hrvatska and Slovenija. In 1988-89 the beleaguered central government has been reforming the reforms, trying to create an open market economy with still considerable state ownership of major industrial plants. These reforms have been moving forward with the advice and support of the International Monetary Fund through a series of tough negotiations. Self-management supposedly is to be replaced by the discipline of the market and by fiscal austerity, ultimately leading to a stable dinar. However, strikes in major plants, hyperinflation, and interregional political jousting have held back progress. According to US economic advisers, only a highly unlikely combination of genuine privatization, massive Western economic investment and aid, and political moderation can salvage this economy.

GNP: $129.5 billion, per capita $5,464; real growth rate −1.0% (1989 est.)

Inflation rate (consumer prices): 2,700% (1989 est.)

Unemployment rate: 15% (1989)

Budget: revenues $6.4 billion; expenditures $6.4 billion, including capital expenditures of $NA (1990)

Exports: $13.1 billion (f.o.b., 1988); *commodities*—raw materials and semimanufactures 50%, consumer goods 31%, capital goods and equipment 19%; *partners*—EC 30%, CEMA 45%, less developed countries 14%, US 5%, other 6%

Imports: $13.8 billion (c.i.f., 1988); *commodities*—raw materials and semimanufactures 79%, capital goods and equipment 15%, consumer goods 6%; *partners*—EC 30%, CEMA 45%, less developed countries 14%, US 5%, other 6%

External debt: $17.0 billion, medium and long term (1989)

Industrial production: growth rate −1% (1989 est.)

Electricity: 21,000,000 kW capacity; 87,100 million kWh produced, 3,650 kWh per capita (1989)

Industries: metallurgy, machinery and equipment, petroleum, chemicals, textiles, wood processing, food processing, pulp and paper, motor vehicles, building materials

Agriculture: diversified, with many small private holdings and large combines; main crops—corn, wheat, tobacco, sugar beets, sunflowers; occasionally a net exporter of corn, tobacco, foodstuffs, live animals

Aid: donor—about $3.5 billion in bilateral aid to non-Communist less developed countries (1966-88)

Currency: Yugoslav dinar (plural—dinars); 1 Yugoslav dinar (YD) = 100 paras; note—on 1 January 1990, Yugoslavia began issuing a new currency with 1 new dinar equal to 10,000 YD

Exchange rates: Yugoslav dinars (YD) per US$1—118,568 (January 1990), 28,764 (1989), 2,523 (1988), 737 (1987), 379 (1986), 270 (1985); note—as of February 1990 the new dinar is linked to the FRG deutsche mark at the rate of 7 new dinars per 1 deustche mark

Fiscal year: calendar year

Communications

Railroads: 9,270 km total; (all 1.435-meter standard gauge) including 926 km double track, 3,771 km electrified (1987)

Highways: 120,747 km total; 71,315 km asphalt, concrete, stone block; 34,299 km macadam, asphalt treated, gravel, crushed stone; 15,133 km earth (1987)

Inland waterways: 2,600 km (1982)

Pipelines: 1,373 km crude oil; 2,900 km natural gas; 150 km refined products

Ports: Rijeka, Split, Koper, Bar, Ploce; inland port is Belgrade

Merchant marine: 270 ships (1,000 GRT or over) totaling 3,608,705 GRT/ 5,809,219 DWT; includes 3 passenger, 4 short-sea passenger, 131 cargo, 3 refrigerated cargo, 16 container, 14 roll-on/roll-off cargo, 3 multifunction large-load carrier, 9 petroleum, oils, and lubricants (POL) tanker, 3 chemical tanker, 3 combination ore/oil, 73 bulk, 8 combination bulk; note—Yugoslavia owns 19 ships (1,000 GRT or over) totaling 229,614 GRT/ 353,224 DWT under the registry of Liberia, Panama, and Cyprus

Civil air: NA major transport aircraft

Airports: 184 total, 184 usable; 54 with permanent-surface runways; none with runways over 3.659 m; 22 with runways 2,440 to 3,659 m; 20 with runways 1,220-2,439 m

Telecommunications: stations—199 AM, 87 FM, 50 TV; 4,107,846 TV sets; 4,700,000 radio receivers; satellite earth stations—1 Atlantic Ocean INTELSAT and 1 Indian Ocean INTELSAT

Defense Forces

Branches: Yugoslav People's Army—Ground Forces, Naval Forces, Air and Air Defense Forces, Frontier Guard, Territorial Defense Force, Civil Defense

Military manpower: males 15-49, 6,135,628; 4,970,420 fit for military service; 188,028 reach military age (19) annually

Defense expenditures: 14.8 trillion dinars, 4.6% of national income (1989 est.); note—conversion of the military budget into US dollars using the official administratively set exchange rate would produce misleading results

Zaire

500 km

Bumba
Kisangani
Mbandaka
Bukavu
KINSHASA · Ilebo · Lake Tanganyika
Matadi · Kananga · Kalemie
Mbuji-Mayi
Kolwezi
Lubumbashi

Boundary representation is not necessarily authoritative.

See regional map VII

Geography

Total area: 2,345,410 km²; land area: 2,267,600 km²
Comparative area: slightly more than one-quarter the size of US
Land boundaries: 10,271 km total; Angola 2,511 km, Burundi 233 km, Central African Republic 1,577 km, Congo 2,410 km, Rwanda 217 km, Sudan 628 km, Uganda 765 km, Zambia 1,930 km
Coastline: 37 km
Maritime claims:
Territorial sea: 12 nm
Disputes: Tanzania-Zaire-Zambia tripoint in Lake Tanganyika may no longer be indefinite since it is reported that the indefinite section of the Zaire-Zambia boundary has been settled; long section with Congo along the Congo River is indefinite (no division of the river or its islands has been made)
Climate: tropical; hot and humid in equatorial river basin; cooler and drier in southern highlands; cooler and wetter in eastern highlands; north of Equator—wet season April to October, dry season December to February; south of Equator—wet season November to March, dry season April to October
Terrain: vast central basin is a low-lying plateau; mountains in east
Natural resources: cobalt, copper, cadmium, crude oil, industrial and gem diamonds, gold, silver, zinc, manganese, tin, germanium, uranium, radium, bauxite, iron ore, coal, hydropower potential
Land use: 3% arable land; NEGL% permanent crops; 4% meadows and pastures; 78% forest and woodland; 15% other; includes NEGL% irrigated
Environment: dense tropical rainforest in central river basin and eastern highlands; periodic droughts in south
Note: straddles Equator; very narrow strip of land is only outlet to South Atlantic Ocean

People

Population: 36,589,468 (July 1990), growth rate 3.3% (1990)
Birth rate: 46 births/1,000 population (1990)
Death rate: 13 deaths/1,000 population (1990)
Net migration rate: NEGL migrants/1,000 population (1990)
Infant mortality rate: 103 deaths/1,000 live births (1990)
Life expectancy at birth: 51 years male, 55 years female (1990)
Total fertility rate: 6.2 children born/woman (1990)
Nationality: noun—Zairian(s); adjective—Zairian
Ethnic divisions: over 200 African ethnic groups, the majority are Bantu; four largest tribes—Mongo, Luba, Kongo (all Bantu), and the Mangbetu-Azande (Hamitic) make up about 45% of the population
Religion: 50% Roman Catholic, 20% Protestant, 10% Kimbanguist, 10% Muslim, 10% other syncretic sects and traditional beliefs
Language: French (official), Lingala, Swahili, Kingwana, Kikongo, Tshiluba
Literacy: 55% males, 37% females
Labor force: 15,000,000; 75% agriculture, 13% industry, 12% services; 13% wage earners (1981); 51% of population of working age (1985)
Organized labor: National Union of Workers of Zaire (UNTZA) is the only trade union

Government

Long-form name: Republic of Zaire
Type: republic with a strong presidential system
Capital: Kinshasa
Administrative divisions: 8 regions (régions, singular—région) and 1 town* (ville); Bandundu, Bas-Zaïre, Equateur, Haut-Zaïre, Kasai-Occidental, Kasai-Oriental, Kinshasa*, Kivu, Shaba; note—there may now be 10 regions with the elimination of Kivu and addition of Maniema, Nord-Kivu, and Sud-Kivu
Independence: 30 June 1960 (from Belgium; formerly Belgian Congo, then Congo/Leopoldville, then Congo/Kinshasa)
Constitution: 24 June 1967, amended August 1974, revised 15 February 1978
Legal system: based on Belgian civil law system and tribal law; has not accepted compulsory ICJ jurisdiction
National holiday: Anniversary of the Regime (Second Republic), 24 November (1965)
Executive branch: president, prime minister, Executive Council (cabinet)

Legislative branch: unicameral National Legislative Council (Conseil Législatif National)
Judicial branch: Supreme Court (Cour Suprême)
Leaders: *Chief of State*—President Marshal MOBUTU Sese Seko Kuku Ngbendu wa Za Banga (since 24 November 1965); *Head of Government*—Prime Minister LUNDA Bululu (since 25 April 1990)
Political parties and leaders: only party—Popular Movement of the Revolution (MPR)
Suffrage: universal and compulsory at age 18
Elections: *President*—last held 29 July 1984 (next to be held July 1991); results—President Mobutu was reelected without opposition;
National Legislative Council—last held 6 September 1987 (next to be held September 1992); results—MPR is the only party; seats—(210 total) MPR 210
Communists: no Communist party
Member of: ACP, AfDB, APC, CCC, CIPEC, EAMA, EIB (associate), FAO, G-77, GATT, IAEA, IBRD, ICAO, ICO, IDA, IFAD, IFC, IHO, ILO, IMF, IMO, INTELSAT, INTERPOL, IPU, ITC, ITU, NAM, OAU, OCAM, UN, UNESCO, UPU, WHO, WIPO, WMO, WTO
Diplomatic representation: Ambassador (vacant), Chargé d'Affaires MUKENDI Tambo a Kabila; Chancery at 1800 New Hampshire Avenue NW, Washington DC 20009; telephone (202) 234-7690 or 7691; *US*—Ambassador William C. HARROP; Embassy at 310 Avenue des Aviateurs, Kinshasa (mailing address is APO New York 09662); telephone [243] (12) 25881 through 25886; there is a US Consulate General in Lubumbashi
Flag: light green with a yellow disk in the center bearing a black arm holding a red flaming torch; the flames of the torch are blowing away from the hoist side; uses the popular pan-African colors of Ethiopia

Economy

Overview: In 1988, in spite of large mineral resources and one of the most developed and diversified economies in Sub-Saharan Africa, Zaire had a GDP per capita of $195, one of the lowest on the continent. Agriculture, a key sector of the economy, employs 75% of the population but generates under 30% of GDP. The main impetus for economic development has been the extractive industries. Mining and mineral processing account for about one-third of GDP and two-thirds of total export earnings. During the period 1983-88 the economy experienced slow growth, high inflation, a rising foreign debt, and a drop in foreign exchange earnings. Recent increases in foreign prices for copper—a key export earner—and other minerals offer some hope of reversing the economic decline. Zaire is the world's largest producer of diamonds.

GDP: $6.5 billion, per capita $195; real growth rate 2.8% (1988)
Inflation rate (consumer prices): 82% (1988)
Unemployment rate: NA%
Budget: revenues $856 million; expenditures $2.3 billion, including capital expenditures of $655 million (1988)
Exports: $2.2 billion (f.o.b., 1988); *commodities*—copper 37%, coffee 24%, diamonds 12%, cobalt, crude oil; *partners*—US, Belgium, France, FRG, Italy, UK, Japan
Imports: $1.9 billion (f.o.b., 1988); *commodities*—consumer goods, foodstuffs, mining and other machinery, transport equipment, fuels; *partners*—US, Belgium, France, FRG, Italy, Japan, UK
External debt: $8.6 billion (December 1989 est.)
Industrial production: growth rate NA%
Electricity: 2,574,000 kW capacity; 5,550 million kWh produced, 160 kWh per capita (1989)
Industries: mining, mineral processing, consumer products (including textiles, footwear, and cigarettes), processed foods and beverages, cement, diamonds
Agriculture: cash crops—coffee, palm oil, rubber, quinine; food crops—cassava, bananas, root crops, corn
Illicit drugs: illicit producer of cannabis, mostly for domestic consumption
Aid: US commitments, including Ex-Im (FY70-88), $998 million; Western (non-US) countries, ODA and OOF bilateral commitments (1970-87), $6.0 billion; OPEC bilateral aid (1979-89), $35 million; Communist countries (1970-88), $263 million
Currency: zaïre (plural—zaïre); 1 zaïre (Z) = 100 makuta
Exchange rates: zaïre (Z) per US$1— 465.000 (January 1989), 381.445 (1989), 187.070 (1988), 112.403 (1987), 59.625 (1986), 49.873 (1985)
Fiscal year: calendar year

Communications

Railroads: 5,254 km total; 3,968 km 1.067-meter gauge (851 km electrified); 125 km 1.000-meter gauge; 136 km 0.615-meter gauge; 1,025 km 0.600-meter gauge
Highways: 146,500 km total; 2,550 km bituminous, 46,450 km gravel and improved earth; remainder unimproved earth

Inland waterways: 15,000 km including the Congo, its tributaries, and unconnected lakes
Pipelines: refined products 390 km
Ports: Matadi, Boma, Banana
Merchant marine: 4 ships (1,000 GRT or over) totaling 41,802 GRT/60,496 DWT; includes 1 passenger cargo, 3 cargo
Civil air: 38 major transport aircraft
Airports: 312 total, 258 usable; 25 with permanent-surface runways; 1 with runways over 3,659 m; 6 with runways 2,440-3,659 m; 71 with runways 1,220-2,439 m
Telecommunications: barely adequate wire and radio relay service; 31,200 telephones; stations—10 AM, 4 FM, 18 TV; satellite earth stations—1 Atlantic Ocean INTELSAT, 14 domestic

Defense Forces

Branches: Army, Navy, Air Force, National Gendarmerie, Logistics Corps, Special Presidential Division
Military manpower: males 15-49, 7,970,619; 4,057,561 fit for military service
Defense expenditures: $67 million (1988)

Zambia

300 km

Boundary representation is not necessarily authoritative

See regional map VII

Geography

Total area: 752,610 km²; land area: 740,720 km²
Comparative area: slightly larger than Texas
Land boundaries: 5,664 km total; Angola 1,110 km, Malawi 837 km, Mozambique 419 km, Namibia 233 km, Tanzania 338 km, Zaire 1,930 km, Zimbabwe 797 km
Coastline: none—landlocked
Maritime claims: none—landlocked
Disputes: quadripoint with Botswana, Namibia, and Zimbabwe is in disagreement; Tanzania-Zaire-Zambia tripoint in Lake Tanganyika may no longer be indefinite since it is reported that the indefinite section of the Zaire-Zambia boundary has been settled
Climate: tropical; modified by altitude; rainy season (October to April)
Terrain: mostly high plateau with some hills and mountains
Natural resources: copper, cobalt, zinc, lead, coal, emeralds, gold, silver, uranium, hydropower potential
Land use: 7% arable land; NEGL% permanent crops; 47% meadows and pastures; 27% forest and woodland; 19% other; includes NEGL% irrigated
Environment: deforestation; soil erosion; desertification
Note: landlocked

People

Population: 8,112,782 (July 1990), growth rate 3.2% (1990)
Birth rate: 49 births/1,000 population (1990)
Death rate: 12 deaths/1,000 population (1990)
Net migration rate: −6 migrants/1,000 population (1990)
Infant mortality rate: 80 deaths/1,000 live births (1990)

Zambia (continued)

Life expectancy at birth: 55 years male, 58 years female (1990)
Total fertility rate: 7.0 children born/woman (1990)
Nationality: noun—Zambian(s); adjective—Zambian
Ethnic divisions: 98.7% African, 1.1% European, 0.2% other
Religion: 50-75% Christian, 1% Muslim and Hindu, remainder indigenous beliefs
Language: English (official); about 70 indigenous languages
Literacy: 75.7%
Labor force: 2,455,000; 85% agriculture; 6% mining, manufacturing, and construction; 9% transport and services
Organized labor: about 238,000 wage earners are unionized

Government

Long-form name: Republic of Zambia
Type: one-party state
Capital: Lusaka
Administrative divisions: 9 provinces; Central, Copperbelt, Eastern, Luapula, Lusaka, Northern, North-Western, Southern, Western
Independence: 24 October 1964 (from UK; formerly Northern Rhodesia)
Constitution: 25 August 1973
Legal system: based on English common law and customary law; judicial review of legislative acts in an ad hoc constitutional council; has not accepted compulsory ICJ jurisdiction
National holiday: Independence Day, 24 October (1964)
Executive branch: president, prime minister, Cabinet
Legislative branch: unicameral National Assembly
Judicial branch: Supreme Court
Leaders: *Chief of State*—President Dr. Kenneth David KAUNDA (since 24 October 1964);
Head of Government—Prime Minister Gen. Malimba MASHEKE (since 15 March 1989)
Political parties and leaders: only party—United National Independence Party (UNIP), Kenneth Kaunda
Suffrage: universal at age 18
Elections: *President*—last held 26 October 1988 (next to be held October 1993); results—President Kenneth Kaunda was reelected without opposition;
National Assembly—last held 26 October 1988 (next to be held October 1993); results—UNIP is the only party; seats—(136 total, 125 elected) UNIP 125
Communists: no Communist party
Member of: ACP, AfDB, CCC, Commonwealth, FAO, G-77, GATT (de facto), IAEA, IBRD, ICAO, IDA, IEA, IFAD, IFC, ILO, ILZSG, IMF, INTELSAT, INTERPOL, IPU, ITU, NAM, OAU, SADCC, UN, UNESCO, UPU, WHO, WIPO, WMO, WTO
Diplomatic representation: Ambassador Paul J. F. LUSAKA; Chancery at 2419 Massachusetts Avenue NW, Washington DC 20008; telephone (202) 265-9717 through 9721; *US*—Ambassador Jeffrey DAVIDOW; Embassy at corner of Independence Avenue and United Nations Avenue, Lusaka (mailing address is P. O. Box 31617, Lusaka); telephone [2601] 214911
Flag: green with a panel of three vertical bands of red (hoist side), black, and orange below a soaring orange eagle, on the outer edge of the flag

Economy

Overview: Despite temporary growth in 1988, the economy has been in decline for more than a decade with falling imports and growing foreign debt. Economic difficulties stem from a sustained drop in copper production and ineffective economic policies. In 1988 real GDP stood only slightly higher than that of 10 years before, while an annual population growth of more than 3% has brought a decline in per capita GDP of 25% during the same period. A high inflation rate has also added to Zambia's economic woes in recent years.
GDP: $4.0 billion, per capita $530; real growth rate 6.7% (1988)
Inflation rate (consumer prices): 55.7% (1988)
Unemployment rate: NA%
Budget: revenues $570 million; expenditures $939 million, including capital expenditures of $36 million (1988 est.)
Exports: $1,184 million (f.o.b., 1988); *commodities*—copper, zinc, cobalt, lead, tobacco; *partners*—EC, Japan, South Africa, US
Imports: $687 million (c.i.f., 1988); *commodities*—machinery, transportation equipment, foodstuffs, fuels, manufactures; *partners*—EC, Japan, South Africa, US
External debt: $6.9 billion (December 1989)
Industrial production: growth rate NA% (1986)
Electricity: 1,900,000 kW capacity; 8,245 million kWh produced, 1,050 kWh per capita (1989)
Industries: copper mining and processing, transport, construction, foodstuffs, beverages, chemicals, textiles, and fertilizer
Agriculture: accounts for 15% of GDP and 85% of labor force; crops—corn (food staple), sorghum, rice, peanuts, sunflower, tobacco, cotton, sugarcane, cassava; cattle, goats, beef, eggs produced; marginally self-sufficient in corn
Aid: US commitments, including Ex-Im (1970-88), $466 million; Western (non-US) countries, ODA and OOF bilateral commitments (1970-87), $4.2 billion; OPEC bilateral aid (1979-89), $60 million; Communist countries (1970-88), $533 million
Currency: Zambian kwacha (plural—kwacha); 1 Zambian kwacha (ZK) = 100 ngwee
Exchange rates: Zambian kwacha (ZK) per US$1—21.7865 (January 1990), 12.9032 (1989), 8.2237 (1988), 8.8889 (1987), 7.3046 (1986), 2.7137 (1985)
Fiscal year: calendar year

Communications

Railroads: 1,266 km, all 1.067-meter gauge; 13 km double track
Highways: 36,370 km total; 6,500 km paved, 7,000 km crushed stone, gravel, or stabilized soil; 22,870 km improved and unimproved earth
Inland waterways: 2,250 km, including Zambezi and Luapula Rivers, Lake Tanganyika
Pipelines: 1,724 km crude oil
Ports: Mpulungu (lake port)
Civil air: 6 major transport aircraft
Airports: 121 total, 106 usable; 13 with permanent-surface runways; 1 with runways over 3,659 m; 4 with runways 2,440-3,659 m; 22 with runways 1,220-2,439 m
Telecommunications: facilities are among the best in Sub-Saharan Africa; high-capacity radio relay connects most larger towns and cities; 71,700 telephones; stations—11 AM, 3 FM, 9 TV; satellite earth stations—1 Indian Ocean INTELSAT and 1 Atlantic Ocean INTELSAT

Defense Forces

Branches: Army, Air Force, Police, Paramilitary
Military manpower: males 15-49, 1,683,758; 883,283 fit for military service
Defense expenditures: NA

Zimbabwe

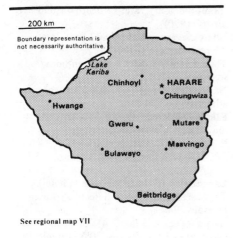

200 km

Boundary representation is not necessarily authoritative

Lake Kariba

Chinhoyi ★ HARARE
• Chitungwiza
• Hwange
Gweru • • Mutare
• Masvingo
• Bulawayo

• Beitbridge

See regional map VII

Geography

Total area: 390,580 km²; land area: 386,670 km²
Comparative area: slightly larger than Montana
Land boundaries: 3,066 km total; Botswana 813 km, Mozambique 1,231 km, South Africa 225 km, Zambia 797 km
Coastline: none—landlocked
Maritime claims: none—landlocked
Disputes: quadripoint with Botswana, Namibia, and Zambia is in disagreement
Climate: tropical; moderated by altitude; rainy season (November to March)
Terrain: mostly high plateau with higher central plateau (high veld); mountains in east
Natural resources: coal, chromium ore, asbestos, gold, nickel, copper, iron ore, vanadium, lithium, tin
Land use: 7% arable land; NEGL% permanent crops; 12% meadows and pastures; 62% forest and woodland; 19% other; includes NEGL% irrigated
Environment: recurring droughts; floods and severe storms are rare; deforestation; soil erosion; air and water pollution; desertification
Note: landlocked

People

Population: 10,392,161 (July 1990), growth rate 3.3% (1990)
Birth rate: 42 births/1,000 population (1990)
Death rate: 9 deaths/1,000 population (1990)
Net migration rate: 0 migrants/1,000 population (1990)
Infant mortality rate: 65 deaths/1,000 live births (1990)
Life expectancy at birth: 59 years male, 63 years female (1990)
Total fertility rate: 5.8 children born/woman (1990)

Nationality: noun—Zimbabwean(s); adjective—Zimbabwean
Ethnic divisions: 98% African (71% Shona, 16% Ndebele, 11% other); 1% white, 1% mixed and Asian
Religion: 50% syncretic (part Christian, part indigenous beliefs), 25% Christian, 24% indigenous beliefs, a few Muslim
Language: English (official); Shona and Ndebele
Literacy: 74%
Labor force: 3,100,000; 74% agriculture, 16% transport and services, 10% mining, manufacturing, construction (1987)
Organized labor: 17% of wage and salary earners have union membership

Government

Long-form name: Republic of Zimbabwe
Type: parliamentary democracy
Capital: Harare
Administrative divisions: 8 provinces; Manicaland, Mashonaland Central, Mashonaland East, Mashonaland West, Matabeleland North, Matabeleland South, Midlands, Victoria (commonly called Masvingo)
Independence: 18 April 1980 (from UK; formerly Southern Rhodesia)
Constitution: 21 December 1979
Legal system: mixture of Roman-Dutch and English common law
National holiday: Independence Day, 18 April (1980)
Executive branch: president, vice president, Cabinet
Legislative branch: unicameral Parliament
Judicial branch: Supreme Court
Leaders: *Chief of State and Head of Government*—Executive President Robert Gabriel MUGABE (since 31 December 1987); Vice President Simon Vengai MUZENDA (since 31 December 1987)
Political parties and leaders: Zimbabwe African National Union-Patriotic Front (ZANU-PF), Robert Mugabe; Zimbabwe African National Union-Sithole (ZANU-S), Ndabaningi Sithole; Zimbabwe Unity Movement (ZUM), Edgar Tekere
Suffrage: universal at age 18
Elections: *President*—last held 28-30 March 1990 (next to be held March 1995); results—President Robert Mugabe 78.3%; Edgar Tekere 21.7%;
Parliament—last held 28-30 March 1990 (next to be held March 1993); results—percent of vote by party NA; seats—(150 total, 120 elected) ZANU 116, ZUM 2, ZANU-S 1, to be determined 1
Communists: no Communist party
Member of: ACP, AfDB, CCC, Commonwealth, FAO, G-77, GATT, IAEA, IBRD, ICAO, IDA, IFAD, IFC, ILO,

IMF, INTERPOL, NAM, OAU, SADCC, UN, UNESCO, UPU, WFTU, WHO, WMO
Diplomatic representation: Counselor (Political Affairs), Head of Chancery, Ambassador Stanislaus Garikai CHIGWEDERE; Chancery at 2852 McGill Terrace NW, Washington DC 20008; telephone (202) 332-7100; *US*—Ambassador-designate Steven RHODES; Embassy at 172 Rhodes Avenue, Harare (mailing address is P. O. Box 3340, Harare); telephone [263] (14) 794-521
Flag: seven equal horizontal bands of green, yellow, red, black, red, yellow, and green with a white equilateral triangle edged in black based on the hoist side; a yellow Zimbabwe bird is superimposed on a red five-pointed star in the center of the triangle

Economy

Overview: Agriculture employs a majority of the labor force and supplies almost 40% of exports. The agro-based manufacturing sector produces a variety of goods and contributes about 25% to GDP. Mining accounts for only 5% of both GDP and employment, but supplies of minerals and metals account for about 40% of exports. Wide year-to-year fluctuations in agricultural production over the past six years resulted in not only an uneven growth rate, but one that did not equal the 3% annual increase in population.
GDP: $4.6 billion, per capita $470; real growth rate 5.3% (1988 est.)
Inflation rate (consumer prices): 7.4% (1988)
Unemployment rate: at least 20% (1988 est.)
Budget: revenues $2.4 billion; expenditures $3.0 billion, including capital expenditures of $290 million (FY90)
Exports: $1.6 billion (f.o.b., 1988); *commodities*—agricultural 34% (tobacco 21%, other 13%), manufactures 19%, gold 11%, ferrochrome 11%, cotton 6%; *partners*—Europe 55% (EC 41%, Netherlands 6%, other 8%), Africa 22% (South Africa 12%, other 10%), US 6%
Imports: $1.1 billion (c.i.f., 1988); *commodities*—machinery and transportation equipment 37%, other manufactures 22%, chemicals 16%, fuels 15%; *partners*—EC 31%, Africa 29% (South Africa 21%, other 8%), US 8%, Japan 4%
External debt: $2.96 billion (December 1989 est.)
Industrial production: growth rate 4.7% (1988 est.)
Electricity: 2,036,000 kW capacity; 5,460 million kWh produced, 540 kWh per capita (1989)

Zimbabwe *(continued)*

Industries: mining, steel, clothing and footwear, chemicals, foodstuffs, fertilizer, beverage, transportation equipment, wood products

Agriculture: accounts for about 15% of GDP and employs over 70% of population; 40% of land area divided into 6,000 large commercial farms and 42% in communal lands; crops—corn (food staple), cotton, tobacco, wheat, coffee, sugarcane, peanuts; livestock—cattle, sheep, goats, pigs; self-sufficient in food

Aid: US commitments, including Ex-Im (FY80-88), $359 million; Western (non-US) countries, ODA and OOF bilateral commitments (1970-87), $2.0 billion; OPEC bilateral aid (1979-89), $36 million; Communist countries (1970-88), $134 million

Currency: Zimbabwean dollar (plural—dollars); 1 Zimbabwean dollar (Z$) = 100 cents

Exchange rates: Zimbabwean dollars (Z$) per US$1—2.2873 (January 1990), 2.1133 (1989), 1.8018 (1988), 1.6611 (1987), 1.6650 (1986), 1.6119 (1985)

Fiscal year: 1 July-30 June

Communications

Railroads: 2,745 km 1.067-meter gauge; 42 km double track; 355 km electrified

Highways: 85,237 km total; 15,800 km paved, 39,090 km crushed stone, gravel, stabilized soil: 23,097 km improved earth; 7,250 km unimproved earth

Inland waterways: Lake Kariba is a potential line of communication

Pipelines: 8 km, refined products

Civil air: 12 major transport aircraft

Airports: 506 total, 420 usable; 23 with permanent-surface runways; 2 with runways over 3,659 m; 3 with runways 2,440-3,659 m; 37 with runways 1,220-2,439 m

Telecommunications: system was once one of the best in Africa, but now suffers from poor maintenance; consists of radio relay links, open-wire lines, and radio communications stations; 247,000 telephones; stations—8 AM, 18 FM, 8 TV; 1 Atlantic Ocean INTELSAT earth station

Defense Forces

Branches: Zimbabwe National Army, Air Force of Zimbabwe, Police Support Unit, People's Militia

Military manpower: males 15-49, 2,173,448; 1,342,920 fit for military service

Defense expenditures: $446.7 million (FY89 est.)

Taiwan

100 km

Taiwan Strait

Chi-lung
Taipei
Su-ao
Chang-hua
Hua-lien
Pescadores
Taiwan
Philippine Sea
Ma-kung
Tai-nan
Kao-hsiung
T'ai-tung

Quemoy and Matsu islands are not shown

See regional map VIII

Geography

Total area: 35,980 km²; land area: 32,260 km²; includes the Pescadores, Matsu, and Quemoy

Comparative area: slightly less than three times the size of Connecticut

Land boundaries: none

Coastline: 1,448 km

Maritime claims:
Extended economic zone: 200 nm
Territorial sea: 12 nm

Disputes: involved in complex dispute over the Spratly Islands with China, Malaysia, Philippines, and Vietnam; Paracel Islands occupied by China, but claimed by Vietnam and Taiwan; Japanese-administered Senkaku-shotō (Senkaku Islands) claimed by China and Taiwan

Climate: tropical; marine; rainy season during southwest monsoon (June to August); cloudiness is persistent and extensive all year

Terrain: eastern two-thirds mostly rugged mountains; flat to gently rolling plains in west

Natural resources: small deposits of coal, natural gas, limestone, marble, and asbestos

Land use: 24% arable land; 1% permanent crops; 5% meadows and pastures; 55% forest and woodland; 15% other; 14% irrigated

Environment: subject to earthquakes and typhoons

People

Population: 20,546,664 (July 1990), growth rate 1.1% (1990)

Birth rate: 16 births/1,000 population (1990)

Death rate: 5 deaths/1,000 population (1990)

Net migration rate: NEGL migrants/1,000 population (1990)

Infant mortality rate: 17 deaths/1,000 live births (1990)

Life expectancy at birth: 72 years male, 77 years female (1990)

Total fertility rate: 1.7 children born/woman (1990)

Nationality: noun—Chinese (sing., pl.); adjective—Chinese

Ethnic divisions: 84% Taiwanese, 14% mainland Chinese, 2% aborigine

Religion: 93% mixture of Buddhist, Confucian, and Taoist; 4.5% Christian; 2.5% other

Language: Mandarin Chinese (official); Taiwanese and Hakka dialects also used

Literacy: 94%

Labor force: 7,880,000; 41% industry and commerce, 32% services, 20% agriculture, 7% civil administration (1986)

Organized labor: 1,300,000 or about 18.4% (government controlled) (1983)

Administration

Long-form name: none

Type: one-party presidential regime; opposition political parties legalized in March, 1989

Capital: Taipei

Administrative divisions: 16 counties (hsien, singular and plural), 5 municipalities* (shih, singular and plural), 2 special municipalities** (chuan-shih, singular and plural); Chang-hua, Chia-i, Chia-i*, Chi-lung*, Hsin-chu, Hsin-chu*, Hua-lien, I-lan, Kao-hsiung, Kao-hsiung**, Miao-li, Nan-t'ou, P'eng-hu, P'ing-tung, T'ai-chung, T'ai-chung*, T'ai-nan, T'ai-nan*, T'ai-pei, T'ai-pei**, T'ai-tung, T'ao-yüan, Yün-lin; note—the Wade-Giles system is used for romanization

Constitution: 25 December 1947

Legal system: based on civil law system; accepts compulsory ICJ jurisdiction, with reservations

National holiday: National Day (Anniversary of the Revolution), 10 October (1911)

Executive branch: president, vice president, premier of the Executive Yüan, vice premier of the Executive Yüan, Executive Yüan

Legislative branch: unicameral Legislative Yüan

Judicial branch: Judicial Yüan

Leaders: *Chief of State*—President LI Teng-hui (since 13 January 1988); Vice President LI Yuan-tzu (will take office 20 May 1990);
Head of Government—Premier (President of the Executive Yüan) HAO Po-ts'un (since May 2 1990); Vice Premier (Vice President of the Executive Yüan) SHIH Ch'i-yang (since NA July 1988)

Political parties and leaders: Kuomintang (Nationalist Party), LI Teng-hui, chairman; Democratic Socialist Party and Young China Party controlled by Kuomintang; Democratic Progressive Party (DPP); Labor Party; 27 other minor parties

Suffrage: universal at age 20

Elections: *President*—last held 21 March 1990 (next to be held March 1996); results—President Li Teng-hui was elected by the National Assembly;
Vice President—last held 22 March 1990 (next to be held March 1996); results—Li Yuan-tzu was elected by the National Assembly;
Legislative Yüan—last held 2 December 1989 (next to be held December 1992); results—KMT 65%, DPP 33%, independents 2%; seats—(304 total, 102 elected) KMT 78, DPP 21, independents 3

Member of: expelled from UN General Assembly and Security Council on 25 October 1971 and withdrew on same date from other charter-designated subsidiary organs; expelled from IMF/World Bank group April/May 1980; member of ADB and PECC, seeking to join GATT and/or MFA; attempting to retain membership in ICAC, ISO, INTELSAT, INTERPOL, IWC—International Wheat Council; suspended from IAEA in 1972, but still allows IAEA controls over extensive atomic development

Diplomatic representation: none; unofficial commercial and cultural relations with the people of the US are maintained through a private instrumentality, the Coordination Council for North American Affairs (CCNAA) with headquarters in Taipei and field offices in Washington and 10 other US cities with all addresses and telephone numbers NA; *US*—unofficial commercial and cultural relations with the people of Taiwan are maintained through a private institution, the American Institute in Taiwan (AIT), which has offices in Taipei at 7 Lane 134, Hsin Yi Road, Section 3 with telephone 002 [886] (2) 709-2000 and in Kao-hsiung at 88 Wu Fu 3rd Road with telephone NA

Flag: red with a dark blue rectangle in the upper hoist-side corner bearing a white sun with 12 triangular rays

Economy

Overview: Taiwan has a dynamic capitalist economy with considerable government guidance of investment and foreign trade and partial government ownership of some large banks and industrial firms. Real growth in GNP has averaged about 9% a year during the past three decades. Export growth has been even faster and has provided the impetus for industrialization. Agriculture contributes about 6% to GNP, down from 35% in 1952. Taiwan currently ranks as number 13 among major trading countries. Traditional labor-intensive industries are steadily being replaced with more capital- and technology-intensive industries.

GNP: $121.4 billion, per capita $6,000; real growth rate 7.2% (1989)

Inflation rate (consumer prices): 5.0% (1989)

Unemployment rate: 1.7% (1989)

Budget: revenues $25.9 billion; expenditures $33.2 billion, including capital expenditures of $NA (FY89)

Exports: $66.2 billion (f.o.b., 1989); *commodities*—textiles 9.7%, electrical machinery 19.0%, general machinery and equipment 14%, telecommunications equipment 9%, basic metals and metal products 7.4%, foodstuffs 0.9%, plywood and wood products 1.3%; *partners*—US 36.2%, Japan 13.7%

Imports: $52.2 billion (c.i.f., 1989); *commodities*—machinery and equipment 15.9%, crude oil 5%, chemical and chemical products 11.1%, basic metals 7.4%, foodstuffs 2.0%; *partners*—Japan 31%, US 23%, Saudi Arabia 8.6%

External debt: $1.0 billion (December 1989 est.)

Industrial production: growth rate 4.1% (1988)

Electricity: 17,000,000 kW capacity; 68,000 million kWh produced, 3,360 kWh per capita (1989)

Industries: textiles, clothing, chemicals, electronics, food processing, plywood, sugar milling, cement, shipbuilding, petroleum

Agriculture: accounts for 6% of GNP and 20% of labor force (includes part-time farmers); heavily subsidized sector; major crops—rice, sugarcane, sweet potatoes, fruits, vegetables; livestock—hogs, poultry, beef, milk, cattle; not self-sufficient in wheat, soybeans, corn; fish catch expanding, 1.1 million metric tons in (1987)

Aid: US, including Ex-Im (FY46-82), $4.6 billion; Western (non-US) countries, ODA and OOF bilateral commitments (1970-87), $439 million

Currency: new Taiwan dollar (plural—dollars); 1 new Taiwan dollar (NT$) = 100 cents

Exchange rates: new Taiwan dollars per US$1—26.3 (March 1990), 26.156 (December 1989), 28.589 (1988), 31.845 (1987), 37.838 (1986), 39.849 (1985)

Fiscal year: 1 July-30 June

Communications

Railroads: about 1,075 km common carrier lines and over 3,800 km industrial lines; common carrier lines consist of the 1.067-meter gauge 708 km West Line and the 367 km East Line; a 98.25 km South Link Line connection is under construction; common carrier lines owned by the government and operated by the Railway Administration under Ministry of Communications; industrial lines owned and operated by government enterprises

Highways: 18,800 km total; 15,800 km bituminous or concrete, 2,500 km crushed stone or gravel, 500 km graded earth

Pipelines: 615 km refined products, 97 km natural gas

Ports: Kao-hsiung, Chi-lung, Hua-lien, Su-ao, T'ai-tung

Merchant marine: 218 ships (1,000 GRT or over) totaling 5,061,960 GRT/ 7,634,074 DWT; includes 1 short-sea passenger, 61 cargo, 13 refrigerated cargo, 71 container, 14 petroleum, oils, and lubricants (POL) tanker, 3 combination ore/oil, 1 specialized tanker, 54 bulk

Airports: 38 total, 37 usable; 32 with permanent-surface runways; 3 with runways over 3,659 m; 16 with runways 2,440-3,659 m; 8 with runways 1,220-2,439 m

Telecommunications: best developed system in Asia outside of Japan; 6,000,000 telephones; extensive microwave transmission links on east and west coasts; stations—91 AM, 23 FM, 15 TV (13 relays); 8,000,000 radio receivers; 6,000,000 TV sets (5,300,000 color, 700,000 monochrome); satellite earth stations—1 Pacific Ocean INTELSAT and 1 Indian Ocean INTELSAT; submarine cable links to Japan (Okinawa), the Philippines, Guam, Singapore, Hong Kong, Indonesia, Australia, Middle East, and Western Europe

Defense Forces

Branches: Army, Navy (including Marines), Air Force, Garrison Command

Military manpower: males 15-49, 5,809,354; 4,534,950 fit for military service; about 185,235 currently reach military age (19) annually

Defense expenditures: 6.8% of GNP, or $8.2 billion (FY90 est.)

Appendix A:

The United Nations System

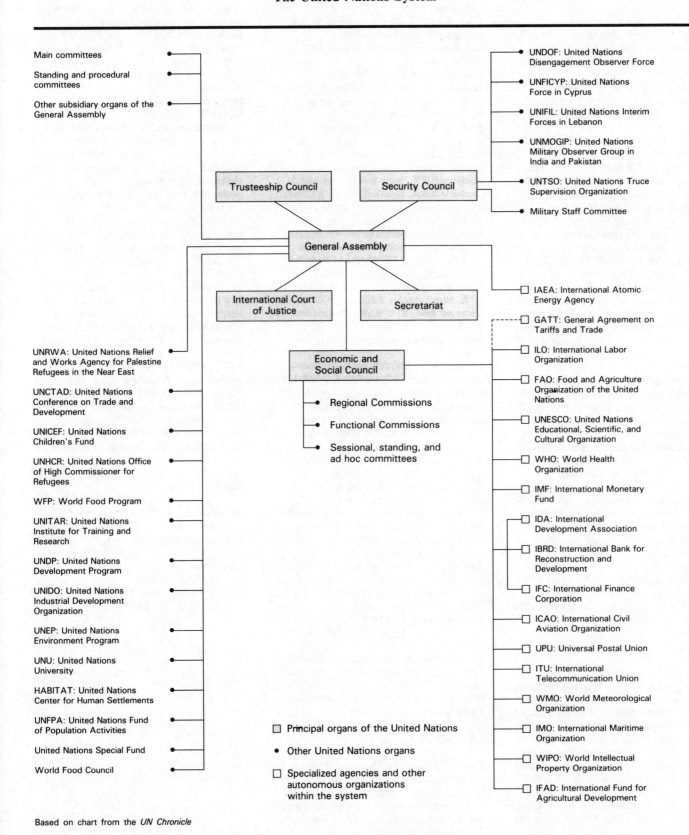

Main committees

Standing and procedural committees

Other subsidiary organs of the General Assembly

UNRWA: United Nations Relief and Works Agency for Palestine Refugees in the Near East

UNCTAD: United Nations Conference on Trade and Development

UNICEF: United Nations Children's Fund

UNHCR: United Nations Office of High Commissioner for Refugees

WFP: World Food Program

UNITAR: United Nations Institute for Training and Research

UNDP: United Nations Development Program

UNIDO: United Nations Industrial Development Organization

UNEP: United Nations Environment Program

UNU: United Nations University

HABITAT: United Nations Center for Human Settlements

UNFPA: United Nations Fund of Population Activities

United Nations Special Fund

World Food Council

Trusteeship Council

Security Council

General Assembly

International Court of Justice

Secretariat

Economic and Social Council

Regional Commissions

Functional Commissions

Sessional, standing, and ad hoc committees

UNDOF: United Nations Disengagement Observer Force

UNFICYP: United Nations Force in Cyprus

UNIFIL: United Nations Interim Forces in Lebanon

UNMOGIP: United Nations Military Observer Group in India and Pakistan

UNTSO: United Nations Truce Supervision Organization

Military Staff Committee

IAEA: International Atomic Energy Agency

GATT: General Agreement on Tariffs and Trade

ILO: International Labor Organization

FAO: Food and Agriculture Organization of the United Nations

UNESCO: United Nations Educational, Scientific, and Cultural Organization

WHO: World Health Organization

IMF: International Monetary Fund

IDA: International Development Association

IBRD: International Bank for Reconstruction and Development

IFC: International Finance Corporation

ICAO: International Civil Aviation Organization

UPU: Universal Postal Union

ITU: International Telecommunication Union

WMO: World Meteorological Organization

IMO: International Maritime Organization

WIPO: World Intellectual Property Organization

IFAD: International Fund for Agricultural Development

□ Principal organs of the United Nations

● Other United Nations organs

□ Specialized agencies and other autonomous organizations within the system

Based on chart from the *UN Chronicle*

352

Appendix B:

International Organizations

A	ACC	Arab Cooperation Council
	ACP	African, Caribbean, and Pacific Countries (associated with the EC)
	ADB	Asian Development Bank
	AfDB	African Development Bank
	AIOEC	Association of Iron Ore Exporting Countries
	. . .	Andean Pact
	ANRPC	Association of Natural Rubber Producing Countries
	ANZUS	ANZUS Council
	APC	African Peanut (Groundnut) Council
	. . .	Arab League (League of Arab States)
	ASEAN	Association of Southeast Asian Nations
	ASPAC	Asian and Pacific Council
	ASSIMER	International Mercury Producers Association
	. . .	Association of Tin Producing Countries
B	Benelux	Belgium, Netherlands, Luxembourg Economic Union
	BLEU	Belgium-Luxembourg Economic Union
C	CACM	Central American Common Market
	CARICOM	Caribbean Community and Common Market
	CCC	Customs Cooperation Council
	CDB	Caribbean Development Bank
	CEAO	West African Economic Community
	CEMA	Council for Mutual Economic Assistance
	CENTO	Central Treaty Organization
	CIPEC	Intergovernmental Council of Copper Exporting Countries
	. . .	Colombo Plan
	. . .	Commonwealth
	. . .	Conference of East and Central African States
	. . .	Council of Europe
D	DAC	Development Assistance Committee (OECD)
E	EAMA	African States associated with the EC
	EC	European Communities
	ECA	Economic Commission for Africa (UN)
	ECE	Economic Commission for Europe (UN)
	ECLA	Economic Commission for Latin America (UN)
	ECOSOC	Economic and Social Council (UN)
	ECOWAS	Economic Community of West African States
	ECWA	Economic Commission for Western Asia (UN)
	EFTA	European Free Trade Association
	EIB	European Investment Bank
	EMS	European Monetary System
	ENTENTE	Council of the Entente
	ESA	European Space Agency
	ESCAP	Economic and Social Commission for Asia and the Pacific (UN)
F	FAO	Food and Agriculture Organization (UN)

G	G-77	Group of 77
	. . .	Group of Eight
	GATT	General Agreement on Tariffs and Trade (UN)
	GCC	Gulf Cooperation Council
I	IADB	Inter-American Defense Board
	IAEA	International Atomic Energy Agency (UN)
	IATP	International Association of Tungsten Producers
	IBA	International Bauxite Association
	IBEC	International Bank for Economic Cooperation
	IBRD	International Bank for Reconstruction and Development (World Bank, UN)
	ICAC	International Cotton Advisory Committee
	ICAO	International Civil Aviation Organization (UN)
	ICCO	International Cocoa Organization
	ICEM	Intergovernmental Committee for European Migration
	ICES	International Cooperation in Ocean Exploration
	ICJ	International Court of Justice (UN)
	ICO	International Coffee Organization
	IDA	International Development Association (IBRD affiliate, UN)
	IDB	Inter-American Development Bank
	IDB	Islamic Development Bank
	IEA	International Energy Agency (associated with OECD)
	IFAD	International Fund for Agricultural Development (UN)
	IFC	International Finance Corporation (IBRD affiliate, UN)
	IHO	International Hydrographic Organization
	ILO	International Labor Organization (UN)
	ILZSG	International Lead and Zinc Study Group
	IMF	International Monetary Fund (UN)
	IMO	International Maritime Organization (UN)
	INRO	International Natural Rubber Organization
	INTELSAT	International Telecommunications Satellite Organization
	INTERPOL	International Criminal Police Organization
	IOOC	International Olive Oil Council
	IPU	Inter-Parliamentary Union
	IRC	International Rice Council
	ISO	International Sugar Organization
	ITC	International Tin Council
	ITU	International Telecommunication Union (UN)
	IWC	International Whaling Commission
	IWC	International Wheat Council
L	. . .	Lake Chad Basin Commission
	LAIA	Latin American Integration Association
M	. . .	Mano River Commission
	. . .	Mekong Committee
N	. . .	Niger River Commission
	NAM	Nonaligned Movement
	NATO	North Atlantic Treaty Organization
	. . .	Nordic Council

O	OAPEC	Organization of Arab Petroleum Exporting Countries
	OAS	Organization of American States
	OAU	Organization of African Unity
	OCAM	Afro-Malagasy and Mauritian Common Organization
	ODECA	Organization of Central American States
	OECD	Organization for Economic Cooperation and Development
	OECS	Organization of Eastern Caribbean States
	OIC	Organization of the Islamic Conference
	OMVS	Organization for the Development of the Senegal River Valley
	OPEC	Organization of Petroleum Exporting Countries
P	PAHO	Pan American Health Organization
S	SAARC	South Asian Association for Regional Cooperation
	SADCC	Southern African Development Coordination Conference
	SELA	Latin American Economic System
	SPC	South Pacific Commission
	SPEC	South Pacific Bureau for Economic Cooperation
	SPF	South Pacific Forum
T	TC	Trusteeship Council (UN)
	TDB	Trade and Development Board (UN)
U	UDEAC	Central African Customs and Economic Union
	UEAC	Union of Central African States
	UN	United Nations
	UNCTAD	UN Conference on Trade and Development
	UNDP	UN Development Program
	UNESCO	UN Educational, Scientific, and Cultural Organization
	UNICEF	UN Children's Fund
	UNIDO	UN Industrial Development Organization
	UPEB	Union of Banana Exporting Countries
	UPU	Universal Postal Union (UN)
W	. . .	Warsaw Pact
	WCL	World Confederation of Labor
	WEU	Western European Union
	WFC	World Food Council (UN)
	WFTU	World Federation of Trade Unions
	WHO	World Health Organization (UN)
	WIPO	World Intellectual Property Organization (UN)
	WMO	World Meteorological Organization (UN)
	WPC	World Peace Council
	WSG	International Wool Study Group
	WTO	World Tourism Organization

Country	ADB	ARAB LEAGUE	ASEAN	CACM	CARICOM	CEMA	EC	G-77	GCC	IDB[a]	IDB[b]	INTELSAT	LAIA	NAM	NATO	OAPEC	OAS
Afghanistan	•							•			•	•		•			
Albania						• d											
Algeria		•						•			•	•		•		•	
Andorra[c]																	
Angola								•				•		•			
Antigua and Barbuda					•			•									•
Argentina								•		•		•	•	•			•
Australia	•											•					
Austria	•									•		•					
Bahamas					•			•		•				•			•
Bahrain		•						•	•		•			•		•	
Bangladesh	•							•			•	•		•			
Barbados					•			•		•		•		•			•
Belgium	•						•			•		•			•		
Belize					•			•									
Benin								•						•			
Bhutan	•							•						•			
Bolivia								•		•		•	•	•			•
Botswana								•						•			
Brazil								•		•		•	•				•
Brunei			•														
Bulgaria						•											
Burkina								•			•	•		•			
Burma	•							•									
Burundi								•						•			
Cambodia	•							•						•			
Cameroon								•			•	•		•			
Canada	•									•		•			•		
Cape Verde								•						•			
Central African Republic								•				•		•			
Chad								•			•	•		•			
Chile								•		•		•	•				•
China, People's Republic of												•					
Colombia								•		•		•	•	•			•
Comoros								•			•			•			
Congo								•				•		•			
Cook Islands[c]	•																
Costa Rica				•				•		•		•					•
Cuba						•		•						•			• f
Cyprus								•				•		•			
Czechoslovakia						•											
Denmark	•						•			•		•			•		
Djibouti		•						•			•			•			
Dominica					•			•									•
Dominican Republic								•		•		•					•
Ecuador								•		•		•	•	•			•
Egypt		•						•			•	•		•		•	
El Salvador				•				•		•		•					•
Equatorial Guinea								•						•			
Ethiopia								•				•		•			

[a] Inter-American Development Bank [b] Islamic Development Bank [c] Not a member of UN

OAU	OECD	OIC	OPEC	SELA	WFTU	FAO	GATT	IAEA	IBRD	ICAO	ICJ	IDA	IFAD	IFC	ILO	IMF	IMO	ITU	UNESCO	UPU	WHO	WMO
		• e			•	•		•	•	•	•	•	•	•	•	•		•	•	•	•	•
					•	•		•			•							•	•	•	•	•
•		•	•			•	•	•	•	•	•	•	•		•	•	•	•	•	•	•	•
																			•			
•					•	•	•		•	•	•		•		•		•	•	•	•	•	•
						•			•	•	•	•			•	•		•	•	•	•	•
			•		•	•	•	•	•	•	•	•	•	•	•	•	•	•	•	•	•	•
	•					•	•	•	•	•	•	•		•	•	•	•	•	•	•	•	•
	•				•	•	•	•	•	•	•	•	•	•	•	•	•	•	•	•	•	•
						•	•	•	•	•	•	•		•	•	•	•	•	•	•	•	•
	•					•	•	•	•	•	•	•	•	•	•	•	•	•	•	•	•	•
	•				•	•	•	•	•	•	•	•	•	•	•	•	•	•	•	•	•	•
			•			•	•	•	•	•	•	•		•	•	•	•	•	•	•	•	•
	•					•	•	•	•	•	•	•		•	•	•	•	•	•	•	•	•
						•	•		•	•	•	•		•	•	•	•	•	•	•	•	•
•		•			•	•	•	•	•	•	•	•	•	•	•	•	•	•	•	•	•	•
						•			•	•	•	•		•	•	•		•	•	•	•	•
			•			•	•	•	•	•	•	•	•	•	•	•	•	•	•	•	•	•
•					•	•		•	•	•	•	•	•	•	•	•	•	•	•	•	•	•
			•		•	•	•	•	•	•	•	•	•	•	•	•	•	•	•	•	•	•
	•																•					
					•	•		•		•	•				•		•	•	•	•	•	•
•	•				•	•	•	•	•	•	•		•	•	•	•	•	•	•	•	•	•
						•		•	•	•	•			•	•	•	•	•	•	•	•	•
•						•	•	•	•	•	•	•	•	•	•	•	•	•	•	•	•	•
			•		•	•	•	•	•	•	•	•		•	•	•	•	•	•	•	•	•
	•					•	•	•	•	•	•	•	•	•	•	•	•	•	•	•	•	•
		•				•	•	•	•	•	•	•	•	•	•	•	•	•	•	•	•	•
•						•	•	•	•	•	•	•	•	•	•	•	•	•	•	•	•	•
•						•	•	•	•	•	•	•	•	•	•	•	•	•	•	•	•	•
						•	•	•	•	•	•	•	•	•	•	•	•	•	•	•	•	•
						•	•	•	•	•	•	•	•	•	•	•	•	•	•	•	•	•
			•		•	•	•	•	•	•	•	•	•	•	•	•	•	•	•	•	•	•
						•		•		•	•			•	•	•		•	•	•	•	•
		•			•	•	•	•	•	•	•	•	•	•	•	•	•	•	•	•	•	•
					•	•		•	•	•	•	•	•	•	•	•	•	•	•	•	•	•
					•	•		•		•	•	•		•	•	•	•	•	•	•	•	•
	•					•	•	•	•	•	•	•	•	•	•	•	•	•	•	•	•	•
•		•			•	•	•	•	•	•	•	•	•	•	•	•	•	•	•	•	•	•
						•	•	•	•	•	•	•	•	•	•	•	•	•	•	•	•	•
		•				•	•	•	•	•	•	•	•	•	•	•	•	•	•	•	•	•
			•		•	•	•	•	•	•	•	•	•	•	•	•	•	•	•	•	•	•
•	•				•	•	•	•	•	•	•	•	•	•	•	•	•	•	•	•	•	•
		•			•	•	•	•	•	•	•	•	•	•	•	•	•	•	•	•	•	•
•						•	•		•	•	•	•	•	•	•	•	•	•	•	•	•	•
•					•	•		•	•	•	•	•	•	•	•	•	•	•	•	•	•	•

d Ceased to participate in 1961   e Suspended   f Excluded since 1962

Country	International Organizations																
	ADB	ARAB LEAGUE	ASEAN	CACM	CARICOM	CEMA	EC	G-77	GCC	IDBa	IDBb	INTELSAT	LAIA	NAM	NATO	OAPEC	OAS
Fiji	•							•				•					
Finland	•									•		•					
France	•						•			•		•			•		
French Guianac																	
Gabon								•			•	•		•			
Gambia, The								•			•			•			
German Democratic Republic						•											
Germany, Federal Republic of	•						•			•		•			•		
Ghana								•				•		•			
Greece							•					•			•		
Grenada					•			•						•			•
Guadeloupec																	
Guatemala				•				•		•		•					•
Guinea								•			•	•		•			
Guinea-Bissau								•			•			•			
Guyana					•			•		•				•			
Haiti								•		•		•					•
Honduras				•				•		•		•					•
Hong Kongc	•																
Hungary						•											
Iceland												•			•		
India	•							•						•			
Indonesia	•		•					•			•	•		•			
Iran								•				•					
Iraq		•						•			•	•		•		•	
Ireland							•					•					
Israel										•		•					
Italy	•						•			•		•			•		
Ivory Coast								•				•		•			
Jamaica					•			•		•		•		•			•
Japan	•									•		•					
Jordan		•						•			•	•		•			
Kenya								•				•		•			
Kiribatic	•																
Korea, Northc								•						•			
Korea, Southc	•							•				•					
Kuwait		•						•	•		•	•		•		•	
Laos	•							•						•			
Lebanon		•						•			•	•		•			
Lesotho								•						•			
Liberia								•						•			
Libya		•						•			•	•		•		•	
Liechtensteinc												•					
Luxembourg							•					•			•		
Madagascar								•				•		•			
Malawi								•				•		•			
Malaysia	•		•					•			•	•		•			
Maldives	•							•			•			•			
Mali								•			•	•		•			

OAU	OECD	OIC	OPEC	SELA	WFTU	United Nations Organizations																
						FAO	GATT	IAEA	IBRD	ICAO	ICJ	IDA	IFAD	IFC	ILO	IMF	IMO	ITU	UNESCO	UPU	WHO	WMO
					•	•	•		•	•	•	•	•	•	•	•	•	•	•	•	•	•
	•					•	•	•	•	•	•	•	•	•	•	•	•	•	•	•	•	•
	•				•	•	•	•	•	•	•	•	•	•	•	•	•	•	•	•	•	•
					•																	
•		•	•			•	•	•	•	•	•	•	•	•	•	•	•	•	•	•	•	•
•	•				•	•	•	•	•	•	•	•	•	•	•	•	•	•	•	•	•	•
					•		•			•					•		•	•	•	•	•	•
	•					•	•	•	•	•	•	•	•	•	•	•	•	•	•	•	•	•
•					•	•	•	•	•	•	•	•	•	•	•	•	•	•	•	•	•	•
	•					•	•	•	•	•	•	•	•	•	•	•	•	•	•	•	•	•
				•		•	•		•	•	•	•	•	•	•	•		•	•	•	•	•
					•																	
				•	•	•		•	•	•	•	•	•	•	•	•	•	•	•	•	•	•
•		•				•			•	•	•	•	•	•	•	•	•	•	•	•	•	•
•		•			•	•	•		•	•	•	•	•	•	•	•	•	•	•	•	•	•
				•	•	•		•	•	•	•	•	•	•	•	•	•	•	•	•	•	•
				•	•	•	•	•	•	•	•	•	•	•	•	•	•	•	•	•	•	•
				•		•	•		•	•	•	•	•	•	•	•	•	•	•	•	•	•
					•												•			•		
					•	•	•	•	•	•	•			•	•	•	•	•	•	•	•	•
	•				•	•	•	•	•	•	•	•	•	•	•	•	•	•	•	•	•	•
		•	•		•	•	•	•	•	•	•	•	•	•	•	•	•	•	•	•	•	•
		•	•			•	•	•	•	•	•	•	•	•	•	•	•	•	•	•	•	•
		•	•		•	•	•	•	•	•	•	•	•	•	•	•	•	•	•	•	•	•
	•				•	•	•	•	•	•	•	•	•	•	•	•	•	•	•	•	•	•
					•	•	•	•	•	•	•	•	•	•	•	•	•	•	•	•	•	•
	•				•	•	•	•	•	•	•	•	•	•	•	•	•	•	•	•	•	•
•					•	•	•	•	•	•	•	•	•	•	•	•	•	•	•	•	•	•
				•	•	•	•	•	•	•	•	•	•	•	•	•	•	•	•	•	•	•
	•				•	•	•	•	•	•	•	•	•	•	•	•	•	•	•	•	•	•
		•				•	•	•	•	•	•	•	•	•	•	•	•	•	•	•	•	•
•						•	•	•	•	•	•	•	•	•	•	•	•	•	•	•	•	•
						•			•											•		
					•	•		•		•	•	•					•	•	•	•	•	•
						•	•	•		•	•	•	•		•	•	•	•	•	•	•	•
		•	•		•	•	•	•	•	•	•	•	•	•	•	•	•	•	•	•	•	•
					•	•		•	•	•	•	•	•	•	•	•		•	•	•	•	•
		•			•	•		•	•	•	•	•	•	•	•	•	•	•	•	•	•	•
•						•	•	•	•	•	•	•	•	•	•	•	•	•	•	•	•	•
•						•		•	•	•	•	•	•	•	•	•	•	•	•	•	•	•
•		•	•			•		•	•	•	•	•	•	•	•	•	•	•	•	•	•	•
											•								•	•		
	•					•		•		•	•	•		•	•	•	•	•	•	•	•	•
					•	•			•	•	•	•	•	•	•	•	•	•	•	•	•	•
		•				•		•	•	•	•	•	•	•	•	•	•	•	•	•	•	•
		•				•	•	•	•	•	•	•	•	•	•	•	•	•	•	•	•	•
•					•	•	•	•	•	•	•	•	•	•	•	•	•	•	•	•	•	•

Country	ADB	ARAB LEAGUE	ASEAN	CACM	CARICOM	CEMA	EC	G-77	GCC	IDB[a]	IDB[b]	INTELSAT	LAIA	NAM	NATO	OAPEC	OAS
Malta								•						•			
Martinique[c]																	
Mauritania		•						•		•	•			•			
Mauritius								•						•			
Mexico								•		•		•	•				•
Monaco[c]												•					
Mongolia						•											
Morocco		•						•		•	•			•			
Montserrat[c]					•												
Mozambique								•						•			
Namibia[c]																	
Nauru[c]																	
Nepal	•							•						•			
Netherlands	•						•			•		•			•		
Netherlands Antilles[c]																	
New Caledonia[c]																	
New Zealand	•											•					
Nicaragua				•				•		•		•		•			•
Niger								•			•	•		•			
Nigeria								•				•		•			
Norway	•											•			•		
Oman		•						•	•		•	•		•			
Pakistan	•							•			•	•		•			
Panama								•		•		•		•			•
Papua New Guinea	•							•				•					
Paraguay								•		•		•	•				•
Peru								•		•		•	•	•			•
Philippines	•		•					•				•					
Poland						•											
Portugal							•			•		•			•		
Qatar		•						•	•		•	•		•		•	
Reunion[c]																	
Romania						•		•									
Rwanda								•						•			
St. Kitts and Nevis					•												•
St. Lucia					•			•						•			•
St. Vincent and the Grenadines					•			•									•
San Marino[c]																	
Sao Tome and Principe								•						•			
Saudi Arabia		•						•	•		•	•		•		•	
Senegal								•			•	•		•			
Seychelles								•						•			
Sierra Leone								•			•			•			
Singapore	•		•					•				•		•			
Solomon Islands	•							•									
Somalia		•						•			•	•		•			
South Africa												•					
Spain							•			•		•			•		
Sri Lanka	•							•				•		•			
Sudan		•						•			•	•		•			

OAU	OECD	OIC	OPEC	SELA	WFTU	FAO	GATT	IAEA	IBRD	ICAO	ICJ	IDA	IFAD	IFC	ILO	IMF	IMO	ITU	UNESCO	UPU	WHO	WMO
						•	•		•	•	•		•		•	•	•	•	•		•	•	•
					•																		
•		•				•	•		•	•	•	•	•	•	•	•	•	•	•		•	•	•
•					•	•	•	•		•	•	•	•	•	•	•	•	•	•		•	•	•
			•			•				•	•	•	•	•	•	•	•	•	•		•	•	•
							•			•									•		•	•	•
					•					•					•				•		•		•
		•				•	•		•	•	•	•	•	•	•	•	•	•	•		•	•	•
																			•			
•						•	•		•	•	•	•		•		•		•	•		•	•	•
					•	•			•						•			•	•		•	•	
									•									•		•		
						•			•	•	•	•	•		•	•	•	•	•		•	•	•
	•					•	•		•	•	•	•	•	•	•	•	•	•	•		•	•	•
																					•		•
					•																		•
	•					•	•	•	•	•	•	•	•	•	•	•	•	•	•		•	•	•
				•	•	•	•	•	•	•	•	•	•	•	•	•	•	•	•		•	•	•
•		•				•	•	•	•	•	•	•	•	•	•	•	•	•	•		•	•	•
•			•			•	•	•	•	•	•	•	•	•	•	•	•	•	•		•	•	•
	•					•	•	•	•	•	•	•	•	•	•	•	•	•	•		•	•	•
	•				•	•	•	•	•	•	•	•	•	•	•	•	•	•	•		•	•	•
	•				•	•	•	•	•	•	•	•	•	•	•	•	•	•	•		•	•	•
				•		•	•	•	•	•	•	•	•	•	•	•	•	•	•		•	•	•
				•	•	•	•	•	•	•	•	•	•	•	•	•	•	•	•		•	•	•
					•	•	•	•	•	•	•	•	•	•	•	•	•	•	•		•	•	•
					•	•	•	•	•	•	•	•	•	•	•	•	•	•	•		•	•	•
	•					•	•	•	•	•	•	•		•	•	•	•	•	•		•	•	•
	•	•				•	•	•	•	•	•	•		•	•	•	•	•	•		•	•	•
					•																		
					•	•	•	•	•	•	•		•		•	•	•	•	•		•	•	•
•						•	•		•	•	•	•	•	•	•	•		•	•		•	•	•
						•			•		•				•			•			•		
					•	•	•		•	•	•	•	•	•	•	•			•		•	•	•
					•	•	•		•	•	•		•			•	•		•		•	•	
					•						•							•	•		•		
•						•	•		•	•	•	•	•	•	•	•		•	•		•	•	•
	•	•				•		•	•	•	•	•	•	•	•	•	•		•		•	•	•
•		•			•	•		•	•	•	•	•	•	•	•	•	•	•	•		•	•	•
•						•	•	•	•	•	•	•	•	•	•	•	•	•	•		•	•	•
•		•				•	•	•	•	•	•	•	•	•	•	•	•	•	•		•	•	•
						•	•	•	•	•		•	•	•	•	•	•	•	•		•	•	•
						•	•	•	•	•	•	•	•	•	•	•					•	•	•
•		•			•	•	•	•	•	•	•	•	•	•	•	•	•	•	•		•	•	•
					•	•	•	•	•	•	•	•	•	•	•	•		•	•				•
	•					•	•	•	•	•	•	•	•	•	•	•	•	•	•		•	•	•
					•	•	•	•	•	•	•	•	•	•	•	•		•	•		•	•	•
•					•	•		•	•	•	•	•	•	•	•	•		•	•		•	•	•

Country	International Organizations																
	ADB	ARAB LEAGUE	ASEAN	CACM	CARICOM	CEMA	EC	G-77	GCC	IDBa	IDBb	INTELSAT	LAIA	NAM	NATO	OAPEC	OAS
Suriname								•		•				•			•
Swaziland								•						•			
Sweden	•									•		•					
Switzerlandc	•									•		•					
Syria		•						•			•	•		•		•	
Tanzania								•				•		•			
Thailand	•		•									•					
Togo								•						•			
Tongac	•																
Trinidad and Tobago					•			•		•		•		•			•
Tunisia		•						•			•	•		•		•	
Turkey											•	•			•		
Tuvalu c																	
Uganda								•			•	•		•			
Union of Soviet Socialist Republics						•											
United Arab Emirates		•						•	•		•	•		•		•	
United Kingdom	•						•			•		•			•		
United States	•									•		•			•		•
Uruguay								•		•		•	•				•
Vanuatu	•							•						•			
Vatican Cityc												•					
Venezuela								•		•		•	•				•
Vietnam	•					•		•				•		•			
Western Samoa	•							•									
Yemen Arab Republic		•						•			•	•		•			
Yemen, People's Democratic Republic of		•						•			•			•			
Yugoslavia								•		•		•		•			
Zaire								•				•		•			
Zambia								•				•		•			
Zimbabwe								•						•			
Taiwan c	•																

						United Nations Organizations																
OAU	OECD	OIC	OPEC	SELA	WFTU	FAO	GATT	IAEA	IBRD	ICAO	ICJ	IDA	IFAD	IFC	ILO	IMF	IMO	ITU	UNESCO	UPU	WHO	WMO
				•		•	•		•	•	•		•		•	•	•	•	•	•	•	•
•						•	•		•	•	•	•	•	•	•	•		•	•	•	•	
	•					•	•	•	•	•	•	•	•	•	•	•	•	•	•	•	•	•
	•					•	•	•	•	•	•		•		•		•	•	•	•	•	•
		•			•	•	•	•	•	•	•	•	•	•	•	•	•	•	•	•	•	•
•						•	•	•	•	•	•	•	•	•	•	•	•	•	•	•	•	•
						•	•	•	•	•	•	•	•	•	•	•	•	•	•	•	•	•
•						•	•	•	•	•	•	•	•	•	•	•	•	•	•	•	•	•
						•	•						•					•	•	•	•	
			•		•	•	•	•	•	•	•			•	•	•	•	•	•	•	•	•
•				•		•	•	•	•	•	•	•		•	•	•	•	•	•	•	•	•
	•		•			•	•	•	•	•	•	•	•	•	•	•	•	•	•	•	•	•
						•														•		
•			•			•	•	•	•	•	•	•	•	•	•	•	•	•	•	•	•	•
					•		•		•	•				•		•	•	•	•	•	•	
	•	•	•			•	•	•	•	•	•	•	•	•	•	•	•	•	•	•	•	•
	•					•	•	•	•	•	•	•	•		•	•			•	•	•	•
	•					•	•	•	•	•	•	•	•	•	•	•	•		•	•	•	•
			•			•	•		•	•	•	•		•	•	•	•	•	•	•	•	•
						•		•	•	•	•	•		•		•		•		•	•	•
								•										•		•		
		•	•	•	•	•		•	•	•	•		•	•	•	•	•	•	•	•	•	•
					•	•		•	•	•	•	•	•	•	•	•		•	•	•	•	•
					•	•			•		•	•	•		•		•		•		•	
	•				•	•			•	•	•	•	•	•	•	•	•	•	•	•	•	•
	•				•	•	•		•	•	•	•	•		•	•	•	•	•	•	•	•
						•	•	•	•	•	•	•	•	•	•	•	•	•	•	•	•	•
•						•	•	•	•	•	•	•	•	•	•	•	•		•	•	•	•
•						•	•	•	•	•	•	•	•	•	•	•		•	•	•	•	•
•				•		•	•	•	•	•	•	•	•	•	•			•	•	•	•	•

Appendix D:

Weights and Measures

Mathematical Power	Name
10^{18} or 1,000,000,000,000,000,000	one quintillion
10^{15} or 1,000,000,000,000,000	one quadrillion
10^{12} or 1,000,000,000,000	one trillion
10^9 or 1,000,000,000	one billion
10^6 or 1,000,000	one million
10^3 or 1,000	one thousand
10^2 or 100	one hundred
10^1 or 10	ten
10^0 or 1	one
10^{-1} or 0.1	one tenth
10^{-2} or 0.01	one hundredth
10^{-3} or 0.001	one thousandth
10^{-6} or 0.000 001	one millionth
10^{-9} or 0.000 000 001	one billionth
10^{-12} or 0.000 000 000 001	one trillionth
10^{-15} or 0.000 000 000 000 001	one quadrillionth
10^{-18} or 0.000 000 000 000 000 001	one quintillionth

Metric Interrelationships

Conversions from a multiple or submultiple to the basic units of meters, liters, or grams can be done using the table. For example, to convert from kilometers to meters, multiply by 1,000 (9.26 kilometers equals 9,260 meters) or to convert from meters to kilometers, multiply by 0.001 (9,260 meters equals 9.26 kilometers)

Prefix	Symbol	Length, weight, capacity	Area	Volume
exa	E	10^{18}	10^{36}	10^{54}
peta	P	10^{15}	10^{30}	10^{45}
tera	T	10^{12}	10^{24}	10^{36}
giga	G	10^9	10^{18}	10^{27}
mega	M	10^6	10^{12}	10^{18}
hectokilo	hk	10^5	10^{10}	10^{15}
myria	ma	10^4	10^8	10^{12}
kilo	k	10^3	10^6	10^9
hecto	h	10^2	10^4	10^6
deka	da	10^1	10^2	10^3
basic unit	—	1 meter, 1 gram, 1 liter	1 meter^2	1 meter^3
deci	d	10^{-1}	10^{-2}	10^{-3}
centi	c	10^{-2}	10^{-4}	10^{-6}
milli	m	10^{-3}	10^{-6}	10^{-9}
decimilli	dm	10^{-4}	10^{-8}	10^{-12}
centimilli	cm	10^{-5}	10^{-10}	10^{-15}
micro	u	10^{-6}	10^{-12}	10^{-18}
nano	n	10^{-9}	10^{-18}	10^{-27}
pico	p	10^{-12}	10^{-24}	10^{-36}
femto	f	10^{-15}	10^{-30}	10^{-45}
atto	a	10^{-18}	10^{-36}	10^{-54}

Equivalents

Unit	Metric Equivalent	US Equivalent
acre	0.404 685 64 hectares	43,560 feet^2
acre	4,046.856 4 meters^2	4,840 yards^2
acre	0.004 046 856 4 kilometers^2	0.001 562 5 miles^2, statute
are	100 meters^2	119.599 yards^2
barrel (petroleum, US)	158.987 29 liters	42 gallons
(proof spirits, US)	151.416 47 liters	40 gallons
(beer, US)	117.347 77 liters	31 gallons
bushel	35.239 07 liters	4 pecks
cable	219.456 meters	120 fathoms
chain (surveyor's)	20.116 8 meters	66 feet
cord (wood)	3.624 556 meters^3	128 feet^3
cup	0.236 588 2 liters	8 ounces, liquid
degrees, celsius	(water boils at 100°C, freezes at 0°C)	multiply by 1.8 and add 32 to obtain °F
degrees, fahrenheit	subtract 32 and divide by 1.8 to obtain °C	(water boils at 212°F, freezes at 32°F)
dram, avoirdupois	1.771 845 2 grams	0.062 5 ounces, avoirdupois
dram, troy	3.887 934 6 grams	0.125 ounces, troy
dram, liquid (US)	3.696 69 milliliters	0.125 ounces, liquid
fathom	1.828 8 meters	6 feet
foot	30.48 centimeters	12 inches
foot	0.304 8 meters	0.333 333 3 yards
foot	0.000 304 8 kilometers	0.000 189 39 miles, statute
foot^2	929.030 4 centimeters^2	144 inches^2
foot^2	0.092 903 04 meters^2	0.111 111 1 yards^2
foot^3	28.316 846 592 liters	7.480 519 gallons
foot^3	0.028 316 847 meters^3	1,728 inches^3
furlong	201.168 meters	220 yards
gallon, liquid (US)	3.785 411 784 liters	4 quarts, liquid
gill (US)	118.294 118 milliliters	4 ounces, liquid
grain	64.798 91 milligrams	0.002 285 71 ounces, avdp.
gram	1,000 milligrams	0.035 273 96 ounces, avdp.
hand (height of horse)	10.16 centimeters	4 inches
hectare	10,000 meters^2	2.471 053 8 acres
hundredweight, long	50.802 345 kilograms	112 pounds, avoirdupois
hundredweight, short	45.359 237 kilograms	100 pounds, avoirdupois
inch	2.54 centimeters	0.083 333 33 feet
inch^2	6.451 6 centimeters^2	0.006 944 44 feet^2
inch^3	16.387 064 centimeters^3	0.000 578 7 feet^3
inch^3	16.387 064 milliliters	0.029 761 6 pints, dry
inch^3	16.387 064 milliliters	0.034 632 0 pints, liquid
kilogram	0.001 tons, metric	2.204 623 pounds, avdp.
kilometer	1,000 meters	0.621 371 19 miles, statute
kilometer^2	100 hectares	247.105 38 acres
kilometer^2	1,000,000 meters^2	0.386 102 16 miles^2, statute
knot (1 nautical mi/hr)	1.852 kilometers/hour	1.151 statute miles/hour
league, nautical	5.559 552 kilometers	3 miles, nautical
league, statute	4.828.032 kilometers	3 miles, statute

Unit	Metric Equivalent	US Equivalent
link (surveyor's)	20.116 8 centimeters	7.92 inches
liter	0.001 meters³	61.023 74 inches³
liter	0.1 dekaliter	0.908 083 quarts, dry
liter	1,000 milliliters	1.056 688 quarts, liquid
meter	100 centimeters	1.093 613 yards
meter²	10,000 centimeters²	1.195 990 yards²
meter³	1,000 liters	1.307 951 yards³
micron	0.000 001 meter	0.000 039 4 inches
mil	0.025 4 millimeters	0.001 inch
mile, nautical	1.852 kilometers	1.150 779 4 miles, statute
mile², nautical	3.429 904 kilometers²	1.325 miles², statute
mile, statute	1.609 344 kilometers	5,280 feet or 8 furlongs
mile², statute	258.998 811 hectares	640 acres or 1 section
mile², statute	2.589 988 11 kilometers²	0.755 miles², nautical
minim (US)	0.061 611 52 milliliters	0.002 083 33 ounces, liquid
ounce, avoirdupois	28.349 523 125 grams	437.5 grains
ounce, liquid (US)	29.573 53 milliliters	0.062 5 pints, liquid
ounce, troy	31.103 476 8 grams	480 grains
pace	76.2 centimeters	30 inches
peck	8.809 767 5 liters	8 quarts, dry
pennyweight	1.555 173 84 grams	24 grains
pint, dry (US)	0.550 610 47 liters	0.5 quarts, dry
pint, liquid (US)	0.473 176 473 liters	0.5 quarts, liquid
point (typographical)	0.351 459 8 millimeters	0.013 837 inches
pound, avoirdupois	453.592 37 grams	16 ounces, avoirdupois
pound, troy	373.241 721 6 grams	12 ounces, troy
quart, dry (US)	1.101 221 liters	2 pints, dry
quart, liquid (US)	0.946 352 946 liters	2 pints, liquid
quintal	100 kilograms	220.462 26 pounds, avdp.
rod	5.029 2 meters	5.5 yards
scruple	1.295 978 2 grams	20 grains
section (US)	2.589 988 1 kilometers²	1 mile², statute or 640 acres
span	22.86 centimeters	9 inches
stere	1 meter³	1.307 95 yards³
tablespoon	14.786 76 milliliters	3 teaspoons
teaspoon	4.928 922 milliliters	0.333 333 tablespoons
ton, long or deadweight	1,016.046 909 kilograms	2,240 pounds, avoirdupois
ton, metric	1,000 kilograms	2,204.623 pounds, avdp.
ton, register	2.831 684 7 meters³	100 feet³
ton, short	907.184 74 kilograms	2,000 pounds, avoirdupois
township (US)	93.239 572 kilometers²	36 miles², statute
yard	0.914 4 meters	3 feet
yard²	0.836 127 36 meters²	9 feet²
yard³	0.764 554 86 meters³	27 feet³
yard³	764.554 857 984 liters	201.974 gallons

Appendix E:

Cross-Reference List of Geographic Names

This list indicates where various names, including all United States Foreign Service Posts, alternate names, former names , and political or geographic portions of larger entities, can be found in **Handbook of the Nations**. Spellings are not necessarily those approved by the United States Board on Geographic Names (BGN). Alternate names are included in parenthesis, additional information is included in brackets.

Name	Entry in *Handbook of the Nations*
A Abidjan [US Embassy]	Ivory Coast
Abu Dhabi [US Embassy]	United Arab Emirates
Acapulco [US Consular Agency]	Mexico
Accra [US Embassy]	Ghana
Adana [US Consulate]	Turkey
Addis Ababa [US Embassy]	Ethiopia
Adelaide [US Consular Agency]	Australia
Adélie Land (Terre Adélie) [claimed by France]	Antarctica
Aden [US post not maintained, representation by British Embassy]	Yemen, People's Democratic Republic of
Aden, Gulf of	Indian Ocean
Admiralty Islands	Papua New Guinea
Adriatic Sea	Atlantic Ocean
Aegean Islands	Greece
Aegean Sea	Atlantic Ocean
Afars and Issas, French Territory of the (F.T.A.I.)	Djibouti
Agalega Islands	Mauritius
Aland Islands	Finland
Alaska	United States
Alaska, Gulf of	Pacific Ocean
Aldabra Islands	Seychelles
Alderney	Guernsey
Aleutian Islands	United States
Alexander Island	Antarctica
Alexandria [US Consulate General]	Egypt
Algiers [US Embassy]	Algeria
Alhucemas, Peñón de	Spain
Alphonse Island	Seychelles
Amami Strait	Pacific Ocean
Amindivi Islands	India
Amirante Isles	Seychelles
Amman [US Embassy]	Jordan
Amsterdam [US Consulate General]	Netherlands
Amsterdam Island (Île Amsterdam)	French Southern and Antarctic Lands
Amundsen Sea	Pacific Ocean
Amur	China; Soviet Union
Andaman Islands	India
Andaman Sea	Indian Ocean
Anegada Passage	Atlantic Ocean
Anglo-Egyptian Sudan	Sudan
Anjouan	Comoros
Ankara [US Embassy]	Turkey
Annobón	Equatorial Guinea
Antananarivo [US Embassy]	Madagascar
Antipodes Islands	New Zealand
Antwerp [US Consulate General]	Belgium
Aozou Strip [claimed by Libya]	Chad
Aqaba, Gulf of	Indian Ocean
Arabian Sea	Indian Ocean
Arafura Sea	Pacific Ocean
Argun	China; Soviet Union
Ascension Island	St. Helena
Assumption Island	Seychelles
Asunción [US Embassy]	Paraguay
Asuncion Island	Northern Mariana Islands

Name	Entry in *Handbook of the Nations*
Atacama	Chile
Athens [US Embassy]	Greece
Attu	United States
Auckland [US Consulate General]	New Zealand
Auckland Islands	New Zealand
Australes Îles (Îles Tubuai)	French Polynesia
Axel Heiberg Island	Canada
Azores	Portugal
Azov, Sea of	Atlantic Ocean

B

Bab el Mandeb	Indian Ocean
Babuyan Channel	Pacific Ocean
Babuyan Islands	Philippines
Baffin Bay	Arctic Ocean
Baffin Island	Canada
Baghdad [US Embassy]	Iraq
Balabac Strait	Pacific Ocean
Balearic Islands	Spain
Balearic Sea (Iberian Sea)	Atlantic Ocean
Bali [US Consular Agency]	Indonesia
Bali Sea	Indian Ocean
Balintang Channel	Pacific Ocean
Balintang Islands	Philippines
Balleny Islands	Antarctica
Baltic Sea	Atlantic Ocean
Baluchistan	Afghanistan; Iran; Pakistan
Bamako [US Embassy]	Mali
Banaba (Ocean Island)	Kiribati
Bandar Seri Begawan [US Embassy]	Brunei
Banda Sea	Pacific Ocean
Bangkok [US Embassy]	Thailand
Bangui [US Embassy]	Central African Republic
Banjul [US Embassy]	Gambia, The
Banks Island	Canada
Banks Islands (Îles Banks)	Vanuatu
Barcelona [US Consulate General]	Spain
Barents Sea	Arctic Ocean
Barranquilla [US Consulate]	Colombia
Bashi Channel	Pacific Ocean
Basilan Strait	Pacific Ocean
Bass Strait	Indian Ocean
Batan Islands	Philippines
Bavaria (Bayern)	Germany, Federal Republic of
Beagle Channel	Atlantic Ocean
Bear Island (Bjørnøya)	Svalbard
Beaufort Sea	Arctic Ocean
Bechuanaland	Botswana
Beijing [US Embassy]	China
Beirut [US Embassy]	Lebanon
Belem [US Consular Agency]	Brazil
Belep Islands (Îles Belep)	New Caledonia
Belfast [US Consulate General]	United Kingdom
Belgian Congo	Zaire
Belgrade [US Embassy]	Yugoslavia
Belize City [US Embassy]	Belize
Belle Isle, Strait of	Atlantic Ocean
Bellinghausen Sea	Pacific Ocean
Belmopan	Belize
Bengal, Bay of	Indian Ocean
Bering Sea	Pacific Ocean
Bering Strait	Pacific Ocean
Berkner Island	Antarctica
Berlin, East [US Embassy]	German Democratic Republic

Name	Entry in *Handbook of the Nations*
Berlin, West [US Mission]	Germany, Federal Republic of
Bern [US Embassy]	Switzerland
Bessarabia	Romania; Soviet Union
Bijagós, Arquipélago dos	Guinea-Bissau
Bikini Atoll	Marshall Islands
Bilbao [US Consulate]	Spain
Bioko	Equatorial Guinea
Biscay, Bay of	Atlantic Ocean
Bishop Rock	United Kingdom
Bismarck Archipelago	Papua New Guinea
Bismarck Sea	Pacific Ocean
Bissau [US Embassy]	Guinea-Bissau
Bjørnøya (Bear Island)	Svalbard
Black Rock	Falkland Islands (Islas Malvinas)
Black Sea	Atlantic Ocean
Boa Vista	Cape Verde
Bogotá [US Embassy]	Colombia
Bombay [US Consulate General]	India
Bonaire	Netherlands Antilles
Bonifacio, Strait of	Atlantic Ocean
Bonin Islands	Japan
Bonn [US Embassy]	Federal Republic of Germany
Bophuthatswana	South Africa
Bora-Bora	French Polynesia
Bordeaux [US Consulate General]	France
Borneo	Brunei; Indonesia; Malaysia
Bornholm	Denmark
Bosporus	Atlantic Ocean
Bothnia, Gulf of	Atlantic Ocean
Bougainville Island	Papua New Guinea
Bougainville Strait	Pacific Ocean
Bounty Islands	New Zealand
Brasilia [US Embassy]	Brazil
Brazzaville [US Embassy]	Congo
Bridgetown [US Embassy]	Barbados
Brisbane [US Consulate]	Australia
British East Africa	Kenya
British Guiana	Guyana
British Honduras	Belize
British Solomon Islands	Solomon Islands
British Somaliland	Somalia
Brussels [US Embassy, US Mission to European Communities, US Mission to the North Atlantic Treaty Organization (USNATO)]	Belgium
Bucharest [US Embassy]	Romania
Budapest [US Embassy]	Hungary
Buenos Aires [US Embassy]	Argentina
Bujumbura [US Embassy]	Burundi

C

Name	Entry in *Handbook of the Nations*
Cabinda	Angola
Cabot Strait	Atlantic Ocean
Caicos Islands	Turks and Caicos Islands
Cairo [US Embassy]	Egypt
Calcutta [US Consulate General]	India
Calgary [US Consulate General]	Canada
California, Gulf of	Pacific Ocean
Campbell Island	New Zealand
Canal Zone	Panama
Canary Islands	Spain
Canberra [US Embassy]	Australia
Cancun [US Consular Agency]	Mexico
Canton (Guangzhou)	China
Canton Island	Kiribati

Name	Entry in *Handbook of the Nations*
Cape Town [US Consulate General]	South Africa
Caracas [US Embassy]	Venezuela
Cargados Carajos Shoals	Mauritius
Caroline Islands	Micronesia, Federated States of; Pacific Islands, Trust Territory of the
Caribbean Sea	Atlantic Ocean
Carpentaria, Gulf of	Pacific Ocean
Casablanca [US Consulate General]	Morocco
Cato Island	Australia
Cebu [US Consulate]	Philippines
Celebes	Indonesia
Celebes Sea	Pacific Ocean
Celtic Sea	Atlantic Ocean
Central African Empire	Central African Republic
Ceuta	Spain
Ceylon	Sri Lanka
Chafarinas, Islas	Spain
Chagos Archipelago (Oil Islands)	British Indian Ocean Territory
Channel Islands	Guernsey; Jersey
Chatham Islands	New Zealand
Cheju-do	Korea, South
Cheju Strait	Pacific Ocean
Chengdu [US Consulate General]	China
Chesterfield Islands (Îles Chesterfield)	New Caledonia
Chiang Mai [US Consulate General]	Thailand
Chihli, Gulf of (Bo Hai)	Pacific Ocean
China, People's Republic of	China
China, Republic of	Taiwan
Choiseul	Solomon Islands
Christchurch [US Consular Agency]	New Zealand
Christmas Island [Indian Ocean]	Australia
Christmas Island [Pacific Ocean] (Kiritimati)	Kiribati
Chukchi Sea	Arctic Ocean
Ciskei	South Africa
Ciudad Juarez [US Consulate General]	Mexico
Cochabamba [US Consular Agency]	Bolivia
Coco, Isla del	Costa Rica
Cocos Islands	Cocos (Keeling) Islands
Colombo [US Embassy]	Sri Lanka
Colon [US Consular Agency]	Panama
Colón, Archipiélago de (Galapagos Islands)	Ecuador
Commander Islands (Komandorskiye Ostrova)	Soviet Union
Conakry [US Embassy]	Guinea
Congo (Brazzaville)	Congo
Congo (Kinshasa)	Zaire
Congo (Leopoldville)	Zaire
Con Son Islands	Vietnam
Cook Strait	Pacific Ocean
Copenhagen [US Embassy]	Denmark
Coral Sea	Pacific Ocean
Corn Islands (Islas del Maíz)	Nicaragua
Corsica	France
Cosmoledo Group	Seychelles
Côte d'Ivoire	Ivory Coast
Cotonou [US Embassy]	Benin
Crete	Greece
Crooked Island Passage	Atlantic Ocean
Crozet Islands (Îles Crozet)	French Southern and Antarctic Lands
Curaçao [US Consulate General]	Netherlands Antilles
Cusco [US Consular Agency]	Peru

D

| Dahomey | Benin |
| Daitō Islands | Japan |

Name	Entry in *Handbook of the Nations*
Dakar [US Embassy]	Senegal
Daman (Damão)	India
Damascus [US Embassy]	Syria
Danger Atoll	Cook Islands
Danish Straits	Atlantic Ocean
Danzig (Gdańsk)	Poland
Dao Bach Long Vi	Vietnam
Dardanelles	Atlantic Ocean
Dar es Salaam [US Embassy]	Tanzania
Davis Strait	Atlantic Ocean
Deception Island	Antarctica
Denmark Strait	Atlantic Ocean
D'Entrecasteaux Islands	Papua New Guinea
Devon Island	Canada
Dhahran [US Consulate General]	Saudi Arabia
Dhaka [US Embassy]	Bangladesh
Diego Garcia	British Indian Ocean Territory
Diego Ramírez	Chile
Diomede Islands	Soviet Union [Big Diomede]; United States [Little Diomede]
Diu	India
Djibouti [US Embassy]	Djibouti
Dodecanese	Greece
Doha [US Embassy]	Qatar
Douala [US Consulate General]	Cameroon
Dover, Strait of	Atlantic Ocean
Drake Passage	Atlantic Ocean
Dubai [US Consulate General]	United Arab Emirates
Dublin [US Embassy]	Ireland
Durango [US Consular Agency]	Mexico
Durban [US Consulate General]	South Africa
Dusseldorf [US Consulate General]	Federal Republic of Germany
Dutch East Indies	Indonesia
Dutch Guiana	Suriname

E

Name	Entry in *Handbook of the Nations*
East China Sea	Pacific Ocean
Easter Island (Isla de Pascua)	Chile
Eastern Channel (East Korea Strait or Tsushima Strait)	Pacific Ocean
East Germany	German Democratic Republic
East Korea Strait (Eastern Channel or Tsushima Strait)	Pacific Ocean
East Pakistan	Bangladesh
East Siberian Sea	Arctic Ocean
East Timor (Portuguese Timor)	Indonesia
Edinburgh [US Consulate General]	United Kingdom
Elba	Italy
Ellef Ringnes Island	Canada
Ellesmere Island	Canada
Ellice Islands	Tuvalu
Elobey, Islas de	Equatorial Guinea
Enderbury Island	Kiribati
Enewetak Atoll (Eniwetok Atoll)	Marshall Islands
England	United Kingdom
English Channel	Atlantic Ocean
Eniwetok Atoll	Marshall Islands
Epirus, Northern	Albania; Greece
Eritrea	Ethiopia
Essequibo [claimed by Venezuela]	Guyana
Estonia	Soviet Union [de facto]
Etorofu	Soviet Union [de facto]

F

Name	Entry in *Handbook of the Nations*
Farquhar Group	Seychelles
Fernando de Noronha	Brazil
Fernando Po (Bioko)	Equatorial Guinea
Finland, Gulf of	Atlantic Ocean

Name	Entry in *Handbook of the Nations*
Florence [US Consulate General]	Italy
Florida, Straits of	Atlantic Ocean
Formosa	Taiwan
Formosa Strait (Taiwan Strait)	Pacific Ocean
Fort-de-France [US Consulate General]	Martinique
Frankfurt am Main [US Consulate General]	Federal Republic of Germany
Franz Josef Land	Soviet Union
Freetown [US Embassy]	Sierra Leone
French Cameroon	Cameroon
French Indochina	Cambodia; Laos; Vietnam
French Guinea	Guinea
French Sudan	Mali
French Territory of the Afars and Issas (F.T.A.I.)	Djibouti
French Togo	Togo
Friendly Islands	Tonga
Fukuoka [US Consulate]	Japan
Funchal [US Consular Agency]	Portugal
Fundy, Bay of	Atlantic Ocean
Futuna Islands (Hoorn Islands)	Wallis and Futuna

G		
	Gaborone [US Embassy]	Botswana
	Galapagos Islands (Archipiélago de Colón)	Ecuador
	Galleons Passage	Atlantic Ocean
	Gambier Islands (Îles Gambier)	French Polynesia
	Gaspar Strait	Indian Ocean
	Geneva [Branch Office of the US Embassy, US Mission to European Office of the UN and Other International Organizations]	Switzerland
	Genoa [US Consulate General]	Italy
	George Town [US Consular Agency]	Cayman Islands
	Georgetown [US Embassy]	Guyana
	Gibraltar, Strait of	Atlantic Ocean
	Gilbert Islands	Kiribati
	Goa	India
	Gold Coast	Ghana
	Golan Heights	Syria
	Good Hope, Cape of	South Africa
	Goteborg [US Consulate General]	Sweden
	Gotland	Sweden
	Gough Island	St. Helena
	Grand Banks	Atlantic Ocean
	Grand Cayman	Cayman Islands
	Grand Turk [US Consular Agency]	Turks and Caicos Islands
	Great Australian Bight	Indian Ocean
	Great Belt (Store Baelt)	Atlantic Ocean
	Great Britain	United Kingdom
	Great Channel	Indian Ocean
	Greater Sunda Islands	Brunei; Indonesia; Malaysia
	Green Islands	Papua New Guinea
	Greenland Sea	Arctic Ocean
	Grenadines, Northern	St. Vincent and the Grenadines
	Grenadines, Southern	Grenada
	Guadalajara [US Consulate General]	Mexico
	Guadalcanal	Solomon Islands
	Guadalupe, Isla de	Mexico
	Guangzhou [US Consulate General]	China
	Guantanamo [US Naval Base]	Cuba
	Guatemala [US Embassy]	Guatemala
	Gubal, Strait of	Indian Ocean
	Guinea, Gulf of	Atlantic Ocean
	Guayaquil [US Consulate General]	Ecuador

H		
	Ha'apai Group	Tonga
	Habomai Islands	Soviet Union [de facto]

Hague, The [US Embassy]	Netherlands
Haifa [US Consular Agency]	Israel
Hainan Dao	China
Halifax [US Consulate General]	Canada
Halmahera	Indonesia
Hamburg [US Consulate General]	Federal Republic of Germany
Hamilton [US Consulate General]	Bermuda
Hanoi	Vietnam
Harare [US Embassy]	Zimbabwe
Hatay	Turkey
Havana [US post not maintained, representation by US Interests Section (USINT) of the Swiss Embassy]	Cuba
Hawaii	United States
Heard Island	Heard Island and McDonald Islands
Helsinki [US Embassy]	Finland
Hermosillo [US Consulate]	Mexico
Hispaniola	Dominican Republic; Haiti
Hokkaido	Japan
Holy See, The	Vatican City
Hong Kong [US Consulate General]	Hong Kong
Honiara [US Consulate]	Solomon Islands
Honshu	Japan
Hormuz, Strait of	Indian Ocean
Horn, Cape (Cabo de Hornos)	Chile
Horne, Îles de	Wallis and Futuna
Horn of Africa	Ethiopia; Somalia
Hudson Bay	Arctic Ocean
Hudson Strait	Arctic Ocean

I

Inaccessible Island	St. Helena
Indochina	Cambodia; Laos; Vietnam
Inner Mongolia (Nei Mongol)	China
Ionian Islands	Greece
Ionian Sea	Atlantic Ocean
Irian Jaya	Indonesia
Irish Sea	Atlantic Ocean
Islamabad [US Embassy]	Pakistan
Islas Malvinas	Falkland Islands (Islas Malvinas)
İstanbul [US Consulate General]	Turkey
Italian Somaliland	Somalia
Iwo Jima	Japan
İzmir [US Consulate General]	Turkey

J

Jakarta [US Embassy]	Indonesia
Japan, Sea of	Pacific Ocean
Java	Indonesia
Java Sea	Indian Ocean
Jeddah [US Consulate General]	Saudi Arabia
Jerusalem [US Consulate General]	Israel; West Bank
Johannesburg [US Consulate General]	South Africa
Juan de Fuca, Strait of	Pacific Ocean
Juan Fernández, Isla de	Chile
Juventud, Isla de la (Isle of Youth)	Cuba

K

Kabul [US Embassy now closed]	Afghanistan
Kaduna [US Consulate General]	Nigeria
Kalimantan	Indonesia
Kamchatka Peninsula (Poluostrov Kamchatka)	Soviet Union
Kampala [US Embassy]	Uganda
Kampuchea	Cambodia
Karachi [US Consulate General]	Pakistan
Kara Sea	Arctic Ocean
Karimata Strait	Indian Ocean
Kathmandu [US Embassy]	Nepal

Name	Entry in *Handbook of the Nations*
Kattegat	Atlantic Ocean
Kauai Channel	Pacific Ocean
Keeling Islands	Cocos (Keeling) Islands
Kerguelen, Îles	French Southern and Antarctic Lands
Kermadec Islands	New Zealand
Khabarovsk	Soviet Union
Khartoum [US Embassy]	Sudan
Khmer Republic	Cambodia
Kiel Canal (Nord-Ostsee Kanal)	Atlantic Ocean
Khuriya Muriya Islands (Kuria Muria Islands)	Oman
Khyber Pass	Pakistan
Kigali [US Embassy]	Rwanda
Kingston [US Embassy]	Jamaica
Kinshasa [US Embassy]	Zaire
Kiritimati (Christmas Island)	Kiribati
Kithira Strait	Atlantic Ocean
Kodiak Island	United States
Kola Peninsula (Kol'skiy Poluostrov)	Soviet Union
Kolonia [US Special Office]	Micronesia, Federated States of
Korea Bay	Pacific Ocean
Korea, Democratic People's Republic of	Korea, North
Korea, Republic of	Korea, South
Korea Strait	Pacific Ocean
Koror [US Special Office]	Pacific Islands, Trust Territory of
Kosovo	Yugoslavia
Kowloon	Hong Kong
Krakow [US Consulate]	Poland
Kuala Lumpur [US Embassy]	Malaysia
Kunashiri (Kunashir)	Soviet Union [de facto]
Kuril Islands	Soviet Union [de facto]
Kuwait [US Embassy]	Kuwait
Kwajalein Atoll	Marshall Islands
Kyushu	Japan

L

Name	Entry
Labrador	Canada
Laccadive Islands	India
Laccadive Sea	Indian Ocean
La Coruna [US Consular Agency]	Spain
Lagos [US Embassy]	Nigeria
Lahore [US Consulate General]	Pakistan
Lakshadweep	India
La Paz [US Embassy]	Bolivia
La Perouse Strait	Pacific Ocean
Laptev Sea	Arctic Ocean
Las Palmas [US Consular Agency]	Spain
Latvia	Soviet Union [de facto]
Lau Group	Fiji
Leningrad [US Consulate General]	Soviet Union
Lesser Sunda Islands	Indonesia
Leyte	Philippines
Liancourt Rocks [claimed by Japan]	Korea, South
Libreville [US Embassy]	Gabon
Ligurian Sea	Atlantic Ocean
Lilongwe [US Embassy]	Malawi
Lima [US Embassy]	Peru
Lincoln Sea	Arctic Ocean
Line Islands	Kiribati; Palmyra Atoll
Lisbon [US Embassy]	Portugal
Lithuania	Soviet Union [de facto]
Lombok Strait	Indian Ocean
Lomé [US Embassy]	Togo
London [US Embassy]	United Kingdom
Lord Howe Island	Australia

Name	Entry in *Handbook of the Nations*
Louisiade Archipelago	Papua New Guinea
Loyalty Islands (Îles Loyauté)	New Caledonia
Lubumbashi [US Consulate General]	Zaire
Lusaka [US Embassy]	Zambia
Luxembourg [US Embassy]	Luxembourg
Luzon	Philippines
Luzon Strait	Pacific Ocean
Lyon [US Consulate General]	France

M Macao	Macau
Macedonia	Bulgaria; Greece; Yugoslavia
Macquarie Island	Australia
Madeira Islands	Portugal
Madras [US Consulate General]	India
Madrid [US Embassy]	Spain
Magellan, Strait of	Atlantic Ocean
Mahé Island	Seychelles
Maíz, Islas del (Corn Islands)	Nicaragua
Majorca (Mallorca)	Spain
Majuro [US Special Office]	Marshall Islands
Makassar Strait	Pacific Ocean
Malabo [US Embassy]	Equatorial Guinea
Malacca, Strait of	Indian Ocean
Malaga [US Consular Agency]	Spain
Malagasy Republic	Madagascar
Male [US post not maintained, representation from Colombo, Sri Lanka]	Maldives
Mallorca (Majorca)	Spain
Malpelo, Isla de	Colombia
Malta Channel	Atlantic Ocean
Malvinas, Islas	Falkland Islands (Islas Malvinas)
Managua [US Embassy]	Nicaragua
Manama [US Embassy]	Bahrain
Manaus [US Consular Agency]	Brazil
Manchukuo	China
Manchuria	China
Manila [US Embassy]	Philippines
Manipa Strait	Pacific Ocean
Mannar, Gulf of	Indian Ocean
Manua Islands	American Samoa
Maputo [US Embassy]	Mozambique
Maracaibo [US Consulate]	Venezuela
Marcus Island (Minami-tori-shima)	Japan
Mariana Islands	Guam; Northern Mariana Islands
Marion Island	South Africa
Marmara, Sea of	Atlantic Ocean
Marquesas Islands (Îles Marquises)	French Polynesia
Marseille [US Consulate General]	France
Martin Vaz, Ilhas	Brazil
Más a Tierra (Robinson Crusoe Island)	Chile
Mascarene Islands	Mauritius; Reunion
Maseru [US Embassy]	Lesotho
Matamoros [US Consulate]	Mexico
Mazatlan [US Consulate]	Mexico
Mbabane [US Embassy]	Swaziland
McDonald Islands	Heard Island and McDonald Islands
Medan [US Consulate]	Indonesia
Mediterranean Sea	Atlantic Ocean
Melbourne [US Consulate General]	Australia
Melilla	Spain
Merida [US Consulate]	Mexico
Messina, Strait of	Atlantic Ocean
Mexico [US Embassy]	Mexico

Name	Entry in *Handbook of the Nations*
Mexico, Gulf of	Atlantic Ocean
Milan [US Consulate General]	Italy
Minami-tori-shima	Japan
Mindanao	Philippines
Mindoro Strait	Pacific Ocean
Minicoy Island	India
Mogadishu [US Embassy]	Somalia
Mombasa [US Consulate]	Kenya
Mona Passage	Atlantic Ocean
Monrovia [US Embassy]	Liberia
Montego Bay [US Consular Agency]	Jamaica
Monterrey [US Consulate General]	Mexico
Montevideo [US Embassy]	Uruguay
Montreal [US Consulate General, US Mission to the International Civil Aviation Organization (ICAO)]	Canada
Moravian Gate	Czechoslovakia
Moroni [US Embassy]	Comoros
Mortlock Islands	Micronesia, Federated States of
Moscow [US Embassy]	Soviet Union
Mozambique Channel	Indian Ocean
Mulege [US Consular Agency]	Mexico
Munich [US Consulate General]	Federal Republic of Germany
Musandam Peninsula	Oman; United Arab Emirates
Muscat [US Embassy]	Oman
Muscat and Oman	Oman
Myanma or Myanmar	Burma

N

Name	Entry in *Handbook of the Nations*
Naha [US Consulate General]	Japan
Nairobi [US Embassy]	Kenya
Nampō-shotō	Japan
Naples [US Consulate General]	Italy
Nassau [US Embassy]	Bahamas, The
Natuna Besar Islands	Indonesia
N'Djamena [US Embassy]	Chad
Netherlands East Indies	Indonesia
Netherlands Guiana	Suriname
Nevis	St. Kitts and Nevis
New Delhi [US Embassy]	India
Newfoundland	Canada
New Guinea	Indonesia; Papua New Guinea
New Hebrides	Vanuatu
New Siberian Islands	Soviet Union
New Territories	Hong Kong
New York, New York [US Mission to the United Nations (USUN)]	United States
Niamey [US Embassy]	Niger
Nice [US Consular Agency]	France
Nicobar Islands	India
Nicosia [US Embassy]	Cyprus
Nightingale Island	St. Helena
North Atlantic Ocean	Atlantic Ocean
North Channel	Atlantic Ocean
Northeast Providence Channel	Atlantic Ocean
Northern Epirus	Albania; Greece
Northern Grenadines	St. Vincent and the Grenadines
Northern Ireland	United Kingdom
Northern Rhodesia	Zambia
North Island	New Zealand
North Korea	Korea, North
North Pacific Ocean	Pacific Ocean
North Sea	Atlantic Ocean
North Vietnam	Vietnam
Northwest Passage	Arctic Ocean

Name	Entry in *Handbook of the Nations*
North Yemen	Yemen Arab Republic
Norwegian Sea	Atlantic Ocean
Nouakchott [US Embassy]	Mauritania
Novaya Zemlya	Soviet Union
Nuevo Laredo [US Consulate]	Mexico
Nyasaland	Malawi

O

Name	Entry in *Handbook of the Nations*
Oahu	United States
Oaxaca [US Consular Agency]	Mexico
Ocean Island (Banaba)	Kiribati
Ocean Island (Kure Island)	United States
Ogaden	Ethiopia; Somalia
Oil Islands (Chagos Archipelago)	British Indian Ocean Territory
Okhotsk, Sea of	Pacific Ocean
Okinawa	Japan
Oman, Gulf of	Indian Ocean
Ombai Strait	Pacific Ocean
Oporto [US Consulate]	Portugal
Oran [US Consulate]	Algeria
Øresund (The Sound)	Atlantic Ocean
Orkney Islands	United Kingdom
Osaka-Kobe [US Consulate General]	Japan
Oslo [US Embassy]	Norway
Otranto, Strait of	Atlantic Ocean
Ottawa [US Embassy]	Canada
Ouagadougou [US Embassy]	Burkina
Outer Mongolia	Mongolia

P

Name	Entry in *Handbook of the Nations*
Pagan	Northern Mariana Islands
Palau	Pacific Islands, Trust Territory of the
Palawan	Philippines
Palermo [US Consulate General]	Italy
Palk Strait	Indian Ocean
Palma de Mallorca [US Consular Agency]	Spain
Pamirs	China; Soviet Union
Panama [US Embassy]	Panama
Panama Canal	Panama
Panama, Gulf of	Pacific Ocean
Paramaribo [US Embassy]	Suriname
Parece Vela	Japan
Paris [US Embassy, US Mission to the Organization for Economic Cooperation and Development (OECD), US Observer Mission at the UN Educational, Scientific, and Cultural Organization (UNESCO)]	France
Pashtunistan	Afghanistan; Pakistan
Pascua, Isla de (Easter Island)	Chile
Peking (Beijing)	China
Pemba Island	Tanzania
Pentland Firth	Atlantic Ocean
Perim	Yemen, People's Democratic Republic of
Perouse Strait, La	Pacific Ocean
Persian Gulf	Indian Ocean
Perth [US Consulate]	Australia
Pescadores	Taiwan
Peshawar [US Consulate]	Pakistan
Peter I Island	Antarctica
Philip Island	Norfolk Island
Philippine Sea	Pacific Ocean
Phoenix Islands	Kiribati
Pines, Isle of (Isla de la Juventud)	Cuba
Piura [US Consular Agency]	Peru
Pleasant Island	Nauru
Ponape (Pohnpei)	Micronesia
Ponta Delgada [US Consulate]	Portugal

Name	Entry in *Handbook of the Nations*
Port-au-Prince [US Embassy]	Haiti
Port Louis [US Embassy]	Mauritius
Port Moresby [US Embassy]	Papua New Guinea
Porto Alegre [US Consulate]	Brazil
Port-of-Spain [US Embassy]	Trinidad and Tobago
Port Said [US Consular Agency]	Egypt
Portuguese Guinea	Guinea-Bissau
Portuguese Timor (East Timor)	Indonesia
Poznan [US Consulate]	Poland
Prague [US Embassy]	Czechoslovakia
Praia [US Embassy]	Cape Verde
Pretoria [US Embassy]	South Africa
Pribilof Islands	United States
Prince Edward Island	Canada
Prince Edward Islands	South Africa
Prince Patrick Island	Canada
Principe	Sao Tome and Principe
Puerto Plata [US Consular Agency]	Dominican Republic
Puerto Vallarta [US Consular Agency]	Mexico
Pusan [US Consulate]	South Korea
P'yŏngyang	Korea, North

Q

Quebec [US Consulate General]	Canada
Queen Charlotte Islands	Canada
Queen Elizabeth Islands	Canada
Queen Maud Land [claimed by Norway]	Antarctica
Quito [US Embassy]	Ecuador

R

Rabat [US Embassy]	Morocco
Ralik Chain	Marshall Islands
Rangoon [US Embassy]	Burma
Ratak Chain	Marshall Islands
Recife [US Consulate]	Brazil
Redonda	Antigua and Barbuda
Red Sea	Indian Ocean
Revillagigedo Island	United States
Revillagigedo Islands	Mexico
Reykjavik [US Embassy]	Iceland
Rhodes	Greece
Rhodesia	Zimbabwe
Rhodesia, Northern	Zambia
Rhodesia, Southern	Zimbabwe
Rio de Janeiro [US Consulate General]	Brazil
Río de Oro	Western Sahara
Río Muni	Equatorial Guinea
Riyadh [US Embassy]	Saudi Arabia
Robinson Crusoe Island (Más a Tierra)	Chile
Rocas, Atol das	Brazil
Rockall [disputed]	United Kingdom
Rodrigues	Mauritius
Rome [US Embassy, US Mission to the UN Agencies for Food and Agriculture (FODAG)]	Italy
Roncador Cay	Colombia
Roosevelt Island	Antarctica
Ross Dependency [claimed by New Zealand]	Antarctica
Ross Island	Antarctica
Ross Sea	Antarctica
Rota	Northern Mariana Islands
Rotuma	Fiji
Ryukyu Islands	Japan

S

Saba	Netherlands Antilles
Sabah	Malaysia
Sable Island	Canada

Name	Entry in *Handbook of the Nations*
Sahel	Burkina; Cape Verde; Chad; The Gambia; Guinea-Bissau; Mali; Mauritania; Niger; Senegal
Saigon (Ho Chi Minh City)	Vietnam
St. Brandon	Mauritius
St. Christopher and Nevis	St. Kitts and Nevis
St. George's [US Embassy]	Grenada
St. George's Channel	Atlantic Ocean
St. John's [US Embassy]	Antigua and Barbuda
St. Lawrence, Gulf of	Atlantic Ocean
St. Lawrence Island	United States
St. Lawrence Seaway	Atlantic Ocean
St. Martin	Guadeloupe
St. Martin (Sint Maarten)	Netherlands Antilles
St. Paul Island	Canada
St. Paul Island	United States
St. Paul Island (Île Saint-Paul)	French Southern and Antarctic Lands
St. Peter and St. Paul Rocks (Penedos de São Pedro e São Paulo)	Brazil
St. Vincent Passage	Atlantic Ocean
Saipan	Northern Mariana Islands
Sakhalin Island (Ostrov Sakhalin)	Soviet Union
Sala y Gómez, Isla	Chile
Salisbury (Harare)	Zimbabwe
Salvador de Bahia [US Consular Agency]	Brazil
Salzburg [US Consulate General]	Austria
Sanaa [US Embassy]	Yemen Arab Republic
San Ambrosio	Chile
San Andrés y Providencia, Archipiélago	Colombia
San Bernardino Strait	Pacific Ocean
San Félix, Isla	Chile
San Jose [US Embassy]	Costa Rica
San Luis Potosi [US Consular Agency]	Mexico
San Miguel Allende [US Consular Agency]	Mexico
San Salvador [US Embassy]	El Salvador
Santa Cruz [US Consular Agency]	Bolivia
Santa Cruz Islands	Solomon Islands
Santiago [US Embassy]	Chile
Santo Domingo [US Embassy]	Dominican Republic
Sao Luis [US Consular Agency]	Brazil
Sao Paulo [US Consulate General]	Brazil
São Pedro e São Paulo, Penedos de	Brazil
Sapporo [US Consulate General]	Japan
Sapudi Strait	Indian Ocean
Sarawak	Malaysia
Sardinia	Italy
Sargasso Sea	Atlantic Ocean
Sark	Guernsey
Scotia Sea	Atlantic Ocean
Scotland	United Kingdom
Scott Island	Antarctica
Senyavin Islands	Micronesia, Federated States of
Seoul [US Embassy]	Korea, South
Serrana Bank	Colombia
Serranilla Bank	Colombia
Severnaya Zemlya (Northland)	Soviet Union
Seville [US Consular Agency]	Spain
Shag Island	Heard Island and McDonald Islands
Shag Rocks	Falkland Islands (Islas Malvinas)
Shanghai [US Consulate General]	China
Shenyang [US Consulate General]	China
Shetland Islands	United Kingdom
Shikoku	Japan
Shikotan (Shikotan-tō)	Japan

Name	Entry in *Handbook of the Nations*
Siam	Thailand
Sibutu Passage	Pacific Ocean
Sicily	Italy
Sicily, Strait of	Atlantic Ocean
Sikkim	India
Sinai	Egypt
Singapore [US Embassy]	Singapore
Singapore Strait	Pacific Ocean
Sinkiang (Xinjiang)	China
Sint Eustatius	Netherlands Antilles
Sint Maarten (St. Martin)	Netherlands Antilles
Skagerrak	Atlantic Ocean
Slovakia	Czechoslovakia
Society Islands (Îles de la Société)	French Polynesia
Socotra	Yemen, People's Democratic Republic of
Sofia [US Embassy]	Bulgaria
Solomon Islands, northern	Papua New Guinea
Solomon Islands, southern	Solomon Islands
Soloman Sea	Pacific Ocean
Songkhla [US Consulate]	Thailand
Sound, The (Øresund)	Atlantic Ocean
South Atlantic Ocean	Atlantic Ocean
South China Sea	Pacific Ocean
Southern Grenadines	Grenada
Southern Rhodesia	Zimbabwe
South Georgia	South Georgia and the South Sandwich Islands
South Island	New Zealand
South Korea	Korea, South
South Orkney Islands	Antarctica
South Pacific Ocean	Pacific Ocean
South Sandwich Islands	South Georgia and the South Sandwich Islands
South Shetland Islands	Antarctica
South Tyrol	Italy
South Vietnam	Vietnam
South-West Africa	Namibia
South Yemen	Yemen, People's Democratic Republic of
Spanish Guinea	Equatorial Guinea
Spanish Sahara	Western Sahara
Spitsbergen	Svalbard
Stockholm [US Embassy]	Sweden
Strasbourg [US Consulate General]	France
Stuttgart [US Consulate General]	Federal Republic of Germany
Suez, Gulf of	Indian Ocean
Sulu Archipelago	Philippines
Sulu Sea	Pacific Ocean
Sumatra	Indonesia
Sumba	Indonesia
Sunda Islands (Soenda Isles)	Indonesia; Malaysia
Sunda Strait	Indian Ocean
Surabaya [US Consulate]	Indonesia
Surigao Strait	Pacific Ocean
Surinam	Suriname
Suva [US Embassy]	Fiji
Swains Island	American Samoa
Swan Islands	Honduras
Sydney [US Consulate General]	Australia

T

Name	Entry in *Handbook of the Nations*
Tahiti	French Polynesia
Taipei	Taiwan
Taiwan Strait	Pacific Ocean
Tampico [US Consular Agency]	Mexico
Tanganyika	Tanzania
Tangier [US Consulate General]	Morocco

Name	Entry in *Handbook of the Nations*
Tarawa	Kiribati
Tartar Strait	Pacific Ocean
Tasmania	Australia
Tasman Sea	Pacific Ocean
Taymyr Peninsula (Poluostrov Taymyra)	Soviet Union
Tegucigalpa [US Embassy]	Honduras
Tehran [US post not maintained, representation by Swiss Embassy]	Iran
Tel Aviv [US Embassy]	Israel
Terre Adélie (Adélie Land) [claimed by France]	Antarctica
Thailand, Gulf of	Pacific Ocean
Thessaloniki [US Consulate General]	Greece
Thurston Island	Antarctica
Tibet (Xizang)	China
Tierra del Fuego	Argentina; Chile
Tijuana [US Consulate General]	Mexico
Timor	Indonesia
Timor Sea	Indian Ocean
Tinian	Northern Mariana Islands
Tiran, Strait of	Indian Ocean
Tobago	Trinidad and Tobago
Tokyo [US Embassy]	Japan
Tonkin, Gulf of	Pacific Ocean
Toronto [US Consulate General]	Canada
Torres Strait	Pacific Ocean
Trans-Jordan	Jordan
Transkei	South Africa
Transylvania	Romania
Trieste [US Consular Agency]	Italy
Trindade, Ilha de	Brazil
Tripoli [US post not maintained, representation by Belgian Embassy]	Libya
Tristan da Cunha Group	St. Helena
Trobriand Islands	Papua New Guinea
Trucial States	United Arab Emirates
Truk Islands	Micronesia
Tsugaru Strait	Pacific Ocean
Tuamotu Islands (Îles Tuamotu)	French Polynesia
Tubuai Islands (Îles Tubuai)	French Polynesia
Tunis [US Embassy]	Tunisia
Turin [US Consulate]	Italy
Turkish Straits	Atlantic Ocean
Turks Island Passage	Atlantic Ocean
Tyrol, South	Italy
Tyrrhenian Sea	Atlantic Ocean
U Udorn [US Consulate]	Thailand
Ulaanbaatar	Mongolia
Ullŭng-do	Korea, South
Unimak Pass [strait]	Pacific Ocean
United Arab Republic	Egypt; Syria
Upper Volta	Burkina
V Vaduz [US post not maintained, representation from Zürich, Switzerland]	Liechtenstein
Vākhān (Wakhan Corridor)	Afghanistan
Valencia [US Consular Agency]	Spain
Valletta [US Embassy]	Malta
Vancouver [US Consulate General]	Canada
Vancouver Island	Canada
Van Diemen Strait	Pacific Ocean
Vatican City [US Embassy]	Vatican City
Vélez de la Gomera, Peñón de	Spain
Venda	South Africa

Name	Entry in *Handbook of the Nations*
Veracruz [US Consular Agency]	Mexico
Verde Island Passage	Pacific Ocean
Victoria [US Embassy]	Seychelles
Vienna [US Embassy, US Mission to International Organizations in Vienna (UNVIE)]	Austria
Vientiane [US Embassy]	Laos
Volcano Islands	Japan
Vostok Island	Kiribati
Vrangelya, Ostrov (Wrangel Island)	Soviet Union

W

Name	Entry
Wakhan Corridor (now Vākhān)	Afghanistan
Wales	United Kingdom
Walvis Bay	South Africa
Warsaw [US Embassy]	Poland
Washington, D. C. [The Permanent Mission of the USA to the Organization of American States (OAS)]	United States
Weddell Sea	Atlantic Ocean
Wellington [US Embassy]	New Zealand
Western Channel (West Korea Strait)	Pacific Ocean
West Germany	Germany, Federal Republic of
West Korea Strait (Western Channel)	Pacific Ocean
West Pakistan	Pakistan
Wetar Strait	Pacific Ocean
White Sea	Arctic Ocean
Windhoek	Namibia
Windward Passage	Atlantic Ocean
Winnipeg [US Consular Agency]	Canada
Wrangel Island (Ostrov Vrangelya)	Soviet Union

Y

Name	Entry
Yaounde [US Embassy]	Cameroon
Yap Islands	Micronesia
Yellow Sea	Pacific Ocean
Yemen (Aden)	Yemen, People's Democratic Republic of
Yemen, North	Yemen Arab Republic
Yemen (Sanaa)	Yemen Arab Republic
Yemen, South	Yemen, People's Democratic Republic of
Youth, Isle of (Isla de la Juventud)	Canada
Yucatan Channel	Atlantic Ocean

Z

Name	Entry
Zagreb [US Consulate General]	Yugoslavia
Zanzibar	Tanzania
Zürich [US Consulate General]	Switzerland

Map I

The World (Guide to Regional Maps)

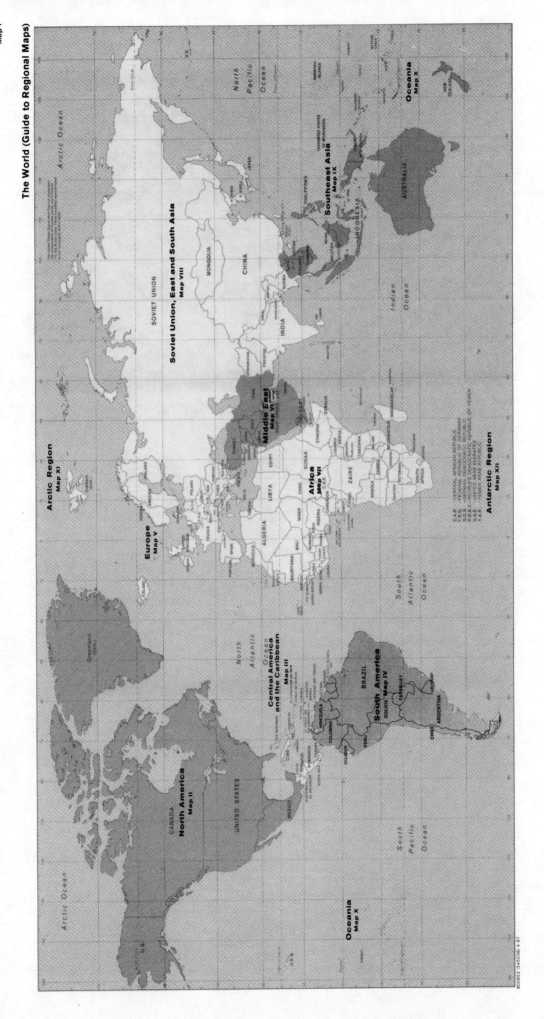

Map II

North America

Greenland Sea

Nord

Danmark
Havn

Itseqqortoormiit

Arctic Ocean

Alert

Greenland
(DENMARK)

Ellesmere
Island

Thule

Denmark
Strait

Queen Elizabeth
Islands

Baffin Bay

Ammassalik

Barrow

Beaufort
Sea

Resolute

Qeqertarsuaq

Nome

Bering
Strait

Prudhoe Bay

Banks
Island

Arctic
Bay

Arctic Circle

Godthåb
(Nuuk)

UNITED STATES
(Alaska)

Bethel

Fairbanks

Victoria
Island

Cambridge
Bay

Baffin
Island

Davis
Strait

Qaqortoq

Anchorage

Dawson

Great
Bear Lake

Echo
Bay

Repulse Bay

Valdez

Gulf of
Alaska

Kodiak

Whitehorse

Frobisher
Bay

Labrador Sea

Juneau

Yellowknife

Ketchikan

Great
Slave Lake

CANADA

Ivugivik

Prince
Rupert

Peace River

Uranium City

Hudson Bay

Scheferville

Goose
Bay

Newfoundland

St. John's

Lake
Athabasca

Churchill

Fort George

St. Pierre
and Miquelon
(FRANCE)

Edmonton

Gulf of St.
Lawrence

North

Vancouver

Calgary

Saskatoon

Lake
Winnipeg

Moosonee

Sydney

Pacific

Seattle

Columbia River

Regina

Winnipeg

Quebec

St.
John

Halifax

Ocean

Portland

Great
Falls

Missouri River

Thunder
Bay

Lake
Superior

Montreal

Bangor

North

Boise

Snake River

Minneapolis

Lake
Michigan

Lake
Huron

Ottawa

Toronto

Boston

Atlantic

San Francisco

Great Salt
Lake

Salt Lake City

Omaha

Chicago

Detroit

Lake
Erie

Lake Ontario

Cleveland

New York

Philadelphia

Ocean

Denver

St. Louis

Ohio River

Washington

Las Vegas

Colorado River

UNITED STATES

Louisville

Norfolk

Bermuda
(U.K.)

Los Angeles

Phoenix

Albuquerque

Arkansas River

Little Rock

Mississippi River

Atlanta

Charleston

San Diego

Nogales

El Paso

Dallas

Jacksonville

Hermosillo

Gulf of California

Rio Grande

Houston

New Orleans

Chihuahua

Miami

Tropic of Cancer

Torreón

Monterrey

Gulf of Mexico

La Paz

Durango

Mazatlán

MEXICO

Tampico

León

Guadalajara

Mérida

Mexico

Puebla

Veracruz

Acapulco

Oaxaca

Scale 1:38,700,000

0   500 Kilometers

0   500 Nautical Miles

Boundary representation is
not necessarily authoritative.

U.S.-Russia 1867
Treaty Convention Line

800853 (545526) 4-87

Map III

Central America and the Caribbean

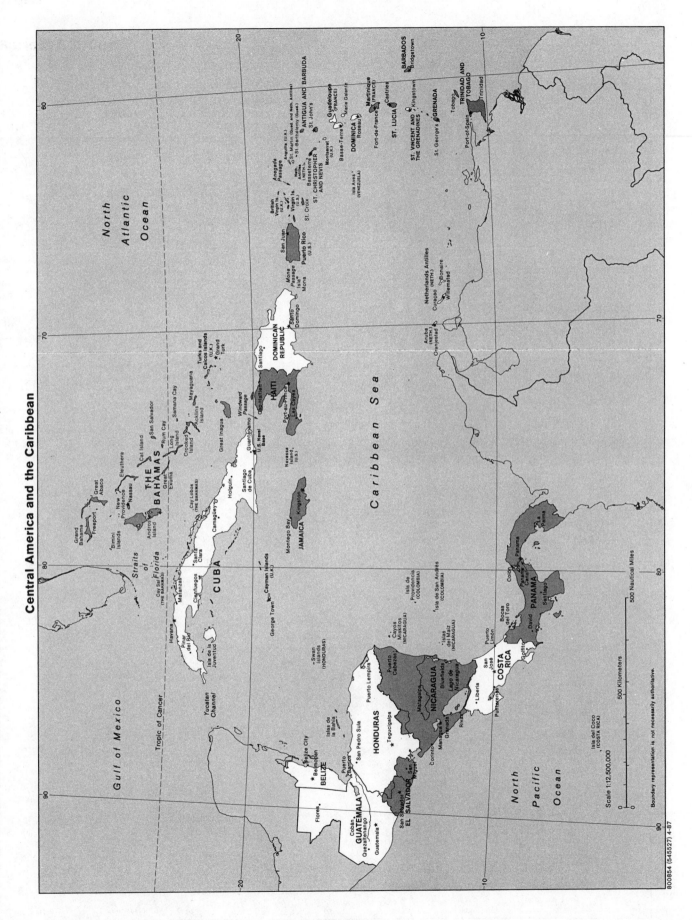

North Atlantic Ocean

Gulf of Mexico

Tropic of Cancer

Straits of Florida

Grand Bahama
Freeport
Bimini Islands
New Providence
Nassau
Andros Island
Cat Island
San Salvador
Rum Cay
Long Island
Exuma
Crooked Island
Acklins Island
Mayaguana
Samana Cay
Turks and Caicos Islands (U.K.)
Grand Turk

THE BAHAMAS
Great Exuma
Cay Lobos (THE BAHAMAS)
Santa Clara
Holguin

Havana
Pinar del Río
Isla de la Juventud
Matanzas
Cienfuegos
CUBA
Camagüey
Cayman Islands (U.K.)
George Town
Santiago de Cuba

Great Inagua
Windward Passage
Guantánamo
U.S. Naval Base
Navassa Island (U.S.)

HAITI
Port-au-Prince
Les Cayes
Santiago
DOMINICAN REPUBLIC
Santo Domingo

Mona Passage
Isla Mona
San Juan
Puerto Rico (U.S.)

Montego Bay
Kingston
JAMAICA

Anegada Passage
British Virgin Is. (U.K.)
Virgin Is. (U.K.)
St. Croix

St. Martin (Guad. and Neth. Antilles)
St-Barthélemy (Guad.)
ANTIGUA AND BARBUDA
St. John's
Neth. Antilles (NETH.)
Basseterre
ST. CHRISTOPHER AND NEVIS
Montserrat (U.K.)
Basse-Terre
Guadeloupe (FRANCE)
Marie Galante
DOMINICA
Roseau
Fort-de-France
Martinique (FRANCE)
Castries
ST. LUCIA
Kingstown
ST. VINCENT AND THE GRENADINES
St. George's **GRENADA**

BARBADOS
Bridgetown

Isla Aves (VENEZUELA)

Tobago
TRINIDAD AND TOBAGO
Port-of-Spain
Trinidad

Netherlands Antilles
Curaçao
Willemstad
Bonaire
Aruba (NETH.)
Oranjestad

Caribbean Sea

Swan Islands (HONDURAS)
Puerto Lempira
Cayos Miskitos (NICARAGUA)
Puerto Cabezas
NICARAGUA
Matagalpa
Bluefields
Lago de Nicaragua
Islas del Maíz (NICARAGUA)
Rivas
Granada
Managua
Corinto
San Miguel

Isla de Providencia (COLOMBIA)
Isla de San Andrés (COLOMBIA)

San José
COSTA RICA
Liberia
Puntarenas
Puerto Limón
Bocas del Toro
David
PANAMA
Santiago
Colón
Panamá
Panama Canal
La Palma

Belize City
Belmopan
BELIZE
Puerto Barrios
Islas de la Bahía
San Pedro Sula
HONDURAS
Tegucigalpa

Flores
Cobán
Quezaltenango
GUATEMALA
Guatemala
San Salvador
EL SALVADOR

North Pacific Ocean

Isla del Coco (COSTA RICA)

Scale 1:12,500,000

500 Kilometers
500 Nautical Miles

Boundary representation is not necessarily authoritative.

800854 (545527) 4-87

Map IV

South America

Caribbean Sea

Barranquilla
Maracaibo
★ Caracas
San Cristobal
VENEZUELA
Ciudad Guayana
Rio Orinoco

Medellín

Bogotá ★
COLOMBIA
Cali

Isla de Malpelo •
(COLOMBIA)

GUYANA
Georgetown ★
Paramaribo ★
SURINAME
Cayenne ★
French Guiana
(FRANCE)

Boa Vista •

Mitú •

Equator

★ Quito
ECUADOR
Guayaquil •

Iquitos •

Rio Negro

Fonte Boa •
Amazon
Manaus •
Macapá

Amazon
Belém •
São Luís •

Piura •
Rio Marañón
Rio Ucayali

Trujillo •
Huánuco •

PERU

Lima ★

Ica •

Cusco •

Arequipa •

Rio Branco •
Pôrto Velho •

South Pacific Ocean

Lago Titicaca
La Paz •
Trinidad •
BOLIVIA
Cochabamba •
Sucre •
Santa Cruz •

Arica •

B R A Z I L

Fortaleza •

Natal •

Recife •

Aracaju •

Salvador •

Teresina •

Pôrto Nacional •
Rio São Francisco

Rio Xingu
Rio Tocantins

Cuiabá •

Goiânia •
Brasília ★

Santarém •

Belo Horizonte •

Vitória •

20

Tropic of Capricorn

Antofagasta •

Isla San Félix
(CHILE)
Isla San Ambrosio
(CHILE)

PARAGUAY

Asunción ★

San Miguel de Tucumán •

Resistencia •

Rio Paraná

Rio de Janeiro
São Paulo •
Curitiba •

Florianópolis •

South Atlantic Ocean

CHILE

Archipiélago Juan Fernández
(CHILE)

Valparaíso •
Santiago ★

Córdoba •
Mendoza •
Rosario •

ARGENTINA

Concepción •

Bahía Blanca •

San Carlos de Bariloche •

Puerto Montt •

Pôrto Alegre •
Salto •
URUGUAY
Buenos Aires •
Montevideo ★
Mar del Plata •

Comodoro Rivadavia •

Scale 1:35,000,000

0   500 Kilometers
0   500 Nautical Miles

Boundary representation is
not necessarily authoritative.

Strait of Magellan
Punta Arenas •

Stanley •
Falkland Islands
(Islas Malvinas)
(administered by U.K.,
claimed by ARGENTINA)

Ushuaia •

South Georgia
(Falkland Islands)

North Atlantic Ocean

South Pacific Ocean

Map V

Europe

Update note: Borders shown for the two German states were as of September 1990. Reunification was scheduled for October 3, 1990.

Map VI

Middle East

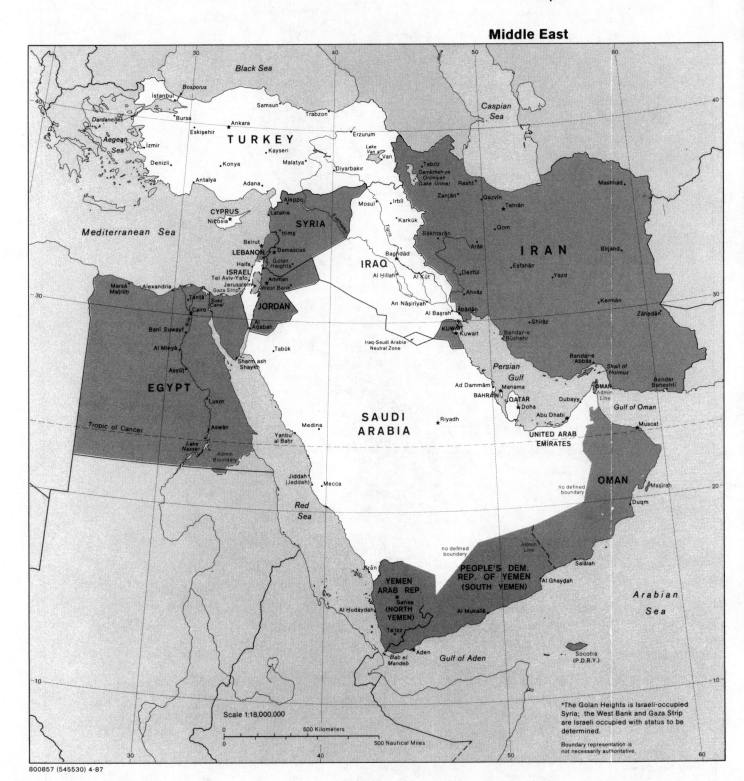

*The Golan Heights is Israeli-occupied Syria; the West Bank and Gaza Strip are Israeli occupied with status to be determined.

Boundary representation is not necessarily authoritative.

Scale 1:18,000,000

500 Kilometers

500 Nautical Miles

800857 (545530) 4-87

Map VII

Africa

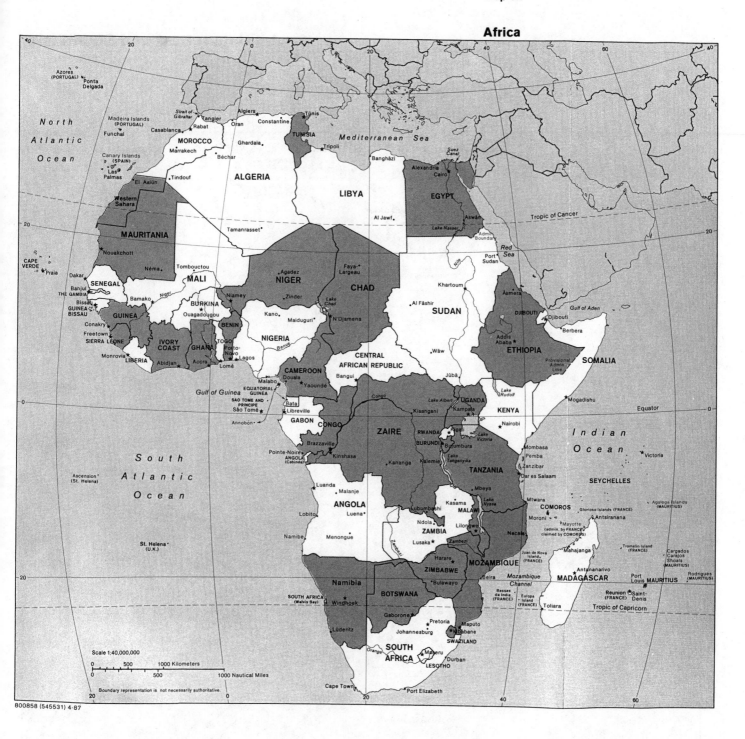

Scale 1:40,000,000

Boundary representation is not necessarily authoritative.

800858 (545531) 4-87

Map VIII

Soviet Union, East and South Asia

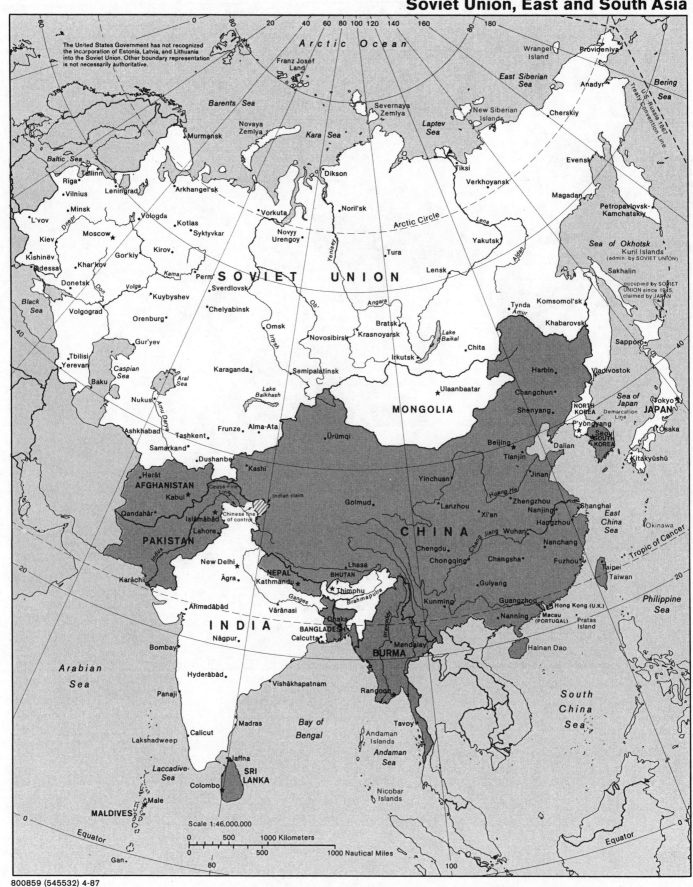

The United States Government has not recognized
the incorporation of Estonia, Latvia, and Lithuania
into the Soviet Union. Other boundary representation
is not necessarily authoritative.

Scale 1:46,000,000

0   500   1000 Kilometers

0   500   1000 Nautical Miles

Southeast Asia

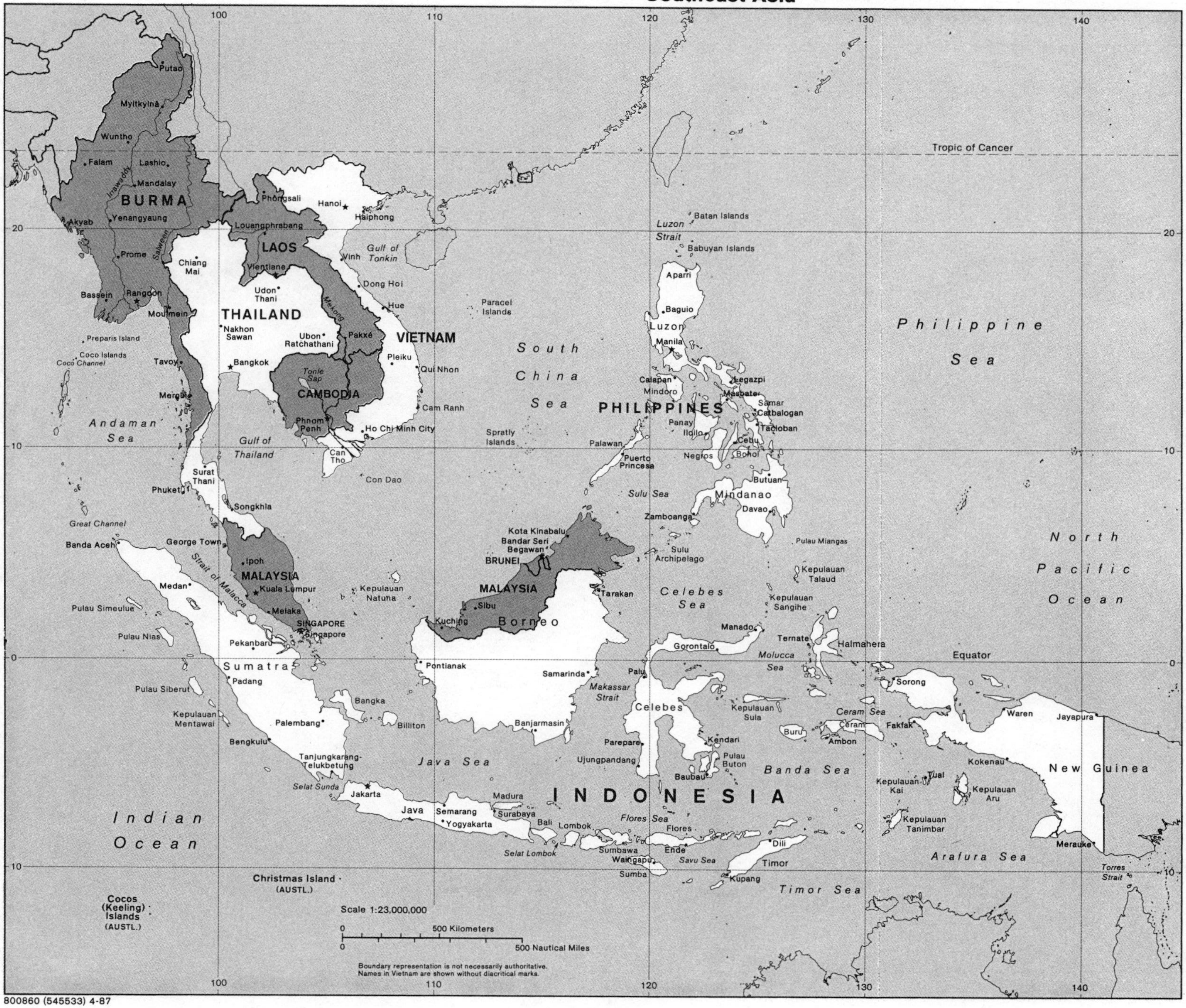

Tropic of Cancer

North Pacific Ocean

Philippine Sea

Pacific Ocean

New Guinea

Jayapura
Merauke
Waren
Sorong
Kokenau
Kepulauan Aru
Fakfak
Kepulauan Kai
Kepulauan Tanimbar

Equator

Arafura Sea

Timor Sea

BURMA
Putao
Myitkyina
Lashio
Mandalay
Wuntho
Falam
Akyab
Yenangyaung
Prome
Rangoon
Bassein
Moulmein
Irrawaddy
Salween
Chiang Mai
Tavoy
Mergui
Prepares Island
Coco Islands
Coco Channel
Great Channel

Andaman Sea

THAILAND
Nakhon Sawan
Bangkok
Udon Thani
Ubon Ratchathani
Phonsali
Louangphrabang
Vientiane

LAOS

VIETNAM
Hanoi
Haiphong
Dong Hoi
Hue
Pleiku
Qui Nhon
Cam Ranh
Ho Chi Minh City
Can Tho
Con Dao

CAMBODIA
Phnom Penh
Paksé
Tonle Sap
Mekong

Gulf of Tonkin

Gulf of Thailand

Surat Thani
Phuket
Songkhla

South China Sea

Paracel Islands

Spratly Islands

PHILIPPINES
Luzon
Batan Islands
Babuyan Islands
Aparri
Baguio
Manila
Luzon Strait
Calapan
Mindoro
Legazpi
Masbate
Samar
Catbalogan
Tacloban
Cebu
Bohol
Panay
Iloilo
Negros
Puerto Princesa
Palawan
Butuan
Mindanao
Davao
Zamboanga

Sulu Sea
Sulu Archipelago

Celebes Sea

MALAYSIA
Kota Kinabalu
BRUNEI
Bandar Seri Begawan
Sibu
Kuching
Borneo
Tarakan
Pontianak
Samarinda
Banjarmasin
Makassar Strait

George Town
Medan
MALAYSIA
Ipoh
Kuala Lumpur
Melaka
Strait of Malacca
Pekanbaru
SINGAPORE
Singapore
Bangka
Billiton
Palembang
Bengkulu
Padang
Sumatra
Pulau Nias
Pulau Siberut
Kepulauan Mentawai
Pulau Simeulue
Banda Aceh
Kepulauan Natuna
Tanjungkarang-Telukbetung
Selat Sunda

INDONESIA

Java Sea
Jakarta
Semarang
Semarang
Yogyakarta
Surabaya
Madura
Java
Bali
Lombok
Selat Lombok

Flores Sea
Sumbawa
Waingapu
Sumba
Savu Sea
Ende
Flores

Celebes
Gorontalo
Manado
Palu
Parepare
Ujungpandang
Pulau Buton
Baubau
Kendari
Molucca Sea
Ternate
Kepulauan Sula
Kepulauan Sangihe
Kepulauan Talaud
Pulau Miangas

Ceram Sea
Ambon
Buru
Ceram
Halmahera
Banda Sea
Dili
Kupang
Timor

Indian Ocean

Christmas Island (AUSTL.)

Cocos (Keeling) Islands (AUSTL.)

Scale 1:23,000,000

0   500 Kilometers
0   500 Nautical Miles

Boundary representation is not necessarily authoritative.
Names in Vietnam are shown without diacritical marks.

800860 (545533) 4-87

Map X

Oceania

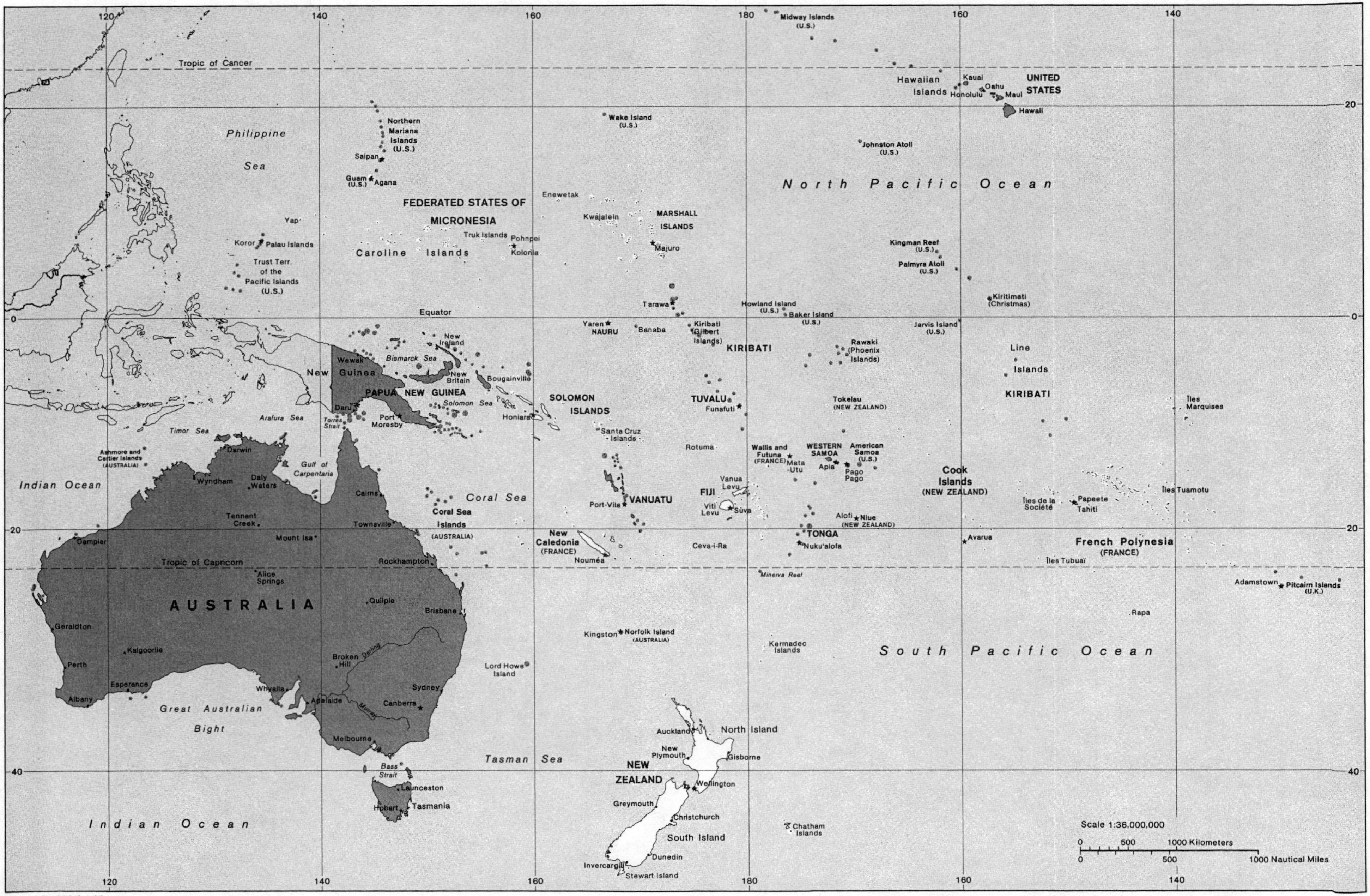

Tropic of Cancer

Philippine Sea

UNITED STATES

Hawaii

Hawaiian Islands (U.S.)

Kauai Oahu Maui
Honolulu

North Pacific Ocean

Midway Islands (U.S.)

Johnston Atoll (U.S.)

Northern Mariana Islands (U.S.)

Saipan
Guam (U.S.) Agana

FEDERATED STATES OF MICRONESIA

Caroline Islands

Truk Islands Pohnpei
Kolonia

Yap

Koror Palau Islands
Trust Terr. of the Pacific Islands (U.S.)

Wake Island (U.S.)

MARSHALL ISLANDS

Kwajalein

Majuro

Enewetak

Equator

KIRIBATI

Kiribati (Gilbert Islands)

Tarawa Banaba

Yaren NAURU

Howland Island (U.S.)
S Baker Island (U.S.)

Kingman Reef (U.S.)
Palmyra Atoll (U.S.)

Jarvis Island (U.S.)

Line Islands

KIRIBATI

Kiritimati (Christmas)

Rawaki Phoenix Islands (U.S.)

Tokelau (NEW ZEALAND)

WESTERN SAMOA American Samoa
Apia Pago Pago

Alofi Niue (NEW ZEALAND)

TONGA
Nukualofa

Wallis and Futuna (FRANCE) Mata-Utu

TUVALU Funafuti

Rotuma

FIJI Vanua Levu
Viti Levu Suva

Ceva-i-Ra

Minerva Reef

Kermadec Islands

Iles Marquises

Iles Tuamotu

French Polynesia (FRANCE)

Papeete Tahiti

Iles de la Société

Iles Tubuai

Rapa

Cook Islands (NEW ZEALAND)

Avarua

South Pacific Ocean

Adamstown Pitcairn Islands (U.K.)

Scale 1:36,000,000

1000 Kilometers
500   500
0

1000 Nautical Miles
500
0

SOLOMON ISLANDS

Bougainville
Honiara

Santa Cruz Islands

VANUATU
Port-Vila

New Caledonia (FRANCE)
Nouméa

PAPUA NEW GUINEA
New Ireland New Britain
Bismarck Sea
Wewak
Daru Port Moresby

New Guinea

Lae

Solomon Sea

Coral Sea

Coral Sea Islands (AUSTRALIA)

Lord Howe Island

Tasman Sea

North Island

NEW ZEALAND

Auckland
New Plymouth
Wellington
Christchurch
South Island
Greymouth
Dunedin
Invercargill Stewart Island

Gisborne

Norfolk Island (AUSTRALIA)

Kingston

Chatham Islands

Gulf of Carpentaria

Arafura Sea

Timor Sea

Torres Strait

Ashmore and Cartier Islands (AUSTRALIA)

Darwin
Wyndham
Daly Waters

Tennant Creek

Mount Isa

Alice Springs

Tropic of Capricorn

AUSTRALIA

Great Australian Bight

Indian Ocean

Dampier
Geraldton
Perth
Kalgoorlie
Esperance
Albany

Whyalla
Adelaide

Broken Hill

Quilpie

Rockhampton

Brisbane

Townsville

Cairns

Sydney
Canberra
Melbourne
Murray

Bass Strait
Launceston
Tasmania
Hobart

Philippine Sea

Map XI

Arctic Region

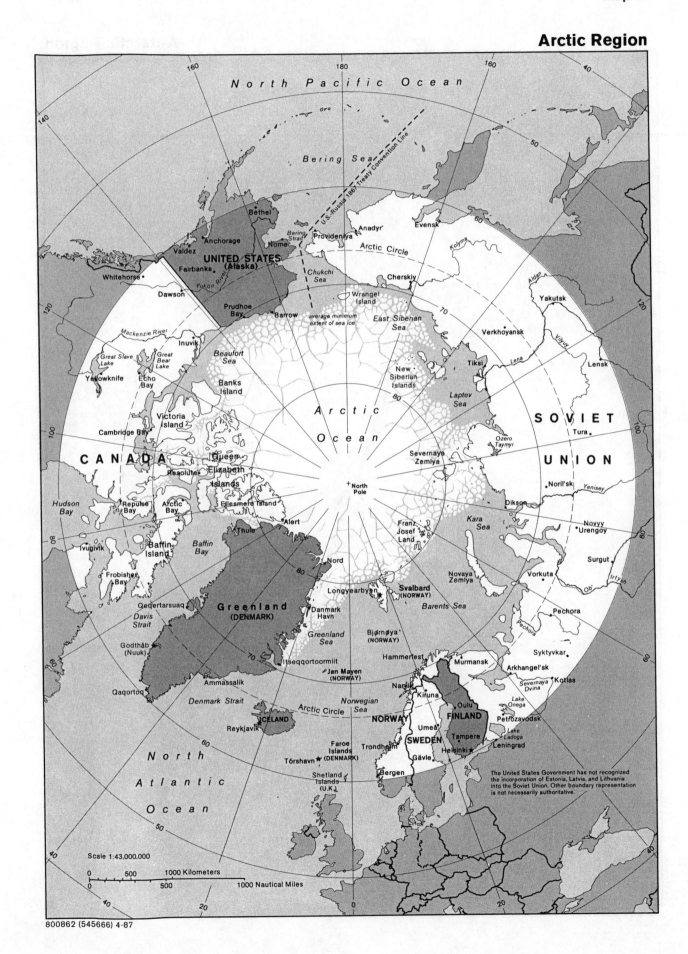

North Pacific Ocean

Bering Sea

Arctic Circle

Bethel
Anchorage
Valdez
UNITED STATES
(Alaska)
Fairbanks
Whitehorse
Dawson
Prudhoe Bay
Barrow

Nome
Bering Strait
Provideniya
Anadyr'
Evensk
Kolyma
Cherskiy
Wrangel Island
average minimum extent of sea ice
East Siberian Sea
Yakutsk
Verkhoyansk
Aldan
Lena
Vilyuy
Lensk

Chukchi Sea
Beaufort Sea
Banks Island
New Siberian Islands
Laptev Sea
Tiksi

Mackenzie River
Inuvik
Great Slave Lake
Great Bear Lake
Yellowknife
Echo Bay
Victoria Island
Cambridge Bay

Arctic Ocean

SOVIET

UNION

Tura
Ozero Taymyr
Severnaya Zemlya
Noril'sk
Yenisey
Dikson
Novyy Urengoy
Surgut
Ob'
Irtysh

Yukon River

North Pole

CANADA

Queen Elizabeth Islands
Resolute
Ellesmere Island
Alert
Thule
Nord

Hudson Bay
Repulse Bay
Arctic Bay
Baffin Island
Baffin Bay

Ivugivik
Frobisher Bay
Qeqertarsuaq
Davis Strait
Godthåb (Nuuk)
Ammassalik
Qaqortoq

Longyearbyen
Svalbard (NORWAY)
Kara Sea
Franz Josef Land
Novaya Zemlya
Vorkuta
Pechora
Pechora

Greenland
(DENMARK)
Danmark Havn
Greenland Sea
Bjørnøya (NORWAY)
Barents Sea

Hammerfest
Murmansk
Arkhangel'sk
Severnaya Dvina
Kotlas

Denmark Strait
Norwegian Sea
Arctic Circle
Jan Mayen (NORWAY)

Syktyvkar

Itseqqortoormiit

ICELAND
Reykjavik
Faroe Islands
Tórshavn ★ (DENMARK)
Shetland Islands (U.K.)
Trondheim
Bergen

Narvik
Kiruna
NORWAY
Umeå
SWEDEN
Gävle
Oulu
FINLAND
Tampere
Helsinki ★
Lake Onega
Petrozavodsk
Lake Ladoga
Leningrad

North

Atlantic

Ocean

The United States Government has not recognized the incorporation of Estonia, Latvia, and Lithuania into the Soviet Union. Other boundary representation is not necessarily authoritative.

U.S.-Russia 1867 Treaty Convention Line

Scale 1:43,000,000

0   500   1000 Kilometers
0   500   1000 Nautical Miles

Map XII

Antarctic Region

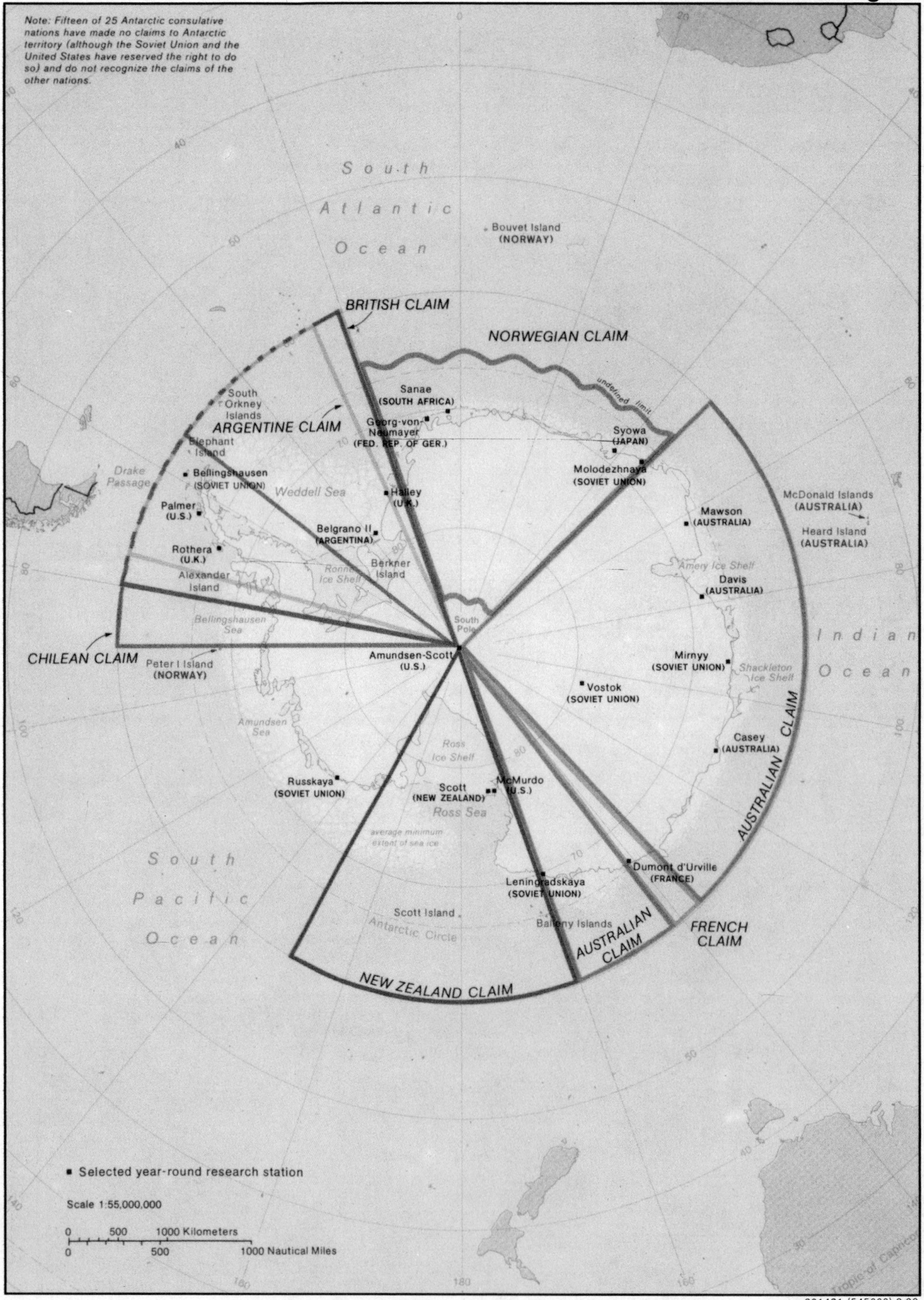

Note: Fifteen of 25 Antarctic consulative nations have made no claims to Antarctic territory (although the Soviet Union and the United States have reserved the right to do so) and do not recognize the claims of the other nations.

South
Atlantic
Ocean

Bouvet Island
(NORWAY)

BRITISH CLAIM

NORWEGIAN CLAIM

undefined limit

South
Orkney
Islands

Sanae
(SOUTH AFRICA)

Syowa
(JAPAN)

ARGENTINE CLAIM

Georg-von-
Neumayer
(FED. REP. OF GER.)

Molodezhnaya
(SOVIET UNION)

Elephant
Island

Drake
Passage

Bellingshausen
(SOVIET UNION)

Weddell Sea

Halley
(U.K.)

Mawson
(AUSTRALIA)

McDonald Islands
(AUSTRALIA)

Heard Island
(AUSTRALIA)

Palmer
(U.S.)

Belgrano II
(ARGENTINA)

Amery Ice Shelf

Davis
(AUSTRALIA)

Rothera
(U.K.)

Ronne
Ice Shelf

Berkner
Island

Alexander
Island

Bellingshausen
Sea

South
Pole

Indian
Ocean

CHILEAN CLAIM

Peter I Island
(NORWAY)

Amundsen-Scott
(U.S.)

Mirnyy
(SOVIET UNION)

Shackleton
Ice Shelf

AUSTRALIAN CLAIM

Amundsen
Sea

Vostok
(SOVIET UNION)

Casey
(AUSTRALIA)

Ross
Ice Shelf

Russkaya
(SOVIET UNION)

Scott
(NEW ZEALAND)

McMurdo
(U.S.)

Ross Sea

South
Pacific
Ocean

average minimum
extent of sea ice

Dumont d'Urville
(FRANCE)

Leningradskaya
(SOVIET UNION)

Scott Island

Antarctic Circle

Balleny Islands

*AUSTRALIAN
CLAIM*

*FRENCH
CLAIM*

NEW ZEALAND CLAIM

■ Selected year-round research station

Scale 1:55,000,000

| 0 | 500 | 1000 Kilometers |
0   500   1000 Nautical Miles

Map XIII

Standard Time Zones of the World

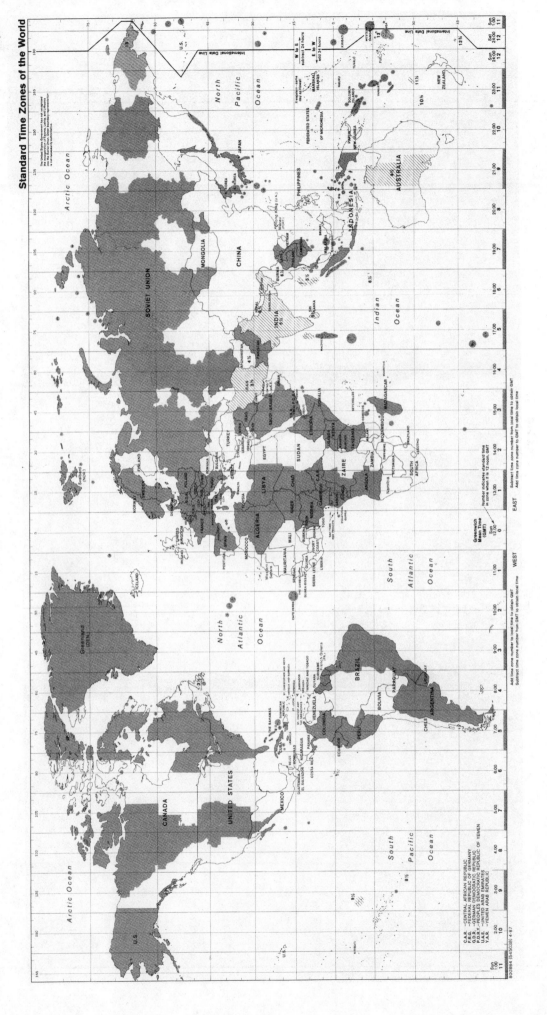